BARRON'S

THE TRUSTED NAME IN TEST PREP

SAT®
Premium
Study Guide
2023

Brian W. Stewart, M.Ed.

Dedication

Dedicated to Caitlin, Andrew, and Eloise—without your love and support, this book would not have been possible. I would like to thank my mom, my dad, Andy, Pam, Leah, Thapasvi, Patrick, Sarah, and Bella. A special thank you to Michal Strawn for her invaluable help. I am grateful to all the support from my publisher, especially Jennifer Goodenough and Angela Tartaro.

Thanks so much to all of my students over the years—I have learned far more from you than you have learned from me.

Published by Kaplan North America, LLC, d/b/a Barron's Educational Series
1515 W Cypress Creek Road
Fort Lauderdale, FL 33309
www.barronseduc.com

ISBN: 978-1-5062-6457-8

Kaplan North America, LLC, d/b/a Barron's Educational Series print books are available at special quantity discounts to use for sales promotions, employee premiums, or educational purposes. For more information or to purchase books, please call the Simon & Schuster special sales department at 866-506-1949.

About the Author

Brian W. Stewart is the founder and president of BWS Education Consulting, Inc., a boutique tutoring and test preparation company based in Columbus, Ohio. Brian is a nationally recognized test preparation expert, having over 30,000 hours of direct instructional experience with a wide variety of learners from all over the world. He has achieved a perfect score on the SAT, helped hundreds of students reach their college admissions goals, and presented on best tutoring practices at national conferences.

Brian has used his experience and expertise to write several best-selling books with Barron's, including *Barron's ACT* and *Barron's PSAT/NMSQT*. He is a former high school teacher and graduate of Princeton University (A.B.) and The Ohio State University (M.Ed.).

Brian resides in Columbus with his wife, two children, and an assortment of pets.

To learn more about Brian's online tutoring and group presentations, please visit www.bwseducationconsulting.com.

Table of Contents

About the Author ... iii
How to Use This Book ... vii

PART 1: INTRODUCTION TO THE SAT

Welcome to the SAT ... 3

PART 2: DIAGNOSTIC TEST

SAT Diagnostic Test ... 11

Reading Test ... 17
Writing and Language Test ... 30
Math Test (No Calculator) ... 41
Math Test (Calculator) ... 47
Answers Explained ... 64

PART 3: READING

Introduction and Strategies ... 89
Question Drills ... 105
Full-Length Passage Drills ... 169
Advanced Drills ... 192

PART 4: WRITING AND LANGUAGE

Introduction and Strategies ... 217
Grammar Review ... 225
Advanced Drills ... 323

PART 5: MATH

Introduction and Strategies ... 343
Heart of Algebra ... 358
Passport to Advanced Math ... 414
Problem Solving and Data Analysis ... 486
Additional Topics in Math ... 556
Advanced Drills ... 610

PART 6: TEST YOURSELF

Practice Test 1 .... **657**
Answer Key 698
Answers Explained 703

Practice Test 2 .... **729**
Answer Key 771
Answers Explained 776

Practice Test 3 .... **803**
Answer Key 845
Answers Explained 850

Practice Test 4 .... **879**
Answer Key 920
Answers Explained 925

Appendix **947**

Index **981**

How to Use This Book

This book is designed to allow for highly targeted preparation for the SAT. Based on your previous SAT scores or the SAT Diagnostic Test in this book, review the strategies and content knowledge that are most relevant to your needs. There are hundreds of drills that range in difficulty from easy to challenging so that you can achieve the very best results for your personal situation.

Diagnostic Test

First, take the Diagnostic Test to gain an understanding of your strengths and weaknesses. It is a complete test with answer explanations and a question-type analysis guide so you know what types of concepts need the most attention.

Review and Practice

The Reading, Writing and Language, and Math sections each have:

- Proven test-taking strategies that allow you to customize your approach
- Extensive review of key concepts, particularly grammar and math knowledge
- Practice questions fully aligned with SAT content
- Advanced practice drills for ambitious students

Practice Tests

The final section of the book offers the opportunity to take four full-length practice tests that include all question types found on the actual SAT for the Reading, Writing and Language, and Math (calculator and non-calculator) sections. Comprehensive answer explanations are provided for all questions.

Online Practice

In addition to the Diagnostic Test and four practice tests within this book, there are also three full-length online practice exams. You may take these exams in practice (untimed) mode or in timed mode. All questions include answer explanations.

For Students

Every strategy and explanation is based on what I have found works best for students on the actual SAT. No matter your personal goals and background knowledge, you will find practice drills and test-taking strategies that are geared toward your situation. Look at the SAT as an opportunity to showcase all of your knowledge and skills for colleges.

Best of luck,
Brian W. Stewart

For Teachers

While many students will like working through this book independently, others will maximize their learning when they have a great teacher or tutor as their guide. Help your students work smarter instead of simply harder by utilizing the concept reviews and drills most appropriate for your students' needs. Also, you can coach your students on which test-taking strategies will be the best fit based on their past performance. I am hopeful that the skills students develop from using this book will help them not just with the SAT, but also with their academic coursework and future careers. If you have any suggestions for future editions, please reach out via the publisher.

Sincerely,
Brian W. Stewart

PART 1
Introduction to the SAT

Welcome to the SAT

The New Digital SAT

In January 2022, the College Board announced that in the spring of 2024, students in the United States are scheduled to switch from a paper SAT to a digital SAT. Students taking the SAT internationally are scheduled to shift to the digital format in the spring of 2023. The fundamental math, reading, and grammar skills and knowledge necessary for success will remain the same, and the test will still be scored out of 1600 points. The most important anticipated changes are that the SAT will take about 2 hours to complete instead of 3, the test sections will be "adaptive" (changing in difficulty based on your performance), and the entire test will be given on a computer. Check out the latest information on the digital exam by accessing Barron's Online Learning Hub via the link provided in the card at the front of the book. The Learning Hub includes online practice materials, and you can find more information on the digital SAT in the Library section.

Frequently Asked Questions

What is the SAT?

The SAT is a standardized test designed to assess your readiness for college-level work. Approximately 2,200,000 students take the exam each year, and most U.S. colleges and universities accept it for admissions consideration. Many schools also use the SAT to determine eligibility for scholarships. The SAT is one of many factors that colleges use to grant admission, along with evaluations of high school coursework, application essays, extracurricular involvement, and more.

What is the format of the SAT?

The SAT takes approximately three hours to complete, and is broken down as follows:

SAT Format		
1. Reading	*65 minutes*	*52 questions*
10-minute break		
2. Writing and Language	*35 minutes*	*44 questions*
3. Math No Calculator	*25 minutes*	*20 questions*
5-minute break		
4. Math with Calculator	*55 minutes*	*38 questions*

How is the SAT scored?

- The SAT score is broken up into two halves:
  1. Evidence-Based Reading and Writing, made of the Reading and Writing and Language sections, is scored between 200–800 points.
  2. Math, made of the Math No Calculator and Math with Calculator sections, is scored between 200–800 points.

- The total SAT score is therefore between 400–1600 points, with a 1600 being a perfect score, and a 1000 being approximately an average score.
- There is no penalty for guessing, so be sure to answer every question.

How do you register for the test? When is it offered?

Go to the College Board website and set up an account here: *https://collegereadiness.collegeboard.org/sat/register*

The SAT is typically offered seven times throughout the year in the following months: March, May, June, August, October, November, and December. Check on the above website link for the most updated information on test dates. Some schools may also offer an in-school test date; check with your guidance counselor for more details.

What is a good SAT score?

There is not a "passing" score on the SAT—a good score for you depends on your specific goals for college admissions. Take a look at this free College Board website for detailed information on typical scores for admitted students at schools throughout the United States: *https://bigfuture.collegeboard.org*

Does the SAT potentially offer accommodations?

For students whose test-taking is impacted by a documented disability, such as ADHD, dyslexia, or visual or motor impairments, the SAT may offer accommodations. The most typical accommodation is extended time, although some students may receive more specific accommodations, like the services of a reader or extended breaks. If you have an IEP or 504 plan with your school, talk to your guidance counselor or school administrator about applying for accommodations on the SAT. Having an IEP or a 504 plan will not necessarily lead to having accommodations on the SAT, but it usually helps. Allow plenty of time to apply for accommodations—at least seven weeks. Go to this website for the latest details on requesting SAT accommodations: *https://accommodations.collegeboard.org*

Does the SAT offer accommodations for English language learners?

Students who are actively enrolled in an English as a Second Language program at their school may be able to take the SAT with 50% extra time, translated test directions, and the use of a bilingual dictionary. This service is currently available on school-day SATs, but not on the national test dates on weekends. Go to this website for further information about SAT supports for English language learners: *https://collegereadiness.collegeboard.org/educators/k-12/english-learner-supports*

What are the similarities and differences between the SAT and ACT?

The SAT and ACT have many similarities:

- They both test English grammar.
- They both test high school math up through precalculus.
- They both test reading comprehension.
- They both assess students' ability to analyze graphs and charts.
- There is no guessing penalty on either test—be sure to answer every question.
- Colleges throughout the United States will accept results from either the SAT or ACT.

There are some important differences:

- **The SAT gives students more time to complete the same amount of material.** For example, on the Writing and Language section of the SAT, students have about nine minutes to complete 11 questions, while on the English section of the ACT, students have nine minutes to complete 15 questions. So, if you are more comfortable taking your time completing the test, the SAT may be a better fit than the ACT.

- **The SAT focuses more deeply on certain math topics**, emphasizing algebra and word problems. **The ACT has a broader array of math topics**, including things like matrices, logarithms, and hyperbolas.
- **The ACT has a Science section, while the SAT tests scientific skills throughout the test.** The final section of the ACT is a stand-alone science reasoning section, which assesses your skill in analyzing experiments, scientific research, and scientific theories. The SAT has questions on each section—even the Writing and Language—that will ask you to interpret graphs and charts.

What should I do right before the SAT?

Immediately before the SAT, prioritize sleep and relaxation. You will do far better on the SAT if you are well-rested and have a positive mindset. In the week before the test, try to get eight to nine hours of sleep a night. Since the SAT is very much a critical thinking test, the better rested you are, the better you will be able to read, problem solve, and edit. Some practice shortly before the test is perfectly fine to do, but make sure you are not staying up late and cramming.

What should I bring with me to the SAT?

- **Admissions ticket**
- **Wooden number 2 pencils** (not mechanical)
- **Calculator with fresh batteries**—most any graphing or scientific calculator is fine.
    - Check to see if your calculator is approved here: *https://collegereadiness.collegeboard.org/sat/taking-the-test/calculator-policy*
- **A watch** (one that doesn't make noise and is not connected to the internet)
- **A snack and a drink** to have during your breaks (don't have food/drink out on your desk)
- **Do not have your cell phone with you during the duration of the test**—you are welcome to use it after the test has concluded, but the proctors do not want to see phones used during the test to prevent possible cheating.

What are some general SAT test-taking strategies?

While there are plenty of strategies applicable to individual sections of the SAT, here are ten strategies that are important throughout the exam:

1. **Answer every question.** There is no penalty for guessing on the SAT, so be sure to enter an answer for every question. Even on the fill-in questions on the SAT Math section, there is no penalty for guessing. Put down some number so you have at least a chance of earning the point.
2. **Know the directions and format ahead of time.** The directions you need to follow and the general format of the test will not change. Familiarize yourself with these so that you do not need to waste time reading directions and reviewing the format on the day of the test.
3. **Focus on understanding the question.** SAT questions are sometimes a paragraph long—if you skim the question, you will likely miss critical details. Break down the question by underlining and circling key words to fully grasp what you are asked to do.
4. **Come back to questions if needed.** Do not look at skipping a question as a sign that you have given up. Instead, use it as an opportunity to let your subconscious mind process the question while you consider other questions. Revisit the question after some time has gone by, and you will likely notice something that you did not previously see. To minimize the amount of time you spend reacquainting yourself with questions in the Reading and the Writing and Language sections, try to come back to questions about each passage prior to going on to the next passage.

5. **Write as much as you would like on the test booklet.** Underline and make notes as you read the reading passages, circle important phrases in the Writing and Language, and draw pictures and write out equations in the Math. Writing will help you clarify what is being asked and notice patterns so that you can arrive at a solution.
6. **Use the full amount of time.** The SAT is not a race—there is no prize for finishing first. Also, since the questions are often challenging, you will be best served by taking your time to do the questions once well instead of doing them over and over again, repeating the same mistakes. Pace yourself so that you finish your work right as time is called.
7. **Do not look at your performance on the SAT as an all-or-nothing situation.** The SAT is very different from typical school tests in which missing a few questions results in a greatly decreased grade. The SAT is graded on a curve, so your score is determined by how other test-takers perform, not just some arbitrary number. If the test is more difficult on a particular day, the curve will be more generous. On most any test, you can likely miss several questions to achieve the score you desire. So, do not look at the SAT as something where you either do great or do poorly—a score that isn't perfect can still be excellent.
8. **Try to figure things out.** Instead of looking at SAT problems as knowledge to be recalled, look at them as puzzles to be solved. Do not be intimidated by a problem that you do not immediately know how to solve—instead, patiently think your way through it. The SAT is a test of your skill in problem solving, not simply a test of memorized knowledge.
9. **Know that there will be one definite answer to each question.** The College Board goes to extraordinary lengths to be sure that test questions are fair and have a definitive answer. Each question is independently reviewed by at least 12 test developers or educators before it makes it onto an actual SAT.[1] In addition, each test question is pre-tested on 1,000–3,000 students to be sure it performs as expected prior to inclusion on a real SAT.[2] Given these checks, you can be assured that the questions are well-crafted. Do not overthink the questions because you are looking for a trick. Instead, give the SAT the benefit of the doubt, and if you do not see a correct answer, review the passages and the questions to be sure you did not miss anything.
10. **What works for one student may not work for another.** This book provides you with a variety of strategic tools—use whatever works best for your personal situation. Students differ in terms of how quickly they read, how much they comprehend, their knowledge of English grammar, how much math they have taken, and their competency with different types of math problems. Just because a strategy worked well for your friend does not necessarily mean it would work well for you. Use this book to fine-tune the strategies and review the content knowledge that *you* need.

How can I manage test anxiety?

Like with other major performances—such as ones in music, athletics, or theater—it is natural to have some anxiety. While some anxiety may release adrenaline that helps sharpen your focus and improve your stamina, too much anxiety can be problematic. Here are some tips to help keep your anxiety under control:

- **Make your practice as realistic as possible.** Take a full-length practice test under timed conditions with the usual breaks. Eat the same food and have the same drink you will have during your break. See how your body and your mind perform under realistic conditions, and then make any needed adjustments. By practicing like this before the actual test, you will both consciously and subconsciously know what to expect.

[1] https://collegereadiness.collegeboard.org/educators/higher-ed/test-validity-design/test-development

[2] https://collegereadiness.collegeboard.org/pdf/sat-suite-assessments-technical-manual.pdf

- **Realize that SAT results are but one part of a college application.** While test results are perhaps the easiest part of the application to quantify, they are one component in a holistic admissions process. If the other parts of your application are quite strong, the test results will be less important. If you have not done as well in school or have not had as many extra-curricular opportunities, the SAT can give you an opportunity to showcase your college readiness.
- **Start early with your testing.** Plan on taking the SAT after you have completed Algebra 2 so you have nearly all the math the test requires. If you take the test early, you will not feel like your entire college application is riding on your performance on a single day; instead, you will know that you have multiple opportunities to retake the exam. Colleges routinely look at your best performance, and if your early performance is not all that great, it should not be an issue.
- **You will likely be able to "superscore."** More and more schools allow superscoring, i.e., taking the best score from each of the two test sections over multiple test dates. For example, if you scored a 700 on the Evidence-Based Reading and Writing and a 500 on the Math on a test in March, and then scored a 600 on the Evidence-Based Reading and Writing and a 700 on the Math on a test in May, your superscore would be $700 + 700 = 1{,}400$. So, if one-half of the test does not go as well, it is okay—you can focus on the more challenging half on the next test date.

How should I use this book to study for the SAT?

Use previous test results to help you target your preparation. If you have previously taken the PSAT or SAT, look at your scores on the College Board website: *https://collegereadiness.collegeboard.org*

For the PSAT, the entire test you took will be made freely available to you in your online account. For the SAT, you may be able to purchase the Question-and-Answer Service for your test date. This gives you full access to the test that you took, your answers, and the correct answers. Learn more about the Question-and-Answer Service here: *https://collegereadiness.collegeboard.org/sat/scores/verifying-scores*

If you have not previously taken the PSAT or SAT, take the Diagnostic Test at the beginning of this book to help you determine the areas that you most need to review. Each chapter in this book has extensive review and drills for each type of question or passage you will face so you can focus on the areas that need the most work. Including the Diagnostic Test, there is a total of eight practice SATs in both the book and its online resources. Practice full-length tests under timed conditions to develop your problem-solving skills and learn to manage your timing.

How should I study given different amounts of time to prepare?

If you only have one day to prepare:

- Review the general SAT strategies in this introductory chapter.
- Skim through an entire SAT practice test to become familiar with the directions, timing, and format.
- Try a few questions from each section (Reading, Writing and Language, Math No Calculator, and Math with Calculator).
- Do not stay up late to cram before the test—get a good night's sleep.

If you have about a week to prepare:

- Review any past PSAT or SAT test results to determine where you need to focus your preparation.
- Read the test-taking strategies in each of the book chapters so you have a clear plan for how to attack the exam.
- Study the specific review and drills that are most relevant given your strengths and weaknesses.
- Take a full-length timed practice test. Score it, review your answers, and analyze what you need to do better in terms of timing and strategy to do your best on the actual test.

If you have a month or more to prepare:

- Take the full-length Diagnostic Test.
- Work through all of the book chapters to review important strategies and content. Pay especially close attention to the areas where you struggled in the Diagnostic Test.
- Take additional full-length practice SAT tests and review the in-depth solutions for each question that you missed.

The bottom line with your preparation—it is not just practice that makes perfect . . . it is *perfect* practice that makes perfect. In particular:

- Actively assess where you need the most help and target your review accordingly. Do not skip over challenging sections to review and do not waste time reviewing concepts you already fully understand.
- Practice using the timing you will use on the actual test. Do not rush through a practice test just to get it done, only to find that you have made a number of careless errors. Pace yourself just as you would want to do on test day.

What are some things I can do beyond this book to prepare?

The SAT assesses your fundamental academic skills and your readiness for college-level work. So, anything you can do to build your reading, writing, and mathematical problem-solving skills will help you perform better on the SAT.

- **Take rigorous courses**, like Advanced Placement and International Baccalaureate classes. The College Board administers the AP exam program, so there is considerable crossover between the skills assessed on AP exams and the skills assessed on the SAT.
- **Read widely on your own.** Students who read for fun tend to find the reading comprehension section easier than students who look at reading as a boring chore. Go to your local library, talk to a librarian, and find a book or magazine that really interests you. Install an e-reader on your phone so that you can easily read when you have spare time.
- **Do additional practice with freely available College Board tests.** The College Board has made eight full-length practice tests available. You can download them directly from their website.

  With the tests and drills in this book along with the free material from College Board, you will have more than enough material to use to get ready for test day.

Let's get to work!

PART 2
Diagnostic Test

SAT Diagnostic Test

A full-length SAT Diagnostic Test is on the pages that follow. Allow about three hours and 15 minutes of uninterrupted time to complete the entire test with breaks. Find a spot to take the test where you will not be distracted. You can take a ten-minute break after the Reading test and another five-minute break after the Math (No Calculator) test.

Completing this Diagnostic Test will help you determine your SAT strengths and weaknesses:

- How was your time management? Did you finish ahead of time or did you need more time?
- Are there certain types of Reading questions you find challenging?
- Do particular reading passages give you more difficulty than others?
- Are there English grammar concepts you need to review?
- Do some types of Writing and Language questions give you more trouble than others?
- Do you need to review or learn some math concepts?
- What kinds of Math questions are toughest for you?

After completing the test, review your answers with the **Diagnostic Test Analysis Guide** to determine what types of questions and concepts you most need to study. The book chapters are aligned with the question types presented in the Diagnostic Test Analysis Guide so you can easily target your preparation.

Good luck!

ANSWER SHEET
Diagnostic Test

Section 1: Reading

1. Ⓐ Ⓑ Ⓒ Ⓓ	**14.** Ⓐ Ⓑ Ⓒ Ⓓ	**27.** Ⓐ Ⓑ Ⓒ Ⓓ	**40.** Ⓐ Ⓑ Ⓒ Ⓓ
2. Ⓐ Ⓑ Ⓒ Ⓓ	**15.** Ⓐ Ⓑ Ⓒ Ⓓ	**28.** Ⓐ Ⓑ Ⓒ Ⓓ	**41.** Ⓐ Ⓑ Ⓒ Ⓓ
3. Ⓐ Ⓑ Ⓒ Ⓓ	**16.** Ⓐ Ⓑ Ⓒ Ⓓ	**29.** Ⓐ Ⓑ Ⓒ Ⓓ	**42.** Ⓐ Ⓑ Ⓒ Ⓓ
4. Ⓐ Ⓑ Ⓒ Ⓓ	**17.** Ⓐ Ⓑ Ⓒ Ⓓ	**30.** Ⓐ Ⓑ Ⓒ Ⓓ	**43.** Ⓐ Ⓑ Ⓒ Ⓓ
5. Ⓐ Ⓑ Ⓒ Ⓓ	**18.** Ⓐ Ⓑ Ⓒ Ⓓ	**31.** Ⓐ Ⓑ Ⓒ Ⓓ	**44.** Ⓐ Ⓑ Ⓒ Ⓓ
6. Ⓐ Ⓑ Ⓒ Ⓓ	**19.** Ⓐ Ⓑ Ⓒ Ⓓ	**32.** Ⓐ Ⓑ Ⓒ Ⓓ	**45.** Ⓐ Ⓑ Ⓒ Ⓓ
7. Ⓐ Ⓑ Ⓒ Ⓓ	**20.** Ⓐ Ⓑ Ⓒ Ⓓ	**33.** Ⓐ Ⓑ Ⓒ Ⓓ	**46.** Ⓐ Ⓑ Ⓒ Ⓓ
8. Ⓐ Ⓑ Ⓒ Ⓓ	**21.** Ⓐ Ⓑ Ⓒ Ⓓ	**34.** Ⓐ Ⓑ Ⓒ Ⓓ	**47.** Ⓐ Ⓑ Ⓒ Ⓓ
9. Ⓐ Ⓑ Ⓒ Ⓓ	**22.** Ⓐ Ⓑ Ⓒ Ⓓ	**35.** Ⓐ Ⓑ Ⓒ Ⓓ	**48.** Ⓐ Ⓑ Ⓒ Ⓓ
10. Ⓐ Ⓑ Ⓒ Ⓓ	**23.** Ⓐ Ⓑ Ⓒ Ⓓ	**36.** Ⓐ Ⓑ Ⓒ Ⓓ	**49.** Ⓐ Ⓑ Ⓒ Ⓓ
11. Ⓐ Ⓑ Ⓒ Ⓓ	**24.** Ⓐ Ⓑ Ⓒ Ⓓ	**37.** Ⓐ Ⓑ Ⓒ Ⓓ	**50.** Ⓐ Ⓑ Ⓒ Ⓓ
12. Ⓐ Ⓑ Ⓒ Ⓓ	**25.** Ⓐ Ⓑ Ⓒ Ⓓ	**38.** Ⓐ Ⓑ Ⓒ Ⓓ	**51.** Ⓐ Ⓑ Ⓒ Ⓓ
13. Ⓐ Ⓑ Ⓒ Ⓓ	**26.** Ⓐ Ⓑ Ⓒ Ⓓ	**39.** Ⓐ Ⓑ Ⓒ Ⓓ	**52.** Ⓐ Ⓑ Ⓒ Ⓓ

Section 2: Writing and Language

1. Ⓐ Ⓑ Ⓒ Ⓓ	**12.** Ⓐ Ⓑ Ⓒ Ⓓ	**23.** Ⓐ Ⓑ Ⓒ Ⓓ	**34.** Ⓐ Ⓑ Ⓒ Ⓓ
2. Ⓐ Ⓑ Ⓒ Ⓓ	**13.** Ⓐ Ⓑ Ⓒ Ⓓ	**24.** Ⓐ Ⓑ Ⓒ Ⓓ	**35.** Ⓐ Ⓑ Ⓒ Ⓓ
3. Ⓐ Ⓑ Ⓒ Ⓓ	**14.** Ⓐ Ⓑ Ⓒ Ⓓ	**25.** Ⓐ Ⓑ Ⓒ Ⓓ	**36.** Ⓐ Ⓑ Ⓒ Ⓓ
4. Ⓐ Ⓑ Ⓒ Ⓓ	**15.** Ⓐ Ⓑ Ⓒ Ⓓ	**26.** Ⓐ Ⓑ Ⓒ Ⓓ	**37.** Ⓐ Ⓑ Ⓒ Ⓓ
5. Ⓐ Ⓑ Ⓒ Ⓓ	**16.** Ⓐ Ⓑ Ⓒ Ⓓ	**27.** Ⓐ Ⓑ Ⓒ Ⓓ	**38.** Ⓐ Ⓑ Ⓒ Ⓓ
6. Ⓐ Ⓑ Ⓒ Ⓓ	**17.** Ⓐ Ⓑ Ⓒ Ⓓ	**28.** Ⓐ Ⓑ Ⓒ Ⓓ	**39.** Ⓐ Ⓑ Ⓒ Ⓓ
7. Ⓐ Ⓑ Ⓒ Ⓓ	**18.** Ⓐ Ⓑ Ⓒ Ⓓ	**29.** Ⓐ Ⓑ Ⓒ Ⓓ	**40.** Ⓐ Ⓑ Ⓒ Ⓓ
8. Ⓐ Ⓑ Ⓒ Ⓓ	**19.** Ⓐ Ⓑ Ⓒ Ⓓ	**30.** Ⓐ Ⓑ Ⓒ Ⓓ	**41.** Ⓐ Ⓑ Ⓒ Ⓓ
9. Ⓐ Ⓑ Ⓒ Ⓓ	**20.** Ⓐ Ⓑ Ⓒ Ⓓ	**31.** Ⓐ Ⓑ Ⓒ Ⓓ	**42.** Ⓐ Ⓑ Ⓒ Ⓓ
10. Ⓐ Ⓑ Ⓒ Ⓓ	**21.** Ⓐ Ⓑ Ⓒ Ⓓ	**32.** Ⓐ Ⓑ Ⓒ Ⓓ	**43.** Ⓐ Ⓑ Ⓒ Ⓓ
11. Ⓐ Ⓑ Ⓒ Ⓓ	**22.** Ⓐ Ⓑ Ⓒ Ⓓ	**33.** Ⓐ Ⓑ Ⓒ Ⓓ	**44.** Ⓐ Ⓑ Ⓒ Ⓓ

ANSWER SHEET
Diagnostic Test

Section 3: Math (No Calculator)

1. Ⓐ Ⓑ Ⓒ Ⓓ
2. Ⓐ Ⓑ Ⓒ Ⓓ
3. Ⓐ Ⓑ Ⓒ Ⓓ
4. Ⓐ Ⓑ Ⓒ Ⓓ
5. Ⓐ Ⓑ Ⓒ Ⓓ
6. Ⓐ Ⓑ Ⓒ Ⓓ
7. Ⓐ Ⓑ Ⓒ Ⓓ
8. Ⓐ Ⓑ Ⓒ Ⓓ
9. Ⓐ Ⓑ Ⓒ Ⓓ
10. Ⓐ Ⓑ Ⓒ Ⓓ
11. Ⓐ Ⓑ Ⓒ Ⓓ
12. Ⓐ Ⓑ Ⓒ Ⓓ
13. Ⓐ Ⓑ Ⓒ Ⓓ
14. Ⓐ Ⓑ Ⓒ Ⓓ
15. Ⓐ Ⓑ Ⓒ Ⓓ

16.

17.

18.

19.

20.

ANSWER SHEET
Diagnostic Test

Section 4: Math (Calculator)

1. Ⓐ Ⓑ Ⓒ Ⓓ
2. Ⓐ Ⓑ Ⓒ Ⓓ
3. Ⓐ Ⓑ Ⓒ Ⓓ
4. Ⓐ Ⓑ Ⓒ Ⓓ
5. Ⓐ Ⓑ Ⓒ Ⓓ
6. Ⓐ Ⓑ Ⓒ Ⓓ
7. Ⓐ Ⓑ Ⓒ Ⓓ
8. Ⓐ Ⓑ Ⓒ Ⓓ
9. Ⓐ Ⓑ Ⓒ Ⓓ
10. Ⓐ Ⓑ Ⓒ Ⓓ
11. Ⓐ Ⓑ Ⓒ Ⓓ
12. Ⓐ Ⓑ Ⓒ Ⓓ
13. Ⓐ Ⓑ Ⓒ Ⓓ
14. Ⓐ Ⓑ Ⓒ Ⓓ
15. Ⓐ Ⓑ Ⓒ Ⓓ
16. Ⓐ Ⓑ Ⓒ Ⓓ
17. Ⓐ Ⓑ Ⓒ Ⓓ
18. Ⓐ Ⓑ Ⓒ Ⓓ
19. Ⓐ Ⓑ Ⓒ Ⓓ
20. Ⓐ Ⓑ Ⓒ Ⓓ
21. Ⓐ Ⓑ Ⓒ Ⓓ
22. Ⓐ Ⓑ Ⓒ Ⓓ
23. Ⓐ Ⓑ Ⓒ Ⓓ
24. Ⓐ Ⓑ Ⓒ Ⓓ
25. Ⓐ Ⓑ Ⓒ Ⓓ
26. Ⓐ Ⓑ Ⓒ Ⓓ
27. Ⓐ Ⓑ Ⓒ Ⓓ
28. Ⓐ Ⓑ Ⓒ Ⓓ
29. Ⓐ Ⓑ Ⓒ Ⓓ
30. Ⓐ Ⓑ Ⓒ Ⓓ

31.

32.

33.

34.

35.

36.

37.

38.

Diagnostic Test

READING TEST

65 MINUTES, 52 QUESTIONS

DIRECTIONS: Each passage or pair of passages is accompanied by several questions. After reading the passage(s), choose the best answer to each question based on what is indicated explicitly or implicitly in the passage(s) or in the associated graphics.

Questions 1–10 are based on the following passage.

The following is an excerpt from the novel The Jungle *by Upton Sinclair, written in 1906.*

During the early part of the winter, the family had had money enough to live and a little over to pay their debts with; but when the earnings of Jurgis fell from nine or ten dollars a week to five or six, there was no longer anything to spare. The winter went, and the spring came, and found them still living thus from hand to mouth, hanging on day by day, with literally not a month's wages between them and starvation. Marija was in despair, for there was still no word about the reopening of the canning factory, and her savings were almost entirely gone. She had had to give up all idea of marrying then; the family could not get along without her—though for that matter she was likely soon to become a burden even upon them, for when her money was all gone, they would have to pay back what they owed her in board. So Jurgis and Ona and Teta Elzbieta would hold anxious conferences until late at night, trying to figure how they could manage this too without starving.

Such were the cruel terms upon which their life was possible, that they might never have nor expect a single instant's respite from worry, a single instant in which they were not haunted by the thought of money. They would no sooner escape, as by a miracle, from one difficulty, than a new one would come into view. In addition to all their physical hardships, there was thus a constant strain upon their minds; they were harried all day and nearly all night by worry and fear. This was in truth not living; it was scarcely even existing, and they felt that it was too little for the price they paid. They were willing to work all the time; and when people did their best, ought they not to be able to keep alive?

There seemed never to be an end to the things they had to buy and to the unforeseen contingencies. Once their water pipes froze and burst; and when, in their ignorance, they thawed them out, they had a terrifying flood in their house. It happened while the men were away, and poor Elzbieta rushed out into the

GO ON TO THE NEXT PAGE

street screaming for help, for she did not even know whether the flood could be stopped, or whether they were ruined for life. It was nearly as bad as the latter, they found in the end, for the plumber charged them seventy-five cents an hour, and seventy-five cents for another man who had stood and watched him, and included all the time the two had been going and coming, and also a charge for all sorts of material and extras. And then again, when they went to pay their January's installment on the house, the agent terrified them by asking them if they had had the insurance attended to yet. In answer to their inquiry he showed them a clause in the deed which provided that they were to keep the house insured for one thousand dollars, as soon as the present policy ran out, which would happen in a few days. Poor Elzbieta, upon whom again fell the blow, demanded how much it would cost them. Seven dollars, the man said; and that night came Jurgis, grim and determined, requesting that the agent would be good enough to inform him, once for all, as to all the expenses they were liable for. The deed was signed now, he said, with sarcasm proper to the new way of life he had learned—the deed was signed, and so the agent had no longer anything to gain by keeping quiet. And Jurgis looked the fellow squarely in the eye, and so the fellow wasted no time in conventional protests, but read him the deed. They would have to renew the insurance every year; they would have to pay the taxes, about ten dollars a year; they would have to pay the water tax, about six dollars a year—(Jurgis silently resolved to shut off the hydrant). This, besides the interest and the monthly installments, would be all—unless by chance the city should happen to decide to put in a sewer or to lay a sidewalk. Yes, said the agent, they would have to have these, whether they wanted them or not, if the city said so.

1. The overall feeling felt by the primary characters throughout the passage can best be summarized as

   (A) unbridled optimism.
   (B) stoic acceptance.
   (C) vengeful rage.
   (D) melancholy hopelessness.

2. Marija's attitude toward her family members is one of

   (A) increasing resentment.
   (B) mild disapproval.
   (C) dutiful obligation.
   (D) outright hostility.

3. As used in line 30, "strain" most closely means

   (A) sifting.
   (B) variety.
   (C) burden.
   (D) filtration.

4. It can be reasonably inferred that a large obstacle to budgetary planning by Jurgis, Ona, and Teta is

   (A) the high likelihood of unforeseen expenses.
   (B) their lack of financial discipline.
   (C) an unwillingness to openly discuss monetary matters.
   (D) the impossibility of finding a place to live.

5. Which option gives the best evidence for the answer to the previous question?

   (A) Lines 12–16 ("She had... upon them")
   (B) Lines 18–21 ("So Jurgis... starving")
   (C) Lines 32–34 ("This was... paid")
   (D) Lines 37–39 ("There seemed... contingencies")

GO ON TO THE NEXT PAGE

6. The passage suggests that the family's overall work ethic is
   (A) rather weak.
   (B) very strong.
   (C) fairly moderate.
   (D) easily satisfactory.

7. The feeling that Jurgis has toward authorities in his community is best described as one of
   (A) humility.
   (B) skepticism.
   (C) appreciation.
   (D) commitment.

8. Which option gives the best evidence for the answer to the previous question?
   (A) Lines 39–42 ("Once... house")
   (B) Lines 56–61 ("In answer... few days")
   (C) Lines 67–71 ("The deed... quiet")
   (D) Lines 82–84 ("Yes... said so")

9. As used in line 72 "squarely" most closely means
   (A) traditionally.
   (B) directly.
   (C) corruptly.
   (D) humbly.

10. The narrative in lines 61–84 ("Poor Elzbieta... said so") primarily serves to illustrate how
    (A) much of a challenge Elzbieta and Jurgis had in securing physically safe employment.
    (B) easy it was for Elzbieta and Jurgis to verify the terms of their housing contracts.
    (C) difficult it was for Elzbieta and Jurgis to determine their precise financial obligations.
    (D) likely it was that Elzbieta and Jurgis would resort to violent confrontation to achieve their goals.

Questions 11–21 are based on the following passage and supplementary material.

The following is an article about bedbugs, authored in 2020.

Many parents, as they lovingly tuck their children into bed, repeat a short rhyme that has been around for centuries: night-night, sleep tight, don't let the bedbugs bite! This phrase refers to a time when even the wealthy had to deal with the constant scourge of bedbugs and other pests that preyed on sleeping humans. With the advent of modern pesticides, bedbugs were, for a time, largely an issue of the past. However, in the past few years they have come back with a vengeance, once again plaguing people rich and poor and proving very difficult to eradicate.

One key reason *C. lecturlarius* (bedbugs) can be so difficult to remove is their physical properties. They are tiny brown bugs that live solely on the blood of other animals, so edible poison traps won't work the way they do for ants. In addition, they can live months without food which makes starving them out nearly impossible, and they lay eggs which are impervious to regular pest control methods and stick in unreachable nooks and crannies. Most methods that work on adults do not work on eggs and vice versa. To add to the difficulty, the microscopic size of the eggs makes early stage infestations nearly impossible to detect. In the 1950s, however, with the development of dichloro-diphenyl-trichloroethane (DDT), bedbugs met their match. This chemical, when sprayed on a bed, allowed for up to a year of protection from bedbugs. Humanity lived for roughly 40 years without a major infestation. In fact, scientists had a tough time finding live specimens to study.

GO ON TO THE NEXT PAGE

Then, in 1990s, amidst concern for its effect on wildlife, DDT was largely banned; bedbugs slowly began their comeback. By 2010 their numbers were spiking. Because of a huge increase in personal travel since the last time the bugs were an issue, they spread faster than ever. Laundromats, hotels, and libraries became vectors for transmission. Bug eggs can get tucked into suitcases when traveling, or into books that you check out from the library. In communal living areas (like apartment buildings) they can crawl from one apartment to another as they look for human hosts on which to feed. Their bites, inflicted on victims as they sleep, are painful and itchy and continue to appear if the infestation goes unchecked.

Because DDT is no longer used, the solution to these pests must be multifaceted. Most poisons and bug bombs will not work as the bugs don't need to eat and the eggs won't be affected by sprays. The first step in the process is to reduce clutter in the home. These bugs like to live in small nooks and crannies: reducing clutter reduces their living space. Then, vacuum as many porous surfaces as possible to remove any active bugs. This won't be hugely helpful since regular vacuum cleaners can't fit into the small spaces where bedbugs choose to reside, but it is a good preliminary step. Finally, the best option for killing both adults and eggs is heat treatment—this needs to be completed by a professional. Eradication specialists will bring portable heaters and temperature sensors into the space to raise the temperature to a level where the bugs can't survive. The temperature must be maintained for several hours. This treatment, combined with less effective pesticides, can lead to a full eradication.

Full eradication is quite expensive, however, and due to the recent resurgence of bedbugs as a problem, many people are unaware of the issue until the infestation in their home reaches incredibly high levels. Education seems to be the best way to help people avoid bed bug infestation as well as its associated costs and stigmas. People should educate themselves as to the best practices to avoid infestations as they travel and bring goods into their homes. Upon suspicion of infection, experts should be called promptly to eradicate the population before it gets out of control and becomes very expensive and time consuming to do so. Only through these methods can individuals have peace of mind that as they sleep that the bedbugs will not bite.

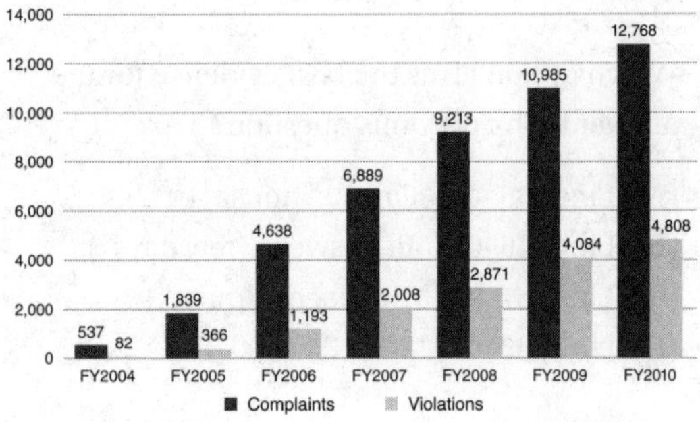

Figure 1

11. Based on the passage as a whole, bedbug infestations over the past century can best be described as

    (A) consistently eradicated with only a recent uptick in prevalence.
    (B) first a major problem, then generally eradicated, and then gradually resurgent.
    (C) steadily declining over time, leading to a widespread eradication today.
    (D) initially a mild concern, then a significant issue, and yet again a mild concern today.

GO ON TO THE NEXT PAGE

12. The main function of lines 1–4 ("Many... bite!") is to
    (A) engage the reader in the passage's topic by referring to likely common knowledge.
    (B) demonstrate the ever-present danger of a household pest.
    (C) show how drawing upon childhood memories can lead to scientific discoveries.
    (D) explain why bedbugs have drawn more investigative interest than other insects.

13. The primary purpose of lines 14–27 ("One key... detect") is to
    (A) explain the exterminating techniques most popular among cleaners today.
    (B) illustrate the unique challenges in attempting to exterminate bedbugs.
    (C) showcase the evolutionary advantages that bedbugs have over other animals.
    (D) demonstrate the health dangers that bedbugs pose to humans.

14. It can be reasonably inferred from the passage that DDT is no longer used today because of
    (A) excessive costs.
    (B) more effective replacement technology.
    (C) environmental concerns.
    (D) no need for its application.

15. Which option gives the best evidence for the answer to the previous question?
    (A) Lines 24–25 ("Most... versa")
    (B) Lines 36–37 ("Then... banned")
    (C) Lines 52–53 ("Because... multifaceted")
    (D) Lines 74–78 ("Full... levels")

16. As used in line 51, "unchecked" most closely means
    (A) unexamined.
    (B) unknown.
    (C) uncontrolled.
    (D) disappointing.

17. The passage suggests that eradication of bedbugs using heat and moderately effective pesticides is
    (A) the only way to effectively control bedbugs.
    (B) less expensive than DDT pesticide treatments.
    (C) most useful when bedbugs are beginning to emerge in a home.
    (D) less preferable to preventative measures.

18. As used in line 82, "practices" most closely means
    (A) methods.
    (B) performances.
    (C) eliminations.
    (D) observations.

19. According to Figure 1, the relationship between bedbug complaints and bedbug violations can best be described as
    (A) inversely related.
    (B) generally proportional.
    (C) somewhat equivalent.
    (D) mostly not correlated.

20. Based on Figure 1, if the number of bedbug violations continued to increase at the same rate, what would be the most reasonable estimation for the approximate number of bedbug violations in New York City in the year 2012?
    (A) 6,500
    (B) 9,000
    (C) 12,500
    (D) 14,000

21. The data from Figure 1 best provide evidence to support which of the following claims from the passage?
    (A) Lines 10–13 ("However... eradicate")
    (B) Lines 32–35 ("Humanity... study")
    (C) Lines 48–51 ("Their bites... unchecked")
    (D) Lines 78–80 ("Education... stigmas")

GO ON TO THE NEXT PAGE

Questions 22–31 are based on the following passage.

Peace, Patriotism, and Fireworks, authored in 2020

The night sky erupted with great displays of sound and light. Every couple of minutes, from dusk till late, the loud, explosive sounds would shake the sky and some unsuspecting and innocent below. It is not lightning or anything nefarious; rather, it is meant to be a symbol of patriotism. It was a week before the Fourth of July, a day meant to celebrate the United States and those who defend it, and the fireworks had already begun. As red, white, and blue colors streaked across the sky, some reveled with pride for their nation, others waited for the explosive reminders of trauma to end, and I sat with my dog as he shivered in fright.

Setting off fireworks in celebration of the independence of the United States is considered a tradition today. This tradition started in Boston during the second celebration of the Fourth of July; these displays continued each year thereafter in more cities across the United States. By the mid-nineteenth century, fireworks had become widely available, making it customary for citizens to blast their own into the night sky. While firework displays were historically limited to one night a year, they now go on for days, even weeks, spouting patriotism and enjoyment as their motivation. Beside these seemingly positive motivations, it can be easy to ignore the consequences.

One consequence is that fireworks may act as a trigger, reminding veterans who suffer from post-traumatic stress disorder (PTSD) of traumatic events from their service. While many veterans are prepared for the explosion-like sounds, firework displays beginning a full week before and continuing a full week after the Fourth of July can be draining. A whopping twenty percent of veterans are thought to suffer from PTSD, and if even a small fraction of them are triggered by fireworks it begs the question: are the joys of fireworks worth the consequences?

Our nation's heroes are not the only ones who may experience the detrimental effects of fireworks. Furry companions also can be frightened by the loud blasts above for nights on end. Veterinary practices, animal shelters, and other animal organizations frequently send out reminders in the weeks leading up to the Fourth of July to protect our pets from running away out of fright. These may include reminders to microchip our pets, keep pets indoors, and take pets on walks early in the day in case they are too afraid to relieve themselves during the fireworks. Their efforts are not without reason. In fact, more pets run away on the night of the Fourth of July than any other night of the year. Add the consecutive days and weeks of firework displays surrounding the Fourth of July, and it is no wonder that animal organizations go to great lengths to keep pet owners informed.

While the light and sound pollution may trigger veterans and frighten pets, the environmental pollution caused by fireworks can harm us all. Those who set off fireworks are at most risk for experiencing the negative respiratory effects, but add up all the firework displays in the weeks surrounding the Fourth of July, and the consequences for air quality are profound. Many fireworks are also set off above bodies of water. Runoff of pollutants from firework displays into lakes and streams can harm the waterways, affecting wildlife and water quality.

The weeks-long displays of fireworks are not sustainable for veterans, pets, or the environment. To truly allow those affected by fireworks peace, it may seem like a harmless option to get rid of fireworks, but this too would have its own consequences. Those who cherish this practice would feel an attack on their patriotic

GO ON TO THE NEXT PAGE

rights, others would be saddened about the end of a tradition, and the remaining would simply continue lighting fireworks. The answer does not seem to be to eradicate fireworks—they do not need to disappear from the night sky—but perhaps their colors, sounds, magic, and consequences could be limited to just that one night in early July.

22. The primary aim of this passage is to
    (A) advocate increased respect for patriotic institutions.
    (B) convince readers of the merits of a particular viewpoint.
    (C) highlight the historical basis for a national holiday.
    (D) encourage widespread civil disobedience to combat an injustice.

23. The main function of the letters in parentheses in line 32, "(PTSD)," is to
    (A) introduce an abbreviation for a key term that will be used throughout the passage.
    (B) remind readers of a definition that had been previously used in the passage.
    (C) highlight the initials of an important contributor to sociological research.
    (D) use a term with which readers will more likely be familiar to identify an artistic concept.

24. As used in line 37, "draining" most closely means
    (A) drying.
    (B) escaping.
    (C) exhausting.
    (D) unloading.

25. The passage suggests that the number of days of summer firework celebrations in the United States has
    (A) steadily decreased over time.
    (B) remained constant since the first Fourth of July.
    (C) greatly increased over the years.
    (D) approached zero due to concerns over negative health consequences.

26. Which option gives the best evidence for the answer to the previous question?
    (A) Lines 15–19 ("Setting... July")
    (B) Lines 24–27 ("While firework... motivation")
    (C) Lines 33–37 ("While many... draining")
    (D) Lines 58–61 ("Add the... informed")

27. It can be reasonably inferred from the passage that the narrator can most personally relate to those who are
    (A) pet owners.
    (B) military veterans.
    (C) patriotic advocates.
    (D) those sensitive to airborne pollutants.

28. Which option gives the best evidence for the answer to the previous question?
    (A) Lines 12–14 ("others... fright")
    (B) Lines 30–33 ("One consequence... service")
    (C) Lines 71–73 ("Runoff... quality")
    (D) Lines 79–83 ("Those who... fireworks")

29. What argumentative techniques does the author utilize in the third paragraph (lines 30–42, "One consequence... consequences")?
    (A) Historical analogies and appeals to authority
    (B) A personal anecdote and political persuasion
    (C) Metaphorical language and a humorous aside
    (D) Statistical evidence and a rhetorical question

30. As used in line 55, "reason" most closely means
    (A) belief.
    (B) justification.
    (C) mindfulness.
    (D) ambition.

GO ON TO THE NEXT PAGE

0 0 0

31. The author of the passage would most likely find which of the following to be an optimal solution to the problems that she raises?
    (A) An increase in historical education programs in schools that teach students about the importance of American independence
    (B) Newer fireworks that are able to explode somewhat higher in the air, providing illumination over a wider area
    (C) The replacement of fireworks with a laser light show that does not make noise or create smoke
    (D) Noise-cancelling headphones for people bothered by large and sudden noises to use during summer evenings

Questions 32–42 are based on the following passages.

Passage 1 is an adaptation of a letter from Daisy Bates, the president of the Arkansas State Conference of the NAACP, to the NAACP executive secretary Roy Wilkins on December 17, 1957. In it she discusses the situation in the Little Rock schools, which had recently been forced by the federal government to integrate. Passage 2 is an adaptation of the decision in the Supreme Court case Brown v. Board of Education *(1954), in which American schools were legally desegregated.*

Passage 1

Conditions are yet pretty rough in the school for the children. Last week, Minnie Jean's mother...asked me to go over to the school with her for a conference with the principal...Subject of the conference: "Firmer disciplinary measures, and the withdrawal of Minnie Jean from the glee club's Christmas program." The principal had informed Minnie Jean in withdrawing her from the program that "When it is definitely decided that [this school will be integrated] and the troops removed, then you will be able to participate in all activities." We strongly challenged this statement, which he denied making in that fashion.

We also pointed out that the treatment of the children had been getting steadily worse for the last two weeks in the form of kicking, spitting, and general abuse. As a result of our visit, stronger measures are being taken against the white students who are guilty of committing these offenses. For instance, a boy who had been suspended for two weeks, ...on his return to school, the first day he knocked Gloria Rey into her locker. As a result of our visit, he was given an indefinite suspension.

The superintendent of schools also requested a conference the same afternoon...Here, again we pointed out that a three-day suspension given Hugh Williams for a sneak attack perpetrated on one of the...boys which knocked him out, and required a doctor's attention, was not sufficient punishment. We also informed him that our investigation revealed that there were many pupils willing to help if given the opportunity, and that President Eisenhower was very much concerned about the Little Rock crisis. He has stated his willingness to come down and address the student body if invited by student leaders of the school. This information was passed on to the principal of the school, but we have not been assured that leadership would be given to children in the school who are willing to organize for law and order. However, we have not abandoned the idea. Last Friday...I was asked to call Washington and see if we could get FBI men placed in the school...

Passage 2

[These students] seek the aid of the courts in obtaining admission to the public schools of their community on a nonsegregated basis. In each instance, they had been denied admission to schools attended by white children under laws requiring or permitting segregation according to race. This segregation was alleged to deprive the plaintiffs of the equal protection of the laws under the Fourteenth Amendment... [In prior cases it was held that] equality of treatment is accorded when the races are provided substantially equal facilities even though these facilities be separate...

The plaintiffs contend that segregated public schools are not "equal" and cannot be made "equal," and that hence they are deprived of the equal protection of the laws...

We come then to the question presented: Does segregation of children in public schools solely on the basis of race, even though the physical facilities and other "tangible" factors may be equal, deprive the children of the minority group of equal educational opportunities? We believe that it does.

Segregation of white and [minority] children in public schools has a detrimental effect upon the [minority] children. The impact is greater when it has the sanction of the law, for the policy of separating the races is usually interpreted as denoting the inferiority of the [minority] group. A sense of inferiority affects the motivation of a child to learn. Segregation with the sanction of law, therefore, has a tendency to [slow] the educational and mental development of [minority] children and to deprive them of some of the benefits they would receive in a racially integrated school system...

We conclude that in the field of public education the doctrine of "separate but equal" has no place. Separate educational facilities are inherently unequal. Therefore, we hold that the plaintiffs and others similarly situated for whom the actions have been brought are, by reason of the segregation complained of, deprived of the equal protection of the laws guaranteed by the Fourteenth Amendment. This disposition makes unnecessary any discussion whether such segregation also violates the Due Process Clause of the Fourteenth Amendment.

32. Which selection from Passage 1 best indicates that Daisy Bates succeeding in convincing school officials of her point of view?

(A) Lines 13–14 ("We strongly...fashion")
(B) Lines 15–18 ("We also...abuse")
(C) Lines 18–25 ("As a...suspension")
(D) Lines 37–39 ("He has...school")

33. It can be most reasonably inferred that the author of Passage 1 has what attitude toward President Eisenhower?

(A) Appreciation for his willingness to intervene in a situation
(B) Disgust with his implementation of policies encouraging segregation
(C) Indifference toward his lack of concern with racial injustice
(D) Respect for his ability to ignore calls for federal interference

34. As used in line 46, "placed" most closely means

(A) settled.
(B) stationed.
(C) planted.
(D) deposited.

35. The students in the Little Rock Schools as described in Passage 1 are

(A) uniformly skeptical of racial diversity.
(B) generally eager to welcome new students.
(C) a mixture of open-mindedness and hostility.
(D) strongly inclined toward deceitful practices.

GO ON TO THE NEXT PAGE

36. If someone were to argue to the author of Passage 2 that the plaintiffs should pursue other avenues besides the Supreme Court to achieve their goals, the author of Passage 2 would most likely respond that

(A) such an attempt is worthwhile given the likelihood that the Supreme Court will be unable to settle the issue.
(B) they had already attempted to resolve the matter through other authorities and were denied.
(C) segregation in this case is best adjudicated by action of the United States Congress.
(D) they are as likely to find success in their current argument before the Supreme Court as they were in their previous arguments.

37. The author of Passage 2 most likely places the term "equal" in quotation marks in line 61 in order to

(A) show the consistency of the plaintiffs' ideas with educational practices.
(B) emphasize the inherent inequality in having segregated schools.
(C) quote the personal accounts of eyewitnesses to injustice.
(D) set aside a largely unfamiliar word for a definition.

38. Passage 2 most strongly suggests that minority students at segregated schools are usually

(A) educationally disadvantaged relative to students at integrated schools.
(B) afforded extracurricular opportunities on par with students at all-white schools.
(C) unaware of the lesser quality of their educational experience.
(D) willing to engage in acts of civil disobedience in order to effect lasting change.

39. Which option gives the best evidence for the answer to the previous question?

(A) Lines 50–53 ("In each... race")
(B) Lines 56–59 ("In prior... separate")
(C) Lines 78–83 ("Segregation... system")
(D) Lines 92–95 ("This disposition... Amendment")

40. Which choice best summarizes the differences in the argumentative approach between the two passages?

(A) Passage 1 appeals to historical precedent, while Passage 2 appeals to the emotions of readers.
(B) Passage 1 relies on observational evidence, while Passage 2 relies on philosophical consistency.
(C) Passage 1 utilizes statistics, while Passage 2 utilizes firsthand accounts.
(D) Passage 1 is sensitive to a lack of equality, while Passage 2 is dismissive of such a concern.

41. Which passage has a wider intended audience and why?

(A) Passage 1 since it is written in a more approachable style than Passage 2.
(B) Passage 1 since it is written as a letter from one official to another.
(C) Passage 2 since it announces and justifies a change to public policy.
(D) Passage 2 since it considers the specific personal hardships of the plaintiffs.

GO ON TO THE NEXT PAGE

42. The author of Passage 1 would most likely argue that the solution to racial inequality outlined in Passage 2 is

    (A) inadequate, because even with shared facilities, unequal treatment can still persist.
    (B) sufficient, because with a common school building, racial hostility will inevitably diminish.
    (C) disappointing, because separate facilities are inherently unequal.
    (D) satisfying, since conflict between students immediately decreased once schools achieved full integration.

Questions 43–52 are based on the following passage and supplementary material.

Friedel-Crafts Reactions, written in 2020

Benzene is an organic compound originally discovered in the early 1800s. It contains six carbon atoms that connect to form an aromatic ring, with each carbon atom also connected to one hydrogen atom. Naturally, it is a by-product of volcanic eruptions and forest fires. Today, it is also a by-product of car exhaust and tobacco smoke. On its own, it is known as a volatile organic compound (VOC) that is carcinogenic to humans. Despite this, chemists have researched ways to modify benzene since its discovery. Scientists hope that by modifying benzene, they can find more uses for the molecule.

One such duo is Charles Friedel and James Crafts who, in the late 1800s, published a technique that they believed added a single alkyl sidechain to the benzene molecule. This modification technique is now known as Friedel-Crafts Alkylation. It was originally thought to be revolutionary, but was soon proven to be ineffective due to one unexpected flaw: the polyalkylation of benzene. Unfortunately, Friedel and Crafts did not realize that by adding a single alkyl sidechain, the benzene ring would become more reactive. This meant that the benzene ring would again react after the first reaction, thus adding another sidechain. This process would repeat until the benzene ring was covered in sidechains. Their technique not only added one sidechain—It added six.

Though Friedel and Crafts discovered a new chemical reaction, this reaction technique was virtually useless to the scientific community because it lacked selectivity. Selectivity causes a reaction to favor one product over another potential product of the reaction. Without selectivity, it is impossible for chemists to isolate the products of their reaction. Not being able to separate one product from another makes a reaction useless because even a small alteration in a molecule can result in adverse effects.

A famous example showing the importance of the selectivity is the case of a drug known as thalidomide. This drug was marketed toward pregnant women in the mid-1900s with promises to alleviate morning sickness. What the pharmaceutical company that marketed this drug and consumers did not know is that the reaction behind the making of this drug produced two products with remarkably similar structures. One structure was a sedative while the other was teratogenic, meaning it could disrupt the development of a fetus. The drug was banned from production after this fact was realized, but not before countless children around the world had been born with severe birth defects. The negative consequences from the use of thalidomide hurt the favorability of Friedel-Crafts reactions for a period of time.

Fortunately, scientists found a way to avoid the negative impact of chemical selectivity by implementing a more controlled reaction process. Scientists modified the benzene reaction to produce a product similar to their original intent, but one that did not add multiple sidechains to the benzene ring. This modified technique came to be known as Friedel-Crafts Acylation, a now widely used technique in the production of benzene-containing products.

This technique adds a single acyl sidechain to a benzene ring. The addition of the acyl sidechain makes the benzene ring less reactive, preventing multiple sidechains from being added to the benzene ring. Though the sidechain formed through this technique is not the single alkyl sidechain Friedel and Craft had intended, chemists are easily able to achieve an alkyl sidechain product using an additional reduction reaction.

Since the transition from alkylation to acylation for benzene reactions, chemists' abilities to safely modify benzene have expanded exponentially. What seemed revolutionary in the late 1800s is now part of undergraduate organic chemistry experiments in courses throughout universities worldwide. Benzene is no longer solely thought of as a carcinogenic and volatile compound. It now used in a variety of products including plastics, drugs, pesticides, detergents, etc. Its importance to modern chemistry, materials science and pharmaceuticals is unquestioned in the scientific community.

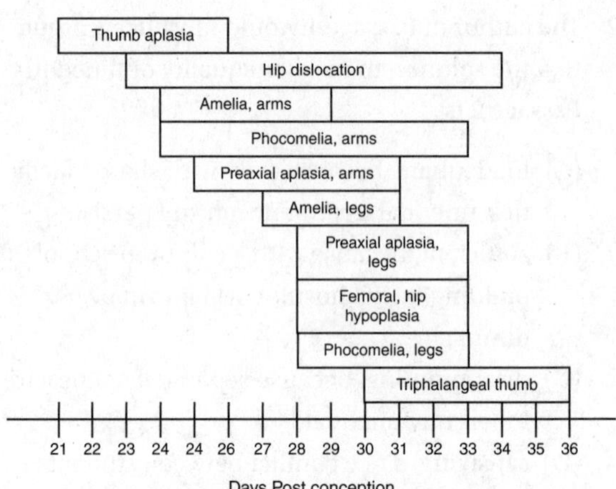

Critical exposure periods for thalidomide-associated developmental defects during human development. Source: *Thalidomide: The Tragedy of Birth Defects and the Effective Treatment of Disease,* by James Kim. Published in 2011.

Figure 2

43. Which of the following best explains why the author most likely included the discussion of thalidomide in the passage?

    (A) To use a specific example to make a general point
    (B) To analyze the success of a scientific technique
    (C) To illustrate an argument with a personal anecdote
    (D) To consider current objections to a newly developed technology

44. Which choice best supports the idea that a failure to break apart the results of a chemical reaction will make the reaction less useful to scientists?

    (A) Lines 5–8 ("Naturally... smoke")
    (B) Lines 15–18 ("One such... molecule")
    (C) Lines 28–31 ("This process... added six)"
    (D) Lines 39–42 ("Not being... effects")

45. As used in line 11, "modify" most closely means
    (A) transform.
    (B) persuade.
    (C) reform.
    (D) pronounce.

46. The author most likely uses the word "virtually" in line 34 to convey the idea that
    (A) benzene alkylation reactions were more useful in practice than anticipated.
    (B) alkylation probably still had some uses despite its general shortcomings.
    (C) selectivity is essential to the possibility of a chemical reaction.
    (D) scientists embraced the findings of Friedel and Crafts for many applications.

47. It is reasonable to infer from the passage that the negative side effects of thalidomide were most likely
    (A) known, yet concealed.
    (B) unintentional.
    (C) needlessly emphasized.
    (D) surprisingly mild.

48. Which option gives the best evidence for the answer to the previous question?
    (A) Lines 43–45 ("A famous . . . thalidomide")
    (B) Lines 45–47 ("This drug . . . sickness")
    (C) Lines 54–58 ("The drug . . . defects")
    (D) Lines 58–60 ("The negative . . . time")

49. It can reasonably be inferred from the fifth paragraph, (lines 61–79), that the primary difference between alkylation and acylation is
    (A) acylation allows for chemical selectivity, while alkylation does not.
    (B) alkylation has wider applicability in scientific processes than acylation.
    (C) acylation has more significantly negative health consequences than does alkylation.
    (D) alkylation is more affordable to implement than is acylation.

50. Lines 84–87, ("What seemed . . . worldwide"), mainly function to suggest that
    (A) the negative consequences of Friedel-Crafts reactions are a major curricular focus today.
    (B) benzene is no longer utilized as chemical compound.
    (C) chemical safety needs to be an increasingly high priority for students to avoid accidents.
    (D) acylation has become a widely accepted practice.

51. The information in Figure 2 is most helpful in better understanding the nature of which of the following terms used in the passage?
    (A) "selectivity" (line 35)
    (B) "morning sickness" (line 47)
    (C) "severe birth defects" (line 57–58)
    (D) "Friedel-Crafts reactions" (line 60)

52. Based on Figure 2, in what range of days after conception would it be most dangerous for a pregnant mother to consume thalidomide due to the likelihood of it interfering with multiple developmental processes?
    (A) Days 21–23
    (B) Days 24–26
    (C) Days 27–31
    (D) Days 32–35

If there is still time remaining, you may review your answers.

WRITING AND LANGUAGE TEST

35 MINUTES, 44 QUESTIONS

DIRECTIONS: The passages below are each accompanied by several questions, some of which refer to an underlined portion in the passage, and some of which refer to the passage as a whole. For some questions, determine how the expression of ideas can be improved. For other questions, determine the best sentence structure, usage, or punctuation given the context. A passage or question may have an accompanying graphic that you will need to consider as you choose the best answer.

Choose the best answer to each question, considering what will optimize the writing quality and make the writing follow the conventions of standard written English. Some questions will have a "NO CHANGE" option that you can pick if you believe the best choice would be to leave the underlined portion as it is.

Questions 1–11 are based on the following passage.

The European Cuckoo

A parasitic relationship is between two ❶ organisms, one of the organisms benefits while the other is harmed. Parasitic relationships are often associated with internal parasites like worms or some species of mites, but parasitic relationships are not limited to organisms residing within a host. ❷ An interesting particular parasite example is the European cuckoo.

❸ Out of deference for her fellow species, a female cuckoo deposits her egg into the nest of another species of bird. She does not randomly deposit her egg though; she chooses the nests of specific species with

1. (A) NO CHANGE
   (B) organisms—one
   (C) organisms, while one
   (D) organisms. If one

2. (A) NO CHANGE
   (B) An interestingly particular
   (C) A particularly interesting
   (D) A particular interesting

3. Which choice most logically introduces the information that follows in the sentence and the paragraph as a whole?
   (A) NO CHANGE
   (B) Much like other organisms that have a mutually beneficial relationship,
   (C) Just as other birds do to European Cuckoo nests,
   (D) Instead of acting as a nurturing mother,

eggs that resemble ❹ those of the European cuckoo. She deposits her egg and leaves it with the other bird's eggs, and that is the extent of her parenting. Since the European cuckoo egg resembles the other species' eggs, the egg goes ❺ unnoticing with the other mother bird.

When the European cuckoo hatches, things take a turn for the worse for the non-cuckoo eggs. Upon hatching, a baby European cuckoo's first instinct is to empty the nest. ❻ Its' back is perfectly shaped to scoop up other eggs and eject them from the nest. If one of the other eggs has already hatched, it will do the same to the hatchling. ❼ The newly hatched European cuckoo essentially attempts to remove all other new life from the nest, eggs and baby birds alike. Even this does not ❽ deter the non-cuckoo mother bird from caring for her "adopted" baby.

{1} In addition, the European cuckoo baby grows to be much larger than similarly aged offspring of the host species. {2} The baby may even quickly grow larger than full-grown adults of the host species. {3} The baby cuckoo's call mimics the sound of several babies of the host species. {4} The mother responds to this call by

4. (A) NO CHANGE
   (B) these of
   (C) this from
   (D) this of

5. (A) NO CHANGE
   (B) unnoticing by
   (C) unnoticed by
   (D) unnoticed with

6. (A) NO CHANGE
   (B) Its
   (C) It's
   (D) It is

7. The writer is considering adding the following sentence.

   While a cuckoo bird feeds off of the ground, it does not walk very gracefully.

   Should the writer make this addition here?
   (A) Yes, because it adds an important detail.
   (B) Yes, because it addresses a likely concern of the reader.
   (C) No, because it repeats a point already made in the essay.
   (D) No, because it is irrelevant to the discussion in this paragraph.

8. (A) NO CHANGE
   (B) instigate
   (C) chill
   (D) incite

gathering enough food for a nest full of babies rather than just enough for one. {5} She will continue to feed this baby even as it vastly outgrows her. 9

This relationship may not seem parasitic in the same sense as internal parasites like tapeworms, 10 but the relationship is indeed benefiting one organism while harming the other. In this case, the host species has fewer of its own offspring, if any survive at all. An organism's fitness is defined by its reproductive output, i.e., how many offspring it produces. The parasitic European cuckoo decreases the mother bird's output and, in some cases, kills all offspring, 11 however decreasing the host bird's fitness. On top of reproductive output, the mother bird must put in additional work to feed the equivalent of a nest full of babies that is actually just one large baby. All the while, the European cuckoo has been provided with food, shelter, and safety.

9. The writer wants to add the following sentence to the last paragraph.

   In order to cause this growth, the bird needs a lot of nutrients.

   The sentence would most logically be placed
   (A) before sentence 1.
   (B) after sentence 2.
   (C) after sentence 3.
   (D) after sentence 4.

10. Which choice most logically follows the statement in the first part of the sentence based on the context of the essay?
    (A) NO CHANGE
    (B) and both organisms benefit equally from the relationship.
    (C) but parasitic relationships are not applicable in the situation of the cuckoo.
    (D) and the cuckoo is taken advantage of by the other bird species.

11. (A) NO CHANGE
    (B) but
    (C) thus
    (D) previously

GO ON TO THE NEXT PAGE

Questions 12–22 are based on the following passage and supplementary material.

Nurse Practitioners and Physician Assistants

With health care professionals more needed than ever, hospitals and universities are working to attract students to their health care programs. Students often head into either a nursing or premed track without ⓬ realizing however that there are many more jobs in healing beyond (or better yet, between) those two positions. Two of the primary positions "between" nurse and doctor ⓭ are those of nurse practitioner and physician assistant.

You can think of a nurse practitioner as a more advanced nurse and a physician assistant as a more restricted doctor. The nurse practitioner will have both attended nursing ⓮ school. Also, they will have completed additional graduate work in order to be licensed as a nurse practitioner. Nurse practitioners use a patient-based model and may work in disease prevention, health education, or patient care. They may diagnose and treat some diseases as part of a health care team, ⓯ might ordering the tests, and may in some cases prescribe medication for patients.

12. (A) NO CHANGE
    (B) realizing however, that
    (C) realizing, however, that
    (D) realizing; however that

13. (A) NO CHANGE
    (B) is
    (C) has
    (D) was

14. Which choice most effectively combines the sentences at the underlined portion?
    (A) school; additionally, they have completed
    (B) school and completed
    (C) school, because they are completing
    (D) school: they complete the extra,

15. (A) NO CHANGE
    (B) order tests,
    (C) may order tests,
    (D) ordering tests,

Table 1: Average Wages for Nurse Practitioners (NP) and Physician Assistants (PA) in 2020

Percentile	10%	25%	50%	75%	90%
NP Annual Wage	$82,960	$94,890	$111,680	$130,240	$156,160
PA Annual Wage	$76,700	$95,730	$115,390	$135,220	$162,470

Data Sources: *www.bls.gov/oes/CURRENT/oes291171.htm*
www.bls.gov/oes/current/oes291071.htm

GO ON TO THE NEXT PAGE

Physician assistants, on the other hand, attend a medical school but do not complete all the requirements that a doctor would. Like nurse practitioners, they work **16** under the supervision of a physician; however, their practice focuses more on disease diagnosis and treatment. They may complete physicals, provide treatment, and advise patients; they may, in some cases, be able to prescribe medication. Both positions allow students to become health care professionals who **17** helps people without the rigors of medical school and the associated student debt.

Compensation is another great reason to seek nurse practitioner or physician assistant education. The median income for a nurse practitioner in the United States in 2020 was **18** $82,960 and the median income for a physician assistant was $76,700. This is much more than the median income for a nurse and even some doctors' incomes depending on experience and specialty. **19** For example, nurse practitioners may make as much as $82,960 in annual compensation.

Another great benefit to seeking a career in health care is the sheer need. With baby boomers aging and health care expanding, we will soon need more workers in the field **20** than ever before. Good health care practitioners should be able to find work in nearly

16. (A) NO CHANGE
(B) under the supervising of
(C) with the supervision on
(D) supervising of

17. (A) NO CHANGE
(B) helping
(C) helped
(D) help

18. Which choice is best supported by the information in Table 1?
(A) NO CHANGE
(B) $156,160 and the median income for a physician assistant was $162,470.
(C) $130,240 and the median income for a physician assistant was $135,220.
(D) $111,680 and the median income for a physician assistant was $115,390.

19. Which choice best uses the information in Table 1 to support the statement made in the previous sentence?
(A) NO CHANGE
(B) What is more, nurse practitioners have salaries that are slightly less than those of physician assistants.
(C) In fact, the top 10 percent of nurse practitioners from the year 2020 could expect to earn at least $156,160 in annual compensation.
(D) Further, the average salaries of nurse practitioners are typically half the average salaries of surgeons.

20. (A) NO CHANGE
(B) then
(C) for
(D) to

any corner of the United **21** States, moreover, they can earn higher pay in less desirable regions like rural areas and other underserved communities.

Students who are empathetic, want to help people, desire flexibility in their location, and are strong in the sciences should consider health care positions. **22** The compensation of physician assistants and nurse practitioners is more competitive than it has been in previous years.

21. (A) NO CHANGE
    (B) States: moreover they can earn higher
    (C) States, moreover they can earn higher
    (D) States; moreover, they can earn higher

22. The writer wants to conclude the essay with a sentence that connects to a general theme laid out in the first paragraph of the essay. Which choice best accomplishes this goal?
    (A) NO CHANGE
    (B) There are many careers in medicine that can satisfy their desires besides those of the traditional doctor and nurse.
    (C) Those who have both strong intellectual and emotional intelligence may be well-suited for these careers.
    (D) It is critical that those in underserved areas of the United States receive the attention they need from health care practitioners.

GO ON TO THE NEXT PAGE

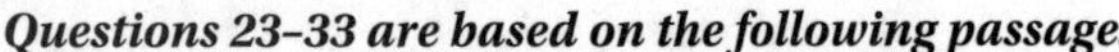

Questions 23–33 are based on the following passage.

J. P. Morgan and Bailouts

Whether they like it or dislike it, most Americans are familiar with the concept of a (23) government bailout: the government swoops in to save a large company that is floundering. The government does this primarily to try to save the economy from potentially crushing bankruptcies of giant corporations that employ thousands of people. While the concept of a government bailout is fairly new, the idea of external powers stepping in to try to boost the economy is not. Prior to the era of governmental intervention, (24) consequently, it was big business who worked to protect the economy and with it, their profits.

Probably the most interesting of these situations was in the years leading up to the Great Depression. A man by the name of J. P. Morgan found himself in a position (25) that enabled him to conduct diplomatic negotiations to bring an end to international conflict. Morgan was a banker—possibly the wealthiest banker of all time. His contemporaries were men like Dale Carnegie and John D. Rockefeller. He (26), as a rich banker, helped create many international corporations that still exist today such as Chase Bank, General Electric, and U.S. Steel. The extent of his wealth and influence (27) can be understated.

23. (A) NO CHANGE
    (B) government bailout, the government swoops
    (C) government; bailout the government swoops
    (D) government bailout the government—swoops

24. (A) NO CHANGE
    (B) also,
    (C) due to this,
    (D) however,

25. The writer wants to include a description of J. P. Morgan that highlights his ability to solve a problem of the United States during the Great Depression, doing so by connecting to the description of his circumstances that takes place later in the passage. Which choice best accomplishes this goal?
    (A) NO CHANGE
    (B) as a well-respected literary artist whose poems would inspire the country.
    (C) where he controlled enough money to make a difference.
    (D) as a politician who had savvy negotiating skills to work out a deal.

26. (A) NO CHANGE
    (B) , as a wealthy financier,
    (C) , as someone with money to burn,
    (D) DELETE the underlined portion.

27. (A) NO CHANGE
    (B) cannot be overstated.
    (C) should not be overstating.
    (D) is overstated.

So, in 1907 when a financial (28) crisis, (one of the foreshocks of the panic that would lead to the Great Depression), took place, Morgan took charge. Banks were on the brink of falling apart. People were going to lose their savings; the situation was dire and the government at the time did not have the power to intervene in a meaningful way. (29) So, Morgan did.

He met with bankers from the (30) derogatory banks as well as others who were doing well. He actually locked them into a room in his mansion and refused to allow anyone to leave until they came up with a plan. They found new sources of revenue, (31) set up new lending credit lines from banks, lent money between themselves, and worked to shore up those floundering corporations. In one situation with a bank's bad investments—Tennessee Coal, Iron, and Railroad

28. (A) NO CHANGE
    (B) crisis; one of the foreshocks of the panic that would lead to the Great Depression, took
    (C) crisis (one of the foreshocks of the panic that would lead to the Great Depression) took
    (D) crisis, one of the foreshocks of the panic that would lead to the Great Depression—took

29. (A) NO CHANGE
    (B) Additionally,
    (C) Formerly,
    (D) Moreover,

30. (A) NO CHANGE
    (B) nasty
    (C) struggling
    (D) combative

31. Which choice provides a second example that is most similar to the examples already in the sentence?
    (A) NO CHANGE
    (B) conducted long-term research into historical causes of financial collapse,
    (C) completely gave up their businesses given the dire circumstances,
    (D) found no helpful resolutions to their significant problems,

Company—Morgan used his own company's money ($30 million) ㉜ to back up the investments and prevent panic. This move is seen as the first private bailout. It's a move that is still being echoed by our government today.

The question then becomes this: is it better to bail out or to let natural market forces self-correct? Should we as a society let large businesses fail ㉝ so that governmental jobs are the only possibility? This would hurt a lot of ordinary workers who rely on big businesses for money, but it would lead to better business decisions in the long term. Or should we follow J. P. Morgan and shore up failing businesses to stabilize the short-term economy?

32. The writer is considering deleting the underlined portion, adjusting the punctuation as needed. Should the underlined portion be kept or deleted?
    (A) Kept, because it provides an explanation of the sources of Carnegie's wealth.
    (B) Kept, because it provides a relevant elaboration on how the money was put into use.
    (C) Deleted, because it shifts the focus of the paragraph away from economic problem solving.
    (D) Deleted, because it is unnecessarily repetitive.

33. Which choice provides the most appropriate context for what follows in the passage?
    (A) NO CHANGE
    (B) in order to encourage only the soundest business practices?
    (C) to foment a revolutionary change to the structure of the economy?
    (D) so that governmental intervention will ensure that no businesses close or jobs are lost?

GO ON TO THE NEXT PAGE

Questions 34–44 are based on the following passage.

Community, Dance, and Happiness

The interconnectedness between mental and physical health has been consistently shown in a variety of fields in research. (34) In the short term mental stress, typically causes relatively minor physical ailments like headaches, digestive issues, and muscle tension. (35) Over long periods of time, from the ancient past to the distant future, however, mental stress can have serious impacts on physical health.

The Roseto Effect is a concept that has expanded scientists' understanding of the effect of mental health on physical health. It has been found that there are some areas in which certain conditions (36) are much less common. Scientists believe this may be due to the feeling of connectedness in the community contributing to greater mental health and thus positively (37) influenced physical health.

The Roseto Effect was first studied in Roseto, Pennsylvania, where there lived a tight-knit community whose diets contained significant levels of fatty acids. (38) Despite members of the town eating high levels of fats, drinking alcohol, and commonly smoking tobacco, the town's residents had significantly lower rates of cardiovascular diseases than (39) this in surrounding areas. It was hypothesized that this was due

34. (A) NO CHANGE
    (B) In the short term, mental stress typically
    (C) In the short term; mental stress typically
    (D) In the short term, mental stress, typically

35. Which choice is the most logical introduction to the sentence that is also stylistically consistent with the paragraph?
    (A) NO CHANGE
    (B) In short periods of time,
    (C) In the long term,
    (D) Over the smallest increments of time,

36. At this point, the writer is considering adding the following.

    , such as heart disease,

    Should the writer make this addition here?
    (A) Yes, because it provides a helpful elaboration on the types of conditions that may be less common.
    (B) Yes, because it explains how the scientists designed their research about the Roseto Effect.
    (C) No, because it repeats information that has already been stated in the paragraph.
    (D) No, because it improperly shifts the main focus of the sentence.

37. (A) NO CHANGE
    (B) influencing
    (C) has influence
    (D) had influenced

38. (A) NO CHANGE
    (B) Because of the
    (C) Given the
    (D) Whenever

39. (A) NO CHANGE
    (B) them
    (C) these
    (D) those

GO ON TO THE NEXT PAGE

to the positive mental benefits from residents interacting with their close-knit community. Over time, when the town began to adopt more mainstream customs with respect to family dynamics, the rate of cardiovascular disease **40** rise.

Like the mental benefits, and thus physical benefits, that have been found from living in close-knit **41** communities, there are many activities that are known to promote physical health due to their impact on mental health. One such activity is dance. While always known to be a good form of exercise, research in the past couple decades **42** suggest that its added mental benefits have a significant impact on the physical health of those that dance.

It is well known that dancing, in all its forms, can evoke a sense of great joy. When research participants were studied over time, researchers found that those who primarily used dance as a form of exercise were less likely to suffer from physical ailments due to old age than those who did not use dance as a form of exercise. Even more meaningful was the finding that when compared to participants who engaged in other forms of exercise, the group of participants who danced were **43** much more likely to have long-term physical limitations.

44 Researchers have found that dance is by far the best way to achieve mental and physical symbiosis. As research on what causes the physical benefits of happiness grows, perhaps communities will further embrace activities, such as dance and close relationships, that promote mental health.

40. (A) NO CHANGE
    (B) risen.
    (C) rose.
    (D) rised.

41. (A) NO CHANGE
    (B) communities there
    (C) communities; there
    (D) communities: there

42. (A) NO CHANGE
    (B) suggests
    (C) had suggested
    (D) has suggesting

43. The writer wants to conclude the paragraph by reinforcing its main claim. Which choice best accomplishes this goal?
    (A) NO CHANGE
    (B) more likely to have difficulty making long-term friendships.
    (C) less likely to continue in artistically focused careers.
    (D) still significantly less likely to have physical ailments.

44. The writer wants a conclusion that restates the main theme of the passage. Which choice best accomplishes this goal?
    (A) NO CHANGE
    (B) In order to maximize overall health, it is vital to prioritize physical well-being over mental well-being.
    (C) The interconnectedness between mental and physical health is profound and can be seen in various fields of study.
    (D) Initial research into the Roseto Effect is necessary in order to see if further research is warranted.

STOP If there is still time remaining, you may review your answers.

MATH TEST (NO CALCULATOR)

25 MINUTES, 20 QUESTIONS

DIRECTIONS: For questions 1–15, solve each problem and choose the best answer from the given options. Fill in the corresponding oval on your answer document. For questions 16–20, solve the problem and fill in the answer in the answer sheet grid. Please use any space in the test booklet to work out your answers.

Notes:

- You **CANNOT** use a calculator on this section.
- All variables and expressions represent real numbers, unless indicated otherwise.
- All figures are drawn to scale, unless indicated otherwise.
- All figures are in a plane, unless indicated otherwise.
- Unless indicated otherwise, the domain of a given function is the set of all real numbers *x* for which the function has real values.

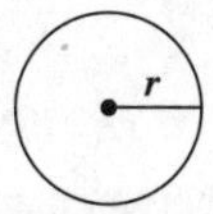

Radius of a circle = r
Area of a circle = πr^2
Circumference of a circle = $2\pi r$

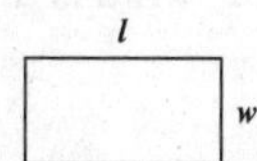

Area of a rectangle = length × width = lw

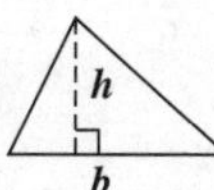

Area of a triangle = $\frac{1}{2}$ × base × height = $\frac{1}{2}bh$

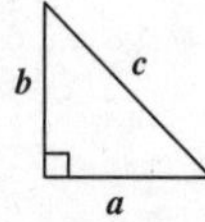

Pythagorean theorem: $a^2 + b^2 = c^2$

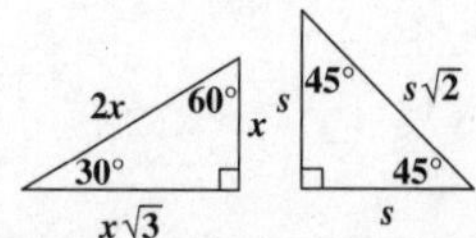

Special right triangles: 30-60-90 and 45-45-90

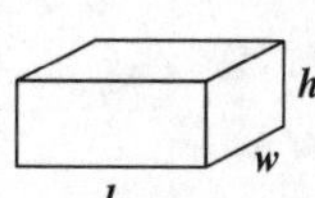

Volume of a box = length × width × height = lwh

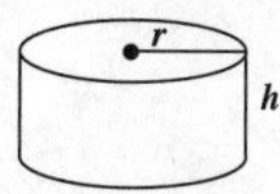

Volume of a cylinder = $\pi r^2 h$

Volume of a sphere = $\frac{4}{3}\pi r^3$

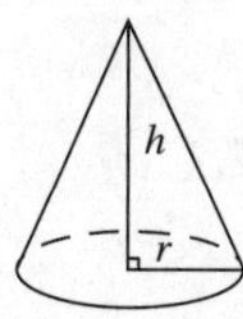

Volume of a cone = $\frac{1}{3}\pi r^2 h$

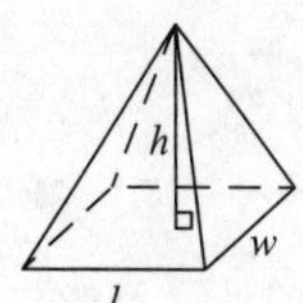

Volume of a pyramid =
$\frac{1}{3}$ × length × width × height = $\frac{1}{3}$ lwh

GO ON TO THE NEXT PAGE

Key Facts:

- **A circle has 360 degrees.**
- **There are 2π radians in a circle.**
- **There are 180 degrees in a triangle.**

1. The graph of a line in the xy plane is totally vertical and has a negative x-intercept. Which of the following could represent a line with these conditions?

   (A) $x = -5$
   (B) $y = -4$
   (C) $y = -x - 2$
   (D) $x = -4y$

2. $\frac{6}{7} \times \frac{14}{3} = ?$

   (A) $\frac{1}{3}$
   (B) 4
   (C) $\frac{27}{4}$
   (D) 9

3. Which of the following is equivalent to $8^{\left(\frac{1}{3}\right)}$?

   (A) 0
   (B) 1
   (C) 2
   (D) 6

4. If $\frac{x}{4} = 6$, what is $\frac{x}{8}$?

   (A) 3
   (B) 4
   (C) 8
   (D) 12

5.

$$2x - 3y = 7$$
$$6x + ky = 21$$

   For what value of the constant k will the above system of equations have infinitely many solutions?

   (A) -9
   (B) -7
   (C) 2
   (D) 13

6. What is the y-intercept of the graph of the function $y = 2^x - 3$?

   (A) -3
   (B) -2
   (C) 0
   (D) 1

7. The relationship between x and y can be modeled using this equation, in which k is a constant:

$$y = \frac{k}{x}$$

   If $x = 4$ when $y = 2$, what is the value of y when x is 8?

   (A) 1
   (B) 8
   (C) 14
   (D) 24

GO ON TO THE NEXT PAGE

8. If $x + 3 = y$ and $xy = 40$, what is the sum of x and y, given that both x and y are positive?

(A) 5
(B) 8
(C) 13
(D) 15

9. What is y in terms of x in the following inequality?

$$12 < -4x + 6y$$

(A) $3 + 2x > y$
(B) $6x - 2 < y$
(C) $\frac{1}{2}x + 3 > y$
(D) $2 + \frac{2}{3}x < y$

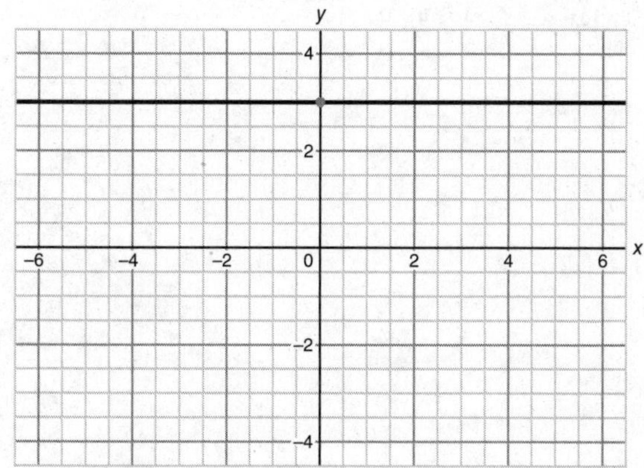

10. The graph of the above line is portrayed by which of the following equations?

(A) $y = 3$
(B) $y = \frac{1}{3}x$
(C) $y = 3x$
(D) $y = x + 3$

11. Which of the following is a solution for x in the equation $4x = 2 - 3x^2$?

(A) $\frac{-3 + \sqrt{10}}{4}$
(B) $\frac{2 - \sqrt{5}}{3}$
(C) $\frac{\sqrt{3}}{4}$
(D) $\frac{-2 - \sqrt{10}}{3}$

12. Given that $i = \sqrt{-1}$, what is the sum of the complex numbers $(4i + 3i^2)$ and $(7 + 2i)$?

(A) $6i + 10$
(B) $4 + 6i$
(C) $28i - 6$
(D) $-5i - 11$

13. A function $g(x)$ has values given in the table below:

x	$g(x)$
-3	-1
-2	0
-1	2
0	1
1	0
2	3

Which of the following would be a factor of $g(x)$?

(A) $(x - 1)(x + 2)$
(B) $(x - 2)(x + 3)$
(C) $(x + 1)(x - 2)$
(D) $(x + 2)(x - 2)$

GO ON TO THE NEXT PAGE

DIAGNOSTIC TEST

14.

$$v_e = \sqrt{\frac{2GM}{r}}$$

The escape velocity for a given spherical body, like a planet or a star, is given by the above formula, in which G is the gravitational constant, r is the distance from the center of the body's mass to the object, and m is the mass of the spherical body. What is M in terms of the other variables?

(A) $M = \frac{(v_e)G}{2r}$

(B) $M = \frac{2G}{(v_e)^2 r}$

(C) $M = \frac{(v_e)^2 r}{2G}$

(D) $M = \frac{2r\sqrt{v_e}}{G}$

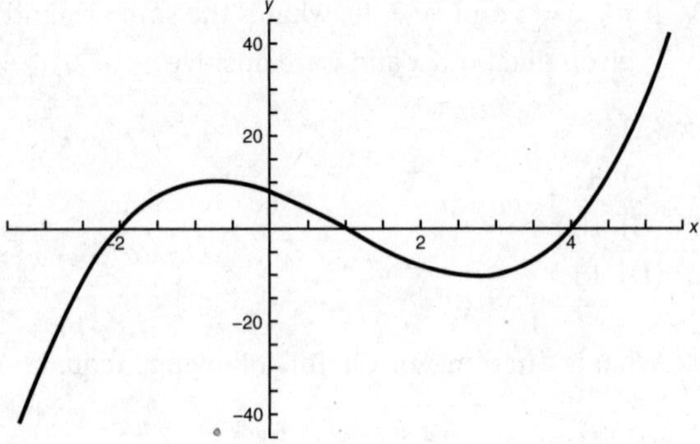

15. Which equation would portray the function graphed above?

(A) $y = (x-2)(x+4)(x-1)$
(B) $y = (x-4)(x+2)(x-1)$
(C) $y = (x-4)(x-2)$
(D) $y = (x+1)(x+2)$

Student-Produced Response Directions

In questions 16–20, first solve the problem, and then enter your answer on the grid provided on the answer sheet. The instructions for entering your answers follow.

- First, write your answer in the boxes at the top of the grid.
- Second, you may grid your answer in the columns below the boxes.
- Use the fraction bar in the first row or the decimal point in the second row to enter fractions and decimals.

Answer: $\frac{8}{15}$ Answer: 1.75 Answer: 100

Write your answer in the boxes

Grid in your answer

Either position is acceptable

- Grid only one space in each column.
- Entering the answer in the boxes is recommended as an aid in gridding but is not required.
- The machine scoring your exam can read only what you grid, so you **must grid-in your answers correctly to get credit**.
- If a question has more than one correct answer, grid-in only one of them.
- The grid does not have a minus sign; so no answer can be negative.
- A mixed number *must* be converted to an improper fraction or a decimal before it is gridded. Enter $1\frac{1}{4}$ as $\frac{5}{4}$ or 1.25; the machine will interpret 11/4 as $\frac{11}{4}$ and mark it wrong.
- **All decimals must be entered as accurately as possible.** Here are three acceptable ways of gridding

$$\frac{3}{11} = 0.272727\ldots$$

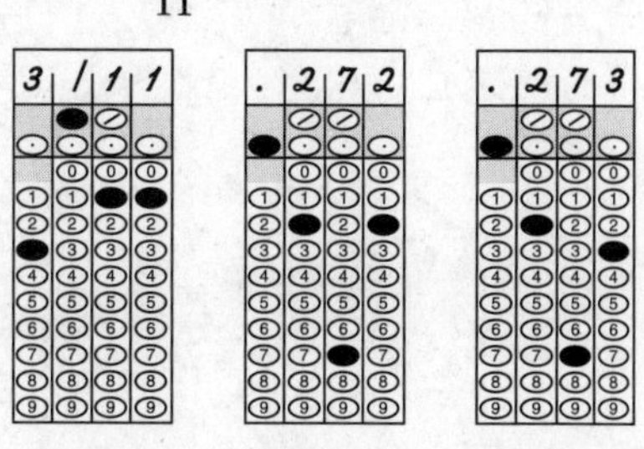

- Note that rounding to .273 is acceptable because you are using the full grid, but you would receive **no credit** for .3 or .27, because they are less accurate.

16. If $\frac{x^2}{6} = \frac{x}{2}$, what is the value of x?

17. A restaurant charges \$5 for a cheeseburger and \$4 for a hamburger. If Connor wants to buy at least 2 of each sandwich and wants to spend a total of between \$20 and \$30 (inclusive) on sandwiches, what is a possible value for the number of cheeseburgers Connor purchased?

18. If $x + y = 7$ and $x - y = 3$, what is the value of $3x^2 - 3y^2$?

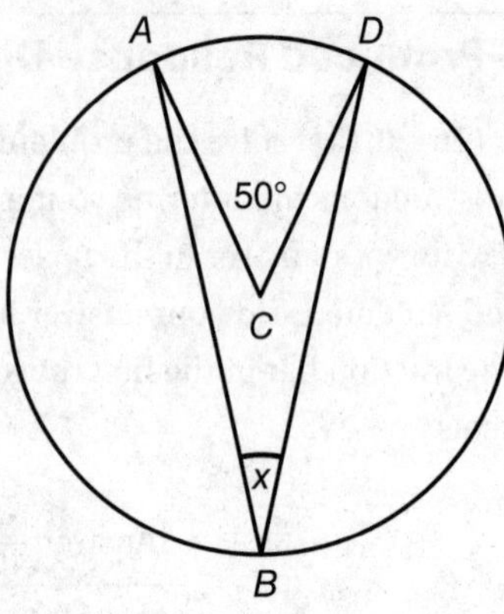

19. What is the measure in degrees of $\angle X$, given that AB and DB are straight lines and C is the center of the circle?

20. A sphere has a volume of 8 cubic feet. What is the volume in cubic feet of a sphere with twice the radius of the original one?

STOP If there is still time remaining, you may review your answers.

MATH TEST (CALCULATOR)

55 MINUTES, 38 QUESTIONS

DIRECTIONS: For questions 1–30, solve each problem and choose the best answer from the given options. Fill in the corresponding oval on your answer document. For questions 31–38, solve the problem and fill in the answer in the answer sheet grid. Please use any space in the test booklet to work out your answers.

Notes:
- You **CAN** use a calculator on this section.
- All variables and expressions represent real numbers, unless indicated otherwise.
- All figures are drawn to scale, unless indicated otherwise.
- All figures are in a plane, unless indicated otherwise.
- Unless indicated otherwise, the domain of a given function is the set of all real numbers x for which the function has real values.

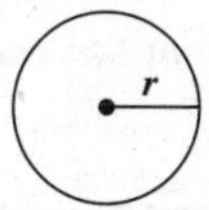

Radius of a circle = r
Area of a circle = πr^2
Circumference of a circle = $2\pi r$

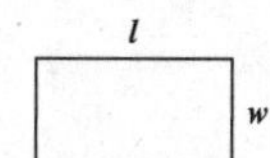

Area of a rectangle = length × width = lw

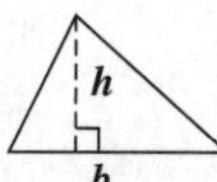

Area of a triangle = $\frac{1}{2}$ × base × height = $\frac{1}{2}bh$

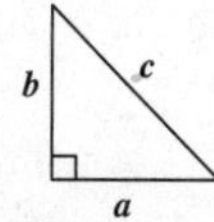

Pythagorean theorem: $a^2 + b^2 = c^2$

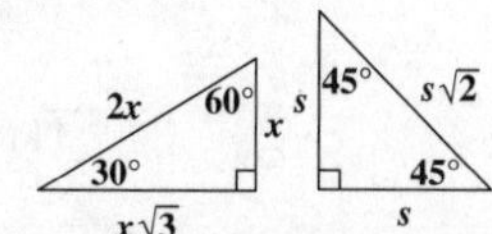

Special right triangles: 30-60-90 and 45-45-90

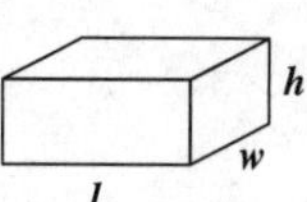

Volume of a box = length × width × height = lwh

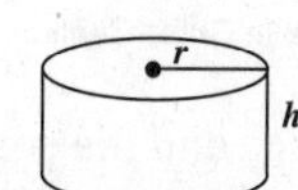

Volume of a cylinder = $\pi r^2 h$

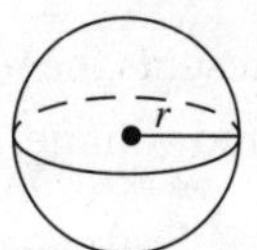

Volume of a sphere = $\frac{4}{3}\pi r^3$

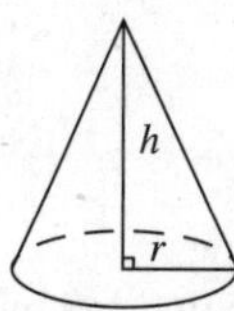

Volume of a cone = $\frac{1}{3}\pi r^2 h$

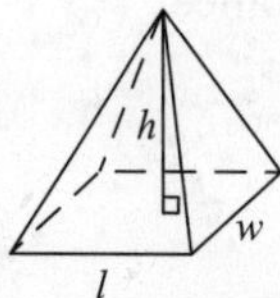

Volume of a pyramid = $\frac{1}{3}$ × length × width × height = $\frac{1}{3}$ lwh

GO ON TO THE NEXT PAGE

Key Facts:

- **A circle has 360 degrees.**
- **There are 2π radians in a circle.**
- **There are 180 degrees in a triangle.**

Questions 1 and 2 refer to the following information.

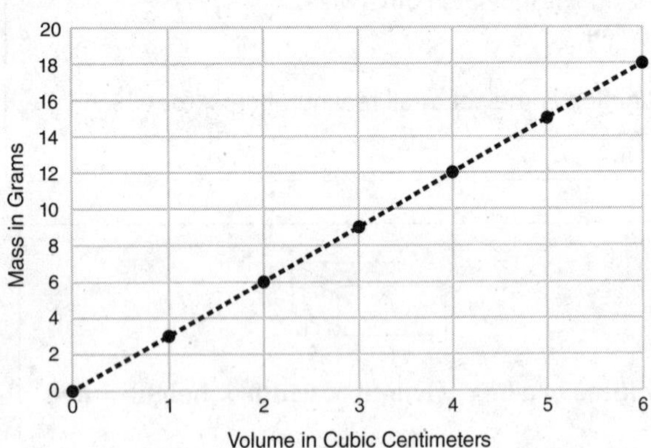

The volume of a substance and the corresponding mass of the substance are graphed above.

1. What equation represents the relationship between mass, m, and volume, v, in the above graph?

   (A) $v = 3m$
   (B) $m = 3v$
   (C) $m = 6v$
   (D) $v = m + 2$

2. Density equals mass divided by volume. What aspect of the function corresponds to the density of the substance?

   (A) slope
   (B) y-intercept
   (C) x-intercept
   (D) domain

3. What is the sum of the following polynomials?

   $$5x^3 - x + 4 \text{ and } 6x^3 + x^2 - 3$$

   (A) $30x^6 + x^3 - x + 1$
   (B) $30x^3 + 2x^2 + x - 1$
   (C) $11x^3 + x^2 - x + 1$
   (D) $11x^3 - x^2 + x - 1$

4. What is the median of this set of numbers?

   $$\{2, 5, 7, 9, 12, 16\}$$

   (A) 7
   (B) 8
   (C) 8.5
   (D) 9

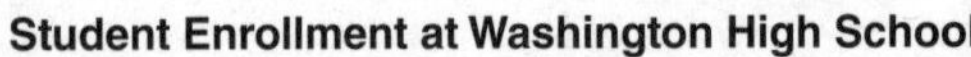

Student Enrollment at Washington High School

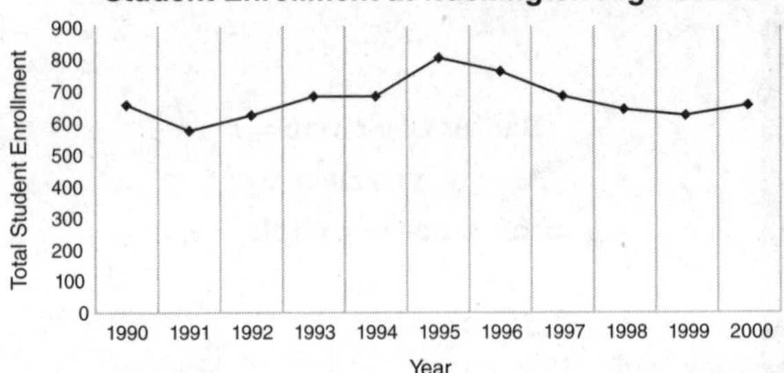

5. Between which years did enrollment stay steady?

   (A) 1990–1991
   (B) 1992–1993
   (C) 1993–1994
   (D) 1996–1997

Questions 6 and 7 refer to the following information.

The equation for gravitational force, F_g, is the following:

$$F_g = G\frac{m_1 m_2}{r^2}$$

G is the gravitational constant, m_1 and m_2 are the masses of objects, and r is the distance between the objects.

6. How would the gravitational force between two objects change if the distance between the objects doubles while all other quantities remain the same?

   (A) It would be twice the original force.
   (B) It would be four times the original force.
   (C) It would be $\frac{1}{2}$ of the original force.
   (D) It would be $\frac{1}{4}$ of the original force.

7. What is the value of m_2 in terms of the other values in the equation?

   (A) $m_2 = \frac{F_g r^2}{G m_1}$
   (B) $m_2 = \frac{F_g r^2 m_1}{G}$
   (C) $m_2 = \frac{\sqrt{r}}{F_g G m_1}$
   (D) $m_2 = \frac{G m_1}{F_g r^2}$

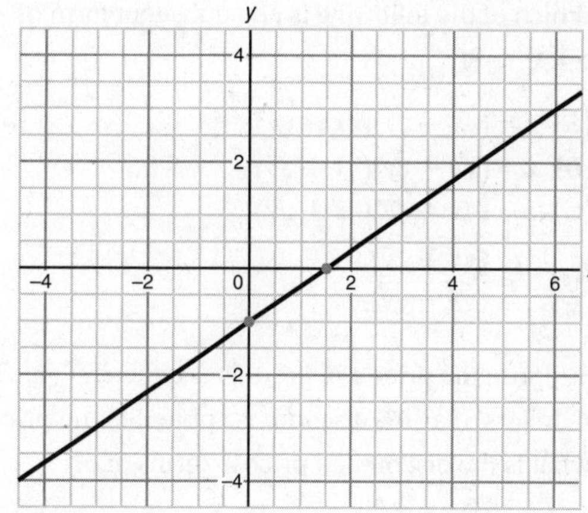

8. If the graph of the above function is written in the form $ax + by = 3$, in which a and b are constants, what is the sum of a and b?

   (A) −3
   (B) −1
   (C) 2
   (D) 5

9. There are 3 teaspoons in a tablespoon and 16 tablespoons in a cup. How much of a cup would there be in 12 teaspoons?

   (A) $\frac{1}{12}$ cup
   (B) $\frac{1}{4}$ cup
   (C) 2 cups
   (D) 6 cups

10. If $a + 2b = 11$ and $3a - 2b = 1$, what is the value of a?

    (A) −3
    (B) 1
    (C) 2
    (D) 3

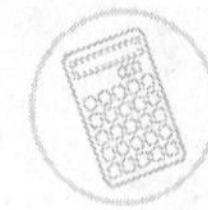

11. Which of the following is an equivalent form of $z = x - y$?

(A) $z = (\sqrt{x} - \sqrt{y})(\sqrt{x} - \sqrt{y})$
(B) $z = (\sqrt{x} - \sqrt{y})(\sqrt{x} + \sqrt{y})$
(C) $z = (\sqrt{x} + \sqrt{y})(\sqrt{x} + \sqrt{y})$
(D) $z = \dfrac{(\sqrt{x} + \sqrt{y})}{(\sqrt{x} - \sqrt{y})}$

12. Suppose the price of a product is typically p dollars. If a 30% discount is applied to the price, what is the discounted price in terms of p?

(A) $0.03p$
(B) $0.3p$
(C) $0.7p$
(D) $1.3p$

13. Tran runs a 5 km (5,000 m) race. Given that there are 0.3048 meters in 1 foot, approximately how many feet did he run in the race?

(A) 0.174
(B) 1,524
(C) 2,088
(D) 16,400

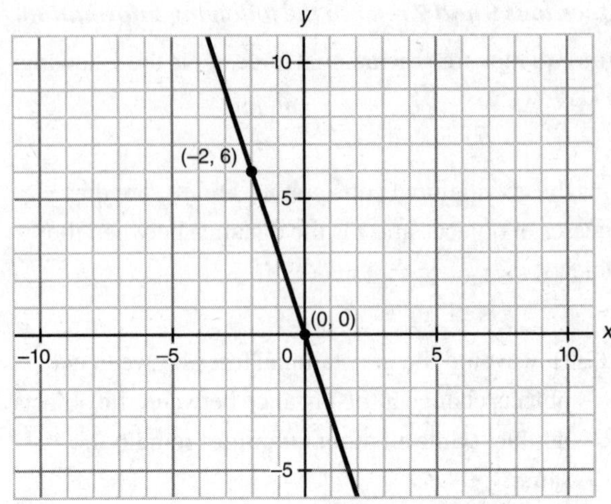

14. If a point on the above line has an x value of a, what is the value of the point's y-coordinate in terms of a?

(A) $-\frac{1}{3}a$
(B) $-\frac{1}{2}a$
(C) $-3a$
(D) $3a$

Pet Owners Who Have Only One Pet

	Dog	Cat	Total
Male	60	40	100
Female	50	38	88
Total	110	78	188

15. If there were a randomly selected pet owner from the table above, what is the probability that it would be a male cat owner?

(A) $\frac{40}{188}$
(B) $\frac{40}{100}$
(C) $\frac{60}{188}$
(D) $\frac{40}{78}$

GO ON TO THE NEXT PAGE

16. Due to radiation, the mass of a substance decreases by 0.5% of that day's mass every day. Which type of function would properly model the mass of the substance as the days go by?

(A) Increasing linear
(B) Decreasing linear
(C) Increasing exponential
(D) Decreasing exponential

17. Jane is watering her garden and spends 5 minutes watering each tree and 2 minutes watering each shrub. If she can spend no more than 30 minutes watering her garden, which inequality represents the number of T trees and S shrubs she can water given these constraints?

(A) $5T + 2S \geq 30$
(B) $5T + 2S \leq 30$
(C) $5 \times T \times S \leq 30$
(D) $5 > 30 \times T \times S$

Questions 18–19 refer to the following information.

Travel Statistics on Journey from Times Square to Harlem in New York City

	Estimated Time	Distance
Subway	17 minutes	5 miles
Car	19 minutes	4.9 miles
Walk	93 minutes	4.6 miles
Bicycle	33 minutes	5.7 miles

18. If Sarah took the subway from Times Square to Harlem, what was her speed in miles per hour, to the nearest tenth?

(A) 0.7 MPH
(B) 3.4 MPH
(C) 17.6 MPH
(D) 204.0 MPH

19. If Johann rode his bicycle to Harlem and then took a car back to Times Square (using the times and distances estimated in the table above), what was his speed in miles per hour for the entire time he travelled, to the nearest tenth?

(A) 9.2 MPH
(B) 12.2 MPH
(C) 14.6 MPH
(D) 551.2 MPH

20. A particular line is graphed in the xy-plane and uses only real numbers. The line has a positive slope and a positive y-intercept. Which of these points could be on the line?

(A) $(-4, 5)$
(B) $(2, 0)$
(C) $(3, -6)$
(D) $(0, -1)$

21. What percentage of 70 is 35?

(A) 40%
(B) 50%
(C) 75%
(D) 200%

22. Kamini wants to make money from recycling aluminum cans and glass bottles. Her local government pays her \$0.10 per can and \$0.16 for each bottle. If she wants to earn a total of at least \$100 and has collected a total of 600 cans (and cannot collect any more cans), what is the minimum number of bottles she would need to collect to reach her goal?

(A) 250
(B) 270
(C) 300
(D) 420

GO ON TO THE NEXT PAGE

Questions 23 and 24 refer to the following material.

Material	Kilograms per Cubic Meter
Cement	1,440
Maplewood	755
Steel	7,850
Cedarwood	380
Glass	2,580
Gravel	2,000

The density of different building materials is presented in the table above.

23. Based on the information in the table above, what is the weight of a solid steel wall that has a volume of 300 cubic meters?

(A) 26 kilograms
(B) 8,150 kilograms
(C) 432,000 kilograms
(D) 2,355,000 kilograms

24. The weight of a 20 cubic meter block of cement is what percent (to the nearest whole number) greater than the weight of a block of cedarwood of the same volume?

(A) 82%
(B) 279%
(C) 288%
(D) 1,282%

25. Students at a university were surveyed as to whether they wanted a new library for the university. Out of the 100 students surveyed, 40% said they wanted a new library. What is justifiable based on this information?

(A) Of the 100 students surveyed, 40 wanted a new library.
(B) Of all people in the university community, 40% want a new library.
(C) Exactly 40 students at the university want a new library.
(D) No more than 40 university students want a new library.

26. The function f is expressed as $f(x) = k$ for all values of x, and k is a constant real number. Which of the following must be true?

I. $f(x)$ forms a line.
II. $f(x)$ has a slope of zero.
III. $f(x)$ has a range from $-\infty$ to $+\infty$.

(A) I only
(B) II only
(C) Only I and II
(D) Only II and III

27. There are 10 cards, each distinctly numbered from 1 to 10. After a card is selected from the set, it is returned to the set. If someone first picks a 3 and then picks a 2, what is the probability that on the third selection the person will pick a 9?

(A) $\frac{1}{20}$
(B) $\frac{1}{10}$
(C) $\frac{1}{9}$
(D) $\frac{1}{6}$

28. In a right rectangular prism, the smallest edge is 2 cm long. The next greatest edge is twice the length of the smallest edge, and the greatest edge is 3 times the length of the smallest edge. What is the surface area of the prism?

(A) 6 sq cm
(B) 24 sq cm
(C) 64 sq cm
(D) 88 sq cm

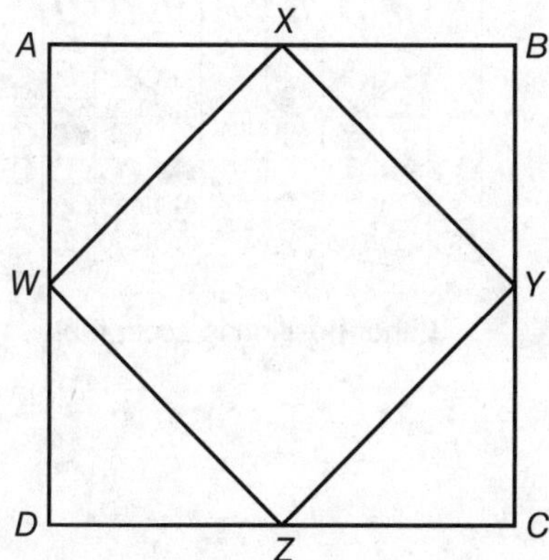

29. If square *ABCD* has an area of 36 square units, what is the perimeter of square *WXYZ*, given that each vertex of square *WXYZ* bisects the side of square *ABCD* that it intersects?

(A) 6
(B) $6\sqrt{3}$
(C) 12
(D) $12\sqrt{2}$

30. The price of a video streaming service increases by 15% each year. If the price, *P*, of the service begins at *v* dollars, what is the value of the constant *c* in the following function that models the price of the service *t* years after it begins?

$$P = vc^t$$

(A) 0.15
(B) 0.85
(C) 1.15
(D) 1.55

Student-Produced Response Directions

In questions 31–38, first solve the problem, and then enter your answer on the grid provided on the answer sheet. The instructions for entering your answers follow.

- First, write your answer in the boxes at the top of the grid.
- Second, you may grid your answer in the columns below the boxes.
- Use the fraction bar in the first row or the decimal point in the second row to enter fractions and decimals.

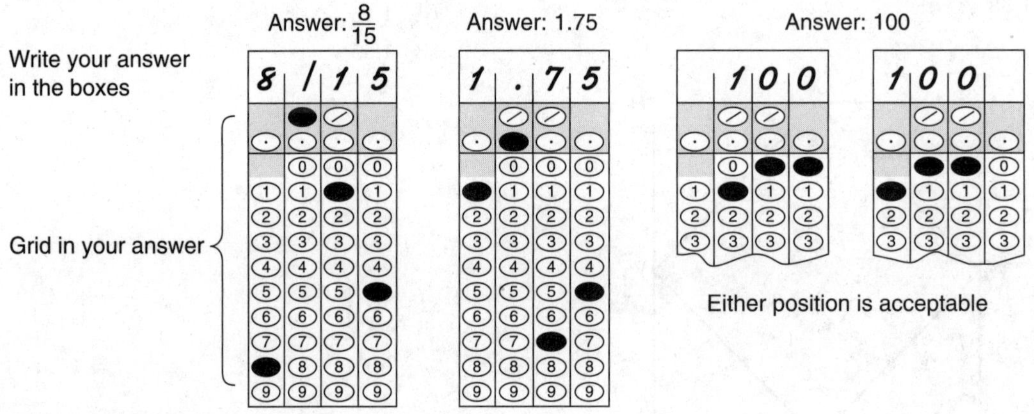

- Grid only one space in each column.
- Entering the answer in the boxes is recommended as an aid in gridding but is not required.
- The machine scoring your exam can read only what you grid, so you **must grid-in your answers correctly to get credit.**
- If a question has more than one correct answer, grid-in only one of them.
- The grid does not have a minus sign, so no answer can be negative.
- A mixed number *must* be converted to an improper fraction or a decimal before it is gridded. Enter $1\frac{1}{4}$ as $\frac{5}{4}$ or 1.25; the machine will interpret 11/4 as $\frac{11}{4}$ and mark it wrong.
- **All decimals must be entered as accurately as possible.** Here are three acceptable ways of gridding

$$\frac{3}{11} = 0.272727\ldots$$

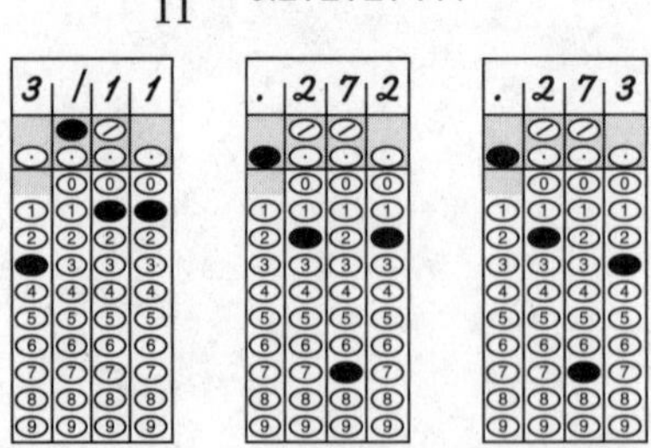

- Note that rounding to .273 is acceptable because you are using the full grid, but you would receive **no credit** for .3 or .27, because they are less accurate.

31. If $\frac{2}{3}x - 1 = \frac{1}{6}x + 4$, what is the value of x?

32. Triangle ABC has a right angle B. If side AB has a length of 7 units and side BC has a length of 24 units, what is the length in units of side AC?

33. The total calories for a particular salad are 1,100. The salad consists of only cheese, vegetables, and dressing. If the total caloric value of the cheese and vegetables is 650, and each packet of dressing used on the salad has 75 calories, how many packets of dressing were used on the salad?

$$2a - 3b = 5$$
$$3a - 2b = 10$$

34. The solution to the above system of equations is (a, b). What is the value of $a - b$?

$$ax + 2 = 3x + 2$$

35. In the above equation, a is a constant. The equation has infinitely many solutions. What is the value of a?

36. Water from the ocean has 3.5% salt, and water from the Dead Sea has 33.7% salt. If someone has 10 gallons of ocean water, how many gallons of water from the Dead Sea (measured to the nearest hundredth of a gallon) need to be added so that the solution has 10% salt?

37. The mean height of 7 teenage boys is 67 inches. If one of the boys has a height of 74 inches, what is the mean height of the remaining boys to the nearest tenth of an inch?

$$h(t) = -16t^2 + 16t + 10$$

38. The function above portrays the height, h, of a projectile t seconds after being thrown. Which of the following would be the time in seconds at which the height of the projectile is at its maximum value?

STOP If there is still time remaining, you may review your answers.

ANSWER KEY
Diagnostic Test

Section 1: Reading Test

1. **D**	14. **C**	27. **A**	40. **B**
2. **C**	15. **B**	28. **A**	41. **C**
3. **C**	16. **C**	29. **D**	42. **A**
4. **A**	17. **D**	30. **B**	43. **A**
5. **D**	18. **A**	31. **C**	44. **D**
6. **B**	19. **B**	32. **C**	45. **A**
7. **B**	20. **A**	33. **A**	46. **B**
8. **C**	21. **A**	34. **B**	47. **B**
9. **B**	22. **B**	35. **C**	48. **C**
10. **C**	23. **A**	36. **B**	49. **A**
11. **B**	24. **C**	37. **B**	50. **D**
12. **A**	25. **C**	38. **A**	51. **C**
13. **B**	26. **B**	39. **C**	52. **C**

Section 2: Writing and Language Test

1. **B**	12. **C**	23. **A**	34. **B**
2. **C**	13. **A**	24. **D**	35. **C**
3. **D**	14. **B**	25. **C**	36. **A**
4. **A**	15. **C**	26. **D**	37. **B**
5. **C**	16. **A**	27. **B**	38. **A**
6. **B**	17. **D**	28. **C**	39. **D**
7. **D**	18. **D**	29. **A**	40. **C**
8. **A**	19. **C**	30. **C**	41. **A**
9. **B**	20. **A**	31. **A**	42. **B**
10. **A**	21. **D**	32. **B**	43. **D**
11. **C**	22. **B**	33. **B**	44. **C**

ANSWER KEY
Diagnostic Test

Section 3: Math Test (No Calculator)

1. **A**
2. **B**
3. **C**
4. **A**
5. **A**
6. **B**
7. **A**
8. **C**
9. **D**
10. **A**
11. **D**
12. **B**
13. **A**
14. **C**
15. **B**
16. **3**
17. **2, 3, or 4**
18. **63**
19. **25**
20. **64**

Section 4: Math (Calculator)

1. **B**
2. **A**
3. **C**
4. **B**
5. **C**
6. **D**
7. **A**
8. **B**
9. **B**
10. **D**
11. **B**
12. **C**
13. **D**
14. **C**
15. **A**
16. **D**
17. **B**
18. **C**
19. **B**
20. **A**
21. **B**
22. **A**
23. **D**
24. **B**
25. **A**
26. **C**
27. **B**
28. **D**
29. **D**
30. **C**
31. **10**
32. **25**
33. **6**
34. **3**
35. **3**
36. **2.74**
37. **65.8**
38. **0.5 or $\frac{1}{2}$**

SAT Scoring Chart

Tally the number of correct answers from the Reading section (out of 52), the Writing and Language section (out of 44), and the combined Math without and with calculator sections (out of 58). Match these numbers of correct answers to the find the Reading Test score, the Writing and Language Test score, and the Math section score.

Number of Correct Answers on Each Test Part (Reading, Writing/Language, Combined Math Sections)	Reading Test Score	Writing and Language Test Score	Math Section Score
0	10	10	200
1	10	10	200
2	10	10	210
3	10	11	220
4	11	11	230
5	12	12	250
6	13	13	270
7	13	14	280
8	14	14	300
9	15	15	310
10	16	16	320
11	16	16	340
12	17	17	350
13	17	17	360
14	18	18	370
15	18	18	380
16	19	18	390
17	19	19	400
18	20	19	410
19	20	20	420
20	21	20	430
21	21	21	440
22	22	21	450
23	22	22	460
24	23	23	470
25	23	23	480
26	24	24	490
27	24	24	500
28	25	25	500
29	25	25	510
30	26	26	520

(Continued)

Number of Correct Answers on Each Test Part (Reading, Writing/Language, Combined Math Sections)	Reading Test Score	Writing and Language Test Score	Math Section Score
31	26	27	520
32	27	27	530
33	28	28	540
34	28	29	540
35	29	29	550
36	29	30	560
37	30	31	570
38	30	31	580
39	31	32	580
40	31	33	590
41	31	34	600
42	32	36	610
43	32	38	610
44	33	40	620
45	33		630
46	34		640
47	35		650
48	36		660
49	36		670
50	37		680
51	39		690
52	40		700
53			710
54			730
55			750
56			770
57			790
58			800

Add the Reading Test score and the Writing and Language Test scores:

________ (Reading Score) + ________(Writing and Language Score) =

__________ (Combined Reading and Writing and Language Score)

Then multiply the Combined Reading and Writing Language score by 10 to find your Evidence-Based Reading and Writing section score:

10 × ___________ (Combined Reading and Writing and Language Score) =

______________ **Evidence-Based Reading and Writing Score (between 200–800)**

The Math section score is also between 200–800. Get this from the table above.

_______________ **Math Section Score (between 200–800)**

Add the Evidence-Based Reading and Writing score and the Math section score to find your total SAT test score:

___________ Evidence-Based Reading and Writing Score +

___________ Math Section Score =

___________ **Total SAT Test Score (between 400–1600)**

Approximate your testing percentiles (1st–99th) using this chart:

Total Score	Section Score	Total Percentile	Evidence-Based Reading and Writing Percentile	Math Percentile
1600	800	99+	99+	99
1500	750	98	98	96
1400	700	94	94	91
1300	650	86	86	84
1200	600	74	73	75
1100	550	59	57	61
1000	500	41	40	42
900	450	25	24	27
800	400	11	11	15
700	350	3	3	5
600	300	1	1	1
500	250	1	1	1
400	200	1	1	1

Diagnostic Analysis Guide

Review the questions you missed to see which question types you should review in the chapter sections. There are extensive strategies, content review, and practice problems fully aligned with each of these question types.

Reading

Question Type	Question Numbers
Interpretation	2, 6, 7, 17, 38, 43, 49
Inference	4, 14, 25, 27, 33, 47
Function/Purpose	10, 12, 13, 23, 37, 50
Evidence	5, 8, 15, 21, 26, 28, 32, 39, 44, 48
Big Picture	1, 11, 22, 35
Critical Thinking	29, 31, 36
Comparative	40, 41, 42
Words in Context	3, 9, 16, 18, 24, 30, 34, 45, 46
Graph Analysis	19, 20, 51, 52

Writing and Language

Question Type	Question Numbers
Number and Tense Agreement	5, 13, 17, 40, 42
Wordiness	7, 26, 32, 36
Punctuation	1, 6, 12, 21, 23, 28, 34, 41
Sentence Structure and Organization	4, 14, 15, 31, 37, 39
Proper Wording	2, 8, 16, 20, 27, 30
Transitions	11, 24, 29, 38
Passage and Paragraph Organization	3, 9, 22, 35, 43
Passage and Paragraph Analysis	10, 25, 33, 44
Graph Analysis	18, 19

Math

Heart of Algebra

Concept Type	Math No Calculator Question Numbers	Math with Calculator Question Numbers
Fundamentals	2	
Solving Equations	4, 5, 8	10, 31, 34
Word Problems and Function Interpretation	6, 7	6, 17, 22, 33, 35
Lines and Slope	1, 10	8, 14, 20

Passport to Advanced Math

Concept Type	Math No Calculator Question Numbers	Math with Calculator Question Numbers
Polynomials and Factoring	16	3, 11
Exponents and Roots	3	
Solving Quadratic Equations	11, 17	
Zeros, Parabolas, and Polynomial Graphing	13, 15	38
Function Interpretation and Manipulation	9, 14, 17	2, 7, 16, 26, 30

Problem Solving and Data Analysis

Concept Type	Math No Calculator Question Numbers	Math with Calculator Question Numbers
Measures of Center		4, 3, 7
Unit Conversion		9, 13, 23
Percentages		12, 21, 24, 36
Surveys		25
Graph and Data Interpretation		1, 5, 15, 18, 19, 27

Additional Topics in Math

Concept Type	Math No Calculator Question Numbers	Math with Calculator Question Numbers
Area, Perimeter, and Volume	20	28
Lines, Angles, and Triangles		29
Right Triangles and Trigonometry		32
Circles	19	
Imaginary Numbers	12	

Answers Explained

Section 1: Reading Test

The Jungle

1. **(D)** Throughout the passage, the characters are offered little opportunity to improve their dismal lives. This is shown though the fact that the characters are unemployed, in debt, and battling starvation. They are hopeless as one issue after another drives them further into poverty. Choice **(D)** is the best option: they are melancholy (sad) and hopeless. Choice (A) would show an upbeat attitude, which is not the case. Choice (B) would indicate that they have found some peace in the acceptance of their situation, which did not occur. Choice (C) would indicate that they are plotting revenge, a concept for which there is no evidence.

2. **(C)** In the first paragraph, the reader learns that Marija is supporting her family using her savings even though she lost her job. Choice **(C)** is the best option because Marija is shown dutifully fulfilling what she views as her family obligations. Choice (A) is incorrect. It would make sense for Marija to resent this obligation, but the passage presents no evidence of this. Choice (B) is incorrect as there is no evidence of disapproval; the passage shows a family working together through a tough situation. Choice (D) is incorrect since Marija seems to love her family—she is not hostile toward them.

3. **(C)** The context for the word "strain" is "there was thus a constant strain upon their minds; they were harried all day and nearly all night by worry and fear." This worry and fear is the strain that they are feeling and can best be described by answer choice **(C)**: burden. Answer choices (A) and (D) are alternative meanings of the word "strain" but do not fit into the context of the sentence. Answer choice (B) does not show the hardship of the worry and fear.

4. **(A)** This question is asking the reader to make an inference based on the passage; the passage doesn't explicitly say what the large obstacle is. Based on the first and second sentences in the third paragraph, choice **(A)** is the best option since we can see there that their lives and budgets are turned upside down by a fairly common issue—a burst pipe. This implies that unforeseen expenses prevent them from staying on budget. It isn't choice (B) because all of the characters are very careful about spending money. It isn't choice (C) since we see that they do discuss their financial issues with one another as they look for solutions. It isn't choice (D) since they have a place to live already.

5. **(D)** Choice **(D)** is the best answer since those lines show how a simple expense from a burst pipe causes great financial distress to the family. Choice (A) shows a consequence of losing a job. Choice (B) showcases the discussions that the family had about their financial situation. Choice (C) shows how difficult life is for the family, but doesn't explain their budgetary obstacles.

6. **(B)** The overall story shows a family that works very hard just to survive. This can be seen in the statement at the end of the second paragraph that tells the reader that they're willing to work all the time. Thus, choice **(B)** is the correct answer. The other choices do not show how much the family is willing to work.

7. **(B)** The only interaction between Jurgis and the authorities is in the final paragraph as Jurgis tries to deal with the man who comes to collect their house payment. Jurgis uses sarcasm in asking the man to be direct about the hidden fees. This shows the skepticism that he has toward the authorities. Jurgis is not humble in his request, therefore choice (A) is incorrect.

Jurgis doesn't appreciate that the authority demands more money from him, so choice (C) is incorrect. While he may be committed to paying what he owes, he is not committed to the authority figure himself, so choice (D) is incorrect.

8. **(C)** Choice **(C)** is correct as it is the location where we can find the sarcastic comment referenced in the previous answer explanation. Choice (A) does not show an interaction with the authorities. Choices (B) and (D) show the authority figure's words, but not Jurgis's approach when dealing with the man.

9. **(B)** In context, the word "squarely" is referring to Jurgis looking someone "squarely in the eye." The best alternate word in this context would be "directly," making choice **(B)** the best option. The other choices do not fit into the context of the sentence or the author's intended meaning. Jurgis is not looking at the man traditionally, corruptly, or humbly.

10. **(C)** Within these lines, the author learns of the many unexpected expenses that the family faces, from burst pipes to insurance and water needs. They highlight how difficult it is for the family to know how much money they will need, since it seems to them that new expenses are always popping up. Thus, choice **(C)** is the best answer. Choice (A) is incorrect since their challenge is in paying for expenses, not in finding physically safe employment. Choice (B) is incorrect since the very opposite is true: they struggle to understand their housing contract. Choice (D) is incorrect since nowhere in the passage is it implied that the characters are considering violence.

Bedbugs

11. **(B)** In the first paragraph, the author shares with the reader a brief history of bedbug infestations, saying that there was a time in the past when all people had to deal with the pests. She then goes on to explain that modern pesticides nearly eradicated the bugs, but that they are making a comeback. This outline clearly makes choice **(B)** the correct answer. Choice (A) is not correct since bedbugs have not been consistently eradicated; there was a time in the past when they were an issue. Choice (C) is incorrect because bedbugs are not eradicated today. Choice (D) is incorrect as it is the opposite of what the author explains.

12. **(A)** The initial few sentences of the passage are not a serious discussion of bedbugs, but rather a small familiar story from many people's childhood. It is most likely that the author included this in order to engage readers by referring to something with which they are familiar. This makes choice **(A)** the best answer. It is not choice (B) since it does not discuss the danger of bedbugs. It is not choice (C) since the story does not lead to scientific discoveries. It is not choice (D) because it does not explain why bedbugs are so heavily studied.

13. **(B)** These lines run through a list of things that make the bedbug difficult to eradicate: size, diet, eggs, and habitat. Therefore, it is best to say that these lines function to help the reader understand why bedbugs are a unique challenge in pest control. This makes choice **(B)** the best answer option. Choice (A) is incorrect because the lines discuss extermination challenges, not extermination techniques. Choice (C) is incorrect because the lines do not address evolutionary advantages. Choice (D) is incorrect because the lines discuss the difficulty of eradication, not the dangers posed to humans.

14. **(C)** The author clearly states at the beginning of the third paragraph that DDT was banned because of its effects on wildlife. This is an environmental concern, making choice **(C)** the best option. Choice (A) is incorrect because wildlife impact is not an excessive cost. Choice (B) is incorrect because the author says the very opposite: the replacement technology is *less* effective. Choice (D) is incorrect because DDT was banned; it did not cease to be necessary.

15. **(B)** At the beginning of the third paragraph, the author explains that DDT was banned because of its effects on wildlife: an environmental concern. This makes choice **(B)** the best option. Choices (A) and (D) include lines that explain the difficulty of eradicating bugs without DDT but do not explain why DDT is no longer used. Choice (C) reiterates that DDT is no longer used but does not explain why.

16. **(C)** The context indicates that the bites continue as long as the bugs are "unchecked." This implies that if the bugs are removed, then the bites will stop. Thus, "unchecked" must mean "not removed." The best answer with this meaning would be choice **(C)**: the bugs are not controlled and removed. Choice (A) is incorrect since an infestation can be examined but not controlled. Choice (B) is incorrect as an infestation can continue whether it is known or unknown. Choice (D) is incorrect as *disappointing* does not fit the context in any way.

17. **(D)** In the last paragraph, the author speaks to the expense and stress of bedbug removal and encourages people to avoid infestations at all costs. This makes choice **(D)** the best answer. Choice (A) is incorrect as there are measures other than prevention that can control bedbugs. Choice (B) is incorrect since we do not know how much prevention and DDT controls would cost. Choice (C) is incorrect as preventative measures are too late once bedbugs are already in the home.

18. **(A)** The author says, "people should educate themselves as to the best practices to avoid infestations." In this context, we aren't talking about practicing something like a sport or a musical instrument (thus eliminating choice (B)), but rather about a practice, meaning a thing that one does. This makes choice **(A)**, methods, the best answer. Choice (C) is incorrect since we are not talking about eliminating bedbugs, but rather preventing them. Choice (D) is incorrect since we are not observing something (like a holiday).

19. **(B)** If we look at the figure, we can see that for each year the complaints and violations grow together. The relationship between the two bars for each year is proportional, thus making choice **(B)** the best answer. Choice (A) is incorrect since the two bars are not inversely related—one is not growing while the other shrinks. Choice (C) is not correct since the two bars are generally not equal. Choice (D) is incorrect since the bars do seem to be growing together, not in an unrelated manner.

20. **(A)** Imagine another two sets of bars were added to this chart—one for 2011 and one for 2012. What would the growth look like if it followed the pattern previously established in the graph? The violations bar would continue to grow at roughly the same rate, ending up most logically around 6,000–7,000, making choice **(A)** the best answer. The other answer options are all far too great.

21. **(A)** In the first paragraph, we can see the author says that bedbug issues are seeing a comeback. In the figure, we can see that each year the number of complaints and violations are growing. This makes choice **(A)** the best answer. The other answers do not provide information that is supported by the figure. Choice (B) talks about a time when there were no infections. Choice (C) talks about the consequences of an infection. Choice (D) talks about solutions that can be used to prevent bedbug infestations.

Peace, Patriotism, and Fireworks

22. **(B)** This passage presents the concept that fireworks should be confined to just one night—July 4th. The author tries to convince readers of this by talking about the negative effects of fireworks on pets, veterans, and the environment. This makes choice **(B)** the best option.

Choice (A) is not correct because the author does not think we need to be more respectful of institutions. Choice (C) is not correct since the origins of the Fourth of July, while mentioned, are not main focus of the passage. Choice (D) is not correct because the author does not advocate for civil disobedience.

23. **(A)** If you pay close attention, you'll notice that "(PTSD)" comes after the phrase "post-traumatic stress disorder." The letters in the parentheses show us a common abbreviation for a long term that would be clunky to write repeatedly. This makes choice **(A)** the best option. This was not used previously in the passage, so it's not choice (B). The letters aren't the initials of a person, so it's not choice (C). It has nothing to do with an artistic concept, so it's not choice (D).

24. **(C)** While "draining" often means "to remove a liquid," in the context here it is speaking more of a draining of energy. This makes choice **(C)** the best option: removing energy would be exhausting. While choices (A), (B), and (D) may all be synonyms for draining within other contexts, they do not fit the context of this line.

25. **(C)** If you look at the end of the second paragraph, you'll see that the author mentions that "while firework displays were historically limited to one night a year, they now go on for days, even weeks." This best supports choice **(C)**, which indicates that firework celebrations have increased over the years. Choice (A) is the opposite of what the author said. Choice (B) implies that there has been no increase when the author insists that there has been an increase. Choice (D) says that there are essentially no fireworks displays anymore, an opinion with which the author disagrees.

26. **(B)** The best evidence for the previous question is toward the end of the second paragraph as quoted in the previous answer explanation. This is choice **(B)**. Choice (A) discusses a tradition. Choice (C) discusses veterans' response to fireworks. Choice (D) mentions how long the fireworks last today, but does not give any indication of how they have changed over time.

27. **(A)** We can see at the very end of the first paragraph that the writer is sitting with his dog, who is scared of the fireworks. This clearly tells us that the author is a pet owner, making choice **(A)** the best option. Choices (B), (C), and (D) are all incorrect, because while they *might* be true, the passage does not imply that is the case.

28. **(A)** In the end of the first paragraph, we get the clearest evidence that the writer owns a dog since he sits with his dog. Choice (B) discusses consequences of fireworks with veterans. Choice (C) discusses the environmental consequences of fireworks. Choice (D) discusses a drawback of banning fireworks.

29. **(D)** In this paragraph, the author reveals the percentage of veterans thought to suffer from PTSD and asks if fireworks are worth the consequences. This makes choice **(D)** the best option. Choice (A) is incorrect since the author does not use analogies nor does he appeal to authority. Choice (B) is incorrect as there is no personal anecdote or story. Choice (C) is incorrect, in part, because no part of this paragraph could be seen as humorous.

30. **(B)** As used within the context of the sentence, the author is saying that veterinarians and animal shelters have a reason for the way they act leading up to the Fourth of July. Reason in this situation most means "justification," making choice **(B)** the best option. It is not choice (A) since this is not merely a belief but a solid reason. It's not choice (C) since that would not fit into the sentence. It's not choice (D) since "reason" does not mean "ambition."

31. **(C)** The issues raised in the passage center around having the noise and pollution from fireworks for weeks on end. Choice **(C)** would best fix these issues because a light show would be both quiet and smoke-free. Choices (A) and (B) do not solve the problem of noise and smoke, and choice (D) only solves the problem of noise but does not address smoke pollution.

Segregation

32. **(C)** At the end of the second paragraph of Passage 1, we learn that because of Daisy's visit to the school, a young man was suspended indefinitely because of his actions against the minority students. This makes choice **(C)** the best option as it shows that Daisy convinced the administration to make this suspension. Choices (A) and (B) simply show Daisy's beliefs and the facts of the situation, not that she persuaded anyone of them. Choice (D) shows that the president is willing to visit, not that Daisy has convinced him of anything.

33. **(A)** We learn in the passage that "President Eisenhower was very much concerned about the Little Rock crisis. He has stated his willingness to come down... we have not abandoned the idea." This shows that Eisenhower is willing to help and the author is willing to take him up on that. Therefore, she must be appreciative of his offer to help, making choice **(A)** the best answer. Choice (B) is the opposite of her feelings. Choice (C) is incorrect as Eisenhower was not lacking concern about the situation. Choice (D) is incorrect as the passage does not say that Eisenhower ignored calls for interference.

34. **(B)** Within the context of the sentence, "placed" is used to describe FBI agents being put into the schools for the protection of the children. This makes choice **(B)** the best option as we would say FBI men are *stationed* at a school. Choice (A) is incorrect since the agents would be there to settle a crisis, but the agents themselves wouldn't be described as *settled*. Choice (C) is incorrect since this wouldn't be a secret operation, so the agents wouldn't be *planted*. Choice (D) is incorrect as *deposited* implies something is being dropped off, which doesn't fit the context of the passage.

35. **(C)** While some students are described as getting into fights—hitting, spitting, and kicking the new students—the author does say in the last paragraph that "our investigation revealed that there were many pupils willing to help if given the opportunity." Thus, choice **(C)** is the best option as some students were open-minded, while others were hostile. Choice (A) is incorrect as there is no uniformity of opinion across the student body. Choice (B) is incorrect because some students were abusive to the new students. Choice (D) is incorrect as we are not told whether the students are deceitful.

36. **(B)** In the first paragraph of the second passage, the author states, "In each instance, they had been denied admission to schools attended by white children under laws requiring or permitting segregation according to race." This tells the author that these children (the plaintiff in this case) had attempted to gain access to the local schools in other ways but were turned away, leaving the Supreme Court as their last resort. Therefore, choice **(B)** is the best option. Choice (A) is incorrect since the author of the passage is a member of the Supreme Court and would likely not say the Court is incapable of settling an issue. Choice (C) is incorrect since Congress cannot strike down state laws and is not discussed in the passage. Choice (D) is incorrect since that response would not logically follow from the argument that the students should seek paths other than the Supreme Court to resolve their issues.

37. **(B)** In the context of this sentence, the author is saying that "equal" treatment isn't actually equal. He therefore puts the word in quotes to show that it doesn't mean what people use it

to mean. This makes choice **(B)** the best option. Choice (A) is the opposite of the intended meaning. Choice (C) is incorrect since the quotation marks do not function to show that it's a personal account. Choice (D) is incorrect because "equal" is not an unfamiliar word to most people.

38. **(A)** Toward the end of the second to last paragraph, the author states, "Segregation with the sanction of law, therefore, has a tendency to [slow] the educational and mental development of [minority] children and to deprive them of some of the benefits they would receive in a racially integrated school." The author is clearly saying that students who are segregated have poorer educational outcomes than those who are integrated, making choice **(A)** the best option. Choice (B) is incorrect since the passage does not address extracurriculars. Choice (C) is incorrect since it is obvious that the students are aware of the discrepancy and have thus gone to the courts to fix the issue. Choice (D) is incorrect since civil disobedience is not addressed in the passage.

39. **(C)** Choice **(C)** is the best option as it is the quote used in the previous answer explanation. Choice (A) presents evidence that the students were segregated, but not the negative consequences of that segregation. Choice (B) presents the old view of segregation being acceptable as long as facilities are equal. Choice (D) simply gives a legal argument.

40. **(B)** Passage 1 is a firsthand account from experience in a school that was being forced to integrate. Passage 2 is a legal and technical argument. Thus, choice **(B)** is the best answer as the first passage is based on observations, while the second relies on more cerebral and philosophical reasoning. Choice (A) is incorrect as Passage 1 is not appealing to the historical precedent of segregation. Choice (C) is incorrect as Passage 2 does not use firsthand accounts. Choice (D) is incorrect as both passages are sensitive to a lack of equality.

41. **(C)** While Passage 1 is a private letter, Passage 2 is a publicly available legal decision. Passage 2 has a wider intended audience because it affects the general public more than Passage 1. This makes choice **(C)** the best option. Choice (A) is incorrect as the approachable writing does not change the intended audience. Choice (B) is incorrect since a letter does not widen the intended audience. Choice (D) is incorrect as the consideration given the plaintiff does not change the intended audience of the document.

42. **(A)** In Passage 1, the author recounts the horrible treatment the minority students must face in the integrated school. This makes choice **(A)** the best answer. Choice (B) is not correct as the author of Passage 1 still sees racial hostility in the school. Choice (C) is not correct as it does not correctly identify the solution. Choice (D) is not correct as conflicts did not seem to cease upon integration.

Friedel-Crafts Reactions

43. **(A)** The example of thalidomide is brought up in the fourth paragraph and introduced with the phrase "A famous example showing the importance of the selectivity is the case of a drug known as thalidomide." This shows the reader that thalidomide is introduced to the passage as an example of the previously discussed issue of selectivity, making choice **(A)** the best answer. Choice (B) is not correct as thalidomide was not successful. Choice (C) is not correct as the thalidomide example is not a personal story. Choice (D) is not correct as this is a historic example, not a current objection.

44. **(D)** Choice **(D)** is the best option as it tells the reader that being unable to separate, or break apart, products makes a reaction useless. Choice (A) tells the reader where benzene comes

from, not about its usefulness. Choice (B) explains the history of Friedel-Crafts alkylation, but it doesn't share its usefulness. Choice (C) tells the reader an issue with Friedel-Crafts alkylation, but doesn't indicate how that issue impacts usefulness.

45. **(A)** In the first paragraph, we learn that benzene is harmful to human health in its natural form but that scientists hope to "modify" it to find more uses for it. This context tells us that "modify" is being used to mean "change," making choice **(A)** the best option. Benzene is a molecule, not a person or institution, meaning it can't be persuaded or reformed, making choices (B) and (C) incorrect. *Pronounce* is similar to *announce*, so choice (D) is incorrect since the scientists aren't announcing anything.

46. **(B)** In the context of the sentence, the word "virtually" is not being used to describe something related to the internet but to mean "essentially." This means that the new reaction was essentially useless, meaning that its use was very limited. This makes choice **(B)** the best option. Choices (A) and (D) convey the opposite of this meaning. Choice (C) simply misinterprets the sentence.

47. **(B)** In the fourth paragraph, it says, "The drug was banned from production soon after this fact was realized." The fact referred to there is that the drug could harm unborn fetuses. This implies that the creators of the drug were unaware of the harm the drug could do until after the drug was released to the public. This makes the negative side effects unintentional, and choice **(B)** the best answer. Choice (A) is incorrect as there is no evidence of a cover-up. Choice (C) is incorrect since the passage does not say that the effects were blown out of proportion. Choice (D) is incorrect as the effects of the drug were very bad, not surprisingly mild.

48. **(C)** Choice (C) is the best option as it is in these lines that we learn that the drug was removed from the market after the side effects were discovered. This shows that those side effects were unintentional. Choice (A) simply introduces the topic of thalidomide but does not address the negative side effects. Choice (B) discusses the intended positive effects of the drug, but doesn't discuss the negatives. Choice (D) connects the side effects of the drug to the chemical reaction being discussed in the passage, but doesn't imply that those side effects were unintentional.

49. **(A)** In the previous paragraphs, we were discussing alkylation and its negative side effects. This paragraph starts by introducing a more controlled reaction process that will avoid the negative impact of chemical selectivity: acylation. This tells the reader that acylation is more useful than alkylation in that the chemical selectivity in acylation is more controlled. This makes choice **(A)** the best answer. Choices (B) and (C) are incorrect as they are the opposite of the relationship that is described in the passage. Choice (D) is incorrect as this passage does not discuss the affordability of the two processes.

50. **(D)** This paragraph functions to show the reader that a once unique process is now taught in basic chemistry classes and is vital in developing the items that we use in our everyday lives. This makes choice **(D)** the best option. This paragraph is not discussing the negative impact, so choice (A) is incorrect. The paragraph tells us that benzene is readily used now, so choice (B) is incorrect. The paragraph does not address the need for more safety measures, so choice (C) is incorrect.

51. **(C)** The information in the figure shows the variety of birth defects that can be seen in babies exposed to thalidomide at various times during gestation. This makes choice **(C)** the best

option. The figure does not address selectivity, morning sickness, or Friedel-Crafts reactions, making the other answer options incorrect.

52. **(C)** Looking at the figure, we can see that exposure to thalidomide in days 27–31 could lead to nine different birth defects (excluding only thumb aplasia). Exposure in this range, therefore, would interfere with the most developmental processes. Choice (A) is incorrect as exposure in this range could only lead to thumb aplasia. Choice (B) is incorrect as exposure in this range would only lead to five different defects. Choice (D) is incorrect as exposure in this range would only lead to six possible birth defects.

Section 2: Writing and Language Test

1. **(B)** Use a dash before the clarification of the relationship between the two organisms since it provides a heavy pause. Choice (A) is a comma splice. Choice (C) incorrectly uses "while" to show a contrast. Choice (D) would result in a sentence fragment for the second part.

2. **(C)** This option uses the adverb "particularly" before the adjective "interesting," thereby describing how interesting the situation is. Choices (A) and (D) both use adjectives, and choice (B) mixes up the order of the words in an illogical way.

3. **(D)** Saying "Instead of acting as a nurturing mother" introduces the information that follows since the female cuckoo does not raise her own child, but instead deposits the egg into the nest of another bird. It is not choices (A) or (B) because these would show a more cooperative relationship between the birds. And it is not choice (C) because there is no evidence that other birds deposit their eggs in the nests of European cuckoos.

4. **(A)** "Those of" correctly represents a logical comparison between the nests of the cuckoo and the plural nests of other birds. Choices (C) and (D) are both singular, and choice (B) incorrectly uses "these," which is improper wording in a comparative situation.

5. **(C)** "Goes unnoticed by" uses the proper verb phrasing in this context. Choices (A) and (B) incorrectly use "unnoticing," and choice (D) uses the incorrect preposition "with."

6. **(B)** "Its" is the correct form of the possessive for the bird's back. Choice (A) would never be correct, and choices (C) and (D) would signify "it is" instead of the possessive.

7. **(D)** The focus of this paragraph is on the hatching of the eggs of European cuckoos. Inserting a sentence about the walking abilities of the bird would be irrelevant. It is not choice (C) because this point has not already been made. It is not choices (A) or (B) because the insertion should not be made.

8. **(A)** The word "deter" is most appropriate given the context. The sentence suggests that even though the European cuckoo acts in a parasitic fashion, the non-cuckoo mother bird is not prevented, or "deterred," from caring for the cuckoo baby bird. It is not choices (B) or (D) because these words mean that the non-cuckoo bird would be aggravated by having to care for a new bird. It is not choice (C) because you cannot say "chill the bird."

9. **(B)** After sentence 2 is the most logical placement since sentence 2 refers to the quick growth of European cuckoo babies, so this inserted sentence would elaborate on the growth. The other possible placements would not follow a statement about European cuckoo growth, making the phrase "this growth" in the inserted sentence unclear.

10. **(A)** The passage describes the European cuckoo as indeed operating in a parasitic fashion, with the children of the non-cuckoo bird destroyed to make room for the European cuckoo

baby. So, a clarification that the relationship is indeed parasitic would be helpful. The other options all fail to accurately represent the parasitic relationship between the European cuckoo and other birds.

11. **(C)** This option is the only choice that shows a cause-and-effect relationship between the European cuckoo acting parasitically toward other birds and the resulting decrease in the host bird's overall fitness. Choices (A) and (B) show a contrast, and choice (D) unnecessarily inserts a time sequence indication.

12. **(C)** The transitional word "however" should be surrounded with commas since the sentence would still be logical if this word were removed. Choices (A) and (B) do not have enough commas, and choice (D) incorrectly uses a semicolon since there is not a complete sentence after the semicolon. Moreover, there is no comma after "however" in choice (D).

13. **(A)** "Are" is the only plural verb out of the options. A plural verb is necessary to match with the plural subject of "two of the primary positions." The other options are all singular verbs.

14. **(B)** There is no need to have the pronoun "they" stand in for the subject since there is no lack of clarity as to who is completing the additional graduate work. Choice **(B)** is the only option to remove the unnecessary "they" and concisely join the two sentences.

15. **(C)** "May order tests" is the only option that is parallel to the other parts of the list in this sentence, namely "may diagnose" and "may . . . prescribe." The other options all lack parallelism with respect to the rest of the sentence.

16. **(A)** "Under the supervision of" is the correct idiom to use in this context. The other phrases are not consistent with generally accepted usage.

17. **(D)** "Help" would match both the plural subject of "professionals" and the present tense of the sentence as indicated by the verb "allow." Choice (A) is a singular verb, and choices (B) and (C) are not present tense plural verbs.

18. **(D)** To find the correct answer, look at the 50th percentile of wages for each profession. The nurse practitioner median wage was at $111,680 and the physician assistant median wage was at $115,390, so the correct answer is **(D)**.

19. **(C)** The previous sentence makes the point that the income levels for nurse practitioners can be quite high. Choice **(C)** gives concrete evidence in support of this claim, showing the relatively high salaries that top professionals in this field can earn. Choice (A) does not cite the highest possible levels of compensation. Choice (B) focuses on comparing nurse practitioners and physician assistants instead of comparing the group of both professions to other medical professions. Choice (D) would show relatively lower compensation by nurse practitioners.

20. **(A)** "Than" is used when making comparisons, making it the logical option to compare how many workers are needed versus how many have been needed before. "Then" is used to mark time. "For" and "to" would not be used to make comparisons in this context.

21. **(D)** When joining two sentences with a conjunctive adverb like "moreover," you need a semicolon before the adverb and a comma after. Choice **(D)** is the only option that joins these sentences in this way.

22. **(B)** The general theme laid out in the first paragraph is that there are many other career options in medicine besides doctor and nurse. Choice **(B)** is the only option that reconnects

to this general theme. Choice (A) focuses more on compensation, which is discussed at a different point in the essay—not in the introductory paragraph. Choice (C) is overly broad, and choice (D) does not focus on the comparison to doctor and nurse careers.

23. **(A)** The colon is appropriate in this case because there is a complete sentence before it and a clarification after it. Choice (B) would result in a comma splice. Choice (C) would not have a complete and logical sentence after the semicolon, and choice (D) has a pause at an awkward spot.

24. **(D)** "However" is the appropriate transition in this context, since the sentence points out the contrast between the current era of governmental intervention and an era in the past when privately based bailouts were more commonplace. Choices (A) and (C) would show cause-and-effect, and choice (B) would be used to list an additional item or idea.

25. **(C)** The later part of the passage describes how Morgan was able to use his financial resources to provide a bailout that helped prevent an economic panic; choice **(C)** would highlight his ability to make a difference during a time of economic strife. Choices (A), (B), and (D) do not directly relate to his economic bailout power.

26. **(D)** In a previous sentence, the author states that Morgan was "possibly the wealthiest banker of all time." It would therefore be repetitive to use the language in choices (A), (B), or (C). Deleting the language will prevent repetition.

27. **(B)** The phrase "cannot be overstated" in this context means that it is impossible to exaggerate the extent of his wealth and influence. It is not choices (A) or (D), because these would suggest that Morgan did not possess much wealth. And it is not choice (C) because this incorrectly uses the common phrase.

28. **(C)** When parentheses are inserted in a sentence, they have no impact on the other punctuation that surrounds them. Choice **(C)** correctly uses parentheses to set aside a phrase that describes the 1907 financial crisis. Choice (A) uses excessive punctuation for the parenthetical phrase—either commas or parentheses could be used to surround it, but not both. Choice (B) incorrectly uses a semicolon, since there is not a complete sentence prior to the semicolon. Choice (D) mixes the punctuation used for the parenthetical phrase; be consistent in how you begin and end a parenthetical phrase.

29. **(A)** "So" correctly expresses a cause-and-effect relationship between the earlier sentence, which says that there was a dire situation with no government help, and the current sentence expresses that Morgan did intervene. The other options do not express a cause-and-effect relationship.

30. **(C)** While all of these options convey negative ideas, "struggling" is the most logical word to express that the banks were in need of financial help. "Derogatory" and "nasty" are associated with insults, and it would not make sense to say that bankers with whom Morgan was willing to meet would be "combative."

31. **(A)** The sentence lists different ways that the bankers resolved to solve the financial crisis. Choice **(A)** provides an example similar to the others, since it gives another concrete action that the bankers took to increase economic activity. Choice (B) would not provide a concrete action, and choices (C) and (D) are overly pessimistic.

32. **(B)** Without this underlined phrase, the sentence would not make clear what Morgan's money was used for; thus, the phrase provides a relevant elaboration and should be kept.

It is not choice (A) because it does not explain how Carnegie made his money. And it is not choices (C) or (D) because the selection should remain in the passage.

33. **(B)** Later in the passage, the author suggests that letting large businesses fail could lead to better business decisions in the long term. It would therefore be most logical to put choice **(B)** in this spot, since it would ask a question that directly connects to this suggestion. It is not choice (A) because the paragraph does not go on to focus on governmental intervention. It is not choice (C) because there is no mention of revolution. And it is not choice (D) because the sentence that follows refers to the suffering that ordinary workers could face.

34. **(B)** This option correctly places a comma after the introductory phrase, separating the dependent clause from the independent clause that follows. Choice (A) would interrupt the independent clause, separating its subject, "mental stress," from the remainder of the sentence. Choice (C) incorrectly uses a semicolon after a dependent clause—a semicolon must have an independent clause on either side of it. Choice (D) has too many commas.

35. **(C)** In the previous paragraph, the sentence begins with the phrase "In the short term." To be consistent with this phrasing, "In the long term" should be used. The other options are inconsistent with the phrasing elsewhere in the paragraph and are overly wordy.

36. **(A)** The phrase "certain conditions" in this sentence is rather broad, so having a specific example like "such as heart disease" would provide a helpful clarification. It is not choice (B) because it does not explain the design of a research study. And it is not choices (C) or (D) because the phrase should be added for clarity.

37. **(B)** "Influencing" is parallel to the earlier phrasing of "contributing." The other options would not maintain this parallel structure.

38. **(A)** "Despite" signifies an oppositional relationship between the first part of the sentence, which states that the diets of the town's residents are not particularly healthy, and the unexpected lack of cardiovascular disease among the residents. The other options do not convey a contrasting relationship.

39. **(D)** The proper wording sets up a logical comparison between the residents of this town and "those" who live in surrounding areas. It is not choice (A) because "this" is singular. It is not choice (B) because "them" is used as a direct object. And it is not choice (C) because "these" is generally used with things that would be figuratively closer (like the word "this"), while "those" is used with things that are figuratively farther away (like "that").

40. **(C)** "Rose" is the correct past tense version of the verb "rise," making its use consistent with the other past tense verb in the sentence, "began." "Rise" is present tense, "risen" is used in conjunction with "have" or "had," and "rised" is not the proper past tense conjugation for the irregular verb "to rise."

41. **(A)** A comma will correctly separate the long dependent clause from the independent clause that follows. Choice (B) provides no pause, and choices (C) and (D) would need a complete sentence preceding their punctuation.

42. **(B)** The subject that corresponds to the verb is the singular word "research." Choice **(B)** correctly uses the present tense and a singular verb. Choice (A) is plural, and choice (C) is not in the present tense. While "has" as used in choice (D) would indicate the present perfect tense, the word "suggesting" is the improper conjugation of "to suggest" in the present perfect form.

43. **(D)** This is the only option that relates to the main claim of the paragraph, namely that dance is an excellent form of exercise for those who are trying to reduce physical ailments as they age. Choices (A) and (B) are overly negative, and choice (C) is not connected to the health and exercise theme of the paragraph.

44. **(C)** This option provides a broad conclusion that would encompass the themes of community and dance. Choices (A) and (B) only focus on physical exercise, and choice (D) only focuses on the Roseto Effect, ignoring the dance theme.

Section 3: Math Test (No Calculator)

1. **(A)** For a line to be totally vertical, the line must have a constant value for x. $x = -5$ works because no matter what the value of y is, the value of x will always be -5. Here is what $x = -5$ looks like when graphed:

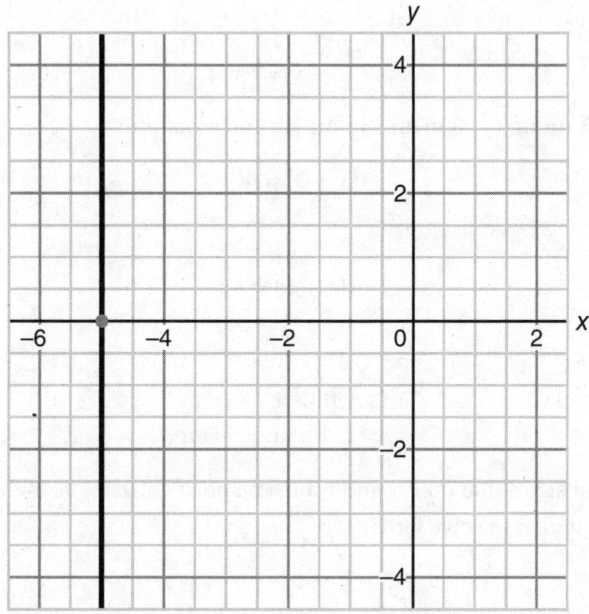

$y = -4$ represents a horizontal line, and the other options are neither horizontal nor vertical.

2. **(B)**

$$\frac{6}{7} \times \frac{14}{3} \rightarrow \text{Reduce the 6 and 3} \rightarrow$$
$$\frac{2}{7} \times \frac{14}{1} \rightarrow \text{Reduce the 14 and 7} \rightarrow$$
$$\frac{2}{1} \times \frac{2}{1} = \frac{4}{1} = 4$$

3. **(C)** $8^{\left(\frac{1}{3}\right)} \rightarrow \sqrt[3]{8} = 2$

4. **(A)**

$$\frac{x}{4} = 6 \rightarrow x = 6 \times 4 \rightarrow x = 24$$

Now that we know $x = 24$, divide 24 by 8 to get the solution:

$$\frac{24}{8} = 3$$

5. **(A)** For the equations to have infinitely many solutions, the two equations should be multiples of each other.

$$2x - 3y = 7$$
$$6x + ky = 21$$

The second equation is three times that of the first equation, since 21 is three times 7 and 6 is three times 2. So, k should be three times -3, which is -9.

6. **(B)** The y-intercept is the point at which the function intersects the y-axis—the value of x at this point must be 0. So, plug 0 in for x in the equation to solve for the y-intercept (keep in mind that a number to the zero power is equal to 1):

$$y = 2^x - 3 \rightarrow y = 2^0 - 3 \rightarrow 1 - 3 = -2$$

7. **(A)** Plug in the first series of values, $x = 4$and $y = 2$, to solve for the constant k:

$$y = \frac{k}{x} \rightarrow 2 = \frac{k}{4} \rightarrow k = 8$$

Now that we know that k is equal to 8, plug 8 in for the constant k and plug 8 in for the value of x:

$$y = \frac{k}{x} \rightarrow y = \frac{8}{8} = 1$$

8. **(C)** Start by substituting $x + 3$ in for y to the second equation:

$$x(x + 3) = 40$$

Now, solve for x:

$$x(x + 3) = 40 \rightarrow$$
$$x^2 + 3x = 40 \rightarrow$$
$$x^2 + 3x - 40 = 0 \rightarrow$$
$$(x + 8)(x - 5) \rightarrow$$
$$x = -8 \text{ or } 5$$

Since the question states that both x and y must be positive, use 5 as the value of x. Then plug 5 in to the first equation to solve for y:

$$x + 3 = y \rightarrow 5 + 3 = 8 = y$$

Now, find the sum of x and y by adding their values together:

$$8 + 5 = 13$$

9. **(D)**

$$12 < -4x + 6y \rightarrow$$

Divide everything by 2 to simplify:

$$6 < -2x + 3y \rightarrow$$

Get y by itself $\rightarrow$

$$6 + 2x < 3y \rightarrow$$

Divide both sides by 3 $\rightarrow$

$$2 + \frac{2}{3}x < y$$

10. **(A)** The line is horizontal, with every value of x giving the same value of y: 3. So, the equation of the line is $y = 3$.

11. **(D)** Looking ahead to the format of the answers, it appears that the quadratic formula will be used to solve for this. Start by putting the equation in quadratic form:

$$4x = 2 - 3x^2 \rightarrow$$
$$3x^2 + 4x - 2 = 0$$

Now, use the quadratic equation to solve for x:

$$x = \frac{-b \pm \sqrt{b^2 - 4ac}}{2a} \rightarrow$$
$$3x^2 + 4x - 2 = 0 \rightarrow$$
$$a = 3,\ b = 4,\ c = -2$$
$$x = \frac{-4 \pm \sqrt{4^2 - 4(3)(-2)}}{2(3)} \rightarrow$$
$$x = \frac{-4 \pm \sqrt{16 + 24}}{6} \rightarrow$$
$$x = \frac{-4 \pm \sqrt{40}}{6} = \frac{-4 \pm \sqrt{4 \times 10}}{6} \rightarrow$$
$$x = \frac{-4 \pm 2\sqrt{10}}{6} = \frac{-2 \pm \sqrt{10}}{3}$$

Out of the two solutions, $\frac{-2 - \sqrt{10}}{3}$ is the only one given, making **(D)** correct.

12. **(B)** Add $(4i + 3i^2)$ and $(7 + 2i)$ to find the sum. Keep in mind that $i^2 = -1$ since $i = \sqrt{-1}$.

$$(4i + 3i^2) + (7 + 2i) \rightarrow$$
$$(4i - 3) + (7 + 2i) \rightarrow$$
$$4 + 6i$$

13. **(A)** Factors of the function can be found at the x-intercepts. Look for the x values where $g(x)$ is equal to 0: -2 and 1. Then see which option would make it so that plugging these two numbers in would result in a value of 0. The only option is choice **(A)**, $(x - 1)(x + 2)$.

14. **(C)** Manipulate the equation so that M is isolated.

$$v_e = \sqrt{\frac{2GM}{r}} \rightarrow \text{Square both sides} \rightarrow$$
$$(v_e)^2 = \frac{2GM}{r} \rightarrow \text{Get } M \text{ by itself} \rightarrow$$
$$\frac{(v_e)^2 r}{2G} = M$$

15. **(B)** The graph of the parabola intersects the x-axis at -2, 1, and 4. So, see which equation would have those as zeros, i.e., plugging in these numbers would cause the value of the function to equal zero. The only one that has all three of these numbers as zeros is

$$y = (x - 4)(x + 2)(x - 1).$$

16. **3**

$$\frac{x^2}{6} = \frac{x}{2} \rightarrow \text{Divide both sides by } x \rightarrow$$
$$\frac{x}{6} = \frac{1}{2} \rightarrow x = \frac{6}{2} \rightarrow x = 3$$

17. **2, 3, or 4** This is easiest to solve by plugging in some possible numbers. If Connor purchases 2 cheeseburgers for \$10, he would need to purchase 3, 4, or 5 hamburgers to be within the \$20–\$30 range. If Connor purchases 3 cheeseburgers for \$15, he would need to purchase 2, 3, or 4 hamburgers to be in the range. If he purchases 4 cheeseburgers for \$20, he could purchase 2 hamburgers to be in the range. And if he purchases more than 4 cheeseburgers, he would fall outside the range since he has to purchase at least 2 hamburgers.

18. **63** Since $(x+y)(x-y)=x^2-y^2$, substitute 7 and 3 in for these expressions and multiply the product by 3 to arrive at the answer:

$$3x^2-3y^2=3(x+y)(x-y)=3(7)(3)=63$$

19. **25** $\angle X$ is an inscribed angle that is across from an intercepted arc that measures 50 degrees. The rule is that an inscribed angle is half the length of the intercepted arc, so take half of 50 to get 25 degrees.

20. **64** Write an equation for the original sphere:

$$V=\frac{4}{3}\pi r^3 \rightarrow$$
$$8=\frac{4}{3}\pi r^3$$

A sphere with a radius of twice this original one would have a radius of $2r$. Calculate the value of this new sphere in terms of r:

$$V=\frac{4}{3}\pi(2r)^3=\frac{4}{3}\pi(8r)$$

So, the volume of the new sphere is 8 times the volume of the original sphere: $8\times 8=64$ cubic feet.

Section 4: Math Test (Calculator)

1. **(B)** Put the equation in slope-intercept form: $y=mx+b$. The y-intercept is 0, and the slope is 3—calculate the slope either by visualizing the rise over the run or by plugging in points to the slope formula. You can use the points (0, 0) and (2, 6):

$$slope=\frac{y_2-y_1}{x_2-x_1}=\frac{6-0}{2-0}=3$$

The mass corresponds to the y value and the v corresponds to the x value. So, the equation will be $m=3v$.

2. **(A)** Since the slope is defined as the change in y divided by the change in x, and since the mass corresponds to the y value and the v corresponds to the x value, the slope will equal the density of the substance.

3. **(C)**

$$(5x^3-x+4)+(6x^3+x^2-3)=$$
$$(5x^3+6x^3)+x^2-x+(4-3)=$$
$$11x^3+x^2-x+1$$

4. **(B)** The numbers are already in order from least to greatest. Since there is an even number of terms and the two middle terms are different from one another, take the average of the two middle terms, 7 and 9, to find the median of the set:

$$\frac{7+9}{2}=8$$

5. **(C)** In 1993 the student enrollment was approximately 680, and in 1994 the student enrollment was also approximately 680. So, the enrollment stayed steady between 1993 and 1994.

6. **(D)** Distance is represented by r in the equation. Double the r to see how the overall force would change:

$$F_g = G\frac{m_1 m_2}{r^2} \rightarrow \text{Double the } r \rightarrow$$

$$F_g = G\frac{m_1 m_2}{(2r)^2} = G\frac{m_1 m_2}{4r^2}$$

So, the force would change such that it is $\frac{1}{4}$ of the original force.

7. **(A)** Manipulate the equation so that you isolate the m_2. Multiply both sides by r^2, then divide both sides by m_1:

$$F_g = G\frac{m_1 m_2}{r^2} \rightarrow F_g r^2 = Gm_1 m_2 \rightarrow \frac{F_g r^2}{Gm_1} = m_2$$

8. **(B)** Use the graph to find the slope and the y-intercept of the line. The y-intercept is at $(0, -1)$. The slope is calculated by finding the change in y divided by the change in x. Use the points $(0, -1)$ and $(1.5, 0)$ to find the slope:

$$slope = \frac{y_2 - y_1}{x_2 - x_1} = \frac{-1 - 0}{0 - 1.5} = \frac{-1}{-1.5} = \frac{2}{3}$$

So, the equation of the line in slope-intercept form is $y = \frac{2}{3}x - 1$. Now, manipulate the equation so that it is in standard form:

$$y = \frac{2}{3}x - 1 \rightarrow y - \frac{2}{3}x = -1$$

Then, multiply both sides by 3 to get it in the form $ax + by = 3$:

$$3\left(y - \frac{2}{3}x\right) = 3(-1) \rightarrow$$

$$3y - 2x = 3$$

So, $a = 3$ and $b = -2$. Add them together to get -1.

You could also solve this by manipulating the equation $ax + by = 3$ and getting it in slope-intercept form:

$$ax + by = 3 \rightarrow by = -ax + 3 \rightarrow y = -\frac{a}{b}x + \frac{3}{b}$$

Using the slope of $\frac{2}{3}$ and y-intercept of -1 derived from the graph, you could solve for a and b and then add them together.

9. **(B)** Convert from teaspoons to tablespoons, and then to cups.

$$12 \text{ teaspoons} \times \frac{1 \text{ tablespoon}}{3 \text{ teaspoons}} \times \frac{1 \text{ cup}}{16 \text{ tablespoons}} \rightarrow$$

$$12 \text{ teaspoons} \times \frac{1 \text{ tablespoon}}{3 \text{ teaspoons}} \times \frac{1 \text{ cup}}{16 \text{ tablespoons}} = \frac{12}{3 \times 16} = \frac{12}{48} = \frac{1}{4} \text{ cup}$$

10. **(D)** Use elimination to solve for a, cancelling out the b terms:

$$\begin{array}{r} a + 2b = 11 \\ \underline{+\,3a - 2b = 1} \\ 4a = 12 \end{array}$$

Then, divide both sides by 4 to solve for a:

$$4a = 12 \rightarrow a = \frac{12}{4} = 3$$

11. **(B)** Choice **(B)** is the only option that will eliminate terms when it is simplified, allowing it to look like $z = x - y$:

$$(\sqrt{x} - \sqrt{y})(\sqrt{x} + \sqrt{y}) \rightarrow \text{FOIL the expression} \rightarrow$$
$$(\sqrt{x})(\sqrt{x}) + (\sqrt{x})(\sqrt{y}) - (\sqrt{x})(\sqrt{y}) - (\sqrt{y})(\sqrt{y}) =$$
$$x + \cancel{(\sqrt{x})(\sqrt{y})} - \cancel{(\sqrt{x})(\sqrt{y})} - y =$$
$$x - y$$

12. **(C)** If there is a 30% discount, the new price of the of the product is $100\,\% - 30\,\% = 70\%$ of the original price. Since the original price is p, take 70% of p. Move the decimal point on 70 to the left two spots, giving you 0.7. Then multiply it by p for the solution: $0.7p$.

13. **(D)** Convert the 5,000 meters to feet:

$$5,000 \text{ meters} \times \frac{1 \text{ foot}}{0.3048 \text{ meters}} \rightarrow$$
$$5,000 \cancel{\text{meters}} \times \frac{1 \text{ foot}}{0.3048 \cancel{\text{meters}}} \approx 16,400 \text{ feet}$$

14. **(C)** The line has a y-intercept of 0, and you can calculate the slope of the line using the points (0, 0) and (−2, 6):

$$slope = \frac{y_2 - y_1}{x_2 - x_1} = \frac{6 - 0}{-2 - 0} = -3$$

So, the equation of the line is $y = -3x$. Thus, if a point on the above line has an x value of a, plug in a for x to see what the y-coordinate would be:

$$y = -3x = -3a$$

15. **(A)** There is a total of 188 people in the table. Out of these 188, there are 40 male cat owners. So, divide 40 by 188 to get the probability that a randomly selected pet owner would be a male cat owner: $\frac{40}{188}$.

16. **(D)** You can eliminate choices (A) and (C) since the mass is going down. And you can eliminate choice (A) because the mass is not decreasing at a steady, linear rate. So, the answer is **(D)** because the mass is both decreasing and doing so at an exponential rate.

17. **(B)** The number of minutes spent watering each tree is 5, and the number of minutes watering each shrub is 2. So, find the total number of minutes spent watering the sum of the plants by multiplying the number of each plant by the amount of time each plant type is watered:

$$5T + 2S$$

This total must be no more than 30 minutes, meaning it can be less than or equal to 30 minutes. Putting this all together, you have this expression:

$$5T + 2S \leq 30$$

18. **(C)** Sarah travelled 5 miles for 17 minutes. So, convert 5 miles per 17 minutes to miles per hour:

$$\frac{5\text{ miles}}{17\text{ }\cancel{\text{minutes}}} \times \frac{60\text{ }\cancel{\text{minutes}}}{1\text{ hour}} = 17.6\text{ miles/hour}$$

19. **(B)** Start by finding the total distance in miles that Johann travels during the two segments of his trip:

$$4.9 + 5.7 = 10.6\text{ miles}$$

Then, calculate the total number of minutes he travels:

$$19 + 33 = 52\text{ minutes}$$

Finally, convert the 10.6 miles per 52 minutes to miles per hour:

$$\frac{10.6\text{ miles}}{52\text{ }\cancel{\text{minutes}}} \times \frac{60\text{ }\cancel{\text{minutes}}}{1\text{ hour}} = 12.2\text{ miles/hour}$$

20. **(A)**

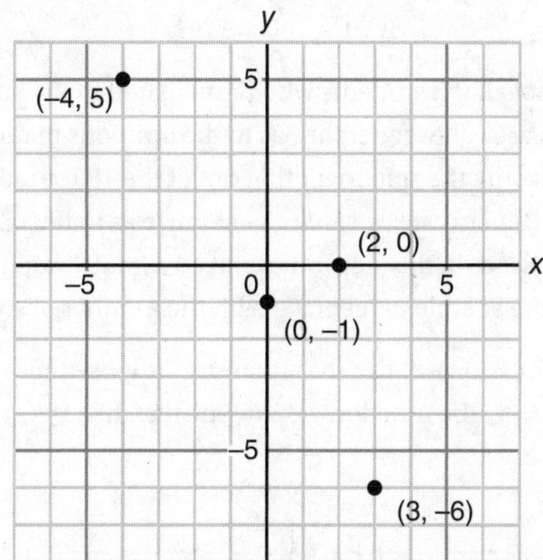

Given that the line has both a positive slope and a positive y-intercept, the line must be above the x-axis for values of x greater than 0. So, choices (B), (C), and (D) will not work since they would fall on or underneath the x-axis for values of x greater than 0. Choice **(A)** would work because it is already above the x-axis even when it has a negative value for x. A line with the point $(-4, 5)$ could continue with a positive slope and also have a positive y-intercept.

21. **(B)** Take 35, divide it by 70, and multiply the result by 100 to determine what percentage 35 is of 70:

$$\frac{35}{70} \times 100 = 50\%$$

22. **(A)** Use a as the number of aluminum cans and g as the number of glass bottles to create an inequality expressing that the total money made is at least \$100.

$$0.1a + 0.16g \geq 100$$

Then, substitute 600 in for a, since we know that she has collected 600 cans, and solve for g:

$$0.1(600) + 0.16g \geq 100 \rightarrow$$
$$60 + 0.16g \geq 100 \rightarrow$$
$$0.16g \geq 40 \rightarrow$$
$$g \geq \frac{40}{0.16} \rightarrow$$
$$g \geq 250$$

So, the least possible value for the number of bottles would be 250.

23. **(D)** Take the 300 cubic meters and multiply it by the density for steel, 7,850 kilograms per cubic meter, to get the total weight of the wall:

$$300 \times 7,850 = 2,355,000 \text{ kilograms}$$

24. **(B)** Since the blocks are the same volume, you can simply compare how much greater a cubic meter of cement is than a cubic meter of cedarwood. First, find the difference in their densities:

$$1,440 - 380 = 1,060$$

Then, divide the difference by the density of a cubic meter of cedarwood to find the percent difference between the two densities:

$$\frac{1,060}{380} \approx 2.79$$

Convert this to a percentage by multiplying it by 100:

$$2.79 \times 100 = 279\%$$

25. **(A)** Since we do not know if the students who participated in the survey were randomly selected, we can only reasonably generalize as to the opinions of those who participated in the survey. So, we can justify the statement that out of the 100 students surveyed, 40 wanted a new library. It is not (B) because we cannot generalize as to the opinions of all university community members based on this non-randomized sample. And it is not (C) or (D) because these options confuse the sample percentage with the number of students.

26. **(C)** Plug in a number for *k* to visualize the situation. Suppose that *k* is equal to 3. Then the function would be $f(x) = 3$. The function would look like this:

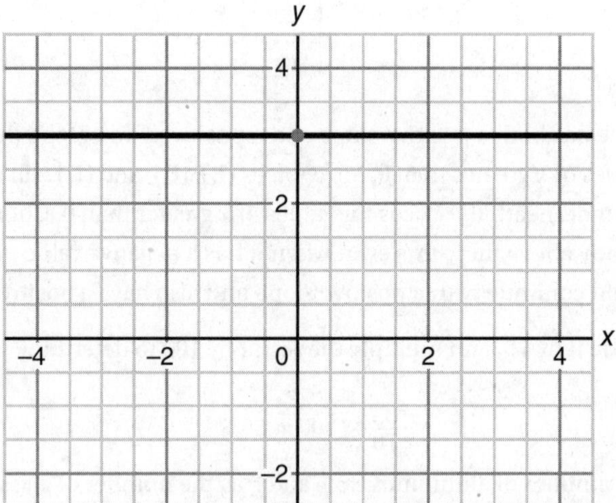

Condition 1 fits, since the function is a line. Condition 2 fits, since the function is flat and has a slope of zero. Condition 3 does not fit because the *domain* (corresponds to *x* values) goes from positive to negative infinity, but the *range* (corresponds to *y* values) is only 3. So, just conditions I and II will apply.

27. **(B)** Since the cards are returned to the set after each selection, the total number of choices will remain at 10. So, the probability that someone would pick a 9 on this selection would simply be $\frac{1}{10}$.

28. **(D)** The smallest edge is 2 cm, the next greatest edge will be 4 cm, and the greatest edge will be 6 cm. The prism will look like this:

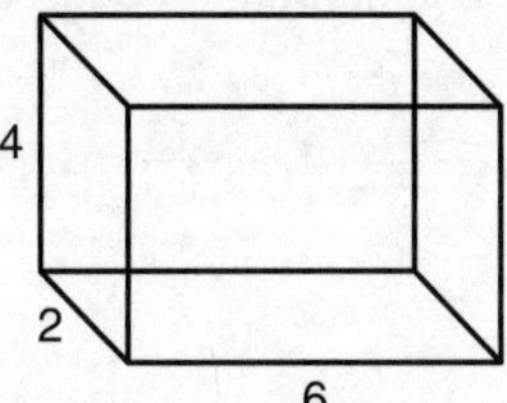

There are two sides with dimensions 2×4, two sides with dimensions 4×6, and two sides with dimensions 2×6. So, add these surfaces areas together to find the total surface area of the prism:

$$2(2 \times 4) + 2(4 \times 6) + 2(2 \times 6) =$$
$$2(8) + 2(24) + 2(12) =$$
$$16 + 48 + 24 = 88$$

29. **(D)** Since the area of the square is 36 square units, the length of each side will be the square root of 36: 6. Label the drawing to visualize the side lengths, and notice that 45-45-90 triangles are inscribed in the larger square, since each side is bisected by a vertex of the inner square.

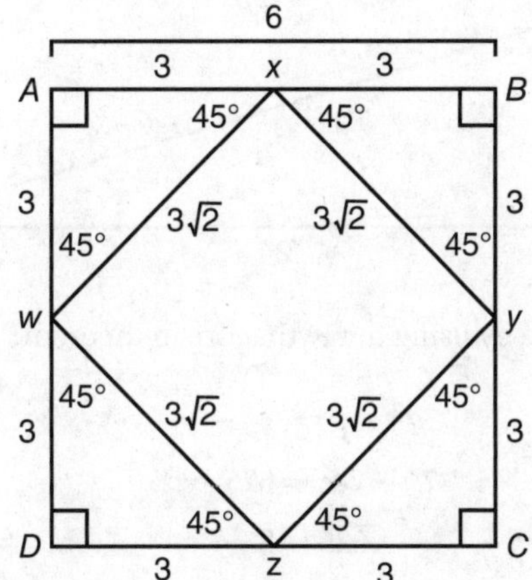

Add the four sides of square *WXYZ* to find its perimeter:

$$3\sqrt{2} + 3\sqrt{2} + 3\sqrt{2} + 3\sqrt{2} = 12\sqrt{2}$$

30. **(C)** Recall the formula for compound interest:

$$A = P\left(1 + \frac{r}{n}\right)^{nt}$$

A = Future Value
P = Initial Value (Principal)
r = Interest Rate Expressed as a Decimal (r is positive if increasing, negative if decreasing)
t = Time
n = Number of Times Interest Is Compounded over Time Period t

Applying this formula to the problem, v would be the initial value, and t would be the number of years. The constant c corresponds to the part in parentheses: $1 + \frac{r}{n}$. Since the price increases 15% each year, the number of times that it is compounded is just one. So, turn 15% into a decimal to determine what $1 + \frac{r}{n}$ will equal:

$$1 + \frac{r}{n} \rightarrow 1 + \frac{0.15}{1} = 1.15$$

So, the constant c will equal 1.15.

31. **10**

$$\frac{2}{3}x - 1 = \frac{1}{6}x + 4 \rightarrow$$
$$\frac{2}{3}x = \frac{1}{6}x + 5 \rightarrow$$
$$\frac{2}{3}x - \frac{1}{6}x = 5 \rightarrow$$
$$\frac{4}{6}x - \frac{1}{6}x = 5 \rightarrow$$
$$\frac{3}{6}x = 5 \rightarrow$$
$$\frac{1}{2}x = 5 \rightarrow x = 10$$

32. **25** The triangle can be drawn as follows:

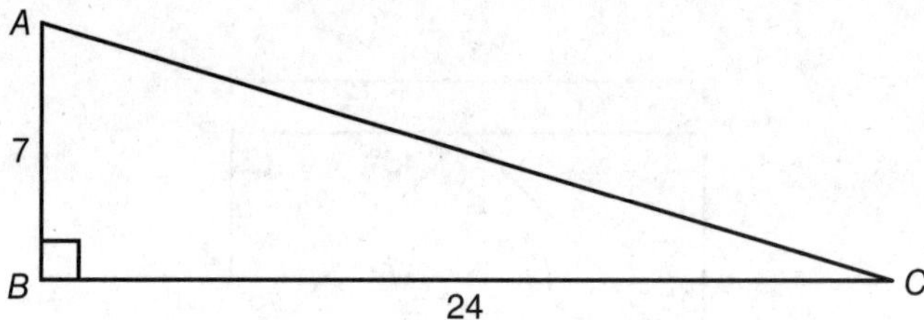

Solve for the unknown side by using the Pythagorean theorem:

$$a^2 + b^2 = c^2 \rightarrow$$
$$7^2 + 24^2 = 625 = c^2 \rightarrow$$
$$\sqrt{625} = 25 = c$$

So, the side $AC = 25$. Alternatively, you can recognize that this is a Pythagorean triple that you could have memorized: 7-24-25.

33. **6** Subtract the calories of the cheese and vegetables from the total calories of the salad to find how many calories come from salad dressing:

$$1{,}100 - 650 = 450$$

Now, divide 450 by 75 to find the number of salad dressing packets used:

$$450 \div 75 = 6$$

So, 6 packets of salad dressing were used.

34. **3** Notice a pattern here—if you add the two equations together, you will be able to simplify the expression so that you can solve for $a - b$.

$$\begin{array}{r} 2a - 3b = 5 \\ +\ \underline{3a - 2b = 10} \\ 5a - 5b = 15 \end{array}$$

Then, divide the whole equation by 5, and you will have the needed expression:

$$\frac{5a - 5b = 15}{5} \rightarrow a - b = 3$$

Thus, $a - b$ is equal to 3.

35. **3** For the equations to have infinitely many solutions, they should be equal to one another. This will cause them to overlap. So, a must equal 3 so that you would have the expression $3x + 2 = 3x + 2$. If needed, you can verify that this works by plugging in any real number for x.

36. **2.74** Set up an equation that uses x as the number of gallons of Dead Sea water that would be needed to add to the 10 gallons of ocean water to get water with 10% salt. The 3.35% is expressed as 0.035 and the 33.7% is expressed as 0.337 since you move the decimal point to the right two spots when calculating percentages. The $10 + x$ represents the total number of gallons.

$$0.035 \times 10 + 0.337x = .1(10 + x) \rightarrow$$
$$0.35 + 0.337x = 1 + 0.1x \rightarrow$$
$$0.337x = .65 + 0.1x \rightarrow$$
$$0.237x = 0.65 \rightarrow$$
$$x = \frac{0.65}{0.237} = 2.74$$

37. **65.8** Calculate the total height of the 7 boys by using the mean formula and solving for the sum:

$$\frac{Sum}{7} = 67 \rightarrow Sum = 469$$

Now, subtract the height of 74 from the total:

$$469 - 74 = 395$$

Finally, find the mean of the 6 boys using 395 as the sum:

$$\frac{395}{6} \approx 65.8$$

38. **0.5 or $\frac{1}{2}$** Solve for the vertex of the parabola, since at that point the projectile will reach its maximum. Use the formula $\frac{-b}{2a}$ to find the time at which it will reach its maximum. The function $h(t) = -16t^2 + 16t + 10$ is already in quadratic form, so you can see the values needed for a and for b. Use -16 for a and 16 for b:

$$\frac{-b}{2a} \rightarrow \frac{-(16)}{2(-16)} = \frac{16}{32} = \frac{1}{2}$$

PART 3
Reading

Introduction and Strategies

What is tested on the SAT Reading?

The SAT Reading section tests your ability to comprehend and analyze reading passages in a variety of styles. No matter your choice of college major or career, it will be important to be skilled in interpreting written material and graphics. While you will not need any specific background knowledge of the passage topics, the more widely and deeply you have read, the easier the SAT Reading will be for you.

How is the SAT Reading section structured?

The Reading section is the first section of the test.

- 65 minutes long
- 5 total reading passages
- 52 total multiple-choice questions (no fill-in)

Each of the five passages is between 500–750 words in length. The passage types are as follows:

- **Fiction/Literature**—this may be a short story or an excerpt from a novel.
- **Social Science**—this may be something you would find in a social studies class, like psychology, sociology, anthropology, or economics.
- **Historical Document**—this may be a selection from a speech, letter, or government document; often, it has a theme related to the struggle for human rights or the foundations of democracy.
- **Two Science Passages**—topics could include most any general scientific area, like biology, astronomy, geology, physics, or chemistry.
- **Passage 1 and Passage 2**—instead of one longer passage, one of the nonfiction texts will have two shorter passages to read and compare.
- **Graphs**—two of the passages will have graphs associated with the passage topic for you to analyze.

The fiction passage is always first, and the nonfiction passages follow in random order. The questions on the SAT Reading are in a random order of difficulty, but are generally presented in the same order that they are found in the reading passage. Here are the types of questions you will find on the SAT Reading:

Question Type	Typical Number of Questions	Example
Interpretation	7	*According to the passage, Kristen felt most comfortable on her voyage when she . . .*
Inference	4–5	*It can reasonably be inferred from the passage that which species was most dominant in the biome?*
Function/Purpose	5	*The main function of the fourth paragraph (lines 40–50) is to . . .*
Evidence	10	*What choice provides the best evidence for the answer to the previous question?*
Big Picture	4–5	*The primary argument of the passage as a whole is . . .*
Critical Thinking	3–4	*What conclusion is best supported by the result of Smith's series of experiments?*
Comparative	2–3	*What choice provides a central difference in how the two passages approach the role of friendship?*
Words in Context	10	*As used in line 24, "compromise" most nearly means . . .*
Graph Analysis	4–5	*According to Figure 2, which year had the greatest increase in gross domestic product?*

How does the SAT Reading differ from typical tests I have taken in school?

If you find yourself frustrated with your performance on the SAT Reading section because you excel in your regular high school coursework, understand that the way you need to approach the SAT Reading is different from how you approach reading textbooks in school.

Typical School Reading for Tests and Quizzes	SAT Reading
Closed Book—rarely can you refer back to the textbook on your in-school tests.	**Open Book**—you can refer back to the passages as often as you need.
Memorize Facts—questions often assess your ability to remember specific information. It is vital to take careful notes and reread so that you can recall the facts on the test.	**Interpret Ideas**—rather than having quite a few factual recall questions, you will be asked about determining the author's purpose, drawing reasonable inferences, and analyzing the main argument.
Small Picture Focus—when you read, you need to absorb all the small bits of information, memorizing important details.	**Big Picture Focus**—when you read, absorb the author's main argument and the overall structure of the passage.

How is the SAT Reading section scored?

Since there is NO penalty for guessing, be certain to answer *every* question on the SAT Reading section. The Reading and the Writing and Language sections (sections #1 and #2 of the test) are combined to give you an Evidence-Based Reading and Writing score out of a maximum of 800 points and minimum of 200 points. The test is curved so that if the test is more difficult, you can miss more questions to get a particular score, and if it is easier, you can miss fewer questions to get a particular score. To give you a rough idea of how many questions you need to answer correctly on the Reading to get a certain score, take a look at this table. Keep in mind that you would need to have a similar score on the Writing and Language section to have the score out of 800 noted below.

Correct Answers Out of 52 Total Reading Questions	Approximate Corresponding Evidence-Based Reading and Writing Score Out of 800 Points (both of these sections will affect this score)
52	800
49	740
46	680
42	620
38	580
34	540
30	500
25	440
20	400
15	360
10	320
5	240
0	200

How can I use this book to prepare for the SAT Reading section?

- Read the Reading test-taking strategies that follow in this section. Consider which specific approaches would work best for you.
- Target your review by practicing with the question types and passage types that you find most challenging. The drills that follow in this chapter are designed with targeted practice in mind.
- Take full-length SAT Reading tests and review your answers afterwards. Reflect on what is working well and what is not working well, then adjust your strategies as needed.
- Challenge yourself with the advanced SAT Reading drills at the end of the chapter to simulate the toughest questions you could encounter.
- If you struggle with the vocabulary found in the passages and the questions, study the Vocabulary Appendix at the end of the book.

Passage Reading Strategies

Read the Passage Actively, Not Passively

It is easy to let yourself become distracted or bored when reading a passage, such that while your eyes may be moving across the page, your mind is somewhere else. Keep this from happening by doing the following:

- **Ask questions about the passage.** The more you ask yourself questions as you read, the easier it will be to answer the questions you are asked. Ask things like: "What is the main point of this passage?" "Who are the characters?" "Is this the argument of the author or is she considering a different point of view?"
- **Make connections to the passage topic.** Just as you would try to find something in common with someone you just met to get to know them, see what experiences or knowledge you have that can relate to the passage topic.
- **Make predictions about what may come next.** Try to anticipate where a story or an argument is headed, then see if you are correct as you read further. Look at the introductory information about a passage to make predictions before even starting. On comparative passages, make an educated guess about what the second passage may argue before you read it.
- **Catch yourself if you begin to lose focus.** If you read the first paragraph and it didn't sink in, give it another quick read. Don't allow yourself to get halfway through the passage with no idea what is going on.
- **Paraphrase the passage.** The more comfortable you are putting the message of the passage in your own words as you read, the easier it will be for you to answer questions that ask you to paraphrase and analyze the selection.
- **Underline key words and make small notations to stay engaged with the passage.** You are able to write all over the passage—no one else needs to use your test booklet. While you do not need to take detailed notes as you would if you were preparing for a big test in school (in which you would have to read lots of material over a longer period of time), some small notations and underlining may help you keep your focus.
- **You will only need the information on the page.** While having background knowledge about the passage topic can be helpful, everything you need to understand the passage is right in front of you. If you read it actively, you will be in excellent shape to answer the questions.
- **Active reading prepares you to make inferences.** If the SAT Reading only had questions about the meaning of specific words and small details, you would not have to read the passage to perform well—you could simply go back to the passage and locate those details. Since so many of the SAT Reading questions require you to think critically and deeply analyze the passage, you will be best served by reading it well before jumping in to the questions.
- **Read at a steady pace, at about 100–150 words per minute.** You can take about five minutes to read each SAT Reading passage. Skimming and speed-reading are not at all necessary. Approximately 100–150 words per minute is the pace at which most students talk, so reading in this way is very doable.

Think of active reading like active listening. In your school classes, you will get much more out of the teacher's lecture if you connect to what they are saying and ask questions. You will be much better prepared for the test if you are mentally active, not passively writing notes while your mind is on other topics.

Adjust How You Read Based on the Type of Passage

Short stories are structured very differently from nonfiction arguments. Change the way you approach each passage to maximize comprehension. It is helpful to give more attention to certain parts of and ask different questions about different types of passages.

Type of Passage	What to Read More Slowly	Types of Questions to Ask to Read Actively
Fiction	Read the first paragraph or two more carefully to fully understand the setting, characters, and beginning of the plot.	*Which character is speaking right now?* *What is the sequence of events? Are there any flashbacks?* *What emotions are being expressed in the story?*
Science (Social and Natural)	Read the first paragraph, topic sentences (first sentence of each of the body paragraphs), and last paragraph more carefully. This will help you understand the thesis and overall structure of the essay.	*Is this an argumentative essay, and if so, what is their argument?* *Is this a presentation of scientific findings? What is a summary of the main discoveries?* *Is the author considering objections? Am I avoiding confusing the author's position and the position of others?* *If there are graphs, how do they relate to what is presented in the passage?*
Historical Document	Since this is also nonfiction, go more slowly on the first paragraph, topic sentences, and last paragraph. Allow a bit more time (including the occasional pause to collect your thoughts) if needed to understand the style of writing since it may be from an earlier time period.	*What type of document is this? A speech, a letter, an editorial, or a government document?* *What is the point of this document? Is it to present an argument or highlight an issue?* *What are the cultural assumptions in the environment in which the document was written? Does the author suggest different views from modern ones about gender, ethnicity, and/or social class?*

(*Continued*)

Type of Passage	What to Read More Slowly	Types of Questions to Ask to Read Actively
Passage 1 & Passage 2	This will be nonfiction, so read the first paragraph and beginning of each body paragraph more slowly. Since the first few questions are about just Passage 1, you may want to read Passage 1 first, do its questions, then do Passage 2 and the comparative questions.	*What is the thesis—the main argument—of each passage? What are they trying to show the reader or convince the reader to believe?* *What is similar about the passages? Do they share any assumptions in terms of facts or opinions?* *What is different about the passages? What would each author think about the other author's argument?*

Active Reading Demonstration: In the right margin alongside the following passage, you will see examples of the types of active reading approaches you might take while reading an SAT passage. You will also see some key words and phrases underlined. Keep in mind that there is not one correct way to read actively—so long as you are thoroughly engaged in what you are reading, you are doing it the right way. *The boxes indicate possible thoughts you could have while reading—there is no need to write out whole sentences as seen in the boxes as that would slow you down.*

> This is a nonfiction passage. I should read the first paragraph, topic sentences, and last paragraph more slowly.

> This introductory sentence gives me a summary of what this passage will be about—an explanation of the Vaccines for Children Program.

Vaccines for Children Program, written in 2020

The Vaccines for Children Program (VFC) was instituted in 1994, as part of the Omnibus Reconciliation Act of 1993, to provide low-income, uninsured, or underinsured children access to childhood vaccinations. Children are eligible to receive immunizations through VFC if they are Medicaid-eligible, uninsured, underinsured, and/or American Indian or Alaska Native. Underinsured means that while someone does have health insurance, it does not cover certain basic things or has a limit on those things. In the case of children and vaccines, underinsured would mean that the health insurance plan either does not cover childhood vaccinations or it might put a limit on how much the plan will pay for vaccinations, which would limit the child's access to vaccines. If their health plan does not fully cover the cost of vaccinations, underinsured children are eligible to receive vaccinations through VFC at certain federally qualified clinics.

> The author is defining an important term: "underinsured." It looks like kids who are underinsured are eligible for the Vaccines for Children Program.

Approximately half of all children are eligible to receive vaccines through VFC. VFC provides vaccines that protect children from sixteen diseases including chickenpox, Hepatitis A, Hepatitis B, diphtheria, flu, Hib, HPV, measles, mumps, polio, rotavirus, whooping cough, tetanus, rubella, pneumococcus, and meningococcus. VFC's primary aims are to reduce vaccine-preventable childhood illness and associated morbidity and mortality by increasing the availability of low-cost vaccines. The Centers for Disease Control and Prevention purchases the vaccines, which are ultimately distributed to approved providers at no cost.

I remember getting vaccinated when I was younger. I did not realize there were so many diseases for which kids can get vaccinated.

VFC was conceived in reaction to a measles outbreak among primarily unvaccinated preschool-age children (19–35 months). Measles is a highly contagious viral infection, which results, among other symptoms, in a rash and high fever. Measles is most dangerous to children under five-years-old, adults over 20-years-old, and people with compromised immune systems. Complications from measles can result in hearing loss, intellectual disability, and respiratory and neurological conditions.

Here the author is showing why the VFC came into existence—in order to prevent outbreaks of serious illnesses like measles.

In the years preceding the 1989 measles outbreak, measles, mumps, and rubella (MMR) vaccination rates among preschool-age children were under 70%. During the outbreak from 1989–1991, more than 18,000 annual cases of measles were diagnosed in contrast to approximately 3,000 annual cases diagnosed in prior years. The outbreak resulted in the deaths of hundreds of children. It was later determined that half of those children who contracted measles had not been vaccinated. The outbreak occurred in part because of a reservoir among children living in high population density areas. Those children were unvaccinated not necessarily because they lacked a primary health care provider, but because continuity of care was lost when that provider referred patients to low-cost clinics for vaccinations.

The author is using statistics to show the extent of a measles outbreak.

It looks like some people may think the reason that kids did not get vaccinated is because they did not have a primary care doctor. The author addresses that objection here.

VFC has had many successes. Since 1995, vaccination rates have increased among all races, ethnicities, and income levels. For children born between 1994 and 2013, VFC has prevented over 70 million cases of measles, over 8 million hospitalizations due to measles, and 57,300 deaths to measles. Among VFC-eligible preschool-age children, the MMR vaccination rate is over 88%. The Centers for Disease Control and Prevention estimates that the overall vaccination of children born between 1994 and 2014 has prevented 419 million illnesses and saved nearly 1 million lives.

The author is focusing on the successes of the VFC. I predict that the passage will also focus on the shortcomings of the program.

The outcomes of VFC are impressive, but the program still faces some challenges in achieving its aims. According to the Centers for Disease Control and Prevention, there are over 44,000 physicians who are VFC providers. A 2012 Department of Health and Human Services report found that 76% of those VFC providers mishandled or stored their vaccines at incorrect temperatures. This could result in medical errors or children being administered vaccines which have been stored incorrectly.

And now the author is shifting to analyzing the challenges of the VFC, like possibly incorrectly storing vaccines. My prediction was correct!

As the program has grown, the Centers for Disease Control and Prevention note that the potential for fraud has increased. To address fraud, providers who receive VFC vaccines are required to have procedures in place to prevent and investigate fraud.

The author notes that as the VFC has grown, it will be vital to have anti-fraud procedures.

Further, while the vaccines themselves are provided at no cost, providers are allowed to charge for an office visit and/or charge to administer the vaccine. The charge to administer the vaccine must be waived if the family cannot afford it, while there is no such requirement for the office visit fee.

Another potential issue—vaccine affordability—is presented. The author suggests fee waivers as a solution.

Additionally, pockets of children underserved by VFC remain. This is thought to be caused not by lack of VFC providers, but potentially by lack of access to transportation and telecommunication services. Additional steps are needed to identify and provide VFC access to these children and their families.

The passage wraps up with a call to action for more access to the VFC.

SAT Reading Questions Dos and Don'ts

Do read the question carefully, underlining and circling important words.
Don't skip key words in the question and misinterpret what is asked.
It is easy to become rushed when you read the SAT Reading questions. Read the questions only as quickly as you can fully understand what is being asked, paying close attention to key words like *infer, primary, function, suggest, NOT,* and *purpose.* Be sure that you are able to explain the question in your own words—if you cannot do so, you probably don't fully understand what is being asked.

Example (based on the passage above):

What is the primary purpose of the sentence in lines 48–49 ("The outcomes . . . aims") in the passage as a whole?

(A) To summarize the specific successes of the VFC program
(B) To dispute the possibility of shortcomings in the program's implementation
(C) To present the author's views on whether the VFC should continue
(D) To provide a transition in the focus of the author's analysis

To fully understand the question, underline and circle key words, taking your time to absorb what is asked:

What is the primary purpose of the sentence in lines 48–49 ("The outcomes . . . aims") in the passage as a whole?

Now you can see that the question asks for the main purpose that this sentence serves with respect to the entire passage. If you did not take your time in reading the question, you might think it is just asking you to summarize the sentence.

Do create an answer in your own words based on the context of the passage. Go back to the passage to paraphrase what is happening and create a broad idea of what you are looking for. It may take more time at first, but it will save you time in the long run since you will be more decisive when choosing your answer. The questions in the passage typically *go in the order* of where they are found, making it easy to find the relevant context. Often, the specific lines are mentioned; other times, you can *identify a key word* in the question and scan the passage for it.

Don't jump into the choices before you are ready. If you look at the choices before you have looked back at the passage or created your own idea of an answer, the choices can often trap you into an incorrect interpretation.

Example (based on the passage above):

What is the primary purpose of the sentence in lines 48–49 ("The outcomes . . . aims") in the passage as a whole?

(A) To summarize the specific successes of the VFC program
(B) To dispute the possibility of shortcomings in the program's implementation
(C) To present the author's views on whether the VFC should continue
(D) To provide a transition in the focus of the author's analysis

Now that you understand what is being asked, create an answer in your own words.

- The paragraph right before this sentence discusses the successes of the VFC program.
- The paragraphs after this sentence focus on shortcomings of the VFC program.
- It looks like this sentence is linking these two parts of the passage together.

Do be flexible as you review the choices, looking for any potential flaw in each option. There are lots of ways a correct answer can be phrased. Keep an open mind as you review the choices, but if you find a flaw in an answer, eliminate it. The correct answer will be 100% correct each and every time.

Don't pick answers simply because they match up with wording in the passage. If you did not fully understand what the passage was about, it will be easy to be fooled by answers that simply match wording. While correct answers often use wording that was in the passage, make sure you are not picking an answer simply because of word matching—instead, pick a choice that properly answers what is asked.

Example (based on the passage above):

What is the primary purpose of the sentence in lines 48–49 ("The outcomes . . . aims") in the passage as a whole?

Let's break down each choice:

(A) To summarize the specific successes of the VFC program
The sentence does not summarize successes of the program; it simply states that the outcomes were impressive. Also, this choice says nothing of the challenges the VFC faces.

(B) To dispute the possibility of shortcomings in the program's implementation
The sentence does not dispute the possibility of shortcomings—instead it suggests that there are shortcomings in the implementation of the VFC.

(C) To present the author's views on whether the VFC should continue
Rather than presenting the author's views on whether the VFC should continue, the focus is on presenting a balanced analysis of the successes and failures of the program.

(D) To provide a transition in the focus of the author's analysis
Considering the big picture of the passage, this sentence does provide a transition between a paragraph that focuses on the successes of the VFC to paragraphs that focus on the shortcomings of the VFC. Therefore, choice **(D)** *is correct.*

Let's practice these strategies with some more questions about this passage.

1. The main function of the sentence in lines 5–6 ("Underinsured . . . those things") is to

   (A) consider an objection.
   (B) define a key term.
   (C) present a hypothesis.
   (D) analyze a finding.

✓ Solution

Start by figuring out what is being asked—you need to find the "main function" of the sentence. In other words, what purpose does this sentence serve in the passage? Take a look at the context that surrounds lines 5–6. In the sentence prior to lines 5–6, the term "underinsured" is used to describe a way to be eligible for immunizations. In the sentence in lines 5–6, the author tells us what "underinsured" means, saying some people who have health insurance may not receive coverage for all the health needs they have. In the sentence after lines 5–6, the author takes the general definition of "underinsured" and explains how it applies to the case of childhood vaccinations. So, it appears that the sentence in lines 5–6 is used to define what "underinsured" means so that we can see how the term can apply to the case of childhood vaccination eligibility.

Now, we can examine the choices. Choice (A) is incorrect because the author is not considering an objection, but clarifying a concept. Choice (C) is incorrect because even though this passage deals with a scientific theme, the author is not presenting a hypothesis at this point. Choice (D) is incorrect because no analysis—examining the reasons behind an idea—is taking place. Choice **(B)** is correct because a key term, "underinsured," is defined.

2. Based on the information in the passage, it can reasonably be inferred that an MMR vaccination rate among children of less than 70% could likely result in

   (A) half the cases of measles present in a fully vaccinated population.
   (B) the same number of cases of measles present in a fully vaccinated population.
   (C) a measles outbreak in a high population density area.
   (D) a measles outbreak in a low population density area.

✓ Solution

What is being asked? We must make an inference—figure out what is indirectly suggested—about the potential results of having a childhood MMR vaccination rate less than 70%. Since this question does not give a specific line reference, you can find a key word in the question and then see where that is mentioned so that you can analyze the relevant context. The most prominent detail in the question is "70%," so see where this is mentioned in the passage—it is in line 30. The sentence in which we find it says that leading up to a 1989 measles outbreak, the vaccination rates among preschool-age children were under 70%. The following sentences elaborate on the large number of cases after 1989 and the resulting deaths of many children. In lines 34–36, the author elaborates further, saying that the children who were unvaccinated were living in "high population density areas."

Based on this information, it is reasonable to infer that having a lower vaccination rate in a high population density area would cause more widespread infection. The answer that corresponds to this idea is choice **(C)**. Choices (A) and (B) are incorrect since there would be more cases of measles in the 70% vaccinated area, not half or an equal number. Choice (D) is incorrect since having a low population density would help prevent the spread of disease.

3. The paragraph in lines 59–65 ("Further . . . visit fee") suggests that the author believes which of the following is a potential obstacle to widespread childhood vaccination?

   (A) Lack of affordable administration
   (B) Lack of parental involvement
   (C) Lack of effective vaccines
   (D) Lack of competent medical providers

✓ Solution

We need to determine what the author would most likely believe would potentially stand in the way of widespread childhood vaccination. Go back to the passage and analyze the paragraph to think about what might be an obstacle to this goal. The paragraph in lines 59–65 discusses how even though the vaccines themselves are free, there may be a fee to administer the vaccine. This added cost may be an obstacle to parents who do not have much money.

Now, let's examine the choices. Choice (B) is incorrect, because while this *could* be true, the author is not suggesting that a lack of parental involvement would be an obstacle to widespread childhood vaccination. Choice (C) is incorrect, because the passage has already suggested that there are effective vaccines—it is a matter of distributing them to children. Choice (D) is incorrect because the author does not suggest that the medical providers lack skill; instead, there is an issue with affordable access to vaccination clinics. Choice **(A)** is correct because the author uses this paragraph to suggest that a potential obstacle to widespread childhood vaccination is a lack of affordable access to the vaccines.

Customize Your SAT Reading Strategy

What do most students find helpful?

- **Take 13 minutes per passage.** Since there are 65 minutes and 5 passages, most students like to take 13 minutes per passage. This includes both reading the passage and doing the questions. If you read at about 100–150 words per minute, that would give you about 5 minutes to read each passage and 8 minutes to do the questions.
- **Do the questions once and do them well.** SAT Reading questions are more complex than many test questions you have previously encountered, so it is generally to your advantage to use the full amount of time to read and attempt the questions once. While double-checking works well on many other tests, on the SAT Reading it may cause you to rush the first time you work through questions or to change answers that you already had correct.

- **Check your pacing when you complete a passage.** If you check your pacing several times during a passage, it can make you more anxious and distracted. If you do not check your pace at all, you could vastly overshoot or undershoot your pacing. Checking your pace upon completing a passage will ensure that you are on track with your pace—if you are going too quickly or slowly, you can adjust your speed on the next passage.

What are some other options?

- **Spend more time on the tougher passages and less time on the easier passages.** If, for example, you find the historical document tougher to comprehend, you could spend 14–15 minutes on that passage and make up your time by spending 11–12 minutes on a science passage. As long as you average 13 minutes a passage, you'll be fine.
- **Go right to the questions on one of the passages, most likely a social or natural science passage.** If you are pretty close to finishing SAT Reading but could benefit from five to six extra minutes, you may want to pick one passage on which you will just go right to the questions. Since the fiction and historical document may have more narrative structures, you may want to go right to the questions on one of the science passages—they are likely to be a bit more straightforward.
- **Guess on one of the passages.** If you have difficulty finishing the SAT Reading section, pick the passage that is most difficult for you and guess on it. There is no guessing penalty, so you are likely to get 25% of the questions right on the passage on which you guess. Since the SAT Reading section is curved, you can still earn a very solid score when you miss several questions. If you guess on one of the passages, you will have about 16 minutes to do each of the other four passages.

Passage Order

What do most students find helpful?

- **Go in the order that the passages are presented.** If you plan on completing all the passages within the time allotted, this will be the most straightforward approach. You can simply do the passages in order and not have to spend time deciding which passage to do first and which to do last.
- **Complete all the questions about a passage when you are on that passage.** On the Math section, it makes sense to revisit questions from earlier in the test, since each question is self-contained. On the Reading, however, you would need to reacquaint yourself with each passage that you were revisiting, and that would potentially eat up valuable time. Instead, complete all the questions about a passage while you are on that passage—that way you do not have to spend time reacquainting yourself with the material.

What are some other options?

- **Start with the easiest passage first, and end with the most difficult one.** Since the Reading section comes first thing in the morning, it may help you to get warmed up with an easier passage. Based on your practice, you may be able to go into the test knowing which passage type—fiction, social science, historical document, or science—is easiest for you. If you have difficulty moving on from a passage on which you did not feel you did so well, this approach may be especially helpful. You can build positive momentum instead of getting down on yourself early in the test.

- **Look at the passage titles and decide which passage is most interesting—start with that one.** If you like the idea of building positive momentum as you do the passages, but the passage that is easiest for you varies from test to test, this may be a more effective option. Take a look at the small blurbs that come before each passage; start with whichever one seems like an interesting topic or one on which you have background knowledge. Try to spend just a few seconds looking over the passage titles so you have plenty of time to actually read the passages and answer the questions.

Question Order

What do most students find helpful?

- **Go in the order that the questions are given.** The SAT Reading questions generally go in the order in which they can be found in the passage. (This is different from the ACT, in which the Reading questions often go out of order). Given this pattern, most students prefer to avoid skipping around and simply do the questions in the order provided.
- **Skip a tough question and come back to it.** Often, the first question you will be asked on a passage involves interpreting the passage as a whole. If you did not fully understand the passage, you will be better off skipping a question like this and focusing on the more specific questions. After working through the more specific questions, you will have a better understanding of the passage as a whole and can revisit that first question. Skipping questions can be good on other challenging questions, such as ones that ask you to make inferences or ask about the function of a selection. Coming back to the question will allow your subconscious mind to process what you have read and what the answer could be, possibly making the question easier when you revisit it.

What are some other options?

- **Skim the questions before reading the passage.** The types of questions on the SAT Reading are quite predictable, so it is not generally necessary to preview the questions before reading. However, some students do find it useful:
  - If you have a hard time focusing on the passage, you may find previewing the questions helpful. You will get a sense of what things you should focus on while reading the passage.
  - If you tend to overthink the reading and want to memorize all the details, you may want to skim the questions. Knowing what you will be asked about might help you relax while reading, enabling you to focus on the big picture instead of trying to remember every fact and figure.
- **Start with the more specific questions, and end with the more general questions.** If you have more difficulty with questions about tone, purpose, inference, and function, you may want to wait on those questions and answer the questions that are about evidence and word meaning, as well as those with specific line references. Doing the more specific questions first will allow you time to put together the overall idea of what is happening in the passage, better positioning you to be successful on the big picture questions.

How can I improve my overall reading comprehension?

In order to strengthen reading skills, it is imperative to read regularly outside of what you might be assigned for school. The type of reading material you select is very important. It should be something that you enjoy learning about or reading so that you are motivated to continue even when it is difficult. The reading should be *slightly more difficult* than what you are used to in order to strengthen your mental abilities. Improving your reading comprehension is similar to lifting weights. If you never add more weight to the bar, you'll never get stronger. Reading is the same—if you never read difficult texts, your reading skills won't improve. On the other hand, texts that are just slightly above your comfort level will help improve your abilities so that difficult texts will eventually feel manageable.

Below are some resources that you can use to find reading materials that you enjoy. By using these resources, you will be able to find reading materials that both interest you and represent the type of text you may find on the SAT. Each resource includes a few sentences to help guide you through using it. Infinite reading possibilities may seem overwhelming, so if that ends up being the case, ask a librarian for help—they can assist you in developing a short list of books and readings that are tailored for you.

One final note: If you don't enjoy the topic you're reading about, if the book seems silly and the characters unbearable, or if you just don't care about the scientific study the article is covering, just stop. Put it down. Find something you're more interested in reading. In personal reading, there is no requirement to finish books you don't like. Forcing yourself to do so will only lead to you dreading your daily reading time and finding excuses to do literally anything else.

Project Gutenberg

www.gutenberg.org

This is an enormous online library of books that are in the public domain (public domain means they're old enough that no one holds copyrights to them anymore—they can be freely used). There are thousands of classics stored there. On the main webpage, there are options for various searches. There is a top 100 list, which will lead you to a list of books you've probably heard of before but never read. The bookshelf feature will allow you to explore by genre or topic—if there is a topic you're interested in, that would be a good place to start.

Internet Archives

https://archive.org

The internet Archives is more than you could read in a lifetime! It describes itself as "a non-profit library of millions of free books, movies, software, music, websites, and more." You'll want to focus on the books. It's easy to get lost on this website, so it might be simplest to stick with the open library collection. From the main page, select "books" off the menu and then "open library." At the top of the open library page, there will be options to browse by subject. You can also browse selections curated by librarians. Be careful on the internet archives—it's endless, and you can easily lose a whole afternoon that you meant to spend studying!

Side note: The open library has a lot of textbooks. If you ever find yourself writing an essay and you left your textbook at school, it can be a lifesaver!

Library of Congress Archives

www.loc.gov/collections

The above link is to the Library of Congress digital collections. These are great for practice on those historical reading passages on the SAT. For example, you can read a selection of papers by Abraham Lincoln, someone whose writings are often used on the SAT.

www.read.gov/teens

This second link is to the Library of Congress's teen page. If browsing the online digital collection is overwhelming or maybe the content is too difficult for your reading level, the teen page has a lot of resources to help you find things that might be interesting to you. You can even email a librarian to ask for suggestions.

Local Library Resources/Phone e-Reader

Most communities have a local library—have you ever been to yours? It's full of reading materials and employees who love reading. They can help you find things you'll love reading too. Go ask your librarian for some help! Something a lot of people don't realize is that libraries have done a great job keeping up with the times. Many are part of online collaborations to allow patrons to check out just about any book in existence, and often those books can be checked out via an app and read entirely on an e-reader or phone. This allows you to take your reading with you anywhere you go so that you can get your reading time in between classes, in waiting rooms, or while stuck in a traffic jam (while someone else is driving, of course).

School Library

In addition to the local library, you likely also have a school library (which many schools now call a resource center). While school libraries are often small, they are in the building where you already spend dozens of hours each week and so are very accessible. They don't have just books and magazines, but also resources geared specifically to students your age. It is likely that there will also be a librarian there who spends a large portion of their work time keeping on top of what students like to read in order make recommendations. Make friends with this person—they can be a huge help to students looking for interesting reading materials.

Magazines

If you're interested in a specific hobby or area of study, magazines are a resource that are often forgotten. Trade publications and more serious magazines (*TIME, Scientific American, National Geographic*, etc.) have a fairly high difficulty level. If you're into robotics, see if you can subscribe to a robotics magazine—when it's delivered to your mailbox, it will remind you to read! You can also read magazines at your local library or often on its website, but the magazine in the mail is a nice reminder.

Audiobooks and Podcasts

It can be difficult to find time to sit down with a good book to read. Audiobooks and podcasts are great ways to consume high-quality media while doing something else, like driving in the car or exercising. The websites *www.librivox.org* and *www.audible.com* have many free audiobooks you can try, and your public library will have a variety of audiobooks you can borrow. Your reading comprehension will increase even if you are listening to someone else read to you instead of reading yourself.

How important is vocabulary study to success on the SAT Reading?

In years past, the SAT Reading section had sentence completion questions and analogies that heavily emphasized the memorization of challenging words. The current SAT Reading section primarily focuses on your ability to decipher the meaning of words in context. Does this mean you should no longer focus on memorizing word definitions? Not necessarily. If you do not have a strong baseline level of vocabulary—you frequently encounter words in the passages and questions that you do not know—some focused vocabulary memorization will be useful to you. Also, if English is not your native language, memorizing words that you will likely encounter on the SAT will help you improve your score. That is why there is a Vocabulary Appendix at the end of this book. It has definitions and examples for 50 common words you will find in SAT test questions and 250 words you will find in SAT passages. Use this valuable tool to help you build your vocabulary so you no longer come across words in the passages and questions you do not understand.

How can I use this book to prepare for the SAT Reading test?

Practice with the specific types of questions that are most challenging for you:

- **Interpretation** (page 105)
- **Inference** (page 111)
- **Function** (page 119)
- **Evidence** (page 125)
- **Big Picture** (page 134)
- **Critical Thinking** (page 140)
- **Comparative** (page 146)
- **Words in Context** (page 153)
- **Graph Analysis** (page 161)

Practice with **full-length passages**, starting on page 169 focusing on the types of passages that are most difficult for you.

Practice with **advanced passages**, starting on page 192, that present the most challenging types of reading and questions you could encounter on the SAT.

Review the **vocabulary appendix**, starting on page 947, to bolster your understanding of the most common challenging words you may come across in the questions and passages of the SAT.

Practice with the **full-length reading tests**, carefully watching your time management.

Good luck!

Question Drills

Interpretation Questions

Interpretation questions ask you to understand what a passage states at a more fundamental level. These questions may ask you to interpret specific selections, determine what a phrase indicates, or identify what the passage states about a topic. How can you do well on these questions?

- **Go back to the passage for context, even if the lines are not given.** The level of specificity you will be expected to remember is fairly elevated. Therefore, it is generally better to review the context in the passage before answering interpretation questions instead of trying to answer them based solely on your memory.
- **Use key words to identify relevant context.** Sometimes the question will present you with lines, making it relatively easy to locate the relevant part of the passage. Other times, the question will give you key words. Find the most prominent key word in the question and scan for where it is mentioned to locate the relevant information to review.
- **Questions generally go in order—use this to your advantage.** If an interpretation question does not give you a line reference, look at the surrounding questions to get a sense of where to look in the passage. This will save you valuable time. If you can't find where the information is, skip the question as you may "stumble" onto the information as you complete other questions. Come back to the question at the end of the passage when you know exactly how much time is left to search for the reference point.
- **Use interpretation questions to strengthen your performance on big picture questions.** If you struggle with questions that ask about the passage as a whole, you may want to do interpretation questions first. That way you will have read the passage *and* completed some more straightforward questions to solidify your passage comprehension before trying the more challenging questions.

Now, try some interpretation questions in the following drills. Read the passages thoroughly before you attempt to answer the questions. Allow about ten minutes total for each drill to both read and answer the questions.

The following is an adaptation from The Three Stages of Clarinda Thorbald *by William T. Hamilton, Jr. In it, young Clarinda is waiting for the day of her wedding to arrive.*

Clarinda sat in an old chair and read a thesis upon love, and she found set forth in this thesis that without love the world would not go around. Further, without love life would be but dross and hideous calamity. She also found therein that men have died from love, and women have languished in torments when it was unrequited.

Even though she was filled with apprehension as she read, she did not wish to eschew love, but was glad she was suffering from its effects . . .

At times when she sat by herself, she was filled with fear that the object of her love might fail her—that what she felt might be a dream and not a real condition.

At times this trepidation was so overwhelming she became frightened. It might occur that she would awake from her blissful state and find it was all a mistake.

Clarinda was young and believed in love, and she had not found out that love dies even as the body, and often becomes stale, that more than often it passed from the soul as the miasma from the fetid lake.

The hour of her wedding came. And when it was at hand she awoke with the sun and sprang from her bed as light as the lark, with her hair hanging in golden strands over her shoulders . . . Clarinda was thrilled, and her heart went out to meet the lover who would come . . .

A fear gripped her. She felt she might be giving up more than she was gaining. It came to her that she was leaving all that had made her. In these surroundings she had grown, and now she was arriving at one end of her life. Further, she knew she was about to take a step into new fields; she would be thrown into a new perspective; a new condition of which she knew nothing and all these things she loved would fade from her and be lost. . . .

Clarinda fitted one pink foot after another pink foot into two pink slippers, then she went from the room out upon the landing to the head of the stairs.

Below her were banked flowers. Men, bearing other masses ran hither and thither, placing them as they were brought in by other men . . .

She went over to her mother and put her arms around her neck, pressing a kiss upon her cheek. They said nothing. Then she walked over to her father and helped him to a chair, and knelt down beside him. Her father smoothed her hair with his hand as if to give her courage. She whispered to him in a shaking voice: "This is joy!" "It is joy," he answered simply.

"I am dying!" she exclaimed still whispering. "I am already dead! Look! Look! Father!" She raised her hand and pointed toward the men who moved about. "The men," she continued, "are decorating the rooms for the corpse. I—I—am the corpse!" and close she shrank to the side of the chair. "My youth is dead!" Clarinda's eyes filled with tears and her body shook from her emotion.

Her father raised her head and tilting her face looked into her eyes.

"No, Clarinda, you are not dead. You are not a corpse. The rooms are not decorated for your death. It is done for your rebirth. Only your youth is dead, and from it has sprung a new and wonderful thing."

Clarinda rose from her knees and put her arms frantically around his neck. "Save me! Save me! Father!" she pleaded. "Save me! You are wonderful!"

"Listen, Clarinda, you mustn't weep. Rather you must be filled with joy, for this is a festival. You have come into something new. A great responsibility grasps you in its hand. You are re-born. Nature calls you and you go—it is inexorable—you cannot help. You must not weep; rather you must sing and dance. You must array yourself in gold and in silk and go forth to meet the bridegroom."

"Is there no way?" she asked with pleading in her voice. With terrible finality, he answered "No!"

1. In the first paragraph, the message in the thesis that Clarinda reads can best be summarized as:

   (A) Love is not important to life, since it leads to trivial distractions.
   (B) Love is essential to life; without it, life would be dreadfully dull.
   (C) Love takes hard work from both parties to be successful.
   (D) Love cannot be fully understood without a literary education.

2. Based on the passage, what is something that Clarinda fears about love?

   (A) The person she loves will not reciprocate her feelings.
   (B) There is no one in the world with whom she could fall in love.
   (C) Her stoic personality would prevent her from feeling any passion.
   (D) Her parents would not permit her to leave their home.

3. According to the passage, where is Clarinda waiting as she converses with her father?
   (A) Adjacent to a polluted lake
   (B) In a ceremonial chapel
   (C) Outside in a meadow
   (D) At the top of a staircase

4. The father's quotation in line 30, "It is joy," represents the father's attempt to
   (A) offer reassurance.
   (B) show remorse.
   (C) promote introspection.
   (D) embrace uncertainty.

5. The passage indicates that Clarinda's attitude toward change can best be described as
   (A) uneasy.
   (B) optimistic.
   (C) neutral.
   (D) self-assured.

6. Based on the final paragraph, Clarinda's father's ultimate attitude toward Clarinda's concerns can best be described as
   (A) indulgent and patient.
   (B) exasperated and dismissive.
   (C) confused and questioning.
   (D) friendly and understanding.

The following is an excerpt from a letter by Mary Wollstonecraft. In it she discusses a trip to Sweden and her observations of the Swedish servant class in the late 19th century.

The population of Sweden has been estimated from two million and a half to three million; a small number for such an immense tract of country, of which only so much is cultivated—and that in the simplest manner—as is absolutely requisite to supply the necessaries of life; and near the seashore, whence herrings are easily procured, there scarcely appears a vestige of cultivation. The scattered huts that stand shivering on the naked rocks, braving the pitiless elements, are formed of logs of wood rudely hewn; and so little pains are taken with the craggy foundation that nothing like a pathway points out the door.

Gathered into himself by the cold, lowering his visage to avoid the cutting blast, is it surprising that the churlish pleasure of drinking drams takes the place of social enjoyments amongst the poor, especially if we take into the account that they mostly live on high seasoned provision and rye bread? Hard enough, you may imagine, as it is baked only once a year. The servants also, in most families, eat this kind of bread, and have a different kind of food from their masters, which, in spite of all the arguments I have heard to vindicate the custom, appears to me a remnant of barbarism.

In fact, the situation of the servants in every respect, particularly that of the women, shows how far the Swedes are from having a just conception of rational equality. They are not termed slaves; yet a man may strike a man with impunity because he pays him wages, though these wages are so low that necessity must teach them to pilfer, whilst servility renders them false and boorish. Still the men stand up for the dignity of man by oppressing the women. The most menial, and even laborious offices, are therefore left to these poor drudges. Much of this I have seen. In the winter, I am told, they take the linen down to the river to wash it in the cold water, and though their hands, cut by ice, are cracked and bleeding, the men, their fellow servants, will not disgrace their manhood by carrying a tub to lighten their burden.

You will not be surprised to hear that they do not wear shoes or stockings, when I inform you that their wages are seldom more than twenty or thirty shillings per annum. It is the custom, I know, to give them a new year's gift and a present at some other period, but can it all amount to just indemnity for their labor? The treatment of servants in most countries, I grant, is very unjust, and in England that boasted land of freedom, it is often extremely tyrannical. I have frequently, with indignation, heard gentlemen declare that they would never allow a servant to answer them; and ladies of the most exquisite sensibility, who were continually exclaiming against the cruelty of the vulgar to the brute creation, have in my presence forgot that their attendants had human feelings as well as forms. I do not know a more agreeable sight than to see servants part of a family. By taking an interest, generally speaking, in their concerns you inspire them with one for yours. We must love our servants, or we shall never be sufficiently attentive to their happiness; and how can those masters be attentive to their happiness who, living above their fortunes, are more anxious to outshine their neighbors than to allow their household the innocent enjoyments they earn?

It is, in fact, much more difficult for servants, who are tantalized by seeing and preparing the dainties of which they are not to partake, to remain honest, than the poor, whose thoughts are not led from their homely fare; so that, though the servants here are commonly thieves, you seldom hear of housebreaking, or robbery on the highway. The country is, perhaps, too thinly inhabited to produce many of that description of thieves termed footpads, or highwaymen. They are usually the spawn of great cities—the effect of the spurious desires generated by wealth, rather than the desperate struggles of poverty to escape from misery.

1. In the first paragraph, how does the author describe Sweden's relationship to its natural resources?

(A) Overly exploiting them
(B) Lacking in them
(C) Not taking full advantage of them
(D) Allowing foreigners to interfere with them

2. According to the passage, what best describes the opinions of both the author and her contemporaries about the food consumed by the servant class?

(A) While many argue the opposite, she believes it is of poor quality.
(B) Many agree with her position that it is of acceptable quality.
(C) While many argue the opposite, she believes it is of good quality.
(D) Many agree with her position that it is of mediocre quality.

3. In the third paragraph, lines 15–24, the passage indicates that servant men in Sweden of this time period treated their fellow women with

(A) mutual respect.
(B) deep affection.
(C) harsh mistreatment.
(D) servile equality.

4. According to the passage, the wages for servants in this time period were
   (A) exceedingly generous.
   (B) quite meager.
   (C) justifiably low.
   (D) nonexistent.

5. Lines 31–33, "ladies . . . forms," indicate that the author believes that some in the upper classes had attitudes that were
   (A) enlightened.
   (B) inconsistent.
   (C) sensible.
   (D) destitute.

6. The passage indicates that an increase in the forms and aggression of robbery is associated with an increase in
   (A) wealth equality.
   (B) gender diversity.
   (C) severe poverty.
   (D) population density.

Answers and Explanations

Three Stages of Clarinda Passage

1. **(B)** The first paragraph indicates that the thesis that Clarinda reads states that "without love, the world would not go around," and that "life would be but dross and hideous calamity." In other words, without love, life would be dull and disastrous. Choice (A) would be the opposite of the intended meaning; choice (C) may be true, but is not suggested in this paragraph; and choice (D) is incorrect because while having an understanding of literature may be helpful to better understanding love, given that Clarinda is reading a thesis, it is not suggested that it cannot be fully understood without a literary education.
2. **(A)** Clarinda found in the thesis that she read that "women have languished in torments when (love) was unrequited," meaning that women have been quite sad when the person they loved did not feel the same way. Also, Clarinda says that she is concerned that "the object of her love might fail her." Both of these statements point to Clarinda's concern that the person whom she loves may not return the feeling. It is not choice (B) because she already feels love toward someone. It is not choice (C) since she clearly feels passion. And it is not choice (D) because her parents are trying to get her to leave the house.
3. **(D)** When Clarinda begins her conversation with her father, she is at the "head of the stairs" with flowers below her. This suggests that she is at the top of a staircase. The other options are not mentioned as possible settings for when the conversation with her father begins.
4. **(A)** Prior to this sentence, the father is smoothing his daughter's hair and trying to give her courage. Although his daughter is speaking in a shaking voice, he reassures her by saying "It is joy." It is not choice (B), because the father is not showing any regret. It is not choice (C) because he is not encouraging Clarinda to think more in-depth about the situation. And it is not choice (D) because he is trying to offer certainty, not encourage her to embrace uncertainty.
5. **(A)** Throughout the passage, Clarinda is quite reluctant to have a change in her life. This is perhaps best seen in the paragraph in which she expresses feelings of "dying" and that her "youth is dead!" as the moment of marriage approaches. She is not optimistic or self-assured, since her feelings are ones of uneasiness. And she is not neutral since she expresses strong emotions about love and marriage.
6. **(B)** Although Clarinda continues to plead with her father, he states with a "terrible finality" that there is no other way than to proceed with meeting the bridegroom. Given that he no longer indulges her concerns and that he is rather abrupt, it makes sense to describe his attitude as "exasperated and dismissive." While he does express patience, questioning, and understanding for Clarinda's worries earlier in the passage, ultimately he stops trying to reason with her and simply states what she must do.

Mary Wollstonecraft Passage

1. **(C)** Wollstonecraft describes Sweden as cultivating only "so much" of the immense tract of its land, suggesting that Sweden is not taking full advantage of its natural resources. It is not choice (A), since she argues they are not using them as much as they could. It is not choice (B) because she mentions Sweden as having plentiful land. And it is not choice (D) because she does not discuss foreign interference with the resources.

2. **(A)** The author considers the kind of bread that the servants eat to be a "remnant of barbarism," even though there are many arguments she has heard to "vindicate the custom," i.e., justify that it is fine. Therefore, it makes sense to say that while many may argue the opposite, the author believes the food is of poor quality. It is not choice (B) or choice (D) because there is no indication that many of her contemporaries agree with her. It is not choice (C) because she does not believe the food is of good quality.
3. **(C)** The passage states that "the men stand up for the dignity of man by oppressing the women," designating the most labor-intensive jobs to them. Thus, it makes sense to describe the way that servant men treated servant women as harsh mistreatment. Choices (A), (B), and (D) are all overly positive in describing the way the women were treated.
4. **(B)** In line 18, the passage describes the wages as "so low that necessity much teach them to pilfer," or steal to get by. Thus, the wages of the servants were extremely low, making *quite meager* a good description. It is not choice (A), since the wages were not generous. It is not choice (C), since the passage does not indicate that the low wages were justifiable. And it is not choice (D) since the servants were in fact paid wages.
5. **(B)** Some of the ladies Wollstonecraft observed spoke about their disdain for cruelty, yet those same ladies treated their servants as though they did not have feelings. This conflict between their thoughts and actions represents an inconsistency. The treatment is neither enlightened nor sensible, since those adjectives are rather positive. And destitute is not a fitting description since the focus is on kindness and a lack thereof, not on poverty.
6. **(D)** Lines 39–45 suggest that thinly inhabited areas do not produce as many thieves, while great cities, which would be more dense in population, would lead to the creation of more thieves. Therefore, the passage indicates that population density is associated with an increase in robbery. It is not choice (A), since the narrator would likely suggest that wealth equality would *decrease* robbery. It is not choice (B), because the narrator does not suggest a clear relationship between gender diversity and an increase in the forms and aggression of robbery. And it is not choice (C), because while the passage indicates that severe poverty is associated with hardship, it does not directly link an increase in the forms and aggression of robbery to extreme poverty, but rather draws this connection in the last paragraph to population density.

Inference Questions

Inference questions will ask you to determine what the author suggests or implies based on different selections of a passage. How can you do well on these questions?

- **Consider the context surrounding the selection in the question.** Often, to determine what a sentence suggests, it is important to see what the sentences surrounding it have to say. If a question asks about what can be reasonably inferred from the sentence in lines 10–12, you should probably also look at lines 7–9 and lines 13–15.
- **Have a general feel of your answer before evaluating the choices.** There are plenty of ways you could state what could be reasonably inferred from a paragraph or sentence in the passage. When creating your own answer on these types of questions, it is better to be broad and flexible than it is to be specific and rigid. Doing so will ensure that you are open-minded as you review the possible options.

- **Be wary of answers that simply match wording from the passage.** If you do not pick up that the question is asking you to make an inference based on a selection, you may instead simply try to summarize the selection. If you make this mistake, you will often pick an answer that happens to match some of the wording in the passage. When making inferences, you will need to draw conclusions based on what is *indirectly* stated, not *directly* stated.
- **There will be a definite answer.** It is easy to dismiss an inference question as being just based on someone's opinion, making it a matter of luck to pick the correct option. This will not be the case on SAT Reading—inference questions (along with all other test questions) will have a definite answer with a clear justification. If you are having difficulty formulating an answer on inference questions, don't assume there must be a test question error.
- **Do not eliminate answers too quickly.** Since you are determining what is indirectly suggested on inference questions, you will be better served by keeping answer choices open as possibilities instead of crossing them off too quickly. Sometimes when you look at an answer choice a second time, you will more fully grasp its meaning and it will make more sense as a possibility.

Now, try some inference questions in the following drills. Read the passages thoroughly before you attempt to answer the questions. Allow about ten minutes total for each drill to both read and answer the questions.

The following is an adaptation from The End of Books *by Octave Uzanne. In this story, a group of gentlemen gathers after dinner to discuss what they think the future holds. Eventually they come to the topic of the future of books and the following monologue is given by one of the group. This story was originally published in* Scribner's *magazine in August of 1894.*

If by books you are to be understood as referring to our innumerable collections of paper, printed, sewed, and bound in a cover announcing the title of the work, I own to you frankly that I do not believe (and the progress of electricity and modern mechanism forbids me to believe) that Gutenberg's invention can do otherwise than sooner or later fall into desuetude as a means of current interpretation of our mental products.

Printing, which Rivarol so judiciously called the artillery of thought, and of which Luther said that it is the last and best gift by which God advances the things of the Gospel—printing, which has changed the destiny of Europe, and which, especially during the last two centuries, has governed opinion through the book, the pamphlet, and the newspaper—printing, which since 1436 has reigned despotically over the mind of man, is, in my opinion, threatened with death by the various devices for registering sound which have lately been invented, and which little by little will go to perfection.

Notwithstanding the enormous progress which has gradually been made in the printing-press, in spite of the already existing composing-machines, easy to run, and furnishing new characters freshly molded in movable matrices, it still appears to me that the art in which printers successively excelled, has attained its acme of perfection, and that our grandchildren will no longer trust their works to this somewhat antiquated process, now become very easy to replace by phonography, which is yet in its initial stage and of which we have much to hope.

I take my stand upon this incontestable fact, that the man of leisure becomes daily more reluctant to undergo fatigue, that he eagerly seeks for what he calls the comfortable, that is to say for every means of sparing himself the play and the waste of the organs. You will surely agree with me that reading, as we practice it today, soon brings on great weariness;

for not only does it require of the brain a sustained attention which consumes a large proportion of the cerebral phosphates but it also forces our bodies into various fatiguing attitudes. If we are reading one of our great newspapers it constrains us to acquire a certain dexterity in the art of turning and folding the sheets; if we hold the paper wide open it is not long before the muscles of tension are overtaxed, and finally, if we address ourselves to the book, the necessity of cutting the leaves and turning them one after another, ends by producing an enervated condition very distressing in the long run.

Our eyes are made to see and reflect the beauties of nature, and not to wear themselves out in the reading of texts; they have been too long abused, and I like to fancy that someone will soon discover the need there is that they should be relieved by laying a greater burden upon our ears. This will be to establish an equitable compensation in our general physical economy.

[In the future] there will be registering cylinders as light as celluloid penholders, capable of containing five or six hundred words and working upon very tenuous axles, and occupying not more than five square inches; all the vibrations of the voice will be reproduced in them; we shall attain to perfection in this apparatus as surely as we have obtained precision in the smallest and most ornamental watches.

As to the electricity, that will be found in the individual himself. Each will work his pocket apparatus by a fluent current ingeniously set in action; the whole system may be kept in a simple opera-glass case, and suspended by a strap from the shoulder.

As for the book, or let us rather say, for by that time books 'will have lived,' as for the novel, or the storyograph, the author will become his own publisher. To avoid imitations and counterfeits he will be obliged, first of all, to go the patent-office, there to deposit his voice, and register its lowest and highest notes, giving all the counter-hearings necessary for the recognition of any imitation of his deposit.

Having thus made himself right with the law, the author will talk his work, fixing it upon registering cylinders. He will himself put these patented cylinders on sale; they will be delivered in cases for the consumption of hearers.

1. It can reasonably be inferred from the passage that the narrator would have most closely predicted which of the following modern inventions?

    (A) The internet
    (B) Audiobooks
    (C) Television
    (D) Video games

2. The narrator suggests in the second paragraph, lines 6–12, that the impact of printing on history up to the time period when the article was written could be described as

    (A) extremely significant.
    (B) largely irrelevant.
    (C) indisputably oppressive.
    (D) uniformly militaristic.

3. The narrator implies that by 1894, the technological development of the printing process was
   (A) in its early stages.
   (B) somewhat developed.
   (C) at its peak.
   (D) destined for continued prominence.

4. It can most reasonably be inferred from the fourth paragraph, lines 20–30, that the narrator considers a major issue with reading to be
   (A) its physical demands.
   (B) its dull subject matter.
   (C) its intellectual requirements.
   (D) its obscure language.

5. In lines 36–43, the narrator suggests that readers may likely have concerns about what aspects of potential recording technology?
   (A) Lack of written material to provide for the recordings
   (B) Uncomfortable vibrations and shoulder discomfort
   (C) Small dimensions and lack of consumer interest
   (D) Size, sound quality, and power source

6. The final two paragraphs suggest that authors need to be concerned with
   (A) ensuring a diversity of viewpoints.
   (B) protecting their intellectual property.
   (C) creating what is artistically beautiful instead of financially viable.
   (D) allowing others to make variations on their original creations.

The following is a portion of an address given by Senator Herbert H. Lehman at the annual membership meeting of the Urban League of Greater New York in June of 1956, as reported in the Arizona Sun.

I take this opportunity to pay my heartfelt tribute to the Urban League, which has been working on the problem of inter-group and inter-racial relations for almost half a century.

Over the years the Urban League has made historic contributions to the solution of many the civil rights problem. One of the League's main achievements has been to help expose and define its roots and manifestations, in terms of housing, schools, recreation facilities, and other phases of segregation and integration.

The Urban League has furnished a framework within which men of good will of all races could work together to achieve steady advances toward the goal of adjustment, focusing their efforts on the neighborhood and the community. This organization has helped to show how vast are the ramifications of inter-group and inter-racial adjustment, what concrete and specific evils flow from discrimination and segregation, and what must and can be done about it.

Some people, including some of the leaders of our government, act as though civil rights were a brand-new problem, which has just arisen and needs nothing so much as to be studied. And they indicate that just as soon as they finish studying it, they will probably do something about it. And, of course, that may take a long time.

Others talk as if the civil rights problems were like a sudden attack of virus and that all that should or can be done is to give the patient plenty of rest, and maybe a dose or two of some patent medicine, like a conference.

You and I know how unrelated to the facts of life these views of the problem are. We know that the problem called civil rights is one of vast complexity, some of whose manifestations will take time to work out, but all of whose aspects need to be worked on, without a moment's needless delay, urgently, deliberately and zealously.

You and I know—and some of you better than I—how galling and intolerable are the many aspects of injustice, discrimination and segregation based on race, and how they involve almost every phase of neighborhood, community, and national life.

In basic respects, the civil rights problem is as much a northern problem as it is a southern. Harlem here is a glaring manifestation of the civil rights problem in the North—and I shall speak more about it in a moment.

But above all, the civil rights problem is one which involves each of us and millions like us—in our personal, everyday lives—either as victims of discrimination and segregation, or as those who, willing or not, or consciously or not, are the victimizers, the discriminators or the segregators.

The civil rights problem is reflected in the house or apartment we live in, in the street or neighborhood we call our own, in the job or profession we work at, in the shops we patronize, in the movie we attend, in the vacation we plan, and in the schools to which we send our children or to which we ourselves go. In short, the civil rights problem touches us all in the most personal and intimate details of our lives, in one way or another, depending upon the racial, social, and economic group to which we belong.

These aspects constitute the real core of the civil rights problem. Around this core are gathered the more dramatic manifestations—the legal and political manifestations which furnish the major approaches to the core and substance aspects of it.

In our concentration on these approaches, which are the obvious instruments of our efforts, we must never lose sight of the core and substance, which are the end objects of these efforts.

1. It can be most reasonably inferred that Senator Lehman's attitude toward the Urban League is

   (A) greatly appreciative.
   (B) moderately admiring.
   (C) generally disappointed.
   (D) somewhat unforgiving.

2. Lines 13–16 most strongly suggest that opponents of civil rights progress will use what approach to achieve their aims?

   (A) Personal attacks
   (B) Increased funding
   (C) Excessive delay
   (D) Social justice

3. The narrator's opinion of the overall attitude that society should have toward civil rights problems is that

   (A) significant additional research is needed to determine the appropriate solutions.
   (B) they should be solved with a sense of urgency.
   (C) patience is key to making lasting progress.
   (D) only those few in society who are directly impacted by the issues should solve them.

4. The narrator suggests that civil rights is an issue

   (A) only in the North.
   (B) only in the South.
   (C) in neither the North nor the South.
   (D) throughout the whole country.

5. In lines 30–39, it is most reasonable to infer that the narrator believes that civil rights issues

   (A) impact nearly every citizen, albeit in different ways.
   (B) impact nearly every citizen in the same way.
   (C) impact very few citizens.
   (D) impact those in other countries more than those in the United States.

6. Based on the last paragraph, it is most reasonable to infer that the narrator is concerned about civil rights advocates

   (A) paying insufficient attention to the prevalence of mental illness.
   (B) becoming distracted from the primary goals of the movement.
   (C) spending too much time devoted to the pursuit of racial equality.
   (D) forbidding outsiders from joining their cause.

Answers and Explanations

The End of Books Passage

1. **(B)** In line 18, the author states that book printing can easily be replaced by "phonography," which is in its "initial stage" and for which the author has a great deal of hope. As described later on, phonography would entail authors recording their books for public consumption—this makes it most like modern audiobooks. There is no discussion of anything resembling the internet, television, or video games.

2. **(A)** In the second paragraph, the author describes the tremendous impact that printing has had on human history, saying that it "changed the destiny of Europe," and that it has "governed opinion," reigning over the mind of man. So, this influence can best be described as "extremely significant." It is not choice (B) because the influence of printing is relevant, not irrelevant. It is not choice (C) because the author suggests that printing has had a widespread influence, not that it has had a serious negative impact on society. In fact, the author wants to replace the printed word with the more advanced technology of voice recordings—not because of any widespread oppression, but because it would be more convenient and easier to use. And it is not choice (D) because the impact of printing is more cultural, not militaristic.

3. **(C)** From the introduction to the passage, you can see that the passage was authored in the year 1894. So when the author says in line 16 that printing has "attained its acme of perfection," he suggests that it has advanced as far as it probably can. Therefore, it is reasonable to infer that the author believes that printing technology is "at its peak." It is not choices (A) or (B) because the author believes that printing is further along in its development. And it is not choice (D) because the author believes that printing will be displaced by audio recordings and is therefore not destined for continued prominence.

4. **(A)** Throughout this paragraph, the author underscores the physical demands of reading in the printed form—needing to have "dexterity" to turn and fold the sheets and to hold the paper wide open. The author suggests that a "man of leisure" will be more and more unwilling to undergo fatigue and would therefore be open to a less physically demanding type of media. So, it is reasonable to infer that the physical demands of reading are what the author considers to be a major issue. Choices (B), (C), and (D) all could represent shortcomings of reading, but they are not mentioned in this paragraph.

5. **(D)** Since printed books are not overly cumbersome and do not require a power source to read, the author is using these two paragraphs to address potential objections that a reader of 1894 may have about the possibility of portable audio recordings. He suggests that by using the same sort of advances that have made small watches possible, small audio recording devices will also be possible, and those devices will be able to precisely record the vibrations of voices. Moreover, he believes that the audio recording could be powered by a device strapped to one's shoulder. So, it is reasonable to infer that the author wanted to address potential concerns about the size, sound quality, and power source of new recording technology. It is not choice (A) because the author does not express any concern about there being a lack of material to record, but rather about how the recordings would be done. It is not choice (B) because the author suggests that the small size of the power device would not pose physical problems. And it is not choice (C) because although the author does discuss the small dimensions of the new technology, he does not discuss a potential lack of consumer interest.

6. **(B)** In the last two paragraphs, the author focuses on how audio authors will be prevented from copying the works of others and on how their recordings can be prevented from being copied. This entails protecting the intellectual property of authors. It is not choice (A) because there is no discussion of ensuring a diversity of viewpoints. It is not choice (C) because the emphasis is on maintaining intellectual property, which would be associated with financial viability. And it is not choice (D) because the author wants recording creators to maintain ownership of their materials through registration in the patent office.

Herbert Lehman Passage

1. **(A)** In the first sentence of the passage, Lehman states that he takes "this opportunity to pay my heartfelt tribute to the Urban League." Paying heartfelt tribute suggests that he greatly appreciates the Urban League, making choice **(A)** correct. Choice (B) is not sufficiently positive, and choices (C) and (D) are overly negative in terms of capturing Lehman's attitude toward the League.
2. **(C)** The paragraph states that government leaders will take too long to analyze civil rights problems, declaring that they need to be studied thoroughly, and that only then can some course of action be taken. Therefore, the author suggests that opponents of civil rights progress will use excessive delay to achieve their aims. There is no mention of personal attacks in this paragraph, making choice (A) incorrect. And choices (B) and (D) are incorrect because they are goals that those *in favor of* civil rights progress would seek, not goals of those opposed to civil rights progress.
3. **(B)** The author states in lines 22–23 that the civil rights issues need to be worked on "without a moment's needless delay, urgently, deliberately, and zealously." Thus, the author believes they should be worked on with a sense of urgency. It is not choices (A) or (C) because these would involve delays. And it is not choice (D) because the author states in 37 that civil rights problems touch "us all," so it would not make sense to have only some groups in society focus on finding solutions.
4. **(D)** In lines 27–28, the author states that "the civil rights problem is as much a northern problem as it is a southern." Therefore, the author suggests that it is a problem throughout the whole country. The other options do not capture the author's belief that there is a nationwide need to address civil rights issues.
5. **(A)** In these lines, the author states that "depending upon the racial, social, and economic group to which we belong," civil rights problems impact everyone in the most "personal and intimate details of our lives." So, the author believes that civil rights issues will impact nearly every citizen, but in different ways depending on the groups to which they belong. It is not choice (B) because the author acknowledges that depending on one's group, the impact of civil rights issues will be different. It is not choice (C) because civil rights would impact all citizens, not just a few. And it is not choice (D) because the focus is on the United States, not on other countries.
6. **(B)** Lehman argues that in working on civil rights progress, we must "never lose sight of the core and substance"—in other words, civil rights leaders must not become distracted by issues that are not related to the core demands of civil rights progress. Choice (A) is a worthy goal, but the author does not focus on mental illness. Choice (C) is incorrect because the author wants people to devote quite a bit of time to pursue racial equality. And it is not choice (D), because there is nothing to suggest that the author would not want others to join the civil rights cause, especially since he suggests that civil rights issues impact everyone in the United States.

Function Questions

Function questions ask you to determine the purpose of parts of a passage. The questions take on many forms, such as asking you what a selection in the passage primarily serves to do or asking you the main purpose of a paragraph. How can you do well on these questions?

- **Understand the passage as a whole to fully grasp the purpose of different selections.** It is difficult to perform well on function questions without reading the passage in its entirety. If you do not comprehend the overall point of the passage, it will be challenging to determine the significance of particular parts. So if you have struggled on function questions and are *not* currently reading the passage in its entirety, try reading the passage beginning to end to see if you improve on these question types. If you have been reading a passage in less than 5 minutes, you may want to slow down and use the full amount of time to improve your performance on these questions.
- **Consider the context before and after the selection in question.** When asked a question about the purpose of a sentence, read at least the sentences before and after so that you have a better sense of what the function of the sentence would be. If the selection in question comes at the beginning or end of a paragraph, the selection may be a transition—be sure to look at what comes before or after to understand how it transitions to or from the surrounding material.
- **If you are asked about the "primary" or "main" purpose, be sure not to choose an overly specific answer.** It is easy to be trapped by choices on primary purpose questions that do provide you with something that is true about the selection, but don't capture the overall significance of the selection. Make certain that you go for an answer that captures the primary purpose, not one that merely presents a specific idea.

Now, try some function questions in the following drills. Read the passages thoroughly before you attempt to answer the questions. Allow about ten minutes total for each drill to both read and answer the questions.

Colony Collapse Disorder, written in 2020

Colony collapse disorder (CCD) is an issue that has, over the last ten years, caused a grave amount of concern as to the feasibility of the continued bee population in North America. Fruit and vegetable crops are pollinated by bees. Should the bee population drop drastically, the availability of these healthy options would be dramatically reduced. No one thing causes the collapse of a colony, and scientists aren't quite sure exactly how a hive collapses. However, it is widely accepted that one contributing factor to CCD is the presence in the colony (or hive) of Varroa Destructor mites (or simply Varroa mites).

Varroa mites are an issue for bee colonies for several reasons. The primary issue is that they attach themselves to the bodies of worker bees and feed on them. This can affect a bee's immune system, ability to flush out pesticides, and regulation of hormones. When the mite abandons the bee for a fresh host, it leaves behind an open wound which often leads to infection by one of the many bee viruses that the mites carry. The overall effect is that the bees are much weaker when mites are present. This weakness means that worker bees are much less able to perform their crucial tasks as they try to maintain the colony.

Another factor in these mites causing such distress to colonies is how they breed. They themselves reproduce within the colony. The female mite plants herself into the brood cells of the honeycomb where the queen has laid an egg. The cell is then sealed as the egg hatches and the larva grows. During that time, the female mite lays her eggs on the larva so that when the new bee emerges from the cell to join the workforce, it already has mites and is in a weakened state. Since worker bees and beekeepers alike can't see into the capped cell, no one knows how many of the capped cells are infested, and once the cell is uncapped, several more mites are able to harm the colony. This reproduction method makes the mites very difficult to get rid of as, at any given time, there are more mites breeding in capped cells that mite treatments may not reach. If a bee keeper wants to treat for mites, they must spray multiple times, exposing the bees to the chemicals over and over again and making the honey in the hive inedible.

Put all of this together and any given hive with mites is in serious danger. However, mites do not necessarily mean the end of bees. These mites are slow to spread in nature, and North America is a big place. However, because of commercial farming practices, there is a major concern that mites and their associated viruses could soon infect most colonies in North America. Most bees, despite what people think, do not just stay in one area. In fact, most hives do not stay in one area. They travel the country. Beekeepers in today's agricultural setting rent out their bees to massive farms. One great example is the almond orchards in California. Natural bees in the area are not populous enough to pollinate the thousands and thousands of almond trees. So, apiarists (beekeepers) rent hives out to the almond farms for a few months each year to get the job done.

What comes next is anyone's guess. Bees from all over the country are brought to a common location. Any disease or mite that one colony carries can be given to another colony that then takes it back across the country to infect still more hives. These traveling hives are quickly and efficiently spreading not just mites but other deadly bee diseases, furthering the progression of colony collapse disorder and putting our supply of fresh fruits and vegetables (as well as honey) at risk.

1. The main purpose of the sentence in lines 3–4, ("Should . . . reduced") is to

    (A) explain the precise mechanism for plant pollination.
    (B) describe a scientific research process.
    (C) outline a potentially negative consequence.
    (D) recount a devastating recent episode.

2. The mentions of "(or hive)" and "(or simply Varroa mites)" serve primarily to

    (A) illustrate alternative nomenclature for certain entities.
    (B) define the scientific theory behind a concept.
    (C) consider alternative scientific evidence.
    (D) provide a rigorous historical foundation for a biological observation.

3. The primary function of the sentence in lines 9–10 ("This can . . . hormones") is to

    (A) describe inherent weaknesses in the bodies of common honeybees.
    (B) show why a mite would abandon the body of a particular bee to find a new host.
    (C) illustrate some of the typical tasks a bee needs to accomplish to benefit its hive.
    (D) elaborate on the specific problems associated with mite attachment to bees.

4. The main purpose of the third paragraph, lines 15–26, is to

(A) demonstrate how the visual system of a mite functions when within a hive.
(B) explain why the method whereby mites breed can be so harmful to bees.
(C) discuss some of the potential consequences of becoming a beekeeper.
(D) present an alternative view on bee reproduction with which the narrator disagrees.

5. The primary function of the sentence in lines 31–32 ("Most bees . . . one area") is to

(A) dispel a common misconception.
(B) describe where bees are most prevalent.
(C) chronicle the migratory journey of bees.
(D) provide results from a scientific survey.

6. The final paragraph serves to suggest that the narrator has what attitude about the future prospects for bees?

(A) Optimism
(B) Confidence
(C) Uncertainty
(D) Progression

The following is the entirety of the fairy tale "The Mouse, the Bird, and the Sausage," by the Brothers Grimm.

Once upon a time, a mouse, a bird, and a sausage entered into a partnership and set up house together. For a long time all went well; they lived in great comfort, and prospered so far as to be able to add considerably to their stores. The bird's duty was to fly daily into the wood and bring in fuel; the mouse fetched the water, and the sausage saw to the cooking.

When people are too well off they always begin to long for something new. And so it came to pass, that the bird, while out one day, met a fellow bird, to whom he boastfully expatiated on the excellence of his household arrangements. But the other bird sneered at him for being a poor simpleton, who did all the hard work, while the other two stayed at home and had a good time of it. For, when the mouse had made the fire and fetched in the water, she could retire into her little room and rest until it was time to set the table. The sausage had only to watch the pot to see that the food was properly cooked, and when it was near dinner-time, he just threw himself into the broth, or rolled in and out among the vegetables three or four times, and there they were, buttered, and salted, and ready to be served. Then, when the bird came home and had laid aside his burden, they sat down to table, and when they had finished their meal, they could sleep their fill till the following morning: and that was really a very delightful life.

Influenced by those remarks, the bird next morning refused to bring in the wood, telling the others that he had been their servant long enough, and had been a fool into the bargain, and that it was now time to make a change, and to try some other way of arranging the work. Beg and pray as the mouse and the sausage might, it was of no use; the bird remained master of the situation, and the venture had to be made. They therefore drew lots, and it fell to the sausage to bring in the wood, to the mouse to cook, and to the bird to fetch the water.

And now what happened? The sausage started in search of wood, the bird made the fire, and the mouse put on the pot, and then these two waited till the sausage returned with the fuel for the following day. But the sausage remained so long away, that they became uneasy, and the bird flew out to meet him. He had not flown far, however, when he came across a dog who, having met the sausage, had regarded him as his legitimate booty, and so seized and swallowed him. The bird complained to the dog of this bare-faced robbery, but nothing he said was of any avail, for the dog answered that he found false credentials on the sausage, and that was the reason his life had been forfeited.

He picked up the wood, and flew sadly home, and told the mouse all he had seen and heard. They were both very unhappy, but agreed to make the best of things and to remain with one another.

So now the bird set the table, and the mouse looked after the food and, wishing to prepare it in the same way as the sausage, by rolling in and out among the vegetables to salt and butter them, she jumped into the pot; but she stopped short long before she reached the bottom, having already parted not only with her skin and hair, but also with life.

Presently the bird came in and wanted to serve up the dinner, but he could nowhere see the cook. In his alarm and flurry, he threw the wood here and there about the floor, called and searched, but no cook was to be found. Then some of the wood that had been carelessly thrown down, caught fire and began to blaze. The bird hastened to fetch some water, but his pail fell into the well, and he after it, and as he was unable to recover himself, he was drowned.

1. What is the main function of the final sentence of the first paragraph in lines 3–4 ("The bird's . . . cooking")?

   (A) To describe the methods whereby each creature carried out its chores
   (B) To convey the primary moral of the fable
   (C) To analyze the individual differences in each creature's motivations
   (D) To outline the daily obligations of the three creatures

2. The conversation with the other bird in the second paragraph, lines 5–16, primarily served to convince the main bird in the story that

   (A) he had the skills necessary to strike out on his own.
   (B) he was being taken advantage of by the other creatures.
   (C) he should feel gratitude for being able to live such a delightful life.
   (D) he could better understand the source of his distress through introspection.

3. The phrase "Influenced by those remarks" in line 17 mainly functions to

   (A) describe the physical setting for a series of events.
   (B) provide a transition from the previous paragraph.
   (C) explain the source of the bird's satisfaction.
   (D) illustrate the merits of interpersonal discussion.

4. The statement in line 20, "Beg and pray . . . no use," primarily serves to illustrate the

   (A) ease with which the animals came to a compromise.
   (B) camaraderie between the bird and the mouse.
   (C) futility of trying to change the bird's mind.
   (D) open-mindedness of the bird with respect to his friends.

5. The dog's response in lines 29–30, "for the . . . forfeited," is most likely used to show

   (A) a dishonest explanation.
   (B) a true excuse for the action.
   (C) the dog's curiosity for the truth.
   (D) an attempt to find common ground.

6. Which statement best describes the purpose of the last paragraph in the context of the passage as a whole?

   (A) To explain how with determination, one can master a brand new task
   (B) To illustrate the negative consequences that can result from dissatisfaction with one's situation
   (C) To provide the moral of the story, namely that honesty is the best policy
   (D) To demonstrate that some tasks can be accomplished more efficiently by an individual than by a group

Answers and Explanations

Colony Collapse Disorder Passage

1. **(C)** In the introduction to the passage, the author is helping the reader understand why colony collapse disorder is something that would be worthy of consideration. In lines 3–4, the author outlines a potentially negative consequence of the collapse of beehives, namely that healthy fruits and vegetables would not be available for consumption. It is not choice (A) because it is providing a general prediction, not a precise explanation. It is not choice (B) because it is outlining a potential consequence, not describing a research process. And it is not choice (D) because it is not showing something that has actually occurred.
2. **(A)** In lines 10–11, the author uses these parenthetical asides to give alternative names (nomenclature) to terms that will be used in the passage. That way if the reader has heard of a beehive but not a bee colony, the reader will understand what is being discussed. The other options do not make sense because these parenthetical mentions simply provide alternative names, not scientific theories, scientific evidence, or a historical foundation.
3. **(D)** In the sentence prior to this selection, the passage states that the main issue is that Varroa mites may attach themselves to the bodies of bees and feed on them. The sentence in lines 9–10 elaborates on this general statement, showing why having the mites feed on the bees will cause significant health problems for the bees. It is not choice (A) because the problems caused by the mites come from the presence of the mites, not anything that is inherently wrong with the bee anatomy. It is not choice (B) because it is demonstrating what a mite would do to a bee, not why the mite would want to leave the bee for a new home. And it is not choice (C) because the sentence lists health problems that would result from mite attacks, not the tasks a bee would need to accomplish for the benefit of the hive as a whole.
4. **(B)** The paragraph begins with a clear statement of its purpose: "Another factor in these mites causing such distress to colonies is how they breed." The paragraph goes on to elaborate on how this takes place. Choices (A) and (C) are mentioned in the paragraph, but do not represent its main purpose. And choice (D) is incorrect since the paragraph focuses on mite reproduction, not bee reproduction.
5. **(A)** The author anticipates that the reader may have a common misconception that bees generally stay in one area. This is made clear by stating "despite what people think." So, the purpose of lines 31–32 is to dispel a common misconception. The other answers are incorrect because the selection does not tell us where we are most likely to find bees, about their migratory path, or about results from a scientific survey.
6. **(C)** The paragraph begins by stating that what happens next to the bee situation is "anyone's guess," suggesting an uncertain attitude. The author goes on in the paragraph to highlight potential problems that could result due to the spread of disease among bee colonies. The other answers are all overly positive, making them incorrect descriptions of the author's attitude in this paragraph.

"The Mouse, the Bird, and the Sausage" Passage

1. **(D)** In this sentence, the particular chores for the creatures are described, helping the reader better understand the story that follows. It is not choice (A) because the chores are simply named, and no discussion of the methods of carrying out the chores is given. It is not choice (B) because this gives us no preview of a moral of the story. And it is not choice (C) because while differences in the chores are given, there is no discussion of the motivations of the creatures.

2. **(B)** This is most clearly seen in the sentence in lines 7–9, in which the other bird makes fun of the main bird, considering him a "poor simpleton" who did all the "hard work" while the other creatures were able to relax. The other bird then explains why he thought the main bird was being taken advantage of by detailing the relatively easy chores that the other creatures had. It is not choice (A) because the other bird doesn't recommend that he completely abandon his home. It is not choice (C) because the other bird does not suggest he should be grateful. And it is not choice (D) because he does not suggest that the main bird should take time to think by himself.
3. **(B)** In the paragraph that precedes line 17, the main bird is told by the other bird that he is being taken advantage of by the mouse and the sausage. In the paragraph that begins with line 17, the main bird takes action to try to correct what he believes to be an imbalance in the work obligations of the creatures. So, the phrase "Influenced by those remarks" provides a transition between these two paragraphs. The phrase does not give a physical setting, explain why the bird is happy, or show why a discussion would have been worthwhile.
4. **(C)** In these lines, we see how the mouse and sausage had tried to convince the bird to change his mind, but they realized that is was useless. It is not choices (A), (B), or (D) because those choices all indicate a more positive and accommodating relationship among the creatures.
5. **(A)** We see earlier in the paragraph that the dog regarded the sausage as "booty" to which he was entitled, and so consumed it. The justification given in lines 28–30 is disingenuous, since the true reason the dog behaved as he did was a desire for food. It is not choice (B) because this is not a true excuse. It is not choice (C) because the dog does not display curiosity for the truth, but rather attempts to hide the truth. And it is not choice (D) because the dog does not seem to care about finding common ground with the bird.
6. **(B)** In the final paragraph, the bird's actions result in his death, illustrating that his earlier dissatisfaction with his circumstances led to unwise choices. As with fables like this, the moral of the story comes at the end. It is not choice (A) because the bird failed to master his task. It is not choice (C) because while this does suggest the moral of the story, the moral does not have to do with honesty. It has to do with what sort of attitude toward one's circumstances will lead to happiness. And it is not choice (D) because the task the bird attempts cannot be accomplished better by him—when he let each member of the group do what it did best, the group as a whole flourished.

Evidence Questions

Evidence questions ask you to determine the best textual evidence to support ideas. Some of the evidence questions come immediately after another question and ask you to determine which choice provides the best evidence to the previous question. Other evidence questions stand alone, asking you to find the best support for an idea mentioned in the question itself. How can you do well on these questions?

- **Evidence questions will typically require you to make an inference, not simply to find a quotation that obviously supports an idea.** For example, if you were looking for evidence to best support the idea that the narrator had concerns about the effects of pollution in a city, you would almost certainly not find a quote in the passage like "I am very concerned about the effects of pollution in the city." Instead, you would likely find something like "the continued presence of industrial chemical runoff in the city's river will likely lead to long-term negative consequences, like decreased life expectancy and increased birth defects." With this statement, the author would definitely be implying that pollution is a concern, so it would constitute evidence that he had concerns about the effects of pollution in a city.

- **You may need to look around the lines to see the significance of the evidence.** Sometimes, all you need to understand the importance of a piece of textual evidence will be the lines a choice presents. Other times, you may need to read a bit before or after a selection to understand the meaning of the given evidence. For example, suppose a question asked to find the best evidence that an author believed that a bridge in a city had recently become more dangerous. Now, suppose that one of the answer choices pointed to lines that stated, "Last year, the number of fatalities on the bridge was at 45." This piece of evidence by itself would not necessarily provide sufficient support for the author's claim. However, their claim would be supported if the passage also stated, "In the previous decade, the average number of fatalities on the bridge was 10 per year." In the context of this additional information, the statement about the number of fatalities rising to 45 becomes significant and would represent evidence in support of the idea that the bridge had become more dangerous.
- **Try treating paired evidence questions like two-part questions.** Often a question is immediately followed by an evidence question that asks, "Which choice provides the best evidence for the answer to the previous question?" In this case, evaluate the evidence in the different line selections to help you formulate an answer for the preceding question. After all, the evidence needed to answer the preceding question will be found in one of the line selections. Consider the evidence in the line selections prior to reading the choices in the first question.

Now, try some evidence questions in the following drills. Read the passages thoroughly before you attempt to answer the questions. Allow about 11 minutes total for each drill to both read and answer the questions.

The following is an excerpt from the Emancipation Day speech given January 2, 1888, by Reverend E.K. Love as reported by the Savannah Tribune *and preserved by the Library of Congress.*

No man is more willing to honor the means which God used in our emancipation than I—but I am not willing to give any man more honor than I candidly believe he deserves. Our people have learned to think that Abraham Lincoln was the greatest champion of our cause. But such is not true. The thing that was uppermost in the mind of Mr. Lincoln was the salvation of the Union. So far as Mr. Lincoln was concerned the Emancipation Proclamation was purely a war measure—for he would "save the Union with or without freeing the slaves." From this single statement, it must be clear to you that our freedom was not first in Mr. Lincoln's mind, yet I thank God for Mr. Lincoln for his election which had much to do with kindling the fire between the two sections, which resulted in a bloody war whose crimson stream washed away the black stain of slavery.

I thank God for a Charles Sumner, whose persistent efforts, sweeping influence, true patriotism and far-seeing sagacity almost compelled Mr. Lincoln to issue the Emancipation Proclamation which we celebrate today. We have never had a truer nor abler friend than Charles Sumner. I honor Mr. Lincoln, but I honor Charles Sumner more.

I thank God for that brave man and soldier Jeff Davis. I thank God for his election. Had the Southern Confederacy placed a coward at its head, we would not have been freed as the results of that four years of bloody war. If Jeff Davis had not been a brave, great man fighting from what he conceived to be a principle of right and justice (although he was wrong) he would have accepted Lincoln's offer of surrender in ninety days. If he had accepted, it is hard for me to see from a human standpoint how or when we would have been freed. The odds were against Jeff Davis. He confronted a greater army than his, far more skilled in the science of war and far more skilled in the manufacture of arms and with all the power the shattered government had at its back. This would have been a sufficient inducement for, perhaps anybody but Jeff Davis to have accepted Mr. Lincoln's [inglorious offer]. I call it inglorious from my stand point, for had Jeff Davis accepted it I do not see how I could have been freed.

The truth of it is that God was using both Abraham Lincoln and Jeff Davis to bring to light this child of freedom the birth of which we celebrate today. Our past is shrouded in shame, degradation, ignominy, ignorance, outrages on our virtue and inexplicable suffering. The Emancipation Proclamation has only served to check some of this treatment. In many instances the suffering has only been changed in form. Emancipation only gave us the key to greatness but did not make us great. It did not unlock the great house of honor, fame, wealth, culture, elevation, moral stamina, civil rights, social equality nor respectability. This we must do for ourselves. The mother may give birth to the child, but cannot give it growth and strength. Neither the Federal army nor the Grand Old Party can give us these things. They are not given. They must be dearly bought by diligent application to business, economy, truthfulness, soberness, honesty, and virtue.

1. The narrator suggests that the primary motivation for Abraham Lincoln to fight the Civil War was

   (A) to end slavery in all its forms.
   (B) to stop the oppression of minorities.
   (C) to maintain the Union of states.
   (D) to establish a new nation.

2. Which choice provides the best evidence for the answer to the previous question?

   (A) Lines 3–4 ("Our people . . . cause")
   (B) Lines 4–5 ("The thing . . . Union")
   (C) Lines 14 ("I honor . . . more")
   (D) Lines 15–17 ("Had the . . . war")

3. Based on the passage, which person was most philosophically aligned with the cause of emancipation?

   (A) Abraham Lincoln
   (B) Jefferson Davis
   (C) Charles Sumner
   (D) All of the above were equally aligned with the cause.

4. Which choice provides the best evidence for the answer to the previous question?

   (A) Lines 5–6 ("So far as . . . slaves")
   (B) Lines 13–14 ("We have . . . Sumner")
   (C) Line 15 ("I thank . . . election")
   (D) Lines 27–28 ("The truth . . . today")

5. Which choice best supports the idea that the Confederacy faced difficult prospects for victory?

   (A) Lines 5–6 ("So far as . . . slaves")
   (B) Lines 13–14 ("We have . . . more")
   (C) Lines 21–23 ("He confronted . . . back")
   (D) Lines 31–34 ("Emancipation . . . respectability")

6. According to the narrator, to what extent did the Emancipation Proclamation solve issues of racial injustice?

   (A) It completely transformed attitudes on race in American society.
   (B) It was an insignificant historical event that should be deemphasized in instruction.
   (C) It was the primary cause of racial oppression and suffering in the years following its passage.
   (D) It was a step in the right direction, but was only a beginning.

7. Which choice provides the best evidence for the answer to the previous question?

   (A) Lines 28–30 ("Our past . . . suffering")
   (B) Line 30 ("The Emancipation . . . treatment")
   (C) Lines 35–36 ("Neither the . . . things")
   (D) Lines 36–37 ("They must . . . virtue")

8. Which choice best supports the idea that without the bloody U.S. Civil War, the narrator would NOT have been emancipated?

   (A) Lines 1–2 ("No man . . . deserves")
   (B) Lines 7–8 ("From this . . . mind")
   (C) Lines 24–26 ("I call . . . freed")
   (D) Lines 28–30 ("Our past . . . suffering")

Classification of Protists, written in 2020

Protists are organisms that have minimal shared characteristics with various organisms like animals, plants, and fungi. Most protists are currently known to be unicellular, mobile, microscopic, and can be found almost anywhere with water. The classification of protists has been a challenge for many decades as scientists did not know what to make of these organisms.

Throughout history, there were many changes and additions to the classifications of organisms as scientists tried to piece together the similarities through evolution. As new technological changes were made, new discoveries appeared, and the classification of protists changed.

The three highest levels of organism classification from broadest to least broad include domain, kingdom, and phylum. Convergent evolution—evolution that occurs independently resulting in organisms having similar characteristics with different species over different periods of time—is one of the reasons different levels of classification were added. Supergroups were added to show common ancestors and explain evolutionary changes of convergent evolution. Supergroups categorize different groups in order to show shared ancestors and to show relationships between the kingdoms and origin of each kind of organism. Rearranging and adding new evolutionary relationships does not demonstrate the connection between organisms, but rather only differences.

A scientist named Leeuwenhoek discovered both protists and bacteria. He discovered them using a single-lensed microscope in 1675, calling them "little animals." Microbes were also discovered, and classification of organisms expanded. In 1820, protists were known as Protozoa and were classified under a class in Kingdom Animalia by Goldfuss. Protozoa were then classified as a phylum in Kingdom Animalia in 1845 by Siebold. In 1858, Owen identified Protozoa as a kingdom. By bringing them up to a kingdom level, there was a difference established between Protozoa versus plants and animals, which were also a part of Kingdom Animalia. The reason for new kingdom classifications is that organisms like protists display a variety of characteristics, making them overlap the previously established kingdom classifications. So as technology increased and more characteristics of these organisms were discovered, they were able to be classified more accurately.

In 1860, Hogg named four kingdoms: Plant, Animal, Mineral, and the Primigenal Kingdom (which consisted of what he called "lower creatures"). In 1866, Haeckel proposed three kingdoms which consisted of Kingdom Plantae and Kingdom Animalia like before, and with an addition of Kingdom Protista. At this time, protists were not identified as eukaryotes; they were merely identified as unicellular organisms. Haeckel then redefined the classification of protists by removing sponges from the kingdom. A discovery about sexual reproduction led him to move Phylum Fungi into Kingdom Protista, which further changed the organisms' classification.

With new discoveries about the characteristics of protists, adjustments were made to their classification. Copeland believed the kingdoms to be Kingdom Monera, Kingdom Protista, Kingdom Plantae, Kingdom Animalia. Later, in 1947, Copeland changed Haeckel's Kingdom Protista to Protoctista instead because he understood that organisms that had a nucleus were completely different from the organisms that did not have this characteristic. Haeckel's Kingdom Protista included organisms in which some had a nucleus and some did not, which Copeland said was incorrect and misleading. Haeckel believed Monera to be a part of Kingdom Protista but in 1969, Whittaker established a five-kingdom system by adding a separate Kingdom Monera. This five-kingdom system remains today.

Later, in the 1990s, Woese established three domains instead of the two domains: prokaryotes and eukaryotes. Woese named Domain Archaea and Bacteria as prokaryotic organisms and Eukarya as all eukaryotic organisms. The three domains were established because of major differences between prokaryotes and eukaryotes.

Through the improvement of technology and microscopy techniques, the differences between prokaryotes and eukaryotes were discovered. Protists previously fell under the category of prokaryotes, which were originally classified as anucleate organisms and unicellular. Technological advances led to the understanding that protists are eukaryotic organisms even though most protists do remain unicellular. Since 1675, there have been around 200,000 species of protists found. Each year, scientists are discovering new species of all sorts.

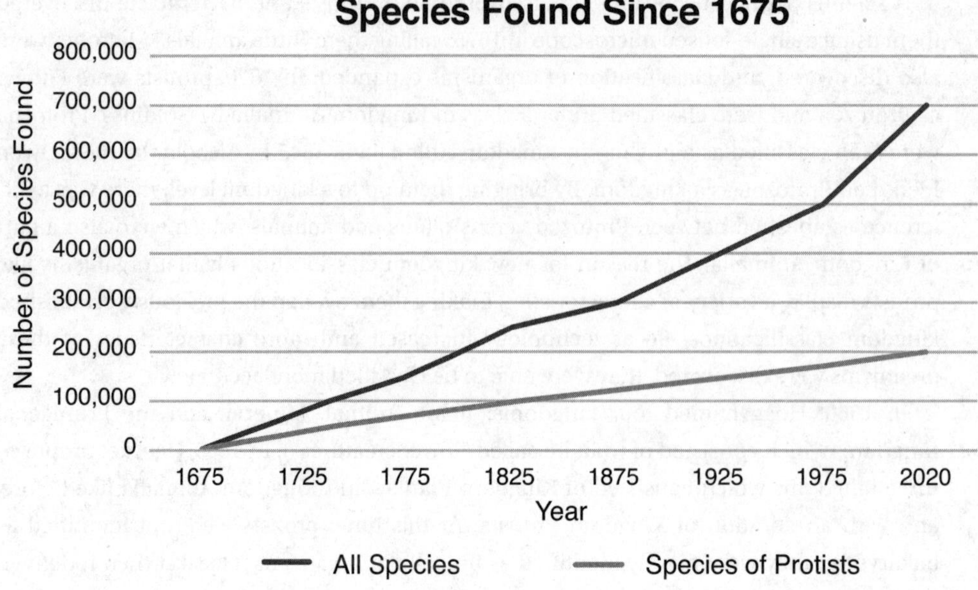

1. The passage most strongly suggests that a human observer would be able to view a protist with
   (A) the naked eye.
   (B) the aid of a microscope.
   (C) the analysis of supergroups.
   (D) telescopic technology.

2. Which choice provides the best evidence for the answer to the previous question?
   (A) Lines 3–4 ("The classification . . . organisms")
   (B) Lines 18–19 ("A scientist . . . animals")
   (C) Lines 34–36 ("A discovery . . . classification")
   (D) Lines 53–54 ("Technological . . . unicellular")

3. The classification of protists over time can best be described as
   (A) steady and constant.
   (B) changing in light of new information.
   (C) decreasingly scientific.
   (D) similar to that of animals and plants.

4. Which choice provides the best evidence for the answer to the previous question?
   (A) Lines 9–10 ("The three . . . phylum")
   (B) Lines 14–16 ("Supergroups . . . organism")
   (C) Lines 37–38 ("With new . . . classification")
   (D) Lines 42–43 ("Haeckel's . . . misleading")

5. At the time of writing, the narrator would most likely divide all species into how many kingdoms?

(A) 2
(B) 3
(C) 4
(D) 5

6. Which choice provides the best evidence for the answer to the previous question?

(A) Line 18 ("A scientist . . . bacteria")
(B) Lines 23–25 ("By bringing . . . Animalia")
(C) Lines 44–45 ("in 1969 . . . today")
(D) Lines 46–47 ("Later . . . eukaryotes")

7. Which choice provides the best support for trends in the slopes of the lines in the accompanying graph?

(A) Lines 6–8 ("As new . . . changed")
(B) Lines 19–20 ("Microbes . . . expanded")
(C) Lines 46–47 ("Later . . . eukaryotes")
(D) Lines 54–56 ("Since . . . sorts")

8. Which choice provides the best evidence of a scientific willingness to change a theory in light of new information?

(A) Lines 1–2 ("Protists . . . fungi")
(B) Lines 9–10 ("The three . . . phylum")
(C) Lines 34–36 ("A discovery . . . classification")
(D) Lines 54–56 ("Since 1675 . . . sorts")

Answers and Explanations

Emancipation Day Passage

1. **(C)** Lines 4–5 state, "The thing that was uppermost in the mind of Mr. Lincoln was the salvation of the Union," making it clear that the narrator believes that Lincoln's primary motivation was to maintain the Union of states. It is not choices (A) or (B) because in the view of this passage, Lincoln was focused on the Union, not on ending slavery and helping minorities. And it is not choice (D) because Lincoln wanted to maintain the current nation, not start a new one.

2. **(B)** Lines 4–5 provide the most direct evidence to support the previous question. It is not choice (A) because these lines focus on a common assumption about Lincoln. It is not choice (C) because these lines focus on Charles Sumner. And it is not choice (D) because these lines refer to Jefferson Davis.

3. **(C)** According to the passage, Lincoln was more concerned with preserving the Union than with ending slavery, and Davis was in favor of slavery. Charles Sumner was most philosophically aligned with the cause of emancipation, because in lines 13–14, the author states that those in favor of emancipation have never had "a truer nor abler friend than Charles Sumner."

4. **(B)** Lines 13–14 most directly support the idea that Sumner was a supporter of emancipation. It is not choice (A) because these lines support a common assumption about Abraham Lincoln. It is not choice (C) because the author expresses thanks for Jefferson Davis, but then goes on to state that he is glad not for his views on emancipation, but because Davis brought the issue of emancipation to a conflict that was then resolved. And it is not choice (D) because although the author is thankful for Davis and Lincoln, he views their actions as indirectly helping the cause of emancipation rather than viewing their philosophies as aligned with emancipation.

5. **(C)** These lines suggest that the odds were against the Confederacy, since their army was smaller and their manufacturing capacity weaker than that of the North. It is not choice (A) because these lines focus on Lincoln's motivations. It is not choice (B) because these lines focus on Charles Sumner. And it is not choice (D) because these lines focus on the long-term need for more civil rights progress.

6. **(D)** In line 30, the author states that "The Emancipation Proclamation has only served to check" some of the racist treatment in society, suggesting a need for further progress. Keep in mind that with evidence questions, sometimes the significance of the evidence is not clear without further context. The sentence immediately before this in lines 28–30 discusses the history of the horrible treatment, helping us understand the significance of the evidence in line 30 (even though lines 28–30 do not provide that evidence themselves). It is not choice (A) because the author argues that it resulted in a partial rather than a complete transformation. It is not choice (B) because the author argues that it was a significant rather than insignificant event. And it is not choice (C) because the author believes the Emancipation Proclamation helped the cause of civil rights, not that it was the cause of further racial oppression.

7. **(B)** Line 30 most directly support the idea that the Emancipation Proclamation was a step in the right direction for the cause of civil rights, although society needed further progress. It is not choice (A) because these lines mention the historical status of civil rights instead of

clarifying the role of the Emancipation Proclamation; lines 28–30 do, however, help us better understand the significance of the evidence in line 30, even though they do not provide the evidence themselves. It is not choices (C) or (D) because these lines highlight the need for citizens to take ownership of solving civil rights problems.

8. **(C)** Be sure you notice the "NOT" in the question. Lines 17–19 suggest that without Jefferson Davis's willingness to fight instead of surrender, the issue of slavery would unlikely have been resolved definitively. It is not choice (A) because these lines do not allude to the necessity of the Civil War. It is not choice (B) because these lines show that Lincoln was not primarily concerned with emancipation. And it is not choice (D) because these lines emphasize the historical horrors of a lack of racial justice.

Protist Passage

1. **(B)** Lines 18–19 state that Leeuwenhoek discovered protists using a microscope, making it a reasonable assumption that a human could observe protists with a microscope. It is not choice (A) because the protists are too small to be seen with the naked eye. It is not choice (C) because supergroups are used to categorize organisms, not observe them. And it is not choice (D) because telescopes are used to observe faraway objects, not small objects close by.
2. **(B)** These lines most directly support the idea that using a microscope would allow protists to be observed. It is not choice (A) because these lines discuss classification, not observation. It is not choice (C) because these lines discuss how a change in classification took place, not the method whereby the organism difference was seen. And it is not choice (D) because these lines mention technological developments that enabled a discovery, but don't mention the observability of protists.
3. **(B)** Throughout the passage, the author outlines the ways that the classification of protists has changed in light of new information. This is clearly seen in lines 37–38, which state that as new discoveries were made about the characteristics of protists, adjustments were made to their classification. It is not choice (A) because there have been changes to classification of protists over time. It is not choice (C) because the categorization is increasingly scientific since adjustments were made with new data. And it is not choice (D) because the protists have at times been categorized under different kingdoms instead of being kingdoms unto themselves, like plants and animals.
4. **(C)** The lines in choice **(C)** most directly state that as new information was discovered, adjustments to protist categorization were made. It is not choice (A) because these lines summarize the way organism classification is done. It is not choice (B) because these lines explain what supergroups were. And it is not choice (D) because these lines show a specific dispute in protist categorization instead of discussing the overall pattern.
5. **(D)** Lines 43–45 indicate that there are five kingdoms of organisms, and the system remains in place today. Therefore, it is reasonable to conclude that there would be five kingdoms of organisms at the time the passage was written. The other options may have been applicable in earlier time periods, but not in the present day.
6. **(C)** These lines indicate that in the present day, scientists categorize organisms into five kingdoms. It is not choices (A) or (B) because these refer to categorization in earlier time periods. And it is not choice (D) because these lines refer to domains instead of kingdoms.

7. **(D)** These lines indicate that each year, more and more species are being found, showing that the slopes of the lines are upward. It is not choice (A) because these lines mention how the classification of protists has changed over the years, but do not mention the increasing number of species discovered. It is not choice (B) because these lines refer to the classification of organisms expanding, but not specifically the number of species increasing. And it is not choice (C) because these lines refer to an increase in domains, not in species discovered.
8. **(C)** In these lines, the author states that when there was a discovery about sexual reproduction, the classification of fungi changed; this change illustrates a willingness to be open to new scientific ideas. It is not choice (A) because these lines define a term. It is not choice (B) because these lines explain general categories for organism classification. And it is not choice (D) because although the scientists are adding new species, there is not an indication that an overall theory is being changed.

Big Picture Questions

Big picture questions ask you to analyze the main ideas of a passage, such as its overall purpose, structure, or tone. How can you do well on these questions?

- **Be certain you have a solid understanding of the passage.** Active and careful reading will really pay off when it comes to big picture questions—take the necessary time to fully grasp the passage in order to be well-prepared for these questions.
- **Focus on meaning, not matching.** Do not pick an answer simply because it matches up with the wording in a small part of the passage. Choose an answer that captures the general meaning of what is needed.
- **Be flexible as you evaluate choices.** There are nearly infinite ways that answers to big picture questions can be phrased, so do not eliminate choices too quickly—keep an open mind.
- **Come back to these questions if needed.** Often, the first question you come across in a passage will be a big picture question. It may be easier to answer a big picture question after completing the more specific questions since you will likely gather a stronger sense of the overall idea of a passage as you examine the details.

Now, try some big picture questions in the following drills. Read the passages thoroughly before you attempt to answer the questions. Allow about nine minutes total for each drill to both read and answer the questions.

The following is an adaptation from the 1919 paper On the Firing Line of Education *by A. J. Ladd, a professor of education at State University of North Dakota. In it, Professor Ladd discusses the future of vocational education in American high schools.*

Much has been said in recent years about vocational education. The schools have been severely criticized for not teaching trades. Many have demanded that that be the dominating motive in all our schools, especially in the high schools . . . Books have been written calling attention to the heavy dropping out of school of pupils even before reaching high school age wholly unfit to do anything above the most menial and lowest-paid work. They have argued strenuously and sometimes logically for better things. To this program the objection has been raised that children in these early years are not yet ready to choose their work of life; that they do not yet sufficiently know themselves—their own tastes and capacities for such serious choice; it has also been urged that to place before children such attractive objective features would result in swerving many from the normal pathway of their development and check it midway. The result has been what might be called a compromise . . . Not vocational education but vocational guidance is now more nearly the thought. And this has a much larger content . . . the social motive in education supplemented by the individual involving the discovery and development of taste and capacity.

I have already called attention to the high mortality rate of high school students. The reasons I have given are the lack of sympathy that the teacher has with the adolescent and the lack of meaning found in the work being done. The same facts account for the heavy elimination that takes place in the upper grades of the elementary school. But both are being remedied to some extent. The first thru the child-study movement and the second thru the matter of vocational guidance . . . Thru the child-study movement the teacher comes to know child nature so well that direct application can be made to the individual child and an intimate knowledge gained of his tastes, capacities, ambitions, and dominant interests. This will enable her to give the subject matter definite meaning in the early years, and, later on, when vocations begin to attract, the guiding may be intelligent and the final choice a suitable one. From the beginning of the adolescent period there should be opportunities furnished by the school or thru its co-operative effort for children to test themselves in various lines—academic lines, vocational lines. They should, in a word, be vocationally tempted in as many different directions as possible so as to come to know themselves so well that the final settling will not be haphazard. In these ways they should be guided into their vocations, definite ones, just as early in life as they can be adequately prepared for them. For example—if his tastes and capacities fit a certain boy for merely a mechanical pursuit that requires but little academic learning, such as carpentry, plumbing, blacksmithing, brick laying, etc., he should, relatively early in the adolescent period, be thus guided, and not forced to attempt an academic course that can have no possible meaning to him. This would send him out, a productive member of society, happy in his work because suited to him and efficient in it because fitted for doing it well. If, on the other hand, tastes and capacities fit for academic or professional careers, such as medicine, law, teaching, or engineering, the principle would remain the same but the program would differ. The academic work, meaningless to the prospective plumber, or dressmaker, would be full of meaning to the embryo lawyer or teacher, and the period of preparation much prolonged.

Such are the points of view that teachers should hold, and such the opportunities that schools should offer . . . The time is not very far distant when something of the kind will be demanded in all our towns. For out in the front ranks the high school is no longer regarded chiefly as a preparatory for college. Out there it is seen to possess a much larger function—assisting the child—every child—to form its own acquaintance and to begin the planning of its future. In other words, the thought on the firing line is that the high school is an institution established by a community for community purposes—to take its young people—all of them—and guide them thru the difficult and transitional period of adolescence, directing, inspiring, shaping, checking, developing for the largest manhood and womanhood possible and providing the community with efficient workmen in various lines.

1. A central idea of the passage is that

   (A) educators are responsible for teaching a uniform curriculum to all students.
   (B) high school should primarily be seen as providing the foundation for college work.
   (C) educators have a duty to focus their instruction on personal ethics and morality.
   (D) schools should help guide students into their most appropriate vocational paths.

2. Which choice best represents the overall structure of the passage?
   (A) A consideration of objections followed by a specific argument for a position
   (B) An analysis of historical events followed by an introspective investigation
   (C) An explanation of the narrator's position followed by a presentation of alternative viewpoints
   (D) A discussion of the perspectives of teachers followed by a discussion of the perspectives of students

3. The narrator of the passage can best be described as
   (A) a concerned citizen who is largely pessimistic about society as a whole.
   (B) a passionate, informed advocate for his position.
   (C) a proponent of teaching all students a hands-on trade.
   (D) a theorist who advocates abstract over concrete solutions.

4. The narrator believes that the link between childhood education and the economy should be
   (A) vitally intertwined.
   (B) mostly disconnected.
   (C) largely adversarial.
   (D) strongly independent.

The following is an excerpt from The Prophet *by Kahlil Gibran. In it, Almustafa contemplates what he should do and say as he leaves a land where he has long been stranded.*

Almustafa, the chosen and the beloved, who was a dawn unto his own day, had waited twelve years in the city of Orphalese for his ship that was to return and bear him back to the isle of his birth. And in the twelfth year, on the seventh day of Lelool, the month of reaping, he climbed the hill without the city walls and looked seaward; and he beheld his ship coming with the mist. Then the gates of his heart were flung open, and his joy flew far over the sea. And he closed his eyes and prayed in the silences of his soul.

But as he descended the hill, a sadness came upon him, and he thought in his heart:

How shall I go in peace and without sorrow? Nay, not without a wound in the spirit shall I leave this city. Long were the days of pain I have spent within its walls, and long were the nights of aloneness; and who can depart from his pain and his aloneness without regret? Too many fragments of the spirit have I scattered in these streets . . . and I cannot withdraw from them without a burden and an ache. It is not a garment I cast off this day, but a skin that I tear with my own hands. Nor is it a thought I leave behind me, but a heart made sweet with hunger and with thirst. Yet I cannot tarry longer. The sea that calls all things unto her calls me, and I must embark.

For to stay, though the hours burn in the night, is to freeze and crystallize and be bound in a mold. Fain would I take with me all that is here. But how shall I? A voice cannot carry the tongue and the lips that gave it wings. Alone must it seek the ether. And alone and without his nest shall the eagle fly across the sun.

Now when he reached the foot of the hill, he turned again towards the sea, and he saw his ship approaching the harbor, and upon her prow the mariners, the men of his own land.

And his soul cried out to them, and he said:

Sons of my ancient mother, you riders of the tides, how often have you sailed in my dreams. And now you come in my awakening, which is my deeper dream. Ready am I to go, and my eagerness with sails full set awaits the wind. Only another breath will I breathe in this still air, only another loving look cast backward. And then I shall stand among you, a seafarer among seafarers.

And you, vast sea, sleepless mother; Who alone are peace and freedom to the river and the stream; only another winding will this stream make, only another murmur in this glade, and then shall I come to you, a boundless drop to a boundless ocean.

And as he walked he saw from afar men and women leaving their fields and their vineyards and hastening towards the city gates. And he heard their voices calling his name, and shouting from field to field telling one another of the coming of his ship.

And he said to himself:

Shall the day of parting be the day of gathering? And shall it be said that my eve was in truth my dawn? And what shall I give unto him who has left his plough in midfurrow, or to him who has stopped the wheel of his winepress? Shall my heart become a tree heavy-laden with fruit that I may gather and give unto them? And shall my desires flow like a fountain that I may fill their cups? Am I a harp that the hand of the mighty may touch me, or a flute that his breath may pass through me? A seeker of silences am I, and what treasure have I found in silences that I may dispense with confidence? If this is my day of harvest, in what fields have I sowed the seed, and in what unremembered seasons? If this indeed be the hour in which I lift up my lantern, it is not my flame that shall burn therein. Empty and dark shall I raise my lantern, And the guardian of the night shall fill it with oil and he shall light it also.

These things he said in words. But much in his heart remained unsaid. For he himself could not speak his deeper secret.

1. The point of view of the passage can best be described as

   (A) third person omniscient with access to multiple perspectives.
   (B) third person limited focused on a single perspective.
   (C) first person with direct viewpoints of multiple characters.
   (D) first person perspective throughout.

2. Over the course of the passage, the main focus of Almustafa's thoughts shift from

   (A) mostly sorrow at saying goodbye, to acceptance of the change, to dread at potential introspection.
   (B) excitement to embark on a voyage, to love for his past adventures, to melancholy about returning to his native land.
   (C) fear of a dangerous journey, to dread at a pending reconciliation, to an internal embrace of a new perspective.
   (D) joy about a new beginning, to fear of meeting his countrymen, to a peaceful resolution.

3. A central theme developed in the passage is

   (A) the embrace of new perspectives.
   (B) the inherent selfishness of mankind.
   (C) the difficulty of transitions.
   (D) the ease of contemplation.

4. Based on the passage as a whole, Almustafa appears to have the least clarity in the feelings he has toward

   (A) the mariners of his own land.
   (B) the sea itself.
   (C) the ship on which he will travel.
   (D) himself.

Answers and Explanations

Education Passage

1. **(D)** As you might expect, the main thesis of the passage is located at its end. In the very last sentence of the passage, the author states that a high school is responsible for taking "its young people" and guiding them through adolescence so that they may provide the community "with efficient workmen in various lines." It is not choice (A) because the passage recommends that the curriculum be differentiated based on student needs and talents. It is not choice (B) because the author argues that some students will not find college work helpful. And it is not choice (C) because the author emphasizes the need to prepare students for the workforce, not to train them in ethics and morality.
2. **(A)** The first paragraph of the essay begins by considering objections to vocational education—e.g., that they don't teach trades, that the students are not ready to choose their careers. The essay goes on to argue that vocational guidance is a worthy goal of education. It is not choice (B) because there is not an introspective investigation (when one looks within one's own thoughts and feelings and analyzes them). It is not choice (C) because the author's position comes after the alternative viewpoints are considered. And it is not choice (D) because a mixture of perspectives is presented throughout the essay.
3. **(B)** The author of the passage presents a clear, well-supported argument in favor of implementing vocational guidance into the curriculum, making him a passionate, informed advocate for his position. It is not choice (A) because the author is not pessimistic about the future, believing that he has a solution that will make a difference. It is not choice (C) because he recognizes that some students will be best served by more abstract educational training for fields like law and education. And it is not choice (D) because he does suggest concrete solutions to the problem.
4. **(A)** The author argues that young people should have educators guide them "into their vocations," indicating that the author believes there is a vital link between education and the economy. Since the author believes there should be a strong connection between childhood education and the economy, the other options will not work since they involve varying degrees of a disconnection between education and the economy.

The Prophet Passage

1. **(B)** The narrator refers to Almustafa using "he" and describing his actions from an outside point of view, making this a third person perspective. Also, the narrator recounts the internal thoughts of Almustafa, but does not do so for other characters—therefore, this is a third person perspective that is limited to a single person. It is not choice (A) because the narrator does not share the internal thoughts of other characters. It is not choices (C) or (D) because the perspective is third person, not first person.
2. **(A)** Almustafa's thoughts initially emphasize sadness at having to say goodbye, as we see most specifically in line 7: "But as he descended the hill, a sadness came upon him." Then he eagerly contemplates his pending voyage back to his homeland, as seen in lines 24–25: "Ready am I to go, and my eagerness with sails full set awaits the wind." Finally, at the end of the passage in lines 45–46, he thinks, "For he himself could not speak his deeper secret." In other words, there is something that has happened that must be so awful that he cannot bring himself to think about it. Thus, he is experiencing dread at potential introspection. It is

not choice (B) because he is not showing melancholy about returning to his native land. It is not choice (C) because he does not fear the journey, nor does he embrace a new perspective. And it is not choice (D) because he is not afraid of meeting his countrymen, and he does not have a peaceful resolution of his thoughts.

3. **(C)** Throughout the passage, although Almustafa expresses excitement at his upcoming journey, he expresses sadness at having to make transitions. For example, in line 8, he states, "How shall I go in peace and without sorrow?" Also, in lines 31–33, he asks himself questions to highlight the bittersweet nature of this change. It is not choice (A) because he has mixed feelings about a change to his life, not an embrace of new perspectives. It is not choice (B) because the narrator does not focus on the theme of selfishness in the passage. And it is not choice (D) because Almustafa finds contemplation challenging, especially at the very end of the passage when he has thoughts that he dare not explore.
4. **(D)** Throughout the paragraph in lines 35–44, Almustafa asks himself questions that illustrate his confused feelings about where he is in his personal journey toward an understanding of himself. It is not choices (A), (B), or (C) because Almustafa expresses positive feelings earlier in the passage toward his country's mariners, the sea, and the ship on which he will sail.

Critical Thinking Questions

Critical thinking questions ask you to analyze the passage in a deeper way, by applying the author's argument to a new situation or considering what information would best support or undermine the author's position. How can you do well on these questions?

- **Paraphrase the author's argument.** Having a clear idea of the author's position will ensure that you can identify further information that would support or undermine that argument.
- **Give yourself time to make sense of the question.** Other SAT Reading questions, like ones that ask you to determine the best meaning for a word, are easily understood in a few seconds. Critical thinking questions may take more time to fully grasp—do not rush through these.
- **Realize that the answer will not be spelled out in the passage.** Since critical thinking questions typically ask you to think about new information or different positions, do not try to "find" the answer in the wording of the passage. Instead, focus on applying the big ideas of the passage to different situations.

Now, try some big picture questions in the following drills. Read the passages thoroughly before you attempt to answer the questions. Allow about nine minutes total for each drill to both read and answer the questions.

The following is an adaptation from Vice-President Al Gore's speech on August 17, 1997, which was the 125th anniversary of the founding of Yellowstone National Park and the national park system.

Some of you may not know this, but this is the only land of its scope and size in the 48 contiguous states that has never been farmed or fenced. In Yellowstone, nature, with all its majesty and power, still reigns supreme. Yellowstone is the Old Faithful of our National Park system.

Native American tribes traveled this land for centuries, and a small tribe of Shoshones made it their home. It was in August of 1805 that the Shoshones first met American citizens—a small band of explorers led by Meriwether Lewis and William Clark. They were the first to cross the continent, and the first to cross the Rockies.

As the day of their return came nearer, one man felt himself drawn back into the wilderness. John Colter knew that there was something he had yet to find—a place more magical than the wonders he had already seen. And so, on August 17, 1806—191 years ago to this very day—Lewis and Clark gave him permission to leave the expedition. They watched as Colter disappeared upstream—into the mists of the mountains, and into the pages of our history as the man who first discovered Yellowstone.

Three years later, when Colter returned to St. Louis with stories of this spectacular land, his tales were mocked as mad hallucinations.

And so it went for more than half a century: all who went to Yellowstone returned to the east with stories of waterfalls that spouted upward and petrified birds and trees—stories too fantastic and too outlandish to be believed. But the stories were repeated.

Every so often, a group of explorers would come back to see for themselves. The most important of these was the Washburn-Doane expedition. All through the summer of 1870, they traveled this region. To a man, each hoped to exploit the land for personal profit.

But then a young man by the name of Cornelius Hedges spoke up. As the story goes, he said this land was put here for the use of all, and should be set aside so that it cannot be damaged by man's heavy hand.

Most importantly, he said that everyone who had the chance to experience the wonders of Yellowstone had the responsibility to safeguard for others that same fortune. Yellowstone had found its first protector.

Two years later—exactly 125 years ago—President Grant signed a law setting aside this land for the "benefit and enjoyment of the people." Yellowstone National Park—and our National Park system—was born.

Parks like Yellowstone still have their protectors. They know what Cornelius Hedges knew—that we must all do our part as protectors of the parks, as inheritors of this eternal gift.

President Clinton and I are committed to doing our part. The fact is, we must protect not just Yellowstone but all of our natural treasures. Under President Clinton, we have preserved and protected millions of acres of America's most cherished natural resources. To President Clinton and me, preserving America's most special places isn't just a commitment—it's a moral obligation.

That is especially important when it comes to our parks, because that is how so many millions of our families enjoy our natural splendor. That is why we increased the operating budget of all of our parks by nearly one-fifth. In our balanced budget, we are increasing our investment in parks by another 12%, with an 8% increase in funds for Yellowstone itself. Our fee demonstration program has raised more than $50 million for park repairs and maintenance, $2 million of which will come to Yellowstone.

Despite the hundreds of millions of people who come here every year, not every American has been to Yellowstone, and not every American has seen its grandeur and its glory. But every American has a stake in this land, because it is part of our heritage. It belongs to us all, and we have an obligation to ensure that it is here for us all, for the next 125 years. So let us leave here today rededicated to preserving nature's home, reconnected to Yellowstone's balance of continuity and change, and resolved to protect all of America's parks—so that we can use them and enjoy them for all of our days.

1. With which statement would the narrator most strongly agree?
   (A) It was monumentally beneficial that Lewis and Clark settled in the Yellowstone region.
   (B) The national parks system would thrive if led by people similar to the leaders of the Washburn-Doane expedition.
   (C) President Grant's military conquests came at too great a cost.
   (D) Nature will benefit if more people think like Cornelius Hedges.

2. Based on the passage, which situation is most similar to that described in lines 15–16 ("Three years . . . hallucinations")?
   (A) An astronaut travels to the far side of the moon, and her factual reports on her findings are widely dismissed as overly fantastical.
   (B) A writer creates an otherworldly fantasy, which her readers consider extraordinarily imaginative.
   (C) An explorer discovers a new island and is widely congratulated for the strength of his scientific prowess.
   (D) An artist paints a widely acclaimed dream-like landscape that is loosely based on places she has travelled over the course of her life.

3. Which of the following statements would most undermine the argument made in lines 48–50 ("But every . . . years")?
   (A) Tourists indicate that they are primarily interested in enjoying the parklands with their younger relatives.
   (B) Some members of the Shoshone tribe considered the lands of Yellowstone their exclusive territory.
   (C) Legal action has prevented mining companies from excavating gold and other precious minerals from Yellowstone.
   (D) While some Americans have been able to visit Yellowstone, not every American has been able to see it.

4. The narrator primarily utilizes what argumentative approach to make his case?
   (A) Considering the objections of industrialists
   (B) Rooting his claims in a historical context
   (C) Appealing to authoritative scientific figures
   (D) Using an analogy to international policy

The following is an adaptation of remarks given by Don Evans (the secretary of commerce under George W. Bush) as part of a panel at an economics conference in December of 2004. Note: A tort is a type of lawsuit.

As I've traveled across America, the one thing that I hear time and time again among manufacturers, as well as service companies, is the burdens of lawsuits—the burdens of junk and frivolous lawsuits and how they continue to weaken our economy and make it harder for us to compete domestically and internationally, and not easier for us to compete domestically and internationally.

And that's the one question we ought to always ask ourselves when we make decisions in this town. Does this make it harder for us to compete and create jobs in America domestically? Or does it make it easier for us to compete? Everything we do should say it makes it easier to compete and create jobs. And what lawsuit abuse has done is not only threaten our competitiveness and innovation in the world, but also harm our health care system; it raises the cost of health care in this country, it stifles innovation, et cetera.

Last year, our department went around the country, and we held roundtable discussions—some small and medium-sized manufacturers all across America. And we heard this same message, with an incredible amount of passion and energy, not just from the manufacturers, but also service companies, as well, and that is how important it is to deal with lawsuit reform and deal with it now, because it's going to impact the creation of jobs in this country for generations to come. It's not only about today's economy, but it's the economy for your children and your grandchildren. And it's time to deal with it now.

Mr. President, you referred to some of the cost of tort reform—or tort costs in this country. It represents over 2 percent of our Gross Domestic Product, over $250 billion in tort costs into our economy. That is a lot more than that of those that we compete with around the world. The manufacturing sector bears a disproportionate share of that, about 4.5 percent. And so when you think of the tort cost in manufacturing products in this country, then compare it with wages and salaries in the manufacturing sector—17.5 percent of the cost of labor and wages is part of the cost, where only—where 4.5 percent is tort claims. So you can see how tort costs are a significant price of cost in everything that we purchase in this country.

I was in Missouri this last year, and I had a chance to really see up close and personal how it's impacting the health care industry. I talked to a David Carpenter, who is the CEO of North Kansas City Hospital, and what he told me was that there had been 30 doctors that had moved from Missouri to Kansas because Kansas had, indeed, passed tort reform and had put some caps in place. So you see it happening all across America, where doctors are moving around and trying to find a more friendly environment.

Lawsuit abuse is just simply piling up cost on the backs of not just companies, but the American people. I like to call it a tort tax. If you take the total cost of tort claims and judgments in our country and divide it by the number of people in the country, it's a tort tax of about $809 per capita. So in everything that we purchase, everything that we buy, in there someplace is a tort tax or a tort cost. And so it's going to continue to drive up the cost of automobiles, groceries that we purchase, work boots that we purchase—whatever it is we purchase, it's going to continue to drive up those costs if we don't do something about it, and it's also going to continue to stifle innovation and the entrepreneurial spirit.

And what we ought to be doing is figuring out ways to lower risk and increase rewards, and that's exactly the opposite of what junk and frivolous lawsuits do in a society. What they do is they increase risk and lower results, and lower rewards.

So for us to continue to be the most competitive economy in the world, the most innovative economy in the world, this is an issue that we must deal with and we must deal with it now.

1. Based on the passage, how would the author most likely characterize the relative impact of tort costs in the United States compared to that in other countries?

(A) Somewhat less significant
(B) More significant
(C) About the same
(D) Much less significant

2. The passage most strongly suggests that there is a causal relationship between a high level of lawsuit costs and

(A) decreased national competitiveness.
(B) increased business employment.
(C) decreased medical needs.
(D) increased corporate innovation.

3. Which of the following findings, if true, would best support the argument presented in the paragraph in lines 28–33 ("I was in . . . environment")?

(A) A survey of medical doctors indicated that 85% of them prefer to work close to the community of patients they treat.
(B) Cities with unlimited caps on business lawsuit payouts had 15% overall greater life satisfaction among residents than cities that limited such payouts.
(C) States with tort reforms in place saw 20% more businesses relocate to their territories than states without such reforms.
(D) Medical practices are 30% more likely to move to states with populations in excess of 10,000,000 residents.

4. Which statement best identifies a weakness in the author's claim in the last sentence of the passage, lines 45–47 ("So for us . . . it now")?

(A) Increased economic progress is unlikely to be of major interest to many readers.
(B) Many other factors besides tort policy likely contribute to overall national competitiveness.
(C) Costs associated with lawsuits ultimately cause increased prices for consumers.
(D) Based on the passage, tort reform has not been successfully implemented anywhere in the United States.

Answer Explanations

Yellowstone Passage

1. **(D)** The narrator tells the story of how Cornelius Hedges successfully convinced his fellow explorers that the land of Yellowstone should be protected rather than exploited. The passage goes on in lines 23–25 to argue that all of us should do our part to be like Cornelius Hedges and help protect precious lands. It is not choice (A) because Lewis and Clark did not settle in the Yellowstone region. It is not choice (B) because the leaders of the Washburn-Doane expedition were primarily interested in personal profit, although they were persuaded by Hedges to refrain from exploiting Yellowstone. And it is not choice (C) because Grant is portrayed in a positive light for helping initiate the national parks system.

2. **(A)** The situation in these lines is that Colter travelled to Yellowstone and came back to report tales of its marvels, but his stories were dismissed as fantastic. This is most similar to the situation outlined in choice **(A)** because this would involve going somewhere that other people had not travelled, reporting back on her findings, and having them dismissed as fantastic. It is not choice (B) because this is not the creation of a fantasy world, but the exploration of the real world. It is not choice (C) because the reaction Colter experienced when sharing his findings was dismissive, not positive. And it is not choice (D) because Colter gave straightforward accounts of what he saw; there is no indication that he used art to express himself.

3. **(B)** These lines state that these lands belong "to us all," indicating that the narrator believes that all Americans have some claim to this land. If there were members of the Shoshone who considered the lands of Yellowstone their exclusive territory, that would hurt the claim that the lands rightly belong to all Americans, thus undermining Gore's argument. It is not choice (A) because tourists wanting to visit national parks would support Gore's argument to preserve these lands for all. It is not choice (C) because it would support the idea that governmental intervention is necessary to preserve the lands from economic exploitation. And it is not choice (D) because Gore acknowledges that not every American has visited Yellowstone, but responds by arguing that Yellowstone remains a part of our country's heritage.

4. **(B)** Gore structures his argument in a chronological fashion, using historical examples ranging from the Lewis and Clark expedition to the Grant proclamation, to show how Yellowstone is connected to the heritage of the United States. It is not choice (A) because he does not spend time responding to the objections of industrialists. It is not choice (C) because he primarily appeals to historical examples, not to scientific authorities. And it is not choice (D) because he focuses on the history of the United States, not on comparing this situation to others in an international forum.

Tort Passage

1. **(B)** The author argues that tort costs in our economy represent over two percent of our Gross Domestic Product, stating that it is "a lot more than that of those that we compete with around the world." This suggests that the relative impact of tort costs in the United States is more significant than that in other countries. The other options do not correspond to the level of significance of this impact.

2. **(A)** In the introduction to the passage, the narrator states that the burdens of lawsuits "make it harder for us to compete domestically and internationally." So, the narrator believes that the cost of lawsuits is linked to decreased national competitiveness. It is not choice (B) because the

passage suggests that employment would be negatively impacted. It is not choice (C) because the passage does not draw a link between a high level of lawsuit costs and a decreased need for medicine. And it is not choice (D) because the author suggests that increased costs would be associated with decreased corporate innovation.

3. **(C)** The author makes an anecdotal argument in favor of lawsuit reform in this paragraph—the argument would be bolstered by using concrete statistics in support. Choice **(C)** would provide direct statistical support to make the case that implementing tort reform would result in businesses relocating to more tort-friendly locations. It is not choice (A) because this does not connect to tort reform. It is not choice (B) because this would undermine the author's argument, showing that having a greater possibility of lawsuit payouts would lead to greater social happiness. And it is not choice (D) because this gives a reason unrelated to tort reform for business relocation.

4. **(B)** The last paragraph of the passage makes a sweeping statement that in order for the United States to be competitive and innovative, it is essential to engage in tort reform. Choice **(B)** identifies a major weakness with this argument, namely that there could be other factors that would influence national competitiveness and innovation that the author does not consider. It is not choice (A) because it is reasonable to assume that most readers would like to live in a prosperous society. It is not choice (C) because this would support the author's argument, illustrating the importance of getting lawsuit costs under control. And it is not choice (D) because the passage already mentions that Kansas had implemented tort reform.

Comparative Questions

You will find comparative questions in the Passage 1 and Passage 2 combinations. They come at the end of the series of questions, and there are usually about two to three on the Reading test. These questions ask you to compare the passages in a variety of ways. How can you do well on these questions?

- **Be clear on the main argument of each passage.** Passage 1 and Passage 2 combinations are typically argumentative—each passage will have a clear thesis that is presented and supported with examples. If you cannot clearly state what the argument of each passage is, go back and look at the introduction and conclusion of each passage, since you will most likely find the thesis statements there.
- **Do not confuse an author's viewpoint with the author's consideration of possible objections.** In argumentative essays, authors frequently present and analyze views with which they do not agree. After all, one of the best ways to convince someone of a position is to show why the opposite position is flawed. When you read the comparative passages, pay close attention to when the author shifts to considering objections. When you do comparative questions, be mindful that not everything in a passage may necessarily represent what the author believes.
- **Realize that the relationships between comparative passages will often be more nuanced.** Instead of having clear pro and con arguments on a topic, the passages often have a number of similarities and very subtle differences. The passages could present somewhat different accounts of the same historical event; one passage could provide an explanation for the events or phenomena described in the other passage; one passage could summarize a topic in a more general way while the other passage investigates the topic in a more specific way. Keep an open mind as you read comparative passages to determine the precise nature of the relationship between the passages.

Now, try some comparative questions in the following drills. Read the passages thoroughly before you attempt to answer the questions. Allow about nine minutes total for each drill to both read and answer the questions.

Passage 1 is titled "The Breakdown of the Digestive System."

Passage 2 is titled "The Horrific Beginning to Gastric Physiology."

Passage 1

Most assume that digestion begins in the stomach, or perhaps, a little lower, in the intestines. But the digestive system kicks into action long before food even touches the lips. As soon as one sees, smells, or even thinks about food, the medulla oblongata, a section of the brain, sends nerve signals throughout the body, triggering salivary glands in the mouth.

Chewing is one of the few parts of the digestive system that requires conscious thought, leading many parents to often remind their children to chew their food. Not only does chewing prevent choking, but it mechanically breaks food apart, creating a greater surface area to volume ratio. This allows for saliva, which contains various digestive enzymes, to coat the food and begin the chemical processes of digestion. This salivation is necessary for mammals to chew, chemically break down, and swallow food.

Once the now saliva-soaked food is swallowed, it moves towards the stomach, where it is further broken down. The stomach's acidity, paired with various digestive enzymes and mechanical contractions, results in a liquid mixture called chyme. At this point, the body has expended a significant amount of energy breaking down and filtering the nutrient-filled food.

In the intestines, the next stage of the digestive system, is where the energy-expenditure pays off for the body in the form of nutrients. As the food moves through the twenty-to thirty-foot-long small intestine and subsequently the large intestine, macromolecules and water are absorbed by the body, providing the molecules needed to survive.

The length of digestion varies and depends on several factors including hydration, type of food eaten, gender, and age. Hydration plays a large role in carrying food through the gastrointestinal tract and making sure there is enough lubrication for excretion. Depending on these factors, the process can take anywhere from forty-eight hours to five days, before releasing the body's unneeded and undigested molecules and completing the process of digestion.

Passage 2

In the early 1800s, William Beaumont was stationed at Mackinac Island as an army surgeon. It was there that he was lucky enough to meet a new patient named Alexis St. Martin, who was being treated for a life-threatening gunshot wound. Though Beaumont did not know it at the time, St. Martin would soon be the key to his success.

When St. Martin healed and survived, he was left in an unlucky spot. His wounds had not healed correctly and had formed what is now known as a gastric fistula. The lining of his stomach and skin had connected while healing, meaning that St. Martin would have a permanent hole in his torso that led straight to his stomach. At the time, the field of medicine was not nearly advanced enough to correct this issue; besides, it was already a miracle St. Martin was alive, so why conduct a surgery that could put his life in peril again? At least, one would hope Beaumont had that thought before deciding to experiment on St. Martin for the next decade.

Beaumont realized he could use St. Martin's unique wound to learn more about the mechanisms behind digestion—he just needed St. Martin to participate. Beaumont decided to ask St. Martin to sign a document, and St. Martin, being unable to read, had no idea he was signing away his rights. As he signed that document, St. Martin became a legally bound test-subject. In the over 200 subsequent experiments on St. Martin, Beaumont was able to gain an understanding of the human digestive system.

In his most well-known experiment, Beaumont tied pieces of food to a string and placed the food in St. Martin's stomach. After a period, he pulled out the food to analyze, recording observations along the way. Because St. Martin's wound also allowed for Beaumont to remove samples of stomach fluid, he was able to identify some of the components of gastric acid. One such component is hydrochloric acid, which has since been found to be a key component of the digestive tract's ability to chemically break down foods.

Through a combination of luck and perhaps cruelty, Beaumont's work has since led several scholarships, awards, and buildings to be named in his honor. Despite his unethical research methods, Beaumont's findings about the digestive tract have paved the way for further research in this field and have even led him to be called the Father of Gastric Physiology.

1. Which choice best describes the relationship between the passages?

(A) Passage 1 gives a historical overview, while Passage 2 is not focused on any historical anecdotes.

(B) Covering a similar topic, Passage 1 provides a general survey, while Passage 2 has a more focused approach.

(C) While both passages discuss the ethics of research, Passage 1 displays more ambivalent opinions on research methods.

(D) Passage 1 mostly analyzes how research was conducted, while Passage 2 mostly presents the findings of research.

2. Which statement best summarizes the respective themes in terms of scientific research for each passage?

(A) Passage 1 emphasizes research results, while Passage 2 emphasizes research methods.

(B) Passage 1 emphasizes research methodology, while Passage 2 emphasizes research theories.

(C) Passage 1 emphasizes research ethics, while Passage 2 emphasizes research funding.

(D) Passage 1 emphasizes research bias, while Passage 2 emphasizes researcher biography.

3. Based on the passages, what best summarizes the connection between William Beaumont from Passage 2 and the information presented in Passage 1?

(A) Beaumont's intellectual curiosity most likely unraveled the mysteries of the conscious components of digestion.

(B) Beaumont's concern for ethical research methods inspired those whose results are presented in Passage 1.

(C) Beaumont's drive to understand the mechanisms of the intestines helped later researchers understand the duration of digestion.

(D) Beaumont's research most likely laid the foundation for some of the findings presented in Passage 1.

4. Based on the emphases of the two passages, both authors would most likely agree that
   (A) whatever it takes to find scientific truth is permissible.
   (B) the pace of gastrointestinal research has quickened.
   (C) the digestive system is a topic worthy of study.
   (D) it is not difficult to find subjects for gastro-physiological research.

Passage 1 is an adaptation from the newspaper The Record-Union *on January 30, 1893. It records the events that occurred in Hawaii that led to the annexation of the island chain for the United States, including the resignation of Hawaii's last monarch, Queen Liliuokalani. Passage 2 is an excerpt from the obituary of Queen Liliuokalani upon her death as recorded in* The Union Times *on November 15, 1917.*

Passage 1

The steamer Claudine arrived from the Hawaiian Islands at an early hour yesterday morning bringing the important news of a revolution in that kingdom. A provisional government has been established by the uprising of the people. Queen Liliuokalani has been deposed from power, the monarchy abrogated, the government buildings seized, and a provisional government placed in power without any serious disturbance.

Annexation to the United States was the chief plank in the proclamation issued by the Committee of Safety and the provisional government lost no time in dispatching five able commissioners to lay their case before the United States government.

The commissioners are here on their way to Washington, and simply state that their instructions are to get the consent of our government to annex the islands . . .

[Upon her abdication, Queen Liliuokalani stated:]

"I, Liliuokalani, by grace of God and under the Constitution of the Hawaiian Kingdom, Queen, do hereby solemnly protest against any and all acts done against myself and the constitutional government of the Hawaiian Kingdom by certain persons claiming to have established a provisional government of and for this Kingdom.

That I yield to the superior force of the United States of America, whose Minister Plenipotentiary, His Excellency John L. Stevens, has caused United States troops to be landed at Honolulu and declared that he would support the said provisional government.

Now to avoid any collision of armed forces and perhaps the loss of life, I do under this protest and impelled by said force yield my authority until such time as the government of the United States shall upon the facts being presented to it undo the action of its representative and reinstate me in the authority which I claim as the constitutional sovereign of the Hawaiian Islands."

Passage 2

With the death of Queen Liliuokalani has passed the last vestige of royalty in the Hawaiian Islands. The eighth and last monarch to hold sway over the entire insular group, she reigned for only two years and that brief flicker of sovereignty was extinguished more than 20 years ago in a revolution which led to the annexation of the islands to the United States . . .

Liliuokalani ascended the throne of Hawaii January 29th, 1891, immediately following the receipt of news from San Francisco that her brother, King Kalakaua, had died there in the Palace Hotel nine days previously . . . it was [prior to her reign] that a coterie of white men, most of whom had been born in Hawaii, organized a league to restore and maintain constitutional government. This league, becoming secretly powerful, made a demonstration which had thoroughly frightened King Kalakaua, who agreed to a new constitution along the lines demanded . . .

Liliuokalani began her reign with [a] determination to abolish restrictions on the power of the crown. Her first move was to appoint a new cabinet with the members of which she made with the condition that she should contend all appointments. Immediate dissatisfaction on the part of the white residents was caused by the manner in which this power was used . . .

Later the queen caused to be drawn up a new constitution, in secret, striking at the rights for the non-Hawaiian residents of the Islands. By this document some of the principle checks upon the power of the crown were to be removed, the existing guarantees of the independence of the supreme court were to be eliminated and only native Hawaiian subjects were to be allowed to vote. [This document was not adopted] . . .

The queen's bold attempt to deprive the white residents of any voice in the affairs of government led to prompt retaliatory measures. The business men of the community named a "committee of safety" which proceeded immediately with the formation of a provisional government and the reorganization of the volunteer military companies which had been disbanded in 1890 . . .

The United States cruiser Boston was in the harbor, having arrived two days before. At the request of United States Minister J.L. Stevens, this vessel landed a force of marines on the evening of the 16th, avowedly to protect the lives of American citizens and to guard their property in case of rioting or incendiarism.

The next day, January 17th, [the provisional government] took possession of the government building, and the reign of Liliuokalani was at an end.

1. The two passages portray the approach to conflict of Liliuokalani

    (A) in a similar way, with Liliuokalani advocating open reconciliation in each passage.
    (B) in a similar way, with Liliuokalani advocating military conflict in each passage.
    (C) in a different way, with Passage 1 describing Liliuokalani as more passive and Passage 2 describing her as more plotting.
    (D) in a different way, with Passage 1 describing Liliuokalani as more aggressive and Passage 2 describing her as more tolerant.

2. Both passages describe the American annexation of Hawaii as

    (A) extremely deadly.
    (B) largely amicable.
    (C) universally respected.
    (D) generally nonlethal.

3. How do the two passages use quotation marks differently in lines 12 and 23 in Passage 1, and in line 47 in Passage 2?

    (A) Passage 1 uses them to quote a historical figure, while Passage 2 uses them to label a term.
    (B) Passage 1 uses them to label a term, while Passage 2 uses them to quote a historical figure.
    (C) Both passages use them to designate quotations from historical figures.
    (D) Both passages use them to label terms.

4. The passages both characterize the attitude of the government of the United States with respect to the concerns of Queen Liliuokalani as

   (A) essentially uninterested.
   (B) quite interested.
   (C) somewhat open-minded.
   (D) mostly tolerant.

Answer Explanations

Digestion Passages

1. **(B)** Both passages cover the general topic of digestion—the first passage gives a broad overview of the digestive process, while the second passage delves deeply into a particular research situation. It is not choice (A) because Passage 2 does focus on a historical anecdote, namely that of Beaumont and St. Martin. It is not choice (C) because the first passage does not focus on the ethics of research. And it is not choice (D) because Passage 1 summarizes the findings of research instead of analyzing how the research was done, and Passage 2 analyzes research methods.

2. **(A)** The first passage presents the latest scientific understanding of the digestive process, thereby emphasizing research results. The second passage explores how Beaumont experimented on St. Martin to gain insights into the digestive system, thereby emphasizing research methods. It is not choice (B) because Passage 1 does not emphasize research methodology. It is not choice (C) because Passage 1 does not emphasize ethics, and Passage 2 does not emphasize research funding. And it is not choice (D) because Passage 1 does not emphasize research bias.

3. **(D)** The first passage states certain findings that Beaumont discovered as well-known facts about the digestive system, such as the acidity of the stomach. So, the connection between Beaumont and the information presented in Passage 1 is that Beaumont's research likely led to the modern understanding of digestion as presented in Passage 1. It is not choice (A) because Beaumont did not focus on the conscious components of digestion. It is not choice (B) because Beaumont did not seem to care about research ethics—his curiosity was paramount. And it is not choice (C) because Beaumont's research focused on the stomach, not the intestines.

4. **(C)** Given their choices of topics—Passage 1 on a summary of the digestive process and Passage 2 on a digestion-related scientific anecdote—it is reasonable to conclude that both authors consider digestion to be a topic worthy of study. It is not choice (A) because Passage 1 does not suggest this. It is not choice (B) because the relative speed of gastrointestinal research over time is not discussed. And it is not choice (D) because Passage 2 emphasizes the difficulty scientists had in finding research subjects, making St. Martin's rare wound an excellent research opportunity.

Hawaii Passages

1. **(C)** The first passage portrays Liliuokalani as more passive, since she protests the creation of the provisional government, yet yields to the forces of the United States. The second passage portrays her as more plotting, focusing on her attempt to draw up a new constitution in secret. It is not choice (A) because she does not advocate open reconciliation in the second passage. It is not choice (B) because she is not portrayed in either passage as advocating military conflict. And it is not choice (D) because she is not portrayed as aggressive in the first passage.

2. **(D)** The first passage portrays the American takeover of Hawaii as taking place "without any serious disturbance," and the second passage portrays the takeover as quick and bloodless, with marines taking possession of a government building leading to the end of Hawaiian independence. It is not choice (A) because there was not a serious loss of life in the takeover.

It is not choice (B) because there was not a friendly exchange of power. And it is not choice (C) because the Hawaiians did not respect the way that the takeover took place.

3. **(A)** Passage 1 uses the quotation marks to quote Liliuokalani, while Passage 2 uses them to label the term "committee of safety." Choice (B) is incorrect because it has the relationship backwards. And choices (C) and (D) are incorrect because the passages differ in how they use quotation marks.
4. **(A)** By the actions of the United States in creating a provisional Hawaiian government to replace the monarchy, it is clear that the United States was essentially uninterested in addressing the concerns of the queen. It is not choices (B), (C), or (D), because if any of these had been true, it is highly unlikely that the United States would have taken over Hawaii so rapidly.

Words in Context Questions

Words in context questions ask you to determine the meaning of a word or phrase based on how it is used in the passage. There are typically two of these types of questions per passage, and they usually have the form of "As used in line 20, 'compromise' most nearly means . . ." How can you do well on these questions?

- **Base your answer on how the word is used in context, not on its dictionary definition.** The answer choices will all typically present meanings that could work well for a word in different situations. Instead of determining your answer only on your recall of the definition of a word, consider at least the sentence the word is in to determine what type of meaning it may have.
- **Realize that the word may take on one of its alternative meanings.** Words usually have several different possible definitions. Be mindful that the appropriate meaning for the word in question may be the third or fourth most common meaning instead of the first.
- **Try plugging in the meanings to the sentence to see what is most logical.** If you are having trouble making a decision on a word meaning question, try taking the different options and substituting them for the word.
- **If you do not know what a particular answer option means, do not immediately eliminate it as a possibility.** When presented with a choice between an option you know versus an option you do not know, you may typically choose the word you know, even if the option is not a good fit. Instead of this approach, realize that whatever the correct answer is will work 100 percent, so even if you do not know what a word means, do not eliminate it as a possibility. Instead, use the fact that if the other options only *partially* work, they are *completely* wrong.

Now, try some words in context questions in the following drills. Read the passages thoroughly before you attempt to answer the questions. Allow about ten minutes total for each drill to both read and answer the questions.

The following is the preface to The White Slaves of England, *a book published in 1854 to decry the horrible working and living conditions among the poor working classes of England.*

The following pages exhibit a system of wrong and outrage equally abhorrent to justice, civilization and humanity. The frightful abuses which are here set forth, are, from their enormity, difficult of belief; yet they are supported by testimony the most impartial, clear and irrefutable. These abuses are time-honored, and have the sanction of a nation which prides itself upon the *freedom of its Constitution*; and which holds up its government to the nations of the earth as a model of *regulated liberty*. Vain, audacious, *false* assumption! Let the refutation be found in the details which this volume furnishes, of the want, misery and starvation—the slavish toil—the menial degradation of nineteen-twentieths of her people. Let her *miners*, her *operatives, the tenants of her workhouses*, her *naval service*, and the millions upon millions in the *Emerald Isle* and in farther India attest its fallacy.

These are the legitimate results of the laws and institutions of Great Britain; and they reach and affect, in a greater or less degree, all her dependencies. Her *church and state*, and her *laws of entail and primogeniture*, are the principal sources of the evils under which her people groan; and until these are changed there is no just ground of hope for an improvement in their condition. The tendency of things is, indeed, to make matters still worse. The poor are every year becoming poorer, and more dependent upon those who feast upon their sufferings; while the wealth and power of the realm are annually concentrating in fewer hands, and becoming more and more instruments of oppression. The picture is already sufficiently revolting. "Nine hundred and ninety-nine children of the same common Father, suffer from destitution, that the thousandth may revel in superfluities. A thousand cottages shrink into meanness and want, to swell the dimensions of a single palace. The tables of a thousand families of the industrious poor waste away into drought and barrenness, that one board may be laden with surfeits."

From these monstrous evils there seems to be little chance of escape, except by flight; and happy is it for the victims of oppression, that an asylum is open to them, in which they can fully enjoy the rights and privileges, from which, for ages, they have been debarred. Let them come. The feudal chains which so long have bound them can here be shaken off. Here they can freely indulge the pure impulses of the mind and the soul, untrammeled by political or religious tyranny. Here they can enjoy the beneficent influences of humane institutions and laws, and find a vast and ample field in which to develop and properly employ all their faculties.

The United States appear before the eyes of the down-trodden whites of Europe as a land of promise. Thousands of ignorant, degraded wretches, who have fled from their homes to escape exhausting systems of slavery, annually land upon our shores, and in their hearts thank God that he has created such a refuge. This is the answer—the overwhelming answer—to the decriers of our country and its institutions. These emigrants are more keenly alive to the superiority of our institutions than most persons who have been bred under them, and to their care we might confidently entrust our defense.

We design to prove in this work that the oligarchy which owns Great Britain at the present day is the best friend of human slavery, and that its system is most barbarous and destructive. Those feudal institutions which reduced to slavery the . . . whites, are perpetuated in Great Britain, to the detriment of freedom wherever the British sway extends. Institutions which nearly every other civilized country has abolished, and which are at least a century behind the age, still curse the British islands and their dependencies. This system of slavery, with all its destructive effects, will be found fully illustrated in this volume.

Our plan has been to quote English authorities wherever possible. Out of their own mouths shall they be condemned. We have been much indebted to the publications of distinguished democrats of England, who have keenly felt the evils under which their country groans, and striven, with a hearty will, to remove them. They have the sympathies of civilized mankind with their cause. May their efforts soon be crowned with success, for the British masses and oppressed nations far away in the East will shout loud and long when the aristocracy is brought to the dust!

1. As used in line 4, "sanction" most nearly means

   (A) tariff.
   (B) condemnation.
   (C) discipline.
   (D) permission.

2. The author most likely uses the italicized terms in the sentence in lines 9–19 ("Let her . . . fallacy") to

   (A) name those who approve of oppression.
   (B) underscore the widespread presence of injustice.
   (C) legitimize the British policy toward social class.
   (D) show the diversity of various empowered groups.

3. As used in line 16, "feast upon" most nearly means

   (A) greatly profit from.
   (B) somewhat quench.
   (C) quickly ingest.
   (D) offer relief to.

4. As used in line 21, "meanness" most nearly means

   (A) spitefulness.
   (B) viciousness.
   (C) shabbiness.
   (D) cruelty.

5. As used in line 29, "enjoy" most nearly means

   (A) savor.
   (B) make use of.
   (C) fancy.
   (D) have freedom from.

6. As used in line 37, "alive to" most nearly means

   (A) opposed to.
   (B) aware of.
   (C) impartial toward.
   (D) ignorant of.

7. As used in line 41, "reduced" most nearly means

   (A) subtracted.
   (B) alleviated.
   (C) stole.
   (D) degraded.

8. The author most likely uses the sentence "Out of their own mouths shall they be condemned" in line 46 to

    (A) share the heartfelt confessions of those who were formerly oppressors.
    (B) consider the objections of those who dismiss democracy.
    (C) express a desire to use the words of authorities against them.
    (D) demonstrate the widespread acceptance of a point of view.

The following is an adaptation of the article "On the Purification of Amorphous Phosphorus," written by M. Ernest Nickles and published in The American Journal of Science and Arts, *22nd volume, in November of 1856.*

It is known that phosphorus not spontaneously inflammable (amorphous phosphorus) is obtained by heating common phosphorus for some time at a temperature between 230 and 250 degrees Celsius, in an atmosphere of nitrogen, hydrogen, or other gas free from oxygen. But however long the treatment be continued, a portion of the phosphorus always escapes the change and must be removed if we would not compromise the essential qualities of the amorphous phosphorus, its innocuity and its inalterability in the air. This mode of purifying is very inconvenient. It is based on the use of sulphuret of carbon which dissolves ordinary phosphorus without acting on the other. The process theoretically seems to be a simple one; but it is in practice attended with much trouble and danger; for the washing are not only interminable and require a large quantity of the sulphuret of carbon, but besides this, the chances of inflaming it increase rapidly with the proportions of phosphorus under treatment. The precautions that have long been proposed do not always suffice to prevent accidents.

Impressed with these difficulties while experimenting with the red phosphorus, I have sought, by a study of the distinctive qualities of the two kinds of phosphorus to arrive at a safer and more expeditious mode of preparations; I have looked more particularly to the physical properties of the two bodies. In this way, I have arrived at a process, which is both simple and rapid, and may be trusted even to inexperienced hands—the last thing of importance since red phosphorus has become an article of commerce.

This process depends on the different specific gravities of the two kinds of phosphorus. It consists in putting the mixture into a liquid of intermediate density: a saline solution with a specific gravity between those of the two types of phosphorus answers well the purpose; the lighter ordinary phosphorus floats on the surface while the heavier red phosphorus remains below; and the former is readily taken up by a little sulphuret of carbon which dissolves it, so that the operation can be performed in a closed vessel.

The following are the details of the process. A little sulphuret of carbon is introduced into the retort in which the transformation has been affected. If the material, which usually adheres strongly, does not detach itself, the bottom of the retort is put into warm water. The disaggregation of the material takes place immediately, and is attended with a slight noise. As soon as the phosphorus is detached, the saline solution is added; the vessel is then closed and shaken, and at the end of ten minutes the separation of the two is accomplished. If the ordinary phosphorus is only one fourth of the whole, it may be removed entirely at a single washing in the manner explained, although it is more prudent to make a second trial, decanting first the phosphuretted sulphuret of carbon, and adding another quantity of pure sulphuret: and this is quite necessary if the two kinds of phosphorus are mixed in equal proportions. Three washings of this kind will remove every trace of the ordinary phosphorus, however large the proportion.

After separating the two liquids by decantation, it is only necessary to turn upon a piece of linen cloth, the saline solution containing the red phosphorus. The purity of the product is so perfect, that it is useless to boil it with a solution of caustic potash, the common method. The whole is completed in half an hour; and what is also important, it is also attended with no danger, for the operation by being carried on in a closed vessel, does not allow of the vaporization of the sulphuret of carbon and a deposition of the inflammable phosphorus.

Recent observations have shown that the inhalation of the vapor of sulphuret of carbon is not without injury to the health; workmen employed in [manufacturing] have suffered severely through this means. Still this sulphuret is the best-known solvent of phosphorus. The process proposed has a double advantage from this point of view, it diminishes the quantity of sulphuret of carbon used and the chances of inhalation.

Chemists will see the value of the mode of separating solid substances of different specific gravities, mentioned above—a method not requiring heat nor a direct solvent, and being both easy and expeditious.

1. As used in line 6, "mode" most nearly means

    (A) method.
    (B) cleaner.
    (C) average.
    (D) ideology.

2. As used in line 9, "attended" most nearly means

    (A) endangered.
    (B) associated.
    (C) researched.
    (D) terminated.

3. As used in lines 15–17, "arrive at" and "arrived at" most nearly mean to

    (A) travel.
    (B) immerse.
    (C) discover.
    (D) believe.

4. In referring to red phosphorus as an "article of commerce" in line 19, the narrator is expressing

    (A) his belief that it will be bought and sold by non-scientists.
    (B) his fear that the supply of red phosphorus will become scarce.
    (C) his faith that commercial applications for red phosphorus will be found.
    (D) his disappointment with the commercialization of scientific discovery.

5. As used in line 24, "below" most nearly means

    (A) less.
    (B) fluid.
    (C) dependent.
    (D) underneath.

6. As used in line 33, “manner” most nearly means

   (A) way.
   (B) politeness.
   (C) presentation.
   (D) removal.

7. As used in line 40, “common” most nearly means

   (A) unnecessary.
   (B) shared.
   (C) typical.
   (D) vulgar.

8. As used in line 48, “chances” most nearly means

   (A) possibility.
   (B) impossibility.
   (C) advantage.
   (D) disadvantage.

Answer Explanations

England Passage

1. **(D)** The narrator is expressing the contradiction between the supposed democratic values in which the people of England take pride and the fact that there are terrible abuses of the working class. As used in this context, "sanction" most nearly means "permission," since the people of England are allowing these abuses to take place. It is not choice (A) because a tariff is a tax on trade. It is not choice (B) because the English are allowing these abusive practices, not condemning them. And it is not choice (C) because these are not acts of rightful punishment, or discipline, but acts of abuse.

2. **(B)** In this paragraph, the narrator introduces the abuses found in 19th-century English society. The italicized selections can be reasonably inferred to be groups that could bear witness to the abuses. Since there are so many different groups that could highlight these abuses, it underscores the widespread presence of injustice in English society at the time. It is not choices (A) or (C) because the narrator is not suggesting these groups would approve or legitimize these practices. And it is not choice (D) because while these groups were diverse, they were not empowered at the time.

3. **(A)** In context, it can be inferred that the narrator is referring to wealthier people who are taking advantage of the poor to enrich themselves. In other words, they are "greatly profiting from" this arrangement. It is not choices (B) or (C) because no actual consumption of food or drink is taking place. And it is not choice (D) because the wealthier members of society are using the poor for their own ends, not offering relief to them.

4. **(C)** The sentence states that cottages are shrinking into "meanness," which when applied to the deterioration of a dwelling could be called *shabbiness*. The other options suggest variations of a negative human attitude, and would not be appropriately applied to a house.

5. **(B)** The narrator uses this sentence to express that people belonging to the lower class in England have no opportunity to escape from their situations and no opportunity to "enjoy," or make use of, rights to which they are entitled. It is not choices (A) or (C) because these associate "enjoy" with pleasure. And it is not choice (D) because the people belonging to the lower class want the freedom *to use* these rights, not freedom *from* these rights (which would suggest they would not want to have the rights).

6. **(B)** The narrator emphasizes that those who have escaped an oppressive system are much more likely to be aware of, or "alive to," the superiority of the institutions of their new country. It is not choice (A) because they would be in favor of the new country's institutions, not opposed to them. It is not choice (C) because they would have strong feelings about the situation, not have neutral feelings of impartiality. And it is not choice (D) because they would know the truth of the matter, not be ignorant of it.

7. **(D)** People belonging to the lower class of England were, according to this sentence, brought down to a system of slavery by the feudal institutions of England. Therefore, they were degraded to extreme poverty. It is not choice (A) because this is not a mathematical operation. It is not choice (B), since alleviate would be to make things better. And it is not choice (C) because one could not properly say "stole to slavery"—it would be appropriate to say "stole freedom."

8. **(C)** In the previous sentence, the narrator says that the plan "has been to quote English authorities wherever possible," indicating a desire to use the words of authorities against them. It is not choice (A) because there would be no need to condemn those who confessed in a heartfelt way. It is not choice (B) because the narrator is not trying to consider the objections of authorities, but to trap them in their contradictions. And it is not choice (D) because the narrator understands that English authorities likely have very different points of view from those whom they oppress.

"Phosphorus" Passage

1. **(A)** In the previous sentences, the author explains the process by which phosphorus can be obtained. Therefore, "mode" stands for a method of purifying phosphorus. It is not choice (B) because this paragraph is describing a process of making phosphorus, not cleaning. It is not choice (C) because this is not a mathematical operation. And it is not choice (D) because this is a scientific process, not a system of beliefs.

2. **(B)** The narrator describes the phosphorus purification process, stating that although it appears to be a simple one, much trouble and danger go along with it. In other words, trouble and danger are associated with it. It is not choice (A) because although the process is dangerous, the process itself is not endangered. It is not choice (C) because the scientists are not researching it with trouble and danger. And it is not choice (D) because they are carrying out the process, not terminating or ending it.

3. **(C)** The narrator explains how he has created a process of preparing red phosphorus that would be safer than the method used previously. So, by arriving at this new method, he has discovered it. It is not choice (A) because he is not suggesting any physical travel. It is not choice (B) because while he likely immersed himself in the problem to find a solution, he is highlighting his discovery. And it is not choice (D) because he doesn't merely believe in his method—he found it.

4. **(A)** Earlier in the sentence, the narrator states that the process he has invented is both "simple and rapid," and "may be trusted even to inexperienced hands." The underlying suggestion is that people who may not have scientific backgrounds may still be able to use the process he has created. It is not choice (B) since the author refers to phosphorus as "common," and the only thing limiting the supply of red phosphorus is how much of it can be created from common phosphorus. It is not choice (C) because if red phosphorus is already an article of commerce, i.e., something bought and sold in the economy, it would likely already have commercial applications. And it is not choice (D) because if he were disappointed in the commercialization of scientific discovery, he would not have created a process to more easily refine red phosphorus for commercial use.

5. **(D)** The narrator describes the process he has developed to refine phosphorus, with the lighter phosphorus floating on the surface, while the heavier red phosphorus would be below, or "underneath." It is not choice (A) because the red phosphorus is separated from the other phosphorus, not decreased in quantity. It is not choice (B) because the next sentence suggests that the red phosphorus needs to be dissolved, making it a solid, not liquid. And it is not choice (C) because the red phosphorus and lighter phosphorus are separated from each other, not dependent on one another.

6. **(A)** The narrator outlines how ordinary phosphorus can be removed through the process he designed—he outlines the steps that must be taken, with the "manner" referring to the way

that this refinement will take place. It is not choice (B) because this is a physical process, not a human interaction. It is not choice (C) because no presentation is taking place. And it is not choice (D) because the removal is mentioned earlier in the sentence, while "manner" must refer to *how* this removal takes place.

7. **(C)** Given that the purity of the product described in this sentence is so perfect, there is no need for a special refining process. Therefore, the typical way of refining the phosphorus will be suitable. It is not choice (A) because the process is in fact necessary to achieve the desired result. It is not choice (B) because "common" in this sense would refer to shared property, not to how usual or unusual something would be. And it is not choice (D) because the author is discussing chemical refinement, not spiritual or intellectual refinement.

8. **(A)** In this paragraph, the narrator discusses the need to minimize the inhalation of a toxic vapor, and is therefore interested in minimizing the "chances," or possibility, of inhalation. It is not choice (B) because impossibility is the opposite of the intended meaning. It is not choice (C) or (D) because the narrator is not considering advantages or disadvantages, but rather the likelihood that something will occur.

Graph Analysis Questions

Graph analysis questions ask you to interpret the data presented in a chart of some kind, relating the data to the argument presented in the passage. You will find the graph analysis questions on two passages—social and/or natural science passages—and they come at the end of the series of questions. How can you do well on these questions?

- **Carefully review the key, labels, and headings of the graph(s).** The graphs will come in a variety of forms—circle graphs, tables, and linear charts. Take time to understand to familiarize yourself with the organization of the graph before you dive into the graph-oriented questions.
- **Watch the scales on the axes.** Sometimes the least value in a graph will be at zero; other times, the least value may be at a higher number. Also, sometimes the spacing between numbers on the *x*-axis may be different from that on the *y*-axis. Avoid careless mistakes on the graph questions by paying close attention to where the numbers begin and the separation between data points.
- **Limit yourself to the evidence provided.** Even if you have background knowledge on the data presented in the graph, base your analysis solely on the information provided. The SAT will not expect you to have specific knowledge of the information in the graphs; the test will provide you with the information you need.
- **Use trends in the chart to make predictions.** If a question asks you to make a prediction for a scenario not pictured in the graph, use the trends evident in the data presented to make a reasonable prediction. See if the numbers are increasing or decreasing, and if they seem to be doing so in a linear or exponential way. The SAT will not try to "trick" you by having you make extremely precise predictions—the answers will be far enough apart from one another that you can make a good estimate to be correct.
- **Integrate the information in the graph with the information in the passage when needed.** Graph analysis questions will often require you to consider what the author of the passage might say about the information in the graph. Be prepared to go back and forth between the graph and the passage to answer graph analysis questions.

Now, try some graph analysis questions in the following drills. Allow about three to four minutes for each graph and its accompanying questions.

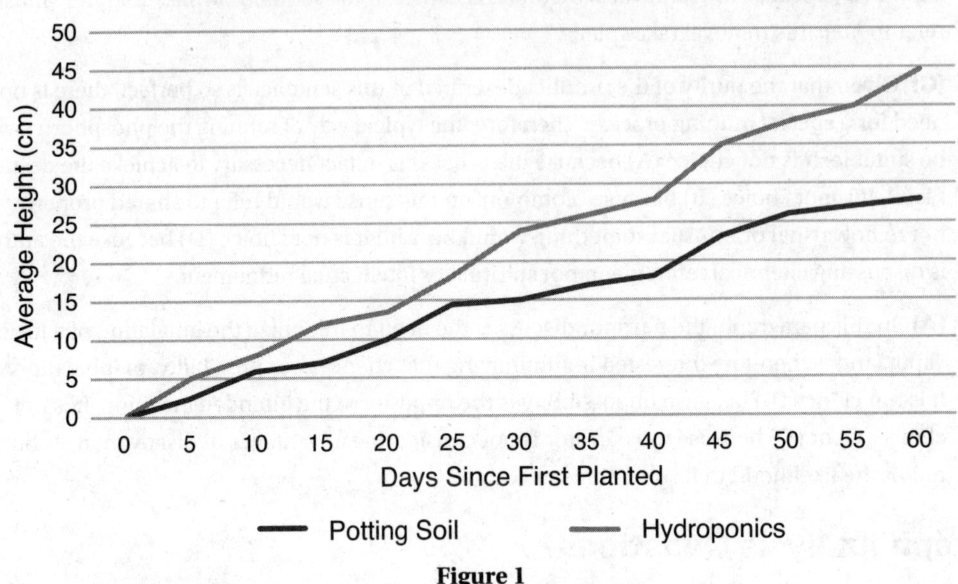

Figure 1

Scientists monitored the growth of French bean plants over a period of two months. The average height of the French bean plants in potting soil versus a hydroponics system was charted over time.

1. According to Figure 1, what was the average height of the French bean plants that were planted in the potting soil 30 days after being planted?

   (A) 12 cm
   (B) 15 cm
   (C) 26 cm
   (D) 30 cm

2. The information in Figure 1 most strongly suggests that

   (A) planting French bean plants in either hydroponics or in potting soil gives similar results.
   (B) planting French bean plants in either hydroponics or in potting soil negatively affects the plant growth.
   (C) planting French bean plants in hydroponics generally results in greater plant height than when French bean plants are planted in potting soil.
   (D) planting French bean plants in potting soil generally results in greater plant height than when French bean plants are planted in hydroponics.

3. Based on Figure 1, at the completion of the observation period, approximately how great a difference was there between the average French bean plant height from the potting soil group and the average French bean plant height from the hydroponics group?

   (A) 12 cm
   (B) 17 cm
   (C) 28 cm
   (D) 45 cm

Average Annual Fuel Wasted Due to Traffic Congestion (Measured in Millions of Gallons of Gasoline)

City Name	City Population Profile	Year 1985	Year 1990	Year 1995	Year 2000	Year 2005	Year 2010
Anchorage, Alaska	*Small*	0.9	1.5	2.3	3.2	3.7	4.0
Boston, Massachusetts	*Very Large*	29.5	38.6	43.9	59.0	65.4	67.3
Dayton, Ohio	*Medium*	2.4	3.5	5.0	6.8	7.2	7.1
Los Angeles, California	*Very Large*	119.9	148.3	182.9	211.6	242.1	238.4
Orlando, Florida	*Large*	3.6	7.1	10.5	15.9	21.3	21.9
Salt Lake City, Utah	*Large*	3.0	4.0	5.7	9.4	12.6	13.2

Source: *www.bts.gov/content/annual-wasted-fuel-due-congestion*

Figure 2

4. Based on Figure 2, between the years 1985 and 2010, the average annual fuel wasted due to traffic congestion in the very large cities in the table roughly

    (A) doubled.
    (B) tripled.
    (C) quadrupled.
    (D) quintupled.

5. Another city is added to Figure 2 and has an average annual fuel wasted due to traffic congestion in the year 2000 of 12 million gallons of gasoline. Based on the overall pattern in the figure, what it is the most likely population category of this city?

    (A) Small
    (B) Medium
    (C) Large
    (D) Very Large

6. An economist hypothesizes that during an economic downturn, some cities may see a decrease in their average annual fuel wasted due to traffic congestion. If that were the case, based on Figure 2, during which of the following years would the economist most likely conjecture that an economic downturn took place?

    (A) 1988
    (B) 1997
    (C) 2000
    (D) 2007

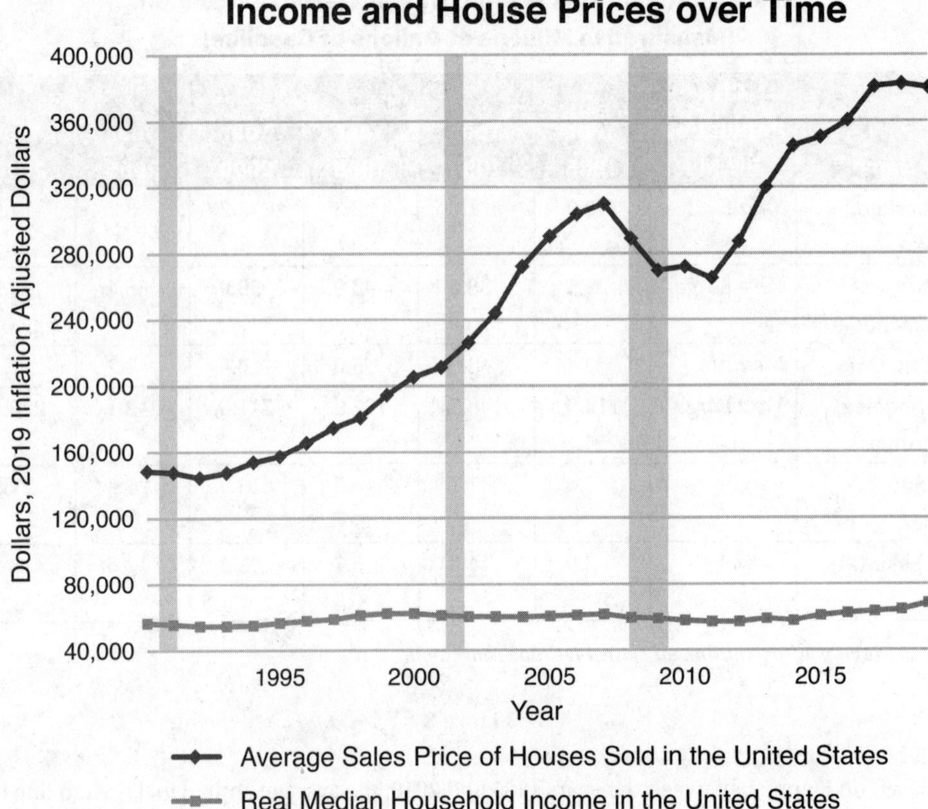

Data and table gathered from the St. Louis Federal Reserve: https://fred.stlouisfed.org
Note: Gray areas indicate economic recessions.

Figure 3

7. Which statement best generalizes the overall trend in Figure 3 in the real median household income in the United States over the time from 1995 to 2010?

   (A) It increases exponentially.
   (B) It decreases exponentially.
   (C) It stays relatively constant.
   (D) There is insufficient information to make a determination.

8. Which of the following is an accurate statement about the trend in Figure 3 in the average sales prices for homes in the United States before and after economic recessions?

   (A) They consistently decrease.
   (B) They consistently increase.
   (C) They remain the same.
   (D) They sometimes increase and sometimes decrease.

9. The information in Figure 3 would lend the greatest direct support to which of the following points of view?
   (A) A home has become increasingly unaffordable for the typical household in the United States.
   (B) Families in the United States would find more affordable housing in other countries.
   (C) The very least expensive houses in the United States have steadily increased in value.
   (D) The monthly payment to purchase a home paid by a typical household in the United States has decreased over the past three decades.

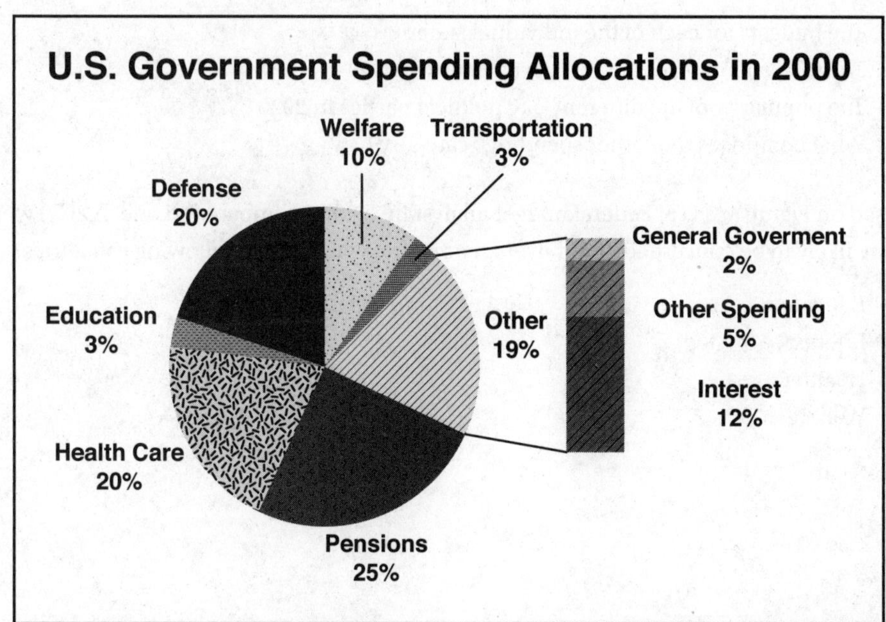

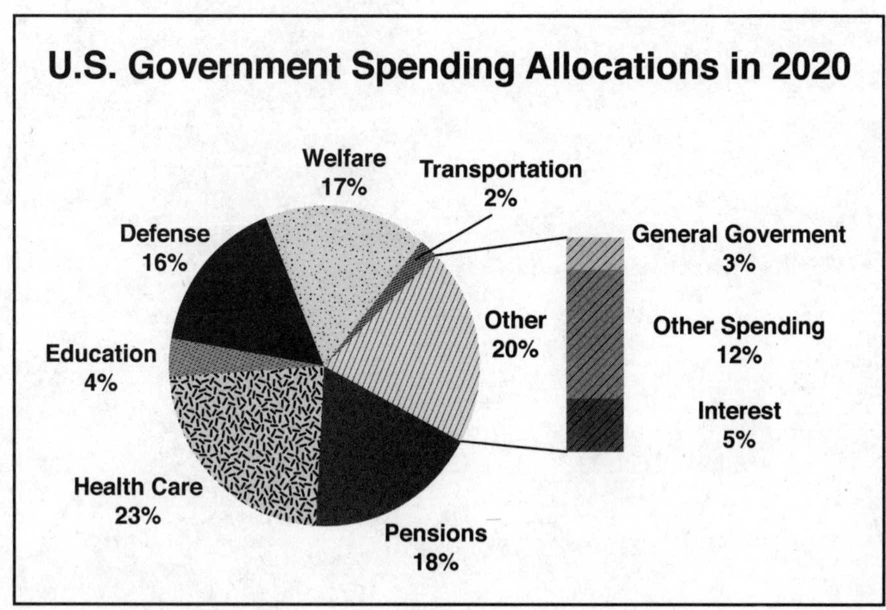

Source: *govinfo.gov*

Figure 4

10. According to Figure 4, which spending categories were the largest in 2000 and in 2020 respectively?

(A) "Other" in both
(B) Pensions, Health Care
(C) Defense, Welfare
(D) Health Care, Defense

11. Which of the following facts, if added to Figure 4, would give the reader a more precise understanding of spending categories of the United States government in the year 2020?

(A) The budgets for each of the individual states
(B) The total spending of the U.S. government in 2010
(C) The popularity of the different U.S. political parties in 2020
(D) What comprises the "other spending" category

12. Based on Figure 4, a U.S. Federal budget analyst in 2000 as compared to one in 2020 would be more likely to be concerned about overspending on which of the following categories?

(A) Education
(B) Interest
(C) Health Care
(D) Welfare

Answer Explanations

1. **(B)** Follow the darker line that represents the potting soil, and find what the *y* value is when the *x* value is at 30—it is 15 cm.

2. **(C)** For all the days after the start of the study, the beans cultivated in the hydroponics system had an average height greater than the beans cultivated in the potting soil. Therefore, the graph most strongly suggests that planting French bean plants in hydroponics generally results in greater plant height than when French bean plants are planted in potting soil. It is not choice (A) because the results diverge, and it is not choice (B) because the plants do indeed grow, suggesting that there is not a negative impact from these environments.

3. **(B)** The graph provides 60 days of observations, so look at the final set of points on the far right side of the graph to compare. At 60 days, the hydroponics sample has an average height of 45, while the potting soil sample has an average height of 28. Subtract 28 from 45 to get 17 cm as the difference in height.

4. **(A)** The two very large cities in the table are Boston and Los Angeles. Their average annual fuel wasted due to traffic congestion roughly doubled between 1985 and 2010, with Boston's going from 29.5 to 67.3, and L.A.'s going from 119.9 to 238.4.

5. **(C)** In the year 2000, the large city of Orlando had 15.9, and the large city of Salt Lake City had 9.4. An unknown city with a level of 12 would come closest to the levels of these large cities.

6. **(D)** Between the years 2005 and 2010, the level in Dayton decreased from 7.2 to 7.1, and the level in Los Angeles decreased from 242.1 to 238.4. Since these are the only examples of a decrease in average annual fuel waste over a period of time, the economist would likely believe that during the interval of 2005–2010, an economic downturn took place. The only option that has a year within this interval is 2007.

7. **(C)** The real median household income is represented by the lower line, and in the interval between 1995 and 2010, it stays relatively constant.

8. **(D)** In the first and third economic recessions indicated in the graph, in the years 1991 and 2008, the average sale price of houses sold in the United States decreased. In the second economic recession in 2001, the average increased. Therefore, it would be accurate to say that the average sales prices for homes in the United States sometimes increase and sometimes decrease after recessions.

9. **(A)** In 1990, the average home price was approximately 150,000, while the average household income was around 55,000—the home price was about three times that of household income. By 2019, the home price was approximately 380,000, while household income was around 70,000—the home price was then about five times that of household income. Given the increase in the ratio over time, it would be reasonable to state that based on this data, a home has become increasingly unaffordable for the typical U.S. household. It is not choice (B) because there is nothing in the graph to compare home prices in the United States to those in other countries. It is not choice (C) because only the average sales prices of homes are presented—there is no breakdown into least expensive vs. most expensive homes. And it is not choice (D) because the amount a household must pay per month to buy a house is not presented; it is possible that factors other than the home price, such as interest rates and taxes, would affect the average monthly payment.

10. **(B)** "Respectively" is a word that sometimes comes up in questions, meaning that the descriptions apply in the order the items are mentioned—in this situation it means that the first adjective will apply to the first item, and the second adjective will apply to the second term. In the year 2000, pensions were the largest category at 25% of government spending. In the year 2020, health care was the largest category at 23% of government spending.

11. **(D)** In the 2020 graph, 12% of the overall government spending is labelled as "other." It would help the reader have a more precise understanding of spending categories in 2020 if a detailed breakdown of what comprised the "other" category were provided. It is not choice (A) because the graph provides information on the overall U.S. government spending, not on individual state spending. It is not choice (B) because while this would help a reader better understand the amount of money spent, it would not help clarify what the spending categories were. And it is not choice (C) because even with an understanding of the popularity of different political parties, there would not necessarily be clarity on the makeup of the government spending.

12. **(B)** In the year 2000, interest represented 12% of U.S. government spending, while in 2020, interest represented 5%. So, it would be reasonable to conclude that a federal budget analyst would be more concerned about overspending on interest in 2000 than in 2020. The other three categories all *increased* in their percentage of federal spending from 2000 to 2020, so it would be more likely that an analyst would be concerned about overspending in these categories in 2020, not in 2000.

Full-Length Passage Drills

The following five drills each represents a passage type you will encounter on the SAT Reading: Fiction, Social Science, Historical Document, Science, and Comparative. If needed, refresh yourself on strategies for reading each type of passage in the introductory part of the Reading chapter. Take a total of 13 minutes to complete each drill—5 minutes for reading and 8 minutes for the questions. Good luck!

Fiction: *Oliver Twist*

In 1838, Charles Dickens published Oliver Twist, *the story of a young orphan who is apprenticed to an undertaker and later runs off to London. Below, Oliver's quick ascent under Mr. Sowerberry incites the jealousy of Noah, another apprentice.*

The month's trial over, Oliver was formally apprenticed. It was a nice sickly season just at this time. In commercial phrase, coffins were looking up; and, in the course of a few weeks, Oliver had acquired a great deal of experience. The success of Mr. Sowerberry's ingenious speculation exceeded even his most sanguine hopes. The oldest inhabitants recollected no period at which measles had been so prevalent, or so fatal to infant existence; and many were the mournful processions which little Oliver headed in a hat-band reaching down to his knees, to the indescribable admiration and emotion of all the mothers in the town. As Oliver accompanied his master in most of his adult expeditions too, in order that he might acquire that unanimity of demeanour and full command of nerve which are so essential to a finished undertaker, he had many opportunities of observing the beautiful resignation and fortitude with which some strong-minded people bear their trials and losses.

For instance, when Sowerberry had an order for the burial of some rich old lady or gentleman, who was surrounded by a great number of nephews and nieces, who had been perfectly inconsolable during the previous illness, and whose grief had been wholly irrepressible even on the most public occasions, they would be as happy among themselves as need be—quite cheerful and contented, conversing together with as much freedom and gaiety as if nothing whatever had happened to disturb them. Husbands, too, bore the loss of their wives with the most heroic calmness; and wives, again, put on weeds for their husbands, as if, so far from grieving in the garb of sorrow, they had made up their minds to render it as becoming and attractive as possible. It was observable, too, that ladies and gentlemen who were in passions of anguish during the ceremony of interment, recovered almost as soon as they reached home, and became quite composed before the tea-drinking was over. All this was very pleasant and improving to see, and Oliver beheld it with great admiration.

That Oliver Twist was moved to resignation by the example of these good people, I cannot, although I am his biographer, undertake to affirm with any degree of confidence; but I can most distinctly say, that for many months he continued meekly to submit to the domination and ill-treatment of Noah Claypole, who used him far worse than ever, now that his jealousy was roused by seeing the new boy promoted to the black stick and hat-band, while he, the old one, remained stationary in the muffin-cap and leathers. Charlotte treated him badly because Noah did; and Mrs. Sowerberry was his decided enemy because Mr. Sowerberry was disposed to be his friend: so, between these three on one side, and a glut of funerals on the other, Oliver was not altogether as comfortable as the hungry pig was, when he was shut up by mistake in the grain department of a brewery.

And now I come to a very important passage in Oliver's history, for I have to record an act, slight and unimportant perhaps in appearance, but which indirectly produced a most material change in all his future prospects and proceedings.

One day Oliver and Noah had descended into the kitchen, at the usual dinner-hour, to banquet upon a small joint of mutton—a pound and a half of the worst end of the neck; when, Charlotte being called out of the way, there ensued a brief interval of time, which Noah Claypole, being hungry and vicious, considered he could not possibly devote to a worthier purpose than aggravating and tantalising young Oliver Twist.

Intent upon this innocent amusement, Noah put his feet on the table-cloth, and pulled Oliver's hair, and twitched his ears, and expressed his opinion that he was a "sneak," and furthermore announced his intention of coming to see him hung whenever that desirable event should take place, and entered upon various other topics of petty annoyance, like a malicious and ill-conditioned charity-boy as he was. But, none of these taunts producing the desired effect of making Oliver cry, Noah attempted to be more facetious still, and in this attempt did what many small wits, with far greater reputations than Noah, notwithstanding, do to this day when they want to be funny;—he got rather personal.

"Work'us," said Noah, "how's your mother?"

"She's dead," replied Oliver; "don't you say anything about her to me!"

1. The passage suggests that the financial interests of undertakers are

(A) more subject to unpredictable social patterns than the interests of other professionals.
(B) the subject of dinner table conversation in homes across the country.
(C) surprisingly in accord with the political goals of the powers that be.
(D) at odds with the overall interests of the population as a whole.

2. As used in line 4, "sanguine" most closely means

(A) trivial.
(B) worldly.
(C) optimistic.
(D) ancient.

3. It is reasonable to infer that what characteristic of Oliver may have made him a better undertaker apprentice than Noah?

(A) His physical presence
(B) His ability to forecast the future
(C) His even-temperedness
(D) His personal wealth

4. Which option gives the best evidence for the answer to the previous question?

(A) Lines 2–3 ("In commercial . . . experience")
(B) Lines 20–22 ("It was . . . over")
(C) Lines 29–31 ("Charlotte . . . his friend")
(D) Lines 46–47 ("But, none . . . Oliver cry")

5. What general attitude toward death does the narrator most strongly suggest that Oliver would respect?
   (A) A joyful one
   (B) A stoic one
   (C) An expressive one
   (D) A melancholy one

6. Which option gives the best evidence for the answer to the previous question?
   (A) Lines 4–7 ("The oldest . . . in the town")
   (B) Lines 12–14 ("For instance . . . illness")
   (C) Lines 20–23 ("It was . . . admiration")
   (D) Lines 26–29 ("but I can . . . leathers")

7. The purpose of the paragraph in lines 34–36 is most likely
   (A) to provide a transition to an important anecdote.
   (B) to introduce the primary characters of the narrative.
   (C) to describe a vital life event.
   (D) to address a likely objection by the reader.

8. As used in line 36, "material" most closely means
   (A) economic.
   (B) significant.
   (C) tactile.
   (D) pessimistic.

9. Noah's taunting of Oliver throughout the passage can best be described as
   (A) increasingly below the belt.
   (B) consistently lighthearted.
   (C) violently physical.
   (D) largely justifiable.

10. It is reasonable to infer that Noah would have ceased his taunting of Oliver had Oliver
    (A) responded with a strong reaction at an earlier provocation.
    (B) kept his calm disposition for longer than he did.
    (C) taken a personal attack to heart.
    (D) been promoted even further in the undertaking business.

Social Science: Social Media Effects, written in 2020

In high school now is a group of students who has never experienced life without the internet. From their very earliest memories, a vast amount of information and interaction has been at their fingertips. Notably, in-person socializing, which used to be the primary way to spend time together, is now far less common than interacting with friends and acquaintances, and even strangers, online. These students will soon be entering the workforce with much of their lives spent online. They spend a significant portion of their time on social media, *and they don't know any differently*. This cohort consists of the guinea pigs of one of the biggest communications revolutions of all time. As they grow and change, their brains can be studied to see how this constant exposure to online social communication affects them.

One of the primary effects of social media use that has already been observed in populations that utilize social media regularly is a decrease in mental health and self-esteem. As far back as 1998, a study showed that increased social media use correlated with decreased in-person interactions with their friends and family. This was hypothesized to lead to issues with symptoms of depression. As modern social media developed, this decrease in personal face-to-face interactions increased. In England a recent study by the National Institute of Health (NIH) found a significant correlation between social media usage and symptoms of depression in high school aged subjects. This correlation was not found among older social media users. Of course, correlation is not causation: already depressed people could just tend to use social media more. However, the preliminary results do seem to indicate that the adolescent brain is negatively impacted by social media use.

The predominant hypothesis as to how this occurs lies within what people choose to post online. In order to cultivate a following, feel popular, and receive the positive attention so many people crave, most people on social media only post the very best part of their lives. Their fancy vacations (one week per year), their designer clothes (two outfits out of 50), and their restaurant meals (one a week). And it's safe to say no one posts any picture of themselves looking anything less than their best. They don't post about the boredom of their internship, their "staying-in" sweat pants, or the ramen noodles they eat most evenings for dinner. This creates a false online environment. People logging into Instagram after school each day see what appears to be all their friends and acquaintances living amazing and exciting lives. As they eat a frozen dinner and try to decide what to watch on Netflix, people scroll through engaging and perfect pictures and feel worse and worse about themselves and their seemingly inferior lives.

It is important to point out that while many studies have been conducted about this phenomenon, there is no conclusive proof that social media causes depression or low self-esteem. In fact, many scientists are working with social media platforms to use social media data to help detect and intervene in cases of depression before they become too advanced. There is hope that outreach through social media may be a new frontier in mental health detection and treatment. However, as with all new technologies, students and parents must be very careful. Research has yet to catch up with our quickly evolving methods of communication: safe practices have yet to be established.

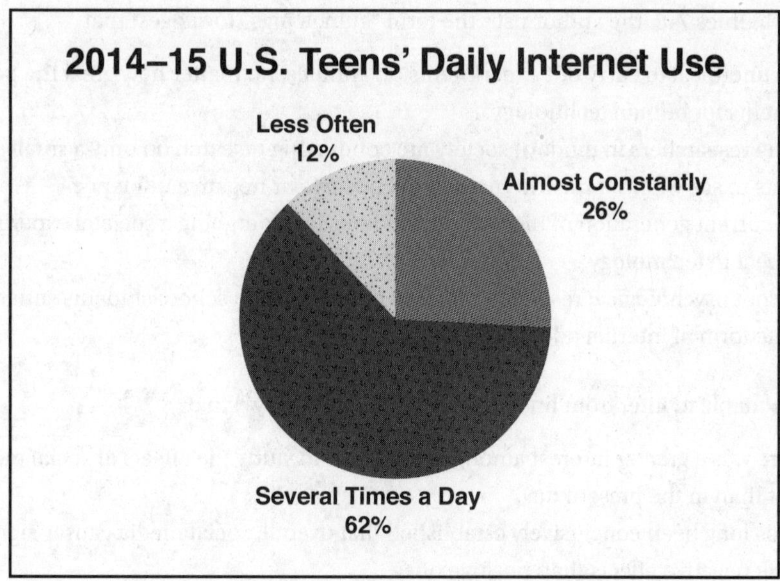

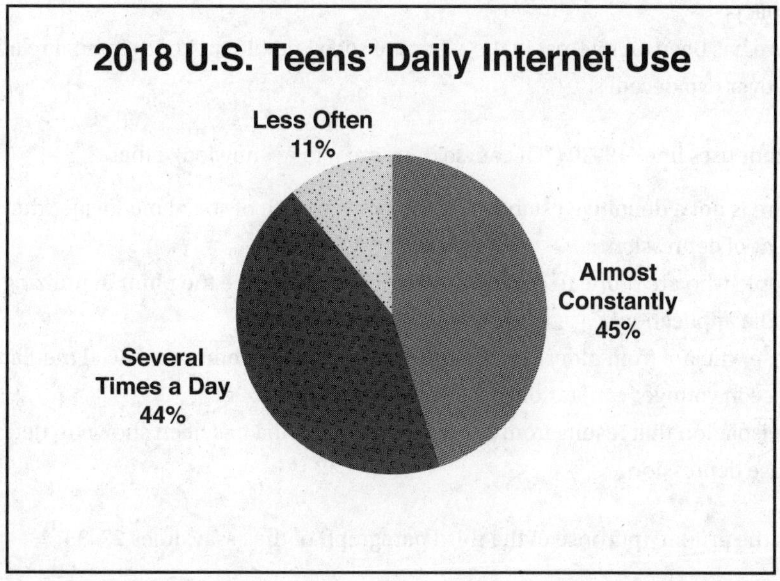

Adapted from *pewresearch.org.*

1. Based on the passage as a whole, the author of the passage would most likely find that research results about the social media effects on teenagers from which of the following years could be most insightful?

(A) 2000
(B) 2010
(C) 2020
(D) 2030

2. As used in lines 7-8, the author uses the term "guinea pigs" to suggest that
   (A) it is unethical to carry out experiments on animals, no matter how great the potential benefits for human technology.
   (B) some researchers in modern society are conducting research on only a small set of students to see whether the internet is a net positive or negative influence.
   (C) the current generation of high school students is undergoing a societal experiment with respect to technology.
   (D) current psychological research indicates that most high school students suffer from some form of internet addiction.

3. It is reasonable to infer from lines 12–14 ("As far . . . family") that
   (A) there was a greater interest among researchers to study the effects of social media in the past than in the present day.
   (B) it has long been conclusively established that overall, social media causes significantly more negative effects than positive ones.
   (C) once individuals begin to use social media, they are unable to control its addictive impacts.
   (D) there has been an interest in the effects of social media on interpersonal relationships for over two decades.

4. The author uses lines 19-20 ("Of course . . . more") to acknowledge that
   (A) there is not a definitive established link between use of social media and the development of depression.
   (B) people who are prone to depression are less likely to see the point in utilizing social media applications.
   (C) those who are from older generations are less likely to embrace social media use than those in younger generations.
   (D) the isolation that results from the use of social media has been shown to definitively cause depression.

5. What is the primary purpose of the third paragraph of the essay, lines 22–33?
   (A) To demonstrate how consumerism is rampant across different age groups
   (B) To provide a possible explanation for the results of a study
   (C) To consider the potential benefits of a new technology
   (D) To elaborate on why older generations find social media appealing

6. In line 37, "advanced" most nearly means
   (A) refined.
   (B) modern.
   (C) severe.
   (D) skillful.

7. What does the author most strongly suggest is the appropriate attitude for users of new technology to have?

    (A) optimism.
    (B) pessimism.
    (C) celebration.
    (D) prudence.

8. Which choice provides the best evidence for the answer to the previous question?

    (A) Lines 1–3 ("In high . . . fingertips")
    (B) Lines 15–19 ("As modern . . . users")
    (C) Lines 22–24 ("The predominant . . . lives")
    (D) Lines 39–41 ("However . . . established")

9. Which choice is supported by the data in the set of figures?

    (A) While approximately half of U.S. teenagers were likely to use the internet constantly in 2014–2015, nearly two-thirds of U.S. teenagers were likely to do so in 2018.
    (B) While approximately one-fourth of U.S. teenagers were likely to use the internet constantly in 2014–2015, nearly half of U.S. teenagers were likely to do so in 2018.
    (C) While approximately one-tenth of U.S. teenagers were likely to use the internet constantly in 2014–2015, nearly three-tenths of U.S. teenagers were likely to do so in 2018.
    (D) While approximately one-fifth of U.S. teenagers were likely to use the internet constantly in 2014–2015, nearly four-fifths of U.S. teenagers were likely to do so in 2018.

10. The information in the two graphs gives the best support for the statement in which of the following selections from the passage?

    (A) Lines 5–6 ("These students . . . online")
    (B) Lines 11–12 ("One of . . . esteem")
    (C) Lines 20–21 ("However. . . use")
    (D) Lines 26–29 ("And it's . . . dinner")

Historical Document: *The Souls of Black Folk*

Below is an excerpt adapted from a section of W. E. B. Du Bois's The Souls of Black Folk *titled "Of Sorrow Songs."*

They that walked in darkness sang songs in the olden days—Sorrow Songs—for they were weary at heart. And so before each thought that I have written in this book I have set a phrase, a haunting echo of these weird old songs in which the soul of the black slave spoke to men. Ever since I was a child these songs have stirred me strangely. They came out of the South unknown to me, one by one, and yet at once I knew them as of me and of mine. Then in after years when I came to Nashville I saw the great temple builded of these songs towering over the pale city. To me Jubilee Hall seemed ever made of the songs themselves, and its bricks were red with the blood and dust of toil. Out of them rose for me morning, noon, and night, bursts of wonderful melody, full of the voices of my brothers and sisters, full of the voices of the past.

Little of beauty has America given the world save the rude grandeur God himself stamped on her bosom; the human spirit in this new world has expressed itself in vigor and ingenuity rather than in beauty. And so by fateful chance the Negro folk-song—the rhythmic cry of the slave—stands to-day not simply as the sole American music, but as the most beautiful expression of human experience born this side the seas. It has been neglected, it has been, and is, half despised, and above all it has been persistently mistaken and misunderstood; but notwithstanding, it still remains as the singular spiritual heritage of the nation and the greatest gift of the Negro people.

Away back in the thirties the melody of these slave songs stirred the nation, but the songs were soon half forgotten. Some, like "Near the lake where drooped the willow," passed into current airs and their source was forgotten; others were caricatured on the "minstrel" stage and their memory died away. Then in war-time came the singular Port Royal experiment after the capture of Hilton Head, and perhaps for the first time the North met the Southern slave face to face and heart to heart with no third witness. The Sea Islands of the Carolinas, where they met, were filled with a black folk of primitive type, touched and moulded less by the world about them than any others outside the Black Belt. Their appearance was uncouth, their language funny, but their hearts were human and their singing stirred men with a mighty power. Thomas Wentworth Higginson hastened to tell of these songs, and Miss McKim and others urged upon the world their rare beauty. But the world listened only half credulously until the Fisk Jubilee Singers sang the slave songs so deeply into the world's heart that it can never wholly forget them again.

What are these songs, and what do they mean? I know little of music and can say nothing in technical phrase, but I know something of men, and knowing them, I know that these songs are the articulate message of the slave to the world. They tell us in these eager days that life was joyous to the black slave, careless and happy. I can easily believe this of some, of many. But not all the past South, though it rose from the dead, can gainsay the heart-touching witness of these songs. They are the music of an unhappy people, of the children of disappointment; they tell of death and suffering and unvoiced longing toward a truer world, of misty wanderings and hidden ways.

1. What is the point of the passage?

   (A) To introduce a topic
   (B) To analyze a disagreement
   (C) To examine an event
   (D) To provide a personal anecdote

2. Du Bois most strongly suggests that general American creativity is focused on

   (A) lyrical beauty.
   (B) musical innovation.
   (C) energetic inventiveness.
   (D) mystical contemplation.

3. Which option gives the best evidence for the answer to the previous question?

   (A) Lines 8–10 ("Out of . . . the past")
   (B) Lines 12–13 ("the human . . . beauty")
   (C) Lines 20–22 ("Some . . . died away")
   (D) Lines 37–39 ("They are . . . hidden ways")

4. As used in line 17, "singular" most closely means

   (A) lonely.
   (B) extraordinary.
   (C) odd.
   (D) remote.

5. Du Bois suggests that the meaning of the slave songs is both

   (A) technical and complex.
   (B) scholarly and esoteric.
   (C) consequential and eloquent.
   (D) eternal and incomprehensible.

6. Which option gives the best evidence for the answer to the previous question?

   (A) Lines 15–17 ("It has been neglected . . . misunderstood")
   (B) Lines 20–22 ("Some, like . . . died away")
   (C) Lines 32–34 ("I know . . . the world")
   (D) Lines 36–37 ("But not . . . these songs")

7. Du Bois implies in lines 22–31 ("Then in . . . them again") that the initial greater public reception to the songs of the slaves of the Sea Islands was

   (A) patiently analytical and systematic.
   (B) blatantly belligerent and argumentative.
   (C) warmly receptive and tolerant.
   (D) overly superficial and dismissive.

8. "They" in line 34 most likely refers to

   (A) slaves.
   (B) society.
   (C) slave owners.
   (D) musicians.

9. As used in line 39, "misty" most closely means

   (A) vaporous.
   (B) cloudy.
   (C) steamy.
   (D) dewy.

10. Based on the final paragraph, it is reasonable to infer that Du Bois's attitude toward those who would suggest that the songs of slaves expressed their happiness and joy is one of

    (A) complete agreement.
    (B) qualified skepticism.
    (C) outright dismissal.
    (D) hopeful optimism.

Science: Calico and Tortoiseshell Cat Genetics, written in 2020

When breeding animals of any kind, different coat colors may be more desired than others. To ensure that a breeder has offspring with the desired coat color or pattern, it is important to understand the genetic basis of inheritance of that trait. In some cases, coat color may be as simple as one gene with a dominant allele and recessive allele, making it very easy to predict what coat color offspring will have based on parental coat colors. A more complicated example of coat color inheritance would be the genetic phenomenon that creates tortoiseshell and calico coat colors in domesticated cats. Tortoiseshell cats have a coat that contains a mixture of orange and black fur, while calico cats have orange, white, and black patches. Cats with these two coat variations have a lot in common, including the reason why they have both orange and black fur.

Nearly all tortoiseshell and calico cats are female. This is because the gene that dictates whether the cat's fur is orange or black is located on the X chromosome. Since male cats have XY chromosomes, they will usually only have one allele coding for either orange fur or black fur. Males would be calico or tortoiseshell if they had two X chromosomes along with a Y, but this is very rare. Since female cats have two X chromosomes, a female cat that is heterozygous for this fur color gene will have one X chromosome with an allele coding for orange and another X chromosome with an allele coding for black.

Every cell in a cat contains a pair of every chromosome, including sex chromosomes (for cats, XX for females and XY for males). In cats, along with other species, having one active X chromosome per cell is considered the adequate number. With this logic, males have a sufficient number of X chromosome genes, while females have double that number. To account for this, every cell in a female cat inactivates one X chromosome; the inactivated chromosome is condensed into a small structure called a Barr body and does not express genes. This is called X-inactivation, and is responsible for the display of both orange and black fur in both tortoiseshell and calico coat colors. Which X chromosome gets inactivated is thought to be a random process in each cell, so neither X is more likely to be selected for inactivation. Additionally, the X chromosome selected for inactivation in one cell does not impact the selection of the X chromosome to be inactivated in another.

Since one X chromosome is inactivated, only one X chromosome remains active and expresses genes in each cell in females. This being said, each cell may have one or the other X chromosome active. If a female cat is heterozygous for the fur color gene (meaning she has one X chromosome with an allele coding orange fur and the other X chromosome coding for black fur), each of her cells will have one of the X chromosomes inactivated. Since only one X chromosome is active per cell, some cells will have the active X chromosome with the allele that codes for orange fur, while others will have an active X chromosome with the allele coding for black fur. This yields the characteristic patches of orange and black fur in tortoiseshell and calico cats.

Whether the cat has white patches or not is dictated by another gene. Calico cats express this trait, which is why they have orange, black, and white patches. Tortoiseshell cats do not express this trait. Calico and tortoiseshell cats act as a great physical representation for the phenomenon of X-inactivation. For some time, scientists have noted that X-inactivation occurs in several species, including humans. The expression of the X-inactivation varies across species—humans do not display this with different colored patches of hair.

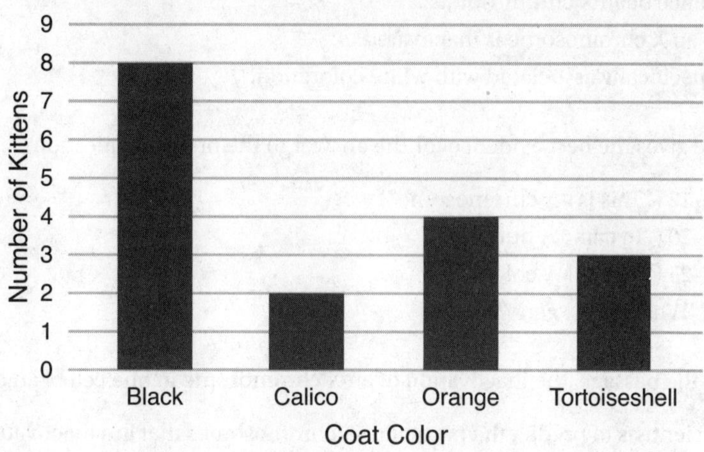

1. The main purpose of this passage is to

(A) argue for a point of view.
(B) explain a phenomenon.
(C) analyze a recent discovery.
(D) challenge conventional wisdom.

2. Based on the information in the passage, the phenomenon of X-inactivation is most likely to occur

(A) only in female felines.
(B) only in male felines.
(C) in females of several different species.
(D) in males of several different species.

3. As used in line 11, "dictates" most nearly means

(A) determines.
(B) obeys.
(C) speaks.
(D) analyzes.

4. It is reasonable to infer from the passage that which of the following combinations of XY chromosomes is least common?

(A) XX
(B) XY
(C) XXY
(D) All of these are equally common.

5. The primary cause for the difference in appearance in calico cats and tortoiseshell cats is

   (A) the gender of the cat.
   (B) the presence of an X chromosome.
   (C) whether an X chromosome is inactivated.
   (D) a gene specifically associated with white coloration.

6. Which choice gives the best evidence for the answer to the previous question?

   (A) Lines 11–12 ("This is . . . chromosome")
   (B) Lines 19–20 ("In cats . . . number")
   (C) Lines 24–25 ("This is . . . colors")
   (D) Line 38 ("Whether . . . gene")

7. According to the passage, the inactivation of an X chromosome in one cell of an organism will

   (A) enable scientists to predict the particular X chromosomes that are inactivated throughout the cells of the organism.
   (B) not affect the particular X chromosomes that are inactivated in other cells of the organism.
   (C) only affect the inactivation of X chromosomes in species genetically similar to house cats.
   (D) be determined by whether the Y chromosome in the cell is also inactivated.

8. Which choice gives the best evidence for the answer to the previous question?

   (A) Lines 14–15 ("Males . . . rare")
   (B) Lines 18–19 ("Every . . . males")
   (C) Lines 27–28 ("Additionally . . . another")
   (D) Lines 42–43 ("The expression . . . hair")

9. Based on the information in the passage, it is most likely that which two groupings of cat color in the graph would have some male members?

   (A) Calico and black
   (B) Tortoiseshell and calico
   (C) Orange and black
   (D) Orange and tortoiseshell

10. Based on the information in the passage and the graph, how many cats from the first litter born as portrayed in the graph would have been calico cats?

    (A) Zero
    (B) One
    (C) Two
    (D) There is insufficient information to make a determination.

Comparative Passages: Ocean Plastics

Passages 1 and 2 are by two scientists discussing the problem of the Pacific garbage islands. Both passages were written in 2020.

Passage 1

The Pacific garbage island, also known as the Pacific trash vortex, is a massive floating garbage island in the Pacific that has an area twice the size of Texas. This is just one of the most visible effects of humans' significant overuse of plastics and their effect on the environment. The great abundance of microplastics in marine and other environments is very detrimental to the ecosystem. The obvious solution would be to stop using so much plastic, but with human nature being what it is, we will probably genetically engineer pigs with wings before that happens. A possible solution is one that nature seems to be providing.

In Japan, plastic-eating bacteria were discovered in a landfill. Since then, much research has been devoted to optimizing these bacteria so that they can eat plastic more quickly. It seems clear that plastic-eating bacteria are the most likely solution to our plastic crisis because the amount of plastic in the environment has built up to a point where it is already damaging the ecosystem. Halting production of plastic simply is insufficient; there is already far too much plastic in the ocean for us to merely discontinue production. The plastic already in the ecosystem has already done and will continue to do massive amounts of damage. Although the current plastic-eating bacteria are very slow, they are just the first generation of this technology.

The fact that these organisms had already evolved naturally in landfills is remarkable and shows the adaptivity of life in the face of new challenges. Modern science can use principles of evolutionary biology and biochemistry to accelerate this important technology so it can be a critical tool in alleviating this crisis.

Passage 2

Microplastics are microscopic particles of plastic that tend to accumulate toxins and are in some cases toxic themselves. Unfortunately, microplastics tend to end up being eaten by various organisms. The primary reason for this problem is that in recent years, approximately 380 million tons of plastic are produced annually. Plastic is not biodegradable, which means that once it enters the environment it can take several hundred years to degrade. Some have proposed plastic-eating microorganisms as a revolutionary solution to this critical issue. I am skeptical of the claims made about this bacteria's utility in consuming massive plastic deposits.

Right now, almost all of the plastics in the ocean are in macroscopic objects, but if they are broken down by plastic-eating bacteria, an explosion in the amount of microplastics in the ocean seems inevitable. This massive accumulation in microplastics could have an extremely detrimental effect on the ocean's ecosystem. Thus, plastic-eating bacteria must be carefully researched before these creatures are released into the ocean.

Additionally, the polymers in PET plastic—the most common type of plastic—are fundamentally different from the sorts of biological molecules that naturally occurring enzymes are meant to break down. These enzymes are simply not well suited to breaking these chemical bonds and will take significant modification to become anything more than an interesting novelty.

Finally, if these bacteria do become sufficiently efficient to be useful, it will be impossible to keep them contained. These bacteria would soon start degrading plastic car parts, packaging, and anything else made of plastic. It would be an economic disaster. That's not even the worst part; as soon as PET plastic becomes biodegradable, industry will simply switch to a different plastic formulation that is not biodegradable and within a few years, we will be in the same place we started.

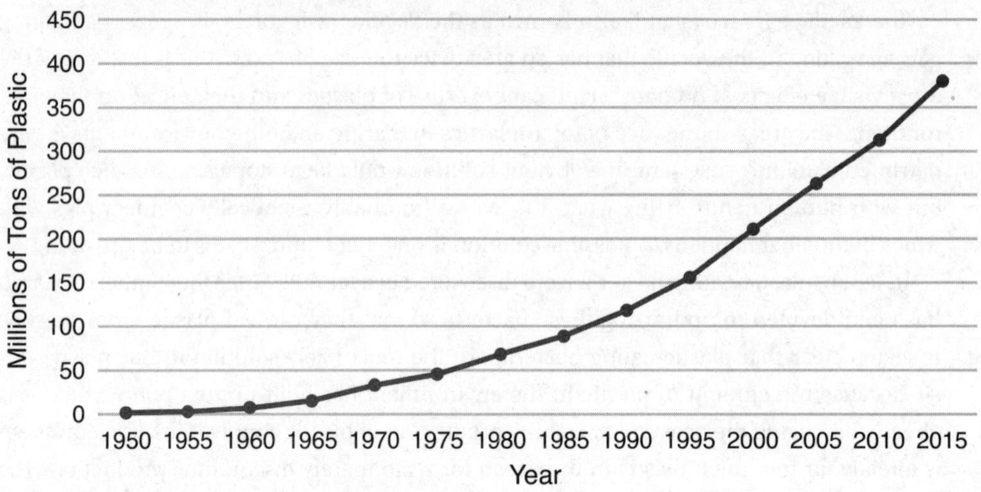

Data gathered from https://ourworldindata.org/plastic-pollution

1. As used in line 27, "critical" most nearly means

   (A) crucial.
   (B) judgmental.
   (C) censorious.
   (D) rapid.

2. It can reasonably be inferred that the author of Passage 1 considers the likeliness that humans will voluntarily reduce their plastic consumption as

   (A) quite possible.
   (B) definitely probable.
   (C) virtually none.
   (D) moderately diminished.

3. Which choice gives the best evidence for the answer to the previous question?

   (A) Lines 2–4 ("This is . . . environment")
   (B) Lines 6–7 ("with human . . . happens")
   (C) Lines 12–13 ("Halting . . . production")
   (D) Lines 17–18 ("The fact . . . challenges")

4. The primary purpose of the final paragraph of Passage 2, lines 39–44, is to

   (A) highlight the findings from recent studies.
   (B) forecast potentially negative outcomes.
   (C) cite what has happened when an approach has been previously attempted.
   (D) encourage the embrace of a new technology.

5. As used in line 40, "degrading" most nearly means

   (A) creating.
   (B) suffering.
   (C) breaking down.
   (D) disassembling.

6. The author of Passage 2 most strongly suggests that a relevant difference between macroscopic and microscopic plastic objects is that macroscopic plastic objects are

   (A) less easily consumed by organisms.
   (B) less prevalent in the ocean.
   (C) composed of different materials.
   (D) more biodegradable.

7. Based on the information in the graph, the author of Passage 2 most likely gathered the data about the amount of plastic production in "recent years" from which particular year?

   (A) 2005
   (B) 2010
   (C) 2015
   (D) 2020

8. The relationship between the two passages is best summarized as

   (A) Passage 1 presents an approach to solving a problem, while Passage 2 is skeptical of this approach.
   (B) Passage 1 considers and addresses each of the objections from Passage 2.
   (C) Passage 1 and Passage 2 largely agree on both the nature of a problem and its best solution.
   (D) Passage 1 dismisses a potential environmental issue, while Passage 2 proposes a method to deal with the environmental issue.

9. Based on the information in the passages, of the plastic shown in the graph that was produced between 1950 and 1960 that was disposed of in the ocean, how much is likely still remaining?

   (A) Nearly all
   (B) About half
   (C) About one-third
   (D) Nearly none

10. Which choice gives the best evidence for the answer to the previous question?

   (A) Lines 4–5 ("The great . . . ecosystem")
   (B) Lines 15–16 ("Although . . . technology")
   (C) Lines 24–26 ("Plastic . . . degrade")
   (D) Lines 41–44 ("That's not . . . started")

Answer Explanations

Fiction: *Oliver Twist*

1. **(D)** This question asks about the financial interests of the funeral business, which in this passage becomes quite prosperous when the measles breaks out and claims a multitude of lives. Hence, the undertaker makes money when people die, making his financial situation very much at odds with the general wishes of people (which of course do not include burying their loved ones). Choice (B) incorrectly links the profits of undertakers with how often people talk about them at dinner. Choice (C) assumes political powers want people dead, which is not evidenced in the passage. Choice (A), albeit tempting, is incorrect because many professions are subject to "social patterns," such as social class and welfare.

2. **(C)** Use context clues here. The "sickly season" increases "commercial" business so that even the undertaker's hopeful expectations are exceeded. "Sanguine" means optimistic in bad situations. "Trivial" means unimportant, and "ancient" means old or belonging to the distant past. Choice (B) implies that the undertaker's hopes were concerned with material gains rather than spiritual existence, which is certainly true. However, it is more accurate to say his hopes were high, or optimistic, than to suggest the author means the undertaker's hopes were in contrast to spiritual endeavors.

3. **(C)** Reword this question. "What qualities does Oliver seem to have that Noah does not?" We know Oliver is dedicated and attentive to his work; his efforts are rewarded in quick advancement and favor. We also know he usually submits willingly to Noah's ill treatment. Of Noah, we know only that he acts jealously and spitefully, often trying to upset Oliver's cool indifference with insults and personal taunts. Thus, we can infer Oliver is normally even-tempered in comparison to Noah's impetuous cruelty. We have no evidence to support choices (A), (B), or (D).

4. **(D)** In lines 46–47, Oliver ignores Noah's incessant taunts and provocations, providing support for the distinction in their respective characters. Choice (A) provides proof of the undertaker's booming business. Choice (B) discusses the differences between the reactions of people when at their loved ones' funerals and when at home. Choice (C) gives us an idea of how people other than Noah treat Oliver.

5. **(B)** Oliver reacts to death quite apathetically; he doesn't seem to show any emotion or feeling either way except in the instance of his own mother. Similarly, he admires those who remain "composed." So, look for the answer that sounds dispassionate or indifferent. Choices (A), (C), and (D) all suggest a strong showing of emotion. Choice **(B)** is the only answer that implies that Oliver respects those who endure death without extended or unnecessary emotional reaction.

6. **(C)** Here we are looking for lines that prove that Oliver respects stoicism, or an endurance without emotion. Choice **(C)** gives evidence of Oliver's "great admiration" for those who "recovered almost as soon as they reached home." Choice (A) tells us why the undertaker's business is doing so well financially, namely the spread of the measles. Choice (B) ends at line 14 and so discusses an emotional reaction to death but never gets to the part that Oliver respects, the "content" that comes soon after. Finally, choice (D) merely depicts Oliver's reaction, or lack thereof, to Noah's cruelty.

7. **(A)** Ask yourself not what this paragraph says but what it does. Before this, we have been hearing about Oliver's experience under Mr. Sowerberry. After this, we move into the particular incident where Noah finally elicits a reaction out of Oliver. This paragraph, then, moves from the broad description of experience to a particular event that proves significant for Oliver, making choice **(A)** correct. The characters are already introduced, ruling out choice (B). Be careful to avoid choice (C): the actual description of the event comes later. This paragraph just tells us we are now moving to that event. Choice (D) wrongfully assumes the reader would oppose or take issue with something that was just said.

8. **(B)** Here, the important act despite its trivial appearance "produced a most material change." We could substitute *significant* or *substantial* for "material," making choice **(B)** the correct answer. Choices (A) and (C) refer to other definitions of "material." Choice (D) wrongly implies that the change itself has feeling and thinks the worst will happen.

9. **(A)** Noah tries everything to upset Oliver and finally succeeds by getting very personal—by mentioning Oliver's dead mother. Hence, Noah's insults get more and more vindictive until Oliver finally reacts. Choices (B) and (D) both imply that Noah is not unnecessarily cruel to Oliver, which we know to be untrue. Choice (C) is incorrect because the passage doesn't evidence "physical" abuse, only verbal.

10. **(A)** Noah keeps taunting Oliver until he elicits a reaction by resorting to a personal attack about Oliver's deceased mother. While he tried to get Oliver to react with less provocative attacks earlier, he kept up his taunting until Oliver finally lost his temper. So, it is reasonable to infer that if Oliver had responded earlier with a strong reaction, Noah would have seen no need to continue to escalate. It is not choice (B) since if Oliver had continued to keep calm, Noah would likely have just continued to tease him. It is not choice (C), because Oliver does take a personal attack to heart when Noah finally does one. And it is not choice (D) since if Oliver had been further promoted, Noah would have likely been further annoyed by their relative difference in status.

Social Science: Social Media Effects

1. **(D)** In lines 40–41, the passage states that "Research has yet to catch up with our quickly evolving methods of communication." The narrator is suggesting that future research results would likely provide the most useful analysis of the impact of social media on teenagers, since there would be more time to determine the long-term impact of these changes. The other options are incorrect since they suggest earlier time frames when the information would not be as helpful.

2. **(C)** The narrator refers to modern teenagers as "guinea pigs" who can be studied to determine how constant exposure to the internet and social media will affect their brains. Therefore, the passage suggests that the current generation of high school students is undergoing a societal experiment with respect to technology. Choice (A) is incorrect since the narrator does not suggest that this experiment or other experiments that involve animals would be unethical. Choice (B) is incorrect because the research is not being conducted on just a small set of students, but rather on most modern teenagers in the United States. And choice (D) is incorrect because the author suggests that as of 2020, the research about the prevalence of internet addiction among teenagers is still in the early stages.

3. **(D)** Since the article was written in 2020, and lines 12–14 mention that a study on the effects of social media use was conducted as far back as the year 1998, it can be reasonably inferred that there has been an interest in analyzing the impact of social media on interpersonal relationships for at least two decades. Choice (A) is incorrect because there is no evidence in the passage that researchers were more interested in studying the impacts of social media in past years than in the present day. Choice (B) is incorrect, since in lines 34–36, the passage states that there has not been conclusive proof that social media causes depression or low self-esteem. And choice (C) is incorrect because the passage does not present evidence that there is uniform addiction to social media among users as soon as they start to use it.

4. **(A)** "Correlation is not causation" means that just because two things happen together, there is not necessarily a cause-and-effect link between those two things. In the case of social media, the passage states that there has not been a causal link established between using social media and becoming depressed; in these lines, the author suggests that the link *could* go in the opposite direction, with more depressed people being more likely to use social media. It is not choice (B) because the passage suggests that it is more likely that those prone to depression would be *more likely* to be attracted to social media. It is not choices (C) or (D) because this selection is not relevant to making generalizations about the habits and preferences of older generations.

5. **(B)** The previous paragraph concludes by stating that preliminary results from a study indicate that the adolescent brain is negatively impacted by social media use. The paragraph starting with line 22 provides a hypothesis and explanation as to why this could be true—namely that users create a false online environment in which the best parts of their lives are highlighted, while the worst parts of their lives are ignored. It is not choice (A) or (D) because the focus is on teenagers, not on different and older age groups. And it is not choice (C) because the negative potential consequences, not the potential benefits, are considered.

6. **(C)** In context, "advanced" refers to a case of depression that would be quite far along, or severe, since the scientists and social media platforms are trying to intervene in cases of depression before they become a concern. The other options are incorrect because they convey positive connotations of the word "advanced," which would not be applicable in the case of the progression of an illness.

7. **(D)** Lines 39–41 suggest that students and parents need to be careful in their use of new social media technology, since the research has not yet established clear guidelines as to its safe use. Therefore, prudence, or cautiousness, would be the appropriate attitude in the mind of the author. Choices (A) and (C) are overly positive, while choice (B) is overly negative.

8. **(D)** These lines provide the best evidence that the appropriate attitude for users of new technology is one of prudence. Choice (A) introduces the overall topic, choice (B) presents results from a study without analyzing them, and choice (C) presents a hypothesis without suggesting an overall attitude about new technology.

9. **(B)** In 2014–2015, 26% (about one-quarter) of teens reported almost constant daily internet use, while in 2018, the number jumped to 45% (nearly one-half). This information corresponds to choice **(B)**. The other options all make incorrect approximations of the internet use changes.

10. **(A)** Lines 5–4 state that high school students will soon enter the workforce having spent much of their lives online. The 2018 graph shows that 89% of teens report using the internet several times a day or almost constantly, which would strongly support the statement made in lines 5–6. The other options all relate to ideas that would not be strongly supported by the information in the graph. Choice (B) connects to mental health impacts; choice (C) connects to adolescent brain development; and choice (D) expands on a hypothesis.

Historical Document: *The Souls of Black Folk*

1. **(A)** This passage introduces sorrow songs and their impact on the writer, making choice **(A)** the correct answer. The passage in its entirety does reference disagreement, specific events, and personal stories but only as details rather than as the main purpose.
2. **(C)** To approach this question, look for what Du Bois says about American creativity. Specifically, he states America has given little beauty to the world (aside from the slave songs, which are the exception to him), instead expressing itself in "vigor and ingenuity." So general American creativity aligns with choice **(C)**. Choices (A), (B), and (D) might describe aspects of the slave songs, but again, these are the exception to "general American creativity."
3. **(B)** Lines 11–13 remark on America's general contribution to the world and thus evidence of what Du Bois sees as its attention to "vigor" (strength and determination) and "ingenuity" (inventiveness and insight) over beauty. Choice (A) illustrates the impact the sorrow songs had on Du Bois. Choice (C) discusses how some songs were lost or forgotten. Choice (D) concludes Du Bois's ideas on the lasting effect and significance of the songs.
4. **(B)** Here Du Bois claims that the slave songs are "the sole American music," remaining "the singular spiritual heritage of the nation." Try to substitute a synonym for "singular." You might pick *unique* or *remarkable*. Surely, Du Bois isn't saying they are the only heritage out there but, instead, that they are truly definitive of the nation and exceptional in their expression of the national history. Choices (A) and (D) imply isolation and distance. Choice (C) evokes a negative connotation meaning strange or peculiar.
5. **(C)** A good approach to this question is process of elimination. Du Bois says he is not concerned with technical aspects of the songs, so get rid of choice (A). Although he undeniably believes they are worthy of study, the songs themselves are not scholarly in meaning, making choice (B) incorrect. You can eliminate choice (D) because although some meaning is lost through the distance of time and language, Du Bois does understand the songs and believes they can tell us a lot. He believes they impact us (consequential) and give an articulate message (eloquent), making choice **(C)** correct.
6. **(C)** These lines specifically reference Du Bois's claim that the songs prove particularly important because they "are the articulate message of the slave to the world." Thus, they provide evidence that the sorrow songs are both consequential and eloquent, the correct answer to the previous question. Choices (A) and (B) do not indicate the meaning of the songs but merely how the songs have been forgotten and misunderstood. Choice (D) doesn't specifically reference what Du Bois sees as the meaning of the songs (that comes in the following lines); instead, these lines evidence the limits to society's message that slavery was mostly carefree for the enslaved.
7. **(D)** We are looking for the initial reaction to the slave songs of the Sea Islands. Despite people like Higginson and McKim, "the world listened only half credulously" at first. So look for an answer that says the songs were largely ignored initially. Choices (A) and (C) suggest that

the songs were given much more attention than is evidenced in the passage. Choice (B) is too extreme since the songs weren't treated seriously.

8. **(B)** The question asks who might have declared "that life was joyous to the black slave" despite proof in the sorrow songs that it was not. Since the passage talks about slavery as something of the past, choices (A) and (C) can be ruled out—also consider that the slaves told a very different story in their songs. The only musicians referenced in the passage are the Jubilee Singers who repeated and ingrained the sorrow songs into the public imagination, ruling out choice (D). Hence, it is most likely that "they" refers broadly to society or the general public.

9. **(B)** Use the other adjectives to make sense of this use of "misty." The music tells of "unvoiced" longing and "hidden" ways. So think *unclear* or *indistinct*, which are closest to *cloudy*. Choices (A), (C), and (D) evoke images nearer to evaporation or sticky humidity.

10. **(B)** In reference to some thinkers who might believe that the slave songs expressed joy for a carefree and happy life, Du Bois states that he can believe it of "some, of many." However, Du Bois goes on to state from his viewpoint, the songs of slaves generally express the "music of an unhappy people." Therefore, he ultimately believes that the songs are largely expressions of the extremely difficult lives that slaves led. So, it is reasonable to infer that Du Bois would have an attitude of qualified skepticism toward these claims, since he acknowledges that there may have been some joy expressed in the songs—this is his "qualification" of the claim. He is primarily skeptical, however, believing that the emotional expressions of the songs are mainly ones of sadness. It will not be choices (A) or (D), since they are overly positive. And it is not choice (C), because he does not completely dismiss those who may think that the songs were happier.

Science: Calico and Tortoiseshell Cat Genetics

1. **(B)** The primary purpose of the passage is to explain the genetic phenomenon that creates tortoiseshell and calico coat colors in domesticated cats, showing how this takes place through X chromosome inactivation. Choice (A) is incorrect because the passage emphasizes explanation over argumentation. Choice (C) is incorrect because there is not a specific recent discovery that is being analyzed. And choice (D) is incorrect because the passage is simply explaining how an unusual phenomenon takes place, not trying to change conventional assumptions.

2. **(C)** The passage indicates that X chromosome inactivation is very rare for males and more common with females since they have two X chromosomes. Also, 19–20 indicates that other species are subject to this phenomenon, not just cats. Therefore, the only logical answer would be that this phenomenon is most likely to occur in females of several different species.

3. **(A)** The sentence is analyzing the gene that "dictates" the coloration of fur—in other words, the gene that causes, or determines, the coloration. Choice (B) would be what someone listening to a dictator may do and would be inappropriate to be used to describe an inanimate object. Choices (C) and (D) refer to the verbal notion of dictation, which would not be applicable in discussing the cause-and-effect relationship between genes and their physical manifestations.

4. **(C)** Lines 14–15 state that a male could be a calico or tortoiseshell cat if it had two X chromosomes and a Y chromosome, but notes that this is very rare. The XX combination is more common as that is the general configuration for females, and the XY combination is also common, since it the general configuration for males.

5. **(D)** The passage spends quite a bit of time analyzing the causes of the orange and black patches of fur in domestic cats; line 38 shifts the discussion to the source of the white patches. Rather than analyzing this particular phenomenon in-depth, the narrator states that the white patches are associated with a different gene. Calico cats have the white patch, while tortoiseshell cats do not have it. Therefore, the difference in appearance between these two types of cats is due to this specific gene. It is not choice (A) because these cats are primarily female. It is not (B) or (C) because the X chromosome does not impact the white coloration—it is affected by some other gene.

6. **(D)** Line 38 provides the most direct support to the fact that the white patches that determine the difference between calico and tortoiseshell cats result from a specific gene. Choices (A) and (C) focus on the similarities between the cats. And choice (B) focuses on X chromosome activation, which is not associated with the white patch.

7. **(B)** Lines 27–28 state that the X chromosome that is selected for inactivation in one cell will not impact the selection of the X chromosome that will be inactivated in another cell—this allows for the color variations seen in the fur of calico and tortoiseshell cats. It is not choice (A) because the inactivation patterns are random rather than predictable. It is not choice (C) because the passage states that X chromosome inactivation is a phenomenon that happens to many different species, not just cats. And it is not choice (D) because the X chromosome is far more likely to be inactivated than the Y chromosome.

8. **(C)** These lines best support the idea that there is no direct connection between the X chromosome inactivated in one cell and the X chromosome inactivated in another cell. Choice (A) describes how a male cat could be tortoiseshell or calico. Choice (B) provides an overview of the chromosomes found in cat cells. And choice (D) discusses the overall characteristics of X chromosome inactivation across different species.

9. **(C)** According to line 11, most tortoiseshell and calico cats are female. Therefore, choices (A), (B), and (D) are unlikely since they all mention the tortoiseshell and/or the calico cats as being male. Choice **(C)** is correct because it has just orange and black coloration, making it more likely that some of its members could be male.

10. **(D)** The graph title summarizes the coloration of two litters of cats—it gives no indication of the breakdown of the first litter and the second litter. Therefore, there is insufficient information to determine the number of cats from the first litter that would have been calico cats.

Comparative Passages: Ocean Plastics

1. **(A)** Passage 1 emphasizes the significant problem that ocean plastics represent, arguing for an innovative solution—plastic-eating bacteria—to the problem. In the final sentence of Passage 1, the narrator argues that science should help accelerate the development of plastic-eating bacteria so that they can be a "critical" tool in helping solve the crisis. Since the bacteria would be extremely helpful to solving this problem, *crucial* is a fitting synonym. Choices (B) and (C) are overly negative, while choice (D) emphasizes speed over importance.

2. **(C)** The author uses lines 5–7 to suggest that humans are as likely to reduce plastic use as pigs are to fly, meaning that there is virtually no chance it will happen. So, *virtually none* is the best description. The other choices all present at least some possibility that it could happen, which is inconsistent with the author's suggestion in lines 5–7.

3. **(B)** These lines best support the idea that humans are highly unlikely to voluntarily reduce plastic consumption. Choice (A) analyzes the impact of humans on the environment rather than examining humans' likelihood to embrace change. Choice (C) considers and then rejects a possible solution to plastic pollution. And choice (D) analyzes the development of plastic-eating bacteria instead of analyzing human behavior.

4. **(B)** This paragraph predicts that plastic-eating bacteria will not limit themselves to consuming plastics in the ocean, but will also consume plastics that humans find economically beneficial. This could be summarized as "forecasting a potentially negative outcome," corresponding to choice **(B)**. It is not choices (A) or (C) because the author is making a prediction, rather than presenting findings from recent studies or analyzing what has already occurred. And it is not choice (D) because the author is *discouraging* the embrace of a new technology, not encouraging it.

5. **(C)** The passage is forecasting the potential pitfalls of plastic-eating bacteria, in particular that they would degrade, or break down, anything made of plastic, including objects that humans found useful. Creating would be the opposite of degrading. Suffering would not apply to inanimate plastic objects. And disassembling is used to describe the step-by-step process of carefully taking apart an object—plastic-eating bacteria would not be disassembling plastic objects, but would be breaking them down indiscriminately.

6. **(A)** Lines 22–23 state that "microplastics tend to end up being eaten by various organisms," suggesting that smaller plastic objects will be more likely to be consumed by organisms than larger plastic objects. It is not choice (B) because in line 29, the narrator states that almost all of the plastic in the ocean is in macroscopic objects. It is not choice (C) because both the macro and micro objects would be composed of plastics. And it is not choice (D) because according to lines 23–24, the microplastics are eaten by various organisms, while there is no mention that this happens to macroscopic plastics. In fact, the need for plastic-eating bacteria to break down these objects underscores that the macroscopic plastics would not be more biodegradable than microscopic plastics.

7. **(C)** In lines 24–26, the author of Passage 2 states that "approximately 380 million tons of plastic are produced annually." This number corresponds to the value found in the year 2015 in the graph. The numbers in 2005 and 2010 are too small, and the year 2020 is not presented in the graph.

8. **(A)** Passage 1 presents plastic-eating bacteria as an approach to solving the problem of plastic pollution in the ocean, while Passage 2 expresses skepticism of plastic-eating bacteria as a solution, arguing that using plastic-eating bacteria will be ineffective and lead to additional problems. It is not choice (B) because Passage 1 does not consider and address each objection mentioned in Passage 2. It is not choice (C) because while they both agree that plastic pollution is a problem, they disagree on a solution. And it is not choice (D) because Passage 1 underscores the environmental problem of plastic pollution and doesn't dismiss it; additionally, Passage 2 does not present an approach to dealing with plastic pollution.

9. **(A)** According to lines 24–26, once plastic enters an environment it can take several hundred years for it to degrade. Since the plastic disposed of between 1950 and 1960 occurred only a few decades ago, nearly all of that plastic would likely still remain in the ocean. The passages are considering plastic-eating bacteria as a potential solution to this issue, but there is no indication that plastic-eating bacteria have been widely introduced into the oceans to tackle the problem of plastic pollution.

10. **(C)** These lines address the length of time it takes for plastics to degrade. Choice (A) is tempting, but it does not directly address the speed with which plastics degrade. Choice (B) analyzes a new technology, but does not consider the length of time current plastics are still in the environment. And choice (D) does not analyze the current situation with plastics, but forecasts a potential negative consequence.

Advanced Drills

The following passages are designed to represent the most difficult sorts of passages and questions you could encounter on the SAT Reading. Take about 13 minutes total for each drill. Good luck!

Fiction

"An Encounter" is part of James Joyce's 1914 short story collection, Dubliners. *A young, unnamed narrator searches for release from the constraints of daily routine.*

It was Joe Dillon who introduced the Wild West to us. He had a little library made up of old numbers of *The Union Jack, Pluck* and *The Halfpenny Marvel.* Every evening after school we met in his back garden and arranged Indian battles. He and his fat young brother Leo, the idler, held the loft of the stable while we tried to carry it by storm; or we fought a pitched battle on the grass. But, however well we fought, we never won siege or battle and all our bouts ended with Joe Dillon's war dance of victory. His parents went to eight-o'clock mass every morning in Gardiner Street and the peaceful odour of Mrs. Dillon was prevalent in the hall of the house. But he played too fiercely for us who were younger and more timid. He looked like some kind of an Indian when he capered round the garden, an old tea-cosy on his head, beating a tin with his fist and yelling:

"Ya! yaka, yaka, yaka!"

Everyone was incredulous when it was reported that he had a vocation for the priesthood. Nevertheless it was true.

A spirit of unruliness diffused itself among us and, under its influence, differences of culture and constitution were waived. We banded ourselves together, some boldly, some in jest and some almost in fear: and of the number of these latter, the reluctant Indians who were afraid to seem studious or lacking in robustness, I was one. The adventures related in the literature of the Wild West were remote from my nature but, at least, they opened doors of escape. I liked better some American detective stories which were traversed from time to time by unkempt fierce and beautiful girls. Though there was nothing wrong in these stories and though their intention was sometimes literary they were circulated secretly at school. One day when Father Butler was hearing the four pages of Roman History clumsy Leo Dillon was discovered with a copy of *The Halfpenny Marvel.*

"This page or this page? This page Now, Dillon, up! *Hardly had the day* . . . Go on! What day? *Hardly had the day dawned* . . . Have you studied it? What have you there in your pocket?"

Everyone's heart palpitated as Leo Dillon handed up the paper and everyone assumed an innocent face. Father Butler turned over the pages, frowning.

"What is this rubbish?" he said. "*The Apache Chief!* Is this what you read instead of studying your Roman History? Let me not find any more of this wretched stuff in this college. The man who wrote it, I suppose, was some wretched fellow who writes these things for a drink. I'm surprised at boys like you, educated, reading such stuff. I could understand it if you were . . . National School boys. Now, Dillon, I advise you strongly, get at your work or . . ."

This rebuke during the sober hours of school paled much of the glory of the Wild West for me and the confused puffy face of Leo Dillon awakened one of my consciences. But when the restraining influence of the school was at a distance I began to hunger again for wild sensations, for the escape which those chronicles of disorder alone seemed to offer me. The mimic warfare of the evening became at last as wearisome to me as the routine of school in the morning because I wanted real adventures to happen to myself. But real adventures, I reflected, do not happen to people who remain at home: they must be sought abroad.

1. A major underlying theme in the essay as a whole is best described as the conflict between

   (A) order and chaos.
   (B) peacefulness and warfare.
   (C) racism and tolerance.
   (D) energy and laziness.

2. According to the first paragraph, Joe Dillon's personality is mostly

   (A) accommodating.
   (B) forceful.
   (C) compromising.
   (D) dishonest.

3. As used in line 12, "incredulous" most closely means

   (A) disappointed.
   (B) skeptical.
   (C) enamored.
   (D) inspired.

4. Joyce uses lines 15–17, "We banded . . . was one," to most directly suggest that the narrator was motivated to play Wild West with his friends because of

   (A) a quest to fight a common enemy.
   (B) a need to satisfy a moral code.
   (C) desire to meet his peers' expectations.
   (D) a reluctance to stand up against prejudice.

5. The narrator's willingness to follow the intellectual requirements of his school can best be described as

   (A) openly rebellious.
   (B) peacefully obedient.
   (C) studiously ignorant.
   (D) half-hearted.

6. Which option gives the best evidence for the answer to the previous question?

   (A) Lines 2–3 ("Every evening . . . battles")
   (B) Lines 24–26 ("This page . . . pocket?")
   (C) Lines 32–33 ("I'm surprised . . . work or")
   (D) Lines 35–37 ("But when . . . offer me")

7. Father Butler uses what approach in lines 32–33 ("I'm surprised . . . School boys") to encourage obedience?

   (A) An appeal to pride
   (B) A fear of failure
   (C) A disgust with learning
   (D) A request for curiosity

8. The most significant role that the Wild West games played in the life of the narrator is best described as

   (A) an introduction to a love of literature.
   (B) a turning point in his choice of careers.
   (C) the way to achieve independence from his parents.
   (D) a gateway to new thinking.

9. Which option gives the best evidence for the answer to the previous question?

   (A) Lines 1–3 ("It was . . . battles")
   (B) Lines 8–10 ("But he . . . yelling")
   (C) Lines 20–23 ("Though there . . . *Marvel*")
   (D) Lines 37–40 ("The mimic . . . sought abroad")

10. The narrator suggests that in order to have genuine adventures, he will need to

   (A) create more interesting games with his peers.
   (B) follow the guidance of his instructors.
   (C) go to another country.
   (D) fight in a war.

Social Science

The Model of Occupational Dysfunction, *written in 2020 by Dr. Caitlin Stewart*

The Model of Occupational Dysfunction (MOOD) is a proposed, theoretical framework for occupational therapists to use in evaluating dysfunctional occupation—addictive behaviors or an occupation the client would like to change—and also for replacing the dysfunctional occupation with functional occupation. Occupation refers to the activities with which individuals fill their time. Often, those occupations are productive or necessary—such as bathing, preparing meals, caring for pets, sleep, and enjoying time with friends and family. But other occupations, like substance abuse, lead to occupational dysfunction. These dysfunctional occupations are not productive and can be detrimental to health and wellness. In addition to identifying occupational dysfunction, the MOOD is a framework for discovering new, productive occupation, enhancing participation in an existing productive occupation, and preventing return to occupational dysfunction.

Like existing applied behavioral and cognitive behavioral frames, the MOOD seeks to follow the client's lead and interests as outcome drivers and change behavior. The MOOD is influenced by rational emotive therapy (RET), social learning theory, cognitive therapy, self-regulation programs, and the Socratic method. What distinguishes the MOOD from existing applied behavioral frames and cognitive behavioral frames is its focus on dysfunctional occupation and replacing those occupations with functional, preferred occupations.

Through this approach, the MOOD disrupts the cycle of occupational dysfunction and directs the occupational therapist and the client towards functional occupation.

The primary driver of change in the MOOD is the development of functional occupation and the extinguishment of dysfunctional occupation through behavioral modification. Behaviors, habits, and performance patterns are changed when dysfunctional occupation is reduced or extinguished and replaced with meaningful, psychologically rewarding functional occupation. Change is not realized through just reduction or extinguishment of the dysfunctional occupation. There must be an intentional replacement of the dysfunctional occupation with functional occupation. If there is not, the time left by the dysfunctional occupation is not devoted to any occupation, and the client may return to occupational dysfunction. Motivation is derived from the client's desire for change and the client's identification of occupational dysfunction. Motivation is guided by the occupational therapist using the Socratic method and the scientific method of therapy.

Evaluation using the MOOD begins with skilled interview, therapeutic use of self, and an occupational profile. Changing dysfunctional occupation and replacing it with functional occupation is challenging for the client; through therapeutic use of self, the occupational therapist can establish the necessary trust and rapport. The client and the occupational therapist will identify the dysfunctional occupation. Additional evaluation of the dysfunctional occupation will be guided by the occupation itself. For example, evaluation of money management skills may be necessary when compulsive shopping is identified as the dysfunctional occupation, while evaluation of stress may be necessary when drug abuse is identified as the dysfunctional occupation. Next, the client and the occupational therapist will identify functional occupation.

Relaxation strategies are used across disciplines to address a wide variety of diagnoses. These strategies are beneficial in managing anxious feelings and feelings of not being in control of one's self. In the scope of the MOOD, relaxation techniques are used to address stress and anxiety management and impulse control. Some approaches may include meditation, progressive muscle relaxation, yoga, deep breathing, progressive muscle relaxation, and personal mantras.

Behavioral strategies are used to extinguish dysfunctional occupation. Depending on the dysfunctional occupation, this may be accomplished in conjunction with a full medical team. For example, if the dysfunctional occupation being extinguished is drug abuse, the client must be closely monitored for seizures and other medical emergencies. In whole or in part, the dysfunctional occupation will be reduced or eliminated through extinguishment. In order for extinguishment to be successful and behavioral change implemented, the reinforcement must be identified and removed. In the case of a client with drug abuse, the reinforcement may be the increased ease with which the client participates in social settings where the temptation to abuse drugs may exist.

Occupation has previously been used as a coping mechanism. Occupation, when using the MOOD, is used to prevent a return to dysfunctional occupation. Self-regulation strategies also include personal awareness of stressors, stress management, and using occupation to reduce stress.

After dysfunctional occupation has been extinguished, the client may need to learn new skills. Skills training teaches the client new habits, roles, performance patterns, and/or routines supportive of the functional occupation. In the case of a client with drug addiction whose social reinforcement from drug use was removed, social skills training in order to be successful in social settings without drug use is necessary.

1. The essence of the *Model of Occupational Dysfunction* can best be summarized as to

(A) eliminate unhealthy behaviors through whatever means necessary.
(B) substitute unhealthy behaviors with healthy ones.
(C) use new relaxation techniques to battle drug addiction.
(D) counsel clients to find jobs about which they are passionate.

2. It is reasonable to infer from lines 4–5 ("Occupation . . . time") that the author believes that her use of the term "occupation" throughout the essay is

(A) different from how the word is more typically used.
(B) consistent with the career-oriented focus of her research.
(C) appropriately synonymous with the presence of serious substance abuse.
(D) well-suited for the use of the term for an international audience.

3. The therapeutic process as outlined by the Model of Occupational Dysfunction is best characterized as

(A) collaborative.
(B) speculative.
(C) confrontational.
(D) remorseful.

4. Which choice gives the best evidence for the answer to the previous question?

(A) Lines 5–7 ("Often . . . dysfunction")
(B) Lines 22–24 ("Behaviors . . . occupation")
(C) Lines 32–35 ("Changing . . . occupation")
(D) Lines 56–59 ("Occupation . . . stress")

5. The primary purpose of the paragraph in lines 31–40 is to

(A) highlight the most prevalent dysfunctional occupations to increase awareness of a problem.
(B) contrast a new therapeutic approach with existing ones by highlighting the differences in outcomes.
(C) cite significant obstacles to a therapist's successful implementation of an approach.
(D) explain how a general theoretical framework can be customized in particular instances.

6. As used in line 48, "in conjunction with" most nearly means

(A) controlled by.
(B) through complete delegation to.
(C) fused with.
(D) together with.

7. It can reasonably be inferred that the author would most likely consider which of the following an example of a successful implementation of the Model of Occupational Dysfunction?

   (A) A person formerly with an addiction to drugs knows how to avoid places that would trigger the addiction to resurface.
   (B) A person formerly with a video game addiction is able to be around those playing video games without succumbing to previous behaviors.
   (C) A person with an addiction to overeating successfully undergoes gastric-bypass surgery to reduce his appetite.
   (D) A person with what he initially thought was an addiction to the internet realizes after consultation with a therapist that his behavior cannot be categorized as an addiction.

8. Which choice gives the best evidence for the answer to the previous question?

   (A) Lines 13–15 ("The MOOD . . . method")
   (B) Lines 29–30 ("Motivation . . . therapy")
   (C) Lines 36–39 ("For example . . . occupation")
   (D) Lines 53–55 ("In the case . . . exist")

9. The author most strongly suggests that relaxation techniques, with respect to the overall approach of the Model of Occupational Dysfunction, are

   (A) of minimal utility.
   (B) largely irrelevant.
   (C) helpful, yet not primary.
   (D) both primary and essential.

10. Which of the following, if true, would provide the best support to the Model of Occupational Dysfunction?

    (A) Research showing the positive impact of a new form of psychiatric medication in lessening the urges for addictive behaviors
    (B) Research demonstrating significantly lower relapses among those who learn a new, productive skill while in rehabilitation
    (C) Research that highlights the common personality characteristics among those who have addictive tendencies
    (D) Research that demonstrates the precise impact that early childhood experiences may have on adult dysfunctional occupations

Historical Document

This passage is adapted from the Library of Congress, Manuscript Division, American Federation of Labor Records. "Image 503 of American Federation of Labor Records: 1918; Jan. 30–Feb. 26." In it, the American Federation of Labor discusses the possible ramifications of labor uprisings and revolts in Europe as the end of World War I approaches.

The Governments of America and Great Britain are doing everything possible to encourage the German Minority Socialists and are apparently inclined to recognize the Bolsheviki as the de facto Government of Russia . . . But such recognition . . . would be taken by the Bolsheviki in Russia and all other countries as an acknowledgement of partial defeat by the "imperialist" governments of Great Britain, France, and America, against which they have declared a world-wide class war.

The direct objective of our government in "establishing a better understanding" with the Bolsheviki is not to encourage them either in their home or their foreign policy but solely to delay and restrict their approach to Germany and above all to encourage their efforts to revolutionize the peoples of Central Europe. We are also endeavoring to appeal directly to these peoples to revolt . . . But we forget that the continuing success of Bolshevism in Russia and the growing strength of pacifist strikes in Germany and Austria immensely aid the already dangerous pacifist movements among the working-men of France, England, and Italy—movements united in the demand for a Stockholm conference to bring about "an immediate democratic peace." As we have seen with the Bolsheviki, the emphasis is on the "immediacy" which involves a recognition of the war map and of the military situation at the time the conference is held.

Entirely independently of German victories, brutal German peace terms, Bolshevik sur renders, or other events, the Stockholm movement grows without . . . interruption. I have watched carefully for the influence of events. It is nil. No German victory or ultimatum can affect the underlying cause, war weariness, accompanied by Utopian dreams fanned into new life by the Russian revolution.

The Stockholm movement grows apace. Sooner or later . . . the conference will occur—or an agreement will be reached without it . . . the overwhelming majority [of delegates] will be for those terms upon which an immediate peace can be obtained. And if the conference is not held a Labor and Socialist entente, including all the parties of Europe, will probably soon be formed and will reach the same conclusion.

The current in this direction is steady and rapid, and is accelerating. The French Socialists are unanimous and the labor unionists nearly unanimous for Stockholm . . . In Italy the situation was similar until the great defeat. After that there was a short revival of the fighting spirit; all later reports indicate a rapid tendency for Socialists and unionists to resume their previous revolutionary pacifist activities. The situation in England is not very much better. . . . a few months more may produce movements far more threatening to the French and Italian armies than are Bolshevism and German Socialism and the armies of Germany and Austria . . . A general European movement would almost certainly spread to England. Nor could it fail to have an effect on Chicago, New York, San Francisco, and other foreign industrial centrals in this country.

Even if—in the midst of such a crisis—the German government were overthrown and the war brought to an end, Germany would keep a very large part of the advantages she has won.

For the danger is that these widespread strikes will begin before the power of America has been fully developed, . . . The German Socialists might voluntarily and magnanimously surrender a certain part of the German gains. But even the Haase and Liebknecht programs do not offer to relinquish German domination over Germany's present allies, nor her economic domination over Russia and all surrounding small nations. Nor does the Haase program offer any solution of the questions of German and Austrian Poland and Alsace-Lorraine or propose any compensation for the vast destruction done by the Kaiser—except very vaguely—and insufficiently—in the case of Belgium.

But it is far more probable that any revolutionary movement in Germany, before her military defeat, would prove either partial or abortive. The result would then be that Germany would have been less weakened by her won upheaval than Italy, and France—and perhaps, less weakened than England.

The peace then offered would be even worse than that of Haase, namely, . . . adaptation of the status quo ante and "no annexations, no indemnities" formula, with neighboring nations bound by coerced economic treaties and "readjustments of the frontiers."

To aid the German Socialists (positively) and the Bolsheviki (negatively) is not only playing with fire, it is almost certain to end the war before German defeat or American victory—with all the consequences that must inevitably follow such an indecisive outcome.

1. The primary purpose of the passage is to

   (A) encourage a more equitable society.
   (B) discourage a particular course of action.
   (C) dispute the veracity of historical claims.
   (D) encourage an immediate resolution to a conflict.

2. The author's general tone toward resolving his primary concerns is one of

   (A) urgency.
   (B) passivity.
   (C) optimism.
   (D) fatigue.

3. Which choice gives the best evidence for the answer to the previous question?

   (A) Lines 10–11 ("We are . . . revolt")
   (B) Lines 19–21 ("No German . . . revolution")
   (C) Lines 22–24 ("The Stockholm . . . obtained")
   (D) Lines 41–43 ("But even . . . nations")

4. As used in lines 20–21, "fanned into new life" most nearly means

   (A) extinguished.
   (B) researched.
   (C) transformed.
   (D) revitalized.

5. The paragraph in lines 27–36 ("The current . . . country") primarily suggests that the author fears

   (A) a rapid international spread of revolutionary ideologies.
   (B) the defeat of American forces by European ones.
   (C) a reemphasis on militaristic tendencies among global powers.
   (D) a coming conflict pitting socialism against Bolshevism.

6. Which choice provides the best evidence that the author is concerned about an imbalance in international power relationships were a peace treaty to be immediately agreed to at the time of the composition of the passage?

   (A) Lines 7–10 ("The direct . . . Europe")
   (B) Lines 17–18 ("Entirely . . . interruption")
   (C) Lines 35–36 ("Nor could . . . country")
   (D) Lines 37–38 ("Even if . . . won")

7. The main point of the author's argument in lines 39–40 ("For the . . . developed") is that

   (A) the military might of the United States will be turned to defeat the threat of Bolshevism.
   (B) a German victory in the war is inevitable, and Europeans would be wise to create a peace treaty.
   (C) the coming American mobilization should dissuade those who seek an immediate peace.
   (D) the existing gains by France, the United Kingdom, and others should be codified in a treaty.

8. Based on the paragraph in lines 47–50 ("But it . . . England"), it is reasonable to infer that the author is concerned that in a future potential European conflict,

   (A) Italy and France would have developed long-term ideological hostility toward one another.
   (B) France would be in a relatively stronger position than other countries.
   (C) England would be in a relatively stronger position than other countries.
   (D) Germany would be in a relatively stronger position than other countries.

9. The author uses the term "playing with fire" in lines 54–55 to underscore

   (A) potentially negative consequences.
   (B) pending physical harm.
   (C) possible sources of reconciliation.
   (D) a coming perpetual peace.

10. Which of the following pieces of information, taken at the time of the composition of the passage, would be most useful in interpreting the strength of the author's argument?

    (A) The percentage of adults in European countries who consider themselves politically aligned with pacifist movements
    (B) The number of casualties experienced by each of the major powers throughout the previous years of the war
    (C) The land area controlled by German forces and French and English forces on the European continent
    (D) The number of Bolshevik-aligned publications composed on the European continent

Science: *Synthetic Intermediates*

It's fair to say that the world in which we live is made up of chemicals, though the cultural emphasis in recent years on natural or "organic" products has somewhat demonized this notion. "Chemophobia," in fact, is a term that has emerged to describe the irrational fear of chemistry and chemical nomenclature. In general, individuals affected by chemophobia tend to view the precisely planned manipulation of molecular compounds with suspicion, and perceive products rendered by these means as both "unnatural" and inherently inferior to those derived through cruder avenues. In reality, nothing could be more natural than the intricate, multi-step reactions of organic chemistry. Life itself could not exist without a constant, dynamic stream of these complicated interactions, and very often the role of industrial chemists has not been to confound the processes we observe in nature, but merely to simplify and refine them.

Retrosynthetic analysis is a quintessential example of this task. Frequently, after isolating and identifying the structure of a valuable biochemical compound, a chemist is confronted with the problem of how to efficiently and effectively reproduce the compound by artificial means. More often than not, the biosynthetic pathways found *in vivo* employ a staggering number of highly specialized enzymes and enzymatic cofactors, and are utterly impractical for a laboratory setting. The task of the chemist, then, is to conceptually deconstruct the compound into successively simpler constituent pieces in such a way as will facilitate its synthesis through the smallest number of individual reactions, and yield an end product with the highest achievable degree of chemical purity.

It is necessary to remember that harvesting biochemical compounds directly from their natural sources is often not only costly, but more wasteful than using artificial synthetic alternatives. Through careful retrosynthetic analysis, chemists can help us to meet the public demand for a product, and in certain cases spare the unnecessary destruction of scarce environmental resources. For instance, paclitaxel is a critically important component of the chemotherapy regimen for breast, ovarian, lung, and pancreatic cancers. Prior to the successful retrosynthesis of paclitaxel—a landmark achievement that took a team of chemists more than twenty years to complete—the only known source of this compound was from the bark of the Pacific Yew tree. Had not artificially synthesized paclitaxel become available when it did, many ecological biologists have projected that the tree would have soon been harvested to extinction.

Still, some will contend that the true problem of retrosynthesis lies not in the end-products, but rather in the byproducts and novel synthetic intermediates required to artificially reproduce biochemical compounds. It must be acknowledged that this is indeed a valid concern. The design of stable synthetic intermediates not found in nature has at times led to unforeseen consequences. Methyldioxymethamphetamine, for example, is a dangerous and highly concerning drug of abuse among youth. It was first designed in 1912 by the Merck Corporation as a synthetic intermediate in the production of the hemostatic agent hydrastine, a compound traditionally extracted from a then-endangered perennial herb.

Even so, there have also been occasions in which the chemical ingenuity required to design new synthetic intermediates has unexpectedly yielded a useful product in and of itself. Aspartame, notably, was among the first non-disaccharide sweeteners to become available as a food additive. Aspartame itself is a derivative of two conjoined amino acids—specifically, aspartic acid, and phenylalanine—but it was originally created as synthetic intermediate in an attempt to make gastrin, a hormone produced by the parietal cells of the stomach that stimulates secretion of hydrochloric acid. Due perhaps to the chemophobic public perception of aspartame as an "unnatural" compound, for nearly half a century the sweetener has been a subject of ongoing controversy, and despite reliable evidence to the contrary, it has been incorrectly associated with both cancer and Alzheimer's disease. Most likely, a segment of the population will never accept the safety of aspartame. It is perhaps worth reflecting, however, that sucrose and fructose—two sweeteners harvested naturally from plant sources—through their exacerbation of diabetes mellitus are known to contribute directly to the leading cause of blindness in the United States, to more than half of all non-traumatic amputations, and to our seventh leading cause of death.

1. What is the author's overall point about synthetic intermediates?

   (A) The dangers of their overuse need to be widely publicized.
   (B) It is time that industries begin using them.
   (C) Further study is needed before they should be used.
   (D) The pros of using them outweigh the cons.

2. Which of the following does the author acknowledge as a negative consequence of synthetic intermediates?

   (A) The production of addictive substances
   (B) Justifiable skepticism about industrial technology
   (C) Decreased professional opportunities for scientists
   (D) Overreliance on large corporations for economic growth

3. Which option gives the best evidence for the answer to the previous question?

   (A) Lines 4–7 ("In general . . . avenues")
   (B) Lines 16–19 ("The task . . . purity")
   (C) Lines 34–36 ("The design . . . youth")
   (D) Lines 36–38 ("It was . . . herb")

4. As used in line 12, "confronted" most closely means

   (A) defied.
   (B) presented.
   (C) tackled.
   (D) rebelled.

5. The second paragraph, lines 11–19, suggests that retrosynthetic analysis is most similar to which of these situations?

   (A) A teacher oversimplifying the explanation of a difficult concept
   (B) A car repair shop using non-brand name parts to craft an inferior product
   (C) Traveling to the same destination but by a less circuitous route
   (D) A political scientist analyzing the pros and cons of a current controversy

6. As used in line 20, "harvesting" most closely means

   (A) farming.
   (B) deriving.
   (C) building.
   (D) deconstructing.

7. What is the author's view on natural substances relative to synthetic ones?
   - (A) Natural substances are inherently superior.
   - (B) Natural substances can sometimes be more harmful.
   - (C) Natural substances are more environmentally friendly.
   - (D) Natural substances are less scientifically linked to disease.

8. Which option gives the best evidence for the answer to the previous question?
   - (A) Lines 20–24 ("It is . . . resources")
   - (B) Lines 25–30 ("Prior . . . extinction")
   - (C) Lines 45–48 ("Due perhaps . . . disease")
   - (D) Lines 49–53 ("It is . . . death")

9. The author primarily uses lines 39–49 ("Even so . . . aspartame") to argue that
   - (A) accidental discoveries are typically more fruitful than sustained scientific research.
   - (B) food additives should be avoided so that healthier, more natural flavorings can be used.
   - (C) the culinary benefits of aspartame outweigh the negative health consequences from its use.
   - (D) fear about synthetic compounds simply due to their artificiality is unwarranted.

10. It is reasonable to infer that if there were further scientific studies that demonstrated the safety of aspartame,
    - (A) aspartame skeptics would be uniformly convinced of its safety.
    - (B) a portion of the population would still be reluctant to use it.
    - (C) scientists would recommend against the consumption of this substance.
    - (D) culinary professionals would embrace widespread substitution of sugar with aspartame.

Comparative Passages

Passage 1 is an adaptation from Edmund Burke's Selections from the Speeches and Writings of Edmund Burke, *specifically the selection under the title "Colonies and British Constitution." This selection is believed to have been written shortly before the American Revolution and discusses the relationship between the United States and Great Britain. Passage 2 is an adaptation of a letter written in April of 1775, shortly before the American Revolution, by John Adams under the pen name Novanglus. In it, he discusses the relationship between Great Britain and her colonies.*

Passage 1

My hold of the colonies is in the close affection which grows from common names, from kindred blood, from similar privileges, and equal protection. These are ties, which, though light as air, are as strong as links of iron.

Let the colonies always keep the idea of their civil rights associated with your government; . . . no force under heaven will be of power to tear them from their allegiance. But let it be once understood that your government may be one thing, and their privileges another; that these two things may exist without any mutual relation; the cement is gone; the cohesion is loosened; and everything hastens to decay and dissolution. As long as you have the wisdom to keep the sovereign authority of this country as the sanctuary of liberty, the sacred temple consecrated to our common faith, wherever the chosen race and sons of England worship freedom, they will turn their faces towards you. The more they multiply, the more friends you will have; the more ardently they love liberty, the more perfect will be their obedience. Slavery they can have anywhere. It is a weed that grows in every soil . . . But, until you become lost to all feeling of your true interest and your natural dignity, freedom they can have from none but you.

This is the commodity of price, of which you have the monopoly. This is the true act of navigation, which binds to you the commerce of the colonies, and through them secures to you the wealth of the world. Deny them this participation of freedom, and you break that sole bond, which originally made, and must still preserve, the unity of the empire. Do not entertain so weak an imagination, as that your registers and your bonds . . . are what form the great securities of your commerce. Do not dream that your letters of office, and your instructions, and your suspending clauses, are the things that hold together the great contexture of this mysterious whole. These things do not make your government. Dead instruments, passive tools as they are, it is the spirit of the English communion that gives all their life and efficacy to them. It is the spirit of the English constitution, which, infused through the mighty mass, pervades, feeds, unites, invigorates, vivifies every part of the empire, even down to the minutest member.

Passage 2

We now come to Jersey and Guernsey, which Massachusetts says "are no part of the realm of England, nor are they represented in parliament, but are subject to its authority." We shall [examine] how these islands came to be subject to the authority of parliament. It is either upon the principle that the king is absolute there, and has a right to make laws for them by his mere will, and therefore may express his will by an act of parliament or an edict at his pleasure, or it is an usurpation. If it is an usurpation, it ought not to be a precedent for the colonies, but it ought to be reformed, and they ought to be incorporated into the realm, by act of parliament, and their own act. Their situation is no objection to this. Ours is an insurmountable obstacle.

Thus we see that in every instance which can be found, the observation proves to be true, that by the common law, the laws of England, and the authority of parliament and the limits of the realm, were confined within seas. That the kings of England had frequently foreign dominions, some by conquest, some by marriage, and some by descent . . . And from this extensive survey of all the foregoing cases, there results a confirmation of what has been so often said, that there is no provision in the common law, in English precedents, in the English government or constitution, made for the case of the colonies. It is not a conquered, but a discovered country. It came not to the king by descent, but was explored by the settlers. It came not by marriage to the king, but was purchased by the settlers . . . It was not granted by the king of his grace, but was dearly, very dearly earned by the planters, in the labour, blood, and treasure which they expended to subdue it to cultivation. It stands upon no grounds then of law or policy, but what are found in the law of nature, and their express contracts in their charters, and their implied contracts in the commissions to governors and terms of settlement.

1. It is reasonable to infer that the most likely intended audience for Passage 1 was

    (A) the common people of Great Britain.
    (B) the king of Great Britain.
    (C) the colonists of North America.
    (D) enslaved persons in Great Britain.

2. The author of Passage 1 most strongly suggests that at the time he wrote the passage, the recognition of civil rights for the citizens of countries around the world was

(A) generally universal.
(B) fairly widespread.
(C) relatively limited.
(D) nonexistent.

3. Which choice gives the best evidence for the answer to the previous question?

(A) Lines 2–3 ("These are . . . iron")
(B) Line 13 ("Slavery . . . soil)
(C) Lines 19–21 ("Do not . . . commerce")
(D) Lines 23–25 ("Dead . . . to them")

4. As used in lines 19–20, "Do not entertain so weak an imagination" most nearly means

(A) do not even consider.
(B) do not even worship.
(C) do not even confide.
(D) do not even confess.

5. It can be reasonably inferred that the author of Passage 2 was aware that some of his contemporaries may likely have used the examples of Jersey and Guernsey to argue that

(A) the British Parliament should return them to another country.
(B) conquering one's countrymen is a worthy pursuit.
(C) marriage alliances are appropriate for empire building.
(D) the colonies should be treated in a similar fashion.

6. The author of Passage 2 most strongly suggests that those most responsible for creating the colonies was/were the

(A) British monarch.
(B) foreign dominions.
(C) settlers.
(D) English government.

7. As used in line 48, "grounds" most nearly means

(A) justification.
(B) lands.
(C) extent.
(D) instruction.

8. The tones of Passage 1 and Passage 2 can best be respectively described as

(A) pessimistic vs. optimistic.
(B) ideological vs. emotional.
(C) rational vs. irrational.
(D) idealistic vs. unsentimental.

9. Which selection from Passage 1, if taken by itself, would best capture the sentiment that the author of Passage 2 has about the relationship between the colonies and Great Britain?

   (A) Lines 2–3 ("These are . . . iron")
   (B) Lines 7–8 ("the cement . . . loosened")
   (C) Lines 10–11 ("wherever . . . towards you")
   (D) Lines 16–17 ("This is . . . colonies")

10. Which of the following characteristics of the argument in Passage 2 would most likely be troubling to the author of Passage 1?

   (A) A recognition of British monarchical rule in noncontiguous territories
   (B) A feeling of respect for the requirements of British common law
   (C) No sense that British governance has strengthened freedom in the colonies
   (D) Outright hostility toward both the British Parliament and the British king

Answers and Explanations

Fiction: *Dubliners*

1. **(A)** The protagonist struggles to find adventure in routine. The appeal of the Wild West tales is that they allow escape from the order and monotony of everyday living, making choice **(A)** the correct option. Our protagonist, although he reenacts battles between American Indians and cowboys with his friends, is not actually involved in warfare or racial intolerance. Choice (D) is incorrect because although excitement and idleness are details within the essay, they are not the focus.

2. **(B)** Joe Dillon is the character who introduces the narrator to the Wild West stories. He is described as fiercer than the other children, making choice **(B)** correct. He doesn't ever allow the enemy side to win, so choices (A) and (C) can be ruled out. No evidence is provided to support choice (D).

3. **(B)** Here, everyone shows surprise and doubt when the boisterous and adventurous Joe Dillon pursues a career within the church. The text suggests that this "boring" choice is contrary to Joe's "excitable" nature. Hence, skeptical is a near synonym for "incredulous" in this instance. "Incredulous" means "unwilling or unable to believe something." Even if you don't know the word's definition, no evidence is provided to suggest that people were disappointed or inspired by Joe's priestly ambitions; instead, they are merely doubtful or confused. Enamored means "in love with" or "showing great admiration for" and, likewise, does not fit.

4. **(C)** In lines 16–17, the narrator situates himself among those reluctant few who play "in fear" because they are "afraid to seem studious." "Studious" might be substituted with *bookish* or *overly academic*. So these lines specifically reference the narrator's desire to fit in, making choice **(C)** the best answer. These lines never specifically mention a common enemy or prejudice among the children playing. Choice (B) seems tempting but fails to capture the narrator's fear of seeming too scholarly among his more popular peers; he is not overly concerned with morality but, instead, desires inclusion.

5. **(D)** Approach this question by asking what we know about our narrator's attitude toward school. He calls his hours spent at school "sober" and begins to "hunger again for wild sensations" because the routine of school is "wearisome." So choice **(D)** best describes his apathy toward schoolwork. Although other students might, the narrator doesn't express open rebellion. Choice (B) is too passive; we know the narrator longs to escape and participates in activities deemed inappropriate. Don't fall for choice (C) just because "studious" is included in the answer. Instead, the narrator's concern over seeming too studious, or academically motivated, discourages any claim that he is ignorant of the school's expectations.

6. **(D)** In these lines, our narrator voices his discontent with the requirements of school and his attention toward other "wild sensations," supporting the idea that his interest toward his studies is only half-hearted. Choices (A), (B), and (C) are incorrect because they do not provide evidence of our character's attitude toward following and participating in school requirements.

7. **(A)** Here, Father Butler calls the American-Indian story "rubbish" and expresses disappointment that boys of high education would show interest in it. He insinuates that the students should take themselves more seriously and read loftier, canonical texts; hence, he appeals to their pride. He is not disgusted by learning but, instead, by what he believes is pointless learning. Likewise, he is not trying to inspire curiosity in the story but quell it. Choice (B) is

a tempting answer because he hints that reading this sort of nonsense would make the students less worthy, but he doesn't actively try to convince them that they'll fail.

8. **(D)** If we look at the last paragraph, we see that the Wild West eventually became dull for the narrator as well. However, the stories did succeed in stirring within him a desire for "real adventures," which he concludes "must be sought abroad." So our narrator develops and ultimately seeks out something he didn't previously want, making choice **(D)** the correct option. Because he doesn't particularly enjoy the Wild West stories, choice (A) is not correct. His career choice is not mentioned at all, making choice (B) incorrect. Although the character's adventures probably do lead to independence, he is concerned less with demanding parents and more with boring day-to-day studies.

9. **(D)** For proof of the narrator's character development, refer to lines 37–40 where we see how the Wild West stories eventually influence him. Choice (A) merely introduces how he became acquainted with the Wild West; choice (B) describes Joe Dillon; choice (C) discusses how Father Butler came to find a specific story among the boys.

10. **(C)** In the final paragraph, the narrator expresses his weariness both with the routines of school and the games that he plays with his peers. He concludes by saying that "real adventures" must be "sought abroad." To go abroad is to go to another country, so choice **(C)** is correct. It is not choices (A) or (B) because he has grown tired of the routines of his current environment. And it is not choice (D) because he merely suggests a desire to go to another country, not necessarily to fight over there.

Social Science: Occupational Dysfunction

1. **(B)** The overall idea of the MOOD is stated in the first sentence of the passage, in which the author states that dysfunctional occupations, i.e., undesirable behaviors, will be replaced with functional occupations, i.e., desirable behaviors. It is not choice (A) because the model does not advocate eliminating unhealthy behaviors by any means necessary, but by replacing them with functional behaviors. It is not choice (C) because relaxation techniques are used to implement the MOOD, but do not represent the MOOD itself. And it is not choice (D) because while this could be an example of a successful implementation of the MOOD, it does not encompass the overall approach of this theory.

2. **(A)** Since in lines 4–5 the author defines "occupation" as the term will be used in the essay, namely that it refers to behaviors, it is reasonable to infer that this use is different from the typical way the term is used, namely to refer to specific professions. choice (B) is incorrect because the focus of the essay is on behavioral change, not on career advisement. Choice (C) is incorrect because not all occupations would necessarily be negative. And choice (D) is incorrect because there is no indication that the audience is international; the clarification she presents of the term "occupation" would be needed even for native English speakers.

3. **(A)** Lines 31–34 state that to implement a change to more functional occupations, the therapist must first establish trust with the client, and then, working together in a collaborative way, the client and therapist will identify the dysfunctional occupation. It is not choice (B) because speculative would suggest guesswork instead of open discussion. It is not choice (C) because the therapeutic model is one of discussion, not confrontation and judgement. And it is not choice (D) because there is no indication that guilt and remorse are components of this approach.

4. **(C)** These lines provide the best evidence that the MOOD is a collaborative enterprise, involving the input of both the therapist and the client. choice (A) clarifies the differences between functional and dysfunctional occupations instead of generalizing about the overall model. choice (B) is also rather specific, describing how behavioral change comes about through replacement of undesirable behaviors with desirable ones. choice (D) focuses on specific strategies that can be used to implement the MOOD without reflecting on its collaborative nature.

5. **(D)** This paragraph explains how the MOOD could be successfully implemented in the case of a client who abused drugs. It is therefore showing how the general theoretical framework of the MOOD could be customized in a particular instance. It is not choice (A) because the author does not indicate that drug abuse is the most prevalent dysfunctional occupation. It is not choice (B) because this paragraph demonstrates how an approach could be implemented, not how it differs from other approaches. And it is not choice (C) because the author illustrates how the obstacles can indeed be successfully overcome.

6. **(D)** In the sentence in lines 75–77, the author recognizes that if a client has a behavior that warrants additional medical support, a therapist should treat the client "in conjunction with," (together with) the support of a full medical team. The therapist would collaborate with the medical team, not be controlled by them or delegate all the tasks to them. And while the therapist and medical team would work together, they would maintain their independence, not be fused together.

7. **(B)** Lines 88–91 show that a successful implementation of the MOOD in the instance of a client who abuses drugs would be that the client could be in a social setting where the temptation to abuse drugs may be present, but the client could easily resist the urge to abuse drugs. This is most like the situation outlined in choice **(B)**, since the person would be able to be around video games without exhibiting addictive behaviors. It is not choice (A) because the person would be isolated from social settings in which people might exhibit dysfunctional behaviors. It is not choice (C) because this would be a surgical solution to the problem instead of a therapeutic solution. And it is not choice (D) because the client would not in fact have a dysfunctional behavior that required intervention.

8. **(D)** These lines demonstrate that if someone could tolerate being in a social setting where the tempting dysfunctional occupations were on display, the person would have done an excellent job implementing the MOOD. choice (A) outlines the intellectual influences on the MOOD, not how the model could be successfully applied. Choice (B) discusses motivation in general terms rather than demonstrating a specific application. And choice (C) focuses on the diagnostic aspect of the MOOD instead of how a treatment would be implemented.

9. **(C)** The passage uses the paragraph in lines 59–66 to show how relaxation techniques can be a valuable supplement to implementing the MOOD. However, the following paragraph goes on to emphasize the behavioral strategies needed to extinguish dysfunctional occupation—the core idea of the theory. So, relaxation techniques would be helpful but not primary to the MOOD. It is not choices (A) or (B) because these would minimize the importance of relaxation techniques, and it is not choice (D) because this would overemphasize the importance of relaxation techniques to the MOOD.

10. **(B)** The essence of the MOOD is to replace unhealthy behaviors with healthy behaviors. If there were significantly lower relapse rates among those who learned a new, productive skill while in rehabilitation, that would demonstrate the effectiveness of an approach that replaced unhealthy behaviors with healthy ones. It is not choice (A) because this would involve medication instead of therapy. It is not choices (C) or (D) because these would focus on the causes of rather than solutions to dysfunctional behaviors.

Historical Document: Labor Uprisings

1. **(B)** This can most clearly be seen in the final paragraph, in which the author summarizes his conclusion that ending the war prematurely before a German defeat or an American victory will lead to an indecisive outcome that will have negative long-term ramifications. So, the primary purpose of the passage is to discourage the course of action—aiding the German Socialists and recognizing the Bolsheviki as the Russian government—that would lead to a premature peace settlement. It is not choice (A) because the author is primarily concerned with preventing a premature peace rather than encouraging a more equitable society. It is not choice (C) because the historical claims are not disputed, but rather what actions should be taken in response. And it is not choice (D) because an immediate resolution to a conflict is the opposite of what the author would like.
2. **(A)** According to lines 22–24, the Stockholm movement was growing "apace" and "sooner or later," an agreement toward an immediate peace would be obtained—this language suggests that the author feels a sense of urgency in resolving his primary concerns about not taking actions that would lead to a premature agreement to end the war. Passivity is not a fitting description, since the author is making a strong argument for a particular course of action instead of sitting idly by while events transpire. *Optimism* does not work since the narrator is concerned about the likelihood of a premature peace. And *fatigue* does not work because the author would like to see the war continue with American participation instead of coming to an end because of weariness.
3. **(C)** These lines best support the idea that the author's general tone toward resolving his primary concerns is one of urgency. It is not choice (A) because these lines present a view with which the author does not agree. It is not choice (B) because these lines analyze the motivations of the Stockholm movement. And it is not choice (D) because these lines present critiques of particular peace plans instead of analyzing the urgency of resolving the author's concerns.
4. **(D)** The paragraph in lines 17–21 argues that the Stockholm movement is growing without anything seeming to stand in its way, and is helped by the example of the Russian revolution. The dreams of the Stockholm movement find the success of the Russian revolution inspiring, with the hopes of European revolutionaries "fanned into new life," or revitalized, by these events. *Extinguished* conveys the opposite of the intended meaning. It is not *researched* because the Stockholm movement followers want action, not more analysis. And it is not *transformed* because the movement does not appear to change into something new, but rather to have new energy behind it from the inspiration from Russia.
5. **(A)** In this paragraph, the narrator forecasts a slippery slope toward the eventual success of revolutionary movements throughout the European continent, as well as in England and the United States. Therefore, it is accurate to say that the author appears to fear a rapid international spread of revolutionary ideologies. It is not choices (B) or (C) because there is a focus

on the spread of ideology in this paragraph, not a focus on military defeats or militaristic tendencies. And it is not choice (D) because the author suggests that Bolshevism appears to inspire many of the socialist, pacifist movements—they are complementary, not at odds.

6. **(D)** Lines 37–38 best accomplish this, since they forecast that if the war were ended prematurely, Germany would keep much of its winnings—this could be reasonably inferred to lead to an imbalance in international power relationships, with Germany more dominant than its counterparts. It is not choice (A) because these lines explore the motivations of the American government. It is not choice (B) because these lines emphasize the concerns the author has about the growth in the Stockholm movement. And it is not choice (C) because these lines forecast potential future consequences of a spreading revolutionary ideology.

7. **(C)** The author uses these lines to suggest that widespread strikes may lead to a premature peace, and that with the development of American military power and its coming influence in the war, no such premature peace would be needed. It is not choice (A) because the author does not suggest that the United States will fight Russia in this war. It is not choice (B) because the author is advocating patience in the war effort so that American military intervention can have an impact against Germany. And it is not choice (D) because the narrator does not want to codify the existing boundaries into a peace treaty, but to spend more time fighting until there is a clear German defeat.

8. **(D)** These lines suggest that if peace were quickly agreed to, Germany would be less weakened than other European countries, thereby putting it in a stronger position in a future conflict. It is not choice (A) because there is nothing here to suggest that Italy and France would be adversaries. And it is not choices (B) or (C) because the author believes that Germany—not France or England—would emerge relatively stronger if there were an early peace.

9. **(A)** In the last paragraph, the author summarizes his argument that aiding the German Socialists and recognizing the Bolsheviki would be "playing with fire"—i.e., would lead to potentially negative consequences due to an indecisive outcome to the war. It is not choice (B) because this is too literal an interpretation. And it is not choices (C) or (D) because this phrase does not refer to making peace or reconciling.

10. **(A)** The author argues that there is a great risk of a revolutionary pacifist ideology that will spread internationally and lead to an indecisive outcome in the war. The author does not provide any concrete data in terms of the number of people who are ideologically aligned with these pacifist movements, so having that information would be useful so that we can interpret the strength of the author's points. If only a small percentage of European adults support revolutionary movements, his argument would not have much merit. However, if the majority of European adults support revolutionary movements, his argument would be quite forceful. Knowledge of war casualties, land area, and Bolshevik-aligned publications would give readers some insights into the possibility of war weariness and the desire for peace, but would not be as effective in directly interpreting the primary line of the author's argument.

Science: Synthetic Intermediates

1. **(D)** Throughout the passage, the author argues that chemophobia is unwarranted. He concedes that creating novel by-products and intermediates can be harmful, as in the case of methyldioxymethamphetamine, but the vast majority of the passage is about the pros of synthesizing chemicals. This makes choice **(D)** correct. Choice (A) is wrong because the author

focuses on the benefits rather than the dangers. Choice (B) is wrong because many industries are already using synthetic intermediates, as evidenced by the passage. Choice (C) is wrong because he thinks that they have their place in society now.

2. **(A)** The author says that certain synthetic intermediates can have unforeseen consequences and then goes on to discuss the case of the addictive methyldioxymethamphetamine, making choice **(A)** correct. Choice (B) is wrong because although he admits that skepticism is justifiable in this industry, this isn't a negative consequence. Choice (C) is wrong because there are plenty of opportunities for scientists in the field of industrial chemistry, as shown in the first paragraph. Choice (D) is wrong because the author doesn't discuss this.

3. **(C)** Choice **(C)** is correct because these lines consider a time when a synthetic intermediate had negative consequences. Choice (A) simply discusses chemophobia. Choice (B) talks about the opportunities for scientists: a pro rather than a con. Choice (D) gives the circumstances surrounding the creation of methyldioxymethamphetamine, but it's more in the context of a pro—that scientists were trying to create a more sustainable source of hydrastine.

4. **(B)** The sentence states that "a chemist is *confronted* with the problem of how to efficiently and effectively reproduce the compound by artificial means." The word "confronted" most nearly means presented because the process of scientific inquiry as described in the passage does not have confrontation or violence associated with it. The other choices all suggest too much negativity and hostility.

5. **(C)** This paragraph describes retrosynthetic analysis as finding the most efficient way of constructing a compound. This is best described by choice **(C)**, which is also maximizing efficiency. Choice (A) is wrong because it's making something overly simple rather than improving efficiency. Choice (B) comes at the cost of quality. Choice (D) is incorrect because it has nothing to do with finding the most efficient way of doing something.

6. **(B)** This line talks about getting biochemical compounds from nature. In terms of chemistry, deriving means exactly this, so choice **(B)** is the correct answer. Choices (A) and (C) don't work because these are more like creating than harvesting. Choice (D) is wrong because it's about obtaining the compounds rather than breaking them down.

7. **(B)** The author thinks that synthetic substances have a largely unsubstantiated bad reputation. He also talks about two natural substances—sucrose and fructose—that have negative impacts on health. Thus, he believes that natural substances can sometimes be more harmful than synthetic substances, choice **(B)**. Choices (A) and (D) express viewpoints that the author explicitly disagrees with. Choice (C) is wrong because he talks about several instances in which harvesting natural substances from plants can have devastating effects on the environment.

8. **(D)** The correct answer is choice **(D)** because it gives a concrete example of when natural substances can be more harmful than synthetic—this is something about which the author is trying to persuade the reader. Choices (A) and (B) talk about when harvesting natural resources is harmful to the environment. Choice (C) discusses the bad reputation that synthetic compounds get but only to disagree.

9. **(D)** The author's main purpose in these lines is to argue that the chemophobic public's unease over synthetic substances—in this case, aspartame—sometimes persists even when science says that the fear is unsubstantiated. This matches the sentiment in choice **(D)**. Choice (A) is wrong because the author simply says that accidental discoveries can be helpful

but not that they're more helpful than more intentional findings. Choice (B) expresses the chemophobic view that the author disagrees with; choice (C) says that aspartame is unhealthy, something the author explicitly disagrees with.

10. **(B)** In lines 48–49, the author states, "Most likely, a segment of the population will never accept the safety of aspartame." So, even if there were further studies demonstrating its safety, these studies would be unlikely to convince a portion of the population. It is not choice (A), since the author suggests that it is unlikely that there would be uniform embrace of aspartame. It is not choice (C), because if scientific evidence showed that aspartame were safe, it is unlikely that scientists would recommend against its consumption. And it is not choice (D), since there is no indication that cooks and restaurant workers would want to embrace substitution of sugar with aspartame.

Passages 1 and 2: Burke and Adams

1. **(B)** Throughout the passage, Burke addresses someone who is implicitly in control of the British government, pleading with the person to bind the colonists to the British Empire through the idea of freedom secured in the British constitution. It is reasonable to infer that the most likely person whom Burke is addressing would be the king of Great Britain, since he would be in a position of power. It is not choice (A) because it would not be logical to address the common people of Great Britain as though this large group would have "letters of office" and governmental "instructions." And it is not choices (C) or (D) because these groups would not likely be in positions of power in the British government.
2. **(C)** In line 13, Burke states that the colonists can have "Slavery . . . anywhere. It is a weed that grows in every soil." The suggestion is that a system of constitutional protections for human freedom must have been relatively limited at the time. Choices (A) and (B) are overly expansive and choice (D) is overly limited.
3. **(B)** These lines provide the most direct support to the idea that at the time of the passage's composition, the recognition of civil rights for the citizens of countries around the world was relatively limited. It is not choice (A) because these lines refer to the connection Burke believes that the colonists and the British people share. And it is not choices (C) or (D) because these lines directly question supposed sources of British governmental authority.
4. **(A)** Burke uses this sentence to argue that the British government should not suppose that "registers" and "bonds" are what form the great securities of commerce; Burke goes on to say that it is the spirit of the British constitution that truly provides the source of strength and unity. Therefore, it is reasonable to conclude by this phrase that Burke does not want the British government to consider this as a possibility. It is not choice (B) because this is a consideration of governmental, not religious matters. And it is not choices (C) or (D) because Burke does not suggest that these beliefs about the source of governmental authority are confidential and private.
5. **(D)** In the beginning of Passage 2, Adams argues that Massachusetts has used the example of Jersey and Guernsey to argue that places with no representation in the British parliament could nonetheless be subject to British parliamentary authority. Toward the end of the first paragraph of Passage 2, he argues that while the situation of Jersey and Guernsey presents no serious problem for the legitimacy of British authority in those territories, the situation of the colonies presents "an insurmountable obstacle." Adams goes on to explain why the colonies are in a unique situation that cannot be considered as needing to be subjected to

British authority. Given that Adams begins his essay by considering the situation of Jersey and Guernsey, it is reasonable to infer that he was aware that some of his political contemporaries may have argued that the colonies would need to be treated in a similar fashion. It is not choice (A) because there is no mention of returning Jersey and Guernsey to some other nation. It is not choice (B) because Adams advocates a legislative process and clear legal rules to establish legitimate authority, not just outright conquest. And it is not choice (C) because there is no mention of Jersey and Guernsey being acquired through a marriage alliance.

6. **(C)** In lines 44–50, Adams clearly states that in his view, the colonies came to be acquired through the diligence of the settlers, not from some other source. The other options would ascribe creation of the colonies to foreign sources, which these lines do not support.
7. **(A)** In the final sentence of the passage, Adams states that there can be no "grounds" but that of the "law of nature" and governmental settlement charters to provide legitimacy for the government of the colonies. Therefore, there would be no justification for the colonial government except for these sources of legitimacy. It is not choices (B) or (C), because these refer to expanses of territory rather than the ideological justification of a governmental system. And it is not choice (D) because to merely instruct does not necessarily suggest that a rationale behind the instructions must be provided.
8. **(D)** The tone of the first passage is quite idealistic, with Burke arguing that the British government should seek bonds with the colonists through the ideals of its constitutional system. The tone of the second passage is unsentimental, with Adams considering legal precedents and how they would or would not apply to the case of the colonies. It is not choice (A) because the first passage is more optimistic than pessimistic. It is not choice (B) because Adams is more rational than emotional. And it is not choice (C) because Adams uses a series of well-reasoned arguments to make his point—it would not be accurate to describe his tone as irrational.
9. **(B)** Adams argues that the settlers of the colonies are responsible for their creation, making "the cement" of "cohesion" between the colonies and the British government far looser than some might believe. Therefore, lines 4–8 would best capture the feeling that Adams has about the relationship between the colonies and Great Britain. It is not choice (A) because Adams does not suggest that there are strong ties between the colonies and Great Britain. It is not choice (C) because Adams does not suggest a worshipful gratitude on the part of the colonists toward the British government. And it is not choice (D) because Adams does not suggest that commerce and navigation provide a great bond between the colonists and British government.
10. **(C)** Burke argues that if the British government can be seen by colonists as the authority that provides a sanctuary of liberty and guarantees freedom, colonists will look toward the British government with appreciation and a sense of belonging. The fact that Adams does not express any sense that British government has strengthened freedom in the colonies would likely be most troubling to Burke. It is not choice (A) because this would not apply to the case of the colonies and their relative sense of affection toward the British government. It is not choice (B) because Adams does seem to show respect for the requirements of British common law given the legal arguments he makes; to Burke, this would suggest some connection, at least an intellectual one, from the colonists to the British government. And it is not choice (D) because Adams does not express outright hostility toward the British government.

PART 4
Writing and Language

Introduction and Strategies

What is tested on the SAT Writing and Language section?

When you write in academic settings and in your future career, you will need to use correct grammar, proper wording, logical organization, and persuasive evidence. The SAT Writing and Language tests your skill in determining which choices lead to the highest quality essays. In addition to your knowledge of specific grammar rules, a broad understanding of written English will ensure you do your very best on this section. When in doubt about your approach to the SAT Writing and Language, keep in mind that if you are using the same skills that would be effective in editing a paper, you are likely doing things the right way.

How is the SAT Writing and Language section structured?

Writing and Language is the second section of the test.

- There are 44 total multiple-choice questions.
- The section is broken into four passages with these themes: History/Social Studies, Humanities, Science, and Careers.
- The passages are approximately 400–450 words each and have the type of writing you would encounter in an academic setting.
- There are 35 minutes to complete the Writing and Language section.
- Spend about 9 minutes for each 11-question passage.
- The questions on the SAT Writing and Language are in a random order of difficulty.

Here are the types of questions you will find on the SAT Writing and Language:

Question Type	Typical Number of Questions	What do these questions cover?
Number and Tense Agreement	4–5	Singular/plural agreement, verb tense usage
Wordiness	4–5	Determining if wording is irrelevant/repetitive or relevant/helpful
Punctuation	8	Proper use of commas, semicolons, colons, dashes, and apostrophes
Sentence Structure and Organization	6–7	Misplaced modifiers, logical comparisons, sentence combinations, parallelism
Proper Wording	5–6	Idioms, proper use of prepositions, and proper word choice
Transitions	4–5	Use of connecting words like *and, but,* and *also* to create logical transitions
Passage and Paragraph Organization	5–6	Determining effective introductions, conclusions, and sentence placements
Passage and Paragraph Analysis	2–3	Determining appropriate tone, support for ideas, and synthesis of passage meaning
Graph Analysis	2	Using evidence in tables and charts to draw conclusions and connect to the argument of a passage

How is the SAT Writing and Language section scored?

There is NO guessing penalty on the SAT, so be certain to answer *every* question. The SAT Writing and Language combines with the SAT Reading section to give you an Evidence-Based Reading and Writing score out of a maximum of 800 points and minimum of 200 points. The test is curved so that if the test is more difficult, you can miss more questions to get a particular score, and if it is easier, you can miss fewer questions to get a particular score. Look at the table on the following page to get an approximate idea of how many questions you need to answer correctly on the Writing and Language section to earn a particular score. Note that you would need to have a similar score on the Reading section to have the score out of 800 as shown.

Correct Answers Out of 44 Total Writing and Language Questions	Approximate Corresponding SAT Reading and Writing & Language Score Out of 800 Points (both sections will affect this score)
44	800
42	750
39	680
36	620
32	580
29	540
25	500
21	440
17	400
13	360
8	320
4	240
0	200

SAT Writing and Language Questions Dos and Don'ts

Do use the full amount of time available. As you probably know from having to edit papers for school, good editing takes time. Take approximately *nine minutes* to complete each of the four passages. When you evaluate longer questions, be sure to underline and circle key words so that you fully understand what the question is asking.

Don't rush and make careless errors. Students are usually aware when they have difficulty with a Math or Reading question. With SAT Writing and Language questions, it is easy to *think* you are doing great but to actually make a careless mistake. Most students feel comfortable checking out the questions as they review the surrounding context (i.e., the material before and after). However, if you are still finishing the Writing and Language section with quite a bit of time left, you may want to adjust by *reading the passage from beginning to end* before starting to evaluate the questions one by one. This would provide you with a broader analysis of the passage context, and is a better use of time than having a few minutes at the end of the section to just sit there.

Example

❶ Since many people enjoy travelling to new places, video streaming services have become increasingly popular in recent years.

1. Which choice best supports the information that follows in the sentence?
   (A) NO CHANGE
   (B) While reading has maintained its universal appeal,
   (C) With their increasing collection of high quality original content,
   (D) Although many scholars are skeptical of the statistics,

Carefully read the question and put it in your own words—we need an introduction to the sentence that will provide support for what follows. Next, look at what follows in the sentence: "video streaming services have become increasingly popular in recent years." The introduction to the sentence should provide support to the assertion that more and more people like video streaming services. Now, carefully review the choices—the issue is not whether the choices are grammatically correct, but whether they support what follows. Choice (A) discusses the popularity of travel, but that would not directly connect to an increased popularity for streaming services. Choice (B) discusses the universal appeal of reading—if anything, this would undermine the remainder of the sentence, drawing a contrast between reading and streaming. Choice (D) strongly undermines the remainder of the sentence, arguing that the statistics that show an increase in the popularity of streaming services cannot be trusted. Choice **(C)** is correct—it gives a clear reason why streaming services would be increasingly popular, thereby providing strong support for the remainder of the sentence. Take your time on questions like these and you will do great; rush through them, and you are much more likely to make careless errors.

Do look at enough context. In general, be sure to read *at least the whole sentence* that the question asks about. With questions involving transitional words, introductions, conclusions, and wordiness, you may need much more context—perhaps a whole paragraph or two. If you have any doubt about whether you have sufficient context to make a decision, check out a bit more just to be sure.

Don't only consider part of a sentence. It is easy to jump to an answer based on just a small part of a sentence. Keep an open mind as you read the entirety of a sentence. If you have difficulty with jumping to answers too quickly, try covering up the answer choices until you have carefully considered the relevant context.

› Example

Marquis went to his ❷ parent's house—he was eager to visit with both his mother and father.

2. (A) NO CHANGE
   (B) parents
   (C) parenting
   (D) parents'

Unless you consider the information later in the sentence, you will have insufficient context to determine the correct option. The second part of the sentence states that Marquis was going to meet with "both his mother and father." This clarifies that he was meeting with both parents, and it is reasonable to infer that his mother and father shared the house. So, since there are two parents, show possession by putting an apostrophe *after* the *s* as found in choice **(D)**. Choice (A) would work if you had a singular parent. Choice (B) would work if you were using *parents* as a noun instead of using the word to show possession. And choice (C) would suggest that Marquis is going to some house where he does his own parenting, which is inconsistent with the later part of the sentence.

Do mouth out the passage as you read it. One of the best strategies for editing a paper is to read it out loud in your head—that way, you will pick up on all sorts of errors that you would miss if you only quickly scanned your paper. Many of the correct answers on the SAT Writing and Language section can be found based on how things sound. In particular, punctuation, proper word choice, and parallel structure all lend themselves well to analysis through hearing. When taking the SAT, your job is not to go in front of a class and precisely explain the grammatical justification for an answer. Instead, you simply need to arrive at the correct answer by any means necessary, including trusting your hearing.

Don't overly rely on intuition—know the rules. While hearing the passage can be extremely helpful, use this approach to *supplement* rather than *replace* careful analysis based on grammar knowledge. Many potential grammar issues—like advanced punctuation concepts, subject-verb agreement, and logical comparisons—won't be clear unless you understand the underlying grammar concepts. Fortunately, this book comprehensively reviews the grammar you need to know.

Example

Teacher letters of recommendation are a key component of a college **3** application; accordingly, it is important for students to develop good relationships with their educators.

3. (A) NO CHANGE
   (B) application, accordingly, it
   (C) application; accordingly it
   (D) application accordingly, it

Mouthing this out can help you determine where natural pauses are needed. First, a pause is needed between the two independent clauses (complete sentences)—after "application" and before "accordingly." Second, a pause is needed after "accordingly," since it is an introductory word before the second independent clause. This intuitive knowledge will only get you so far. It is important to know that a comma cannot join two independent clauses together unless it has a conjunction like *for*, *and*, or *but* along with it. Also, conjunctive adverbs like "accordingly" must have a semicolon precede them when they are used to join two independent clauses. So, the correct answer is choice **(A)** since it has a semicolon to separate the two independent clauses and a comma to separate the introductory word "accordingly" from the following independent clause. Intuition and grammar knowledge together make for an unstoppable combination on the SAT Writing and Language.

Do use the choices to help clarify your thinking. The choices can help you see where a question is headed—look at what is different among the choices to determine what concept is being evaluated. If the choices use different verbs, watch out for subject-verb agreement. If the choices use different punctuation, watch for independent and dependent clauses. And if the choices have different lengths, watch for wordiness. Also, if two or more choices mean essentially the same thing, that is a clue that it will not be those options. For example, since both a semicolon and a period can be used to separate two independent clauses, if you see two options that only differ in that one uses a period and one uses a semicolon, it is likely *neither* of the options.

Don't jump to a choice too quickly. Keep an open mind as you review the choices. Be sure you have considered what the question is asking, what the surrounding context says, and what the subtle differences among the choices entail. Do not treat the SAT Writing and Language as a recall test you may find in school, in which you can quickly remember the answer from class. Instead, take your time.

Example

I stayed up late last night studying for my test. ❹ <u>However,</u> I am rather tired this morning.

4. (A) NO CHANGE
   (B) In contrast,
   (C) Additionally,
   (D) Consequently,

The primary way you should attack this problem is to consider the logical relationship between what comes before the transitional word and what comes after it. The sentence before says that the narrator stayed up late studying for a test, and the part after says that the narrator is now rather tired. A transition that expresses a cause-and-effect relationship would be best, since it is because the narrator stayed up late that now the narrator is tired. "Consequently" in choice **(D)** signifies a cause-and-effect relationship, and it is correct. In addition to attacking the problem this way, you can look at the choices to see what clues are evident. First, all the words are transitional, making it clear that you will need to look at what comes before and after the underlined word to determine the correct answer. Second, you can look for similarities among the answers. "However" and "in contrast" are synonymous, both meaning that what comes before and what comes after are opposites. Since these two options are synonymous, you are able to eliminate them both. While this strategy is likely applicable on just a handful of problems, it can be a powerful tool if you are trying to break the tie between a couple of options.

<u>Do</u> consider widely agreed upon grammar rules. There will be one definite answer. The makers of the SAT ensure that when they ask a question, it has been thoroughly evaluated so that it clearly has a single answer. The SAT Writing and Language section will ask you about core grammatical concepts where there is widespread agreement, like subject-verb agreement, proper verb tense, and correct use of punctuation. It is especially important for students who are strong in math to keep this in mind, since they are used to the definitive answers found in math and sometimes feel that grammar rules are a matter of opinion. Keep in mind that while there are many ways that an essay can be crafted, out of the four options given for each SAT Writing and Language question, there will be *one and only one correct answer*.

<u>Don't</u> worry about stylistic preferences and pet peeves. Here are some examples of pet peeves that some people have, which are not considered widely agreed upon grammar rules:

- Using the Oxford comma—a comma before the *and* in a list of three or more items
- Never starting a sentence with *because*
- Never using the more informal second person, *you*, and always using the more formal third person, *he*, *she*, *they*, in papers

The SAT will not test you on concepts like this because not everyone agrees on them. So, you should give the SAT Writing and Language the benefit of the doubt—instead of overthinking a question because you think it is testing some random rule, know that there is indeed one correct answer and look at enough context until you clearly see what that correct answer is.

Example

The school board decided that it would be **5** forcible to wear uniforms at school.

5. (A) NO CHANGE
   (B) mandatory
   (C) coercive
   (D) imperative

The SAT will have several questions asking you to evaluate the proper wording in a sentence. It would be easy to think that this question is trying to trick you and has multiple correct answers. Instead of overthinking this, realize that there will be just one correct answer and carefully think through the problem until you see it for yourself. The sentence is referring to a policy that a school board would have about uniforms. While all of these answers in some way mean "required," in the context of a school policy, "mandatory," choice **(B)**, is most suitable. "Forcible" and "coercive" are overly violent. And "imperative" would mean it is important to wear the uniforms, but not necessarily required by the school policy. So, by realizing that there is one definite answer, you will be able to keep an open mind as you evaluate the subtle differences among the choices.

How can I improve my overall grammar knowledge?

- **Read widely.** Reading will, of course, help you improve your reading comprehension. However, it will also greatly help you with grammar. By reading high-quality books and articles, you will develop an intuitive sense of what language sounds proper and what arguments are logically organized. This is especially important when building a sense of what word choices are most appropriate. If you rely too much on a thesaurus when coming up with synonyms, you may have difficulty identifying the word that is best to use in a given context.
- **Write as much as you can.** The more you write, the better you will be at determining what arguments flow well and what organization of your essays is most appropriate. You will have a better sense of how to avoid repetition, maintain parallel structure, and maintain subject-verb agreement. When you have had to be on the lookout for good writing strategies in your own writing, you will be much more in tune with looking for good strategies in the writing of other material.
- **Take rigorous courses that encourage you to write and read high-quality material as much as possible.** While it is tempting to take easier courses where it will not be difficult to earn an A, this will ultimately be a disservice to you when it comes to SAT Writing and Language. Take courses like AP Language and Composition, AP Literature and Composition, and any of the other AP humanities courses. All of these courses will require you to read challenging, high-quality material and to write organized essays. The stronger your reading and writing skills, the better you will do on the SAT Writing and Language.
- **Practice writing in your daily life.** Do not limit your writing to the classroom. Look for opportunities to write recreationally. Instead of texting, try sending an email with full paragraphs. Instead of only video chatting with a distant friend or relative, try writing a letter. Instead of just scanning online articles, give your opinions in the online comments. If you are more ambitious, try entering writing contests, writing a blog of your own, or sending well-crafted correspondence to public officials with your opinions on important issues.

Rather than waiting to the last minute to write your college application essays, begin working on them in your junior year so that you can both write the best possible essays and improve your writing and editing skills.

- **Practice editing.** Use a cloud-based word processing program so that you can easily have your papers edited—encourage your friends to do the same. If you and your friends practice editing one another's papers, not only will your papers be far better, but you will also sharpen the skills needed for success on the SAT Writing and Language section.

How can I use this book to prepare for the SAT Writing and Language test?

Practice with the specific types of questions that are most challenging for you:

- **Number and Tense Agreement** (pages 231–233)
- **Wordiness** (pages 233–240)
- **Punctuation** (pages 240–255)
- **Sentence Structure and Organization** (pages 255–269)
- **Proper Wording** (pages 269–276)
- **Transitions** (pages 277–284)
- **Organization** (pages 285–292)
- **Passage and Paragraph Analysis** (pages 293–299)
- **Graph Analysis** (pages 299–305)

Practice with **full-length passages**, starting on page 306, reviewing the types of material you will encounter on the actual test.

Practice with **advanced passages**, starting on page 323, that present the most challenging types of Writing and Language questions you could encounter on the SAT.

Practice with the **full-length Writing and Language tests**, carefully watching your time management.

Good luck!

Grammar Review

Subject-Verb Agreement

The SAT Writing and Language section tests your skill in determining whether nouns, pronouns, and verbs agree numerically. A singular subject should be paired with a singular verb, and a plural subject should be paired with a plural verb.

Example 1

Incorrect: My friend's brand new car need to be washed.

Correct: My friend's brand new car **needs** to be washed.

Explanation: The subject is what is doing the action. In this case, the car is the thing that has to be washed. Since the subject "car" is singular, it requires a singular verb, "needs."

Example 2

Incorrect: The pack of wolves are howling.

Correct: The pack of wolves **is** howling.

Explanation: The subject is the singular word "pack," not "wolves." Even though there are multiple wolves within a pack, the subject is still just the singular "pack." "Pack" is an example of a *collective noun*—the word refers to the singular group instead of the plural members of the group. Some other examples of collective nouns include *group, flock, class, herd, company,* and *collection.*

Example 3

Incorrect: The smoke detector has dead batteries, which is why they are beeping.

Correct: The smoke detector has dead batteries, which is why **it is** beeping.

Explanation: The earlier nouns in the sentence are "detector" and "batteries." Which of these could most logically be described as "beeping?" It would have to be a detector—batteries don't beep. So, both the pronoun and the verb must change to be the singular "it is" instead of the plural "they are."

Example 4

Incorrect: When Darnell and Liam go to the game, he always insists on paying for the tickets.

Correct: When Darnell and Liam go to the game, **Darnell** always insists on paying for the tickets.

Explanation: If a pronoun is vague, it must be clarified. In this case, the "he" could have referred to either Darnell or Liam. By revising it to have the person's actual name, the sentence becomes clear. Sometimes students worry about replacing a pronoun, thinking that they cannot be certain as to its substitute. Do not worry about that—if a pronoun needs to be replaced because it is vague, consider the potential replacements to be true.

Example 5

Incorrect: Everybody in the school are excited for the assembly.

Correct: Everybody in the school **is** excited for the assembly.

Explanation: "Everybody" is singular, even though it refers to several people. Other singular pronouns include *everyone, anybody, no one, someone, another, either, neither,* and *each.* If you are unsure if a pronoun is singular or plural, simply take the pronoun and place it next to the verb to see if it makes sense. For example, you would say "anybody is here" instead of "anybody are here."

Singular and Plural Agreement Practice—select the correct choice given the context.

1. The food for both of my dogs (A) is *or* (B) are expensive.
2. My friend Andrew forgot (A) its *or* (B) his lunch money.
3. (A) These *or* (B) This books are really interesting.
4. All the cars, including mine, (A) is *or* (B) are legally parked on the street and will not be towed.
5. The flock of geese (A) are *or* (B) is migrating south for the winter.
6. My English teacher and my math teacher always (A) give *or* (B) gives detailed instructions in class.
7. The lamp, which has three light bulbs, (A) is *or* (B) are in need of some maintenance.
8. I discovered in my studies that while I enjoyed painting and sculpture, (A) it was *or* (B) they were music I found most appealing.
9. The sights and sounds of the World's Fair (A) were *or* (B) was truly memorable.
10. A dog that can still walk on all fours (A) are *or* (B) is considered mobile.
11. When starting the car, be sure that (A) the emergency brake *or* (B) it is deactivated.
12. (A) Those *or* (B) This plants really have to be watered.
13. The captain of the team (A) has led *or* (B) have led her team to victory.
14. When one is speaking to one's friends online, one should be certain that the chat is from one's friends (A) themselves *or* (B) oneself and not from a bot.
15. The car and truck were in a close race, with (A) the one *or* (B) the truck currently in the lead.
16. Anyone who loves the great outdoors (A) is *or* (B) are excited for good weather.
17. Neither terrible snow nor awful rain (A) keeps *or* (B) keep the mail from being delivered.
18. Halley's Comet, one of the solar system's short period comets, (A) is *or* (B) are projected to pass by Earth in the year 2061.
19. Since (A) it *or* (B) they will not be available on the trail, bring food and water with you for the backpacking journey.
20. Zaha Hadid, an architect known for her parametric designs (i.e., ones that embrace adaptive shapes and forms), (A) are *or* (B) is a native of Iraq.

✓ Solutions

1. The food for both of my dogs (A) is expensive. "Food" is the subject and is singular.

2. My friend Andrew forgot (B) his lunch money. "Andrew" is a singular person, so "his" would be appropriate.

3. (A) These books are really interesting. "Books" is a plural word and "these" is used in reference to plural nouns.

4. All the cars, including mine, (B) are legally parked on the street and will not be towed. In this case, "all" is referring to the entire set of cars and is plural.

5. The flock of geese (B) is migrating south for the winter. "Flock" is a collective noun and is singular.
6. My English teacher and my math teacher always (A) give detailed instructions in class. There is a compound subject with both the English teacher and the math teacher, so the plural verb "give" is needed.
7. The lamp, which has three light bulbs, (A) is in need of some maintenance. The subject is "lamp," not "light bulbs," and "lamp" is a singular word that needs the singular verb "is."
8. I discovered in my studies that while I enjoyed painting and sculpture, (A) it was music I found most appealing. The singular subject "music" comes later in the sentence, but it is in fact the thing that the narrator finds most appealing.
9. The sights and sounds of the World's Fair (A) were truly memorable. There is a compound subject—sights and sounds—that requires a plural verb, "were."
10. A dog that can still walk on all fours (B) is considered mobile. The subject is the singular "dog," not the plural "fours." Thus, the singular verb "is" would be correct.
11. When starting the car, be sure that (A) the emergency brake is deactivated. In this case, there is a vague pronoun, so clarifying it by saying "the emergency brake" would be appropriate.
12. (A) Those plants really have to be watered. The word "plants" is plural, so the word "those" would be correct.
13. The captain of the team (A) has led her team to victory. The subject is "captain," which is singular. A singular verb "has" is needed.
14. When one is speaking to one's friends online, one should be certain that the chat is from one's friends (A) themselves and not from a bot. The word "themselves" refers to the word "friends," which is plural.
15. The car and truck were in a close race, with (B) the truck currently in the lead. The pronoun would be vague in this case, so clarify with "the truck."
16. Anyone who loves the great outdoors (A) is excited for good weather. The word "anyone" is considered to be singular, so the singular "is" would match.
17. Neither terrible snow nor awful rain (A) keeps the mail from being delivered. "Neither" and "nor" refer to objects one at a time instead of collectively, and require a singular verb; "keeps" is singular and would work.
18. Halley's Comet, one of the solar system's short period comets, (A) is projected to pass by Earth in the year 2061. The verb must agree with the singular "comet," not the plural "comets," since it is the "comet" that will be coming by Earth in the future.
19. Since (B) they will not be available on the trail, bring food and water with you for the backpacking journey. The plural word "they" refers to the plural "food and water" that should go on the trail with a hiker.
20. Zaha Hadid, an architect known for her parametric designs (i.e., ones that embrace adaptive shapes and forms), (B) is a native of Iraq. Go back to the beginning of the sentence to see that the subject is the singular person Zaha Hadid, and not the other possible nouns like "designs," "shapes," or "forms."

Verb Agreement

The SAT Writing and Language section will test your skill in verb usage. You will often be asked to determine whether a verb is used in the correct tense. Be aware of the basics of verb conjugation, as outlined in this table (you may have learned quite a bit of verb conjugation in a world language course).

Present	Past	Future
She is They are I am	She was They were I was	She will They will I will
Present Perfect	**Past Perfect**	**Future Perfect**
She has been They have been I have been	She had been They had been I had been	She will have been They will have been I will have been

Example 1

Incorrect: I went on a trip to Florida, and I have a memorable experience.

Correct: I went on a trip to Florida, and I **had** a memorable experience.

Explanation: Make sure that the verbs are used consistently in the sentence. Change "have" to "had" so that the sentence is all in the past tense.

Example 2

Incorrect: My friend's group has been working hard on the school project, while most of the other groups are not doing so.

Correct: My friend's group has been working hard on the school project, while most of the other groups **have not been** doing so.

Explanation: The project has not yet been completed—it is an ongoing activity, so the present perfect tense is appropriate.

Example 3

In addition to ensuring that verbs are in the correct tense, the SAT Writing and Language will ask questions to check for both tense *and* number agreement.

Incorrect: When Eli lived across from two excellent parks, he have ample opportunities for outdoor recreation.

Correct: When Eli lived across from two excellent parks, he **had** ample opportunities for outdoor recreation.

Explanation: In the first version, "have" is incorrect with subject-verb agreement and tense. In the corrected version, "had" uses the correct past tense and is numerically consistent with the subject "Eli."

Verb Agreement Practice—select the correct choice given the context.

1. Yesterday, I (A) ate *or* (B) eat lunch at home.
2. Whenever I walk past that store, I always (A) felt *or* (B) feel like making a purchase.
3. My two aunts have always (A) taken *or* (B) took the bus to work.
4. The large boulder fell into the river and (A) diverted *or* (B) divert the water out of its typical path.
5. You should leave a nice review for a travel guide who (A) do *or* (B) does a good job.
6. Before watching the sequel, I (A) watching *or* (B) watched the prequel.
7. They have been swimming since early this morning and (A) is *or* (B) are continuing to do so now.
8. If you have the instructions, assembly of the new bicycle (A) were *or* (B) is easy.
9. It would (A) have *or* (B) had been an easy test if I had studied some more.
10. My neighbor will not (A) entertained *or* (B) entertain any new offers to purchase his old car.
11. When she flew to visit her relatives overseas, she (A) took *or* (B) takes only two flights.
12. The Renaissance artist (A) draws *or* (B) drew pencil sketches before he turned his ideas into paintings.
13. I will read my textbook this evening after I (A) had completed *or* (B) complete my other homework.
14. An infant may have trouble falling asleep, while teenagers rarely (A) has *or* (B) have any difficulty doing so.
15. The guard dog barked at a predator that (A) approached *or* (B) will approach the herd of sheep.
16. My father is unsure of what dish to (A) brought *or* (B) bring to the potluck dinner.
17. The flock of birds (A) have *or* (B) has taken off from the steep cliff to find food.
18. Emma did a great job on her last assignment, and I am confident she (A) will do *or* (B) had done well on the one due next week.
19. Jesse Owens, winner of four Olympic gold medals, (A) was *or* (B) were born in Oakville, Alabama.
20. What colleges have you (A) chose *or* (B) chosen for your in-person visits?

✓ Solutions

1. Yesterday, I (A) ate lunch at home.
   "Ate" is in the past tense, which makes sense given that the sentence begins with "yesterday," putting the event in the past.

2. Whenever I walk past that store, I always (B) feel like making a purchase.
   "Feel" is in the present tense, consistent with the earlier present tense verb "walk."

3. My two aunts have always (A) taken the bus to work.
   "Have taken" is the correct conjugation, while "have took" would not work; "took" by itself is fine to express the past tense, but not in conjunction with "have."

4. The large boulder fell into the river and (A) diverted the water out of its typical path.
   The earlier verb "fell" is in the past tense, so use "diverted" to be consistent throughout the sentence.

5. You should leave a nice review for a travel guide who (B) does a good job.
   The noun "guide" is singular and therefore requires a singular verb, "does."

6. Before watching the sequel, I (B) watched the prequel.
Using "watched" is logical given that this is a past series of events; also, using "watching" would prevent this from being a complete sentence.

7. They have been swimming since early this morning and (B) are continuing to do so now.
"Are" is consistent with the earlier subject "they."

8. If you have the instructions, assembly of the new bicycle (B) is easy.
"Is" will keep the sentence in the present tense, and it will be consistent with the singular subject "assembly."

9. It would (A) have been an easy test if I had studied some more.
Use "have" in conjunction with "would have." It can be fine to say "if it had," but do not use the word "would" along with "had."

10. My neighbor will not (B) entertain any new offers to purchase his old car.
"Will not entertain" is the proper conjugation to express that this will take place in the future; "entertained" is fine as a past tense option, but not along with "will not."

11. When she flew to visit her relatives overseas, she (A) took only two flights.
"Took" is consistent with the earlier past tense verb "flew."

12. The Renaissance artist (B) drew pencil sketches before he turned his ideas into paintings.
Look later in the sentence to see that it is in the past tense given the verb "turned"; therefore, use the past tense "drew" for consistency.

13. I will read my textbook this evening after I (B) complete my other homework.
Since the textbook reading is happening in the future after the completion of the homework, it is appropriate to use the present tense for "complete."

14. An infant may have trouble falling asleep, while teenagers rarely (B) have any difficulty doing so.
"Have" will be consistent with the plural subject "teenagers."

15. The guard dog barked at a predator that (A) approached the herd of sheep.
"Approached" is consistent with the past tense verb "barked" earlier in the sentence.

16. My father is unsure of what dish to (B) bring to the potluck dinner.
"To bring" is the correct infinitive form of the verb, not "to brought."

17. The flock of birds (B) has taken off from the steep cliff to find food.
The subject is the singular noun "flock," so "has" would be consistent with it.

18. Emma did a great job on her last assignment, and I am confident she (A) will do well on the one due next week.
Based on context clues, the correct verb will be "will do" since the next assignment is one that has not yet been evaluated.

19. Jesse Owens, winner of four Olympic gold medals, (A) was born in Oakville, Alabama.
The subject is the singular person "Jesse Owens," not the plural "medals"; therefore, use the singular verb "was."

20. What colleges have you (B) chosen for your in-person visits?
"Have chosen" is the correct conjugation of the verb, not "have chose."

Number and Tense Agreement Practice Passage

Take approximately six to seven minutes to complete this exercise if you are doing it timed.

An adaptation of the introduction of Animal Figures in the Maya Codices *by Alfred M. Tozzer and Glover M. Allen as published by the Peabody Museum of American Archeology and Ethnology (Vol IV No. 3) in February of 1910.*

The various peoples inhabiting Mexico and Central America in early pre-Columbian times **1** is accustomed to record various events, especially in regard to their calendar and the religious ceremonials in relation to **2** it, on long strips of skin or bark. These were usually painted on both sides and folded together like a screen. Several of these codices are still in existence from the Nahua and Zapotec areas in Mexico, but only three have **3** came down to us from the Maya region. These three manuscripts are the Dresden Codex in the Royal Public Library at Dresden, the Tro-Cortesianus (formerly considered to have been two, the Troano and the Cortesianus) in the National Archaeological Museum at Madrid, and the Peresianus in the National Library at Paris. **4** This pre-Columbian manuscripts have all been published in facsimile.

These remains of a once extensive literature **5** shows evidence not only of considerable intellectual attainments on the part of their authors but also of a high degree of artistic skill in the drawings and hieroglyphics. The frequent occurrence in these manuscripts of representations of animals showing various degrees of elaboration and conventionalization **6** has led us to undertake the task of identifying these figures as far as possible and studying the uses and significance of the several species, a field practically untouched. Förstemann in his various commentaries on the Maya codices, Brinton, and DeRosny have only commented briefly upon this side of the study **7** of them. Seler and some others have written short papers on special animals.

1. (A) NO CHANGE
   (B) was
   (C) were
   (D) will be

2. (A) NO CHANGE
   (B) them
   (C) those
   (D) these

3. (A) NO CHANGE
   (B) come
   (C) comed
   (D) camed

4. (A) NO CHANGE
   (B) Them
   (C) These
   (D) A

5. (A) NO CHANGE
   (B) showing
   (C) will show
   (D) show

6. (A) NO CHANGE
   (B) have
   (C) will have
   (D) having

7. (A) NO CHANGE
   (B) of it.
   (C) of the manuscripts.
   (D) of this.

In making our identifications, we **8** have given the reasons for our determinations in some detail and have stated the characteristics employed to denote the several species.

We have not **9** limit ourselves entirely to the Maya manuscripts as we have drawn upon the vast amount of material available in the stone carvings, the stucco figures, and the frescoes found throughout the Maya area. This material has by no means been exhausted in the present paper. In addition to the figures from the Maya codices and a comparatively few from other sources in the Maya region, we have introduced for comparison in a number of cases figures from a few of the ancient manuscripts of the Nahuas and the Zapotecs to the north. The calendar of **10** this two peoples is fundamentally the same as that of the Mayas. The year is made up in the same way, being composed of eighteen months of twenty days each with five days additional at the end of the year. There is therefore a more or less close connection as regards subject matter in all the pre-Columbian codices of Mexico and Central America, but the manner of presentation **11** differs among the different peoples of this region.

8. (A) NO CHANGE
   (B) has given
   (C) have give
   (D) has giving

9. (A) NO CHANGE
   (B) limits
   (C) limiting
   (D) limited

10. (A) NO CHANGE
    (B) these
    (C) it's
    (D) its

11. (A) NO CHANGE
    (B) had differs
    (C) differ
    (D) have differ

✓ Solutions

1. **(C)** "Were" matches up with the plural subject of "peoples." It is not choice (A) or (B) because those are both singular verbs. And it is not choice (D) because the events are not taking place in the future.

2. **(A)** The pronoun "it" matches the singular word "calendar." The other options are all plural and therefore incorrect.

3. **(B)** "Have come" is the correct conjugation in the present perfect of "to come." Choice (A), "came," is the past tense and does not go along with "have." Choices (C) and (D) are not considered words.

4. **(C)** "These" corresponds to the plural "manuscripts." Choices (A) and (D) would be singular, and choice (B), "Them," is not used as an adjective.

5. **(D)** "Show" matches with the plural subject "remains." Choice (A) is a singular verb, choice (B) would prevent this from being a complete sentence, and choice (C) incorrectly places the events in the future.

6. **(A)** The subject is the singular "occurrence," so the singular "has" would work. Choices (B) and (C) would be plural, and choice (D) would make this sentence into a fragment.

7. **(C)** The pronoun is vague, so it is necessary to clear it up with a noun, making "of the manuscripts" the only logical possibility.

8. **(A)** The proper conjugation along with "we" is "have given." Choice (B) is for a singular subject, and choices (C) and (D) use improper conjugation.

9. **(D)** "We have not limited" uses the proper present perfect conjugation of "to limit." The other options cannot go along with "have" as verbs.

10. **(B)** "These" is plural, corresponding to the two "peoples." The other options are all singular.

11. **(A)** "Differs" matches the singular subject of "manner." Choices (B) and (D) use improper conjugation, and choice (C) is for a plural subject.

Wordiness

In order to write an excellent paper, it is critical to be able to tell the difference between wordy writing and descriptive writing. Wordy writing can be repetitive and include information that is irrelevant to the point being made. Descriptive writing, on the other hand, provides clear details about what is taking place. The SAT Writing and Language section will assess your skill in determining whether something is wordy or descriptive.

Example 1

Incorrect: The previous and former principal was more strict than the current one.

Correct: The previous ~~**and former**~~ principal was more strict than the current one.

Explanation: Watch out for repetition. "Previous" and "former" mean the same thing, so to have both would be repetitive.

Example 2

Rare earth elements **2** have become more popular to mine in recent years.

2. At this point, the writer is considering adding the following.

   , metals that are used in many electronic devices,

   Should the writer make this addition here?

   (A) Yes, because it explains how the elements are used in electronic devices.
   (B) Yes, because it clarifies an important term.
   (C) No, because it presents an irrelevant detail.
   (D) No, because it contradicts the information elsewhere in the sentence.

Explanation: This is an example of how more description would be helpful. The correct answer is **(B)**. The insertion would clarify a term that would be unfamiliar to many readers: "rare earth elements." Generally speaking, if an additional phrase provides a helpful clarification to a less familiar idea, it will be useful. It is not choice (A) because the selection does not provide an explanation for how the metals are used in electronic devices—it simply states that they are used in such a way. It is not choice (C) because the selection is relevant, and it is not choice (D) because there is nothing in the selection that contradicts information found elsewhere in the sentence.

Wordiness Practice—select the better sentence out of the two options.

1. (A) The previous coach of the team, who formerly was in charge, did a better job than the current coach.
   (B) The previous coach of the team did a better job than the current coach.
2. (A) While walking and going for a stroll, I saw some beautiful birds fly past.
   (B) While going for a stroll, I saw some beautiful birds fly past.
3. (A) The 1950 champion oak, the largest known specimen of the tree at that time, was very impressive.
   (B) The 1950 champion oak was very impressive.
4. (A) The towering building cast a long shadow over the city park.
   (B) The towering and sky-high building cast a long shadow over the city park.
5. (A) People who are strong proponents of and advocates for their positions can often be very determined to persuade others.
   (B) People who are strong advocates for their positions can often be very determined to persuade others.
6. (A) I like pizza that is delicious and affordable.
   (B) I like pizza that is delicious.
7. (A) My uncle had no difficulty helping me finish baking the cake.
   (B) My uncle, a professionally trained chef, had no difficulty helping me finish baking the cake.
8. (A) During the Olympic torch relay, large crowds lined the streets of the city.
   (B) During the Olympic torch relay, large crowds and enormous groups of people lined the streets of the city.
9. (A) Keep in mind the conditions and circumstances facing the country before judging its policy choices.
   (B) Keep in mind the circumstances facing the country before judging its policy choices.
10. (A) The engineer's original creation had a positive impact on the progress of the project.
    (B) The engineer's original creation, which was of her own invention, had a positive impact on the progress of the project.
11. (A) My aunt Gia is a philologist—someone who studies the history of languages.
    (B) My aunt Gia is a philologist.
12. (A) Large boats and enormous ships were better able to traverse the canal after it had been dredged.
    (B) Large boats were better able to traverse the canal after it had been dredged.
13. (A) I would like to have cereal for breakfast, which is a meal that takes place during the morning.
    (B) I would like to have cereal for breakfast.
14. (A) The medical treatment actually exacerbated the patient's condition.
    (B) The medical treatment actually exacerbated the patient's condition, making things worse.

15. (A) A total solar eclipse—an astronomical event that occurs when the sun is completely covered by the moon in the sky—is something I hope to witness in my lifetime.
(B) A total solar eclipse is something I hope to witness in my lifetime.

16. (A) Between 1930 and 1935, my ancestor lived in Seattle.
(B) Between the years of 1930 and 1935, my ancestor lived in Seattle.

17. (A) Scientist Jane Goodall, considered the world's foremost expert on chimpanzees, was born in London, England.
(B) Scientist Jane Goodall was born in London, England.

18. (A) Try to minimize and keep down the amount of consumer debt you have in order to get ahead financially.
(B) Try to minimize the amount of consumer debt you have in order to get ahead financially.

19. (A) Throw the soiled, filthy napkin in the garbage.
(B) Throw the filthy napkin in the garbage.

20. (A) On the road trip through the American West, we saw beautiful canyons and vast deserts.
(B) On the road trip through the American West, we saw beautiful canyons, impressive mountains, and vast deserts.

✓ Solutions

1. **(B)** The previous coach of the team did a better job than the current coach.
Since "previous" and "formerly" mean the same thing, it is fine to eliminate "who formerly was in charge."

2. **(B)** While going for a stroll, I saw some beautiful birds fly past.
"Walking" and "going for a stroll" are synonymous, so eliminate the repetition.

3. **(A)** The 1950 champion oak, the largest known specimen of the tree at that time, was very impressive.
The idea of a champion tree is a specialized idea that may be unfamiliar to most readers, so it is appropriate to define it.

4. **(A)** The towering building cast a long shadow over the city park.
"Towering" and "sky-high" are synonymous, so eliminate the repetition.

5. **(B)** People who are strong advocates for their positions can often be very determined to persuade others.
An "advocate" and a "proponent" are synonymous, so only one of these words is needed.

6. **(A)** I like pizza that is delicious and affordable.
This version of the sentence provides details as to what the narrator may want in a pizza without being repetitive.

7. **(B)** My uncle, a professionally trained chef, had no difficulty helping me finish baking the cake.
Having the clarification about the uncle's professional background helps the reader better understand why he had no difficulty helping the narrator finish baking the cake.

8. **(A)** During the Olympic torch relay, large crowds lined the streets of the city.
"Large crowds" and "enormous groups of people" are synonymous, so eliminate the repetition.

9. **(B)** Keep in mind the circumstances facing the country before judging its policy choices.
"Conditions" and "circumstances" are synonymous, so only one of them is needed.

10. **(A)** The engineer's original creation had a positive impact on the progress of the project.
If the engineer had an "original creation," it would by definition be of her own invention; so, we can eliminate the repetition.

11. **(A)** My aunt Gia is a philologist—someone who studies the history of languages.
"Philologist" is a more challenging academic term, so it will be helpful to readers to clarify its meaning.

12. **(B)** Large boats were better able to traverse the canal after it had been dredged.
"Large boats" and "enormous ships" mean the same thing, so it is appropriate to eliminate one of these phrases.

13. **(B)** I would like to have cereal for breakfast.
"Breakfast" is an easy, widely known term, so there is no need for clarification of its meaning.

14. **(A)** The medical treatment actually exacerbated the patient's condition.
To "exacerbate" is defined as "making things worse," so there is no need to have this final phrase in the sentence.

15. **(A)** A total solar eclipse—an astronomical event that occurs when the sun is completely covered by the moon in the sky—is something I hope to witness in my lifetime.
Since the precise definition of a total solar eclipse is a technical, scientific idea, it would be helpful to the reader to have it defined.

16. **(A)** Between 1930 and 1935, my ancestor lived in Seattle.
It is reasonable to infer that 1930 and 1935 refer to years, so there is no need to say "between the years of."

17. **(A)** Scientist Jane Goodall, considered the world's foremost expert on chimpanzees, was born in London, England.
Having an idea of Goodall's area of expertise is more helpful than simply knowing that she was a "scientist."

18. **(B)** Try to minimize the amount of consumer debt you have in order to get ahead financially.
"Minimize" and "keep down" are synonymous, so eliminate the repetition.

19. **(B)** Throw the filthy napkin in the garbage.
A "soiled" and a "filthy" napkin are both considered dirty, so there is no need for this repetition.

20. **(B)** On the road trip through the American West, we saw beautiful canyons, impressive mountains, and vast deserts.
The phrase "impressive mountains" provides a helpful description of what was seen on the road trip, and it does not repeat any of the other points of description, so it is appropriate to include it.

Wordiness Practice Passage

Take approximately nine minutes to complete this exercise if you are doing it timed.

A Looming Threat to a Popular Fruit

Bananas have a surprisingly unfortunate history. ❶ They have been the cause of wars and clandestine military operations in Central America. In the early 20th century, the most popular variety of bananas almost died off due to disease. This particular banana variety was called "Gros Michel"; it was widely considered to be a tastier ❷ variety and type than the currently popular Cavendish variety. The only reason that the Cavendish banana is now the one widely sold in grocery stores is that it was resistant to the strain of Panama disease that swept through Central America, killing almost all ❸ of the Gros Michel variety. Recently a new strain of Panama disease has emerged that threatens the Cavendish variety and may disrupt the world's banana supply. ❹

1. The writer is considering deleting the underlined sentence. Should the sentence be kept or deleted?
   (A) Kept, because it explains how the banana led to a military conflict.
   (B) Kept, because it elaborates on the statement made in the preceding sentence.
   (C) Deleted, because it provides an irrelevant detail.
   (D) Deleted, because it contradicts a point made elsewhere in the essay.

2. (A) NO CHANGE
   (B) species, type, and variety
   (C) variety
   (D) specific species of plant

3. (A) NO CHANGE
   (B) of them.
   (C) the bananas.
   (D) DELETE the underlined portion

4. At this point, the writer is considering adding the following sentence.

   Many people, including myself, enjoy eating bananas for breakfast.

   Should the writer make this addition here?
   (A) Yes, because it is helpful to know the narrator's personal opinions.
   (B) Yes, because an analysis of banana consumption habits provides a welcome transition.
   (C) No, because it distracts from the primary focus of the paragraph.
   (D) No, because it is inconsistent with the first person style of the essay.

It has long been known to **5** persons of a scientific area of study that genetic diversity is a key factor in a population's resistance to the threat of mass extinction from disease. Without genetic diversity, most of the individuals in a population will be susceptible to the same pathogens. Thus, when a deadly pathogen enters a more homogenous population, it will tend to **6** rapidly move through it quickly and with a high mortality rate. Every gardener is well aware of this, and most experienced gardeners will vary the types of crops they plant each year to help reduce the chance that last year's pests will gain a foothold in the current growing season.

The new Panama disease can kill Cavendish bananas. Given the extremely low genetic diversity of the Cavendish banana, there is no reason to think that this disease will not make the Cavendish banana **7** go the way of the Gros Michel. The only way to stop this disease from disrupting the world banana supply is to start growing and selling more **8** varieties of bananas. The main obstacle to creating more banana varieties is the fact that banana trees are difficult to grow from seeds. Moreover, Cavendish bananas are seedless, **9** decreasing the genetic variation and making the genetic diversity in this variety very low. Being seedless, most of the current banana plants are clones of another banana plant from which a branch was taken and planted to produce a new tree. This means that most current banana plants are not merely closely related to each other—they are genetically identical. Although most people have become used to the **10** taste, flavor, and texture of the Cavendish banana, the world has become used to new bananas before and can do so again.

5. (A) NO CHANGE
   (B) those who are passionate about studying the sciences
   (C) people who follow scientific logic
   (D) scientists

6. (A) NO CHANGE
   (B) speedily
   (C) rather briskly
   (D) DELETE the underlined portion

7. The writer is considering deleting the underlined potion, adjusting the punctuation as needed. Should the underlined portion be kept or deleted?
   (A) Kept, because it elaborates on how the Cavendish variety would thrive.
   (B) Kept, because it clarifies what would otherwise be an illogical ending to the sentence.
   (C) Deleted, because it shifts the focus to a different species of banana.
   (D) Deleted, because it does not support the argument made in the sentence.

8. (A) NO CHANGE
   (B) various types
   (C) different species that can be found in nature
   (D) DELETE the underlined portion

9. (A) NO CHANGE
   (B) defined as being without seeds and
   (C) are considered edible by humans and
   (D) DELETE the underlined portion

10. (A) NO CHANGE
    (B) flavoring and taste
    (C) taste and texture
    (D) sense

Hopefully, the world will have a wake-up call that leads to ⓫ something.

The writer is considering making the following revision to the underlined portion.

11. The writer is considering revising the underlined portion, changing it to the following phrase.

    greater banana diversity.

    Should the writer make this revision?
    (A) Yes, because it provides a more precise idea.
    (B) Yes, because it clarifies the source of the demise of the Cavendish species.
    (C) No, because is overly repetitive.
    (D) No, because fails to adequately conclude the essay.

✓ Solutions

1. **(B)** The previous sentence states that bananas have an "unfortunate history" without elaborating on that statement. The sentence in question would add details to support the narrator's claim about the unfortunate history of bananas. It is not choice (A) because it does not *explain* how the banana led to a conflict, merely that there were conflicts about bananas. It is not choice (C) because the detail is in fact relevant. And it is not choice (D) because the information does not contradict anything else in the passage.
2. **(C)** "Variety" expresses the point sufficiently. All the other options introduce synonyms for "variety," and are thus repetitive.
3. **(A)** Without the full statement that it was the Gros Michel variety that was nearly killed off, the sentence would lack an essential detail. The other options would result in unnecessary vagueness.
4. **(C)** The focus of the surrounding sentences is on the susceptibility of the banana to disease, so inserting this personal statement from the narrator would be inappropriate. It is not choice (A) because it is not helpful to know the narrator's personal opinions in a more formal essay like this. It is not choice (B) because the next paragraph focuses on the need for genetic diversity, not on personal eating habits. And it is not choice (D) because the essay is written in the third person, not first person.
5. **(D)** "Scientists" is perfectly fine in concisely expressing who is aware that genetic diversity is important to disease prevention. The other options are unnecessarily wordy.
6. **(D)** The sentence goes on to say that the disease will move "quickly," so there is no need to state this earlier. The other options would all result in repetition.
7. **(B)** Without this phrase, the sentence would end abruptly without clarifying what the Cavendish banana is being made to do. It is not choice (A) because it does not tell us how the banana would live, but rather how it might die. It is not choices (C) or (D) because the selection does need to remain in the sentence for clarity.
8. **(A)** "Varieties" is needed for clarity, especially given the "of" that immediately follows the underlined portion. Choices (B) and (C) are repetitive, and choice (D) would lack clarity.

9. **(D)** There is no need to clarify the simple term "seedless," so the underlined portion can be deleted. Choices (A), (B), and (C) would all result in unneeded wordiness.

10. **(C)** "Taste and texture" express two different aspects of the banana, making this the correct choice. It is not choice (A) because "taste" and "flavor" are synonymous. It is not choice (B) because "taste" and "flavoring" are synonymous. And it is not choice (D) because "sense" is overly vague.

11. **(A)** "Something" would be too vague, but "greater banana diversity" would provide needed description. It is not choice (B) because the Cavendish species has not become extinct. It is not choice (C) because "something" is not repetitive, just imprecise. And it is not choice (D) because the change is in fact needed.

Punctuation

Commas

When it comes to comma questions on the SAT, it is important to know both *when* to use a comma and *when NOT* to use a comma. You may be able to intuitively tell when to use a comma by mouthing out the sentence in your head and "hearing" where a small breath or pause would be. However, it is helpful to know specific rules about when and when not to use commas so that you can do your best.

<u>Do</u> use a comma to separate an introductory phrase (dependent clause) from a complete sentence (independent clause).

Correct: Whenever my brother sleeps, he snores loudly.

Correct: If you are happy with your grade, put the paper on your refrigerator.

Explanation: In both of these examples, there is an introductory phrase followed by a complete sentence. A comma is great for separating dependent clauses (incomplete thoughts that cannot stand on their own) from complete sentences (a complete idea with both a subject and a verb).

<u>Don't</u> use a comma by itself to join two complete sentences (independent clauses).

Incorrect: Jean went for a walk around town, she saw many different neighborhoods.

Correct: Jean went for a walk around town, **<u>and</u>** she saw many different neighborhoods.

Incorrect: My friend loves to paint, he makes large messes when doing so.

Correct: My friend loves to paint, **<u>but</u>** he makes large messes when doing so.

Explanation: A comma by itself cannot separate one complete sentence from another—this error is called a *comma splice.* If you had a word like *and, but,* or *yet* along with the comma, that would be fine. Also, a semicolon, period, and sometimes a dash or colon can work to separate complete sentences.

<u>Do</u> use a comma before and after a parenthetical phrase (i.e., words that are added to a sentence without changing the original sentence's grammar or meaning).

Correct: The first person to walk on the moon, Neil Armstrong, is a native of the state of Ohio.

Correct: Jigsaw puzzles, unlike crossword puzzles, involve visual pattern recognition.

Correct: A box of my favorite cereal, which I purchased on sale, is what my family will have for breakfast this week.

Explanation: The phrases "Neil Armstrong," "unlike crossword puzzles," and "which I purchased on sale" could be removed from the original sentences and the sentences would remain complete with their original meanings. Note that parenthetical phrases will often start with *which*. (If *which* is used without a parenthetical phrase, like "the building in which I will take the SAT," no comma before *which* is needed).

Don't use a comma to separate the subject from the verb in a sentence.

Incorrect: My best friend, is moving out of town.

Correct: My best friend is moving out of town.

Incorrect: Football players and basketball players, both use locker rooms to get ready.

Correct: Football players and basketball players both use locker rooms to get ready.

Incorrect: The book, that I have almost finished is very suspenseful.

Correct: The book that I have almost finished is very suspenseful.

Explanation: These sentences would work if the commas were removed. Just because a sentence has a long subject does not mean that it requires a comma. Note that phrases that do not require a comma will often start with *that*. *That* indicates that a phrase is restrictive, or essential, to the sentence's meaning.

Do use a comma to separate words within a list.

Correct: I will pick up apples, bananas, and oranges at the fruit stand.

Don't use a comma right *before* a list begins.

Incorrect: At the fruit stand, I will pick up, oranges, apples, and bananas.

Correct: At the fruit stand, I will pick up oranges, apples, and bananas.

Explanation: There is no need for a comma after "pick up" in the second sentence. Just use commas to separate the items within the list.

Note: The SAT uses the Oxford comma with lists: the comma before the *and* that comes before the final item. However, since the Oxford comma is more of a stylistic choice than a grammar rule, they most likely will not test you on this concept.

Do use a comma along with coordinating conjunctions to connect two complete sentences. Coordinating conjunctions provide a strong connection between sentences. *Remember coordinating conjunctions with the acronym FANBOYS (For, And, Nor, But, Or, Yet, So).*

Correct: My sister was hungry, so she grabbed a snack from the kitchen.

Correct: I studied quite a bit for the test, but I did not perform as well as I would have liked.

Don't just use a comma to connect two complete sentences joined by a conjunctive adverb (e.g., however, indeed, nevertheless, moreover, namely, meanwhile, subsequently, thus, furthermore). Conjunctive adverbs provide a weaker connection between sentences. Instead, use a semicolon with a comma.

Incorrect: He was delighted to be promoted, however, he was not happy with the new work schedule.

Correct: He was delighted to be promoted; however, he was not happy with the new work schedule.

Incorrect: The tour started at the museum, subsequently, it went to the park.

Correct: The tour started at the museum; subsequently, it went to the park.

Note: It is fine to use conjunctive adverbs with just commas so long as they are not used to connect two complete sentences:

Correct: My friend wanted me to come to his house. Instead, I decided to stay home.

Correct: Most birds can fly. The penguin, however, cannot.

Explanation: While a comma by itself is not enough to join two complete sentences, a comma along with one of the FANBOYS words *will* be enough. Be sure that the word joining the two complete sentences is one of these FANBOYS words—if it is one of the conjunctive adverbs, use a semicolon before the conjunctive adverb and a comma after the conjunctive adverb to make the connection.

Do use commas to separate adjectives if the order of the adjectives *does not* matter.

Correct: The fluffy, friendly puppy likes to wag its tail.

Correct: The friendly, fluffy puppy likes to wag its tail.

Explanation: It does not change the meaning of the sentence whether "fluffy" or "friendly" comes first.

Don't use commas to separate adjectives if the order of the adjectives *does* matter.

Incorrect: The first, female governor won a large majority of the vote.

Incorrect: The female, first governor won a large majority of the vote.

Correct: The first female governor won a large majority of the vote.

Explanation: The order of the adjectives "first" and "female" does matter—"first" must come before "female" in order for the sentence to be logical. In this situation, do not use commas to separate the adjectives.

Comma Practice—select the better sentence out of the two options.

1. (A) Once upon a time, the kingdom was under attack.
   (B) Once upon a time the kingdom was under attack.
2. (A) My Advanced Placement World History class, is very interesting.
   (B) My Advanced Placement World History class is very interesting.
3. (A) I needed a quiet place to read, so I went to the library.
   (B) I needed a quiet place to read so I went to the library.
4. (A) The pedestal onto, which you place the trophies should be sturdy.
   (B) The pedestal onto which you place the trophies should be sturdy.
5. (A) If you are going to do well on your test, be sure to get a good night's sleep.
   (B) If you are going to do well on your test be sure to get a good night's sleep.
6. (A) One example of a large animal, is the blue whale.
   (B) One example of a large animal is the blue whale.
7. (A) The first person to walk across Antarctica without any assistance Colin O'Brady took 54 days to do so.
   (B) The first person to walk across Antarctica without any assistance, Colin O'Brady, took 54 days to do so.

8. (A) Essential ingredients for the cake are flour, sugar, and eggs.
(B) Essential ingredients for the cake are flour sugar and eggs.

9. (A) The results of the study, indicate that the medicine is highly effective.
(B) The results of the study indicate that the medicine is highly effective.

10. (A) The saw is extremely precise, cutting each edge flawlessly.
(B) The saw is extremely precise cutting each edge flawlessly.

11. (A) Broccoli, though not my friend's favorite, is something I love to eat whenever I can.
(B) Broccoli though not my friend's favorite is something I love to eat whenever I can.

12. (A) The chair that is by the window is extremely comfortable.
(B) The chair, that is by the window, is extremely comfortable.

13. (A) Each morning, I like to take a shower, eat breakfast, and gather my things for school.
(B) Each morning, I like to take a shower eat breakfast, and gather my things for school.

14. (A) Inflation is largely attributable to the ever-increasing prices of different goods and services.
(B) Inflation is largely attributable, to the ever-increasing prices of different goods and services.

15. (A) The ping-pong table in the middle of the gymnasium, is where I spend my time after eating lunch.
(B) The ping-pong table in the middle of the gymnasium is where I spend my time after eating lunch.

16. (A) Our house, which we moved into last year, is still in good condition.
(B) Our house which we moved into last year is still in good condition.

17. (A) The job of a lifeguard, is to vigilantly keep watch over the beach.
(B) The job of a lifeguard is to vigilantly keep watch over the beach.

18. (A) You did an excellent job on your group project; moreover, you aced your final exam.
(B) You did an excellent job on your group project, moreover, you aced your final exam.

19. (A) My newest neighbor Jian, loves to play basketball in his driveway.
(B) My newest neighbor, Jian, loves to play basketball in his driveway.

20. (A) If you are passionate about your profession, work will not feel like "work."
(B) If you are passionate about your profession work will not feel like "work."

21. (A) The new volleyball coach, was excited for the team's first game.
(B) The new volleyball coach was excited for the team's first game.

22. (A) Cold-brewed coffee, though not my personal favorite, has become increasingly popular.
(B) Cold-brewed coffee, though not my personal favorite has become increasingly popular.

23. (A) The traffic, that clogged up the highway for eight straight miles, was quite a nuisance.
(B) The traffic that clogged up the highway for eight straight miles was quite a nuisance.

24. (A) My videoconferencing software which I just updated helped me to meet with faraway relatives.
(B) My videoconferencing software, which I just updated, helped me to meet with faraway relatives.

25. (A) Several thousand years ago, people, along with many animals, traversed an ice bridge from Eurasia to the Americas.
(B) Several thousand years ago people, along with many animals traversed an ice bridge from Eurasia to the Americas.

✓ Solutions

1. **(A)** Once upon a time, the kingdom was under attack.
Place a comma after the introductory phrase.
2. **(B)** My Advanced Placement World History class is very interesting.
Don't separate the subject from the verb with a comma.
3. **(A)** I needed a quiet place to read, so I went to the library.
"So" is one of the FANBOYS words, and can therefore be used to join two sentences along with a comma.
4. **(B)** The pedestal onto which you place the trophies should be sturdy.
This is an example of using "which" when it does not precede a parenthetical phrase—thus, no comma is needed.
5. **(A)** If you are going to do well on your test, be sure to get a good night's sleep.
Use a comma to separate the introductory phrase from the complete sentence that follows.
6. **(B)** One example of a large animal is the blue whale.
There is no need to separate the subject and the verb.
7. **(B)** The first person to walk across Antarctica without any assistance, Colin O'Brady, took 54 days to do so.
Surround the name with commas since the sentence will maintain its meaning and grammar without it.
8. **(A)** Essential ingredients for the cake are flour, sugar, and eggs.
Use commas to separate the items in the list.
9. **(B)** The results of the study indicate that the medicine is highly effective.
There is no need to separate the subject and the verb with a comma.
10. **(A)** The saw is extremely precise, cutting each edge flawlessly.
Use a comma to separate the complete sentence from the dependent clause that follows.
11. **(A)** Broccoli, though not my friend's favorite, is something I love to eat whenever I can.
Surround the parenthetical phrase with commas.
12. **(A)** The chair that is by the window is extremely comfortable.
The is no need for commas when using "that" to describe something essential to the subject.
13. **(A)** Each morning, I like to take a shower, eat breakfast, and gather my things for school.
Use commas to separate the items in the list.
14. **(A)** Inflation is largely attributable to the ever-increasing prices of different goods and services.
Do not use a comma to break up the phrase "attributable to."

15. **(B)** The ping-pong table in the middle of the gymnasium is where I spend my time after eating lunch.
Even though there is a long subject in the sentence, do not use a comma to separate the subject from the verb.

16. **(A)** Our house, which we moved into last year, is still in good condition.
Use commas around the parenthetical phrase that begins with "which."

17. **(B)** The job of a lifeguard is to vigilantly keep watch over the beach.
Do not separate the subject from the verb.

18. **(A)** You did an excellent job on your group project; moreover, you aced your final exam.
Use a semicolon, not a comma, to separate two sentences joined by a conjunctive adverb.

19. **(B)** My newest neighbor, Jian, loves to play basketball in his driveway.
"Jian" is the same person as "my newest neighbor," so his name can be set off with commas.

20. **(A)** If you are passionate about your profession, work will not feel like "work."
Use commas to separate the introductory phrase from the complete sentence that follows.

21. **(B)** The new volleyball coach was excited for the team's first game.
Do not separate the subject from the verb.

22. **(A)** Cold-brewed coffee, though not my personal favorite, has become increasingly popular.
Surround the parenthetical phrase with commas.

23. **(B)** The traffic that clogged up the highway for eight straight miles was quite a nuisance.
No commas are needed to surround an essential phrase starting with "that."

24. **(B)** My videoconferencing software, which I just updated, helped me to meet with faraway relatives.
Surround the parenthetical, nonessential phrase that begins with "which" with commas.

25. **(A)** Several thousand years ago, people, along with many animals, traversed an ice bridge from Eurasia to the Americas.
Use a comma after "people" to separate the introductory phrase, and also use commas around the parenthetical phrase "along with many animals."

Semicolons

Use a semicolon (;) to separate two complete, related sentences from one another. While a period could be substituted for a semicolon in most cases, using the semicolon allows for more stylistic variety in one's writing.

Correct: I am excited to go to the concert; I will show up early to be first in line.

Incorrect: While I am excited to go to the concert; there is no way I want to show up early to wait.

Correct: While I am excited to go to the concert, there is no way I want to show up early to wait.

Explanation: If there are complete sentences on either side of the semicolon, it is appropriate to use one. If there is a sentence fragment on either side of the semicolon, change the sentence structure (perhaps by substituting a comma for the semicolon) to make it work.

Semicolon Practice—select the better sentence out of the two options.

1. (A) This is the best book I have ever read, I simply cannot put it down.
   (B) This is the best book I have ever read; I simply cannot put it down.
2. (A) A positive attitude can help you overcome adversity, no matter the circumstances.
   (B) A positive attitude can help you overcome adversity; no matter the circumstances.
3. (A) It was supposed to be a cloudy day, however, the weather forecast was fortunately incorrect.
   (B) It was supposed to be a cloudy day; however, the weather forecast was fortunately incorrect.
4. (A) The ride on the bus was bumpy; I spilled my drink on the floor.
   (B) The ride on the bus was bumpy, I spilled my drink on the floor.
5. (A) If the grass is dry, water the lawn.
   (B) If the grass is dry; water the lawn.

✓ Solutions

1. **(B)** This is the best book I have ever read; I simply cannot put it down.
   Use a semicolon to separate the two complete sentences.
2. **(A)** A positive attitude can help you overcome adversity, no matter the circumstances.
   "No matter the circumstances" is not a complete sentence, so separate it from the complete sentence that comes before it with a comma.
3. **(B)** It was supposed to be a cloudy day; however, the weather forecast was fortunately incorrect.
   Recall that with conjunctive adverbs (like "however") that join two complete sentences, use a semicolon followed by a comma.
4. **(A)** The ride on the bus was bumpy; I spilled my drink on the floor.
   Use a semicolon to separate the two complete sentences.
5. **(A)** If the grass is dry, water the lawn.
   A comma will work to separate the introductory phrase from the complete sentence.

Colons

Use a colon (:) if it comes after a complete sentence and introduces a clarification or a list. If an idea is not fully expressed, the colon can set off the information that will complete the thought.

Correct: After many years of hard work, I have achieved my lifelong dream: hiking up a tall mountain.

Correct: French mirepoix uses these ingredients: carrots, onions, and celery.

Colon Practice—select the better sentence out of the two options.

1. (A) My houseplant requires the following to thrive sunlight, fertilizer, and water.
   (B) My houseplant requires the following to thrive: sunlight, fertilizer, and water.
2. (A) The office workers finally agreed on the setting for the thermostat: 72 degrees.
   (B) The office workers finally: agreed on the setting for the thermostat 72 degrees.

3. (A) You should take: your suitcase, backpack, and wallet with you on the trip.
   (B) You should take your suitcase, backpack, and wallet with you on the trip.

4. (A) We were delighted to see two of our favorite animals at the zoo: elephants and tigers.
   (B) We were delighted to see two of our favorite animals at the zoo elephants and tigers.

5. (A) No matter how you choose to season your food, salt and pepper are recommended items to have on a dinner table.
   (B) No matter how you choose to season your food: salt and pepper are recommended items to have on a dinner table.

✓ Solutions

1. **(B)** My houseplant requires the following to thrive: sunlight, fertilizer, and water.
   The colon comes before the list of items the plant requires to thrive.

2. **(A)** The office workers finally agreed on the setting for the thermostat: 72 degrees.
   This is the correct placement for the colon since it comes after a complete sentence and before a clarification.

3. **(B)** You should take your suitcase, backpack, and wallet with you on the trip.
   Not every list will require a colon to come before it. In this case, a colon would cause a very abrupt pause.

4. **(A)** We were delighted to see two of our favorite animals at the zoo: elephants and tigers.
   The colon comes before the clarification of which animals were at the zoo.

5. **(A)** No matter how you choose to season your food, salt and pepper are recommended items to have on a dinner table.
   Since "No matter how you choose to season your food" is not a complete sentence, having a colon after it would not work. Use a comma instead.

Dashes

Use a dash (—) to indicate a change of thought or change of voice in a sentence.

Correct: I would not go down that alley—it looks very spooky.

Correct: Wait—I am not ready to go.

Use dashes to surround a parenthetical phrase. Start and finish the parenthetical phrase using the same punctuation, like commas, dashes, or parentheses.

Correct: Las Vegas—a major tourist town—is surprisingly surrounded by desert.

Incorrect: Las Vegas—a major tourist town, is surprisingly surrounded by desert.

Note: With the above examples, other forms of punctuation could have been used instead of the dash. You have a great deal of flexibility in your punctuation choices in more complex sentences. *However, do not worry about whether the SAT will have two correct options.* If a colon could be used for a dash and vice versa, only one of these options will be presented.

Dash Practice—select the better sentence out of the two options.

1. (A) My favorite food—pizza—is easily found at many restaurants.
   (B) My favorite food, pizza—is easily found at many restaurants.

2. (A) The backpacking journey looks quite challenging—be prepared.
(B) The backpacking journey looks quite challenging be prepared.

3. (A) My science teacher—a former government researcher—is excellent at helping us see the applications of what we learn.
(B) My science teacher—a former government researcher is excellent at helping us see the applications of what we learn.

4. (A) Based on the latest data, the geologists could only come to one conclusion—a volcanic eruption was imminent.
(B) Based on the latest data, the geologists could only come to one conclusion a volcanic eruption was imminent.

5. (A) My friends Sharon and Maria are coming over to my house this evening.
(B) My friends Sharon—and Maria—are coming over to my house this evening.

✓ Solutions

1. **(A)** My favorite food—pizza—is easily found at many restaurants.
Be consistent in using the same type of punctuation on either side of parenthetical phrases.

2. **(A)** The backpacking journey looks quite challenging—be prepared.
Have a dash toward the end of the sentence to indicate the change of thought.

3. **(A)** My science teacher—a former government researcher—is excellent at helping us see the applications of what we learn.
Surround the clarification about the science teacher's background with dashes.

4. **(A)** Based on the latest data, the geologists could only come to one conclusion—a volcanic eruption was imminent.
Have a dash before the clarification of what the conclusion was.

5. **(A)** My friends Sharon and Maria are coming over to my house this evening.
There is no need for dashes in this situation because there is no parenthetical phrase. Instead, "Maria" is part of the subject.

Apostrophes

Common Situations

Use an apostrophe (') *before* an *s* to show singular possession.

- One pet's dish
- A person's house
- Caitlin's shoes
- My car's steering wheel

Use an apostrophe *after* an *s* to show plural possession.

- Three pets' fence
- Seven cars' parking lot spaces
- Our books' shelf
- Three families' neighborhood

Note: It does not matter how many things are possessed/owned; it matters *how many owners* there are.

Less Common Situations

Use an apostrophe *before* an *s* to show possession if the word is already plural.

- The women's organization
- The children's playground

Use just one apostrophe if both of the nouns in a compound subject *jointly* own something.

- Pam and Andy's family (they share a family)
- The cat and dog's toys (they share the toys)

Use apostrophes after each of the nouns in a sequence if each noun *individually* possesses an item.

- Aliyah's and Olivia's report cards were each excellent. (Aliyah and Olivia have their own report cards.)
- My sister's and my brother's rooms are both messy. (The sister and brother individually have messy rooms.)

TIP

Another way to keep these rules straight is to realize that if you remove the apostrophe and what comes after it, you will get the original non-possessive word.

Note: Do not worry about apostrophe placement exceptions for names ending in s. The SAT will stick to widely agreed upon apostrophe rules.

For example:

Possessive Form	What to Remove	Original Word
Dog's	's	Dog
Friends'	'	Friends
Men's	's	Men

Apostrophes and Pronouns

Do use an apostrophe on pronoun contractions—ones that have a pronoun and verb together.

- It's a beautiful day outside. (same as "it is")
- They're coming over this evening. (same as "they are")
- You're doing well with your homework. (same as "you are")

Don't use an apostrophe with pronouns that show possession.

- The bicycle needs its tires inflated. (The tires belong to the bicycle.)
- Their clothes are now clean. (The clothes belong to the implicit people.)
- You should mind your manners at dinner. (The manners belong to you.)

Apostrophe Practice—select the better sentence out of the two options.

1. (A) One persons' trash is another person's treasure.
(B) One person's trash is another person's treasure.

2. (A) The teachers' are meeting to share their best lesson ideas.
(B) The teachers are meeting to share their best lesson ideas.

3. (A) The natural history museum's planetarium is extremely impressive.
(B) The natural history museums planetarium is extremely impressive.

4. (A) Whenever my relatives come over, we need to order extra food.
(B) Whenever my relatives' come over, we need to order extra food.

5. (A) Humpback whales love to swim in the open ocean.
(B) Humpback whales' love to swim in the open ocean.

6. (A) The Broadway show's sets are difficult to move.
(B) The Broadway show's set's are difficult to move.

7. (A) When the new coach helped the men's soccer team, he made significant adjustments to the lineup.
(B) When the new coach helped the mens' soccer team, he made significant adjustments to the lineup.

8. (A) As you read the joint paper by the scientists, note how Watson's and Crick's results match their hypothesis.
(B) As you read the joint paper by the scientists, note how Watson and Crick's results match their hypothesis.

9. (A) His backpack needs it's straps repaired.
(B) His backpack needs its straps repaired.

10. (A) The three farmers' fields encompassed over 500 acres.
(B) The three farmers fields encompassed over 500 acres.

✓ Solutions

1. **(B)** One person's trash is another person's treasure.
Since it is just one person who possesses the trash, have the apostrophe before the *s*.

2. **(B)** The teachers are meeting to share their best lesson ideas.
No apostrophe is needed since the teachers are not showing possession.

3. **(A)** The natural history museum's planetarium is extremely impressive.
The planetarium belongs to the singular museum.

4. **(A)** Whenever my relatives come over, we need to order extra food.
The relatives are doing the action of coming over, not possessing anything, so no apostrophe is needed.

5. **(A)** Humpback whales love to swim in the open ocean.
The whales are acting as a subject, not possessing anything, so no apostrophe is required.

6. **(A)** The Broadway show's sets are difficult to move.
The sets belong to the show; the sets do not possess anything.

7. **(A)** When the new coach helped the men's soccer team, he made significant adjustments to the lineup.
Since "men" is already plural, put the apostrophe before the *s*.

8. **(B)** As you read the joint paper by the scientists, note how Watson and Crick's results match their hypothesis.
Since Watson and Crick collectively own the results, just put an apostrophe before the *s* in the final name.

9. **(B)** His backpack needs its straps repaired.
Show possession with the pronoun "it" by *not* using the apostrophe.

10. **(A)** The three farmers' fields encompassed over 500 acres.
Three farmers collectively own the fields, so show possession by putting an apostrophe after the *s*.

Parentheses

Parentheses ( ) do not affect the grammar and meaning of the surrounding sentence.

Without Parentheses	With Parentheses
Once I finish the test, I will read my book for fun.	Once I finish the test (it should take about 30 minutes), I will read my book for fun.
Your next-door neighbor is really nice.	Your next-door neighbor (the one with the unusual mailbox) is really nice.
My teacher gave everyone the opportunity to earn extra credit after the difficult test.	My teacher gave everyone the opportunity to earn extra credit after the difficult test (only a handful of students took advantage of it).

In all the above examples, the parentheses do not affect the usage of the commas and periods that surround them.

Parentheses Practice—select the better sentence out of the two options.

1. (A) The large dog eats quite a bit of food each day (mainly food from a bag).
   (B) The large dog eats quite a bit of food each day (mainly food from a bag.)
2. (A) When you eat breakfast (considered the most important meal of the day,) you have energy for several hours.
   (B) When you eat breakfast (considered the most important meal of the day), you have energy for several hours.
3. (A) Cricket (once an Olympic game,) is one of my favorite sports.
   (B) Cricket (once an Olympic game) is one of my favorite sports.

✓ Solutions

1. **(A)** The large dog eats quite a bit of food each day (mainly food from a bag).
   Put the period outside of the parentheses since the parentheses will not affect the surrounding punctuation.
2. **(B)** When you eat breakfast (considered the most important meal of the day), you have energy for several hours.
   Have the comma outside of the parentheses.
3. **(B)** Cricket (once an Olympic game) is one of my favorite sports.
   There is no need for a comma within the parentheses since the parentheses already provide a needed pause.

Question Marks

<u>Do</u> use a question mark (?) at the end of a sentence that directly asks a question.

- Why did you bring that toy to school with you?
- What is he planning on doing in the future?
- "Who is knocking at the door?" my father asked.

<u>Don't</u> use a question mark if the sentence *indirectly* asks a question.

- I would like to find out who my teacher will be.
- He is excited to find out what happens next in the play.
- The article addresses the central question of whether nature or nurture ultimately has a greater impact.

Question Mark Practice—select the better sentence out of the two options.

1. (A) If you want to do well in class, be sure to ask your teacher questions?
   (B) If you want to do well in class, be sure to ask your teacher questions.
2. (A) Where is the nearest subway station.
   (B) Where is the nearest subway station?
3. (A) While many students are quiet in class, I prefer to ask my teacher what I need to know.
   (B) While many students are quiet in class, I prefer to ask my teacher what I need to know?

✓ Solutions

1. **(B)** If you want to do well in class, be sure to ask your teacher questions.
   This is an indirect question, so no question mark is needed.
2. **(B)** Where is the nearest subway station?
   This is a direct question, so use a question mark.
3. **(A)** While many students are quiet in class, I prefer to ask my teacher what I need to know.
   This is an indirect question, so no question mark is needed.

Punctuation Practice Passage

Take approximately six to seven minutes to complete this exercise if you are doing it timed.

An adaptation from Bird-Lore, *published in spring of 1916 for the Audubon Society, edited by Frank M. Chapman*

The migration of birds at Raleigh, N.C., during the spring of 1915 was so unusual that it is believed that a short (1) account, together with a list of the records, will be of interest to the readers of *Bird-Lore*. In considering the following (2) remarks: it may be well to bear in mind that records of the bird migration in this locality have been made each year for the past thirty-one years. Also, the amount of time spent in making observations during the past (3) season, is significant. Observations were typically made independently by each of the writers and on lands differing somewhat in general character. It is believed that (4) the great majority of species: were recorded on as near the actual date of their arrival as it would ordinarily be possible to obtain them.

1. (A) NO CHANGE
   (B) account, together with a list of the records will
   (C) account—together with a list of the records, will
   (D) account together with a list of the records; will
2. (A) NO CHANGE
   (B) remarks; it may
   (C) remarks, it may
   (D) remarks it may
3. (A) NO CHANGE
   (B) season is significant.
   (C) season is, significant.
   (D) season—is significant.
4. (A) NO CHANGE
   (B) the great majority of species were recorded
   (C) the great majority of species, were recorded
   (D) the great majority of species; were recorded

The most remarkable fact in connection with the season was the earlier **5** <u>migrant's,</u> greatly delayed arrival. This was probably due almost entirely to the unusual weather conditions that seemed to prevail throughout the South during March and early April, affecting the migration of these birds. March was abnormally **6** <u>cool; especially so during</u> the latter part of the month. Six new records were established for late departures of **7** <u>winter birds: Loggerhead Shrike,</u> Fox Sparrow, American Pipit, Brown Creeper, Song Sparrow, and White-throated Sparrow. Two former records were duplicated, and seven of the remaining fourteen species noted were from four to fourteen days later than the average. It is plain that species that normally leave before the sixth of April could have been delayed a few days by the severe weather of late March **8** <u>and early April; however, it is not</u> easy to understand how it could have affected, to any marked extent, the species that depart in late April and in May.

The migration at Raleigh was also characterized by an unusually great variety of species, including a number of very rare birds. The total number of species whose arrival was observed amounted to no less than sixty-eight **9** <u>in all which is the</u> largest number yet recorded at Raleigh during a single season. This fact can probably in no way be attributed to the abnormal weather conditions before **10** <u>mentioned (except possibly in the case of the Night Herons,) but rather</u> to the large amount of time spent in making observations. Additionally, the fact that two observers were in the field did not play so large a part in this as might be **11** <u>expected; as one of them</u> alone observed all but one of the sixty-eight species recorded.

5. (A) NO CHANGE
   (B) migrant's,
   (C) migrant
   (D) migrants'

6. (A) NO CHANGE
   (B) cool especially so during
   (C) cool, especially so during
   (D) cool. Especially so during

7. (A) NO CHANGE
   (B) winter birds Loggerhead Shrike,
   (C) winter birds, Loggerhead Shrike,
   (D) winter birds; Loggerhead Shrike,

8. (A) NO CHANGE
   (B) and early April; however it is not
   (C) and early April, however, it is not
   (D) and early April, however it is not

9. (A) NO CHANGE
   (B) in all; which is the
   (C) in all. Which is the
   (D) in all, which is the

10. (A) NO CHANGE
    (B) mentioned (except possibly in the case of the Night Herons), but rather
    (C) mentioned—except possibly in the case of the Night Herons, but rather
    (D) mentioned, except possibly in the case of the Night Herons—but rather

11. (A) NO CHANGE
    (B) expected as one of them
    (C) expected, as one of them
    (D) expected, as one, of them

✓ Solutions

1. **(A)** Surround the parenthetical phrase, "together with a list of the records," with commas. Choice (B) only begins the parenthetical phrase with a comma, but does not have one at the end. Choice (C) is inconsistent in how it starts and finishes the parenthetical punctuation. And (D) incorrectly uses a semicolon when no complete sentence follows it.
2. **(C)** Use a comma to separate the introductory phrase from the complete sentence that follows. A semicolon or colon will not work, as in choices (A) and (B), since there is not a complete sentence beforehand. No comma whatsoever, as in choice (D), would not allow for a needed pause.
3. **(B)** Do not separate the subject "the amount of time spent in making observations during the past season" from the verb "is." All the other options give an unnecessary pause.
4. **(B)** Do not separate the subject "the great majority of species" from the verb "were recorded." The other options incorrectly separate the subject from the verb.
5. **(D)** Based on the context, there are multiple birds that are migrating. So, show possession of the "arrival" by putting the apostrophe after migrants. It is not choice (A) or (B) since there are multiple migrants, and it is not choice (C) because this does not show possession.
6. **(C)** Use a comma to separate the complete sentence from the phrase that follows. It is not choices (A) or (D) because what follows is not a complete sentence. And it is not choice (B) because a brief pause is needed.
7. **(A)** Use a colon after a complete sentence to introduce the list that follows. Also, the list of birds clarifies what is meant by "winter birds" at the end of the first part of the sentence. The other options do not provide the break needed before the clarifying list.
8. **(A)** When a conjunctive adverb like "however" joins two complete sentences, it needs a semicolon before it and a comma after it. Choice **(A)** is the only option that does this.
9. **(D)** Use a comma to introduce the dependent clause that begins with "which." Choice (A) provides no pause at all, and choices (B) and (C) do not work since the phrase starting with "which" is not a complete sentence.
10. **(B)** This option correctly inserts parentheses such that they do not affect the surrounding grammar or punctuation. Choice (A) incorrectly puts the comma before the second parenthesis. Choices (C) and (D) inconsistently start and finish the parenthetical phrase—it is necessary to start and finish parenthetical phrases with the same type of punctuation.
11. **(C)** This option correctly separates the independent clause at the beginning of the sentence from the dependent clause at the end of the sentence. Choice (A) is incorrect since a complete sentence does not follow the semicolon. Choice (B) has insufficient pauses, while choice (D) has too many.

Sentence Structure and Organization

Parallelism

Even though the meaning of a sentence may be clear, unless it is written in a way that has stylistic consistency, it will not flow how it should. Have stylistic consistency by looking out for *parallel structure.*

Example 1

Incorrect: Two of my hobbies are riding bicycles and to watch movies.

Correct: Two of my hobbies are riding bicycles and **watching** movies.

Explanation: Maintain the same way of describing the hobbies so that the sentence has a parallel structure.

Example 2

Incorrect: Covered in mud, leaves, and in grass, he really needed a shower.

Correct: Covered in mud, leaves, and ~~**in**~~ grass, he really needed a shower.

Explanation: If all the items in the list started with "in," then it would be fine to maintain that phrasing. Since the "in" that goes with "mud" also goes with "leaves," it can also apply to "grass" so there is no need to have "in" again.

Example 3

As of 2021, the countries with the greatest number of Nobel prize winners are the United States (375), United Kingdom (131), and **3** Germany, 108.

3. Which choice completes the sentence with an example most similar to the ones already in the sentence?
   (A) NO CHANGE
   (B) Germany's 108.
   (C) Germany (108).
   (D) the 108 prizes of the Germans.

Explanation: The correct answer is **(C)**. The previous examples in the sentence have the structure of "country" followed by "(number of prizes)," and choice **(C)** is the only one that maintains this structure.

Parallelism Practice—select the better sentence out of the two options.

1. (A) Choose a teacher to write your letter of recommendation who knows you well, likes the work you have done, and has the time to do a good job.
   (B) Choose a teacher to write your letter of recommendation who knows you well, likes the work you have done, and time to do a good job.
2. (A) To win or losing is not really important—just enjoy the game.
   (B) Winning or losing is not really important—just enjoy the game.
3. (A) Neither the children nor the adults were ready to leave the amusement park.
   (B) Neither the children or those who were adults were ready to leave the amusement park.

4. (A) To get the most out of class, listen carefully, write detailed notes, and ask pointed questions.
(B) To get the most out of class, listen carefully, write detailed notes, and asking pointed questions.

5. (A) Dressed in tuxedos, ballgowns, and additionally in jewels, the celebrities were ready for the awards banquet.
(B) Dressed in tuxedos, ballgowns, and jewels, the celebrities were ready for the awards banquet.

6. (A) Having a diversified portfolio, including investments in domestic growth stocks and international items, is a sound financial strategy.
(B) Having a diversified portfolio, including investments in domestic growth stocks and international value stocks, is a sound financial strategy.

7. (A) Ben, a country music lover, and Kim, an appreciator of the musical genre of classical, surprisingly found a radio station they both liked.
(B) Ben, a country music lover, and Kim, a classical music lover, surprisingly found a radio station they both liked.

8. (A) Be sure to pack these items for the bus trip: delicious snacks, entertaining movies, and good books.
(B) Be sure to pack these items for the bus trip: delicious snacks, movies that you find entertaining, and good books.

9. (A) To clean his apartment, Henry vacuumed the floor and dusting the shelves.
(B) To clean his apartment, Henry vacuumed the floor and dusted the shelves.

10. (A) My brother, a football fan, and my sister, a baseball fan, both enjoy watching sports in autumn.
(B) My brother, a football fan, and my sister, who is a baseball fan, both enjoy watching sports in autumn.

✓ Solutions

1. **(A)** Choose a teacher to write your letter of recommendation who knows you well, likes the work you have done, and has the time to do a good job.
Use "has the" with the final item in the list since all the listed items begin with a verb.

2. **(B)** Winning or losing is not really important—just enjoy the game.
"Winning" and "losing" use the same phrasing.

3. **(A)** Neither the children nor the adults were ready to leave the amusement park.
"Neither" and "nor" go together, while "either" and "or" go together.

4. **(A)** To get the most out of class, listen carefully, write detailed notes, and ask pointed questions.
"Asking" is not parallel with the other verbs.

5. **(B)** Dressed in tuxedos, ballgowns, and jewels, the celebrities were ready for the awards banquet.
Using "additionally in" interrupts the parallel structure.

6. **(B)** Having a diversified portfolio, including investments in domestic growth stocks and international value stocks, is a sound financial strategy.
"International items" does not match the previous example of "domestic growth stocks."

7. **(B)** Ben, a country music lover, and Kim, a classical music lover, surprisingly found a radio station they both liked.
Simply using "lover" is sufficient and maintains the parallel structure.

8. **(A)** Be sure to pack these items for the bus trip: delicious snacks, entertaining movies, and good books.
Maintain the parallel listing structure of *adjective-noun* by saying "entertaining movies."

9. **(B)** To clean his apartment, Henry vacuumed the floor and dusted the shelves.
"Vacuumed" and "dusted" maintain a parallel style.

10. **(A)** My brother, a football fan, and my sister, a baseball fan, both enjoy watching sports in autumn.
Since the first parenthetical in the list does not have "who is," maintain that style for the next parenthetical.

Modifier Placement

Make sure sentences follow a logical order, with descriptions and subjects in a clear sequence. Be certain that the *literal* meaning matches up with the *intended* meaning.

› Example 1

Incorrect: After completing the long hike, a three-hour nap did Xavier take.

Correct: After completing the long hike, Xavier took a three-hour nap.

Explanation: The first sentence does not name the subject until the very end, making it difficult to follow. The second sentence makes it clear that Xaiver took the hike.

› Example 2

Incorrect: Once we left the stadium, traffic was directed.

Correct: Once we left the stadium, the police directed the traffic.

Explanation: The first sentence is vague as to who or what directed the traffic. The second sentence makes it clear that the police did so.

› Example 3

Incorrect: Your book will not become damaged, covered with a brown paper book cover.

Correct: Your book, covered with a brown paper book cover, will not become damaged.

Explanation: The description of the book—that it is covered with a brown paper book cover—should come after the book, as the second sentence does.

Modifier Placement Practice—select the better sentence out of the two options.

1. (A) I helped when dinner was over to clear the table.
(B) When dinner was over, I helped to clear the table.

2. (A) The deer encountered a bear eating grass in the meadow.
(B) While eating grass in the meadow, the deer encountered a bear.

3. (A) My friend Jordan, an art aficionado, loves to go to the latest museum openings.
(B) My friend Jordan loves to go to the latest museum openings, an art aficionado.

4. (A) Widely embraced as an ethical practice, recycling is required in many municipalities.
(B) Recycling is required in many municipalities, widely embraced as an ethical practice.

5. (A) The 1960s (a decade of much social upheaval) made my relatives the people they are today.
(B) The 1960s made my relatives the people (a decade of much social upheaval) they are today.

6. (A) My classmate is very generous when I forget my own, always shares his extra pencils and erasers with me.
(B) My classmate is very generous, since he always shares his extra pencils and erasers with me when I forget my own.

7. (A) Despite my reservations about going on the trip, I ended up having a wonderful time.
(B) I ended, despite my reservations about going on the trip, up having a wonderful time.

8. (A) Astrophysicists, a mysterious force in the universe, are excited to discover the true identity of dark energy.
(B) Astrophysicists are excited to discover the true identity of dark energy, a mysterious force in the universe.

9. (A) The diameter of a circle goes through the center of the circle, which is twice the circle's radius.
(B) The diameter of a circle, which is twice the circle's radius, goes through the center of the circle.

10. (A) Even though they were delicious, the habanero peppers were so spicy they hurt my eyes.
(B) The habanero peppers were so spicy they hurt my eyes, even though they were delicious.

✓ Solutions

1. **(B)** When dinner was over, I helped to clear the table.
This makes it clear that the narrator helped with clearing the table *after* dinner was over.
2. **(B)** While eating grass in the meadow, the deer encountered a bear.
This makes it clear that it is the deer that is eating grass, not the bear.
3. **(A)** My friend Jordan, an art aficionado, loves to go to the latest museum openings.
Jordan, not the museum openings, is the art aficionado (someone who appreciates art).
4. **(A)** Widely embraced as an ethical practice, recycling is required in many municipalities.
The ethical practice is recycling, not municipalities.

5. **(A)** The 1960s (a decade of much social upheaval) made my relatives the people they are today.
The 1960s, not the people, were the decade of much social upheaval.
6. **(B)** My classmate is very generous, since he always shares his extra pencils and erasers with me when I forget my own.
This sentence makes sense, putting the reason the classmate is generous immediately after stating that he is generous, and making the subject "he" clear in the later part of the sentence.
7. **(A)** Despite my reservations about going on the trip, I ended up having a wonderful time.
The other option breaks up the phrase "I ended up," making the sentence confusing.
8. **(B)** Astrophysicists are excited to discover the true identity of dark energy, a mysterious force in the universe.
Dark energy, not astrophysicists, can logically be described as a mysterious force in the universe.
9. **(B)** The diameter of a circle, which is twice the circle's radius, goes through the center of the circle.
This makes it clear that the diameter is twice the circle's radius, not that the circle is twice its own radius.
10. **(A)** Even though they were delicious, the habanero peppers were so spicy they hurt my eyes.
The habanero peppers were delicious, not the narrator's eyes.

Logical Comparisons

When making comparisons, be sure that the things being compared match one another in their type and number. As with other sentence structure and organization ideas, be sure that the *intended* meaning corresponds to the *literal* meaning.

Example 1

Incorrect: The salaries at the first business are comparable to the other business.

Correct: The salaries at the first business are comparable to **those of** the other business.

Explanation: The salaries, not the businesses, are what are being compared. Putting "those of" in the second part of the sentence makes this clear.

Example 2

Incorrect: Pollen affects me the same way that ragweed.

Correct: Pollen affects me the same way that ragweed **does**.

Explanation: The ways that pollen and ragweed affect the narrator are what are being compared. Without putting "does" at the end, the sentence would compare "pollen affects" to the noun "ragweed."

Logical Comparisons Practice—select the better sentence out of the two options.

1. (A) The downtown park in my city is better than any park.
(B) The downtown park in my city is better than any other park.

2. (A) Your assignment is better than him.
   (B) Your assignment is better than his.
3. (A) The principal at my middle school was tougher than the one at my elementary school.
   (B) The principal at my middle school was tougher than my elementary school.
4. (A) I hope that my job application is better than the other applicants.
   (B) I hope that my job application is better than the other applicants'.
5. (A) Nurse practitioners provide many of the same treatments that doctors.
   (B) Nurse practitioners provide many of the same treatments that doctors provide.
6. (A) I was disappointed to learn that students who did less work in the class earned better grades than students who put in more effort.

   (B) I was disappointed to learn that students who did less work in the class earned better grades than students of effort.
7. (A) Relative to the collection of my local town's art museum, that of the Louvre is far more impressive.

   (B) Relative to the collection of my local town's art museum, the Louvre is far more impressive.
8. (A) Algebra is better understood as a study of mathematical principles than simply studying letters.

   (B) Algebra is better understood as a study of mathematical principles than simply a study of letters.
9. (A) A general is typically more experienced than a lieutenant.
   (B) A general is typically more experienced than a lieutenant does.
10. (A) I find walking far easier than running.
    (B) I find walking far easier than the times in which I run.

✓ Solutions

1. **(B)** The downtown park in my city is better than any other park.
   Without the "other," the sentence would be comparing the downtown park to itself.
2. **(B)** Your assignment is better than his.
   Compare the assignment to another assignment, not to a person.
3. **(A)** The principal at my middle school was tougher than the one at my elementary school.
   Compare the principal to another principal, not to a school.
4. **(B)** I hope that my job application is better than the other applicants'.
   Using the apostrophe at the end of "applicants" makes the word a substitute for the "applications of other applicants," giving us a logical comparison.
5. **(B)** Nurse practitioners provide many of the same treatments that doctors provide.
   Compare the providing of the nurse practitioners to the providing of the doctors, not the doctors themselves.
6. **(A)** I was disappointed to learn that students who did less work in the class earned better grades than students who put in more effort.
   Keep the phrasing of "who did less work" consistent by using the verb "put in."

7. **(A)** Relative to the collection of my local town's art museum, that of the Louvre is far more impressive.
   "That of" provides a stand-in for the collection of the Louvre, so that you are comparing a collection of one museum to the collection of the other.
8. **(B)** Algebra is better understood as a study of mathematical principles than simply a study of letters.
   "A study of" is consistent with the earlier phrasing, not "studying."
9. **(A)** A general is typically more experienced than a lieutenant.
   The general is described with the adjective "experienced," and there is no need to use a verb like "does."
10. **(A)** I find walking far easier than running.
    This comparison concisely maintains the style, ending in "ing." The other option is overly wordy and confusing.

Sentence Combinations

The SAT Writing and Language has questions that ask you to effectively combine two sentences, giving the combined sentences appropriate punctuation, transitions, and word choice.

Example:

When Stanley applied for the new position at the company, he provided three professional **5** references. The references verified his previous employment history.

5. Which choice most effectively combines the sentences at the underlined portion?
   (A) references; and these references
   (B) references who
   (C) references, and these people
   (D) references: references are the persons who

The correct answer is **(B)**. Saying "references who" most concisely joins these two sentences while avoiding unneeded repetition. Choice (A) incorrectly uses the semicolon, since a semicolon must have two complete sentences on either side. Choices (C) and (D) are overly wordy, since there is no need to mention the people or references again.

Sentence Combinations Practice—select the best choice out of the four options.

1 Coaches who recruit top athletes to their schools are able to build winning programs. This enables them to recruit even more top athletes.

1. Which choice most effectively combines the sentences at the underlined portion?
   (A) programs; this fact is enables them
   (B) programs, this recruiting prowess enables them
   (C) programs, enabling them
   (D) programs; which enables them

Saving for your retirement can also help you start ❷ a business in the future. Starting a business in the future is easier if you have assets you can use as collateral.

While eating at a Brazilian steakhouse, you are given a card ❸ with a green and red side. The green side informs the waiter that you would like more food, while the red side indicates that you do not want more food.

❹ The paper had so many errors. Therefore, the teacher advised the student, from scratch, to redo the paper.

2. Which choice most effectively combines the sentences at the underlined portion?
   (A) a business that in the future; this process that you would entail
   (B) a business in the future, which
   (C) a business in the future;
   (D) a business in the future, that idea of doing so
3. Which choice most effectively combines the sentences at the underlined portion?
   (A) with a green side and a side that is red; the green side instructs the waiter that you would like more food,
   (B) both a green and a red side: in contrast to the red side, the green side informs the waiter that you would like more food,
   (C) two different sides: first, the green side informs the waiter that you would like more food; second,
   (D) two sides: the green side informs the waiter that you would like more food,
4. Which choice most effectively combines the underlined sentences?
   (A) While the paper had so many errors, the teacher advocated the redoing of it from scratch by the student.
   (B) If the paper had so many errors, the student redoing it from scratch, the teacher advised.
   (C) Thus having so many errors in the paper, the student needed to redo the paper, from scratch, as the teacher advised.
   (D) Since the paper had so many errors, the teacher advised the student to redo the paper from scratch.

Salvador Dalí, a surrealist artist, painted works that commonly ❺ featured melting clocks. In Dalí's works, these clocks symbolize the power that time has over humanity.

❻ Advocates of year-round schooling argue that with no summer break, students would avoid a major obstacle to learning. They would no longer have the need to review forgotten material at the beginning of each school year.

❼ The popularity of arcade games diminished. This came as a result of home video game consoles being more widespread.

John Maynard Keynes, the founder of the Keynesian school of economics, argued that high unemployment was connected to a ❽ lack of economic demand. So that economic demand could be bolstered, Keynes advocated that governments should provide fiscal and monetary stimulus as needed to increase economic demand.

5. Which choice most effectively combines the sentences at the underlined portion?
   (A) featured melting clocks; these symbolize
   (B) featured melting clocks; that symbolizes
   (C) featured melting clocks, these artistic representations symbolize
   (D) featured melting clocks, these symbolize

6. Which choice most effectively combines the sentences at the underlined portion?
   (A) learning—the need
   (B) learning; they would successfully avoid the requirement
   (C) learning
   (D) learning, that is the need

7. Which choice most effectively combines the underlined sentences?
   (A) When the popularity of arcade games diminished, home video game consoles became more widespread as a result.
   (B) When home video game consoles became more popular; this caused the popularity of arcade games to diminish.
   (C) As home video game consoles became more widespread, the popularity of arcade games diminished.
   (D) While arcade games have diminished in popularity, home video game consoles, as a result of this, have become more widespread.

8. Which choice most effectively combines the sentences at the underlined portion?
   (A) lack of economic demand—so that economic demand could be bolstered and improved, Keynes advocated that
   (B) lack of economic demand; Keynes advocated that
   (C) lack of economic demand: in order for there to be an increased economic demand, Keynes advocated that
   (D) lack of economic demand; Keynes advocated that when confronted with a lack of economic demand,

While supersonic air transport would provide greatly decreased travel times between cities, the major obstacle to its use over land is **9** the sonic boom. The sonic boom is an extremely loud noise created by the shock wave an airplane makes when travelling faster than the speed of sound.

Aluminum, **10** which is now common, used to be a metal that was only used by the very wealthiest people in society. In a similar way, broadband internet access will someday be widely available to everyone, no matter what their social class may be.

9. Which choice most effectively combines the sentences at the underlined portion?
   (A) the sonic boom; the sonic boom is an extremely
   (B) the sonic boom, and the sonic boom is an extremely
   (C) the sonic boom; the sonic boom being an extremely
   (D) the sonic boom, which is an extremely

10. Which choice most effectively combines the underlined sentences?
    (A) The now-common aluminum, which used to be only used by the very wealthiest people in society, is similar to broadband internet access, which no matter what their social class may be, will be someday widely available to everyone.
    (B) Much like the now-common aluminum was a metal used only by the very wealthiest people in society, broadband internet access will someday be widely available to everyone, no matter their social class.
    (C) Similar to the now-common aluminum, broadband internet access, which was only used by the very wealthiest people in society, aluminum will someday be widely available to everyone, no matter what their social class might be.
    (D) Broadband internet access, much like the now-common aluminum, will, in a similar way, be widely available to, no matter the social class, everyone in society.

Solutions

1. **(C)** This option concisely joins the two sentences. Choices (A) and (B) are repetitive, and choice (D) incorrectly uses the semicolon, since there is no complete sentence after the semicolon.
2. **(B)** This option avoids repetition and joins the two sentences with "which," giving a dependent clause after the independent clause. Choices (A) and (D) insert unneeded words like "process" and "idea of doing so." Choice (C) would cause there to be a sentence fragment, with no subject present, after the semicolon.
3. **(D)** Since the sentence already states that there are two sides, referring to the red side and the green side is perfectly fine. Choices (A) and (B) unnecessarily repeat information about the two sides, and choice (C) unnecessarily inserts "first" and "second" to describe the sides.
4. **(D)** This option puts the words in a logical sequence. Choice (A) uses the passive voice, i.e., "redoing it . . . by the student." Choice (B) places the phrase "the student redoing it from scratch" too early in the sentence for it to make sense. Choice (C) incorrectly breaks up the phrase "redo from scratch."
5. **(A)** This option correctly uses a semicolon to separate two independent clauses and correctly uses the plural "these" in reference to the plural "clocks." Choice (B) uses the singular "that," and choice (C) uses the wordy language "artistic representations." Choice (D) has a comma splice.
6. **(A)** This option uses a dash before a clarification of what the educational obstacle is. Choice (B) is too wordy, choice (C) has no connection to the phrase that follows, and choice (D) incorrectly uses "that" when "which" would be appropriate after a comma.
7. **(C)** This option logically states the cause-and-effect relationship between the increase in home game consoles and the decrease in arcade game popularity. Choice (A) puts the cause-and-effect relationship backwards. Choice (B) has a sentence fragment before the semicolon. And choice (D) places the phrase "as a result of this" in an awkward spot.
8. **(B)** This option does not restate "economic demand," which is already clear from elsewhere in the sentence, especially where it states that the governments will provide stimulus "as needed." The other options all unnecessarily repeat the phrase "economic demand" in varying ways.
9. **(D)** This option concisely joins the two parts of the sentence without unneeded repetition. The other options all restate "the sonic boom."
10. **(B)** This option makes it clear that the situations between aluminum and broadband internet access are analogous. Choice (A) uses the awkward phrasing "which no matter what their social class may be" immediately after internet access, which does not make sense. Choice (C) mentions aluminum again later in the sentence, making for an illogical meaning. And choice (D) has awkward and abrupt pauses, in particular by placing "no matter the social class" before "everyone in society."

Sentence Structure and Organization Practice Passage

Take approximately nine minutes to complete this exercise if you are doing it timed.

An adaptation from Agriculture *(No. 2) as printed in* The Economist.

❶ A chemical investigation of the soil and subsoil will frequently provide the most useful indications of the value of land. It may be laid down as an axiom that fertile soil must contain all the chemical ingredients that a plant can only obtain from the soil, and chemistry ought to be able to inform us of the ingredients that are wanting in unproductive soils. ❷ It also is able to inform us if any poisonous substance exists in the soil. Also, it can determine how the poisonous substance may be neutralized.

The Royal Agricultural Society say that chemistry is unable to explain the productivity of soils. But why is it unable? One reason is that everything required by the plant is present in the soil, yet the soil is either too wet ❸ or overly dry, too cohesive or too loose; thus, the plant does not flourish. Chemical analysis does not declare ❹ this. The reason for this is that it affords no information respecting the mechanical division in which substances

1. (A) NO CHANGE
   (B) Frequently providing the most useful indications of the value of land, soil and subsoil with a chemical investigation of them.
   (C) A chemical investigation, the most useful indications of the value of land, of the soil and subsoil.
   (D) The soil and subsoil will frequently provide the most useful indications of the value of land with a chemical investigation.

2. Which choice most effectively combines the underlined sentences?
   (A) While able to inform us if any poisonous substance exists in the soil: how may it be neutralized?
   (B) It is also able to inform us if any poisonous substance exists in the soil; how it may be neutralized.
   (C) It also is able to inform us if any poisonous substance exists in the soil and how it may be neutralized.
   (D) It is also able to inform us both if the poisonous substance can be neutralized and also whether any poisonous substance exists in the soil.

3. (A) NO CHANGE
   (B) or dry
   (C) or dryer
   (D) or too dry

4. Which choice most effectively combines the sentences as the underlined portion?
   (A) this, because the reason is that it affords no information
   (B) this, for it affords no information
   (C) this and it affords no information
   (D) this; however, it affords no information

exist in the soil. Again, the chemical analysis of soils, to be worth anything, must be conducted with more rigorous accuracy **5** <u>than those published by English writers.</u>

Chemistry, however, outsteps its province when it attempts to explain how vegetable productions are formed in the plants by chemical forces; for the recent discoveries of Schwann, Henle, **6** <u>and the person called Schleiden</u> prove that all the functions of the plant are performed by the means of simple vesicles and cells. Hence it may be stated that all the vegetable productions that are formed in the plant are caused by a series of vital actions through the agency of cells.

All the different tissues in vegetables are formed **7** <u>from a particular process. The process is that there are different transformations</u> that these cells undergo. Schwann showed that the formation of tissues in animals went through exactly the same progress, a fact that has been confirmed by microscopic observations. Thus vessels, glands, the brain, nerves, muscles, and even **8** <u>bones and teeth</u> are all formed from metamorphosed cells.

What are the implications of this discovery? **9** <u>If it is true, it obliges us to modify our notions of organization and life, and there can be little doubt.</u> It compels us to recognize that vegetables and animals are not simple beings, but composed of a greater or less number of individuals, of which thousands may exist in a

5. (A) NO CHANGE
   (B) than English writers.
   (C) than the others.
   (D) than the ones that are published by writers of an English background.

6. (A) NO CHANGE
   (B) and the discovery of Schleiden
   (C) and Schleiden's discocvery
   (D) and Schleiden

7. Which choice most effectively combines the underlined sentences at the underlined portion?
   (A) from an interesting process: this process is known as the one
   (B) from a process known as the different transformations
   (C) from the different transformations
   (D) from an interesting process; the transformations

8. Which choice provides a supporting example that is most similar to the examples already in the sentence?
   (A) NO CHANGE
   (B) feelings and thoughts
   (C) oxygen and carbon
   (D) molecules and DNA

9. (A) NO CHANGE
   (B) If it is true it obliges us to modify, and there can be little doubt, our notions of organization and life.
   (C) If it is true, it obliges us to modify our notions, and there can be little doubt, of organization and life.
   (D) If it is true, and there can be little doubt, it obliges us to modify our notions of organization and life.

mass not larger than a grain of sand, each having a vital center and separate life **10** these are independent of the ones around it. Each of these individuals, or organized cells, should be regarded as a living being, which has its particular vital center of absorption, assimilation, and growth, and which continues to vegetate, to increase, and **11** to undergoing transformations as if it were an isolated individual. At all events, a knowledge of the existence of the cell-life of plants will explain several phenomena respecting the vegetation, growth, and ripening of corn, and may hereafter lead to some valuable practical results.

10. (A) NO CHANGE
    (B) independent of those around it.
    (C) independent of them.
    (D) these are independent of them.

11. (A) NO CHANGE
    (B) undergoing
    (C) also to undergo
    (D) to undergo

✓ Solutions

1. **(A)** This option puts the words in a logical sequence with the subject made clear at the beginning. Choice (B) is incorrect because it makes it seem that the soil is the item that provides the most useful indication of land. Choice (C) interrupts the phrase "A chemical investigation of the soil and subsoil." And choice (D) doesn't mention the chemical investigation until the very end.
2. **(C)** This option avoids repeating "poisonous substance," making the sentence more concise. Choice (A) is incorrect because there is not a complete sentence before the colon. Choice (B) is incorrect because there is not a complete sentence after the semicolon. And choice (D) is incorrect because it is overly wordy.
3. **(D)** All of the other items in the list, "too wet," "too cohesive," and "too loose," all start with "too" before the adjective. Choice **(D)** is the only option that maintains this parallel structure.
4. **(B)** This option concisely joins the two sentences with an appropriate transition, "for," that shows a cause-and-effect relationship. Choice (A) is too wordy. Choices (C) and (D) do not have a correct transition to connect the parts of the sentence.
5. **(A)** This option makes a logical comparison with "chemical analysis of soils." Choices (B) and (C) do not match up with the most logical item to which this should be compared, and choice (D) is too wordy.
6. **(D)** This is the only option that is parallel to the other listed names in the sentence, "Schwann" and "Henle."
7. **(C)** Choice **(C)** concisely joins the two sentences, since a "transformation" is itself a process. The other options are all overly wordy.
8. **(A)** The other items listed in the sentence are all parts of the bodies of animals that are formed by cells. Therefore, "bones and teeth" would fit. The other options are not consistent with the previously listed items.
9. **(D)** This option logically places "and there can be little doubt" immediately after "true," which it modifies. The other options place this phrase in illogical and awkward spots.

10. **(B)** This option concisely makes a clear and logical comparison. Choice (A) is overly wordy, choice (C) is too vague, and choice (D) would lead to a comma splice.

11. **(D)** This is the only option that maintains the parallel structure of listing "to" before each word: "to vegetate, to increase, and to undergo."

Proper Wording

The SAT Writing and Language section will assess your skill in picking the appropriate word or phrase for a given situation. First, review these words that writers commonly confuse.

- **Accept**—*receive*; **Except**—*exclude*: I cannot accept the package except for when I am at home.
- **Advice** *(noun)—recommendation*; **Advise** *(verb)—to recommend*: She advised me to follow my best friend's advice.
- **Affect**—*usually a verb*; **Effect**—*usually a noun*: A major effect of the new grading system was how it affected student motivation.
- **Allude**—*indirectly refer to*; **Elude**—*escape from*: The diner alluded to how the mouse eluded the chef.
- **Amount**—*usually not countable*; **Number**—*usually countable*: The number of students gathered in the cafeteria caused a large amount of noise.
- **Beside**—*next to*; **Besides**—*in addition to*: Besides cleaning up the kitchen, please clean up the mess beside the dining room table.
- **Choose**—*present tense*; **Chose**—*past tense*: The last time I chose poorly when selecting a movie; this time I will let you choose.
- **Complement/Complementary**—*adding to or completing something*; **Compliment**—praise; **Complimentary**—*given free of charge*: I complimented the waiter for giving us a complimentary dessert. I told him that it really complemented the meal, making it feel complete.
- **Elicit**—*obtain or evoke*; **Illicit**—*illegal*: It is unlikely you will elicit the truth from someone who is involved in illicit activity.
- **Have** *(verb)—"I have an idea"*; **Of** *(preposition)—Do not say "I could of," say "I could have."* When you have an idea of the answer, enter it on the sheet.
- **I**—*subject of a sentence*; **Me**—*object of a sentence*: I have great rapport with my teacher; he likes having me as his student. When he involves my friends and me in class discussions, my friends and I always enjoy participating.
- **Its**—*possession*; **It's**—*it is*: It's a nice day, so we should go to the park and check out its trails. (Note that **its'** is *always* incorrect.)
- **Less/Much**—*usually not countable*; **Fewer/Many**—*usually countable*: When there are many pizzas, there is less hunger. When there are fewer pizzas, there is much hunger. (It is easy to count up the number of pizzas, but it is difficult to count hunger.)
- **Loose**—*does not fit tightly*; **Lose**—*has a loss*: You will lose your balance if your shoes are too loose.
- **Precede**—*come before*; **Proceed**—*go ahead*: Proceed to the questions after reviewing the preceding passage.
- **Principle**—*belief or rule*; **Principal**—*high-ranking person or school official*: The main principle every high school principal should follow is to treat all the students fairly.
- **Sight**—*seeing*; **Site**—*location*: If you have good sight, you will be able to find the site of the hidden treasure.
- **Than**—*used to compare*; **Then**—*used for time*: Back then, money was worth more than it is now.
- **There**—*physical place or statement of fact*; **They're**—*"they are"*; **Their**—possession: They're the nicest neighbors; there is no doubt you will have fun when you visit their home.

- **To**—*connecting preposition*; **Too**—*used to compare things ("too many") or mean "also" ("I like pizza too")*; **Two**—*number*: Two men went to the mall, but left because it was too busy.
- **Who**—*used as a subject (does the action), can substitute "I," "he," "she," or "they" to see if "who" works*; **Whom**—*used as an object (directly or indirectly receives the action), can substitute "me," "him," "her," or "them" to see if "whom" works*:

  Who is walking on the sidewalk? *You could say "He is walking on the sidewalk."*
  To whom are you talking? *You could say "I am talking to him."*
  Who is winning the race? *You could say "She is winning the race."*
  From whom did you receive that gift? *You could say "I received that gift from him."*

- **Whose**—*possession*; **Who's**—*"who is:"* Who's going to help me figure out whose project is the best?
- **Your**—*possession*; **You're**—*"you are"*: Your positive attitude is the reason you're doing so well in the game.

Next, review the following list and memorize any phrases with which you are unfamiliar. The more you read, the more comfortable you will be with the proper use of prepositional phrases and the more likely you will be able to intuitively select the proper choice.

adhere to
at a high rate
at the outset
at a disadvantage
at all costs
at any rate
at least
at length
at play
at the beginning
at the expense of
at times
at work
benefit from
by all means
by chance
by check
by definition
by force
by hand
by mistake
by no means
by process of
by request
by surprise
by way of
capable of
cheaper than
cling to
correlates with

for a change
for certain
for granted
for hire
for lack of
for the good of
for the sake of
from experience
from memory
in a hurry
in abundance
in addition to
in advance
in agony
in bulk
in character
in charge of
in code
in collaboration with
in command of
in common
in conclusion
in confidence
in confusion
in conjunction with
in connection with
in contact with
in contrast to
in fear of
in contrast with

in control of
in danger
in demand
in detail
in doubt
in effect
in error
in essence
in exchange for
in existence
in facing
in fact
in fairness
in favor of
in general
in good faith
in memory of
in mind
in moderation
in opposition to
in origin
in other words
in particular
in practice
in preparation for
in principle
in private
in public
in pursuit of
in quantity

in question
in reality
in recognition of
in relation to
in reply to
in reserve
in residence
in response to
in retrospect
in return
in search of
in secret
in self-defense
in silence
in suspense
in tears
in terms of
in the absence of
in the course of
in the event of
in the interests of
in the lead
in the making
in the mood for
in the wrong
in theory
in time for
in trouble
in tune with
in turmoil
in turn
in vain
in view of
in which
in whom
of the opinion
on the record
on a trip
on a regular basis
on account of
in the name of
on average
on behalf of
on board
on display
on file
on fire
on good terms
on hand
on impulse
on leave
on loan
on no account
on occasion
on order
on purpose
on reflection
on the move
out of context
out of duty
out of order
out of the question
to an extent
to date
to excess
to the location
to protect
to the satisfaction of
under consideration
under cover of
under discussion
under pressure
under strain
under stress
with regard to
within limits
within reason
without delay
without fail
without precedent
without question

Proper Tone and Meaning

The SAT will also test your skill in determining which word best matches the passage's tone and captures the author's intended meaning. This is an especially important skill for students who are heavily reliant on using a thesaurus when they write—even though words may have somewhat similar dictionary definitions, they may have very different practical uses.

Example 1

Incorrect: The author was abundant, writing many novels and short stories.

Correct: The author was **prolific**, writing many novels and short stories.

Explanation: While "abundant" and "prolific" are similar in meaning, both having to do with something being plentiful, "prolific" is used to describe a creator having produced quite a bit of something. Since the sentence focuses on an author's creations, "prolific" is more suitable.

Example 2

Incorrect: The chemist created a solution that gave off gross fumes.

Correct: The chemist created a solution that gave off **noxious** fumes.

Explanation: The SAT passages will almost always have a more formal tone. The word "gross" is overly informal, while "noxious" is a more suitable word to express that the solution gave off fumes with a foul odor.

Proper Wording Practice—select the better sentence out of the two options.

1. (A) I hope they find what their missing.
(B) I hope they find what they're missing.

2. (A) Increased sleep will positively effect your attentiveness while awake.
(B) Increased sleep will positively affect your attentiveness while awake.

3. (A) When looking for professional help, be sure to find someone with an exemplary track record.
(B) When looking for professional help, be sure to find someone with a humdrum track record.

4. (A) When looking at the roof, its clear that it's shingles need to be repaired.
(B) When looking at the roof, it's clear that its shingles need to be repaired.

5. (A) It is important to eliminate the infectious patient from the other patients.
(B) It is important to isolate the infectious patient from the other patients.

6. (A) Good engineers are intimately familiar with the best processes to manufacturing.
(B) Good engineers are intimately familiar with the best processes for manufacturing.

7. (A) Be careful when you hike over the difficult terrain in the National Park.
(B) Be careful when you hike over the difficult spread in the National Park.

8. (A) To much worrying will lead too problems.
(B) Too much worrying will lead to problems.

9. (A) The car dealership upraised my trade-in at a reasonable value.
(B) The car dealership appraised my trade-in at a reasonable value.

10. (A) We went to the flea market in search of a bargain.
(B) We went to the flea market in search to a bargain.

11. (A) Moving the tree off the road will allow the traffic to precede.
(B) Moving the tree off the road will allow the traffic to proceed.

12. (A) Evidence against the accused is nothing short of conclusive; a conviction is assured.
(B) Evidence against the accused is nothing short of potent; a conviction is insured.

13. (A) Whomever addresses the letter needs to start with "to who it may concern."
(B) Whoever addresses the letter needs to start with "to whom it may concern."

14. (A) The scientific study demonstrated that an increase in the dosage strongly correlates with a decrease in illness.
(B) The scientific study demonstrated that an increase in the dosage strongly links on a decrease in illness.

15. (A) Take your friend's advice and apologize to your parents.
(B) Take your friend's advise and apologize to your parents.

16. (A) The attorney's reasoning in the courtroom was bogus, helping her convince the jury of her position.
(B) The attorney's reasoning in the courtroom was valid, helping her convince the jury of her position.

17. (A) Customers are prohibited from taking their own food into the movie theater.
(B) Customers are prohibitive from taking their own food into the movie theater.

18. (A) Increasing your doses of fruits and vegetables will lead to better health.
(B) Increasing your portions of fruits and vegetables will lead to better health.

19. (A) Good managers cling to the highest standards in their personal conduct.
(B) Good managers adhere to the highest standards in their personal conduct.

20. (A) If you cheat on a test, you are only hurting yourself.
(B) If you hoax on a test, you are only hurting yourself.

✓ Solutions

1. **(B)** I hope they find what they're missing.
It should be *they are*. "Their" shows possession.

2. **(B)** Increased sleep will positively affect your attentiveness while awake.
Use the verb "affect" instead of the noun "effect."

3. **(A)** When looking for professional help, be sure to find someone with an exemplary track record.
"Exemplary" is more formal in tone than the casual "humdrum."

4. **(B)** When looking at the roof, it's clear that its shingles need to be repaired.
"It's" stands for *it is*, and "its" shows possession.

5. **(B)** It is important to isolate the infectious patient from the other patients.
It makes sense to simply keep the infectious patient away from the other patients to prevent contagion; there is no need to "eliminate" the other patient.

6. **(B)** Good engineers are intimately familiar with the best processes for manufacturing.
"For" is the correct preposition to use in this situation.

7. **(A)** Be careful when you hike over the difficult terrain in the National Park.
"Terrain" more appropriately describes the land you would find in a park; "spread" could be used to describe the area of the land, but not so much the land itself.

8. **(B)** Too much worrying will lead to problems.
"Too" is used for comparisons, while "to" is a connecting preposition.

9. **(B)** The car dealership appraised my trade-in at a reasonable value.
"Appraise" means to assess the price of something, while "upraised" means to raise something to a higher level.

10. **(A)** We went to the flea market in search of a bargain.
"In search of" uses the correct preposition.

11. **(B)** Moving the tree off the road will allow the traffic to proceed.
"Proceed" means to move forward, while "precede" means to come before.

12. **(A)** Evidence against the accused is nothing short of "potent"; a conviction is assured. "Assure" means to convince someone, while "insure" means to provide money in case of a loss.

13. **(B)** Whoever addresses the letter needs to start with "to whom it may concern."
"Whoever" works because it is acting as a subject, and "to whom" works because "whom" is acting as an object.

14. **(A)** The scientific study demonstrated that an increase in the dosage strongly correlates with a decrease in illness.
"Correlates with" is an appropriate phrase, while "links on" does not use the right preposition.

15. **(A)** Take your friend's advice and apologize to your parents.
"Advice" is used as a noun, while "advise" is a verb.

16. **(B)** The attorney's reasoning in the courtroom was valid, helping her convince the jury of her position.
"Bogus" is an overly casual word, while "valid" is more formal.

17. **(A)** Customers are prohibited from taking their own food into the movie theater.
"Prohibited" appropriately would be a verb in this context, while "prohibitive" would be an adjective.

18. **(B)** Increasing your portions of fruits and vegetables will lead to better health.
"Portion" works to describe the amount of food you are consuming, while "dose" works better to describe the amount of medicine consumed.

19. **(B)** Good managers adhere to the highest standards in their personal conduct.
"Cling" has more of a negative connotation when used like this, while "adhere" would mean the managers uphold the highest standards.

20. **(A)** If you cheat on a test, you are only hurting yourself.
"Cheat" is used as a verb here, while "hoax" would be a noun.

Proper Wording Practice Passage

Take approximately six to seven minutes to complete this exercise if you are doing it timed.

House Plants and Humidity

House plants are often thought of as a curious hobby: something that older folks or recluses care for instead of pets. However, plants are not just an easy way to **1** past time. Besides giving residents something to do and something nice to look at, having a large number of house plants in a home can positively **2** affect the health of the residents by reducing the number of pollutants and microbes in the air (especially in well-sealed, modern buildings).

Newer buildings and buildings that have been renovated to be "green" are essentially sealed up. This causes the building's air to remain trapped so as **3** for minimize HVAC costs and maximize energy efficiency. Unfortunately, this sealing of buildings also traps inside anything that we might *want* to escape: carbon dioxide, dust, allergens, microbes, and other airborne particles that are **4** wicked to human health.

1. (A) NO CHANGE
(B) passed
(C) pass
(D) pest

2. (A) NO CHANGE
(B) effect
(C) infect
(D) defect

3. (A) NO CHANGE
(B) of minimizing
(C) for minimizing
(D) to minimize

4. (A) NO CHANGE
(B) cruel
(C) detrimental
(D) nefarious

While several studies had previously examined plant benefits in small sealed spaces, in 1996, two scientists, both **5** by the name of Wolverton, published a study that examined the impact of house plants on a well-sealed home. Using a plant-filled sun room as a test group and a plant-free bedroom as a control group, they **6** seized several three-month studies to investigate the effect of the plants on indoor air quality.

The Wolvertons knew that a moderate humidity level in the home would optimize the residents' health. Modern sealed buildings typically have low humidity, since water vapor from the outside cannot **7** undertake. The Wolvertons found that the plants did indeed increase humidity within the plant room. In addition, they increased the humidity and air quality in the room next door when the door was left open a majority of the time. This was **8** in contrast to the much drier bedroom that was devoid of vegetation. In addition, the plants helped to clear the air of the rooms of various microbes.

This means that for the average homeowner, having houseplants is more helpful to health **9** then having a humidifier. The plants increase the humidity, leading to microbe growth; the plants also clear the air of contaminants. A humidifier will increase a room's humidity without the added benefit of **10** clarification with harmful microbes. Consequently, as people are making interior decorating choices, they should consider the benefits that house plants offer. In addition to being green, they are more beautiful and healthy than the traditional humidifier. Having house plants is good **11** with the mental and physical health of humans, and for the health of the planet.

5. (A) NO CHANGE
(B) to
(C) for
(D) on

6. (A) NO CHANGE
(B) conducted
(C) escorted
(D) demeaned

7. (A) NO CHANGE
(B) enter.
(C) infest.
(D) swarm.

8. (A) NO CHANGE
(B) of contrast with
(C) to contrast in
(D) for contrasting of

9. (A) NO CHANGE
(B) than
(C) to
(D) of

10. (A) NO CHANGE
(B) clarity of
(C) clearance toward
(D) clearing away

11. (A) NO CHANGE
(B) in
(C) for
(D) on

✓ Solutions

1. **(C)** "Pass time" means to make the time go by. "Past" refers to a previous time, "passed" means "threw," and "pest" means "nuisance."
2. **(A)** "Affect" works since a verb is needed. "Effect" would be a noun in this case, and "infect" and "defect" have negative connotations.
3. **(D)** The infinitive "to minimize" is appropriate here since it goes along with "so as . . ." The other choices do not use an appropriate preposition.
4. **(C)** "Detrimental" means "harmful" in the sense that an inanimate air particle could be harmful. The other options could describe people and their intentions, but not lifeless air particles.
5. **(A)** "By the name of" means that the scientists have that name. The other options would not convey this correct meaning.
6. **(B)** A scientist "conducts" studies—the other options do not serve to describe a scientist running studies.
7. **(B)** Vapor could best be described as "entering" another room. "Seize" is used with physical touch, and "infest" and "swarm" are used to describe insects or other living things entering a place.
8. **(A)** "In contrast to" uses the correct prepositions; the other options do not use prepositional phrases that are acceptable.
9. **(B)** "Than" is used to make a comparison. "Then" is used to express time. "To" and "of" would not be used to make a comparison in this context.
10. **(D)** It is idiomatically correct to say that a humidifier would "clear away" harmful microbes; the other options use incorrect variations of "clear."
11. **(C)** The proper phrase to indicate that something is beneficial is "good for." The other options use incorrect prepositions.

Transitions

The SAT tests your proficiency with transitional words—words like "but," "also," and "because" that connect phrases and sentences together. An understanding of transitional words will ensure that your writing is well-organized. Here is a list of some of the most common transitional words you will encounter on the SAT:

General Meaning	Transitional Words
Additional Information	Also, and, besides, further, furthermore, in addition, what's more
Cause and Effect	As a result, because, consequently, therefore, thus, to that end
Clarification	At any rate, in other words, in fact
Comparison	Likewise, similarly, by the same token
Contrast	After all, alternately, although, but, by contrast, even though, however, instead, meanwhile, nevertheless, nonetheless, on the other hand, rather, still, whereas
Give an Example	For example, for instance
Obviously	Of course
Time Sequence	Eventually, finally, in the first place, next, ultimately
Typically	Traditionally

Example 1

Incorrect: The kitchen had virtually no food in it. Also, we managed to make dinner.

Correct: The kitchen had virtually no food in it. **Still**, we managed to make dinner.

Explanation: Even though the kitchen did not have much food, the group was still able to make dinner. Thus, a contrast is needed between the two sentences—"Still" works well. When working through transition questions, be certain to consider the surrounding context so you can determine the best logical relationship.

In the above example, you needed to look at the sentence before and after the transitional word. In some sentences, the transition is based just on what comes after the transitional word, like "Although I was excited to watch the movie, I had difficulty finding time to do so." Err on the side of considering a bit too much context just to be sure you fully understand what logical relationship is needed.

Example 2

When school begins in the fall, seniors often ask their past teachers to write letters of recommendation on their behalf. The best teachers are typically inundated with requests, and usually have to limit the number of letters they can write. ❷ Also, it is a good idea to ask teachers in the spring or summer for letters of recommendation so that the teachers have adequate time to do them.

2. Which choice provides the best transition from the previous sentences to the current sentence in this paragraph?
   (A) NO CHANGE
   (B) For instance,
   (C) Therefore,
   (D) Furthermore,

Explanation: The correct answer to this question is **(C)**, "Therefore." This is the only option that provides a cause-and-effect relationship between the first two sentences and the final sentence of the paragraph. A cause-and-effect relationship is necessary here since it is because good teachers are flooded with letter of recommendation requests that it is sensible to ask teachers earlier to write letters on your behalf.

Transitions Practice—select the better sentence(s) out of the two options.

1. (A) Even though I had plenty of sleep, I still felt tired.
   (B) Consequently I had plenty of sleep, I still felt tired.
2. (A) A part-time job during high school is a great way to make extra money. Furthermore, it can help you develop skills that will serve you well in college and in your career.
   (B) A part-time job during high school is a great way to make extra money. In contrast, it can help you develop skills that will serve you well in college and in your career.
3. (A) When making bread, first preheat the oven. Therefore, put the well-kneaded dough into the oven to bake.
   (B) When making bread, first preheat the oven. Next, put the well-kneaded dough into the oven to bake.
4. (A) The yard was completely covered with weeds. Nevertheless, the gardener happily tackled the weeding and turned the yard into a beautiful site.
   (B) The yard was completely covered with weeds. Also, the gardener happily tackled the weeding and turned the yard into a beautiful site.
5. (A) Majoring in two different areas may allow for a natural synergy between subjects. For instance, a business major with an engineering major could help you learn both how to make a product and how to market it.
   (B) Majoring in two different areas may allow for a natural synergy between subjects. Whereas a business major with an engineering major could help you learn both how to make a product and how to market it.
6. (A) He did not have a good reason to run for office, and, by the same token, he did not have a reason to avoid running.
   (B) He did not have a good reason to run for office, and, in the first place, he did not have a reason to avoid running.
7. (A) A perfect score would, of course, be preferable; thus, a 99 out of 100 is truly excellent.
   (B) A perfect score would, of course, be preferable; however, a 99 out of 100 is truly excellent.
8. (A) We did not do very well in the game; consequently, our coach made us run extra laps.
   (B) We did not do very well in the game; and our coach made us run extra laps.
9. (A) The roller coaster had an awesome first hill, and what's more, it had three incredible loops.
   (B) The roller coaster had an awesome first hill and despite this, it had three incredible loops.
10. (A) The wildlife sanctuary had elephants and rhinos. In contrast, it had zebra, giraffes, and water buffalo.
    (B) The wildlife sanctuary had elephants and rhinos. Further, it had zebra, giraffes, and water buffalo.

11. (A) His anger at his neighbor was understandable. Therefore, it was no justification for vandalism of his neighbor's house.
(B) His anger at his neighbor was understandable. However, it was no justification for vandalism of his neighbor's house.

12. (A) The world-renowned orchestra conductor is nonetheless an excellent violinist.
(B) The world-renowned orchestra conductor is likewise an excellent violinist.

13. (A) I did not eat breakfast. As a result, I was really hungry for lunch.
(B) I did not eat breakfast. Moreover, I was really hungry for lunch.

14. (A) Thanksgiving is, in other words, a day on which people eat quite a bit of food.
(B) Thanksgiving is traditionally a day on which people eat quite a bit of food.

15. (A) Her parents did not think she wanted to join the club. In fact, she was the first one to sign up for the club at the school fair.
(B) Her parents did not think she wanted to join the club. Typically, she was the first one to sign up for the club at the school fair.

16. (A) Best friends are forever; despite this, you will stay connected to your best friend over many decades and great distances.
(B) Best friends are forever; in other words, you will stay connected to your best friend over many decades and great distances.

17. (A) At first, the athlete resisted the advice of his coach. Ultimately, he took the coach's advice and improved immensely.
(B) Initially, the athlete resisted the advice of his coach. At first, he took the coach's advice and improved immensely.

18. (A) I am excited for the first day of school. On the other hand, I am worried about a pop quiz over the summer reading.
(B) I am excited for the first day of school. Consequently, I am worried about a pop quiz over the summer reading.

19. (A) We climbed up the mountain and still reached the summit.
(B) We climbed up the mountain and eventually reached the summit.

20. (A) The doctor said you should eat more fruits and vegetables. Therefore, you should come to the farmer's market to buy some healthy produce.
(B) The doctor said you should eat more fruits and vegetables. Whereas you should come to the farmer's market to buy some healthy produce.

✓ Solutions

1. **(A)** Even though I had plenty of sleep, I still felt tired.
"Even though" shows contrast between having plenty of sleep and still feeling tired.

2. **(A)** A part-time job during high school is a great way to make extra money. Furthermore, it can help you develop skills that will serve you well in college and in your career.
"Furthermore" makes sense since the idea of skill development would be an additional benefit of having a part-time job.

3. **(B)** When making bread, first preheat the oven. Next, put the well-kneaded dough into the oven to bake.
   "Next" demonstrates the sequence of events that one would find in a recipe.

4. **(A)** The yard was completely covered with weeds. Nevertheless, the gardener happily tackled the weeding and turned the yard into a beautiful site.
   "Nevertheless" shows a contrast between the fact that the yard was covered with weeds and the fact that the gardener could still make the yard into something beautiful.

5. **(A)** Majoring in two different areas may allow for a natural synergy between subjects. For instance, a business major with an engineering major could help you learn both how to make a product and how to market it.
   "For instance" is a logical way to join the two sentences, since the second sentence provides an example of how a double major could make sense.

6. **(A)** He did not have a good reason to run for office, and, by the same token, he did not have a reason to avoid running.
   "By the same token" means that the man both had a good reason to run for office *and* had a reason not to run.

7. **(B)** A perfect score would, of course, be preferable; however, a 99 out of 100 is truly excellent.
   "However" shows a contrast between the acknowledgement that a perfect score would be better, but that a 99 is still outstanding.

8. **(A)** We did not do very well in the game; consequently, our coach made us run extra laps.
   "Consequently" states the cause-and-effect relationship between not doing well in the game and the coach's decision to make the players run laps.

9. **(A)** The roller coaster had an awesome first hill, and what's more, it had three incredible loops.
   "What's more" shows that in addition to the awesome first hill, the roller coast had three incredible loops.

10. **(B)** The wildlife sanctuary had elephants and rhinos. Further, it had zebra, giraffes, and water buffalo.
    "Further" shows that along with the elephants and rhinos, the sanctuary also had other animals.

11. **(B)** His anger at his neighbor was understandable. However, it was no justification for vandalism of his neighbor's house.
    "However" shows that while the man was understandably angry at his neighbor, he had no good reason to vandalize his neighbor's home.

12. **(B)** The world-renowned orchestra conductor is likewise an excellent violinist.
    "Likewise" shows that the conductor is both excellent with the orchestra and with the piano.

13. **(A)** I did not eat breakfast. As a result, I was really hungry for lunch.
    "As a result" shows a direct cause-and-effect relationship between not eating breakfast and being hungry for lunch.

14. **(B)** Thanksgiving is traditionally a day on which people eat quite a bit of food.
    "In other words" does not make sense since the sentence is not rephrasing anything; "traditionally" works because the sentence says what typically happens on this holiday.

15. **(A)** Her parents did not think she wanted to join the club. In fact, she was the first one to sign up for the club at the school fair. "In fact" clarifies that despite what her parents thought, the daughter was actually interested in joining the club.

16. **(B)** Best friends are forever; in other words, you will stay connected to your best friend over many decades and great distances.
    The part of the sentence after the semicolon clarifies what is meant by the statement that "best friends are forever," so "in other words" is logical.

17. **(A)** At first, the athlete resisted the advice of his coach. Ultimately, he took the coach's advice and improved immensely.
    This sentence puts the sequence of events in a logical order, with the athlete initially resisting the coach's advice and eventually following it.

18. **(A)** I am excited for the first day of school. On the other hand, I am worried about a pop quiz over the summer reading.
    "On the other hand" suggests a contrast between the excitement of the student and the worry over a quiz.

19. **(B)** We climbed up the mountain and eventually reached the summit.
    This option shows a logical sequence of events with "eventually" used to mark the final part of the journey.

20. **(A)** The doctor said you should eat more fruits and vegetables. Therefore, you should come to the farmer's market to buy some healthy produce.
    "Therefore" shows a cause-and-effect relationship between the doctor's recommendation about how to eat and the action necessary to acquire the recommended foods.

Transitions Practice Passage

Take approximately nine minutes to complete this exercise if you are doing it timed.

Sunscreen

"Ladies and gentlemen of the class of '97, wear sunscreen. If I could only offer you one tip for the future, that would be it." **1** Whereas begins a well-known commencement speech; the speaker goes on to explain why his advice about careers and life goals may or may not be helpful to the students, but the advice to wear sunscreen will always be applicable. **2** By and large, he is correct. When used properly in everyday life, sunscreen can help people avoid sunburn, prevent aging, and escape skin cancer; it does this by mitigating the effects of sunlight on skin.

1. (A) NO CHANGE
   (B) Additionally
   (C) Thus
   (D) Also

2. Which choice provides the best transition from the previous sentences in the paragraph to the remainder of the paragraph?
   (A) NO CHANGE
   (B) Unquestionably,
   (C) On the other hand,
   (D) Unexpectedly,

Sunlight is different from the light that a person experiences from a fire or a light bulb. Sunlight is mostly UV light, which has a much shorter wavelength than the light we turn on when we use the bathroom in the middle of the night. **3** Meanwhile, if the earth's protective ozone layer didn't filter out much of the UV light, humans would risk their health just by going about their everyday lives during daylight hours. Astronauts in space have this issue and need special equipment to prevent serious injury from sun exposure. **4** When we are lucky most of the radiation doesn't reach us, enough still makes it to earth to do harm: anyone who has ever suffered a sunburn can attest to that. **5** Since the sun poses only a mild threat to most people, these rays can cause permanent sun damage to the skin and eyes if proper precautions are not taken.

Enter sunscreen. UV-A (which causes sunburn) and UV-B (which can cause permanent damage) can both be stopped by sunscreen, which generally has two different types of active ingredients. The first group is from inorganic materials, such as titanium dioxide or zinc oxide, which form a literal barrier to the sun. Old pictures of beach goers often show people with what looks like white paint smeared across their nose. **6** The antiquated practice of using sunscreen is no longer embraced, and rightly so. Today, these active ingredients have been manufactured to be significantly smaller and thus clear to avoid the paint look, but they function in the same way.

3. (A) NO CHANGE
   (B) Nonetheless,
   (C) Indeed,
   (D) As a result,

4. (A) NO CHANGE
   (B) While
   (C) Since
   (D) Thus

5. Which choice provides the best transition from the previous sentence to the current sentence?
   (A) NO CHANGE
   (B) Beyond the discomfort of a short-term sunburn,
   (C) While many people are unaware of the dangers of sun exposure,
   (D) Given the widespread prevalence of sun-related illness,

6. Which choice provides the best transition from the previous sentences in the paragraph to the sentence that follows?
   (A) NO CHANGE
   (B) Scientists have developed techniques to eliminate the use of these ingredients in sunscreen.
   (C) Today, beachgoers are more concerned about their personal aesthetics than proper sun protection.
   (D) This paint-like sunscreen physically prevents the sun from accessing the skin by reflecting it away.

❼ New sunscreens do away with the paint-like look found in the sunscreens of past generations. These are organic compounds that work in a slightly different way than the inorganic materials. ❽ Instead of simply reflecting the UV rays away from skin, they actively absorb the rays and then release the energy as heat.

Working together, these two classes of active ingredients can protect you from the damaging UV rays of the sun for some time. A good broad range sunscreen can, when used properly, prevent sunburn for hours. ❾ Despite this, if a product has a sun protection factor (SPF) of 30, that means that skin can be exposed for 30 times longer without burning than if no protection was used. ❿ However, when sweating or swimming, these products can be easily washed away. ⓫ Subsequently, a new application will not set the timer to zero: only time out of the sun will do that. What this means is that frequent applications (at least every two hours) and breaks from the sun are important.

7. Which choice provides the best transition from the previous paragraph?
   (A) NO CHANGE
   (B) People today find that they no longer wish to use sunscreens with inorganic materials.
   (C) Most sunscreens also have a second set of active ingredients.
   (D) To maximize dietary health, a shift from inorganic foods to organic foods is essential.

8. (A) NO CHANGE
   (B) In addition to
   (C) As a result of
   (D) For the purpose of

9. (A) NO CHANGE
   (B) For example,
   (C) In contrast,
   (D) Also,

10. (A) NO CHANGE
    (B) Consequently,
    (C) Likewise,
    (D) Due to this,

11. (A) NO CHANGE
    (B) Meanwhile,
    (C) To that end,
    (D) In addition,

✓ Solutions

1. **(C)** "Thus" is used to make the idiomatic phrase "Thus begins"; this phrase provides a logical transition between the quotation that started the speech and the clarification of the significance of the speech. It is not choice (A) because there is no contrast, and it is not choices (B) or (D) because this is not an additional piece of information, but a clarification.

2. **(A)** "By and large" means "for the most part"; the next sentence states that *if* sunscreen is used properly, *then* it will have positive effects. So, it is possible that if sunscreen is not properly applied to the skin, then it will fail to have positive effects. It is not choice (B) because the narrator qualifies the assertion, acknowledging that it is possible for the sunscreen to be ineffective. And it is not choices (C) or (D) because there is not a contrast.

3. **(C)** "Indeed" is used to introduce a further point that elaborates on the previous point made; in this case, "indeed" connects the previous sentence that states that sunlight is mostly UV light and the current sentence that underscores the potential danger from UV light to humans. It is not choices (A) or (B) because there is not a contrast, and it is not choice (D) because there is not a cause-and-effect relationship.

4. **(B)** "While" shows a contrast within the sentence between the acknowledgment that it is good we don't have more exposure to UV light and the statement that enough UV light reaches us to potentially cause harm.

5. **(B)** This statement provides the most logical connection between the previous sentence, which states that sunburns can be harmful, to a more severe statement in the current sentence, which states that permanent damage can result from too much sun exposure. Choice (A) does not align with the negative health consequences the narrator mentions. Choice (C) contradicts the previous sentence, since the narrator suggests that familiarity with sunburn is widespread. And choice (D) is not supported by the conditional nature of the statement (emphasizing a possibility rather than a certain outcome) in the current sentence.

6. **(D)** This option elaborates on the previous sentence, which asserts that older sunscreen resembled paint, and connects it to the next sentence, which asserts that the paint look is no longer prevalent in modern sunscreen. It is not choice (A) because the practice of sunscreen is different today, not abandoned. It is not choice (B) because the following sentence states that the active ingredients have been made smaller, not eliminated. And it is not choice (C) because the next sentence does not suggest that there has been a deemphasis in the use of sunscreen.

7. **(C)** The previous paragraph refers to "the first group" of "inorganic materials," so the current paragraph should refer to a second group of ingredients to continue this line of argument. None of the other options mentions a second set of ingredients, and so would not provide a logical transition.

8. **(A)** This is the only option that provides a contrast between "simply reflecting the UV rays" and "actively absorb the rays." Choice (B) provides an additional point, choice (C) provides a cause-and-effect relationship, and choice (D) provides an elaboration.

9. **(B)** "For example" is appropriate since the current sentence provides an example of what makes a high quality sunscreen. It is not choices (A) or (C) because there is not contrast, and it is not choice (D) because the current sentence provides an example, not simply an extra point.

10. **(A)** "However" gives a needed contrast between a discussion of what makes for a high-quality sunscreen and a statement of how the sunscreen can be improperly used, rendering it ineffective. It is not choices (B) or (D) because there is not a contrast, and it is not choice (C) because the current statement is not similar to the previous statement.

11. **(D)** This sentence provides an additional explanation that helps the reader understand how sunscreen is not a perfect solution in and of itself—responsible behavior, like taking breaks from the sun, is essential to sun safety. It is not choice (A) because this is not a subsequent, or next, event. It is not choice (B) because the previous and current sentences do not contrast with one another. And it is not choice (C) because the current sentence is not simply elaborating on the previous sentence, but providing a new point.

Organization

To be an effective writer, you must be able to have well-organized sentences and paragraphs. The SAT Writing and Language section will assess your skill in determining effective paragraph introductions and conclusions, as well as proper arrangement of sentences and paragraphs. To perform well on these types of questions, focus on the meaning of what you are considering and what will provide a logical argument.

Example 1: Setting Up Information

Consumers are increasingly conscientious about generating excess waste that will simply sit in a landfill. **1** While some consumers are not environmentally conscientious, coffee pod manufacturers provide consumers with prepaid bags to return used coffee pods so they may be recycled.

1. Which choice most effectively sets up the information that follows in the sentence?
   (A) NO CHANGE
   (B) In order to meet the demand to minimize waste,
   (C) Since coffee is a popular beverage among commuters,
   (D) Although coffee is not an environmentally friendly beverage,

Explanation: Paraphrase what comes before the underlined portion and what comes after the underlined portion to think about what phrase would best set up the second sentence. The correct answer is **(B)**—it connects the previous sentence that outlines the increasing consumer demand for environmentally responsible choices to the current sentence that shows a way that coffee pod manufacturers are giving consumers a way to minimize excess waste. Choice (A) contradicts the previous sentence's statement about consumers' increased environmental conscientiousness. Choice (C) focuses on the preferences of commuters, which does not connect to the surrounding information. And choice (D) is not supported by what follows in the sentence, where there is a suggestion about how coffee pods can indeed be used responsibly.

Practice

Every liquid has a vapor pressure, which is the amount of pressure the liquid exerts on the environment at a given temperature. The temperature in the liquid determines how fast molecules in the liquid are moving. In fact, temperature is simply a measure of how fast the molecules of a substance are moving on average. **5** Temperature can be measured in both Celsius and Fahrenheit, which is why liquid evaporates more quickly and eventually boils at high temperatures.

5. Which choice most effectively sets up the information that follows in the sentence?
   (A) NO CHANGE
   (B) Molecules are invisible to the naked eye,
   (C) Faster molecules are more likely to escape,
   (D) Boiling points are lower when at higher altitudes,

Explanation: The correct answer is **(C)**, since mentioning the escape of faster molecules would logically connect to the evaporation of liquids. It is not choice (A) because the paragraph is not focused on the units of temperature measurement. Choice (B) provides an irrelevant detail. And choice (D) does not make a connection to the relationship between temperature and molecular behavior, focusing instead on the relationship between altitude and boiling point.

Example 2: Sentence Placement

{1} Essays are a key component of your college applications. {2} Doing so will allow you plenty of time to brainstorm ideas that will make for interesting essay topics. {3} Instead of procrastinating on coming up with a topics, begin thinking about what you will write several weeks ahead of the application deadline. {4} If you have difficulty determining what to write, talk to you friends and family about what stories about your background would be most intriguing to an admissions evaluator. ❽

8. To make this paragraph most logical, sentence 2 should be placed
   (A) where it is now.
   (B) before sentence 1.
   (C) after sentence 3.
   (D) after sentence 4.

Explanation: On placement questions like these, take your time and look at how placing a sentence in a particular spot will connect to what comes before and after. The correct answer is **(C)** because sentence 3 encourages the reader to begin the brainstorming process early, and sentence 2 elaborates on why that would be a good idea. The "Doing so" in sentence 2 would refer to taking several weeks to begin thinking about essay topics. The other potential placements would make the "Doing so" in sentence 2 unclear.

Practice

{1} Free association is a process in which the patient freely expresses their thoughts, while the therapist analyzes those thoughts to determine what in the patient's childhood caused them to feel the way they currently do. {2} The therapist actively engages in conversation with a patient to pinpoint a childhood experience that may have had a serious effect. {3} Many therapists use this technique today to help patients recover from anxiety and depression. {4} One of the most important components of Sigmund Freud's approach to psychoanalysis is a technique called free association. ❼

7. To make this paragraph most logical, sentence 4 should be placed
   (A) where it is now.
   (B) before sentence 1.
   (C) before sentence 2.
   (D) before sentence 3.

Explanation: The correct answer is **(B)**. Sentence 4 provides an introduction to the paragraph, putting the subject of "free association" in a greater historical context. Sentence 1 would then immediately elaborate on what free association is. Putting the sentence in any of the other spots would not allow it to provide the needed introduction.

Example 3: Introductions

3 It is clear that textbooks are far superior to computer tablets when it comes to effective student learning. Computer tablets take up less space, so students can have all their school materials in a handheld device instead of a heavy backpack. Tablets also provide more interactive multimedia—graphics, videos, and quizzes—than a paper textbook can provide. Textbooks do, however, have some potential advantages over tablets. Students will be less likely to be distracted by internet surfing while reading a textbook. Also, many students like being able to highlight and make notes in the margins of textbooks. Schools should carefully weigh the benefits and drawbacks of textbooks and tablets when determining whether textbooks should be replaced with tablets.

3. Which choice best introduces the topic of the paragraph?
   (A) NO CHANGE
   (B) Tablets are the wave of the future and should be universally embraced by students and educators.
   (C) Innovations in educational technology are creating a revolution in student learning.
   (D) Replacing school textbooks with computer tablets has several pros and cons.

Explanation: While many Writing and Language questions can be answered by simply considering the context of a single sentence, on questions like these, it is critical to consider the entirety of the paragraph. The paragraph presents arguments for and against textbooks and tablets. Choice **(D)** is correct because it comprehensively introduces what the paragraph as a whole discusses. The other options only introduce the tablet aspect of the paragraph, underscoring how it is important to not merely look at the sentences that immediately follow the introduction, but to consider everything the paragraph goes on to say.

Practice

9 It has been found that major life events rarely have the effect on happiness or unhappiness that is expected by the person who goes through them. For instance, it has been found that people who win the lottery are on average no happier than they were before winning the lottery. In the case of winning the lottery, there are also many examples of this event ruining the life of the winner in contrast to the expected boost to happiness. Luckily, this phenomenon also applies to events that people expect will be dreadful. Bad events are also less detrimental to one's happiness than one tends to expect. For instance, people that fall ill with chronic diseases tend to report similar levels of happiness years after the initial shock of getting the disease has passed.

9. Which choice best introduces the main idea of the paragraph?
   (A) NO CHANGE
   (B) A person who is fortunate enough to win the lottery is assured of a lifetime of financial security.
   (C) Upon entering adulthood, humans have the experience to accurately gauge how positive or negative a life event will be.
   (D) Those who win the lottery inevitably end up far worse than they would have been had they continued with the trajectory of their less financially prosperous lives.

Explanation: The correct answer is **(A)**. The paragraph as a whole discusses how for both positive and negative life events, people are often unable to accurately predict the emotional impact that will result. Choice (B) is contradicted later in the paragraph, when the author states that some people's lives are ruined with this financial windfall. Choice (C) is contradicted by the paragraph's argument that people are in fact unable to accurately predict the emotional impact of certain life events. And choice (D) is overly definitive in stating the inevitability of negative outcomes from winning the lottery.

Example 4: Conclusions

When children learn to read, a whole world of incredible stories opens up to them. They realize that the greater detail found in a novel typically far exceeds the superficial presentation in a movie or television show. Unfortunately, as many children turn into teenagers, their love of reading often fades. Instead of reading for pleasure, teenagers find themselves having to read assigned texts for school. To remedy this problem, schools should allow students as much freedom as possible when selecting reading materials. **4** Doing so will help teenage students recapture the love of reading they had as children.

4. Which choice provides the most effective conclusion to the paragraph?
   - (A) NO CHANGE
   - (B) Schools must ensure that students read the necessary textbooks for workplace success.
   - (C) When teachers have the freedom to choose what subjects they cover, they will focus on areas where they have more background knowledge, making for much more effective instruction.
   - (D) Reading materials should be carefully aligned with national content standards.

Explanation: Consider the entirety of the paragraph before making a decision. The paragraph as a whole argues that while young kids thoroughly enjoy reading, teenagers often lose that love of reading since reading is more of a chore than something they choose to do. To effectively conclude the paragraph, choice **(A)** is the best option—it ties the later part of the paragraph back to the initial part, arguing that if teenagers can feel the sense of wonder they had as children when they read books, the love of reading may come back. Choices (B) and (D) incorrectly emphasize the need to standardize what students read, instead of giving them more freedom. And choice (C) focuses on teacher choice in curriculum instead of student choice in reading material.

Practice

Why does water boil at 208 degrees Fahrenheit instead of 212 degrees Fahrenheit in Colorado? Colorado is at a higher altitude than most of the rest of the United States, which means that the air pressure is lower in Colorado. The same effect can be noticed when one's ears pop from ascending in an airplane because as altitude increases, pressure decreases. This effect can become so extreme that on the summit of Mount Everest, water boils at 154 degrees Fahrenheit, while in space it boils while freezing at the same time. Water boils when its vapor pressure is equal to the pressure of its surrounding environment. The vapor pressure at a given temperature is a constant value that is independent of environmental pressure; so if the pressure drops while the temperature remains the same, the **6** water will turn from a liquid to a solid.

6. Which choice provides the most logical conclusion to the paragraph?
   (A) NO CHANGE
   (B) water will maintain its liquid form no matter how far the pressure drops.
   (C) water will change its form while the temperature changes.
   (D) water that was not previously boiling may start to do so.

Explanation: The correct answer is choice **(D)**. Based on the earlier discussion in the paragraph, if there is a decrease in air pressure because the altitude decreases, the boiling point of a liquid will also decrease. So, in this sentence, it is logical to state that if air pressure goes down while temperature is constant, some of the water could come to a boil. It is not choice (A) because the paragraph supports the idea that if pressure drops while temperature is constant, the liquid would turn into a gas, not into a solid. It is not choice (B) because earlier examples in the paragraph state that if the air pressure is lower because of higher altitudes, water will boil at a lower temperature. And it is not choice (C) because this contradicts the phrase that immediately precedes it in the sentence: "if the pressure drops while the temperature remains the same."

Organization Practice Passage

Take approximately nine minutes to complete this exercise if you are doing it timed.

What Should Become of Museum Artifacts?

The collection and preservation of ancient cultural artifacts is a topic that, on its surface, seems quite straightforward. Important pieces of human history should be kept, preserved, and displayed for all to see in museums and other display places so that all of humanity can learn from its past. **1** The consensus among scholars and government officials is that artifacts are best kept in museums.

1. Which choice best introduces the topic of the passage?
   (A) NO CHANGE
   (B) Tourist demand to see ancient artifacts outweighs the demands of those who would like to see artifacts returned to their countries of origin.
   (C) Unfortunately, due to a lack of funding and neglect, these artifacts are unlikely to survive for future generations to enjoy.
   (D) The reality, however, is far from this idealistic and straightforward approach.

{1} In capital cities across Europe, there are museums that host thousands of artifacts from around the world. {2} ❷ The British Museum in London is perhaps the best example. {3} The artifacts hosted there are at the center of a controversy around their path to Britain. {4} ❸ There can be no justification for not returning these artifacts to their native lands. {5} But scholars in lands far from the British Isles have been pointing out for a while now that many of the artifacts were not purchased, but taken during Britain's colonial past. {6} During a time when the British Empire covered huge portions of the world, artifacts from colonized lands were often dug up and shipped to the British Museum without the permission of the governments of the colonized lands. {7} ❹ Sculptures are among the most revered artifacts by museum-goers today.

{1} While it may seem obvious to a casual observer that these treasures should be returned to the places from which they originated, ❺ it is vital that the artifacts be returned to their native lands. {2} Supporters of the British Museum are quick to point out that many of the treasures housed there may never have been found or may not have been preserved if they hadn't been kept in a museum. {3} In addition, they are all displayed together so that people who wish to experience human history don't have to fly to all corners of the

2. The underlined sentence would most logically be placed
   (A) where it currently is.
   (B) after sentence 3.
   (C) after sentence 5.
   (D) after sentence 6.

3. Which choice most effectively sets up the point made in the next sentence?
   (A) NO CHANGE
   (B) The path many of these artifacts have taken remains a mystery.
   (C) Fortunately, there is widespread consensus on the best path forward.
   (D) Some were purchased, yes.

4. Which choice best concludes the paragraph?
   (A) NO CHANGE
   (B) Now, those countries understandably want their treasures back.
   (C) The disparity in wealth between Britain and its former colonies is substantial.
   (D) The British Empire once included lands ranging from Oceania to Africa to Asia.

5. Which choice best introduces the material the follows in the paragraph?
   (A) NO CHANGE
   (B) nothing can match the outstanding aesthetics of their displays in museums.
   (C) it is important to consider the work that was put into finding and saving those artifacts.
   (D) Britain is but one location with world-renowned museums.

world, but rather can view them easily and simply online, or by traveling to just one place: London. ❻

❼ <u>Despite all the positives of this preservation work, the pressure is mounting for museums all over Europe to return artifacts to their original lands:</u> the sarcophagi back to Egypt, the marble statues back to Greece, and Sumerian scrolls back to Iraq. While some archeologists worry that these relics will not be properly safeguarded if removed from the confines of the museum, a clear fact remains: artifacts may be human history, but they don't belong to us all. Rather, they belong to the places where they were found.

Some museum pieces have already been returned to their countries of origin. As precedents like these mount, more and more pieces will go back to where they belong. Some will survive, others may be lost forever. ❽ <u>Clearly, a melancholy future awaits those who value the preservation of ancient treasures.</u>

6. The writer wants to insert the following sentence:

   Artifacts that might otherwise have been lost to time, war, and incorrect storage are instead well preserved.

   To make the paragraph most logical, where should the sentence be placed?

   (A) Before sentence 1
   (B) Before sentence 2
   (C) Before sentence 3
   (D) After sentence 3

7. Which choice best introduces the material that follows in the paragraph?

   (A) NO CHANGE
   (B) The British Museum is packed with marvelous antiquities that any lover of history would thoroughly enjoy seeing in person:
   (C) World travelers are wise to see architectural treasures in their lands of origin, instead of in Great Britain:
   (D) When scholars assess the quality of ancient art pieces, they try to follow the criteria of previous evaluations so that consistency can be maintained:

8. Which choice provides the most effective conclusion for the passage?

   (A) NO CHANGE
   (B) We must hope that when new artistic treasures are unearthed, they are treated with more care than they have been up to this point in human history.
   (C) Ultimately, full compensation for the plundered artifacts must be a part of any international settlement.
   (D) We can only hope that both historical preservation and social justice will be served by these changes.

✓ Solutions

1. **(D)** The passage as a whole does not take a stand one way or the other on the issue of whether artifacts should be returned to their countries of origin. Instead, the passage presents both sides of the argument. It is not choices (A) or (B) because they favor keeping the artifacts in museums. And it is not choice (C) because it is overly pessimistic.

2. **(A)** It is necessary to keep sentence 2 in its current location because it introduces the location represented by "there" that is mentioned in sentence 3. If sentence 2 were placed in any of the other possible locations, sentence 3 would be illogical and unclear.

3. **(D)** This option introduces one side of the debate, acknowledging that some of the artifacts were purchased instead of stolen. This leads into the next sentence that points out that many of the artifacts were in fact stolen. Choice (A) is incorrect because it is too one-sided. Choice (B) doesn't work because the following sentence explains how many of the artifacts did come to be in museums. And it is not choice (C) because the passage goes on to show how there is not a clear consensus on the best path forward.

4. **(B)** The previous sentence, which outlines how the British Empire took artifacts without permission, would best lead into the sentence in choice **(B)**. The other options are all unrelated to the core focus of the paragraph, namely that many of the artifacts in European museums were taken from their native lands without permission.

5. **(C)** This paragraph considers an opposing view from the one expressed in the preceding paragraph; it focuses on the good aspects of historical artifacts being stored in museums. Choice **(C)** is the best option in terms of leading in to the discussion of the positive aspects of museum storage. Choice (A) is the opposite of the point of view expressed in this paragraph. Choice (B) incorrectly focuses on the aesthetics of museum displays instead of the difficult labor that went into the artifacts' preservation. And choice (D) provides an irrelevant aside.

6. **(C)** It is most logical to place this sentence before sentence 3 because it elaborates on the general assertion about how many museum treasures would not have survived. The other potential placements would not allow for this needed elaboration.

7. **(A)** No change is needed because this sentence transitions from the previous paragraph, which outlines the good aspects of museum preservation, to the current paragraph, which acknowledges the inevitability of many of these artifacts being returned to their lands of origin. In addition to not making this transition, the other options would be illogical in terms of what immediately follows in the sentence, with the mention of different artifacts going "back to" their lands of origin.

8. **(D)** This option underscores the two primary concerns of the narrator—acknowledging the need to return artifacts to their lands of origin and also expressing a hope that these transfers will not result in the artifacts' destruction. Choice (A) is overly pessimistic. Choice (B) is contradicted by the earlier discussion of the quality of museum preservation. And choice (C) is not mentioned elsewhere in the passage as something that the countries of the artifacts' origins are seeking—they seem to simply want the artifacts to be returned.

Passage and Paragraph Analysis

SAT Writing and Language will have a handful of questions that ask you to analyze the larger meaning and style of the passage. On questions like these, you will likely need to review more context than you typically do on other question types. You may need to analyze at least the paragraph the question is in, and perhaps scan through the passage as a whole to have sufficient information. Fortunately, since time management on the Writing and Language section is rarely a major concern, do not hesitate to take enough time to get a full sense of the context of the passage. Also, it can be worthwhile to come back to questions like these if you are able to gather further context while answering other questions in the passage.

Example 1: Accomplishing a Goal

Have you ever had a broken bone and required an X-ray? You have the scientist Marie Curie to thank for our understanding of the theory of radioactivity. Not only did she help the theoretical construct of radioactivity, she was able to successfully isolate radioactive isotopes to discover new elements. **1** While radiation has many good applications, the overuse of radiation can result in negative side effects for human health.

1. The writer wants a conclusion that places the paragraph's discussion within a larger historical context. Which choice best accomplishes this goal?
   - (A) NO CHANGE
   - (B) Curie was married to another scientist, Pierre, with whom she partnered in conducting research.
   - (C) After receiving an X-ray, patients are able to receive a much more accurate diagnosis from orthopedic surgeons.
   - (D) For her work, Curie is the only person to be awarded Nobel prizes in two different scientific fields.

Explanation: These questions do not focus on the grammar of the different selections, but on their meaning. Underline and circle the key words in the question to help you focus on the writer's goal. Then, consider the necessary context to arrive at your answer—you will typically need much more context than you often do to answer questions like these. The correct answer is **(D)**. The primary focus of the paragraph is on the scientific contributions of Marie Curie—choice (D) places this discussion in a larger historical context, with Curie having the significant status of being the only person to be awarded Nobel prizes in two different scientific fields. Choice (A) incorrectly focuses just on radiation, choice (B) does not provide a sufficiently large historical context, and choice (C) focuses too much on the medical aspects of X-rays.

Practice

In order to prepare students for the workplace, schools should enforce a dress code. In a place of business, employees will not be able to wear whatever they like, because it could be offensive to their fellow employees and to their customers. Similarly, regulating what students wear will ensure that teachers and other students are not offended by particular choices of outfits. ❼ <u>In addition to places of business, the military requires strict dress codes for soldiers.</u>

7. At this point, the narrator would like to acknowledge a potential objection to how the conclusion was reached. Which choice most effectively accomplishes this goal?
   (A) NO CHANGE
   (B) It is critical, however, that allowances be made for students to wear clothing that aligns with their religious and moral beliefs.
   (C) Businesses typically outline their expectations for dress code in their employee manuals.
   (D) While dress code is an important component of school policy, social media use regulations are also vital.

Explanation: The correct answer is choice **(B)**. To acknowledge a potential objection, consider a likely criticism of the author's argument and think about an effective response to that criticism. The critique that choice **(B)** addresses is that some students, due to their religious and moral beliefs, may not feel wearing a particular outfit is appropriate. So, by stating that allowances must be made for students in these situations, the writer would accomplish the goal of addressing this criticism. It is not choices (A) or (C) because these simply build upon the previous argument instead of considering an objection. And it is not choice (D) because it shifts the focus to a different topic: social media use.

Example 2: Developing Ideas

Learning a world language can help students in a number of ways. First, proficiency in another language will help students communicate with native speakers. For example, a doctor who is proficient in a patient's native language will be much more effective in understanding the patient's illness. Second, knowing a world language helps students understand other cultures. There are some cultural concepts that cannot be adequately expressed in English, so one's intellectual horizons will grow significantly with an understanding of new ideas. Third, understanding another language helps native English speakers better understand English. ❷ <u>Finally, students who are proficient in another language will be much more comfortable with international travel.</u>

2. Which choice best supports the point made in the previous sentence in a style consistent with the rest of the paragraph?
   (A) NO CHANGE
   (B) Among the most popular world languages to study are Spanish, Chinese, and French.
   (C) For instance, learning the grammatical terms in another language will help English speakers better understand English grammar.
   (D) Many world language teachers also advise clubs associated with their language, providing additional opportunities for enrichment.

Explanation: Focus on what the question is asking—you need a sentence that supports the point made in the previous sentence. Choice **(C)** best develops the idea that those who learn a world language will better understand the English language; it suggests that when you learn a world language, you have to learn the fundamentals of grammar, which would make your understanding of English much more solid. Choice (A) does not develop the idea from the previous sentence, but introduces a new idea. Choices (B) and (D) mention world language, but are not relevant to the focus of the paragraph—how learning world languages is beneficial.

Practice

The investor sold off some of her stock investments after having held them for a decade. ⓬ Among the stocks that she has in her portfolio are ones in banking, travel, and energy.

12. Which choice provides the most effective explanation for the action described in the previous sentence?
    (A) NO CHANGE
    (B) Stocks represent shares of different companies, giving investors a stake in the success or failure of these companies.
    (C) In addition to stocks, investors can put money into bonds, money market accounts, and real estate.
    (D) She felt that they had appreciated adequately and wanted to lock in some financial gains.

Explanation: Ask yourself why it would make sense for an investor to sell off some of her stocks. Choice **(D)** provides the best explanation out of any of the options—the investments had "appreciated," or gone up in value, and she wanted to sell them so that she could be sure to make profits off of her sales. The other options all provide information related to stocks and investing, but they fail to provide an explanation as to why she would have wanted to sell off some of her investments.

Example 3: Tone

Cover letters are a key component of any job application. A good cover letter explains the specific reasons why you are interested in an employer, and what about your background makes you an excellent fit for a position. A poor cover letter is generic—it is clearly not written for a particular employer, instead reading as though it were written for a number of different job applications.

Which choice helps maintain the tone and style of the passage?
(A) NO CHANGE
(B) nasty
(C) a dime a dozen
(D) ill-mannered

Explanation: A major component of good writing is to realize that it is not just *what* you say but *how* you say it. Being mindful of the tone and style will ensure that the emotional mood that the author conveys is consistent throughout an essay. The paragraph presented has a more formal style and serious tone. The only option that works is choice **(A)**, since it expresses the idea that a poor cover letter will not stand out—it will be "generic." Choice (C) also expresses this idea, but it is too casual. And choices (B) and (D) are overly negative given the objective tone of the paragraph.

Practice

Violent revolutions are commonly recognized as a way to overthrow unjust political regimes. Nonviolent protesters, however, can often be more effective in accomplishing their goals than violent protestors. Many important historical figures, like Mahatma Gandhi and Dr. Martin Luther King, Jr., used nonviolent protests to accomplish their goals for social reform. Through nonviolent means, like sit-ins, boycotts, and hunger strikes, protestors can (8) destroy the status quo in a way that underscores the moral strength of their position.

8. Which choice best maintains the tone established in the paragraph?
   (A) NO CHANGE
   (B) challenge
   (C) annihilate
   (D) crush

Explanation: As in most of the SAT Writing and Language passages you will encounter, the tone of this passage is formal and serious. The author is expressing how nonviolent protests can be an effective way of creating social change. Since the focus is on nonviolence, "challenge" in choice **(B)** would work since it does not have a connotation of violence. The other options all have a connotation of violence, making them inconsistent with the tone of the paragraph.

Analysis Practice Passage

Take approximately six minutes to complete this exercise if you are doing it timed.

For many groups, the fights for voting rights and representation in governmental matters are intertwined. (1) After the Civil War in the United States, there were great debates on how to extend the right to vote to newly freed slaves. Jeanette Rankin got her start as a suffragette in her home state of Montana. Montana was one of the first states to allow women the right to vote due, in part, to Rankin's efforts with the National American Woman Suffrage Association.

1. Which choice most effectively establishes the main idea of the passage?
   (A) NO CHANGE
   (B) The right to vote has been extended to U.S. citizens ages 18 years old and up.
   (C) Women's suffrage came after a multi-decade struggle to ratify the 19th Amendment to the U.S. Constitution.
   (D) The same was true for the first woman to serve in the United States House of Representatives.

❷ Indeed, Montana was far ahead of the curve and allowed women the vote years before the 19th Amendment made female suffrage a national right. The women of Montana responded by sending Rankin to congress in 1916. Rankin served one term, but was not reelected due to a change in Montana's policy that set up districts and made it difficult for her to ❸ gather support. However, she did run again much later and was elected again in 1941, allowing her to spread her legacy over two nonconsecutive terms. By the time of her second term, she was not the only woman in the House of Representatives.

Rankin is probably best known for voting against involvement in both world wars. History seemed to repeat itself for her as in her second term, a call for a war vote swept the nation following the Japanese attack on the U.S. naval base at Pearl Harbor. The vote for World War I had been slightly disputed with 55 representatives voting against going to war; Rankin received a lot of hate and disagreement for voting against it, but things were mostly ❹ fairly relaxed.

2. Which choice provides the most appropriate context for the discussion that follows in the paragraph?
   (A) NO CHANGE
   (B) Montana has one of the largest land areas of any state in the contiguous lower 48 states, and features many beautiful landscapes.
   (C) The constitutional amendment to legalize female suffrage was fully adopted by the entire United States in 1920.
   (D) The National American Woman Suffrage Association had chapters throughout many states in the United States and played a key role in fighting for women's rights.

3. Which choice best maintains the tone established in the passage?
   (A) NO CHANGE
   (B) find those who would obey.
   (C) crush her opposition.
   (D) win over fans.

4. Which choice is most consistent with the style used throughout the passage?
   (A) NO CHANGE
   (B) chilled out.
   (C) piped down.
   (D) civil.

Her World War II vote was different. The United States had been directly attacked. The entire nation seemed to support going to war. Certainly, her constituents did. **5** Rankin justifiably felt that a vote for the United States to enter the second World War was not only politically, but morally, appropriate. When the vote was taken, she was the only dissenter out of 389 representatives. Her vote was met with a chorus of boos and jeers.

This stance ostracized her in Congress. Her fellow congressmen and congresswomen would not talk to her and barely deigned to work with her. **6** The people of the state of Montana made it clear that they did not support her and did not want her as their representative. She chose not to run for reelection. Had she not been the first woman in Congress, she would likely have been forgotten by history. But the suffragette spirit that got her elected to Congress in the first place also cemented her place in history. She opened up the door for women to serve the United States in the highest political offices.

5. Which choice provides the most effective explanation for Rankin's action given the context in this paragraph?
   (A) NO CHANGE
   (B) World War II was the most violent and deadly conflict in human history, and Rankin wanted to be viewed by posterity as having chosen the winning side in this global war.
   (C) However, Rankin, as a woman, felt that since she could not go and fight and risk her life, she could not, in good conscience, send anyone else to do the same.
   (D) In contrast to the public feelings about World War I, public feelings about World War II were far more nuanced and complex.

6. The writer wants to reinforce the assertion made in the previous sentence. Which choice best accomplishes this goal?
   (A) NO CHANGE
   (B) Many of her fellow Montanans were highly supportive of her courageous stand for her beliefs.
   (C) While many in Montana did not support her position, those in Congress were far more enthusiastic in backing her vote.
   (D) Since she did not yet have the right to vote, such a protest was noted by members of the media for its sincerity and passion.

✓ Solutions

1. **(D)** For a question like this, you should look ahead to the remainder of the passage, at least reading the topic sentences of each paragraph to understand the ideas conveyed in the passage. The main idea of the passage is that Jeanette Rankin was a trailblazing figure who broke gender barriers and stood for her moral beliefs despite criticism. Choice **(D)** is the only option that aligns with this idea. The other choices all provide historical information that is not related to the main focus of the paragraph.

2. **(A)** The paragraph goes on to describe how Rankin was able to successfully run for congressional office in Montana and details her political biography. Choice **(A)** would best provide the context needed to understand how she was able to use the unique circumstances in Montana to advance her career. Choice (B) focuses more on the state of Montana than on Rankin's career. Choice (C) would not help us understand how Rankin was able to run for office, given that she went to Washington four years before women's suffrage was legalized on a national level. And choice (D) focuses on the National American Woman Suffrage Association instead of on Rankin's biography.

3. **(A)** Rankin is running for elected office, so she would want to "gather support." Choices (B) and (C) would be more appropriate for a dictatorship, not a democracy. And choice (D) would be more appropriate for a celebrity, not for a politician.

4. **(D)** The style of the passage is more formal and serious, so describing the reaction to Rankin's vote as "civil" would be most appropriate. The other options are all overly informal.

5. **(C)** Choice **(C)** provides a logical reason why Rankin did not want to vote to enter the second World War despite the feelings of many at the time—she felt it would be morally wrong to ask others to sacrifice their lives when she couldn't do the same. Choice (A) is inconsistent with the fact that she did not vote in favor of the war. Choice (B) is incorrect because Rankin's dilemma was not in picking a particular side, but whether she should require others to fight when she could not. And choice (D) is inconsistent with the stronger feelings people had about World War II based on the passage.

6. **(A)** Choice **(A)** best reinforces the assertion made in the previous sentence that Rankin's decision was not politically popular. The other options all suggest that her position was in fact politically popular and respected—these options would contradict rather than reinforce the assertion made in the previous sentence.

Graph Analysis

There are typically two graph analysis questions on the SAT Writing and Language section. Unlike many of the other questions that ask you about grammar or writing techniques, these questions ask you to analyze the evidence in the graph. How can you be successful on these types of questions?

- **Take time to understand the organization of the graph.** A variety of graph types could be presented—line graphs, bar graphs, tables, circle graphs, and more. Give yourself time to analyze the labels and headings of the graph and any trends in the data.
- **Avoid careless errors by reading the choices carefully.** The answer choices will often have very subtle differences in the numbers presented—it is very easy to rush and make careless errors. Instead, slow down and be sure your choice fully aligns with both what the question is asking and what the data is presenting.
- **Limit yourself to the evidence directly presented by the graph and passage.** The SAT Writing and Language will not ask you to use background knowledge to answer graph analysis questions. Use the evidence in the graph and the passage to draw reasonable inferences.
- **Consider how the statistics are related to the argument of the passage as a whole.** Each graph is connected to a passage, and the questions about the graph will often ask how the information in the graph can be best used to support the argument. Review the necessary selections of the passage to ensure you understand the connection between the statistics in the graph and the ideas in the passage.

Example

Worldwide Internet Users

	2005	2010	2017	2019
World Population	6.5 billion	6.9 billion	7.4 billion	7.75 billion
Internet Users as a Percent of World Population	16%	30%	48%	53.6%
Percent of internet Users in the Developing World	8%	21%	41.3%	47%
Percent of internet Users in the Developed World	51%	67%	81%	86.6%

Source: International Telecommunications Union

1. Which choice provides accurate information from the above table?

   (A) In 2019, 86.6% of citizens in the United States used the internet.
   (B) There were 43% more internet users in the developed world than in the developing world in 2005.
   (C) The percentage of internet users in the developed world was greater than the percentage of internet users in the developing world in 2005 and 2010.
   (D) E-commerce became a dominant component of the economies in developing countries by the year 2019.

   Explanation: Limit yourself to the data directly presented in the table. Choice **(C)** is correct because in both 2005 and 2010, the percentage of internet users in the developed world was greater than that in the developing world. It is not choice (A) because the table does not specify statistics about individual countries. It is not choice (B) because the table does not give the total numbers of internet users there were in the developed vs. developing countries—it just compares percentages of internet users. And it is not choice (D) because the table provides no direct information about the importance of e-commerce.

2. Which choice most effectively uses data from the table to support the argument that a majority of the world's people were internet users in 2019?

   (A) Between 2005 and 2019, the number of internet users in all countries throughout the world steadily increased.
   (B) By 2019, 53.6% of the world population used the internet.
   (C) In 2019, the population of the world had increased to a staggering 7.75 billion people.
   (D) In 2019, 86.6% of people in the developed world were internet users, a vast majority.

   Explanation: Choice **(B)** uses a concrete statistic from the table to make the point that over half of the world's people were internet users in 2019. It is not choice (A) because we do not know if there was a steady increase of internet users in all countries because the table does not provide individual country data. It is not choice (C) because although this is an accurate piece of information from the table, it does not directly state anything about the number of global internet users. And it is not choice (D) because this statistic is only about people in the developed world, not in the world as a whole.

Practice

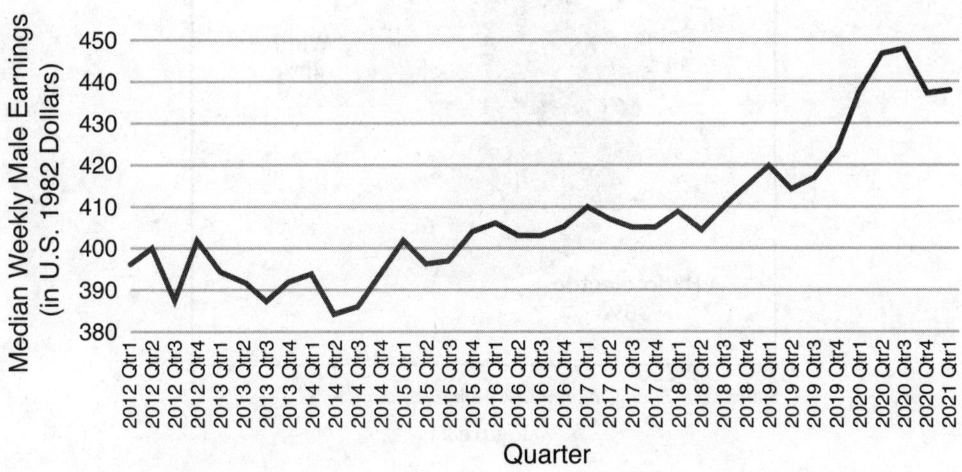

Source: The Bureau of Labor and Statistics

Figure 1

1. Which choice accurately reflects the information in Figure 1?

   (A) In the fourth quarter of 2012, the median weekly earnings for males in the United States exceeded $400 (held steady in 1982 dollars).
   (B) In the third quarter of 2015, the median weekly earnings for males in the United States was less than $380 (held steady in 1982 dollars).
   (C) In the second quarter of 2017, the median weekly earnings for males in the United States exceeded $410 (held steady in 1982 dollars).
   (D) In the first quarter of 2020, the median weekly earnings for males in the United States exceeded $450 (held steady in 1982 dollars).

2. Which choice most effectively uses information from the graph to support the idea that average wages for males have remained relatively constant?

   (A) Over the span of 2019 and 2020, average weekly wages for males in the United States increased from $414 to $447.
   (B) The average weekly wages for males in the United States in the third quarter of 2012 were merely $387.
   (C) Between the first quarter of 2012 and the second quarter of 2015, average weekly wages for males in the United States fluctuated just a bit, holding fairly steady at around $396.
   (D) From the end of the year in 2012 to the end of the year in 2014, average weekly wages for males in the United States decreased from $402 to $394.

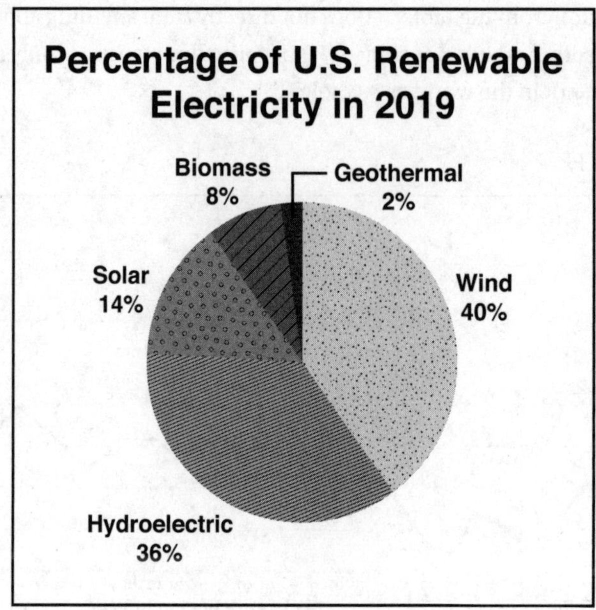

Source: U.S. Energy Information Administration

Figure 2

3. Which choice best reflects the data presented in Figure 2?
   (A) In 2019, 40% of U.S. energy generation came from wind power.
   (B) Hydroelectric power contributed over twice the amount of U.S. renewable electricity in 2019 as did solar.
   (C) Wind and hydroelectric together generated the majority of U.S. electricity in the year 2019.
   (D) The relative share of U.S. renewable electricity generation that comes from solar and wind steadily increased leading up to 2019.

4. Which choice most effectively uses information from Figure 2 to support an argument in favor of the role of wind power as an energy source in the United States?
   (A) Wind power provided the majority of U.S. renewable electricity generation in the year 2019.
   (B) With 40% of the share of U.S. renewable electricity generation in 2019, wind is the safest and most popular energy source in the country.
   (C) In the year 2019, wind generated a greater amount of electricity than any other generating source for U.S. residents.
   (D) Approximately two-fifths of U.S. renewable electricity generation in 2019 came from wind power.

If net migration is positive, it indicates an excess of people entering a country (i.e., immigrating). If net migration is negative, it indicates an excess of people leaving a country (i.e., emigrating).

Country	Average yearly net migration per 1,000 inhabitants in the years 2010–2014	Average yearly net migration per 1,000 inhabitants in the years 2015–2020
Argentina	0.1	0.1
Cambodia	−2.0	−1.9
Ethiopia	0.8	0.3
Maldives	28.4	22.8
Peru	−4.2	3.1
Western Samoa	−12.8	−14.3

Source: The CIA World Factbook

Figure 3

5. Which choice most accurately reflects the data in Figure 3?

   (A) There was an excess of people entering Peru in the years 2010–2014.
   (B) Average net migration in Argentina was generally steady in the decade between 2010 and 2020.
   (C) The population of Cambodia decreased between the years 2010 and 2020.
   (D) Average net migration in Ethiopia in the year 2017 was less than it was in 2014.

6. Which choice most effectively uses the data in Figure 3 to make an accurate comparison between two countries?

   (A) In the decade between 2010 and 2020, the Maldives had greater immigration per 1,000 inhabitants than did Cambodia.
   (B) Between 2010 and 2020, more people left Western Samoa than left Cambodia.
   (C) During the interval from 2010 to 2020, more residents of Western Samoa emigrated to the United States than did residents of Ethiopia.
   (D) By 2020, the share of immigrants in the population of Peru was greater than the share of immigrants in the population of Argentina.

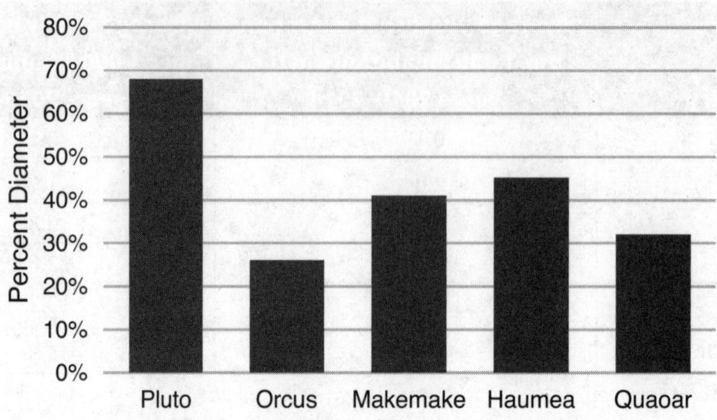

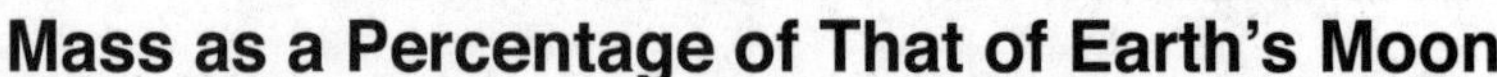
Figure 4: Possible Dwarf Planet Examples from the Solar System

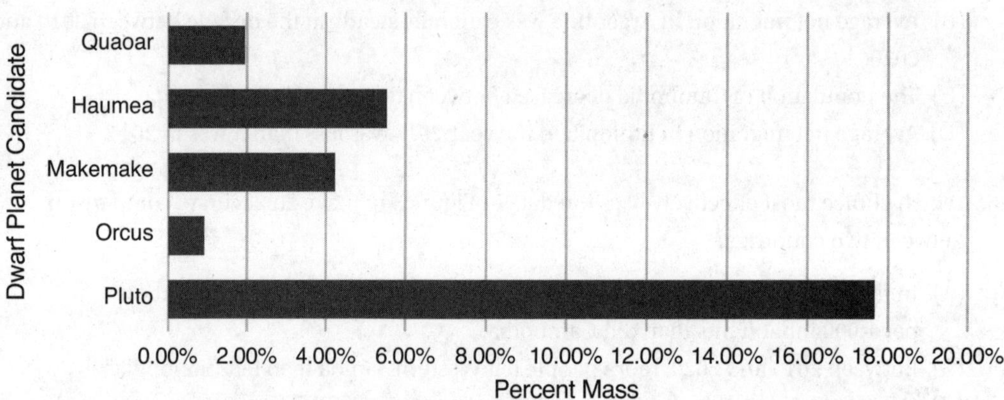

Source: www.go-astronomy.com

Figure 5

7. Which choice most accurately reflects the data in Figures 4 and 5 above?

   (A) The radius of Quaoar is greater than the radius of Makemake.
   (B) Earth's moon has a mass that is greater than that of all dwarf planets combined.
   (C) The mass of Pluto is greater than the mass of Orcus.
   (D) Haumea's volume is approximately 1.4 times that of Quaoar.

8. Which choice most effectively uses information from Figures 4 and 5 to support an accurate generalization about dwarf planets?

   (A) The time it takes to orbit the sun is typically far greater for a dwarf planet than it is for Earth's moon.
   (B) It is reasonable to expect that another dwarf planet would have a mass less than that of Earth's moon.
   (C) There are more dwarf planets in the solar system than there are planetary moons.
   (D) A typical dwarf planet will have a planetary diameter that is greater than half that of Earth's moon.

Solutions

1. **(A)** In the fourth quarter of 2012, the median weekly earnings for males in the United States was at approximately $402, thereby exceeding $400. The other options all misread the data in the graph.
2. **(C)** In order to support the idea that wages have remained relatively constant, it makes the most sense to select data that shows a steady level of wages over time. Choice **(C)** best accomplishes this, since on these two dates the wages were both at $396. Choice (A) shows an increase, choice (B) does not show any change over time, and choice (D) shows a decrease.
3. **(B)** According to the graph, electricity from wind power, at 40%, exceeded that from solar power, at 14%, by over two times in the year 2019. It is not choices (A) or (C) because we are not told how much of total U.S. electricity generation comes from renewable sources. And it is not choice (D) because the graph does not provide information about what happened in the years prior to 2019.
4. **(D)** This choice accurately uses the information in the graph to illustrate that two-fifths, or 40%, of renewable electricity generation in 2019 came from wind power. It is not choice (A) because 40% would not be a majority, even of just the renewable energy sources. It is not choice (B) because the graph does not provide information about the safety or popularity of energy sources. And it is not choice (C) because the graph only provides information about renewable electricity, not about all sources of electricity generation.
5. **(B)** Since the average net migration in Argentina was 0.1 in both intervals in the graph, it is reasonable to conclude that average net migration remained fairly steady during this time. It is not choice (A) because net migration was negative in Peru during this time. It is not choice (C) because the graph does not provide information about the total population of the countries—just about their immigration and emigration. And it is not choice (D) because the table only provides information about the whole intervals of five years, not about individual years.
6. **(A)** The average yearly net migration in the Maldives was quite a bit larger than that of Cambodia during these years. It is not choice (B) because we would need to know the populations of these countries to make a comparison. It is not choice (C) because the table does not provide information on the locations to which residents moved. And it is not choice (D) because we do not know how many immigrants were in each country at the start of these periods.
7. **(C)** Since Pluto has a mass that is almost 18% of Earth's moon while Orcus has a mass that is less than 1% of Earth's moon, the mass of Pluto would be greater than that of Orcus. It is not choice (A) because the diameter (and therefore the radius) of Makemake is actually greater than the diameter of Quaoar. It is not choice (B) because the table does not claim to provide the mass of all the dwarf planets—it provides examples of dwarf planets. And it is not choice (D) because while this would be true about the diameter, it would not necessarily be true about a three-dimensional volume calculation for potentially spherical planets.
8. **(B)** Since all the example dwarf planets presented have masses that are substantially smaller than that of Earth's moon, it is reasonable to expect that other dwarf planets would have smaller masses than that of the moon. It is not choice (A) because there is no information in the table about orbital times. It is not choice (C) because there is no information presented about the total numbers of planetary moons or dwarf planets. And it is not choice (D) because most of the example dwarf planets have diameters less than half that of Earth's moon.

Practice Writing and Language Passages

On the SAT Writing and Language test, you will see four passages. Each one will be from a different content area: careers, history/social sciences, humanities, and science. One passage from each of these categories is presented below, giving you the same number of passages/questions you will have on the actual SAT Writing and Language test. After each passage, detailed solutions to the questions follow. Take about 9 minutes to complete each passage.

Electroconvulsive Therapy

Despite its sinister and somewhat draconian reputation, electroconvulsive therapy ❶ (ECT) is making a rather magnificent return in the treatment of chronic clinical depression. Like many of its pharmaceutical counterparts, the exact physiological mechanism responsible for ECT's alleviation of the symptoms of depression remains fairly elusive, ❷ and its results are inarguably remarkable. The idea itself—which in many ways seems like the fever dream of a 19th-century medical quack—was in fact spawned from the careful observation by two Italian physicians in the 1930s of patients who suffered from both depression and epilepsy. Doctors Lucio Bini and Ugo Cerletti ❸ noted that with, startling consistency, many of their patients experienced an extended reprieve from their depression symptoms following a grand mal seizure. Concluding that seizures and depression were, somehow, pathologically incompatible—and after some extensive animal testing—the two cautiously began experimenting ❹ in the treatment of severely depressed patients.

1. Should the underlined phrase be kept or deleted?
   (A) Kept, because it defines the term immediately before it.
   (B) Kept, because it clarifies the abbreviation that will be used throughout the passage.
   (C) Deleted, because it provides an unnecessary parenthetical reference.
   (D) Deleted, because it restates an acronym that is widely present elsewhere in the passage.

2. (A) NO CHANGE
   (B) since
   (C) with
   (D) but

3. (A) NO CHANGE
   (B) noted that, with startling, consistency many
   (C) noted that, with startling consistency, many
   (D) noted that with startling consistency many

4. (A) NO CHANGE
   (B) for the treating on
   (C) of the treatment for
   (D) to the treating with

The procedural sophistication of ECT has evolved tremendously in the past 25 years. Innovations in muscle relaxants have eliminated the violent, involuntary spasms that contributed to ECT's notorious character. **5** The administration of ECT which once required heavy restraints and at least six orderlies to prevent the patient from causing harm to himself or others can now be carried out by as few as two medical **6** professionals: one to operate the equipment, another to monitor the patient's vitals and electroencephalogram. Theories seeking to explain the physiological cause for ECT's impressive outcomes **7** is limited by the impossibility of directly observing a patient's brain activity during and immediately following treatment. However, the prevailing consensus suggests that the induced electrical current stimulates a release of certain neurotransmitters in the brain—perhaps endorphins—and temporarily **8** overwhelm the chemical imbalances of depression.

More contentious than ECT's neurological mechanism **9** are their potential to produce long-term or permanent results. Despite its essentially immediate results following treatment, roughly half of the patients undergo an ECT relapse within six months. Some proponents of the therapy have suggested that this is in part due to the severity and chronicity of the depression typical of patients following a

5. (A) NO CHANGE
   (B) The administration of ECT—which once required heavy restraints and at least six orderlies to prevent the patient from causing harm to himself or others—can now
   (C) The administration of ECT; which once required heavy restraints and at least six orderlies to prevent the patient from causing harm to themselves or others, can now
   (D) The administration of ECT, which once required heavy restraints, and at least six orderlies to prevent the patient from causing harm to themselves or others can now

6. (A) NO CHANGE
   (B) professionals one to operate the equipment, another
   (C) professionals—one to operate the equipment another
   (D) professionals, one to operate the equipment another

7. (A) NO CHANGE
   (B) is limiting
   (C) are limiting
   (D) are limited

8. (A) NO CHANGE
   (B) overwhelms
   (C) overwhelming
   (D) provides an overwhelming effect on

9. (A) NO CHANGE
   (B) is their
   (C) are its
   (D) is its

course of treatment in ECT; (10) scientists are hopeful that ECT will, in the not too distant future, provide a long-term solution for most types of mental illness. Perhaps one day—with its surprising efficacy and minimal side effects—ECT will become as commonplace as the pharmacological giants Prozac and Zoloft in the treatment of depression. However, until the skeptical public perception of ECT catches up with its modern medical reality, we can do little more than (11) speculate.

10. Which choice would give an optimistic and logical clarification of the first part of the sentence that is supported by the information in this paragraph?
    (A) NO CHANGE
    (B) there is a scientific consensus that further experiments will demonstrate that ECT is a lasting cure for victims of the most intense depression.
    (C) it is possible that the treatment will prove more effective in the long term for patients suffering from milder cases of depression.
    (D) many researchers contend that due to this ineffectiveness, ECT should be abandoned in all its forms in favor of therapeutic approach

11. (A) NO CHANGE
    (B) convert.
    (C) venture.
    (D) optimize.

 **Solutions**

Answers Explained

1. **(B)** Later in the passage, the author uses "ECT" to refer to electroconvulsive therapy. If this underlined portion were deleted, the meaning of the abbreviation would not be clear. Choice (A) is not correct because it provides an abbreviation, not a definition. Choices (C) and (D) are incorrect because without including this abbreviation in the passage, the reader would be confused by its subsequent use throughout the essay.

2. **(D)** The word "but" is the appropriate transition. The sentence contains a contrast—scientists do not know exactly how ECT works, but they do know that the results are remarkable. The transitions in choices (A), (B), and (C) do not indicate a contrast.

3. **(C)** It is best to place the breaks around the clarifying parenthetical phrase "with startling consistency." The sentence can function as a logical sentence without this phrase, so the phrase can be set aside, although it does provide an important clarification. Choices (A) and (B) break up the phrase "with startling consistency," and choice (D) does not have any needed pauses.

4. **(A)** Choice **(A)** uses the correct prepositions given the context since it is proper to say "experimenting in." Additionally, this choice uses the proper wording of "treatment." Choices (B) and (D) use improper prepositions ("for" and "to") to introduce the phrase, and they also use "treating" instead of "treatment." Choice (C) uses the incorrect preposition since it is improper to say "began experimenting of" something.

5. **(B)** Choice **(B)** uses dashes to set apart the long parenthetical phrase from the rest of the sentence. The sentence can function without this parenthetical phrase, so the phrase can be placed aside. In addition, since "patient" is singular, "himself" must be used in order to have singular numerical agreement. The word "themselves," although often used in conversation in such a context, does not work in this situation because it is plural. Choice (A) does not set aside the parenthetical phrase. Choices (C) and (D) improperly use "themselves" instead of "himself."

6. **(A)** Choice **(A)** uses the colon to set off a list that clarifies what the medical professionals used to carry out the procedure. Choice (B) does not have a pause before the list. Choices (C) and (D) do not have a comma separating the two items listed.

7. **(D)** Choice **(D)** correctly matches the plural subject of "theories" by using "are." This answer also uses the proper verb since it is correct to say "are limited by" instead of "are limiting by." Choices (A) and (B) use the singular "is." Choice (C) is incorrect since saying "they are limiting by" is improper.

8. **(B)** "Overwhelms" matches up with the singular subject of "current." Choice (A) is for a plural subject. Choice (C) does not maintain the parallel structure with "suggests" and "stimulates" from earlier in the sentence. Choice (D) is too wordy.

9. **(D)** "Is" matches with the singular subject of "potential," and "its" matches with the singular noun of "ECT." Choices (A) and (B) both improperly use the plural "their." Choices (A) and (C) improperly use the plural "are."

10. **(C)** Prior to this statement, the author gives a hypothetical explanation as to why so many of the patients who undergo ECT go back to having the illness they previously had—the fact that so many ECT patients had severe, long-term depression, skewing the results toward negativity. If ECT is used on patients who have more mild depression, perhaps research will demonstrate that ECT is much more effective. Choices (A) and (B) are incorrect because the paragraph indicates that researchers have found this treatment does not work for many patients since so many relapse. Choice (D) is not correct because although many patients relapse, some do benefit, making this option far too pessimistic.

11. **(A)** The author does not know whether ECT will one day become as widespread as other mental illness treatments. Therefore, the author can only "speculate" (guess) about what might happen in the future. The author is not going to "convert" anything from one form to another, making choice (B) incorrect. If choice (C) had said "venture a guess," it could work. However, the word "venture" alone is insufficient. Choice (D) is incorrect because although scientists might want to optimize their understanding, they can hardly do so given the status of public perception.

Summer Break

Why is it that our modern schools still operate on a preindustrial calendar? How many students need to spend three months of the year helping the family with the crop harvest? **1** Only about 2 percent of the U.S. population is involved in agriculture. The modern school calendar should be updated to reflect our modern lifestyles, and summer break should be ended in favor of several longer breaks throughout the school year.

2 Teachers spend approximately two months, out of the nine-month school year on reviewing the material from the last academic year. If school were operated on a year-round basis, student retention of material would be strengthened since it is much easier to forget material over a three-month break **3** then over a two-week one. Material retention is especially vital for subjects like math and foreign language in which more advanced units will not make sense without a sound basis in the earlier material. **4** However, if students have more frequent breaks from the rigors of school, they are less likely to burn out. This will help minimize behavioral issues due to student fatigue and maximize student learning since students will be more physically rejuvenated throughout the academic year.

1. Which choice most specifically builds upon the argument of the previous sentence?
   (A) NO CHANGE
   (B) Not very many students are familiar with raising crops themselves, having familiarity with food only from groceries and restaurants.
   (C) Three months is far too long to spend farming; instead, time could be better focused on academic learning.
   (D) Although many students might do gardening as a hobby, few students plan on pursuing agriculture as their primary career.

2. (A) NO CHANGE
   (B) Teachers spend approximately two months, out of the nine-month school year, on reviewing the material, from the last academic year.
   (C) Teachers spend, approximately two months out of the nine-month school year on reviewing the material from the last academic year.
   (D) Teachers spend approximately two months out of the nine-month school year on reviewing the material from the last academic year.

3. (A) NO CHANGE
   (B) than
   (C) moreover
   (D) for

4. (A) NO CHANGE
   (B) Consequently,
   (C) Additionally,
   (D) On the other hand,

Some will argue that students need time to do sports and camps over the ❺ summer why can't camps and sports adjust to take advantage of breaks throughout the year? ❻ It makes no sense that camps cannot shift to accommodate the needs of the new school calendar. Some sports and activities, like football, do benefit from having summer to prepare for the fall season. ❼ Other sports and activities however, are primarily done in the winter like basketball. Basketball players could greatly benefit from having a two to three week break from academics to focus on their practice. Also, not all students are financially able to benefit from being able to do summer camps and the like. ❽ When he or she is not in school, they are not going to academic enrichment camps; odds are, they are spending time at home watching television and letting their minds deteriorate. For students who cannot afford summer enrichment, a year-round school schedule would be especially helpful in keeping them from falling ❾ from their peers.

5. (A) NO CHANGE
   (B) summer. Why
   (C) summer, why
   (D) summer, this is why

6. The writer is considering deleting the underlined sentence. Should the sentence be kept or deleted?
   (A) Kept, because it elaborates on the argument of the previous sentence.
   (B) Kept, because it provides specific details that demonstrate how camps will adjust to the new circumstances.
   (C) Deleted, because it contradicts information presented elsewhere in the passage.
   (D) Deleted, because it unnecessarily repeats the idea presented in the previous sentence.

7. (A) NO CHANGE
   (B) Other sports and activities, however, are primarily done in the winter like basketball.
   (C) Other sports and activities, however, are primarily done in the winter, like basketball.
   (D) Other sports and activities however are primarily done in the winter, like basketball.

8. (A) NO CHANGE
   (B) When he or she is not in school, he or she is not
   (C) When they are not in school, they are not
   (D) When one is not in school, one is not

9. (A) NO CHANGE
   (B) down
   (C) beneath
   (D) behind

10 [1] When adults have full-time jobs, they take periodic breaks during the year. [2] By having a year-round school calendar, students will be preparing for the real-world schedules they will face as grown-ups. [3] It is time that our society moves from a calendar based on a 19th-century schedule to one based on a 21st-century schedule and shifts to year-round school.

10. The writer would like to insert this sentence into the paragraph.

"Doing so helps them refresh and recharge so that they are able to perform their occupational tasks well when they return."

What would be the best placement of this sentence?

(A) Before sentence 1
(B) Before sentence 2
(C) Before sentence 3
(D) After sentence 3

11. Suppose the author presents her paper to her colleagues. They argue that, rather than eliminating summer break in favor of the same amount of vacation throughout the year, the school board should merely add hours of instruction to the school year in order to improve academic performance. The author could best dispute this counterargument by citing information about which two states from the table?

State*	Hours of Elementary School Instructional Time in a Year	Average SAT Reading/ Writing Score	Average SAT Math Score
California	840	501	516
Florida	900	496	498
New York	900	484	489
Texas	1,260	484	505
Massachusetts	900	512	526

**Source: www.centerforpubliceducation.org/Main-Menu/Organizing-a-school/Time-in-school-How-does-the-US-compare http://www.publicagendaarchives.org/charts/state-state-sat-and-act-scores*

(A) California and Florida
(B) Massachusetts and New York
(C) Texas and Massachusetts
(D) New York and California

Answers Explained

1. **(A)** The previous sentence rhetorically argues that since very few people are involved in agriculture, building the school calendar around the old agricultural economy does not make sense. Choice **(A)** most specifically builds on this argument by giving statistical evidence in support. Choice (B) is specific but does not directly relate to the argument. Choice (C) repeats information from the previous sentence. Although choice (D) is relevant to the argument, it is not as specific as choice **(A)**.

2. **(D)** Choice **(D)** deletes the unnecessary comma. Just because this is a long sentence does not mean that a comma is required. Choices (A) and (B) break up the phrase "two months out of the nine-month school year." Choice (C) breaks up the phrase "spend approximately." This is a good example of a problem where quietly mouthing the words will help you determine when a pause is needed.

3. **(B)** The word "than" properly compares how it is easier to forget something over a longer break *than* over a shorter one. Choice (A) incorrectly uses "then," which refers to time, not comparison. Choice (C), "moreover," is synonymous with "also." Choice (D), "for," provides more of a direct connection rather than a separation between compared terms. So out of the options, choice **(B)** is the only one that can be used in this context to provide a comparison.

4. **(C)** The word "Additionally" correctly indicates that this sentence builds upon the argument in the previous sentences. Choice (B), "Consequently," indicates a cause-and-effect relationship. Choice (A), "However," and choice (D), "On the other hand," both indicate a contrast.

5. **(B)** Without a period between the two independent clauses (i.e., complete sentences), this is a run-on sentence. All of the other choices would form run-ons because two independent clauses are joined by either nothing, as in choice (A), or by a comma, as in choices (C) and (D). A comma without a conjunction, like "but" or "and," is insufficient to join two independent clauses.

6. **(D)** The previous sentence rhetorically asks, "Why can't camps and sports adjust to take advantage of breaks throughout the year?" This is the same general point made by the underlined sentence, so the underlined sentence should be deleted in order to avoid repetition. Choices (A) and (B) both incorrectly leave this redundant sentence in the paragraph. Choice (C) is incorrect because the idea in the underlined portion is repetitive, not contradictory.

7. **(C)** Choice **(C)** properly sets aside a transitional word, "however," and a clarifying phrase, "like basketball," with commas since the sentence would function as a complete and logical sentence without these two insertions. Choices (A) and (B) do not have a needed pause before "like basketball." Choice (D) does not set aside the word "however."

8. **(C)** "They" correctly refers to the "students," which is plural. Choices (A) and (B) both use "he or she," which would be fine if the paragraph was referring to each student as an individual. However, the paragraph is referring to them as a group. Choice (D) uses "one," which is also singular.

9. **(D)** The phrase "falling behind" refers to people's failure to keep up with something, which is applicable to academic progress in this sentence. Falling "from," "down," or "beneath" indicate falling in a physical sense.

10. **(B)** This sentence should be placed before sentence 2 because it clarifies how taking periodic breaks helps adults perform better in their jobs. Choice (A) is not correct because the phrase "Doing so" would lack the intended meaning without sentence 1 coming beforehand. Choices (C) and (D) are incorrect because "occupational tasks" more appropriately refers to the work of adults, not the schooling of children.

11. **(C)** Comparing the SAT results of Texas and Massachusetts would best counter this argument. Texas provides significantly more hours of instructional time than Massachusetts, yet the average SAT Reading and Writing and Math scores for students in Texas are lower than those of students in Massachusetts. The data for the states in choices (A), (B), and (D) are all too similar to one another with respect to the hours of elementary school instructional time, making citing any of these pairs unhelpful to countering the argument.

The Sur-Surrealist

Easily one of the most distinctive painters associated with the surrealist movement of the early 20th century, Frida Kahlo **1** consequently insisted adamantly throughout her career that she was by no means a surrealist herself. It is true enough that she had personal contact with many brazen members of the movement, and her work is **2** soundly featured as a triumph in any compilation study of surrealist imagery. However, Kahlo sought to distinguish herself from artists such as Dali and de Chirico, **3** affirming that rather than painting from dreams or imagination she explored exclusively her own reality.

The infamous social eccentricities of her surrealist counterparts are, perhaps, partly responsible for why so many scholars have too frequently taken **4** Kahlos self-proclaimed distinction so lightly—a superficial glance at her work exposes a world where skyscrapers erupt from volcanoes, electric lamps possess umbilical cords, and **5** a shattered Roman Column is the thing which replaces the human spine. These are, one might easily suppose, undeniably the stuff of dreams. However, a more **6** biased evaluation of the works coupled with a little knowledge of Kahlo's life history may help to reveal how such fantastical and, often, unsettling images became intertwined with Kahlo's personal reality. So inward was her artistic focus that she often dismissed

1. (A) NO CHANGE
   (B) moreover
   (C) accordingly
   (D) nonetheless

2. Which choice best expresses the great renown of Kahlo's work in a tone consistent with the context?
   (A) NO CHANGE
   (B) somewhat respected by scholars
   (C) plainly disregarded as mediocrity
   (D) really liked a lot

3. (A) NO CHANGE
   (B) affirming that, rather than painting from dreams or imagination she
   (C) affirming that, rather than painting from dreams or imagination, she
   (D) affirming that rather than painting, from dreams or imagination, she

4. (A) NO CHANGE
   (B) Kahlo's self proclaimed
   (C) Kahlo's self-proclaimed
   (D) Kahlos' self-proclaimed

5. (A) NO CHANGE
   (B) by a shattered Roman Column is the human spine substituted.
   (C) the human spine was being replaced with a destroyed Roman Column.
   (D) the human spine is replaced with a shattered Roman column.

6. (A) NO CHANGE
   (B) sober
   (C) troublesome
   (D) confusing

the work, saying that her paintings were "all small and unimportant, with the same personal subjects that only appeal to me and nobody else." ❼ Kahlo was in fact able to create images that were rather physically large in size.

The fantastical elements of her paintings are invariably symbolic of Kahlo's personal experiences; this distinguishes her, to some degree, from so many surrealists ❽ who sought to distort reality for the sheer sake of invention. It is well known that throughout her life, Kahlo suffered tremendously both physically and emotionally. At the age of eighteen, Kahlo was involved in a bus accident that left her with significant permanent damage to her spinal column and organs and caused frequent relapses into chronic pain throughout her life. Kahlo's relationship with her husband, artist ❾ Diego Rivera was another source of inner turmoil: some of Kahlo's most despairing works can be traced to the time of

7. Which choice would best express a view that is contradictory toward Kahlo's sentiments about her own paintings?
   (A) NO CHANGE
   (B) Kahlo was greatly mistaken in supposing her powerful images would resonate with no one but herself.
   (C) Kahlo is a shining example of an artist who looked to her own inner thoughts for creative inspiration.
   (D) Kahlo was truly despondent about her personal abilities, much like many perfectionists have a tendency to be.

8. Should the underlined portion be kept or deleted?
   (A) Kept, because it provides a helpful clarification.
   (B) Kept, because it details the experiences of the surrealists.
   (C) Deleted, because it is irrelevant to the focus of the paragraph.
   (D) Deleted, because it shifts the discussion to other artists instead of Kahlo.

9. (A) NO CHANGE
   (B) Diego Rivera, was another source of inner turmoil, some of
   (C) Diego Rivera was another source of inner turmoil. Some of
   (D) Diego Rivera, was another source of inner turmoil; some of

their brief divorce in 1939. Recurring symbols of these ⑩ tribulations—such as blood, dry and cracked landscapes, and even orthopedic corsets—are prevalent throughout her work, though their correlation should seem perfectly natural to one familiar with Kahlo's life and her need to express a synthesis of her emotional and physical pain. To the untrained eye, such juxtapositions may easily betoken the randomness of a ⑪ weird and odd dream.

10. (A) NO CHANGE
    (B) tribulations—such as blood, dry and cracked landscapes, and even orthopedic corsets, are prevalent
    (C) tribulations, such as blood dry and cracked landscapes, and even orthopedic corsets, are prevalent
    (D) tribulations: such as blood, dry and cracked landscapes, and even orthopedic corsets, are prevalent

11. (A) NO CHANGE
    (B) pitiful
    (C) surreal
    (D) evil

Answers Explained

1. **(D)** "Nonetheless" is used to show a contrast between the fact that Frida Kahlo is considered a surrealist by society, yet she did not consider herself a surrealist. Choice (A), "consequently," and choice (C), "accordingly," show cause and effect. Choice (B), "moreover," is synonymous with "also." This is a good example where you can use the similarities among choices (A) and (C) to eliminate them.
2. **(A)** "Great renown" refers to significant respect, and stating that something is "soundly . . . a triumph" best captures the feeling of respect for Kahlo's work. Choice (B) does not go far enough in its praise. Choice (C) is far too negative based on the context. Choice (D) is inconsistent with the tone since "really liked a lot" is far too informal.
3. **(C)** Choice **(C)** properly uses commas to surround the parenthetical phrase that contrasts with the rest of the sentence. Choice (A) has no pauses at all. Choice (B) has only one comma at the start of the parenthetical phrase and does not have a comma at the end of the phrase. Choice (D) has a comma that interrupts the phrase "painting from dreams."
4. **(C)** Kahlo is a singular person who possesses the "distinction," so there should be an apostrophe before the *s*. In addition, "self-proclaimed" is an adjective describing the distinction, so it should be hyphenated. Choice (A) does not show possession. Choice (B) lacks hyphenation. Choice (D) places the apostrophe where it would be placed with a plural noun.
5. **(D)** Choice **(D)** puts the words in the most logical order, making clear that the human spine is replaced by the column in the painting. It also correctly lowercases "column." Choices (A) and (C) are too wordy, and choice (B) is inverted.
6. **(B)** "Sober" in this context means "serious" and "careful." This is the best fit given that the essay argues that if one gets past the initial notion that Kahlo's paintings are merely the stuff of dreams, one will find a much deeper meaning. If we evaluated Kahlo's work in a "biased," "troublesome," or "confusing" way, we would not have these insights.

7. **(B)** The previous sentence states that Kahlo thought that her work would appeal only to herself. To contrast with this, choice **(B)** is the best since it points out that many people actually do find her work interesting. Choices (A) and (C) do not relate to Kahlo's attitude toward her paintings. Choice (D) further develops the sentiment Kahlo expresses in the previous sentence rather than contradicting it.

8. **(A)** Without this information, we would not fully understand what distinguished Kahlo's paintings from those of other surrealist painters—she symbolized her personal experiences, while many surrealists painted unrealistically just to be unrealistic. Choice (B) is incorrect because we do not see details about what surrealists experienced. Choices (C) and (D) are not correct because this phrase needs to stay in the sentence for clarification.

9. **(D)** Choice **(D)** properly places a comma after Rivera, which is needed since it is an appositive (a helpful yet not essential clarification of a title). Choice (D) also puts a needed semicolon between the two independent clauses. Choices (A) and (C) do not place a comma after the appositive. Choice (B) makes this a run-on sentence.

10. **(A)** Choice **(A)** places dashes around the parenthetical description of what the symbols were. It clearly distinguishes among the individual symbols by separating each item in the list with commas. Choice (B) does not finish the parenthetical phrase in the same way it started—it uses a dash at the beginning and a comma at the end. Choice (C) does not separate "blood" with a comma from the next item in the list. Choice (D) improperly and inconsistently uses a colon to start off the parenthetical phrase and uses a comma to finish it.

11. **(C)** The paragraph describes Kahlo's images with words like "randomness" and refers to unusual symbols, like an orthopedic corset. Such visuals are best described as "surreal" since they are imaginative rather than realistic. Choice (A) is incorrect because these words are too informal in tone and are repetitive. Choice (B) is not correct because Kahlo's images most likely do not arouse pity but do evoke imaginative musings. Choice (D) is incorrect because although many negative things happened to Kahlo in her life, "evil" takes the description of these images to a negative extreme since evil is not necessarily associated with "randomness."

Resumes

A professional and error-free resume helps you stand out ❶ in a sea of applicants. How a resume should be organized and presented is fairly static across fields, with the notable exception being the art and design industries. For these positions, it may be acceptable to ❷ conform with the traditionally accepted format to showcase your individual design skills and creativity.

For all other ❸ fields; however, resume structure for recent graduates is very much the same. Paper should be white or cream, and ink should be black. Choose a commonly used font, such as Times New Roman or Arial. Headings should be a visually pleasing mix of capitalization and bolded font. ❹ Most jobs to which people will apply will have a similar resume-writing format.

Begin with contact information, including ❺ name, phone number, address, email address, and, if appropriate, professional networking information. Objectives or goal statements are not typically used. Your resume should make your qualifications clear, and any other job-related topics can be addressed in the cover letter. List education and major educational accomplishments beginning with your most recent school. If your grade point average overall or within your major is impressive, include it.

1. (A) NO CHANGE
   (B) between the different applications.
   (C) among applications submitted by students worldwide.
   (D) OMIT the underlined portion.

2. Which choice would most logically build upon the previous sentence?
   (A) NO CHANGE
   (B) try
   (C) break with
   (D) seize upon

3. (A) NO CHANGE
   (B) fields, however, resume
   (C) fields: however, resume
   (D) fields, however resume

4. The writer is considering deleting the underlined sentence. Should the underlined sentence be kept or deleted?
   (A) Kept, because it elaborates on common resume-writing techniques.
   (B) Kept, because it clarifies the general characteristics of well-written resumes.
   (C) Deleted, because it repeats an idea previously stated in the paragraph.
   (D) Deleted, because it diverges from the primary focus of the paragraph.

5. (A) NO CHANGE
   (B) name phone number, address, email
   (C) name, phone, number, address email
   (D) name, phone number address, email

❻ Finally include clinical experience or specialized training programs if you have any. Then move on to work experience. Begin with either the most recent experience and work backward chronologically, or begin with the most relevant work experience and list from most relevant to least relevant experience. For each position, include the name of the company, dates you worked there, your position, and two or three bullet points about your responsibilities. Begin your bullet points with active verbs such as ❼ "implemented" or "managed" instead of less-impressive words such as "helped" or "worked on."

If you have more experience related to the position but it is not quite as important, put it under an "Additional Experience" heading. Here, list the ❽ company and organization the dates, and your position.

6. (A) NO CHANGE
   (B) Finally, include
   (C) Next include
   (D) Next, include

7. The writer is considering removing the quotation marks from the words in the underlined sentence. Should the writer make this change?
   (A) Yes, because these are not quotations from actual people.
   (B) Yes, because these words do not possess other items and so do not require quotations.
   (C) No, because the writer is referring to the words themselves rather than to what the words represent.
   (D) No, because they are referring to formal titles that must be placed in quotations.

8. (A) NO CHANGE
   (B) company and organization,
   (C) company or organization
   (D) company or organization,

If you have still more relevant and important awards or activities, choose the most important ones and put them under an "Additional Selected Activities, Leadership, and Honors" heading. **9** The word "selected" emphasizes that you have earned these prestigious honors due to being "selected" by outside organizations for your professional excellence. Include the organization or award, the date, and any leadership position held.

When **10** your finished, review your resume for visual appeal. It should not look cluttered and should be a mix of white space and black text. If your resume looks cluttered, continue on to a second page. Make sure you have enough information to fill **11** at least half of the second page. If you do not, review the information you have included and reduce it until your resume fits on one page.

9. Which sentence should be used in the underlined portion to logically support why the writer uses "Selected" in the heading discussed in the previous sentence?
   (A) NO CHANGE
   (B) The use of "Selected" is important as it shows the person reading your resume that this is just a sample of your most important honors.
   (C) Writing "Selected" indicates that you have confidence in your abilities to get the job done.
   (D) Specifying that these are "Selected" honors demonstrates that you have a masterful command of the English language, impressing potential companies with your ability to communicate.

10. (A) NO CHANGE
    (B) you were
    (C) you are
    (D) you felt

11. (A) NO CHANGE
    (B) half at least with
    (C) of least at half
    (D) at least of half

Answers Explained

1. **(A)** Choice **(A)** gives a grammatically proper and concise clarification of how exactly a resume will help you stand out. Choice (B) is incorrect because "between" is used when comparing just two things—there would surely be more than two applicants for a typical job. Choice (C) is too wordy. Choice (D) is incorrect because without this phrase, the sentence would be unclear about how a well-crafted resume would help you stand out.

2. **(C)** "Break with" is the best option since it establishes a contrast between the recommended resume styles for traditional career fields and for more creative ones. The other options all keep with the traditional resume format, which do not make sense given that art and design are described as exceptions to how resumes should be organized.

3. **(B)** A semicolon or colon would not work, as in choices (A) and (C), since there is not a complete sentence beforehand. Choice **(B)** correctly sets aside the transitional "however" with commas, unlike choice (D), which has a comma only before the word.

4. **(C)** The underlined sentence repeats the idea expressed in the first sentence of the paragraph, i.e., that resumes are mostly formatted in the same way across career fields. Choice (D) is not correct because the sentence is focused on the topic of the paragraph. In fact, it repeats a point already made in the paragraph, which is problematic. Choices (A) and (B) are not correct because these would both keep this redundant sentence in the paragraph.

5. **(A)** Choice **(A)** places commas at the appropriate spots between each whole item in the list. Choice (B) makes "name phone number" into one object. Choice (C) makes "address email" into one object. Choice (D) makes "phone number address" into one object.

6. **(D)** As the second major point in the body of the essay, "Next" is more appropriate than "Finally." Also, a comma is needed immediately after the introductory transition of "Next" to provide a small pause.

7. **(C)** When you refer to a word itself, put quotation marks around the word. When you refer to what the word actually represents, no quotation marks are needed. For example, *I drive a car* vs. *"Car" rhymes with "star."* The writer is describing what words should be placed on a resume, so quotation marks are appropriate. Choice (D) is incorrect because these words are not formal titles of things like books or people. Choices (A) and (B) are not correct because they would unnecessarily remove the quotation marks.

8. **(D)** Since you would list either the company or the organization, depending on whether you worked for a business or a nonprofit, it is correct to say *or* and not to separate the two terms with commas. So you will list three things: the group for which you worked (company/organization), the dates, and the position. Choices (A) and (B) are incorrect because these use *and* when you would have either a company or an organization, but not both. Choice (C) is not correct because the needed pause between "company or organization" and "the dates" would be missing.

9. **(B)** The reader might wonder why the author recommends that you write "Selected" in the previous sentence. Choice **(B)** provides the most logical support. It clarifies that you have many awards that you could mention but that you are choosing to list only some of the most significant, or selected, ones. Choice (A) does not make sense, because the idea that you were given these awards by outside organizations would still be expressed without "Selected" in the title. Choice (C) does not make sense. If you said you had been selected for something,

you would be expressing confidence. However, this use of "Selected" pertains to choosing which awards to mention, not directly to your confidence in your abilities. Choice (D) does not make sense. There is no strong reason that inserting this word primarily demonstrates mastery of the English language.

10. **(C)** This should be in the present tense to be consistent with the rest of the essay, making choices (B) and (D) incorrect. It also should be a subject and verb, not possession, making choice (A) incorrect since "your" indicates possession. "You are" is in the correct tense and gives the proper subject and verb.

11. **(A)** Choice **(A)** puts the words into the most logical order since the correct expression is "fill at least half." The other options make this phrase nonsensical and inconsistent with common practice.

Advanced Drills

Passages

The following passages are designed to represent the most difficult sorts of passages and questions you could encounter on the SAT Writing and Language. Take about nine minutes total for each drill. Good luck!

A Tricky Feline

Isaac Newton and Albert Einstein are probably the only theoretical physicists to ever become household names, **1** because of the fictional character of physicist Sheldon Cooper. The layperson merely associates Newton with gravity and laws of motion, and Einstein with relativity and mass-energy equivalence, failing to understand the magnitude of **2** either scientist's contribution. In fact, "Einstein" is used more often as a synonym for "genius" than actually to reference his work. **3** Erwin Schrödinger a lesser recognized name, however, sought to tackle many of the same issues in physics as Einstein himself.

1. (A) NO CHANGE
   (B) notwithstanding
   (C) aside with
   (D) stemming in

2. (A) NO CHANGE
   (B) either scientists'
   (C) each scientists
   (D) each scientists'

3. (A) NO CHANGE
   (B) Erwin Schrödinger, a lesser recognized name, however sought
   (C) Erwin Schrödinger, a lesser recognized name however sought
   (D) Erwin Schrödinger, a lesser recognized name, however, sought

Schrödinger won the Nobel Prize in Physics in 1933 for his work in quantum mechanics, ❹ since he is most remembered for a theoretical experiment he proposed two years later. In this thought experiment, Schrödinger hoped to illustrate the absurdity of the Copenhagen interpretation, a widely accepted notion of quantum physics that Einstein had an equally difficult time ❺ smelling. Schrödinger offered a paradox that came to be known as Schrödinger's Cat. In this paradox, a cat is placed into a steel box with a vial of poison and a radioactive substance. When the radioactive substance decays, an internal monitor releases the poison and subsequently kills the cat.

[1] The trick here ❻ lies in the unpredictability of radioactive material. [2] Called "superposition" by scientists, the decay is completely random, existing simultaneously in a state of decay and not. [3] The subatomic event simply may or may not occur. [4] Since the cat's fate is tied to the atom's, the cat would then exist in this same superposition, simultaneously dead and alive. [5] Yet, we know that the cat is not both dead *and* alive. [6] Schrödinger, then, posited the issue of when superposition collapses into reality—when multiple occupying states simultaneously ❼ becomes one or the other. ❽

4. (A) NO CHANGE
   (B) for
   (C) but
   (D) and

5. Which ending to the sentence is most consistent with the sentence's meaning?
   (A) NO CHANGE
   (B) chewing.
   (C) tasting.
   (D) swallowing.

6. (A) NO CHANGE
   (B) lies to
   (C) lays in
   (D) lays on

7. (A) NO CHANGE
   (B) become
   (C) have becoming
   (D) had becoming

8. The author wishes to insert the following sentence into the previous paragraph:

   "Hence, the flaw in this line of thinking."

   Where would it most logically be placed?
   (A) Before sentence 2
   (B) Before sentence 3
   (C) Before sentence 5
   (D) Before sentence 6

(9) Quantum theory is carried about by specialists known as theoretical physicists. Since physicists know that particles as small as electrons do not follow the rules of Newton's laws, they account for all possible states that particles could be in at one time with the wave function. You cannot say, without direct observation, what subatomic particles are doing; instead, you say there is a combination of the multiple states in which the particle could possibly be. Schrödinger, a father of quantum mechanics himself, surely understood the uses of quantum superposition but also sought to bring attention to (10) its shortcomings.

Although Schrödinger will never be as widely referenced as Einstein, he too was dissatisfied with quantum randomness. (11) It is truly a shame that Schrödinger's accomplishments are unknown to other scientists.

9. Which of the following provides the most logical introduction to the paragraph?
   (A) NO CHANGE
   (B) Quantum theory is concerned with the study of subatomic behaviors.
   (C) Quantum theory confirms the findings of those physicists who were apostles to Newton's theories.
   (D) Quantum theory focuses on the behavior of large physical entities, such as galaxies.

10. (A) NO CHANGE
    (B) it's
    (C) their
    (D) there

11. Which of the following would provide the most logical ending to this paragraph and to the essay as a whole?
    (A) NO CHANGE
    (B) The cat, after all, is either dead or alive—never both.
    (C) Both men were instrumental in confirming the Newtonian theoretical construct.
    (D) While Schrödinger was not recognized in his lifetime, that has finally begun to change.

To Test or Not to Test

❶ I find myself in a catch-22, an advocate of critical pedagogies who desperately, wishes to see my students succeed in high-stakes testing. Training to become a teacher is being assigned the texts of John Dewey, Paulo Freire, and Ira Shor, and then being handed a thirty-page mandated curriculum to be followed to the letter. The clash ❷ among pedagogy and practice is not a new one, nor is the contradiction between teaching stance and accountability measurements. By this, I mean that many scholars have addressed the underlying issues between what they believe the classroom should look like and what the institution says it must look like. As teachers, we empower our students, open their minds, and encourage social justice—a job not done well when teaching-to-the-test. Yet, assessment signifies what we value in the classroom and how we assign that value. ❸ In other words, to stop testing a subject is to see it all but disappear from the curriculum.

[1] Many argue that high-stakes testing is antithetical to the critical classroom. [2] An increase in required courses and standardized tests, for them, ❹ equating to the disempowerment of students. [3] Today's student, under this line of thinking, is told what is important and what is not, who is in authority and who will never be, and whose perspective is heard and whose is silenced. [4] Ira Shor, literacy and composition scholar, suggests that all education is, and has always been, political. [5] Whereas a traditional English teacher might assign canonical texts and then assess a ❺ classes understanding of plot, setting, and character analyses, a critical English teacher assigns literature with a goal in mind of what the class will get from that particular text, and then encourages the class to talk about how the social issues reflect their own lives,

1. (A) NO CHANGE
   (B) I find myself in a catch-22: an advocate of critical pedagogies who desperately wishes to see my students succeed in high-stakes testing.
   (C) I find myself in a catch-22—an advocate of critical pedagogies—who desperately wishes to see my students succeed in high-stakes testing.
   (D) I find myself in a catch-22; an advocate of critical pedagogies, who desperately wishes to see my students succeed in high-stakes testing.

2. (A) NO CHANGE
   (B) between
   (C) through
   (D) in

3. (A) NO CHANGE
   (B) For these reasons,
   (C) Due to this,
   (D) Henceforth,

4. (A) NO CHANGE
   (B) equation
   (C) equate
   (D) equates

5. (A) NO CHANGE
   (B) class'es
   (C) class's
   (D) classes'

whose voices weren't heard, and how the story might be told differently from another perspective. ❻

❼ Yet, testing is not without its benefits. Educators agree that assessments encourage better instruction, improve motivation, and help teachers identify students' needs. Inside the classroom, students, their parents, and administrators all want high test scores. Effective schools are continually aligned with those ❽ that adequately prepare students for testing. And, when done correctly, tests should operate as an assessment of what is practiced on a daily basis inside the classroom. Classrooms that teach to well-written standards ❾ assure that students are prepared for the next grade level. Imagine the student who moves from grade to grade (or worse, school to

6. The author would like to insert the following sentence into the previous paragraph:

   "Critical pedagogies, therefore, are committed to democracy and the questioning of power structures."

   Where would it most logically be placed?
   (A) After sentence 2
   (B) After sentence 3
   (C) After sentence 4
   (D) After sentence 5

7. Which of the following would provide the most logical introduction to this paragraph?
   (A) NO CHANGE
   (B) The problems with widespread testing are clear.
   (C) Scholars are in agreement when it comes to the shortcomings of testing.
   (D) In fact, the time has come for educators to take a stand.

8. (A) NO CHANGE
   (B) for which
   (C) whom
   (D) OMIT the underlined portion.

9. (A) NO CHANGE
   (B) insure
   (C) ensure
   (D) reassure

school) without standards. While testing might not be perfect, it is necessary. ⑩ Testing is critical to assessing what people are capable of doing. ⑪

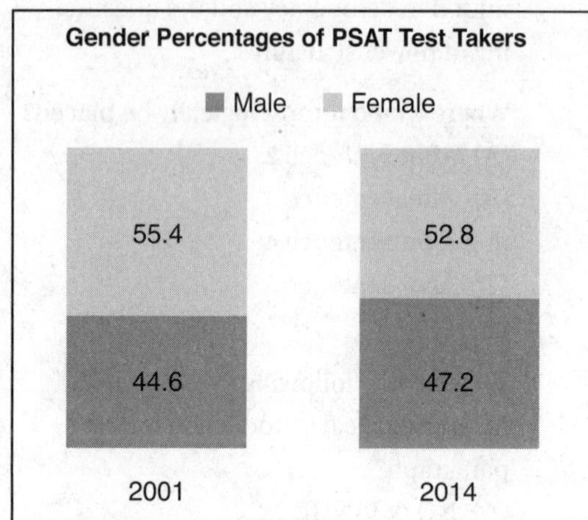

Source: The College Board

10. Which of the following sentences most effectively and specifically builds off of the statement made in the previous sentence?
    (A) NO CHANGE
    (B) I cannot think of one career path that doesn't require a series of tests.
    (C) Can someone think of a reasonable alternative to the tried and true avenue of testing?
    (D) Students are far more than just a number based on a random assessment.

11. The author is considering incorporating information from the accompanying graph into her essay. Should she utilize this information?
    (A) Yes, because it provides relevant facts on standardized testing.
    (B) Yes, because it demonstrates cultural shifts over time.
    (C) No, because it is only loosely related to the major theme of the passage.
    (D) No, because it contradicts the author's principal claim.

Truman and MacArthur

Many of the greatest battles in history can be simplified to microcosmic struggles **1** among two strong characters. Take Grant and Lee, for instance. Or consider David and Goliath if you prefer an older story. But not often **2** do such a struggle occur when both Great Men are on the same side. And in those instances, you see, are when the fireworks really commence to combust. The old saying is that it's best to avoid having **3** "a chicken in every pot"; it is best to have only one person making executive decisions and delegating orders to inferiors. General Douglas MacArthur and President Harry **4** Truman—Great Men, by all accounts—were both American leaders in the late 1940s and early 1950s in the aftermath of the Allied victory during World War II. Naturally, only one of them could emerge victorious from the rubble of **5** there power struggle.

MacArthur, so distinguished a war hero that he was awarded the illustrious and unparalleled Congressional Medal of Honor for his heroism during WWII, was the Army's most powerful and decorated general. He had been a Republican presidential candidate during the elections of 1944 and 1948, and was currently serving as the Supreme Commander of the Allied Powers **6** —an office created specifically for General MacArthur in which he would oversee the Allied occupation of Japan after the war victory.

1. (A) NO CHANGE
   (B) between
   (C) within
   (D) throughout

2. (A) NO CHANGE
   (B) doing
   (C) does
   (D) OMIT the underlined portion.

3. What colloquial expression would be most appropriate, given the content of the sentence as a whole?
   (A) NO CHANGE
   (B) "a chip on your shoulder";
   (C) "too many cooks in the kitchen";
   (D) "a wild goose chase";

4. (A) NO CHANGE
   (B) Truman—Great Men, by all accounts, were
   (C) Truman: Great Men, by all accounts—were
   (D) Truman; Great Men, by all accounts—were

5. (A) NO CHANGE
   (B) their
   (C) his
   (D) one's

6. The author is considering deleting the underlined portion. Should it be kept or removed?
   (A) Kept, because it clarifies a key title
   (B) Kept, because it states the author's point of view
   (C) Removed, because it provides an unnecessary detail
   (D) Removed, because it distracts from the primary message of the sentence

❼ Truman, a man now generally viewed by political scholars and historians as one of the finest commanders in chief of the 20th century had a military foundation of his own: he had served in the first World War and later held a reserve commission as colonel. ❽ As a result, Truman distrusted the current crop of military executives at his disposal. He once remarked on his confusion that the U.S. Army could "produce people such as Lee, Pershing, Eisenhower and Bradley, and at the same time produce Custer, Patton, and MacArthur."

[1] The start of the Korean War in 1950 ❾ made happen the cataclysm. [2] General MacArthur, often superseding orders by Truman, had instituted deft military strategic policy that prevented South Korea (a U.S. ally) from being overrun by North Korea ❿ (which was being supported both militarily and financially by Communist China). [3] Momentum in the war began to shift, however, and soon South Korea was in a position to attack. [4] MacArthur assured Truman that a U.S.-led offensive into North Korea to eradicate Communism there would be met with little resistance from China.

7. (A) NO CHANGE
   (B) Truman, a man now generally viewed by political scholars, and historians as one of the finest commanders in chief of the 20th century, had
   (C) Truman, a man now generally viewed by political scholars and historians as one of the finest commanders in chief of the 20th century, had
   (D) Truman a man now generally viewed by political scholars and historians as one of the finest commanders in chief of the 20th century had

8. (A) NO CHANGE
   (B) An observation:
   (C) Chronologically,
   (D) Nonetheless,

9. (A) NO CHANGE
   (B) precipitated
   (C) impeded
   (D) destroyed

10. The author is considering deleting the underlined portion. Should this selection be kept or deleted?
    (A) Kept, because it explains the Chinese motivations for supporting North Korea
    (B) Kept, because it makes a chain of events analyzed later in the paragraph more clear
    (C) Deleted, because it provides an irrelevant aside
    (D) Deleted, because it overuses the already utilized parenthetical phrase

[5] China lashed back. [6] MacArthur proceeded to disobey numerous Truman orders and even began to publicly criticize Truman to the media. [7] Alas, the president had no choice, and MacArthur was relieved of his command on April 11, 1951. ⓫

11. The author would like to insert the following sentence into the previous paragraph:

    "This, unfortunately, was a grave miscalculation."

    Where would it most logically be placed?
    (A) Before sentence 4
    (B) Before sentence 5
    (C) Before sentence 6
    (D) After sentence 7

The Y-Bridge

States can best be characterized by their natural intricacies. Florida has its powdered sugar beaches; Nebraska, its butterscotch **1** cornfields; and Arizona it's Grand Canyon. Cities, on the other hand, are known better by their man-made marvels. Everybody knows San Francisco as the Golden Gate City, just as Seattle is synonymous with the Space Needle and Saint Louis is famous for the Golden Gate Arch. Zanesville, Ohio, may not be as large or as recognizable as those three municipal behemoths, but its quirky Y-Bridge serves as its focal point **2** once upon a time.

Zanesville natives often joke about the **3** looks of incredulity they receive when visitors to the town ask for directions. "Go to the middle of the bridge and turn left" is a command to which most are unaccustomed, but it is commonplace in Zanesville. The Y-Bridge (named for its distinctive Y-shape) was designed to span the confluence of the Muskingum and Licking rivers. **4** For it crosses both rivers, Ripley's Believe It Or Not once claimed that the Y-Bridge was the only bridge in the world where it was possible to cross and still end up on the same side

1. (A) NO CHANGE
   (B) cornfields: Arizona its Grand Canyon.
   (C) cornfields; and Arizona, its Grand Canyon.
   (D) cornfields, and Arizona, it's Grand Canyon.

2. Which of the following would be the most logical conclusion to this sentence?
   (A) NO CHANGE
   (B) for better or for worse.
   (C) just the same.
   (D) much to one's surprise.

3. Which of the following would be the most reasonable phrase to have at this point in the sentence?
   (A) NO CHANGE
   (B) casting of aspersions
   (C) dearth of piety
   (D) outright hostility

4. (A) NO CHANGE
   (B) Because
   (C) While
   (D) When

of the river, and Amelia Earhart once called Zanesville **5** "the most recognizable city on the country" because of the bridge.

Construction on the Y-Bridge began in 1812, and it opened officially in 1814. However, the first edition was riddled with issues: it required ceaseless **6** repairs; and due, to its frailness, was destroyed by a flood in 1818. Construction on the second bridge began soon after, and it then officially opened in 1819 before being declared unsafe just 12 short years after. The third edition of the Y-Bridge **7** enjoyed much greater longevity, spanning from 1832–1900. This third bridge, unlike the previous two, was a covered structure.

What doomed the third bridge, interestingly enough, was not **8** public panic so much as hysteria; rumors began circulating that the bridge was unsafe, and locals voted to erect a new structure. This fourth Y-Bridge was completed in 1902, and was the first version to be constructed of concrete rather than wood. It stood until 1983 but was torn down and replaced by the fifth version, **9** that still stands today. The fifth version, formed from steel and concrete, was designed to look like the fourth bridge.

While the greater part of this lengthy history is unknown by most Zanesvillians, all who **10** reside there are proud of the bridge's legacy nonetheless. **11** So, if you ever find yourself passing through Central Ohio, be sure and make a quick stop in Zanesville. Just be sure to keep your poise when a local tells you to drive to the center of the Y-bridge and turn left!

5. (A) NO CHANGE
(B) "the most recognizing city for the country"
(C) "the most recognizing city of the country"
(D) "the most recognizable city in the country"

6. (A) NO CHANGE
(B) repairs and—due to its frailness, was
(C) repairs and—due to its frailness—was
(D) repairs, and due to its frailness; was

7. Which of the following options provides the most fitting ending to the introductory phrase in the sentence?
(A) NO CHANGE
(B) failed to accomplish its goals,
(C) was much like its predecessor,
(D) captured the imaginations of passersby,

8. What word would be most appropriate given the context of the essay?
(A) NO CHANGE
(B) fear-mongering
(C) obsolescence
(D) decomposition

9. (A) NO CHANGE
(B) where it
(C) which
(D) when it

10. (A) NO CHANGE
(B) resides there is
(C) reside there is
(D) residing there are

11. (A) NO CHANGE
(B) However,
(C) Inevitably,
(D) Paradoxically,

Answer Explanations

A Tricky Feline

1. **(B)** "Notwithstanding" means "in spite of" or "despite," which fits the meaning of this sentence perfectly. Choice (A) attempts to draw a causal relationship that is absent. "Aside with" should read *aside from,* and "stemming in" should read *stemming from,* which would still be incorrect in context. *Aside from* would be acceptable, but it is not an option.

2. **(A)** This needs a possessive to match the idea: *the contribution of either scientist.* As possession and an apostrophe are required, eliminate choice (C). Eliminate choices (B) and (D) for using the plural word "scientists" since the initial idea was *the contribution of either scientist,* not *the contribution of both scientists.*

3. **(D)** This sentence is a rare instance in which there are *two* uses of extra wording. Both "a lesser recognized name" and "however" can be removed from the sentence and still have the sentence function perfectly well. Accordingly, we must surround each phrase with a set of dashes or commas to isolate them from the rest of the sentence. Choice (A) omits the comma after "Schrödinger," which ruins the first phrase. Choice (B) ruins the second instance by forgetting the comma after "however." Choice (C) botches both instances. Choice **(D)**, however, perfectly surrounds both instances with the required punctuation.

4. **(C)** To determine the correct conjunction to use, analyze the relationship between the two clauses. Here, the second clause contrasts with the first. Essentially, *although* Schrödinger won the Nobel Prize, he is more famous for something else. *Although,* like "but," is a contrasting term. Choice **(C)** is the correct answer. Choices (A) and (B) emphasize a causal relationship. Choice (D) is not contrasting but, rather, conjoining.

5. **(D)** *To swallow* has an alternative meaning outside of simple ingestion that most closely aligns with the verb *to accept.* In the context of the question, Einstein had a difficult time *accepting* the Copenhagen interpretation. "Swallowing" is the correct answer. None of the other choices has either a denotation or a connotation that matches the context of the sentence.

6. **(A)** At the core of this question is *lie* vs. *lay.* In context, the sentence most clearly means *the trick here rests upon the unpredictability of radioactivity. Rests upon* corresponds to "lies," so we can eliminate choices (C) and (D). The correct idiom is *lies in* rather than *lies on,* so the correct answer is choice **(A)**. Choice (B) improperly uses "to."

7. **(B)** The verb refers to the plural "states" and so requires a plural verb—"become." Choice (A) is singular, and choices (C) and (D) use incorrect verb tense.

8. **(D)** Sentence 5 mentions the mutually exclusive states of being dead and alive, which obviously *can't* occur simultaneously. "Hence the flaw in this line of thinking" follows that sentence perfectly as its presumption is certainly flawed. Choice **(D)** is the correct answer.

9. **(B)** The main theme of the paragraph is subatomic particles. Choice **(B)**, particularly with its mention of "subatomic behaviors," is the best introduction to this paragraph. The paragraph mentions nothing of "theoretical physicists" or "large physical entities." Choice (C) is flawed in that subatomic particles go *against* Newton's theories.

10. **(A)** We need a possessive to serve as a stand-in for "quantum superposition," which is a singular noun. "Its" is the best substitute for *quantum superposition's.* Choices (B) and (D) are not possessive, and choice (C) refers to *multiple* people or things. Quantum superposition is one thing.

11. **(B)** Although the passage briefly touches on Schrödinger's fame (or lack thereof), it is not the main idea. Eliminate choices (A) and (D) because they focus on the wrong theme and thus provide ineffective conclusions. Similarly, the "Newtonian theoretical construct" is not the main idea, so eliminate choice (C). Choice **(B)**, however, is ideal. It mentions Schrödinger (the main character in the passage). It also refers to the cat, which is a key component of the article and its focus on quantum theory. Moreover, the very title of the article is "A Tricky Feline," further illustrating the significance of the cat.

To Test or Not to Test

1. **(B)** Choice (A) inserts an unnecessary comma after "desperately," separating verb and adverb. Choice (C) incorrectly treats an appositive. Choice (D)'s semicolon is incorrect since a semicolon requires an independent clause on both sides of the semicolon. The second clause is not complete. Choice **(B)** is perfect, inserting neither excessive commas nor improper punctuation.

2. **(B)** When a conflict occurs with two things/parties, "between" must be used. When it occurs with three or more parties, "among" must be used. As "pedagogy" and "practice" are two things, "between" is the correct answer. "Through" and "in" are not valid options.

3. **(A)** Analyze the relationship between this sentence and the previous statement. Essentially, the second sentence is a restatement of the previous sentence. "In other words" serves to introduce a restatement. Choices (B) and (C) create a cause-and-effect relationship that is not apparent here. "Henceforth" is often used chronologically to signify *from this point forward.*

4. **(D)** The subject is "increase," which is a singular noun that requires a singular verb. Eliminate choice (C) because it uses a plural verb. Choice (A) is a fragment. Choice (B) does away entirely with the required predicate.

5. **(C)** The difficult part here is that the correct answer simply looks odd, despite being flawless. A possessive form of *understanding of the class* is needed: "class's" understanding is the proper way to illustrate this. Choice (A) is both plural and lacking an apostrophe. Choice (B) is an improper way to indicate possession. Choice (D) indicates multiple "classes," whereas there is actually only one class.

6. **(C)** Sentence 4, particularly with its mention of the "political," is the perfect sentence to precede the insertion. The insertion refers to politics, which is most apparent with its discussion of "democracy." Thus, sentence 4 acts as an introduction to the insertion, making choice **(C)** the correct answer.

7. **(A)** Analyze the content of the entire paragraph to answer this question. Notice that this paragraph acts as a shift away from the detriments of testing; the passage is now presenting *good things* about testing. "Benefits" are *good things,* and choice **(A)** is the correct answer. Choices (B), (C), and (D) fail to act as acceptable transitions from criticism to praise of testing.

8. **(A)** Choice (D) does away with the connector, ultimately leading to a broken clause. Choice (C), "whom," can be used only with people, whereas the author is discussing schools, not people. Choice (B) uses awkward wording, interjecting an unnecessary "for." This is a restrictive clause, so "that" makes sense.

9. **(C)** This question is all about vocabulary. To "assure" is to remove doubt, and it is generally done to another person. *I assured my father that I would be home by curfew.* To "ensure" means to make sure a thing will or won't happen. *I studied last night to ensure that I wouldn't fail the test.* To "insure" refers to car insurance, life insurance, health insurance, etc. To "reassure" is simply to "assure" someone multiple times. In this sentence, the classrooms are *ensuring* that something will happen: students will be prepared for the next grade. Choice **(C)** is the correct answer.

10. **(B)** The previous sentence says that testing, despite its flaws, is necessary. We need to find an option that "specifically" and "effectively" builds on that previous sentence. Choice (D) is most flawed in that it *refutes* entirely the previous sentence. Choices (A), (B), and (C) are all valid options at first glance. Look more closely, though, and see that choice **(B)** is both more *specific* and more *effective*. Choices (A) and (C) are more general and somewhat blasé. Choice **(B)**'s connection between education and life after education is the most attention grabbing.

11. **(C)** The graph refers to testing by gender. As the passage itself has nothing to do with gender, the graph data isn't relevant to the passage and should not be included. Eliminate choices (A) and (B) because they incorrectly state that the graph should be included. Eliminate choice (D), as gender data contradicts nothing in the passage but, rather, is mostly irrelevant to the passage's main claim. Choice **(C)** is the correct answer.

Truman and MacArthur

1. **(B)** If a struggle occurs with three or more parties, that would be a *struggle among them*. We only have "two men," though. Something occurring with two parties happens *between them*, so choice **(B)** is the correct answer. Choices (C) and (D) are not acceptable usage.

2. **(C)** The subject here is "a struggle," which is a singular noun. We will need a singular verb to match. "Does" is the correct answer. "Do" is a plural verb in this context, "doing" leads to gibberish, and choice (D) eliminates a principal part of the predicate.

3. **(C)** This question requires knowledge of colloquialisms. Choice (A) is used to symbolize prosperity for everybody. Choice (B) signifies a feeling of being slighted in some way and motivated by that slight. Choice (C) refers to a situation in which there are too many people giving orders and not enough people *taking* orders. Choice (D) refers to undertaking a frenetic—and often futile—task. Since the second part of the sentence refers to giving and taking orders, choice **(C)** is the correct answer.

4. **(A)** "Great Men, by all accounts" is a parenthetical statement. If you remove it from the sentence, the clause still functions perfectly well. The general rule with parenthetical statements is that there can be either two commas or two dashes separating the statement from the rest of the sentence. Choice (B) is close, but it starts with a dash and concludes with a comma, which breaks with parallelism.

5. **(B)** We need a possessive word to serve as a stand-in for *Truman and MacArthur*. Eliminate choices (C) and (D) for being singular possessives. Eliminate choice (A) for not being a possessive at all. "Their" is the correct answer.

6. **(A)** If we were to delete the underlined portion, the reader would be left wondering, *What does that title mean? It sounds illustrious, but what* is *it?* Choice **(A)**, therefore, is correct as it "clarifies a key title." Choices (B), (C), and (D) all make erroneous statements.

7. **(C)** "A man now generally viewed by political scholars and historians as one of the finest commanders in chief of the 20th century" is an *appositive*: the phrase can be removed, and the sentence still functions perfectly well. So we must separate the appositive from the rest of the sentence using either two dashes or two commas. Eliminate choice (A) for neglecting the second comma, and eliminate choice (D) for neglecting both commas. Choice (B) executes the appositive correctly, but it inserts an unnecessary comma after "scholars" since there is no need to place a comma between two things in a list.

8. **(D)** Analyze the relationship between this sentence and the preceding sentence. When paraphrased, the sentences are *Truman was a military man,* but *he still was distrustful of military leadership. But* is a contrasting term, and "nonetheless" is also a contrasting term. Choice (A) implies a cause and effect that does not exist. Choice (B) is out of place. *Who is observing and why are you telling me you're observing?* Choice (C) deals with the progression of time and is illogical.

9. **(B)** *Precipitate* is a synonym for *cause, trigger,* or *spark.* The start of the Korean War *triggered* the cataclysm, so "precipitated" is the best answer. Choice (C) means "prevented" or "blocked," which is the opposite of what occurred. Choice (D) is illogical since the meltdown wasn't destroyed. Choice (A) is a wordy and unacceptably informal way of saying *caused.*

10. **(B)** If we were to delete this portion, the conflict with China would be unexplained. The role of the Chinese government in the proceedings would be unclear. Choice **(B)** is the correct answer because "it makes a chain of events analyzed more clear." Choice (A) is flawed in that it mentions the Chinese support but *doesn't explain why they were supporting North Korea.* Choices (C) and (D) make wholly false claims.

11. **(B)** The "grave miscalculation" mentioned in the question refers to sentence 4, which mentions MacArthur's certainty that China would not interfere in an invasion of North Korea. Sentence 5 mentions the consequences of that "grave miscalculation." Thus, it is sensible to insert this sentence between sentences 4 and 5, as described in choice **(B)**.

The Y-Bridge

1. **(C)** Notice the parallelism of listing: as each item in the list has a comma inside the item, it is proper to separate the items using semicolons. Choices (B) and (D) do not have the proper structure. Now notice the comma after each state in the previous items. Choice (A) omits that comma after "Arizona." Additionally, choice (A) makes use of "it's," meaning it is, where the correct answer should use the possessive form "its."

2. **(C)** It is probably easiest to determine the correct answer simply by eliminating all of the wrong answers. Choice (A) is a phrase used to refer to the past, whereas the verbs in this sentence are present tense. Choice (B) implies an ambivalence that does not match the author's tone; he is wholly enthusiastic about the bridge. Choice (D) is flawed in that there is nothing inherently *surprising* about this fact. We examine the remaining choice, "just the same," and realize that the author was making a comparison between the bridge and the collection of other notable landmarks of larger cities.

3. **(A)** To cast aspersions is to make rude or insulting remarks. Eliminate choice (B) primarily because it is too similar to the "outright hostility" of choice (D). There can only be one correct answer, so these two interchangeable choices are incorrect by default. Choice (C) means a lack of religious devotion, which is entirely irrelevant. "Looks of incredulity" is most appropriate here: the visitors, upon being told to go to the middle of the bridge and turn left, look at the locals in utter disbelief.

4. **(B)** This transition refers to the relationship between the first and second clauses in this sentence, where the first clause is the *cause* and the second clause is the *effect.* In essence, "because" of clause one, then clause two. Choice (A) leaves the sentence disjointed and lacking fluidity. Choice (C) is used to introduce simultaneous (but often contradictory) clauses, while choice (D) is also generally a lead-in for two actions occurring at the same time.

5. **(D)** First, "recognizable," essentially *able to be recognized,* is superior to "recognizing." "Recognizing" means that the city would be recognizing others as opposed to *being* recognized by others. Eliminate choices (B) and (C). Now, it is far superior to say "in the country" than "on the country." Unfortunately, there is no true rule behind this; preposition recognition in certain phrases often requires familiarity with the phrase, without substitute. Because choice (A) is not something commonly said and choice **(D)** is, the correct answer is choice **(D)**.

6. **(C)** "Due to its frailness" is a parenthetical phrase. If you remove it, the sentence still functions perfectly well. In order to denote our parenthetical phrase, we can surround it with two commas or two dashes. Choices (A) and (D) improperly use semicolons without having independent clauses on both sides of the semicolon. Choice (B) begins the parenthetical phrase with a dash but then breaks with parallelism by switching to a comma on the back end.

7. **(A)** It is important to analyze not only the entire sentence but also the qualities of this bridge relative to those of other bridges. The largest exception is that this bridge lasted much longer than the previous bridges. "Enjoyed much greater longevity" simply means lasted longer, so choice **(A)** is the best option. Choices (B) and (C) make incorrect statements. Choice (D), though possibly correct in its statement, is illogical and out of context in conjunction with the rest of the sentence.

8. **(C)** Knowledge of vocabulary is critical here, particularly with choice **(C)**; obsolescence means the state of no longer being useful. In context, this is our best choice: the bridge was still perfectly usable, but the public felt a safer bridge was needed, ultimately dooming the bridge. Choices (A) and (B) are synonyms for the "hysteria" mentioned next and thus do not function in context. "Decomposition" is a term traditionally used to mean the breakdown of organic matter.

9. **(C)** This is a *nonrestrictive* clause (i.e., describing a nonessential characteristic) rather than a *restrictive* clause (i.e., describing an essential characteristic), so "which" is preferable to "that." Choice (B) can be used only after mentioning a place, while choice (D) must be preceded by a chronological term (e.g., *in 1983* or *on Tuesday*).

10. **(A)** "Zanesvillians" is a plural noun referring to citizens of Zanesville, so a plural verb must be used to maintain subject-verb agreement. Eliminate choices (B) and (C) because they use "resides" and/or "is," which are singular verbs that do not agree with "Zanesvillians." "Residing," a gerund, does not provide an acceptable, complete sentence. Choice **(A)** is the only remaining option, and it ultimately matches the aforementioned criteria.

11. **(A)** "However" implies a contrast that is not apparent. "Inevitably" makes it sound as if the reader will *certainly* find herself/himself in Zanesville at some point. There is no paradox, as in choice (D). In common usage, a paradox refers to things that, in combination with each other, are ironic, unexpected, or sometimes self-contradictory. "So" is the best choice. It serves as a tidy way to conclude an argument, followed by another claim that is logical based on that argument. Such is the case with this sentence.

PART 5
Math

Introduction and Strategies

What is tested on the SAT Math? What math classes should I have taken?

The SAT Math focuses on the core math skills that you will need to be successful in a variety of college majors and future careers. No matter if you are an engineer, a nurse, a teacher, a graphic designer, or a business manager, it will be important to know how to work with numbers and interpret data. Here is a big picture summary of what is tested:

SAT Math Question Type	Definition	Math Class(es) That Covers It
Heart of Algebra	Interpretation of linear equations and solving systems of equations	Mostly covered in Pre-Algebra and Algebra 1
Problem Solving and Data Analysis	Demonstration of literacy with data and graphs with real-world applications	Covered throughout your Pre-Algebra, Algebra 1, and Algebra 2 coursework Science classes can also provide helpful data interpretation skills.
Passport to Advanced Math	Working with more complicated equations	Mostly covered in Algebra 2
Additional Topics in Math	Geometry, trigonometry, and other advanced math	Mainly in Geometry and Pre-Calculus

How is the SAT Math section structured?

The Math sections are the third and fourth sections of the test, with a non-calculator section followed by a calculator-permitted section.

Non-Calculator Section:

- 25 minutes
- 20 questions
  - 15 multiple-choice, 5 fill-in

Calculator Section:

- 55 minutes
- 38 questions
  - 30 multiple-choice, 8 fill-in

The questions generally become more difficult as you go. The typical organization of difficulty is as follows:

- Non-Calculator Section—The multiple-choice questions 1–15 go from easy to hard; the fill-in questions 16–20 go easy to hard.
- Calculator Section—The multiple-choice questions 1–30 go from easy to hard; the fill-in questions 31–38 go easy to hard.

This is the breakdown of specific question types on the non-calculator and calculator sections, and SAT Math test as a whole:

SAT Math Question Type	Non-Calculator Section	Calculator Section	Total Number of Questions
Heart of Algebra	8	11	19
Problem Solving and Data Analysis	0	17	17
Passport to Advanced Math	9	7	16
Additional Topics in Math	3	3	6
Total Number of Questions	20	38	58

What is *not* tested on the SAT Math? What do I *not* need to worry about?

If you have taken the ACT, you may recall how that test has quite a few more advanced math concepts. Some of the concepts you will NOT need to know for the SAT that are tested on the ACT include:

- Matrices
- Logarithms
- Hyperbolas
- Ellipses
- Cosecant, Secant, Cotangent
- Permutations and Combinations

How does the SAT Math differ from typical math tests I have taken in school?

Often, students have difficulty with the SAT Math because they approach it the same way as they would typical school math tests and quizzes. This is especially true for high-achieving students who consistently earn A's in their math classes—after all, if their approach works well on one math test, why wouldn't it work well on another math test like the SAT? By realizing that the SAT Math is quite a bit different from typical school math tests, students are empowered to have a different mindset to help them be successful.

	Typical School Math Tests/ Quizzes	SAT Math
Time Management	▪ Typically, you don't have to worry much about time management. ▪ Tests often do not take the entire class period, or you may be allowed to stay after class to finish up.	▪ You will likely need the full amount of time to finish. ▪ Move through the test carefully and efficiently to complete every question.
Scoring Curve	▪ If you miss a couple of questions, your grade may drop quite a bit. ▪ To get an A, you may need to aim for perfection.	▪ Since the test is heavily curved, do not worry about missing a couple questions. ▪ To get a good score, you do not need to aim for perfection.

(*Continued*)

	Typical School Math Tests/ Quizzes	SAT Math
Concepts Tested	■ Usually highly focused on a particular set of concepts you have recently studied ■ For example, a test on your factoring unit will focus just on factoring. You have a good sense of what each question will likely be about.	■ Tests on a variety of concepts from multiple years of coursework ■ Cannot go on "autopilot" and just start solving the problem—have to figure out what the question is about
Problem Solving Process	■ Often, if you do not "know" the formula or problem-solving process from class, you will have trouble coming up with the answer.	■ While there is a good bit you need to know, the emphasis on SAT Math problems is to "figure them out" by any means necessary. ■ Unconventional methods like using estimation, intuition, and plugging in answers are much more applicable.
Possible Test Errors	■ If there is an error on your test or quiz, just let your teacher know and it can easily be fixed.	■ SAT Math problems go through multiple rounds of review before they are put on an actual test. ■ Rather than trying to find the flaw in the question, give the question the benefit of the doubt.
Need to Explain Answer	■ Your teacher may expect you to solve the problem in the way you were taught, clearly writing out every step so you can earn full credit.	■ You are evaluated simply on whether you answered the question correctly. ■ Use whatever problem-solving method works best for you.

How is the SAT Math section scored?

There is NO penalty for guessing, so it is definitely in your interest to answer every question on the SAT Math, including the fill-in questions. The SAT Math is scored out of a maximum of 800 points and minimum of 200 points, with the number of questions you need to answer correctly for a particular score changing from test to test based on the curve. If a certain test is more difficult for students, the curve will be more generous and you can miss more questions to get a good score. If a test is easier, the curve will be less generous and you will need to answer more questions correctly to get a good score. Here is a rough estimate of how many questions you need to answer correctly to score at different levels.

Correct Answers Out of 58 Total Math Questions	Math Section Score Out of 800 Points
58	800
54	750
50	700
44	650
39	600
32	550
26	500
20	450
16	400
12	350
8	300
4	250
0	200

Can I use a calculator?

You are permitted to use a calculator on the fourth section of the test, but not on the third section of the test. The non-calculator portion of the test will not ask questions where having a calculator would make a significant difference to your speed in solving the problem. The SAT is fairly generous in terms of permitted calculators. Most scientific and graphing calculators are permitted—for a complete, updated list of approved calculators, check here: *https://collegereadiness.collegeboard.org/sat/taking-the-test/calculator-policy*.

How do the fill-in questions work?

The SAT Math has a total of **13 fill-in questions**: five on the non-calculator section and eight on the calculator section. You will enter your answer in a grid like this:

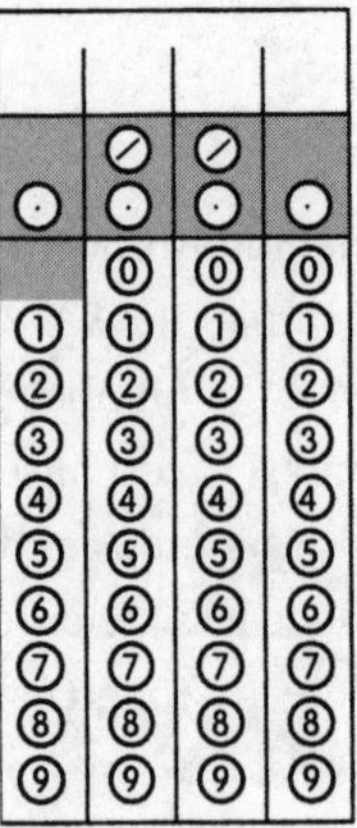

Here are some special rules about these problems:

- **It is sometimes possible to have more than one correct answer**—if you fill in any of the correct answers, you will be fine. For example, if the correct answer could be any number between 4 and 6, if you entered 5.5 you would be correct.
- **There will never be a negative answer.** As you can see above, there is no way to enter a negative sign; therefore, if you come up with a negative answer on a fill-in, redo the problem.

- Decimals that continue past the four spots allowed for gridding **can be rounded or shortened**, as long as you use all of the spaces on the grid. You can also express the decimal as a fraction. For example, you can write $\frac{7}{9}$ as 7/9, .777 or .778 (Note that 0.8, 0.77, or 0.78 would be considered incorrect.).
- **You don't need to reduce fractions.** For example, since $\frac{2}{3}$, $\frac{4}{6}$, and $\frac{6}{9}$ are equivalent, any of them would work as an answer.

The bottom line on fill-ins: The SAT will not *trick* you into missing the problem. If you have a reasonable answer and enter it, you will be in good shape.

Do they provide any formulas?

The SAT will provide some of the most important geometry and trigonometry formulas. However, since most of the test covers algebra, you will need to commit algebraic formulas to memory. Here are the formulas you will be given at the beginning of each Math section:

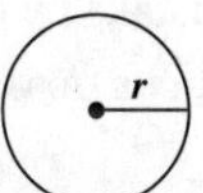

Radius of a circle = r
Area of a circle = πr^2
Circumference of a circle = $2\pi r$

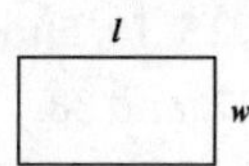

Area of a rectangle = length × width = lw

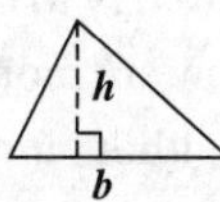

Area of a triangle = $\frac{1}{2}$ × base × height = $\frac{1}{2}bh$

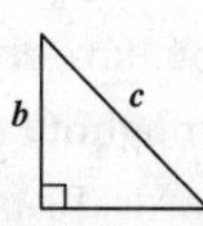

Pythagorean theorem: $a^2 + b^2 = c^2$

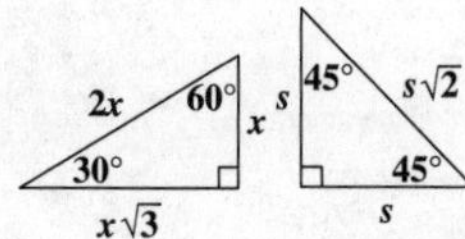

Special right triangles: 30-60-90 and 45-45-90

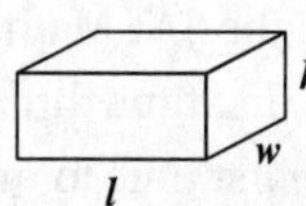

Volume of a box =
length × width × height = lwh

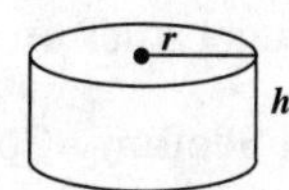

Volume of a cylinder = $\pi r^2 h$

Volume of a sphere = $\frac{4}{3}\pi r^3$

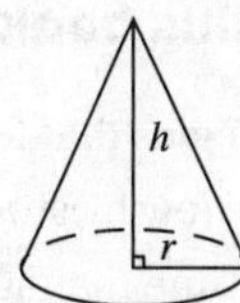

Volume of a cone = $\frac{1}{3}\pi r^2 h$

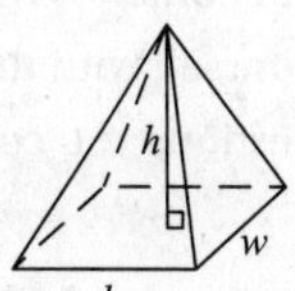

Volume of a pyramid =
$\frac{1}{3}$ × length × width × height = $\frac{1}{3}lwh$

KEY FACTS:

- **A circle has 360 degrees.**
- **There are 2π radians in a circle.**
- **There are 180 degrees in a triangle.**

How should I pace myself on the SAT Math?

On the non-calculator section, you have an average of 1 minute and 15 seconds per question, and on the calculator section, you have an average of 1 minutes and 27 seconds per question. Keep in mind that the questions do increase in difficulty as you progress through the multiple-choice questions and then again through the fill-in questions. So, instead of trying to set a stopwatch for each individual question, use these general guidelines:

- **Take between 1 and 1.5 minutes a question. If it is an easier/earlier question, go closer to a minute; if it is a harder/later question, go closer to 1.5 minutes.**
- **Check your pace at reasonable intervals—each time you turn a page is generally a good time to see if you are on pace.** If you check your pace with each problem, you will waste time looking at your watch. On the other hand, if you do not check your pace at all, you will only have the proctor's verbal reminders to help you (they give you two reminders of time per math section; at 15 minutes and 5 minutes remaining on the non-calculator section and at 30 minutes and 5 minutes remaining on the calculator section).
- **Try to do the problems <u>once</u> and <u>well</u> instead of rushing to the end.** With so many word problems on the SAT Math, it is very easy to make a careless mistake by misreading the problem the first time through. Instead of rushing to the end, focus on doing the problems carefully the first time to maximize your score.

If you cannot finish the test in a reasonable amount of time, **guess on the most difficult questions** (remember that the questions restart the order of difficulty from easy to hard with the fill-ins, so don't get stuck on the last multiple-choice questions and ignore the easy fill-ins):

Non-Calculator Section—Consider guessing on questions 13, 14, 15, 19, and 20.
Calculator Section—Consider guessing on 26, 27, 28, 29, 30, 36, 37, and 38.

Also, if you find an earlier question to be overly difficult, go ahead and guess on it—you do not want to spend two to three minutes on a problem and not get anywhere. Try to be decisive when guessing on a problem; if there are certain problem types that you know are more difficult for you, like long word problems or particular math concepts, guess on those without investing lots of time.

How can I use this book to prepare for the SAT Math?

- Read the strategies that follow in this section to help you with your test-taking mindset.
- Target your review by studying the math content areas where you have struggled.
- Practice your time management with the SAT problem drills throughout the chapter.
- Take full-length SAT Math tests and review your answers afterwards. Brush up on weak areas through content review.
- Challenge yourself with the advanced math drills at the end of the chapter to simulate the toughest questions you could encounter.

SAT Math Dos and Don'ts

<u>Do</u> fully understand the question, actively checking understanding as you go. Read slowly and carefully, doing the problem one time well.

<u>Don't</u> go on to the next sentence unless you fully understand the previous one. Don't let a desire to finish quickly ultimately make you go more slowly and less accurately.

Example

Four roommates are splitting the rent equally on an apartment. Currently, each roommate's share is $500 a month. If they were to add one more roommate with whom they would equally split the monthly rent, by how much would the monthly rent for each of the original four roommates decrease?

(A) $80
(B) $100
(C) $120
(D) $400

Solution

Fully understand each sentence of the question.

1. The total rent for an apartment is divided into four equal shares.
2. Each share is currently $500. This means that the total amount of rent for the apartment is $4 \times 500 = 2{,}000$.
3. If one more roommate is added, the total rent must now be divided by 5 instead of 4. So, the new rent per person is $\frac{2{,}000}{5} = 400$.

Now does this mean the correct answer is choice (D)? No—the question asks us how much each person's monthly rent would *decrease*. So, subtract the new share from the original share to find the per-person decrease: $500 - 400 = 100$. Therefore, the correct answer is **(B)**.

Do pay attention to key details by underlining and circling key words in the question. You are able to write all over the test booklet, so take advantage of it!

Don't get bogged down in clarifying information. Some of the information in a question may be given so there is no room for misinterpretation—do not dwell on clarifying information like this.

Example

The formula for compound interest is $A = P\left(1 + \frac{r}{n}\right)^{nt}$ where A is the amount accumulated, P is the principal, r is the interest rate, n is the number of times interest is applied in a compounding period, and t is the number of compounding periods. What is the principal in terms of the other variables?

(A) $P = \frac{1}{A\left(1 + \frac{r}{n}\right)^{nt}}$

(B) $P = \frac{1}{A\left(1 + \frac{r}{n}\right)^{-nt}}$

(C) $P = A\left(1 + \frac{r}{n}\right)^{-(nt)}$

(D) $P = A\left(1 + \frac{r}{n}\right)^{nt}$

✓ Solution

So that there is no room for misinterpretation (e.g., thinking that the constants could represent variables or imaginary numbers), the SAT clarifies what each constant represents in this question. You can ignore information like this and instead focus on what the questions asks you to do. The most important parts of the question are underlined below:

The formula for compound interest is $A = P\left(1+\frac{r}{n}\right)^{nt}$ where A is the amount accumulated, P is the principal, r is the interest rate, n is the number of times interest is applied in a compounding period, and t is the number of compounding periods. What is the principal in terms of the other variables?

So, the problem is much easier to solve than it appears at first glance. All we must do is divide both sides by $\left(1+\frac{r}{n}\right)^{nt}$ so that the P is by itself, then simplify the expression:

$$A = P\left(1+\frac{r}{n}\right)^{nt} \rightarrow$$

$$\frac{A}{\left(1+\frac{r}{n}\right)^{nt}} = \frac{P\left(1+\frac{r}{n}\right)^{nt}}{\left(1+\frac{r}{n}\right)^{nt}} \rightarrow$$

Cancel out the like terms to simplify →

$$\frac{A}{\left(1+\frac{r}{n}\right)^{nt}} = \frac{P\cancel{\left(1+\frac{r}{n}\right)^{nt}}}{\cancel{\left(1+\frac{r}{n}\right)^{nt}}} \rightarrow$$

$$\frac{A}{\left(1+\frac{r}{n}\right)^{nt}} = P \rightarrow$$

Use a negative exponent to show the part that was in the denominator:

$$A\left(1+\frac{r}{n}\right)^{-(nt)} = P$$

Do watch out for key words that will change what you are asked to do. In longer word problems and in questions where terms are easily confused, be especially careful.

Don't just assume that because your calculated answer is an option, you must be correct. The SAT will have answer choices based on common misreadings of the questions, so do not jump to conclusions.

Exercise—Spot the difference between the two very similarly worded questions.

1A. A drink stand charges $2 for a glass of iced tea and $1.50 for a glass of lemonade. If during an hour of operation, the stand sold a combined total of 14 glasses of tea and lemonade for a total revenue of $25, how many glasses of lemonade were sold?

1B. A drink stand charges $2 for a glass of iced tea and $1.50 for a glass of lemonade. If during an hour of operation, the stand sold a combined total of 14 glasses of tea and lemonade for a total revenue of $25, how many glasses of iced tea were sold?

2A. If the diameter of a circle is 10 units, what is the numerical difference between the area and circumference of the circle (ignore squared units)?

2B. If the radius of a circle is 10 units, what is the numerical difference between the area and circumference of the circle (ignore squared units)?

3A. Given that $i = \sqrt{-1}$, what is the product of the complex numbers $(1 + i)$ and $(1 - i)$?

3B. Given that $i = \sqrt{-1}$, what is the sum of the complex numbers $(1 + i)$ and $(1 - i)$?

✓ Solutions

1. Glasses of lemonade vs. glasses of iced tea
2. Diameter vs. radius
3. Product vs. sum

Do write out your work. Writing out your work will help you avoid careless errors and recognize patterns that you might otherwise miss.

Don't do everything in your head. You will ultimately save time and be more accurate if you write out your work. Common incorrect answers are based on common miscalculations.

› Example

Which of the following expressions is equivalent to the polynomial below?

$$(x^2 - 3x) + (2x - 3x^2)$$

(A) $-2x^2 - x$
(B) $3x^2 - 2x$
(C) $-3x^4 + 11x^3 - 6x^2$
(D) $3x^4 - 11x^3 + 6x^2$

✓ Solution

This problem is not that difficult, yet it is easy to miss if you make an error with negative signs or combining exponents. If you do make a common error, it is highly likely that one of the answer choices will have your incorrect solution. Students who are good at math yet impatient to finish the test are susceptible to this sort of error. So, write out your work step-by-step to get it right:

$$(x^2 - 3x) + (2x - 3x^2) \rightarrow$$

Remove the parentheses since you are not multiplying:

$$x^2 - 3x + 2x - 3x^2 \rightarrow$$

Group like terms together and simplify:

$$x^2 - 3x^2 - 3x + 2x \rightarrow$$

$$-2x^2 - x$$

Do use whatever is given in the problem, like scaled drawings and formulas. All the drawings on the SAT are to scale and problems often have formulas given within them, so take advantage of what you have in front of you.

Don't let yourself be intimidated by longer, more challenging questions. Use whatever knowledge and skills you have to attack the problem.

Example

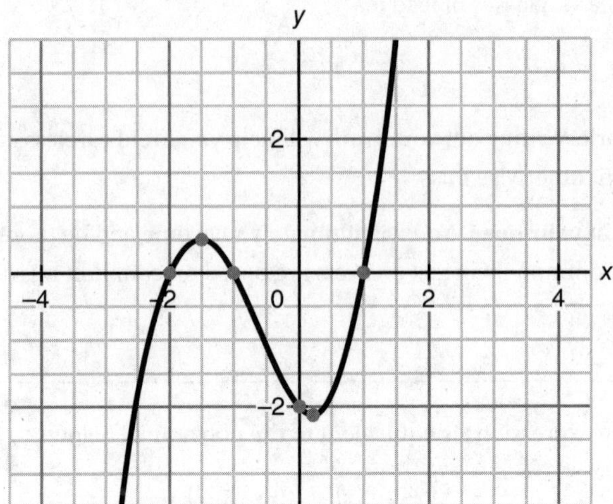

Consider the function $f(x)$ as portrayed in the xy-coordinate plane in the above graph. For how many values does $f(x)$ equal zero?

(A) 0
(B) 1
(C) 2
(D) 3

✓ Solution

Suppose that you do not remember how to work with complex functions and find zeros. You can still solve this problem without that specific knowledge. The question asks to find how many times the $f(x)$ equals zero—remember that $f(x)$ is the same as the y-coordinate. Circle the points on the graph where the y value is equal to zero:

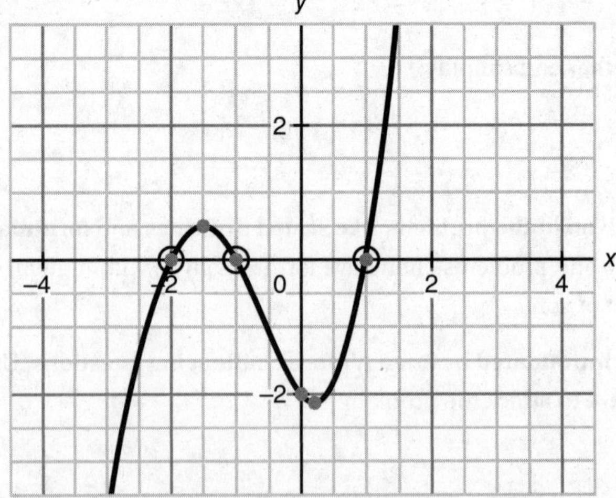

There are a total of three points where the function is equal to zero because it intersects the x-axis. Therefore, the correct answer is **(D)**. While this problem could also have been solved by creating an equation that had the zeros in it, make things easier for yourself and do not be intimidated.

<u>Do</u> approach the problems like a puzzle that you *figure out*. You may need to write out some work before you see the ultimate steps to solving the problem.

<u>Don't</u> just give up and say you *don't know*. The SAT Math emphasizes the core concepts from early high school math—in all likelihood, you have the background knowledge necessary to solve the problem.

Example

$$(3x-5)(3x+5)+25=ax^2$$

In the equation above, what is the value of the constant a?

Fill-in: ______________

Solution

This is not likely a problem you have typically worked with in your math classes. However, you can solve it by using concepts you probably already know—in this case, FOILing and simplifying. You do not need to know any advanced concepts about constants or equation equivalence.

$$(3x-5)(3x+5)+25=ax^2$$

FOIL the part in parentheses:

$$9x^2+15x-15x-25+25=ax^2\rightarrow$$

Add the x terms and the numbers to simplify:

$$9x^2+\cancel{15x-15x-25+25}=ax^2\rightarrow$$

$$9x^2=ax^2$$

Divide both sides to eliminate the $x^2\rightarrow$

$$\frac{9x^2}{x^2}=\frac{ax^2}{x^2}\rightarrow\frac{9\cancel{x^2}}{\cancel{x^2}}=\frac{a\cancel{x^2}}{\cancel{x^2}}\rightarrow 9=a$$

The correct answer is therefore **9**.

<u>Do</u> use the choices to help see what a solution may look like. Recognize that the answers typically go from least to greatest, so if you need to work your way backwards from the choices, start with answer (B) or (C) and then work your way up or down. Also, use the choices to recognize helpful clues as to your problem-solving process.

<u>Don't</u> jump into the choices too quickly. While plugging in the options does work sometimes, it won't be as frequent as you might like. You will be best served by carefully reading and setting up the problem step-by-step.

Example

For what values of x does $|x - 3| = 5$?

(A) 8 and 2
(B) 8 and −2
(C) −8 and 2
(D) −8 and −2

Solution

While you could set up two absolute value equations to solve, a glance at the answer choices tells you that plugging in the possible answers will probably save you time. Because each of the numbers 8, −8, 2, and −2 is in each answer twice, you can eliminate choices more rapidly. First, let's try −8:

$$|x - 3| = 5 \rightarrow |-8 - 3| = 11 \neq 5$$

Since −8 does NOT work, we can eliminate choices (C) and (D).

Now, try −2 since it is in choice (B) and not in choice (A):

$$|x - 3| = 5 \rightarrow |-2 - 3| = 5$$

This does work, so the correct answer is choice **(B)**. There is no need to also try 8 since both choices (A) and (B) have 8 as a possibility, so trying it out would give us no new information.

Do review and practice in a targeted way. Focus on the problem types and math concepts that are most challenging for you.

Don't practice by simply taking test after test, repeating the same mistakes. Remember that practice doesn't make perfect; "perfect practice" makes perfect. Use this book to focus on areas of weakness so you may turn them into areas of strength.

Here are the major concepts and formulas you will need to know, along with where they are covered in the book:

Heart of Algebra—Fundamentals

- Order of Operations (page 358)
- FOIL (page 359)
- Least Common Multiple (LCM) and Greatest Common Factor (GCF) (page 361)
- Solving Fractions (page 362)

Heart of Algebra—Solving Equations

- Substitution (page 364)
- Elimination (page 365)
- Pattern Recognition (page 366)
- Plugging in Choices (page 367)
- Inequalities (page 372)
- Absolute Value (page 373)
- Function Notation (page 374)

Heart of Algebra—Word Problems and Function Interpretation

- Setting Up Word Problems (page 386)
- Distance, Rate, and Time (page 388)
- Interpreting Variables and Constants (page 389)
- Functions in Table Form (page 390)

Heart of Algebra—Lines and Slope

- Slope Formula (page 403)
- Slope-Intercept Form of a Line (page 404)
- Overlapping and Intersecting Lines (page 405)
- Parallel and Perpendicular Lines (page 406)

Passport to Advanced Math—Polynomials and Factoring

- Polynomial Manipulation (page 414)
- Common Factoring Patterns (page 416)

Passport to Advanced Math—Exponents and Roots

- Exponent Rules (page 421)
- Problems with Exponents and Roots (page 423)

Passport to Advanced Math—Solving Quadratic Equations

- Factoring Quadratic Equations (page 429)
- Square Root Method (page 431)
- Quadratic Formula (page 432)
- Completing the Square (page 434)
- Plugging in the Answers (page 436)
- Undefined Functions (page 438)
- Extraneous Solutions (page 439)
- Synthetic Division (page 441)

Passport to Advanced Math—Zeros, Parabolas, and Polynomial Graphing

- Zeros of a Function (page 452)
- Parabola Graphing (page 455)
- Function Transformations (page 460)
- Visualizing Polynomial Graphs (page 463)

Passport to Advanced Math—Function Interpretation and Manipulation

- Putting Variables in Terms of Other Variables (page 473)
- Identifying Constants (page 474)
- Interpreting Functions (page 475)

Problem Solving and Data Analysis—Measures of Center

- Mean (page 486)
- Median (page 487)
- Mode (page 488)
- Outliers (page 488)
- Range and Standard Deviation (page 489)

Problem Solving and Data Analysis—Unit Conversion

- Conversion with Proportions (page 496)
- Conversion with Unit Cancellation (page 497)

Problem Solving and Data Analysis—Percentages

- Percentage Essentials (page 502)
- Percent Increase and Decrease (page 505)
- Simple Interest (page 508)
- Compound Interest (page 509)

Problem Solving and Data Analysis—Surveys

- Sampling Methods (page 519)
- Drawing Conclusions (page 520)

Problem Solving and Data Analysis—Graphs and Data Interpretation

- Probability (page 525)
- Graph Interpretation (page 527)
- Scatterplots (page 529)
- Histograms (page 532)
- Tables (page 535)
- Box Plots (page 538)
- Linear and Exponential Growth (page 540)
- Interpreting Constants and Functions (page 543)

Additional Topics in Math—Area, Perimeter, and Volume

- Rectangle Area (page 558)
- Triangle Area (page 558)
- Perimeter of Polygons (page 559)
- Parallelogram Area (page 560)
- Trapezoid Area (page 560)
- Surface Area (page 561)
- Volume of a Box, Cylinder, Sphere, Cone, and Pyramid (pages 563–565)

Additional Topics in Math—Lines, Angles, and Triangles

- Supplementary Angles (page 572)
- Vertical Angles (page 573)
- Parallel Lines and a Transversal (page 573)
- Equilateral Triangles (page 575)
- Isosceles Triangles (page 575)
- Similar Triangles (page 576)
- Angles in a Quadrilateral (page 577)

Additional Topics in Math—Right Triangles and Trigonometry

- Pythagorean Theorem and Special Right Triangles (page 583)
- Sine, Cosine, Tangent (page 586)
- Area of an Equilateral Triangle (page 587)
- Sine and Cosine of Complementary Angles (page 588)

Additional Topics in Math—Circles

- Radius and Diameter (page 593)
- Area and Circumference (page 594)
- 360 Degrees in a Circle (page 594)
- Inscribed Angle (page 595)
- Arc Length (page 596)
- Sector Area (page 597)
- Circle Formula (page 598)
- Radians (page 599)

Additional Topics in Math—Imaginary Numbers

- Imaginary Number Essentials (page 606)

Heart of Algebra

This section contains comprehensive review and strategies for all of the concepts below:

Heart of Algebra—Fundamentals

- Order of Operations
- FOIL
- Least Common Multiple and Greatest Common Factor
- Fractions

Heart of Algebra—Solving Equations

- Substitution
- Elimination
- Pattern Recognition
- Plugging in Choices
- Inequalities
- Absolute Value
- Function Notation

Heart of Algebra—Word Problems and Function Interpretation

- Setting Up Word Problems
- Distance, Rate, and Time
- Interpreting Variables and Constants
- Functions in Table Form

Heart of Algebra—Lines and Slope

- Slope Formula
- Slope-Intercept Form of a Line
- Overlapping and Intersecting Lines
- Parallel and Perpendicular Lines

Heart of Algebra—Fundamentals

Order of Operations

To remember the correct order of operations, use the popular acronym **PEMDAS**: *Please Excuse My Dear Aunt Sally.*

Please Excuse	My Dear	Aunt Sally
Parentheses ( ) and other grouping symbols, like $\sqrt{\ }$ or { } Exponents x^y	Multiplication $x \times y$ Division $x \div y$	Addition $x + y$ Subtraction $x - y$

Example 1

$$3(2+5)^2 - 4 = ?$$

Solution

To simplify the above expression, calculate what is within the parentheses first and square it. Then multiply that number by 3. Finally, subtract 4 to get your answer.

$$3(2+5)^2 - 4 \rightarrow 3(7)^2 - 4 \rightarrow$$
$$3 \times 49 - 4 \rightarrow 147 - 4 = 143$$

Example 2

$$-\sqrt{\frac{64}{9}} = ?$$

Solution

Calculate the square root of the numerator and denominator, and multiply the total by -1.

$$-\sqrt{\frac{64}{9}} \rightarrow -\frac{\sqrt{64}}{\sqrt{9}} \rightarrow -\frac{8}{3}$$

Practice

Simplify the following expressions.

1. $2x + 3x = ?$
2. $5(2 - 4x) = ?$
3. $5(x^2) + 2(x - 3) = ?$
4. $\frac{3+7}{2} - \frac{4}{2} = ?$
5. $(4+2)^2 - \frac{12}{2} = ?$

Solutions

1. $2x + 3x = 5x$
2. $5(2 - 4x) = 5 \times 2 - 5 \times 4x = 10 - 20x$
3. $5(x^2) + 2(x - 3) = 5x^2 + 2x - 6$
4. $\frac{3+7}{2} - \frac{4}{2} = \frac{10}{2} - 2 = 5 - 2 = 3$
5. $(4+2)^2 - \frac{12}{2} = (6)^2 - 6 = 36 - 6 = 30$

FOIL

Simplify polynomials by "**FOIL**ing" the parts of an expression like $(a+b)(c+d)$ in this order: **First, Outer, Inner, Last**.

$$(a+b)(c+d) = ?$$

First $= ac$ Outer $= ad$ Inner $= bc$ Last $= bd$

Combine them: $ac + ad + bc + bd$

Example

$$(2 + x)(3 - y) = ?$$

Solution

$$(2 + x)(3 - y) \rightarrow$$
$$\text{First} = 2 \times 3 \;\; \text{Outer} = 2 \times (-y)$$
$$\text{Inner} = x \times 3 \;\; \text{Last} = x \times (-y)$$
$$\text{So, it equals } 6 - 2y + 3x - xy$$

Practice

1. $(x + 1)(x + 2) = ?$
2. $(-3 + x)(-4 + x) = ?$
3. $(2 - y)(3 + y) = ?$
4. $(2x + 1)(2x - 1) = ?$
5. $(2x - 5)(3 + 4x) = ?$

Solutions

1. $(x + 1)(x + 2) =$
   $x^2 + 2x + 1x + 2 =$
   $x^2 + 3x + 2$
2. $(-3 + x)(-4 + x) =$
   $(-3)(-4) + (-3)x + (-4)x + x^2 =$
   $12 - 7x + x^2$
3. $(2 - y)(3 + y) =$
   $2 \times 3 + 2 \times y + (-y) \times 3 + (-y) \times y =$
   $6 + 2y - 3y - y^2 =$
   $6 - y - y^2$
4. $(2x + 1)(2x - 1) =$
   $(2x)(2x) - 1(2x) + 1(2x) - 1^2 =$
   $4x^2 - 2x + 2x - 1 =$
   $4x^2 - 1$
5. $(2x - 5)(3 + 4x) =$
   $3(2x) + (2x)(4x) + (-5)(3) + (-5)(4x) =$
   $6x + 8x^2 - 15 - 20x =$
   $8x^2 - 14x - 15$

Least Common Multiple and Greatest Common Factor

A multiple of a number is the result when the number is multiplied by a whole number, i.e., an integer. For example, multiples of 3 include 3, 6, 9, and 12.

The least common multiple (LCM) of two numbers is the *least* value that some numbers share as a *common multiple.*

Example

What is the least common multiple of 6 and 8?

Solution

Multiples of 6 include 6, 12, 18, and 24.

Multiples of 8 include 8, 16, and 24.

So, the least number that 6 and 8 have in common as a multiple is 24.

Factors of a number are numbers that can be multiplied together to give that number. For example, factors of 10 include 1, 2, 5, and 10 since $1 \times 10 = 10$ and $2 \times 5 = 10$.

The greatest common factor (GCF) of two numbers is the *greatest factor* that the numbers have in *common.*

Example

What is the greatest common factor of 8 and 12?

Solution

Factors of 8 are 1, 2, 4, and 8. Factors of 12 are 1, 2, 3, 4, 6, and 12.

So the greatest common factor between the two is 4 since it is the greatest factor that 8 and 12 share.

Practice

1. What are five multiples of the number 4?
2. What are the factors of the number 15?
3. How many factors does 7 have?
4. What is the least common multiple of 4 and 5?
5. What is the greatest common factor of 6 and 9?

Solutions

1. Multiples of 4 could include 4, 8, 12, 16, 20, 24, 28, and so on.
2. 1, 3, 5, and 15
3. 7 is a prime number, which has just *two* factors—1 and itself (7).
4. Multiples of 4: 4, 8, 12, 16, 20, etc. Multiples of 5: 5, 10, 15, 20, etc. So, the least common multiple between them is 20.
5. Factors of 6 are 1, 2, 3, and 6. Factors of 9 are 1, 3, and 9. So the greatest common factor between them is 3.

Solving Fractions

Examples of fractions include numbers like $\frac{1}{3}$, $\frac{5}{7}$, and $\frac{6}{11}$. The *numerator* is on *top* of a fraction, and the *denominator* is on the *bottom*:

$$\frac{\text{Numerator}}{\text{Denominator}}$$

For example, in the fraction $\frac{2}{3}$, 2 is the numerator and 3 is the denominator.

Fractions equal one another as long as the ratio of the numerator to the denominator is equivalent. For example, $\frac{3}{4}$, $\frac{6}{8}$, and $\frac{9}{12}$ are all equivalent since they are all equal to 0.75. Putting a fraction in its "lowest term" simplifies the fraction so that the numerator and denominator only have 1 as a common factor. For the group of $\frac{3}{4}$, $\frac{6}{8}$, and $\frac{9}{12}$, $\frac{3}{4}$ is the lowest term since 3 and 4 only share 1 as a common factor.

If fractions have the same denominator, the fractions can be added or subtracted by adding or subtracting the numerators.

Example 1

$$\frac{5}{13}+\frac{3}{13}=?$$

Solution

$$\frac{5}{13}+\frac{3}{13}=\frac{5+3}{13}=\frac{8}{13}$$

To add and subtract fractions that do not have the same denominator, change the fractions so they have a *common denominator*.

Example 2

$$\frac{2}{3}+\frac{1}{4}=?$$

Solution

To provide a common denominator, 3 and 4 can be multiplied together. So that the fractions retain their values, multiply both the numerator and denominator of each fraction by a ratio equivalent to 1 (i.e., $\frac{4}{4}$ or $\frac{3}{3}$).

$$\frac{2}{3}+\frac{1}{4}=\frac{2}{3}\times\frac{4}{4}+\frac{1}{4}\times\frac{3}{3}=$$

$$\frac{2\times 4}{3\times 4}+\frac{1\times 3}{4\times 3}=\frac{8}{12}+\frac{3}{12}=\frac{11}{12}$$

Example 3

The time it takes Henry to mop a certain floor is 10 minutes, and the time it takes Tanner to mop the same floor is 8 minutes. What is the time it takes to mop the floor if both of them work together the full amount of time to do so (use the combined work formula below to solve)?

Combined Work Formula:

$$\frac{1}{t_c} = \frac{1}{t_a} + \frac{1}{t_b}$$

t_a = Time for *a* to complete the work
t_b = Time for *b* to complete the work
t_c = Time for both *a* and *b* to complete the work

Solution

Using the combined worked formula above, we can calculate the time it will take both Henry and Tanner to complete the mopping. We can use 10 minutes as time *a* and 8 minutes as time *b*.

$$\frac{1}{t_c} = \frac{1}{t_a} + \frac{1}{t_b} \rightarrow$$

$$\frac{1}{t_c} = \frac{1}{8} + \frac{1}{10} \rightarrow \text{Use 40 as the least common denominator} \rightarrow$$

$$\frac{1}{t_c} = \frac{5}{5} \times \frac{1}{8} + \frac{4}{4} \times \frac{1}{10}$$

$$\frac{1}{t_c} = \frac{5}{40} + \frac{4}{40} \rightarrow$$

$$\frac{1}{t_c} = \frac{9}{40} \rightarrow \text{Flip the fractions to solve} \rightarrow$$

$$t_c = \frac{40}{9}$$

So, it will take $\frac{40}{9}$ minutes, or about 4.44 minutes, for both of them working together to mop the floor.

Use this rule to *multiply* fractions:

$$\frac{a}{b} \times \frac{c}{d} = \frac{ac}{bd} \quad \text{(Neither } b \text{ nor } d \text{ can equal zero, or it will be undefined.)}$$

Example 4

$$\frac{4}{7} \times \frac{2}{5} = ?$$

Solution

$$\frac{4}{7} \times \frac{2}{5} = \frac{4 \times 2}{7 \times 5} = \frac{8}{35}$$

Use this rule to *divide* fractions—flip the second fraction and multiply the first one by it:
$\frac{a}{b} \div \frac{c}{d} = \frac{a}{b} \times \frac{d}{c}$ (*b*, *c*, and *d* cannot equal zero, or it will be undefined.)

Example 5

$$\frac{4}{5} \div \frac{1}{2} = ?$$

Solution

$$\frac{4}{5} \div \frac{1}{2} = \frac{4}{5} \times \frac{2}{1} = \frac{4 \times 2}{5 \times 1} = \frac{8}{5}$$

Practice

1. $\frac{1}{2} + \frac{1}{2} = ?$
2. $\frac{3}{4} - \frac{1}{4} = ?$
3. $\frac{2}{5} \times \frac{3}{5} = ?$
4. $\frac{3}{7} \div \frac{2}{5} = ?$
5. $\frac{3}{5} + \frac{1}{10} = ?$
6. $\frac{2}{3} - \frac{1}{6} = ?$

Solutions

1. $\frac{1}{2} + \frac{1}{2} = \frac{1+1}{2} = \frac{2}{2} = 1$
2. $\frac{3}{4} - \frac{1}{4} = \frac{3-1}{4} = \frac{2}{4} = \frac{1}{2}$
3. $\frac{2}{5} \times \frac{3}{5} = \frac{2 \times 3}{5 \times 5} = \frac{6}{25}$
4. $\frac{3}{7} \div \frac{2}{5} = \frac{3}{7} \times \frac{5}{2} = \frac{15}{14}$
5. $\frac{3}{5} + \frac{1}{10} = \frac{3}{5} \times \frac{2}{2} + \frac{1}{10} = \frac{6}{10} + \frac{1}{10} = \frac{7}{10}$
6. $\frac{2}{3} - \frac{1}{6} = \frac{2}{3} \times \frac{2}{2} - \frac{1}{6} = \frac{4}{6} - \frac{1}{6} = \frac{3}{6} = \frac{1}{2}$

Heart of Algebra—Solving Equations

Substitution

When there is a system of two equations and two variables, it is often easiest to substitute an expression in terms of the other variable for one of the variables. That way, there is just one variable to work with.

Example

What is the value of x in the set of equations below?

$$y = x + 1$$
$$x + y = 3$$

✓ Solution

To solve for x, use substitution of y in terms of x. Use the first equation, $y = x + 1$, to put everything in terms of x in the second equation:

$$x + y = 3 \rightarrow$$
$$x + (x + 1) = 3 \rightarrow$$
$$2x + 1 = 3 \rightarrow 2x = 2 \rightarrow x = 1$$

Elimination

If two equations have similar formats, eliminating variables can be the easiest approach to solving the system of equations. Use multiplication to reformat one of the equations so that it can be easily added or subtracted from the other equation, eliminating one of the variables.

› Example 1

$$2x + y = 7$$
$$3x - y = 3$$

What is the value of x in the above system of equations?

✓ Solution

Recognize that if you add the two equations together, the y values will cancel, leaving you only with x.

$$2x + y = 7$$
$$+\underline{(3x - y = 3)}$$
$$5x + 0 = 10 \rightarrow 5x = 10 \rightarrow x = 2$$

› Example 2

What are the values of x and y in the system of equations below?

$$3x + 4y = 1$$
$$2x - 2y = 10$$

✓ Solution

Use elimination to solve this. If you multiply the second equation by 2, you will be able to eliminate the y variables and can then solve for x.

$$3x + 4y = 1$$
$$\underline{+2 \times (2x - 2y = 10)} \rightarrow$$

$$3x + 4y = 1$$
$$\underline{+4x - 4y = 20}$$
$$7x + 0 = 21 \rightarrow$$

$$7x = 21 \rightarrow x = 3$$

Then, plug 3 in for x into one of the equations to solve for y:

$$3x + 4y = 1 \rightarrow$$
$$3(3) + 4y = 1 \rightarrow$$
$$9 + 4y = 1 \rightarrow 4y = -8 \rightarrow y = -2$$

So, the solution set is $x = 3$ and $y = -2$.

Pattern Recognition

An excellent shortcut you can use to solve equations is to see if there is a pattern that will allow you to easily rearrange the equations without having to use substitution or elimination. If the SAT asks you to solve a problem in terms of an *expression* rather than just a *variable*, odds are that you can use pattern recognition to figure it out.

› Example

Given that $3(x + 4) = 2(x + 4) + 5$, what is the value of $x + 4$?

✓ Solution

While you could distribute the 3 and the 2 through the values in the parentheses and solving for x by itself, make things easier by just solving for $x + 4$ as a whole.

$$3(x + 4) = 2(x + 4) + 5 \rightarrow$$

Subtract $2(x + 4)$ from both sides $\rightarrow$

$$3(x + 4) - 2(x + 4) = 2(x + 4) - 2(x + 4) + 5 \rightarrow$$
$$x + 4 = 5$$

You will find far more pattern recognition types of problems on the SAT Math than you are accustomed to finding in your typical math class questions. Be on look out for them to save you time.

Pattern Recognition: Infinite Solutions

Building off the material in the Heart of Algebra Fundamentals, be able to recognize when there are infinite solutions to a system of equations.

If two equations with two variables can be simplified to be the same equation, there will be infinite solutions. Another way to think about it—if the lines have the same slopes and the same y-intercepts, they will overlap and there will be infinitely many solutions.

› Example

How many solutions does the following system of equations have?

$$x - 2y = 4$$
$$2x - 4y = 8$$

✓ **Solution**

Divide the second equation by 2 and you will see that it is identical to the first equation:

$$2x - 4y = 8 \rightarrow \frac{2x - 4y}{2} = \frac{8}{2} \rightarrow$$
$$x - 2y = 4$$

Since the two equations can be written the same way, there will be infinitely many sets of points that can be plugged in for x and y to be solutions for the set of equations.

Pattern Recognition: Zero Solutions

If two equations written in linear form have identical slopes and different y-intercepts, they will be parallel to each other and never intersect. Therefore, there will be zero solutions between them.

› **Example**

How many solutions does the following system of equations have?

$$y = 3x - 4$$
$$y = 3x + 12$$

✓ **Solution**

Recall the slope-intercept form of a line: $y = mx + b$. If the lines have the same slope and different y-intercepts, they will run parallel to each other.

$$y = mx + b$$
$$y = 3x - 4$$
$$y = 3x + 12$$

These two lines have the same slope of 3, and different y-intercepts of -4 and 12. So, they will run parallel to each other, resulting in no solutions to the system of equations.

Plugging in Choices

Sometimes it can save you time to simply plug in the answer choices to see what the answer would be. Do this when it looks like plugging in the choices will ultimately take you less time than solving the problem using algebra.

› **Example**

1. $|3x + 1| = 7$

   What value of x is a positive number that would be a solution to the above equation?

   (A) 1
   (B) 2
   (C) 3
   (D) 4

✓ Solution

While it would be possible to solve this using algebra, you will likely save time by working backwards from the choices. Since the choices on the SAT Math are consistently in order from least to greatest, start with one of the middle choices like (B) or (C). That way, if your answer is too big you can try the smaller answers, and if it is too small you can try the larger answers.

Plug in choice (C) first:

$$|3x + 1| = 7 \rightarrow$$
$$|3(3) + 1| = 10$$

So, 3 is too large of an answer. Let us now try the next smallest answer, choice (B):

$$|3x + 1| = 7 \rightarrow$$
$$|3(2) + 1| = 7$$

SAT Math Strategy

Save time by recognizing when substitution, elimination, pattern recognition, or plugging in choices will be the most efficient way to solve a system of equations.

This works, so the correct answer is choice **(B)**.

This table breaks down how to recognize which strategy will likely be most efficient.

	When to Use	Example	Solution
Substitution	If one variable can easily be expressed as the other variable, use substitution.	What is x in the system of equations below? $y = 7x - 4$ $3x + 2y = 5$	*Plug $y = 7x + 4$ in for y in the second equation to solve.* $3x + 2(7x - 4) = 5 \rightarrow$ $3x + 14x - 8 = 5 \rightarrow$ $17x = 12 \rightarrow x = \frac{12}{17}$
Elimination	If one equation can be easily modified so that one variable will cancel when the equations are combined, use elimination.	What is x in the system of equations below? $6x - 3y = 7$ $4x + 3y = 5$	*Add the two equations together to eliminate the y components.* $6x - 3y = 7$ $+ 4x + 3y = 5$ $10x + 0 = 12 \rightarrow$ $x = \frac{12}{10} = \frac{6}{5}$
Pattern Recognition	If the question asks for the value of an expression instead of a variable, watch out for pattern recognition.	What is the value of $5x - 1$ in the equation below? $\frac{5x-1}{3} = 4$	*Simplify the equation to look like by $5x - 1$ multiplying both sides by 3.* $\frac{5x-1}{3} = 4 \rightarrow$ $5x - 1 = 4 \times 3 = 12$

(Continued)

	When to Use	Example	Solution
Plugging in Choices	When you can more easily plug in the answers than solve the problem with algebra, plug in the choices starting with the middle values.	What is a possible value for x in this inequality? $5x > -2x - 4$ (A) 0 (B) −1 (C) −2 (D) −3	Since the algebra could be a little tricky, you could work backwards from the choices and find that choice (A), 0, is the only option that will make this true.

Practice

1. What is the value of x in this series of equations?

$$y = x - 3$$
$$y + 2x = 9$$

2. What is the value of y in this series of equations?

$$3x - 2y = 6$$
$$-6x + 5y = 4$$

3. What is the value of $3x^2$ in the equation $6x^2 - 4 = 8$?

4. What is the value of x in this series of equations?

$$3x = 6y + 9$$
$$x + 2y = 7$$

5. What is the solution set for (x, y) in this series of equations?

$$4x - 3y = 5$$
$$8x = 6y + 10$$

6. What is the value of y in this series of equations?

$$\frac{1}{2}x + 2y = -1$$
$$2x - 3y = 7$$

7. How many solutions are there in this series of equations?

$$y = 5x + \frac{1}{2}$$
$$2y + 8 = 10x$$

8. If $|x - 4| \leq 2$, what is a possible value of x?

✓ Solutions

1. Substitute $x - 3$ in for y in the second equation to solve:

$$(x - 3) + 2x = 9 \rightarrow$$
$$3x - 3 = 9 \rightarrow 3x = 12 \rightarrow x = 4$$

2. Double the first equation and then add it to the second to eliminate the x components:

$$2(3x - 2y = 6)$$
$$-6x + 5y = 4 \rightarrow$$

$$\begin{array}{r} 6x - 4y = 12 \\ +(-6x + 5y = 4) \\ \hline 0 + y = 16 \rightarrow y = 16 \end{array}$$

3. Recognize that you can manipulate the equation fairly easily to isolate $3x^2$:

$$6x^2 - 4 = 8 \rightarrow$$
$$6x^2 = 12 \rightarrow$$

Divide both sides by 2 $\rightarrow$

$$3x^2 = 6$$

4. Simplify the first equation by dividing it by 3, then substitute it in to the second equation:

$$3x = 6y + 9 \rightarrow \text{Divide by } 3 \rightarrow$$
$$x = 2y + 3$$

Substitute this in the second equation $\rightarrow$

$$(2y + 3) + 2y = 7 \rightarrow$$
$$4y + 3 = 7 \rightarrow 4y = 4 \rightarrow y = 1$$

Plug 1 in for y to solve for x:

$$x = 2y + 3 \rightarrow$$
$$x = 2(1) + 3 = 5$$

5. With a little bit of manipulation, you can see the pattern, which makes this easier to solve:

$$4x - 3y = 5$$
$$8x = 6y + 10$$

Manipulate the second equation to make it look like the first one:

$$8x = 6y + 10 \rightarrow 8x - 6y = 10 \rightarrow$$

Divide both sides by 2 $\rightarrow$

$$4x - 3y = 5$$

So, since the second equation is equivalent to the first equation, there are infinitely many solutions.

6. Use elimination to solve—multiply the first equation by -4 to make it possible to add and eliminate the x components:

$$-4\left(\frac{1}{2}x + 2y = -1\right) = -2x - 8y = 4 \rightarrow$$
$$-2x - 8y = 4$$
$$\underline{+2x - 3y = 7}$$
$$0 - 11y = 11 \rightarrow y = -1$$

7. Recognize the pattern here by simplifying the second equation to get it in slope-intercept form:

$$2y + 8 = 10x \rightarrow 2y = 10x - 8 \rightarrow y = 5x - 4$$

Once this equation is in slope-intercept form, you can see that it has the same slope as the first equation, 5, and a different y-intercept. Therefore, the lines created by these two equations will never overlap or intersect, resulting in no solutions.

8. Although this is a fill-in question, you could still try plugging in potential answers to find one that would make this statement true. Since we know that $|x - 4| \leq 2$, we could pick a value that is less than 2 and plug that in: $|x - 4| = 1$. Based on this, 5 would be a possible value for x.

Alternatively, you could do this algebraically as follows:

$$|x - 4| \leq 2 \rightarrow$$

Break up the absolute value like this:

$$-2 \leq x - 4 \leq 2 \rightarrow$$

Add 4 to all parts of the expression:

$$-2 + 4 \leq x - 4 + 4 \leq 2 + 4 \rightarrow$$
$$2 \leq x \leq 6$$

So, any number greater than or equal to 2 and less than or equal to 6 would work. As you can see, plugging in potential solutions would likely save you time.

Inequalities

An inequality indicates which value is greater than or less than another value. The open end of the $>$ goes toward the larger number. For example:

$$-3 < 0 \text{ and } 10 > 4$$

A line underneath a greater/less than sign indicates that the terms on either side can possibly equal one another. For example:

$8 \geq n$ means that n is less than or equal to 8, or alternatively, that 8 is greater than or equal to n.

Inequalities can be solved like typical equations, with an important exception:

If multiplying or dividing a side of the inequality by a negative number, change the direction of the inequality sign.

Example

Simplify the expression $-4x > 3$.

Solution

$$-4x > 3$$

Divide both sides by -4 and turn the $>$ around to $<$.

$$\frac{-4x}{-4} < \frac{3}{-4}$$

$$\frac{\cancel{-4}x}{\cancel{-4}} < \frac{3}{-4}$$

$$x < -\frac{3}{4}$$

Practice

1. How would one express that x represents all the numbers greater than or equal to 14?
2. If $x > 4$ and $x < 9$, what is a possible value for x?
3. Simplify $-2x + 4 > 6$.

Solutions

1. $x \geq 14$
2. The values of x must be greater than 4 and less than 9, so any number between 4 and 9 would work. (Note—it would not include 4 or 9 themselves since the expressions do not indicate equality.)
3. $-2x + 4 > 6 \rightarrow$

   $-2x > 2 \rightarrow$

   Divide both sides by -2 and flip the sign:

$$x < \frac{2}{-2} \rightarrow x < -1$$

Absolute Value

When you take the absolute value of a number, it represents how far that number is from zero. If you took the absolute value of −6 or 6, both would be 6 since they are both 6 units away from zero.

Absolute value is written by putting two lines around the number—for example, the absolute value of 4 would be written as |4|. Calculate the absolute value of an expression by making the expression positive, no matter if the expression is originally positive or negative. Here are some absolute value expressions:

$$|8| = 8$$
$$|-5| = 5$$
$$\left|-\frac{1}{2}\right| = \frac{1}{2}$$

To solve an absolute value equation, set it up as two equations—one with a positive and one with a negative value.

Example

What are the possible values for x in the equation $|x + 1| = 5$?

Solution

$|x + 1| = 5$ can be set up as two different equations:

$$x + 1 = 5$$
$$x + 1 = -5$$

Solve each equation for x to find the solutions:

$$x + 1 = 5 \rightarrow x = 4$$
$$x + 1 = -5 \rightarrow x = -6$$

So x could be either 4 or −6.

Practice

1. What is the value of $|4 - 7|$?
2. What are the possible values of x in the equation $|x - 1| = 5$?
3. Given that x is a real number, what is the least possible value for $|x|$?

Solutions

1. $|4 - 7| \rightarrow |-3| \rightarrow 3$
2. Set it up as two separate equations:

$$x - 1 = 5$$
$$x - 1 = -5$$

Then solve each equation for x:

$$x - 1 = 5 \rightarrow x = 6$$
$$x - 1 = -5 \rightarrow x = -4$$

So, x could be either 6 or −4.

3. If you take the absolute value of any real number, it will be the positive value of that number. So, the least possible value for x is found when you take the absolute value of zero: $|0| = 0$. Therefore, zero is the least possible value for $|x|$.

Function Notation

Many of the expressions you encounter on the SAT Math will be equations with x and y values. However, be sure you understand function notation:

$f(x) = 2x + 1$ is the same as $y = 2x + 1$; $f(x)$ corresponds to the y value.

If you were told that $f(x) = 3x - 5$ and asked to find the value of $f(4)$, simply plug 4 in for x into the function:

$$f(x) = 3x - 5$$

$$f(4) = 3(4) - 5 = 12 - 5 = 7$$

Finally, you may be asked to combine functions together. Be sure you work from the "inside out" to solve these.

Example

If $f(x) = 4x - 3$ and $g(x) = 2x + 1$, what is $g(f(2))$?

Solution

Start by calculating the value of $f(2)$:

$$f(x) = 4x - 3$$

$$f(2) = 4(2) - 3 = 8 - 3 = 5$$

Then, take 5 and plug it into $g(x)$:

$$g(x) = 2x + 1$$

$$g(5) = 2(5) + 1 = 11$$

Practice

1. If x is 4, what is $f(x)$ if $f(x) = 2x - 5$?
2. If x is 8 and $f(x) = x - 4$, what is the value of $3\,f(x)$?
3. If $f(x) = x^2$ and $g(x) = \frac{x}{2}$, what is $f(g(4))$?

Solutions

1. Plug 4 in for x to the function:

$$f(x) = 2x - 5$$

$$f(4) = 2(4) - 5 = 8 - 5 = 3$$

2. First, determine the value of $f(x)$ by plugging in 8 for x:

$$f(x) = x - 4$$

$$f(8) = 8 - 4 = 4$$

Then, multiply 4 by 3 to see what $3f(x)$ would be:

$$4 \times 3 = 12$$

3. Work inside out to solve. First, determine $g(4)$:

$$g(x) = \frac{x}{2}$$
$$g(4) = \frac{4}{2} = 2$$

Then, plug 2 into $f(x)$:

$$f(x) = x^2$$
$$f(x) = 2^2 = 4$$

SAT Math Questions Practice Drill #1—Solving Equations

(If timing, take about 12 minutes to complete.)

1. $6 = 5x + 1$

   What is the solution for x in the equation above?

   (A) 0
   (B) 1
   (C) 2
   (D) 3

2. What value of x satisfies the equation $13x + 3 = 42$?

   (A) 3
   (B) 5
   (C) 7
   (D) 10

3. $1.2x - 2.4 = 3.6$

   What value of x is a solution to the above equation?

   (A) 4
   (B) 5
   (C) 6
   (D) 7

4. $-|y + 5| = -4$

   What are the solutions to the equation above?

   (A) 1 or -3
   (B) 1 or -9
   (C) -1 or 9
   (D) -1 or -9

5. What is the solution set for x and y at which these two lines would intersect?

$$3x - y = 2$$
$$-4x + 2y = 2$$

(A) (3, 7)
(B) (1, 6)
(C) (−4, 5)
(D) (2, −1)

$$5(a - 1) - 2(a + 2) = \frac{3}{4}a$$

6. What is the value of a in the above equation?

(A) 2
(B) 3
(C) 4
(D) 5

$$3x - 2y = 7$$
$$-6y + 4x = 12$$

7. Consider the system of equations above. What is the value of $7x - 8y$?

(A) 7
(B) 8
(C) 14
(D) 19

8. $3x - 2 \leq 2x + 3$

What is the greatest possible number that would work for x in the above inequality?

(A) 3
(B) 5
(C) 8
(D) 9

9. $2y = -6x + 14$

$\frac{2}{3}y = -2x + 1$

How many solutions are there to the above system of equations?

(A) Zero
(B) One
(C) Two
(D) Infinite

10. $\frac{1}{2}x - \frac{2}{3}y = 18$

$\frac{3}{4}x + 2y = 36$

Based on the system of equations above, what is the product of x and y?

(A) 30
(B) 80
(C) 120
(D) 180

✓ Solutions

1. **(B)** $6 = 5x + 1 \rightarrow$
$5 = 5x \rightarrow$
$1 = x$

2. **(A)** $13x + 3 = 42 \rightarrow$
$13x = 39 \rightarrow$
$x = 3$

3. **(B)** $1.2x - 2.4 = 3.6 \rightarrow$
$1.2x = 6.0 \rightarrow$
$x = \frac{6.0}{1.2} = 5$

4. **(D)** $-|y + 5| = -4 \rightarrow$
$|y + 5| = 4 \rightarrow$

Make two separate equations and solve:

$$y + 5 = 4 \rightarrow y = -1$$

or

$$y + 5 = -4 \rightarrow y = -9$$

5. **(A)** Use elimination to solve this series of equations, since the y's can be easily cancelled if you multiply the first equation by 2:

$$2(3x - y) = 2 \times 2 \rightarrow$$
$$6x - 2y = 4$$

Then, add this to the second equation to eliminate:

$$\begin{array}{r} 6x - 2y = 4 \\ \underline{-4x + 2y = 2} \\ 2x + 0 = 6 \rightarrow 2x = 6 \rightarrow x = 3 \end{array}$$

Fortunately, the only answer that has a 3 for the x value is choice **(A)**, so you do not need to bother solving for y.

6. **(C)** $5(a - 1) - 2(a + 2) = \frac{3}{4}a \rightarrow$

$$5a - 5 - 2a - 4 = \frac{3}{4}a \rightarrow$$

$$3a - 9 = \frac{3}{4}a \rightarrow$$

$$-9 = \frac{3}{4}a - 3a \rightarrow$$

$$-9 = \frac{3}{4}a - \frac{12}{4}a \rightarrow$$

$$-9 = -\frac{9}{4}a \rightarrow$$

$$-9 \times -\frac{4}{9} = 4 = a$$

7. **(D)** Although the equations present the x and y values in different orders, do your best to recognize that if you add these two equations together you will have the expression $7x - 8y$:

$$3x - 2y = 7$$

$$-6y + 4x = 12$$

Change the order of the second equation, and add it to the first one:

$$3x - 2y = 7$$

$$\underline{+\,4x - 6y = 12}$$

$$7x - 8y = 19$$

8. **(B)** Simplify the inequality in order to see what the largest potential value for x could be:

$$3x - 2 \leq 2x + 3 \rightarrow$$

$$3x \leq 2x + 5 \rightarrow$$

$$x \leq 5$$

Since x can be any value less than or equal to 5, the largest possible value it could be is 5.

9. **(A)** The two equations can be simplified to be in slope-intercept form:

$$2y = -6x + 14$$

$$y = -3x + 7$$

And:

$$\frac{2}{3}y = -2x + 1 \rightarrow$$

$$y = \frac{3}{2}(-2x + 1) \rightarrow$$

$$y = -3x + 1.5$$

So, the lines have the same slope, which makes them parallel. They also have different y-intercepts, which means they do not intersect or overlap. Therefore, there are no points of intersection for the two lines and zero solutions.

10. **(C)** Multiply the first equation by 3 so that you can add the equations together and eliminate y.

$$\frac{1}{2}x - \frac{2}{3}y = 18 \rightarrow$$

$$\frac{3}{2}x - 2y = 54$$

Now, add this equation to the second equation to eliminate the y's:

$$\begin{array}{r} \frac{3}{2}x - 2y = 54 \\ +\frac{3}{4}x + 2y = 36 \\ \hline \end{array}$$

$$\frac{9}{4}x + 0 = 90 \rightarrow \frac{9}{4}x = 90 \rightarrow \frac{4}{9} \times 90 = 40 = x$$

Now, plug 40 back in for x to one of the equations to solve for y:

$$\frac{1}{2}x - \frac{2}{3}y = 18 \rightarrow$$

$$\frac{1}{2}(40) - \frac{2}{3}y = 18 \rightarrow$$

$$20 - \frac{2}{3}y = 18 \rightarrow -\frac{2}{3}y = 18 - 20 \rightarrow$$

$$-\frac{2}{3}y = -2 \rightarrow \left(-\frac{3}{2}\right) \times -2 = 3 = y$$

Now, multiply 3 and 40 together to give you 120.

SAT Math Questions Practice Drill #2—Solving Equations

(If timing, take about 12 minutes to complete.)

1. $5x + 4 = -6$

   In the equation above, what is the value of x?

   (A) –2
   (B) –1
   (C) 0
   (D) 1

2. If $-5(x - 3) + 2(x + 6) = 12$, what is the value of x?

   (A) 3
   (B) 5
   (C) 8
   (D) 9

3. If $\frac{5a}{2} = \frac{3}{7}$, what is the value of a?

   (A) $\frac{6}{35}$
   (B) $\frac{10}{21}$
   (C) $\frac{14}{15}$
   (D) $\frac{7}{6}$

4. $y > 7$ and $y - 4 < 3x$

Based on the system of inequalities above, what are the possible values for x?

(A) $x < 0$
(B) $x > 3$
(C) $x < -11$
(D) $x > 1$

5. If $y + 1 > 2x$ and $y > 3x + 2$, which ordered pair would satisfy the system of inequalities?

(A) $(-3, 5)$
(B) $(2, -4)$
(C) $(1, 2)$
(D) $(4, 0)$

Fill-In Practice: Write your answer in the underlined blank under each question.

6. $11x + 3y = 7$
$6x + 8y = 5$

If (x, y) is a solution to the above system of equations, what is the value of $5x - 5y$?

Answer: ________

7. Consider this series of equations:

$x + 2y = 5$
$y - x = -2$

What is the value of y?

Answer: ________

8. $2x - y = -1$
$2x + y = 7$

If (x, y) is a solution to the above series of equations, what is the value of x?

Answer: ________

9. For the function g, if $g(5x - 1) = x + 4$, what is the value of $g(4)$?

Answer: ________

10. $3x - 2y = 7$
$x + y = 9$

In the system of equations above what is the value of x?

Answer: ________

Solutions

1. **(A)** $5x + 4 = -6 \rightarrow$

$$5x = -10 \rightarrow$$

$$x = -\frac{10}{5} = -2$$

2. **(B)** $-5(x - 3) + 2(x + 6) = 12 \rightarrow$

$$-5x + 15 + 2x + 12 = 12 \rightarrow$$

$$-3x + 27 = 12 \rightarrow$$

$$-3x = -15 \rightarrow x = 5$$

3. **(A)** $\frac{5a}{2} = \frac{3}{7} \rightarrow$ Cross Multiply the 2 $\rightarrow$

$5a = \frac{6}{7} \rightarrow$ Divide Both Sides by 5 $\rightarrow$

$$a = \frac{6}{7 \times 5} = \frac{6}{35}$$

4. **(D)** Simplify $y - 4 < 3x$ to put it in terms of y:

$$y - 4 < 3x \rightarrow y = 3x + 4$$

Then combine the two inequalities, $y > 7$ and $y < 3x + 4$, and simplify:

$$7 < y < 3x + 4 \rightarrow$$

$$7 < 3x + 4 \rightarrow$$

$$3 < 3x \rightarrow 1 < x \rightarrow x > 1$$

5. **(A)** This is a good example of plugging in the choices to solve. Choice (A) is the only option that will be true for both the x and y values in the pair:

$$y + 1 > 2x \rightarrow$$

$$(5) + 1 > 2(-3) \rightarrow$$

$$6 > -6$$

And:

$$y > 3x + 2 \rightarrow$$

$$(5) > 3(-3) + 2 \rightarrow$$

$$5 > -9 + 2 \rightarrow$$

$$5 > -7$$

6. **2** This is a great example of a pattern recognition problem. If you subtract the second equation from the first one, you will get it to look like $5x - 5y$:

$$\begin{array}{r} 11x + 3y = 7 \\ \underline{-(6x + 8y = 5)} \\ 5x - 5y = 2 \end{array}$$

7. **1** If you add the two equations together, the x's will cancel, leaving you with only the y term to analyze. Rearrange the second equation, $y - x = -2$, so that the x term comes first and it can be more easily added to the first equation:

$$\begin{array}{r} x + 2y = 5 \\ \underline{+(-x + y = -2)} \\ 0 + 3y = 3 \rightarrow 3y = 3 \rightarrow y = 1 \end{array}$$

8. **1.5 or $\frac{3}{2}$** This is a great example of an elimination question. Add the two equations together to eliminate the y:

$$\begin{array}{r} 2x - y = -1 \\ \underline{+\,2x + y = 7} \\ 4x + 0 = 6 \rightarrow 4x = 6 \rightarrow x = 1.5 \end{array}$$

9. **5** Since $g(4) = g(5x - 1)$, find out what the value of x is by solving the equation $4 = 5x - 1$:

$$4 = 5x - 1 \rightarrow 5 = 5x \rightarrow x = 1$$

Then, plug 1 in for x in the right-hand side of the function:

$$x + 4 \rightarrow 1 + 4 \rightarrow 5$$

So, the value of $g(4)$ is 5.

10. **5** If you double the second equation, $x + y = 9$, you can eliminate the y terms and solve for x:

$$\begin{array}{r} 3x - 2y = 7 \\ \underline{+2x + 2y = 18} \\ 5x + 0 = 25 \rightarrow 5x = 25 \rightarrow x = 5 \end{array}$$

SAT Math Questions Practice Drill #3—Solving Equations

(If timing, take about 12 minutes to complete.)

1. If $x - 3 = 0.5x$, what is the value of x?

(A) 2
(B) 4
(C) 6
(D) 8

2. If $5(x + 4) - 3(x + 4) = 3x - 2$, what is the value of x?

(A) 3
(B) 4
(C) 7
(D) 10

3. If $3x$ is 5 less than 20, what is $x + 4$?

(A) 4
(B) 6
(C) 8
(D) 9

$y + 5n = 3$

4. In the equation above, if $y = 2$, what is the value of n?

(A) $\frac{1}{5}$
(B) 2
(C) $\frac{7}{2}$
(D) 6

5. If $\frac{4}{3y} = \frac{2}{3}$, what is the value of y?

(A) 1
(B) 2
(C) 6
(D) 12

6. $y = 3x - 5$
$y = 3x + k$

Consider the system of equations above. What must the value of the constant k be so that the system of equations has infinitely many solutions?

(A) −15
(B) −8
(C) −5
(D) 0

7. $4x + y = 3$
$-3x - 2y = 4$

In the above system of equations, what is the point in the xy-coordinate plane at which the lines formed by the equations would intersect?

(A) (2, −5)
(B) (6, −3)
(C) (9, 0)
(D) (12, 6)

8. $y = x + 5$
$2x + y = 11$

In the system of equations above, what is the value of x?

(A) 0
(B) 2
(C) 4
(D) 6

9. If $|x + 2| > 0$, which of the following statements must be true?

(A) $x = -6$
(B) $x = 5$
(C) $x \neq -2$
(D) $x \neq 0$

10. If $f(x) = 2x - 1$, and $g(x) = 3f(x)$, what is the slope and y-intercept of the line formed by $g(x)$?

(A) Slope = 3, y-intercept = −1
(B) Slope = 4, y-intercept = −2
(C) Slope = 6, y-intercept = 3
(D) Slope = 6, y-intercept = −3

✓ Solutions

1. **(C)** $x - 3 = 0.5x \rightarrow$

$-3 = 0.5x - x \rightarrow$

$-3 = -0.5x \rightarrow x = 6$

2. **(D)** $5(x + 4) - 3(x + 4) = 3x - 2 \rightarrow$

$5x + 20 - 3x - 12 = 3x - 2 \rightarrow$

$2x + 8 = 3x - 2 \rightarrow$

$8 = x - 2 \rightarrow x = 10$

3. **(D)** Turn the words into an algebraic expression. "If $3x$ is 5 less than 20" is equivalent to:

$$3x = 20 - 5 \rightarrow$$

$$3x = 15$$

Since $3x = 15 \rightarrow x = 5$

Therefore, $x + 4 = 5 + 4 = 9$

4. **(A)** Plug 2 in for y and then solve for n:

$$y + 5n = 3 \rightarrow$$

$$2 + 5n = 3 \rightarrow$$

$$5n = 1 \rightarrow n = \frac{1}{5}$$

In the equation above, if $y = -2$, what is the value of n?

5. **(B)** $\frac{4}{3y} = \frac{2}{3} \rightarrow$ Cross Multiply $\rightarrow$

$4 = \frac{2}{3} \times 3y \rightarrow$ Cancel the 3s $\rightarrow$

$4 = 2y \rightarrow 2 = y$

6. **(C)** Two equations will have infinitely many solutions if they overlap one another. Equations that have the same slope and y-intercept will overlap. Therefore, since the equations are already in slope-intercept form, make the constant k identical to the y-intercept in the first equation:

$$y = 3x - 5$$

So, the y-intercept is -5 and k should be -5.

7. **(A)** Use elimination to find the point of intersection. Double the first equation and add it to the second equation to eliminate the y values:

$$2(4x + y) = 2(3) \rightarrow 8x + 2y = 6$$

Now add this to the second equation:

$$\begin{array}{r} 8x + 2y = 6 \\ \underline{+(-\,3x - 2y = 4)} \\ 5x + 0 = 10 \rightarrow 5x = 10 \rightarrow x = 2 \end{array}$$

Fortunately, the only option that has 2 as the x value is choice **(A)**, so you do not have to continue to solve for y.

8. **(B)** Use substitution to solve this series of equations.

$$y = x + 5$$
$$2x + y = 11$$

Plug the first equation into the second one, then solve for x:

$$2x + (x + 5) = 11 \rightarrow$$
$$2x + x + 5 = 11 \rightarrow$$
$$3x + 5 = 11 \rightarrow$$
$$3x = 6 \rightarrow x = 2$$

9. **(C)** Given that $|x + 2| > 0$, choices (A), (B), and (D) all *could* be true. However, the only choice that *must* be true is choice **(C)**. If x were equal to -2, then the inequality would say that $0 > 0$, which cannot be the case.

10. **(D)** Plug $f(x) = 2x - 1$ into $g(x)$:

$$g(x) = 3(2x - 1) \rightarrow 6x - 3$$

Now, it is in slope-intercept form, and we can see that the slope is 6 and the y-intercept is -3.

Heart of Algebra—Word Problems and Function Interpretation

Setting Up Word Problems

SAT Math Strategy

Know which wording corresponds to which mathematical operations to help you solve word problems.

So far in this section, you have worked with how to execute algebraic operations. However, many SAT Math problems have you set up the algebra by asking detailed word problems. Here are some of the most common word problem phrases along with their corresponding mathematical operations.

Wording Examples for Common Mathematical Operations	Operation
is, are, was, were, will be, equals, gives, yields, results in, costs, sells for	$=$
sum, plus, increased by, more than, together, combined, total(s), added to, greater than, older than, farther than	$+$
difference, decreased by, less than, fewer than, minus, after, left over, younger than, shorter than, smaller than	$-$
multiplied by, times, of, product of, twice, triple, quadruple	$\times$
Divided by, per, out of, split, average, ratio of, half of, one third of	$\div$ or $\frac{x}{y}$

Example 1

Translate this sentence into an algebraic expression:

There are a total of 40 pets at a store, with x dogs and y cats.

Solution

$$40 = x + y$$

Example 2

Translate these sentences into algebraic expressions:

Caitlin is 6 years older than Allison, and the sum of Allison's age and Caitlin's age is 60 years.

✓ Solution

Let's use C for Caitlin's age and A for Allison's age. Be careful to not to make the equation go in the order of the words if the algebra does not correspond. For the first half of the sentence, "Caitlin is 6 years older than Allison," the equation would be:

$$C = A + 6$$

The second half of the sentence, "the sum of Allison's age and Caitlin's age is 60 years," would look like this algebraically:

$$A + C = 60$$

› Example 3

A stoplight is always green, yellow, or red. It is green $\frac{3}{5}$ of the time and yellow $\frac{1}{4}$ of the remaining time. What fraction of the entire time is the light red?

Fill in: ________

✓ Solution

Read the question one step at time, writing out the relevant information. Since the stoplight is always green, yellow, or red, we can determine the fraction of time it *is not* red by subtracting the green, yellow, and red fractions from 1; the remaining fraction will indicate the fraction of the time it *is* red.

The light is green $\frac{3}{5}$ of the time. The time that it is remaining would be $1 - \frac{3}{5} = \frac{5}{5} - \frac{3}{5} = \frac{2}{5}$ of the time. Out of the $\frac{2}{5}$ of time remaining, it is yellow $\frac{1}{4}$ of time time. So, calculate the fraction of time it is yellow by multiplying $\frac{2}{5}$ and $\frac{1}{4}$:

$$\frac{2}{5} \times \frac{1}{4} = \frac{2}{20} = \frac{1}{10}$$

Then calculate the time it is red by subtracting $\frac{3}{5}$, the fraction of time it is green, and $\frac{1}{10}$, the fraction of time it is yellow, from 1:

$$1 - \frac{3}{5} - \frac{1}{10} \rightarrow$$

Use 10 as the least common denominator:

$$\frac{10}{10} - \frac{6}{10} - \frac{1}{10} = \frac{3}{10}$$

So, the light is red $\frac{3}{10}$ of the entire time.

Practice

Turn these sentences into algebraic expressions.

1. Pam read 40 pages of her book on Monday, 30 pages of her book on Tuesday, and x pages of her book on Wednesday for a total of 120 pages.
2. If Yusuf did 1 hour of homework on Sunday and twice as much homework on Monday, how many hours did he do on both of those days?
3. Dog x is 5 years older than dog y.
4. Sofia spends two-thirds out of the 24 hours in a day awake. How would you calculate the number of hours, h, she is asleep in a day?
5. The average weight of person A, B, and C is 150 pounds.

Solutions

1. $40 + 30 + x = 120$
2. $1 + 2(1) = 3$ total hours of homework
3. Be sure you don't just read this left to right. It should be set up as the following:

$$x = y + 5$$

4. From this expression, you can see that x is 5 greater than y.
5. $24 - \frac{2}{3} \times 24 = h \rightarrow$
   $24 - 16 = h \rightarrow$
   $8 = h$
6. $\frac{A + B + C}{3} = 150$

NOTE

Averages will be covered in-depth in the Problem Solving and Data Analysis section.

Distance, Rate, and Time

The relationship among distance, rate (speed), and time is given by the following formula:

$$DISTANCE = RATE \times TIME\text{, or } D = RT$$

For example, if you were driving at 60 miles per hour for two hours, you would travel a total of 120 miles:

$$D = RT$$

$$120 \text{ Miles} = 60 \text{ MPH} \times 2 \text{ Hours}$$

Example

Julia's family took a road trip in which they drove 8 hours a day and averaged a driving speed of 50 miles per hour. If they spent a total of 6 days on the trip, how far in total did they drive?

✓ Solution

Start by figuring out how far they drove on a given day:

$$D = RT \rightarrow$$
$$D = 50 \times 8 \rightarrow$$
$$\text{Distance} = 400 \text{ Miles}$$

Then, multiply the daily number of miles by 6 days to find the total number of miles travelled:

$$400 \times 6 = 2{,}400$$

So, they drove a total of 2,400 miles on the trip.

Interpreting Variables and Constants

Sometimes, SAT word problems will not simply ask for you to solve for the value of a variable, but to interpret the significance of a constant or a variable.

> **SAT Math Strategy**
>
> Create your own idea of the meaning of a constant or variable before jumping into the options.

› Example 1

A teacher is counting up his classroom supplies for inventory at the end of the year. T is equal to the number of textbooks in his classroom at the end of the year, and L is the equal to the number of laptop computers in his classroom at the end of the year. In the equation

$T + L = 60$, what does the number 60 represent?

(A) The product of the number of the laptops and the number of the textbooks at the end of the year in the teacher's classroom

(B) The combined total number of laptops and textbooks at the end of the year in the teacher's classroom

(C) The difference between the number of laptops and number of textbooks in the teacher's classroom at the end of the year

(D) The predicted value of the number of laptops and textbooks a year from now

✓ Solution

Following our strategy for problems like these, do not jump into the choices before we have considered the meaning independently. T represents the number of textbooks at the end of the year, and L represents the number of laptops at the end of the year. If we add these together, we would get the sum of the textbooks and laptops the teacher has at the end of the year.

$$T + L = \text{Total number of textbooks and laptops}$$

This total is 60 in the problem. So, we can check out the choices and see that choice **(B)**, "The combined total number of laptops and textbooks at the end of the year in the teacher's classroom," corresponds to this idea.

Example 2

The height of water in inches, h, in a classroom's fish tank after w weeks is given by the function below.

$$h(w) = -\frac{1}{2}w + 25$$

Over a three-week period, by how much does the height of water in the tank change?

(A) Increases by .5 inches
(B) Increases by 25 inches
(C) Decreases by 1.5 inches
(D) Decreases by 2.5 inches

Solution

To answer this, we must first understand the meaning of the numbers in the function before diving into the choices. The function is written in slope-intercept form. The y-intercept is 25, indicating the initial height of water in the tank before any weeks have gone by. The slope is $-\frac{1}{2}$, indicating that each week that goes by, the height of the water in the tank will decrease by $\frac{1}{2}$ an inch.

So, over a three-week period, we can see by how much the height in the tank has changed by taking $-\frac{1}{2}$ and multiplying it by 3:

$$-\frac{1}{2} \times 3 = -\frac{3}{2} = -1.5$$

Therefore, the height in the tank after three weeks have passed will decrease by 1.5 inches, corresponding to choice **(C)**.

Functions in Table Form

Most functions you will encounter will be in the form of an equation. Sometimes, however, the SAT will provide the values of the function in a table. Here is how you attack a problem formatted in this way:

Example

The linear function f is defined by $f(x) = ax + b$, where a and b are constants. The values in the table below represent ordered pairs for the function:

x	$f(x)$
10	700
20	1200

What is the value of the constant b?

Fill In ______

✓ **Solution**

The way to read the table is to understand that each row represents an ordered pair: (10, 700) and (20, 1,200). You can solve for the constant b by first calculating the value of the constant a, which corresponds to the slope of the line:

$$\frac{\text{Change in } y}{\text{Change in } x} = \frac{1{,}200 - 700}{20 - 10} = \frac{500}{10} = 50$$

Now we know that the function can be written as $f(x) = 50x + b$. Next, solve for b by plugging in an ordered pair—let's use (10, 700) since it is smaller.

$$f(x) = 50x + b \rightarrow$$
$$700 = 50 \times 10 + b \rightarrow$$
$$700 = 500 + b \rightarrow b = 200$$

So, the value of the constant b is 200.

SAT Math Questions Practice Drill #1—Word Problems and Function Interpretation

(If timing, take about 12 minutes to complete.)

1. The total number of pages in a book is T. Eloise will read P pages each day for exactly D days until she completes the book at the end of the final day. Which of the following expresses the relationship between these values?

   (A) $T = PD$
   (B) $T = \frac{P}{D}$
   (C) $T = P + D$
   (D) $T = P - D$

2. Mary rented a boat that cost a $100 flat fee plus $3 for each gallon of gasoline used. If Mary paid a total of $130 to rent the boat, how many gallons of gasoline did she use?

   (A) 10
   (B) 15
   (C) 30
   (D) 45

3. An average pace for a backpacker on a certain trail is to hike 10 miles per day. If Joseph is taking a weeklong backpacking trip in which he wants his average pace over the entire week to exceed this average pace each day, which inequality represents the number of miles, m, he will travel on his trip?

   (A) $m > 10$
   (B) $m < 10$
   (C) $m < 70$
   (D) $m > 70$

4. A bread recipe calls for 6 eggs for every 10 cups of flour. If Martin wants to use a total of 15 eggs, how many cups of flour will he need to make this larger amount of bread using this recipe?

(A) 15
(B) 16
(C) 25
(D) 60

5. The number of windmills at a windfarm starts at 200, with 6 new windmills added each year and 2 mills removed each year due to wear and tear. What function represents the number of windmills, w, on the windfarm t years after the windfarm opens?

(A) $w(t) = 200 + 6t$
(B) $w(t) = 200 + 4t$
(C) $w(t) = 6 + 200t$
(D) $w(t) = 200 - 4t$

6. A catalog weighs enough that it requires 4 stamps for the post office to mail it. If a business is sending 500 catalogs, and each book of stamps has 20 stamps in it, how many books of stamps would the business need to purchase to mail all the catalogs?

(A) 24
(B) 80
(C) 100
(D) 2,000

7. Each student on a school trip packs 2 suitcases, 1 backpack, and 1 personal object. If there are 65 students on the trip, how many total items would the students pack?

(A) 69
(B) 130
(C) 196
(D) 260

8. The cost in dollars, C, of installing a sewer pipe that is L feet long is modeled by the function below:

$$C(L) = 300 + 20L$$

Given that function, what is the most logical interpretation of the following equation?

$$C(20) = 700$$

(A) The cost to install a 700-foot sewer pipe is 20 dollars.
(B) 20 times the cost of a typical pipe is equivalent to 700 dollars.
(C) The cost to install a 20-foot-long sewer pipe is 700 dollars.
(D) 20 typical sewer pipes have a total installation cost of 700 dollars.

9. A plumber's compensation is $50 per hour plus a $5,000 profit-share at the end of the year. Which inequality represents the number of hours, n, she will need to work in order to make at least $50,000 total compensation for the year?

(A) $50{,}000 \leq 50n + 5{,}000$
(B) $50{,}000 \geq 50n + 5{,}000$
(C) $\frac{n}{50} \geq 5{,}000$
(D) $\frac{n}{50} \leq 5{,}000$

10. The height in feet of an airplane, A, and a balloon, B, are modeled by these two equations, in which t is the number of minutes after 12:00 P.M.

$$A = 10{,}000 - 180t$$
$$B = 20t$$

At what time that same day would the airplane and the balloon be at the same height?

(A) 12:30 P.M.
(B) 12:50 P.M.
(C) 1:00 P.M.
(D) 1:45 P.M.

✓ Solutions

1. **(A)** Since she will read P pages each day for D days, multiply P and D together to get the total number of pages read:

$$T = PD$$

2. **(A)** Using x as the number of gallons of gasoline used, set up an equation modeling the situation like this:

$$130 = 100 + 3x$$

This means that the $100 flat fee plus $3 times each gallon of gas used will equal a total amount of $130. Then, solve for x:

$$130 = 100 + 3x \rightarrow$$
$$30 = 3x \rightarrow$$
$$x = 10$$

So, 10 gallons of gas were used.

3. **(D)** If Joseph exceeds the average pace of 10 miles per day over the 7-day period, he will travel in excess of $10 \times 7 = 70$ miles all together. Express this as an inequality by making the number of miles, m, be greater than 70: $m > 70$.

4. **(C)** Set up a proportion to solve this. There are 6 eggs for every 10 cups of flour, and this ratio needs to equal the ratio when there are 15 eggs (put the flour in the numerator since you are solving for flour, making you have to use fewer steps):

$$\frac{\text{Flour}}{\text{Eggs}} = \frac{10}{6} = \frac{x}{15} \rightarrow \text{Cross multiply to solve for } x \rightarrow$$
$$\frac{10}{6} \times 15 = x \rightarrow x = 25$$

5. **(B)** Since the number of windmills begins at 200, this number can be a constant. Each year, a net of 4 windmills are added to the windfarm, since 6 are added and 2 taken away. Therefore, the function that portrays the situation is:

$$w(t) = 200 + 4t$$

6. **(C)** The business will need to purchase a total of 4 stamps for each of 500 catalogs, so to get the total number of stamps needed, multiply 4 and 500 together:

$$4 \times 500 = 2{,}000$$

Then, calculate the number of stamp books needed by taking the total of 2,000 stamps and dividing it by the number of stamps in each stamp book, 20:

$$\frac{2{,}000}{20} = 100$$

So, 100 books of stamps would be needed.

7. **(D)** Each student packs a total of $2 + 1 + 1 = 4$ personal items. Therefore, simply multiply 4 by 65 to find the total items the students would pack:

$$65 \times 4 = 260$$

8. **(C)** Consider the original equation:

$$C(L) = 300 + 20L$$

Now, take a look at the other equation:

$$C(20) = 700$$

The 20 goes in the place of the variable L, which represents the length of the pipe. Therefore, the length of the pipe in consideration is 20 feet. $C(L)$ represents the cost to install a pipe of length L, so 700 is the cost of installation for a pipe of 20 feet.

9. **(A)** The plumber's compensation is the sum of \$5,000 plus \$50 per each of n hours worked. This total compensation needs to be at least \$50,000, meaning the sum of the hourly wages and the profit sharing needs to be greater than or equal to 50,000. Multiply 50 by n to get the total from the hourly wages, and then add it to the \$5,000.

$50,000 \leq 50n + 5,000$ represents this situation.

10. **(B)** Set the two heights equal to each other to solve for the number of minutes after 12:00 P.M., t, at which they meet in the air:

$$A = 10{,}000 - 180t$$
$$B = 20t$$

Set them equal to each other and solve for t:

$$10{,}000 - 180t = 20t \rightarrow$$
$$10{,}000 = 200t \rightarrow$$
$$\frac{10{,}000}{200} = t \rightarrow$$
$$50 = t$$

So, take 50 minutes past 12:00 to get 12:50 P.M.

SAT Math Questions Practice Drill #2—Word Problems and Function Interpretation

(If timing, take about 12 minutes to complete.)

1. If a cat eats x cups of food per day, how many cups of food will the cat eat in y days?

   (A) $x - y$
   (B) $x + y$
   (C) xy
   (D) $\frac{x}{y}$

2. The relationship between distance, D, rate, R, and time, T, is modeled by the equation $D = RT$. If the rate increases but the distance remains the same, what must happen to the time?

   (A) It decreases.
   (B) It increases.
   (C) It remains constant.
   (D) It cannot be determined.

3. The average price of a gallon of milk is modeled by the function C, in which y is the number of years after the year 2000.

   $$C(y) = 2.00 + 0.08y$$

   What does the number 0.08 in the function represent?

   (A) The number of gallons of milk sold
   (B) The average yearly increase in price per gallon of milk
   (C) The unit price for each gallon of milk
   (D) The total number of gallons of milk sold in a given year

4. Out of the 50 states in the United States, all but 1, Nebraska, have bicameral legislatures—i.e., there are two legislative chambers. Nebraska has a unicameral legislature—i.e., there is just one legislative chamber. What fraction of the states in the United States are bicameral?

   (A) $\frac{1}{50}$
   (B) $\frac{1}{25}$
   (C) $\frac{24}{25}$
   (D) $\frac{49}{50}$

5. Tabitha works as a cell phone salesperson. Her pay is \$10 per hour plus \$20 commission for each new cell phone she sells. If H represents the number of hours she works in a given week and C represents the number of cell phones she sells that week, which equation represents her total salary (expressed in dollars before any deductions for taxes, etc.) for the week?

   (A) $Salary = 20H + 10C$
   (B) $Salary = 10H + 20C$
   (C) $Salary = 10H - 20C$
   (D) $Salary = 20H - 10C$

6. A movie theater concession counter sells a large popcorn for $5 and a small popcorn for $3. If the total number of both types of popcorn sold in a given day is 150, and the total revenue from the popcorn sales is $570, how many small popcorns were sold? (Ignore sales tax in your calculations.)

(A) 15
(B) 30
(C) 45
(D) 90

7. The cost in dollars to operate a lemonade stand, C, is given by the function $c(x) = .25x + 20$, in which x represents the number of cups of lemonade sold. What does the number 20 represent in this situation?

(A) The fixed cost to set up the lemonade stand
(B) The cost per each cup of lemonade sold
(C) The total number of cups of lemonade sold
(D) The revenue from setting up the lemonade stand

8. The linear function $f(x) = kx + b$ has constants k and b. What is the y-intercept of the function based on the values of x and $f(x)$ in the table below?

x	$f(x)$
16	−28
21	−38

(A) 2
(B) 4
(C) 6
(D) 10

9. John has $20 to spend on his school lunch each week. A meal costs $3 and a milk costs $0.50. If he purchases one meal each day on Monday through Friday, what is the greatest number of milks he could purchase that week given his budget (note that sales tax is not applied to his purchases)?

(A) 3
(B) 7
(C) 10
(D) 20

10. In store A, 3 out of every 4 items are sold at a discount. In store B, 1 out of every 3 items is sold at a discount. If each store has 240 total items it is selling (both full price and at a discount), how many more discounted items will there be in store A than in store B?

(A) 80
(B) 100
(C) 120
(D) 480

✓ Solutions

1. **(C)** Take the x cups of food and multiply it by the y days the cat eats it:

$$x \times y = xy$$

2. **(A)** Take the original expression and isolate the time variable, T, to better understand what would happen:

$$D = RT \rightarrow \frac{D}{R} = T$$

So, if the rate increases while the distance remains the same, the fraction will decrease because the denominator will increase. Therefore, the time will decrease.

3. **(B)** In the function $C(y) = 2.00 + 0.08y$, C represents the price of the gallon of milk, and y is the number of years after 2000. So, 2.00 would be the price of the milk in the year 2000, and each year after 2000, the price of a gallon of milk would increase by 8 cents. Thus, the number 0.08 represents the average yearly increase in the price per gallon of milk.

4. **(D)** Since there is just 1 state, Nebraska, that does *not* have a bicameral legislature, there are 49 states that *do* have a bicameral legislature. To find the fraction, divide the number of states with a bicameral legislature, 49, by the total of 50 states:

$$\frac{49}{50}$$

5. **(B)** Tabitha makes \$10 for each of the H hours a week she works and \$20 for each of the C cell phones she sells in a week. Put this together to find her total salary for the week:

$$Salary = 10H + 20C$$

6. **(D)** Set up a series of equations to solve for the number of small popcorns sold. First, the sum of the large popcorns, which we can label L, and the small popcorns, which we can label S, is 150. In equation form, it is:

$$L + S = 150$$

The total revenue from the popcorn sales, \$570, is equivalent to what we get when multiplying 5 by the number of large popcorns and 3 by the number of small popcorns:

$$5L + 3S = 570$$

Now, use substitution to solve for the number of small popcorns:

$$L + S = 150 \rightarrow L = 150 - S$$

Plug this in to the second equation:

$$\begin{aligned} 5L + 3S &= 570 \rightarrow \\ 5(150 - S) + 3S &= 570 \rightarrow \\ 750 - 5S + 3S &= 570 \rightarrow \\ -2S &= -180 \rightarrow \\ S &= 90 \end{aligned}$$

So, 90 small popcorns were sold.

This problem can also be solved using elimination. Take the two equations $L + S = 150$ and $5L + 3S = 570$. Since we are solving for S, eliminate the L by multiplying $L + S = 150$ by -5 and adding this to the other equation:

$$\begin{array}{r} -5L - 5S = -750 \\ \underline{+5L + 3S = 570} \\ 0 - 2S = -180 \rightarrow S = 90 \end{array}$$

7. **(A)** In the function $C(x) = .25x + 20$, if zero cups of lemonade were sold, there would still be a cost of \$20 to operate the stand. Since this cost is fixed, no matter how many cups of lemonade are sold, the \$20 would be the cost to set up the lemonade stand.

8. **(B)** Since the function is a line, you can start by solving for the slope of the line using the ordered pairs presented in the table: (16, −28) and (21, −38).

$$\frac{\text{Change in } y}{\text{Change in } x} = \frac{-38 - (-28)}{21 - 16} = \frac{-10}{5} = -2$$

Since the function, $f(x) = kx + b$, is already in slope-intercept form, we now know that -2 is the slope and can be plugged in for the constant k:

$$f(x) = kx + b \rightarrow$$
$$f(x) = -2x + b$$

Now, we can solve for the constant b, which corresponds to the y-intercept of the function. Do so by plugging in an ordered pair for x and $f(x)$. Let us use (16, −28) since it is smaller:

$$f(x) = -2x + b \rightarrow$$
$$-28 = -2(16) + b \rightarrow$$
$$-28 = -32 + b \rightarrow$$
$$4 = b$$

Therefore, the y-intercept of the function is 4.

9. **(C)** If John purchases 1 meal each day on Monday through Friday, he will purchase a total of 5 meals. The cost for 5 meals is:

$$5 \times 3 = 15$$

He then has $20 - 15 = 5$ dollars remaining to purchase milks. Take the \$5 and divide it by \$0.50 to see the maximum number of milks he could purchase:

$$\frac{5}{0.50} = 10$$

Thus, John can purchase a maximum of 10 milks that week given his budget.

10. **(B)** Since there are 240 items in store A, find out how many items are being sold at a discount by multiplying $\frac{3}{4}$ by the total number of items:

$$\frac{3}{4} \times 240 = 180$$

For the discounted items in store B, do a similar calculation:

$$\frac{1}{3} \times 240 = 80$$

Then, find the difference in the number of discounted items for each store by subtracting:

$$180 - 80 = 100$$

SAT Math Questions Practice Drill #3—Word Problems and Function Interpretation

(If timing, take about 12 minutes to complete.)

1. If $2x + k = 2(x + 3)$, what is the value of the constant k?

(A) 2
(B) 3
(C) 5
(D) 6

2. The price of a painting, p, is modeled by the equation $p = 800 + 20y$, in which y is the number of years after the painting was created. What is the most logical interpretation of the number 20 in the equation?

(A) The price of the painting in y years
(B) The initial price of the painting
(C) The yearly increase in the painting's price
(D) The change in the painting's price over a 20-year period

3. Rental of a video game costs a flat fee of $20 plus $3 for each hour the video game is used. Which equation provides the total cost, C, of using the game for H hours?

(A) $C(H) = 3H - 20$
(B) $C(H) = H + 60$
(C) $C(H) = 3H + 20$
(D) $C(H) = 20H + 3$

x	y
6	0
4	$-\frac{2}{3}$
2	$-\frac{4}{3}$
0	-2
-2	$-\frac{8}{3}$

4. The table above provides pairs of values for x and y. Which equation below correctly shows the linear relationship between these values?

(A) $y = \frac{1}{3}x - 2$
(B) $y = \frac{2}{3}x - 1$
(C) $y = \frac{1}{2}x - 5$
(D) $y = \frac{1}{4}x$

5. A baker sells cupcakes for \$3 each and cookies for \$2 each. If he sells a total of 200 cookies and cupcakes and the total amount of revenue from selling the cookies and cupcakes is \$460, which set of equations could be used to solve for x cupcakes sold and y cupcakes sold?

(A) $x + y = 460$ and $2x + 3y = 200$
(B) $x + y = 200$ and $3x + 2y = 460$
(C) $3x + 2y = 200$ and $x + y = 460$
(D) $x \times y = 200$ and $(3x) \times (2y) = 460$

6. A discount bookstore sells books for \$6 each and magazines for \$3 each. In a given week, the store sells a combined total of 750 books/magazines and makes a total of \$3,600 from the book and magazine sales. In that week, how many magazines were sold?

(A) 300
(B) 450
(C) 900
(D) 10,800

7. A house is initially purchased for \$150,000 and increases in value by \$3,500 each year. Which of these expressions gives the price, P, of the house t years after purchase?

(A) $P = 3,500 + 150,000t$
(B) $P = 3,500t - 150,000$
(C) $P = 150,000 + 3,500t$
(D) $P = 150,000 - 3,500t$

8. In the following equation, $3x + 5 = 3x + k$, what must be true about the constant k equal in order for there to be no real solutions for x?

(A) $k = 3$
(B) $k = 5$
(C) $k \neq 3$
(D) $k \neq 5$

9. In an art class, a bin contains C crayons and M markers. If there are twice as many markers as crayons, and the total number of markers and crayons in the bin is 90, which of these sets of equations could be used to solve for C and M?

(A) $C + M = 90$
$M = 2C$

(B) $C \times M = 90$
$M = \frac{C}{2}$

(C) $\frac{C}{M} = 90$
$2M = C$

(D) $C \times M = 2C$
$M - 2C = 90$

10. Chris took a bike ride through the hills near his home. On his ride, he either went uphill or downhill. His total ride was 30 miles and took 1.6 hours. If half of the distance of his journey was uphill and the other half of the distance was downhill, and his downhill speed was an average of 25 mph, what was his average uphill speed?

    (A) 10 MPH
    (B) 12 MPH
    (C) 15 MPH
    (D) 18 MPH

✓ Solutions

1. **(D)** Simplify the expression so that the k is isolated to see its value:

$$2x + k = 2(x + 3) \rightarrow$$

$$2x + k = 2x + 6 \rightarrow$$

Subtract the $2x$ from both sides $\rightarrow$

$$k = 6$$

2. **(C)** The price of the painting is found with the equation $p = 800 + 20y$. At the year of the painting's creation, y equals zero and p will be 800. After one year, the price of the painting will increase by 20. So, the 20 represents the yearly increase in the painting's price.

3. **(C)** There is a flat fee of \$20, so no matter how many hours the video game is rented, there will be a constant \$20 fee. Then, for each hour the game is rented, there is a charge of \$3. The total cost is found by adding the flat fee of \$20 to the cost of \$3 for each hour it is rented:

$$C(H) = 3H + 20$$

4. **(A)** Save yourself time on this question by recognizing that all the answer choices are written in slope-intercept form, and have different y-intercepts. Fortunately, we can determine the y-intercept of the function by looking at the table: when the x value is 0, the y value is -2. Therefore, the only plausible option is choice (A): $y = \frac{1}{3}x - 2$.

5. **(B)** The total number of cupcakes sold is 200, so this equation fits the problem:

$$x + y = 200$$

The total revenue is \$460, and each of the x cupcakes sells for \$3 each, and each of the y cupcakes sells for \$2 each. Therefore, this equation fits the situation:

$$3x + 2y = 460$$

6. **(A)** Let's use the variable B for books and M for magazines and create equations to model what is described. First, there are a total of 750 books and magazines sold:

$$B + M = 750$$

Next, the total revenue from selling books at \$6 each and magazines at \$3 each is \$3,600:

$$6B + 3M = 3,600$$

Now, we can use elimination to solve for the magazines sold. Take the first equation and multiply it by −6 so that the B term can be eliminated, then add it to the second equation:

$$\begin{array}{r} -6B - 6M = -4{,}500 \\ \underline{+\,6B + 3M = 3{,}600} \\ 0 - 3M = -900 \end{array}$$

Then, solve for the number of magazines:

$$-3M = -900 \rightarrow$$
$$M = 300$$

This can also be solved using substitution. Take the two equations $B + M = 750$ and $6B + 3M = 3{,}600$. Since we want M, substitute for B so everything is in terms of M:

$$B + M = 750 \rightarrow$$
$$B = 750 - M$$

Plug this in for B into the other equation:

$$6B + 3M = 3{,}600 \rightarrow$$
$$6(750 - M) + 3M = 3{,}600 \rightarrow$$
$$4{,}500 - 6M + 3M = 3{,}600 \rightarrow$$
$$-3M = -900 \rightarrow$$
$$M = 300$$

7. **(C)** The price starts at 150,000 (i.e., when the years are zero), and each year it goes up by \$3,500. So, the y-intercept of the function is 150,000, and the slope (yearly change) of the function is 3,500. Putting this in slope-intercept form, $P = 150{,}000 + 3{,}500t$ is correct even though the y-intercept comes first in the expression.

8. **(D)** In order for there to be no solutions, the equation must result in something that is not true for any value of x. If we simplify the equation, we can see that if k is 5, there will be infinitely many solutions:

$$3x + 5 = 3x + k \rightarrow$$

Subtract $3x$ from both sides →

$$5 = k$$

So, if $k \neq 5$, there would not be any solutions.

9. **(A)** The total number of markers and crayons in the class is 90, which can be represented by this equation:

$$C + M = 90$$

For the next equation, be careful to not just read it left to right. The correct representation of the phrase "there are twice as many markers as crayons" is:

$$M = 2C$$

Plug in a sample for M and a sample for C to see that this makes sense. If M is 40 and C is 20 then $M = 2C$. These two equations together correspond to choice **(A)**.

10. **(C)** Since half of the distance of the journey is uphill and the other downhill, 15 miles would be uphill, and 15 downhill. Let us first find how long it took to make the downhill journey—this portion would be at 25 mph. Plug it into the equation $D = RT$ and solve for time.

$$D = RT \rightarrow$$
$$15 = 25 \times T \rightarrow$$
$$\frac{15}{25} = .6 = T$$

Now that we know that .6 of an hour was spent going downhill, we know that $1.6 - .6 = 1$ hour was spent going uphill. Since this part of the journey is 15 miles, the average uphill speed will simply be 15 miles per hour.

Heart of Algebra—Lines and Slope

Slope Formula

The slope of a line represents its vertical increase, *rise*, divided by the horizontal increase, *run*. Calculate the slope between two points, (x_1, y_1) and (x_2, y_2), by plugging the coordinates of the points into this formula:

$$\text{Slope} = \frac{\text{Change in } y}{\text{Change in } x} = \frac{(y_2 - y_1)}{(x_2 - x_1)}$$

Example

What is the slope of a line that has the points (8, 3) and (5, 1)?

Solution

Be consistent in which point is point 2 and which point is point 1. In this case, let's use (8, 3) as point 2 and (5, 1) as point 1—doing so will make for an easier calculation that does not involve negative values. So, $y_2 = 3$, $y_1 = 1$, $x_2 = 8$, and $x_1 = 5$.

$$\frac{(y_2 - y_1)}{(x_2 - x_1)} = \frac{(3 - 1)}{(8 - 5)} = \frac{2}{3}$$

Thus, the slope of this line would be $\frac{2}{3}$.

Practice

1. What is the slope of a line with the points (4, 3) and (6, 1)?
2. What is the slope of a line with the points (2.5, 7) and (−4, −8)?
3. Consider a line in the *xy*-coordinate plane in which to get from point *A* to point *B*, one must go up +5 units vertically and go over +3 units horizontally. What is the slope of this line?

Solutions

1. $\frac{(y_2 - y_1)}{(x_2 - x_1)} = \frac{(3 - 1)}{(4 - 6)} = \frac{2}{-2} = -1$

2. $\frac{(y_2 - y_1)}{(x_2 - x_1)} = \frac{(7 - (-8))}{(2.5 - (-4))} = \frac{7 + 8}{2.5 + 4} = \frac{15}{6.5} \approx 2.31$

3. The "rise" of the line is +5 units and the "run" of the line is +3 units. So, the slope is the rise divided by the run:

$$\frac{\text{Rise}}{\text{Run}} = \frac{\text{Change in } y}{\text{Change in } x} = \frac{5}{3}$$

Slope-Intercept Form of a Line

In order to graph a line, put its equation in **slope-intercept** form:

$y = mx + b$

$m =$ slope of the line, the "rise" over the "run"

$b = y$-intercept of the line, i.e., where the line intersects the y-axis

Example 1

What is the slope and y-intercept of a line with the equation $y = 5x - 7$?

Solution

The equation is already in slope-intercept form, so just match up the numbers in the equation to their corresponding values.

$$y = mx + b$$
$$y = 5x - 7$$
$$m = 5$$
$$b = -7$$

So, the slope of this line is 5, and the y-intercept of the line is -7.

Example 2

What is the equation of the line with the graph below?

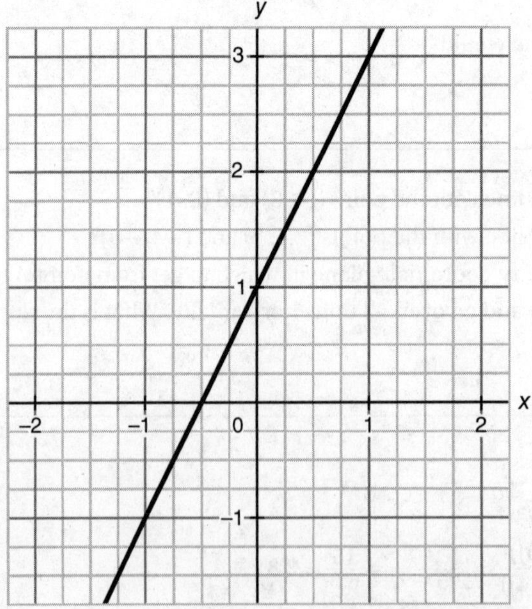

✓ **Solution**

The line intersects the y-axis at (0, 1), making this point the y-intercept. The line "rises" 2 units for every 1 unit it "runs," giving a slope of 2. So, the equation for the line is:

$$y = 2x + 1$$

Overlapping and Intersecting Lines

Lines that have *equivalent* equations, although in different forms, will *overlap* one another. For example, $y = 3x + 4$ and $2y = 6x + 8$ overlap since the second equation is simply two times the first equation.

Lines that *meet at a single point intersect* one another. For example, $y = 2x + 3$ and $y = -2x + 1$ will intersect in the xy-coordinate plane when graphed:

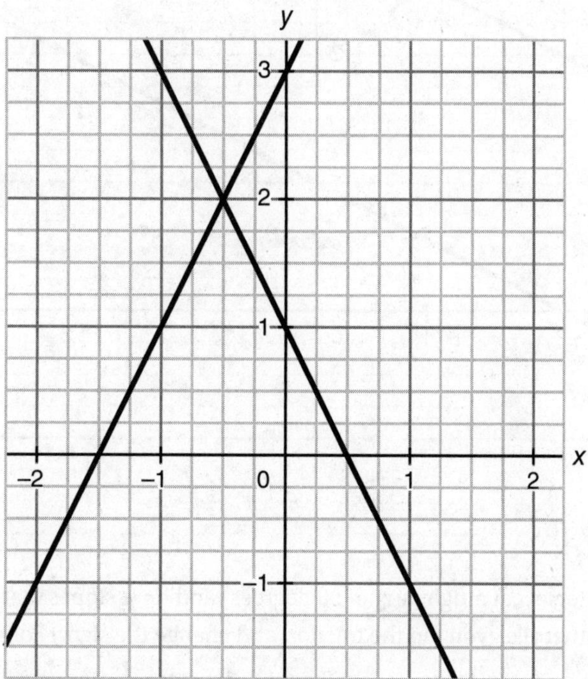

Parallel and Perpendicular Lines

Lines that are *parallel* to one another will have the *same slope*, but different *y*-intercepts—they will never intersect or overlap one another. For example, the lines with the equations $y = \frac{1}{2}x + 1$ and $y = \frac{1}{2}x + 3$ are parallel to one another:

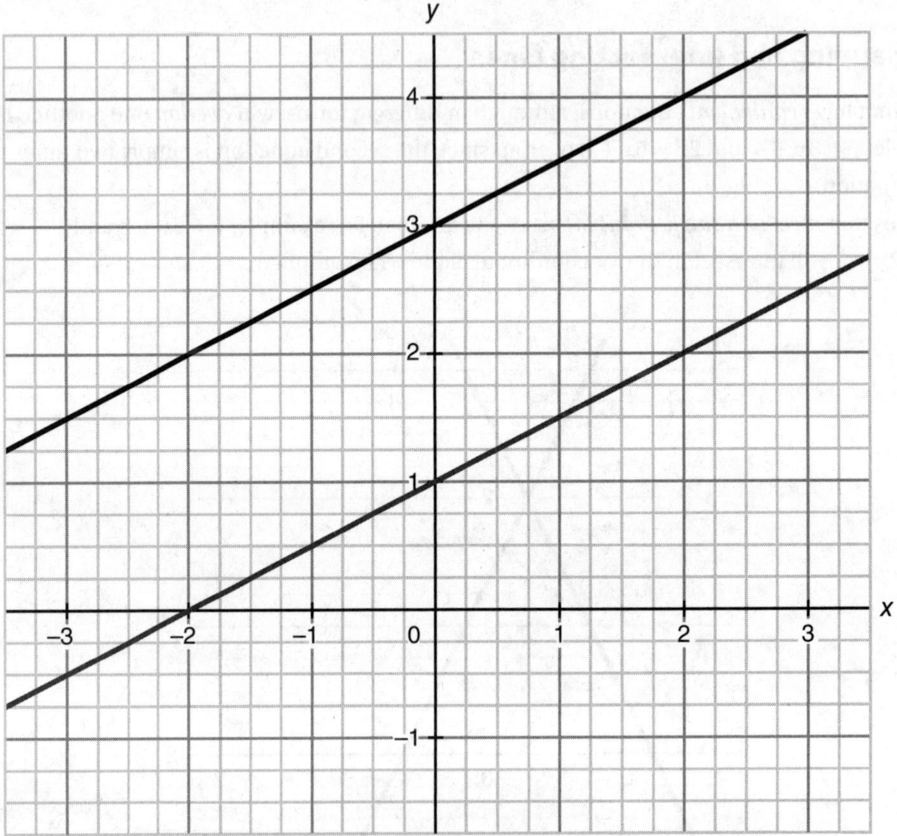

Perpendicular lines intersect at a right angle (90 degrees) and have slopes that are *negative reciprocals* of one another (i.e., you filp the fraction and change the sign.) For example, if one line has a slope of 3, the line perpendicular to it will have a slope of $-\frac{1}{3}$. Consider two perpendicular lines: $y = -\frac{1}{2}x + 1$ and $y = 2x + 2$.

Their graph in the *xy*-coordinate plane would be as follows:

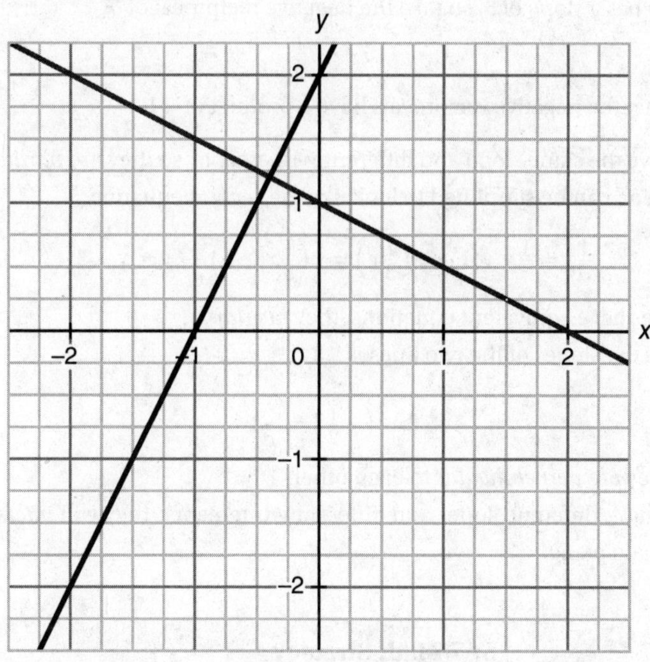

Practice

1. What is the slope of a line with the equation $y = -3x + 8$?
2. What is the *y*-intercept of a line with the equation $y = 2x + 5$?
3. What is the slope of a line with the equation $2y = 3x + 4$?
4. What is the *y*-intercept of a line with the equation $y - 3 = 2x + 1$?
5. If the slope of a line is 4, what is the slope of a line parallel to it?
6. If a line has the equation $y = 5x - 4$, what is the slope of a line perpendicular to it?
7. Would the following sets of lines *overlap, intersect,* be *parallel,* or be *perpendicular* to each other?
   (A) $y = 2x + 9$ and $y = 2x - 4$
   (B) $\frac{1}{3}y = \frac{1}{3}x - 1$ and $y = x - 3$
   (C) $y = 2x$ and $y = -\frac{1}{2}x - 2$
   (D) $y = 4x - 1$ and $y = 3x + 2$

Solutions

1. −3.
2. 5.
3. Divide both sides of the equation by 2 to put it in slope-intercept form.

$$2y = 3x + 4 \rightarrow \frac{2y}{2} = \frac{3x + 4}{2} \rightarrow y = \frac{3}{2}x + 2$$

   Now that it is in slope-intercept form, find the slope: $\frac{3}{2}$.

4. Put the equation in slope-intercept form to determine the *y*-intercept.

$$y - 3 = 2x + 1 \rightarrow y = 2x + 1 + 3 = y = 2x + 4$$

   Now that it is in slope-intercept form, you can see that the *y*-intercept is 4.

5. Parallel lines have the same slopes as one another, so it would just be 4.
6. The current line has a slope of 5, so take the negative reciprocal of 5:

$$5 \rightarrow -\frac{1}{5}$$

Keep in mind that the negative reciprocals have a product of −1.

7A. These lines have the same slope and different y-intercepts, so they are *parallel*.

7B. The first equation can be simplified to look like the second equation:

$$\frac{1}{3}y = \frac{1}{3}x - 1 \rightarrow 3\left(\frac{1}{3}y\right) = 3\left(\frac{1}{3}x - 1\right) \rightarrow y = x - 3$$

Since the lines have equivalent equations, they *overlap*.

7C. The product of the slopes of the two lines is −1.

$$2 \times \left(-\frac{1}{2}\right) = -1$$

Therefore, they are *perpendicular* to each other.

7D. The two lines have different slopes and different y-intercepts. They will *intersect* each other in the xy-coordinate plane.

SAT Math Strategy

Memorize the key slope and line formulas so you can avoid being intimidated.

SAT Math questions using the above concepts will often integrate multiple ideas about slope and lines. If you know the formulas well, you can write out what you need to think through the problem.

Example 1

If $ax + by = 5$ is a line in the xy-coordinate plane in which a and b are constants, which of the following expresses the slope of the line?

(A) a

(B) $-\frac{a}{b}$

(C) $-\frac{b}{a}$

(D) 5

Solution

Do not let yourself be intimidated by the unusual formatting presented in the problem.

Remember the fundamental concept:

- Slope-intercept form is $y = mx + b$.

So, take the equation and put it in slope-intercept form to find the slope of the line:

$$ax + by = 5 \rightarrow by = -ax + 5 \rightarrow \frac{by}{b} = \frac{-ax + 5}{b} \rightarrow y = -\frac{a}{b}x + \frac{5}{b}$$

So, the correct answer is **(B)**, $-\frac{a}{b}$.

Example 2

a	4	*x*	10	13
b	1	2	3	4

Given that the relationship between a and b is linear, what is the value of x in the table above?

Fill in: ___________

Solution

The information is presented in a table instead of the usual (x, y) style. Since the problem states that the relationship between a and b is linear, the *slope* of the line will be constant. We can treat a as we would normally treat x and treat b as we would normally treat y. If we find the slope of the line between two points, it will be the same as it would be for two different points on the line. Let's take the point (13, 4) and (10, 3) to see what the slope of the line would be:

$$\frac{(y_2 - y_1)}{(x_2 - x_1)} = \frac{(4 - 3)}{(13 - 10)} = \frac{1}{3}$$

We can then set up an equation to solve for the unknown value of x. The slope of $\frac{1}{3}$ will be the same if we pick a different set of points. So, let's pick (4, 1) and $(x, 2)$ and set it equal to $\frac{1}{3}$ so that we can solve for x:

$$\frac{2-1}{x-4} = \frac{1}{3} \rightarrow \frac{1}{x-4} = \frac{1}{3} \rightarrow \text{Cross Multiply} \rightarrow$$

$$3 = x - 4 \rightarrow x = 7$$

Keep in mind that in a line, the y-value changes by the same amount with each unit increase in x; so the the problem can be answered by inspection (just follow the pattern and add 3 to 4).

SAT Math Questions Practice Drill—Lines and Slope

(If timing, take about 12 minutes to complete.)

1. Which of the following equations represents a line in the xy-coordinate plane with a y-intercept of 6 and a slope of -3?

   (A) $y = 3x + 6$
   (B) $y = 6x - 3$
   (C) $y = 6x + 3$
   (D) $y = -3x + 6$

2. In the xy-plane, which of these linear equations has a y-intercept of 12?

   (A) $y = 4x + 12$
   (B) $12y = 4x - 1$
   (C) $y = 4x - 12$
   (D) $12 + y = 4x$

3. A linear equation in the xy-plane intercepts the y-axis at -3. For every 2 units the y-coordinate of the line increases, the x-coordinate decreases by 7 units. Which of the following is the correct equation for this line?

(A) $y = \frac{7}{2}x + 3$
(B) $y = \frac{2}{7}x - 3$
(C) $y = -\frac{2}{7}x - 3$
(D) $y = \frac{3}{2}x - 7$

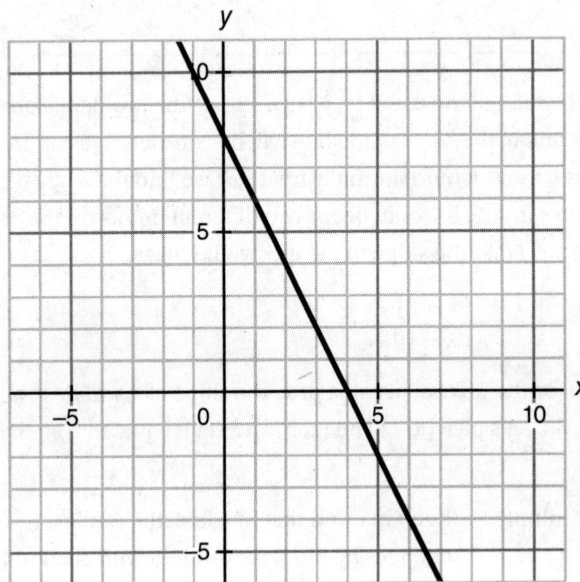

4. Consider the graph of the line above as graphed in the xy-coordinate plane. What is the value of b if the line is presented in the equation $y = mx + b$, in which both m and b are constants?

(A) 4
(B) 8
(C) −2
(D) $-\frac{1}{2}$

5. What is the slope of a line with the equation $5x + 4y = 2$?

(A) $-\frac{1}{2}$
(B) $\frac{4}{5}$
(C) $-\frac{5}{4}$
(D) 2

6. For the equation $\frac{1}{2}y = \frac{2}{3}x - 4$, what is the x-intercept?

(A) −8
(B) $-\frac{4}{3}$
(C) 3
(D) 6

7. Two lines are graphed in the *xy*-plane. The lines have the same slope and different *y*-intercepts. How many solution(s) would the equations represented by this pair of lines have?

(A) None
(B) One
(C) Two
(D) Infinite

8. Which of these represents a linear equation in the *xy*-plane that has the points (5, 17) and (2, 5)?

(A) $y = -4x - 3$
(B) $y = -3x + 4$
(C) $y = 4x - 3$
(D) $y = 3x + 4$

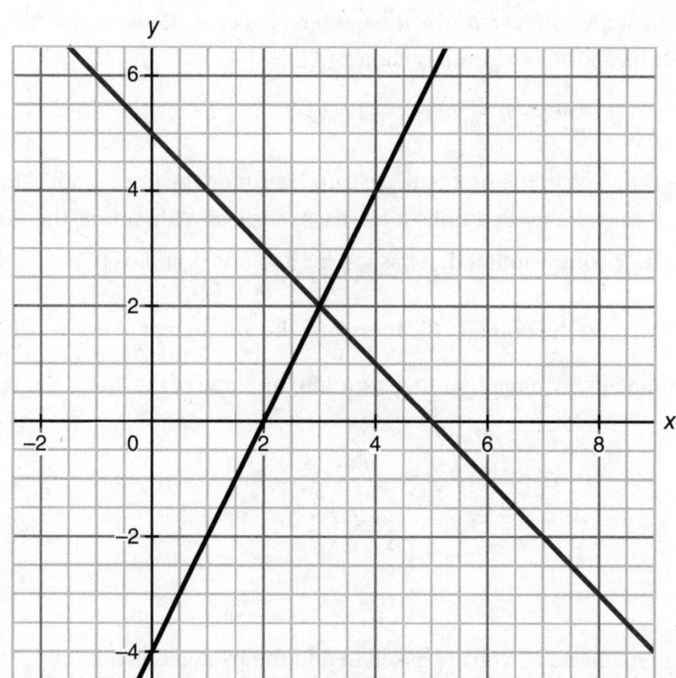

9. The above graph is represented by which of these sets of equations?

(A) $y = -4x + 2$
$y = 5x + 1$
(B) $y = 2x - 4$
$y = -x + 5$
(C) $y = \frac{1}{2}x - 4$
$y = -5x + 1$
(D) $y = \frac{1}{4}x - 1$
$y = -2x + 5$

10. Which of the following equations has a slope perpendicular to the slope of a line with the equation $y = ax + b$, given that a and b are constants?

(A) $y = -\frac{1}{a}x + 2b$
(B) $y = -ax + 2b$
(C) $y = -\frac{1}{b}x + 2a$
(D) $y = -bx - 2a$

✓ Solutions

1. **(D)** Use the slope-intercept form of a line, and plug in the value for the slope, m, and the y-intercept, b.

$$y = mx + b \rightarrow y = -3x + 6$$

2. **(A)** When a line is written in slope-intercept form, the y-intercept corresponds to the constant b. The only option that has positive 12 for b is choice **(A)**.

$$y = mx + b \rightarrow y = 4x + 12$$

3. **(C)** From the description of the line in the problem, we can determine the line's slope. The line decreases horizontally 7 units for every 2 units it increases vertically. Therefore, the slope of the line will be $\frac{2}{(-7)} = -\frac{2}{7}$. The only option that has $-\frac{2}{7}$ for its slope is choice **(C)**.

4. **(B)** The line intersects the y-axis at the point (0, 8). Therefore, the y-intercept of the line is 8.

5. **(C)** Put the line in slope-intercept form in order to determine the slope of the line:

$$5x + 4y = 2 \rightarrow$$
$$4y = -5x + 2 \rightarrow$$
$$y = -\frac{5}{4}x + \frac{2}{4} \rightarrow y = -\frac{5}{4}x + \frac{1}{2}$$

So, the slope of the line is $-\frac{5}{4}$.

6. **(D)** This is an easy question to misread—you are asked to find the x-intercept, not the y-intercept. The x-intercept is the point at which the line intersects the x-axis; for this to happen, the y value at the point must be zero. So, plug zero in for y and see what the value of x is:

$$\frac{1}{2}y = \frac{2}{3}x - 4 \rightarrow$$
$$\frac{1}{2}(0) = \frac{2}{3}x - 4 \rightarrow$$
$$0 = \frac{2}{3}x - 4 \rightarrow 4 = \frac{2}{3}x \rightarrow$$
$$x = 4 \times \left(\frac{3}{2}\right) \rightarrow x = \frac{12}{2} = 6$$

7. **(A)** Lines that have the same slope and different y-intercepts run parallel to one another. At no point will they intersect, so the answer is "none."

8. **(C)** Looking ahead to the answers, all of the choices have different values for the line's slope. So, calculate the slope of the line with the given information and see which of the options matches:

$$\text{Slope} = \frac{y_2 - y_1}{x_2 - x_1} = \frac{17 - 5}{5 - 2} = \frac{12}{3} = 4$$

The only one of the lines that has 4 as its slope is choice **(C)**, $y = 4x - 3$.

9. **(B)** Fortunately, the different options given have different y-intercepts. So you can save time in solving this by identifying the y-intercepts of the two lines and then matching them with a choice. The two y-intercepts are 5 and −4, and the only option that has both of those values as y-intercepts is choice **(B)**:

$$y = 2x - 4$$
$$y = -x + 5$$

10. **(A)** Since the equation of the line is already in slope-intercept form, we can see that its slope is a. We then can take the negative reciprocal of a to get the slope of a line perpendicular to it:

$$a \rightarrow -\frac{1}{a}$$

The only option that has $-\frac{1}{a}$ as its slope is choice **(A)**.

Passport to Advanced Math

This section contains comprehensive review and strategies for all of the concepts below:

Passport to Advanced Math—Polynomials and Factoring

- Polynomial Manipulation
- Common Factoring Patterns

Passport to Advanced Math—Exponents and Roots

- Exponent Rules
- Problems with Exponents and Roots

Passport to Advanced Math—Solving Quadratic Equations

- Factoring Quadratic Equations
- Square Root Method
- Quadratic Formula
- Completing the Square
- Plugging in the Answers
- Undefined Functions
- Extraneous Solutions
- Synthetic Division

Passport to Advanced Math—Zeros, Parabolas, and Polynomial Graphing

- Zeros of a Function
- Parabola Graphing
- Function Transformations
- Visualizing Polynomial Graphs

Passport to Advanced Math—Function Interpretation and Manipulation

- Putting Variables in Terms of Other Variables
- Identifying Constants
- Interpreting Functions

Passport to Advanced Math—Polynomials and Factoring

Polynomial Manipulation

SAT Math Strategy

When simplifying polynomials, write out all your steps to avoid making careless errors.

The SAT Math section will have you simplify polynomial expressions using addition, subtraction, multiplication, and division. How should you approach these types of problems?

Students typically miss polynomial simplification problems not because of their mathematical difficulty, but because of careless mistakes, like with manipulating negative signs.

Example

$(-2x^2 + 3x + 1) - (x^2 + x + 2)$ is equivalent to which of these expressions?

(A) $x^2 + 3x - 1$
(B) $-x^2 + 3x + 1$
(C) $-3x^2 + 2x - 1$
(D) $-3x^2 - 2x - 1$

Solution

Combine the x^2 components, the x components, and the numerical components in order to simplify. Write out all your steps to avoid careless errors.

$$(-2x^2 + 3x + 1) - (x^2 + x + 2)$$

Remove the parentheses, and distribute the -1 throughout the second half of the expression:

$$-2x^2 + 3x + 1 - x^2 - x - 2$$

Now, group like terms together to simplify:

$$(-2x^2 - x^2) + (3x - x) + (1 - 2) \rightarrow$$
$$-3x^2 + 2x - 1$$

This corresponds to answer choice (C).

Practice

Simplify the following expressions.

1. $2x + 6x - 9x$
2. $3x^2 - 4x^2$
3. $2x^2 - x + x^2$
4. $3x^3 - 2x + x^3 + 4x$
5. $8x^4 + 2(x^2 - 3x^4)$
6. $3(4x^2 - 2x) - 2(3x^2 + 5)$
7. $x(-x + 4) - 2x(x + 3)$

Solutions

1. $2x + 6x - 9x \rightarrow 8x - 9x \rightarrow -x$
2. $3x^2 - 4x^2 \rightarrow -x^2$
3. $2x^2 - x + x^2 \rightarrow (2x^2 + x^2) - x \rightarrow 3x^2 - x$
4. $3x^3 - 2x + x^3 + 4x \rightarrow$
   $(3x^3 + x^3) + (-2x + 4x) \rightarrow$
   $4x^3 + 2x$
5. $8x^4 + 2(x^2 - 3x^4) \rightarrow$
   $8x^4 + 2x^2 - 6x^4 \rightarrow$
   $(8x^4 - 6x^4) + 2x^2 \rightarrow$
   $2x^4 + 2x^2$

6. $3(4x^2 - 2x) - 2(3x^2 + 5) \rightarrow$
$12x^2 - 6x - 6x^2 - 10 \rightarrow$
$(12x^2 - 6x^2) - 6x - 10 \rightarrow$
$6x^2 - 6x - 10$
7. $x(-x + 4) - 2x(x + 3) \rightarrow$
$-x^2 + 4x - 2x^2 - 6x \rightarrow$
$(-x^2 - 2x^2) + (4x - 6x) \rightarrow$
$-3x^2 - 2x$

Common Factoring Patterns

SAT Math Strategy

The SAT math consistently has problems in form that can be easily factored. Be on the lookout for common factoring patterns.

Since the SAT primarily evaluates your skill in problem solving and pattern recognition, as opposed to evaluating your skill in doing tedious calculations, memorize these common factoring patterns so that you can solve the problems most efficiently.

Square of Binomial (with plus sign)

$$(a + b)(a + b) = a^2 + 2ab + b^2$$

Example

$$(x + 5)(x + 5) = x^2 + 10x + 25$$

Difference of Squares

$$(a + b)(a - b) = a^2 - b^2$$

Example

$$(x + 5)(x - 5) = x^2 - 25$$

Square of Binomial (with negative sign)

$$(a - b)(a - b) = a^2 - 2ab + b^2$$

Example

$$(x - 5)(x - 5) = x^2 - 10x + 25$$

Sum of Cubes

$$(a + b)(a^2 - ab + b^2) = a^3 + b^3$$

Example

$$(x + 5)(x^2 - 5x + 25) = x^3 + 5^3 = x^3 + 125$$

Difference of Cubes

$$(a - b)(a^2 + ab + b^2) = a^3 - b^3$$

Example

$$(x - 5)(x^2 + 5x + 25) = x^3 - 5^3 = x^3 - 125$$

Practice

Write the following expressions in factored form.

1. $n^2 + 2n + 1 = ?$
2. $a^2 - 14a + 49 = ?$
3. $y^2 - 16 = ?$
4. $4x^2 - 9y^2 = ?$
5. $27 - n^3 = ?$
6. $9x^2 - 25y^2 = ?$
7. $\frac{1}{4}x^2 - \frac{1}{9}y^2 = ?$
8. $125a^3 + 64b^3 = ?$

Solutions

1. $n^2 + 2n + 1 = (n + 1)(n + 1)$
2. $a^2 - 14a + 49 = (a - 7)(a - 7)$
3. $y^2 - 16 = (y + 4)(y - 4)$
4. $4x^2 - 9y^2 = (2x)^2 - (3y)^2 = (2x + 3y)(2x - 3y)$
5. $27 - n^3 = \rightarrow$
   $a^3 - b^3 = (a - b)(a^2 + ab + b^2) \rightarrow$
   $3^3 - n^3 = (3 - n)(9 + 3n + n^2)$
6. $9x^2 - 25y^2 = (3x)^2 - (5y)^2 = (3x + 5y)(3x - 5y)$
7. $\frac{1}{4}x^2 - \frac{1}{9}y^2 = ?$
   $\left(\frac{1}{2}x + \frac{1}{3}y\right)\left(\frac{1}{2}x - \frac{1}{3}y\right)$
8. $(a + b)(a^2 - ab + b^2) = a^3 + b^3$
   $125a^3 + 64b^3 = (5a)^3 + (4b)^3 \rightarrow$
   $a^3 + b^3 = (a + b)(a^2 - ab + b^2) \rightarrow$
   $(5a + 4b)(25a^2 - 20ab + 16b^2)$

SAT Math Questions Practice Drill—Polynomials and Factoring

(If timing, take about 12 minutes to complete.)

1. Which of the following is equivalent to $3n(n^2 + 2n - 1)$?

   (A) $3n^3 + 6n^2 - 3n$
   (B) $3n^2 + 6n - 3$
   (C) $3n^3 + 6n^2 + 3n$
   (D) $3n^6 + 6n^4 - 3n^2$

$x^3 + 6x^2 + 9x$

2. Which of the following is equivalent to the above expression?

(A) $x(x + 3)(x - 3)$
(B) $(x + 3)^3$
(C) $x(x + 3)^2$
(D) $(x + 3)(x + 3)$

3. $x^2 + 12x = -36$ is equivalent to which of the following?

(A) $(x + 6) = (x - 6)$
(B) $x(x + 12 + 36) = 0$
(C) $(x + 6)^2 = 0$
(D) $(x - 6)^2 = 4$

4. Which of the following expresses the result when $x^3 + x$ is subtracted from $3x^3 + 2x^2$?

(A) $2x^3 + 2x^2 - x$
(B) $4x^3 + 2x^2 + x$
(C) $-2x^3 - 2x^2 + x$
(D) $4x^3 + 2x^2 - x$

5. The expression $-(x^2 + 2)(-x - 1)$ is equivalent to which of the following?

(A) $x^3 - x^2 + 2x - 2$
(B) $x^3 + 2x^2 - x - 2$
(C) $x^3 + x^2 + 2x + 2$
(D) $-x^3 - x^2 + 2x + 1$

$(x + y^2)(-x - y^2)$

6. Which of the following options is an equivalent form of the expression above?

(A) $x^2 - 2xy^2 + y^4$
(B) $-x^2 - 2xy^2 - y^4$
(C) $2x^2 - xy^2 - 4y^4$
(D) $-x^2 - y^4$

7. $\frac{5}{3} + \frac{2}{x - 3}$ is equivalent to which of the following, given that $x \neq 3$?

(A) $\frac{7}{3x}$

(B) $\frac{7}{3x - 9}$

(C) $\frac{10}{3(x - 3)}$

(D) $\frac{5x - 9}{3x - 9}$

Fill-In Practice: Write your answer in the underlined blank under each question.

8. For the function $f(x) = (2x - 10)^2$, what is the value of $f(13)$?

   Answer: ________

9. If $\frac{2x}{5} - \frac{3y}{10} = 0$, what is the value of $\frac{x}{y}$?

   Answer: ________

10. If $\frac{3}{9 + 6x + x^2} = \frac{3}{4}$, what is the value of $(x + 3)$ if $(x + 3) > 0$?

    Answer: ________

✓ Solutions

1. **(A)**

   $3n(n^2 + 2n - 1) \rightarrow$

   Distribute the $3n \rightarrow$

   $3n^3 + 6n^2 - 3n$

2. **(C)**

   $x^3 + 6x^2 + 9x \rightarrow$

   Factor out an $x \rightarrow$

   $x(x^2 + 6x + 9) \rightarrow$

   Factor the part in parentheses $\rightarrow$

   $x(x + 3)(x + 3) \rightarrow x(x + 3)^2$

3. **(C)**

   $x^2 + 12x = -36 \rightarrow$

   $x^2 + 12x + 36 = 0 \rightarrow$

   $(x + 6)(x + 6) = 0 \rightarrow (x + 6)^2 = 0$

4. **(A)** Be careful to put this in the correct order. It should look like this:

   $(3x^3 + 2x^2) - (x^3 + x) \rightarrow$

   $3x^3 + 2x^2 - x^3 - x \rightarrow$

   $2x^3 + 2x^2 - x$

5. **(C)**

   $-(x^2 + 2)(-x - 1) \rightarrow$

   FOIL the parts within the parentheses $\rightarrow$

   $-(-x^3 - x^2 - 2x - 2) \rightarrow$

   Distribute the $-1 \rightarrow$

   $x^3 + x^2 + 2x + 2$

6. **(B)**

$(x + y^2)(-x - y^2) \rightarrow$

FOIL the expression $\rightarrow$

$-x^2 - xy^2 - xy^2 + y^4 \rightarrow$

$-x^2 - 2xy^2 - y^4$

7. **(D)** Make each fraction have a common denominator and then add them together.

$\frac{5}{3} + \frac{2}{x-3} \rightarrow$

$\frac{5(x-3)}{3(x-3)} + \frac{2(3)}{3(x-3)} \rightarrow$

$\frac{5(x-3)+6}{3(x-3)} \rightarrow$

$\frac{5x-15+6}{3(x-3)} \rightarrow$

$\frac{5x-9}{3(x-3)} \rightarrow$

$\frac{5x-9}{3x-9}$

8. **256**

$f(x) = (2x - 10)^2 \rightarrow$

$f(13) = (2(13) - 10)^2 \rightarrow$

$f(13) = (26 - 10)^2 \rightarrow$

$f(13) = 16^2 = 256$

9. **$\frac{3}{4}$ or 0.75**

$\frac{2x}{5} - \frac{3y}{10} = 0 \rightarrow$

$\frac{2x}{5} = \frac{3y}{10} \rightarrow$

Divide both sides by $y \rightarrow$

$\frac{2x}{5y} = \frac{3}{10} \rightarrow$

Multiply both sides by $\frac{5}{2} \rightarrow$

$\frac{x}{y} = \frac{3}{10} \times \frac{5}{2} = \frac{15}{20} = \frac{3}{4}$

10. **2** Recognize that the denominator is the square of $(x + 3)$, and this will be much easier to solve:

$\frac{3}{9+6x+x^2} = \frac{3}{4} \rightarrow$

$\frac{3}{(x+3)(x+3)} = \frac{3}{4} \rightarrow$

$\frac{3}{(x+3)^2} = \frac{3}{4} \rightarrow$

Divide both sides by 3 $\rightarrow$

$\frac{1}{(x+3)^2} = \frac{1}{4} \rightarrow$

Cross multiply to bring the values to the numerator →

$4 = (x + 3)^2 \rightarrow$

Take the square root of both sides →

$2 = x + 3$

Fortunately, we don't need to worry about imaginary solutions since the value of $(x + 3)$ is greater than zero.

If you do not see the pattern, you can also solve this by finding the value of x:

$\frac{3}{9 + 6x + x^2} = \frac{3}{4} \rightarrow$

$\frac{1}{9 + 6x + x^2} = \frac{1}{4} \rightarrow$

$9 + 6x + x^2 = 4 \rightarrow$

$x^2 + 6x + 5 = 0 \rightarrow$

$(x + 5)(x + 1) = 0$

$x = -5$ or $x = -1$

Since $(x + 3)$ must be greater than zero, the only possible solution for x is -1. Plugging this in to the expression gives us the same answer of 2:

$(x + 3) \rightarrow -1 + 3 = 2$

Passport to Advanced Math—Exponents and Roots

Exponent Rules

Memorize these exponent rules that are frequently tested on the SAT Math:

Exponent Rule	Example	How to Remember
$x^a x^b = x^{(a+b)}$	$x^2 x^3 = x^{(2+3)} = x^5$	*Use the acronym* ***MADSPM*** <u>M</u>ultiply exponents, <u>A</u>dd them
$\frac{x^a}{x^b} = x^{a-b}$	$\frac{x^5}{x^2} = x^{5-2} = x^3$	<u>D</u>ivide exponents, <u>S</u>ubtract them
$(x^a)^b = x^{(ab)}$	$(x^2)^3 = x^{(2 \times 3)} = x^6$	<u>P</u>arentheses with exponents, <u>M</u>ultiply them
$x^{-a} = \frac{1}{x^a}$	$x^{-3} = \frac{1}{x^3}$	"Negative" things go to the bottom.
$x^{\frac{a}{b}} = \sqrt[b]{x^a}$	$x^{\frac{2}{3}} = \sqrt[3]{x^2}$	The <u>root</u> of a tree is on the <u>bottom.</u> The bottom part of the fraction is identical to the <u>root</u>.

Practice

Write these expressions in simplified, alternative forms.

1. $a^2 a^6 = ?$
2. $\frac{x^7}{x^4} = ?$
3. $y^{\left(\frac{3}{4}\right)} = ?$
4. $b^{-4} = ?$
5. $(n^3)^4 = ?$
6. $(x^2 x^3)^2 = ?$
7. $\frac{1}{a^{-3}} = ?$
8. $\sqrt[3]{216x^{12}} = ?$

Solutions

1. $a^2 a^6 = a^{(2+6)} = a^8$
2. $\frac{x^7}{x^4} = x^{(7-4)} = x^3$
3. $y^{\left(\frac{3}{4}\right)} =$ the fourth root of $y^3 = \sqrt[4]{y^3}$
4. $b^{-4} = \frac{1}{b^4}$
5. $(n^3)^4 = n^{(3\times 4)} = n^{12}$
6. $(x^2 x^3)^2 = \left(x^{(2+3)}\right)^2 = (x^5)^2 = x^{(5\times 2)} = x^{10}$
7. $\frac{1}{a^{-3}} \rightarrow$

   Bring the denominator up to the top since it has a negative exponent $\rightarrow$

   $\rightarrow a^3$
8. $\sqrt[3]{216x^{12}} \rightarrow$

   $\sqrt[3]{(6\times 6\times 6)\times (x^4)(x^4)(x^4)} \rightarrow$

   $6x^4$

Problems with Exponents and Roots

SAT Math problems that involve exponents and roots will often ask you to integrate multiple concepts to arrive at a solution.

Example

If $x^{\left(-\frac{1}{3}\right)} = y$ and x is positive, what is x in terms of y?

(A) $y = x^3$

(B) $y = \sqrt[3]{x}$

(C) $x = \frac{1}{y^3}$

(D) $x = y^3$

Solution

When a problem asks you to put x in terms of y, it means that you should have x by itself and an expression in terms of y on the other side. So, we should isolate the x variable to arrive at a solution:

$$x^{\left(-\frac{1}{3}\right)} = y \rightarrow$$

Take each side to the -3 power to get a simple $x \rightarrow$

$$\left(x^{\left(-\frac{1}{3}\right)}\right)^{(-3)} = y^{-3} \rightarrow$$

$$x^{\left(-\frac{1}{3} \times -3\right)} = y^{-3} \rightarrow$$

$$x^1 = y^{-3} \rightarrow$$

$$x = \frac{1}{y^3}$$

The SAT Math heavily emphasizes pattern recognition and does *not* emphasize tedious calculations. As a result, you will frequently find that problems involving exponents and roots will involve simple numbers and their exponential values and roots. Memorizing these equivalences will save you time.

SAT Math Strategy

Memorize the values of simple numbers to different powers to more easily recognize patterns.

$x^0 = 1$ Anything to the zero power is simply one. $1^0 = 1$ $2^0 = 1$ $10^0 = 1$

$2^1 = 2$ Anything to the 1st power is simply itself. $3^1 = 3$ $20^1 = 20$ $(-5)^1 = -5$

$2^2 = 4$ $2^3 = 8$ $2^4 = 16$ $2^5 = 32$ $2^6 = 64$

$\sqrt{4} = 2$ $\sqrt[3]{8} = 2$ $\sqrt[4]{16} = 2$ $\sqrt[5]{32} = 2$ $\sqrt[6]{64} = 2$

$3^2 = 9$ $3^3 = 27$ $3^4 = 81$

$\sqrt{9} = 3$ $\sqrt[3]{27} = 3$ $\sqrt[4]{81} = 3$

$4^2 = 16 \quad 4^3 = 64 \quad 4^4 = 256$

$\sqrt{16} = 4 \quad \sqrt[3]{64} = 4 \quad \sqrt[4]{256} = 4$

$5^2 = 25 \quad 5^3 = 125$

$\sqrt{25} = 5 \quad \sqrt[3]{125} = 5$

$6^2 = 36 \quad 6^3 = 216$

$\sqrt{36} = 6 \quad \sqrt[3]{216} = 6$

$7^2 = 49 \quad 8^2 = 64 \quad 9^2 = 81$

$\sqrt{49} = 7 \quad \sqrt{64} = 8 \quad \sqrt{81} = 9$

$10^2 = 100 \quad 10^3 = 1,000 \quad 10^4 = 10,000$

$\sqrt{100} = 10 \quad \sqrt[3]{1,000} = 10 \quad \sqrt[4]{10,000} = 10$

Example 1

If $2^{(x-5)} = 8$, what is the value of x?

(A) 4
(B) 5
(C) 7
(D) 8

Solution

Use your knowledge of the exponential values of 2 to see a shortcut. Since $2^3 = 8$, simply set the exponent of 2 equal to 3 to solve for x:

$$x - 5 = 3 \rightarrow x = 8$$

So, choice **(D)** is correct. Alternatively, you could work your way backwards from the answer choices. When you plug in choice (D), you will also arrive at the correct answer:

$$2^{(x-5)} = 8 \rightarrow \text{Plug in 8 for } x \rightarrow$$
$$2^{(8-5)} = 8 \rightarrow 2^3 = 8$$

Your knowledge of the exponential values of 2 will also help you quickly see the correct answer when you solve by plugging in the answer choices.

Example 2

x	$f(x)$
1	1
2	4
3	9
4	16

In the table above, which of the following defines the function $f(x)$?

(A) $f(x) = x + 3$
(B) $f(x) = x^2$
(C) $f(x) = -x^2$
(D) $f(x) = x^3$

Solution

Use your knowledge of the exponential values of simple numbers to recognize the pattern.

$$1^2 = 1$$
$$2^2 = 2$$
$$3^2 = 9$$
$$4^2 = 16$$

Choice **(B)**, $f(x) = x^2$, therefore correctly models this relationship.

SAT Math Questions Practice Drill—Exponents and Roots

(If timing, take about 12 minutes to complete.)

1. Which of these expressions is equivalent to $\sqrt[4]{x^3}$?

(A) $x^{\left(\frac{4}{3}\right)}$
(B) $\frac{x^3}{x^4}$
(C) $\frac{x^4}{x^3}$
(D) $x^{\left(\frac{3}{4}\right)}$

2. If $3x^2 - 27 = 0$, and $x > 0$, what is the value of x?

(A) 1
(B) 2
(C) 3
(D) 4

$$f(x) = \frac{5^x}{2^x}$$

3. What is the value of $f(2)$ in the function above?

(A) $\frac{25}{4}$
(B) $\frac{5}{2}$
(C) $\frac{10}{4}$
(D) 8

4. If $f(x) = \frac{\sqrt{x}}{x}$, what is $f(9)$?

(A) $\frac{1}{9}$
(B) $\frac{1}{3}$
(C) 1
(D) 3

5. If x is positive, which expression is equivalent to $\sqrt[3]{27x^6}$?

(A) $3x$
(B) $3x^2$
(C) $6x^2$
(D) $9x^3$

x	f(x)
1	2
2	5
3	10
4	17
5	26

6. Based on the values in the table above, which of the following correctly expresses the value of $f(x)$?

(A) $f(x) = x + 1$
(B) $f(x) = x^2$
(C) $f(x) = x^3$
(D) $f(x) = x^2 + 1$

$$\frac{x^a y^{-b}}{x^{-a} y^b}$$

7. Consider the expression above, in which x and y are both positive, and a and b are positive constants. Which of the following would be an equivalent form of the expression?

(A) $\frac{x^a}{y^b}$

(B) $\frac{x^{(a^2)}}{y^{(b^2)}}$

(C) $\frac{x^{2a}}{y^{2b}}$

(D) $\frac{y}{x}$

Fill-In Practice: Write your answer in the underlined blank under each question.

8. $\sqrt[3]{125} + \sqrt[3]{64} = x^2$

Given that $x > 0$, what is the value of x in the above equation?

Answer: ________

9. If $x^{-2}y^{-1} = \frac{1}{5}$, what is the value of x^4y^2?

Answer: ________

10. If $\sqrt{\frac{x}{2}} = 4$, what is $\sqrt[5]{x}$?

Answer: ________

✓ Solutions

1. **(D)**

$\sqrt[4]{x^3}$ → The root, 4, is on the outside →

$= x^{\left(\frac{3}{4}\right)}$

2. **(C)**

$3x^2 - 27 = 0$ →

$3x^2 = 27$ →

$x^2 = 9$ →

$x = 3$

Alternatively, you could have tried plugging in the answer choices to the original equation.

3. **(A)**

$f(x) = \frac{5^x}{2^x}$ →

$f(2) = \frac{5^2}{2^2}$ →

$f(2) = \frac{25}{4}$

4. **(B)**

$f(x) = \frac{\sqrt{x}}{x} \rightarrow$

$f(9) = \frac{\sqrt{9}}{9} \rightarrow$

$f(9) = \frac{3}{9} = \frac{1}{3}$

5. **(B)**

$\sqrt[3]{27x^6} \rightarrow$

Take the cube root of both 27 and $x^6 \rightarrow$

$= 3x^2$

6. **(D)** Try plugging some sample values into the answer choices to determine the answer. When you try the first ordered pair, (1, 2), choices (B) and (C) can be eliminated. When you try the next ordered pair, (2, 5), choice (A) can be eliminated. Only choice **(D)**, $f(x) = x^2 + 1$, correctly models the function.

7. **(C)** On a problem like this, it can be helpful to look ahead to the answers to have a sense of what the answer might look like. It appears we want a solution that has only the *x* values on either the numerator or denominator and only the *y* values on the opposite side. With that in mind, simplify the expression:

$\frac{x^a y^{-b}}{x^{-a} y^b} \rightarrow$

$\frac{x^a x^a}{y^b y^b} \rightarrow$

$\frac{x^{2a}}{y^{2b}}$

8. **3**

$\sqrt[3]{125} + \sqrt[3]{64} = x^2 \rightarrow$

$5 + 4 = 9 = x^2 \rightarrow 3 = x$

9. **25**

$x^{-2}y^{-1} = \frac{1}{5} \rightarrow$

Flip both sides $\rightarrow$

$x^2 y = 5 \rightarrow$

Square both sides to make it the desired expression $\rightarrow$

$x^4 y^2 = 25$

10. **2**

$\sqrt{\frac{x}{2}} = 4 \rightarrow$

Square both sides $\rightarrow$

$\frac{x}{2} = 16 \rightarrow$

$x = 32$

Take the fifth root of 32 $\rightarrow$

$\sqrt[5]{32} = 2$

Passport to Advanced Math—Solving Quadratic Functions

Factoring Quadratic Equations

If a quadratic function can be easily factored to identify the solutions, use factoring to solve.

Example 1

$$x^2 - 9x + 20 = 0$$

What are the solutions for x in the equation above?

Solution

Factor the expression to solve for the solutions.

$$x^2 - 9x + 20 = 0 \rightarrow$$
$$(x - 4)(x - 5) = 0$$

With the equation in this form, you can identify which values of x will make the expression zero:

$$x - 4 = 0 \rightarrow x = 4$$

or

$$x - 5 = 0 \rightarrow x = 5$$

So, x could equal 4 or 5.

Example 2

$$3x^2 - 3x = 6$$

What are the solutions for x in the equation above?

✓ Solution

Even though this equation is not as obviously factorable as the previous example, with a little bit of manipulation you can get it in a factorable form:

$$3x^2 - 3x = 6 \rightarrow$$

Divide both sides by 3 →

$$x^2 - x = 2 \rightarrow$$

$$x^2 - x - 2 = 0$$

Factor the expression →

$$(x - 2)(x + 1) = 0$$

Based on this, the two values that would be solutions are 2 and −1, since either value if plugged in for x would make the entire expression equal to zero.

› Practice

Use factoring to find the solutions to the equations.

1. $x^2 - 6x + 8 = 0$
2. $x^2 - 10x + 21 = 0$
3. $x^2 - 6x - 16 = 0$
4. $x^3 - 4x = 0$
5. $x^3 + 5x^2 + 6x = 0$

✓ Solutions

1. $x^2 - 6x + 8 = 0 \rightarrow$
   $(x - 4)(x - 2) = 0 \rightarrow$
   $x = 4$ or $x = 2$

2. $x^2 - 10x + 21 = 0 \rightarrow$
   $(x - 7)(x - 3) = 0 \rightarrow$
   $x = 7$ or $x = 3$

3. $x^2 - 6x - 16 = 0 \rightarrow$
   $(x - 8)(x + 2) = 0 \rightarrow$
   Solutions: 8, −2

4. $x^3 - 4x = 0 \rightarrow$
   $x(x^2 - 4) = 0 \rightarrow$
   $x(x + 2)(x - 2) = 0$
   Solutions are 0, −2, or 2

5. $x^3 + 5x^2 + 6x = 0 \rightarrow$
   $x(x^2 + 5x + 6) = 0 \rightarrow$
   $x(x + 3)(x + 2) = 0$
   Solutions are 0, −3, or −2

Square Root Method

If a quadratic equation does *not* have an x term, you may want to use the square root method—take the square root of both sides of the equation to arrive at the solution(s). The positive and negative cases will be solutions.

Example

$$x^2 - 16 = 0$$

What are the solutions for x in the equation above?

Solution

This equation lacks an x term, so we can use the square root method to solve:

$$x^2 - 16 = 0 \rightarrow$$

$$x^2 = 16 \rightarrow$$

$$x = \pm 4$$

Practice

Use the square root method to solve these equations.

1. $x^2 = 81$
2. $y^2 - 64 = 0$
3. $(x - 3)^2 = 25$

Solutions

1. $x^2 = 81 \rightarrow$
   $\sqrt{x^2} = \sqrt{81} \rightarrow$
   $x = \pm 9$

2. $y^2 - 64 = 0 \rightarrow$
   $\sqrt{y^2} = 64 \rightarrow$
   $y = \pm 8$

3. $(x - 3)^2 = 25 \rightarrow$
   $\sqrt{(x - 3)^2} = \sqrt{25} \rightarrow$
   $x - 3 = \pm 5$

   Then, set up two equations to solve for the potential values of x:

   $$x - 3 = 5 \rightarrow x = 8$$

   or

   $$x - 3 = -5 \rightarrow x = -2$$

   So, the solutions are 8 and -2.

Quadratic Formula

An equation with constants a, b, and c and a variable x that is written in the form $ax^2 + bx + c = 0$ may be solved using the *quadratic formula*:

$$x = \frac{-b \pm \sqrt{b^2 - 4ac}}{2a}$$

Use the quadratic formula when factoring the equation looks challenging, often when the x^2 term has a constant other than 1 in front of it (examples: $6x^2$ or $\frac{1}{3}x^2$).

Example

$$3x^2 + 5x - 2 = 0$$

What are the solutions for x in the equation above?

Solution

The values of the constants are $a = 3$, $b = 5$, and $c = -2$. Plug these values into the quadratic formula to solve for x.

$$x = \frac{-b \pm \sqrt{b^2 - 4ac}}{2a} \rightarrow$$

$$x = \frac{-5 \pm \sqrt{5^2 - 4(3)(-2)}}{2(3)} \rightarrow$$

$$x = \frac{-5 \pm \sqrt{25 + 24}}{6} \rightarrow$$

$$x = \frac{-5 \pm \sqrt{49}}{6} \rightarrow$$

$$x = -\frac{5}{6} \pm \frac{\sqrt{49}}{6} \rightarrow -\frac{5}{6} \pm \frac{7}{6}$$

So, the solutions are:

$$-\frac{5}{6} + \frac{7}{6} = \frac{2}{6} = \frac{1}{3}$$

or

$$-\frac{5}{6} - \frac{7}{6} = -\frac{12}{6} = -2$$

Practice

1. $3x^2 + 5x + 2 = 0$
2. $2x^2 - 5x - 7 = 0$
3. $5x^2 + 3x = 2$
4. $3x^2 + 4x - 5 = 0$
5. How many real solutions does the equation $5x^2 - 3x + 2 = 0$ have?

Solutions

1. $x = \dfrac{-b \pm \sqrt{b^2 - 4ac}}{2a}$

$3x^2 + 5x + 2 = 0 \rightarrow$

$x = \dfrac{-5 \pm \sqrt{5^2 - 4(3)(2)}}{2(3)} \rightarrow$

$x = \dfrac{-5 \pm \sqrt{25 - 24}}{6} \rightarrow$

$x = \dfrac{-5 \pm 1}{6} \rightarrow x = -1 \text{ or } -\dfrac{2}{3}$

2. $2x^2 - 5x - 7 = 0 \rightarrow$

$x = \dfrac{-b \pm \sqrt{b^2 - 4ac}}{2a} \rightarrow$

$x = \dfrac{-(-5) \pm \sqrt{(-5)^2 - 4(2)(-7)}}{2(2)} \rightarrow$

$x = \dfrac{5 \pm \sqrt{25 + 56}}{4} \rightarrow$

$x = \dfrac{5 \pm \sqrt{81}}{4} \rightarrow$

$x = \dfrac{5 \pm 9}{4} \rightarrow$

$x = \dfrac{5 + 9}{4} = 3.5 \text{ or } x = \dfrac{5 - 9}{4} = -1$

3. $5x^2 + 3x = 2 \rightarrow$

$5x^2 + 3x - 2 = 0 \rightarrow$

$x = \dfrac{-b \pm \sqrt{b^2 - 4ac}}{2a} \rightarrow$

$x = \dfrac{-3 \pm \sqrt{3^2 - 4(5)(-2)}}{2(5)} \rightarrow$

$x = \dfrac{-3 \pm \sqrt{9 + 40}}{10} \rightarrow$

$x = \dfrac{-3 \pm \sqrt{49}}{10} \rightarrow$

$x = \dfrac{-3 \pm 7}{10} \rightarrow$

$x = \dfrac{-3 + 7}{10} = \dfrac{4}{10} = 0.4$

or

$x = \dfrac{-3 - 7}{10} = \dfrac{-10}{10} = -1$

4. $3x^2 + 4x - 5 = 0 \rightarrow$

$$x = \frac{-b \pm \sqrt{b^2 - 4ac}}{2a} \rightarrow$$

$$x = \frac{-4 \pm \sqrt{4^2 - 4(3)(-5)}}{2(3)} \rightarrow$$

$$x = \frac{-4 \pm \sqrt{16 + 60}}{6} \rightarrow$$

$$x = \frac{-4 \pm \sqrt{76}}{6} \rightarrow$$

Simplify the $\sqrt{76}$ by factoring out the square root of 4 $\rightarrow$

$$x = \frac{-4 \pm \sqrt{4(19)}}{6} \rightarrow \frac{-4 \pm 2\sqrt{19}}{6} \rightarrow \frac{-2 \pm \sqrt{19}}{3}$$

So, x can be:

$$-\frac{2}{3} + \frac{\sqrt{19}}{3} \text{ or } -\frac{2}{3} - \frac{\sqrt{19}}{3}$$

5. To see how many real solutions there are, find the value of the *discriminant*, i.e., the component of the quadratic formula underneath the square root sign: $b^2 - 4ac$. If it is positive, there are two real solutions. If it is zero, there is just one real solution. And if it is negative, there are no real solutions since you would have to take the square root of a negative number.

   In the equation $5x^2 - 3x + 2 = 0$, $b^2 - 4ac = (-3)^2 - 4(5)(2) = 9 - 40 = -31$.

   So, there are *zero* real solutions to the equation.

Completing the Square

Use completing the square particularly to work with problems involving parabolas. Completing the square will enable you to more easily identify key information about the parabola. (Note—parabolas will be covered later in the chapter.)

> Example

$$x^2 + 8x = 20$$

What are the values for x in the above equation?

✓ Solution

Here is how you can use *completing the square* to solve this equation.

First, take half of 8 (which is 4), square it, and add it to both sides of the equation.

$$x^2 + 8x = 20 \rightarrow$$
$$x^2 + 8x + 16 = 20 + 16 \rightarrow$$
$$x^2 + 8x + 16 = 36$$

Now, you can factor the left-hand side in a squared form:

$$(x + 4)^2 = 36$$

Then, take the square root of both sides:

$$\sqrt{(x+4)^2} = \sqrt{36} \rightarrow$$
$$x + 4 = \pm 6$$

Finally, solve for x:

$$x + 4 = 6 \rightarrow x = 6 - 4 = 2$$

or

$$x + 4 = -6 \rightarrow x = -6 - 4 = -10$$

So, x could be either 2 or -10.

Practice

Solve each of these using completing the square.

1. $x^2 + 6x = -8$
2. $x^2 + 8x = 9$
3. $4x^2 + 3x = 1$

Solutions

1. $x^2 + 6x = -8 \rightarrow$
   $x^2 + 6x + 9 = -8 + 9 \rightarrow$
   $(x+3)^2 = 1 \rightarrow$
   $x + 3 = \pm 1$
   So, x could equal -4 or -2.

2. $x^2 + 8x = 9 \rightarrow$
   $x^2 + 8x + 16 = 9 + 16 \rightarrow$
   $(x+4)^2 = 25 \rightarrow$
   $x + 4 = \pm 5$
   So, x could equal 1 or -9.

3. $4x^2 + 3x = 1 \rightarrow$
   $x^2 + \frac{3}{4}x = \frac{1}{4} \rightarrow$
   Take half of $\frac{3}{4}$, $\frac{3}{8}$, square it, and add to both sides:
   $x^2 + \frac{3}{4}x + \left(\frac{3}{8}\right)^2 = \frac{1}{4} + \left(\frac{3}{8}\right)^2 \rightarrow$
   $x^2 + \frac{3}{4}x + \frac{9}{64} = \frac{1}{4} + \frac{9}{64} \rightarrow \frac{16}{64} + \frac{9}{64} = \frac{25}{64} \rightarrow$
   $\left(x + \frac{3}{8}\right)^2 = \frac{25}{64} \rightarrow \sqrt{\frac{25}{64}} = +/-\frac{5}{8}$
   So, x could equal:
   $x + \frac{3}{8} = \frac{5}{8} \rightarrow x = \frac{2}{8} = \frac{1}{4}$
   or
   $x + \frac{3}{8} = -\frac{5}{8} \rightarrow x = -\frac{8}{8} = -1$

Plugging in the Answers

Try plugging in the answer choices in a quadratic equation if solving the problem algebraically will take longer than working backwards from the four options.

Example

$$\frac{1}{x+2}+\frac{3}{2x+4}=\frac{1}{2}$$

What is the value of x in the equation above?

(A) 1
(B) 2
(C) 3
(D) 4

Solution

While this problem could be solved algebraically, it will likely save you time to work backwards from the answer options. Since the answers are in order from least to greatest, start with one of the middle options to minimize the potential trial and error.

Start with 2:

$$\frac{1}{x+2}+\frac{3}{2x+4}=\frac{1}{2}\rightarrow$$

$$\frac{1}{2+2}+\frac{3}{2(2)+4}=\frac{1}{2}\rightarrow$$

$$\frac{1}{4}+\frac{3}{8}=\frac{5}{8}\neq\frac{1}{2}$$

This option did not work. Since the sum was larger than $\frac{1}{2}$, we should try another answer choice that will make the expression have a smaller fraction—this comes from having a larger denominator. So, we will next try choice (C), 3:

$$\frac{1}{x+2}+\frac{3}{2x+4}=\frac{1}{2}\rightarrow$$

$$\frac{1}{3+2}+\frac{3}{2(3)+4}=\frac{1}{2}\rightarrow$$

$$\frac{1}{5}+\frac{3}{10}=\frac{2}{10}+\frac{3}{10}=\frac{5}{10}=\frac{1}{2}$$

This checks out, so choice **(C)**, 3, is correct.

Practice

Use plugging in the answers to solve.

1. $4(x-2)^2+2=2x$

   Which of the following is a value of x?

   (A) 1
   (B) 2
   (C) 3
   (D) 4

2. $\frac{1}{x+2}+\frac{1}{x+3}=\frac{3}{2}$

   Which of the following is a value of x?

   (A) −2
   (B) −1
   (C) 0
   (D) 1

3. Which of the following is/are solutions for x in the following equation?

   $8x^2-7x=x^3$

   I. Zero
   II. One
   III. Two

   (A) I only
   (B) II only
   (C) I and II only
   (D) All of the above

Solutions

1. $4(x-2)^2+2=2x \rightarrow$
   $4(3-2)^2+2=2(3) \rightarrow$
   $4(1)^2+2=6 \rightarrow$
   $6=6$

   So, choice **(C)**, 3, works.

2. $\frac{1}{x+2}+\frac{1}{x+3}=\frac{3}{2} \rightarrow$

   $\frac{1}{-1+2}+\frac{1}{-1+3}=\frac{3}{2} \rightarrow$

   $\frac{1}{1}+\frac{1}{2}=\frac{3}{2}$

   So, choice **(B)**, −1, works.

3. First, let's try zero:

   $8x^2 - 7x = x^3 \rightarrow$

   $8(0)^2 - 7(0) = 0^3 \rightarrow$

   $0 = 0$

   So, option I, zero, does work.

   Next, let's try 1:

   $8x^2 - 7x = x^3 \rightarrow$

   $8(1)^2 - 7(1) = 1^3 \rightarrow$

   $8 - 7 = 1 \rightarrow$

   $1 = 1$

   So option II, 1, does work.

   Finally, let's try 2:

   $8x^2 - 7x = x^3 \rightarrow$

   $8(2)^2 - 7(2) = 2^3 \rightarrow$

   $32 - 14 = 8 \rightarrow$

   $18 \neq 8$

   So option III, 2, does NOT work. Therefore, the correct answer is choice **(C)**. You could also approach this in an efficient way by realizing that if option III DOES work, choice (D) will have to be the answer since it is the only option with option III. Further, if you are evaluating quadratics on the calculator section, you may want to graph the function to more quickly identify its roots.

Undefined Functions

When a function is divided by zero, it may be undefined—that is, it will have no solutions. If you were to divide a number like 3 by 0, it would be undefined since it is impossible to divide 3 into zero parts.

Example

When is this function undefined?

$$f(x) = \frac{x^3 - x^2 + 2}{x - 4}$$

Solution

Determine the value of x that would cause the function to have zero in the denominator. Set the denominator equal to zero and solve for x:

$$x - 4 = 0 \rightarrow x = 4$$

Therefore, the function is undefined when x is equal to 4.

Practice

Find the values of x that will make the expression undefined.

1. $\frac{5}{x}$
2. $\frac{12x+1}{x+4}$
3. $\frac{7}{x^2-9}$

Solutions

1. $\frac{5}{x} \rightarrow \frac{5}{0}$

   So, the function is undefined when x is 0.

2. $\frac{12x+1}{x+4} \rightarrow \frac{12x+1}{0} \rightarrow$

   $x+4=0 \rightarrow x=-4$

   So, the function is undefined when x is -4.

3. $\frac{7}{x^2-9} \rightarrow \frac{7}{0} \rightarrow$

   $x^2-9=0 \rightarrow$

   $x^2=9 \rightarrow x=\pm 3$

   So, the function is undefined when x is 3 or -3.

Extraneous Solutions

When dealing with equations involving roots, it is a good idea to test the solutions to see if they are *extraneous*—meaning, they do not work in the original equation. The reason they typically do not work is that they would require taking the square root of a negative number, which would result in an imaginary solution.

Example

$$\sqrt{x-1}=x-7$$

What are the solutions for x in the equation above?

Solution

Start by squaring both sides to get rid of the radical sign:

$$\sqrt{x-1}=x-7 \rightarrow$$
$$x-1=x^2-14x+49$$

Then, simplify the equation and factor to find the potential solutions:

$$x-1=x^2-14x+49 \rightarrow$$
$$x^2-15x+50=0 \rightarrow$$
$$(x-10)(x-5)=0$$

So, the potential solutions are 10 and 5. Now, to be sure we don't have any extraneous solutions, plug 10 and 5 back in to the original equation to see if they work:

$$\sqrt{x-1} = x - 7 \rightarrow$$
$$\sqrt{10-1} = 10 - 7 \rightarrow$$
$$\sqrt{9} = 3$$

So, 10 works in the original equation. Now let's try 5.

$$\sqrt{5-1} = 5 - 7 \rightarrow$$
$$\sqrt{5-1} = 5 - 7 \rightarrow$$
$$\sqrt{4} \neq -2$$

The square root of 4 cannot be equal to -2 in this case, since we would need an imaginary number to make it work. Therefore, 5 is an extraneous solution and the only solution is 10.

Practice

Solve each of these equations for *x*, watching out for extraneous solutions.

1. $x = \sqrt{12 - x}$
2. $\sqrt{x+1} + 5 = x$
3. $\sqrt{x-6} = x - 8$

Solutions

1. $x = \sqrt{12 - x} \rightarrow$

   $x^2 = 12 - x \rightarrow$

   $x^2 + x - 12 = 0 \rightarrow$

   $(x + 4)(x - 3)$

   So, -4 and 3 are potential solutions. Check to see if either is extraneous.

   $-4 = \sqrt{12 - (-4)} \rightarrow$

   $-4 \neq 4$

   So, -4 does NOT work.

   $3 = \sqrt{12 - 3} \rightarrow$

   $3 = 3$

   So, 3 does work.

2. $\sqrt{x+1} + 5 = x \rightarrow$

   $\sqrt{x+1} = x - 5 \rightarrow$

   $x + 1 = x^2 - 10x + 25 \rightarrow$

   $0 = x^2 - 11x + 24 \rightarrow$

   $0 = (x - 8)(x - 3)$

   8 and 3 are potential solutions. Check to see if either is extraneous.

   $\sqrt{8+1} + 5 = 8 \rightarrow$

   $3 + 5 = 8 \rightarrow$

   $8 = 8$

8 does work.

$\sqrt{3+1}+5=3 \rightarrow$

$\sqrt{4}+5=3 \rightarrow$

$2+5 \neq 3$

3 does NOT work.

3. $\sqrt{x-6}=x-8 \rightarrow$

$x-6=(x-8)^2 \rightarrow$

$x-6=x^2-16x+64 \rightarrow$

$0=x^2-17x+70 \rightarrow$

$0=(x-10)(x-7)$

10 and 7 are potential solutions. Check to see if either is extraneous.

$\sqrt{x-6}=x-8 \rightarrow$

$\sqrt{10-6}=10-8 \rightarrow$

$\sqrt{4}=2$

So, 10 does work.

$\sqrt{x-6}=x-8 \rightarrow$

$\sqrt{7-6}=7-8 \rightarrow$

$\sqrt{1}=1 \neq -1$

So, 7 does NOT work.

Synthetic Division

On occasion, the SAT will ask you to divide a polynomial. The easiest way to do this is using synthetic division.

Example 1

What is the result when $2x^2+5x-3$ is divided by $x-4$?

Solution

Set up the problem by taking the coefficients of the terms of the polynomial and placing the numerical term of the divisor to the left of them like this:

$$\begin{array}{r|rrr} 4 & 2 & 5 & -3 \\ \hline \end{array}$$

Next, bring down each of the coefficients, multiplying the columns one-by-one by the divisor 4, and create sums to see what the divided polynomial and remainder would be:

$$\begin{array}{r|rrr} 4 & 2 & 5 & -3 \\ & & 8 & 52 \\ \hline & 2 & 13 & 49 \end{array}$$

The answer would be $2x+13$ with a remainder of $\frac{49}{x-4}$.

Example 2

Based on the previous problem, is $x - 4$ a factor of $2x^2 + 5x - 3$?

Solution

For an expression to be a factor of the polynomial, you must be able to divide the polynomial by that expression and NOT have a remainder, i.e., the remainder must be zero. Since there is a remainder of $\frac{49}{x-4}$ when the expression is divided, $x - 4$ is NOT a factor of $2x^2 + 5x - 3$.

Practice

1A. What is the result when $x^2 + 2x - 15$ is divided by $x + 5$?
1B. Is $x + 5$ a factor of $x^2 + 2x - 15$?
2A. What is the result when $4x^2 - 3x - 5$ is divided by $x - 3$?
2B. Is $x - 3$ a factor of $4x^2 - 3x - 5$?

Solutions

1A.

$$\begin{array}{r|rrr} -5 & 1 & 2 & -15 \\ & & -5 & 15 \\ \hline & 1 & -3 & 0 \end{array}$$

Therefore, the answer is $x - 3$.

1B. Since there was no remainder when it was divided, this is a factor of the expression.

2A.

$$\begin{array}{r|rrr} 3 & 4 & -3 & -5 \\ & & 12 & 27 \\ \hline & 4 & 9 & 22 \end{array}$$

So, the result is $4x + 9$ with a remainder of $\frac{22}{x-3}$.

2B. Since there was a remainder when it was divided, this is NOT a factor of the expression.

SAT Math Strategy

Many SAT quadratic function problems can be solved in different ways. Use whatever approach is easiest for you.

Example

If $2x^2 - 6x = 20$, what are the solutions for x?

(A) -2 or -5
(B) -2 or 5
(C) 2 or -5
(D) 2 or 5

✓ Solution

Method 1: Factoring. If you notice that all the numbers in the problem have 2 as a factor, you can take a 2 out of everything to simplify. Then factoring will probably appear to be the easiest method.

$$2x^2 - 6x = 20 \rightarrow$$
$$2x^2 - 6x - 20 = 0 \rightarrow$$
$$x^2 - 3x - 10 = 0 \rightarrow$$
$$(x + 2)(x - 5) = 0$$

The correct answer is therefore **(B)**, -2 or 5.

Method 2: Quadratic Formula. If you do not see an easy way to factor the equation, you can put the equation in standard form and use the quadratic formula to solve. This can be a good approach if you are quick and careful with your calculations.

$$2x^2 - 6x = 20 \rightarrow$$
$$2x^2 - 6x - 20 = 0 \rightarrow$$
$$x = \frac{-b \pm \sqrt{b^2 - 4ac}}{2a} \rightarrow$$
$$x = \frac{-(-6) \pm \sqrt{(-6)^2 - 4(2)(-20)}}{2(2)} \rightarrow$$
$$x = \frac{6 \pm \sqrt{36 + 160}}{4} \rightarrow$$
$$x = \frac{6 \pm \sqrt{196}}{4} \rightarrow$$
$$x = \frac{6 \pm 14}{4}$$

So, x could be either $\frac{6 + 14}{4} = \frac{20}{4} = 5$ or $\frac{6 - 14}{4} = \frac{-8}{2} = -2$

Method 3: Plug in the Answers. Look ahead to the answer choices to notice that all of them are variations of ± 2 and ± 5. So, you essentially just have four numbers to plug in to the original equation.

$2(-2)^2 - 6(-2) = 20 \rightarrow$
$8 + 12 = 20$
-2 works.

$2(2)^2 - 6(2) = 20 \rightarrow$
$8 - 12 \neq 20$
2 does NOT work.

$2(-5)^2 - 6(-5) = 20 \rightarrow$
$2(25) + 30 = 20 \rightarrow$
$50 + 30 \neq 20$
-5 does NOT work.

$2(5)^2 - 6(5) = 20 \rightarrow$
$2(25) - 30 = 20 \rightarrow$
$50 - 30 = 20$
5 does work.

If there were more numbers to plug in, this approach would have been more difficult.

SAT Math Strategy

Do not go on autopilot with the questions—carefully consider what you are asked to do.

On school tests, you can often get in a rhythm with the questions you are solving. Each question on a test or quiz may be a variation of "solve for x." On the SAT Math, be careful on quadratic function questions to first understand what the question is asking, then start working on the solution.

Example

Variables x and y are related to each other in a quadratic function of the form $y = kx^2$, in which k is a constant. If y is 12 when x is 2, and y is 48 when x is 4, what is the value of y when x is 5?

(A) 30
(B) 45
(C) 60
(D) 75

Solution

This is not a problem that can be solved in a typical fashion, like using the quadratic formula or factoring. We must fully understand what the question tells us.

- The variables are related to each other in an equation like $y = kx^2$.
- x and y are variables while k is a constant.
- We have ordered pairs of values—(2, 12) and (4, 48)—that we can plug in to see what the constant k would be.

Given that information, let's plug in the ordered pair (2, 12) into the equation, since it is smaller and easier to work with than (4, 48):

$$y = kx^2 \rightarrow$$
$$12 = k(2)^2 \rightarrow$$
$$12 = 4k \rightarrow$$
$$k = 3$$

So, the function in the question is $y = 3x^2$. We now can see what the value of y is when x is 5:

$$y = 3x^2 \rightarrow$$
$$y = 3(5)^2 \rightarrow$$
$$y = 3(25) = 75$$

The answer is therefore **(D)**, 75.

SAT Math Questions Practice Drill #1—Solving Advanced Equations

(If timing, take about 12 minutes to complete.)

1. For what positive value of x is this function undefined?

$$f(x) = \frac{1}{x^2 - 1}$$

(A) 1
(B) 2
(C) 3
(D) 4

2. If $x^2 - 3x - 10 = 0$, for what value of x is this equation true given that $x > 0$?

(A) 3
(B) 4
(C) 5
(D) 6

3. Which of the following would be a solution to this equation?

$$21 - \sqrt{x} = 10$$

(A) 11
(B) 18
(C) 55
(D) 121

4. Which of the following provides the two solutions to this equation?

$$3x^2 + 5x + 2 = 0$$

(A) $-\frac{2}{3}$ or -1
(B) $\frac{1}{6}$ or $\frac{2}{5}$
(C) $-\frac{3}{4}$ or 7
(D) $\frac{6}{11}$ or -8

$x^2 - 15 = x + 5$

5. What is the product of the solutions to the above equation?

(A) -35
(B) -20
(C) 1
(D) 9

6. $\frac{x^2 - y^2}{3} = 0$

What value of y would always make the above equation true?

(A) x
(B) x^2
(C) $4x$
(D) $8x$

Fill-In Practice: Write your answer in the underlined blank under each question.

7. If $\frac{(x+2)}{(x-3)} - 2 = \frac{7}{(x-3)}$, what is the solution for x?

Answer: ________

8. If $2\sqrt{x} + 1 = 10 - \sqrt{x}$, what is the solution for x?

Answer: ________

9. $(x + b)(x + b) = x^2 + 4x + 4$

If the above equation has infinitely many solutions, what is the value of the constant b?

Answer: ________

10. If $\frac{6x^2 - 5x + 8}{2} = x^2 - 3$, how many real solutions are there for x?

Answer: ________

✓ Solutions

1. **(A)** For the function $f(x) = \frac{1}{x^2 - 1}$ to be undefined, we need a value of x that will make the denominator equal to zero. So, set up an equation to solve for the positive value of x needed:

$$x^2 - 1 = 0 \rightarrow$$
$$(x + 1)(x - 1) = 0$$

So, x could equal 1 or -1. Since we need a positive value of x, the correct answer is 1.

2. **(C)** Solve this by factoring:

$$x^2 - 3x - 10 = 0 \rightarrow$$
$$(x - 5)(x + 2) = 0$$

So, x could be either 5 or -2. Since the answer must be positive, the correct answer is 5.

3. **(D)** Use the square root method to solve:

$$21 - \sqrt{x} = 10 \rightarrow$$
$$11 - \sqrt{x} = 0 \rightarrow$$
$$11 = \sqrt{x} \rightarrow$$
$$121 = x$$

4. **(A)** Given that there is a 3 in front of the x^2 term, the quadratic formula will be the best way to solve this:

$$3x^2 + 5x + 2 = 0 \rightarrow$$

$$x = \frac{-b \pm \sqrt{b^2 - 4ac}}{2a} \rightarrow$$

$$x = \frac{-5 \pm \sqrt{5^2 - 4(3)(2)}}{2(3)} \rightarrow$$

$$x = \frac{-5 \pm \sqrt{25 - 24}}{6} \rightarrow$$

$$x = \frac{-5 \pm 1}{6} \rightarrow$$

$$x = -\frac{5}{6} + \frac{1}{6} = -\frac{4}{6} = -\frac{2}{3}$$

and

$$x = -\frac{5}{6} - \frac{1}{6} = -\frac{6}{6} = -1$$

5. **(B)** Simplify and factor the equation to determine the two solutions, then multiply them together to find their product:

$$x^2 - 15 = x + 5 \rightarrow$$

$$x^2 - x - 20 = 0 \rightarrow$$

$$(x - 5)(x + 4) = 0$$

The solutions are therefore 5 or -4. The product of them is $5 \times (-4) = -20$.

6. **(A)** Solve for y by simplifying the equation, then using the square root method:

$$\frac{x^2 - y^2}{3} = 0 \rightarrow$$

$$x^2 - y^2 = 0 \rightarrow$$

$$x^2 = y^2 \rightarrow$$

$$\sqrt{x^2} = \sqrt{y^2} \rightarrow$$

$$x = y$$

7. **1** Multiply the equation by $(x - 3)$ to remove the $(x - 3)$ from the denominator:

$$(x - 3) \times \left(\frac{(x + 2)}{(x - 3)} - 2\right) = (x - 3) \times \left(\frac{7}{(x - 3)}\right) \rightarrow$$

$$(x + 2) - 2(x - 3) = 7 \rightarrow$$

$$x + 2 - 2x + 6 = 7 \rightarrow$$

$$-x + 8 = 7 \rightarrow$$

$$-x = -1 \rightarrow x = 1$$

8. **9** Simplify and use the square root method:

$$2\sqrt{x}+1=10-\sqrt{x}\rightarrow$$

$$3\sqrt{x}=9\rightarrow$$

$$\sqrt{x}=3\rightarrow$$

$$(\sqrt{x})^2=3^2\rightarrow$$

$$x=9$$

9. **2** For there to be infinitely many solutions, the equation must be equivalent on both sides. FOIL the left-hand side to see what the value of b must be for this to be true.

$$(x+b)(x+b)=x^2+4x+4\rightarrow$$

$$x^2+2bx+b^2=x^2+4x+4$$

If b is equal to 2, both sides are equivalent, giving us infinitely many solutions.

10. **0** Simplify this equation to get it in standard form.

$$\frac{6x^2-5x+8}{2}=x^2-3\rightarrow$$

$$6x^2-5x+8=2x^2-6\rightarrow$$

$$4x^2-5x+14=0$$

Now, use the quadratic formula to solve:

$$x=\frac{-b\pm\sqrt{b^2-4ac}}{2a}\rightarrow$$

$$x=\frac{-(-5)\pm\sqrt{(-5)^2-4(4)(14)}}{2(4)}\rightarrow$$

$$x=\frac{5\pm\sqrt{25-224}}{8}$$

Since the discriminant (the $\sqrt{25-224}$ term) is negative, there will be 0 real solutions.

SAT Math Questions Practice Drill #2—Solving Advanced Equations

(If timing, take about 12 minutes to complete.)

1. If $x^2-14x+49=0$, what is the value of x?

(A) 3
(B) 5
(C) 7
(D) 9

2. If $n^2-6n+9=25$, which of the following is a possible value of $n-3$?

(A) 4
(B) 5
(C) 6
(D) 9

3. If $\frac{3x}{6-x} = x$, what are the value(s) of x that would satisfy the equation?

(A) 1 and −6
(B) 2 and −3
(C) 3 and 0
(D) 6 and 4

4. What is the largest value of n that satisfies the following equation?

$$\frac{(n+4)(n-6)}{2} = 0$$

(A) −4
(B) −6
(C) 4
(D) 6

5. $f(x) = \frac{2x - 13}{2x^2 - 16x + 32}$

For what value of x is the above function $f(x)$ undefined?

(A) −8
(B) −4
(C) 2
(D) 4

6. What are the solutions to the equation $5x^2 - 7x + 1 = 0$?

(A) $\frac{5 \pm \sqrt{23}}{14}$

(B) $\frac{7 \pm \sqrt{29}}{10}$

(C) $\frac{3 \pm \sqrt{37}}{11}$

(D) $\frac{12 \pm \sqrt{43}}{7}$

7. $\sqrt{x+4} = -4$

What is the set of real solutions for the above equation?

(A) 2 only
(B) 2 and −4
(C) 4 and −2
(D) There are no real solutions.

8. What is the remainder when $2x^2 + 3x - 1$ is divided by $x - 4$?

(A) $\frac{43}{x-4}$

(B) $\frac{22}{x-4}$

(C) $\frac{16}{x-1}$

(D) 0

9. If $\sqrt{x+5} = 4$, what is the value of x?

(A) −9
(B) −5
(C) 2
(D) 11

10. $\dfrac{3x^2 - 27}{3x - 9} = 5$

What value of x is a solution to the equation above?

(A) 2
(B) 5
(C) 6
(D) 18

✓ Solutions

1. **(C)** Solve by factoring:

$$x^2 - 14x + 49 = 0 \rightarrow$$
$$(x-7)(x-7) = 0$$

So, 7 is the only solution.

2. **(B)** Factor the expression, then use the square root method:

$$n^2 - 6n + 9 = 25 \rightarrow$$
$$(n-3)(n-3) = 25 \rightarrow$$
$$\sqrt{(n-3)^2} = \sqrt{25} \rightarrow$$
$$n - 3 = 5$$

3. **(C)** Plugging and chugging would be a viable approach on this problem, but you can also solve it fairly easily by cross multiplying and then solving for x.

$$\frac{3x}{6-x} = x \rightarrow$$
$$3x = x(6-x) \rightarrow$$
$$3x = 6x - x^2 \rightarrow$$
$$x^2 - 3x = 0 \rightarrow$$
$$x^2 = 3x \rightarrow$$

So zero is a solution.
Also, 3 is a solution because

$$x^2 = 3x \rightarrow x = 3.$$

4. **(D)** This is easiest to solve by plugging in the answers. Start with the largest choice and work your way smaller if needed:

$$\frac{(n+4)(n-6)}{2}=0 \rightarrow$$

$$\frac{(6+4)(6-6)}{2}=0 \rightarrow$$

$$\frac{10 \times 0}{2}=0$$

So, 6 works. Alternatively, keep in mind that a polynomial written in factored form automatically shows what the zeroes are.

5. **(D)** For the function $f(x)=\frac{2x-13}{2x^2-16x+32}$ to be undefined, the denominator must be zero. So, set up an equation in which just the denominator is equal to zero.

$$2x^2-16x+32=0 \rightarrow$$

$$x^2-8x+16=0 \rightarrow$$

$$(x-4)(x-4)=0$$

So, if x equals 4, the denominator will equal zero and the function will be undefined.

6. **(B)** Use the quadratic formula to solve this equation.

$$5x^2-7x+1=0 \rightarrow$$

$$x=\frac{-b \pm \sqrt{b^2-4ac}}{2a} \rightarrow$$

$$x=\frac{-(-7) \pm \sqrt{(-7)^2-4(5)(1)}}{2(5)} \rightarrow$$

$$x=\frac{7 \pm \sqrt{49-20}}{10} \rightarrow$$

$$x=\frac{7 \pm \sqrt{29}}{10}$$

7. **(D)** Plugging in the potential answers of 2, 4, −2, and −4 is an excellent way to solve the problem. You can also solve it algebraically:

$$\sqrt{x+4}=-4 \rightarrow$$

$$(\sqrt{x+4})^2=(-4)^2 \rightarrow$$

$$x+4=16 \rightarrow$$

$$x=12$$

Now, when you plug 12 back in to the original equation, you can see that it does not work:

$$\sqrt{x+4}=-4 \rightarrow$$

$$\sqrt{12+4}=-4 \rightarrow$$

$$4 \neq -4$$

In fact, if you notice that in the original equation it states that the square root of $x+4$ must equal a negative number, you can stop right there since the least that the square root of the number could be would be zero. We would need imaginary numbers to arrive at a negative solution.

8. **(A)** Use synthetic division to solve:

$$\begin{array}{r|rrr} 4 & 2 & 3 & -1 \\ & & 8 & 44 \\ \hline & 2 & 11 & 43 \end{array}$$

Take the 43 and divide it by $x - 4$ to get the remainder of $\frac{43}{x-4}$.

9. **(D)** Plugging in the answers will work well on this problem. Also, you can solve it algebraically:

$$\sqrt{x+5} = 4 \rightarrow$$

$$(\sqrt{x+5})^2 = 4^2 \rightarrow$$

$$x + 5 = 16 \rightarrow$$

$$x = 11$$

10. **(A)** You could use plugging in the answers to solve this, but you could also do it algebraically.

$$\frac{3x^2 - 27}{3x - 9} = 5 \rightarrow$$

Divide the numerator and the denominator of the left side by 3 →

$$\frac{x^2 - 9}{x - 3} = 5 \rightarrow$$

$$\frac{(x+3)(x-3)}{(x-3)} = 5 \rightarrow$$

$$\frac{(x+3)\cancel{(x-3)}}{\cancel{(x-3)}} = 5 \rightarrow$$

$x + 3 = 5 \rightarrow x = 2$ (Note that 3 is an extraneous solution if you plug it back into the original equation.)

Passport to Advanced Math—Zeros, Parabolas, and Polynomial Graphing

Zeros of a Function

The *root* or *zero* of a function is the value of x for which a function like $f(x)$ has a value of zero. When an equation of the function is provided, you can identify the zeros by solving for when $f(x)$ is 0 (i.e., finding the x-intercepts or solutions). When a graph of the function is provided, you can identify the zeros by looking at the values of x for which the $f(x)$values have coordinates at 0.

Example

What are the zeros of the parabola of the equation $f(x) = x^2 - 6x + 5$ and with the graph below?

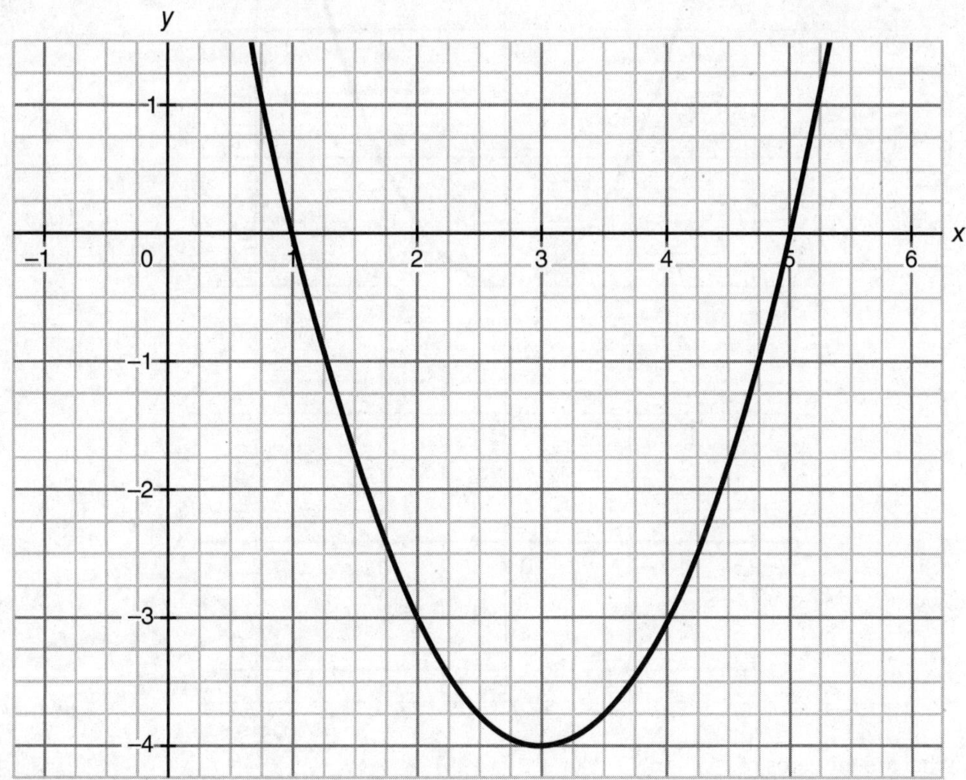

Solution

The first way you can find the zeros is by factoring the equation:

$$f(x) = x^2 - 6x + 5 \rightarrow$$

$$f(x) = (x - 5)(x - 1)$$

So, there are zeros at x values of 5 and 1 since plugging those two values in to the function will cause the value of $f(x)$ to be 0.

The second way you can find the zeros is by examining the graph above. Look at the points where the function intersects the x-axis, since the value of $f(x)$, or y, will be zero there. At points (1, 0) and (5, 0), the function intersects the x-axis, so 5 and 1 are zeros of the function.

Practice

1. What are the zeros of the function $y = (x + 3)(x - 5)$?
2. What are the zeros of the function $f(x) = x^2 + 4x - 12$?

3. What are the zeros of the function graphed below?

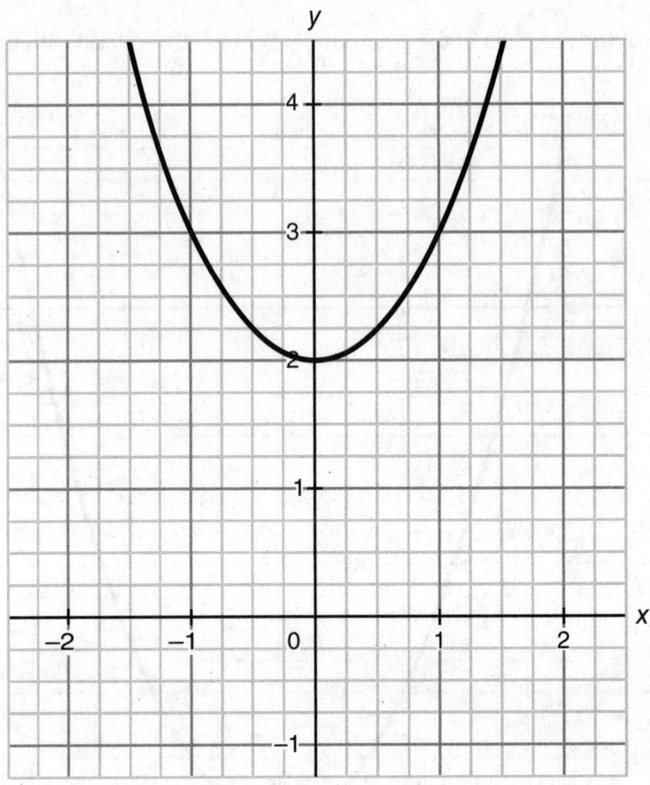

4. What are the zeros of $f(x) = x(x - 1)(x + 2)(x - 9)$?

✓ Solutions

1. Since the function is already in factored form, it is easy to identify which values of x would make y have a value of zero. If x is either -3 or 5, y will be zero. Therefore, the zeros are -3 and 5.

2. Factor the equation to identify the zeros:

$$f(x) = x^2 + 4x - 12 \rightarrow$$
$$f(x) = (x + 6)(x - 2)$$

So, the zeros are at -6 and 2.

3. Since the function does not intersect the x-axis, there are no points at which y will be zero. Therefore, there are NO real zeros in the function.

4. Examine the equation to determine the values of x that will make $f(x) = 0$. Fortunately, the equation is already factored, $f(x) = x(x - 1)(x + 2)(x - 9)$, making it easier to identify the zeros. 0, 1, -2, and 9 if plugged in for x would all make the function equal to 0, so these numbers are all zeros of the function.

Parabola Graphing

A parabola is a function with a u-shaped curve that has certain properties. Here is an example of a parabola with the equation $y = 2(x - 3)^2 + 1$:

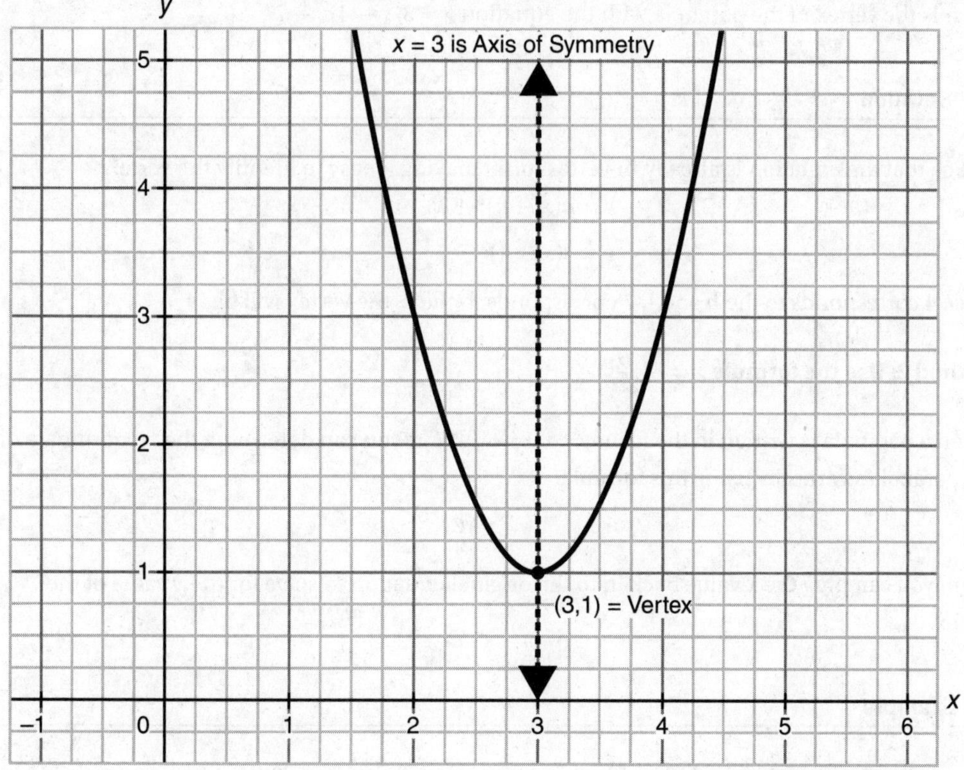

- The vertex form of a parabola is $y = a(x - h)^2 + k$. In the above example, $y = 2(x - 3)^2 + 1$ is written in vertex form, with $a = 2$, $h = 3$, and $k = 1$.
- The value of the constant a determines the direction of the parabola—if it is positive, it opens upward, and if it is negative, it opens downward. In the example, a is $+2$, so the parabola opens upward.
- The vertex (the bottom point of the u-shape) has the coordinates (h, k). The vertex of the parabola in the example is $(3, 1)$.
- The x-coordinate of the vertex gives the *axis of symmetry* for the parabola. The axis of symmetry in the example is $x = 3$.

The SAT Math questions involving parabolas focus heavily on identify the vertex of a parabola. There are four major approaches to doing this.

Method 1: Identify points *h* and *k* when the parabola is in vertex form.

Example

What is the vertex of the parabola with the equation $y = 3(x - 4)^2 - 7$?

Solution

Notice that the equation is already in vertex form, making it easy to identify the vertex:

$$y = a(x - h)^2 + k \rightarrow$$

$$y = 3(x - 4)^2 - 7$$

Since 4 corresponds to the h and -7 corresponds to the k, the vertex will be $(4, -7)$.

Method 2: Use the formula $x = -\frac{b}{2a}$.

When a parabola is written in the form $y = ax^2 + bx + c$, you can determine the x-coordinate of the parabola's vertex by using this formula:

$$x = -\frac{b}{2a}$$

Then, you can plug the x value back in to the original equation to solve for the y value of the vertex.

Example

What is the vertex of the parabola with the equation $y = 4x^2 - 2x - 3$?

Solution

Find the a and b values in the equation and then plug them into the formula. Constant a is 4 and constant b is -2. Now, plug them in:

$$x = -\frac{b}{2a} \rightarrow$$

$$x = -\frac{(-2)}{2(4)} = \frac{2}{8} = \frac{1}{4}$$

Now that we know the x-coordinate of the vertex, we can plug this value back into the original equation to solve for the y-coordinate of the vertex:

$$y = 4x^2 - 2x - 3 \rightarrow$$

$$y = 4\left(\frac{1}{4}\right)^2 - 2\left(\frac{1}{4}\right) - 3 \rightarrow$$

$$y = 4\left(\frac{1}{16}\right) - \frac{1}{2} - 3 \rightarrow$$

$$y = \frac{1}{4} - \frac{1}{2} - 3 = -3\frac{1}{4}$$

So, the vertex of the parabola is $\left(\frac{1}{4}, -3\frac{1}{4}\right)$.

Method 3: Identify the *x* value halfway between the zeros.

Example

What is the *x*-coordinate of the vertex of the parabola with the equation $y = (x - 6)(x - 2)$?

Solution

The zeros of the parabola are at *x*-coordinates of 6 and 2. The *x*-coordinate of the vertex comes halfway between these two zeros. So the *x*-coordinate of the vertex will be at 4 since it is halfway between 6 and 2. Here is a graph of the parabola to more easily visualize this:

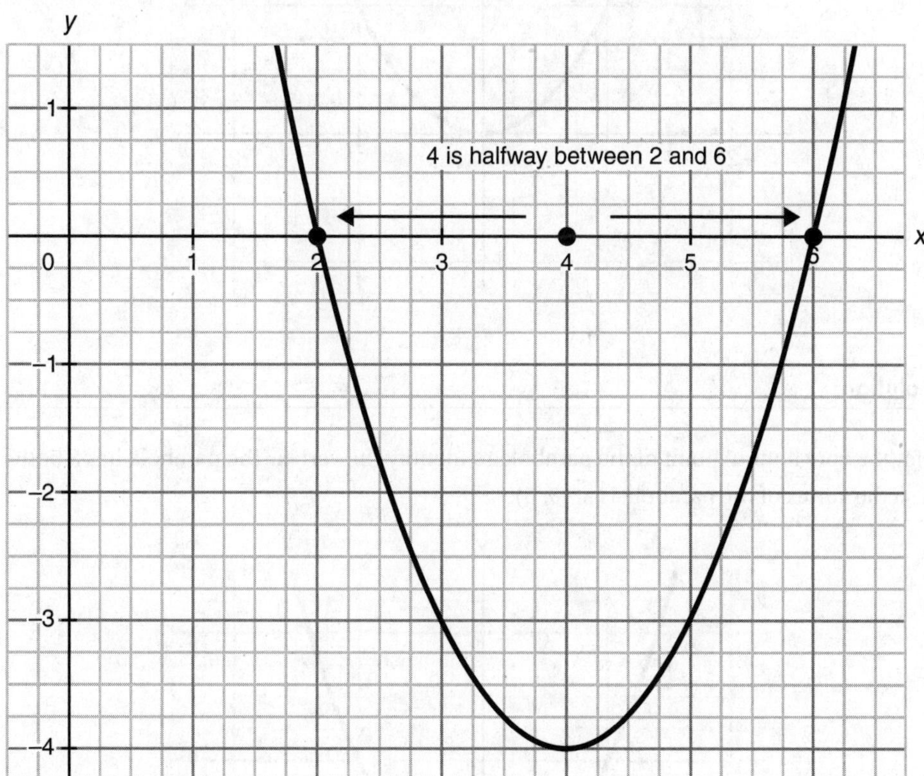

Method 4: Identify the vertex from the graph.

Example

What is the vertex of the parabola with the graph below?

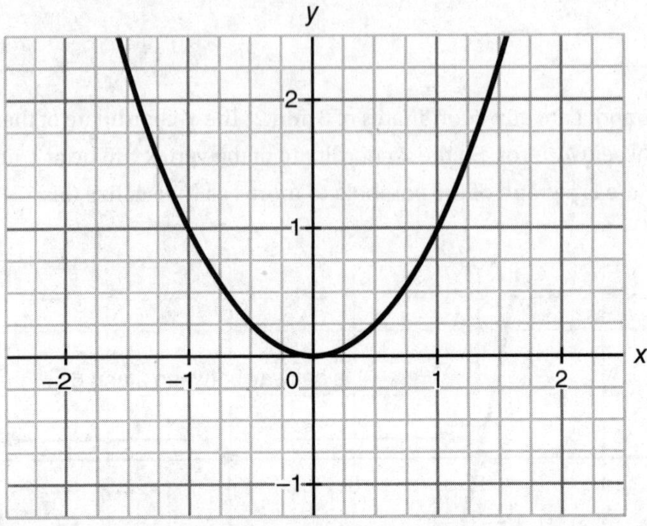

Solution

Look for the very bottom point of the parabola to identify the vertex. The parabola has a bottom at (0, 0), so the vertex of the parabola is at (0, 0):

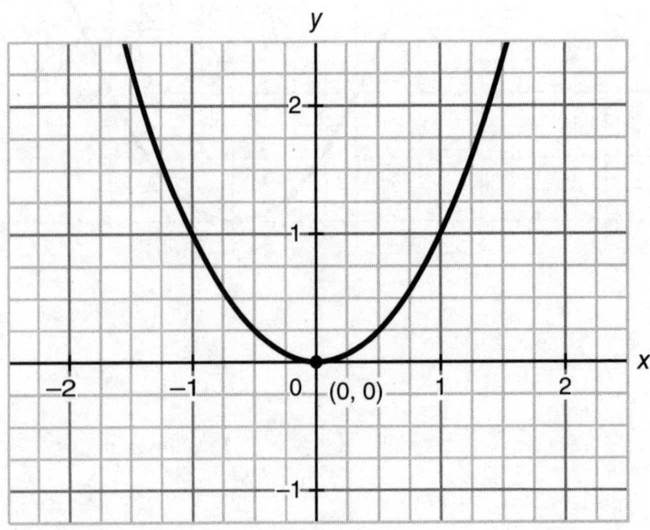

Practice

1. Does the parabola $y = 3(x - 2)^2 + 9$ open upwards or downwards?
2. What is the vertex of the parabola with the equation $y = 4(x - 1)^2 + 6$?
3. What is the x-coordinate of the vertex of a parabola with the equation $y = (x + 4)(x - 8)$?
4. What is the x-coordinate of the vertex of a parabola with the equation $y = 3x^2 - 8x + 4$?
5. What is the vertex of the parabola graphed below?

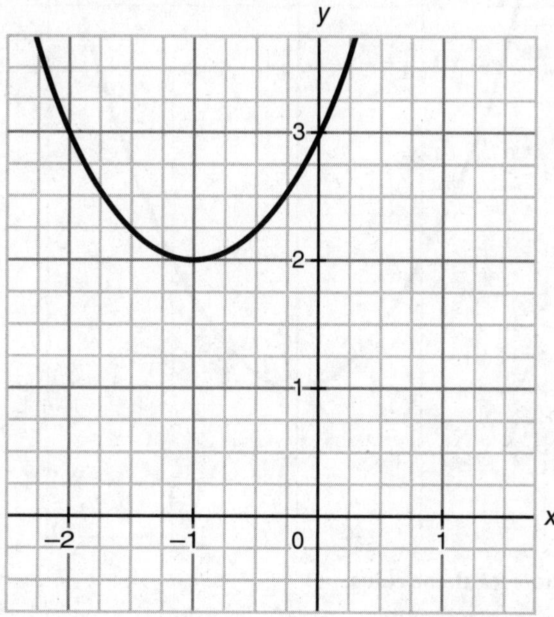

Solutions

1. The parabola is already in the form $y = a(x - h)^2 + k$, with 3 equalling a. Since a is positive, the parabola will open upwards.
2. The parabola is in the form $y = a(x - h)^2 + k$. From this, we can identify the values of the constants h and k to identify the vertex.

$$y = a(x - h)^2 + k \rightarrow$$
$$y = 4(x - 1)^2 + 6 \rightarrow ?$$
$$(h, k) = (1, 6)$$

3. Since the equation is already in factored form, we can identify the zeros of $y = (x + 4)(x - 8)$ as -4 and 8. The x-coordinate of the vertex will be the midpoint of these two values:

$$\frac{-4 + 8}{2} = \frac{4}{2} = 2$$

4. Use the formula $x = -\frac{b}{2a}$ to solve:

$$y = ax^2 + bx + c \rightarrow$$
$$y = 3x^2 - 8x + 4 \rightarrow$$
$$x = -\frac{b}{2a} \rightarrow \frac{-8}{2(3)} = \frac{8}{6} = \frac{4}{3}$$

5. From the graph, we can identify that the vertex of the parabola is at its lowest point, $(-1, 2)$.

Function Transformations

It is useful on some SAT Math problems to know how changes to a function's equation can impact its graph. Here are some key relationships to know.

Suppose we have the function $y = x^2$ with the graph below:

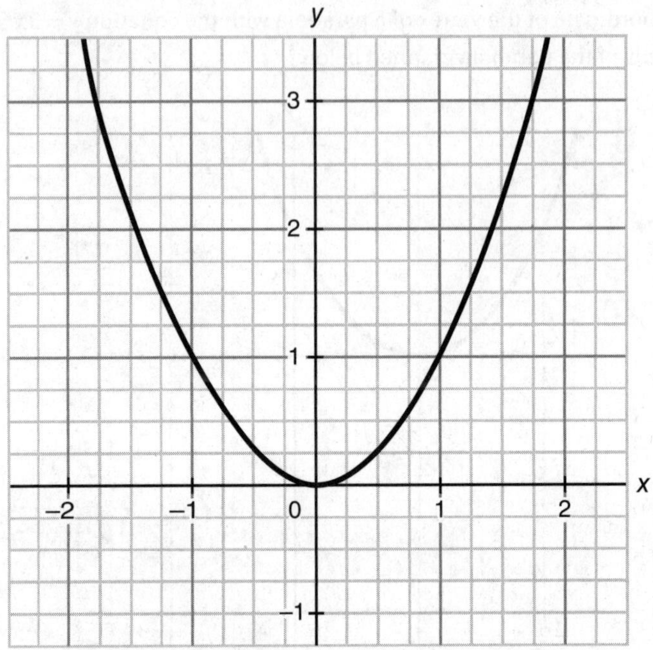

Treat h and k as constants for these rules.

Rule 1: If you transform $f(x)$ to $f(x) + k$, the function will shift UP k units.

The graph of $y = x^2 + 2$ is this:

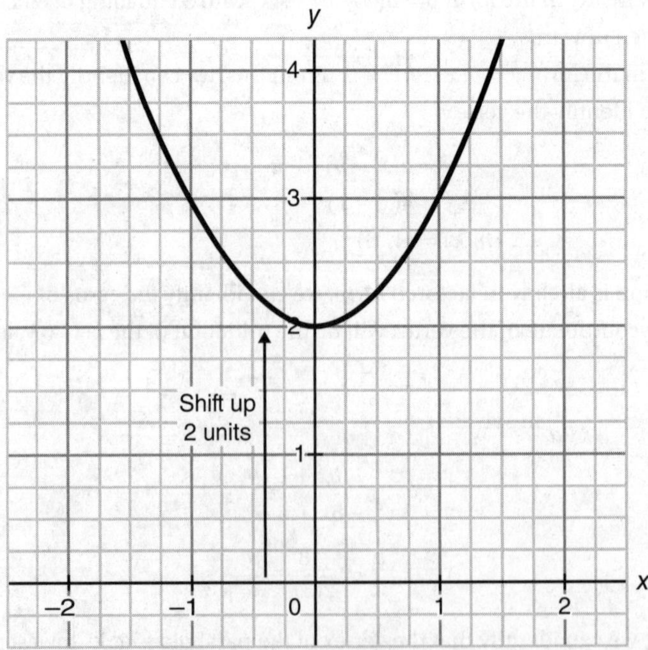

Rule 2: If you transform $f(x)$ to $f(x) - k$, the function will shift DOWN k units.

The graph of $y = x^2 - 2$ is this:

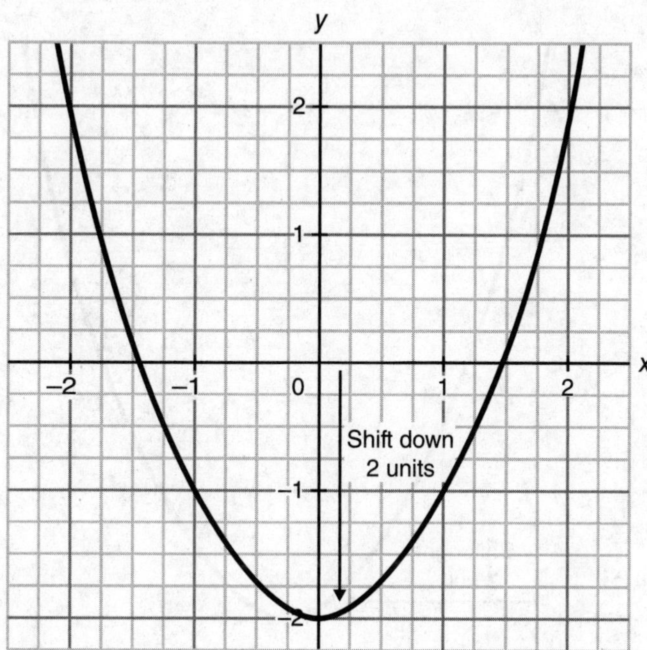

Rule 3: If you transform $f(x)$ to $f(x + h)$, the function will shift LEFT h units.

The graph of $y = (x + 2)^2$ is this:

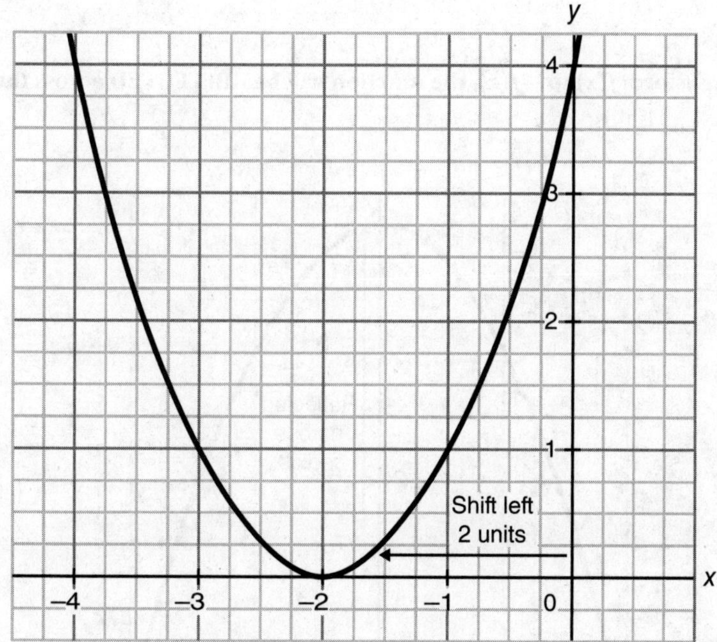

Rule 4: If you transform $f(x)$ to $f(x-h)$, the function will shift RIGHT h units.

The graph of $y = (x-2)^2$ is this:

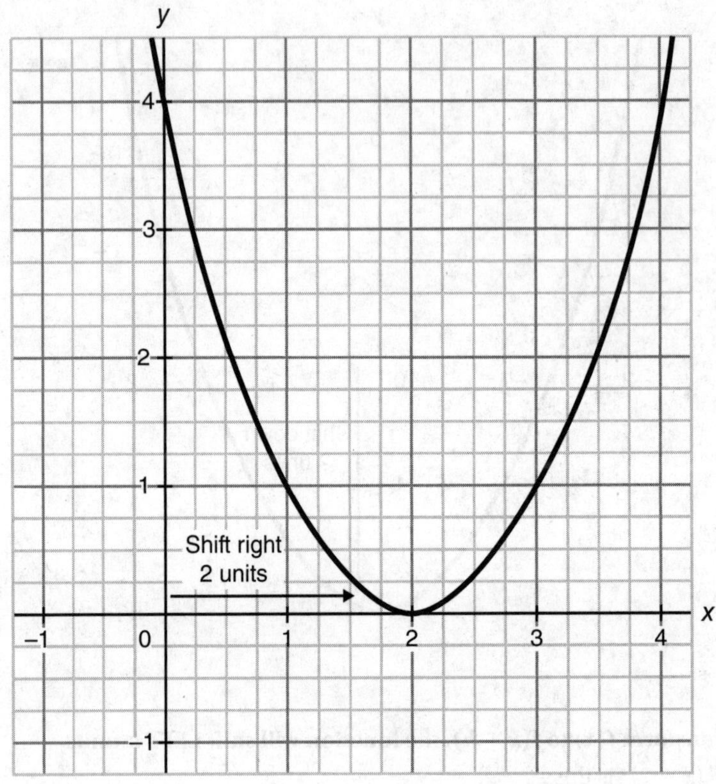

Rule 5: If you transform $f(x)$ to $-f(x)$, the function will be REFLECTED across the x-axis.

The graph of $y = -x^2$ is this:

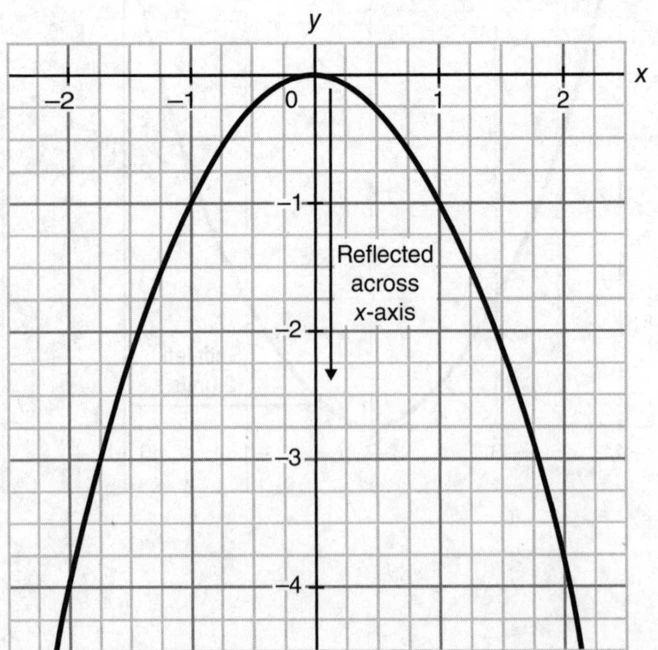

Practice

1. If $y = 3x^3$, how will the graph of $y = 3x^3 - 5$ compare?
2. If $y = 4x^2$, how will the graph of $y = 4(x + 2)^2$ compare?
3. If $y = -2x^3$, how will the graph of $y = 2x^3$ compare?
4. If $y = 6x^2 - 5$, how will the graph of $y = 6(x - 1)^2 - 8$ compare?
5. If $y = 2(x - 4)^5 + 5$, how will the graph of $y = 2(x + 1)^5 - 5$ compare?

Solutions

1. It will be shifted 5 units down.
2. It will be shifted 2 units to the left.
3. It will be reflected across the x-axis.
4. It will be 1 unit to the right and 3 units down.
5. It will be 5 units to the left and 10 units down.

Visualizing Polynomial Graphs

Most of the functions you will encounter on the SAT Math are lines or parabolas. Occasionally, there will be questions involving more advanced concepts about the graphs of polynomial functions. Here are some key things to know.

Consider a polynomial with the term with the highest power term ax^n.

- The greatest possible number of turns (changes in y direction) of this function will be at most $n - 1$.
- If the constant a is positive, the function will ultimately point upwards as the x values increase; if the constant a is negative, the function will ultimately point downwards as the x values increase.
- If the exponent n is even, the ends of the function go the same direction; if the exponent n is odd, the ends of the function go in different directions.

Example 1

Consider the polynomial $y = x^3 - 7x^2 + 7x + 15$.

- How many times will the polynomial turn with respect to its y values?
- Will the function ultimately point upwards or downwards?
- Will the ends of the function go in the same or different directions?

Solutions

The greatest number exponential value in the polynomial is x^3; so the greatest possible number of turns it can have will be $3 - 1 = 2$.

Since the coefficient of x^3 is positive 1, the function will ultimately increase as the x values increase.

Since the greatest exponent in the function, 3, is odd, the ends of the function go in different directions.

All of this is easiest to see in the graph below:

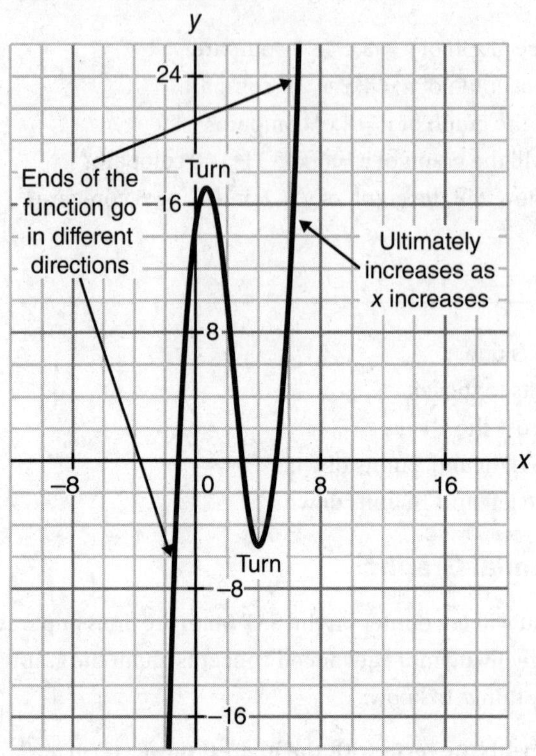

Example 2

Consider the polynomial $y = -x^4 + 5x^3 - 5x^2 - 5x + 6$.

- How many times will the polynomial turn with respect to its y values?
- Will the function ultimately point upwards or downwards?
- Will the ends of the function go in the same or different directions?

Solution

The greatest number exponential value in the polynomial is x^4, so the greatest number of turns it can have will be $4 - 1 = 3$.

Since the coefficient of x^4 is negative 1, the function will ultimately decrease as the x values increase.

Since the greatest exponent in the function, 4, is even, the ends of the function go in the same direction.

All of this is easiest to see in the graph below:

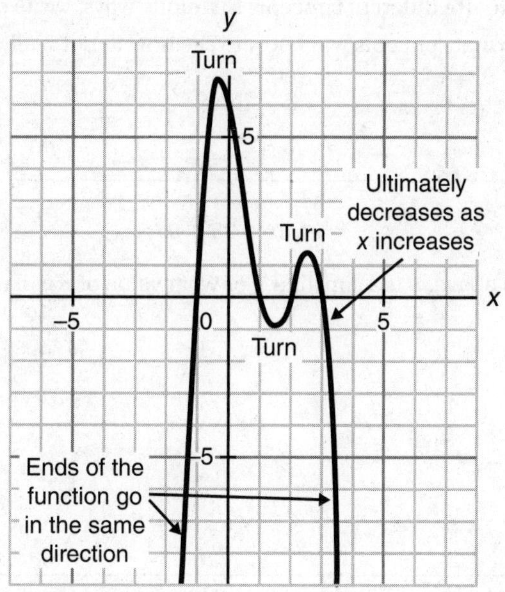

Practice

1. What is the most number of turns a function of the form $f(x) = ax^2$ can have?
2. Will the end values of the function $f(x) = x^3$ go in the same or different directions?
3. Will the y values in $y = 4x^5$ ultimately point upwards or downwards as x increases?
4. Will the end values of the function $f(x) = x^6 + 3x^5 - 2x$ go in the same or different directions?
5. Will the y values in $y = -6x^5 + 3x^4 + 7x^2 - 9$ ultimately point upwards or downwards as x increases?

Solutions

1. The greatest number exponential value in the polynomial is x^2; so the greatest number of turns it can have will be $2 - 1 = 1$.
2. Since the greatest exponent in the function, 3, is odd, the ends of the function go in different directions.
3. Since the coefficient of x^5 is positive 4, the function will ultimately increase as the x values increase.
4. Since the greatest exponent in the function, 6, is even, the ends of the function go in the same direction.
5. Since the coefficient of x^5 is negative 6, the function will ultimately decrease as the x values increase.

SAT Math Strategy

Integrate your knowledge about zeros, parabolas, and polynomial graphing to solve problems.

Many SAT Math problems involving zeros and parabolas will require you to use different concepts in unique ways. Write out what is given and what concepts you know to see how to put it all together.

Example 1

$$x^2 + nx + 25 = 0$$

In the quadratic equation above, n is a constant. For what value of n will the function intersect the x-axis only once?

(A) -13
(B) -12
(C) -11
(D) -10

Solution

This question does not ask us to do something straightforward like identifying the zeros or the vertex. We need to find out what value of the constant n will make the function have only one point of intersection with the x-axis.

To have only one point of intersection with the x-axis, the function should have *only one zero*. So, if we could factor the equation and it would have only one zero in factored form, that would tell us what the constant would need to be. Notice that 25 is a perfect square—the square root of it is 5. So, if we were to write the equation in factored form, it would look like this:

$$(x - 5)(x - 5) = 0$$

When the equation is in this form, it has only ONE zero—the number 5. Next, to identify the constant n, we can FOIL the equation to see what it looks like in the form described by the problem.

$$(x - 5)(x - 5) = 0$$
$$x^2 - 10x + 25 = 0$$

Based on this, n is -10, choice **(D)**. So, we were able to integrate some of the different concepts we know about zeros to solve this problem.

Example 2

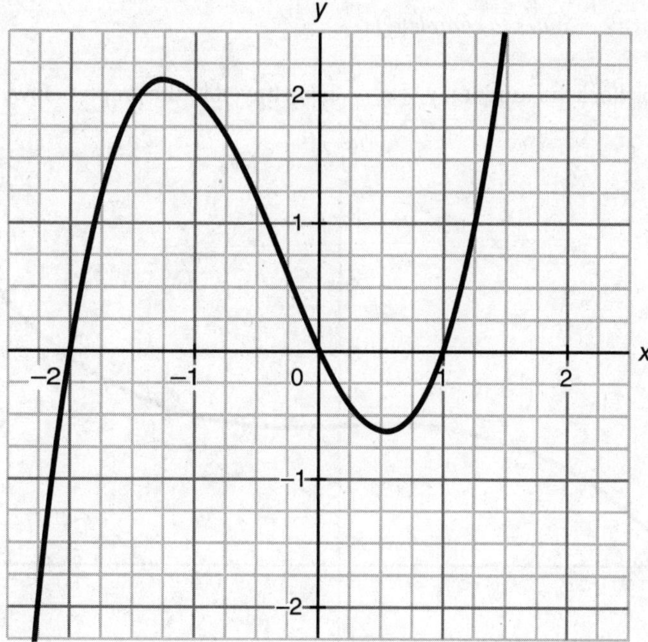

The graph above is represented by which of the following equations?

(A) $y = x(x + 2)(x - 1)$
(B) $y = x^2(x + 1)(x - 2)$
(C) $y = x(x - 2)(x + 1)$
(D) $y = x^2(x + 2)(x - 1)$

Solution

We can integrate our knowledge about zeros and polynomial graphing to solve this problem. First, the ends of the function go in *different* directions, so the largest exponential value in the function must be *odd*. Based on this, we can eliminate choices (B) and (D) since when they are written in expanded form, the largest exponential value would be x^4. Choices (A) and (C) could potentially work since when they are written in expanded form, the largest exponential value would be x^3.

Now that we know it must be either choice (A) or (C), we can identify the zeros of the function from the graph: they are −2, 0, and 1. This makes choice **(A)** correct with respect to zeros of the function, since the outside term x would work with 0, the term $(x + 2)$ would work with −2, and the term $(x - 1)$ would work with 1. Therefore, the correct answer is **(A)**.

SAT Math Questions Practice Drill—Zeros, Parabolas, and Polynomial Graphing

(If timing, take about 12 minutes to complete.)

1. How many zeros does the function $y = x^3 + 2$, portrayed in the graph below, have?

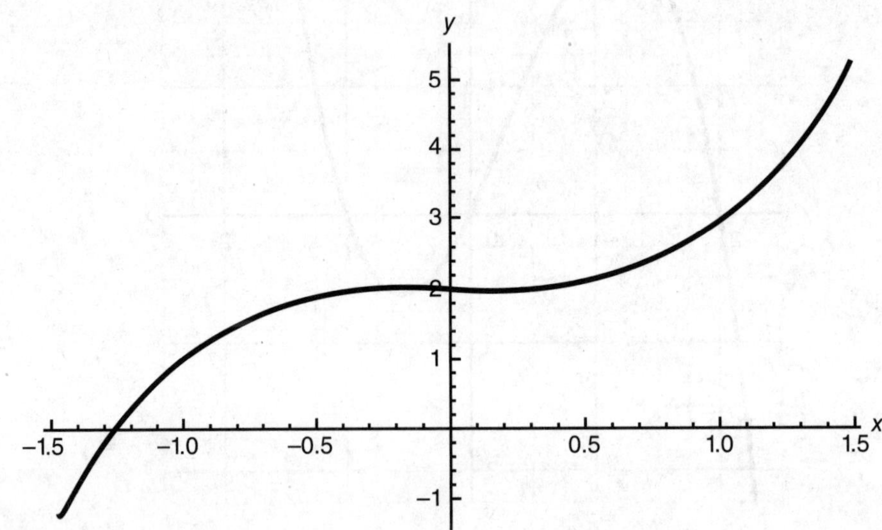

(A) 0
(B) 1
(C) 2
(D) 3

2. $f(x) = (x + 4)(x - 6)$

In the function above, what is the straight-line distance in units in the *xy*-coordinate plane between the function's zeros?

(A) 4
(B) 6
(C) 10
(D) 24

3. What is the *y*-intercept of the function $y = x^2 - 4$?

(A) −4
(B) −2
(C) 1
(D) 4

4. What is the vertex in the parabola with the equation $\frac{y+4}{2} = (x - 5)^2$?

(A) (5, 4)
(B) (−5, −4)
(C) (−5, 4)
(D) (5, −4)

5. What are the x-intercepts of the function $f(x) = x^2 - 3x - 10$?

(A) -2 and 5
(B) -2 and -5
(C) 2 and 5
(D) 10 and 2

6. $y = (x - 3)(x + 5)$

The function above has a vertical axis of symmetry on which line?

(A) $x = -5$
(B) $x = -3$
(C) $x = -1$
(D) $x = 15$

7. Which of the following is a graph of the equation $y = x^2 - 3$?

(A)

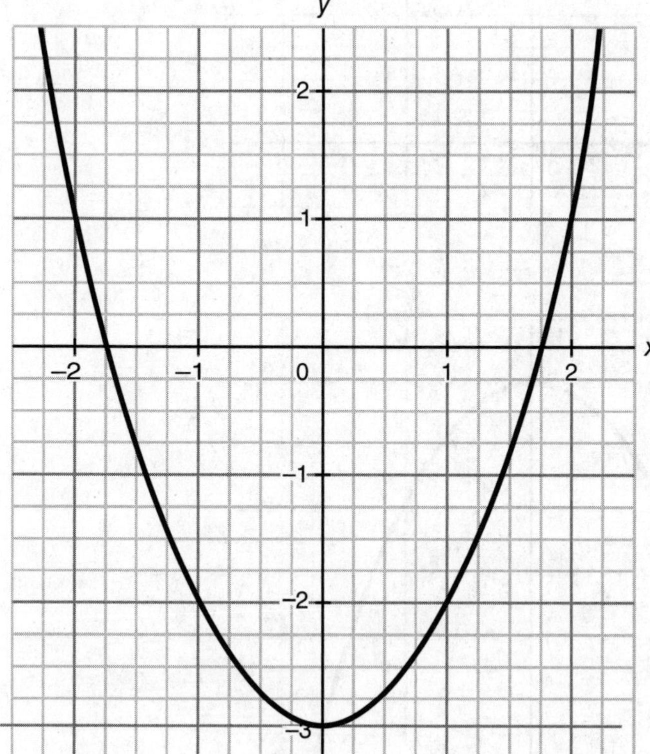

(B)

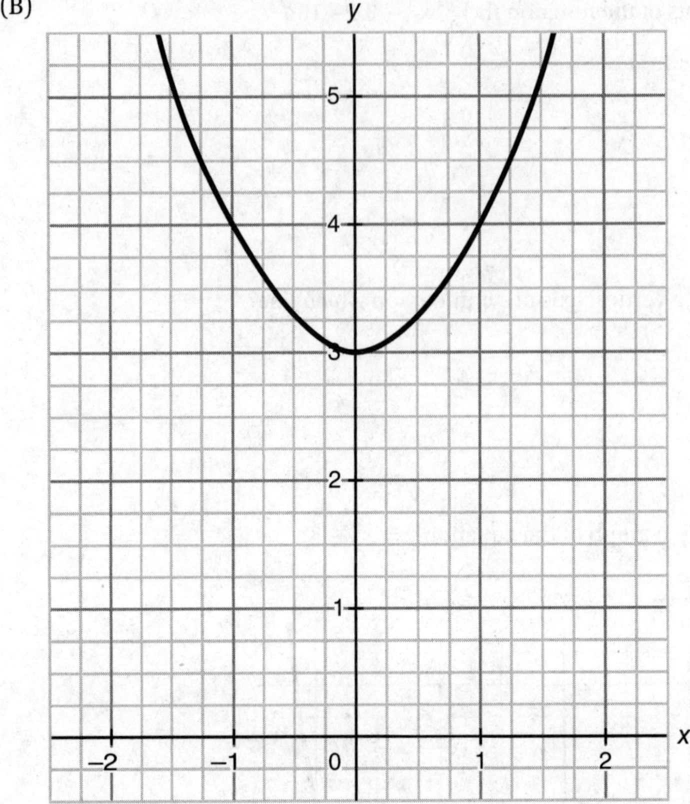

(C)

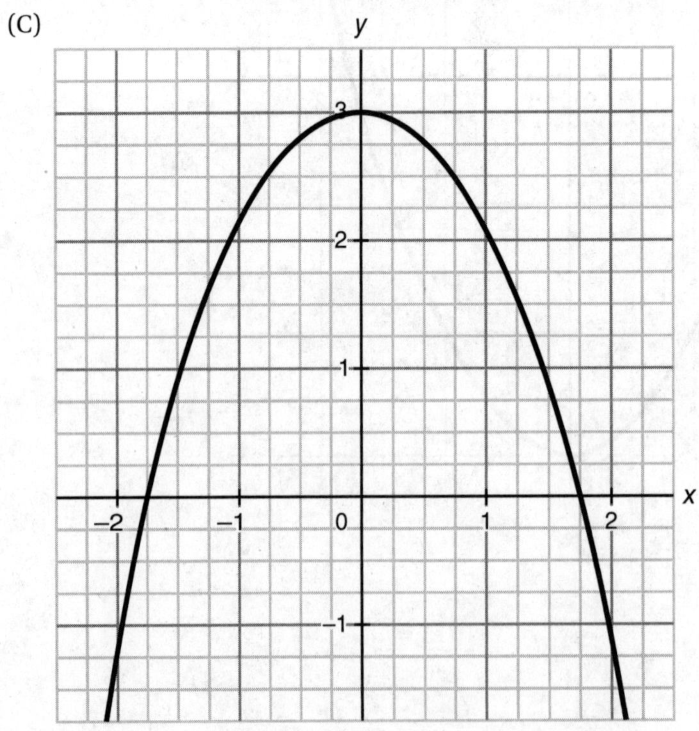

(D)

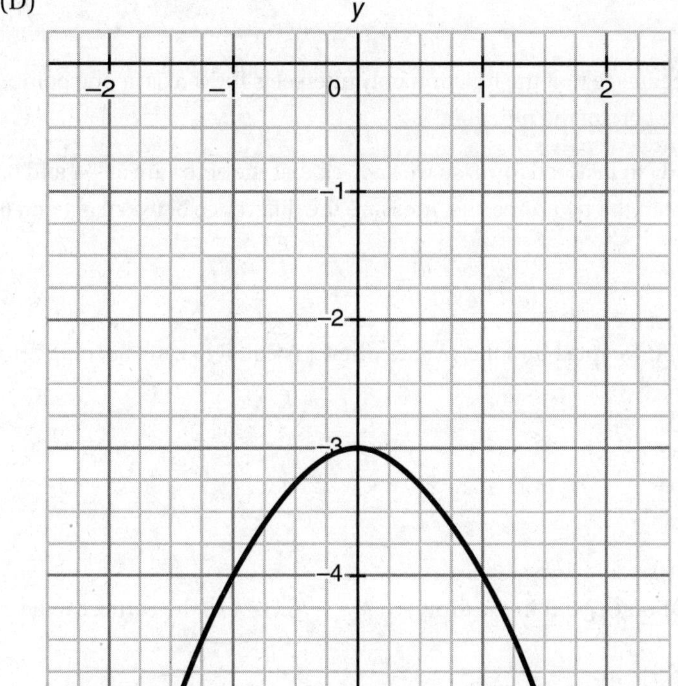

8. Which of the following functions intersects the x-axis at exactly 3 points?

(A) $y = x^2 - 3$
(B) $y = x(x - 2)(x + 3)$
(C) $y = (x + 4)^3$
(D) $y = 5(x - 2)(x - 2)$

9. What is the y value of the y-intercept of the function $y = (5)^x$?

(A) 0
(B) 1
(C) 2
(D) 3

10. If $f(x) = (x - 5)^2 + 4$ and $g(x)$ is a line with a slope of zero that intersects $f(x)$ at only one point, what is the point at which the two functions intersect?

(A) (−3, −4)
(B) (−2, 5)
(C) (0, 8)
(D) (5, 4)

✓ Solutions

1. **(B)** From the graph, you can see that the function only intersects the x-axis at one point. Therefore, there is just one zero of the function.

2. **(C)** The function is already in factored form, so we can see that the zeros are at -4 and 6. So, to find the distance between the two zeros, just measure the difference between -4 and 6 on the x-axis. This will be:

$$6-(-4) = 10$$

3. **(A)** To find the y-intercept, we must find the y value when x is equal to zero. So, plug zero in for x to solve:

$$y = x^2 - 4 \rightarrow$$
$$y = 0^2 - 4 \rightarrow$$
$$y = -4$$

4. **(D)** Manipulate the equation to get it in the form $y = a(x - h)^2 + k$ so the vertex can be easily identified:

$$\frac{y+4}{2} = (x-5)^2 \rightarrow$$
$$y + 4 = 2(x-5)^2 \rightarrow$$
$$y = 2(x-5)^2 - 4$$

Since the vertex corresponds to (h, k), the vertex will be $(5, -4)$.

5. **(A)** Factor the function to identify the zeros—these are the same as the x-intercepts of the function since they are the points at which the y value is zero.

$$f(x) = x^2 - 3x - 10 \rightarrow$$
$$f(x) = (x-5)(x+2)$$

Therefore, the x-intercepts are -2 and 5.

6. **(C)** The vertical axis of symmetry will be the line that bisects the parabola through the vertex. Find the x-coordinate of the vertex and make an equation in which every x value is equal to that point. The zeros of $y = (x - 3)(x + 5)$ are 3 and -5, so the x-coordinate of the vertex will be halfway between them at -1. So, the vertical axis of symmetry will be $x = -1$.

7. **(A)** The equation is already in the form $y = a(x - h)^2 + k$, which makes it easy to identify the vertex and the direction of the parabola. The vertex is $(0, -3)$ and a is $+1$, so the parabola will open upward. The parabola graphed in choice **(A)** has this vertex and direction.

8. **(B)** Determine which of the four functions has three zeros:

$y = x^2 - 3$ has 2 zeros at $\sqrt{3}$ and $-\sqrt{3}$.

$y = x(x - 2)(x + 3)$ has 3 zeros at 0, 2, and -3.

$y = (x + 4)^3$ has 1 zero at -4.

$y = 5(x - 2)(x - 2)$ has 1 zero at $+2$.

So, choice **(B)** is correct.

9. **(B)** The y-intercept for this function is the point at which the x value is 0. So, plug 0 in for x to see the corresponding y value.

$$y = (5)^x \rightarrow$$

$$y = 5^0 = 1$$

10. **(D)** The two functions will intersect at the vertex of the parabola—if the flat, horizontal line intersected above the vertex, it would intersect at two points. Since the function is already in the form $y = a(x - h)^2 + k$, the vertex of $f(x) = (x - 5)^2 + 4$ can be identified as (5, 4). This is the point at which the functions will intersect.

Passport to Advanced Math—Function Interpretation and Manipulation

Putting Variables in Terms of Other Variables

SAT Math Strategy

When asked for the value of a variable or an expression, manipulate the equation to isolate that variable or expression.

Example 1

The energy, E, of a planet in an elliptical orbit around the sun is given by the equation

$$E = -\frac{GmM}{2a}$$

in which G is the gravitational constant, M is the mass of the sun, m is the mass of an orbiting planet, and a is the length of the semimajor axis of the ellipse made by the planetary orbit. What is the value of a planet's mass in terms of the other values?

Solution

Typically, when you solve an equation, you find the numerical value of x or some other variable. In a question like this, you should isolate the variable for mass, m, to see what m is "in terms of" the other variables.

$$E = -\frac{GmM}{2a} \rightarrow$$

Multiply both sides by $2a \rightarrow$

$$2aE = -GmM \rightarrow$$

Divide both sides by $-GM \rightarrow$

$$m = -\frac{2aE}{GM}$$

Example 2

What is the value of $2n - 1$ in the equation below?

$$\frac{2n-1}{3} + 11 = 8n - 4$$

Solution

As a general rule, *when the SAT asks you to find the value of an expression, there will be a straightforward way to find it by treating the expression as a whole unit.* This problem is no exception. We do not need to solve for n individually—instead, we can manipulate the equation to isolate the expression $2n - 1$:

$$\frac{2n-1}{3} + 11 = 8n - 4 \rightarrow$$

Factor the right side $\rightarrow$

$$\frac{(2n-1)}{3} + 11 = 4(2n - 1) \rightarrow$$

Multiply both sides by 3 $\rightarrow$

$$(2n - 1) + 33 = 12(2n - 1) \rightarrow$$

Subtract $(2n - 1)$ from both sides $\rightarrow$

$$33 = 11(2n - 1) \rightarrow$$

$$3 = (2n - 1)$$

So, the value of $2n - 1$ is 3.

Identifying Constants

SAT Math Strategy

Recognize that the SAT will make it easy to identify constant terms.

Example 1

If $(x + 4)^2 + 5 = ax^2 + bx + c$, what is the sum of the constants a, b, and c?

Solution

You do not need to use any special formulas to solve this. Just expand the left side of the expression and simplify so you can identify the constants a, b, and c:

$$(x + 4)^2 + 5 \rightarrow$$

$$(x + 4)(x + 4) + 5 \rightarrow$$

$$x^2 + 4x + 4x + 16 + 5 \rightarrow$$

$$x^2 + 8x + 16 + 5 \rightarrow$$

$$x^2 + 8x + 21$$

So,

$$a = 1,\ b = 8,\ \text{and}\ c = 21$$

$$1 + 8 + 21 = 30$$

Example 2

$$f(x) = (x - 4)(x + 11)$$

In the equation above, which of these values is displayed as a constant or constants?

(A) y-intercepts
(B) x-intercepts
(C) x-coordinate of the vertex
(D) y-coordinate of the vertex

Solution

In the function, we see the numbers 4 and 11 displayed as constants. What do we know about this function based on what we have previously covered? The *zeros* of the function are going to be 4 and -11. Since a zero is where the function intersects the x-axis, we can say that the x-intercepts are displayed as constants in the function.

Interpreting Functions

SAT Math Strategy

Apply what you have already learned about algebra and graphs to interpret functions—you will only be tested on what is reasonable to know.

Example 1

A company's profit, P, for selling n products is modeled by the following function:

$$P = -10n^2 + 300n - 1{,}000$$

How many products should the company sell to achieve its maximum profit?

(A) 10
(B) 12
(C) 15
(D) 18

Solution

While it would be possible to work your way backwards from the solutions, that could be time-consuming in this case. Instead, use your knowledge of quadratic functions to solve. The maximum of a parabola that is facing downwards can be found at the vertex of the parabola. The n^2 term is the largest power term, and it has -10 as its coefficient, meaning the parabola will face downwards. So, if we can find the vertex of the parabola, we can find the x-coordinate at which the parabola is at its maximum.

Use the formula $x = -\frac{b}{2a}$ to find the vertex since the equation is in standard form. The constant a will be -10, and the constant b will be 300, and we can substitute n for x.

$$x = -\frac{b}{2a} \rightarrow$$

$$n = -\frac{b}{2a} \rightarrow$$

$$n = -\frac{300}{2(-10)} = \frac{300}{20} = 15$$

Thus, the number of products that should be sold to maximize the profit is 15, choice **(C)**.

Example 2

In the equation $nx^2 + m = 5x^2 + 4$, there are infinitely many solutions for x. What is the product of the constants m and n?

(A) 10
(B) 14
(C) 18
(D) 20

✓ Solution

Think through what you know about equations. For there to be infinitely many solutions, the equation can be formatted so that what is on the left side and the right side are identical. For example, $x + 5 = x + 5$ would have infinitely many solutions since any number can be plugged in for x to make this equation true.

So, let's apply the same idea to this problem. For this equation to have infinitely many solutions, the two sides should be equal:

$$nx^2 + m = 5x^2 + 4 \rightarrow$$

$$5x^2 + 4 = 5x^2 + 4$$

Therefore, n equals 5 and m equals 4. The product comes from multiplying the two numbers together. Thus, the product of 5 and 4 is $5 \times 4 = 20$, choice **(D)**.

SAT Math Questions Practice Drill #1—Function Interpretation and Manipulation

(If timing, take about 12 minutes to complete.)

1. In the equation $E = mc^2$, what is the value of c in terms of the other values?

(A) Em
(B) $\frac{m}{E}$
(C) $\sqrt{\frac{E}{m}}$
(D) $\sqrt{\frac{m}{E^2}}$

2. The formula to model the height, h, in meters of an object t seconds after being dropped is $h(t) = -4.9t^2 + h_0$ in which h_0 is the height from which the object is dropped. If the height of an object 3 seconds after being dropped is 0, what is the initial height of the object?

(A) 9.8 meters
(B) 17.2 meters
(C) 24.4 meters
(D) 44.1 meters

3. Body mass index is calculated by taking the mass of a person in pounds and the height of a person in inches and plugging these values into this formula:

$$BMI = \frac{mass}{height^2} \times 703$$

What is the mass of a person in terms of the other values?

(A) $mass = \frac{BMI \times height^2}{703}$

(B) $mass = \frac{BMI \times height}{703}$

(C) $mass = \frac{703}{BMI \times height^2}$

(D) $mass = \frac{703}{BMI \times height}$

4. The height of a rock thrown off a ledge relative to the ground beneath the ledge is graphed below.

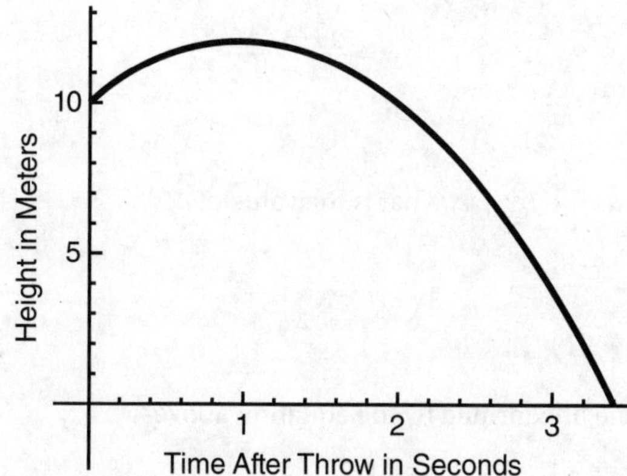

At what time did the rock reach its maximum height?

(A) At the time of the throw
(B) 1 second after the throw
(C) 2 seconds after the throw
(D) 3.5 seconds after the throw

5. If $x - 5 = \frac{2x^2 + ax - 20}{2x + 4}$, what is the value of the constant a?

   (A) -6
   (B) -3
   (C) $\frac{1}{2}$
   (D) 8

6. The moon orbits Earth once approximately every 27 days. Titan, a moon of the planet Saturn, orbits Saturn once approximately every 16 days. For every full planetary orbit the moon of Earth makes, M, how many orbits of Saturn (or fractions thereof) will Titan make of Saturn, T?

   (A) $T = \frac{16}{27}M$
   (B) $T = \frac{4}{9}M$
   (C) $T = \frac{27}{16}M$
   (D) $T = \frac{9}{4}M$

Fill-In Practice: Write your answer in the underlined blank under each question.

7. The number of geese at a lake tripled each year, when compared to the number of geese on January 1 of each year between January 1, 2017, and January 1, 2020. If there were 810 geese on January 1, 2020, how many geese would there have been on January 1, 2017?

   Answer: ______

8. What is the y-intercept of the graph of the following equation?

$$y = \frac{2x^2 - 18}{x - 3}$$

   Answer: ______

9. If $2(3x^2 - 4x + 2) = ax^2 + bx + c$, what is the value of c?

   Answer: ______

10. $y = \frac{4x^2 - 36}{2x + 6}$

    What is the slope of the line formed by the equation above?

    Answer: ______

✓ Solutions

1. **(C)** Isolate the c to arrive at your solution:

$$E = mc^2 \rightarrow$$

$$\frac{E}{m} = c^2 \rightarrow$$

$$\sqrt{\frac{E}{m}} = \sqrt{c^2} \rightarrow$$

$$c = \sqrt{\frac{E}{m}}$$

2. **(D)** The value of h_0 is the initial height of the object. So, plug in 3 for t and 0 for the final height, $h(t)$:

$$h(t) = -4.9t^2 + h_0 \rightarrow$$
$$0 = -4.9(3)^2 + h_0 \rightarrow$$
$$0 = -44.1 + h_0 \rightarrow$$
$$h_0 = 44.1$$

3. **(A)** Manipulate the equation until mass is isolated.

$$BMI = \frac{mass}{height^2} \times 703 \rightarrow$$
$$\frac{BMI}{703} = \frac{mass}{height^2} \rightarrow$$
$$mass = \frac{BMI \times height^2}{703}$$

4. **(B)** Find the point on the graph where the height is at its maximum:

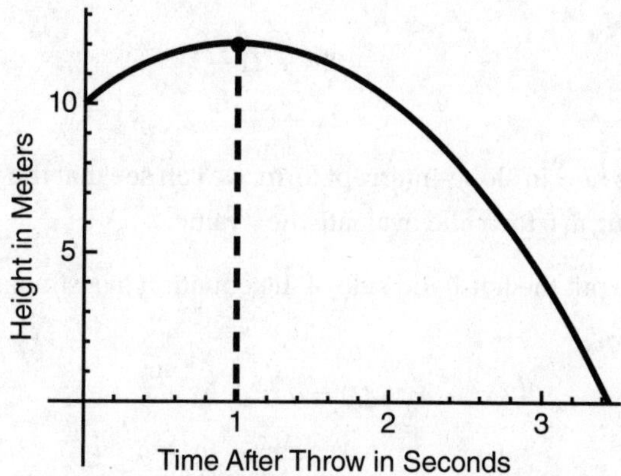

So, the rock reached its maximum height at 1 second after the throw.

5. **(A)**

$$x - 5 = \frac{2x^2 + ax - 20}{2x + 4} \rightarrow$$
$$(x - 5)(2x + 4) = 2x^2 + ax - 20 \rightarrow$$
$$2x^2 - 10x + 4x - 20 = 2x^2 + ax - 20 \rightarrow$$
$$2x^2 - 6x - 20 = 2x^2 + ax - 20$$

The constant a corresponds to -6.

6. **(C)** It takes the moon 27 days to make a complete orbit of Earth, and it takes Titan 16 days to make a complete orbit of Saturn. So, if the moon has made one full orbit, 27 days have gone by—in that time, Titan would have made nearly two orbits since it orbits more quickly.

To be precise, it would make $\frac{27}{16}$ orbits. Therefore, the answer is choice **(C)**, $T = \frac{27}{16}M$.

Another way to think about this: Titan makes $\frac{1}{16}$ of an orbit in one day. Since it takes the moon 27 days to make a complete orbit, Titan would make $\frac{1}{16} \times 27 = \frac{27}{16}$ of an orbit in the time it takes the moon to make a single orbit.

7. **30** Since the number of geese triples each year, work your way backwards to the number of geese in 2017 by taking $\frac{1}{3}$ of each previous year's total.

   In 2020, there were 810 geese.

   In 2019, there would be $\frac{1}{3}$ of 810, which is 270.

   In 2018, there would be $\frac{1}{3}$ of 270, which is 90.

   And in 2017, there would be $\frac{1}{3}$ of 90, which is 30.

8. **6**

$$y = \frac{2x^2 - 18}{x - 3} \rightarrow$$

$$y = \frac{2(x + 3)(x - 3)}{x - 3} \rightarrow$$

   Cancel the $x - 3 \rightarrow$

$$y = 2(x + 3) \rightarrow$$

$$y = 2x + 6$$

   Since the equation is now in slope-intercept form, we can see that the y-intercept is 6. Alternatively, just plug in 0 for x and evaluate the y value.

9. **4** Distribute the 2 to put the left-hand side of the equation in a similar form to the right-hand side:

$$2(3x^2 - 4x + 2) = ax^2 + bx + c \rightarrow$$

$$6x^2 - 8x + 4 = ax^2 + bx + c$$

   So, the constant c is equal to the constant 4.

10. **2** Manipulate this equation to get it in slope-intercept form:

$$y = \frac{4x^2 - 36}{2x + 6} \rightarrow$$

$$y = \frac{4(x^2 - 9)}{2(x + 3)} \rightarrow$$

$$y = 2\frac{(x + 3)(x - 3)}{(x + 3)} \rightarrow$$

$$y = 2\frac{\cancel{(x + 3)}(x - 3)}{\cancel{(x + 3)}} \rightarrow$$

$$y = 2x - 6$$

   So, the slope, m, of the line is 2 since the equation is in the form $y = mx + b$.

SAT Math Questions Practice Drill #2—Function Interpretation and Manipulation

(If timing, take about 12 minutes to complete.)

1. In physics, force, F, is equal to the mass, m, multiplied by acceleration, a:

$$F = ma$$

What is acceleration in terms of force and mass?

(A) $a = F + m$

(B) $a = \frac{m}{F}$

(C) $a = \frac{1}{Fm}$

(D) $a = \frac{F}{m}$

2. In a sphere, the surface area, S, is calculated using the formula $S = 4\pi r^2$, where r is the radius of the sphere. What is the value of the radius in terms of the surface area?

(A) $r = \frac{S}{4\pi}$

(B) $r = 16\pi S^2$

(C) $r = \sqrt{\frac{S}{4\pi}}$

(D) $r = \sqrt{\frac{4\pi}{S}}$

3. If a is a positive constant, what is the value of a in the equation below?

$$(2x + a)(3x + a) = 6x^2 + 5ax + 16$$

(A) 4
(B) 5
(C) 6
(D) 30

4. The solute potential of a solution Ψ_S is calculated as follows:

$$\Psi_S = -iCRT$$

In this equation, i is the ionization constant, C is the molar concentration, R is the pressure constant, and T is the temperature in degrees Kelvin. What is the molar concentration in terms of the other values?

(A) $C = -\frac{R\Psi_S}{iT}$

(B) $C = -\frac{TR}{i\Psi_S}$

(C) $C = -\frac{iRT}{\Psi_S}$

(D) $C = -\frac{\Psi_S}{iRT}$

5. The height, h, of a ball thrown from the top of a ladder that is 10 feet above the ground, and t seconds after being thrown, is calculated using this function:

$$h(t) = -16t^2 + 20t + 10$$

After how many seconds would the ball reach its maximum height?

(A) 0.25 seconds
(B) 0.48 seconds
(C) 0.625 seconds
(D) 0.895 seconds

6. $(2x - 3y)(4x + y) = 8x^2 + axy + bxy - 3y^2$

In the equation with variables x and y above, what is the sum of the constants a and b?

(A) -10
(B) -6
(C) 4
(D) 12

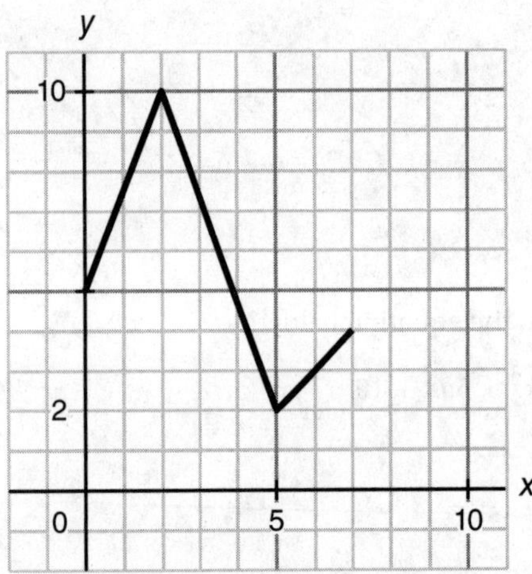

7. The graph above represents all the values for the function $g(x)$ as graphed in the xy-coordinate plane. What is the difference between the minimum and the maximum value of the function?

(A) 5
(B) 7
(C) 8
(D) 10

8. $k(ax^2 + bx + 5) = 6x^2 - 21x + 15$

In the expression above, in which k, a, and b are constants, what is the value of k?

(A) 3
(B) 7
(C) 21
(D) 75

9. If $f(x) = x^2 - 4$ and $f(x + n) = x^2 + 6x + 5$, what is the value of the constant n?

(A) 1
(B) 2
(C) 3
(D) 4

10. If $2y = 3x - 4$ and $y + 1 = z - 5$, what is x in terms of z?

(A) $x = \frac{2}{3}z - \frac{8}{3}$
(B) $x = \frac{4}{5}z + 2$
(C) $x = -\frac{3}{5}z - \frac{4}{9}$
(D) $x = -3z + \frac{1}{4}$

✓ Solutions

1. **(D)** Manipulate the equation so that a is isolated:

$$F = ma \rightarrow$$

Divide both sides by $m \rightarrow$

$$a = \frac{F}{m}$$

2. **(C)** Solve the equation for the radius, r: In a sphere, the surface area, S, is calculated using the formula $S = 4\pi r^2$, where r is the radius of the sphere. What is the value of the radius in terms of the surface area?

$$S = 4\pi r^2 \rightarrow$$

$$r^2 = \frac{S}{4\pi} \rightarrow$$

$$\sqrt{r^2} = \sqrt{\frac{S}{4\pi}} \rightarrow$$

$$r = \sqrt{\frac{S}{4\pi}}$$

3. **(A)** FOIL the left-hand side of the equation so you can identify what values are equivalent:

$$(2x + a)(3x + a) = 6x^2 + 5ax + 16 \rightarrow$$

$$6x^2 + 2ax + 3ax + a^2 = 6x^2 + 5ax + 16 \rightarrow$$

$$6x^2 + 5ax + a^2 = 6x^2 + 5ax + 16 \rightarrow$$

$$a^2 = 16$$

So, a could equal 4. Plugging this back in, you can see that having 4 for a makes the equation work:

$$(2x + a)(3x + a) = 6x^2 + 5ax + 16 \rightarrow$$

$$(2x + 4)(3x + 4) = 6x^2 + 5(4)x + 16 \rightarrow$$

$$6x^2 + 8x + 12x + 16 = 6x^2 + 20x + 16 \rightarrow$$

$$6x^2 + 20x + 16 = 6x^2 + 20x + 16$$

4. **(D)** Manipulate the equation to isolate for C, the molar concentration.

$$\Psi_S = -iCRT \rightarrow$$

Divide both sides by $-iRT \rightarrow$

$$C = -\frac{\Psi_S}{iRT}$$

5. **(C)** The function is a parabola that is facing downwards, given the -16 in front of the largest power term, t^2. The maximum value for the height will therefore be at the parabola's vertex. To find the value of t at the vertex, the easiest way to proceed is to use the formula $x = -\frac{b}{2a}$. The constant a is -16, and the constant b is 20. Instead of x, we can use the variable t:

$$x = -\frac{b}{2a} \rightarrow$$

$$t = -\frac{b}{2a} \rightarrow$$

$$t = -\frac{20}{2(-16)} \rightarrow$$

$$t = \frac{20}{32} = 0.625$$

6. **(A)** FOIL the left-hand side of the equation so you can identify the components that correspond to the values on the right side:

$$(2x - 3y)(4x + y) = 8x^2 + axy + bxy - 3y^2 \rightarrow$$

$$8x^2 + 2xy - 12xy - 3y^2 = 8x^2 + axy + bxy - 3y^2 \rightarrow$$

Subtract the $8x^2$ and $-3y^2$ from both sides $\rightarrow$

$$2xy - 12xy = axy + bxy \rightarrow$$

Divide both sides by $xy \rightarrow$

$$2 - 12 = a + b \rightarrow$$

$$-10 = a + b$$

So, -10 equals the sum of a and b.

7. **(C)** The y value of the highest point on the function is 10, and the y value of the lowest point on the function is 2. So, the difference between the maximum and the minimum of the function will be $10 - 2 = 8$.

8. **(A)** Distribute the k to see potential equivalences:

$$k(ax^2 + bx + 5) = 6x^2 - 21x + 15 \rightarrow$$

$$kax^2 + kbx + 5k = 6x^2 - 21x + 15$$

Based on this, we have three different equivalences:

$$ka = 6,\ kb = -21, \text{ and } 5k = 15$$

Since we do not know the values of a and b, the easiest way to solve this is to solve $5k = 15$:

$$5k = 15 \rightarrow$$
$$\frac{5k}{5} = \frac{15}{5} \rightarrow$$
$$k = 3$$

9. **(C)** Plug $x + n$ into $f(x) = x^2 - 4$, then make this expression equivalent to $x^2 + 6x + 5$ to solve for n:

$$(x + n)^2 - 4 \rightarrow$$
$$(x + n)(x + n) - 4 \rightarrow$$
$$x^2 + 2xn + n^2 - 4 = x^2 + 6x + 5$$

Given this equation, the easiest way to proceed is probably to set $2xn$ equal to $6x$ and solve for n:

$$2xn = 6x \rightarrow$$
$$2n = 6 \rightarrow$$
$$n = 3$$

10. **(A)** Solve this by making an equation that has only x and z in it, eliminating the y.

$$2y = 3x - 4 \rightarrow$$
$$y = \frac{3}{2}x - 2 \rightarrow$$

Substitute this for y in the other equation:

$$\left(\frac{3}{2}x - 2\right) + 1 = z - 5 \rightarrow$$
$$\frac{3}{2}x - 1 = z - 5 \rightarrow$$
$$\frac{3}{2}x = z - 4 \rightarrow$$
$$x = \frac{2}{3}z - \frac{8}{3}$$

Problem Solving and Data Analysis

This section contains comprehensive review and strategies for all of the concepts below:

Problem Solving and Data Analysis—Measures of Center

- Mean
- Median
- Mode
- Outliers
- Range and Standard Deviation

Problem Solving and Data Analysis—Unit Conversion

Problem Solving and Data Analysis—Surveys

- Sampling Methods
- Drawing Conclusions

Problem Solving and Data Analysis—Percentages

- Percentage Essentials
- Percent Increase and Decrease
- Simple Interest
- Compound Interest

Problem Solving and Data Analysis—Graphs and Data Interpretation

- Probability
- Graph Interpretation
- Scatterplots
- Histograms
- Tables
- Box Plots
- Linear and Exponential Growth
- Interpreting Constants and Functions

Problem Solving and Data Analysis—Measures of Center

The SAT Math will assess your understanding of different ways of calculating averages. Mean, median, and mode are the three major concepts to know.

Mean

$$\frac{\text{Sum of Items}}{\text{Number of Items}} = \text{Mean}$$

This is what you typically would do if asked to find the average of a set of terms.

Example 1

What is the mean of the numbers 2, 4, 7, 12, 14, and 18?

Solution

$$\frac{\text{Sum of Items}}{\text{Number of Items}} = \frac{2+4+7+12+14+18}{6} = \frac{57}{6} = 9.5$$

Example 2

There are four numbers in a set: 4, 10, 12, and x. If the mean of the four terms is 10, what is the value of x?

Solution

Set up an equation for the mean of the set, keeping x as an unknown value:

$$\frac{\text{Sum of Items}}{\text{Number of Items}} = \text{Mean} \rightarrow$$

$$\frac{4 + 10 + 12 + x}{4} = 10 \rightarrow$$

$$\frac{26 + x}{4} = 10 \rightarrow$$

$$26 + x = 40 \rightarrow$$

$$x = 14$$

So, the value of x is 14.

Median

The *middle term* of a set of numbers when arranged from *least to greatest.* (If there is an even number of terms and the two middle terms are different, take the mean of the two middle terms to find the median of the set of numbers.)

Example 1

What is the median of this set of numbers? {1, 3, 6, 9, 12, 17, 22}

Solution

The numbers are already arranged from least to greatest, so find the middle term. In this case, since there are seven terms, the fourth term will be the middle term. The answer is therefore 9.

Example 2

What is the median of this set of numbers? {6, 4, 3, 10, 13, 14}

Solution

First, arrange the numbers from least to greatest.

{3, 4, 6, 10, 13, 14}

Notice that there are six numbers, and the two middle numbers are different. So, to find the median of this set, we must take the mean of 6 and 10:

$$\frac{6 + 10}{2} = \frac{16}{2} = 8$$

Mode

This is the *most frequent* number in a set. (Note that if a set of numbers has each number appear just once, there will be zero modes. If a set of numbers has two or more numbers tied for appearing the most times, it will have multiple modes.)

Example

What is the mode of this set of numbers? {1, 5, 3, 9, 2, 4, 8, 9}

Solution

Every number in the set appears just once, except for 9, which appears twice. Therefore, 9 is the mode of the set.

Outliers

A number in a set that is quite different from the other values in the set.

Example

Which value in this set would be considered an outlier? {2, 3, 5, 6, 8, 240}

Solution

While the first five numbers in the set are rather small, 240 is far larger than the others and would be considered an outlier.

Practice

1. What is the mean of this set of numbers? {1, 4, 9, 10}
2. What is the median of this set of numbers? {2, 4, 8, 9, 12}
3. What is the mode of this set of numbers? {4, 5, 7, 8, 4, 2, 9}
4. There are a total of four numbers in a set. The sum of the three smallest terms is 80. If the average of the set of four numbers is 30, what is the value of the largest number in the set?
5. What is the median of 4, 3, 8, 10, 20, and 12?
6. In this set of numbers, {1, 2, 4, 5, 5, 20, 56), is the mean, median, or mode the largest?
7. If an outlier is added to a set of numbers, would it most likely affect the mode, median, or mean of the set?

Solutions

1. $\frac{\text{Sum of Items}}{\text{Number of Items}} = Mean \rightarrow$

   $\frac{1+4+9+10}{4} = \frac{24}{6} = 6$

2. There are five terms in the set, with 8 being the middle term since they are already in order from least to greatest. Therefore, 8 is the median.

3. All the numbers appear just once, except for 4 which appears twice. Thus, 4 is the mode of the set.
4. Calculate the value of the missing term, which we can call x, using the mean formula. Since the smallest three terms add up to 80, we can add 80 and x to get the sum of the items.

$$\frac{\text{Sum of Items}}{\text{Number of Items}} = \text{Mean} \rightarrow$$

$$\frac{80 + x}{4} = 30 \rightarrow$$

$$80 + x = 120 \rightarrow$$

$$x = 40$$

5. Put the numbers in order from least to greatest:

3, 4, 8, 10, 12, 20

There are six terms and the third and fourth terms are different. So, to calculate the median of the set, we must take the mean of 8 and 10:

$$\frac{8 + 10}{2} = \frac{18}{2} = 9$$

6. Rather than calculating the individual values of the median, mean, and mode for the set—{1, 2, 4, 5, 5, 20, 56}—you can take a shortcut. Since the set has two numbers, 20 and 56, that are far greater than the others, they will cause the mean to be greater than the mode and median.

Alternatively, you can calculate the individual values of the mean, median, and mode:

The mean is $\frac{1 + 2 + 4 + 5 + 5 + 20 + 56}{7} \approx 13.3$

The median is 5 since the fourth number out of the set of seven numbers is 5.

The mode is 5 since it appears most frequently.

So, however you find it, the mean will be the greatest.

7. An outlier would most likely affect the *mean* of a set of numbers, since it would be included in the mathematical calculation of the average. It is possible that an outlier would not change the median, so long as the middle value remained the same. It is also possible that an outlier would not change the mode, so long as the outlier was not repeated.

Range and Standard Deviation

To analyze properties of data sets, understand the concepts of range and standard deviation. *Range* is the difference between the smallest and largest values in a set of data.

› Example

What is the range of this set of numbers? {1, 3, 7, 9, 15}

✓ Solution

Take the difference between the largest and smallest values in the set to find the range:

$$15 - 1 = 14$$

Therefore, the range is 14.

Standard deviation indicates how significant the *spread* of the data in a set is.

Mathematically, it is calculated as:

$$\sqrt{\text{Average of the squared distances of the data points from their mean}}$$

Fortunately, instead of having you calculate the precise value of the standard deviation, the SAT tests your understanding of the *concept* of standard deviation.

If the standard deviation in a set of numbers is *small*, there is little variation in the data.

If the standard deviation in a set of numbers is *large*, there will be greater variation in the data.

› Example

Which of the following sets will have a greater standard deviation?

Set X: {5, 6, 7, 8, 9}
Set Y: {1, 20, 40, 80, 95}

✓ Solution

Set Y will have a greater standard deviation because the numbers deviate more greatly from its mean. The values in Set X are much more closely clustered around one another.

› Practice

1. What is the range of this set of numbers? {−5, 3, 8, 20, 28}
2. Which of the following numbers, if added to the set {2, 5, 8, 11, 15} would most likely *decrease* its standard deviation?

   (A) 2
   (B) 5
   (C) 8
   (D) 15

3. What positive number could be added to the set {2, 4, 8, 9, 18} to double its range?
4. Would a sample of ages among students in an elementary school or a sample of ages among residents of a city more likely have a greater standard deviation?

✓ Solutions

1. Find the difference between the least and greatest values in the set to calculate the range:

$$28 - (-5) = 28 + 5 = 33$$

2. Since the standard deviation is calculated by the

$$\sqrt{\text{Average of the squared distances of the data points from their mean}}$$

if you add a data point that *is equal* to the mean, that would certainly reduce the standard deviation of the set. Since the number 8 is equal to the mean, adding it would ensure that the average of the squared distances of the data points from their mean would decrease. So, the answer is **(C)**, 8.

3. First, let's calculate the original range of the set by subtracting the least value from the greatest value:

$$18 - 2 = 16$$

Now, let's double this range:

$$16 \times 2 = 32$$

Since the question asks us to find a *positive* number that could be added to the set that would cause it to have this doubled range of 32, we can add the least value to this range to find the needed value to be added:

$$2 + 32 = 34$$

So, if 34 were added to the set, the range of the set would double.

4. Standard deviation provides a measure of the *spread* of data points—the greater the spread, the greater the standard deviation. In an elementary school, the ages of students would most likely be clustered around lower ages, like 5–12. In a town, the residents would range in age from very young to very old. So, it is more likely that the standard deviation of ages in the town would be greater.

SAT Math Questions Practice Drill—Measures of Center

(If timing, take about 12 minutes to complete.)

1. $\{2, 7, 9, x, 12, 15\}$

Consider the data set above. What must the value of x be so that the median of the data set is 10?

(A) 9
(B) 10
(C) 11
(D) 12

2. What is the mean of the fractions $\frac{1}{3}$, $\frac{1}{4}$, and $\frac{1}{6}$?

(A) $\frac{1}{5}$

(B) $\frac{3}{13}$

(C) $\frac{1}{4}$

(D) $\frac{1}{3}$

3. For a fundraiser, 8 students sold fewer than 5 coupon books. Ten students sold at least 5 and no more than 10 coupon books. Fifteen students sold 11 or more coupon books. Assuming that the previously mentioned students represent the entire set of students, which of the following could have been the median number of coupon books for this group based on this information?

(A) 4
(B) 8
(C) 10.5
(D) 12

Number of Apps on a Phone (Range of Values)	How Many Students with Number of Apps in Range
0–5	2
6–10	5
11–15	7
16–20	4
More than 20	2

4. Twenty students were asked how many apps they had on their phones. The results are provided in the table above. If two students are added to this set, one of whom has just 3 apps and the other of whom has 26 apps, how would the median number of apps per student be affected?

(A) Increases
(B) Decreases
(C) Remains the same
(D) Cannot determine from the given information

5. Five students purchased a computer that costs \$1,000. The students split the cost equally among themselves. In order for the share per person to decrease by \$75, how many additional students would they need to share in the purchase, given that they would all share the cost equally?

(A) 3
(B) 4
(C) 6
(D) 8

6. {1, 4, 5, 5.5, 6, 6.5, 9.5}

   In the above set of numbers, the two values that are the greatest outliers from the others are removed. Once these two values are removed, what is the range of the remaining values?

   (A) 2.5
   (B) 3
   (C) 7
   (D) 8.5

7. The maximum weight a certain elevator can hold is 3,000 pounds. For a group of 15 people to go on the elevator, what is the maximum the mean of their weights could be?

   (A) 170 pounds
   (B) 190 pounds
   (C) 200 pounds
   (D) 240 pounds

8. A student had scores of 80, 90, 85, 100, 75, and 85 on his tests in a history class. If the teacher threw out his worst test grade, which of these values describing the set of his scores would change?

   (A) Mean
   (B) Median
   (C) Mode
   (D) None of the above

9. Jake has a smartwatch that helps him keep track of the number of steps he takes each day. On Monday, he walked 8,000 steps; Tuesday, 13,000; Wednesday, 7,000; and Thursday, 8,500. Which inequality expresses the number of steps, *n*, that Jake could walk on Friday so that the average for the 5 days is at least 10,000 steps per day?

   (A) $\frac{8,000+13,000+7,000+8,500+n}{5} \leq 10,000$

   (B) $\frac{8,000+13,000+7,000+8,500+n}{5} \geq 10,000$

   (C) $\frac{8,000+13,000+7,000+8,500}{n} \geq 10,000$

   (D) $\frac{8,000+13,000+7,000+8,500+n}{4} \leq 10,000$

10. The heights in inches of 10 people in a room is given below:

    {60, 49, 72, 75, 54, 58, 76, 44, 51, 53, 62}

    If someone new comes in to the room and has a height of 74 inches, which of these is an accurate statement about the range and standard deviation of the set?

    (A) Only the standard deviation would change.
    (B) Only the range would change.
    (C) Both the standard deviation and range would change.
    (D) Neither the standard deviation nor range would change.

✓ Solutions

1. **(C)** There are 6 numbers in this set, so the median will be the average of the two middle terms. If the two middle terms were 7 and 9, the median would be 8; if the two middle terms were 9 and 12, the median would be 10.5. So, x must be between 9 and 12 and must average out to 10. You can therefore solve for x by solving the following equation:

$$\frac{x+9}{2}=10 \rightarrow$$

$$x+9=20 \rightarrow$$

$$x=11$$

Thus, 11 would be the value of x that would cause the set of numbers to have a median of 10.

2. **(C)** First, modify all the fractions so they have the same denominator, 12:

$$\frac{1}{3}=\frac{4}{12}, \frac{1}{4}=\frac{3}{12}, \text{ and } \frac{1}{6}=\frac{2}{12}$$

Then, add the fractions together and divide by 3 to solve for the mean.

$$\frac{\left(\frac{4}{12}+\frac{3}{12}+\frac{2}{12}\right)}{3}=\frac{\left(\frac{9}{12}\right)}{3}=\frac{3}{12}=\frac{1}{4}$$

3. **(B)** Let us find the total number of students in the set: $8+10+15=33$. The middle value will be the 17th value, since there would be 16 values less than it and 16 values greater than it.

Since there are 8 who sold fewer than 5, and 10 students who sold between 5–10 books, the 17th term if the terms were placed in order from least to greatest would be within the range of 5–10 books. The answer is therefore 8 because it is the only number within this range.

4. **(C)** Because there are 20 students, the initial median will be the average of the 10th and 11th terms. The 10th and 11th terms will both fall between the range of 11–15 apps based on the table. If a student with 3 apps and a student with 26 apps were added to this set, they would balance each other out and there would be no impact on the median of the set. Therefore, the median of the set would remain the same.

5. **(A)** First, let's find the original cost per student by calculating the mean when there are 5 students and a total price of \$1,000:

$$\frac{1,000}{5}=200$$

So, the initial share per student is \$200. If the amount of the share per student is to decrease by \$75, the new share per student would be $200-75=125$ dollars. Set up a new calculation of the mean to solve for the number of students, x, who would need to be added to the initial 5 students to get a new average of \$125:

$$\frac{1,000}{5+x}=125 \rightarrow$$

$$1,000=125(5+x) \rightarrow$$

$$1,000=625+125x \rightarrow$$

$$375=125x \rightarrow$$

$$x=3$$

Therefore, if 3 students were added to the total, there would be a total of 8 students who could share the cost at an equal amount of \$125 a person.

6. **(A)** The two greatest outliers in the set are the values that are farthest from the mean: 1 and 9.5. If we remove these values, the new set is {4, 5, 5.5, 6, 6.5}. To calculate the range of this new set, subtract the smallest value from the largest value:

$$6.5 - 4 = 2.5$$

7. **(C)** Since the maximum weight is 3,000 pounds, divide 3,000 by 15 to find the mean under these conditions:

$$\frac{3,000}{15} = 200$$

8. **(A)** Let's see how the mean, median, and mode will be affected by this change of removing the score of 75, the worst test grade, from the set. The original set, when the numbers are put in order from least to greatest, is {75, 80, 85, 85, 90, 100}. The new set would be {80, 85, 85, 90, 100}.

Original Set: {75, 80, 85, 85, 90, 100}	New Set: {80, 85, 85, 90, 100}
Original Mean: $\frac{75+80+85+85+90+100}{6} = \frac{515}{6} \approx 85.83$	New Mean: $\frac{80+85+85+90+100}{5} = \frac{440}{5} = 88$
Original Median: {75, 80, 85, 85, 90, 100}: The third and fourth terms are both 85, so the median is 85.	New Median: {80, 85, 85, 90, 100}: The third term is 85, so the median is still 85.
Original Mode: 85 is the most frequent term.	New Mode: 85 is still the most frequent term.

Therefore, only the mean of the set will change. If you notice that the mode and median will not be affected, you can see that just the mean will be affected since removing one value that is less than the original mean will inevitably change the mean of the set.

9. **(B)** This is a question where looking ahead to the answers can help, since the answers show that you just need to set up the calculation, rather than doing it all the way to completion. Be careful to avoid careless mistakes, especially with the direction of the inequality sign. Jake wants to average *at least* 10,000 steps per day, so the average number of steps must be *greater than or equal to* 10,000: *average* ≥ 10,000. The average is calculated by adding the known values together and treating *n* as the one day that is not known. There are 5 total days including *n*. Therefore, the calculation will be:

$$\frac{8,000 + 13,000 + 7,000 + 8,500 + n}{5} \geq 10,000$$

10. **(A)** The range of the set is the difference between the least and greatest terms in the set: $76 - 44 = 32$. The range will not change if 74 were added to the set, since the values of the least and greatest numbers in the set would remain at 44 and 76.

    The standard deviation of the set *would* change since the variation of the numbers from the mean will be different with the relatively large value of 74 added to the group. Therefore, the answer is **(A)**.

Problem Solving and Data Analysis—Unit Conversion

SAT Math Strategy

Use proportions to solve simple unit conversions, and use unit cancellation to solve more complex unit conversions.

If an SAT Math problem involves a straightforward calculation between just two units, you can probably solve it using a proportion.

Example 1

There are 5,280 feet in 1 mile. If Susan runs 3.5 miles, how many feet did she run?

✓ Solution

Set up a proportion to solve for the x number of feet that Susan ran in the race. It is easier if you place the variable for which you are solving *in the numerator* so the algebra is less complex.

$$\frac{5,280 \text{ feet}}{1 \text{ mile}} = \frac{x \text{ feet}}{3.5 \text{ miles}} \rightarrow$$

Multiply both sides by 3.5 miles to solve for $x \rightarrow$

$$\frac{5,280 \text{ feet}}{1 \text{ mile}} \times 3.5 \text{ miles} = \frac{x \text{ feet}}{3.5 \text{ miles}} \times 3.5 \text{ miles} \rightarrow$$

Cancel out the miles units and the 3.5 on the right side $\rightarrow$

$$\frac{5,280 \text{ feet}}{1 \cancel{\text{mile}}} \times 3.5 \cancel{\text{miles}} = \frac{x \text{ feet}}{\cancel{3.5 \text{ miles}}} \times \cancel{3.5 \text{ miles}} \rightarrow$$

$$5,280 \text{ feet} \times 3.5 = x$$

$$18{,}480 \text{ feet} = x$$

Example 2

Ahmad has 300 U.S. dollars that he wants to convert to euros. His bank offers an exchange rate of 0.83 euros for 1 U.S. dollar. Assuming there are no fees or taxes, if Ahmad converts all 300 of his dollars to euros, how many euros will he have?

✓ Solution

Set up a proportion to solve for euros:

$$\frac{0.83 \text{ Euros}}{1 \text{ Dollar}} = \frac{x \text{ Euros}}{300 \text{ Dollars}} \rightarrow$$

Multiply both sides by 300 dollars to solve for $x \rightarrow$

$$\frac{0.83 \text{ Euros}}{1 \text{ Dollar}} \times 300 \text{ Dollars} = \frac{x \text{ Euros}}{300 \text{ Dollars}} \times 300 \text{ Dollars} \rightarrow$$

Cancel out the dollars units and the 300 on the right side →

$$\frac{0.83 \text{ Euros}}{1 \cancel{\text{Dollar}}} \times 300 \cancel{\text{Dollars}} = \frac{x \text{ Euros}}{\cancel{300 \text{ Dollars}}} \times \cancel{300 \text{ Dollars}} \rightarrow$$

$$0.83 \text{ Euros} \times 300 = x$$

$$249 \text{ Euros} = x$$

So, Ahmad would have 249 euros after the currency conversion.

Example 3

Emily took a bike ride that was 8 kilometers long. Given that there are approximately 0.6214 miles in a kilometer and 5,280 feet in a mile, approximately how many *feet* was Emily's bike ride?

Solution

Ultimately, your unit conversion will end with feet. Use *dimensional analysis* or the *unit-factor method* (different ways of labelling the same idea) to cancel out units and end with the desired unit. The ride is 8 kilometers, and there are 0.6214 miles in a kilometer and 5,280 feet in a mile. So, set up the unit conversion like this:

$$8 \text{ kilometers} \times \frac{0.6214 \text{ miles}}{1 \text{ kilometer}} \times \frac{5,280 \text{ feet}}{1 \text{ mile}} \rightarrow$$

Cancel out units that are in both the numerator and denominator:

$$8 \cancel{\text{kilometers}} \times \frac{0.6214 \cancel{\text{miles}}}{1 \cancel{\text{kilometer}}} \times \frac{5,280 \text{ feet}}{1 \cancel{\text{mile}}} \rightarrow$$

$$8 \times 0.6214 \times 5,280 \approx 26,248 \text{ feet}$$

Example 4

Timothy has 1 gallon of milk. There are approximately 3.785 liters in 1 gallon. How many milliliters of milk does Timothy have?

Solution

While the SAT will give you many conversion ratios, there are some that it will be helpful to memorize:

- 12 inches in 1 foot
- 60 seconds in 1 minute
- 60 minutes in 1 hour
- 100 centimeters in 1 meter (Prefix *centi* means "one-hundredth.")
- 1,000 millimeters in 1 meter (Prefix *milli* means "one-thousandth.")
- 1,000 milliliters in 1 liter (Prefix *milli* means "one-thousandth.")
- 1,000 meters in 1 kilometer (Prefix *kilo* means "thousand.")

In this problem, we will ultimately end up with milliliters. Use *dimensional analysis* or the *unit-factor method* to cancel out units and end with the desired unit of milliliters:

$$1\text{ gallon} \times \frac{3.785\text{ liters}}{1\text{ gallon}} \times \frac{1,000\text{ milliliters}}{1\text{ liter}} \rightarrow$$

$$1\ \cancel{\text{gallon}} \times \frac{3.785\ \cancel{\text{liters}}}{1\ \cancel{\text{gallon}}} \times \frac{1,000\text{ milliliters}}{1\ \cancel{\text{liter}}} \rightarrow$$

$$1 \times 3.785 \times 1,000 = 3,785\text{ milliliters}$$

SAT Math Questions Practice Drill—Problem Solving and Data Analysis: Unit Conversion

(If timing, take about 12 minutes to complete.)

1. Approximately how many kilometers are in a marathon, given that a marathon is 26.22 miles and that there are 1.609 kilometers in a mile?

   (A) 16.3 km
   (B) 27.8 km
   (C) 42.2 km
   (D) 74.5 km

2. The Empire State Building in New York City has a height of 1,250 feet, while if its pinnacle is included, it has a height of 1,454 feet. What is the height of just the pinnacle to the nearest whole meter given that there are 3.28 feet in 1 meter?

   (A) 62 meters
   (B) 85 meters
   (C) 204 meters
   (D) 669 meters

3. If 1 ounce of platinum sells for $700 and 1 ounce of gold sells for $1,700, how much more expensive would a pound of gold be than a pound of platinum, given that there are 16 ounces in a pound?

   (A) $7,000
   (B) $16,000
   (C) $27,200
   (D) $38,400

4. A barrel has a volume of 42 gallons. If you have 105 gallons of a liquid, what would be the equivalent number of barrels of the liquid?

   (A) 0.4 barrels
   (B) 1.5 barrels
   (C) 2.5 barrels
   (D) 6.8 barrels

5. The depth in *feet* of water, D, in a lake x days after it was dammed is given by this equation:

$$D = 0.5x + 30$$

Based on this equation, how many *inches* does the depth of the water in the lake increase each day?

(A) 0.5
(B) 3.5
(C) 6
(D) 30

6. In 1875, Matthew Webb was the first person to successfully swim across the English Channel. He took about 22 hours to make the roughly 22-mile swim. Given that there are about 1.61 kilometers in a mile, what was his approximate average swimming speed for this trip in kilometers per hour?

(A) 0.62 km/hour
(B) 1.61 km/hour
(C) 35 km/hour
(D) 44 km/hour

7. The speed of sound as it travels through rubber is approximately 60 meters per second. How fast does sound travel through rubber in kilometers per hour?

(A) Approximately 216 km/hour
(B) Approximately 642 km/hour
(C) Approximately 36,000 km/hour
(D) Approximately 216,000 km/hour

Fill-In Practice: Write your answer in the underlined blank under each question.

8. Mark rides his bicycle 30 feet in 2 seconds. At that rate, how many feet would he travel in 1 minute on his bicycle?

Answer: ________

9. The key on a map indicates that 1 inch on the map corresponds to ½ of a mile in actual distance. If the distance on the map between two points is 6 inches, how many miles apart would they be in real life?

Answer: ________

10. The number of cloves in a head of garlic is between 10 and 12. If a recipe called for 3.5 heads of garlic, what would a possible value for the number of cloves that would meet this requirement?

Answer: ________

✓ Solutions

1. **(C)** Use a proportion to solve for the number of kilometers in a marathon:

$$\frac{1.609 \text{ kilometers}}{1 \text{ mile}} = \frac{x \text{ kilometers}}{26.22 \text{ miles}} \rightarrow$$

Cross Multiply:

$$\frac{1.609 \text{ kilometers}}{1 \text{ mile}} \times 26.22 \text{ miles} = x$$

Cancel out the miles:

$$\frac{1.609 \text{ kilometers}}{1 \cancel{\text{mile}}} \times 26.22 \cancel{\text{miles}} = x \rightarrow$$

$$1.609 \text{ kilometers} \times 26.22 \approx 42.2 \text{ kilometers}$$

2. **(A)** First, determine the height of the pinnacle by itself by subtracting the height of just the building from the height of the building and pinnacle combined:

$$1,454 - 1,250 = 204$$

Then, set up a proportion to solve for the height of the pinnacle in meters:

$$\frac{1 \text{ meter}}{3.28 \text{ feet}} = \frac{x \text{ meters}}{204 \text{ feet}} \rightarrow$$

$$\frac{1 \text{ meter}}{3.28 \text{ feet}} \times 204 \text{ feet} = x \rightarrow$$

$$\frac{1 \text{ meter}}{3.28 \cancel{\text{feet}}} \times 204 \cancel{\text{feet}} = x \rightarrow$$

$$\frac{204}{3.28} \approx 62 \text{ meters}$$

3. **(B)** First, recognize that we need to convert the difference between the price of gold and platinum:

$$1,700 - 700 = 1,000$$

Then, multiply $1,000 by 16 ounces to find the total difference in price per pound:

$$1,000 \times 16 = 16,000$$

4. **(C)** Use a proportion to solve this problem:

$$\frac{1 \text{ barrel}}{42 \text{ gallons}} = \frac{x \text{ barrels}}{105 \text{ gallons}} \rightarrow$$

$$\frac{1 \text{ barrel}}{42 \text{ gallons}} \times 105 \text{ gallons} = x \rightarrow$$

$$\frac{1 \text{ barrel}}{42 \cancel{\text{gallons}}} \times 105 \cancel{\text{gallons}} = x \rightarrow$$

$$\frac{105}{42} = 2.5 \text{ barrels} = x$$

5. **(C)** The equation is written in slope-intercept form, so to see how much the depth is increasing in feet each day, look at the slope—0.5. Then, convert .5 feet to inches. Since there are 12 inches in a foot, multiply 0.5 feet by 12 inches to get the converted number of inches:

$$0.5 \times 12 = 6$$

So, each day the depth of water increases by 6 inches.

6. **(B)** We want to have the units result in kilometers per hour, so use unit cancellation to determine this speed:

$$\frac{22 \text{ miles}}{22 \text{ hours}} \times \frac{1.61 \text{ kilometers}}{1 \text{ mile}} \rightarrow$$

$$\frac{22 \cancel{\text{miles}}}{22 \text{ hours}} \times \frac{1.61 \text{ kilometers}}{1 \cancel{\text{mile}}} \rightarrow$$

$$\frac{22}{22} \times 1.61 = 1.61 \frac{\text{km}}{\text{hr}}$$

Alternatively, you could have noticed that the speed is 1 mile per hour, so just multiply 1 mile per hour by 1.61.

7. **(A)** Use unit-cancellation to solve for the speed in kilometers per hour:

$$\frac{60 \text{ meters}}{1 \text{ second}} \times \frac{1 \text{ kilometer}}{1{,}000 \text{ meters}} \times \frac{3{,}600 \text{ seconds}}{1 \text{ hour}} =$$

$$\frac{60 \cancel{\text{meters}}}{1 \cancel{\text{second}}} \times \frac{1 \text{ kilometer}}{1{,}000 \cancel{\text{meters}}} \times \frac{3{,}600 \cancel{\text{seconds}}}{1 \text{ hour}} \approx 216 \frac{\text{km}}{\text{hr}}$$

8. **900** Use unit-cancellation to solve for the distance he will travel in 1 minute:

$$\frac{30 \text{ feet}}{2 \text{ seconds}} \times \frac{60 \text{ seconds}}{1 \text{ minute}} \rightarrow$$

$$\frac{30 \text{ feet}}{2 \cancel{\text{seconds}}} \times \frac{60 \cancel{\text{seconds}}}{1 \text{ minute}} \rightarrow$$

$$\frac{30 \times 60}{2} = 900 \frac{\text{feet}}{\text{minute}}$$

9. **3** Use a proportion to solve for the miles:

$$\frac{0.5 \text{ mile}}{1 \text{ inch}} = \frac{x \text{ miles}}{6 \text{ inches}} \rightarrow$$

$$\frac{0.5 \text{ mile}}{1 \text{ inch}} \times 6 \text{ inches} = x \rightarrow$$

$$\frac{0.5 \text{ mile}}{1 \cancel{\text{inch}}} \times 6 \cancel{\text{inches}} = x \rightarrow$$

$$0.5 \times 6 = 3 \text{ miles} = x$$

10. **Any number greater than or equal to 35 and less than or equal to 42.** Find the lower number by multiplying 10 by 3.5, and the greater number by multiplying 12 by 3.5:

$$10 \times 3.5 = 35$$

$$12 \times 3.5 = 42$$

So, the range of garlic cloves would be between 35 and 42, inclusive (meaning including 35 and 42 also).

Problem Solving and Data Analysis—Percentages

Percentage Essentials

Percent calculations are heavily emphasized on the SAT Math. To be successful on percent problems, there are several key formulas it is helpful to memorize.

$$\boxed{\frac{\text{Part}}{\text{Whole}} \times 100 = \text{Percent}}$$

In most situations you will come across, the "part" will be the smaller number and the "whole" will be the larger number.

Example 1

If there are 200 students in a graduating class, and 40 of them graduated with honors, what percent of students in the class graduated with honors?

Solution

The "part" is 40, and the "whole" is 200. Plug these values into the above formula to calculate the percent:

$$\frac{\text{Part}}{\text{Whole}} \times 100 = \text{Percent} \rightarrow$$

$$\frac{40}{200} \times 100 = 0.2 \times 100 = 20\%$$

Example 2

If 60% is considered a passing grade on a particular test, and the test has 30 questions, how many questions would a test taker have to answer correctly to pass the test?

Solution

Use 60% as the "percent," and use 30 as the "whole," since 30 represents the total number of questions. Then, use the percent formula to solve for the "part"—the number of questions that must be answered correctly to pass:

$$\frac{\text{Part}}{\text{Whole}} \times 100 = \text{Percent} \rightarrow$$

$$\frac{\text{Part}}{30} \times 100 = 60 \rightarrow$$

$$\text{Part} = \frac{60 \times 30}{100} = \frac{1,800}{100} = 18$$

So, one would need to answer at least 18 questions correctly to pass the test.

Example 3

If 30% of the cars in a parking lot have bumper stickers, what fraction of the cars in the parking lot would have bumper stickers?

✓ Solution

Manipulate the percent formula so we can convert this situation to a fraction:

$$\frac{\text{Part}}{\text{Whole}} \times 100 = \text{Percent} \rightarrow$$

$$\frac{\text{Part}}{\text{Whole}} = \frac{\text{Percent}}{100}$$

Use 30 as the percent, then reduce the fraction:

$$\frac{30}{100} = \frac{3}{10}$$

So, $\frac{3}{10}$ of the cars in the parking lot have bumper stickers.

› Example 4

Michal took a test that had 20 points, and she earned 2 points of extra credit in addition to a perfect score on the test. What was her percentage score?

✓ Solution

In this situation, the "part" will be 22 to include the perfect score and the extra credit. The "whole" will be 20, given that total number of points on the test. So, calculate her percentage scores as follows:

$$\frac{\text{Part}}{\text{Whole}} \times 100 = \text{Percent} \rightarrow$$

$$\frac{22}{20} \times 100 = 110\%$$

For problems like these, it can be helpful to know the conversions of fractions to percentages off the top of your head:

$$10\% = \frac{1}{10}$$

$$25\% = \frac{1}{4}$$

$$50\% = \frac{1}{2}$$

$$75\% = \frac{3}{4}$$

The part/whole formula will always work, so you can stick to that approach if you are more comfortable. There are, however, a number of ways to work with percentages more efficiently depending on the type of problem.

> When asked to find the percent of a number, take the percent and move the decimal point *to the left two spots and then multiply.*

Example 1

What is 75% of 500?

Solution

Rather than using the previous percent formula to solve, start by taking the 75% and moving the decimal point to the left by two spots:

$$75.0 \rightarrow 0.75$$

Now multiply by 500:

$$500 \times 0.75 = 375$$

So, 375 represents 75% of 500.

Example 2

What is 4% of 20?

Solution

Move the decimal point of 4% to the left by two spots:

$$4.0 \rightarrow 0.04$$

Now multiply by 20:

$$0.04 \times 20 = 0.8$$

So, 0.8 is 4% of 20.

Example 3

What is 150% of 70?

Solution

Move the decimal point of 150 to the left by two spots:

$$150.0 \rightarrow 1.5$$

Then, multiply by 70:

$$70 \times 1.5 = 105$$

Practice

1. What is 40% of 240?
2. Two out of every five students at a school pack their lunches each day. What percent of students at the school pack their lunches each day?

3. What is 5% of 125?
4. With extra credit, Chris had a 105% as his grade for the semester in a class. If he scored 100% on every assignment throughout the semester, and there were a total of 400 points from all the regular assignments (not including extra credit), how many points in extra credit did he get that semester?
5. If 60 employees in a business work part-time, and these employees represent 30% of all the employees at the business, how many total employees does the business have?

✓ Solutions

1. $0.4 \times 240 = 96$
2. $\frac{2}{5} \times 100 = 40\%$
3. $0.05 \times 125 = 6.25$
4. Just take 5% of the total points from the regular assignments to find the points in extra credit he earned:

$$0.05 \times 400 = 20$$

5. Plug in values to the general percentage formula to solve for the total number of employees:

$$\frac{\text{Part}}{\text{Whole}} \times 100 = \text{Percent} \rightarrow$$

$$\frac{60}{\text{Whole}} \times 100 = 30 \rightarrow$$

Cross multiply →

$$\frac{60}{30} \times 100 = \text{Whole} \rightarrow$$

$$200 = \text{Whole}$$

So, the business has a total of 200 employees.

Percent Increase and Decrease

To find the percent by which something has increased or decreased, use this formula, being careful on what you plug in for the "original" and "new" values:

$$\frac{\text{New} - \text{Original}}{\text{Original}} \times 100 = \text{Percent Change}$$

If the value of the percent change is positive, the change is increasing. If the value is negative, the change is decreasing.

› Example 1

Melanie's height is 40 inches. A year later, her height is 44 inches. By what percent did her height increase?

✓ Solution

The original value is 40, and the new value is 44, so the calculation is

$$\frac{\text{New} - \text{Original}}{\text{Original}} \times 100 = \text{Percent Change}$$

$$\frac{44 - 40}{40} \times 100 = \frac{4}{40} \times 100 = 10\%$$

So, Melanie's height has increased by 10%.

› Example 2

William has \$800 in his checking account. If he spends \$200 out of his checking account, by what percent did his checking account decrease?

✓ Solution

The new value is \$600 (\$800 – \$200), and the original value is \$800, so the calculation is

$$\frac{\text{New} - \text{Original}}{\text{Original}} \times 100 = \text{Percent Change} \rightarrow$$

$$\frac{600 - 800}{2} \times 100 = \text{Percent Change} \rightarrow$$

$$\frac{-200}{800} \times 100 = -25\%$$

Since this value is *negative*, there has been a 25% *decrease* in his checking account.

What are easy ways to calculate the new amount if we know the percent by which something has increased or decreased?

When the percentage is expressed as a decimal, r:
Increased Total = (Original Amount) × $(1 + r)$
Decreased Total = (Original Amount) × $(1 - r)$

› Example 1

If the cost of a gallon of milk, originally at \$2 a gallon, increased by 20%, what would be the new cost of a gallon of milk?

✓ Solution

Use the increased total formula, plugging in 2 for the original amount, and using 0.20 as the r since we must express 20% as a decimal:

$$\text{Increased Total} = (\text{Original Amount}) \times (1 + r) \rightarrow$$

$$\text{New Price} = (2) \times (1 + 0.2) = 2 \times 1.2 = 2.40$$

So, the new price of a gallon of milk would be \$2.40.

Example 2

If a toy is originally \$30 and is on sale for 40% off, what would its new price be?

Solution

Use the decreased total formula, plugging in 30 for the original amount and 0.40 for r since 40% must be expressed as a decimal:

$$\text{Decreased Total} = (\text{Original Amount}) \times (1 - r) \rightarrow$$
$$\text{Decreased Total} = (30) \times (1 - 0.40) = 30 \times 0.6 = 18$$

Therefore, the discounted price of the toy is \$18.

Practice

1. What number is 60% more than 40?
2. The amount of monthly rainfall in a town in January was 10 inches, and in February it was 7 inches. By what percent did the monthly rainfall decrease?
3. A car originally sells for \$20,000, but is on sale for 10% off. How much money would a buyer save by purchasing the car on sale? (Do not include sales tax in your calculations.)
4. During the school year, Ashra would read 3 hours a week for fun. Over the summer, she would read 9 hours a week for fun. By what percent did her weekly leisure reading in the summer increase compared to what she did during the school year?
5. A book typically sells for \$30, but there is a 20% discount. After including a 7% sales tax, what is the sale price of the book?

Solutions

1. Use this formula, Increased Total = (Original Amount) × (1 + r), plugging in 40 as the original amount and 0.4 as r, since the percent must be expressed as a decimal:

$$\text{Increased Total} = (\text{Original Amount}) \times (1 + r) \rightarrow$$
$$\text{Increased Total} = (40) \times (1 + 0.6) = 40 \times 1.6 = 64$$

2. Use this formula, $\frac{\text{New} - \text{Original}}{\text{Original}} \times 100 = \text{Percent Change}$, plugging in 10 as the original amount and 7 as the new amount to solve for the percent it has changed:

$$\frac{\text{New} - \text{Original}}{\text{Original}} \times 100 = \text{Percent Change} \rightarrow$$
$$\frac{7 - 10}{10} \times 100 = \frac{-3}{10} \times 100 = -30\%$$

Since this is negative, the monthly rainfall has decreased by 30%.

3. Rather than using the percent change formula, recognize that you simply need to calculate 10% of \$20,000 to find the amount saved:

$$20,000 \times 0.10 = 2,000$$

So, the amount of money saved is \$2,000.

4. Calculate the percent increase using this formula, $\frac{\text{New} - \text{Original}}{\text{Original}} \times 100 = \text{Percent Change}$, plugging in 3 for the original amount and 9 for the new amount:

$$\frac{\text{New} - \text{Original}}{\text{Original}} \times 100 = \text{Percent Change} \rightarrow$$

$$\frac{9-3}{3} \times 100 = \frac{6}{3} \times 100 = 200\%$$

Since this is positive, there is a 200% increase in her weekly leisurely reading.

5. First, use this formula to find the discounted price:

$$\text{Decreased Total} = (\text{Original Amount}) \times (1 - r)$$

Use 30 as the original amount and r as 0.2 to represent the 20% discount:

$$\text{Decreased Total} = (30) \times (1 - 0.2) \rightarrow$$

$$\text{Decreased Total} = 30 \times 0.8 = 24$$

Now, use Increased Total = (Original Amount) $\times (1 + r)$ to find the price after adding the 7% sales tax, using 24 as the original amount and 0.07 as the r (since 7% would be expressed as a decimal):

$$\text{Increased Total} = (\text{Original Amount}) \times (1 + r) \rightarrow$$

$$\text{Increased Total} = (24) \times (1 + 0.07) = 24 \times 1.07 = 25.68$$

So, the sale price after tax is added is \$25.68.

Simple Interest

The SAT will frequently test your skill in calculating how interest applied over time will affect the amount. First, *simple interest* enables you to calculate the interest over a set period of time.

Simple Interest

$$I = P \times r \times t$$

I = Amount of Interest
P = Principal (Original Amount)
r = Interest rate expressed as a decimal
t = Time period the interest is applied (usually years)

Example 1

Andrew has \$500 in his savings account, and it receives 1% interest over a year. How much interest would he have accumulated after the end of the year?

✓ Solution

Use the formula $I = P \times r \times t$ to solve for the amount of interest. The principal is \$500, the interest rate expressed as a decimal is 0.01, and the time period is one year.

$$I = P \times r \times t \rightarrow$$

$$I = 500 \times 0.01 \times 1 = 5$$

So, Andrew would earn \$5 in interest in one year.

› Example 2

Bridget's home price increases by 4% in simple interest (not compounded) over a three-year period. If her home at the beginning of the three-year period costs $100,000, what is the price at the end of the period?

✓ Solution

Use $I = P \times r \times t$ to find the amount of interest over the three-year period. The principal is $100,000, the rate is 0.04, and the time period is 3:

$$I = P \times r \times t \rightarrow$$
$$I = 100{,}00 \times 0.04 \times 3 = 12{,}000$$

Then, add 12,000 to the original price to find out the price of the house at the end of the period:

$$100{,}000 + 12{,}000 = 112{,}000$$

So, the price of her house after three years would be $112,000.

Compound Interest

More frequently, the SAT Math will ask about *compound interest*:

> **Compound Interest**
>
> $$A = P\left(1 + \frac{r}{n}\right)^{nt}$$
>
> $A =$ Future Value
>
> $P =$ Initial Value (Principal)
>
> $r =$ Interest Rate Expressed as a Decimal (r is positive if increasing, negative if decreasing)
>
> $t =$ Time
>
> $n =$ Number of Times Interest is Compounded over Time Period t

› Example 1

A savings bond has an initial value of $500. The interest on the bond is 4%, compounded annually. What is the value of the savings bond after 2 years?

✓ Solution

Use the compound interest formula to solve. The initial value is $500, the interest rate expressed as a decimal is 0.04, the time is 2 years, and the number of times it is compounded each year is 1.

$$A = P\left(1 + \frac{r}{n}\right)^{nt} \rightarrow$$
$$A = 500\left(1 + \frac{.04}{1}\right)^{(1\times 2)} \rightarrow$$
$$A = 500(1.04)^2 = 540.80$$

So, the savings bond would have a value of $540.80 after a 2-year time period.

Example 2

The depth in a lake is 40 meters, and is decreasing by 1.2% each month, compounded. After 1 year, what will the depth of the lake be to the nearest hundredth of a meter?

Solution

Use the compound interest formula, with 40 as P, -0.012 as r (since the depth is decreasing), n as 12 (since there are 12 months in a year), and t as 1 since there is 1 year.

$$A = P\left(1+\frac{r}{n}\right)^{nt} \rightarrow$$

$$A = 40\left(1+\frac{-0.012}{12}\right)^{12(1)} \rightarrow$$

$$A = 40(0.999)^{12} \approx 39.52$$

So, the depth of the lake after 1 year to the nearest hundredth of a meter is 39.52 meters.

SAT Math Strategy

In order to visualize percentage changes with variables, use 100 as an initial value.

Example

The price, P, after n years for a television that initially costs x dollars is given in the function below.

$$P = xk^n$$

If the price of a television decreases by 10% each year, what is the value of the constant k?

(A) 0.1
(B) 0.9
(C) 10
(D) 90

Solution

Most of the SAT Math problems you encounter will have concrete numbers in them. On the occasion that you have one with pure variables, it can often be difficult to visualize the potential changes. To make things easier, use 100 as an initial value—that way you can efficiently calculate the percent change from the initial value.

With this problem, let's then use 100 as the initial value for x. If the initial value decreases by 10%, it would be 90 the following year. So, we can plug in 90 for P, 100 for x, and 1 for n, then solve for k:

$$P = xk^n \rightarrow$$

$$90 = 100k^1 \rightarrow$$

$$90 = 100k \rightarrow$$

$$\frac{90}{100} = k \rightarrow$$

$$k = 0.9$$

So, the answer is **(B)**, 0.9 as the k value.

SAT Math Questions Practice Drill #1—Problem Solving and Data Analysis: Percentages

(If timing, take about 12 minutes to complete.)

1. What is 150% of 3,000?

(A) 1,500
(B) 2,000
(C) 4,500
(D) 5,500

2. At a certain university, 25% of graduating seniors earned an honors diploma. What is the number of students graduating with an honors diploma if there were a total of 480 graduating seniors at the university?

(A) 100
(B) 120
(C) 200
(D) 600

3. If a computer that regularly costs $800 is on sale for 20% off, what would its sale price be (do not include sales tax in your calculation)?

(A) $160
(B) $200
(C) $600
(D) $640

Average Commute Time from Home to Work	Percentage of Respondents
Less than 10 minutes	25%
10–30 minutes	45%
Over 30 minutes	30%

4. If the number of respondents with an average commute of greater than 30 minutes is 240, how many people all together responded to this survey?

(A) 480
(B) 620
(C) 800
(D) 960

5. Sam purchases a total of 25 gift cards for his friends, with the gift cards being for retail stores or for restaurants. If he purchases 50% more retail store gift cards than restaurant gift cards, how many retail store gift cards did he purchase?

(A) 12.5
(B) 15
(C) 20
(D) 37.5

6. In a park, 15% of the parkgoers were children, 45% were male adults, and the remaining 8 were adult females. How many parkgoers were there all together?

(A) 20
(B) 24
(C) 30
(D) 36

7. Chelsea has a temperature of 98.6°F. The next day, she has a fever, with a temperature of 103.2°F. By what percentage, calculated to the nearest tenth of a percent, did her temperature increase from the first day to the second day?

(A) 4.5%
(B) 4.7%
(C) 5.1%
(D) 5.4%

8. The U.S. stock market has returned a historical average of approximately 10% per year. If this rate of return were to continue into the future, what function would model the value, V, of an initial investment of V_O in the stock market t years from now?

(A) $V(t) = V_O(10)^t$
(B) $V(t) = V_O(110)^t$
(C) $V(t) = V_O(1.1)^t$
(D) $V(t) = V_O(0.1)^t$

9. A new car is on sale for 15% off the sticker price. Maxwell is trading in his old car for a total of $5,000—all of this counts as a credit toward the price paid for a new car purchase. Assuming there is no sales tax, if the car has a sticker price of x dollars, what amount will Maxwell have to pay, P, for a new car, accounting for the sale discount and the trade-in credit?

(A) $P = 0.85x - 5,000$
(B) $P = 0.85 + 5,000$
(C) $P = 0.15x - 5,000$
(D) $P = 0.15x + 5,000$

10. The gravitational force, F, is related to the gravitational constant, G, mass of one object, m_1, and mass of another object, m_2, and the distance between the centers of the objects, r, using the following equation:

$$F = \frac{Gm_1m_2}{r^2}$$

By what percent would the gravitational force between two objects change if the distance between them were doubled and the other quantities remained the same?

(A) It would decrease by 50%.
(B) It would decrease by 75%.
(C) It would increase by 100%.
(D) It would increase by 200%.

✓ Solutions

1. **(C)** Take 150 and move the decimal point over two spots to the left. Then multiply this by 3,000:

$$1.5 \times 3,000 = 4,500$$

2. **(B)** Calculate 25% of 480 by moving the decimal point two spots to the left in 25, then multiplying it by 480:

$$0.25 \times 480 = 120$$

3. **(D)** Use the formula Decreased Total = (Original Amount) × $(1 - r)$, with 800 as the original amount and r as 0.2:

$$\text{Decreased Total} = (\text{Original Amount}) \times (1 - r) \rightarrow$$
$$\text{Decreased Total} = 800 \times (1 - 0.2) = 800 \times 0.8 = 640$$

4. **(C)** Use the formula $\frac{\text{Part}}{\text{Whole}} \times 100 = \text{Percent}$ to calculate the total number of survey participants. Let's use x as the unknown number of total survey participants, 30 as the percent, and 240 as the "part":

$$\frac{\text{Part}}{\text{Whole}} \times 100 = \text{Percent} \rightarrow$$
$$\frac{240}{x} \times 100 = 30 \rightarrow$$

Cross multiply →

$$\frac{240}{30} \times 100 = x \rightarrow$$
$$8 \times 100 = x \rightarrow$$
$$800 = x$$

5. **(B)** Set up an equation modeling the situation. The total number of gift cards is 25, and he purchased 50% more retail cards than restaurant cards. Use x as the number of restaurant cards and use $1.5x$ as the number of retail cards, since it is 50% more:

$$x + 1.5x = 25 \rightarrow$$
$$2.5x = 25 \rightarrow$$
$$x = 10$$

Then, using the formula Number of Retail Gift Cards = (Original Amount) × $(1 + r)$, calculate the number of retail gift cards purchased; 10 will be the original amount, and r will be 0.5:

$$\text{Number of Retail Gift Cards} = (\text{Original Amount}) \times (1 + r) \rightarrow$$
$$\text{Number of Retail Gift Cards} = 10 \times 1.5 = 15$$

Therefore, he will purchase 15 retail store gift cards. You could also try plugging in the answers to see which would fit the criteria.

6. **(A)** The percent of female parkgoers will be what remains after subtracting the children and males:

$$100\% - 45\% - 15\% = 40\%$$

So, 40% of the parkgoers are female, and this number will be 8. Now, we can solve for the total number of parkgoers by using the equation $\frac{\text{Part}}{\text{Whole}} \times 100 = \text{Percent}$; let's use x as the "whole," 40 as the "percent," and 8 as the "part."

$$\frac{\text{Part}}{\text{Whole}} \times 100 = \text{Percent} \rightarrow$$

$$\frac{8}{x} \times 100 = 40 \rightarrow$$

Cross Multiply →

$$\frac{8}{40} \times 100 = x \rightarrow$$

$$0.2 \times 100 = x \rightarrow$$

$$20 = x$$

So, the total number of parkgoers is 20.

7. **(B)** Use the formula $\frac{\text{New} - \text{Original}}{\text{Original}} \times 100 = \text{Percent Change}$ to calculate the percent change. The original value is 98.6 and the new value is 103.2:

$$\frac{\text{New} - \text{Original}}{\text{Original}} \times 100 = \text{Percent Change} \rightarrow$$

$$\frac{103.2 - 98.6}{98.6} \times 100 \rightarrow$$

$$\frac{4.6}{98.6} \times 100 \approx 4.7\%$$

8. **(C)** Use the formula $A = P\left(1 + \frac{r}{n}\right)^{nt}$ to model the future value of the investment. $V(t)$ will be A, P will be V_O, r will be 0.1, n will be 1, and t will stay as a variable.

$$A = P\left(1 + \frac{r}{n}\right)^{nt} \rightarrow$$

$$V(t) = V_O\left(1 + \frac{0.1}{1}\right)^{1(t)} \rightarrow$$

$$V(t) = V_O(1.1)^t$$

You could also solve this by looking at what makes the answer choices different and noticing that the only one that would show a 10% increase is choice **(C)**.

9. **(A)** Take a 15% discount off the price of the new car to find what he will have to pay before the trade-in value is included:

$$\text{Decreased Total} = (\text{Original Amount}) \times (1 - r) \rightarrow$$

$$\text{Discounted Price} = x \times (1 - 0.15) = 0.85x$$

Then, subtract $5,000 from the price paid to include the trade-in value:

$$P = 0.85x - 5{,}000$$

10. **(B)** In doing the comparison, keep everything constant that remains constant, and change only what is different. The gravitational force, F, and the distance, r, are the only things that will change. Consider the original force:

$$F = \frac{Gm_1 m_2}{r^2}$$

Now, double the distance, r, and see how the original force would change:

$$F = \frac{Gm_1 m_2}{r^2} \rightarrow$$

$$\text{New } F = \frac{Gm_1 m_2}{(2r)^2} = \frac{Gm_1 m_2}{4r^2} = \frac{1}{4}\left(\frac{Gm_1 m_2}{r^2}\right) = \frac{1}{4}F$$

So, the new force is $\frac{1}{4}$ of the original value, which means it has decreased by $\frac{3}{4}$ its original value. Convert $\frac{3}{4}$ to a percentage by using a proportion:

$$\frac{3}{4} = \frac{x}{100} \rightarrow$$

$$0.75 = \frac{x}{100} \rightarrow$$

$$75\% = x$$

Therefore, the gravitational force between the two objects would decrease by 75% if the distance between them were doubled.

SAT Math Questions Practice Drill #2—Problem Solving and Data Analysis: Percentages

(If timing, take about 12 minutes to complete.)

Fill-In Practice: Write your answer in the underlined blank under each question.

1. What number is 130% of 50?

   Answer: ________

2. In the United States in 2019, approximately 62% of utility electricity came from fossil fuels, 20% from nuclear, and 18% from renewable sources. What fraction of U.S. utility electricity in 2019 came from nuclear?

   Answer: ________

3. A wind turbine has a maximum electrical generating capacity of 200 kilowatts per hour, and it operates on average at 25% of this maximum capacity. If the turbine operates at its average capacity for an entire day, how many kilowatts of electricity would it produce?

   Answer: ________

Mascot Preference	Percent of Students Who Prefer Mascot
Tiger	10%
Lion	15%
Bear	30%
Eagle	25%
Dog	20%

4. A college had all of its students vote on their preference for a new school mascot. If the number of students who preferred Bear exceeded the number who preferred Dog by 240 students, how many students selected Eagle?

   Answer: ________

5. A toy store sells only dolls and games; 70% of the toys it sells are dolls and 30% are games. The store sells a total of 400 toys. How many more dolls than games does the store sell?

   Answer: ________

Multiple-Choice Practice

6. A house was initially listed for sale at \$200,000. After three months, the sellers still had not sold it and decided to drop the price by 15%. What would the new price be?

   (A) \$170,000
   (B) \$185,000
   (C) \$215,000
   (D) \$230,000

7. A school district is doing a ten-year projection of its student enrollment. If at the start of the ten years there are 2,000 students in the district, and the student enrollment increases by 5% each year, what would be the enrollment *t* years from now?

   (A) $2,000(1.5)^t$
   (B) $2,000(1.05)^t$
   (C) $2,000(.05)^t$
   (D) $2,000(5)^t$

8. In the year 2010, New York City had a population density of 27,016 people per square mile, and San Francisco had a population density of 17,246 people per square mile. The population density in San Francisco was what percent lower than the population density in New York in 2010, calculated to the nearest tenth of a percent?

   (A) 36.2%
   (B) 41.6%
   (C) 53.4%
   (D) 63.8%

9. The elimination half-life of a medicine is the amount of time it takes for the concentration of the medicine in the body to be reduced by half. If a particular medicine starts at a dose of 100 mg that is fully absorbed in the body and has an elimination half-life of 8 hours, how much of the medicine remains in the body after 1 day?

   (A) 6.25 mg
   (B) 12.5 mg
   (C) 25 mg
   (D) 36 mg

10. One serving of a cereal is $\frac{2}{3}$ of a cup and has 20% of the daily recommended amount of only fiber, which is 6 grams. If another cereal has a serving size of 1 cup, how many grams of fiber should it have to provide 30% of the daily value of fiber?

   (A) 4 grams
   (B) 6 grams
   (C) 9 grams
   (D) 12 grams

✓ Solutions

1. **65** Move the decimal point in 130 to the left two spots, then multiply by 50:

$$1.3 \times 50 = 65$$

2. **0.2 or $\frac{1}{5}$** Convert the 20% from nuclear to a percentage by reducing the fraction to its simplest form:

$$\frac{20}{100} \rightarrow \frac{1}{5}$$

This could also be expressed as a decimal, 0.2.

3. **1,200** Multiply the number of kilowatts per hour, 200, by 0.25 to get the 25% operational level. Then, multiply this by 24 since there are 24 hours in a day:

$$200 \times 0.25 \times 24 = 1,200$$

So, it would produce 1,200 kilowatts of electricity in a day.

4. **600** The Bear students are 30% of the total, and the Dog students are 20% of the total. The difference between them is 10%, so 10% of the total is 240. Multiply 240 by 10 to get the total number of students (since 10% multiplied by 10 is 100%):

$$240 \times 10 = 2,400$$

Then, take 25% of the total:

$$0.25 \times 2,400 = 600$$

5. **160** Calculate the number of dolls sold (70% of 400):

$$0.7 \times 400 = 280$$

Then, calculate the number of games sold (30% of 400):

$$0.3 \times 400 = 120$$

Then, subtract 120 from 280 to find how many more dolls are sold than games:

$$280 - 120 = 160$$

Alternatively, if you notice the difference between them must equal 40% of the total toys sold, you could just take 40% of 400 and get the same result of 160.

6. **(A)** Calculate the discounted price by using this formula,

Decreased Total = (Original Amount) × (1 − *r*), with 200,000 as the original amount and *r* as 0.15:

$$\text{Decreased Total} = (\text{Original Amount}) \times (1 - r) \rightarrow$$
$$\text{Sale Price} = 200,000 \times (1 - 0.15) = 200,000 \times 0.85 = 170,000$$

7. **(B)** Use the formula $A = P\left(1 + \frac{r}{n}\right)^{nt}$ to determine what the enrollment would be. *A* represents the enrollment, *P* is the original number of 2,000 students, *r* is 0.05 (5% expressed as a decimal), *n* is 1 since the compounding is annual, and *t* will remain a variable:

$$A = P\left(1 + \frac{r}{n}\right)^{nt} \rightarrow$$
$$\text{Enrollment} = 2,000\left(1 + \frac{0.05}{1}\right)^{(1)t} \rightarrow$$
$$\text{Enrollment} = 2,000(1.05)^{t}$$

8. **(A)** Use the formula $\frac{\text{New} - \text{Original}}{\text{Original}} \times 100 = \text{Percent Change}$ to calculate the percent difference between the population density of New York City and San Francisco. The "original" value will be 27,016 and the "new" will be 17,246:

$$\frac{\text{New} - \text{Original}}{\text{Original}} \times 100 = \text{Percent Change} \rightarrow$$
$$\frac{17,246 - 27,016}{27,016} \times 100 \rightarrow$$
$$\frac{-9,770}{27,016} \times 100 \approx -36.2\%$$

Since this is negative, the population density in San Francisco is about 36.2% lower than it is in New York City.

9. **(B)** During a one-day period of 24 hours, the medicine will have gone through three half-life cycles, since each half-life cycle is 8 hours and 8 goes into 24 three times. So, to find out how much of the medicine is left after three half-life cycles, take 50% of the original amount of 100 three times:

$$100 \times 0.5 \times 0.5 \times 0.5 = 12.5$$

10. **(C)** Sort out the essential information here, as there is irrelevant information given. The serving sizes of the cereal are not important—what is important is providing the correct amount of fiber. The first cereal provides 20% of the daily value of fiber in its serving; the second cereal provides 30% of the daily value of fiber in its serving. Set up a proportion to solve for *x*, the number of grams of fiber in the second cereal:

$$\frac{30}{20} = \frac{x}{6} \rightarrow$$
$$1.5 = \frac{x}{6} \rightarrow$$
$$6 \times 1.5 = 9 = x$$

Problem Solving and Data Analysis—Surveys

Surveys are a part of everyday life, and the SAT will assess your skill in interpreting surveys. One of the biggest things emphasized will be determining whether a sampling method is appropriate.

Sampling Methods

> **SAT Math Strategy**
>
> In general, to get the best results in a survey, have the sample be as large and as random as possible. The larger and more random the survey, the less the potential bias will be in the results.

Let's first look at some ways a survey could be POORLY conducted.

- **Sample is chosen non-randomly:**
  - Example: Researcher interviews only parents and caregivers at a playground on their thoughts about increased funding for extracurricular activities at schools to determine what all the citizens in the community think about increased extracurricular funding. *Why is this problematic?* If the researcher is interested in sampling the community as a whole, by limiting the respondents to parents and caregivers who have congregated at a playground, the researcher will oversample those who are already interested in children's activities and/or have children.
  - Example: A city worker samples city residents who have memberships to the city's community center about whether they would support a tax levy for an additional city community center. *Why is this problematic?* If the respondents are all members of the city's community center, they are using this service already. So, it is more likely they will support increased funding for a city service they enjoy. The worker should instead include respondents who are not already members of the community center.
- **Participants can volunteer:**
  - Example: A politician has a survey on her website asking whether she or her opponent won a political debate. *Why is this problematic?* Supporters are more likely to be on her website and believe their preferred candidate—i.e., the politician conducting the survey—won the debate. This will result in a sample of respondents skewed toward those who already supported the candidate.
  - Example: A theme park worker asks people who are leaving the theme park to complete a ten-minute customer survey about their experience. *Why is this problematic?* This will result in a sample skewed toward those who have the time to complete the survey and feel passionately enough about their experience (for good or for bad) to want to answer questions.
- **Sample size is too small:**
  - Example: A student, who lives in a city of 100,000 people, surveys four city residents about their favorite restaurant in the city and draws conclusions about the city's favorite restaurant. *Why is this problematic?* Four people is too small of a sample when the population of the city is 100,000.

Now, let's consider some ways a survey could be conducted WELL.

- **Responses are randomly collected.**
  - Example: To survey a group of 1,000 people, a random number generator selects which of the 1,000 people will be respondents.
  - Example: To select 100 respondents for a political survey in a state, a researcher randomly selects phone numbers from a database of all mobile phones and landlines in the state.
- **The sample size is sufficiently large.**
  - Example: To predict the winner of an upcoming senatorial election, a random sample of 1,000 likely voters is conducted.

- **All groups in a survey are fairly represented.**
  - Example: To test the effectiveness of a medicine in the population as a whole, a university ensures that there are sufficient patients in the study from different genders, ages, and ethnicities.
  - Example: To determine the popularity of a shift in the school schedule among staff members, a school superintendent ensures that adequate representation from all types of school district workers is given—teachers, administrators, custodians, bus drivers, etc.

Use *margin of error* to quantify the quality of a survey's conclusions. Margin of error is the maximum expected difference between the actual parameter and the sample parameter. If a survey is conducted poorly, it will have a HIGH margin of error. If it is conducted well, it will have a LOW margin of error.

Example

If a pollster conducts a poll that says 40% of the voters will vote in favor of Candidate 1, with a 3% margin of error, which of the following could be the actual value of the percent of votes cast in the election for Candidate 1?

(A) 35%
(B) 38%
(C) 44%
(D) 47%

Solution

Since the margin of error is 3%, that means that the actual results are projected to be between $\pm 3\%$ of 40%, so between 37% and 43%. So, the correct answer is choice **(B)**, since 38% falls within this range.

Drawing Conclusions

SAT Math Strategy

Limit generalizations about a survey to what is directly supported by the results.

Example 1

A researcher asks 100 randomly selected survey participants in a city their favorite place for outdoor exercise. The survey has a low response rate, and the researcher concludes that the residents are not exercising sufficiently and that a "Get Outdoors Health Campaign" is needed to motivate city residents to exercise outdoors. Is this conclusion warranted based on the given information?

✓ **Solution**

No, it is not supported by the given information since there are many potential reasons why the response rate to the survey could be low:

- Perhaps the deadline to return the survey was too short.
- Perhaps the surveys did not reach the participants.
- Perhaps the potential respondents did not want to participate in research.

Moreover, the survey did not ask participants if they exercise outside—instead, it only asked their favorite location to do so. Given what the survey asked, a conclusion about whether or not city residents are exercising outside and need to be motivated with an advertising campaign cannot be drawn.

› **Example 2**

A city worker wants to determine the percent of the city's residents that are fluent in both Spanish and English. The worker writes the survey in Spanish and mails it to 400 randomly selected addresses in the city. Thirty of the surveys are returned, and 90% of them state that their household members are fluent in both Spanish and English. Would it be correct to generalize that 90% of the town's residents are fluent in both Spanish and English?

✓ **Solution**

No, because of the survey design. If household members were not able to read Spanish, they would not be able to understand the survey and could not respond. Therefore, households in which the residents were only fluent in English would be far less likely to be included in the results. Households that were able to read Spanish would understand the instructions and would be much more likely to respond, skewing the results to show a higher proportion of bilingual households.

SAT Math Questions Practice Drill—Problem Solving and Data Analysis: Surveys

(If timing, take about 12 minutes to complete.)

1. To find out which world language they wanted to study in high school, 250 junior high students were surveyed. Of the students surveyed, 75 indicated they wanted to study Chinese. Which conclusion is best supported by this data?

   (A) Approximately 30% of the junior high students surveyed were interested in studying Chinese.

   (B) Approximately 75% of the junior high students surveyed were interested in studying Chinese.

   (C) Approximately 25% of all students in the town were interested in studying Chinese.

   (D) Approximately 35% of all students in the town were interested in studying Chinese.

2. According to a recent student survey, 40% of high school seniors in the United States have taken a college credit class while in high school. If there are 3.7 million students in this year's high school graduating class in the United States, approximately how many of these graduating students likely took a college credit class while in high school?

(A) 148,000
(B) 222,000
(C) 1,480,000
(D) 2,220,000

3. For an upcoming election, a pollster estimates that 55% of voters will vote for Ballot Issue #1, given a margin of error of $\pm 3\%$. If there are 200,000 voters in the upcoming election, what would the pollster estimate to be the number, x, who will vote for Ballot Issue #1?

(A) $90,000 < x < 96,000$
(B) $104,000 < x < 116,000$
(C) $120,000 < x < 124,000$
(D) $224,000 < x < 248,000$

4. A newspaper surveyed 2,000 likely voters about their preference for a candidate in the upcoming election. The results are compiled in the table below:

Candidate	Vote Total
Candidate A	980
Candidate B	764
Candidate C	155
No Preference	101

Based on these results, which of the following would be a true statement?

(A) 49% of the survey respondents preferred candidate A.
(B) 98% of the survey respondents preferred candidate A.
(C) 16% of survey respondents preferred candidate C.
(D) 46% of survey respondents preferred candidate C.

5. A randomly selected survey of 2,000 dentists finds that 600 prefer Brand A dental floss. Based on this information, out of a group of 1,000 randomly selected dentists, how many will likely prefer Brand A dental floss?

(A) 200
(B) 300
(C) 800
(D) 900

6. A political scientist conducts a survey about approval for a state's governor. The results of the random sample of registered voters in the state are given in the table below:

% Who Approve	% Who Disapprove	Margin of Error
55	45	5

What action by the political scientist would most likely decrease the survey's margin of error?

(A) Conduct an identical survey in a different state
(B) Conduct an identical survey in a different country
(C) Decrease the survey sample size
(D) Increase the survey sample size

7. A travel agency wanted to determine which types of vacation destinations would be most popular for potential clients. They randomly sampled 100 adults within the boundaries of the travel agency's city and found that the majority of the respondents preferred a beach destination. What is the largest group for which these results of the market survey could accurately be generalized?

(A) The child residents of the travel agency's city
(B) The adult residents of the travel agency's city
(C) All residents of the travel agency's city
(D) All citizens of the travel agency's country

8. A medical researcher surveyed a random sample of nursing home residents and estimated between 46% and 54% of the residents had a family member who lived within 25 miles. What is another way she could report her estimate?

(A) 25% with an 8% margin of error
(B) 46% with an 8% margin of error
(C) 50% with a 4% margin of error
(D) 54% with a 4% margin of error

9. At an arboretum, a botanist found that out of 100 randomly selected trees from the arboretum, 30 were evergreen and 70 were deciduous. If there were a total of 1,000 trees in the arboretum, which inequality expresses how many of the remaining trees, E, would have to be evergreen if more than half of all the trees in the arboretum were evergreen?

(A) $E > 470$
(B) $E < 470$
(C) $E > 590$
(D) $E < 590$

10. One hundred randomly selected users of a television streaming service were surveyed as to their preferred use for the service. Of these, 35% preferred to "binge watch" one show until they had seen all the episodes for that show, and 65% preferred to skip around to watch different shows. What is the most accurate conclusion based on these results?

    (A) It is more likely that a randomly selected user of the service prefers binge watching to show skipping.
    (B) It is more likely that a randomly selected user of the service prefers show skipping to binge watching.
    (C) Exactly 65% of all users of the streaming service prefer binge watching over show skipping.
    (D) Exactly 65% of all users of the streaming service prefer show skipping over binge watching.

✓ Solutions

1. **(A)** We can eliminate choices (C) and (D) since the survey is limited to students at the junior high and would not be representative of all students in the town. The correct answer is choice **(A)** because 75 of the 250 junior high students said they wanted to study Chinese—this equates to 30%.

$$\frac{75}{250} \times 100 = 30\%$$

2. **(C)** Based on the survey data, 40% of high school seniors in the United States have taken a college credit class. Therefore, if we take 40% of the total number of students in the United States who are graduating from high school, we will get the approximate number of the graduating students who likely took a college credit class:

$$0.40 \times 3,700,000 = 1,480,000$$

3. **(B)** Since the margin of error is 3%, the likely number of voters will be between 52% and 58% of the 200,000 total.

$$0.52 \times 200,000 = 104,000$$
$$0.58 \times 200,000 = 116,000$$

So, the estimated number of voters who will vote for Ballot Issue #1 is $104,000 < x < 116,000$.

4. **(A)** There are 2,000 total respondents to the survey, so determine what percent of this total Candidate A would be:

$$\frac{980}{2,000} \times 100 = 49\%$$

Thus, 49% of survey respondents preferred Candidate A. The other options are based on incorrect calculations with the vote totals in the table.

5. **(B)** Set up a proportion to solve for the number of dentists out of the 1,000 randomly selected ones who will prefer Brand A:

$$\frac{600}{2,000} = \frac{x}{1,000} \rightarrow$$

Cross multiply →

$$\frac{600}{2,000} \times 1,000 = x \rightarrow$$

$$300 = x$$

6. **(D)** To decrease the margin of error, make the survey sample as large and as random as possible. Choices (A) and (B) are incorrect because conducting the same survey in a different location will not better inform us about the approval within the state; they would be conducting the studies outside the considered population. Choice **(D)** is correct because increasing the sample size will make the survey data set larger, therefore decreasing the margin of error.

7. **(B)** The travel agency did a random sample of adults within the boundaries of the travel agency's city, so the generalization will be for adult residents of that city. It will not be choice (A) since children were not surveyed. It will not be choice (C) because that would include both children and adults in the generalization. And it will not be choice (D) because we do not know the specifics of other areas in the country and how they would respond.

8. **(C)** The number 50 is halfway between 46 and 54, with 4 units separating 46 from 50 and 4 units separating 54 from 50. So, the researcher could report the estimate as 50% with a 4% margin of error since this would encompass values between 46% and 54%.

9. **(A)** One hundred trees have already been selected, so there would be $1,000 - 100 = 900$ trees remaining. Half of all the trees in the arboretum would be 500. In the survey sample, there were 30 evergreen trees. So, there must be enough evergreen trees in the remaining 900 to give a total of over 500. Solve this inequality to reach the solution:

$$E > 500 - 30 \rightarrow$$
$$E > 470$$

10. **(B)** Choices (C) and (D) assert too much precision by stating that "exactly" 65% of the users must have a particular preference. Since 65% of the survey respondents said they like to skip around to different shows, and only 35% of the respondents preferred to binge watch, it would be reasonable to conclude that a randomly selected user of the service prefers show skipping to binge watching.

Problem Solving and Data Analysis—Graphs and Data Interpretation

Probability

Probability is defined as "the likelihood that a given event will happen," expressed as a decimal or fraction.

- If the probability that it will rain tomorrow is 0.5, there is a 50% chance it will rain.
- If the probability that it will snow tomorrow is 0, there is a 0% chance it will snow.
- If the probability that it will be cloudy tomorrow is 1, there is a 100% chance it will be cloudy.

To calculate probability, take the number of ways an event can happen and divide it by the total number of possible outcomes:

$$\frac{\text{Number of Ways Event Can Happen}}{\text{Total Number of Possible Outcomes}} = \text{Probability of Event}$$

Example

If I have a total of 30 books on my bookshelf and 10 of them are novels, what is the probability that a randomly selected book from my bookshelf would be a novel?

Solution

The "number of ways an event can happen" is 10 and the "total number of possible outcomes" is 30, so divide 10 by 30 to determine the probability:

$$\frac{10}{30} = \frac{1}{3}$$

So, the probability that a randomly selected book from the bookshelf would be a novel is $\frac{1}{3}$.

Practice

1. On a multiple-choice test, there are four choices per question: (A), (B), (C), and (D). What is the probability that on a given question a test taker who is randomly selecting his answer will select choice (B)?
2. In John's wallet, he has five 1 dollar bills, two 5 dollar bills, and three 10 dollar bills. If a bill is selected at random from his wallet, what is the possibility it will be a 5 dollar bill?
3. An advertiser finds that for 200 randomly selected online ad placements, six users will click through to the business website. Based on this data, what is the probability that a randomly selected ad placement will result in the user clicking through to the business website?

Solutions

1. There are a total of four possible events, and choice (B) is one of the potential outcomes. So, divide 1 by 4 to find the probability: $\frac{1}{4}$.
2. John has a total of $5 + 2 + 3 = 10$ bills in his wallet. Out of these ten bills, two are 5 dollar bills. So, divide 2 by 10 to find the probability:

   $$\frac{2}{10} = \frac{1}{5}$$

3. There are 6 possible events out of 200 potential outcomes, so divide 6 by 200 to determine the probability:

   $$\frac{6}{200} = 0.03$$

   So, the probability that a randomly selected ad placement will result in the user clicking through to the business website is 0.03.

Graph Interpretation

SAT Math Strategy

Carefully examine the units on the axes to avoid careless errors.

The SAT will assess your skill in interpreting a variety of graphs—you will be asked to find maximums, minimums, overall trends, and more.

Example

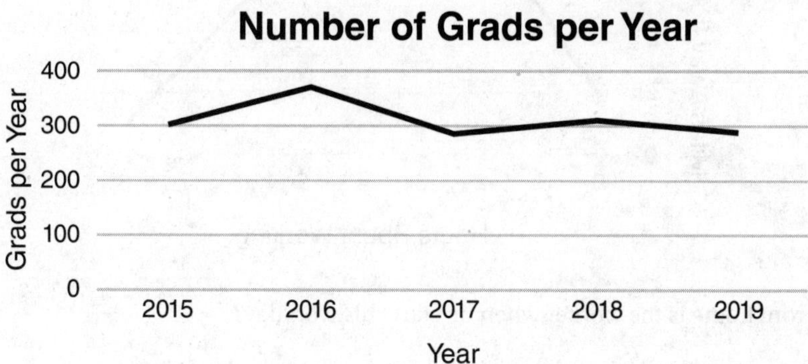

The number of graduates per year from Jackson High School are given in the line graph above. During what year of this time period was the number of graduates the greatest?

Solution

Examine the graph to see that the x-axis has the "years" and the y-axis has "grads per year." So, we need to find where the "grads per year" are at their highest value and the corresponding year.

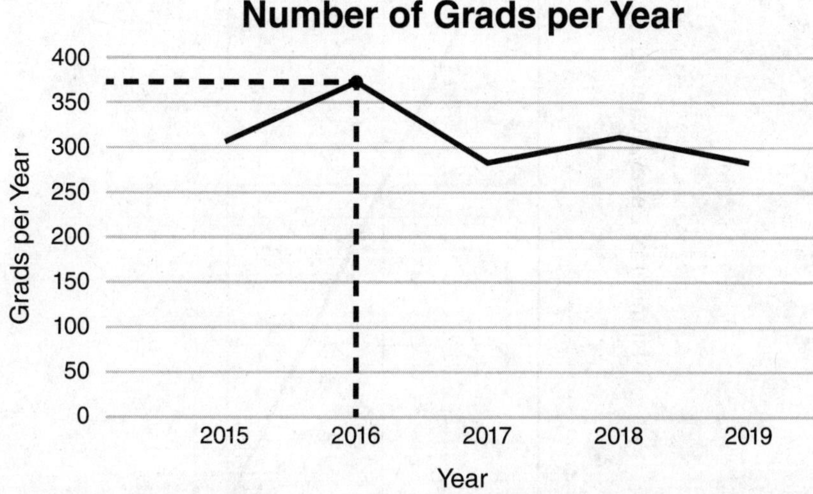

Drawing on the graph will help you visualize that the greatest number of grads per year is approximately 370, and that this occurs in year 2016. So, the answer is 2016.

Practice

A delivery driver plots how far he is from his home throughout his workday.

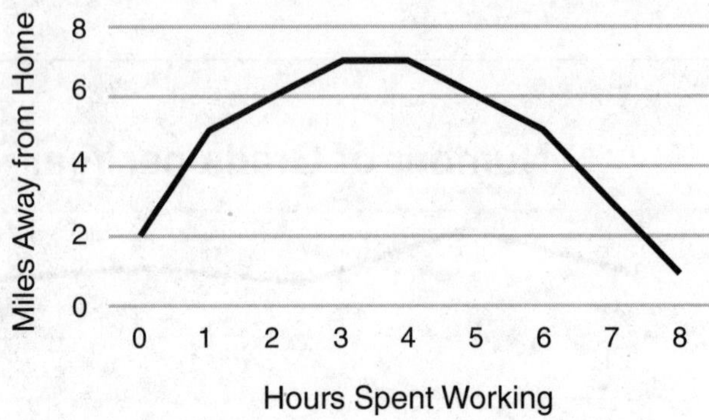

1. How far from home is the worker when he starts his workday?
2. For approximately how long is the driver at least 5 miles from home?

A teacher has a total of 100 minutes he can spend grading essays and group projects. The various ways he could allocate his time are graphed below:

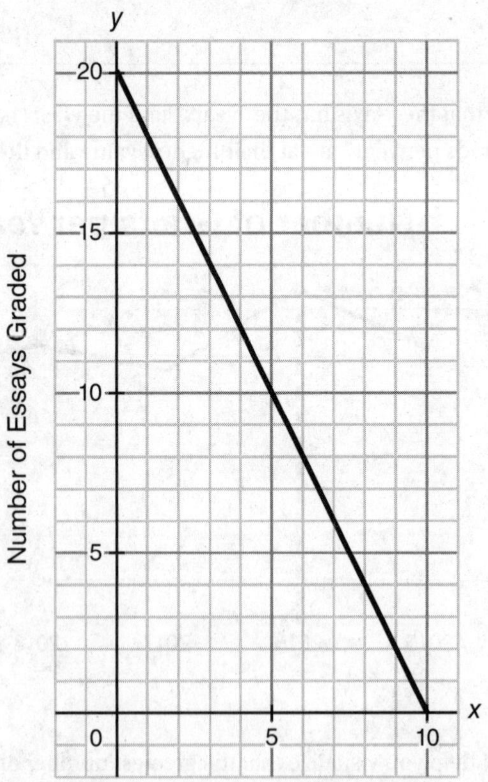

3. If the teacher spends the full 100 minutes grading projects and essays, and he grades 5 group projects, how many essays will he grade within this time?
4. How long does it take for him to grade an essay?

Solutions

1. **2 miles.** Zero hours of working would correspond to the beginning of the driver's workday. At an x value of 0, the y value is 2 for the number of miles away from home. So, he will be 2 miles from home when he starts his workday.
2. **5 hours.** From 1 hour spent working to 6 hours spent working, the miles away from home is at least 5. So, there will be a total of $6 - 1 = 5$ hours he is at least 5 miles from home.
3. **10 essays.** Examine the line and find that when there are 5 group projects graded, the y- value representing the number of essays graded is 10. So, there will be 10 essays graded in this time.
4. **5 minutes.** To find this, look at the situation when the teacher does nothing but grade essays. This is at the point (0, 20)—no group projects are graded, and 20 essays would be graded. Since the teacher is spending a total of 100 minutes grading, find the number of minutes it takes to grade a single essay by dividing 100 minutes by 20 essays:

$$\frac{100}{20} = 5$$

Scatterplots

Scatterplots provide a graph of different points that together will show a relationship among data. To see the relationship among the data, draw a **line of best fit** that shows a line that would best approximate the data points. (On the SAT, the edge of your answer document can give you a great way to approximate a straight line.) Here is an example of a scatterplot with a line of best fit:

Examples

Consider the line of best fit for the scatterplot graphed below.

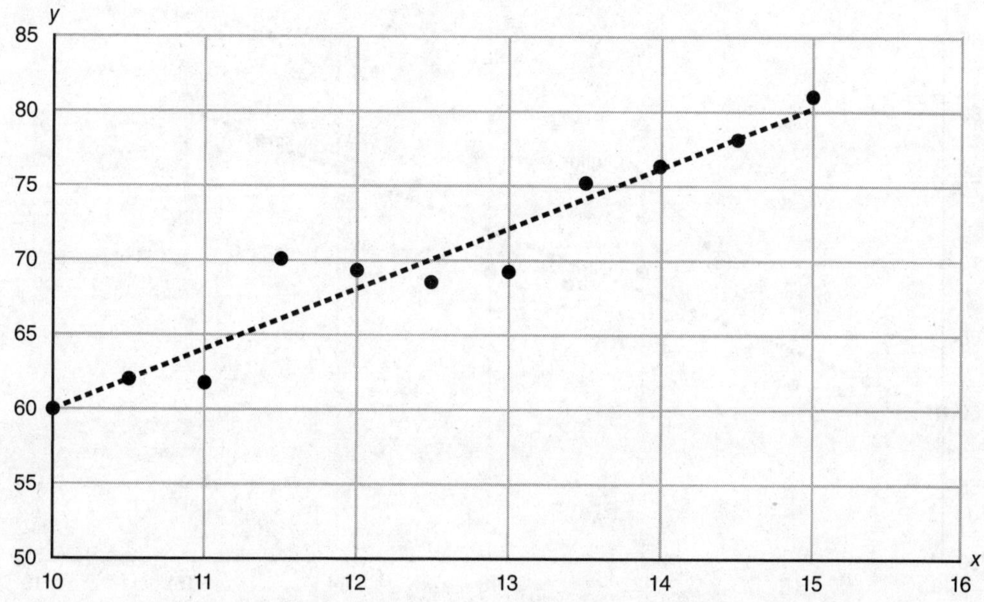

1. What is the equation for the line of best fit, with the slope and y-intercept rounded to the nearest whole integer values?

✓ Solution

Be careful to examine the *x*- and *y*-coordinates in the graph—they do not begin at (0, 0). First, pick two points for which it will be easy to find the slope: (10, 60) and (15, 80) will work.

$$\frac{\text{Change in Y}}{\text{Change in X}} = \frac{80 - 60}{15 - 10} = \frac{20}{5} = 4$$

So, the slope of the line is 4. Now, plug in a point that is in the line of best fit, such as (10, 60), to solve for the *y*-intercept:

$$y = mx + b \rightarrow$$

Plug in 4 for *m*, the slope:

$$y = 4x + b \rightarrow$$

Plug in (10, 60) as a point to solve for *b*:

$$60 = 4(10) + b \rightarrow$$
$$60 = 40 + b \rightarrow$$
$$20 = b$$

So, the equation for the line of best fit is $y = 4x + 20$ since the line has a slope of 4 and a *y*-intercept of 20.

2. Which point is an "outlier"—an observation that lies farthest from the values predicted by the line of best fit?

✓ Solution

Find the point that is most distant from the line of best fit:

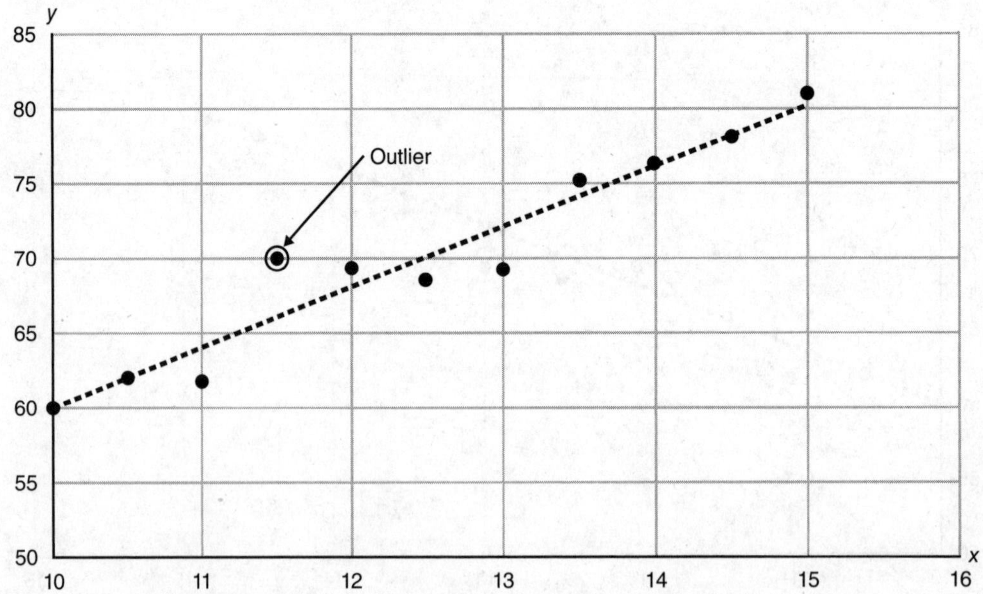

(11.5, 70) is about 4 units above the predicted value for the line of best fit. So, this would be an outlier in the graph.

Practice

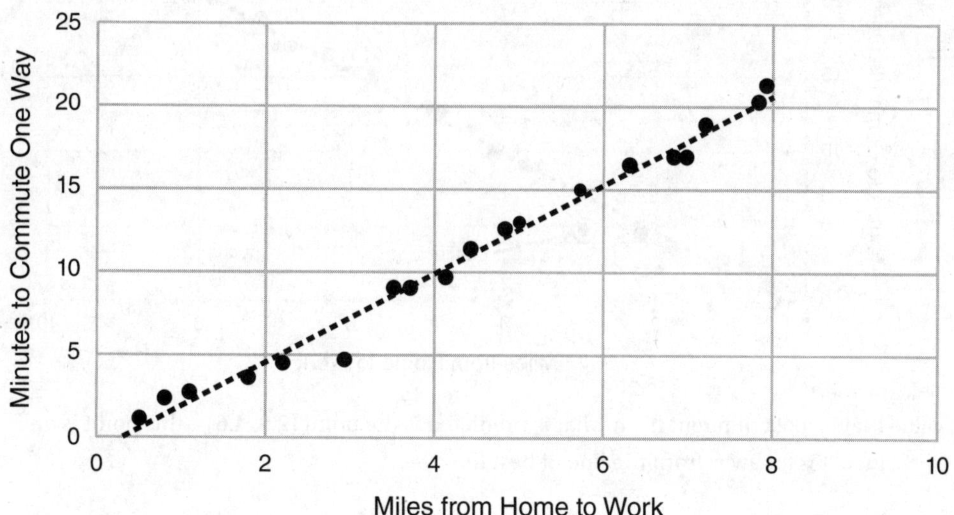

Twenty commuters recorded the distance from their homes to work and the time of their commutes on a particular day.

1. Based on the line of best fit, if someone lived 4 miles from work, how long would their commute time most likely be?
2. What value on the graph is most different from what would be predicted based on the trend?
3. For how many of the commuters was their actual commute time shorter than what would be predicted?

Solutions

1.

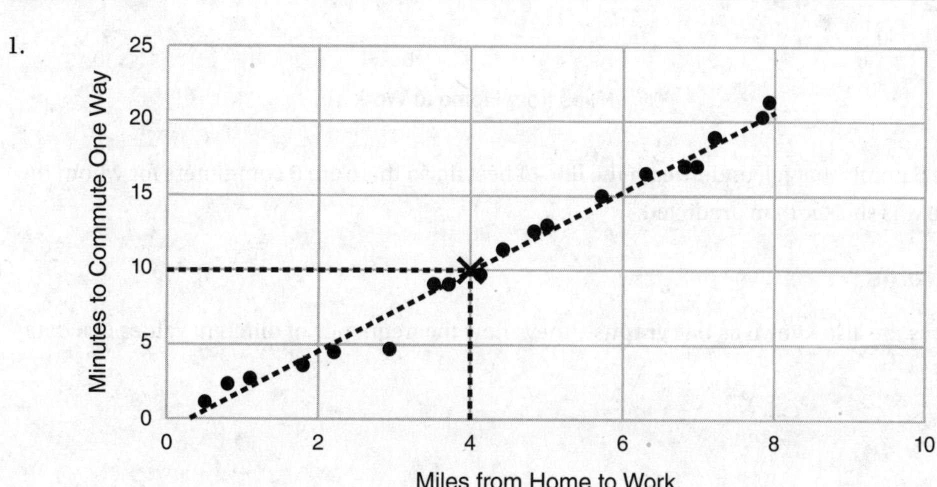

At 4 miles from home to work, the predicted number of commuting minutes is approximately 10, as you can see in the graph above.

2.

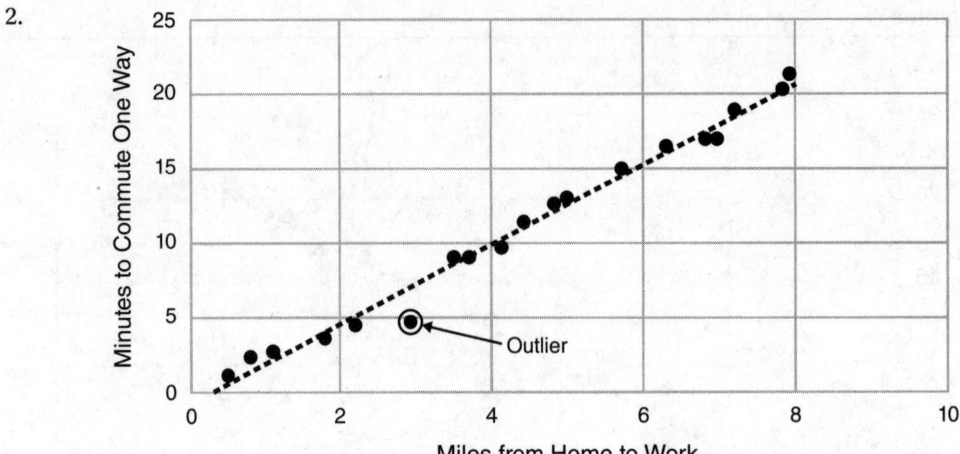

The value that is most different from what is predicted is the point (2.9, 4.6)—this point is an "outlier" since it is far away from the line of best fit.

3. Mark and count the number of points that fall *underneath* the line of best fit:

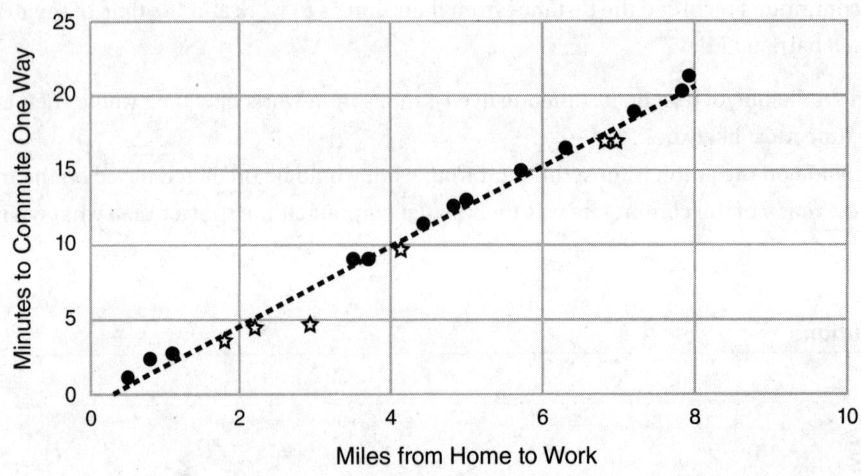

There are 6 points that fall underneath the line of best fit, so there are 6 commuters for whom the commute was shorter than predicted.

Histograms

Histograms are also known as **bar graphs**—they show the frequency of different values in a data set.

Example

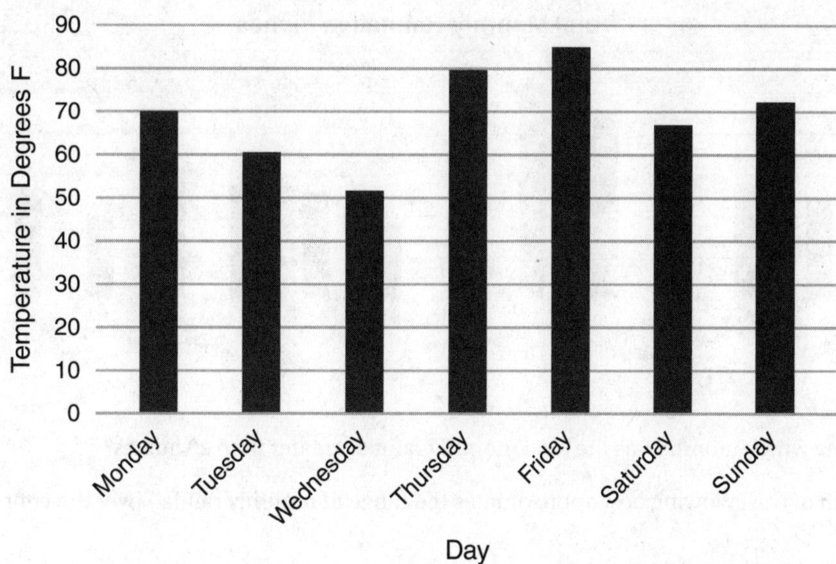

Based on the above graph, between what two days was there the largest increase in temperature?

Solution

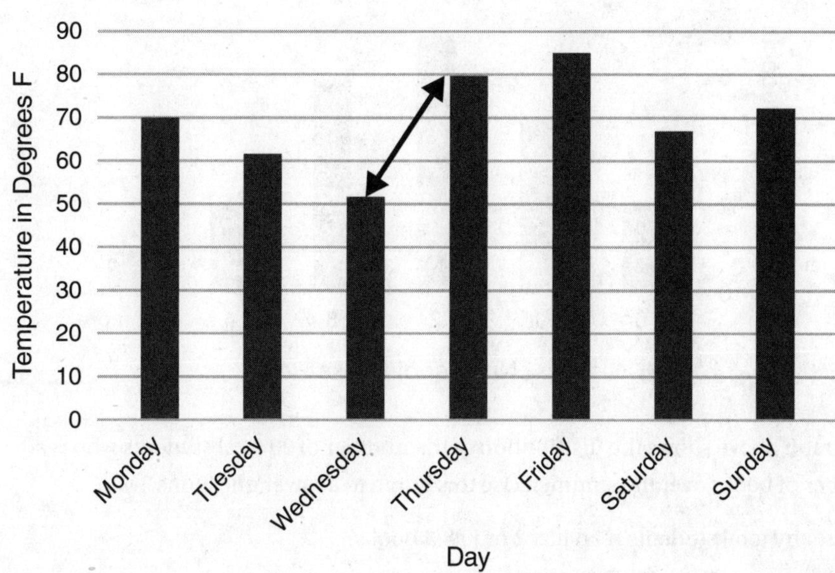

From Wednesday to Thursday, the temperature increases from approximately 52 degrees to 80 degrees. From the graph, this is clearly the largest increase from day to day.

Practice

1.

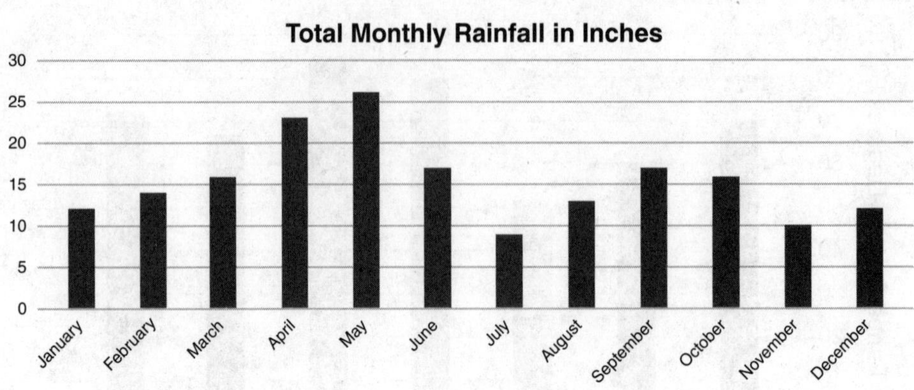

During which months was the total monthly rainfall greater than 20 inches?

2. Which of the following best approximates the range in monthly rainfall over the course of a year?

(A) 9
(B) 17
(C) 22
(D) 26

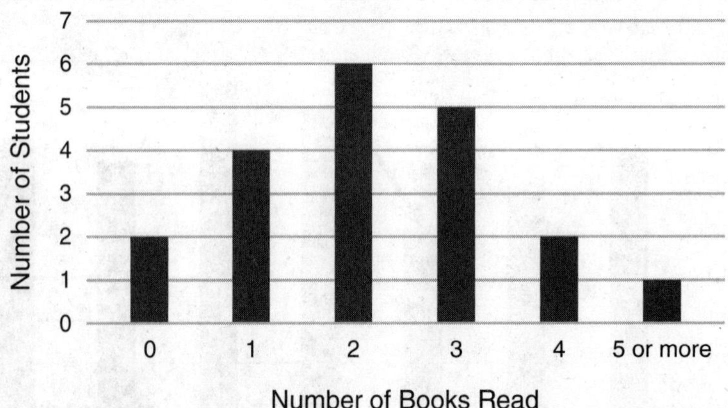

The graph above shows the distribution of the number of 20 total students who read a certain number of books over the summer. Use this graph to answer questions 3–4.

3. How many total students read just 2 or just 3 books?

4. If another student is added to the set who read 7 books over the summer, what will be the effect on the median number of books read and mean number of books read?

(A) Median decreases, while the mean remains the same.
(B) Both the median and the mean decrease.
(C) Median remains the same, and the mean increases.
(D) Both the median and the mean increase.

✓ Solutions

1. April has rainfall of 23 inches, and May has rainfall of 26 inches, while all the other months have less than 20 inches of rain. So, just April and May would have total monthly rainfall greater than 20 inches.
2. The range of a data set is defined as the difference between the largest and smallest values in the set. May has the most rainfall at 26 inches, and July has the least rainfall at 9 inches. So, the difference between the two is $26 - 9 = 17$ giving a range for the data of choice **(B)**, 17.

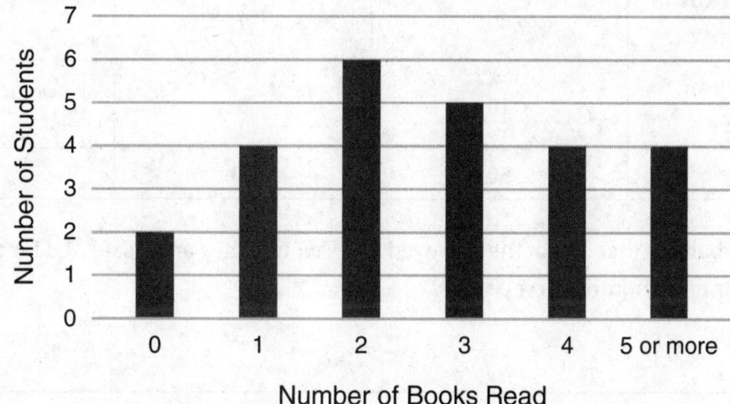

The graph above shows the distribution of the number of students who read a certain number of books over the summer.

3. Six students read 2 books and 5 students read 3 books, so the total number of students who read just 2 or 3 books is $6 + 5 = 11$.
4. Given that there are 20 students total, the median will fall between the 10th and 11th terms in the set. In this case, the 10th and 11th terms are both students who read 2 books, so the median number of books read will not change even if a greater value is added to the set since a new median with 21 total students will remain at 2 books read. The mean, however, will change since it is a calculation of the average number of books read. An additional student who read 7 books would slightly increase the mean since the sum of all the books read would be greater. Thus, the answer is **(C)**.

Tables

The SAT will frequently present data in a table form. When analyzing tables, be sure you clearly understand what the numbers in each cell represent. Do so by carefully matching the cells up with the corresponding descriptions.

Example

Air Quality Index, or AQI, is a measure used to determine how safe it is to be outside given the air pollution that is in an area. The index ranges between 0 and 500, and measures of 151 or above are considered unsafe for the general public. Sixty cities in a country had their average AQI for two months measured, with the results tabulated below:

	AQI less than 151 in February	AQI greater than 151 in February	Total
AQI less than 151 in January	40	4	44
AQI greater than 151 in January	10	6	16
Total	50	10	60

What is the probability that one of the surveyed cities would have an unsafe AQI for the general population over both months surveyed?

Solution

Let's be clear about what the numbers in the table represent (don't worry—you don't need to be this thorough for every problem; this is so you can clearly see how these tables work):

- 40 is the number of cities that had the lower AQI in both January and February.
- 10 is the number of cities that had a greater AQI in January and a lower AQI in February.
- 4 is the number of cities that had a greater AQI in February and a lower AQI in January.
- 6 is the number of cities that had a greater AQI in both January and February.
- 44 is the total number of cities that had a lower AQI in January.
- 16 is the total number of cities that had a higher AQI in January.
- 50 is the total number of cities that had a lower AQI in February.
- 10 is the total number of cities that had a higher AQI in February.
- There are 60 cities all together that were presented.

So, to calculate the probability that one of the surveyed cities would have an *unsafe* AQI (over 151) over *both* months, first see how many cities had the greater AQI in both January and February—there were 6 such cities. Then, divide this by the total number of cities presented, 60.

$$\frac{6}{60} = 0.1$$

So the probability that one of the surveyed cities would have an unsafe AQI over both months is

0.1.

Practice

Type of Math Class and Type of Class Instructor at a University

	Graduate Student	Professor	Totals
Lower-Level Class	80	40	120
Upper-Level Class	20	45	65
Totals	100	85	185

1. How many instructors in total taught lower-level classes?
2. How many instructors were there all together at the university?
3. What percent of all the math classes are taught by professors, calculated to the nearest whole percent?
4. If a math class is taught by a graduate student, what is the probability the class is an upper-level class?

Solutions

1. **120.** Match up the Lower-Level Class with the Totals and see that there are 120 total instructors for lower-level classes.

2. **185.** The bottom right cell shows how many total instructors of all types and all classes were at the university—185.

3. **46%.** There are a total of 185 classes, and out of these 185 classes, 85 are taught by professors. So, calculate the percent of classes taught by professors like this:

$$\frac{85}{185} \times 100 \approx 46\%$$

4. **0.2.** There are 100 total math classes taught by graduate students, and 20 of these classes are upper level. So, to calculate the probability, divide 20 by 100:

$$\frac{20}{100} = 0.2$$

Box Plots

On occasion, you may come across box plots (a.k.a. whisker plots) on the SAT Math, called this because the two quartiles (fourths) of the data that are in the middle make a box (the least and most quartiles make "whiskers" on either side). These plots break up the values in the data set into four quadrants so you can more easily visualize the spread of the data and the median.

Example

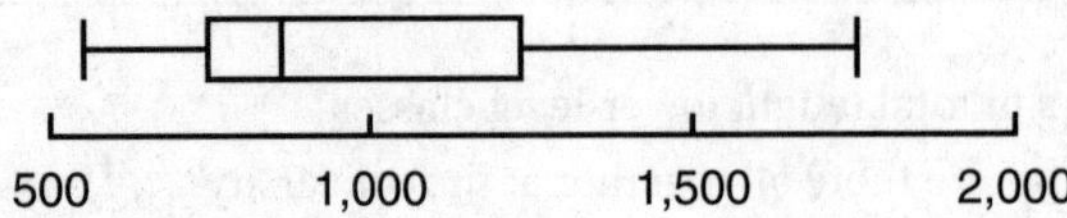

The box plot above summarizes the values for the average monthly apartment rental price in a particular neighborhood. Which of the following would be closest to the median monthly apartment rental price in this neighborhood?

(A) 500
(B) 600
(C) 800
(D) 1,200

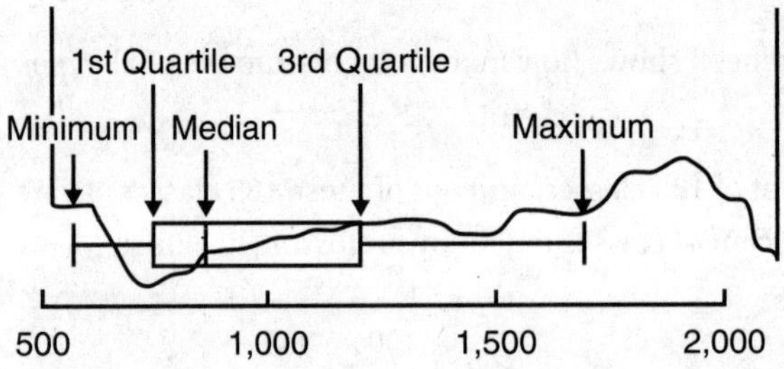

Solution

From this, you can see that the median value would be approximately 800, making choice **(C)** the correct answer.

Practice

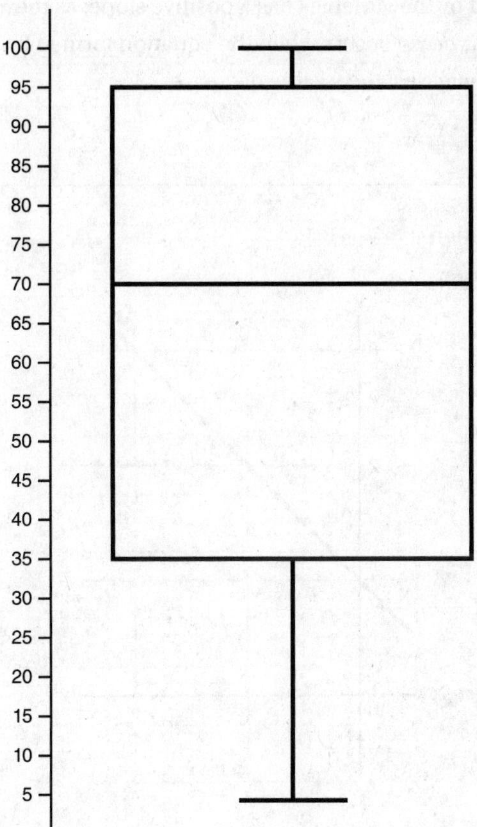

The above box plot summarizes the test results from a group of 300 seniors at a high school.

1. What is the minimum test score?
2. What is the median test score?
3. Which expression would give the test results, x, between the 50th and 75th percentiles?

   (A) $5 < x < 35$
   (B) $35 < x < 70$
   (C) $70 < x < 95$
   (D) $95 < x < 100$

Solutions

1. The very least value in the plot is 5.
2. In the middle of the box is the value 70, which would represent the median.
3. The test results between the 50th and 75th percentiles would be between the 2nd and 3rd quartiles. This would be between the median, 70, and the 3rd quartile, 95. So, the correct answer is choice **(C)**.

Linear and Exponential Growth

A constant relationship between two variables is called a *linear relationship.* Linear *growth* occurs when the equation formed by the variables has a positive slope; as the x value increases, the y value also increases. Linear *decay* occurs when the equation formed by the variables has a negative slope; as the x value increases, the y value decreases.

Example 1

Linear growth for the equation $y = x + 1$

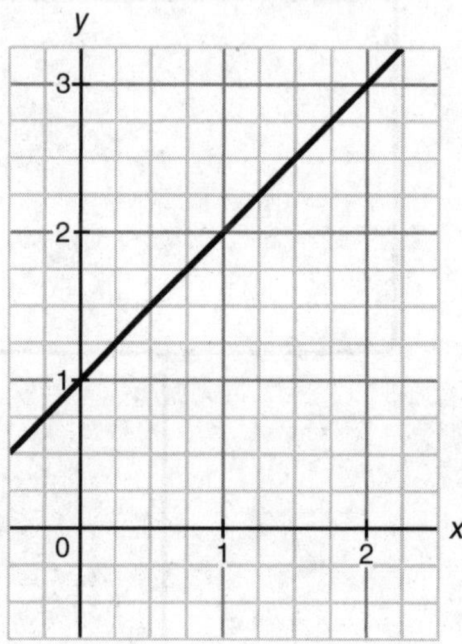

Example 2

Linear decay for the equation $y = -x + 3$

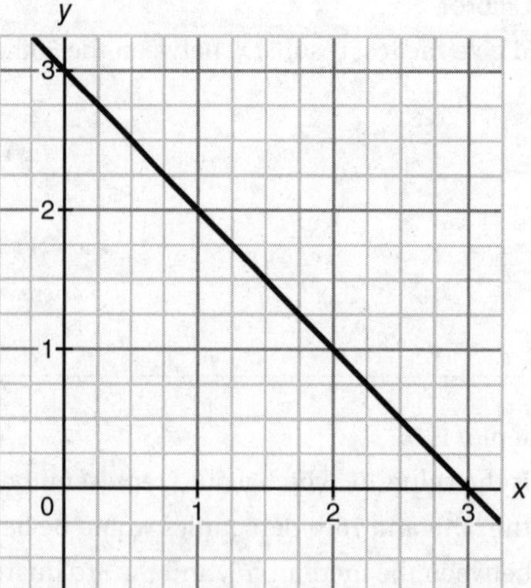

A relationship between two variables x and y that is expressed in the form $y = ab^x$ or $y = ab^x + c$ is *exponential.* Exponential *growth* occurs when as the x value increases, the y value increases exponentially. Exponential *decay* occurs when as the x value increases, the y value decreases exponentially.

Example 3

Twenty sheep were introduced to an island where they had no natural predators. The population of the sheep on the island over time is given in the table below.

Year	Number of Sheep
1800	20
1810	28
1820	38
1830	51
1840	65

If a function were made with the year as the x value and the number of sheep as $f(x)$, what would best describe the relationship between x and $f(x)$ if it were graphed in the xy-coordinate plane?

(A) Exponential growth
(B) Exponential decay
(C) Linear growth
(D) Linear decay

Solution

Let's examine how much the number of sheep changes from year to year:

Year	Number of Sheep	Increase from 10 Years Prior
1800	20	Not applicable
1810	28	+8
1820	38	+10
1830	51	+13
1840	65	+14

We can see that not only is the number of sheep *increasing*, the number by which it is increasing in each interval is also *increasing*. If this had been linear growth, the number by which it increases in each interval would remain the same. So, the correct answer is choice **(A)**, exponential growth.

Practice

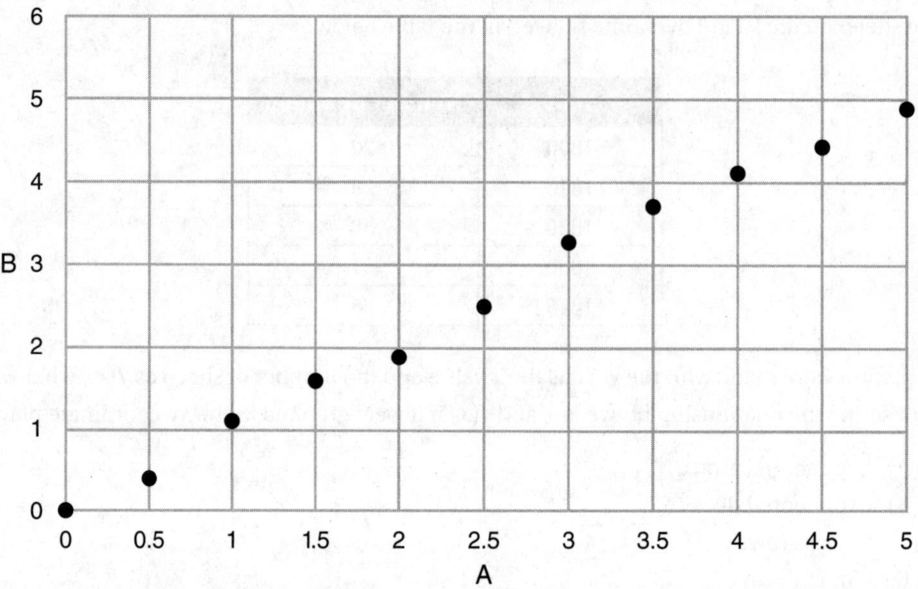

1. The line of best fit for the points given in the graph above would show what type of relationship between *A* and *B*?

   (A) Negative linear association
   (B) Positive linear association
   (C) Negative exponential association
   (D) Positive exponential association

2. If the trend given in the above graph were to continue, what would be closest to the projected value of B when A is 6?

   (A) 5
   (B) 5.5
   (C) 6
   (D) 6.5

3. John wishes to place $1,000 in an investment. Which of these circumstances would provide him with the greatest amount of money after a ten-year period?

   (A) An investment that grows linearly at 7% of the original amount each year
   (B) An investment that has exactly $60 added each year
   (C) An investment in which 2% of the original amount and $45 is added each year
   (D) An investment that grows exponentially at 6% a year, compounded annually

✓ **Solutions**

1. As the x values increase, the y values also increase at a steady rate. Therefore, this will be choice **(B)**, a positive linear association.
2. Be careful to notice that the increments on the x-axis are different from those on the y-axis. For each increase in 1 whole unit of x, the y value increases by about 1 whole unit. So, when A is 6, the B value would be 1 more than what it was at the point (5, 5). So, the projected value for B would be choice **(C)**, 6, since the new point would be approximately (6, 6).
3. Choices (A), (B), and (C) would all result in linear growth—a set amount of money would be added each year. Choice **(D)** is correct because with exponential growth, the amount by which the investment increases will *increase*, resulting in far greater growth over time.

Interpreting Constants and Functions

In order to assess your skill in understanding the meaning of functions, the SAT Math will frequently ask you to interpret constants and other components of functions.

› **Example**

Mary's investment in a stock portfolio, S, is modeled by the function

$$S(y) = 1000(1.15)^y$$

in which y is the number of years Mary holds the stock. What is the best interpretation of the number 1.15 in the context of this function?

(A) When Mary holds the investment for 1.15 years, her overall investment increases by $1,000.
(B) When Mary holds the investment for 0.15 years, her overall investment decreases by $1,000.
(C) For each year that Mary owns the stock portfolio, her investment balance increases by $15.
(D) For each year that Mary owns the stock portfolio, her investment balance increases by 15% compounded annually.

✓ **Solution**

Use your knowledge of other concepts to help you interpret the meaning of constants in functions. Recall from the review of percentages that the formula for compound interest is $A = P\left(1 + \frac{r}{n}\right)^{nt}$, which has the same structure as the function $S(y) = 1000(1.15)^y$. The number 1.15 will correspond to $1 + \frac{r}{n}$. Since the intervals at which the investment value is compounded are one year, given the exponent y, $1 + \frac{r}{n}$ will equal $1 + \frac{0.15}{1} = 1.15$. This means that the percent increase each year is 15%. Therefore, the correct answer is choice **(D)**, since each year that she owns the portfolio, her investment balance will increase by 15%.

You could also use process of elimination to figure this out, since choices (A), (B), and (C) would all correspond to linear growth.

› Practice

A chemist measured the amount of caffeine in different volumes of coffee:

Fluid Ounces	Milligrams of Caffeine
2	25
5	60
8	95
12	143

1. Which of the following functions best approximates the relationship between fluid ounces, F, and milligrams of caffeine, C?

   (A) $C = 4F$
   (B) $C = 8F$
   (C) $C = 12F$
   (D) $C = 16F$

2. Given the relationship in the above table, which of the following would best approximate the milligrams of caffeine in 15 fluid ounces of coffee?

   (A) 150
   (B) 165
   (C) 180
   (D) 195

Questions 3–4 refer to the following information:

The half-life formula for a given substance is

$$N(t) = N_0\left(\frac{1}{2}\right)^{\frac{t}{h}}$$

in which $N(t)$ is how much of the original amount of a substance, N_0, remains after a certain amount of time t elapsed, and h is the half-life of the substance.

3. What would the value of $N(5)$represent?

   (A) How long it takes for half of a substance to decay
   (B) How much of the substance would remain after 5 years had elapsed
   (C) The number of years it takes for a substance to fully decay
   (D) The original mass of a substance before calculation of its half-life

4. Suppose that a particular substance has a half-life of 20 years. What fraction of the substance in the year 2000 would remain in the year 2080?

   (A) $\frac{1}{16}$

   (B) $\frac{1}{8}$

   (C) $\frac{1}{4}$

   (D) $\frac{1}{2}$

✓ Solutions

1. Glance ahead to the solutions to see that all of them are written in slope-intercept form. Determine which equation is correct by approximating the slope of the line. Let's use the points (2, 25) and (5, 60):

$$\frac{60-25}{5-2}=\frac{35}{3}\approx 11.67$$

   This corresponds to choice **(C)**, since 12 is the closest slope value to 11.67.

2. When there is an increase of 3 fluid ounces from 5 to 8, the milligrams of caffeine increases by 35, from 60 to 95. So, when going from 12 fluid ounces to 15 fluid ounces, the milligrams of caffeine will increase by a similar amount: $143 + 35 = 178$. This is closest to choice **(C)**, 180.

   Alternatively, you could have used the equation from the previous problem to solve for the number of milligrams, plugging in 15 for F.

3. $N(5)$ would represent the choice **(B)** since t is the amount of time that would go by, and if t is 5, then $N(5)$ would represent how much of the substance would remain after 5 half-lives had elapsed.

4. If the half-life is 20 years, according to the equation, half of the original amount of the substance would decay in a 20-year period. Since the time span is 80 years, going from 2000 to 2080, the original amount of the substance would be halved a total of 4 times:

$$\frac{1}{2}\times\frac{1}{2}\times\frac{1}{2}\times\frac{1}{2}=\frac{1}{16}$$

   So, the correct answer is **(A)** since there would be $\frac{1}{16}$ of the original amount.

SAT Math Questions Practice Drill #1—Problem Solving and Data Analysis Graphs and Data Interpretation

(If timing, take about 12 minutes to complete.)

The complete distribution of letter grades on a final exam are given in the table below:

Letter Grade	Number of Students
A	12
B	16
C	10
D	7
F	5

1. What is the total number of students who completed the exam?

(A) 40
(B) 50
(C) 60
(D) 70

2. Which set of grades represents $\frac{3}{10}$ of the total number of students?

(A) A and B
(B) A and D
(C) C and D
(D) C and F

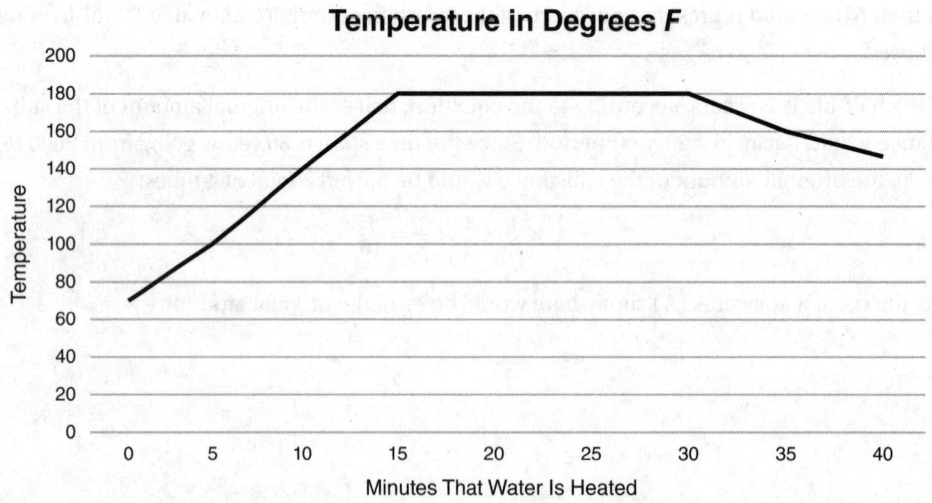

3. According to the graph above, what best approximates the initial temperature of the water?

(A) 70 degrees
(B) 90 degrees
(C) 100 degrees
(D) 120 degrees

4. Consider the graph above. A cook wanted to cook pasta during a 15-minute time period when the water temperature was steady. To accomplish this goal, between what times after starting to heat the water did the cook have the pasta in the water?

   (A) 0–10 minutes
   (B) 10–15 minutes
   (C) 15–30 minutes
   (D) 30–40 minutes

Questions 5–7 are about the following information.

A marketing agency surveyed clients from different online businesses to find the e-commerce conversion rate, i.e., what percentage of website visitors purchased something from the business. The results are compiled below:

Business Type	Conversion Rate
Industrial Supplies	4%
Pet Supplies	9%
Booksellers	10%
Electronics	26%
Toys	12%
Business Supplies	21%

5. Based on the above table, what is the probability that a visitor to an online bookstore will make a purchase?

   (A) 0.1
   (B) 0.2
   (C) 0.3
   (D) 0.4

6. If an online electronics business has 2,000 visitors to its site in a month, how many of them would most likely purchase something?

   (A) 440
   (B) 520
   (C) 650
   (D) 860

7. What is the median conversion rate for the business types presented in the table?

   (A) 5%
   (B) 7%
   (C) 9%
   (D) 11%

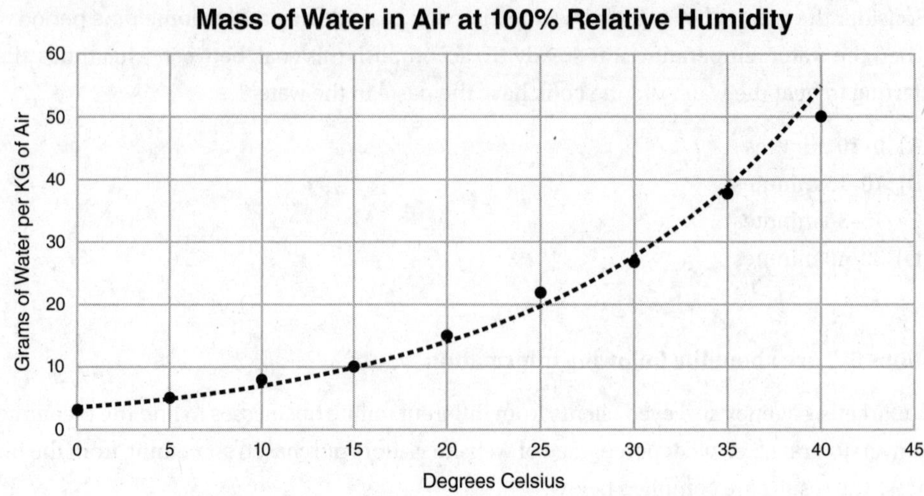

8. The relationship between temperature and grams of water per kilogram of air in the above graph is best described as which of the following?

(A) Exponentially increasing
(B) Exponentially decreasing
(C) Linear increasing
(D) Linear decreasing

9. What is the predicted value of grams of water per kilogram of air at 25 degrees C?

(A) 16
(B) 20
(C) 24
(D) 28

10. The greatest outlier presented in the above graph is found at what temperature?

(A) 10 degrees
(B) 20 degrees
(C) 30 degrees
(D) 40 degrees

✓ Solutions

1. **(B)** Add up the total number of students from the right column to find the total number of students who completed the exam:

$$12 + 16 + 10 + 7 + 5 = 50$$

2. **(D)** Find what $\frac{3}{10}$ of the total of 50 students would be:

$$\frac{3}{10} \times 50 = 15$$

Then, examine which combination will add up to 15. The only one that does is choice **(D)**, *C and F*, since $10 + 5 = 15$.

3. **(A)** The initial temperature of the water is the temperature when 0 minutes have passed. At an *x* value of 0, the *y* value for temperature is closest to 70 degrees.

4. **(C)** For the temperature to be steady, the line must be horizontal, having a slope of zero. Between 15 and 30 minutes, the line is horizontal, so it is in that range that the cook should cook the pasta.

5. **(A)** Look at the percentage of conversion for booksellers—10%. Then, expresses this as a probability:

$$\frac{10}{100} = \frac{1}{10} = 0.1$$

6. **(B)** The conversion rate for electronics businesses is 26% according to the table. So, find 26% of 2,000 to predict how many of the business's visitors will likely purchases something:

$$0.26 \times 2,000 = 520$$

7. **(D)** Put the percentages in order from least to greatest:

$$4, 9, 10, 12, 21, 26$$

Since there are an even number of terms, and the two middle terms are different, find the median of the set by averaging 10 and 12:

$$\frac{10 + 12}{2} = 11$$

So, the median conversion rate is 11%.

8. **(A)** As the temperature increases, the grams of water per kg of air increase more and more. Had this been a constant increase, it would be linear. Since the increase accelerates, it would be an exponential increase.

9. **(B)** The predicted value and measured value differ—the measured value is indicated by the dot, while the predicted value will be on the curved, dotted line. At 25 degrees Celsius, the grams of water per kilogram of air would be 20.

10. **(D)** The greatest outlier is the value that most differs from the predicted value; in other words, it is the measured value that is farthest from the curve. At 40 degrees, the measured value of the grams is 50, while the curve would predict approximately 55. This point is farther away from the predicted values than any of the other dots presented in the graph.

SAT Math Questions Practice Drill #2—Problem Solving and Data Analysis Graphs and Data Interpretation

(If timing, take about 12 minutes to complete.)

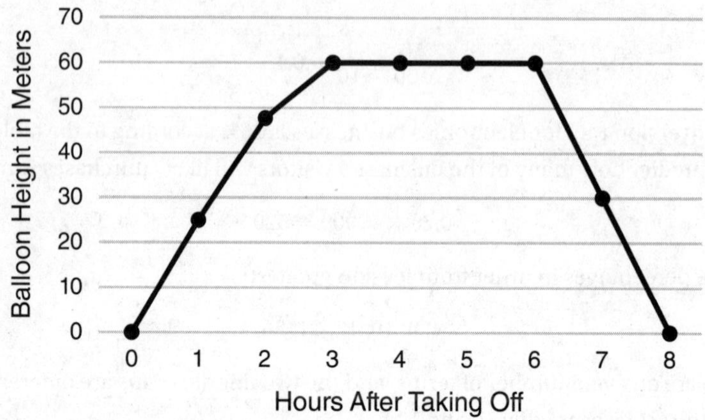

1. Sam took a balloon ride, in which he ascended to a height of 60 meters and remained there for a period of time. His height in meters above the ground as it relates to hours after taking off is graphed above.

   For how many hours in his ride did he stay at his maximum height?

   (A) 1
   (B) 2
   (C) 3
   (D) 4

2. During what interval did Sam's height make the greatest change?

   (A) Between 0–2 hours
   (B) Between 2–4 hours
   (C) Between 4–6 hours
   (D) Between 6–8 hours

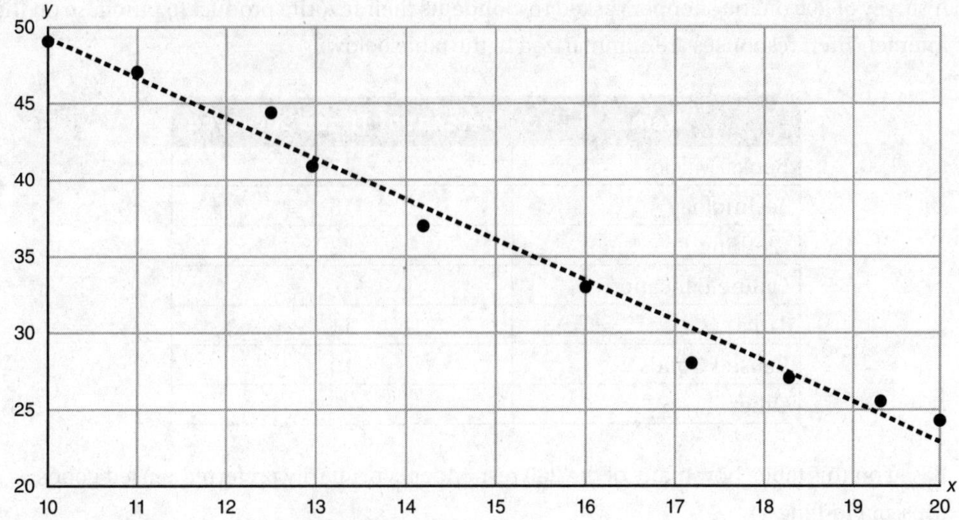

3. Consider the set of data in the scatterplot above.

   Assuming the trend in the above graph were to continue, what would most likely be the *y* value of the predicted point with an *x* value of 25?

   (A) 5
   (B) 10
   (C) 15
   (D) 20

4. If a linear equation were made to represent this data, which of the following would most closely estimate its *y*-intercept?

   (A) 48
   (B) 60
   (C) 75
   (D) 90

A survey of 200 online shoppers asked respondents their favorite product to purchase on the internet. Their responses are summarized in the table below.

Item	Percent of Those Surveyed
Books/Music	17
Technology	18
Clothing	22
Online Education	6
Trips	11
Reused Goods	19
Other	7

5. Based on this table, how many of the 200 respondents primarily preferred reused goods, trips, or clothing?

   (A) 104
   (B) 132
   (C) 150
   (D) 178

Fund Name	Share Price	Expected Yearly Management Expenses per Share
Fund A	$140	$1.12
Fund B	$80	$0.64
Fund C	$200	$1.60
Fund D	$64	$0.51
Fund E	$50	$0.40

6. The table above shows the price per share and the estimated yearly expenses for five different actively managed mutual funds (investment products that purchase stocks in many different companies).

   If Jennifer purchased 200 shares of Fund C, what would her yearly fund expenses most likely be?

   (A) $100
   (B) $190
   (C) $240
   (D) $320

7. Which function best approximates the relationship between the share price, *S*, and expenses, *E*, given that the two quantities have a linear relationship?

   (A) $(0.008)S = E$
   (B) $(0.08)S = E$
   (C) $(0.8)S = E$
   (D) $(8)S = E$

8. If William purchased 100 shares of Fund D, what inequality shows the percentage return on the investment that would allow him to make enough money to cover his expected yearly management expenses, calculated to the nearest tenth of a percent?

   (A) Percent ≤ 0.8
   (B) Percent ≥ 0.8
   (C) Percent ≥ 1.2
   (D) Percent ≤ 1.2

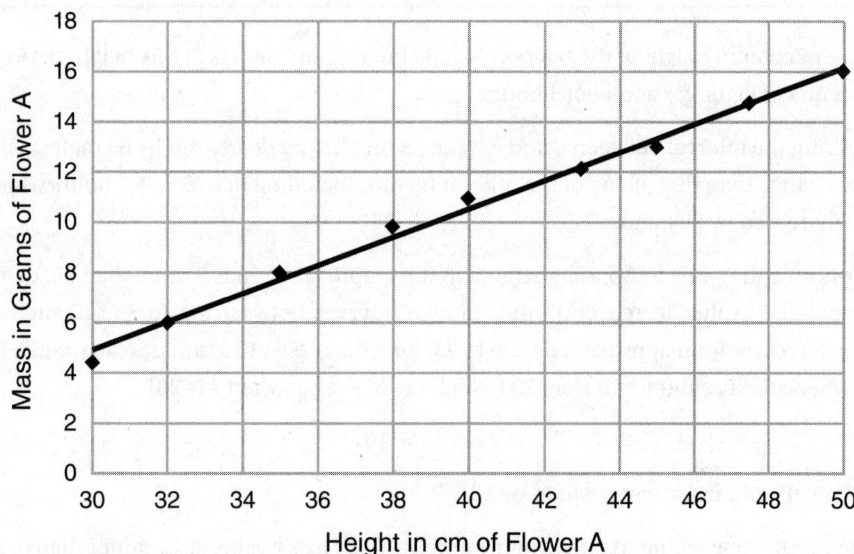

Figure 1

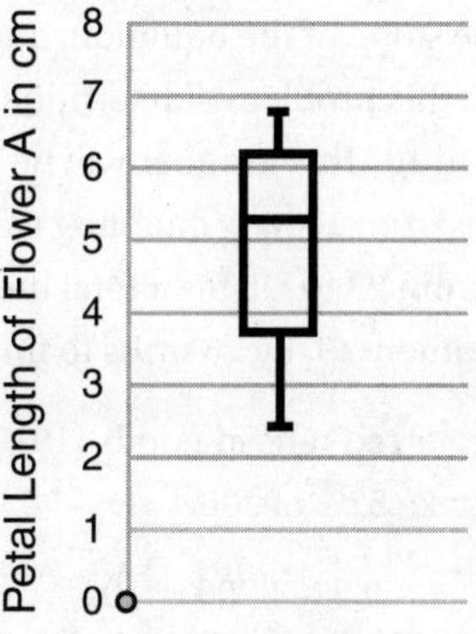

Figure 2

9. Assuming the trend of the best fit line in Figure 1 continues, what would be the mass of flower A if it has a height of 55 cm?

(A) Approximately 12.5 grams
(B) Approximately 16 grams
(C) Approximately 19.5 grams
(D) Approximately 24 grams

10. Based on Figure 2, in which of the following ranges would one find the median petal length of flower A?

(A) 3–4 cm
(B) 4–5 cm
(C) 5–6 cm
(D) 6–7 cm

✓ Solutions

1. **(C)** The maximum height of the balloon is at 60 meters, and Sam is at this height between 3 and 6 hours of flight, for a total of 3 hours.

2. **(D)** During the interval between 6 and 8 hours, Sam's height decreased by 60 meters. This is a greater change than that of any of the other intervals, including between 0–2 hours when Sam's height increased by 50 meters.

3. **(B)** Continue the same trend as illustrated in the graph. Since 25 is 5 more than 20, determine how much the y value decreases during a similar interval. Between x values of 15 and 20, the y value decreases from approximately 36 to 23, for a decrease of 13 units. So, to predict the y value when x is 20, subtract 13 from 23 (which is the y value when x is 20):

$$23 - 13 = 10$$

Therefore, the predicted value would be 10.

4. **(C)** Be careful to examine the units of the graph—the x-axis begins at 10 rather than 0. So, to find the y-intercept, we need to determine what that point of intersection on the y-axis would be if we expanded the graph by 10 lesser x units. This could be accomplished by plugging in sample values, finding the slope of the equation, and then solving for the y-intercept. Fortunately, you can save time in this problem—determine how much the y value increases as the x value decreases from 20 to 10. This number will be identical to how much the y value increases as the x value decreases from 10 to 0, enabling us to find the y-intercept. Between 20 and 10, the y value increases from 23 to 49, for a total increase of $49 - 23 = 26$. So, increase the y value at the x value of 10, namely 49, by 26 units to find the y-intercept: $49 + 26 = 75$.

5. **(A)** Add the percentages who preferred reused goods (19), trips (11), and clothing (22): $19\% + 11\% + 22\% = 52\%$. Then, take 52% of 200:

$$0.52 \times 200 = 104$$

6. **(D)** Each share of Fund C has a per-share management expense of $1.60. So, multiply 1.60 by 200 to find her likely yearly fund expenses:

$$1.6 \times 200 = 320$$

Therefore, her yearly fund expenses would most likely be $320.

7. **(A)** Find the relationship between share price and expenses by setting up an equation using sample values. Let's use a share price of 200 and a corresponding expense amount of 1.60, and call k the constant for which we are solving (since the terms have a linear relationship):

$$kS = E \rightarrow$$

$$k(200) = 1.60 \rightarrow$$

$$k = \frac{1.60}{200} = 0.008$$

So, $(0.008)S = E$ would best approximate the relationship between the share price and expenses.

8. **(B)** For a single share of Fund D, the percent of fund expenses are calculated as follows:

$$\frac{0.51}{64} \times 100 \approx 0.797$$

The percent of fund expenses would remain the same no matter how many shares William had. So, to express the percentage return on his investment that he would need to have to cover his expected yearly management expenses, William would need Percent ≥ 0.8, since 0.8 would approximate 0.797 to the nearest tenth.

9. **(C)** When the height of the flower increases from 45–50 centimeters, the mass of the flower increases by approximately 3 grams, going from 13.5 to 16.5 grams. So, increase the flower's mass when it is at 50 cm in height by a similar amount of 3 grams, since there is a steady, linear relationship between the flower's height and mass. $16.5 + 3 = 19.5$ grams, corresponding to choice **(C)**.

10. **(C)** In a box plot, the line at which the two boxes meet is the median. In this graph, this occurs at approximately 5.25 cm. Therefore, the median will be within the range of 5–6 cm.

Additional Topics in Math

This section contains comprehensive review and strategies for all of the concepts below:

Additional Topics in Math—Area, Perimeter, and Volume

- Rectangle Area
- Triangle Area
- Perimeter of Polygons
- Parallelogram Area
- Trapezoid Area
- Surface Area
- Volume of a Box, Cylinder, Sphere, Cone, and Pyramid

Additional Topics in Math—Lines, Angles, and Triangles

- Supplementary Angles
- Vertical Angles
- Parallel Lines and a Transversal

Additional Topics in Math—Angles, Triangles, and Quadrilaterals

- Equilateral Triangles
- Isosceles Triangles
- Similar Triangles
- Angles in a Quadrilateral

Additional Topics in Math—Right Triangles and Trigonometry

- Pythagorean Theorem and Special Right Triangles
- Sine, Cosine, Tangent
- Area of an Equilateral Triangle
- Sine and Cosine of Complementary Angles

Additional Topics in Math—Circles

- Radius and Diameter
- Area and Circumference
- 360° in a Circle
- Inscribed Angle
- Arc Length
- Sector Area
- Circle Formula
- Radians

Additional Topics in Math—Imaginary Numbers

- Imaginary Number Essentials

Additional Topics in Math—Area, Perimeter, and Volume

At the beginning of each math test section, the SAT will provide you with a formula sheet that covers much of what you will need for problems related to area, perimeter, and volume.

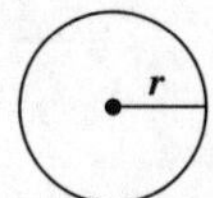

Radius of a circle $= r$
Area of a circle $= \pi r^2$
Circumference of a circle $= 2\pi r$

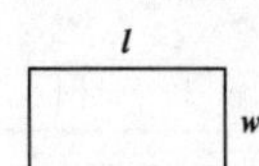

Area of a rectangle $=$ length $\times$ width $= lw$

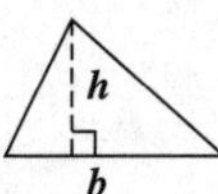

Area of a triangle $= \frac{1}{2} \times$ base $\times$ height $= \frac{1}{2}bh$

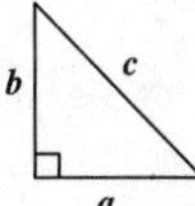

Pythagorean theorem: $a^2 + b^2 = c^2$

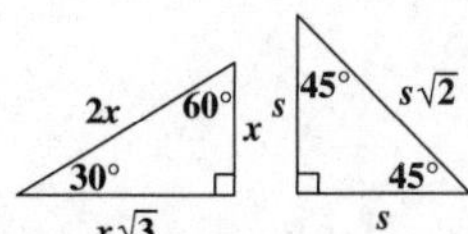

Special right triangles: 30-60-90 and 45-45-90

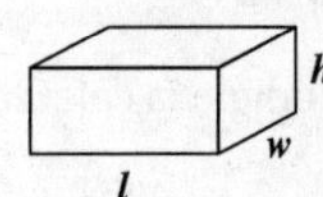

Volume of a box $=$ length $\times$ width $\times$ height $= lwh$

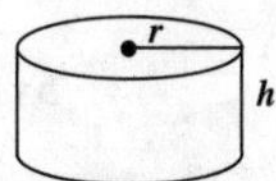

Volume of a cylinder $= \pi r^2 h$

Volume of a sphere $= \frac{4}{3}\pi r^3$

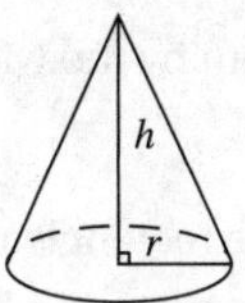

Volume of a cone $= \frac{1}{3}\pi r^2 h$

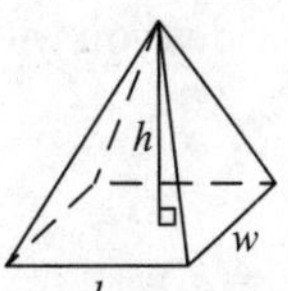

Volume of a pyramid $=$
$\frac{1}{3} \times$ length $\times$ width $\times$ height $= \frac{1}{3} lwh$

KEY FACTS:

- **A circle has 360 degrees.**
- **There are 2π radians in a circle.**
- **There are 180 degrees in a triangle.**

SAT Math Strategy

Even though many geometry formulas are provided, you should memorize these formulas so you have them at your fingertips. Memorizing the formulas will help you quickly remember what formula you will need for a given problem. Also, if you memorize the formulas, you will have a better sense of what all the variables and constants mean and how to apply them.

As you can see from above, the SAT provides you with area formulas for two important shapes: the rectangle and the triangle.

Rectangle Area

The area of a rectangle is calculated as follows:

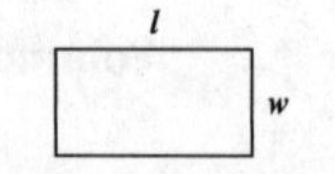

Area of a rectangle = length × width = lw

Example

What is the area of a rectangle with a length of 6 units and a width of 4 units?

Solution

Multiply the length by the width to find the area:

$$6 \times 4 = 24$$

So, the area of the rectangle would be 24 square units.

Triangle Area

The SAT also provides you with the formula for the area of a triangle:

h

b

$$\textbf{Area of a triangle} = \frac{1}{2} \times \textbf{base} \times \textbf{height} = \frac{1}{2}bh$$

Note: In your math class, you may have learned this formula as $A = \frac{bh}{2}$. This formula is perfectly fine to use as well.

Example

What is the area of the triangle drawn below?

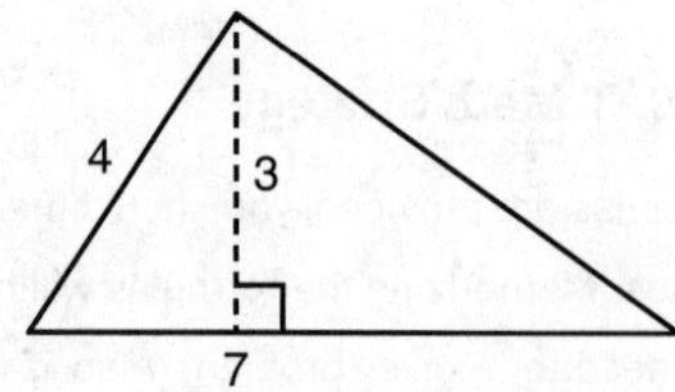

✓ **Solution**

When calculating the area of triangles, parallelograms, and trapezoids, remember that the **height is perpendicular to the base**. On this particular problem, the base is 7 and the height is 3 (not 4). To calculate the area of the triangle, use the triangle area formula:

$$\text{Area} = \frac{1}{2} \times \text{Base} \times \text{Height} \rightarrow$$

$$\text{Area} = \frac{1}{2} \times 7 \times 3 = \frac{21}{2} = 10.5$$

So, the triangle's area will be 10.5 square units.

Now, let's consider the polygon concepts the SAT expects you to know, but for which you **do not** receive formulas.

Perimeter of Polygons

The *perimeter* of a shape is the length of its sides added together.

› **Example 1**

What is the perimeter of the rectangle below?

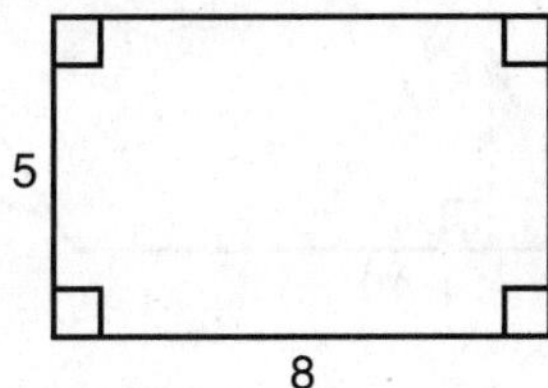

✓ **Solution**

In a rectangle, the sides opposite one another are equal. So the total length of the sides of the rectangle would be $5 + 5 + 8 + 8 = 26$ units.

› **Example 2**

What is the perimeter for the triangle below?

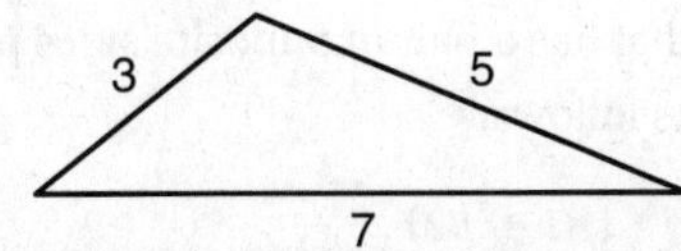

✓ **Solution**

Add the three side lengths of the triangle to find the perimeter:

$$3 + 5 + 7 = 15 \text{ units}$$

Parallelogram Area

A parallelogram is a four-sided figure that has opposite sides that are parallel. (A rectangle is a special form of a parallelogram that has only 90° angles.) The area for a parallelogram is given below:

Base × Height = Area

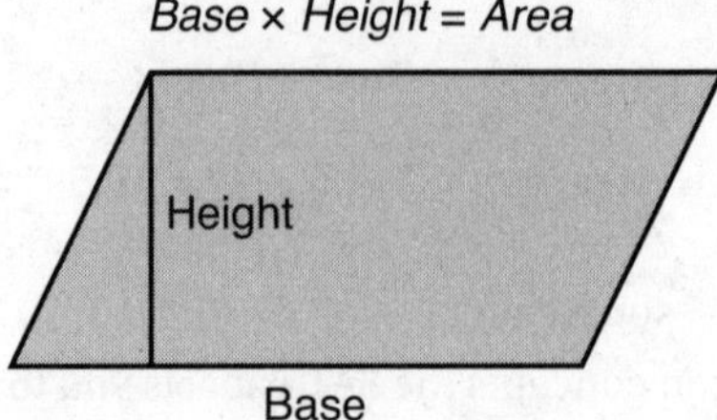

Be careful that you do not count one of the slanted edges as the height. Like with the triangle, the height will always be perpendicular to the base.

Example

What is the area of the parallelogram drawn below?

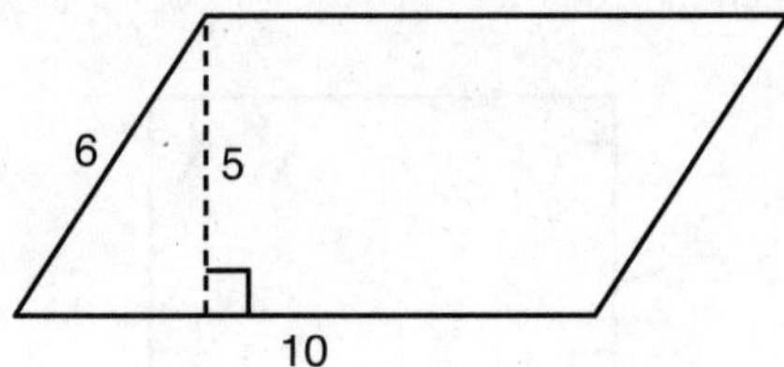

Solution

The base of the parallelogram is 10, and the height is 5 since it is perpendicular to the base. (The height is not 6 since this side is not perpendicular to the base.) So, the area is the base multiplied by the height:

$$\text{Base} \times \text{Height} = 10 \times 5 = 50$$

The area is therefore 50 square units.

Trapezoid Area

A trapezoid is a four-sided figure that has a pair of opposite sides parallel to one another. The area for a trapezoid is calculated as follows:

$$\frac{(B1 + B2)}{2} height = Area$$

B1 (Base 1)

Height

B2 (Base 2)

In essence, you are finding the "average" of the two bases and multiplying this average by the height of the trapezoid. As with the triangle and parallelogram, be mindful that the height must be perpendicular to the base.

Example

What is the area of the trapezoid drawn below?

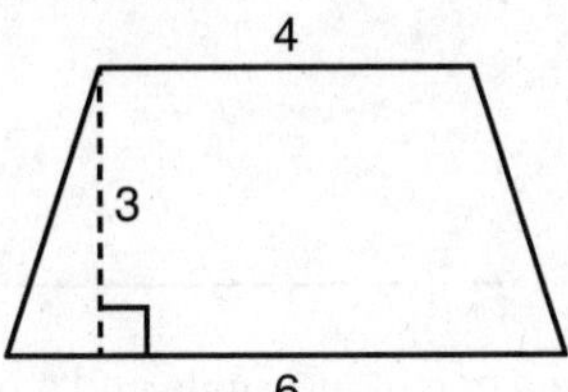

Solution

Use 4 as B1, 6 as B2, and 3 as the height, plugging these values into the trapezoid formula:

$$\frac{(B1 + B2)}{2} height = Area \rightarrow$$

$$\frac{(4 + 6)}{2} \times 3 = 5 \times 3 = 15$$

So, the area of the trapezoid is 15 square units.

Surface Area

The SAT may ask you to calculate the surface area of a *right rectangular prism*—this is a fancy way of saying *box.* To calculate the surface are of a box, take the area of each face of the box and add them together using this formula:

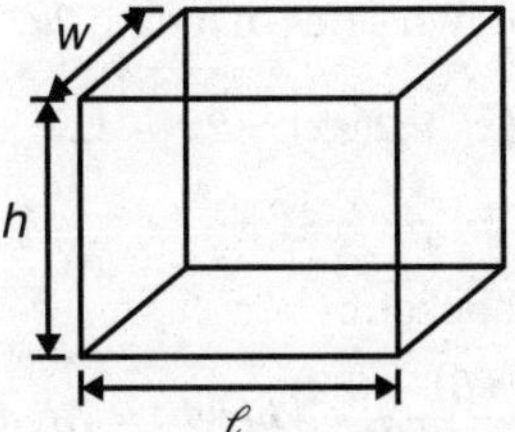

Surface Area = $2(lw) + 2(lh) + 2(wh)$

Example

What is the surface area of a right rectangular prism with a height of 3 units, a length of 5 units, and a width of 4 units?

✓ Solution

Carefully plug 3, 4, and 5 into the surface area formula to find the surface area:

$$\text{Surface Area} = 2(lw) + 2(lh) + 2(wh) \rightarrow$$
$$\text{Surface Area} = 2(5 \times 4) + 2(5 \times 3) + 2(4 \times 3) \rightarrow$$
$$2(20) + 2(15) + 2(12) =$$
$$40 + 30 + 24 = 94$$

So, the surface area is 94 square units.

› Practice

1. What is the area of a triangle with a height of 3 units and a base of 4 units?
2. What is the perimeter of a rectangle with a width of x and length of $2x$?
3. What is the area of the parallelogram below?

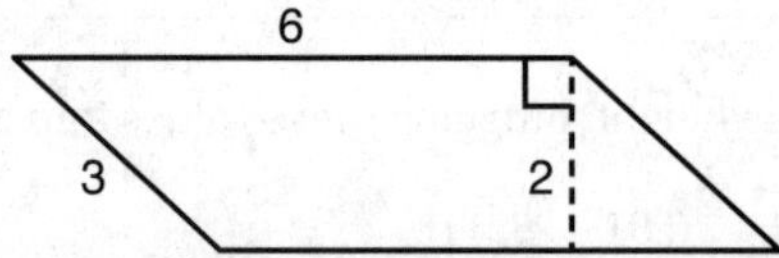

4. If a trapezoid has a height h and an area of $6h$ square units, what would be the area of a trapezoid with bases of the same length but a height twice that of the original?
5. What is the surface area of a cube with an edge length of 3?
6. If the perimeter of a rectangle is 24 inches, what would be the value of the length and the width of the rectangle in order to *maximize* the rectangle's area?

✓ Solutions

1. $\frac{1}{2} \times \text{Base} \times \text{Height} = \frac{1}{2} \times 4 \times 3 = 6$
2. There are two sides of length x and two sides of length $2x$:

$$2(x) + 2(2x) = 2x + 4x = 6x$$

3. $\text{Base} \times \text{Height} = 6 \times 2 = 12$
4. Consider the area formula for a trapezoid:

$$\frac{(B1 + B2)}{2} height = Area$$

   If the bases remain the same, and the height is doubled, the original area will be doubled since the only thing that changes is the height. So, the new area would be $12h$.
5. In a cube, all the edges are of the same length:

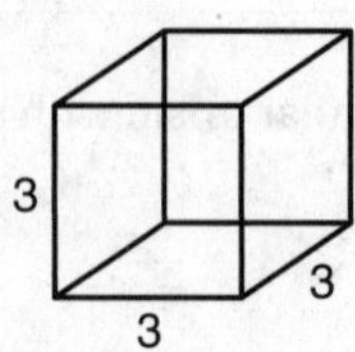

So, plug 3 in for length, width, and height in the surface area formula:

$$\text{Surface Area} = 2(lw) + 2(lh) + 2(wh) \rightarrow$$
$$\text{Surface Area} = 2(3^2) + 2(3^2) + 2(3^2) \rightarrow$$
$$\text{Surface Area} = 18 + 18 + 18 = 54$$

Alternatively, you could calculate the surface area for one of the sides, $3 \times 3 = 9$, and multiply this by 6 since there are 6 total sides: $6 \times 9 = 54$ square units.

6. To maximize the area of the rectangle while minimizing the perimeter, the rectangle should be a *square*. You can see why this would be by trying out some sample values for length and width (that would allow for a perimeter of 24):
Length: 6 inches, width: 6 inches. Area is 36 square inches.
Length: 7 inches, width 5 inches. Area is 35 square inches.
Length: 8 inches, width 4 inches. Area is 32 square inches.
Length: 9 inches, width 3 inches. Area is 27 square inches.
So, the length and width should each be 6 inches in order to maximize the area of the rectangle.

Volume Calculations

The volume formulas you need to know are all provided at the beginning of each math section. Here are examples showing how to apply each of these formulas.

Volume of a Box (Right Rectangular Prism)

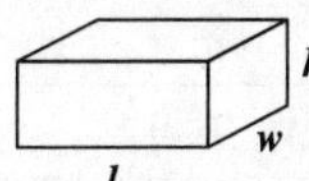

Volume of a box = length × width × height = $\boldsymbol{lwh}$

A common error students make is to confuse area and volume. Area will only be a calculation of two dimensions, like length × width. Volume will be a calculation of three dimensions, as we can see above.

Example

What is the volume of box with a length $2x$ inches, a width of $3x$ inches, and a height of y inches?

Solution

Even though this asks you to calculate expressions with x and y, you can still use the same formula as above and multiply the length, width, and height together.

$$lwh = (2x)(3x)(y) = 6x^2y$$

So, the volume would be $6x^2y$ cubic inches.

Volume of a Cylinder

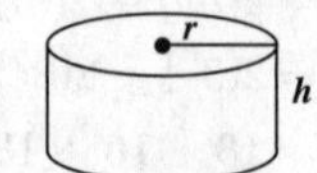

Volume of a cylinder $= \pi r^2 h$

Think about calculating the volume of a cylinder as taking the area of the circle on top, then multiplying it by the height all the way down.

Example

What is the volume of a cylinder with a height of 8 inches and a diameter of 4 inches, as shown below?

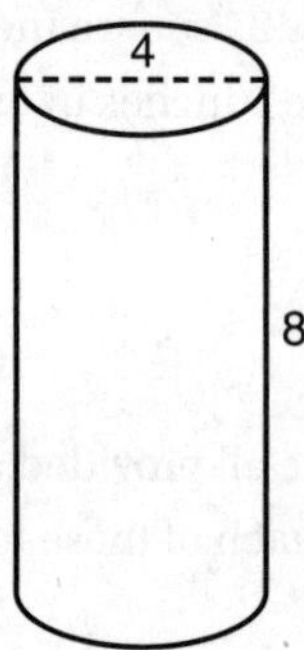

Solution

Be careful to distinguish between the radius and the diameter. The radius is *half* the length of the diameter, so the radius for the above cylinder would be 2. Then, plug 2 in for the radius and 8 in for the height to solve for the volume:

$$\pi r^2 h = \pi(2)^2(8) = 32\pi$$

So, the volume would be 32π cubic inches.

Volume of a Sphere

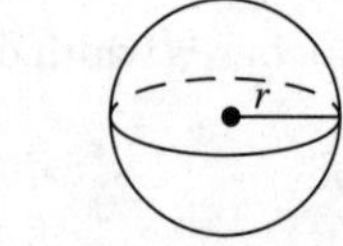

Volume of a sphere $= \frac{4}{3}\pi r^3$

Example

Consider the volume of a sphere with a radius of x units. How much greater will the volume of a sphere with double the radius be?

✓ **Solution**

The volume of the original sphere will be $\frac{4}{3}\pi x^3$ cubic units. The radius of the second sphere will be 2*x*, so its volume will be $\frac{4}{3}\pi(2x)^3 = \frac{4}{3}\pi(8x^3)$ cubic units. Divide the second volume by the first to see the multiple by which it is greater than the first:

$$\frac{\frac{4}{3}\pi(8x^3)}{\frac{4}{3}\pi x^3} \rightarrow \frac{\cancel{\frac{4}{3}}\cancel{\pi}(8\cancel{x^3})}{\cancel{\frac{4}{3}}\cancel{\pi}\cancel{x^3}} = 8$$

So, the volume of the second sphere will be 8 times greater than the first. If you realize that the only thing that will change from one sphere to the next is the radius, you can simply calculate the ratio of the cubes of the radii to arrive at your solution.

Volume of a Cone

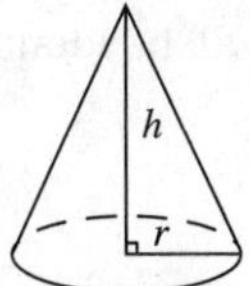

Volume of a cone $= \frac{1}{3}\pi r^2 h$

› **Example**

How many cones of with radius 4 and height 6 will have the same total volume as a cylinder with the same radius and height?

✓ **Solution**

The SAT will frequently test your proficiency in manipulating algebraic expressions instead of doing long calculations. This question is a great example of this. Rather than calculating the volume of each cone, look at the relationship between the two formulas:

$$\text{Cone Volume} = \frac{1}{3}\pi r^2 h$$
$$\text{Cylinder Volume} = \pi r^2 h$$

The cylinder volume is three times that of the cone volume, since everything in the two formulas is the same except for the $\frac{1}{3}$ in front of the cone volume formula. Since $\frac{1}{3}$ goes into 1 three times, three cones could fit into a cylinder with the same radius and height as the cone.

Volume of a Pyramid

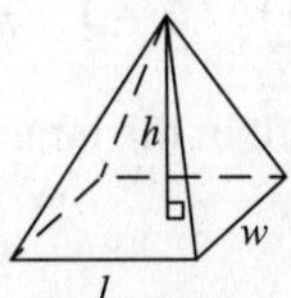

Volume of a pyramid =
$\frac{1}{3}$ **× length × width × height** $= \frac{1}{3}lwh$

Example

Consider a pyramid with a volume of 20 cubic inches. If the width is cut in half and the height is doubled, what would be the volume of the resulting pyramid?

Solution

Focus on how the changes to the width and height would affect the volume calculation.
For the original pyramid, the volume calculation would be as follows:

$$20 = \frac{1}{3}lwh$$

For the second pyramid, the new width is $\frac{1}{2}w$ and the new height is $2h$. So, the volume would be:

$$\frac{1}{3}l\left(\frac{1}{2}w\right)(2h) = \frac{1}{3}l\left(\frac{\cancel{1}}{\cancel{2}}w\right)(\cancel{2}h) = \frac{1}{3}lwh$$

Therefore, the volume of the new pyramid will be identical to the volume of the first: 20 cubic inches.

Practice

1. What is the volume of a box with dimensions 3 inches by 2 inches by 5 inches?
2. What is the volume of a cone with a radius and height both of y centimeters?
3. What is the volume of a sphere with a diameter of 6 inches?
4. How many pyramids with dimensions 1 by 1 by 1 inch would fit in a box with dimensions 1 inch by 2 inches by 2 inches?
5. If the height of a cylinder were tripled and its radius halved, what would the volume of the new cylinder be as a multiple of the volume of the original?

Solutions

1. $lwh = 3 \times 2 \times 5 = 30$ cubic inches
2. Cone Volume $= \frac{1}{3}\pi r^2 h \rightarrow \frac{1}{3}\pi y^2 y = \frac{1}{3}\pi y^3$
3. Be sure to use the radius and not the diameter—the radius for this sphere is 3 inches. Plug 3 in to the sphere volume formula:

$$\text{Volume} = \frac{4}{3}\pi r^3 \rightarrow \frac{4}{3}\pi 3^3 = \left(\frac{4}{3}\right)(27)\pi = 36\pi \text{ cubic inches}$$

4. Divide the volume of a 1 by 2 by 2 inch pyramid by that of a 1 by 1 by 1 inch pyramid to see how many of the smaller pyramids would fit within the larger one.

$$\frac{\left(\frac{1}{3}(1 \times 2 \times 2)\right)}{\left(\frac{1}{3}(1 \times 1 \times 1)\right)} = \frac{\frac{1}{3} \times 4}{\frac{1}{3} \times 1} = \frac{\frac{\cancel{1}}{\cancel{3}} \times 4}{\frac{\cancel{1}}{\cancel{3}} \times 1} = \frac{4}{1} = 4$$

So, four of the smaller pyramids would fit in the larger pyramid.

5. Use the formula for Cylinder Volume $= \pi r^2 h$. For the original cylinder, let's just use r as the radius and h as the height, making the volume $\pi r^2 h$. For the new cylinder, the height is tripled and the radius is halved. So, use $3h$ for the height and $\frac{1}{2}r$ for the radius and calculate the new volume:

$$\pi\left(\frac{1}{2}r\right)^2(3h) = \pi\left(\frac{1}{4}r^2\right)(3h) = \frac{3}{4}\pi r^2 h$$

So, the volume of the new cylinder would be $\frac{3}{4}$ the volume of the original one.

SAT Math Questions Practice Drill—Additional Topics in Math: Area, Perimeter, and Volume

(If timing, take about 12 minutes to complete.)

Fill-In Practice: Write your answer in the underlined blank under each question.

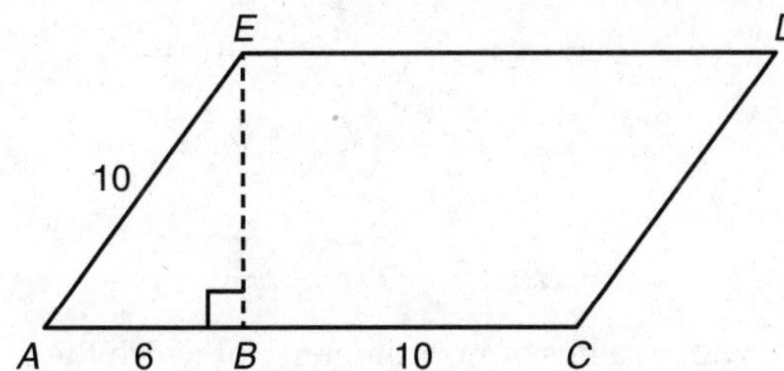

1. $AEDC$ is a parallelogram, with the length of $\overline{AB}$ 6 units, the length of $\overline{BC}$ 10 units, and the length of $\overline{AE}$ 10 units. Point B is on $\overline{AC}$ and $\overline{BE}$ is perpendicular to $\overline{AC}$. What is the area of the parallelogram in square units?

   Answer: ____________

2. A rectangular plot of land has a length twice its width. If the perimeter of the land is 90 feet, what is its area in square feet?

   Answer: ____________

3. If a cube has a volume of 125 cubic centimeters, what is the combined length of all the edges of the cube in centimeters?

   Answer: ____________

4. A cylinder has a volume of 150π square units and a height of 6 units. What is the diameter of the base of the cylinder in units?

   Answer: ____________

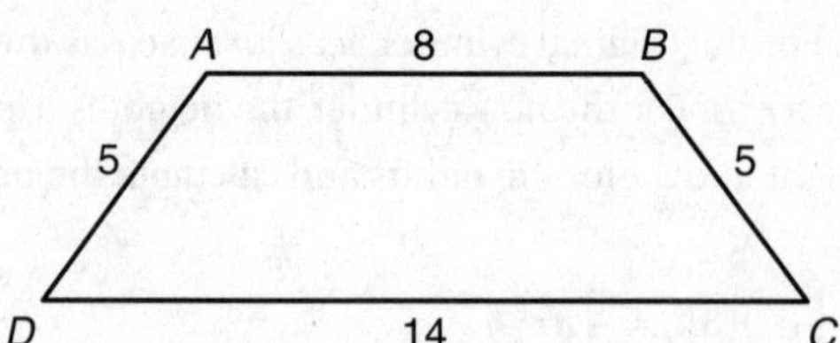

5. What is the area in square units of the trapezoid above, in which $\overline{AB}$ and $\overline{CD}$ are parallel?

Answer: ____________

Multiple-Choice Practice

6. Each gallon of wall paint that Julius purchases covers 400 square feet. If Julius is going to paint 3 walls, each with dimensions 40 feet by 12 feet, what is the minimum number of gallons of paint he needs to purchase, assuming he can only buy whole gallons and that there are no windows or other irregularities on the walls?

(A) 2
(B) 3
(C) 4
(D) 5

7. A basket maker designs cylindrical baskets with a radius of x centimeters, for which the height of the basket is twice the radius of the basket. Which of the following would correctly express the volume, V, in cubic centimeters, of such baskets?

(A) $V = 2\pi x^3$
(B) $V = \pi x^2$
(C) $V = 4\pi x^2$
(D) $V = 4\pi x^3$

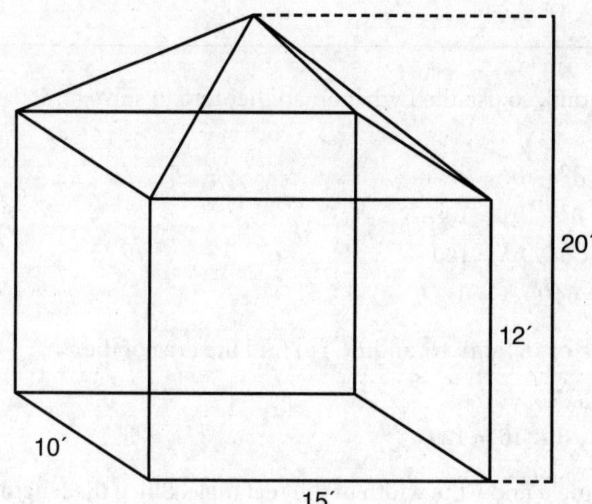

8. In the three-dimensional figure above, a rectangular prism with dimensions 12 feet by 10 feet by 15 feet has a pyramid with a base of 10 by 15 feet on top of it. The height of the rectangular prism and pyramid together is 20 feet. What is the volume of this entire figure?

(A) 900 cubic feet
(B) 1,460 cubic feet
(C) 2,200 cubic feet
(D) 3,000 cubic feet

9. A shoebox in the shape of a rectangular prism is supposed to have a volume between 432 and 504 cubic inches, inclusive. The box needs to have a length of 12 inches and a width of 6 inches. What is the range for a possible value for the height of the box?

(A) 5–6 inches inclusive
(B) 6–7 inches inclusive
(C) 7–8 inches inclusive
(D) 8–9 inches inclusive

10. A cylindrical swimming pool is 3 meters deep and has a diameter of 10 meters. If the density of water is 997 $\frac{kg}{m^3}$, how would one correctly calculate the mass in kilograms of the water in the pool if it is filled to the top with nothing but water?

(A) $\pi \times (10^2) \times 3 \times 997$
(B) $\pi \times (10^2) \times (1.5) \times 997$
(C) $\pi \times (5^2) \times (1.5) \times 997$
(D) $\pi \times (5^2) \times 3 \times 997$

✓ Solutions

1. **128** $\overline{BE}$ is the height of the parallelogram, so use the Pythagorean theorem to solve for its length:

$$a^2 + b^2 = c^2 \rightarrow$$
$$6^2 + b^2 = 10^2 \rightarrow$$
$$36 + b^2 = 100 \rightarrow$$
$$b^2 = 64 \rightarrow b = 8$$

Then, multiply the height 8 by the base of 16 (add $\overline{AB}$ and $\overline{BC}$) to find the area of the parallelogram:

$$8 \times 16 = 128$$

2. **450** Let's call x the length of the rectangle and y the width of the rectangle. Since the length is twice that of the width, we can say that $x = 2y$. The perimeter of the rectangle is $2x + 2y$, and since $x = 2y$, we can use substitution to solve for either the width or length—let's solve for the width:

$$2x + 2y = 90 \rightarrow$$
$$2(2y) + 2y = 90 \rightarrow$$
$$4y + 2y = 90 \rightarrow$$
$$6y = 90 \rightarrow$$
$$y = 15$$

So, the width of the rectangle is 15, and the length would be twice 15: 30. Then multiply 30 and 15 together to find the area of the rectangle:

$$15 \times 30 = 450$$

3. **60** The volume, V, of a cube of side length x is $V = x^3$. Solve for x given that the volume is 125 cubic centimeters:

$$V = x^3 \rightarrow$$
$$125 = x^3 \rightarrow$$
$$\sqrt[3]{125} = x \rightarrow$$
$$5 = x$$

There are 12 total edges in a cube, so multiply 5 by 12 to find the combined length of all the edges of the cube:

$$5 \times 12 = 60$$

4. **10** Plug the volume and the height into the cylinder volume formula:

$$\text{Cylinder Volume} = \pi r^2 h \rightarrow$$
$$150\pi = \pi r^2(6) \rightarrow$$
$$150 = r^2(6) \rightarrow$$
$$25 = r^2 \rightarrow r = 5$$

Now, double the radius to solve for the base diameter:

$$5 \times 2 = 10$$

5. **44** First, determine the height of the trapezoid. The trapezoid is isosceles which makes it easier to find the height using the Pythagorean theorem, since $3^2 + 4^2 = 5^2$.

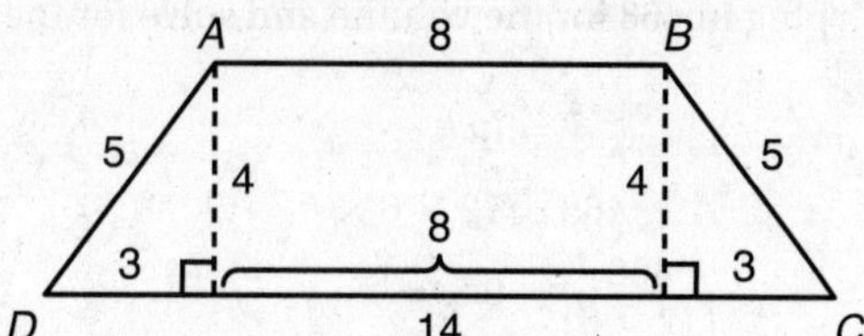

Now, use the area formula for a trapezoid to solve:

$$\frac{(B1 + B2)}{2} height = Area \rightarrow$$

$$\frac{(8 + 14)}{2}(4) = \frac{22}{2}(4) = 11 \times 4 = 44$$

6. **(C)** Find the surface area of each individual wall:

$$40 \times 12 = 480$$

Then multiply 480 by 3 to get the total area of the three walls:

$$480 \times 3 = 1{,}440$$

Now, divide 1,440 by 400 to see how many gallons of paint would be needed:

$$\frac{1{,}440}{400} = 3.6$$

Since Julius cannot purchase a partial gallon of paint, he must buy 4 full gallons to accomplish his task.

7. **(A)** Since the height of the basket is twice the radius of the basket, the height will be $2x$. Plug x in for the radius and $2x$ in for the height to express the volume:

$$V = \pi r^2 h \rightarrow$$
$$V = \pi x^2 (2x) \rightarrow$$
$$V = 2\pi x^3$$

8. **(C)** The figure is a box with dimensions 12 by 10 by 15 with a pyramid on top of it. The pyramid has a base of 10 by 15 and a height of 8, since $20 - 12 = 8$. Find the volumes of these two figures and add them together. First, the volume of the box:

$$lwh = 10 \times 15 \times 12 = 1{,}800$$

Next, the volume of the pyramid:

$$V = \frac{1}{3} lwh = \frac{1}{3} \times 10 \times 15 \times 8 = 400$$

Finally, add these separate volumes together to find the total volume:

$$1{,}800 + 400 = 2{,}200$$

9. **(B)** Pick a value that is within the range of 432 and 504 and solve for the possible height. Halfway between 432 and 504 is 468, so we can use that as a sample volume. The length and width are given, so let's plug in 468 for the volume and solve for the potential height:

$$V = lwh \rightarrow$$
$$468 = 12 \times 6 \times h \rightarrow$$
$$\frac{468}{(12 \times 6)} = 6.5 = h$$

The only option that has 6.5 as a possibility for the height is choice **(B)**.

10. **(D)** Multiply the density by the volume of the pool so we can find the mass of water in the pool—when doing this, we are left with kilograms as the resulting unit. Use 5 meters as the radius, since radius is half the diameter:

$$\pi r^2 h \times \text{Density} \rightarrow$$
$$\pi \times (5^2) \times 3 \times 997$$

Additional Topics in Math—Lines, Angles, and Triangles

SAT Math Strategy

Unless the question states otherwise, the drawings on the SAT math will all be done to scale, so do not hesitate to estimate based on the drawings. The angle rules below are very helpful to know, but if you forget them on test day, making estimates is an excellent backup plan.

Supplementary Angles

Supplementary angles add up to 180 degrees. The most common example of supplementary angles is when two angles are formed with a straight line across the bottom.

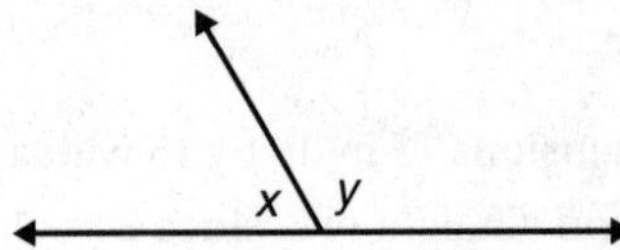

The sum of x and y is 180 degrees.

Example

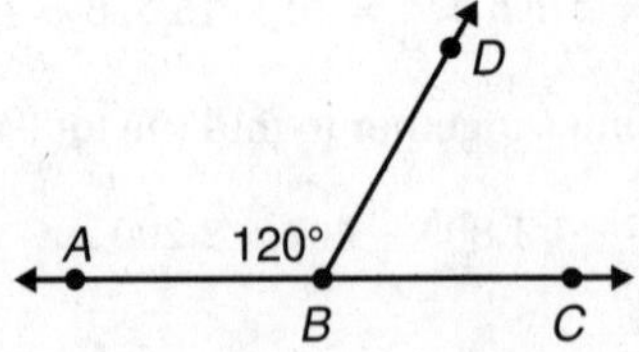

Given that $\overline{ABC}$ is a straight line that is intersected at point B by $\overline{BD}$, and that $\angle ABD$ is 120°, what is the measure of $\angle DBC$?

✓ **Solution**

The two angles add up to 180°, so subtract to find the answer, using x as the unknown angle measure:

$$x + 120 = 180 \rightarrow$$

$$x = 180 - 120 = 60$$

So, $\angle DBC = 60°$

Vertical Angles

When two lines intersect, the angles that are across from one another are called *vertical angles*. Vertical angles are equal to one another.

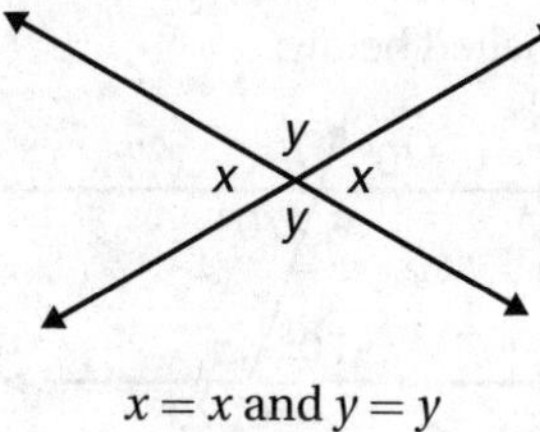

$x = x$ and $y = y$

› **Example**

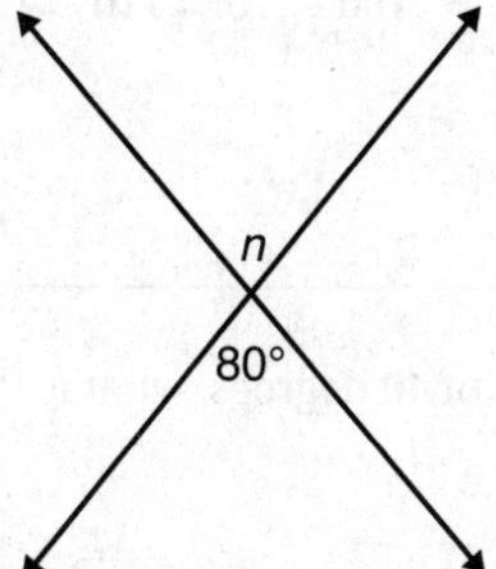

Two lines intersect one another in the figure above. What is the measure of $\angle n$?

✓ **Solution**

Since $\angle n$ is a vertical angle to the angle of 80° across from it, $\angle n$ will be equal to this angle and will therefore have a measure of 80°.

Parallel Lines and a Transversal

When two parallel lines are cut by a *transversal*, a line that intersects both lines, there are angle equivalencies as labelled below:

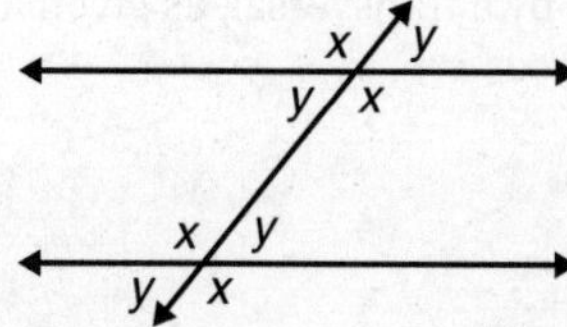

It can help to remember that the "big" angles (in this case x) are all equivalent and the "small" angles (in this case y) are all equivalent.

Example

Two parallel lines have a transversal running through them, as indicated in the drawing below. What is the measure of $\angle a$?

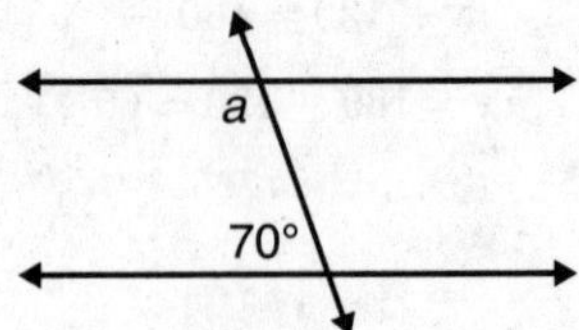

Solution

The measures of all the angles are labelled below:

As you can see, the "big" angles are all equivalent and the "small" angles are all equivalent. To calculate the value of a, subtract 70° from 180° since a and 70° are supplementary:

$$180 - 70 = 110$$

So, a is equal to 110°.

Practice

1. If $\angle x$ is supplementary to an angle of 40 degrees, what is the measure of $\angle x$?

2. 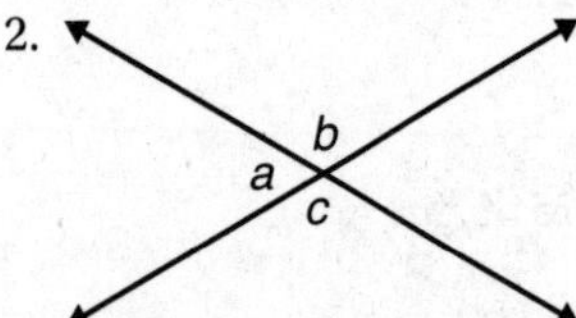

   Two lines intersect above, forming angles with measures a, b, and c degrees. If $\angle b$ is twice the measure of $\angle a$, what is the measure of $\angle c$?

3. 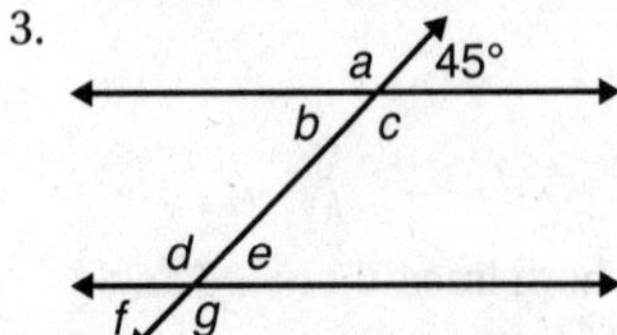

   Two parallel lines are intersected by a transversal, as given above. What are the measures of the labelled angles?

Solutions

1. **140** Since $\angle x$ is supplementary to 40°, $\angle x$ is equal to 180° minus 40°.

$$180 - 40 = 140$$

2. **120** $\angle b$ and $\angle a$ are supplementary, so they will add up to 180°. Since $\angle b$ is twice the measure of $\angle a$, $b = 2a$. Now, plug $2a$ in for b to solve for the angle measure of a:

$$b + a = 180 \rightarrow$$
$$(2a) + a = 180 \rightarrow$$
$$3a = 180 \rightarrow$$
$$a = 60$$

Since $\angle b$ and $\angle a$ are supplementary, find the value of $\angle b$ by subtracting 60 from 180: $180 - 60 = 120$. $\angle b$ is 120°, and since $\angle c$ and $\angle b$ are vertical angles, $\angle c$ is also equal to 120°.

3. $\angle a$ is supplementary to 45°, so it has a measure of $180 - 45 = 135$. $\angle b$, $\angle e$, and $\angle f$ are all equal to 45°, given that these are parallel lines with a transversal. $\angle a$, $\angle c$, $\angle d$, and $\angle g$ are all equal to 135°. This is an excellent example of a problem in which you can think it through using the facts that the "big" angles are equal and the "small" angles are equal.

Additional Topics in Math—Angles, Triangles, and Quadrilaterals

The SAT gives you this important information on the formula sheet at the beginning:

The sum of the measures in degrees of the angles of a triangle is 180.

Even though this is given, it is extremely helpful to commit this fundamental concept to memory.

Example

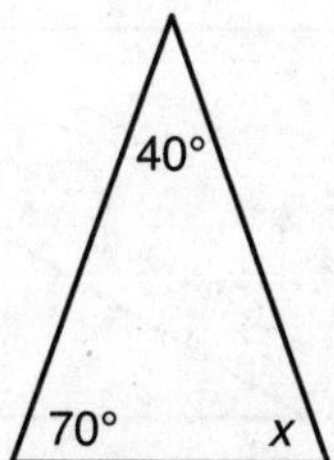

In the triangle above, what is the measure of $\angle x$?

Solution

Subtract 70 and 40 from 180 to find the measure of $\angle x$:

$$180 - 70 - 40 = 70$$

So, $\angle x$ is 70°.

The SAT does NOT give you reminders of these concepts—be sure you memorize them.

- **Equilateral** triangles have all three angles equal (each measuring 60 degrees) and all three sides equal.
- **Isosceles** triangles have only two angles equal and two sides equal.

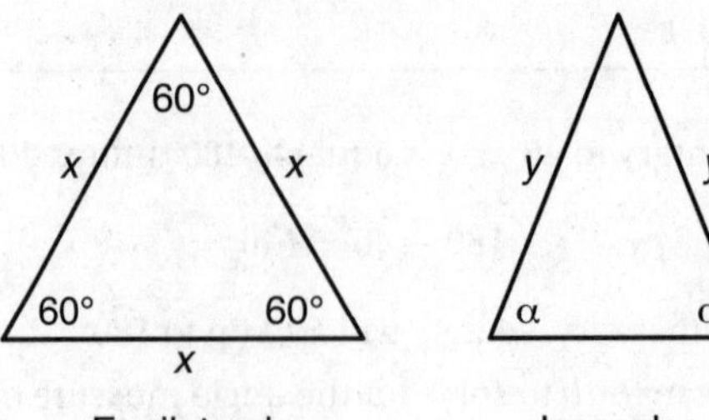

Example

Is an equilateral triangle also isosceles?

Solution

Yes—it is a special form of an isosceles triangle. If two of the angles and corresponding sides are equivalent, the triangle is isosceles. An equilateral triangle does have two angles and sides equivalent. This situation is similar to saying that a square is a special form of a rectangle.

Similar triangles are ones with the same angles, but not necessarily the same sides.

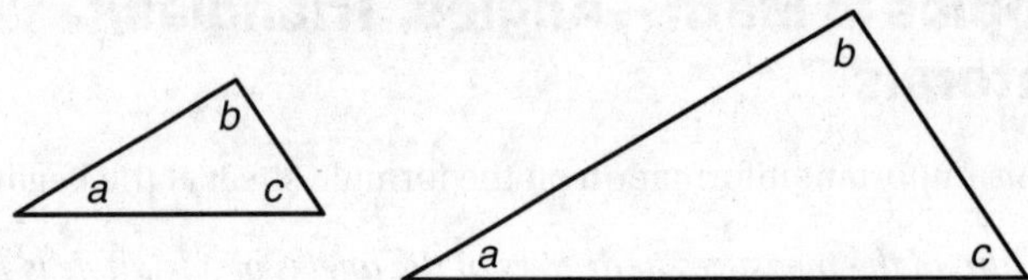

The triangle on the right is larger than the one on the left, yet they are similar—they have the same angle measures and their sides are *proportional* to each other.

Example

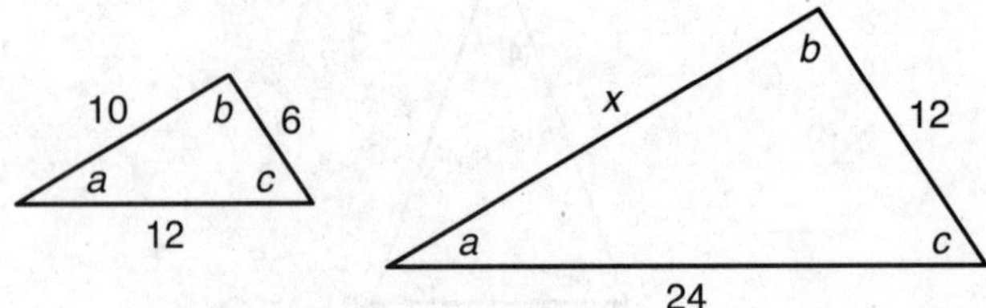

Suppose that the two triangles above are similar to one another. What is the length of side x?

Solution

Since the triangles are similar, their corresponding sides are proportional:

$$10:6:12$$

$$x:12:24$$

So, set up a proportion to solve for x:

$$\frac{x}{12} = \frac{10}{6} \rightarrow$$

$$x = \frac{12 \times 10}{6} = 20$$

x is therefore 20 units long. You could also have used a different proportion to solve this given the numbers provided.

A final important fact to know about angles is that **a quadrilateral has internal angles that add up to 360 degrees**. This is true for squares, rectangles, parallelograms, trapezoids, and so on.

Example

In the parallelogram below, what is the measure of $\angle x$?

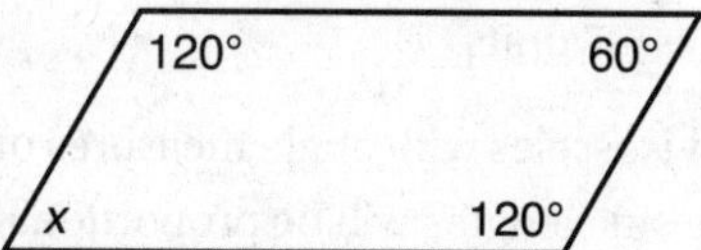

Solution

Subtract the other angles from 360° to find the measure of $\angle x$:

$$360 - 120 - 60 - 120 = 60$$

$\angle x$ is equal to the angle opposite it, 60°.

Practice

1. If three of the angles in a trapezoid add up to 300°, what is the measure of the fourth angle?
2. If an isosceles triangle has one angle of 100°, what are the measures of the other two angles?
3. A triangle has two sides with a length of 7 units and two angles that each measure 60°. Based on this information, what is the length of the third side of the triangle?

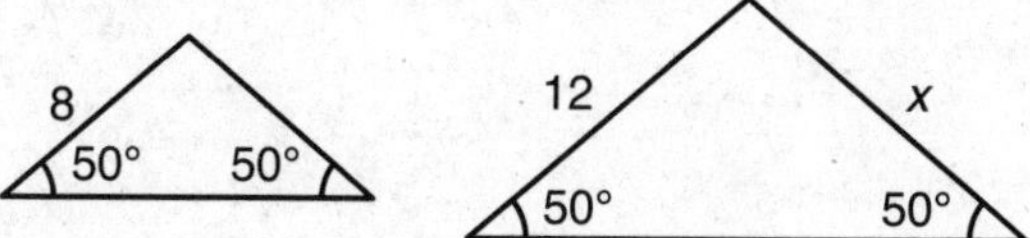

4. Based on the drawing of the two triangles above, what is the measure of side x?

Solutions

1. **60°** Since a trapezoid is a quadrilateral, its internal angles will add up to 360°. To find the measure of the fourth angle, subtract 300 from 360:

$$360 - 300 = 60$$

So, the fourth angle has a measure of 60°.

2. **40°** A triangle has a total internal degree measure of 180°. Since one of the angles is 100°, it must be the case that the other two angles are equivalent and would add up to 80°. (If the 100° angle were duplicated, the total sum of the internal angles in the isosceles triangle would exceed 200°, which is not possible.) So, subtract 100 from 180 to find the sum of the other two angles:

$$180 - 100 = 80$$

Then, divide 80 by 2 to find the measure of each of the other two angles:

$$\frac{80}{2} = 40$$

So, each of the other two angles will measure 40°.

3. **7** Since two of the angles in the triangle are each 60°, the measure of the third angle must also be 60° so that the three angles can have a sum of 180°. Since all the angles are equivalent, the triangle must be equilateral. By definition, an equilateral triangle will have equal angles *and* equal sides. Therefore, the measure of the third side of the triangle will be equivalent to the measures of the other two sides—7 units.

4. **12** The two triangles are both isosceles with angle measures of 50°, 50°, and 100°. Since they are similar to one another, the side lengths will be proportional.

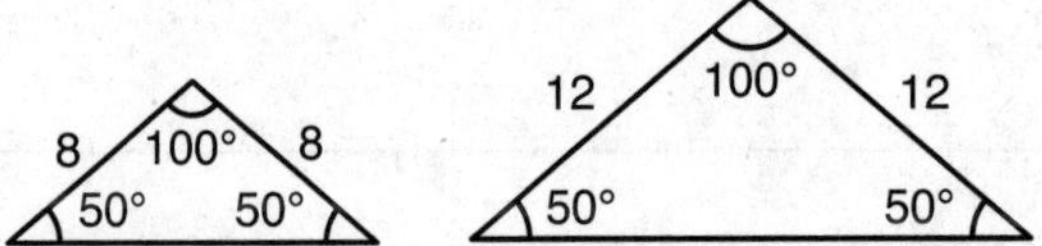

As you can see from the drawings above, the measure of side x will therefore be 12.

SAT Math Questions Practice Drill—Additional Topics in Math: Lines, Angles, and Triangles

(If timing, take about 12 minutes to complete.)

Fill-In Practice: Write your answer in the underlined blank under each question.

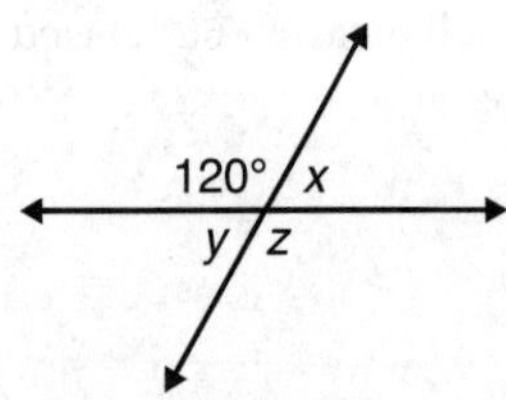

1. In the drawing above of the two intersecting lines, how many of the angles x, y, and z is/are equal to 120°?

   Answer: ____________

2. An equilateral triangle has sides of the following lengths in units: 8, $x - 7$, and $-2x + 38$. What is the value in units of x?

   Answer: ____________

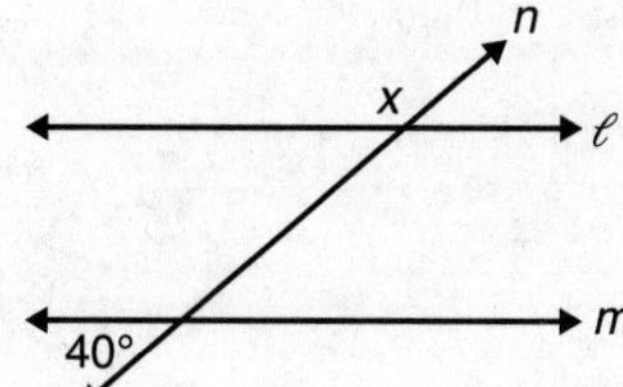

3. For parallel lines *l* and *m* with an intersecting line *n*, what is the measure of angle *x* in degrees?

Answer: ________

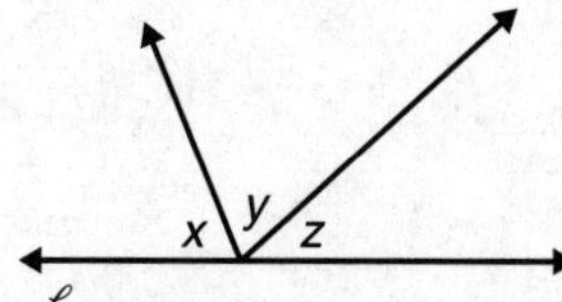

4. Given that *l* is a straight line, what is the mean of the measures of angles *x*, *y*, and *z* in degrees?

Answer: ________

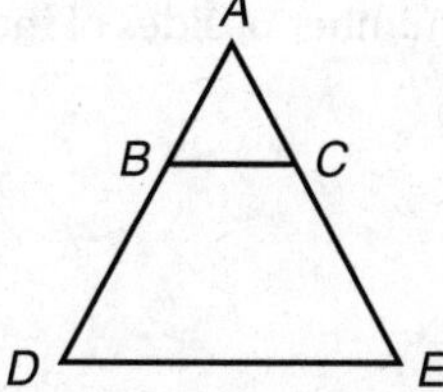

5. In ΔADE, *B* is a point on $\overline{AD}$ and *C* is a point on $\overline{AE}$, and $\overline{BC}$ and $\overline{DE}$ are parallel. If $\overline{AE}$ is 12 units, $\overline{AC}$ is 4 units, and $\overline{BC}$ is 3 units, what is the measure of $\overline{DE}$ in units?

Answer: ________

Multiple-Choice Practice

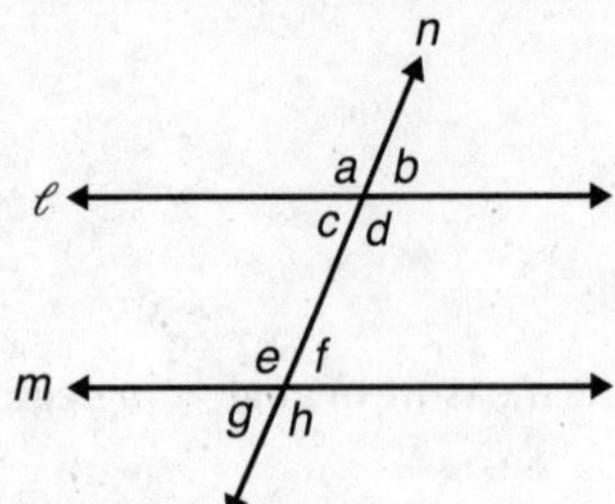

6. If lines l and m are parallel, and line n intersects both line l and line m, which pairs of angles must be congruent?

    I. $\angle a$ and $\angle h$

    II. $\angle c$ and $\angle f$

    III. $\angle e$ and $\angle b$

    (A) I only
    (B) III only
    (C) I and II only
    (D) All of the above

7. If triangle ABC has one angle greater than 90°, what is the maximum number of sides of the triangle that can be equal in length?

    (A) 1
    (B) 2
    (C) 3
    (D) Cannot be determined with the given information

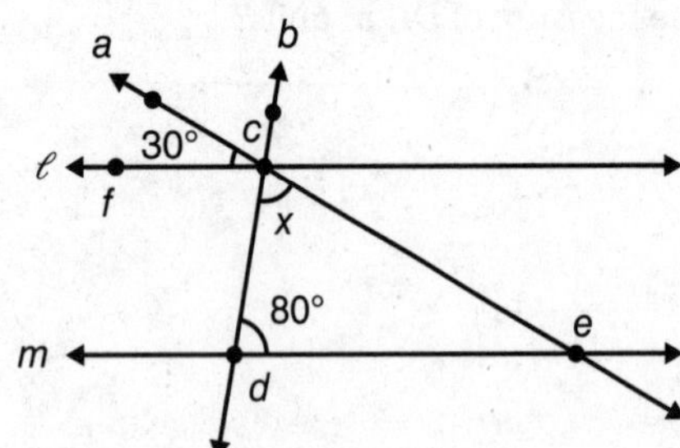

8. In the above figure, lines l and m are parallel, and lines a and b intersect at point C. If $\angle CDE$ is 80° and $\angle ACF$ is 30°, what is the measure of $\angle x$?

    (A) 70°
    (B) 80°
    (C) 100°
    (D) 150°

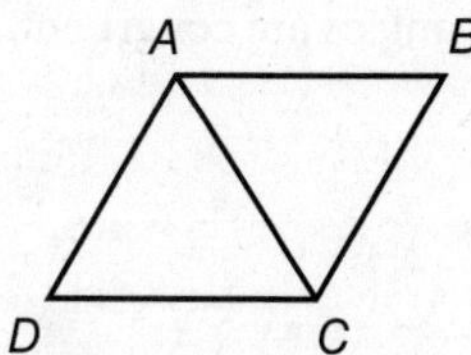

9. In parallelogram *ABCD* above, $\overline{AB}$, $\overline{BC}$, $\overline{CD}$, $\overline{DA}$, and $\overline{AC}$ are all congruent. What is the measure of angle $\angle BAC$?
   (A) 60°
   (B) 80°
   (C) 90°
   (D) 120°

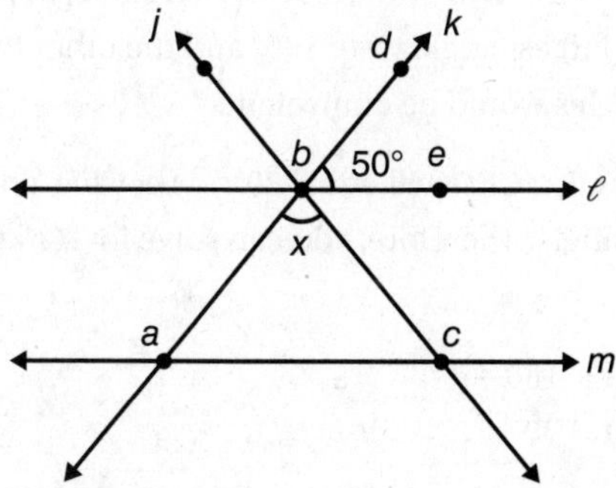

10. In the graph above, lines *l* and *m* are parallel, $\overline{AB}$ and $\overline{BC}$ are congruent, $\angle DBE$ is 50°, and lines *j* and *k* intersect at point *B*. What is the measure of angle *x*?
    (A) 60°
    (B) 80°
    (C) 100°
    (D) 120°

✓ Solutions

1. **1** Only the vertical angle that is across from the angle of 120° will also have a measure of 120°. $\angle x$ and the angle across from it each measure 60°.

2. **15** All of the sides in an equilateral triangle are equivalent, so set up an equation to solve for *x*:

$$8 = x - 7 \rightarrow$$
$$8 + 7 = x \rightarrow$$
$$15 = x$$

3. **140** $\angle x$ is identical to the angle that is supplementary to 40°. Therefore,

$$40 + x = 180 \rightarrow$$
$$x = 140$$

4. **60** All three of the angles add up to 180°, so calculate the mean by dividing 180 by 3:

$$\frac{180}{3} = 60$$

5. **9** Triangles *ABC* and *ADE* are similar to one another because their angles are congruent, so their sides are proportional. Set up a proportion to solve for $\overline{DE}$.

$$\frac{\overline{AC}}{\overline{AE}} = \frac{\overline{BC}}{\overline{DE}} \rightarrow$$

$$\frac{4}{12} = \frac{3}{x} \rightarrow$$

$$x = \frac{3 \times 12}{4} = \frac{36}{4} = 9$$

6. **(C)** With parallel lines and a transversal, match up the "large" and the "small" angles to establish equivalences. $\angle a$ and $\angle h$ are alternate exterior angles that are congruent, and $\angle c$ and $\angle f$are alternate interior angles that are congruent. $\angle e$ and $\angle b$ are not congruent, which you see from estimation in addition to knowing the general rule.

7. **(B)** It will be impossible for the triangle to have all sides equal, since an equilateral triangle has all angles equal to 60°. However, it is possible to have two of the sides equal since an isosceles triangle could be formed. For example, if the largest angle were 100° and the other two angles were both 40°, the sides opposite the 40° angles would be equivalent.

8. **(A)** Since lines *l* and *m* are parallel with a transversal, $\angle CED$ will equal 30°. $\angle x$, $\angle CED$, and $\angle CDE$ add up to 180° because they are within a triangle. Therefore, you can solve for $\angle x$ as follows:

$$x + 80 + 30 = 180 \rightarrow$$

$$x = 180 - 80 - 30 = 70$$

9. **(A)** If all the sides are equivalent, two equilateral triangles, *ABC* and *ACD*, will form. Since all the angles in an equilateral triangle are equal to 60°, $\angle BAC$ will equal 60°.

10. **(B)** Use the fact that vertical angles are equal and the angles across from equal sides in an isosceles triangle (i.e., *ABC*) are equal to establish equivalences as drawn below:

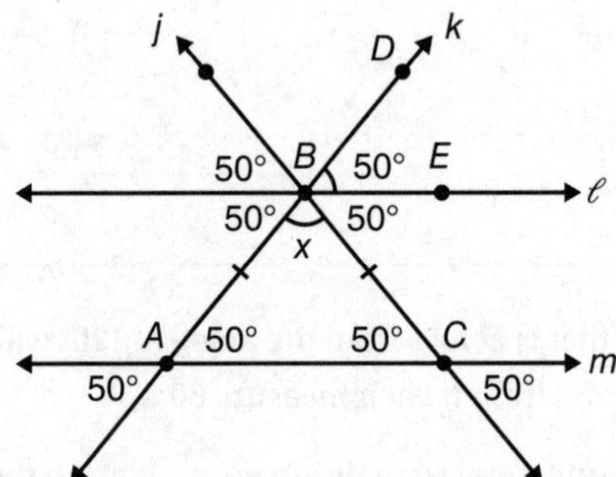

Since $\overline{AB}$ and $\overline{BC}$ are congruent, $\angle BAC = \angle BCA$ (triangle *ABC* is isosceles). Since lines *l* and *m* are parallel and $\angle KBE$ and $\angle BAC$ are corresponding angles, $\angle BAC = 50°$. Therefore, $\angle BCA = 50°$ and $\angle x = 180° - 50° - 50° = 80°$.

Additional Topics in Math—Right Triangles and Trigonometry

Pythagorean Theorem and Special Right Triangles

The SAT provides you with these two important right triangle formulas that enable you to determine the side lengths and even some angles in right triangles (triangles that have a 90° angle):

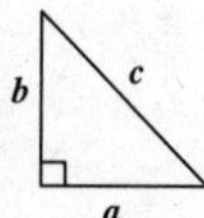

Pythagorean theorem: $a^2 + b^2 = c^2$

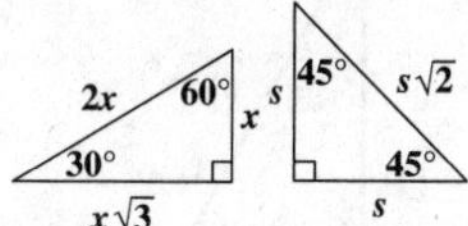

Even though they are provided, it is extremely helpful to have these formulas memorized so that you can more instantaneously and intuitively determine right angle relationships.

Example 1

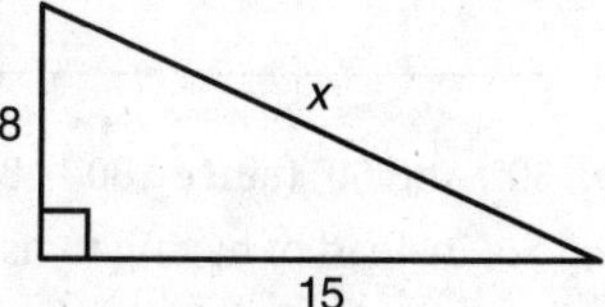

What is the length of x in the right triangle above?

Solution

Use the Pythagorean theorem to solve. Sides a and b are both "legs" of the right triangle (the sides NOT across from the 90° angle), and side c is the hypotenuse (the side that is across from the 90° angle). Let's use 8 as side a, 15 as side b, and x as side c.

$$a^2 + b^2 = c^2 \rightarrow$$
$$8^2 + 15^2 = x^2 \rightarrow$$
$$64 + 225 = 289 = x^2 \rightarrow$$
$$\sqrt{289} = 17 = x$$

So, side x is equal to 17 units.

Example 2

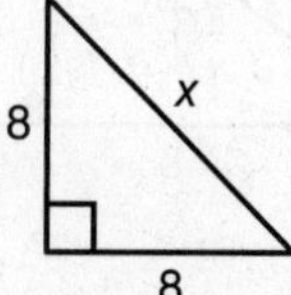

What is the length of side x in the right triangle above?

Solution

While you could use the Pythagorean theorem to solve for x, it will be more efficient to recognize that this is a special right triangle in which the sides have a relationship of s, s, $s\sqrt{2}$. The legs of the triangle are both 8, so you can find the hypotenuse of the triangle by multiplying 8 by $\sqrt{2}$. Therefore, the length of x is $8\sqrt{2}$.

Example 3

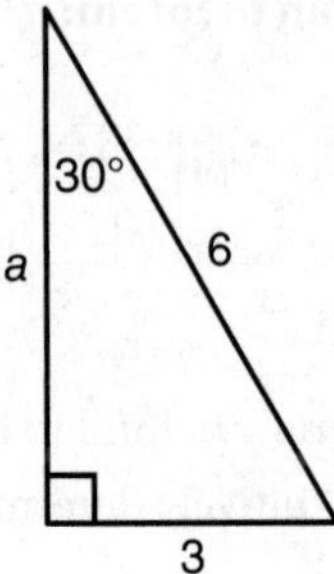

What is the length of side a in the right triangle above?

Solution

The above triangle has angles of 90°, 30°, and 60° (since $180 - 30 - 90 = 60$). So, the sides will have a relationship of x, $x\sqrt{3}$, and $2x$. So, instead of having to use the Pythagorean theorem to solve for a, realize that a will simply be $\sqrt{3}$ multiplied by 3, given where the sides are in the triangle. Therefore, $a = 3\sqrt{3}$.

Another way of solving for the unknown sides of right triangles is to use **Pythagorean triples**. These are combinations of side lengths in right triangles for which each value is an integer. The most important ones to know are the following:

3-4-5, 5-12-13, and 7-24-25

Not only will the above combinations work as sides for right triangles, but *multiples* of them will also work. Just as 5-12-13 could be sides of a right triangle, 10-24-26 could also be sides of a right triangle, since each side is twice the value of the sides in the original triple.

Example

What is the measure of side x in the triangle below?

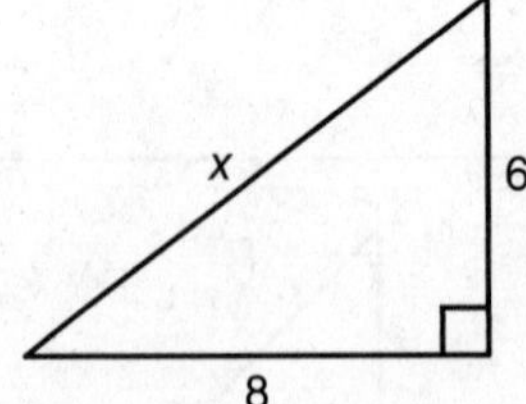

✓ Solution

While you could solve for x by using the Pythagorean theorem, you can solve this more quickly by recognizing that the sides in this triangle are multiples of a 3-4-5 triple. The 6 is twice 3, the 8 is twice 4, so the x is twice 5. So, to solve for x, just double 5:

$$2 \times 5 = 10$$

Side x therefore has a length of 10 units.

› Practice

1. If two legs in a right triangle are 9 and 40, what is the length of the hypotenuse?
2. If the hypotenuse in a right triangle is 61 and one of the legs is 60, what is the length of the other leg?
3. Two legs in a right triangle are equal to y. What is the value of the hypotenuse in terms of y?
4. If the hypotenuse in a right triangle is equal to 50 and the smaller leg is equal to 14, what is the length of the third side?
5. If the sides in a right triangle are 4, $4\sqrt{3}$, and 8, what is the measure of the smallest angle in the triangle?

✓ Solutions

1. Use the Pythagorean theorem to solve:

$$a^2 + b^2 = c^2 \rightarrow$$
$$9^2 + 40^2 = c^2 \rightarrow$$
$$81 + 1{,}600 = 1{,}681 = c^2 \rightarrow$$
$$\sqrt{1{,}681} = 41 = c$$

So, the hypotenuse has a length of 41 units.

2. Use the Pythagorean theorem to solve for the unknown leg. Use 61 as the c and 60 as a:

$$60^2 + b^2 = 61^2 \rightarrow$$
$$3{,}600 + b^2 = 3{,}721 \rightarrow$$
$$b^2 = 121 \rightarrow$$
$$b = 11$$

So, the unknown side has a length of 11 units.

3. With two of the legs equal in this triangle, we know that the relationship of the sides is s, s, $s\sqrt{2}$. Plugging in y for s, the hypotenuse will be $y\sqrt{2}$.

4. While you could use the Pythagorean theorem to solve this, you will save time if you recognize that these values are twice what we would find in the Pythagorean triple of 7-24-25. So, double the 24 to find the third side: $24 \times 2 = 48$.

5. Since the sides have the ratios x, $x\sqrt{3}$, and $2x$ (with $x = 4$), the triangle will have angles of 30°, 60°, and 90°. The smallest angle will therefore have a measure of 30°.

Sine, Cosine, Tangent

In a right triangle (a triangle with a 90° angle), the three sides are called the following:

Hypotenuse: This side is across from the 90° angle, and is always the longest side of the triangle.

Opposite: The side that is opposite, or across from, a particular angle. It could be either of the legs of the triangle depending on where the angle is.

Adjacent: The side that is adjacent to, or next to, a particular angle. It also could be either of the legs of the triangle depending on where the angle is and will never be the hypotenuse.

For example, in the right triangle below, the hypotenuse and the sides opposite and adjacent to angle *x* are labelled:

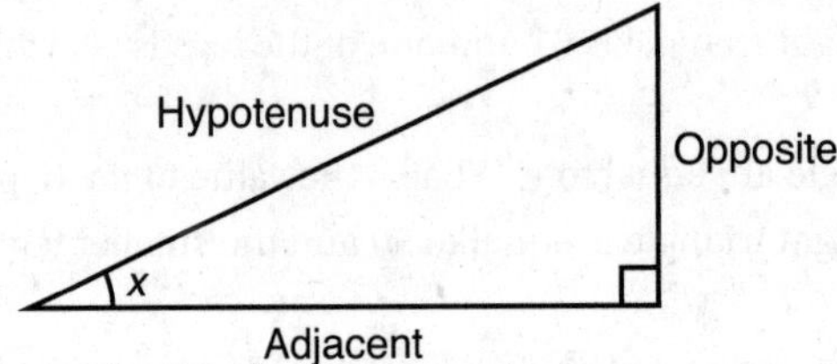

The popular acronym SOH-CAH-TOA will help you remember which sides to use when calculating *sine, cosine,* and *tangent.*

S-O-H	C-A-H	T-O-A
$\sin\theta = \frac{\text{Opposite}}{\text{Hypotenuse}}$	$\cos\theta = \frac{\text{Adjacent}}{\text{Hypotenuse}}$	$\tan\theta = \frac{\text{Opposite}}{\text{Adjacent}}$

Let's take a look at an example to see what the different trigonometry values would be.

$$\sin\theta = \frac{a}{c}$$

$$\cos\theta = \frac{b}{c}$$

$$\tan\theta = \frac{a}{b}$$

Example

What is the tangent for angle *x* in the right triangle below?

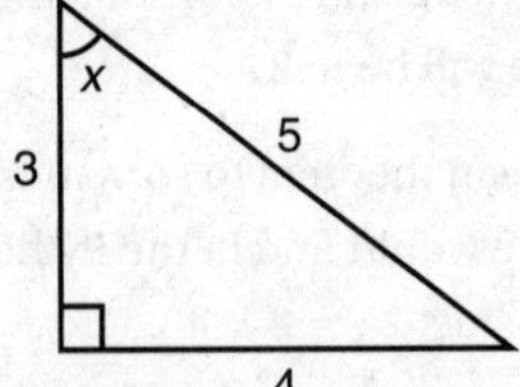

✓ Solution

To find the tangent, we need the opposite side and the adjacent side. The side of length 4 is opposite $\angle x$, and the side of length 3 is adjacent to $\angle x$. So, calculate the tangent of $\angle x$ as follows:

$$\tan\theta = \frac{\text{Opposite}}{\text{Adjecent}} \rightarrow$$

$$\tan x = \frac{4}{3}$$

› Practice

Consider the triangle below:

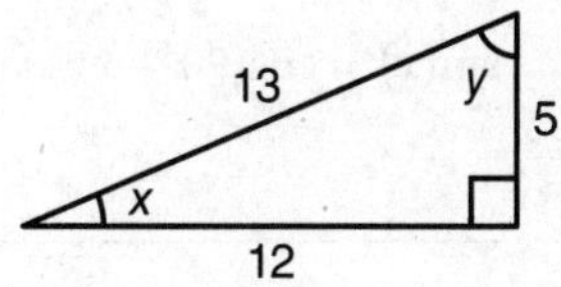

1. What is $\sin x$?
2. What is $\cos y$?
3. What is $\tan y$?
4. In a 45-45-90 triangle, which values will be identical?
   I. $\cos 45$
   II. $\sin 45$
   III. $\tan 45$

✓ Solutions

1. $\sin x = \frac{\text{Opposite}}{\text{Hypotenuse}} = \frac{5}{13}$
2. $\cos y = \frac{\text{Adjacent}}{\text{Hypotenuse}} = \frac{5}{13}$
3. $\tan y = \frac{\text{Opposite}}{\text{Adjacent}} = \frac{12}{5}$
4. In a 45-45-90 triangle, the sides have a ratio of $s{:}s{:}s\sqrt{2}$. I and II are equal since $\cos(45)$ and $\sin(45)$ are both $\frac{1}{\sqrt{2}}$. III is not equal to the others since $\tan(45)$ is just 1.

Area of an Equilateral Triangle

While it is manageable to solve for the area of an equilateral triangle without knowing this formula, memorizing it will save you time should you come across a problem that asks about it.

The area, A, of an equilateral triangle with sides of length a is:

$$A = \frac{\sqrt{3}}{4}a^2$$

› Example

What is the area of an equilateral triangle with sides that are 4 inches long?

 **Solution**

Plug 4 in for a into the equilateral triangle area formula:

$$A = \frac{\sqrt{3}}{4}a^2 \rightarrow$$

$$A = \frac{\sqrt{3}}{4}(4)^2 = \frac{\sqrt{3}}{4}(16) = 4\sqrt{3}$$

So, the area of the triangle would be $4\sqrt{3}$ square inches.

Sine and Cosine of Complementary Angles

Complementary angles add up to 90°. The relationship of the sine and cosine of complementary angles is:

$$\sin(x) = \cos(90° - x)$$

 **Example**

If the sine of 30° is 0.5, what is the cosine of 60°?

✓ **Solution**

While you could use a calculator for a problem like this on the calculator-permitted test section, if this were on the non-calculator test section you would have to know an alternative way to approach it. Use the relationship between the sine and cosine of complementary angles to solve. Since $30 + 60 = 90$, 30° and 60° are complementary. Because $\sin(x) = \cos(90° - x)$, $\sin(30) = \cos(60)$, and the cosine of 60° will also equal 0.5.

SAT Math Questions Practice Drill—Additional Topics in Math: Right Triangles and Trigonometry

(If timing, take about 12 minutes to complete.)

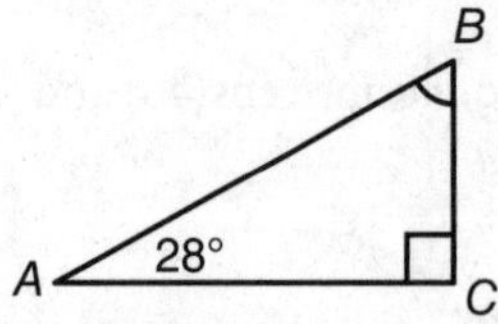

1. Triangle ABC is portrayed above. If triangle DEF is similar to triangle ABC, and angle B corresponds to angle E, what is the measure of angle E?

   (A) 28°
   (B) 52°
   (C) 62°
   (D) 84°

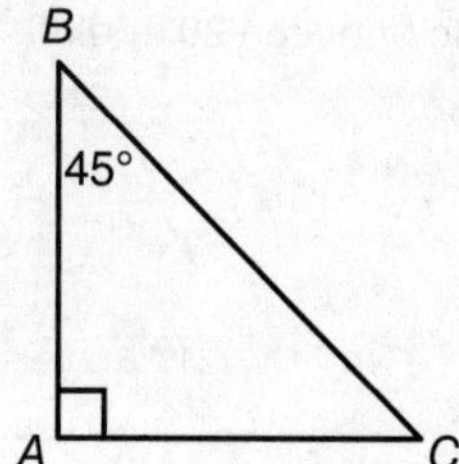

2. In ΔABC, $\angle A$ is 90° and $\angle B$ is 45°. If $\overline{BC}$ has a length of 4 units, what is the length of $\overline{AC}$?

(A) 2
(B) $2\sqrt{2}$
(C) $2\sqrt{3}$
(D) 4

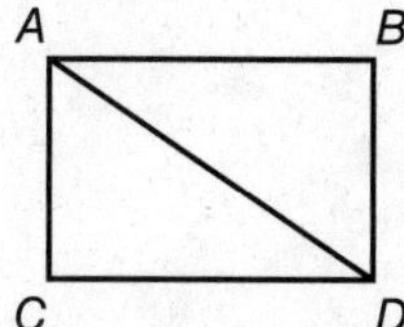

3. If rectangle *ABCD* has a side length of 7 for *AC* and a side length of 24 for *CD*, what is the length of the diagonal *AD*?

(A) 14
(B) 25
(C) 28
(D) 35

4. For an equilateral triangle with a side length of 8 units, what is the triangle's area in square units?

(A) $8\sqrt{2}$
(B) $8\sqrt{3}$
(C) $16\sqrt{2}$
(D) $16\sqrt{3}$

5. Triangle *DEF* is similar to triangle *ABC*, with vertex *D* corresponding to vertex *A*, vertex *E* corresponding to vertex *B*, and vertex *F* corresponding to vertex *C*. The measure of $\angle C$ is 90° and the measure of $\angle B$ is 30°. What is the cosine of $\angle D$?

(A) $\frac{1}{3}$
(B) $\frac{1}{2}$
(C) $\frac{2}{3}$
(D) $\frac{3}{4}$

6. What is the difference between sin(x) and cos(90° − x) if x is an angle between 20 and 30 degrees?

(A) 0
(B) $\frac{1}{2}$
(C) $\frac{3}{5}$
(D) $\frac{3}{4}$

7. What is the sine of the smallest angle in a right triangle with sides 7, 24, and 25?

(A) $\frac{7}{25}$
(B) $\frac{7}{24}$
(C) $\frac{24}{7}$
(D) $\frac{25}{7}$

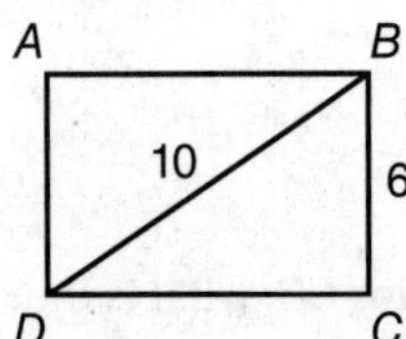

8. In rectangle $ABCD$ above, diagonal $\overline{DB}$ is 10 units long, and side $\overline{BC}$ is 6 units long. What is the area of the rectangle $ABCD$?

(A) 30 square units
(B) 36 square units
(C) 48 square units
(D) 60 square units

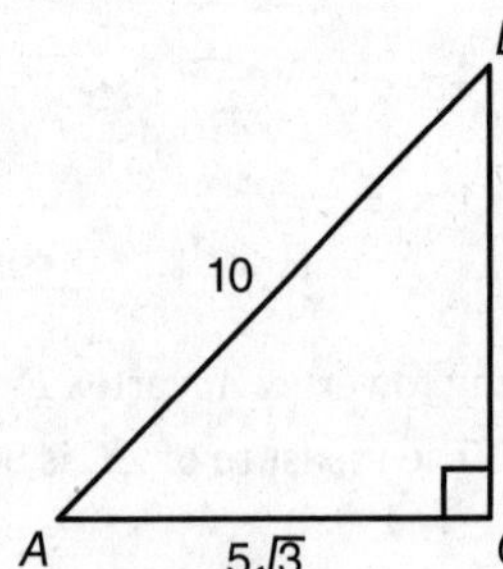

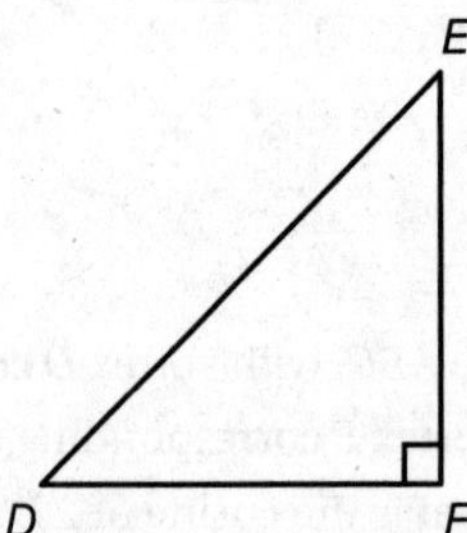

9. Right triangles ABC and DEF are similar to each other. What is the tangent of $\angle EDF$?

(A) $\frac{1}{\sqrt{3}}$
(B) $\frac{\sqrt{2}}{3}$
(C) $\frac{1}{2}$
(D) 2

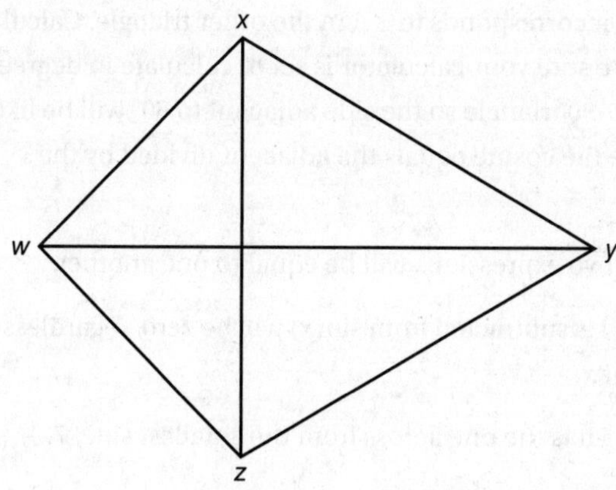

10. In the figure above, $\overline{XZ}$ and $\overline{WY}$ are perpendicular, and $\overline{WY}$ bisects $\overline{XZ}$. $\overline{XY}$ and $\overline{ZY}$ are of equal length, $\overline{WX}$ and $\overline{WZ}$ are of equal length, and $\angle XWY = 45°$. If $\overline{XY}$ is 4 and $\overline{WX}$ is $2\sqrt{2}$, what is the length of $\overline{WY}$?

    (A) $2\sqrt{2}$
    (B) $2\sqrt{3}$
    (C) 4
    (D) $2 + 2\sqrt{3}$

✓ Solutions

1. **(C)** Calculate $\angle B$ as follows:

$$90 - 28 = 62$$

Since $\angle B$ and $\angle E$ correspond to one another, $\angle E$ will have the same measure of 62°.

2. **(B)** In a 45-45-90 triangle, the hypotenuse is $\sqrt{2}$ multiplied by the length of one of the legs. So, in this situation, solve for the length of one of the legs by using a proportion:

$$\frac{\overline{BC}}{\overline{AC}} = \frac{\sqrt{2}}{1} \rightarrow$$

$$\frac{4}{\overline{AC}} = \frac{\sqrt{2}}{1} \rightarrow$$

$$\overline{AC} = \frac{4}{\sqrt{2}} = 2\sqrt{2}$$

3. **(B)** Use the Pythagorean theorem to solve for the length of the diagonal:

$$a^2 + b^2 = c^2 \rightarrow$$
$$7^2 + 24^2 = c^2 \rightarrow$$
$$625 = c^2 \rightarrow$$
$$\sqrt{625} = 25 = c$$

Alternatively, you could recognize that this is a Pythagorean triple of 7-24-25, thereby avoiding the need to calculate.

4. **(D)** Plug 8 in for a into the area formula for an equilateral triangle:

$$A = \frac{\sqrt{3}}{4}a^2 \rightarrow$$

$$A = \frac{\sqrt{3}}{4}(8)^2 = \frac{\sqrt{3} \times 64}{4} = 16\sqrt{3}$$

5. **(B)** $\angle D$ will have a measure of 60°, since it corresponds to $\angle A$ in the other triangle. Calculate the cosine of $\angle D$ using your calculator (be sure your calculator is set to calculate in degrees, not radians), or realize that this is a 30-60-90 triangle so the side adjacent to 60° will be like 1 and the hypotenuse will be like 2. Since the cosine equals the adjacent divided by the hypotenuse, its value will be $\frac{1}{2}$.

6. **(A)** Given that $\sin(x) = \cos(90° - x)$, the two expressions will be equal to one another.

   Therefore, the value when the $\cos(90° - x)$ is subtracted from $\sin(x)$ will be zero, regardless of what particular value you would select for x.

7. **(A)** The smallest angle is marked below—it is the one across from the smallest side, 7.

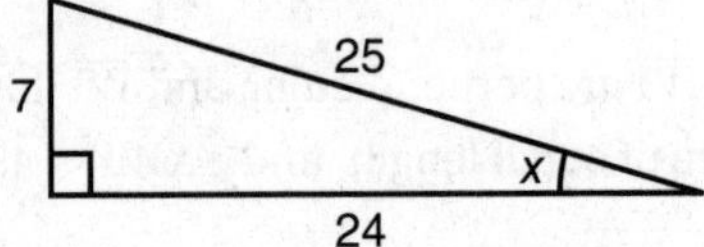

   The sine of this angle is equal to the opposite side divided by the hypotenuse: $\frac{7}{25}$.

8. **(C)** Solve for the length of the rectangle so that you can then multiply by the width of 6 to find the rectangle's area. Save time by recognizing that the numbers 10 and 6 are double the values found in the 3-4-5 Pythagorean triple. So, the length will be twice 4: 8. Then, multiply 8 by 6 to find the area of the rectangle: $8 \times 6 = 48$.

9. **(A)** Because the triangles are similar to one another, their corresponding sides will be proportional. The tangent of $\angle EDF$ will be the same as the tangent of $\angle BAC$. Recognize that triangle ABC is a special right triangle: 30-60-90 with sides relating to each other as x, $x\sqrt{3}$, and $2x$. Therefore, the unknown side in the triangle ABC will be 5. You can then calculate the tangent of $\angle BAC$ by dividing the oppposite side of 5 by the adjacent side of $5\sqrt{3}$:

$$\frac{5}{5\sqrt{3}} = \frac{1}{\sqrt{3}}$$

10. **(D)** Label the figure below to find the angle and side values based on the 30-60-90 triangles and 45-45-90 triangles within:

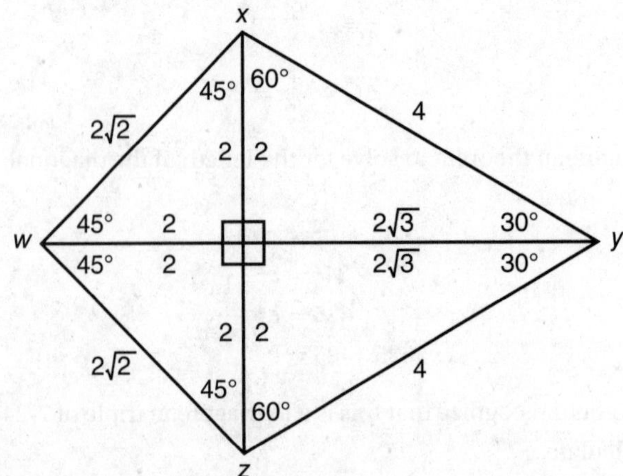

   The length of $\overline{WY}$ is therefore $2 + 2\sqrt{3}$.

Additional Topics in Math—Circles

At the beginning of each math test section, you are provided with these facts and formulas about circles:

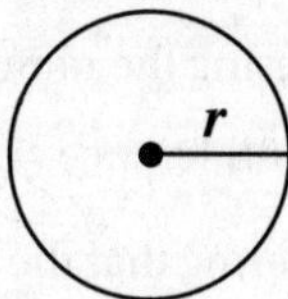

- **r = Radius of the Circle**
- **Area of a Circle = πr^2**
- **Circumference of a Circle = $2\pi r$**
- **A circle has 360 degrees.**

Memorize these facts so you do not have to flip back to the beginning of the section. Here is how to apply these essential concepts.

Radius and Diameter

- The *radius* goes the distance from the center of the circle to the circle itself, and is half the length of the diameter.
- The *diameter* goes from one side of a circle to another side through the center, and is twice the measure of the radius.

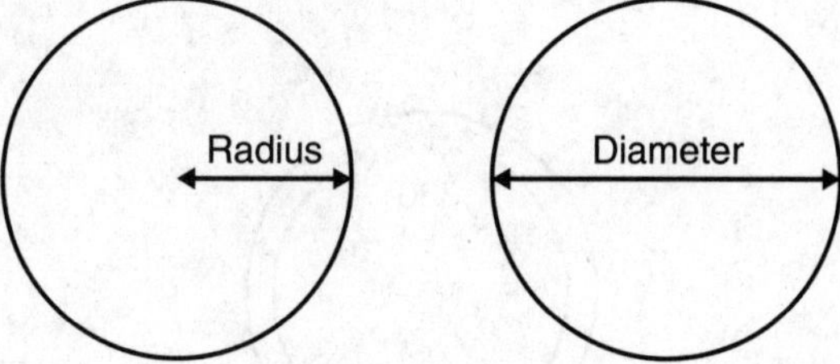

Example

What is the radius and the diameter in the circle drawn below?

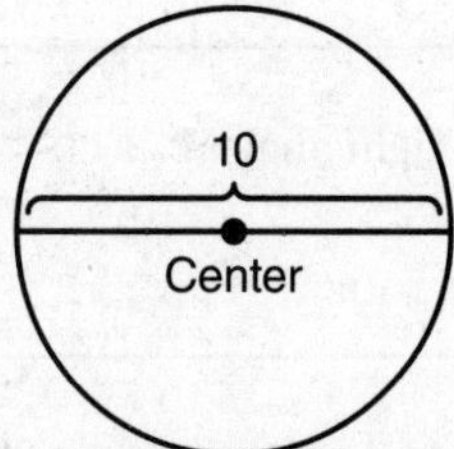

Solution

The diameter is 10 and the radius will be half the diameter, so the radius is 5.

Area and Circumference

The *area* of a circle is calculated using the radius, *r*:

$$\text{Area} = \pi r^2$$

The *circumference* of a circle is calculated using the radius, *r*:

$$\text{Circumference} = 2\pi r$$

Keep these two concepts clear by remembering that the area will give you square units, while the circumference will give you units of length.

Note: It is fine to use the formula Circumference $= \pi \times$ Diameter if you would prefer.

Example

What is the area and the circumference of a circle with a radius of 5 inches?

Solution

Calculate each value using the above formulas, plugging 5 in for *r*.

$$\text{Area} = \pi r^2 \rightarrow \pi 5^2 = 25\pi \text{ square inches}$$

$$\text{Circumference} = 2\pi r = 2 \times \pi \times 5 = 10\pi \text{ inches}$$

360° in a Circle

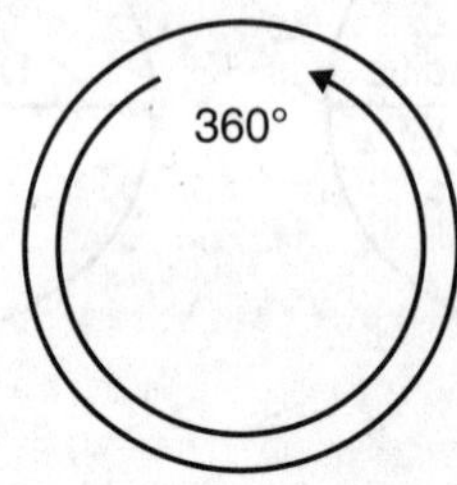

A full rotation of a circle will be 360°.

Example

A circle can be divided into how many right angles?

Solution

Since there is a total of 360° in a circle, and a right angle is 90°, a circle can be divided into $\frac{360}{90} = 4$ right angles.

Inscribed Angle

This is a less common concept related to degree measure that is good to understand, just in case a problem about it comes up.

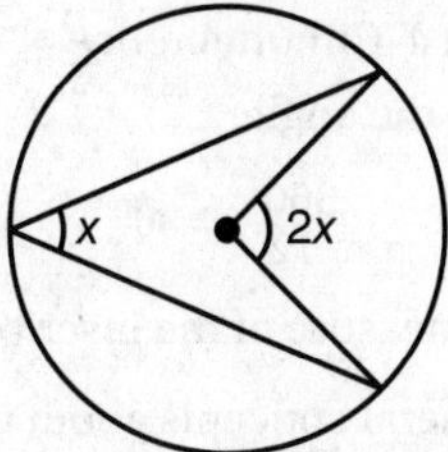

In the graph above, 2x corresponds to a central angle and x corresponds to an inscribed angle. When the inscribed angle and the central angle have the same arc, the central angle is *twice* the measure of the inscribed angle.

Example

In the circle graphed below with a central angle of 80°, what is the measure of $\angle x$?

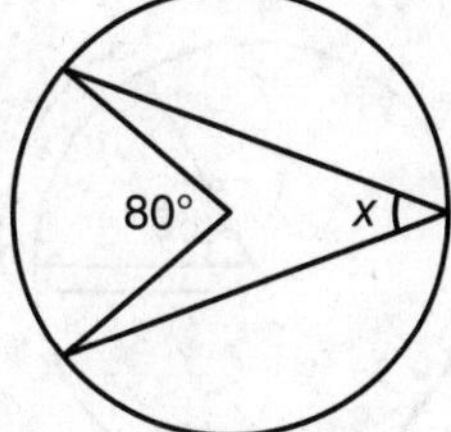

Solution

Given that $\angle x$ is an inscribed angle that shares the same arc as the central angle of 80°, $\angle x$ will be half the measure of 80°:

$$\frac{80^\circ}{2} = 40^\circ$$

Practice

1. If the radius of a circle is x units, what will be the diameter of the circle in terms of x?
2. What is the area of a circle with a radius of 10 inches?
3. What is the circumference of a circle with a diameter of 4 inches?
4. If a circular pie is to be divided into 12 equal pieces, what will be the measure of the angle formed at the central tip of each piece of pie after the pieces are cut?
5. What is the measure of the central angle a of the sector drawn in the figure below?

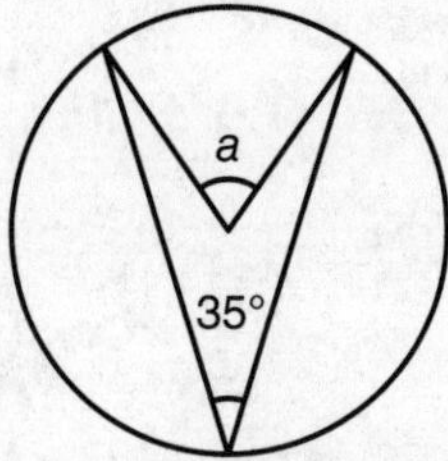

Solutions

1. The diameter of a circle is twice that of the radius, so the diameter will be $2x$.
2. Area $= \pi r^2 \rightarrow \pi 10^2 = 100\pi$
3. Be sure you use 2 for the radius, not 4. Circumference $= 2\pi r \rightarrow 2 \times \pi \times 2 = 4\pi$
4. Take 360° and divide it by 12 to find the angle:
$$\frac{360°}{12} = 30°$$
5. The central angle will be twice the measure of the inscribed angle, 35°. So $35° \times 2 = 70°$.

   The SAT will have you apply the general concepts about circle area, circumference, and degree measure to calculate the length of an arc or the area of a sector.

Arc Length

$$\frac{\text{Part}}{\text{Whole}} = \frac{\text{Angle}}{360°} = \frac{\text{Length of Arc}}{\text{Circumference}}$$

Example

In a circle of radius 3 with an arc of 60°, what is the length of the arc?

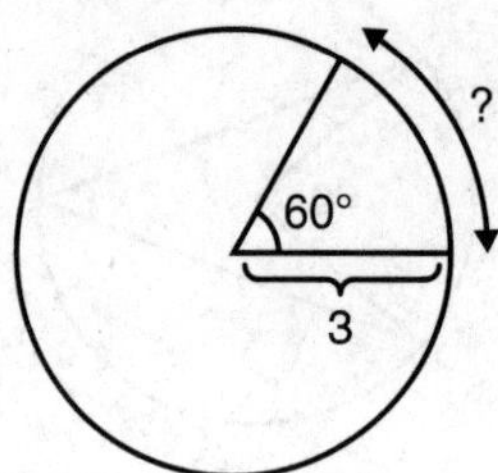

Solution

$$\frac{\text{Part}}{\text{Whole}} = \frac{60°}{360°} = \frac{1}{6} = \frac{\text{Length of Arc}}{\text{Circumference}} = \frac{x}{2 \times \pi \times 3}$$

So, set up a proportion to solve for the arc length:

$$\frac{1}{6} = \frac{x}{6\pi} \rightarrow \frac{6\pi}{6} = x \rightarrow \pi = x$$

The length of the arc is therefore π units.

Sector Area

$$\frac{\text{Part}}{\text{Whole}} = \frac{\text{Angle}}{360°} = \frac{\text{Area of Sector}}{\text{Area of Circle}}$$

Example

In a circle with a radius of 3 and a sector of 60°, what is the area of the sector?

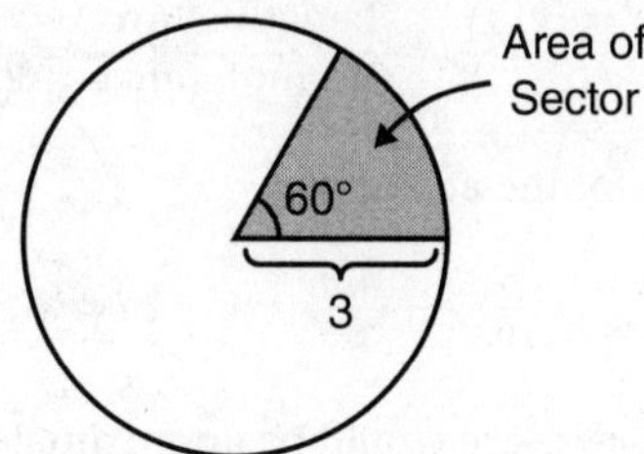

Solution

$$\frac{\text{Part}}{\text{Whole}} = \frac{60°}{360°} = \frac{1}{6} = \frac{\text{Area of Sector}}{\text{Area of Circle}} = \frac{x}{\pi 3^2} = \frac{x}{9\pi}$$

So, set up a proportion to solve for the sector area:

$$\frac{1}{6} = \frac{x}{9\pi} \rightarrow \frac{9\pi}{6} = x \rightarrow \frac{3}{2}\pi = x$$

The area of the sector is therefore $\frac{3}{2}\pi$ square units.

Practice

1. What is the length of a 45° arc in a circle that has a radius of 5 inches?
2. What is the area of a 30° arc in a circle with a radius of 4 inches?
3. A circular pizza has a surface area of 64π square inches. If the pizza is divided into 8 equal pieces made by cutting along the diameter through the center point of the pizza, what is the length of the crust on the edge of each piece?

Solutions

1. $$\frac{\text{Part}}{\text{Whole}} = \frac{45°}{360°} = \frac{1}{8} = \frac{\text{Length of Arc}}{\text{Circumference}} = \frac{x}{2 \times \pi \times 5}$$

   So, set up a proportion to solve for the arc length:

   $$\frac{1}{8} = \frac{x}{10\pi} \rightarrow \frac{10\pi}{8} = x \rightarrow \frac{5}{4}\pi = x$$

2. $$\frac{\text{Part}}{\text{Whole}} = \frac{30°}{360°} = \frac{1}{12} = \frac{\text{Area of Sector}}{\text{Area of Circle}} = \frac{x}{\pi 4^2} = \frac{x}{16\pi}$$

   So, set up a proportion to solve for the sector area:

   $$\frac{1}{12} = \frac{x}{16\pi} \rightarrow \frac{16\pi}{12} = x \rightarrow \frac{4}{3}\pi = x$$

3. First, solve for the radius of the pizza by using its area:

$$64\pi = \pi r^2 \rightarrow 64 = r^2 \rightarrow 8 = r$$

Next, find the angle for the sector formed by each of the 8 pieces:

$$\frac{360°}{8} = 45°$$

Then, calculate the length of a sector in a circle with a radius of 8 inches and a sector angle of 45°:

$$\frac{\text{Part}}{\text{Whole}} = \frac{45°}{360°} = \frac{1}{8} = \frac{\text{Length of Arc}}{\text{Circumference}} = \frac{x}{2 \times \pi \times 8}$$

So, set up a proportion to solve for the arc length:

$$\frac{1}{8} = \frac{x}{16\pi} \rightarrow \frac{16\pi}{8} = x \rightarrow 2\pi = x$$

So, the length of the crust on each piece would be approximately 6.3 inches.

Circle Formula

To graph a circle in the *xy*-coordinate plane, use this formula:

$$(x - h)^2 + (y - k)^2 = r^2$$
$$(h, k) = \text{Center}$$
$$r = \text{Radius}$$

Example

What is the graph of a circle with the equation $(x - 3)^2 + (y - 2)^2 = 16$?

✓ Solution

Based on the equation, the center of the circle will be (3, 2), and the radius will be the square root of 16, which is 4. Here is the graph of this circle:

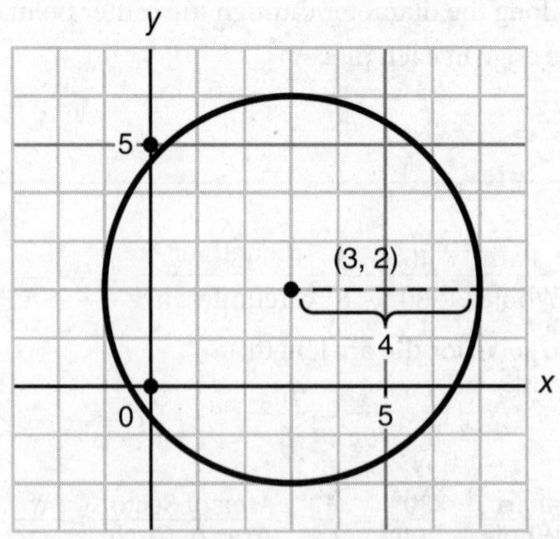

Practice

1. What is the radius of a circle with the equation $(x-2)^2 + (y+5)^2 = 81$?
2. What is the center of a circle with the equation $(x+5)^2 + (y-6)^2 = 14$?
3. What is the equation of the circle graphed below?

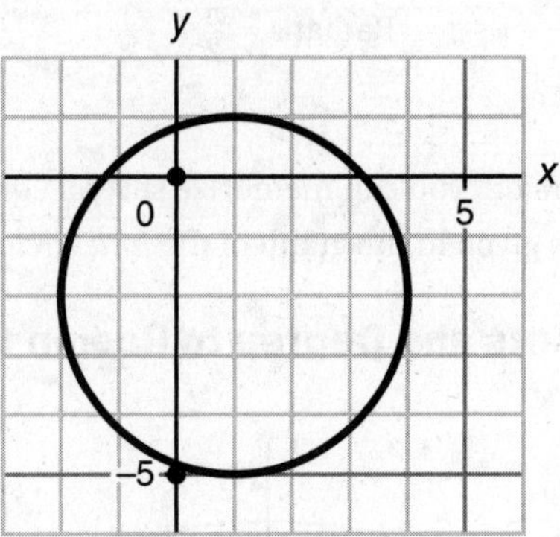

Solutions

1. Take the square root of 81 to find the radius:

$$\sqrt{81} = 9$$

2. Be careful with the negative signs, keeping in mind that in the original circle formula, there are negative signs in front of the h and k. So, +5 will give an x-coordinate for the center of -5 and -6 will give a y-coordinate for the center of +6. Therefore, the center point (h, k) will be $(-5, 6)$.
3. The center of the circle is at $(1, -2)$ and the radius is 3 units. So, the equation for the circle will be $(x-1)^2 + (y+2)^2 = 9$.

Radians

A radian is a different way of measuring angles. The SAT says the following at the beginning of the test section:

- **There are 2π radians in a circle.**

Since there are 360° in a circle, 360° corresponds to 2π radians. Divide this by 2 to find:

$$180° = \pi \text{ radians}$$

While you could figure out radian to degree conversion based just on what the SAT provides at the beginning of the section, it might be easier for you to memorize this conversion formula:

$$\frac{\text{Radians}}{\pi} = \frac{\text{Degrees}}{180}$$

Example

How many radians are in 90 degrees?

Solution

$$\frac{\text{Radians}}{\pi} = \frac{90}{180} \rightarrow$$
$$\frac{\text{Radians}}{\pi} = \frac{1}{2} \rightarrow$$
$$\text{Radians} = \frac{\pi}{2}$$

So, there are $\frac{\pi}{2}$ radians in 90°.

In addition to doing this conversion, you can memorize several common unit circle points and radian to degree conversions as given in the graph of the *unit circle* below.

Common Unit Circle Points and Degree to Radian Conversions:

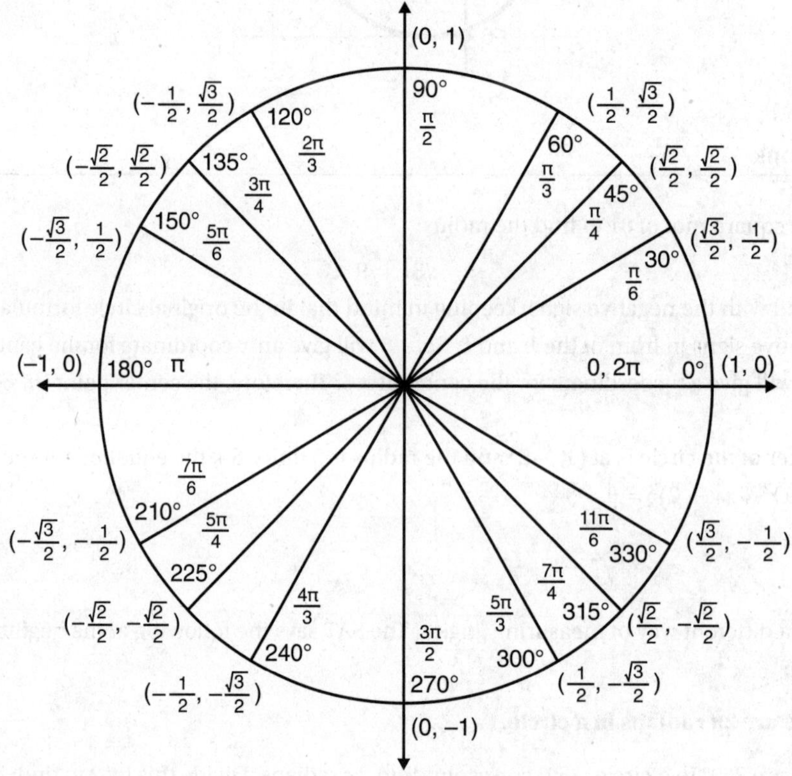

Practice

1. How many radians are in 270°?
2. How many degrees are in π radians?
3. How many total radians would there be in two circles?

✓ Solutions

1.
$$\frac{\text{Radians}}{\pi} = \frac{270}{180} \rightarrow$$
$$\frac{\text{Radians}}{\pi} = \frac{3}{2} \rightarrow$$
$$\text{Radians} = \frac{3\pi}{2}$$

You could also use the graph of the circle with the radian to degree conversions.

2.
$$\frac{\text{Radians}}{\pi} = \frac{\text{Degrees}}{180} \rightarrow$$
$$\frac{\pi}{\pi} = \frac{\text{Degrees}}{180} \rightarrow$$
$$1 = \frac{\text{Degrees}}{180} \rightarrow$$
$$180 = \text{Degrees}$$

You could also memorize that 180° are in π radians.

3. A single circle has 2π radians, so two circles will have twice this: 4π radians.

SAT Math Questions Practice Drill—Additional Topics in Math: Circles

(If timing, take about 12 minutes to complete.)

1. If a circle has an area of 64π units, how many units long is its circumference?

   (A) 8π
   (B) 12π
   (C) 16π
   (D) 32π

2. Consider the circle defined by the equation $(x + 4)^2 + (y - 8)^2 = 144$. What is the radius of this circle?

   (A) 4
   (B) 8
   (C) 12
   (D) 72

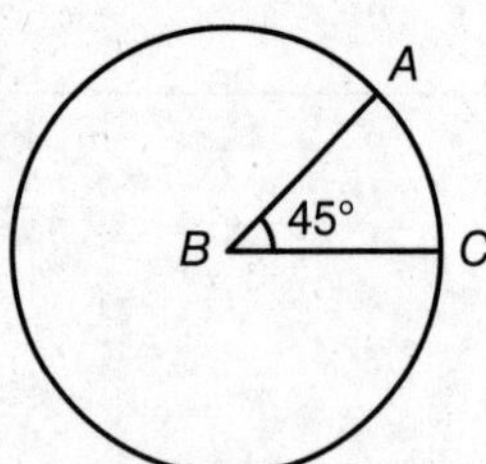

3. The above circle has points A and C and a center of B. What percentage of the circle's area is within the sector designated by the central angle $\angle ABC$?

(A) 8%
(B) 12.5%
(C) 14.5%
(D) 25%

4. A square with a perimeter of 16 inches is inscribed within a circle, all of the square's vertices intersecting the circle itself. What is the diameter of the circle?

(A) 4
(B) $4\sqrt{2}$
(C) $4\sqrt{3}$
(D) 8

5. Circle A has a radius of 2 units and an area of x square units. If circle B has a radius twice that of circle A, and the area of circle B is expressed in the form nx, in which n is a constant, what is the value of n?

(A) 1
(B) 2
(C) 3
(D) 4

6. A circle has a diameter of 10 units. The function graphed below could represent what about the circle?

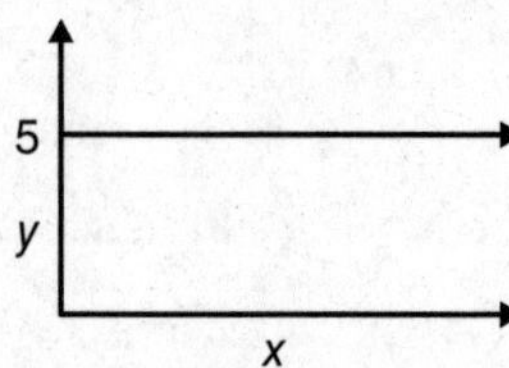

(A) The distance y from a point x on the circle to its center.
(B) The area of the circle, y, depending on its radius, x.
(C) The circumference of the circle, y, depending on its diameter, x.
(D) The diameter of the circle measured at different points in the coordinate plane, (x, y).

7. What is the radius of the circle with the equation $x^2 - 4x + y^2 + 2y = 11$?

(A) 3
(B) 4
(C) 6
(D) 7

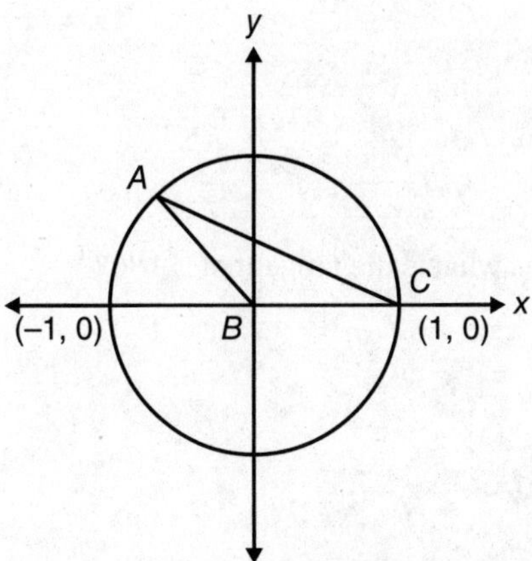

8. The circle above is centered at the origin with a radius of 1 unit; $\overline{AB}$ and $\overline{BC}$ are both radii of the circle. In triangle ABC above, $\angle BAC$ is 40°. What is the measure of $\angle ACB$ in radians?

(A) $\frac{2}{9}\pi$
(B) $\frac{3}{4}\pi$
(C) π
(D) $\frac{7}{6}\pi$

9. At what point will a circle with the equation $(x - 4)^2 + (y - 5)^2 = 9$ and the line $y = -2$ intersect?

(A) $(-5, -2)$
(B) $(3, -2)$
(C) $(4, 5)$
(D) They will not intersect.

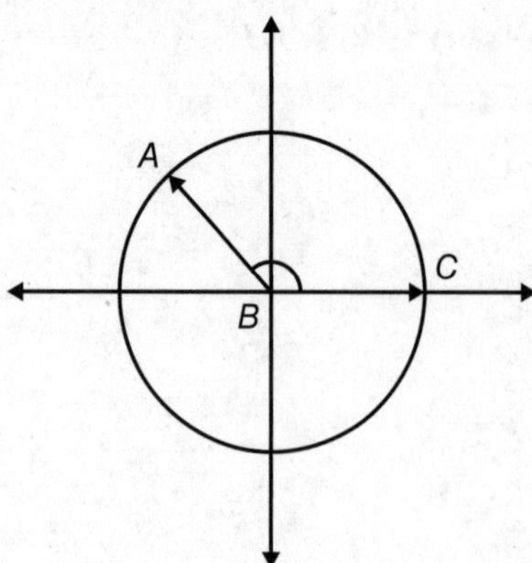

10. If the cosine of $\angle ABC$ in the unit circle above is $-\frac{1}{\sqrt{2}}$, what is the tangent of $\angle ABC$?

    (A) -1
    (B) -0.5
    (C) 1
    (D) 1.8

✓ Solutions

1. **(C)** Use the formula for area to find the radius of the circle:

$$\pi r^2 = 64\pi \rightarrow$$
$$r^2 = 64 \rightarrow r = 8$$

   Now, use the formula for circumference, using 8 as the radius:

$$2\pi r \rightarrow 2 \times \pi \times 8 = 16\pi$$

2. **(C)** In the circle formula, the right side is the radius squared. So, find the square root of 144 to find the radius: $\sqrt{144} = 12$.

3. **(B)** There are 360° in a circle, so find the percentage that 45° is out of 360°:

$$\frac{45}{360} \times 100 = 12.5\%$$

4. **(B)** If the square has a perimeter of 16 inches, each side on the square is 4 inches. The square is inscribed within the circle, making the situation look like this:

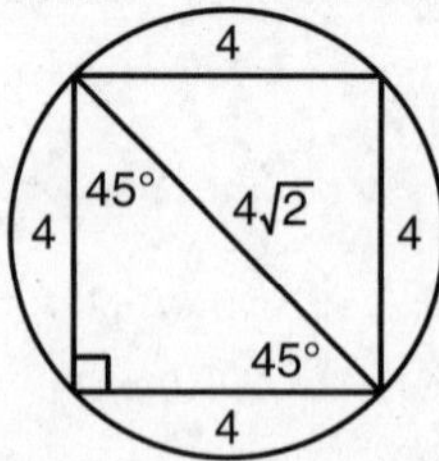

   The triangle formed by two of the sides and the diameter of the circle is a 45-45-90 triangle, so the diameter will be $4\sqrt{2}$ units.

5. **(D)** Circle A will have an area of 4π square units, since it has a radius of 2 and the area of a circle is πr^2. Circle B has twice the radius of circle A, meaning 4 units, thereby having 16π square units of area. Comparing the two areas, if $x = 4\pi$, and the area of B is 16π, then n must equal 4 since $\frac{16\pi}{4\pi} = 4$.

6. **(A)** Since the diameter of the circle is 10, the radius is 5. From any point on the circle, the distance from the point to the center of the circle will be 5. The graph does portray this relationship. It is not going to be choice (B) because the area of this circle would be 25π. It is not going to be choice (C) because the circumference of the circle would be 10π. And it is not going to be choice (D) because the diameter is 10, not 5.

7. **(B)** Complete the square for both the x and y components to get the equation into the format of the circle formula, enabling you to see the radius:

$$x^2 - 4x + y^2 + 2y = 11 \rightarrow$$
$$x^2 - 4x + 4 + y^2 + 2y + 1 = 11 + 4 + 1 \rightarrow$$
$$(x-2)^2 + (y+1)^2 = 16$$

The radius is the square root of 16, 4.

8. **(A)** Sides $\overline{AB}$ and $\overline{BC}$ are equivalent, since they are both radii of the circle. Therefore, triangle ABC is isosceles, with $\angle BAC$ and $\angle ACB$ both 40°. So, we need to convert 40° to radians using the radian conversion formula:

$$\frac{\text{Radians}}{\pi} = \frac{\text{Degrees}}{180} \rightarrow$$
$$\frac{\text{Radians}}{\pi} = \frac{40}{180} \rightarrow$$
$$\frac{\text{Radians}}{\pi} = \frac{2}{9} \rightarrow$$
$$\text{Radians} = \frac{2}{9}\pi$$

9. **(D)** The circle has a center at (4, 5) and a radius of 3. So, it has no points that will be below the x-axis, and therefore will never intersect the line $y = -2$.

10. **(A)** We can label the graph as following given the information in the problem, since sides of this ratio will form a 45-45-90 triangle:

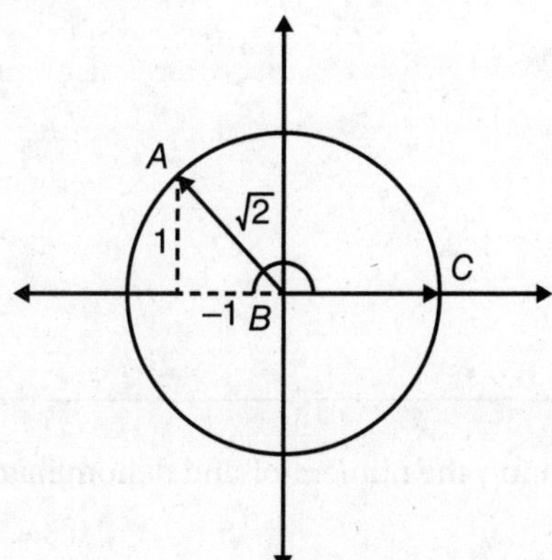

The tangent of $\angle ABC$ will therefore be the opposite divided by the adjacent, which is $\frac{-1}{1} = -1$. You could also calculate the value by using your calculator and solving $\tan(135) = -1$.

Additional Topics in Math—Imaginary Numbers

Imaginary Number Essentials

When taking the square root of a negative number, use the imaginary number i, which represents $\sqrt{-1}$. For example:

$$\sqrt{-9} = 3\sqrt{-1} = 3i$$

Going backwards →

$$(3i)(3i) = 9i^2 = -9$$

SAT problems involving imgainary numbers typically state that $i = \sqrt{-1}$ to help you get started. Here are some examples of how you would do some essential mathematical operations with i:

$$3i + 2i = 5i$$
$$8i - 2i = 6i$$
$$i \times i = -1$$
$$\frac{3i}{1i} = 3$$

A helpful fact to know about using imaginary numbers is that they have a recurring pattern when they are in exponential form, repeating the same value every 4th power:

$i^1 = i$	$i^5 = i$	$i^9 = i$
$i^2 = -1$	$i^6 = -1$	$i^{10} = -1$
$i^3 = -i$	$i^7 = -i$	$i^{11} = -i$
$i^4 = 1$	$i^8 = 1$	$i^{12} = 1$

In addition to having you do arithmetic operations with imaginary numbers, the SAT may ask you to use imaginary number concepts to solve problems.

Example 1

Which of the following would be an equivalent form of the expression $\frac{5}{3 - i}$?

(A) $\frac{2 - i}{5}$

(B) $\frac{3 + i}{2}$

(C) $\frac{4 - i}{3}$

(D) $\frac{1 + i}{4}$

Solution

To simplify this expression, multiply the numerator and denominator by the *conjugate* of $3 - i$, $3 + i$.

This will cause the imaginary numbers in the denominator to be cancelled:

$$\frac{5}{3-i}\times\frac{3+i}{3+i}=\frac{15+5i}{(3-i)(3+i)}\rightarrow$$

$$\frac{15+5i}{9-3i+3i-i^2}\rightarrow$$

$$\frac{15+5i}{9-i^2}\rightarrow$$

$$\frac{15+5i}{9-(-1)}\rightarrow$$

$$\frac{15+5i}{10}\rightarrow$$

$$\frac{3+i}{2}$$

Example 2

In the equation $x^2+bx+4=0$, what are the possible values of b that would cause the equation to have only *imaginary* solutions?

Solution

Use the quadratic formula to visualize the potential solutions:

$$x=\frac{-b\pm\sqrt{b^2-4ac}}{2a}\rightarrow$$

$$x=\frac{-b\pm\sqrt{b^2-4(1)(4)}}{2(1)}\rightarrow$$

$$x=\frac{-b\pm\sqrt{b^2-16}}{2}$$

Use the *discriminant,* i.e., the part of the quadratic equation that is underneath the square root sign, to determine what will cause there to be imaginary solutions. The discriminant in this example is b^2-16. If the discriminant is negative, then there would be only imaginary solutions since the equation would result in an i as part of the solution. So, make the discriminant less than zero to determine what values of b would result in only imaginary values for i.

$$b^2-16<0\rightarrow$$
$$b^2<16\rightarrow$$
$$b<4 \text{ and } b>-4$$

So, any value of b that is between -4 and 4 will work.

Practice

1. What is $4i+12i$?
2. What is $15i-20i$?
3. What is $3\,i^4$?
4. What is the sum of $(2i+1)$ and $(4i-5)$?
5. What is the product of $(5-i)$ and $(5+i)$?

6. What is an equivalent form of $-(2i^2 - 3i + 1)$?

(A) $1 + 3i$
(B) $2 - 3i$
(C) $4 + 5i$
(D) $5 - 4i$

7. Which of the following is equivalent to the product of $(1 + 2i)$ and $3i^2$?

(A) $3 + 12i$
(B) $-6 + 3i$
(C) $3 + 6i$
(D) $-3 - 6i$

8. Which of the following is an equivalent form of $\frac{1+i}{4-i}$?

(A) $\frac{1+3i}{15}$

(B) $\frac{3-5i}{16}$

(C) $\frac{3+5i}{17}$

(D) $\frac{5-3i}{17}$

✓ Solutions

1. $4i + 12i = 16i$
2. $15i - 20i = -5i$
3. $3i^4 = 3i^2 i^2 = 3(-1)(-1) = 3$
4. $(2i + 1) + (4i - 5) = (2i + 4i) + (1 - 5) = 6i - 4$
5. $(5 - i)(5 + i) = 25 - 5i + 5i - i^2 = 25 - (-1) = 26$
6. **(A)**

$$-(2i^2 - 3i + 1) =$$
$$-2i^2 - (-3i) - 1 =$$
$$-2(-1) + 3i - 1 =$$
$$2 + 3i - 1 =$$
$$1 + 3i$$

7. **(D)** Multiply the two expressions to find the product.

$$3i^2 \times (1 + 2i) =$$
$$3i^2 + 6i^3 =$$
$$-3 - 6i$$

8. **(C)** Multiply the numerator and denominator of the fraction by the conjugate of the denominator, $4 + i$, so that you can eliminate the imaginary numbers in the denominator:

$$\frac{(1+i)}{(4-i)} \times \frac{(4+i)}{(4+i)} =$$

$$\frac{4 + i + 4i + i^2}{16 + 4i - 4i - i^2} =$$

$$\frac{4 + 5i - 1}{16 - (-1)} =$$

$$\frac{3 + 5i}{17}$$

Advanced Drills

Use these drills to push yourself with the toughest types of problems you are likely to encounter on SAT test day. Each drill has ten questions, with solutions that follow.

- Heart of Algebra, Calculator
- Heart of Algebra, No Calculator
- Passport to Advanced Math, Calculator
- Passport to Advanced Math, No Calculator
- Problem Solving and Data Analysis
- Additional Topics in Math
- Calculator Problems Mixed

If you are doing a drill under timed conditions, allow about 15 minutes to complete (longer than the chapter drills because of the increased average difficulty of the problems). Good luck!

Heart of Algebra Drill (Calculator)

1. Solve for x:

$$1\frac{7}{8}x + \frac{5}{32} = 3\frac{3}{4}x - 1\frac{1}{4}$$

(A) $\frac{3}{4}$
(B) $2\frac{17}{32}$
(C) $\frac{15}{16}$
(D) $-\frac{45}{76}$

2. When 2 times a number is subtracted from 14, the result is 2 greater than the number. What is the number in question?

(A) $\frac{16}{3}$
(B) 4
(C) 12
(D) 16

3. In 2015, Andre had 210 coins in his collection. If Andre adds 5 new coins a year starting in 2015 through the end of 2022 and then adds 8 coins a year starting in 2023, how many coins will he have in his collection at the end of 2045?

(A) 224
(B) 421
(C) 429
(D) 434

4. How many pairs (x, y) satisfy both $x - y > 3$ and $y - 5 > x$?

(A) 0
(B) 1
(C) 2
(D) Infinitely many

5. What is the solution (x, y) to the following set of equations?

$$4x - 3y = \frac{11}{3} \text{ and } -\frac{2}{3}x + \frac{1}{4}y = -\frac{13}{18}$$

(A) $\left(\frac{4}{3}, \frac{5}{4}\right)$
(B) $\left(\frac{5}{4}, \frac{4}{9}\right)$
(C) $\left(-\frac{37}{12}, -\frac{16}{3}\right)$
(D) $\left(\frac{7}{4}, 10\right)$

6. How many ordered pairs (x, y) satisfy the following system of equations?

$$(x - 2)(y + 5) = 0 \text{ and } 3x + y = 1$$

(A) 0
(B) 1
(C) 2
(D) Infinitely many

7. What are the solutions to the following series of equations?

$$\frac{3}{8}a + \frac{2}{3}b = 4.3 \text{ and } -12.9 + 1.125a = -2b$$

(A) $a = 0.8$ and $b = 6$
(B) $a = 16.8$ and $b = -3$
(C) No solutions
(D) Infinitely many solutions

8. Candidate M and Candidate N are the only candidates running for city mayor. If the total number of votes the two candidates receive is 50,000 and if Candidate M receives 3 times as many votes as Candidate N, what is the total number of votes Candidate N receives?

(A) 12,500
(B) 16,667
(C) 21,500
(D) 37,500

9. Jennifer's yearly salary, S, is modeled using the equation $S = 2{,}500Y + 40{,}000$, where Y represents how many years she has been working at the company. What does the number 2,500 represent in this equation?

(A) The amount Jennifer's salary increases for each year she has been working
(B) Jennifer's starting salary
(C) The amount of money Jennifer has made in year Y
(D) The number of hours Jennifer has worked in year Y

10. If Avinash reads 2 fiction articles per day and 14 nonfiction articles per week, which expression models the total number of articles he would read in w weeks?

    (A) $2w + 14$
    (B) $16w$
    (C) $28w$
    (D) $112w$

✓ Solutions

1. **(A)** To make solving this problem a bit easier, let's convert all of our mixed numbers into improper fractions:

$$\frac{15}{8}x + \frac{5}{32} = \frac{15}{4}x - \frac{5}{4}$$

We eventually want to combine our x terms and combine our constant terms. So our x terms need a common denominator (8), and our constant terms need a common denominator (32). Thus, let's rewrite our fractions with these common denominators. Our full equation is now:

$$\frac{15}{8}x + \frac{5}{32} = \frac{30}{8}x - \frac{40}{32}$$

To avoid dealing with negatives, let's bring the constants to the left by adding $\frac{40}{32}$ to both sides:

$$\frac{15}{8}x + \frac{45}{32} = \frac{30}{8}x$$

We then want to get all x terms on the right by subtracting $\frac{15}{8}x$ from both sides:

$$\frac{45}{32} = \frac{15}{8}x$$

To solve for x, divide both sides by $\frac{15}{8}$ (in other words, multiply both sides by $\frac{8}{15}$):

$$\frac{45(8)}{32(15)} = x \text{ so } \frac{360}{480} = x$$

This reduces to $\frac{3}{4} = x$, which is choice **(A)**.

2. **(B)** Let x be the number we are trying to find.

"2 times a number is subtracted from 14" can be written as $14 - 2x$. (We are subtracting 2 times a number, or $2x$, from the 14.)

"The result is" means an equals sign.

"2 greater than the number" can be written as $x + 2$. Thus, the whole sentence can be written as:

$$14 - 2x = x + 2$$

Add $2x$ to both sides to get all x terms on the right. Then subtract 2 from both sides to get all constants on the left:

$$12 = 3x$$

Dividing by 3 tells us that $x = 4$, which is answer **(B)**.

3. **(D)** Between 2015 and 2022, Andre adds 5 coins 8 times:

2015, 2016, 2017, 2018, 2019, 2020, 2021, and 2022

Adding 5 coins 8 times means he added a total of $5(8) = 40$ coins in those years.

Between 2023 and 2045, he added 8 coins 23 times:

2023, 2024, 2025, 2026, 2027, 2028, 2029, 2030, 2031, 2032, 2033, 2034, 2035, 2036, 2037, 2038, 2039, 2040, 2041, 2042, 2043, 2044, and 2045

Thus, from 2023 to 2045, he added a total of $8(23) = 184$ coins.

Andre started with 210 coins. So the sum of the coins in his collection will be the original 210 plus the number of coins he added:

$$210 + 40 + 184 = 434$$

This is choice **(D)**.

4. **(A)** Since we have two inequalities, we can use elimination to get rid of one variable. Let's add both equations together:

$$\begin{array}{r} x - y > 3 \\ + \underline{\; y - 5 > x \;} \\ x - 5 > 3 + x \end{array}$$

Subtracting x from both sides and adding 5 to both sides leaves you with $0 > 8$. Because we know that under no circumstances is 0 greater than 8, there are no solutions.

5. **(B)** In a system of two equations, we can either use substitution or elimination to solve.

If we multiply the second equation by 12 and add the equations together, our y terms will cancel out. Start by multiplying the second equation by 12:

$$12\left(-\frac{2}{3}x + \frac{1}{4}y = -\frac{13}{18}\right) = -8x + 3y = -\frac{26}{3}$$

Now we can add this equation to the first equation:

$$\begin{array}{r} 4x - 3y = \frac{11}{3} \\ + -8x + 3y = -\frac{26}{3} \\ \hline -4x = -\frac{15}{3} \end{array}$$

To solve for x, divide by -4:

$$x = \frac{15}{12} = \frac{5}{4}$$

This is enough to narrow down the answer to choice (B). However, you could plug this x value into one of your functions to solve for y if you wanted.

Alternatively, you could have used substitution by solving for x in the first equation and then plugging that equation back into the second equation.

To solve for x, first add $3y$ to both sides:

$$4x = 3y + \frac{11}{3}$$

Then divide both sides by 4 to isolate x:

$$x = \frac{3y}{4} + \frac{11}{12}$$

Now you can plug this expression into the second equation for x:

$$-\frac{2}{3}\left(\frac{3y}{4} + \frac{11}{12}\right) + \frac{1}{4}y = -\frac{13}{18}$$

Next, distribute the $-\frac{2}{3}$:

$$-\frac{6}{12}y - \frac{22}{36} + \frac{1}{4}y = -\frac{13}{18}$$

Some of these fractions can be reduced. For our purposes, though, it doesn't really matter. Next, we need to combine our y terms, but first we need a common denominator.

Let's convert $\frac{1}{4}y$ to $\frac{3}{12}y$:

$$-\frac{6}{12}y - \frac{22}{36} + \frac{3}{12}y = -\frac{13}{18}$$

Now combine like terms:

$$-\frac{1}{4}y - \frac{22}{36} = -\frac{13}{18}$$

To add $\frac{22}{36}$ to both sides, we need to first convert $-\frac{13}{18}$ to $-\frac{26}{36}$ so that our constants have a common denominator:

$$-\frac{1}{4}y - \frac{22}{36} = -\frac{26}{36}$$
$$-\frac{1}{4}y = -\frac{1}{9}$$

To solve for y, divide both sides by $-\frac{1}{4}$ (multiply both sides by -4):

$$y = \frac{4}{9}$$

This is enough to narrow it down to choice **(B)**. However, we can solve for x by plugging the y value into our equation for x:

$$x = \frac{3}{4}y + \frac{11}{12} = \frac{3}{4}\left(\frac{4}{9}\right) + \frac{11}{12} = \frac{12}{36} + \frac{11}{12} = \frac{12}{36} + \frac{33}{36} = \frac{45}{36} = \frac{5}{4}$$

Finally, we could have solved this problem by plugging each answer choice into the two equations to see which set of points work. If using this method, be careful to check that the points satisfy BOTH equations. For instance, choice (C) works when plugged into the first equation but not the second.

6. **(B)** In the first equation, one of those factors must equal 0 for the whole equation to equal 0. Therefore, we will find the possible solutions by setting each factor equal to 0:

$$x - 2 = 0$$

Adding 2 to both sides tells us that $x = 2$ is a possible solution:

$$y + 5 = 0$$

Subtracting 5 from both sides tells us that $y = -5$ is another possible solution.

Plugging these values into the second equation will tell us the solutions to it:

$$3(2) + y = 1$$

So $6 + y = 1$.

Subtracting 6 from both sides tells us that $y = -5$, which is the original y value we got from the first equation.

Let's try the y value that we already determined:

$$3x + -5 = 1$$

So $3x = 6$. Dividing by 3 tells us that $x = 2$. However, this is the x solution that we already tried. Therefore, there is only one solution:

$$(2, -5)$$

This is choice **(B)**.

7. **(D)** Let's use substitution. Solve for b in the second equation by dividing both sides by -2:

$$6.45 - 0.5625a = b$$

Let's now plug the left side of this equation into the first equation for b:

$$\frac{3}{8}a + \frac{2}{3}(6.45 - 0.5625a) = 4.3$$

Distributing the $\frac{2}{3}$ leaves us with:

$$\frac{3}{8}a + 4.3 - 0.375a = 4.3$$

Let's get that $\frac{3}{8}a$ into decimal form so that we can easily combine our like terms:

$$0.375a + 4.3 - 0.375a = 4.3$$

Combining both a terms results in:

$$4.3 = 4.3$$

We know that this is always true, meaning we have an infinite number of solutions.

Alternatively, you may have noticed that if you multiply the second equation by $-\frac{1}{3}$ and convert any fractions in the two equations into decimals, the two equations are exactly the same. Since they are the same line, there are infinitely many solutions.

8. **(A)** Let's turn what we know into equations. Let m equal the number of votes that Candidate M receives and let n equal the number of votes that Candidate N receives.

First, we know that the sum of the votes that the two candidates receive is 50,000. In other words:

$$m + n = 50{,}000$$

Additionally, we know that the number of votes Candidate M receives is 3 times the number of votes that Candidate N receives. This can be expressed by the equation

$$m = 3n$$

Now we can plug in $3n$ for m in the first equation:

$$3n + n = 50{,}000$$

Combining like terms results in:

$$4n = 50{,}000$$

We can solve for n by dividing both sides by 4:

$$n = 12{,}500$$

This is choice **(A)**.

9. **(A)** We're told that Y is the number of years Jennifer has worked at the company. We can see that each time Y increases by 1, her salary goes up \$2,500. For instance, when $Y = 0$, Jennifer's salary is \$40,000. When $Y = 1$, her salary is \$42,500. When $Y = 2$, her salary is \$45,000. Therefore, choice **(A)** is correct.

   Choice (B) is incorrect because it can be shown that Jennifer's starting salary (when $Y = 0$) is \$40,000.

   Choice (C) is incorrect because the amount of money made is given by the variable S.

   Choice (D) is incorrect because the equation tells us nothing about the number of hours Jennifer worked.

10. **(C)** We want to know how many articles Avinash reads in w weeks. So we first need to figure out how many articles he reads per week. We can then multiply this number by w to give the number of articles he reads in w weeks.

    Avinash reads 2 fiction articles per day. Since there are 7 days in a week, he reads $2(7) = 14$ fiction articles per week. He also reads 14 nonfiction articles per week. So Avinash reads $14 + 14 = 28$ fiction and nonfiction articles per week.

    Therefore, the number of articles Avinash reads in w weeks is given by the expression $28w$, which is choice **(C)**.

Heart of Algebra Drill (No Calculator)

1. If $-(2x - 4) + 3(x - 5) = -4$, what is the value of x?

   (A) -3
   (B) 5
   (C) 7
   (D) 15

2. If $g(x + 2) = 5x - 4$, what is the value of $g(7)$?

   (A) 21
   (B) 29
   (C) 31
   (D) 41

3. John is having an undetermined number of people over for dinner. He needs to have 6 serving utensils (used by everyone collectively), plus a knife, fork, and spoon for each diner. Which of the following equations correctly models the total number of utensils, U, John will need for x number of diners, himself included?

   (A) $U = 3x$
   (B) $U = 9x$
   (C) $U = 3x + 6$
   (D) $U = 6x + 3$

4. If $f(x) = 4x + 7$ and if $g(x) = -3x + 2$, what is the value of $f(g(3))$?
(A) -27
(B) -21
(C) -7
(D) 19

5. Under a new state law, a massage therapist will be required to charge sales tax on her services. If the sales tax rate is 7%, by what ratio would she need to multiply the current price of her services to determine the new total amount customers will pay under the new law?
(A) $\frac{7}{100}$
(B) $\frac{7}{10}$
(C) $\frac{107}{100}$
(D) $\frac{170}{100}$

6. If $6(2a - b) = 4b$, what is the ratio of b to a?
(A) $\frac{2}{3}$
(B) $\frac{5}{6}$
(C) $\frac{6}{5}$
(D) $\frac{12}{5}$

7. The total operational costs C for a restaurant are modeled by the equation $C = 2M + 50{,}000$, where M represents the number of meals served. What does the 50,000 represent in the equation?
(A) The total operational costs
(B) The fixed operational costs
(C) The cost per meal
(D) The minimum number of meals served

8. The total costs C to operate a factory are represented by the function $C(n) = an + b$, where n is the number of days the factory is operational. If the daily operations costs were to increase beyond the given rate and if the initial startup costs were to decrease beyond the given rate, how would this affect the constants a and b?
(A) a would increase, and b would increase.
(B) a would increase, and b would decrease.
(C) a would decrease, and b would increase.
(D) a and b would remain the same.

9. How will the function $f(x) = 4x - 5$ be affected by the translation

$$g(x) = f(x - 1) + 2?$$

(A) It will be shifted up 2 units and 1 unit to the left.
(B) It will be shifted down 1 unit and 2 units to the left.
(C) It will be shifted up 2 units and 1 unit to the right.
(D) It will be shifted down 1 unit and 2 units to the right.

10. A company is conducting an online campaign to increase its social media followers. The number of social media followers, N, is estimated by the equation $N = 30W + 250$, where W represents the number of weeks of the campaign (and $W > 0$). What does the number 250 represent in the equation?

    (A) The number of weeks of the campaign
    (B) The number of new social media followers each week
    (C) The number of social media followers at the start of the campaign
    (D) The number of social media followers at the end of W weeks

✓ Solutions

1. **(C)** First, we need to distribute. Don't forget to distribute the negative sign to the$(2x - 4)$ term. Distributing gives us:

$$-2x + 4 + 3x - 15 = -4$$

Combining like terms on the left side gives:

$$x - 11 = -4$$

Adding 11 to both sides tells us that $x = 7$, which is choice **(C)**.

Note that you could also plug each answer choice into the equation to see which one gives the correct equality, but doing this could be more time-consuming.

2. **(A)** First, we must determine what number we should plug in for x. Our original function is $g(x + 2)$, and we're looking for $g(7)$. That means that we want x such that $x + 2 = 7$. Subtracting 2 from both sides gives $x = 5$. So to find $g(7)$, we simply plug in 5 for x in the original function:

$$g(5 + 2) = 5(5) - 4 = 25 - 4 = 21$$

The correct answer is choice **(A)**.

3. **(C)** John needs 6 utensils no matter how many people come, so +6 will be a constant. He also needs 3 utensils per person, which can be represented as $3x$. Thus, he needs $3x + 6$ utensils, choice **(C)**.

Choice (A) is incorrect because although it correctly depicts the 3 utensils needed for each person, it neglects the 6 serving utensils.

Choice (B) is incorrect because it states that each person needs 9 utensils.

Choice (D) is incorrect because it states that there are 3 utensils needed no matter how many people come, rather than the 6 utensils actually needed.

Alternatively, you could have imagined a scenario in which John invited 1 other person over, making a total of 2 people at dinner. They need 6 serving utensils, plus each one of them needs a knife, spoon, and fork. This makes a total of 2 knives, 2 spoons, and 2 forks, or 6 more utensils. The total number of utensils needed in this case is $6 + 6 = 12$.

You could have then plugged in 12 for U, plugged in 2 for x, and chosen the answer choice that worked, which is choice **(C)**:

$$12 = 3(2) + 6$$

4. **(B)** First, we have to find the value of $g(3)$ by plugging in 3 wherever there's an x in $g(x)$:

$$g(3) = -3(3) + 2 = -9 + 2 = -7$$

Now we have to find $f(-7)$ by plugging in -7 wherever there is an x in $f(x)$:

$$f(-7) = 4(-7) + 7 = -28 + 7 = -21$$

The answer is choice **(B)**.

5. **(C)** Let's imagine that a massage therapist currently charges \$100 for a massage. If the tax rate is 7%, or 0.07, tax on that service will be:

$$0.07(\$100) = \$7$$

Therefore, the price of the massage including the sales tax will be:

$$\$100 + \$7 = \$107$$

The ratio of the new price to the old price is:

$$\frac{107}{100}$$

The massage therapist can find the new prices for all of her services by multiplying the old prices by this ratio.

6. **(C)** First, distribute the 6:

$$12a - 6b = 4b$$

Bring the b terms to the right side by adding $6b$ to both sides:

$$12a = 10b$$

To find the ratio of b to a, we want to solve for $\frac{b}{a}$. First, divide both sides by a:

$$12 = 10\frac{b}{a}$$

To isolate $\frac{b}{a}$, we need to divide both sides by 10:

$$\frac{b}{a} = \frac{12}{10} = \frac{6}{5}$$

The correct ratio is choice **(C)**.

7. **(B)** This \$50,000 is some sort of cost that stays the same whether the restaurant serves 0 meals or serves 1,000 meals. Because the \$50,000 doesn't vary with the variable meals, it's a fixed cost, which is choice **(B)**.

Choice (A) is incorrect because C represents the total costs, and C varies with the number of meals served.

Choice (C) is incorrect because 2 is the cost per meal, as shown by the $2M$ in the equation.

Choice (D) is incorrect because the minimum number of meals served could be any positive integer.

8. **(B)** Total cost is found by adding together the variable costs and the fixed costs. In this problem, the variable cost is an since this value depends on n, the number of days the factory is operational. Since an is a cost and since n is a number of days, it follows that the daily operational cost is given by a. Therefore, if the daily operational cost increases, a will increase.

The initial startup costs, or fixed costs, are given by variable b because b is a constant that isn't affected by the variable n. Therefore, if the startup costs decrease, b will decrease.

The correct scenario is depicted in choice **(B)**.

9. **(C)** In general, if $f(x)$ is our original function and if c is a constant, then:

   - $f(x-c)$ shifts $f(x)$ to the right by c units.
   - $f(x+c)$ shifts $f(x)$ to the left by c units.
   - $f(x)+c$ shifts $f(x)$ up by c units.
   - $f(x)-c$ shifts $f(x)$ down by c units.

   In this particular problem, $g(x)=f(x-1)+2$. Using the above properties, $f(x-1)$ tells us that $f(x)$ is shifted to the right by 1 unit. The $+2$ in the expression tells us that $f(x)$ is shifted up by 2 units. This corresponds to choice **(C)**.

10. **(C)** The number 250 is in the equation regardless of the value of W. Therefore, it makes sense that 250 would be the initial number of followers the campaign had. We can see this by plugging 0 in for W in the equation. This gives us the initial number of followers before the company starts campaigning:

    $$N=30(0)+250=0+250=250$$

    So we can see that when $W=0$, $N=250$.

Passport to Advanced Math Drill (No Calculator)

1. An element's half-life is the amount of time that it takes for the element to decay by half. If there is x amount of element Z initially, which of the following represents the amount A of Z that would remain after n whole half-lives of Z had passed?

   (A) $A=\frac{x}{2n}$
   (B) $A=\frac{x}{2^n}$
   (C) $A=\frac{n}{2x}$
   (D) $A=\frac{x}{2^{n-1}}$

2. $\sqrt[5]{32x^8y^{11}}$ is equivalent to which of the following?

   (A) $2xy^2\sqrt[5]{x^3y}$
   (B) $2x^5y^{10}\sqrt[5]{x^3y}$
   (C) $2x^3y^6\sqrt[5]{xy}$
   (D) $2xy^2\sqrt[5]{2x^3y^2}$

3. If $x>0$, then $\frac{1}{2x}+\frac{1}{3x}$ is equivalent to which of the following?

   (A) $\left(\frac{25}{6x^2}\right)^{\frac{1}{2}}$
   (B) $\left(\frac{4}{25x^2}\right)^{\frac{1}{2}}$
   (C) $\left(\frac{5}{6x}\right)^{2}$
   (D) $\left(\frac{25}{36x^2}\right)^{\frac{1}{2}}$

4. If $x^2 + ax = b$, where a and b are constants, what are the solutions for x?

(A) $x = -\frac{a}{2} \pm \sqrt{2b + \frac{a^2}{2}}$

(B) $x = -\frac{a}{2} \pm \sqrt{b + \frac{a^2}{4}}$

(C) $x = -\frac{b}{2} \pm \sqrt{\frac{a^2}{2} - 2b}$

(D) $x = -\frac{a}{2} \pm \sqrt{b^2 + \frac{a^2}{4}}$

5. $6x^2 + 15xy + 6y^2 = ?$

(A) $3(2x + y)^2$
(B) $(3x + y)(x + 3y)$
(C) $(3x + 3y)(2x + 2y)$
(D) $3(x + 2y)(2x + y)$

6. What are the solution(s) for x in the equation below?

$$x - 6 = \sqrt{75 - 2x}$$

(A) 13
(B) 13 and −3
(C) −3 and 3
(D) No solution

7. At what points will $f(x) = 8x^2 - 22x + 15$ intersect the x-axis?

(A) 15
(B) $\frac{3}{2}$ and $\frac{5}{4}$
(C) $-\frac{5}{4}$ and $-\frac{3}{2}$
(D) $\frac{5}{4}$ and $\frac{15}{2}$

8. Which value of n will cause the value of $f(x) = xn$ to be consistently positive and increase the most rapidly, given that x is greater than 1 and that n is an even integer?

(A) −2
(B) −1
(C) 1
(D) 2

9. To see if two sets of data are correlated, one can calculate the correlation coefficient between two populations, r_{xy}, using the formula $r_{xy} = \frac{s_{xy}}{s_x s_y}$, where s_{xy} is the covariance of the population, s_x is the standard deviation of population x, and s_y is the standard deviation of population y. If the dispersion of population x and the dispersion of population y both increase while the covariance between the populations remains the same, what would happen to the correlation coefficient of the two populations?

(A) It would decrease.
(B) It would increase.
(C) It would stay the same.
(D) It cannot be determined.

10. If the function $f(x) = x^n + 3^{xm}$ has 5 zeros and if $f(x)$ is multiplied by -1, how many zeros will the resulting function have?

    (A) -5
    (B) 4
    (C) 5
    (D) 6

✓ Solutions

1. **(B)** The amount after one half-life is $\frac{1}{2}x$. After the second half-life, half of this new amount decays, and we're left with:

$$\frac{1}{2}\left(\frac{1}{2}x\right) = \frac{1}{4}x = \left(\frac{1}{2^2}\right)x$$

After the third half-life, half of that amount left decays. We now have left:

$$\frac{1}{2}\left(\frac{1}{4}x\right) = \frac{1}{8}x = \left(\frac{1}{2^3}\right)x$$

We can start to see a pattern: each time a half-life passes, we multiply the amount we previously had by $\frac{1}{2}$. So after n half-lives, $A = \left(\frac{1}{2^n}\right)x$ remains, or $A = A = \frac{x}{2^n}$. This matches choice **(B)**.

2. **(A)** $\sqrt[5]{32} = 2$. So go ahead and bring a 2 outside of the radical before dealing with the variables:

$$\sqrt[5]{32x^8y^{11}} = 2\sqrt[5]{x^8y^{11}}$$

Let's deal with the x term under the root next. Notice the following:

$$\sqrt[5]{x^8} = \sqrt[5]{x^5x^3} = \sqrt[5]{x^5}\sqrt[5]{x^3} = x\sqrt[5]{x^3}$$

Similarly, we can rewrite the y term under the root as follows:

$$\sqrt[5]{y^{11}} = \sqrt[5]{y^5y^5y} = \sqrt[5]{y^5}\sqrt[5]{y^5}\sqrt[5]{y} = y \cdot y\sqrt[5]{y} = y^2\sqrt[5]{y}$$

Thus, the entire expression can be rewritten as:

$$\sqrt[5]{32x^8y^{11}} = 2\sqrt[5]{x^8y^{11}} = 2\sqrt[5]{x^8}\sqrt[5]{y^{11}} = 2xy^2\sqrt[5]{x^3y}$$

This is choice **(A)**.

3. **(D)** All of the answer choices are a single fraction. So first find a common denominator and add the two fractions. The least common denominator is $6x$. Multiply the first fraction by $\frac{3}{3}$ and the second by $\frac{2}{2}$:

$$\frac{3}{6x} + \frac{2}{6x} = \frac{5}{6x}$$

We can rule choice (C) out because it's our answer squared, so it will not equal our answer.

The rest of the answers are being raised to the $\frac{1}{2}$ power, which is equivalent to taking the square root. In order to find out what should be inside the parentheses, we must work backward by doing the opposite to our function. Because the answer choices take the square root of an expression, we must square our expression to find what should go inside the parentheses:

$$\left(\frac{5}{6x}\right)^2 = \frac{5^2}{(6x)^2} = \frac{25}{36x^2}$$

Therefore, the answer is choice **(D)**.

Alternatively, we could have taken the square root of choices (A), (B), and (D) to see which one is equivalent to $\frac{5}{6x}$:

$$\left(\frac{25}{6x^2}\right)^{\frac{1}{2}} = \frac{\sqrt{25}}{\sqrt{6x^2}} = \frac{5}{\sqrt{6}x}$$

So, choice (A) is incorrect.

$$\left(\frac{4}{25x^2}\right)^{\frac{1}{2}} = \frac{\sqrt{4}}{\sqrt{25x^2}} = \frac{2}{5x}$$

So, choice (B) is incorrect.

$$\left(\frac{25}{36x^2}\right)^{\frac{1}{2}} = \frac{\sqrt{25}}{\sqrt{36x^2}} = \frac{5}{6x}$$

This matches the expression we obtained, so choice **(D)** is correct.

4. **(B)** In their structure, the answer choices all look like the quadratic formula. So subtract b from both sides:

$$x^2 + ax - b = 0$$

Now you can use the quadratic formula:

$$x = \frac{-b \pm \sqrt{b^2 - 4ac}}{2a}$$

We have to be careful, though. Our equation has a and b coefficients, but they don't match up exactly with the a and b given in the quadratic formula. In the quadratic formula, a is the coefficient in front of the x^2 term, b corresponds to the coefficient in front of the x term, and c represents the constant. In our case, however, the coefficient in front of the x^2 term is 1, the coefficient of the x term is a, and the constant is b. Keep this in mind while using the quadratic formula to get:

$$x = \frac{-a \pm \sqrt{a^2 - 4(1)(-b)}}{2(1)} = \frac{-a \pm \sqrt{a^2 + 4b}}{2}$$

This doesn't match any of the answer choices, so we need to simplify further. All of the answer choices have the leading term over 2, so let's divide this into two fractions:

$$\frac{-a \pm \sqrt{a^2 + 4b}}{2} = -\frac{a}{2} \pm \frac{\sqrt{a^2 + 4b}}{2}$$

From the leading term, you can narrow it down to choices (A), (B), and (D). It looks like the answer choices have pulled the denominator of the second term into the square root. Because 2 equals $\sqrt{4}$, we can change the denominator to $\sqrt{4}$:

$$-\frac{a}{2} \pm \frac{\sqrt{a^2 + 4b}}{2} = -\frac{a}{2} \pm \frac{\sqrt{a^2 + 4b}}{\sqrt{4}} = -\frac{a}{2} \pm \sqrt{\frac{a^2 + 4b}{4}}$$

In all of the answer choices, the fraction inside the square root appears to be broken up, so do that:

$$-\frac{a}{2} \pm \sqrt{\frac{a^2 + 4b}{4}} = -\frac{a}{2} \pm \sqrt{\frac{a^2}{4} + \frac{4b}{4}} = -\frac{a}{2} \pm \sqrt{\frac{a^2}{4} + b}$$

Reordering what's inside the root gives you choice **(B)**.

5. **(D)** One easy way to solve this problem is to use FOIL on the answer choices and see which matches the original:

Choice (A):

$$3(2x + y)^2 = 3[(2x + y)(2x + y)] = 3(4x^2 + 4xy + y^2) = 12x^2 + 12xy + 3y^2$$

This does not match our expression, so we can rule out this choice.

Choice (B):

$$(3x + y)(x + 3y) = 3x^2 + 10xy + 3y^2$$

This does not match the original.

Choice (C):

$$(3x + 3y)(2x + 2y) = 6x^2 + 12xy + 6y^2$$

This does not quite match the original.

Choice (D):

$$3(x + 2y)(2x + y) = 3(2x^2 + 5xy + 2y^2) = 6x^2 + 15xy + 6y^2$$

This matches the original expression, so the answer is choice **(D)**.

Another way to solve the problem is to factor. Since each term is divisible by 3, we can factor out a 3 to get:

$$3(2x^2 + 5xy + 2y^2)$$

Next, we factor the expression inside the parenthesis as follows:

$$3(2x + y)(x + 2y)$$

This matches choice **(D)**.

6. **(A)** Look at the answer choices. There are only three possible x values in the answer choices (13, 3, and −3), so it's probably easiest to just plug in these three values for x in our original equation to see which ones work:

$$13 - 6 = \sqrt{75 - 2(13)}$$

$$7 = \sqrt{49}$$

The square root of 49 is 7, so 13 works.

$$-3 - 6 = \sqrt{75 - 2(-3)}$$

$$-9 = \sqrt{81}$$

Square roots always give nonnegative answers, so this one doesn't work.

$$3 - 6 = \sqrt{75 - 2(3)}$$

$$-3 = \sqrt{69}$$

Only 13 works, so the answer is choice **(A)**.

You could also solve this directly by squaring both sides of the equation:

$$(x - 6)^2 = (\sqrt{75 - 2x})^2$$

Squaring gives:

$$x^2 - 12x + 36 = 75 - 2x$$

This is a quadratic equation. So we move everything over to one side, combine like terms, and factor:

$$x^2 - 10x - 39 = 0$$

Factoring gives:

$$(x - 13)(x + 3) = 0$$

So $x = 13$ or $x = -3$. Since we initially squared our equation, we have to check our answers since this procedure can lead to extraneous answers. Indeed, only $x = 13$ works. So 13 is the only solution to the equation.

7. **(B)** Functions intersect the x-axis at their zeros. Zeros can be found by setting the function equal to 0 and either factoring or using the quadratic formula to solve for possible values of x.

   The polynomial can be factored to $(4x - 5)(2x - 3) = 0$. Set each factor equal to 0 and solve for x:

   $$4x - 5 = 0$$

   Adding 5 to both sides and then dividing by 4 gives you $x = \frac{5}{4}$.

   $$2x - 3 = 0$$

   Adding 3 to both sides then dividing by 2 gives you $x = \frac{3}{2}$.

   Choice **(B)** is the answer.

   Alternatively, you could have used the quadratic formula:

   $$x = \frac{-b \pm \sqrt{b^2 - 4ac}}{2a} = \frac{22 \pm \sqrt{(-22)^2 - 4(8)(15)}}{2(8)} = \frac{22 \pm \sqrt{4}}{16} = \frac{22 \pm 2}{16}$$

   $$x = \frac{24}{16} = \frac{3}{2} \text{ or } x = \frac{20}{16} = \frac{5}{4}$$

8. **(D)** We are told that x is greater than 1, so the function will always be positive regardless of n. We are also told that n is an even integer, so this narrows down the answer to 2 or -2. In order for the function to increase most rapidly, you want the exponent n to be the largest even number possible, which is choice **(D)**.

9. **(A)** If the dispersion of population x increases, the standard deviation of x increases. If the dispersion of population y increases, the standard deviation of y increases. Therefore, you'd be holding the numerator constant while increasing the denominator. Therefore, the correlation coefficient would decrease, which is choice **(A)**.

10. **(C)** Multiplying a function by -1 will flip it about the x-axis. The new function will still cross the x-axis the same number of times at the same values of x as the original function. So the zeros will not change. If $f(x)$ has 5 zeros, $-f(x)$ will also have 5 zeros.

    Consider this simpler function to see how multiplying it by -1 would affect its graph.

The graph of $y = x^2 - 5$ is shown:

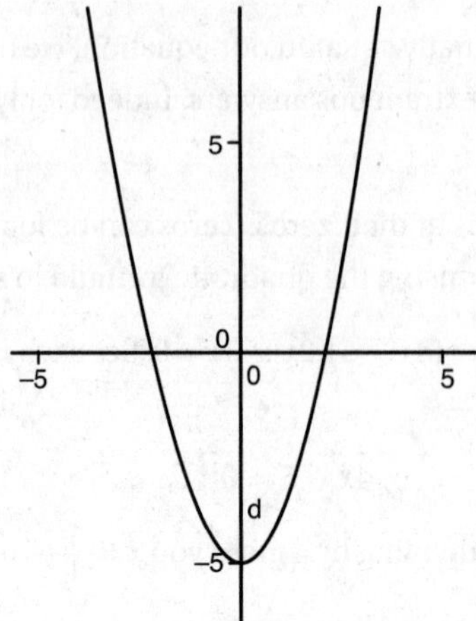

If the function is multiplied by -1 on the right-hand side, it will give the function $y = -x^2 + 5$, which is shown:

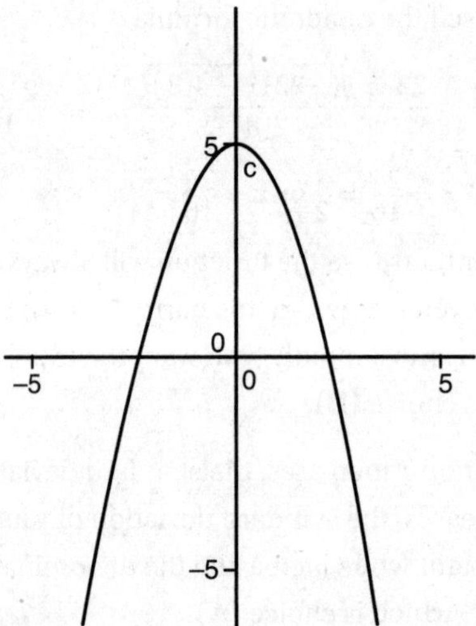

So the functions have the same zeros even though they are mirror images of one another.

Passport to Advanced Math (No Calculator)

1. A particular savings account provides no interest in the first year of a deposit and 3% annual compounded interest on a deposit for each year thereafter. If x dollars are deposited initially, which of the following equations expresses the total amount of money $A(n)$ in the account n years later, where n is an integer greater than 2?

   (A) $A(n) = x\,[(0.03)^n]$
   (B) $A(n) = x\,[(0.97)^n]$
   (C) $A(n) = x\,[(0.03)^{n-1}]$
   (D) $A(n) = x\,[(1.03)^{n-1}]$

2. What is the value of x in the following equation?

$$x^2 + 9 = -6x$$

(A) -3
(B) 0
(C) 3
(D) No solution

3. For $y < 0$, which of the following is equivalent to $\frac{3}{x^2 y}$?

(A) $\frac{3x^{-2}}{\sqrt[4]{y^2}}$

(B) $\frac{3x^{-2}}{-\sqrt[4]{y^4}}$

(C) $\frac{3x^{\frac{1}{2}}}{\sqrt[4]{y^4}}$

(D) $\frac{3x^{-2}}{\sqrt[4]{y^4}}$

4. For positive x and y, $x^{-\frac{3}{4}} y^{\frac{4}{3}}$ is equivalent to

(A) $-\frac{x^3 y^4}{x^4 y^3}$

(B) $\frac{\sqrt[4]{y^3}}{\sqrt[3]{x^4}}$

(C) $\frac{y\sqrt[3]{y}}{\sqrt[4]{x^3}}$

(D) $\frac{y^4\sqrt[3]{y}}{x^3\sqrt[4]{x}}$

5. What are the possible values of x in the following equation?

$$3x^2 + 12x + 6 = 0$$

(A) $-12 \pm \sqrt{3}$
(B) $-2 \pm \sqrt{2}$
(C) $-2 \pm \sqrt{3}$
(D) $2 \pm \sqrt{2}$

6. If $x^2 + x - 12 = 0$ and if $x < 0$, what is the value of x?

(A) -6
(B) -4
(C) -3
(D) 3

7. $64x^6 - 16y^8$ is equivalent to which of the following expressions?

(A) $16(4x^3 + y^4)(x^3 - y^4)$
(B) $16(4x^3 - y^4)(x^3 - y^4)$
(C) $16(2x^3 + y^4)(2x^3 - y^4)$
(D) $16(2x^6 - y^8)(2x - y)$

8. Solve the following equation for all possible x values.

   (A) 3
   (B) 3 and 8
   (C) −3 and −8
   (D) Infinitely many solutions

9. The graph of $x - 4 = y^4$ has a minimal x value that compares in what way to the minimal x value of the graph $x = y^4$?

   (A) It is 4 less.
   (B) It is 4 greater.
   (C) They are the same.
   (D) The answer cannot be determined.

10. Which of the following functions represents the reflection across the x axis of

$$y = 3(x - 5)^2 + 4?$$

   (A) $y = -3(x + 5)^2 - 4$
   (B) $y = -3(x - 5)^2 - 4$
   (C) $y = 3(-x - 5)^2 + 4$
   (D) $y = 3(-x + 5)^2 + 4$

✓ Solutions

1. **(D)** If 3% is added annually after the first year is complete, after the second year, 3% will have been added. Thus, after 2 years, the total amount of money in the account can be represented as:

$$x + 0.03x$$

By combining like terms, it can also be expressed as:

$$1.03x = x(1.03)^1$$

After three years, another 3% is added to the new amount:

$$1.03x + 0.03(1.03x) = 1.03(x + 0.03x) = 1.03(1.03x) = x(1.03)^2$$

Continue in this manner. So after the fourth year, the amount of money in the account is $x(1.03)^3$.

Keeping this pattern in mind, the money in the account after n years is $x(1.03)n^{-1}$, which is choice **(D)**.

Note that raising 1.03 to the $n - 1$ power means that you're multiplying x by 1.03 one time less than the number of years that have passed. This is because no interest is added in the first year.

2. **(A)** Add the $6x$ to both sides so that the polynomial is equal to 0:

$$x^2 + 6x + 9 = 0$$

You can either factor this or use the quadratic formula. This is easily factorable:

$$(x + 3)(x + 3) = 0$$

You can set each factor equal to 0 to solve for the possible values of x. However, since they're the same factor, you need to do it only once:

$$x + 3 = 0$$

Subtracting 3 from both sides tells you that $x = -3$, which is choice **(A)**.

3. **(B)** The key here is to notice that in the problem, $y < 0$. In the original expression, x is squared. So regardless of its sign, x^2 will be positive. Therefore, $\frac{3}{x^2 y}$ will be negative when y is negative. Thus, the new expression must also be negative.

Simplify the answer choices to see which matches the original expression.

Choice (A):

Negative exponents get sent to the denominator:

$$\frac{3x^{-2}}{\sqrt[4]{y^2}} = \frac{3}{x^2\sqrt[4]{y^2}}$$

Roots can be expressed as fractional exponents:

$$\frac{3}{x^2\sqrt[4]{y^2}} = \frac{3}{x^2 y^{\frac{2}{4}}}$$

However, $y^{\frac{2}{4}} \neq y$. So this is different than our original expression. We can rule out choice (A).

Choice (B):

Following the same process as the previous answer choice, we can rewrite this answer as:

$$\frac{3x^{-2}}{-\sqrt[4]{y^4}} = -\frac{3}{x^2\sqrt[4]{y^4}}$$

Now consider $\sqrt[4]{y^4}$. It is tempting to say that this just equals $y^{\frac{4}{4}} = y$, but we have to be careful not to ignore a subtle point. When we take the fourth root of something, or in general the even root of something, we necessarily get a result that is nonnegative. In particular, $\sqrt[4]{y^4}$ must be nonnegative. However, y is negative, so the expression can't equal y. The expression actually equals $-y$, which is positive since y is negative.

(Convince yourself of this. For example, let $y = -2$ and consider $\sqrt[4]{y^4} = \sqrt[4]{(-2)^4}$. This expression is equal to $\sqrt[4]{16} = 2 = -(-2) = -y$ since $y = -2$.)

Thus, plugging in $-y$ for $\sqrt[4]{y^4}$ in our expression gives the following after canceling out the negative signs:

$$\frac{3x^{-2}}{-\sqrt[4]{y^4}} = -\frac{3}{x^2\sqrt[4]{y^4}} = -\frac{3}{x^2(-y)} = \frac{3}{x^2 y}$$

This is our original expression, so choice **(B)** must be the correct answer.

If you wanted to explore the other answer choices, you could.

Choice (C):

By the same logic as before, this simplifies to:

$$\frac{3x^{\frac{1}{2}}}{\sqrt[4]{y^4}} = \frac{3\sqrt{x}}{-y} = -\frac{3\sqrt{x}}{y}$$

This clearly doesn't match the original expression, so it can be eliminated.

Choice (D):

Simplifying gives:

$$\frac{3x^{-2}}{\sqrt[4]{y^4}} = \frac{3}{x^2(-y)} = -\frac{3}{x^2y}$$

This is close to our original expression but has a negative sign in front, so we can eliminate this choice.

4. **(C)** Remember that negative exponents can be made positive by moving whatever is being raised to that exponent to the denominator:

$$x^{-\frac{3}{4}}y^{\frac{4}{3}} = \frac{y^{\frac{4}{3}}}{x^{\frac{3}{4}}}$$

Fractional exponents are the same as roots:

$$\frac{y^{\frac{4}{3}}}{x^{\frac{3}{4}}} = \frac{\sqrt[3]{y^4}}{\sqrt[4]{x^3}}$$

This doesn't match any answer choices, so we need to simplify further. The y is being raised to a power higher than its root, so we should be able to pull something out of the root.

Since y is positive:

$$\sqrt[3]{y^4} = \sqrt[3]{y^3y} = \sqrt[3]{y^3}\sqrt[3]{y} = y\sqrt[3]{y}$$

Therefore, our whole expression can be rewritten as:

$$\frac{y\sqrt[3]{y}}{\sqrt[4]{x^3}}$$

Choice **(C)** is the correct answer.

5. **(B)** Factor out a 3:

$$3(x^2 + 4x + 2) = 0$$

Divide both sides by 3:

$$x^2 + 4x + 2 = 0$$

This isn't easily factorable, so use the quadratic formula:

$$x = \frac{-b \pm \sqrt{b^2 - 4ac}}{2a} = \frac{-4 \pm \sqrt{4^2 - 4(1)(2)}}{2(1)} = \frac{-4 \pm \sqrt{8}}{2} = \frac{-4 \pm 2\sqrt{2}}{2} = -2 \pm \sqrt{2}$$

Choice **(B)** is the answer.

6. **(B)** We need to find all solutions less than 0. This equation is easily factorable:

$$x^2 + x - 12 = (x + 4)(x - 3) = 0$$

If $x + 4$ or $x - 3$ equaled 0, the whole expression would equal 0. Therefore, setting both factors equal to 0 will tell us the two potential values of x:

$$x + 4 = 0 \text{ so } x = -4$$

$$x - 3 = 0 \text{ so } x = 3$$

The question asks for only the value of x that's less than 0, so the answer is $x = -4$, which is choice **(B)**.

7. **(C)** All of the answers have a 16 factored out, so do that first:

$$64x^6 - 16y^8 = 16(4x^6 - y^8)$$

When anything is in the form $(a^2 - b^2)$, it can be factored using the difference of squares formula: $(a + b)(a - b)$. The trick to this problem is figuring out what a and b are. Set $4x^6$ equal to a^2 to find a:

$$4x^6 = a^2$$
$$a = \sqrt{4x^6}$$

Take the square root of both 4 and the x term:

$$a = 2x^{\frac{6}{2}} = 2x^3$$

Next, set y^8 equal to b^2 to solve for b:

$$y^8 = b^2$$
$$b = \sqrt{y^8} = y^{\frac{8}{2}} = y^4$$

Therefore, if you wanted to express $(4x^6 - y^8)$ in the form of $(a + b)(a - b)$, it would be:

$$(2x^3 + y^4)(2x^3 - y^4)$$

Putting the 16 in front gives you choice **(C)**.

8. **(B)** Get rid of the square root by squaring both sides:

$$x^2 = 11x - 24$$

To find the possible values of x, subtract $11x$ and add 24 to both sides, setting the left side equal to 0. Then factor or use the quadratic formula to solve:

$$x^2 - 11x + 24 = 0$$

This equation factors as:

$$(x - 3)(x - 8) = 0$$

This statement would hold true if $x - 3 = 0$ or if $x - 8 = 0$. In other words, the statement would hold true if $x = 3$ or if $x = 8$, which is choice **(B)**.

Be careful, though. When we squared both sides of the equation, we were no longer guaranteed to get the same exact solutions as our original equation. In other words, because we square both sides, it is possible that we get extraneous solutions. So we should get in the habit of checking that both of our solutions are indeed solutions. We can do this by plugging both answer choices into our original equation:

$$x = 3$$
$$\sqrt{11(3) - 24} = \sqrt{9} = 3 = x$$

This solution checks out.

$$x = 8$$
$$\sqrt{11(8) - 24} = \sqrt{64} = 8 = x$$

This solution checks out as well.

In this problem, both solutions check out. However, you should be cautious in general when squaring equations.

9. **(B).** The first function can be expressed as $y = \sqrt[4]{x-4}$. It's an even root. This means that the value within the root must be greater than or equal to 0 since we can find only the even root of a nonnegative number:

$$x - 4 \geq 0$$
$$x \geq 4$$

Therefore, the domain of the function is $[4, \infty)$.

The second function can be expressed as $y = \sqrt[4]{x}$. Again, it's an even root. So what's within the root must be greater than or equal to 0:

$$x \geq 0$$

The domain of this function then is $[0, \infty)$.

Therefore, the minimal x value of the first function is 4 more than the minimal x value of the second function. Choice **(B)** is the answer.

10. **(B).** To reflect something across the x-axis, multiply the entire equation by -1:

$$-y = -[3(x-5)^2 + 4] = -3(x-5)^2 - 4$$

Alternatively, notice that our original function gives the equation of a parabola; think about what this parabola looks like. Recall that the vertex form of a parabola is $y = a(x-h)^2 + k$. Our original parabola will open upward since $a = 3$ is positive. This parabola will also have a vertex at $(h, k) = (5, 4)$. If you want to reflect this across the x- axis, it would need to open downward and have a vertex at $(5, -4)$. Therefore, the vertex form of this new parabola would be:

$$y = -3(x-5)^2 - 4$$

The answer is choice **(B)**.

Problem Solving and Data Analysis Drill (Calculator)

1. If there are 4 cars for every 5 trucks in the parking lot (with no other types of vehicles), what is the ratio of cars to the total number of vehicles in the parking lot?

(A) 1 to 5
(B) 4 to 9
(C) 5 to 9
(D) 4 to 5

2. On Monday, the highest temperature reached was 70 degrees Fahrenheit. On Tuesday, the highest temperature increased by 20%. On Wednesday, the highest temperature decreased by 25% from the previous day. What was the difference between Monday's and Wednesday's highest temperatures in degrees Fahrenheit?

(A) 5
(B) 7
(C) 14
(D) 21

3. A recipe calls for 3 cups of sugar. There are 16 tablespoons in a cup and 3 teaspoons in a tablespoon. If a cook has 1.5 cups of sugar available in the pantry, how many teaspoons of sugar must the cook obtain from other sources to follow the recipe?

(A) 72
(B) 104
(C) 144
(D) 216

Price per Gallon of Milk	Number of Gallons Sold
$1.50	650
$0.90	780
$1.95	530
$2.80	330
$3.40	190

4. Which of these functions best models the relationship between the number of gallons of milk sold, $N(g)$, and the price per gallon of milk, g?

(A) $N(g) = 530 + 590(g - 1.95)^2$
(B) $N(g) = 1{,}000 - 240g$
(C) $N(g) = 1{,}000 + 240g$
(D) $N(g) = 780 - 360(g - 0.9)^2$

	Employed	Unemployed
Population X	890	112
Population Y	748	205

5. What is the difference between the unemployment percentage in Population Y and the unemployment percentage in Populations X and Y combined, calculated to the nearest tenth?

(A) 5.0%
(B) 5.3%
(C) 5.8%
(D) 6.2%

Questions 6–7 use the following table.

Election Results

	Candidate A	Candidate B	Total
Columbus	350,000	270,000	620,000
Cleveland	180,000	195,000	375,000
Total	530,000	465,000	995,000

6. Of all eligible voters in Columbus, 40% actually voted in the election. How many total eligible voters did Columbus have?

(A) 248,000
(B) 875,000
(C) 1,550,000
(D) 2,487,500

7. Suppose that a survey of total 200 randomly selected voters from both cities accurately predicted the results of the election. How many of the people surveyed would have been supporters of Candidate A from Columbus?

(A) 50
(B) 70
(C) 113
(D) 132

Questions 8–9 use the following table.

Grade	Test 1	Project 1	Test 2	Project 2	Total
A	5	8	9	7	29
B	7	6	5	10	28
C	6	7	4	5	22
D	4	1	3	2	10
F	1	1	3	0	5
Total	23	23	24	24	94

8. The median letter grade for assignments in the class is:

(A) A
(B) B
(C) C
(D) D

9. For which assignment is the standard deviation of the grade results the least?

(A) Test 1
(B) Project 1
(C) Test 2
(D) Project 2

10. An online shopping site allows customers to post 1-star, 2-star, 3-star, 4-star, and 5-star reviews for products. If an item currently has an average star rating of 2.3 based on a total of 10 reviews, what is the minimum number of reviews that could bring up the overall average rating to at least a 3.0?

(A) 2
(B) 3
(C) 4
(D) 5

✓ Solutions

1. **(B)** Let's imagine the simplest version of this ratio: there are only 4 cars and 5 trucks in the parking lot. So how many total vehicles are there?

$$4 \text{ cars} + 5 \text{ trucks} = 9 \text{ vehicles}$$

So the ratio of cars to vehicles is 4 cars to 9 vehicles, choice **(B)**.

2. **(B)** If the highest temperature on Tuesday increased 20% from the highest temperature on Monday, then the highest temperature on Tuesday was 120%, or 1.2, of Monday's temperature. Find 120% of 70 degrees:

$$1.2(70) = 84$$

So Tuesday's high temperature was 84 degrees Fahrenheit. Wednesday's high was 25% lower than Tuesday's temperature, so it was only 75%, or 0.75, of Tuesday's temperature. Find 75% of 84 degrees:

$$0.75(84) = 63$$

The highest temperature on Wednesday was 63 degrees Fahrenheit. We want to know the difference between Monday's high temperature and Wednesday's high. The difference is given by $70 - 63 = 7$, which is choice **(B)**.

3. **(A)** If a cook has 1.5 cups of sugar in the pantry but needs 3 cups, he needs $3 - 1.5 = 1.5$ more cups from other sources. We want to convert this to teaspoons:

$$1.5 \text{ cups} \times \frac{16 \text{ tablespoons}}{\text{cup}} \times \frac{3 \text{ teaspoons}}{\text{tablespoon}} = 72 \text{ teaspoons}$$

The answer is choice **(A)**.

4. **(B)** Test the answer choices.

Choice (A):

$$N(1.50) = 530 + 590(1.50 - 1.95)^2 = 649.48$$

This is a fairly good estimate, so let's try another value:

$$N(0.90) = 530 + 590(0.90 - 1.95)^2 = 1{,}180.48$$

We can rule out choice (A).

Choice (B):

$$N(1.50) = 1{,}000 - 240(1.50) = 640$$

This is also a fairly good estimate, so let's try the other values:

$$N(0.90) = 1{,}000 - 240(0.90) = 784$$
$$N(1.95) = 1{,}000 - 240(1.95) = 532$$
$$N(2.80) = 1{,}000 - 240(2.80) = 328$$
$$N(3.40) = 1{,}000 - 240(3.40) = 184$$

All of these values are pretty close to the actual values, so this answer choice may be correct. However, the question asks for the best model, so we need to make sure that there are no better models.

Choice (C):

$$N(1.50) = 1{,}000 + 240(1.50) = 1{,}360$$

We can rule out choice (C).

Choice (D):

$$N(1.50) = 780 - 360(1.50 - 0.9)^2 = 650.4$$
$$N(0.90) = 780 - 360(0.90 - 0.9)^2 = 780$$
$$N(1.95) = 780 - 360(1.95 - 0.9)^2 = 383.1$$

We can rule out choice (D).

Choice **(B)** is the best model of the relationship.

5. **(B)** In Population Y, 205 of the $748 + 205 = 953$ people are unemployed. Therefore, the unemployment percentage is:

$$\frac{205}{953} \times 100\% = 21.51\%$$

In both populations combined, there are a total of $112 + 205 = 317$ unemployed people, and a total population of $890 + 112 + 748 + 205 = 1{,}955$. Therefore, the unemployment rate is:

$$\frac{317}{1{,}955} \times 100\% = 16.21\%$$

The difference between the two unemployment rates is $21.51\% - 16.21\% = 5.3\%$, which is choice **(B)**.

6. **(C)** The number of people who voted in Columbus was 620,000. If this number represents only 40% of eligible voters, you can set up a proportion to solve for 100% of the number of eligible voters:

$$\frac{620{,}000}{40} = \frac{x}{100}$$

In the proportion, x represents the number of eligible voters in Columbus. Cross multiply to get:

$$620{,}000(100) = 40x$$
$$62{,}000{,}000 = 40x$$

Dividing by 40 tells you that $x = 1{,}550{,}000$, which is choice **(C)**.

Another way we can solve this problem is as follows. We know that 620,000 is 40% of the eligible voters, x, in Columbus. In other words, $620{,}000 = 0.4x$. Dividing by 0.4 gives 1,550,000, which is choice **(C)**.

7. **(B)** Since there are 350,000 Columbus voters who support Candidate A and 995,000 voters in the two cities combined, we know that $\frac{350{,}000}{995{,}000} = 0.352$ of the voters in the table were supporters of Candidate A from Columbus. We would expect the same proportion of the 200 randomly surveyed voters to be supporters of Candidate A from Columbus. This can be found by taking $0.352(200) = 70.4$. Thus, we could expect about 70 of the randomly surveyed to fall into this category. So the correct answer is choice **(B)**.

8. **(B)** There are 94 total grades. To find the median term in a series with an even number of terms, you have to take the mean of the two middle terms. To find these two middle terms, first divide the total number of terms by 2. This will tell you the number of the 1st term you'll use in your average. Then add 1 to that number to find the number of the 2nd term you'll use in your average.

If we listed all 94 grades starting with the lowest grades, the F's, and ending with the highest grades, the A's, the median terms would be the average of the $\frac{94}{2} = 47$th term and the $\frac{94}{2} + 1 = 48$th term.

F's take us through the first 5 terms.

D's take us through 10 more, to the 15th term.

C's take us through another 22, to the $15 + 22 = 37$th term.

B's take us through another 28 to the $37 + 28 = 65$th term. The 47th and 48th terms will then both be B's, so the median grade is a B, which is choice **(B)**.

9. **(D)** Standard deviation is usually lowest when range is lowest because it means that more values are centered near the mean. Because no one received an F on project 2, the range was only between an A and a D, with only two people receiving D's. Because this project has a rather small range, it will have a rather small standard deviation. In all of the other assignments, at least one student earned an A and at least one earned an F, so the ranges will be higher for all other answer choices. Thus, choice **(D)** is the best choice.

10. **(C)** An average (in other words, a mean) is given by the following expression:

$$\text{Mean} = \frac{\text{Sum}}{n}$$

In the expression, "sum" is the total of the terms you're averaging and n is the number of terms you're averaging. In order to calculate the minimum number of reviews needed to raise the mean to a 3.0, we'll need to know the sum of the current ratings. Plugging the numbers into the equation gives:

$$2.3 = \frac{\text{Sum}}{10}$$

Therefore, the sum of the current ratings is $2.3(10) = 23$.

In order to raise the average with the minimum number of reviews, the reviews need to all be as high as possible, so they must all be 5-star reviews.

Let's test our answer choices. When plugging in answer choices, start with one of the middle answers since answers tend to be arranged from smallest to largest or from largest to smallest.

Choice (B):

If the product gets 3 new 5-star reviews, this will add $3(5) = 15$ to our current sum. This will also add 3 to our current n:

$$\text{Mean} = \frac{23 + 15}{10 + 3} = \frac{38}{13} = 2.92$$

The mean is not high enough yet, so we need more reviews.

Choice (C):

If the product gets 4 new 5-star reviews, this will add $4(5) = 20$ to our current sum and 4 to our current n:

$$\text{Mean} = \frac{23 + 20}{10 + 4} = \frac{43}{14} = 3.07$$

This mean is higher than our desired mean, so 4 is the minimum number of reviews needed, choice **(C)**.

Alternatively, you could have solved this algebraically. Adding x more 5-star reviews will add $5x$ to the sum and x to n, the total number of reviews. Therefore, the mean can be represented with the following equation:

$$\text{Mean} = \frac{23 + 5x}{10 + x}$$

Since we know we want the mean to be 3.0, we can set the right side of our equation equal to 3.0:

$$3.0 = \frac{23 + 5x}{10 + x}$$

Let's get rid of the denominator by multiplying both sides by $(10 + x)$:

$$30 + 3.0x = 23 + 5x$$

Combine like terms by subtracting $3.0x$ and 23 from both sides:

$$7 = 2.0x$$

Dividing both sides by 2.0 tells you that the minimum number of new reviews needed is 3.5. Recall that we want the minimum number of reviews needed to raise the average to a 3.0. Since 3 reviews would not be enough and a person can't give 0.5 of a review, we must round up to the nearest integer, 4. Therefore, to raise the average to a 3.0, you need 4 new reviews.

Additional Topics in Math Drill

1. A box in the shape of a rectangular prism has dimensions 20 inches by 30 inches by 12 inches. Inside the box are four solid cubes, each with edge lengths of 4 inches. If the inside of the larger box is empty except for the solid cubes, what is the volume of empty space in the box?

   (A) 248 cubic inches
   (B) 1,800 cubic inches
   (C) 6,944 cubic inches
   (D) 7,200 cubic inches

2. Given that $i = \sqrt{-1}$, which of the following is equivalent to $-(6i^2 - 4i + 1)$?

   (A) $5 + 4i$
   (B) $-6i + 1$
   (C) $5 - 4i$
   (D) $7 - i$

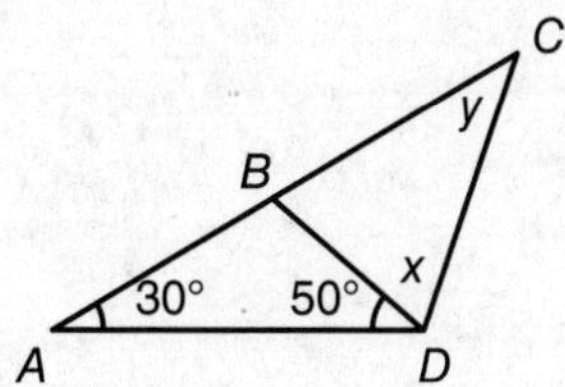

3. In triangle *ACD* above, point *B* is on $\overline{AC}$, and *B* and *D* form a line. What is the sum of $\angle x$ and $\angle y$ in degrees?

(A) 100
(B) 110
(C) 120
(D) 140

4. If a circle has the equation $(x-4)^2+(y-6)^2=9$, what is the equation of the circle if it is reflected directly across the *x*-axis?

(A) $(x+4)^2+(y+6)^2=-9$
(B) $(x-4)^2-(y+6)^2=-9$
(C) $(x+4)^2-(y+6)^2=9$
(D) $(x-4)^2+(y+6)^2=9$

5. If the area of an equilateral triangle is $2\sqrt{3}$ square units, what is the perimeter of the triangle?

(A) 6
(B) $4\sqrt{3}$
(C) $6\sqrt{2}$
(D) $6\sqrt{3}$

6. Given that $\angle X$ is between 0 and 90 degrees, and that $\cos X = Y$, what is the *sine* of an angle with the measure $(90-X)$ degrees?

(A) $90-Y$
(B) Y
(C) $\frac{2}{3}$
(D) 90

7. An angle measuring 3π radians would be equivalent to how many angles with a measure of 45°?

(A) 4
(B) 8
(C) 9
(D) 12

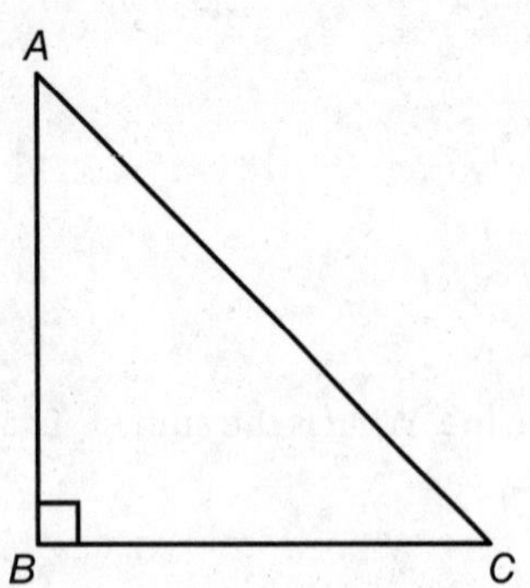

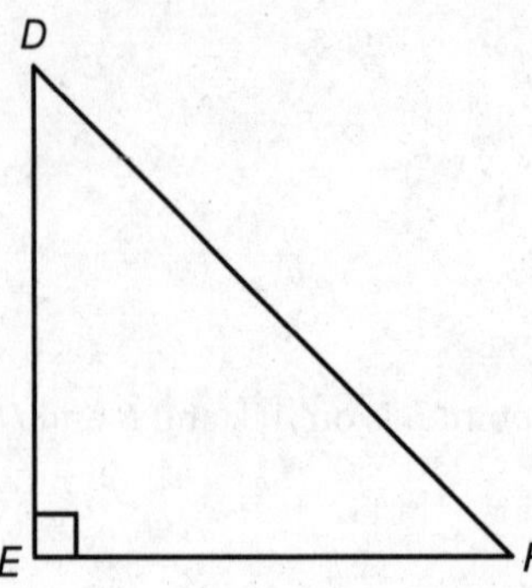

8. Triangles ABC and DEF are similar to one another. If the cosine of $\angle BAC$ is $\frac{12}{13}$, and the length of $\overline{DE}$ is 24 units, what is the length of $\overline{DF}$?

(A) 14
(B) 20
(C) 26
(D) 30

9. Over a 20-second time period, Jeff runs in a circle of 8 feet in radius around a pole. Assuming that Jeff starts the time period at a radius of 8 feet from the pole, the graph during this interval of his time (as the x-coordinates) and his distance from the pole (as the y-coordinates) would have a slope of what?

(A) -1
(B) 0
(C) 1
(D) 2

10. A rectangular dog park is x feet wide and y feet long. The park is to be fenced in along its sides with wooden material, except for part of one side where there will be a metal gate that is g feet long. How long must the fence material be in order to meet these conditions?

(A) $2x + 2y - g$
(B) $2x + 2y + g$
(C) $xy - g$
(D) xyg

✓ Solutions

1. **(C)** Calculate the volume of the larger box, and then subtract the volume of the 4 solid cubes to find the volume of empty space. Use $V = lwh$ to calculate the volume of each rectangular prism.

$$\text{Volume of larger prism} - \text{Volume of 4 smaller cubes} \rightarrow$$
$$(20 \times 30 \times 12) - 4(4 \times 4 \times 4) =$$
$$7,200 - 256 = 6,944$$

2. **(A)**

$$-(6i^2 - 4i + 1) \rightarrow$$
$$-6i^2 + 4i - 1 \rightarrow$$
$$6 + 4i - 1 \rightarrow$$
$$5 + 4i$$

3. **(A)** The angles with measures 30°, 50°, x, and y all add up to form 180° since they are angles within the triangle ACD. Therefore, you can solve for the sum of x and y by subtracting 30 and 50 from 180:

$$180 - 30 - 50 = 100$$

4. **(D)** Based on the circle equation, in which $(x - h)^2 + (y - k)^2 = r^2$, with (h, k) as the center and r as the radius, the original circle will have a center at (4, 6) and radius of 3. To reflect this circle, which is entirely in the first quadrant, across the x-axis, just change the y-coordinate of its center to -6. The reflected circle will have an equation of $(x - 4)^2 + (y + 6)^2 = 9$ and the reflection is drawn below:

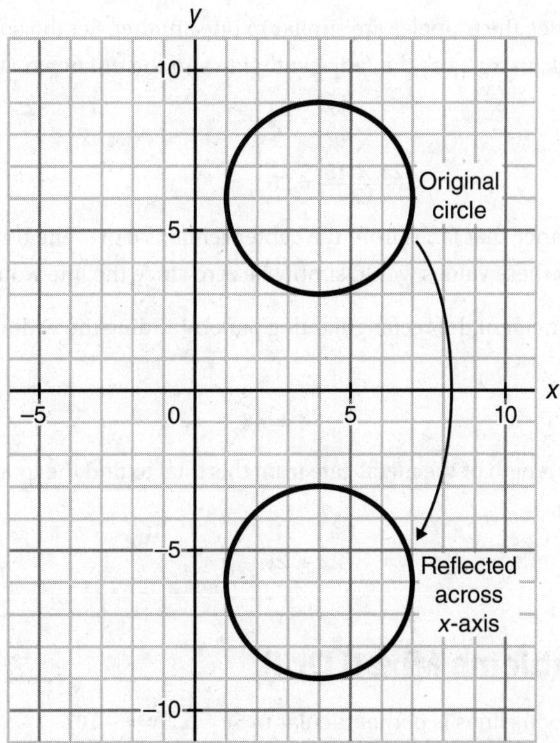

5. **(C)** To find the perimeter of the of the triangle, we must add up the three side lengths of the triangle. The formula for the area of an equilateral triangle is $A = \frac{\sqrt{3}}{4}a^2$, in which a is the side length. So, solve for the side length of the triangle given that we know its area:

$$2\sqrt{3} = \frac{\sqrt{3}}{4}a^2 \rightarrow$$
$$2 = \frac{a^2}{4} \rightarrow$$
$$8 = a^2 \rightarrow$$
$$2\sqrt{2} = a$$

Now, just triple the side length to find the perimeter:

$$3 \times (2\sqrt{2}) = 6\sqrt{2}$$

6. **(B)** Since X and $(90 - X)$ are complementary, the sine of one will equal the cosine of the other. Therefore, the sine of $(90 - X)$ is simply Y.

7. **(D)** There are π radians in 180°, so set up a proportion to make a conversion to the total number of degrees in an angle measuring 3π radians:

$$\frac{180}{\pi} = \frac{x}{3\pi} \rightarrow$$

$$\frac{180}{\pi} \times (3\pi) = x \rightarrow$$

$$180 \times 3 = x \rightarrow$$

$$540 = x$$

Now, divide 540 by 45 to see how many angles of 45° would go into 540:

$$\frac{540}{45} = 12$$

8. **(C)** Set up a proportion to solve for the length of $\overline{DF}$. The cosine of $\angle BAC$ is the same as the cosine of $\angle EDF$ since the triangles are similar to one another. Set the cosine of $\angle BAC$ equal to the cosine of $\angle EDF$, using 24 as the "adjacent" side and the unknown $\overline{DF}$ as the hypotenuse:

$$\frac{12}{13} = \frac{24}{x} \rightarrow$$

$$x = \frac{24 \times 13}{12} = 26$$

9. **(B)** Since the distance that Jeff is from the center remains 8 over the time period, the slope of the line formed by these values would simply be zero since the line would be horizontal.

10. **(A)** Find the perimeter of the rectangular dog park by adding the width twice and the length twice:

$$2x + 2y$$

Then, subtract the length of the metal gate from this total to find the total amount of wooden material required:

$$2x + 2y - g$$

Calculator Problems Mixed Drill

1. Which of the following lines is perpendicular to $5y - 2.5x = -10$?

   (A) $y = -2x + 8$
   (B) $y = 0.5x + 2$
   (C) $y = 2x - 7$
   (D) $y = 0.4x + 10$

Questions 2-3 use the following table.

Hours of Sleep per Night

	More than 8	6–8	Less than 6	Total
Under Age 13	15	8	1	24
Ages 13–18	13	17	14	44
Ages 19–22	18	12	20	50
Total	46	37	35	118

2. The least possible median age of those surveyed would be which of the following?

   (A) 13
   (B) 15
   (C) 19
   (D) Cannot be determined from the given information

3. The mean number of hours of sleep of all those surveyed is

   (A) 6.5
   (B) 7.5
   (C) 8.5
   (D) Cannot be determined from the given information

4. For values of a not equal to zero, $\left(\frac{2}{\sqrt[3]{a}}\right)^6$ equals

   (A) 2a−2
   (B) 12a−2
   (C) $64a\frac{1}{2}$
   (D) $64a^{-2}$

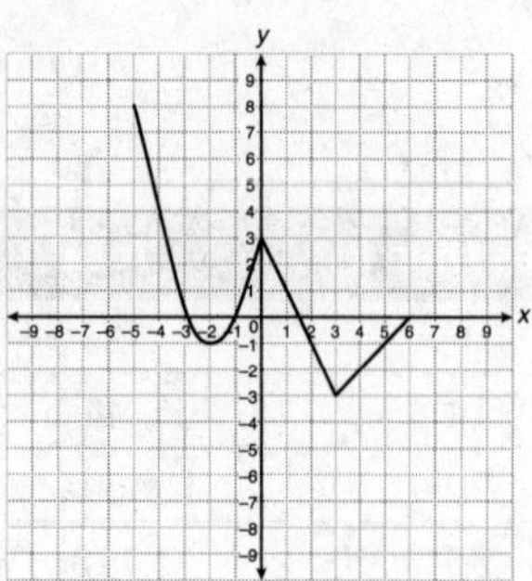

5. The graph of $y = f(x)$ is shown above. Which of the following graphs best represents the graph of $y = |f(x)|$?

(A)

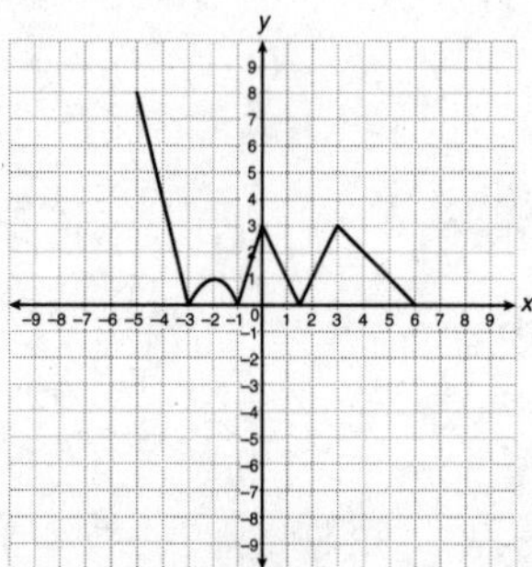

(B)

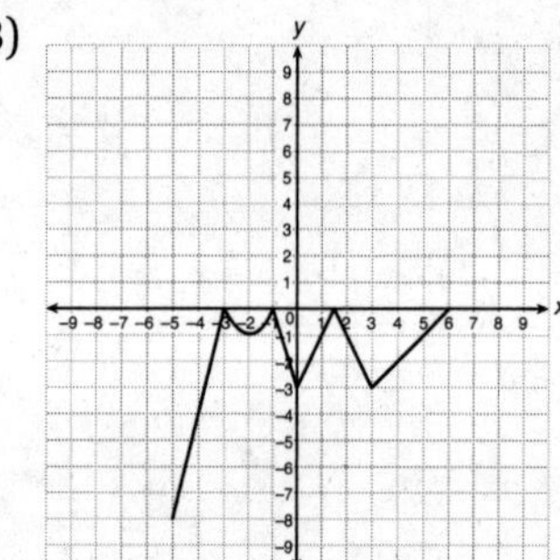

(C)

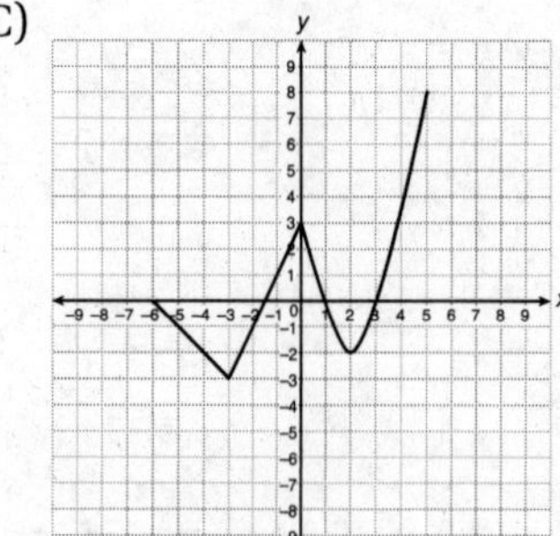

(D)

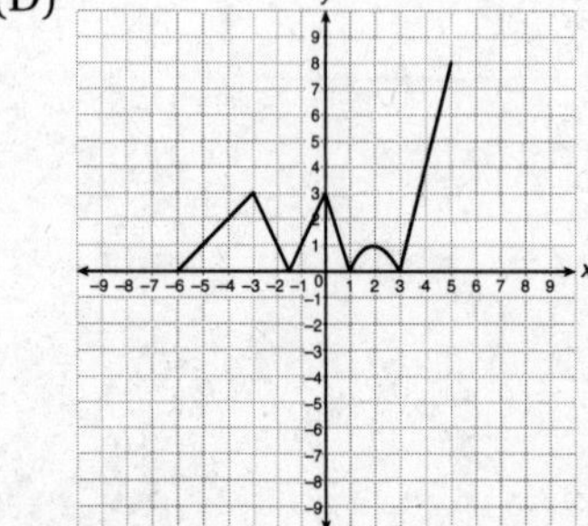

6. Which of the following is equivalent to $(6x^3 + 3x^2 - 1) + (4x^3 - 4x^2 + 2x + 3)$?

(A) $11x^6 + 2$
(B) $10x^3 - 7x^2 + 2x + 2$
(C) $10x^3 - x^2 + x + 3$
(D) $10x^3 - x^2 + 2x + 2$

7. Peter makes \$15 per hour when he works 40 hours a week. For each hour exceeding 40, he is paid 50% more than his usual hourly rate. Assuming that Peter has worked at least 40 hours in a particular week, which inequality properly expresses the range of hours, h, he must work to make over \$800 in that week?

(A) $800 < 600 + 22.5 \times (h - 40)$
(B) $800 < 600 + 22.5h$
(C) $800 < 600 + 7.5 \times (h - 40)$
(D) $800 < 40 + 15h$

8. In the xy-plane below, ABC is an equilateral triangle with sides of length 2. If point A has coordinates $(-2, 0)$, what are the coordinates of point B?

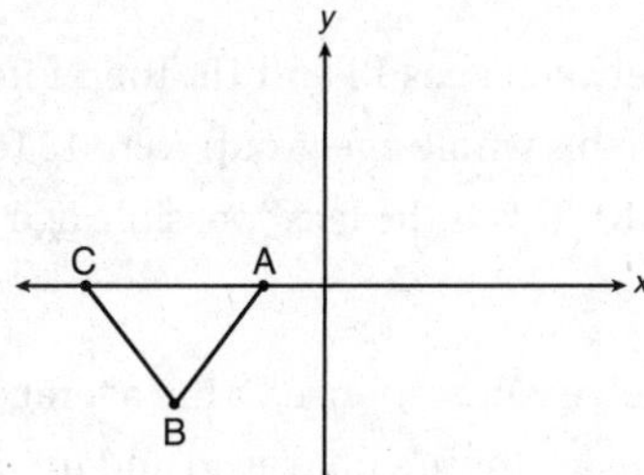

(A) $(-\sqrt{3}, -3)$
(B) $(-2, -\sqrt{3})$
(C) $(-3, \sqrt{2})$
(D) $(-3, -\sqrt{3})$

9. In a pet store with 30 customers, 60% of the customers like dogs and 11 customers like cats. What is the minimum number of customers who like both cats and dogs?

(A) 0
(B) 1
(C) 4
(D) 7

10. The function f is defined below. If $f(n)$ and n are both integers, what is the largest value that n can be?

$$f(n) = \frac{2}{\sqrt[4]{n - 300}}$$

(A) 0
(B) 301
(C) 316
(D) 426

✓ Solutions

1. **(A)** We first need to get the given line into slope-intercept form, i.e., $y = mx + b$, so that we can easily see the slope. Begin by adding $2.5x$ to both sides:

$$5y = 2.5x - 10$$

Now divide by 5:

$$y = \frac{1}{2}x - 2$$

The slope of this line is $\frac{1}{2}$. The slope of a line perpendicular to this will have a slope that is the negative reciprocal of $\frac{1}{2}$. The negative reciprocal of $\frac{1}{2}$ is -2, and only choice (A) has a slope of -2.

2. **(A)** There were 118 people surveyed. If you lined up the people by age, the median age would be the average of the 59th and 60th persons. (Prove this to yourself. If you have a series of four terms, the median is between your second and third term. Divide your even number by 2 to get the first term, and add 1 to get the next.)

The first 24 people are younger than 13.

People numbered 25–68 are between ages 13 and 18. Therefore, the 59th and 60th people are both within this age category. If this whole age group were 13 (or even if all but 8 of them were), then the median age would be 13. This is the least possible age in this category, so it is the least possible median age.

3. **(D)** Without knowing everyone's exact response or the average number of hours slept per group, we can't calculate the mean. There's no way to add up the responses without knowing the responses or averages of the responses.

4. **(D)** Raising a fraction to an exponent raises both the numerator and the denominator to that exponent:

$$\left(\frac{2}{\sqrt[3]{a}}\right)^6 = \frac{2^6}{\sqrt[3]{a^6}}$$

Roots can be written as fractional exponents. So the expression can be rewritten as:

$$\frac{64}{a^{\frac{6}{3}}}$$

$a^{\frac{6}{3}}$ simplifies to a^2:

$$\frac{64}{a^{\frac{6}{3}}} = \frac{64}{a^2}$$

An exponent in the denominator of a fraction can be expressed as a negative exponent in the numerator:

$$\frac{64}{a^2} = 64a^{-2}$$

Choice **(D)** is the answer.

5. **(A)** If the new function is the absolute value of the old function, the graphs should be the same in all of the places where y is already 0 or positive. This includes the intervals from $-5 \leq x \leq -3$ and from $-1 \leq x \leq 1.5$. The values for when the function is below the x-axis, $-3 < x < -1$ and $1.5 < x < 6$, will simply be their positive counterparts; they will be reflected above the x-axis.

   The only graph that shows this relationship is choice **(A)**.

6. **(D)** There's nothing to distribute, so you can just get rid of the parentheses and combine like terms:

$$6x^3 + 3x^2 - 1 + 4x^3 - 4x^2 + 2x + 3$$

   It's probably easiest if you start with the highest degree of x and move downward:

   There's a $6x^3$ term and a $4x^3$ term. Combine these:

$$10x^3 + 3x^2 - 1 - 4x^2 + 2x + 3$$

   Next, there's $3x^2$ and $-4x^2$:

$$10x^3 - x^2 - 1 + 2x + 3$$

   There's only one term with an x in it, so move on to the constant terms: -1 and 3:

$$10x^3 - x^2 + 2x + 2$$

   This corresponds to choice **(D)**.

7. **(A)** If Peter wants to make at least \$800, we can come up with an expression for the amount of money that he'll make working h number of hours and set that expression greater than 800:

$$\text{Amount of money Peter makes weekly} > 800$$

   The problem states that he makes \$15/hour for his first 40 hours, and we assume that he's already worked 40 hours this week. Thus, Peter will make $\$15(40) = \$600$ for those 40 hours. This is a fixed constant.

   For every hour after his 40th hour, he makes 50% more than his original hourly wage, for a total of 150% of his hourly wage. Thus, every hour Peter works after his 40th hour, he makes $1.5(\$15) = \$22.50$.

   However, we can't just express this as $22.5h$, because that would imply that Peter makes \$22.50 for every single hour that he works rather than for just the hours past 40. Thus, it must be expressed as $22.5(h - 40)$.

   To see that this is true, we can plug 41 in for h to see that for the 41st hour he works, Peter makes an extra:

$$22.5(41 - 40) = 22.5(1) = 22.5$$

   This is what we would expect.

   Our total expression for the amount of money Peter makes for working h hours, then, is:

$$600 + 22.5(h - 40)$$

   Plug this into our original inequality to get:

$$600 + 22.5(h - 40) > 800$$

   This is the same as choice **(A)**.

8. **(D)**

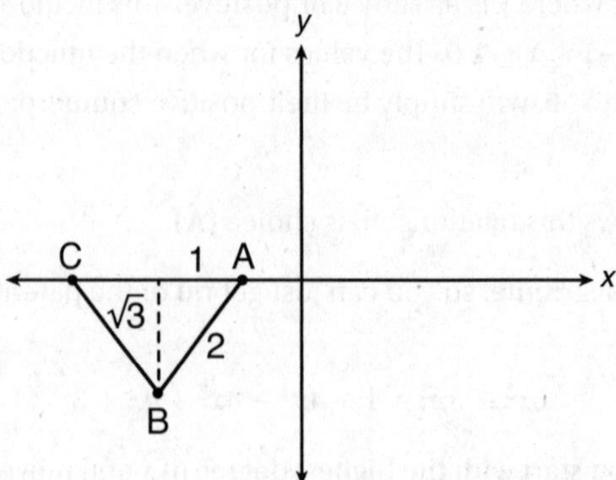

We are told that this triangle is equilateral, so each of the three angles is 60°. We are also told that point *A* has coordinates (−2, 0). Since point *C* is on the *x*-axis and is 2 units to the left of point *A*, point *C* must have coordinates (−4, 0). By drawing a line that starts halfway between points *A* and *C* and bisects the angle at point *B*, as shown in the drawing, we can split this equilateral triangle into two 30-60-90 triangles. Because the equilateral triangle has side lengths of 2 and the line splits the side along the *x*-axis in half, the new triangles have side lengths of 1 along the *x*-axis.

You can see, then, that point *B* has an *x* value 1 unit from both point *A*'s and point *C*'s *x* values. Because points *A* and *C* have *x* values of −2 and −4, respectively, point *B* will have an *x* value of −3.

You may remember that a 30-60-90 triangle is a special right triangle that has opposite side lengths of 1, $\sqrt{3}$, and 2, respectively. Since you've already found side lengths of 1 and 2, the dotted line will have a length of $\sqrt{3}$. Because it's in the negative *y* direction, it will have a *y*-coordinate of $-\sqrt{3}$. Therefore, the coordinates for point *B* are $(-3, -\sqrt{3})$.

Alternatively, if you didn't remember the 30-60-90 triangle, you could have used the Pythagorean theorem with the two known side lengths to find the third length:

$$a^2 + b^2 = c^2$$
$$(1)^2 + b^2 = (2)^2$$
$$1 + b^2 = 4$$

Subtract 1 from both sides:

$$b^2 = 3$$

To find *b*, take the square root of both sides:

$$b = \sqrt{3}$$

So the third side has a length of $\sqrt{3}$.

9. **(A)** We are told that 60% of the customers like dogs. Since there are 30 customers, $0.6(30) = 18$ customers like dogs. We are also told that 11 people like cats. It is possible that 18 customers like only dogs, 11 people like only cats, and $30 - 18 - 11 = 1$ person likes neither. Thus, the minimum number of customers who necessarily like both is 0, choice **(A)**.

10. **(C)** If $f(n)$ needs to be an integer and we want a number in the denominator (n) to be as large as possible, that means we're looking for the smallest possible integer for $f(n)$. This integer must be positive. Because the numerator is positive and the denominator is being raised to an even root, the denominator must be positive as well. The smallest possible positive integer is 1, so set $f(n)$ equal to 1. If $f(n)$ is 1, the denominator must be 2 since $\frac{2}{2}$ is the only fraction with a numerator of 2 that equals 1. Thus, set the denominator equal to 2:

$$2 = \sqrt[4]{n - 300}$$

Raise both sides to the fourth power:

$$16 = n - 300$$

Add 300 to both sides:

$$n = 316$$

You can plug this number back in to the original expression to verify.

PART 6
Test Yourself

ANSWER SHEET

Practice Test 1

Section 1: Reading Test

1. Ⓐ Ⓑ Ⓒ Ⓓ	14. Ⓐ Ⓑ Ⓒ Ⓓ	27. Ⓐ Ⓑ Ⓒ Ⓓ	40. Ⓐ Ⓑ Ⓒ Ⓓ
2. Ⓐ Ⓑ Ⓒ Ⓓ	15. Ⓐ Ⓑ Ⓒ Ⓓ	28. Ⓐ Ⓑ Ⓒ Ⓓ	41. Ⓐ Ⓑ Ⓒ Ⓓ
3. Ⓐ Ⓑ Ⓒ Ⓓ	16. Ⓐ Ⓑ Ⓒ Ⓓ	29. Ⓐ Ⓑ Ⓒ Ⓓ	42. Ⓐ Ⓑ Ⓒ Ⓓ
4. Ⓐ Ⓑ Ⓒ Ⓓ	17. Ⓐ Ⓑ Ⓒ Ⓓ	30. Ⓐ Ⓑ Ⓒ Ⓓ	43. Ⓐ Ⓑ Ⓒ Ⓓ
5. Ⓐ Ⓑ Ⓒ Ⓓ	18. Ⓐ Ⓑ Ⓒ Ⓓ	31. Ⓐ Ⓑ Ⓒ Ⓓ	44. Ⓐ Ⓑ Ⓒ Ⓓ
6. Ⓐ Ⓑ Ⓒ Ⓓ	19. Ⓐ Ⓑ Ⓒ Ⓓ	32. Ⓐ Ⓑ Ⓒ Ⓓ	45. Ⓐ Ⓑ Ⓒ Ⓓ
7. Ⓐ Ⓑ Ⓒ Ⓓ	20. Ⓐ Ⓑ Ⓒ Ⓓ	33. Ⓐ Ⓑ Ⓒ Ⓓ	46. Ⓐ Ⓑ Ⓒ Ⓓ
8. Ⓐ Ⓑ Ⓒ Ⓓ	21. Ⓐ Ⓑ Ⓒ Ⓓ	34. Ⓐ Ⓑ Ⓒ Ⓓ	47. Ⓐ Ⓑ Ⓒ Ⓓ
9. Ⓐ Ⓑ Ⓒ Ⓓ	22. Ⓐ Ⓑ Ⓒ Ⓓ	35. Ⓐ Ⓑ Ⓒ Ⓓ	48. Ⓐ Ⓑ Ⓒ Ⓓ
10. Ⓐ Ⓑ Ⓒ Ⓓ	23. Ⓐ Ⓑ Ⓒ Ⓓ	36. Ⓐ Ⓑ Ⓒ Ⓓ	49. Ⓐ Ⓑ Ⓒ Ⓓ
11. Ⓐ Ⓑ Ⓒ Ⓓ	24. Ⓐ Ⓑ Ⓒ Ⓓ	37. Ⓐ Ⓑ Ⓒ Ⓓ	50. Ⓐ Ⓑ Ⓒ Ⓓ
12. Ⓐ Ⓑ Ⓒ Ⓓ	25. Ⓐ Ⓑ Ⓒ Ⓓ	38. Ⓐ Ⓑ Ⓒ Ⓓ	51. Ⓐ Ⓑ Ⓒ Ⓓ
13. Ⓐ Ⓑ Ⓒ Ⓓ	26. Ⓐ Ⓑ Ⓒ Ⓓ	39. Ⓐ Ⓑ Ⓒ Ⓓ	52. Ⓐ Ⓑ Ⓒ Ⓓ

Section 2: Writing and Language Test

1. Ⓐ Ⓑ Ⓒ Ⓓ	12. Ⓐ Ⓑ Ⓒ Ⓓ	23. Ⓐ Ⓑ Ⓒ Ⓓ	34. Ⓐ Ⓑ Ⓒ Ⓓ
2. Ⓐ Ⓑ Ⓒ Ⓓ	13. Ⓐ Ⓑ Ⓒ Ⓓ	24. Ⓐ Ⓑ Ⓒ Ⓓ	35. Ⓐ Ⓑ Ⓒ Ⓓ
3. Ⓐ Ⓑ Ⓒ Ⓓ	14. Ⓐ Ⓑ Ⓒ Ⓓ	25. Ⓐ Ⓑ Ⓒ Ⓓ	36. Ⓐ Ⓑ Ⓒ Ⓓ
4. Ⓐ Ⓑ Ⓒ Ⓓ	15. Ⓐ Ⓑ Ⓒ Ⓓ	26. Ⓐ Ⓑ Ⓒ Ⓓ	37. Ⓐ Ⓑ Ⓒ Ⓓ
5. Ⓐ Ⓑ Ⓒ Ⓓ	16. Ⓐ Ⓑ Ⓒ Ⓓ	27. Ⓐ Ⓑ Ⓒ Ⓓ	38. Ⓐ Ⓑ Ⓒ Ⓓ
6. Ⓐ Ⓑ Ⓒ Ⓓ	17. Ⓐ Ⓑ Ⓒ Ⓓ	28. Ⓐ Ⓑ Ⓒ Ⓓ	39. Ⓐ Ⓑ Ⓒ Ⓓ
7. Ⓐ Ⓑ Ⓒ Ⓓ	18. Ⓐ Ⓑ Ⓒ Ⓓ	29. Ⓐ Ⓑ Ⓒ Ⓓ	40. Ⓐ Ⓑ Ⓒ Ⓓ
8. Ⓐ Ⓑ Ⓒ Ⓓ	19. Ⓐ Ⓑ Ⓒ Ⓓ	30. Ⓐ Ⓑ Ⓒ Ⓓ	41. Ⓐ Ⓑ Ⓒ Ⓓ
9. Ⓐ Ⓑ Ⓒ Ⓓ	20. Ⓐ Ⓑ Ⓒ Ⓓ	31. Ⓐ Ⓑ Ⓒ Ⓓ	42. Ⓐ Ⓑ Ⓒ Ⓓ
10. Ⓐ Ⓑ Ⓒ Ⓓ	21. Ⓐ Ⓑ Ⓒ Ⓓ	32. Ⓐ Ⓑ Ⓒ Ⓓ	43. Ⓐ Ⓑ Ⓒ Ⓓ
11. Ⓐ Ⓑ Ⓒ Ⓓ	22. Ⓐ Ⓑ Ⓒ Ⓓ	33. Ⓐ Ⓑ Ⓒ Ⓓ	44. Ⓐ Ⓑ Ⓒ Ⓓ

ANSWER SHEET

Practice Test 1

Section 3: Math (No Calculator)

1. Ⓐ Ⓑ Ⓒ Ⓓ **5.** Ⓐ Ⓑ Ⓒ Ⓓ **9.** Ⓐ Ⓑ Ⓒ Ⓓ **13.** Ⓐ Ⓑ Ⓒ Ⓓ

2. Ⓐ Ⓑ Ⓒ Ⓓ **6.** Ⓐ Ⓑ Ⓒ Ⓓ **10.** Ⓐ Ⓑ Ⓒ Ⓓ **14.** Ⓐ Ⓑ Ⓒ Ⓓ

3. Ⓐ Ⓑ Ⓒ Ⓓ **7.** Ⓐ Ⓑ Ⓒ Ⓓ **11.** Ⓐ Ⓑ Ⓒ Ⓓ **15.** Ⓐ Ⓑ Ⓒ Ⓓ

4. Ⓐ Ⓑ Ⓒ Ⓓ **8.** Ⓐ Ⓑ Ⓒ Ⓓ **12.** Ⓐ Ⓑ Ⓒ Ⓓ

16. **17.** **18.**

19. **20.**

ANSWER SHEET
Practice Test 1

Section 4: Math (Calculator)

1. Ⓐ Ⓑ Ⓒ Ⓓ	**9.** Ⓐ Ⓑ Ⓒ Ⓓ	**17.** Ⓐ Ⓑ Ⓒ Ⓓ	**25.** Ⓐ Ⓑ Ⓒ Ⓓ
2. Ⓐ Ⓑ Ⓒ Ⓓ	**10.** Ⓐ Ⓑ Ⓒ Ⓓ	**18.** Ⓐ Ⓑ Ⓒ Ⓓ	**26.** Ⓐ Ⓑ Ⓒ Ⓓ
3. Ⓐ Ⓑ Ⓒ Ⓓ	**11.** Ⓐ Ⓑ Ⓒ Ⓓ	**19.** Ⓐ Ⓑ Ⓒ Ⓓ	**27.** Ⓐ Ⓑ Ⓒ Ⓓ
4. Ⓐ Ⓑ Ⓒ Ⓓ	**12.** Ⓐ Ⓑ Ⓒ Ⓓ	**20.** Ⓐ Ⓑ Ⓒ Ⓓ	**28.** Ⓐ Ⓑ Ⓒ Ⓓ
5. Ⓐ Ⓑ Ⓒ Ⓓ	**13.** Ⓐ Ⓑ Ⓒ Ⓓ	**21.** Ⓐ Ⓑ Ⓒ Ⓓ	**29.** Ⓐ Ⓑ Ⓒ Ⓓ
6. Ⓐ Ⓑ Ⓒ Ⓓ	**14.** Ⓐ Ⓑ Ⓒ Ⓓ	**22.** Ⓐ Ⓑ Ⓒ Ⓓ	**30.** Ⓐ Ⓑ Ⓒ Ⓓ
7. Ⓐ Ⓑ Ⓒ Ⓓ	**15.** Ⓐ Ⓑ Ⓒ Ⓓ	**23.** Ⓐ Ⓑ Ⓒ Ⓓ	
8. Ⓐ Ⓑ Ⓒ Ⓓ	**16.** Ⓐ Ⓑ Ⓒ Ⓓ	**24.** Ⓐ Ⓑ Ⓒ Ⓓ	

31. **32.** **33.** **34.**

35. **36.** **37.** **38.**

Practice Test 1

READING PRACTICE TEST 1

65 MINUTES, 52 QUESTIONS

DIRECTIONS: Each passage or pair of passages is accompanied by several questions. After reading the passage(s), choose the best answer to each question based on what is indicated explicitly or implicitly in the passage(s) or in the associated graphics.

Questions 1–10 are based on the following passage.

Excerpt from "The Last Man," by Mary Shelley, 1826

I am the native of a sea-surrounded nook, a cloud-enshadowed land, which, when the surface of the globe, with its shoreless ocean and trackless continents, presents itself to my mind, appears only as an inconsiderable speck in the immense whole; and yet, when balanced in the scale of mental power, far outweighed countries of larger extent and more numerous population. So true it is, that man's mind alone was the creator of all that was good or great to man, and that Nature herself was only his first minister. England, seated far north in the turbid sea, now visits my dreams in the semblance of a vast and well-manned ship, which mastered the winds and rode proudly over the waves. In my boyish days she was the universe to me. When I stood on my native hills, and saw plain and mountain stretch out to the utmost limits of my vision, speckled by the dwellings of my countrymen, and subdued to fertility by their labors, the earth's very center was fixed for me in that spot, and the rest of her orb was as a fable, to have forgotten which would have cost neither my imagination nor understanding an effort.

My fortunes have been, from the beginning, an exemplification of the power that mutability may possess over the varied tenor of man's life. With regard to myself, this came almost by inheritance. My father was one of those men on whom nature had bestowed to prodigality the envied gifts of wit and imagination, and then left his bark of life to be impelled by these winds, without adding reason as the rudder, or judgment as the pilot for the voyage. His extraction was obscure; but circumstances brought him early into public notice, and his small paternal property was soon dissipated in the splendid scene of fashion and luxury in which he was an actor. During the short years of thoughtless youth, he was adored by the high-bred triflers of the day, nor least by the youthful sovereign, who escaped from the intrigues of party, and the arduous duties of kingly business, to find never-failing amusement and exhilaration of spirit in his society. My father's impulses, never under his own control, perpetually led him into difficulties from which his ingenuity alone could

0 0 0

extricate him; and the accumulating pile of debts of honor and of trade, which would have bent to earth any other, was supported by him with a light spirit and tameless hilarity; while his company was so necessary at the tables and assemblies of the rich, that his derelictions were considered venial, and he himself received with intoxicating flattery.

This kind of popularity, like every other, is evanescent: and the difficulties of every kind with which he had to contend, increased in a frightful ratio compared with his small means of extricating himself. At such times the king, in his enthusiasm for him, would come to his relief, and then kindly take his friend to task; my father gave the best promises for amendment, but his social disposition, his craving for the usual diet of admiration, and more than all, the fiend of gambling, which fully possessed him, made his good resolutions transient, his promises vain. With the quick sensibility peculiar to his temperament, he perceived his power in the brilliant circle to be on the wane. The king married; and the haughty princess of Austria, who became, as queen of England, the head of fashion, looked with harsh eyes on his defects, and with contempt on the affection her royal husband entertained for him. My father felt that his fall was near; but so far from profiting by this last calm before the storm to save himself, he sought to forget anticipated evil by making still greater sacrifices to the deity of pleasure, deceitful and cruel arbiter of his destiny.

1. A central theme developed in the passage is that of
   (A) the struggle between self-discipline and the pursuit of pleasure.
   (B) the greater opportunities available to men than women in the 19th century.
   (C) the importance of spreading one's native culture to countries around the world.
   (D) the consequences of not being truthful to authority figures.

2. The narrator describes England as a country that
   (A) is limited in its influence due to its unfavorable geography.
   (B) he has not personally visited, but dreams of with great frequency.
   (C) has exceeded what might be expected of it given its size and location.
   (D) has weather that made him determined to seek a more pleasant climate.

3. The main purpose of the statement in lines 28–29 ("With regard... inheritance") is most likely to show that the narrator
   (A) shares many of his father's personality characteristics.
   (B) received considerable financial resources to ensure a comfortable life.
   (C) has the same self-reliant and self-disciplined mindset as his ancestors.
   (D) is rather fortunate in how the nature of chance seems to favor him.

4. The author uses the words "rudder" and "pilot" in lines 33–34 to symbolize the idea of
   (A) self-mastery.
   (B) a love of travel.
   (C) scientific knowledge.
   (D) leadership.

5. It can most reasonably be inferred from the passage that the narrator believes he has what degree of control over his own life?

(A) Significant control, given his strong willpower
(B) Limited control, given the influence of changing external factors
(C) Moderate control, given his connections to the royal family
(D) No control, given his ignorance of his culture and family

6. Which option gives the best evidence for the answer to the previous question?

(A) Lines 9–12 ("So true... minister")
(B) Lines 25–28 ("My fortunes... life")
(C) Lines 60–63 ("At such... amendment")
(D) Lines 77–80 ("he sought... destiny")

7. As used in line 57, "evanescent" most closely means

(A) respected.
(B) intimidating.
(C) enticing.
(D) fleeting.

8. What does the narrator suggest is the greatest obstacle to his father's success?

(A) A lack of friendship
(B) His lack of fashionable taste
(C) An inability to perceive imminent threats
(D) A penchant for gambling

9. Which option gives the best evidence for the answer to the previous question?

(A) Lines 39–41 ("During... sovereign")
(B) Lines 65–68 ("and more... vain")
(C) Lines 68–70 ("With the... wane")
(D) Lines 70–75 ("The king... for him")

10. Based on the final sentence of the passage in lines 75–80 ("My father... destiny"), it is most likely that in the next part of this story the father

(A) manages to be well prepared for what is about to transpire.
(B) has little sense of the fate that awaits him.
(C) lets his vices get the better of him.
(D) uses his religious faith to overcome difficulties.

Questions 11–21 are based on the following passage and supplementary material.

Antibiotics, written in 2020

Since the advent of penicillin from mold, antibiotics have become an expected part of many doctor visits. Indeed, the use of antibiotics to treat any number of maladies is one of the most common interventions in modern medicine. Most people will take antibiotics without a second thought as to their potential consequences. However, there are serious consequences of frequent antibiotic use, both to the individual patient and to society.

Societally, the biggest issue with over-prescription of antibiotics is the creation of antibiotic resistant bacteria. No antibiotic can kill all bacteria. Think about your hand sanitizer and cleaning products that advertise that they kill 99.99% of bacteria. Think about the .01% left behind. That .01% is the bacteria that are immune to the antibiotic that was just utilized. These bacteria now have plenty of space to reproduce and grow since their natural competitors have been wiped out. Their "children" will also be able to withstand antibiotic treatment in most cases. The emergence of these resistant strains of bacteria can put our healthcare system right back to where it was prior to penicillin: without any recourse to heal the infected.

Most people do not consider the effect on society in general when asking their doctor for antibiotics. However, they do want to know about any side effects to themselves personally. There can be grave personal consequences to strict antibiotic regimes, especially when patients are in a hospital on a very strong dosage. The problem with antibiotics is that they do not necessarily target one specific bacteria. While some will target certain classes, many simply kill indiscriminately. This means that all the good bacteria within a patient's microbiome are also killed. We are then left with the issue of the .01% again. Quite often in humans the .01% of bacteria left in a person on a high dose of antibiotics is *C. difficile* (*C. diff*).

C. diff is an often fairly innocuous bacteria that is sometimes found in humans and can be picked up from the environment. In small amounts and balanced with other bacteria that keep it under control, *C. diff* can be carried by humans without serious repercussions to health. However, when human gut flora (bacteria and fungi that live in the digestive tract) is wiped out due to antibiotic treatments, the *C. diff* that remain can flourish and essentially take over the intestinal tract of the patient. The bacteria in large amounts produce toxins that attack and weaken the lining of the intestines, and cause the patient to fall seriously ill. Because of *C. diff*'s resistance to antibiotic treatment, it is very difficult to eradicate and can lead to fever, diarrhea, and severe abdominal pain.

C. diff is just one example of how the overuse of antibiotics can harm individuals. Within hospitals, it is a serious issue. This does not mean that we should cease use of antibiotics. In fact, the lack of antibiotics would kill far more people than *C. diff* likely ever will. However, in recent years, a new and more aggressive strain has emerged among people who never were in a hospital or on antibiotics. The bacteria is adapting and changing in response to our attempts to quash it, and is consequently becoming more of a threat than ever before. Doctors and patients should be cautious and should ensure that antibiotics are *truly* necessary before contributing to this issue. Fewer antibiotics prescribed will mean less of a chance for *C. diff* for each individual patient and a greater chance that that antibiotics will remain effective for the people who genuinely need them.

Table 1

Antibiotic	Year Discovered	Year Resistant Bacteria Discovered
Penicillin	1941	1942 Penicillin-resistant *Staphylococcus aureus*
		1967 Penicillin-resistant *Streptococcus pneumoniae*
		1976 Penicillinase-producing *Neisseria gonorrhoeae*
Vancomycin	1958	1988 Plasmid-mediated vancomycin-resistant *Enterococcus faecium*
	2002	Vancomycin-resistant *Staphylococcus aureus*
Amphotericin B	1959	2016 Amphotericin B-resistant *Candida auris*
Methicillin	1960	1960 Methicillin-resistant *Staphylococcus aureus*
Azithromycin	1980	2011 Azithromycin-resistant *Neisseria gonorrhoeae*
Caspofungin	2001	2004 Caspofungin-resistant *Candida*
Daptomycin	2003	2004 Daptomycin-resistant methicillin-resistant *Staphylococcus aureus*
Ceftazidime-avibactam	2015	2015 Ceftazidime-avibactam-resistant KPC-producing *Klebsiella pneumoniae*

Information in table sourced from https://www.cdc.gov/drugresistance/about.html

11. The primary purpose of the passage is to convince readers that

    (A) antibiotics are dangerous to patient health.
    (B) overuse of antibiotics may have detrimental effects.
    (C) they should be more concerned about personal hygiene.
    (D) homeopathic remedies may be more effective than traditional medicine.

12. The author most likely places quotation marks around the term "children" in line 21 in order to

    (A) suggest a figurative rather than literal meaning.
    (B) cite a scientific authority on the subject.
    (C) distance herself from a superstitious belief.
    (D) consider an objection to her line of argumentation.

13. It can be reasonably inferred that an outcome that the author of the passage strongly fears is that

    (A) patients will be overly skeptical of the benefits of antibiotics.
    (B) fewer bacteria like *C. diff* will emerge through natural selection.
    (C) bacteria will emerge that cannot be treated with medicine.
    (D) there will be a lack of research into the history of antibiotic treatment.

14. Which option gives the best evidence for the answer to the previous question?

    (A) Lines 8–10 ("However... society")
    (B) Lines 11–13 ("Societally... bacteria")
    (C) Lines 49–53 ("However... patient")
    (D) Lines 60–62 ("*C. diff*... issue")

15. The author most likely uses the two introductory sentences in the third paragraph in lines 27–31 ("Most people... personally") to acknowledge that
    (A) some patients are overly concerned with how their medical choices will impact the health of their fellow citizens.
    (B) unfortunately, there are patients who are unnecessarily skeptical of medical intervention.
    (C) side effects are the most important consideration by medical professionals when deciding on a course of action.
    (D) many people will be more persuaded by their personal interests than by an appeal to the greater good.

16. The author of the passage most strongly suggests that microorganisms, with respect to their impact on humans, can be
    (A) occasionally helpful.
    (B) uniformly dangerous.
    (C) consistently beneficial.
    (D) mostly irrelevant.

17. Which option gives the best evidence for the answer to the previous question?
    (A) Lines 31–34 ("There can... dosage")
    (B) Lines 36–39 ("While some... killed")
    (C) Lines 53–56 ("The bacteria... ill")
    (D) Lines 65–68 ("However... antibiotics")

18. As used in line 70, "quash" most closely means
    (A) eliminate.
    (B) blend.
    (C) cover.
    (D) smooth.

19. Which of the following situations is most similar to what happens when *C. diff* thrives in a patient after a heavy treatment with antibiotics?
    (A) One business emerges as the most successful after an open and free market competition.
    (B) A student loses interest in a particular course of study, giving in to more distracting entertainment options.
    (C) All plants in a tract of forest are treated with a controlled burn, and a weed becomes dominant in the aftermath.
    (D) During a war between two countries, one country successfully beats the other using advanced espionage techniques.

20. Suppose that a new antibiotic is introduced in the year 2030. Based on the trend in the most recent years in the table, in approximately how many years would it be reasonable to expect that a bacteria resistant to that antibiotic would emerge?
    (A) 0–5 years
    (B) 10–15 years
    (C) 20–30 years
    (D) 50–70 years

21. Based on the data in the table, what is the general pattern when it comes to the availability of the antibiotic and the resistant bacteria that are associated with it?
    (A) More antibiotic-resistant strains of bacteria have emerged in the most recent forms of bacteria.
    (B) Later antibiotics are more popular for medical professionals to use than earlier ones because of their strength against resistant bacteria.
    (C) When an antibiotic has been available for only a short period of time, it causes fewer side effects for patients who are attempting to avoid resistant bacteria.
    (D) The longer the antibiotic has been around, the more resistant bacteria have emerged.

Questions 22–31 are based on the following passage.

The following is an adaptation from The New York Tenement-House Evil and Its Cure *by Ernest Flagg as it was published in* Scribner's Magazine *in 1894. In it, Flagg discusses the deplorable living conditions in the tenements, how the tenements came to be, and how the issue might be solved.*

The greatest evil which ever befell New York City was the division of the blocks into lots of 25 × 100 feet, for from this division has arisen the New York system of tenement-houses, the worst curse which ever afflicted any great community.

The houses are built on lots 25 × 100 feet and generally about five stories high. The Board of Health regulates that there is a space of ten feet by the width of the lot at the rear for light. This is doubled when similar houses are erected back to back. In addition, there is usually a diamond-shaped court, at the sides, about four feet wide, when the houses are built side by side. That is to say, each owner leaves a recess at the side of about two feet by forty. Each floor is arranged for two families in the better class of houses, but more generally four families occupy each floor. Each family has a room facing the street or the yard, and from two to three rooms lighted, or rather not lighted, from the central slit or well. The front rooms measure about twelve feet square. The others about seven by ten feet.

When the city was first laid out, the division of blocks into lots 25 × 100 feet was entirely unobjectionable. The people generally built houses of moderate dimensions, lighted at the front from the street, and in the rear from the yard. If a larger dwelling was required, more land was taken and the house was made wider; but as the city grew, the land increased so greatly in value that an effort was made to occupy more of the 25 × 100 foot lot than was consistent with the proper lighting of the interior. As a result, the central part of many of our so-called fine houses is unfit to live in. If this desire to cover too much of the land proved objectionable in houses occupied by one family, its results have been simply disastrous in houses occupied by several families.

The fashionable quarter of town has moved steadily and rapidly to the north. As the rich people vacated their houses to go farther uptown, they were turned over to the poor. Houses built for one family were occupied by twice as many families as the building had floors. As the older houses were comparatively shallow, another house, known as a rear tenement, was erected on the back of the lot, a space being left between the old building and the new. The city grew at such a rate that it soon became necessary to erect new houses as tenements. The builders, having been in the habit of building houses 25 × 100 feet, saw no better way than to continue the practice. The first houses to be built were lighted only at the front and the rear; all the central rooms being dark as well as the hall and stairs.

Since then, there has been no radical change in the plan of these houses. Acres upon acres have been covered by them, all constructed on the same general plan based upon the shape of the 25 × 100 foot lot. No attempt is ever made to depart from the stereotyped plan. It never seems to have occurred to anyone that this is an extremely extravagant and wasteful way of building, for the system involves the erection of an unnecessary amount of wall, partitions, and corridor, also an unnecessary number of entrances, halls etc. and consequent loss of room. So great is the loss of room from these causes, that it is possible to plan buildings of a different type which, while having the same amount of rentable space in rooms, shall over so much less of the lot as to leave an abundant space free for light and air. The buildings covering a smaller area will cost less to erect, so that properly lighted and well-ventilated apartments

can be supplied at less than it costs to build the dreadful affairs which we now have.

The tenement-house evil is staring us in the face, and the community is daily becoming more and more alive to the imperative necessity for reform. A desperate disease needs a desperate remedy. It should be made unprofitable to erect the kind of tenements we now have. If it is clearly shown that the present evils can be overcome by the adoption of a different type of building, erected on larger lots, certain restrictions established by law would in time bring about the desired change.

22. The main purpose of the passage is to

(A) analyze the nature of human avarice.
(B) describe architectural trends in the late 1800s.
(C) highlight a difficult issue and propose a solution.
(D) suggest how urban poverty may be overcome.

23. It is reasonable to infer from the passage that when compared to earlier housing built on the 25 × 100 lots, later housing was less likely to have

(A) exposure to sunshine for those in the interior rooms.
(B) walls to separate the different rooms in the house.
(C) a location in a densely populated part of the city.
(D) poor ventilation due to improvements in air flow.

24. The sentence in lines 23–25 ("When the... unobjectionable") primarily serves to

(A) illustrate how sound urban planning provides a long-term foundation for success.
(B) acknowledge that something that would become problematic later was initially acceptable.
(C) explain the thought process behind the chosen dimensions of city lots.
(D) show how the needs of lower-class workers were respected by city planners.

25. Which option gives the best evidence for the answer to the previous question?

(A) Lines 40–43 ("The fashionable... poor")
(B) Lines 54–57 ("The first... stairs")
(C) Lines 66–70 ("for the system... room")
(D) Lines 75–79 ("The buildings... now have")

26. The author most likely uses the sentences in lines 62–70 ("No attempt... loss of room") to express

(A) anger at oppression.
(B) disgust for prejudice.
(C) satisfaction with the status quo.
(D) frustration with inflexibility.

27. The sentence in lines 75–79 serves to show that

(A) urban density should be increased.
(B) higher quality can be achieved at a lower price.
(C) some changes are worth a significant financial sacrifice.
(D) faithfulness will lead to stronger communities.

28. As used in line 82, "alive to" most closely means
    (A) swarming with.
    (B) lethargic toward.
    (C) organic in.
    (D) aware of.

29. The passage suggests that those who built the tenement housing were motivated to do so by their
    (A) contempt for their fellow man.
    (B) hope for a better city.
    (C) desire to make money.
    (D) concern for the poor.

30. Which option gives the best evidence for the answer to the previous question?
    (A) Lines 35–39 ("If this . . . families")
    (B) Lines 59–62 ("Acres upon . . . foot lot")
    (C) Lines 80–83 ("The tenement-house . . . reform")
    (D) Lines 84–85 ("It should . . . now have")

31. The repetition of the word "desperate" in line 83 helps to convey a sense of
    (A) urgency.
    (B) greed.
    (C) apathy.
    (D) healing.

Questions 32–41 are based on the following passages.

Passage 1 and Passage 2, both written in 2020, discuss the issue of chronic traumatic encephalopathy and its impact on athletes.

Passage 1

Chronic traumatic encephalopathy (CTE) is a progressive neurodegenerative brain disease that is largely difficult to diagnose and treat. Indeed, since accurate diagnosis can only be done by looking at portions of the brain under a microscope, a true CTE diagnosis can't be made until an autopsy is done on a deceased sufferer. Under a microscope, small lesions can be seen in the proteins of the brain. These lesions are seen only in CTE sufferers and are the only way to definitively give a CTE diagnosis.

Despite the difficulty in officially diagnosing CTE, many families of sufferers and sufferers themselves can see the results of the disease prior to death. Symptoms include headache, irritability, depression, and memory issues. While these symptoms can be treated, the brain lesions themselves have no treatment. However, CTE is easily prevented from ever forming. All known cases of CTE have formed in patients who had repeated blows to the head. These blows often come from sports like football (helmet-to-helmet contact), boxing (punches to the head), and soccer (repeated headers), but they can also form from army combat or even long-term domestic abuse situations.

While many people seem to think that multiple concussions must have been sustained for CTE to form, research indicates that instead, a long period where brains (especially those still under the age of 25 and thus still forming) experience multiple sub-concussive blows is to blame. In fact, in a 2018 study, researchers at the VA-BU-CLF Brain Bank found that vast majority of football players' brains were afflicted with CTE. To be precise, it was 190 out of the 202 brains examined, or 94 percent. CTE was not found in any of the 198 control brains that were examined[1]. To combat CTE, youth sports (and many adult sports as well) should be greatly changed to avoid *any and all* blows to the head, even those that are not strong enough to cause a noticeable concussion.

Passage 2

While chronic traumatic encephalopathy (CTE) is indeed a scary disease which leads to serious issues and sometimes even death, the reports about its frequency are greatly over-exaggerated. The issue lies with the fact that examining for CTE in an autopsy is only ever done in select populations. An average person who is irritable, depressed, or having memory issues generally won't be examined for CTE upon their death. Rather, the irritability may be linked to their personality, depression to hormone issues, and memory loss to advancing age. It is only in former athletes who have these symptoms that CTE is suspected, and thus their brains are examined upon death.

The most famous study on CTE stated that 94% of the brains of football players examined had CTE. However, what people often don't know was that this was not a study of a cross section of players' brains, but rather a study of *donated* brains. It follows logically that only families that *already suspected* CTE would donate the brains of their loved ones to science. The thousands of contact sport players who never develop symptoms will also never be examined. Thus, the numbers are artificially inflated to indicate that CTE is much more prevalent than it likely actually is.

While CTE is a serious issue, there is no reason to reconfigure the whole sports to avoid it. Changing rules in any given sport will simply switch the type of injuries sustained, and adding protective equipment often leads to *more* blows to the head since player feel protected. Instead of reconfiguring the sports landscape, all we need to do is educate players about the dangers of hits to the head and let the players do the rest.

[1]https://concussionfoundation.org/CTE-resources/what-is-CTE

32. Passage 1 argues that the only way to achieve a clear diagnosis of CTE is to

(A) observe only obvious symptoms, like depression and memory loss.
(B) examine the brain of a patient after his or her death.
(C) use a microscope to analyze the tissue of a patient while under anesthesia.
(D) determine the number of severe concussions a patient has suffered.

33. Which option gives the best evidence for the answer to the previous question?

(A) Lines 6–7 ("a true...sufferer")
(B) Lines 8–9 ("Under...brain")
(C) Lines 12–15 ("Despite...death")
(D) Lines 30–33 ("especially...blame")

34. The author of Passage 1 primarily uses the sentence in lines 36–37 ("To be...percent") to

(A) underscore the cultural importance of sports.
(B) dispute the results of a study.
(C) clarify a term from the preceding sentence.
(D) introduce a new concept to the reader.

35. The words "*any and all*" in line 41 are most likely italicized to

(A) emphasize a point.
(B) define a key term.
(C) acknowledge a source of information.
(D) consider a perspective.

36. The author of Passage 2 would consider which of the following already-deceased subjects to be most likely to undergo CTE testing?

(A) A musician suffering from depression
(B) A painter who is unable to walk
(C) A soccer player who has memory problems
(D) A football player with a hormone imbalance

37. It can be reasonably inferred from lines 61–64 ("However ... brains") that the author of Passage 2 believes that the public's understanding of the statistics about CTE is

(A) well informed.
(B) uniformly ignorant.
(C) charitable.
(D) incomplete.

38. As used in line 70, "inflated" most closely means

(A) filled.
(B) dilated.
(C) aerated.
(D) exaggerated.

39. Passage 1 and Passage 2 differ in their opinion of the study primarily discussed in the passage in what way?

(A) Passage 1 considers it to be unquestionably definitive, while Passage 2 considers it to be artificially optimistic.
(B) Passage 1 shows that it needed a larger set of test subjects, while Passage 2 argues that the number of test subjects was sufficient.
(C) Passage 1 portrays it as extremely important, while Passage 2 portrays it as insufficiently rigorous.
(D) Passage 1 acknowledges its imprecision, while Passage 2 demonstrates that it is appropriately precise.

40. The author of Passage 2 would most likely disagree with which statement made by the author of Passage 1?

(A) Lines 1–3 ("Chronic ... treat")
(B) Lines 8–9 ("Under a ... brain")
(C) Lines 36–37 ("To be precise ... percent")
(D) Lines 39–43 ("To combat ... concussion")

41. Which option gives the best evidence for the answer to the previous question?

(A) Lines 44–48 ("While chronic ... overexaggerated")
(B) Lines 48–50 ("The issue ... populations")
(C) Lines 59–61 ("The most ... had CTE")
(D) Lines 72–73 ("While CTE ... avoid it")

0 0 0

Questions 42–52 are based on the following passage and supplementary material.

An Introduction to Family Stress Theory

While family stress is hardly a new topic, research in this field of family science did not begin until the 1930s. Considering the deep economic and social turmoil of those times, it is unsurprising that family stress was at an all-time high. There was no greater time than the Great Depression for researchers to study stress within a family. Intrigued by the events of their time, family scientists took this opportunity to learn how families respond to serious stressors. By doing so, they laid the foundation for what is now known as family stress theory.

In the early years of family stress research, scholars developed the truncated rollercoaster model of family stress. This model assumed that families would respond to stressors with a period of disorganization. After this period of disorganization, families would have a period of recovery, and eventually readjust to the new normal. The rollercoaster model was short-lived and quickly replaced, by the same group of researchers who created it, with the ABC-X model. This model has come to be considered foundational for understanding family stress theory.

The ABC-X model predicts that the resources a family has and the perception the family has of a stressor event will determine whether the stressor will lead to a crisis within the family. The theory differentiates stressors as normative or nonnormative. Normative stressors, such as buying a home, are stressors that are expected parts of life. In contrast, nonnormative stressors, such as a serious car crash, are those that are not expected, and are thus more likely to turn into a family crisis.

While stressors are generally assumed to be negative, they are not always considered so. Some normative events, such as caring for a newborn infant, can be considered a stressor while still being positive events. The way a family perceives any kind of stressor can be based on a variety of factors. While one family may perceive the responsibilities of caring for a newborn overwhelming, another may consider these same responsibilities as overly joyous. In both instances, the stressor was the same, but each family's perception of it was significantly different. Because of this, the ABC-X theory is praised for its incorporation of families' perceptions of stressor events.

In recent years, the ABC-X model has been utilized in a variety of fields, from social science research to clinical psychology. Social scientists have recently begun applying this theory to groups that face stressors unique to their population. One such population is families with an elderly relative for whom to care. By applying the ABC-X model to such studies, researchers have been able to determine the factors that contribute to these family's ability to manage. Such research can offer insight into which resources will best be able to aide families facing these unique stressors.

Similarly, recent case studies on military families have found it quite useful to utilize the ABC-X model in family therapy. Like families who must care for an elderly relative, military families are a population that regularly face significant and unique stressors. When working with this population, research from family stress theorists can be applied to best identify resources and support systems that have worked for families in similar situations avoid a crisis. By utilizing the ABC-X model in their work, helping professionals such as case workers can then develop plans of treatment for these families that are experiencing serious stressor events.

Despite the wide applicability of the ABC-X model, like any other theory, it has faced critiques of its usefulness. One of the major critiques is its focus on serious stressor events and inaccessibility to smaller, everyday stressors. Another drawback is its inability to consider how multiple stressors may affect the current stressor situation. In spite of these issues, the ABC-X model of family stress is useful in understanding families' abilities to cope with significant acute family stressors. By applying the model to family stressors, scientists can continue to build an understanding of the resources that best aide families in stressful situations.

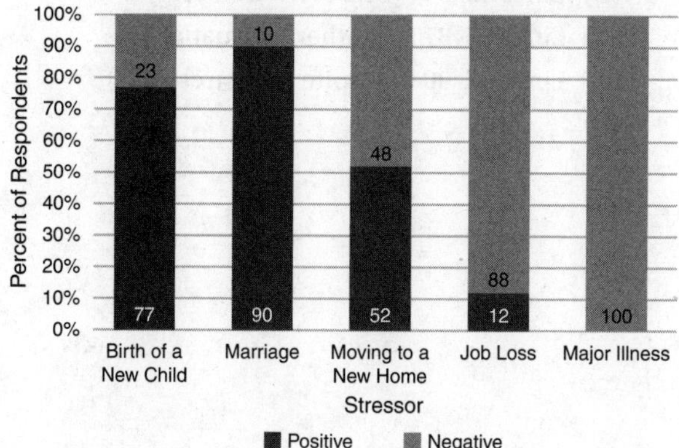

Scientists studied 164 families over a period of five years. During that time, the researchers recorded the families' perceptions of well-known stressors as positive or negative. The results of this study are summarized in the figure above.

42. Over the course of the passage, the main focus shifts from

(A) a general overview to an in-depth description.
(B) a detailed analysis to a broad conclusion.
(C) a persuasive introduction to a review of alternative theories.
(D) a consideration of objections to a recommendation for further research.

43. As used in line 3, "deep" most closely means

(A) significant.
(B) far.
(C) cavernous.
(D) obscure.

44. It is reasonable to infer that in the future, researchers would most likely find which of the following situations optimal to study family stress theory more in-depth?

(A) During a time with a mostly stable environment with respect to property crimes
(B) During a time of unusually high financial and societal hardship
(C) When a major shift in the popularity of particular political leaders occurred
(D) When economic growth is rapidly increasing and unemployment is quite low

45. Which option gives the best evidence for the answer to the previous question?

(A) Lines 1–3 ("While family... 1930s")
(B) Lines 6–8 ("There was... family")
(C) Lines 13–15 ("In the early... stress")
(D) Lines 17–20 ("After... normal")

46. The passage most strongly suggests that the main shortcoming of the rollercoaster model of family stress was its

(A) complexity.
(B) differentiation.
(C) sophistication.
(D) oversimplicity.

47. As used in line 50, "incorporation" most closely means

(A) consolidation.
(B) reinforcement.
(C) unification.
(D) inclusion.

48. As described in the passage, the primary difference between normative and nonnormative events is the extent of their

(A) effect on different age groups.
(B) monetary impact.
(C) predictability.
(D) accuracy.

49. Based on the figure, which of the following stressors is the most difficult to predict as to whether a given family would consider it to be positive or negative?

(A) Birth of a new child
(B) Marriage
(C) Moving to a new home
(D) Job loss

50. According to the figure, about how many of the families surveyed generally indicated that they perceived marriage to be a positive stressor?

(A) 18
(B) 80
(C) 148
(D) 164

51. A critic of the ABC-X model would most likely find which aspect of the figure a shortcoming?

(A) Its emphasis on only normative stressors and not on nonnormative stressors
(B) Its focus on major life events instead of on more normal occurrences
(C) Its portrayal of optimism as a personal weakness instead of as a source of strength
(D) Its stressors being limited to only those that would affect those with families and not to single households

52. Which option gives the best evidence for the answer to the previous question?

(A) Lines 80–82 ("Despite... usefulness")
(B) Lines 82–84 ("One of... stressors")
(C) Lines 85–87 ("Another... situation")
(D) Lines 87–90 ("In spite of... stressors")

STOP If there is still time remaining, you may review your answers.

WRITING AND LANGUAGE PRACTICE TEST 1

35 MINUTES, 44 QUESTIONS

DIRECTIONS: The passages below are each accompanied by several questions, some of which refer to an underlined portion in the passage, and some of which refer to the passage as a whole. For some questions, determine how the expression of ideas can be improved. For other questions, determine the best sentence structure, usage, or punctuation given the context. A passage or question may have an accompanying graphic that you will need to consider as you choose the best answer.

Choose the best answer to each question, considering what will optimize the writing quality and make the writing follow the conventions of standard written English. Some questions will have a "NO CHANGE" option that you can pick if you believe the best choice would be to leave the underlined portion as it is.

Questions 1–11 are based on the following passage.

Edith Wilson

It may come as a surprise to many to learn that in the early twentieth century, the United States had a woman act **1** with a time as President. History seems to have forgotten Edith Wilson, the spouse of Woodrow Wilson, the 28th president of the United States. **2** Edith Wilson's educational pedigree gave her the confidence she needed to forcibly seize power.

{1} Born in 1872, Edith had little formal schooling. {2} For twelve years, she lived as Edith Galt until her husband passed away leaving her with a large business, little debt, and a good income. {3} She came from an educated family, received informal education at

1. (A) NO CHANGE
   (B) of a time
   (C) for a time
   (D) on time

2. Which choice most effectively introduces the passage as a whole?
   (A) NO CHANGE
   (B) Even though Edith Wilson's accomplishments are quite well known to laypeople, she clearly deserves more historical recognition.
   (C) While she never took the oath of office, she did the job and deserves to go down in history as the first female president of the United States.
   (D) Woodrow Wilson's service as president of the United States was marked by the country's involvement in the First World War and the subsequent quest for a lasting peace.

home, and was briefly enrolled at a few **3** different and varying girls' schools. {4} Once she was of marrying age for that time period, she wed Norman Galt. **4**

Several years later, she came to know Woodrow Wilson who was, at the time, the president of the United States and recently widowed. **5** The pair hit it off and were soon married. At that point, they made the history books as the first (and only) presidential couple to be married while in office.

For a time, **6** Edith, now Edith Wilson, performed the regular duties of the First Lady. She was an excellent hostess and a role model for the nation as she **7** rationalized supplies on the president's table during World War I.

After the war had ended, however, tragedy struck and, due to a stroke, President Wilson was unable to fulfill his duties. Confined to his bed, he was paralyzed and weak. Edith **8** taken the reins. Edith and close allies hid the extent of the president's illness from the public and from key members of the government. She organized his priorities and only consulted him on the

3. (A) NO CHANGE
   (B) differences
   (C) various and multitudinous
   (D) different

4. To make this paragraph most logical, sentence 2 should be placed
   (A) where it is now.
   (B) before sentence 1.
   (C) after sentence 3.
   (D) after sentence 4.

5. Which choice most effectively combines the sentences at the underlined portion?
   (A) in a state of marriage, making
   (B) married, entering
   (C) marrying, entered
   (D) about to be married, making

6. (A) NO CHANGE
   (B) Edith now Edith Wilson, performed
   (C) Edith now Edith Wilson performed
   (D) Edith, now Edith Wilson performed

7. (A) NO CHANGE
   (B) ratioed
   (C) radiated
   (D) rationed

8. (A) NO CHANGE
   (B) took
   (C) takes
   (D) has taken

most important issues so that he could preserve his strength. **9** <u>For a year and a half, Edith carried out the regular duties of the office.</u>

Edith would later describe her role as that of a steward. She insisted that she made no decisions outside of choosing what was important enough to require her husband's direct input. However, she did wield her power, filling out paperwork for the president, barring people from seeing him, and **10** <u>pushed for changing in the Cabinet.</u> She even was given security clearance for classified documents and access to codes and encryptions that were far beyond the purview of the First Lady.

After a year and a half, Wilson's term ended and Edith became again just his wife. However, her role should be remembered by history. Whoever ends up being the first woman to take the oath of the office of president will **11** <u>not be alone she will be standing in Ediths shadow.</u>

9. Which choice best sets up the information that follows in the next paragraph?
   (A) NO CHANGE
   (B) President Wilson's stroke caused nothing less than national chaos, with no one able to fill his place.
   (C) Unfortunately, it had become apparent to members of the public that an illegal transfer of power had taken place.
   (D) When Edith Wilson was unable to consult with her husband, she deferred to officials in the president's cabinet for guidance.

10. (A) NO CHANGE
    (B) pushing for the change for the Cabinet.
    (C) pushed on the changes of the Cabinet.
    (D) pushing for changes to the Cabinet.

11. (A) NO CHANGE
    (B) not be alone, she will be standing, in Edith's shadow.
    (C) not be alone; she will be standing in Edith's shadow.
    (D) not be alone, she will be standing in Ediths shadow.

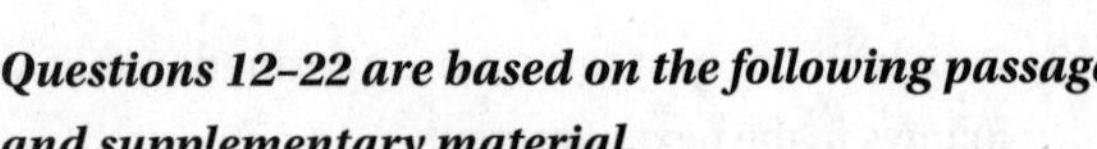

Questions 12–22 are based on the following passage and supplementary material.

The College Career Office

For many students approaching the end of their collegiate studies, the ⓬ prospects of finding a job is daunting. While some will already have leads based on professor recommendations or internship work, others will look at thousands of posts on online job boards and ⓭ felt overwhelmed. Writing a resume, succeeding in an interview, and creating a cover letter all become needed skills that may not have been taught in class. ⓮ For these concerns and most other job search concerns most colleges have a wonderful resource that is vastly underutilized; the career office.

The career office is called by different names on different campuses, but its job remains the same—⓯ a job upon graduation to help students secure. Colleges are invested in helping graduates secure positions, since having large numbers of graduates without jobs makes the colleges look bad and can lead to declining applications and enrollment. ⓰ Thus, it is in the best interest of the college for all students to be employed shortly after graduation.

In order to further this goal, the office will offer many services to help students. One of these services is offering mock interviews to students. Many job candidates dread ⓱ interviews; their very often the deciding factor among a handful of good candidates. What should you wear? How should you answer

12. (A) NO CHANGE
    (B) prospect
    (C) prospective
    (D) prospector

13. (A) NO CHANGE
    (B) felt overwhelming.
    (C) feel overwhelming.
    (D) feel overwhelmed.

14. (A) NO CHANGE
    (B) For these concerns and most other job search concerns, most colleges have a wonderful resource that is vastly underutilized: the career office.
    (C) For these concerns and most other job search concerns; most colleges have a wonderful resource that is vastly underutilized, the career office.
    (D) For these concerns and most other job search concerns, most colleges have a wonderful resource that is vastly underutilized the career office.

15. (A) NO CHANGE
    (B) helping upon graduation to secure a student job.
    (C) to help students secure jobs upon graduation.
    (D) helping secure upon graduation for students jobs.

16. (A) NO CHANGE
    (B) In addition,
    (C) However,
    (D) Moreover,

17. (A) NO CHANGE
    (B) interviews: there
    (C) interviews, they're
    (D) interviews—they are

vague questions? What should you ask when given the opportunity to pose questions? (18) Why should you even seek out a job in the first place when further school may be a better option for many students? Some career offices will even go so far as to partner with local human resources professionals to offer more realistic mock interviews so that students obtain interview experience *and* make a connection in a local office.

(19) Connections to local business owners are essential to securing a high-paying job. An expert in the career office can help not just with mechanics and grammar on the resume, but also with content questions that a student might have. Should you include the job you had (20) in high school? How do you include extra-curricular activities? What exactly should a cover letter look like? This can be especially helpful as candidates should be adjusting the cover letter and resume for each job to which they apply.

18. Which sentence provides the best transition from the previous part of the paragraph to what follows in the paragraph?
    (A) NO CHANGE
    (B) Career offices lack the necessary connections that students need to find postgraduation employment.
    (C) Doing a practice interview with a professional from the career office can help alleviate such concerns.
    (D) Most students, however, find that their academic training is more than sufficient to prepare them for whatever interview questions they may face.

19. Which choice best introduces the information that follows in the paragraph?
    (A) NO CHANGE
    (B) Excellent grammar is essential when presenting yourself in a professional manner.
    (C) Be prepared to have well-researched questions to ask the human resources professional who is interviewing you.
    (D) Another very helpful career service is the proofreading of resumes and cover letters.

20. (A) NO CHANGE
    (B) during the time that you were in high school?
    (C) for the years that you were educated in high school?
    (D) DELETE the underlined portion.

Career services can only be helpful to the extent that students use them. Unfortunately, **21** 55.4% of college students surveyed in 2017 used college office interview services, while 69.9% of students who took advantage of this found the service helpful. While 74.5% of students used the more fundamental resume services, **22** only 29.4% used the potentially helpful career skills testing services. Just as students should not skip college classes, students should not skip the excellent services that career services can provide.

Career Office Service	Percent of Students Who Used Service	Percent of Students Who Found Service Helpful
Practice interviewing	31.2%	69.9%
Resume assistance	74.5%	68.4%
Workshops	37.8%	63.0%
Job listings	55.4%	62.1%
Researching employers	32.2%	60.5%
Career skills testing	29.4%	52.4%

Information adapted from the *Class of 2017 Student Survey*, National Association of Colleges and Employers

21. Which choice is best supported by information in the graph?
    (A) NO CHANGE
    (B) just 31.2% of college students surveyed in 2017 used college office interview services,
    (C) just 37.8% of students used the workshops career service,
    (D) an impressive 74.5% of students used the resume assistance workshops,

22. Which choice most effectively uses information from the graph to demonstrate a contrast with the information in the first part of the sentence?
    (A) NO CHANGE
    (B) 69.9% of students found interview practicing to be helpful.
    (C) 68.4% of whom found the service useful.
    (D) this represented a sizeable majority of respondents to the survey.

Questions 23–33 are based on the following passage.

Ergot Fungus

Some types of food have occasionally altered the course of history in unexpected ways. Rye, a grain which dates to the beginning of civilization, is one such food. **23** It comes from the fertile crescent and was one of the earliest grains used to produce bread. Now it is almost exclusively used to make toast, but long ago it was a major staple crop for many civilizations. Historians believe that after rye became widely cultivated, the parasitic ergot fungus began to **24** wreck the havoc of unsuspecting communities.

Ergot fungus was infecting rye grain and **25** it's natural precursor long before humans began cultivating rye crops. **26** Also scientists speculate that the evolutionary purpose of the toxins in ergot fungus was to discourage animals from eating it, humans were unable to prevent its consumption. **27** Rye, like other grains, was harvested en masse and was only rarely sorted to remove ergot fungus. In most ancient rye bread loaves, there likely would have been some amount of the ergot fungus, though in some cultures the nobility **28** were intent on the discontinuation of the presence of this organism in their sustenance.

23. The writer wants to elaborate on the origin and history of rye grain. What choice best accomplishes this goal?
    (A) NO CHANGE
    (B) Rye is used in many different sandwiches, including the Reuben.
    (C) It originated in what is today southwestern Asia.
    (D) While not as commonly used as wheat and corn, rye is a popular crop throughout much of the world.

24. (A) NO CHANGE
    (B) wreck havoc with
    (C) wreak havoc on
    (D) wreak havoc toward

25. (A) NO CHANGE
    (B) its
    (C) its'
    (D) their

26. (A) NO CHANGE
    (B) If
    (C) For
    (D) While

27. (A) NO CHANGE
    (B) Rye, like other grains was
    (C) Rye—like other grains—were
    (D) Rye—like other grains, was

28. Which choice is most consistent with the tone of the passage as a whole?
    (A) NO CHANGE
    (B) fully blockaded the encroachment of this invader into their food stores.
    (C) laid off eating this since they didn't feel like it.
    (D) took steps to ensure that it was not in their grain.

Ergot has **29** many effects on the human body, the most peculiar of which is that it induces visions and hallucinations. In addition to hallucinations, there were also major physical effects such as convulsions, heart attacks, and restrictions in blood flow so extreme that limbs would sometimes have to be amputated. **30** The ancients called the disease caused by ergot "St. Antony's Fire" because of the burning sensation it caused in the limbs. Until this fungus was discovered as the cause of this strange disease in the 1500s, plagues would tear through whole nations causing an odd mixture of a horrible disease and very strange behaviors in those afflicted. Many unusual historical events have been speculated to have been **31** triggered by this fungus, the Salem witch trials; the siege of Hamburg; and the dancing plagues. The dancing plagues are an interesting case because these would consist of hundreds of people dancing in the streets uncontrollably for hours.

29. (A) NO CHANGE
    (B) much effects
    (C) many affects
    (D) much affects

30. At this point, the writer is considering adding the following sentence.

    Heart attacks are one of the top causes of death for people in the United States today.

    Should the writer make this addition here?
    (A) Yes, because it provides a relevant detail.
    (B) Yes, because it elaborates on a key term from the previous sentence.
    (C) No, because it distracts from the discussion in the paragraph.
    (D) No, because it repeats a point made earlier in the essay.

31. (A) NO CHANGE
    (B) triggered by this fungus: the Salem witch trials, the siege of Hamburg, and the dancing plagues.
    (C) triggered by this fungus, the Salem witch trials the siege of Hamburg and the dancing plagues.
    (D) triggered by this fungus—the Salem witch trials—the siege of Hamburg, and the dancing plagues.

In recent history, a scientist was altering the structure of some ergot molecules and noticed that he felt a bit strange. After further investigation, he found that some of the compounds in ergot are closely related to those in the drug LSD. While scientists (32) hope to find therapeutic uses for the compound, it ultimately became an illegal substance after its widespread abuse. (33) Illegal substances have become a major issue for governmental authorities to effectively regulate.

32. (A) NO CHANGE
    (B) have hoped
    (C) are hoping
    (D) hoped

33. Which choice best provides a summary of the main idea of this passage?
    (A) NO CHANGE
    (B) With this knowledge of ergot chemistry, historians better understand the source of some previously inexplicable human behaviors from the past.
    (C) Most of what has transpired in history can be attributed to the dietary choices of those in positions of power.
    (D) Further research into other unexplained behavior from history should be carried out by scientific historians.

Questions 34–44 are based on the following passage.

Graffiti

In the now excavated streets of Pompeii, (34) the Roman city buried by a volcano nearly two thousand years ago, archeologists have found something more commonly associated with modernity—graffiti. This graffiti is extraordinary in how very ordinary it is. Much of it reads like something you would see today, proclaiming that a certain person was there, or (35) which someone loved someone else. This graffiti, due to its historic nature, is now being preserved as ancient art. This raises an important question: When should graffiti be painted over, and when is it art to be preserved?

Modern day graffiti creates the same questions. Most people would agree that a quickly spray-painted tag is not art, but some graffiti is very elaborate, well planned, and objectively beautiful. Some graffiti (36) quiets the value of an area by making it appear abandoned and unkempt. Other graffiti spruces up a blank wall, adds much needed color, and creates art in an otherwise dismal space. (37) How are cities supposed to decide what to leave; and what to paint over? Also, if cities allow some nicer graffiti to remain, will that not encourage the creation of even more graffiti, both good and bad? Is good graffiti not still vandalism?

On the one hand, cities across the United States spend about 12 billion dollars each year cleaning up graffiti. (38) They do this to improve neighborhoods. This occurs because graffiti tends to make many

34. Should the underlined portion be kept or deleted?
    (A) Kept, because it provides clarifying details.
    (B) Kept, because it explains the process of excavation.
    (C) Deleted, because it is inconsistent with the tone of the passage.
    (D) Deleted, because it is irrelevant to archeological research.

35. (A) NO CHANGE
    (B) that someone loved someone else.
    (C) that someone else was loved by someone.
    (D) which someone else was loved by someone.

36. (A) NO CHANGE
    (B) recedes
    (C) lowers
    (D) muffles

37. (A) NO CHANGE
    (B) How are cities supposed to decide, what to leave and what to paint over?
    (C) How are cities supposed to decide: what to leave and what to paint over?
    (D) How are cities supposed to decide what to leave and what to paint over?

38. Which choice most effectively combines the sentences at the underlined portion?
    (A) neighborhoods, because they
    (B) neighborhoods, the process resulting in graffiti that
    (C) neighborhoods, it
    (D) neighborhoods, since graffiti

people believe a neighborhood is decaying or undesirable. This results in property values sinking. Some point to a correlation between quick removal and the lack of (39) reoccurrence; moreover, graffiti is indeed illegal in most areas.

(40) In addition, some people see graffiti as a nonviolent outlet for bored young people. Ninety percent of graffiti in the United States is connected not to criminal activity, (41) and to individuals merely trying to express themselves in some way.[2] Graffiti advocates point out that creating graffiti is a far less harmful outlet (42) than other potential activities. They can also point to statistics that show that involvement in art improves positive outcomes for young people and argue that graffiti is one of the most accessible and inexpensive artistic outlets.

39. (A) NO CHANGE
(B) reoccurrence, moreover graffiti is indeed illegal in most areas.
(C) reoccurrence. Moreover graffiti is indeed illegal in most areas.
(D) reoccurrence moreover, graffiti is indeed illegal in most areas.

40. Which choice provides the best transition from the previous paragraph?
(A) NO CHANGE
(B) On the other hand,
(C) Because of this,
(D) As a matter of fact,

41. (A) NO CHANGE
(B) also
(C) but
(D) for

42. (A) NO CHANGE
(B) then other activities.
(C) then those of other activities.
(D) DELETE the underlined portion, adjusting the punctuation accordingly.

[2]Statistics from: *www.statisticsdatabase.com/facts/graffiti-statistics-united-states/*

43 Meeting the demands of the body politic is essential to making society harmonious. The United States is, after all, a laboratory of democracy. Different cities and states will handle the issue differently, and by watching the outcomes of the many different policies 44 enacted, we may eventually be able to answer once and for all the question of whether graffiti is art or vandalism.

43. Which choice best introduces the material that follows in the paragraph?
    (A) NO CHANGE
    (B) In the end, it's up to individual municipalities to decide how they want to handle the issue of cleanup.
    (C) Ultimately, graffiti is a significant problem for many municipalities, for which they need increased funding to remove.
    (D) While some may consider graffiti to be an eyesore, different cities across the board have found that preserving it leads to better outcomes.

44. (A) NO CHANGE
    (B) enacted, therefore we may
    (C) enacted; as a result, we may
    (D) enacted, which causes us to

STOP If there is still time remaining, you may review your answers.

MATH TEST 1 (NO CALCULATOR)

25 MINUTES, 20 QUESTIONS

DIRECTIONS: For questions 1–15, solve each problem and choose the best answer from the given options. Fill in the corresponding oval on your answer document. For questions 16–20, solve the problem and fill in the answer in the answer sheet grid. Please use any space in the test booklet to work out your answers.

Notes:

- You **CANNOT** use a calculator on this section.
- All variables and expressions represent real numbers, unless indicated otherwise.
- All figures are drawn to scale, unless indicated otherwise.
- All figures are in a plane, unless indicated otherwise.
- Unless indicated otherwise, the domain of a given function is the set of all real numbers *x* for which the function has real values.

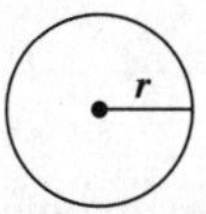

Radius of a circle = r
Area of a circle = πr^2
Circumference of a circle = $2\pi r$

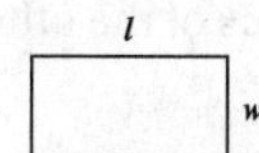

Area of a rectangle = length × width = lw

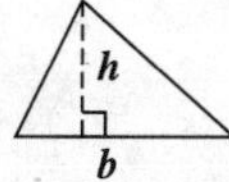

Area of a triangle = $\frac{1}{2}$ × base × height = $\frac{1}{2}bh$

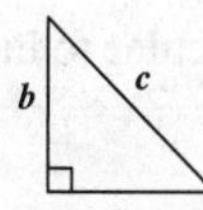

Pythagorean theorem: $a^2 + b^2 = c^2$

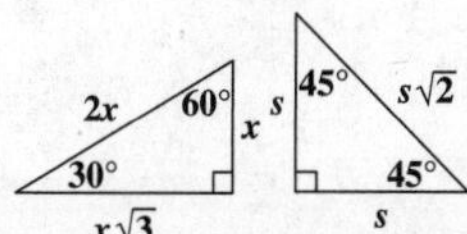

Special right triangles: 30-60-90 and 45-45-90

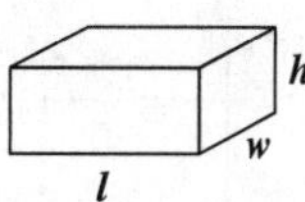

Volume of a box = length × width × height = lwh

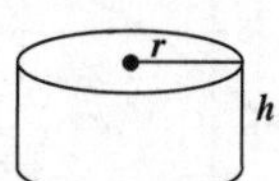

Volume of a cylinder = $\pi r^2 h$

Volume of a sphere = $\frac{4}{3}\pi r^3$

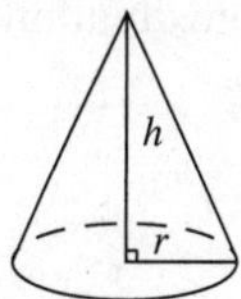

Volume of a cone = $\frac{1}{3}\pi r^2 h$

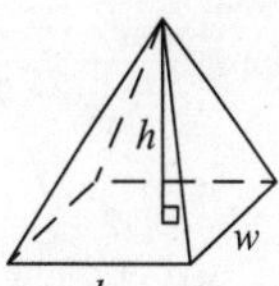

Volume of a pyramid =
$\frac{1}{3}$ × length × width × height = $\frac{1}{3}$ lwh

Key Facts:

- **A circle has 360 degrees.**
- **There are 2π radians in a circle.**
- **There are 180 degrees in a triangle.**

1. Which of the following expressions is equivalent to $\frac{1}{2}x^3(x^2 - 4)$?

(A) $\frac{1}{2}x^6 - 2x^2$
(B) $\frac{1}{2}x^6 - 2$
(C) $\frac{1}{2}x^5 - 2x^3$
(D) $\frac{1}{2}x^5 - 4x^2$

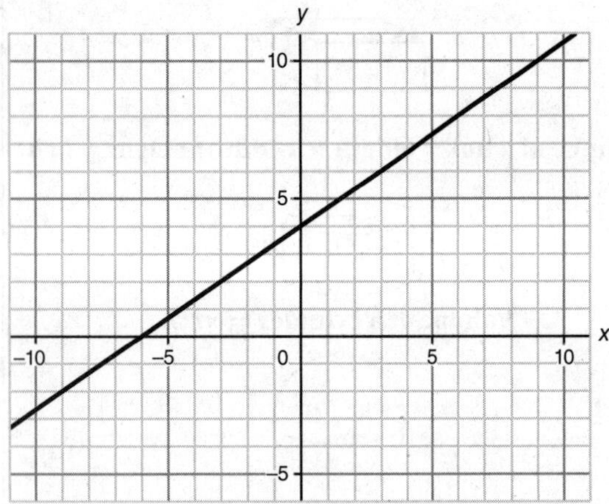

2. What is the best approximation of the slope of the line graphed above?

(A) $\frac{1}{2}$
(B) $\frac{2}{3}$
(C) $\frac{4}{3}$
(D) 2

3. $2x - 5y = 3$
$x + 2y = 6$

If (a, b) is the solution to the system of equations above, what is the value of a?

(A) 1
(B) 2
(C) 3
(D) 4

4. Which of the following expressions is equivalent to $2(x - 4) + 4$?

(A) $2x - 4$
(B) $2x + 4$
(C) $4x - 4$
(D) $4x + 4$

5. $A = \frac{v^2}{R}$

The acceleration of an object moving in a circle is determined by the equation above, in which v is the velocity of the object, A is its acceleration, and R is the radius of the circle. What is the value of the radius in terms of the other variables?

(A) $R = \frac{2v}{A}$
(B) $R = \frac{v^2}{A}$
(C) $R = Av^2$
(D) $R = \frac{1}{Av^2}$

6. For the line l, $y = ax + n$, where a and n are distinct nonzero constants. Which of these lines must be perpendicular to line l?

(A) $y = nx + a$
(B) $y = ax - n$
(C) $y = -\frac{1}{a}x - n$
(D) $y = -ax + n$

7. If $y = bx^2 + 5$ when $x = 2$ and $y = 17$, what is the value of the constant b?

(A) −5
(B) 3
(C) 4
(D) 12

8. Francisco is packing two bags for his trip. The capacity of the small bag is $\frac{1}{3}$ that of the larger bag. If the total capacity of the two bags together is 80 liters, what is the capacity of the smaller bag?

(A) 5 liters
(B) 8 liters
(C) 12 liters
(D) 20 liters

9. The function f is determined by $f(x) = \frac{x^3}{4} + 3$. What is the value of $f(2)$?

(A) 1
(B) 5
(C) 6
(D) 9

10. If $\frac{x^{\frac{2}{3}}}{x^{\frac{1}{6}}} = \frac{x^a}{\sqrt{x}}$, what is the value of a?

(A) 1
(B) 2
(C) 3
(D) 6

11. Given that $i = \sqrt{-1}$, the expression $2i^2 - 3i^4$ is equivalent to which of the following?

(A) −5
(B) −3
(C) −1
(D) 1

12. $\frac{2x - 6}{2} = x + k$

If the equation above has infinitely many solutions, what is the value of the constant k?

(A) $k = -7$
(B) $k = -3$
(C) $k = 0$
(D) $k = 2$

13. In the equation $3 = |x - 1|$, how many solutions are there?

(A) Exactly 1
(B) Exactly 2
(C) None
(D) Infinite

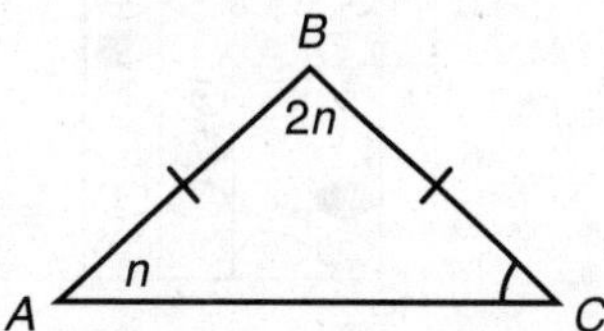

14. In triangle ABC above, $\overline{AB}$ and $\overline{BC}$ are congruent, and $\angle A$ is n degrees and $\angle B$ is $2n$ degrees. What is the measure of $\angle C$ in degrees?

(A) 20°
(B) 35°
(C) 45°
(D) 70°

15. Which of these linear equations has no solutions?

(A) $x + 2 = 3x - 1$
(B) $5x + 4 = 5x + 4$
(C) $x = x - 3$
(D) $2x = \frac{1}{2}x + 5$

Student-Produced Response Directions

In questions 16–20, first solve the problem, and then enter your answer on the grid provided on the answer sheet. The instructions for entering your answers follow.

- First, write your answer in the boxes at the top of the grid.
- Second, you may grid your answer in the columns below the boxes.
- Use the fraction bar in the first row or the decimal point in the second row to enter fractions and decimals.

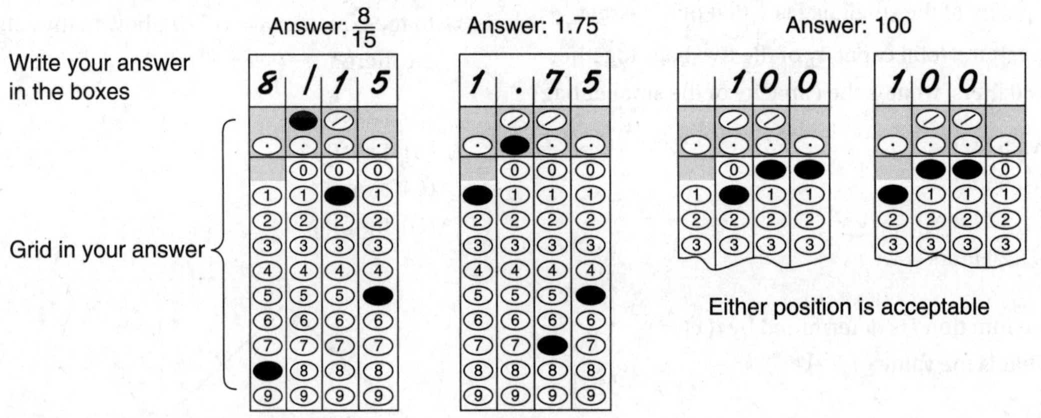

- Grid only one space in each column.
- Entering the answer in the boxes is recommended as an aid in gridding but is not required.
- The machine scoring your exam can read only what you grid, so you **must grid-in your answers correctly to get credit**.
- If a question has more than one correct answer, grid-in only one of them.
- The grid does not have a minus sign, so no answer can be negative.
- A mixed number *must* be converted to an improper fraction or a decimal before it is gridded. Enter $1\frac{1}{4}$ as $\frac{5}{4}$ or 1.25; the machine will interpret 11/4 as $\frac{11}{4}$ and mark it wrong.
- **All decimals must be entered as accurately as possible.** Here are three acceptable ways of gridding $\frac{3}{11} = 0.272727\ldots$

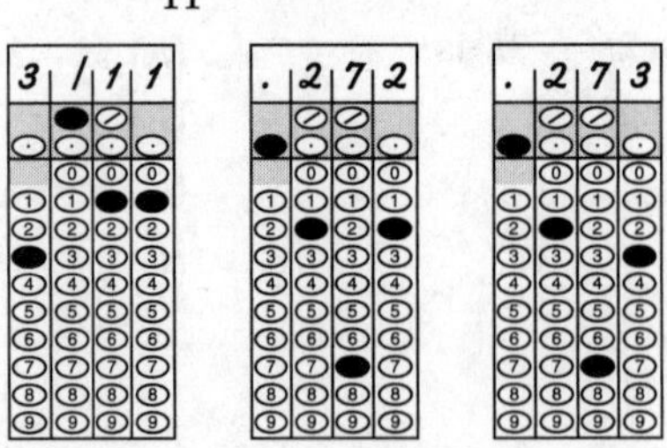

- Note that rounding to .273 is acceptable because you are using the full grid, but you would receive **no credit** for .3 or .27, because they are less accurate.

16. An airplane travels a distance of 3,000 miles in a time of 10 hours. What is its speed in miles per hour?

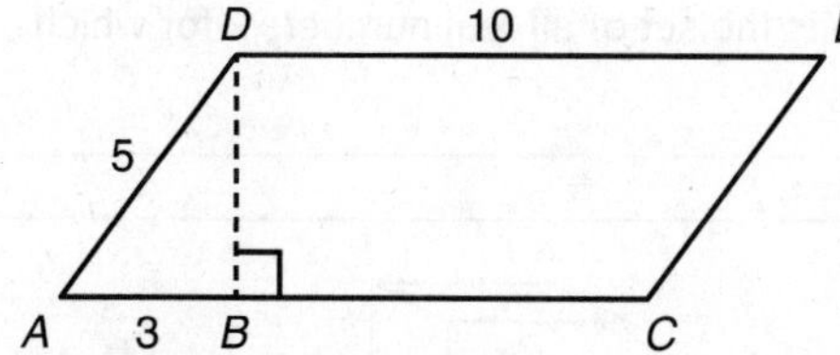

17. Parallelogram *ADEC* has a side of $\overline{DE}$ of length 10 units and a side of $\overline{DA}$ of length 5 units. The length from *A* to *B* is 3 units. What is the area of the parallelogram in square units?

18. $x^2 - x - 20 = 0$

What is the sum of the solutions to the equation above?

19. If $f(x) = 3^x - 1$, for what value of *x* will $f(x)$ intercept the *y*-axis when graphed in the *xy*-coordinate plane?

20. How much greater is the diameter of circle *A* than that of circle *B*?

Circle *A*: $(x - 2)^2 + (y - 7)^2 = 49$

Circle *B*: $(x + 5)^2 + (y - 3)^2 = 25$

STOP If there is still time remaining, you may review your answers.

MATH PRACTICE TEST 1 (CALCULATOR)

55 MINUTES, 38 QUESTIONS

DIRECTIONS: For questions 1–30, solve each problem and choose the best answer from the given options. Fill in the corresponding oval on your answer document. For questions 31–38, solve the problem and fill in the answer in the answer sheet grid. Please use any space in the test booklet to work out your answers.

Notes:

- You **CAN** use a calculator on this section.
- All variables and expressions represent real numbers, unless indicated otherwise.
- All figures are drawn to scale, unless indicated otherwise.
- All figures are in a plane, unless indicated otherwise.
- Unless indicated otherwise, the domain of a given function is the set of all real numbers x for which the function has real values.

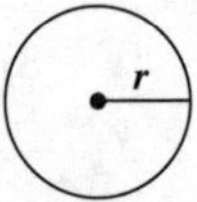

Radius of a circle = r
Area of a circle = πr^2
Circumference of a circle = $2\pi r$

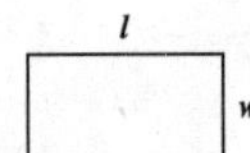

Area of a rectangle = length × width = lw

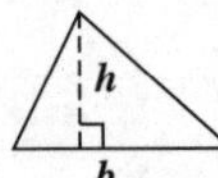

Area of a triangle = $\frac{1}{2}$ × base × height = $\frac{1}{2}bh$

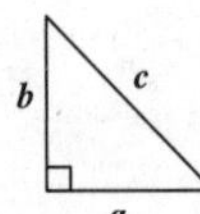

Pythagorean theorem: $a^2 + b^2 = c^2$

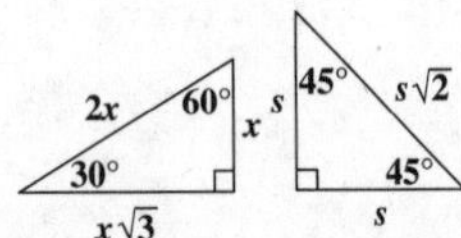

Special right triangles: 30-60-90 and 45-45-90

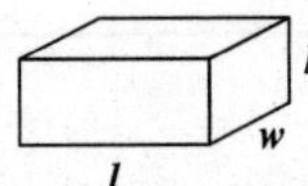

Volume of a box = length × width × height = lwh

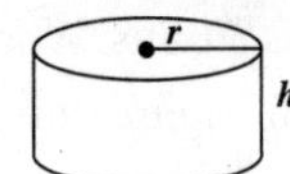

Volume of a cylinder = $\pi r^2 h$

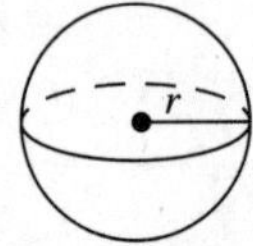

Volume of a sphere = $\frac{4}{3}\pi r^3$

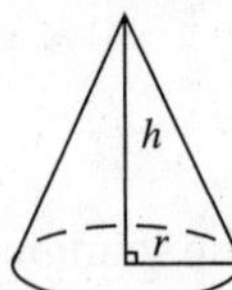

Volume of a cone = $\frac{1}{3}\pi r^2 h$

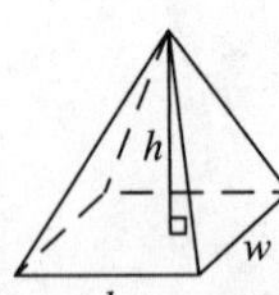

Volume of a pyramid =
$\frac{1}{3}$ × length × width × height = $\frac{1}{3}$ lwh

Key Facts:

- **A circle has 360 degrees.**
- **There are 2π radians in a circle.**
- **There are 180 degrees in a triangle.**

Questions 1–2 refer to the following information.

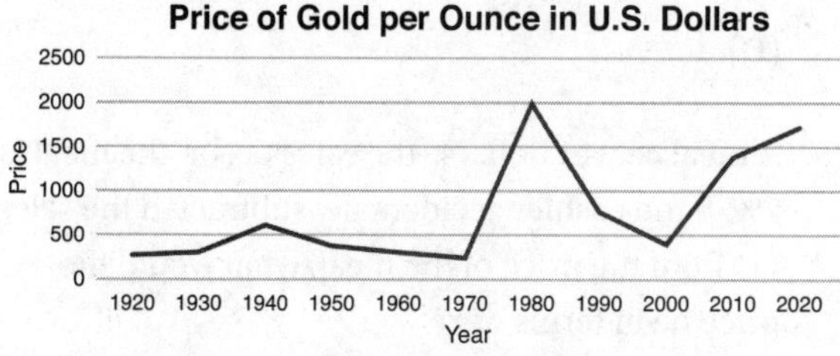

1. Which of the following is closest to the price in U.S. dollars of an ounce of gold in the year 1970?

(A) \$245
(B) \$520
(C) \$610
(D) \$1,225

2. What fraction of the gold price in the year 1980 is the gold price in the year 2000, measured to the nearest tenth?

(A) $\frac{1}{5}$
(B) $\frac{3}{10}$
(C) $\frac{2}{5}$
(D) $\frac{2}{3}$

---

3. Walter is going backpacking on a trail. The total distance of the trail is 300 miles. If he has already traveled 100 miles on the trail, how many miles per day, m, will he need to travel in order to complete his journey in D days?

(A) $m = \frac{200}{D}$
(B) $m = 300D$
(C) $m = \frac{D}{300}$
(D) $m = 200 + D$

4. In normal atmospheric conditions, the speed of sound through dry air can be approximated with the following equation, in which V represents the velocity in meters per second and T represents the air temperature in degrees Celsius.

$$V = 331.4 + 0.6T$$

What is the speed of sound in air that is 15 degrees Celsius?

(A) −537.3 meters per second
(B) 14.8 meters per second
(C) 340.4 meters per second
(D) 423.5 meters per second

5. A museum gift shop provides a 10% discount for museum members. If a customer who is a museum member purchases a book from the store for \$18, what was the original price of the book prior to the discount (ignore sales tax)?

(A) \$12
(B) \$20
(C) \$22
(D) \$26

6. The number of dollars, C, it costs for Halle to run a restaurant is modeled by the function $C(m) = 10m + 10,000$, in which m is the number of meals served. What is the meaning of the 10 in this function?

(A) The total cost for all the meals sold.
(B) The fixed costs for the restaurant to operate.
(C) The profit the restaurant has for each meal sold.
(D) The additional cost to the restaurant for each additional meal.

7. Which of the following represents the graph of $\frac{1}{2}y + 2 = -x$?

(A)
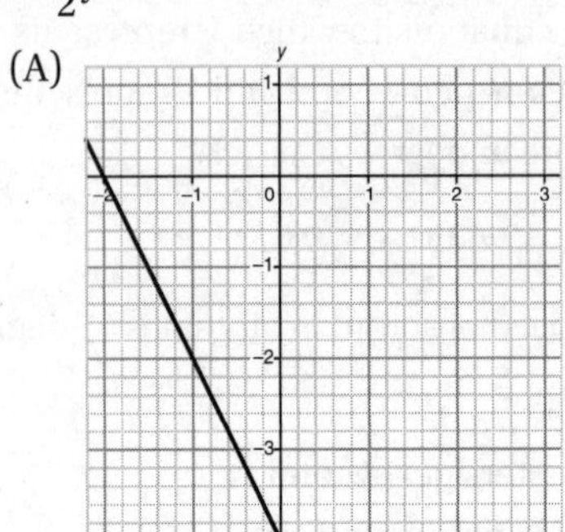

(B)
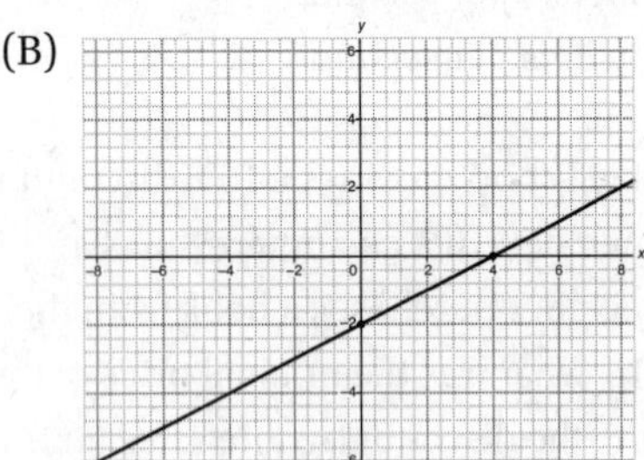

(C)
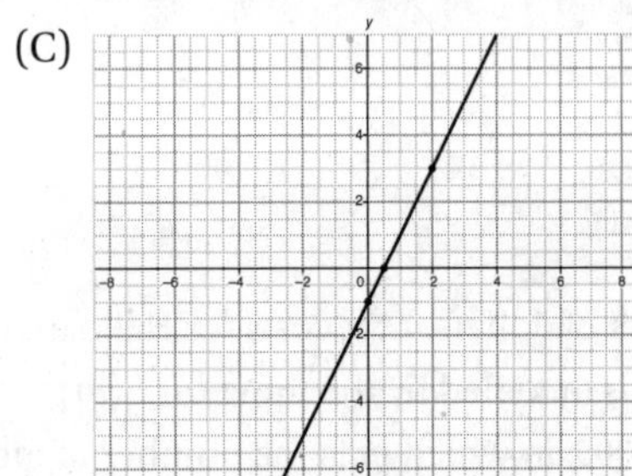

(D)
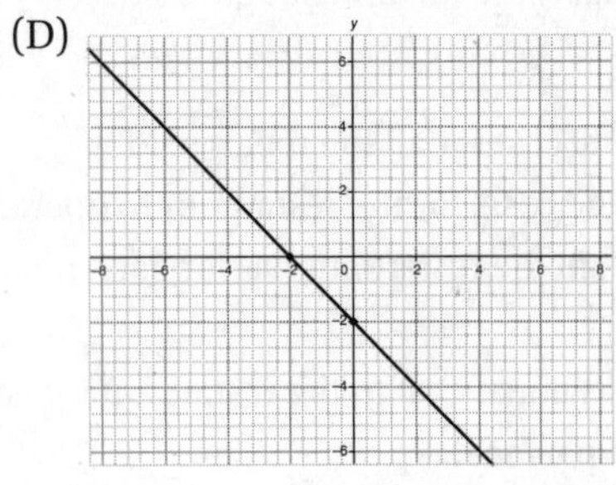

8. In a survey of 1,000 likely voters, $\frac{1}{2}$ like Candidate A, $\frac{1}{3}$ like Candidate B, and the remainder like neither candidate. If a likely voter is selected at random, what is the probability that they will like neither candidate?

(A) $\frac{1}{12}$
(B) $\frac{1}{6}$
(C) $\frac{1}{4}$
(D) $\frac{1}{3}$

9. A meal costs x dollars. The sales tax on the meal is 7%. If the cashier accidentally subtracted the sales tax from the price of the meal, what would the price be in terms of x?

(A) $0.07x$
(B) $0.7x$
(C) $0.93x$
(D) $1.07x$

x	$f(x)$
1	1^C
2	2^C
3	3^C

10. In the function with values given above, in which C is a constant, if $f(2) = 8$, what is the value of $f(3)$?

(A) 16
(B) 27
(C) 64
(D) 81

Questions 11–12 refer to the following information.

Traffic density is measured in vehicles/mile/lane. The traffic density in a city is portrayed in the graph below.

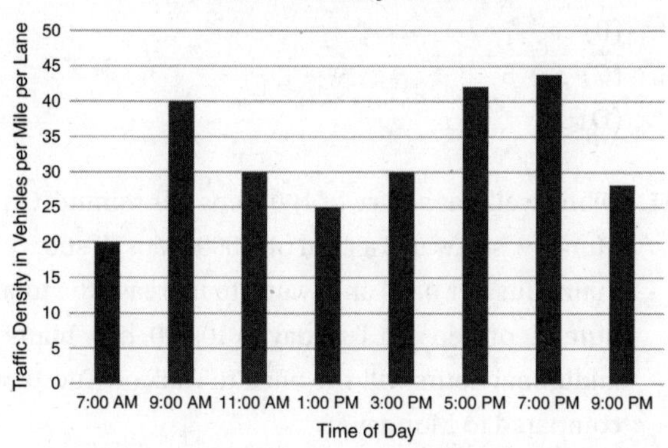

11. Between what two hours does the traffic density increase the most?

(A) Between 7 A.M. and 9 A.M.
(B) Between 9 A.M. and 11 A.M.
(C) Between 1 P.M. and 3 P.M.
(D) Between 3 P.M. and 5 P.M.

12. How many vehicles would one most likely find at 1 P.M. in one mile on a typical two-lane road in the city?

(A) 25 vehicles
(B) 30 vehicles
(C) 40 vehicles
(D) 50 vehicles

---

13. The Statue of Liberty has a height of 93 meters. A model toy version (done to scale) of the Statue of Liberty is 1/500th the height of the actual statue. Given that there are 100 centimeters in a meter, what is the height of the model in centimeters, calculated to the nearest whole centimeter?

(A) 19 cm
(B) 86 cm
(C) 186 cm
(D) 320 cm

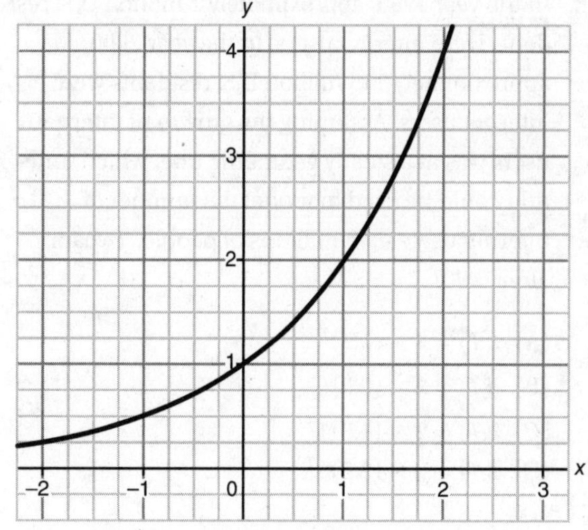

14. Which of the following models the function as presented in the graph above?

(A) $f(x) = x^2$
(B) $f(x) = x^2 + 1$
(C) $f(x) = 2^x$
(D) $f(x) = 3^x + 1$

15. Nyla is driving X miles per hour. Given that there are 5,280 feet in a mile, what is her speed in feet per second?

(A) $\left(\frac{60}{5,280}\right)X$
(B) $\left(\frac{3,600}{5,280}\right)X$
(C) $\left(\frac{5,280}{60}\right)X$
(D) $\left(\frac{5,280}{3,600}\right)X$

16. In the year 1990, approximately 2 million U.S. residents were internet users. In the year 2000, approximately 115 million U.S. residents were internet users. Assuming the growth of internet users was at a steady geometric rate, which function could be used to model the number of internet users, *I*, in millions of people, *T* years after 1990?

(A) $I(T) = 2 \times (1.5)^T$
(B) $I(T) = 2 \times (0.5)^T$
(C) $I(T) = 2 \times (1.5)^{-T}$
(D) $I(T) = 2 \times (2.5)^{-T}$

17. $\angle X$ is measured in degrees. If the cosine of $\angle X$ is $\frac{\sqrt{2}}{2}$, what is the sine of $(90 - \angle X)$?

(A) $\frac{1}{2}$
(B) $\frac{\sqrt{2}}{2}$
(C) $\frac{\sqrt{3}}{2}$
(D) $\frac{2}{\sqrt{3}}$

18. At exactly how many points will the function $f(x) = x^2 - 3x - 4$ intersect the *x*-axis?

(A) 0
(B) 1
(C) 2
(D) 3

19. If $2x^2 + bx + 4 = 0$, for what values of *b* will there be no real solutions?

(A) $b \geq \sqrt{2}$
(B) $|b| \leq -\sqrt{2}$
(C) $b \geq 4$
(D) $|b| \leq 4\sqrt{2}$

20. $x^3 + x^2 - 20x$

Which of the following is NOT a factor of the above expression?

(A) $x - 4$
(B) $x - 7$
(C) $x + 5$
(D) x

21. Diana walks at a pace of 100 steps per minute. On Monday, she walks a total of 6,000 steps. If she maintains her pace and wants to increase the total number of steps on Tuesday to 10,000, how many additional hours will she need to walk on Tuesday compared to Monday?

(A) $\frac{1}{6}$ of an hour
(B) $\frac{1}{4}$ of an hour
(C) $\frac{2}{3}$ of an hour
(D) 1 hour

22. A car dealership begins the year with an inventory of 60 cars and adds 3 cars to its inventory each month. If the number of cars were to be written in slope-intercept form as the *y* value with the number of months after the beginning of the year as the *x* value, what would the slope and *y*-intercept of the function be?

(A) Slope: 3, *y*-intercept 60
(B) Slope: 2, *y*-intercept 90
(C) Slope: −3, *y*-intercept 20
(D) Slope: $-\frac{1}{3}$, *y*-intercept 30

23. A city's population at the beginning of 2010 was 50,000 residents. At the beginning of 2011, its population was 45,000 residents, and at the beginning of 2012, its population was 40,500 residents. If the city's population has continued to change at the same rate each year, which function models the city's population T years after 2010?

(A) $P(T) = 50,000 \times (0.9)^T$
(B) $P(T) = 40,500 \times (0.09)^T$
(C) $P(T) = 50,000 \times (1.1)^T$
(D) $P(T) = 45,000 \times (1.09)^T$

	Less Than 8 Hours of Sleep	8 Hours or More Sleep	Total
Middle-Schoolers	a	b	400
High-Schoolers	300	200	500

24. A sociologist surveyed 400 randomly selected middle-schoolers and 500 randomly selected high-schoolers about the number of hours of sleep they had on a daily basis. If the middle-schoolers are half as likely as the high-schoolers to get less than 8 hours of sleep, what would be the value for a?

(A) 90
(B) 120
(C) 135
(D) 160

25. The linear function g can be written in the form $g(x) = mx + b$, in which m and b are constants. If $g(1) = 7$ and $g(3) = 11$, what is the value of m?

(A) -3
(B) -1
(C) 2
(D) 6

26. In the equation $3x - 6 = 3(x - a)$, the constant a is greater than 2. Which of the following statements must be true?

(A) The equation has exactly one solution.
(B) The equation has exactly two solutions.
(C) The equation has infinitely many solutions.
(D) The equation has no solutions.

Consider these two histograms showing the frequency of 70 integers between 1–9:

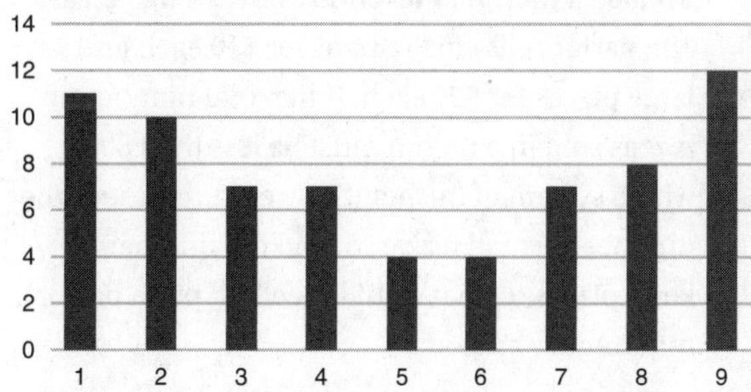

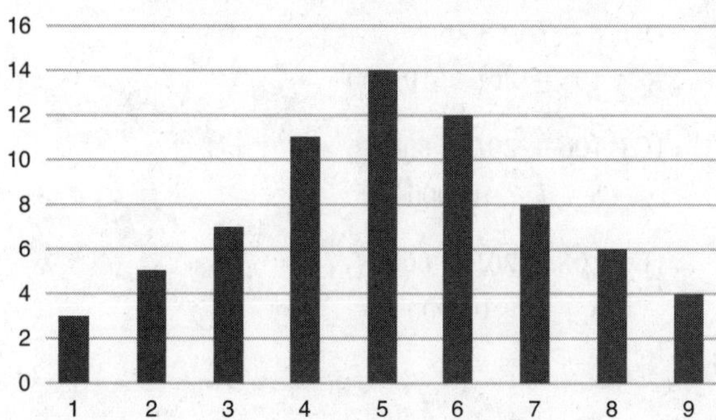

27. Which of the following quantities would be the largest amount greater for set A than for set B?

(A) Median
(B) Standard deviation
(C) Range
(D) Mean

28. {2, 3, 6, 6, 7}

Which expression gives the complete set of potential values of a single number x that can be inserted in the above set of data *without* changing the median of the set?

(A) $x \geq 7$
(B) $x < 2$
(C) $x < 6$
(D) $x \geq 6$

29. A pizza parlor has a goal of making at least $10,000 a month in revenue from selling pizzas. The parlor sells small pizzas for $10 each and large pizzas for $20 each. If the total number of pizzas sold in a month must be less than 800, which system of inequalities would represent the number of small pizzas, S, and the number of large pizzas, L, that would meet the pizza parlor's requirements?

(A) $S + L < 800$
$10S + 20L > 10,000$

(B) $S + L \geq 800$
$10S + 20L < 10,000$

(C) $10S + 20L < 800$
$S + L < 10,000$

(D) $10S + 20L \geq 800$
$S + L > 10,000$

30. The reproduction number, called R_O, is used to calculate the spread of disease. If a virus has an R_O of 6, an infected person will likely directly infect 6 other people. Based on this, if 20 people are infected with a virus that has an R_O of 4.2, how many people will these 20 people most likely directly infect?

(A) 46
(B) 54
(C) 84
(D) 98

Student-Produced Response Directions

In questions 31–38, first solve the problem, and then enter your answer on the grid provided on the answer sheet. The instructions for entering your answers follow.

- First, write your answer in the boxes at the top of the grid.
- Second, you may grid your answer in the columns below the boxes.
- Use the fraction bar in the first row or the decimal point in the second row to enter fractions and decimals.

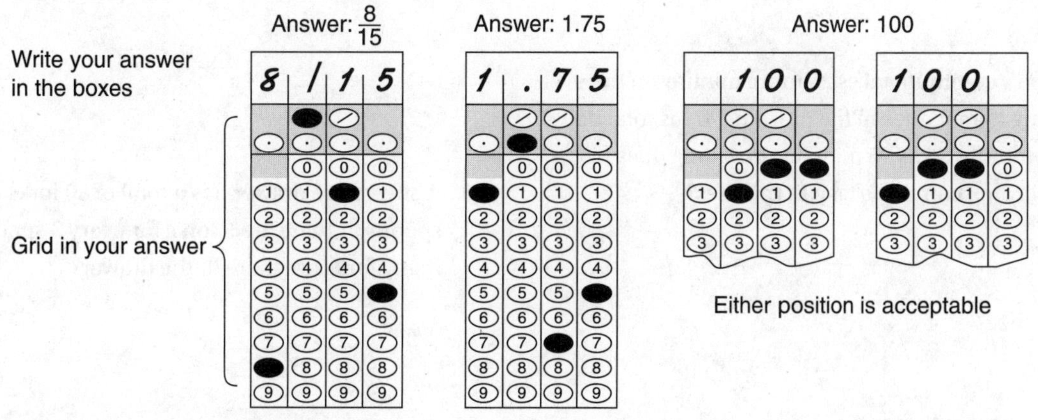

- Grid only one space in each column.
- Entering the answer in the boxes is recommended as an aid in gridding but is not required.
- The machine scoring your exam can read only what you grid, so you **must grid-in your answers correctly to get credit**.
- If a question has more than one correct answer, grid-in only one of them.
- The grid does not have a minus sign, so no answer can be negative.
- A mixed number *must* be converted to an improper fraction or a decimal before it is gridded. Enter $1\frac{1}{4}$ as $\frac{5}{4}$ or 1.25; the machine will interpret 11/4 as $\frac{11}{4}$ and mark it wrong.
- **All decimals must be entered as accurately as possible.** Here are three acceptable ways of gridding

$$\frac{3}{11} = 0.272727\ldots$$

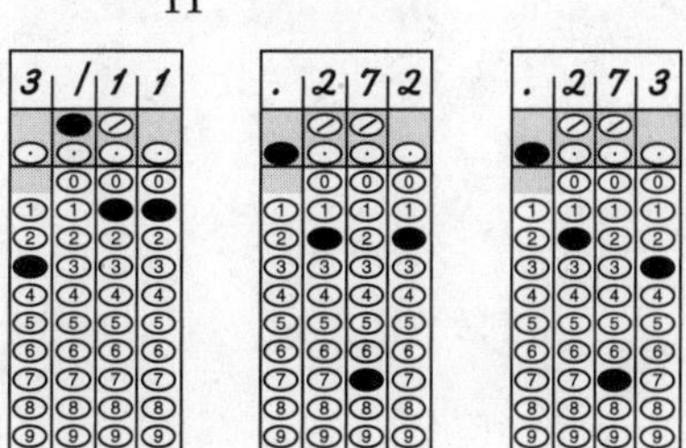

- Note that rounding to .273 is acceptable because you are using the full grid, but you would receive **no credit** for .3 or .27, because they are less accurate.

31. What number is 5% greater than 200?

32. Ken's commute takes 25 more minutes in the evening than it does in the morning. If his total daily commute takes 95 minutes, how long does his morning commute take in minutes?

33. $2x - 3y = 5$
    $4x + y = 17$

    If (x, y) is a solution to the above system of equations, what is the value of y?

34. A line that is perpendicular to the line with the equation $y = -3x + 5$ has a y-intercept of 4. What is the y value of a point in this perpendicular line when its x value is 3?

35. A silverware drawer has a total of 80 forks and spoons. If there are 5 forks for every 3 spoons, how many forks are there in the drawer?

36. The height of a certain triangle is twice the width of its base. If the area of the triangle is 25 square units, what is the height of the triangle?

Heartbeats per Minute	Breaths per Minute
60	12
70	15
80	18

37. Assuming Baahir's heartbeats per minute and breaths per minute have a linear relationship with one another, what would Baahir's pulse (heartbeats per minute) be if he is breathing at a rate of 24 breaths per minute?

38. If a square has a diagonal of $7\sqrt{2}$ units long, how many units would the radius be of the largest possible circle that fits within the square (with the circle tangent to the sides of the square)?

STOP If there is still time remaining, you may review your answers.

ANSWER KEY
Practice Test 1

Section 1: Reading

1. **A**
2. **C**
3. **A**
4. **A**
5. **B**
6. **B**
7. **D**
8. **D**
9. **B**
10. **C**
11. **B**
12. **A**
13. **C**
14. **B**
15. **D**
16. **A**
17. **B**
18. **A**
19. **C**
20. **A**
21. **D**
22. **C**
23. **A**
24. **B**
25. **B**
26. **D**
27. **B**
28. **D**
29. **C**
30. **D**
31. **A**
32. **B**
33. **A**
34. **C**
35. **A**
36. **C**
37. **D**
38. **D**
39. **C**
40. **D**
41. **D**
42. **A**
43. **A**
44. **B**
45. **B**
46. **D**
47. **D**
48. **C**
49. **C**
50. **C**
51. **B**
52. **B**

Section 2: Writing and Language

1. **C**
2. **C**
3. **D**
4. **D**
5. **B**
6. **A**
7. **D**
8. **B**
9. **A**
10. **D**
11. **C**
12. **B**
13. **D**
14. **B**
15. **C**
16. **A**
17. **D**
18. **C**
19. **D**
20. **A**
21. **B**
22. **A**
23. **A**
24. **C**
25. **B**
26. **D**
27. **A**
28. **D**
29. **A**
30. **C**
31. **B**
32. **D**
33. **B**
34. **A**
35. **B**
36. **C**
37. **D**
38. **D**
39. **A**
40. **B**
41. **C**
42. **A**
43. **B**
44. **A**

ANSWER KEY
Practice Test 1

Section 3: Math (No Calculator)

1. **C**	6. **C**	11. **A**	16. **300**
2. **B**	7. **B**	12. **B**	17. **40**
3. **D**	8. **D**	13. **B**	18. **1**
4. **A**	9. **B**	14. **C**	19. **0**
5. **B**	10. **A**	15. **C**	20. **4**

Section 4: Math (Calculator)

1. **A**	11. **A**	21. **C**	31. **210**
2. **A**	12. **D**	22. **A**	32. **35**
3. **A**	13. **A**	23. **A**	33. **1**
4. **C**	14. **C**	24. **B**	34. **5**
5. **B**	15. **D**	25. **C**	35. **50**
6. **D**	16. **A**	26. **D**	36. **10**
7. **A**	17. **B**	27. **B**	37. **100**
8. **B**	18. **C**	28. **D**	38. **3.5 or $\frac{7}{2}$**
9. **C**	19. **D**	29. **A**	
10. **B**	20. **B**	30. **C**	

SAT Scoring Chart

Tally the number of correct answers from the Reading section (out of 52), the Writing and Language section (out of 44), and the combined Math without and with calculator sections (out of 58). Match these numbers of correct answers to the find the Reading Test score, the Writing and Language Test score, and the Math section score.

Number of Correct Answers on Each Test Part (Reading, Writing/Language, Combined Math Sections)	Reading Test Score	Writing and Language Test Score	Math Section Score
0	10	10	200
1	10	10	200
2	10	10	210
3	10	11	220
4	11	11	230
5	12	12	250
6	13	13	270
7	13	14	280
8	14	14	300
9	15	15	310
10	16	16	320
11	16	16	340
12	17	17	350
13	17	17	360
14	18	18	370
15	18	18	380
16	19	18	390
17	19	19	400
18	20	19	410
19	20	20	420
20	21	20	430
21	21	21	440
22	22	21	450
23	22	22	460
24	23	23	470
25	23	23	480
26	24	24	490
27	24	24	500
28	25	25	500
29	25	25	510
30	26	26	520

(Continued)

Number of Correct Answers on Each Test Part (Reading, Writing/Language, Combined Math Sections)	Reading Test Score	Writing and Language Test Score	Math Section Score
31	26	27	520
32	27	27	530
33	28	28	540
34	28	29	540
35	29	29	550
36	29	30	560
37	30	31	570
38	30	31	580
39	31	32	580
40	31	33	590
41	31	34	600
42	32	36	610
43	32	38	610
44	33	40	620
45	33		630
46	34		640
47	35		650
48	36		660
49	36		670
50	37		680
51	39		690
52	40		700
53			710
54			730
55			750
56			770
57			790
58			800

Add the Reading Test Score and the Writing and Language Test scores:

________ (Reading Score) + ________ (Writing and Language Score) =

__________ (Combined Reading and Writing and Language Score)

Then multiply the Combined Reading and Writing Language score by 10 to find your Evidence-Based Reading and Writing section score:

10 × ____________ (Combined Reading and Writing and Language Score) =

______________ **Evidence-Based Reading and Writing Score (between 200–800)**

The Math section score is also between 200–800. Get this from the table above.

_______________ **Math Section Score (between 200–800)**

Add the Evidence-Based Reading and Writing score and the Math section score to find your total SAT test score:

___________ Evidence-Based Reading and Writing Score +

___________ Math Section Score =

___________ **Total SAT Test Score (between 400–1600)**

Approximate your testing percentiles (1st–99th) using this chart:

Total Score	Section Score	Total Percentile	Evidence-Based Reading and Writing Percentile	Math Percentile
1600	800	99+	99+	99
1500	750	98	98	96
1400	700	94	94	91
1300	650	86	86	84
1200	600	74	73	75
1100	550	59	57	61
1000	500	41	40	42
900	450	25	24	27
800	400	11	11	15
700	350	3	3	5
600	300	1	1	1
500	250	1	1	1
400	200	1	1	1

Answers Explained

Section 1: Reading Test

The Last Man

1. **(A)** The passage highlights the issues that the speaker's father had throughout his life as the father sought out pleasure and acclaim. This makes choice **(A)** the best option. The passage does not heavily address work options of the sexes, spreading cultures, or speaking truth to authority figures. While those may be briefly mentioned, they cannot be described as central themes, making choices (B), (C), and (D) incorrect.

2. **(C)** In the first half of the first paragraph, the speaker discusses the "sea-surrounded nook" on which he lives. Later in the paragraph, this "nook" is revealed to be England. All of the first paragraph is a discussion of England. In discussing England, the speaker says that it "appears only as an inconsiderable spec in the immense whole; and yet, when balanced in the scale of mental power, far outweighed countries of larger extent and more numerous population." In short, he is saying that while England is small, it is disproportionately powerful. This makes **(C)** the best choice. Choice (A) is incorrect because while the geography *is* unfavorable, its influence hasn't been limited. Choice (B) is incorrect because the speaker lives in England. Choice (D) is incorrect as we have no evidence that the speaker wants to move to a better climate.

3. **(A)** In these lines, the narrator is not talking about an inheritance of money or items. Rather, he goes on in the rest of the paragraph to describe his father as a means of informing the reader of the personality or situation he inherited. This makes choice **(A)** the best option. Choice (B) is incorrect as there is no evidence of a monetary inheritance. Choice (C) is incorrect as the father is not described as self-reliant or self-disciplined, so the author would not have inherited that. Choice (D) is incorrect as we are not led to believe that this inheritance makes the speaker fortunate.

4. **(A)** In the context of the sentence, the speaker discusses the father's lack of "reason as the rudder, or judgement as the pilot." This means that the father has neither reason nor judgment as he makes his way through life. He lacks the skills necessary for self-mastery, making choice **(A)** the best option. We are not talking about a literal rudder or pilot, so choices (B) and (C) are wrong. We are talking only about being able to lead oneself, not others, so choice (D) is wrong.

5. **(B)** At the beginning of the second paragraph, the speaker says that his "fortunes have been... an exemplification of the power that mutability may possess over the varied tenor of man's life." In other words, some power other than himself does have *some* measure of control over his life. This makes choices (A) and (D) wrong as he does not have *significant control* nor *no control*. Choice (C) is also wrong since it is not the royal family that is impacting him—rather, less concrete forces like fate impact him. Choice **(B)** is the best answer as he seems to believe that he does have some control within the framework of external factors which influence him.

6. **(B)** The lines in choice **(B)**, as quoted in the previous answer's explanation, best show that mutability (changeability) does exert some control over life. Choice (A) is discussing England and creation. Choice (C) discusses the king and his influence on the speaker's father, but not the speaker. Choice (D) again is discussing the father, not the speaker.

7. **(D)** The word "evanescent" describes the popularity that is further explained throughout the paragraph. The reader learns that the father's popularity, while strong at one point, was always on the verge of slipping away. This makes choice **(D)** the best option. The popularity of the father is not respected, intimidating, or enticing, which means that choices (A), (B), and (C) incorrect.

8. **(D)** The speaker describes his father in the last paragraph saying that "gambling...which fully possessed him, made his good resolutions transient, his promises vain." This was a great barrier to success as breaking resolutions and promises is never a good way to stay popular. Choice (A) is incorrect as the father is portrayed as having many friends, even the king. Choice (B) is incorrect as the father's fashion is never discussed. Choice (C) is incorrect as we see that the father does indeed perceive the threat that the new queen of England poses to his position.

9. **(B)** Choice **(B)**, as quoted in the explanation to question 8, best shows that the speaker believes his father's greatest obstacle to be gambling. Choice (A) describes the father's early adulthood, but does not indicate that it is his greatest obstacle. Choices (C) and (D) show a single obstacle his father faced (the declining favor of the king), but does not indicate that this was a large overall issue in his life.

10. **(C)** This last sentence indicates that the father could have taken advantage of his foresight and "profited by this last calm before the storm to save himself," but the father didn't do that and instead threw himself into "the deity of pleasure." He gave in to his bad habits and thus sealed his destiny. This makes choice **(C)** the best option. Choice (A) is the opposite of what the father did. Choice (B) is incorrect as the father did have an idea of what was about to happen. Choice (D) is incorrect as we have no evidence of the father's religion.

Antibiotics

11. **(B)** In this passage, the author presents the issues that can stem from the overuse of antibiotics, both for individuals and for society as a whole. Choice (A) is incorrect: While the author does mention some side effects of antibiotics, those side effects are not the main purpose of the passage. Choices (C) and (D) are not mentioned in the passage. This only leaves choice **(B)**—the author is not speaking against *all* antibiotics, but rather the *overuse* of antibiotics.

12. **(A)** The terms "child" and "children" are used to refer to human offspring. To use this term to refer to bacterial reproduction would be to use it figuratively instead of literally. This makes choice **(A)** the best option. The author is not citing a source, nor addressing a superstition, making choices (B) and (C) incorrect. The author is not considering someone's objection to her argument, so choice (D) is incorrect.

13. **(C)** The author speaks throughout the passage of the dangers of the 0.1 percent. She discusses how those bacteria remaining when most are wiped out will grow back stronger and more resistant to antibiotics. This shows the reader that the author fears antibiotic-resistant strains of bacteria emerging as a danger to humans. This makes choice **(C)** the best option. The author does not present patients' disbelief of the efficacy of antibiotics as an issue, so choice (A) is incorrect. The author is worried that *more* bacteria like *C. diff* will emerge, so choice (B) is incorrect. The author does not seem concerned about the research of the history of antibiotics, but rather the research for the *future* of antibiotics, so choice (D) is incorrect.

14. **(B)** Choice **(B)** is the correct option as these lines best showcase the author's fear of antibiotic resistant bacteria by saying, "the biggest issue with over-prescription of antibiotics is the creation of antibiotic resistant bacteria." Choice (A) is incorrect as it mentions serious consequences but does not clarify what those consequences are. Choices (C) and (D) are wrong as they discuss the issue of *C. diff*, which is merely an example of the bigger issue the author fears.

15. **(D)** The author here is transitioning from discussing the societal consequences of antibiotic use to discussing its personal ramifications. The author uses these sentences to transition and to point out that many people may not be swayed by societal issues, but they will be swayed by things that directly impact them. The following paragraph is about those direct impacts. This makes choice **(D)** the best option. Choice (A) is incorrect as it is the exact opposite of what the author is trying to say. Choice (B) is incorrect because the author does not imply that these patients are skeptical of medical treatment, just that the individuals may take personal cost into account more than societal cost. Choice (C) is incorrect as those sentences are not discussing side effects from the doctor's perspective.

16. **(A)** In the third paragraph, the author discusses the idea that good bacteria and bad bacteria are both killed by antibiotics. This tells us that not all microorganisms (bacteria) are bad, making choice **(A)** the best option. Choice (B) is incorrect as the author says that some are helpful, so they aren't *all* dangerous. Choice (C) is incorrect as the author implies that some are bad, making them not *all* beneficial. Choice (D) is incorrect—if microorganisms were irrelevant, then we would have no need of antibiotics.

17. **(B)** Choice **(B)** is the best answer as this selection mentions to the reader that there are good bacteria in the gut alongside the bad bacteria that might need to be killed by an antibiotic. Choice (A) is incorrect as these lines mention negative consequences, but don't clarify that those consequences include killing good bacteria. Choices (C) and (D) are incorrect as these lines only talk about bad bacteria, but don't mention that there are good bacteria as well.

18. **(A)** Within the context of the sentence, the author says that "the bacteria is adapting and changing in response to our attempts to quash it." When put within the context of the passage, we can see that the attempts that are being made have the intent of eliminating *C. diff.* This makes "quash" synonymous with *eliminate*, so choice **(A)** is the best option. The other answer options are incorrect as none of the choices mean to get rid of or to eliminate.

19. **(C)** The passage talks about the issues of *C. diff* in the second half of the paragraph. The author discusses the issue of antibiotics wiping out all of the other bacteria in the human gut, leaving plenty of room and a lack of competition for resources. It is in this ideal environment that the *C. diff* population can thrive, having negative health consequences for the human host. This situation is the most similar to choice **(C)**. The controlled burn is similar to an antibiotic—the plants throughout the forest are the bacteria in the gut, and the weed that takes over is *C. diff.* The other options are incorrect as they do not include the element of the controlled burn—purposefully killing off many helpful things for one reason and accidentally creating the possibility for a bad thing to take their place.

20. **(A)** Looking at the table, you can see a general trend in the amount of time it takes for new drug resistant bacteria to emerge. As we progress through the table toward modern day, bacteria are taking less and less time to adapt to new antibiotics that are made. The most recent antibiotics in the table had drug resistant bacteria emerge within 0–1 year. This makes choice **(A)** the best option as the trend seems to indicate that bacteria can now adapt fairly quickly. The other answer options would have been true some time ago.

21. **(D)** We can see in the table that the oldest antibiotic—penicillin—has three resistant bacteria. The next oldest has two resistant bacteria. The more recent ones have only one resistant bacteria. This indicates that the longer we use an antibiotic as a society, the more types of resistant bacteria will emerge, making choice **(D)** the best option. Choice (A) is the opposite of this pattern. Choice (B) is not supported in the table, which does not discuss antibiotic popularity among healthcare professionals. Choice (C) is incorrect as the table does not discuss side effects.

Tenement Houses

22. **(C)** The message throughout the passage is that tenement houses, as they stand at the time of the writing of the passage, are dismal places to live. The author lays out the issues of lack of light and airflow and then proposes a solution: a different style of building along with monetary incentive to build the new buildings instead of the old. This problem with the solution setup best matches choice **(C)**. Choice (A) is incorrect because while the passage does mention the issue of avarice (greed for monetary gain), its discussion is not the main purpose of the passage, but merely something that contributes to the larger issues of tenements. Choice (B) is incorrect as the passage does not describe architectural trends in general, but rather one type of building. Choice (D) is incorrect as the solution will not overcome urban poverty, but rather just provide better housing for the same cost for the urban poor.

23. **(A)** The question here is asking what the earlier housing had that the later housing had less of. Notice the description of early houses in the first few sentences of the second paragraph. Those early houses are described as having "houses of moderate dimensions, lighted at the front from the street, and in the rear from the yard." This implies that there was plenty of light within these older houses. The newer houses, however, are described throughout the passage as not having enough light. This makes choice **(A)** the best answer. Choices (B) and (D) are incorrect because they both describe things that would be *more* prevalent in later houses, not less. Choice (C) is incorrect as common sense tells us that the more a house is divided to hold more people, the higher the population density would be.

24. **(B)** This sentence within the paragraph shows that the 25 × 100 foot lots were not an issue at first. Throughout the rest of the passage the reader learns how they later become an issue. Choice (A) is incorrect as the author is saying that the originally sound urban planning later became an issue. Choice (C) is incorrect as we are not shown the architect's thought process in this sentence. Choice (D) is incorrect as the lots were not originally planned for lower-class workers, but rather for the single-family homes of the wealthy.

25. **(B)** Choice **(B)** is the best option as it clearly describes the new houses as having little light. This, combined with the evidence in the second paragraph about the older houses having more light, would indicate that something that was not originally a problem later became an issue. Choice (A) is incorrect as it describes how the population has changed, but not how the houses have changed. Choice (C) is incorrect as it describes the erection of walls, not the consequences thereof: lack of light. Choice (D) is incorrect as it provides a solution to a problem, but does not show how the problem came to be.

26. **(D)** These lines show us the frustration of the author. He sees the issue with the current building plan and sees a solution, yet the issue persists. This occurs seemingly without any of the involved parties even attempting to fix it. Instead, they simply follow the status quo and continue doing what they've always done even though there is a better way to do it. This

makes choice **(D)** the best answer. Choice (A) is incorrect because while we might say that the author is angry, he is not angry at oppression, but rather at an inefficient system that isn't being changed. Choice (B) is incorrect as the author may be disgusted, but again, it's at a system of building, not at a prejudice. Choice (C) is incorrect as the author is the opposite of satisfied with the status quo.

27. **(B)** In these lines, the author points out that the buildings will be cheaper to build and have proper lighting and ventilation: higher quality at a lower price. This makes choice **(B)** the best option. Choice (A) is incorrect as the author is not discussing urban density. Choice (C) is incorrect since the author is saying that builders could save money, not spend more of it. Choice (D) is incorrect as there is no discussion of faith.

28. **(D)** Within the context of the passage, the author says that "The... evil is staring us in the face and [people] are becoming more and more alive to the... necessity for reform." Reform would be what gets rid of the evil—people are becoming alive to the need to be rid of the evil. The best substitution for "alive to" in this sentence is *aware of*. The people are becoming aware of the need for reform. This makes choice **(D)** the best option.

29. **(C)** In the last paragraph, the author asserts that building tenement houses should be made unprofitable. The author implies that this will stop the building of such houses. This leads to the conclusion that these houses are only being built for profit, which makes choice **(C)** the best answer. Choice (A) is incorrect as there is no evidence that the builders dislike their fellow man. Choice (B) is incorrect as the author indicates that tenements clearly make the city worse, not better. Choice (D) is incorrect as concern for the poor would lead to better houses being built for them.

30. **(D)** Choice **(D)** is the best option because in these lines the author shares his solution for ending the building of tenements: making them unprofitable. This leads us to the conclusion that they are only built because they are profitable. Choice (A) is incorrect as it discusses the desire to build tenement style houses, but not why the desire exists. Choice (B) is incorrect as it talks about the unchanging style of the tenements, but again, not about why they don't change. Choice (C) is incorrect because it discusses the public perception of tenement houses, but not why they are built.

31. **(A)** Repetition with writing serves to emphasize a point. When something is "desperate," it is urgent—repeating the word "desperate" makes it even more urgent, which makes choice **(A)** the best answer. Choices (B), (C), and (D) are not shown in the repetition.

Chronic Traumatic Encephalopathy

32. **(B)** This is a detail location question. The author says directly in the first paragraph that "accurate diagnosis can only be done by looking at portions of the brain under a microscope, a true CTE diagnosis can't be made until an autopsy is done on a deceased sufferer." This makes choice **(B)** the only correct option. All other options incorrectly portray the diagnosis process.

33. **(A)** The lines in choice **(A)** explain the diagnostic process for CTE, giving the answer to question 32. Choices (B), (C), and (D) do not explain how CTE is diagnosed.

34. **(C)** The author starts this sentence with the words "To be precise," which shows that her intention is to clarify something from the preceding sentence. This makes choice **(C)** the best option. This sentence does not discuss the importance of sports, so choice (A) is incorrect.

Choice (B) is incorrect since this sentence is clarifying a study, not disputing it. Choice (D) is incorrect as the author has already introduced this study: It is not a new concept.

35. **(A)** Choice **(A)** is the best answer as the italicized words function to emphasize that absolutely no blows to the head should be tolerated in youth sports, even if they don't lead to concussion. The italics do not define a term, give a source, or consider a perspective, making the other choices incorrect.

36. **(C)** The author of the passage makes it clear that only subjects who are suspected of having CTE (athletes who experienced symptoms and had a history of hits to the head) will ever be examined for CTE. This means that an athlete with memory problems (a symptom of CTE) would be the most likely candidate to undergo testing, making choice **(C)** the best answer. Choices (A) and (B) describe people who would not have a history of blows to the head, and choice (D) depicts someone who has no symptoms.

37. **(D)** This sentence points out that public knowledge may not include the selection bias that is apparent in the study of CTE. In other words, people may have heard about the dangers of CTE, but may not realize that the study being quoted is flawed in that it does not have a random sample. Choice **(D)** is the best option as the author is trying to point out the incomplete information that most people are working with. Choice (A) is the opposite of what the author is saying. Choice (B) is incorrect as people aren't completely ignorant—they're just missing some information. Choice (C) is incorrect as charitability is not mentioned in the passage.

38. **(D)** In the context here, "artificially inflated" means "built up to seem worse than it is." This makes choice **(D)** the best option as something that is exaggerated in a bad way is "built up to seem worse than it is." Choice (A) is incorrect as the author is not talking about physically inflating something like a balloon. Choice (B) is incorrect as the author is not talking about physically dilating something to make it bigger. Choice (C) is incorrect as the author is not talking about inserting air into something.

39. **(C)** In the third paragraph, Passage 1 quotes the study to show the dangers of CTE. Passage 2 shows how the study has issues in its methodology, thereby downplaying its results. This relationship is best shown in choice **(C)**. Choice (A) is incorrect as the second passage does not consider the study to be optimistic. Choice (B) is incorrect as it flips the passages around. Choice (D) is incorrect in that Passage 1 does not acknowledge that the study is imprecise.

40. **(D)** In the final paragraph, the author of Passage 2 tells us that she does not believe that sports should be drastically changed to prevent CTE. This directly contradicts the final paragraph of the first passage where the author calls for changes to sports to avoid head blows. This makes choice **(D)** the best option. The author of Passage 2 would not disagree with the quote in choice (A) (a simple explanation of what CTE is) or choice (B) (a simple explanation of how to diagnose CTE). She would also not disagree with choice (C), which is a synopsis of the study that they both reference.

41. **(D)** Choice **(D)** directly calls for changes to youth sports—something that the second author is against. The other options do not set up direct disagreement between the authors.

Family Stress Theory

42. **(A)** In the first few paragraphs of this passage, the author is giving a general history of how family stress theory evolved. In the later paragraphs, he is examining in-depth how that theory is used today. This makes choice **(A)** the best option. Choice (B) is incorrect as the

passage starts broad and then becomes more detailed. Choice (C) is incorrect because the later parts of the passage do not review alternative theories; they dive deep into one theory. Choice (D) is incorrect as there is no recommendation for further research.

43. **(A)** A knowledge of history will help you out with the context for this question. The Great Depression could be described as creating "great economic and social turmoil," so we are looking for an answer that means "great." This makes choice **(A)** the best option. Choices (B), (C), and (D) do not fit into the context or accurately describe the Great Depression.

44. **(B)** In the first paragraph, the author explains that the Great Depression was a perfect time to study family stress because most families were experiencing stress due to the poor economic conditions of the time. It would make the most sense, then, to pick an answer that would exert a similar amount of stress on families. This makes choice **(B)** the best answer. Choices (A) and (D) are incorrect as family stress would be low in such positive situations. Choice (C) is incorrect as shifting popularity of a political figure might cause some stress, but it would not stress society as a whole in the way the Great Depression did.

45. **(B)** Choice **(B)** is the best option as it is in these lines that the author states that the Great Depression made such a good environment for the study of family stress. The other answer options do not show what kind of an environment would make for the most effective study of family stress.

46. **(D)** In the second paragraph, the author describes the rollercoaster model. The author describes this model as "truncated," which means shortened, or brief. This indicates that the model was not in-depth enough to provide a proper understanding of family stress. Choice **(D)** is the best option to illustrate this overly shortened model. Choices (A) and (C) are the opposite of the intended meaning of the author. Choice (B) does not reflect the shortcomings of the rollercoaster model.

47. **(D)** In the context of the paragraph, the inclusion of how different family members feel about the stress is discussed. The ABC-X model is praised for including or incorporating each of the members' feelings. This makes choice **(D)** the best option. Choices (A), (B), and (C) do not reflect the idea that all of the feelings of the family members are being included.

48. **(C)** In the third paragraph, the author defines normative and nonnormative events. She says in part that "normative stressors... are stressors that are expected parts of life. In contrast, nonnormative stressors... are those that are not expected." This tells the reader that the main difference is whether or not the stressor can be anticipated. Thus, choice **(C)** is the best option. Their impact on people or money is not a big difference, making choices (A) and (B) incorrect. Stressors are not things that can be accurate or inaccurate, making choice (D) incorrect.

49. **(C)** The graph shows what percentage of people consider certain stressors to be positive or negative. The central bar on the graph is labeled "Moving to a New Home" and is split nearly in half. This tells us that about half of people find moving to be a positive stressor while the other half find it to be a negative stressor. This would make it difficult to predict how any given person would feel about moving. The other stressors shown on the graph all have clear majorities, which would make it much easier to predict how a person would feel about that event. This makes choice **(C)** the best option and the other choices incorrect.

50. **(C)** When looking at the graph, we can see that 90% of the surveyed families found that marriage was a positive stressor. By reading the information under the graph, we can learn that

164 families were surveyed. Choices (A) and (B) are far too low to be 90% of 164, and choice (D) would be 100%. Therefore, those answers are all incorrect, leaving choice **(C)** as the best answer.

51. **(B)** The final paragraph of the essay discusses the shortcomings of the ABC-X model. Chief among these shortcomings is the inability for the model to deal with everyday stressors. This leads to choice **(B)** as the best option. Choice (A) is incorrect since ABC-X deals with both normative and nonnormative stressors. Choice (C) is incorrect as the passage does not discuss optimism. Choice (D) is incorrect as the difference between families and single households is not discussed.

52. **(B)** Choice **(B)** points out the largest issue with the ABC-X model. "One of the major critiques is its focus on serious stressor events and inaccessibility to smaller, everyday stressors." Choices (A) simply points out that there are issues but does not name any of them specifically. Choice (C) names a smaller, less major issue. Choice (D) discusses how the model is still helpful despite the issues it has.

Section 2: Writing and Language Test

1. **(C)** The phrase "for a time" indicates that something took place for a period of time. While the other options can be used in different contexts, the only option that is idiomatically appropriate is choice **(C)**.

2. **(C)** The passage as a whole explains how Edith Wilson acted as president of the United States when Woodrow Wilson was incapacitated; choice **(C)** would therefore introduce this topic quite well. Choice (A) incorrectly states that Wilson forcibly seized power. Choice (B) incorrectly states that Edith Wilson's accomplishments are widely known. And choice (D) focuses on Woodrow Wilson instead of Edith Wilson.

3. **(D)** This option avoids the unnecessary repetition found in choices (A) and (C). Also, it uses the adjective "different" to describe "schools," unlike choice (B), which uses the noun "differences."

4. **(D)** The paragraph follows a chronological order that outlines Edith's biography. It makes sense for sentence 2, which explains the aftermath of her marriage, to come after sentence 4, which states that she married. The other sentence placements would not follow the chronological order.

5. **(B)** By saying "married, entering," there is no unnecessary wording; the subject of "pair" would carry over to "entering." Choice (C) would need a subject restated before "entered." Choices (A) and (D) are overly wordy.

6. **(A)** This option uses commas to surround a parenthetical phrase that clarifies Edith's change of last names. The other options do not surround this parenthetical phrase with commas.

7. **(D)** "Rationed" means that she would divide and distribute supplies to help with shortages as a result of the war. "Rationalized" means "to justify." "Ratioed" is not a proper word, and "radiated" refers to giving off heat or radiation.

8. **(B)** "Took" is consistent with the simple past tense verbs elsewhere in the previous sentences, like "ended," "was," and "confined." The other verbs are not in the simple past tense.

9. **(A)** The next paragraph goes into detail about Edith Wilson's thoughts about her time helping with the duties of the presidency. Choice **(A)** would most logically lead into this

discussion. Choices (B) and (C) are overly negative and are not supported by the surrounding context. And choice (D) is not supported by the information about Edith's independent decision making.

10. **(D)** "Pushing" keeps the phrase parallel with "filling" and "barring." Also, changes *to* the Cabinet makes sense since she wanted the Cabinet itself to change. The other options either do not maintain parallelism or do not use the correct preposition.

11. **(C)** The semicolon prevents a run-on sentence or comma splice; there is a complete sentence both before and after the semicolon. In addition to the key error of not breaking up two complete sentences, the other options have different problems: Choice (A) has no breaks whatsoever, choice (B) has an unnecessary comma after "standing," and choice (D) does not have an apostrophe with "Edith" to show possession.

12. **(B)** "Prospect" is a noun that means "possibility." This fits in this context since the sentence is describing the potential for students to find a job. "Prospects" is plural, which would not work since the verb "is" that is used later in the sentence would require a singular noun. "Prospective" is an adjective, and a "prospector" is someone who searches for things.

13. **(D)** "Feel" works along with the future tense to say they *will feel*; "felt" is in the past tense and would be inconsistent with the other verbs in the sentence. Also, the correct phrase is to "feel overwhelmed," i.e., that one is intimidated by all of the work one has to do. "Overwhelming" can be used to describe a situation—*my work load is overwhelming*—but not to describe how one feels.

14. **(B)** Choice **(B)** puts a comma after a dependent clause and a colon before a clarification. Choice (A) incorrectly uses the semicolon, since there is no complete sentence after the semicolon. Choice (C) also uses the semicolon incorrectly, since there is not a complete sentence before the semicolon. Choice (D) needs some sort of pause before the phrase "the career office."

15. **(C)** Choice **(C)** puts the wording in a logical sequence. The other options do not have word sequences that flow logically, making it difficult for the reader to fully grasp what is happening.

16. **(A)** "Thus" shows a cause-and-effect relationship. It would be appropriate in this context to show that in order for colleges to minimize the possibility of having graduates without jobs, the colleges should make every effort to ensure that its students find employment. Choices (B) and (D) are similar to *also*, which is not cause-and-effect, and choice (C) shows a contrast.

17. **(D)** This option correctly uses a dash to break up two complete sentences and also uses the wording "they are" to have both a pronoun and a verb. Choice (A) uses the possessive "their." Choice (B) uses the location-oriented "there," and choice (C) incorrectly uses a comma to break up two complete sentences while having no transitional word.

18. **(C)** The paragraph is focused on ways that career offices can help students prepare for job interviews. Choice **(C)** clarifies how the career office can help students who have the sorts of concerns about job interviews mentioned in the paragraph. Also, choice **(C)** would connect to the next sentence, which explains that some offices would go a step beyond merely offering mock interviews within a career office. Choices (A) and (B) do not focus on the interview aspect of the paragraph. And choice (D) contradicts the idea that many students would feel the need to seek out interview preparation assistance.

19. **(D)** The paragraph focuses on how a career office professional can assist students with editing resumes and cover letters, so choice **(D)** effectively introduces this topic. Choice (A) focuses on networking help outside of the career office. Choice (B) is too specifically focused on aspects of grammar. Choice (C) focuses on the interview instead of the resume.

20. **(A)** Choice **(A)** conveys a helpful clarification without unnecessary repetition, which is found in choices (B) and (C). Choice (D) would remove the clarification as to what type of job should or should not be included.

21. **(B)** According to the first row of values in the table, 31.2% of students used the career service office to have help with practice interviewing, and out of this group, 69.9% found the service helpful. While the other values are mentioned in the table, they do not have a corresponding number of 69.9% who found them helpful.

22. **(A)** The first part of the sentence shows how a substantial majority of students used the resume services, so in order to make a contrast, it is most helpful to show how a small percentage of students took advantage of another career service. Choice **(A)** does this since it shows that only 29.4% of students used the career skills testing service. Choices (B) and (C) show large majorities of students taking advantage of career services, and choice (D) does not set up a contrast.

23. **(A)** Focus on what will best elaborate on the origin and history of rye grain. Choice **(A)** shows that it originated in the fertile crescent and elaborates on its history by saying it was one of the earliest grains used to produce bread. Choices (B) and (D) elaborate on the history, but not the origin. Choice (C) elaborates on the origin, but not the history.

24. **(C)** "Wreak havoc" means to cause destruction and chaos. The other options use improper phrasing. Choices (A) and (B) use "wreck" instead of "wreak," and choice (D) uses the incorrect preposition "toward."

25. **(B)** "Its" correctly shows possession, with the "grain's" possession of the "natural precursor." Choice (A) is used to show "it is." Choice (C) is always incorrect. Choice (D) is plural and would be inconsistent with the singular "grain."

26. **(D)** "While" shows a contrast within the sentence between the evolutionary purpose of the ergot fungus and the inability of humans to prevent its consumption. The other options do not show a contrast.

27. **(A)** Choice **(A)** uses a comma both before and after the parenthetical phrase *like other grains,* correctly setting this clarifying phrase aside. Choice (B) does not have a comma at the end of the phrase. Choice (C) incorrectly uses the plural verb "were." And choice (D) is inconsistent in the punctuation used before and after the parenthetical phrase.

28. **(D)** Choice **(D)** matches the more analytical tone of the passage. Choices (A) and (B) are overly stuffy and formal in their choice of wording, and choice (C) is too informal.

29. **(A)** *Many* is generally used with things that can be counted, and *effects* is generally used as a noun to signify the consequence of something. *Much* is typically used for things that cannot be easily counted, like *much love,* and *affect* is typically used as a verb, like *he affected my performance.*

30. **(C)** The primary focus of the paragraph is on the effects that ergot fungus have on the human body. This sentence does not need to be inserted because it distracts from this focus, instead shifting the discussion to heart attacks. It is not choice (D) because this point has not already been made. It is not choices (A) or (B) because the insertion should not be made.

31. **(B)** Choice **(B)** correctly has a colon come after a complete sentence and before a list; also, the items in the list are all separated by commas. It is not choice (A) because a stronger form of punctuation is needed to separate "fungus" and "the Salem." It is not choice (C) because there is not separation between the listed items. And it is not choice (D) because there is no need to treat "the Salem witch trials" as a parenthetical phrase.

32. **(D)** "Hoped" is the only verb in the past tense. This matches the other past tense verbs in the paragraph. Choices (A) and (C) are present tense, and choice (B) is present perfect.

33. **(B)** The passage as a whole shows how the ergot fungus most likely was the cause of previously inexplicable actions in human history; therefore, choice **(B)** would be most effective. It is not choice (A) because there is not a focus on the governmental regulation of illegal substances. It is not choice (C) because the author does not attempt to claim that dietary choices are the primary cause of most of what has happened in human history—just certain instances. And it is not choice (D) because this sentence would not summarize the main idea of the passage.

34. **(A)** Without this phrase, the reader would not understand essential details about the city of Pompeii. It is not choice (B) because it does not explain how the city was excavated. It is not choices (C) or (D) because the selection should not be deleted.

35. **(B)** This option correctly begins the phrase with "that," maintaining parallel structure with the earlier "proclaiming that." Also, it is not overly wordy nor does it use the passive voice, like choice (C). Choices (A) and (D) use "which," making them not parallel to the earlier wording in the sentence.

36. **(C)** "Lowers" would be the most appropriate word to describe the monetary value of a neighborhood changing. "Quiets" and "muffles" are typically used with sounds, and "recedes" with erosion or physically moving away from something.

37. **(D)** Since just two questions are asked, there is no need for any punctuation to break up the sentence. All of the other options inappropriately incorporate extra punctuation.

38. **(D)** The original sentences have the cause-and-effect transition "because" between them. Choice **(D)** best shows cause-and-effect with "since" and also clarifies the subject, "graffiti," in the second part of the sentence. Choice (A) incorrectly uses "they," a plural pronoun that would not match with the singular "tends." Choice (B) is overly wordy, and choice (C) is overly vague.

39. **(A)** A semicolon successfully breaks up the two independent clauses in the sentence. Also, a conjunctive adverb like "moreover" needs a comma after it when it is used in this fashion. Choices (B) and (D) do not have a semicolon or period to break up the independent clauses, and choice (C) does not have a comma after "moreover."

40. **(B)** The previous paragraph discusses the negative aspects of graffiti, such as the costs of cleaning it up and the decline in property values. The current paragraph discusses the positive aspects of graffiti, such as giving people a nonviolent outlet to express themselves and giving them a way to create art. So, the best transition between these two paragraphs is one that shows contrast, which "On the other hand" provides. The other options do not provide a contrasting transition.

41. **(C)** "But" would help logically clarify how graffiti is not connected to criminal activity but to individual expression. The other options do not provide a transition that would give a contrast leading to this clarification.

42. **(A)** "Than" is needed to set up a comparison, unlike "then" which is used to express time. Choices (B) and (C) both use "then." Choice (D) would remove the thing to which the creation of graffiti is being compared, making the statement "less harmful outlet" miss an important clarification.

43. **(B)** The paragraph elaborates on how different cities and states will try various ways to deal with graffiti, making choice **(B)** an appropriate introduction. Choice (A) is too broadly focused on general social harmony instead of the specifics of graffiti. Choices (C) and (D) take strong positions for and against graffiti, while the remainder of the paragraph focuses on how different approaches can be suitable.

44. **(A)** There already is a cause-and-effect transition from the word "by" earlier in the sentence, so no transitional words like "therefore," "as a result," or "which causes" would be needed.

Section 3: Math Test (No Calculator)

1. **(C)** Distribute the $\frac{1}{2}x^3$ to simplify:

$$\frac{1}{2}x^3(x^2 - 4) \rightarrow$$

$$\left(\frac{1}{2}x^3\right)(x^2) + \left(\frac{1}{2}x^3\right)(-4) \rightarrow$$

$$\frac{1}{2}x^5 - 2x^3$$

2. **(B)** Two points that are easy to identify are $(-6, 0)$ and $(0, 4)$. So, take the slope using these two points.

$$slope = \frac{y_2 - y_1}{x_2 - x_1} = \frac{4 - 0}{0 - -6} = \frac{4}{6} = \frac{2}{3}$$

3. **(D)** Use elimination to solve for *a*, which is the value of *x* in this series of equations. First, eliminate the *x* by multiplying the second equation by -2 and adding it to the first equation.

$$2x - 5y = 3$$
$$x + 2y = 6 \rightarrow$$

$$2x - 5y = 3$$
$$+ \underline{-2x - 4y = -12}$$
$$0 - 9y = -9$$

Then, solve for *y*:

$$-9y = -9 \rightarrow$$
$$y = 1$$

Now, plug 1 in for *y* in one of the equations to solve for *x*. Use the second equation since it is simpler.

$$x + 2y = 6 \rightarrow x + 2(1) = 6 \rightarrow x = 4$$

4. **(A)** Distribute and simplify:

$$2(x-4)+4 \rightarrow$$
$$2x-8+4 \rightarrow$$
$$2x-4$$

5. **(B)** Manipulate the equation to get R by itself:

$$A=\frac{v^2}{R} \rightarrow A \times R=\frac{v^2 R}{R} \rightarrow A \times R=v^2 \rightarrow R=\frac{v^2}{A}$$

6. **(C)** Since this line is written in slope-intercept form, $y=mx+b$, recognize that the slope is going to be a. A line that is perpendicular to this one will have a slope that is the negative reciprocal of a: $-\frac{1}{a}$. The only option that has this as its slope is choice **(C)**.

7. **(B)** Plug in 2 for x and 17 for y, then solve for b:

$$y=bx^2+5 \rightarrow$$
$$17=b(2)^2+5 \rightarrow$$
$$17=4b+5 \rightarrow$$
$$12=4b \rightarrow$$
$$b=3$$

8. **(D)** Use x as the capacity for the smaller bag and y as the capacity for the larger bag. Set up two equations to solve. First, make an equation that expresses the capacities in terms of each other:

$$x=\frac{1}{3}y$$

Then, make an equation expressing the total capacity of the two bags:

$$x+y=80$$

Then, simplify and use substitution to solve for the capacity of the smaller bag, x:

$$x=\frac{1}{3}y \rightarrow 3x=y$$

Plug $3x$ into the second equation to solve:

$$x+y=80 \rightarrow x+3x=80 \rightarrow 4x=80 \rightarrow x=20$$

So, the capacity of the smaller bag is 20 liters.

9. **(B)** Plug 2 in for x to find the value of $f(2)$:

$$f(x)=\frac{x^3}{4}+3 \rightarrow$$
$$f(2)=\frac{2^3}{4}+3=\frac{8}{4}+3=2+3=5$$

10. **(A)** When dividing exponential expressions that have the same base, subtract the exponents from one another:

$$\frac{x^{\frac{2}{3}}}{x^{\frac{1}{6}}}=\frac{x^a}{\sqrt{x}} \rightarrow \frac{x^{\frac{4}{6}}}{x^{\frac{1}{6}}}=\frac{x^a}{\sqrt{x}} \rightarrow x^{\left(\frac{4}{6}-\frac{1}{6}\right)}=\frac{x^a}{\sqrt{x}} \rightarrow x^{\left(\frac{3}{6}\right)}=\frac{x^a}{\sqrt{x}} \rightarrow x^{\left(\frac{1}{2}\right)}=\frac{x^a}{\sqrt{x}}$$

The square root of x is equivalent to $x^{\frac{1}{2}}$. Substitute this in to the equation and simplify:

$$x^{\left(\frac{1}{2}\right)}=\frac{x^a}{\sqrt{x}} \rightarrow x^{\left(\frac{1}{2}\right)}=\frac{x^a}{x^{\left(\frac{1}{2}\right)}} \rightarrow x^{\left(\frac{1}{2}\right)}x^{\left(\frac{1}{2}\right)}=x^a \rightarrow x^1=x^a$$

So, $x=1$.

11. **(A)** $2i^2 - 3i^4 = 2(-1) - 3(1) = -2 - 3 = -5$

12. **(B)** For the equation to have infinitely many solutions, the two sides of the equation should be equivalent. Simplify the left-hand side by dividing everything on that side by 2:

$$\frac{2x-6}{2} = x + k \rightarrow$$
$$x - 3 = x + k$$

So, for the equation to have equivalent sides, the constant k must equal -3.

13. **(B)** For an absolute value equation $3 = |x - 1|$, set up two separate equations to represent both the possible positive and negative values of what is inside the absolute value symbol:

Equation 1:

$$3 = x - 1 \rightarrow x = 4$$

Equation 2:

$$-3 = x - 1 \rightarrow x = -2$$

So, there will be two solutions to the equation, 4 or -2.

14. **(C)** Since this is an isosceles triangle, the angles that are opposite the congruent sides are equivalent.

So, angle C has a measure of n.

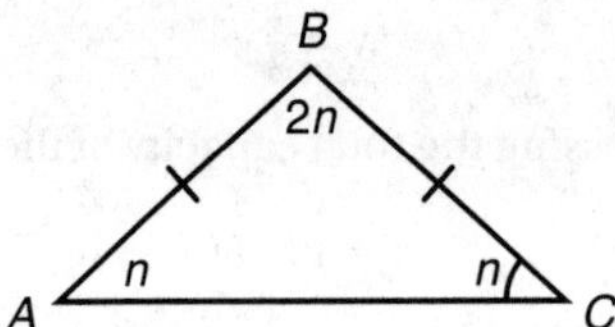

All of the internal angles in a triangle add up to 180°, so solve for n to find the measure of angle C:

$$n + n + 2n = 180 \rightarrow 4n = 180 \rightarrow n = 45$$

Thus, the measure of $\angle C$ is 45°.

15. **(C)** Choices (A) and (D) would have one solution each, and choice (B) would have infinitely many solutions. Choice **(C)** would have no solutions as you can see if the equation is simplified:

$$x = x - 3 \rightarrow$$

Subtract x from both sides $\rightarrow$

$$0 = -3$$

This is not true, so there are no solutions to this equation.

16. **300** Divide 3,000 miles by 10 hours to solve for the speed in miles per hour:

$$\frac{3{,}000 \text{ miles}}{10 \text{ hours}} = 300 \text{ miles per hour}$$

17. **40**

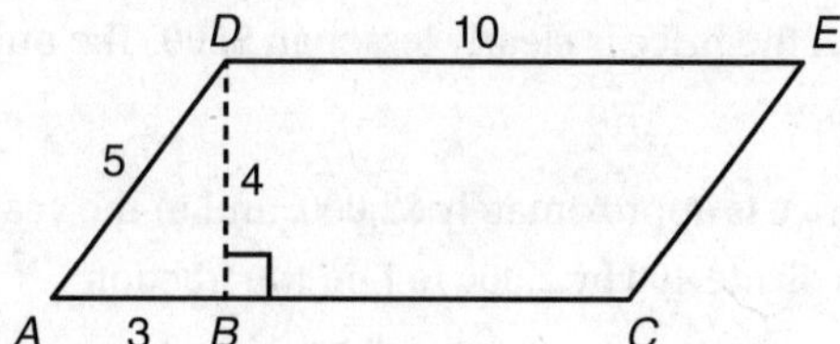

The area of a parallelogram is the base multiplied by the height. The base of the parallelogram is 10, and the height is 4 since it is part of a 3-4-5 special right triangle. Therefore, the area of the parallelogram is $4 \times 10 = 40$ square units.

18. **1** Factor the equation to solve for the possible values of x:

$$x^2 - x - 20 = 0 \rightarrow$$
$$(x + 4)(x - 5) = 0$$

The possible values of x are therefore -4 and 5 since each of these would make the entire left-hand side of the equation equal to zero. Then, add -4 and 5 to find the sum:

$$-4 + 5 = 1$$

19. **0** For the function $f(x)$ to intercept the y-axis, it must have a value of 0 for x. Here is what the function looks like when graphed:

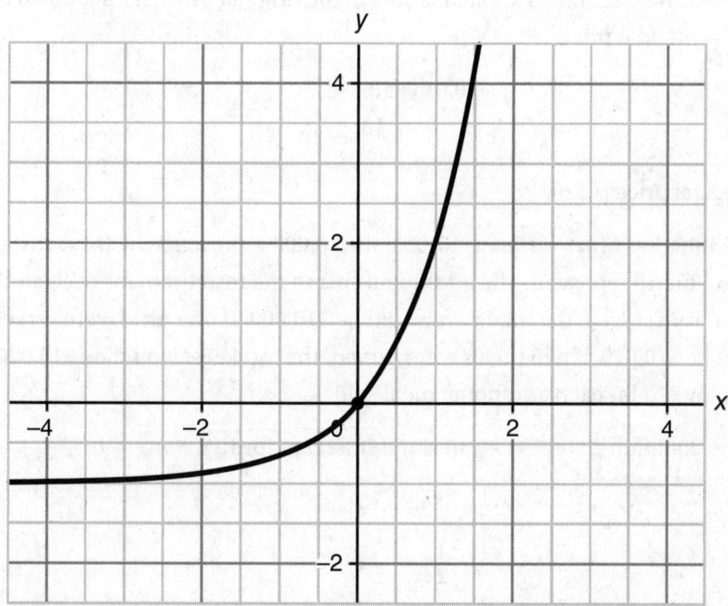

So, do not overthink this question—x simply needs to be 0 for the function to intercept the y-axis.

20. **4** The equation for a circle is $(x - h)^2 + (y - k)^2 = r^2$, in which (h, k) is the center and r is the radius. Memorize this equation because the SAT does not give it to you. The diameter of a circle is twice that of its radius. Take the square root of 49 to find the radius of circle A: $\sqrt{49} = 7$. The diameter of circle A will be twice 7: 14. Next, take the square root of 25 to find the radius of circle B: $\sqrt{25} = 5$. The diameter of circle B will be twice 5: 10. Finally, find the difference between the diameters of the two circles to arrive at the solution:

$$14 - 10 = 4$$

Section 4: Math Test (Calculator)

1. **(A)** In 1970, the value of the price is clearly less than \$500. The only option that is less than \$500 is choice (A), \$245.

2. **(A)** In 1980, the gold price is approximately \$2,000, and in the year 2000, the gold price is approximately \$400. So divide 400 by 2,000 to find the fraction:

$$\frac{400}{2,000}=\frac{1}{5}$$

3. **(A)** Since the total distance of the trail is 300 and Walter has already traveled 100 miles, he has $300-100=200$ miles remaining on his journey. Use the equation Rate $=\frac{\text{Distance}}{\text{Time}}$ to solve. He has to travel a total of 200 miles in D days, and we are solving for the m miles per day he is travelling. So, the equation will be:

$$\text{Rate}=\frac{\text{Distance}}{\text{Time}}\rightarrow$$
$$m=\frac{200}{D}$$

4. **(C)** Plug 15° in for T to solve for the corresponding speed:

$$V=331.4+0.6T\rightarrow$$
$$V=331.4+0.6(15)=340.4$$

5. **(B)** Call x the original price of the book prior to the discount. Since there was a 10% discount, the price after the discount is applied is 90% of the original price. So, set up an equation to solve for the original price:

$$0.9x=18\rightarrow$$
$$x=\frac{18}{0.9}=20$$

So, the original price is \$20.

6. **(D)** In the function $C(m)=10m+10,000$, the 10,000 represents the fixed cost to run the restaurant, and the 10 represents the additional cost to the restaurant for each additional meal. If no meals were served, the total cost would be \$10,000. If one meal were served, the total cost would be \$10,010. If two meals were served, the total cost would be \$10,020. So, the cost is going up by \$10 for each additional meal sold.

7. **(A)** Put the equation $\frac{1}{2}y+2=-x$ in slope-intercept form, $y=mx+b$:

$$\frac{1}{2}y+2=-x\rightarrow$$
$$\frac{1}{2}y=-x-2\rightarrow$$
$$y=-2x-4$$

The equation therefore has a slope of -2 and a y-intercept of -4. This corresponds to choice **(A)**, as graphed below:

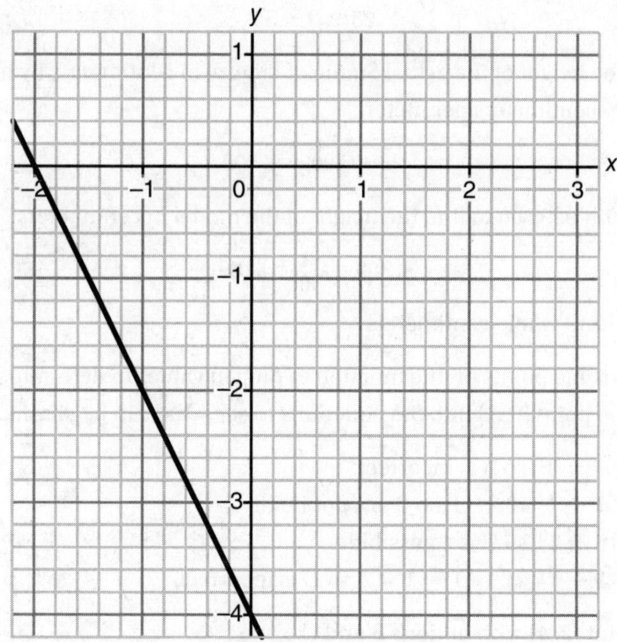

8. **(B)** Subtract the fractions from 1 (which represents the total set of voters) to find the fraction of voters who do not like either candidate:

$$1 - \frac{1}{2} - \frac{1}{3} \rightarrow$$

Put everything in terms of the least common denominator, 6:

$$\frac{6}{6} - \frac{3}{6} - \frac{2}{6} = \frac{1}{6}$$

So, the probability that a randomly selected voter will like neither candidate is $\frac{1}{6}$.

9. **(C)** Since the cashier accidentally subtracted the sales tax from the price of the meal, the new percentage will be 100% – 7% = 93%. Therefore, the price of the meal in terms of x will be $0.93x$.

10. **(B)** Use the fact that $f(2) = 8$ to find what the constant C is. According to the table, $f(2) = 2^C$. So, solve for C:

$$f(2) = 2^C \rightarrow$$
$$8 = 2^C \rightarrow$$
$$2^3 = 2^C \rightarrow$$
$$C = 3$$

Now that we know that $C = 3$, we can solve for $f(3)$:

$$f(3) = 3^C = 3^3 = 27$$

11. **(A)** Between the hours of 7 A.M. and 9 A.M., the traffic density increases from 20 vehicles per mile per lane to 40 vehicles per mile per lane. This is the largest increase in traffic density between any of the intervals.

12. **(D)** According to the graph, at 1:00 PM, the traffic density in vehicles per mile per lane is 25. So, to find the likely number of vehicles in one mile of a typical two-lane road, multiply 25 by the 2 lanes:

$$25 \times 2 = 50$$

13. **(A)** First, find the height of the actual Statue of Liberty in centimeters by multiplying 93 meters by 100 centimeters per meter:

$$93 \times 100 = 9,300$$

Then, find 1/500th of 9,300 to find the height of the model in centimeters:

$$9,300 \times \frac{1}{500} = 18.6$$

18.6 rounds up to 19 whole centimeters.

14. **(C)** Use easily visible points on the function to plug in values to determine the correct equation. First, try the point (0, 1) into the equations to see what can be eliminated.

(A) $f(x) = x^2 \rightarrow 1 \neq 0^2$, so A is incorrect.
(B) $f(x) = x^2 + 1 \rightarrow 1 = 0^2 + 1$, so B is a possibility.
(C) $f(x) = 2^x \rightarrow 1 = 2^0$, so C is a possibility.
(D) $f(x) = 3^x + 1 \rightarrow 1 = 3^0 + 1 \rightarrow 1 \neq 2$, so D is incorrect.

Now, try the point (2, 4) with options B and C:

(B) $f(x) = x^2 + 1 \rightarrow 4 \neq 2^2 + 1$, so B is incorrect.
(C) $f(x) = 2^x \rightarrow 4 = 2^2$, so **C** is correct.

15. **(D)** Convert the miles per hour to feet per second by cancelling out terms:

$$\left(X\frac{\text{miles}}{\text{hour}}\right) \times \frac{5,280 \text{ feet}}{1 \text{ mile}} \times \frac{1 \text{ hour}}{3,600 \text{ seconds}} \rightarrow$$

$$\left(X\frac{\cancel{\text{miles}}}{\cancel{\text{hour}}}\right) \times \frac{5,280 \text{ feet}}{1 \cancel{\text{mile}}} \times \frac{1 \cancel{\text{hour}}}{3,600 \text{ seconds}} \rightarrow$$

$$= X\left(\frac{5,280}{3,600}\right)$$

This corresponds to choice **(D)**.

16. **(A)** Look at the differences among the answer choices to save yourself time. We need a function that will show an exponential increase over time. In the function $I(T) = 2 \times (1.5)^T$, as T increases, $I(T)$ would also increase at an exponential rate. With all of the other options, however, as T increases, the value of $I(T)$ would consistently *decrease*. Choice (B) would involve multiplying by an ever-smaller fraction, and choices (C) and (D) would involve dividing by ever-larger numbers. So, the only logical option is choice **(A)**.

17. **(B)** $\angle X$ and $(90 - \angle X)$ are complementary angles, since they would add up to 90°. Recall that the sine of one angle is equal to the cosine of the angle that is complementary to it; similarly, the cosine of one angle is equal to the sine of the angle that is complementary to it. Thus, the sine of $(90 - \angle X)$ will simply be the same as the cosine of $\angle X$: $\frac{\sqrt{2}}{2}$.

18. **(C)** Factor the function to identify its zeros:

$$f(x) = x^2 - 3x - 4 \rightarrow (x - 4)(x + 1)$$

So, the function will intersect the x-axis at x values of 4 and −1. Therefore, there are two points at which the function will intersect the x-axis.

19. **(D)** Use the quadratic formula to approach this problem:

$$x = \frac{-b \pm \sqrt{b^2 - 4ac}}{2a}$$

If the value of $b^2 - 4ac$ is negative, there will be no real solutions to the problem since the equation would require you to take the square root of a negative number. So, see what values of b would make it such that there would be a negative value for $b^2 - 4ac$.

The equation $2x^2 + bx + 4 = 0$ is already in quadratic form, so you can identify that $a = 2$, $b = b$, and $c = 4$ for the purposes of plugging numbers in to the quadratic formula. We can just look at the value of $b^2 - 4ac$ to determine what values of b would cause there to be only a negative value of the expression.

$$b^2 - 4ac < 0 \rightarrow$$
$$b^2 - 4(2)(4) < 0 \rightarrow$$
$$b^2 - 32 < 0 \rightarrow$$
$$b^2 < 32$$

Take the square root of both sides, adjusting for the potentially negative value of b:

$$b < +\sqrt{32} \text{ or } b > -\sqrt{32} \rightarrow$$
$$\sqrt{32} = \sqrt{16 \times 2} = 4\sqrt{2} \rightarrow$$
$$b < 4\sqrt{2} \text{ or } b > -4\sqrt{2}$$

The option that expresses this range of possible values is $|b| \leq 4\sqrt{2}$, since the absolute value would account for both possible negative and positive values for b in this range.

20. **(B)** Factor the expression to determine what *would* be factors:

$$x^3 + x^2 - 20x \rightarrow$$
$$x(x^2 + x - 20) \rightarrow$$
$$x(x - 4)(x + 5)$$

So, choices (A), (C), and (D) would all be factors. Choice **(B)**, $x - 7$, would not be, so choice **(B)** is correct.

21. **(C)** Diana will need to walk an additional 4,000 steps since $10,000 - 6,000 = 4,000$. Since she walks 100 steps in a minute, determine the number of additional minutes she will need to walk by dividing 4,000 by 100:

$$\frac{4,000}{100} = 40$$

Now, convert 40 minutes to hours:

$$40 \text{ minutes} \times \frac{1 \text{ hour}}{60 \text{ minutes}} = \frac{2}{3} \text{ hour}$$

So, Diana will need to walk an additional $\frac{2}{3}$ of an hour on Tuesday.

22. **(A)** When zero months have passed in the year, the car dealership has an inventory of 60 cars—this means that the y-intercept would be 60. Since the dealership is adding 3 cars to its inventory each month, this means that the slope of the function would be 3—each month that goes by, the number of cars goes up by 3. This makes choice **(A)** the correct answer.

23. **(A)** The population of the city is decreasing exponentially, so choices (C) and (D) can be eliminated since they would model exponential increase. Choice **(A)** portrays the correct initial population of 50,000 and also correctly models a 10% decrease by multiplying by 0.9. Choice (B) has an incorrect initial population and far too great an exponential decrease.

24. **(B)** The likelihood of high-schoolers getting less than 8 hours of sleep is found by dividing the number of high school students who get less than 8 hours of sleep by the total number of high school students:

$$\frac{300}{500} = 0.6$$

Half of 0.6 is 0.3—there is therefore a 0.3 probability of the middle-schoolers having less than 8 hours of sleep. Now find what 0.3 of 400 is to determine the number of middle school students who get less than 8 hours of sleep:

$$0.3 \times 400 = 120$$

25. **(C)** The value of m is equivalent to the slope of the function. Based on the fact that $g(1) = 7$ and $g(3) = 11$, use the ordered pairs (1, 7) and (3, 11) to calculate the slope of the line:

$$slope = \frac{y_2 - y_1}{x_2 - x_1} = \frac{11 - 7}{3 - 1} = \frac{4}{2} = 2$$

So, the value of m is 2.

26. **(D)** Simplify the equation to visualize what is happening:

$$3x - 6 = 3(x - a) \rightarrow$$
$$3x - 6 = 3x - 3a$$

If the constant a is greater than 2, then $3a$ would be greater than 6. This would result in an absurd situation, since the equation would no longer express an equivalence. For example, if a were 3 (a value greater than 2), look at what happens to the equation:

$$3x - 6 = 3x - 3a \rightarrow$$
$$3x - 6 = 3x - 9 \rightarrow$$
$$-6 \neq -9$$

Thus, the equation would have no solutions if the constant a is greater than 2.

27. **(B)** The standard deviation for set A would be greater than that for set B, since in set A, the values are clustered toward greater and lesser numbers, while in set B, the values are clustered around the average. Since the standard deviation corresponds to the typical deviation from the average, it would be much greater in set A than in set B. The range would be the same from set to set, and based on estimating from the graph, the mean and median would be relatively identical from set to set.

28. **(D)** Since the median of the set is currently 6, inserting a number that is 6 or greater would not change the median of the set. For example, if we inserted 6, the new set would be {2, 3, 6, 6, 6, 7}. This would still have a median of 6. If we inserted a number greater than 6, that too would be fine. For example, if we inserted 100 in the set, the set would be {2, 3, 6, 6, 7, 100}. The median of the new set would still be 6. Therefore, the correct answer is $x \geq 6$.

29. **(A)** Use S as the number of small pizzas and L as the number of large pizzas. The total number of pizzas sold in a month must be less than 800, so one inequality will be $S + L < 800$. The parlor needs to make at least \$10,000, so calculate the total revenue from the small pizzas by multiplying each small pizza by 10, and calculate the total revenue from the large pizzas by multiplying each large pizza by 20. This total needs to be greater than 10,000. So, the second inequality will be $10S + 20L > 10,000$.

30. **(C)** Based on the definition of R_O as provided in the question, an R_O of 4.2 means that one infected person will infect 4.2 other people. Thus, to determine the number of people that will be infected by 20 people who are infected with a virus of R_O of 4.2, simply multiply 4.2 by 20:

$$4.2 \times 20 = 84$$

31. **210** Five percent of 200 is found as follows:

$$0.05 \times 200 = 10$$

Then, add 10 to 200 to find the number that would be 5% greater than 200:

$$10 + 200 = 210$$

32. **35** Call x the number of minutes for Ken's morning commute. The commute in the evening would be $x + 25$. So, add the morning and evening commute times together to equal the 95 total minutes, then solve for x:

$$x + (x + 25) = 95 \rightarrow$$
$$2x + 25 = 95 \rightarrow$$
$$2x = 70 \rightarrow$$
$$x = 35$$

So, the number of minutes for the morning commute is 35.

33. **1** Use elimination to solve for y. Multiply the top equation by -2 so you can eliminate the x values when you add the equations together:

$$-2 \times (2x - 3y = 5) \rightarrow -4x + 6y = -10$$

Then, add this equation to the second equation to eliminate the x values:

$$\begin{array}{r} -4x + 6y = -10 \\ + \ 4x + y = 17 \\ \hline 0 + 7y = 7 \end{array}$$

Then, solve for y:

$$7y = 7 \rightarrow y = 1$$

So, the value of y is equal to 1.

34. **5** Find the equation of the new line by calculating its slope—we already know that the y-intercept is 4. Take the negative reciprocal of the slope of the first line, -3, by flipping it and changing the sign.

$$-3 \rightarrow \frac{1}{3}$$

So, the equation of the new line is $y = \frac{1}{3}x + 4$. Calculate the value of a point on this line when the x value is 3 by plugging 3 in for x:

$$y = \frac{1}{3}x + 4 \rightarrow$$
$$y = \frac{1}{3}(3) + 4 \rightarrow$$
$$y = 1 + 4 = 5$$

The y value will thus be 5 for this point.

35. **50** Let x represent the number of forks and y represent the number of spoons. The first equation could be for the total number of forks and spoons:

$$x + y = 80$$

The second equation would show the ratio of forks to spoons:

$$\frac{x}{y} = \frac{5}{3}$$

Now, simplify the second equation and substitute into the first equation to solve for x.

$$\frac{x}{y} = \frac{5}{3} \rightarrow 3x = 5y \rightarrow y = 0.6x$$

Plug $0.6x$ in for y in the first equation:

$$x + y = 80 \rightarrow x + 0.6x = 80 \rightarrow 1.6x = 80 \rightarrow x = \frac{80}{1.6} = 50$$

So, there are 50 forks in the drawer.

36. **10** Let h represent the height of the triangle and let b represent the width of the base of the triangle. Express the idea that the height of the triangle is twice its width with this equation:

$$h = 2b$$

The formula to calculate the area of a triangle is $A = \frac{1}{2}bh$. Substitute 25 for the area and $\frac{h}{2} = b$ from manipulating the above equation, then solve for the height:

$$A = \frac{1}{2}bh \rightarrow 25 = \frac{1}{2}\left(\frac{h}{2}\right)h \rightarrow 25 = \frac{h^2}{4} \rightarrow 100 = h^2 \rightarrow 10 = h$$

The height is therefore 10 units.

37. **100** Since the heartbeats and breaths have a linear relationship, you can solve for the number of heartbeats per minute by noticing that the breaths go up by 3 for every increase of 10 heartbeats per minute. So, if Baahir breathes 24 breaths per minute, add $10 + 10$ to 80 to get 100 heartbeats for minute as his pulse.

38. **3.5 or $\frac{7}{2}$** In a square with a diagonal of $7\sqrt{2}$ units, the sides are 7 units long since the triangle formed by two sides and the diagonal is a 45-45-90 triangle, which would have sides in a ratio of x, x, $x\sqrt{2}$.

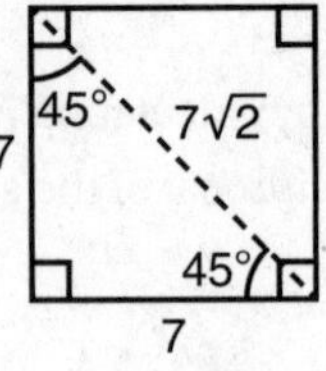

So, the largest possible circle that would fit within the square would have a diameter of 7 units, since it would go from one side to the other. Take half of 7 to find the radius: 3.5.

Answer: 3.5 or $\frac{7}{2}$

ANSWER SHEET
Practice Test 2

Section 1: Reading

1. Ⓐ Ⓑ Ⓒ Ⓓ	14. Ⓐ Ⓑ Ⓒ Ⓓ	27. Ⓐ Ⓑ Ⓒ Ⓓ	40. Ⓐ Ⓑ Ⓒ Ⓓ
2. Ⓐ Ⓑ Ⓒ Ⓓ	15. Ⓐ Ⓑ Ⓒ Ⓓ	28. Ⓐ Ⓑ Ⓒ Ⓓ	41. Ⓐ Ⓑ Ⓒ Ⓓ
3. Ⓐ Ⓑ Ⓒ Ⓓ	16. Ⓐ Ⓑ Ⓒ Ⓓ	29. Ⓐ Ⓑ Ⓒ Ⓓ	42. Ⓐ Ⓑ Ⓒ Ⓓ
4. Ⓐ Ⓑ Ⓒ Ⓓ	17. Ⓐ Ⓑ Ⓒ Ⓓ	30. Ⓐ Ⓑ Ⓒ Ⓓ	43. Ⓐ Ⓑ Ⓒ Ⓓ
5. Ⓐ Ⓑ Ⓒ Ⓓ	18. Ⓐ Ⓑ Ⓒ Ⓓ	31. Ⓐ Ⓑ Ⓒ Ⓓ	44. Ⓐ Ⓑ Ⓒ Ⓓ
6. Ⓐ Ⓑ Ⓒ Ⓓ	19. Ⓐ Ⓑ Ⓒ Ⓓ	32. Ⓐ Ⓑ Ⓒ Ⓓ	45. Ⓐ Ⓑ Ⓒ Ⓓ
7. Ⓐ Ⓑ Ⓒ Ⓓ	20. Ⓐ Ⓑ Ⓒ Ⓓ	33. Ⓐ Ⓑ Ⓒ Ⓓ	46. Ⓐ Ⓑ Ⓒ Ⓓ
8. Ⓐ Ⓑ Ⓒ Ⓓ	21. Ⓐ Ⓑ Ⓒ Ⓓ	34. Ⓐ Ⓑ Ⓒ Ⓓ	47. Ⓐ Ⓑ Ⓒ Ⓓ
9. Ⓐ Ⓑ Ⓒ Ⓓ	22. Ⓐ Ⓑ Ⓒ Ⓓ	35. Ⓐ Ⓑ Ⓒ Ⓓ	48. Ⓐ Ⓑ Ⓒ Ⓓ
10. Ⓐ Ⓑ Ⓒ Ⓓ	23. Ⓐ Ⓑ Ⓒ Ⓓ	36. Ⓐ Ⓑ Ⓒ Ⓓ	49. Ⓐ Ⓑ Ⓒ Ⓓ
11. Ⓐ Ⓑ Ⓒ Ⓓ	24. Ⓐ Ⓑ Ⓒ Ⓓ	37. Ⓐ Ⓑ Ⓒ Ⓓ	50. Ⓐ Ⓑ Ⓒ Ⓓ
12. Ⓐ Ⓑ Ⓒ Ⓓ	25. Ⓐ Ⓑ Ⓒ Ⓓ	38. Ⓐ Ⓑ Ⓒ Ⓓ	51. Ⓐ Ⓑ Ⓒ Ⓓ
13. Ⓐ Ⓑ Ⓒ Ⓓ	26. Ⓐ Ⓑ Ⓒ Ⓓ	39. Ⓐ Ⓑ Ⓒ Ⓓ	52. Ⓐ Ⓑ Ⓒ Ⓓ

Section 2: Writing and Language

1. Ⓐ Ⓑ Ⓒ Ⓓ	12. Ⓐ Ⓑ Ⓒ Ⓓ	23. Ⓐ Ⓑ Ⓒ Ⓓ	34. Ⓐ Ⓑ Ⓒ Ⓓ
2. Ⓐ Ⓑ Ⓒ Ⓓ	13. Ⓐ Ⓑ Ⓒ Ⓓ	24. Ⓐ Ⓑ Ⓒ Ⓓ	35. Ⓐ Ⓑ Ⓒ Ⓓ
3. Ⓐ Ⓑ Ⓒ Ⓓ	14. Ⓐ Ⓑ Ⓒ Ⓓ	25. Ⓐ Ⓑ Ⓒ Ⓓ	36. Ⓐ Ⓑ Ⓒ Ⓓ
4. Ⓐ Ⓑ Ⓒ Ⓓ	15. Ⓐ Ⓑ Ⓒ Ⓓ	26. Ⓐ Ⓑ Ⓒ Ⓓ	37. Ⓐ Ⓑ Ⓒ Ⓓ
5. Ⓐ Ⓑ Ⓒ Ⓓ	16. Ⓐ Ⓑ Ⓒ Ⓓ	27. Ⓐ Ⓑ Ⓒ Ⓓ	38. Ⓐ Ⓑ Ⓒ Ⓓ
6. Ⓐ Ⓑ Ⓒ Ⓓ	17. Ⓐ Ⓑ Ⓒ Ⓓ	28. Ⓐ Ⓑ Ⓒ Ⓓ	39. Ⓐ Ⓑ Ⓒ Ⓓ
7. Ⓐ Ⓑ Ⓒ Ⓓ	18. Ⓐ Ⓑ Ⓒ Ⓓ	29. Ⓐ Ⓑ Ⓒ Ⓓ	40. Ⓐ Ⓑ Ⓒ Ⓓ
8. Ⓐ Ⓑ Ⓒ Ⓓ	19. Ⓐ Ⓑ Ⓒ Ⓓ	30. Ⓐ Ⓑ Ⓒ Ⓓ	41. Ⓐ Ⓑ Ⓒ Ⓓ
9. Ⓐ Ⓑ Ⓒ Ⓓ	20. Ⓐ Ⓑ Ⓒ Ⓓ	31. Ⓐ Ⓑ Ⓒ Ⓓ	42. Ⓐ Ⓑ Ⓒ Ⓓ
10. Ⓐ Ⓑ Ⓒ Ⓓ	21. Ⓐ Ⓑ Ⓒ Ⓓ	32. Ⓐ Ⓑ Ⓒ Ⓓ	43. Ⓐ Ⓑ Ⓒ Ⓓ
11. Ⓐ Ⓑ Ⓒ Ⓓ	22. Ⓐ Ⓑ Ⓒ Ⓓ	33. Ⓐ Ⓑ Ⓒ Ⓓ	44. Ⓐ Ⓑ Ⓒ Ⓓ

ANSWER SHEET
Practice Test 2

Section 3: Math (No Calculator)

1. Ⓐ Ⓑ Ⓒ Ⓓ **5.** Ⓐ Ⓑ Ⓒ Ⓓ **9.** Ⓐ Ⓑ Ⓒ Ⓓ **13.** Ⓐ Ⓑ Ⓒ Ⓓ

2. Ⓐ Ⓑ Ⓒ Ⓓ **6.** Ⓐ Ⓑ Ⓒ Ⓓ **10.** Ⓐ Ⓑ Ⓒ Ⓓ **14.** Ⓐ Ⓑ Ⓒ Ⓓ

3. Ⓐ Ⓑ Ⓒ Ⓓ **7.** Ⓐ Ⓑ Ⓒ Ⓓ **11.** Ⓐ Ⓑ Ⓒ Ⓓ **15.** Ⓐ Ⓑ Ⓒ Ⓓ

4. Ⓐ Ⓑ Ⓒ Ⓓ **8.** Ⓐ Ⓑ Ⓒ Ⓓ **12.** Ⓐ Ⓑ Ⓒ Ⓓ

16.

17.

18.

19.

20.

ANSWER SHEET
Practice Test 2

Section 4: Math (Calculator)

1. Ⓐ Ⓑ Ⓒ Ⓓ
2. Ⓐ Ⓑ Ⓒ Ⓓ
3. Ⓐ Ⓑ Ⓒ Ⓓ
4. Ⓐ Ⓑ Ⓒ Ⓓ
5. Ⓐ Ⓑ Ⓒ Ⓓ
6. Ⓐ Ⓑ Ⓒ Ⓓ
7. Ⓐ Ⓑ Ⓒ Ⓓ
8. Ⓐ Ⓑ Ⓒ Ⓓ
9. Ⓐ Ⓑ Ⓒ Ⓓ
10. Ⓐ Ⓑ Ⓒ Ⓓ
11. Ⓐ Ⓑ Ⓒ Ⓓ
12. Ⓐ Ⓑ Ⓒ Ⓓ
13. Ⓐ Ⓑ Ⓒ Ⓓ
14. Ⓐ Ⓑ Ⓒ Ⓓ
15. Ⓐ Ⓑ Ⓒ Ⓓ
16. Ⓐ Ⓑ Ⓒ Ⓓ
17. Ⓐ Ⓑ Ⓒ Ⓓ
18. Ⓐ Ⓑ Ⓒ Ⓓ
19. Ⓐ Ⓑ Ⓒ Ⓓ
20. Ⓐ Ⓑ Ⓒ Ⓓ
21. Ⓐ Ⓑ Ⓒ Ⓓ
22. Ⓐ Ⓑ Ⓒ Ⓓ
23. Ⓐ Ⓑ Ⓒ Ⓓ
24. Ⓐ Ⓑ Ⓒ Ⓓ
25. Ⓐ Ⓑ Ⓒ Ⓓ
26. Ⓐ Ⓑ Ⓒ Ⓓ
27. Ⓐ Ⓑ Ⓒ Ⓓ
28. Ⓐ Ⓑ Ⓒ Ⓓ
29. Ⓐ Ⓑ Ⓒ Ⓓ
30. Ⓐ Ⓑ Ⓒ Ⓓ

31.

32.

33.

34.

35.

36.

37.

38.

Practice Test 2

READING PRACTICE TEST 2

65 Minutes, 52 Questions

DIRECTIONS: Each passage or pair of passages is accompanied by several questions. After reading the passage(s), choose the best answer to each question based on what is indicated explicitly or implicitly in the passage(s) or in the associated graphics.

Questions 1–10 are based on the following passage.

The following is an adaptation from The Life and Adventures of Robinson Crusoe *by Daniel Defoe. In it, the title character has left home despite his parents' wishes and sets out to find adventures on the sea.*

We worked on; but the water increasing in the hold, it was apparent that the ship would founder; and though the storm began to abate a little, yet it was not possible she could swim till we might run into any port; so the master continued firing guns for help; and a light ship, who had rid it out just ahead of us, ventured a boat out to help us and so we were saved and, partly rowing and partly driving, our boat went away to the northward, sloping towards the shore almost as far as Winterton Ness.

We were not much more than a quarter of an hour out of our ship till we saw her sink, and then I understood for the first time what was meant by a ship foundering in the sea. I could hardly watch, for from the moment that they rather put me into the boat than that I might be said to go in, my heart was, as it were, dead within me, partly with fright, partly with horror of mind, and the thoughts of what was yet before me.

We got all safe on shore, where, as unfortunate men, we were used with great humanity, as well by the magistrates of the town, who assigned us good quarters, as by particular merchants and owners of ships, and had money given us sufficient to carry us either to London or back to Hull as we thought fit.

Had I now had the sense to have gone back to Hull, and have gone home, I had been happy, and my father, had even celebrated my return; for hearing the ship I went away in was cast away in Yarmouth Roads, it was a great while before he had any assurances that I was not drowned.

But my ill fate pushed me on now with an obstinacy that nothing could resist; and though I had several times loud calls from my reason and my more composed judgment to go home, yet I had no power to do it.

My comrade, who had helped to harden me before, and who was the master's son, was now less forward than I. He asked me how I did, and telling his father who I was, and how I had come this voyage only for a trial, in order to go further abroad, his father, turning to me with a very grave and concerned tone "Young man," says he, "you ought never to go to sea anymore; you ought to take this for a plain and visible token that you are not to be a seafaring man. Perhaps this has all befallen us on your account, like Jonah in the ship of Tarshish. Pray," continues he, "what are you; and on what account did you go to sea?" Upon that I told him some of my story; at the end of which he burst out into a strange kind of passion: "What had I done," says he, "that such an unhappy wretch should come into my ship? I would not set my foot in the same ship with thee again for a thousand pounds." This indeed was, as I said, an excursion of his spirits, which were yet agitated by the sense of his loss, and was farther than he could have authority to go. However, he afterwards talked very gravely to me, exhorting me to go back to my father, and not tempt Providence to my ruin, "And, young man," said he, "depend upon it, if you do not go back, wherever you go, you will meet with nothing but disasters and disappointments, till your father's words are fulfilled upon you."

Having some money in my pocket, I travelled to London by land; and there, as well as on the road, had many struggles with myself what course of life I should take, and whether I should go home or to sea.

In this state of life, however, I remained some time, uncertain what measures to take, and what course of life to lead. An irresistible reluctance continued to going home; and as I stayed away a while, the remembrance of the distress I had been in wore off, and as that abated, the little motion I had in my desires to return wore off with it, till at last I quite laid aside the thoughts of it, and looked out for a voyage.

1. Which statement best summarizes the attitude the narrator displays regarding listening to the advice of others?

    (A) He ignores the warnings of others, choosing to instead follow his own desires.
    (B) He eagerly seeks out the seafaring wisdom of his more experienced elders.
    (C) He is more willing to listen to the suggestions of his family than those of new acquaintances.
    (D) He fails to consider the possible outcomes presented by colleagues and family.

2. As used in line 3, "abate" most closely means

    (A) intensify.
    (B) precipitate.
    (C) verify.
    (D) subside.

3. Based on the passage, the word "it" in line 7 is used to refer to

    (A) a boat.
    (B) a storm.
    (C) a ship.
    (D) a port.

4. The narrator uses the paragraph in lines 22–28 ("We got . . . thought fit") to suggest that those who experience shipwrecks are treated in what way?

    (A) With scorn
    (B) With hospitality
    (C) With envy
    (D) With humor

5. The sentence in lines 60–63 ("This indeed . . . to go") demonstrates that the narrator considers the statement in lines 56–60 ("What had . . . pounds") to be
   (A) convincing.
   (B) disingenuous.
   (C) malicious.
   (D) exaggerated.

6. After some time has passed since his shipwreck, the narrator eventually has what attitude toward future sea travels?
   (A) Despite the wreck, he is undeterred.
   (B) Due to the wreck, he has resolved to stay on land.
   (C) Given the wreck, he no longer has the financial resources for travel.
   (D) Since the wreck only partially damaged the ship, his companions are confident in his good fortune.

7. Which option gives the best evidence for the answer to the previous question?
   (A) Lines 33–35 ("it was . . . drowned")
   (B) Lines 36–37 ("But my . . . resist")
   (C) Lines 67–70 ("if you . . . upon you")
   (D) Lines 71–72 ("Having some . . . land")

8. The author of the passage primarily uses the selection in lines 47–70 ("Young man . . . upon you") to convey a sense of
   (A) compassion.
   (B) nostalgia.
   (C) foreboding.
   (D) reverence.

9. As used in line 68, the phrase "meet with" most closely means
   (A) converse.
   (B) remember.
   (C) encounter.
   (D) compete.

10. Which choice provides the best evidence that a character in the story believes in ill omens?
   (A) Lines 41–43 ("My comrade . . . than I")
   (B) Lines 48–50 ("you ought . . . man")
   (C) Lines 76–78 ("In this . . . to lead")
   (D) Lines 83–84 ("till at . . . voyage")

Questions 11–20 are based on the following passage and supplementary material.

Crop Rotation, written in 2020

Many Native American tribes had a unique way of planting crops in what today are the Northeastern and Midwestern regions of the United States. They would plant corn, climbing beans, and winter squash together on a mound of earth. The corn acted as a pole for the beans to grow on, and the vine of the squash would spread along the ground, helping to keep weeds down and preventing soil erosion. But besides the convenience of these crops helping each other in an observably physical way, and whether indigenous peoples realized it or not, planting in this manner also helped the crops and the soil chemically. Today's farmers employ a similar but much more complex system to ensure the continued fertility of soil: crop rotation.

Without crop rotation or the diversification of the plants on a given plot of land, soil quickly becomes tired. Different crops drain and replace nutrients at different rates. Any hobby gardener can tell you that planting corn in the same spot every year will, over several years, lead to poor harvests because the nitrogen will be stripped from the soil. This may be a minor annoyance for a gardener, but for a farmer, this issue could lead to the loss of livelihood. In addition to issues with nutrient depletion, continued use of a single crop can cause issues with soil erosion and weed management. Consequently, the farming industry has developed scientific methods for ensuring soil health.

In general, crop rotation is fairly simple. In one year, a nitrogen-fixing plant, like a legume, will be planted. These crops deposit nitrogen into the soil. The following year a nitrogen-depleting crop can be planted and will thrive. This process can be repeated with different crops all of which will either fix or deposit nitrogen and other nutrients into the soil. The farmer can then also work to rotate in crops that provide ground cover (to reduce weeds) and have deep roots (to reduce erosion). These effects (with the exception of erosion reduction) can also be created by applying various fertilizers and herbicides to the fields. However, that method comes with drawbacks.

While fertilizers and herbicides are very effective at providing nutrients to crops and reducing weeds, they are quite expensive not just to purchase, but also to apply. Farmers who wish to apply herbicides and fertilizers must make extra passes through their fields; this costs the farmer's time as well as wear and tear on equipment that can cost upwards of a million dollars. In addition, both fertilizer and herbicides can have negative environmental consequences in the form of runoff. Whereas a good crop rotation will keep weeds down organically and deposit nutrients into the soil, applications of fertilizer and herbicides are merely topical. When heavy rains fall after these products are applied, they can be washed away, which obviously reduces their effectiveness on the fields. Products washed off fields contain excessive amounts of nitrogen that can clog waterways and have serious negative effects on humans and wildlife. In one particularly bad example in 2014, 400,000 people in Northwest Ohio had their water supply tainted by an algae bloom which was caused in part by fertilizer runoff in Lake Erie.

Because of these negative side effects, environmentally and cost-conscious planters use more modern solutions only when absolutely necessary. Modern technology allows farmers to test soil in various parts of a field and apply topical treatments as minimally as possible only in areas where it is needed. This process allows crop rotation and soil treatment to work together. However, the drones, testing machines, and high-end equipment for GPS fertilizer applications are very expensive for the average family farm. Consequently, crop rotation remains the staple choice for everyday soil management.

Table 1

Crop	Yield (Unit/Acre)	Nitrogen Removal (Pounds/Acre)
Barley	40	30
Corn	50	35
Soybeans	30	103
Wheat	40	42
Corn Silage	15	116
Grass-Legume Hay	2	87

All data is sourced from the University of Delaware, *Nitrogen Removal by Delaware Crops*.

11. Which of the following best summarizes the passage?
    (A) Despite its many shortcomings, crop rotation is preferable to fertilization when planting crops.
    (B) Fertilization and crop rotation provide equally appealing methods of reducing pollution.
    (C) While it is more expensive to implement than other methods of soil improvement, crop rotation is ultimately the safest available option.
    (D) Because of its safety and simplicity, crop rotation represents a great way to manage crop soil.

12. The author of the passage primarily uses the phrase in lines 12–13 ("and whether . . . or not") to show that
    (A) Native Americans lacked a plan for how to grow their crops.
    (B) pesticides were an unknown technology to Native Americans.
    (C) scientific concerns outweighed agricultural concerns in earlier periods.
    (D) a way of arranging crops happened to be chemically advantageous.

13. As used in line 20, "tired" most closely means
    (A) drowsy.
    (B) depleted.
    (C) jaded.
    (D) uninspired.

14. The passage most strongly suggests that nitrogen depletion poses the greatest risk to those who are
    (A) part-time gardeners.
    (B) Native American leaders.
    (C) career farmers.
    (D) scientific researchers.

15. Which option gives the best evidence for the answer to the previous question?
    (A) Lines 1–2 ("Many . . . crops")
    (B) Lines 25–26 ("This may . . . gardener")
    (C) Lines 26–27 ("but for . . . livelihood")
    (D) Lines 30–31 ("Consequently . . . health")

16. The sentence in lines 68–72 ("In one . . . Lake Erie") mainly serves to
    (A) elaborate on a general claim made in the previous sentence.
    (B) explain the shortcomings of the crop rotation method.
    (C) describe a steady pattern in Midwestern agriculture in recent years.
    (D) underscore the decline in an agricultural method in the 21st century.

17. As used in line 85, "staple" most closely means
    (A) consumable.
    (B) fastened.
    (C) specific.
    (D) principal.

18. According to Table 1, which of the following crops would produce the least number of units if planted in the entirety of a 10-acre farm?
    (A) Barley
    (B) Soybeans
    (C) Corn Silage
    (D) Grass-Legume Hay

0 0 0

19. Based on the information in the passage and the table, in a growing season after soybeans have been planted in a field, which of these types of plants would likely be most helpful to plant to optimize the level of nutrients in a given soil sample?

    (A) Corn
    (B) Squash
    (C) Legumes
    (D) Corn silage

20. Which option gives the best evidence for the answer to the previous question?

    (A) Lines 6–7 ("The corn . . . grow on")
    (B) Lines 7–9 ("vine of . . . erosion")
    (C) Lines 14–17 ("Today's . . . rotation")
    (D) Lines 33–36 ("In one . . . the soil")

Questions 21–30 are based on the following passage.

Stress and Love: The Physiological Response to Heartbreak, written in 2020

The heart has long been considered a symbol of love. To describe a loss of love, one may be labeled as heartbroken, and when describing euphoria, one may say one's heart is full. These expressions capture the cultural significance of the heart—one of the body's most vital organs. For centuries, many have believed it contains the soul, symbolically resting in the center of the body. But from where did this significance originate? Surely, it cannot be coincidental that the heart has symbolized these traits across cultures and time.

Recent research suggests that the heart's connection to emotion is more than just symbolic, finding that it is indeed physically affected by a loss of love. Researchers have noted that individuals with recent lost loves are more likely to experience mild to severe physical discomfort in their chest. This phenomenon has come to be known as broken-heart syndrome. The idea of broken-heart syndrome is nothing new; in common language, these symptoms can be described as a heartache. Since this is a rather common occurrence in the world's population, it could explain the cultural connection between the heart and love.

But broken-heart syndrome does not only occur in cases of lost romantic love; any type of severe emotional or physical distress can trigger this physiological response. This is not surprising, as the body's response to stress is the same regardless of the stressor. When faced with stress, the body responds by releasing hormones into the bloodstream. Each hormone released into the body is meant to affect the body in a specific way. For instance, when epinephrine—also known as adrenaline—is released into the bloodstream, it causes blood vessels to shrink, thus increasing blood pressure and heart rate.

The release of stress hormones, such as adrenaline, is an adaptive trait meant to prepare the body for a "fight or flight" response when presented with a stressor. For instance, when cortisol, another stress hormone, is released, energy-containing molecules are made available to the body in preparation for sudden physical exertion. Long ago, the body may have exhibited this response when faced with a predator, preparing to run or fight to survive. Today, stressors are quite different, oftentimes lasting far longer than the seconds-long altercation between our ancestors and a sabre-tooth tiger.

When faced with extreme and prolonged stress, the brain may trigger a greater release of hormones than that to which the body is accustomed. An excess of stress hormones, such as epinephrine and cortisol, can cause extreme effects. While the exact mechanism behind broken-heart syndrome is not known, scientists believe it may be a defense mechanism to protect the heart from the excess of

stress hormones that accompany extreme psychological distress.

Physicians note that this condition often presents symptoms similar to a heart attack, but without the defining arterial blockage. Instead of plaque blocking the arteries, scientists believe surrounding muscles constrict the arteries, reducing the flow of blood to the heart and mimicking a heart attack. Unlike a heart attack, broken-heart syndrome is rarely fatal, and can even resolve itself within hours to weeks. Although patients often recover from this condition quickly, the stress that is thought to cause this condition may persist long after their so-called recovery. Unlike broken-heart syndrome, prolonged stress can have consequences on long-term heart health, resulting in heart disease, hypertension and even stroke. Such consequences exemplify the importance of psychological health, as it can significantly affect one's physical health.

The heart not only signifies love but demonstrates the interconnectedness of mental and physical health. Perhaps this connection is why it is considered the center of the soul in cultures around the world. As research expands to understand the role of hormones on heart health, perhaps the philosophical discussion of love and the heart will grow as well.

21. Based on the passage, the term "broken-heart syndrome" can best be described as

(A) an allegorical idea to express deep emotional pain.
(B) a precise term to represent a common phenomenon.
(C) an alternative to language used to designate severe heart attacks.
(D) a concept useful in analyzing an exclusively psychological event.

22. The author most likely mentions the phrases "heartbroken" and "one's heart is full" in lines 3–4 in order to

(A) connect common idioms to the ideas discussed in the passage.
(B) explain the scientific grounding behind key research terminology.
(C) share the author's personal experiences with lost love.
(D) use metaphorical language to consider objections to the argument of the passage.

23. The author uses the paragraph in lines 41–53 ("The release . . . tiger") to demonstrate that

(A) while many people no longer live in fear of wild animal attacks, they remain a concern for people in some regions.
(B) the duration of stressful events has fundamentally altered the human body's physical response to those events.
(C) humans have adapted in modern times to be able to carefully differentiate between physical and emotional stress.
(D) while the catalyst of stress may be different, the physical manifestation of the stress can remain the same.

24. As used in line 66, "presents" most closely means

(A) bestows.
(B) announces.
(C) exhibits.
(D) contributes.

25. It can be reasonably inferred from the paragraph in lines 65–83 ("Physicians . . . health") that a heart doctor could most effectively differentiate between broken-heart syndrome and a heart attack by analyzing

    (A) if there is a reduction in blood flow to the heart.
    (B) if there are long-term health impacts.
    (C) whether plaque is blocking the arteries.
    (D) whether there is the presence of physical pain.

26. Which selection from the passage provides the best evidence with respect to the mortality risk of broken-heart syndrome?

    (A) Lines 27–30 ("But broken . . . response")
    (B) Lines 50–53 ("Today . . . tiger")
    (C) Lines 71–74 ("Unlike . . . weeks")
    (D) Lines 88–91 ("As research . . . well")

27. Based on the context of the passage, scientific knowledge as to the "defense mechanism" that causes broken-heart syndrome can best be described as

    (A) definitive.
    (B) unsettled.
    (C) polarized.
    (D) paranoid.

28. The passage most strongly expresses that the relationship between physical and mental health is

    (A) disjointed.
    (B) figurative.
    (C) deferential.
    (D) interconnected.

29. Which option gives the best evidence for the answer to the previous question?

    (A) Lines 7–9 ("For centuries . . . body")
    (B) Lines 36–40 ("For instance . . . rate")
    (C) Lines 74–77 ("Although . . . recovery")
    (D) Lines 81–83 ("Such . . . health")

30. Based on the final paragraph in lines 84–91, the author would most likely agree that further research into broken-heart syndrome may be

    (A) complete.
    (B) unnecessary.
    (C) interdisciplinary.
    (D) obsolete.

Questions 31–41 are based on the following passages.

Passage 1 is adapted from a historical oration by Bishop B.W. Arnett on the occasion of the Centennial Jubilee of Freedom in Columbus, Ohio, on September 22nd, 1888. Passage 2 is adapted from a speech given by Frederick Douglass in the Congregational Church in Washington D.C. on April 16th, 1888, on the 21st anniversary of Emancipation.

Passage 1

The recognition of [former slaves] to equal rights in this country, was one of those questions that could not be got out of the way by resolutions, nor by silence; it must be met at every step of the highway . . . There was nowhere to get away from him, nor any way to get around the question asked: "Am I not a man and a brother?" The questions was propounded to all, and some would answer, others would not say a word, but pass on, only to meet the question in the church and in the state; for this last of the great battles is still going on . . . [our population] has taken an active part or a silent part in every religious, political, social conflict since the corner-stone of the national government was laid by the Father of his Country, or he

0 0 0

has been taking some part in the affairs of the nation since the pilgrims landed at Plymouth . . . in 1620. Think of it! What wonderful things he has accomplished.

He has always had a place *under* the Democratic platform. He was *in* the platform of the Whig's until 1852, when General Scott led the last charge for power and office. But, since 1856, when the Republican party was organized, he had an invitation to come *on* the platform; but the Constitution was too small for him, so they amended it and gave him three amendments, the Thirteenth, Fourteenth and Fifteenth. Thus the whites have had twelve amendments and we have had three; but the twelve were just to fit for us, and since 1870 we have been on the platform, and so, thank God, all the parties have a place on their platforms for us. Some of them have a very little place for us, but we have a place . . . When we have more houses and more land, when our bank accounts are larger, then the platform will increase and we can sit with more comfort on all of them than now. So let us get the material to enlarge the platforms of the parties in and out of power.

Passage 2

No matter what the Democratic party may say; no matter what the old master class of the South may say; no matter what the Supreme Court of the United States may say, the fact is beyond question that the loyal American people, in view of the services of [our population] in the national hour of peril, meant to make him, in good faith and according to the letter and spirit of the Constitution of the United States, a full and complete American citizen.

The amendments to the Constitution of the United States mean this, or they are a cruel, scandalous and colossal sham, and deserve to be so branded before the civilized world. What Abraham Lincoln said in respect of the United States is as true of the colored people as of the relations of those States. They cannot remain half slave and half free. You must give them all or take from them all. Until this half-and-half condition is ended, there will be just ground of complaint. You will have an aggrieved class, and this discussion will go on. Until the public schools shall cease to be caste schools in every part of our country, this discussion will go on. Until the colored man's pathway to the American ballot box, North and South, shall be as smooth and as safe as the same is for the white citizen, this discussion will go on . . . Until the courts of the country shall grant the colored man a fair trial and a just verdict, this discussion will go on. Until color shall cease to be a bar to equal participation in the offices and honors of the country, this discussion will go on . . . Until the American people shall make character, and not color, the criterion of respectability, this discussion will go on . . . In a word, until truth and humanity shall cease to be living ideas, and mankind shall sink back into moral darkness, and the world shall put evil for good, bitter for sweet, and darkness for light, this discussion will go on. Until all humane ideas and civilization shall be banished from the world, this discussion will go on.

There never was a time when this great lesson could be more easily learned than now.

31. It can be reasonably inferred that the "He" in line 21 represents those who were

(A) Civil War generals.
(B) former slaves.
(C) pilgrims.
(D) political party leaders.

32. Passage 1 most strongly suggests that after the passage of the 13th, 14th, and 15th amendments, all political parties in the United States were interested in

    (A) having former slaves serve as party leaders.
    (B) changing the religious beliefs of former slaves.
    (C) passing additional Constitutional amendments to achieve equality.
    (D) representing former slaves to at least some degree.

33. Which option gives the best evidence for the answer to the previous question?

    (A) Lines 7–12 ("Am I not . . . going on")
    (B) Lines 12–16 ("our population . . . Country")
    (C) Lines 27–30 ("but the . . . Fifteenth")
    (D) Line 33–34 ("and so . . . a place")

34. As used in line 60, the phrase "half-and-half" most closely means

    (A) discounted.
    (B) equivalent.
    (C) segregated.
    (D) populist.

35. It can reasonably be inferred that the author of Passage 2 believes that issues of racial equality should be approached with a sense of

    (A) harshness.
    (B) violence.
    (C) urgency.
    (D) intellectualism.

36. Which option gives the best evidence for the answer to the previous question?

    (A) Lines 42–43 ("No matter . . . may say")
    (B) Lines 47–51 ("in the . . . citizen")
    (C) Lines 55–58 ("What . . . States")
    (D) Lines 85–86 ("There never . . . than now")

37. As used in line 79, the phrase "sink back" most closely means

    (A) submerge.
    (B) excavate.
    (C) embed.
    (D) regress.

38. In Passage 2, the author repeats the phrase "this discussion will go on" in starting the sentences in lines 63–67 most likely to

    (A) emphasize the amount of work still needed to achieve racial justice.
    (B) showcase the most common oral traditions used in the time period.
    (C) consider objections that some readers may have to his argument.
    (D) declare his willingness to reconsider his fundamental assumptions.

39. The author of Passage 1 differs from the author of Passage 2 in his discussion of the U.S. Constitution by

    (A) treating the Amendments as a whole set.
    (B) grouping Amendments into categories.
    (C) arguing for the importance of social equality.
    (D) considering it an important governmental document.

40. When compared to the tone of Passage 1, the tone of Passage 2 is more

    (A) grateful.
    (B) celebratory.
    (C) forceful.
    (D) introspective.

41. The authors of Passage 1 and Passage 2 differ in their recommendations for solutions to the problem of racial inequality in the extent they focus on
    (A) internal and external factors with respect to former slaves.
    (B) the need for former slaves to have political rights.
    (C) gender equality as vital to social harmony.
    (D) the need for slavery to immediately end.

Questions 42–52 are based on the following passage and supplementary material.

Car Safety, written in 2020

With state-of-the-art seats, airbags, seatbelts, and other safety features, our cars are much safer today than they were at any time in the past. However, due to the way in which safety features are tested, any person who falls outside of certain demographics is at an elevated risk of serious injury. Crash test dummies are generally calibrated to measure injuries on people who fit the 50th percentile of men from a certain point in time. This means that men who are smaller or larger than average, as well as most women, are at an elevated risk for injury. While men travel more miles, engage in more risky behavior, and are therefore in more crashes and more likely to die in car accidents, in any given crash a woman is much more likely to sustain fatal and non-fatal injuries than a man is.

The issue of cars not being tested for women also shows itself in driving habits. The height of the driver's seat in most cars is placed so that an average man can sit comfortably with his feet on the pedals and hands on the wheel and still see over the wheel. When women sit in the same seat, they have a few options. They can elevate the seat so that they can see (which puts the pedals dangerously far away), they can elevate the seat and move it forward (which allows them to reach the pedals and see, but puts them far too close to the airbag), or they can leave the seat away from the airbag and the pedals (which means they struggle to see). Most women choose something in the middle which means they have lowered visibility and may struggle to park or change lanes safely, and also place themselves too close to the airbags.

These along with dozens of other small safety issues—like headrest, seatbelt, airbag placement and seat size—all add up to a 73 percent greater chance of a seatbelt-wearing woman to be seriously injured and 17 percent more likely to die in a given accident, according to Consumer Reports. The issue is car testers just don't use female dummies. A female dummy was first requested by testers in the 1980s and wasn't incorporated into tests by the National Highway Safety and Traffic Administration (NHSTA) until 2003. That female dummy is not adjusted in any way to make up for the difference in shape and composition between men and women—it is just a very scaled down model of the male dummy. In fact, it is so scaled down that it only represents the smallest five percent of women. In addition, it is only used as a passenger in testing, never as a driver. [1]

Testers seemingly refuse to admit that women aren't just short men. Female bone structure, neck strength, and tissue placement are different from those of males. Car manufacturers adjust car design for safety according to these tests, so since there isn't any data for women, there aren't any safety adjustments for women. Failing to account for the differences leads to women being twenty to thirty percent more likely to sustain injuries to the head, chest, and abdomen, forty to fifty percent more likely to be injured in the neck, fifty to sixty percent

[1]Data in paragraph pulled from article: *www.consumerreports.org/car-safety/crash-test-bias-how-male-focused-testing-puts-female-drivers-at-risk/*

more likely to suffer injury on the arms, and *seventy to eighty* percent more likely have leg injuries.

These elevated risks should not be tolerated. Car manufacturers as well as consumers should demand that the NHSTA develop dummies that represent not just men and women but a variety of sizes of men and women as well as a variety of sizes of children. In addition, safety ratings that are available to consumers should break down the safety of any given car for different demographics. A five foot four woman should be able to find data that can inform her of the safest car for *her*, not for a man who will never drive her car. Car safety has come a long way in the past thirty years; now it's time to take the next step toward keeping *all* travelers safe.

Table 1 Fatal passenger vehicle crash involvements per 100 million miles traveled by driver age and gender, 2017

	Male			Female			Total*		
Age	Crash Involvements	Miles	Rate	Crash Involvements	Miles	Rate	Crash Involvements	Miles	Rate
16-19	2,003	31,732,691,896	6.3	959	30,677,731,652	3.1	2,963	62,410,423,548	4.7
20-29	7,119	187,497,565,846	3.8	3,225	198,148,511,278	1.6	10,346	385,646,077,124	2.7
30-59	12,958	785,270,175,131	1.7	6,162	558,224,868,022	1.1	19,124	1,343,495,043,154	1.4
60-69	2,929	207,918,951,320	1.4	1,354	136,711,746,704	1.0	4,283	344,630,698,024	1.2
≥70	3,034	401,684,593,355	2.9	1,488	66,739,614,422	2.2	4,522	171,424,207,778	2.6
Total*	28,053	1,317,103,977,548	2.1	13,191	990,502,472,079	1.3	41,277	2,307,606,449,627	1.8

*Total includes other and/or unknowns

Graph source: *www.iihs.org/topics/fatality-statistics/detail/gender*

42. The main objective of the author in writing this passage is most likely to
    (A) explain the procedures used in running a car crash test.
    (B) convince readers of the need to make car safety more equitable.
    (C) suggest that automobiles should be phased out due to significant safety shortcomings.
    (D) argue that the population as a whole should have a greater tolerance for risk.

43. It is reasonable to infer from the passage that the author of the passage would argue that cars in use 50 years prior to the year the passage was written were
    (A) likely less safe.
    (B) more fuel efficient.
    (C) more likely to incorporate seat belts.
    (D) crash tested with dummies representative of different genders.

44. Which option gives the best evidence for the answer to the previous question?

(A) Lines 1–4 ("With state . . . past")
(B) Lines 10–12 ("This means . . . injury")
(C) Lines 43–47 ("A female . . . 2003")
(D) Lines 75–78 ("In addition . . . demographics")

45. The author most likely uses the phrases in parentheses in lines 25–26 in order to

(A) clarify the method whereby a seating adjustment can be made.
(B) demonstrate how car seating is ultimately gender-neutral.
(C) explain why females are safer drivers than are male drivers.
(D) show the shortcomings of possible solutions to a seating problem.

46. The passage most strongly suggests that which type of person would most likely have a typically designed car optimized for their safety?

(A) A female with above-average size
(B) A female of an average size
(C) A male with below average size
(D) A male with average size

47. Which option gives the best evidence for the answer to the previous question?

(A) Lines 4–7 ("However . . . injury")
(B) Lines 7–10 ("Crash test . . . in time")
(C) Lines 31–35 ("Most women . . . airbags")
(D) Lines 47–50 ("That female . . . women")

48. Based on the data in lines 62–69 ("Failing to . . . injuries"), which of the following would be a fair generalization if a female and a male were in the same car accident (assuming other factors like seating position and car type remain the same)?

(A) The male and female would likely have similar injury outcomes.
(B) The female would be more likely to suffer from leg injuries than the male.
(C) The male would be more likely to suffer from abdominal injuries than the female.
(D) The female would be less likely to suffer a neck injury than the male.

49. As used in line 77, "break down" most closely means

(A) analyze.
(B) disable.
(C) collapse.
(D) disintegrate.

50. According to the table, which age group generally has the safest drivers?

(A) 16–19 years old
(B) 20–29 years old
(C) 30–59 years old
(D) 60–69 years old

51. Among a group of randomly sampled males in the age group of 30–59, it would be reasonable to infer from the table that if the group collectively drove a total of one billion miles in the year 2017, there would likely be how many total car crashes among the group members?

(A) 1.4
(B) 17
(C) 425
(D) 129,580

52. Which statement would best utilize the information in the table to provide an argument against the one provided in the passage?
    (A) Given the higher crash rate of male drivers as compared to female drivers, it is understandable that car manufacturers may prioritize male crash test dummies.
    (B) Since drivers over 70 years of age are over twice as likely to get in vehicle crashes as those in their 60s, increased regulations about the maximum driver age should be implemented.
    (C) Teenage drivers are far more likely to get in car accidents than those in other age groups, so the age to earn a driver's license should be increased.
    (D) Female drivers represent the majority of miles driven in a given year, so it is critical that there be a higher priority on their safety.

STOP If there is still time remaining, you may review your answers.

WRITING AND LANGUAGE PRACTICE TEST 2

35 MINUTES, 44 QUESTIONS

DIRECTIONS: The passages below are each accompanied by several questions, some of which refer to an underlined portion in the passage, and some of which refer to the passage as a whole. For some questions, determine how the expression of ideas can be improved. For other questions, determine the best sentence structure, usage, or punctuation given the context. A passage or question may have an accompanying graphic that you will need to consider as you choose the best answer.

Choose the best answer to each question, considering what will optimize the writing quality and make the writing follow the conventions of standard written English. Some questions will have a "NO CHANGE" option that you can pick if you believe the best choice would be to leave the underlined portion as it is.

Questions 1–11 are based on the following passage.

Adaptations and Characteristics of Platypuses

❶ *Ornithorhynchus anatinus* also known as platypuses are semi-aquatic mammals that live in the Eastern region of Australia and in Tasmania. Platypuses typically live in bodies of freshwater ❷; however, they have been known to live in brackish—a combination of fresh and salt water—estuaries as well.

1. (A) NO CHANGE
   (B) *Ornithorhynchus anatinus,* also known as platypuses are semi-aquatic mammals
   (C) *Ornithorhynchus anatinus*—also known as platypuses, are semi-aquatic mammals
   (D) *Ornithorhynchus anatinus,* also known as platypuses, are semi-aquatic mammals

2. At this point, the writer is considering adding the following description.

   like rivers, wetlands, billabongs, and estuaries

   Should the writer make this addition here?
   (A) Yes, because it addresses a likely objection the reader may have.
   (B) Yes, because it clarifies the preceding term.
   (C) No, because it digresses from the primary focus of the sentence.
   (D) No, because it is unnecessarily repetitive.

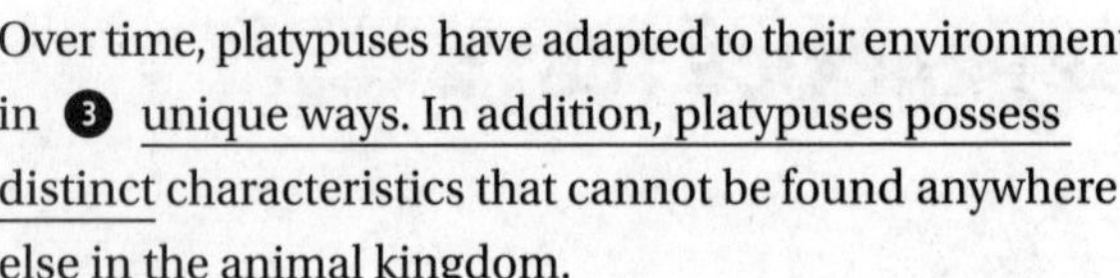

Over time, platypuses have adapted to their environment in **3** unique ways. In addition, platypuses possess distinct characteristics that cannot be found anywhere else in the animal kingdom.

Unlike most other aquatic life, platypuses **4** have adapted over time to hunt herbivorous organisms like insect larvae and crayfish. Because they live in dark and murky habitats, they must rely solely on their duck-shaped bills to find their prey. Platypuses use their bills to sense electrical fields, which enables them to find their prey; **5** platypuses have bills that feel quite smooth, almost like a piece of luxurious clothing. The electroreceptors located on the top and bottom of their bills are responsible for "track[ing] electrical signals produced by the muscular contractions of the small prey," whereas the push-rod mechanoreceptors that are located throughout the bill "detect shifts in the pressure and motion of the water."[1] While hunting, platypuses store their prey in their cheeks and break down their food using gravel or dirt from the water **6** while they have grinding plates instead of teeth.

{1} Additionally, platypuses are one of **7** the few mammals that are capable of laying eggs which is a trait that is advantageous to the survival of the organism; explaining why platypuses did not evolve to have live births like their other mammal ancestors. {2} Therefore, because the platypuses' ability to lay eggs enabled them to continue dominating aquatic environments, they did not evolve to have live births. {3} After platypuses first appeared in Australia about 100 million

3. Which choice most effectively combines the sentences at the underlined portion?
   (A) unique ways that possess distinct
   (B) unique ways, possessing distinct
   (C) unique ways; in addition, they possess distinct
   (D) unique ways which possess distinct

4. (A) NO CHANGE
   (B) has adapting
   (C) has adapted
   (D) have adapting

5. Which choice provides the most relevant and specific elaboration on the first part of the sentence?
   (A) NO CHANGE
   (B) it is impressive that platypuses can survive in the wild, given their diminutive size with weights of only around 5 pounds.
   (C) this is made possible through the stripes on their bills that consist of about 40,000 electroreceptors and 60,000 mechanoreceptors.
   (D) these majestic creatures are among the natural treasures found in the eastern part of Australia.

6. (A) NO CHANGE
   (B) whenever
   (C) but
   (D) since

7. (A) NO CHANGE
   (B) the few mammals that are capable of laying eggs: which is a trait that is advantageous to the survival of the organism explaining
   (C) the few mammals that are capable of laying eggs, which is a trait that is advantageous to the survival of the organism, explaining
   (D) the few mammals that are capable of laying eggs—which is a trait that is advantageous to the survival of the organism, explaining

[1] *www.amnh.org/explore/news-blogs/news-posts/to-hunt-the-platypus-uses-its-electric-sixth-sense*

years ago, they took over the country's **8** <u>panorama;</u> however, when marsupials appeared in Australia 54 to 71 million years ago, they became the country's dominant species everywhere but in the water. {4} **9** <u>The reasoning for why marsupials could not overtake aquatic environments is because</u> "when [marsupials] are born, they need to suckle milk constantly for weeks," and "newborn marsupials would drown if their mothers ever had to venture into the water."[2] {5} **10** <u>In addition,</u> female platypuses only have to incubate their eggs for about ten days until they hatch and feed their offspring for only three to four months. **11**

[2]*www.livescience.com/5746-odd-egg-laying-mammals-exist.html*

8. (A) NO CHANGE
   (B) perspective;
   (C) landscape;
   (D) agriculture;

9. (A) NO CHANGE
   (B) Marsupials could not overtake aquatic environments because
   (C) The reason, more or less, that marsupials could not overtake aquatic environments is due to
   (D) In order to better understand the situation, it is helpful to realize that marsupials could not overtake aquatic environments resulting from

10. (A) NO CHANGE
    (B) What is more,
    (C) As a result,
    (D) In contrast,

11. To make the paragraph most logical, sentence 2 should be placed where?
    (A) Where it currently is
    (B) Before sentence 1
    (C) After sentence 3
    (D) After sentence 5

Questions 12–22 are based on the following passage.

Careers in Engineering

To become an engineer, one should earn a bachelor's degree specializing in a field like mechanical, chemical, or electrical engineering. **12** Probably the most popular engineering major is mechanical engineering. One of the main reasons for this flexibility is that the curriculum for all major types of engineering is identical for the first two years. In the last two years of their training, much of the coursework across engineering specialties **13** are very similar, aside from a few classes that are particular to each branch of engineering. This is why engineers from one major, like chemical engineering, may end up landing jobs in fields that are more suitable for another major, **14** like mechanical or electrical engineering.

A degree in engineering is more or less an education in how to apply the scientific method, mathematics, and computer programming to solve problems or design useful objects. **15** The majority of any undergraduate engineering education is spent developing the skills needed to accomplish those goals. Specific

12. The writer wants to make the point that prospective engineering students can be flexible in determining their engineering major in college. Which choice most effectively accomplishes this goal?
    (A) NO CHANGE
    (B) Colleges offer a variety of potential majors, from ones in the sciences to ones in the humanities.
    (C) Career analysts have found that petroleum engineering is perhaps the most highly compensated major directly after graduation.
    (D) The engineering specialty for the bachelor's degree is not as important as one may expect.

13. (A) NO CHANGE
    (B) have being
    (C) were
    (D) is

14. (A) NO CHANGE
    (B) such as those in the majors of mechanical or electrical engineering.
    (C) like the possible majors of mechanical or electrical engineering.
    (D) like the ones found in mechanical and electrical engineering.

15. Which choice is the most effective version of the underlined portion?
    (A) NO CHANGE
    (B) Spending time developing the necessary skills, the majority of any undergraduate engineering education develops by these goals.
    (C) In spending time developing the needed skills to accomplish goal, the majority of any undergraduate engineering education is done by students.
    (D) The majority of any undergraduate engineering education develops the goals that skills accomplish.

disciplines focus on particular types of physical problems. (16) However, aerospace engineering is mostly concerned with optimizing the performance of airplanes, while civil engineering is mostly concerned with improving physical structures and public works. Each discipline has its own focus, but the thought process and science underlying all engineering problems are more similar than different. (17) This empowers an engineer; to think in an interdisciplinary way.

Because of the generality and flexibility in engineering, many career advisors generally recommend that students (18) do not over-specialize in their undergraduate engineering degrees. For instance, degrees in petroleum and nuclear engineering exist. However, both of these fields could be considered subdisciplines of chemical engineering, and jobs or graduate degree programs can be entered in both of these fields with a bachelor's in chemical engineering. (19) Similarly aerospace jobs, and graduate degree programs can be entered with a bachelor's in mechanical engineering. Thus, it may be advisable to earn a bachelor's in mechanical engineering, then specialize in aerospace later on.

The basic engineering degrees—mechanical, electrical, chemical, and civil—are consistently ranked in the top ten degrees in terms of (20) expenditure after graduation. As such, someone who wants to earn a high salary in a job after graduation may find an engineering degree to be a good fit. Though the long

16. (A) NO CHANGE
    (B) In addition,
    (C) For instance,
    (D) Surprisingly,

17. (A) NO CHANGE
    (B) This empowers an engineer—to think in an interdisciplinary way.
    (C) This empowers an engineer to think in an interdisciplinary way.
    (D) This empowers, an engineer, to think in an interdisciplinary way.

18. Which choice most effectively introduces the paragraph?
    (A) NO CHANGE
    (B) concentrate on the branch of engineering most likely to lead to immediate financial rewards.
    (C) opt to postpone engineering studies until graduate school.
    (D) seek out internships in a variety of fields so that they can determine their ultimate career passion.

19. (A) NO CHANGE
    (B) Similarly aerospace jobs—and graduate degree programs
    (C) Similarly, aerospace jobs and graduate degree programs;
    (D) Similarly, aerospace jobs and graduate degree programs

20. (A) NO CHANGE
    (B) compensation
    (C) enterprises
    (D) reimbursement

nights of studying to earn an engineering degree may be challenging, **21** it is still possible to change one's major to a different field should one wish to do so. In addition to the financial benefits, many graduates of engineering programs find their professional work intellectually stimulating and personally fulfilling. While there certainly are many potential careers that students may find rewarding, students with a math and science **22** aptitude should give engineering serious consideration.

21. The writer wants to emphasize the potential for engineering students to earn financial rewards for their hard work. Which choice most effectively accomplishes this goal?
    (A) NO CHANGE
    (B) the price may very be well worth it when it comes time to bargain for one's postgraduate salary.
    (C) the time in college spent developing lifelong friendships and connections will be worthwhile.
    (D) it is also important for students to have a well-rounded education so that they can effectively communicate about technical issues.

22. (A) NO CHANGE
    (B) warmth
    (C) hankering
    (D) frenzy

Questions 23–33 are based on the following passage and supplementary material.

Bystander Effect

The bystander effect is a psychological phenomenon that prevents people from helping those in need. The psychology behind this phenomenon is actually fairly simple. (23) When several people observe a situation that calls for intervention, the responsibility to help feels less pressing since it is diffused among all the observers. In a crowded place such as a stadium, people may think "I couldn't get there in time," or, "there are so many people who are closer to the scene of distress." In a situation where CPR is being administered in a public space, oftentimes no one calls medics because they assume someone else already (24) have. {1} This is psychologically very different from a situation with only one or two bystanders in which the injured person is more likely to (25) inherit assistance. {2} As an example, imagine going for a run in a fairly empty park. {3} If you were to see another jogger sitting to the side clutching her ankle, you would likely stop and offer assistance. {4} Now, (26) instead of running in your local park, imagine you're running a race with thousands of other people. {5} If you see a woman sitting on the curb holding her ankle, do you still stop? {6} There are organizers and other competitors who should call the medics; you would likely keep running. (27)

23. (A) NO CHANGE
    (B) When several people observe a situation that calls for intervention: the responsibility to help feels less pressing since it is diffused among all the observers.
    (C) When several people observe a situation that calls for intervention; the responsibility to help feels less pressing, since it is diffused among all the observers.
    (D) When several people observe a situation that calls for intervention—the responsibility to help feels—less pressing since it is diffused among all the observers.

24. (A) NO CHANGE
    (B) have had.
    (C) has.
    (D) are.

25. (A) NO CHANGE
    (B) receive
    (C) endure
    (D) extract

26. (A) NO CHANGE
    (B) unlike running through the confines of your local park,
    (C) instead of taking a run through the park that is within your city,
    (D) unlike running and jogging through your park in your town,

27. The writer wants to add the following sentence to the paragraph.

    You would be unlikely to do so.

    The sentence would be most logically placed after
    (A) sentence 1.
    (B) sentence 3.
    (C) sentence 5.
    (D) sentence 6.

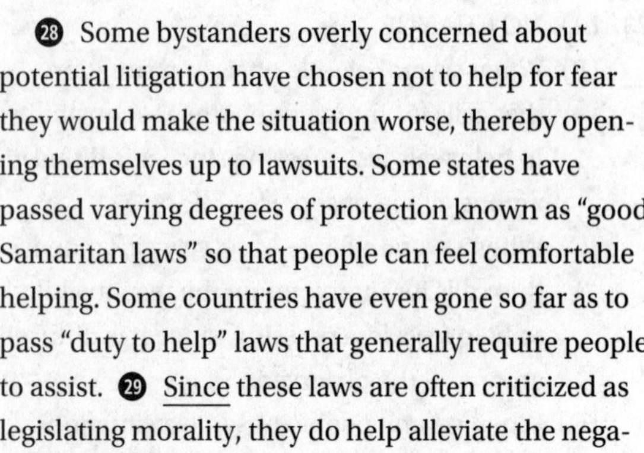

(28) Some bystanders overly concerned about potential litigation have chosen not to help for fear they would make the situation worse, thereby opening themselves up to lawsuits. Some states have passed varying degrees of protection known as "good Samaritan laws" so that people can feel comfortable helping. Some countries have even gone so far as to pass "duty to help" laws that generally require people to assist. (29) Since these laws are often criticized as legislating morality, they do help alleviate the negative (30) impacts of the bystander effect.

Education can also help end the bystander effect. (31) Young children are trained to speak up to those who are bullying others CPR training teaches

28. Which choice most effectively introduces the topic of this paragraph?
    (A) Unfortunately, most people have little interest in doing what they can to be helpful to their fellow human.
    (B) Bystanders often make excuses to justify not helping—how do we fix this problem and encourage people to do the right thing?
    (C) Bystanders have no plausible reasons as to why they would choose not to help those who are suffering.
    (D) The core motivation for deciding not to help someone is personal selfishness.

29. (A) NO CHANGE
    (B) When
    (C) If
    (D) While

30. (A) NO CHANGE
    (B) collisions
    (C) clashes
    (D) accomplishments

31. (A) NO CHANGE
    (B) Young children are trained to speak up, to those who are bullying others;
    (C) Young children are trained to speak up to those who are bullying others,
    (D) Young children are trained to speak up to those, who are bullying others:

PRACTICE TEST 2

that the person administering CPR should point to an individual and tell them to call medics (thus assigning specific responsibilities), and workplace professional development encourages people to report harassment and abuse. People should also be made aware of the positive impact of not being a bystander. According to a recent survey, (32) about 7% of respondents felt that third-party involvement helped scare off an offender, while only 0.2% of respondents felt that the involvement made the offender angrier.

Also, respondents noted that third-party involvement (33) could lead to scaring off an offender and to helping a victim escape. Through greater awareness of the bystander effect, people will understand the need to take action.

32. Which choice accurately reflects information from the tables on the following page?
    (A) NO CHANGE
    (B) about 18% of respondents felt that third-party involvement helped prevent injury, while only 1.1% of respondents felt that the involvement contributed to injury.
    (C) about 1.3% of respondents felt that third-party involvement helped the victim escape, while only 0.2% of respondents felt that the involvement contributed to additional property loss.
    (D) about 3.5% of respondents felt that third-party involvement helped protect property, while only 4.3% of respondents felt that the involvement made the offender angrier.

33. Which choice most effectively interprets information from the tables on the following page to support the main idea of the paragraph?
    (A) NO CHANGE
    (B) could cause significant property damage and injuries to victims.
    (C) could make the offender far more angry, escalating a previously calm situation.
    (D) could cause bystanders to become injured themselves.

Survey results about how third-party involvement helped or worsened the situation during the commitment of a crime.

Helpful consequence of third-party involvement	Percentage of victims who said this consequence resulted from third-party involvement in their situation
Prevented injury	18.0
Scared offender off	7.0
Victim escaped	7.7
Protected property	1.3
Protected other people	3.5
Helped other ways	12.8

Unhelpful consequence of third-party involvement	Percentage of victims who said this consequence resulted from third-party involvement in their situation
Victim injured	1.1
More property loss	0.2
Others hurt worse	0.7
Offender got away	0.2
Made offender angrier	8.7
Harmed other ways	4.3

Adapted from U.S. DOJ Bureau of Justice Statistics Special Report, 2002
https://bjs.ojp.gov/content/pub/pdf/tpivc99.pdf

PRACTICE TEST 2

Questions 34–44 are based on the following passage.

Art Restoration

When visiting museums, most people take for granted the rooms upon rooms of historic paintings, often hundreds of years old, that (34) is carefully preserved for the public's view. (35) What is not visible in these museums are the thousands of paintings that are lost to time for each one that survives. For example,

34. (A) NO CHANGE
(B) are
(C) has
(D) was

35. (A) NO CHANGE
(B) What is not visible, in these museums are the thousands, of paintings that
(C) What is not visible in these museums, are the thousands of paintings that
(D) What is, not visible in these museums are the thousands of paintings, that

a vast majority of the works from the Renaissance period about 500 years ago—even those of the most well-known painters—have been lost **36**. This, of course, makes those that survive today even more precious and worthy of careful preservation. However, despite the most careful care, many such pieces eventually become dirty and faded, making it necessary for them to be restored.

Restoration starts with a thorough inspection of the piece. The restorationist may simply observe closely but may also use x-ray and infrared imaging to see what type of fabric is in the painting's canvas, how the piece was constructed, **37** <u>the paint has absorbed into the canvas,</u> and where paint has chipped or is missing. The goal is to have a good idea of what colors were used on what layers of the painting so that that exact work can be restored, and the restorationist doesn't simply create something that on the outside looks like the old art but is actually new. **38**

39 <u>Once observations are complete; the layer of varnish on the top of the paint must be removed.</u> Varnish protects paint, but it also discolors over time, leaving paintings dull and dark. It must be

36. At this point, the writer is considering making the following addition.

    to war, fire, floods, insects, and sunlight

    Should the writer make this addition here?
    (A) Yes, because it provides specific details to elaborate on a point.
    (B) Yes, because it clarifies a term that follows.
    (C) No, because it distracts from the primary focus of the paragraph.
    (D) No, because it repeats information already stated in the paragraph.

37. (A) NO CHANGE
    (B) absorbing the paint into the canvas,
    (C) where the paint has absorbed into the canvas,
    (D) in which the canvas of the paint had been absorbing,

38. The writer is considering adding the following sentence.

    Some of the most popular colors used in Renaissance art include an extensive palette of blues, greens, browns, and yellows.

    Should the writer make this addition here?
    (A) Yes, because it provides relevant details.
    (B) Yes, because it gives a useful definition.
    (C) No, because it distracts from the focus of the paragraph.
    (D) No, because it repeats information stated elsewhere in the essay.

39. (A) NO CHANGE
    (B) Once observations are complete the layer of varnish: on the top of the paint must be removed.
    (C) Once observations are complete the layer of varnish on the top of the paint, must be removed.
    (D) Once observations are complete, the layer of varnish on the top of the paint must be removed.

removed not only to restore the painting to its original (40) brightness. In addition, it is important to gain access to any damaged paint underneath the surface that needs repair.

(41) After the varnish is removed, repair can finally begin. New varnish can be applied and, before it dries, new paint can be mixed into the varnish on damaged areas to replace damaged paint. This method (42) allowed for the old paint to be preserved under the varnish, but for the painting to have a "face lift" and look like new on the surface.

Of course, this is a very difficult job. In the past few years, more than one horribly botched painting has made the news when it was delivered back to the owner looking nothing like the original. (43) If the restorationist working on the painting is not both top-notch and very well trained in artistic techniques from the time period of the piece, the results of a restoration attempt can be disastrous. (44) Given these threats to the preservation of artistic treasures, it is greatly preferable to avoid any attempts at artistic restoration.

40. Which choice most effectively combines the sentences at the underlined portion?
   (A) brightness, and to gain
   (B) brightness, for the purpose of gaining
   (C) brightness, but also to gain
   (D) brightness, if one were to gain

41. (A) NO CHANGE
   (B) After removing the varnish, the repair can at last begin by the person.
   (C) Beginning the repair, the varnish is finally removed.
   (D) Once the repair can begin, this follows the varnish being removed.

42. (A) NO CHANGE
   (B) would of allowed
   (C) will have allowed
   (D) allows

43. (A) NO CHANGE
   (B) While
   (C) Because
   (D) Since

44. Which choice provides the most effective conclusion for the passage?
   (A) NO CHANGE
   (B) Artistic restoration is a process that can be quite costly—only those with sufficient resources to undertake the restoration should attempt it.
   (C) Artists today should continue to seek inspiration from the masterworks of Renaissance artists as they craft their own pieces.
   (D) Nevertheless, since restoration is the only way to ensure that great pieces of art remain for future generations to enjoy, it is a risk worth taking.

STOP If there is still time remaining, you may review your answers.

MATH TEST 2 (NO CALCULATOR)

25 MINUTES, 20 QUESTIONS

DIRECTIONS: For questions 1–15, solve each problem and choose the best answer from the given options. Fill in the corresponding oval on your answer document. For questions 16–20, solve the problem and fill in the answer in the answer sheet grid. Please use any space in the test booklet to work out your answers.

Notes:
- You **CANNOT** use a calculator on this section.
- All variables and expressions represent real numbers, unless indicated otherwise.
- All figures are drawn to scale, unless indicated otherwise.
- All figures are in a plane, unless indicated otherwise.
- Unless indicated otherwise, the domain of a given function is the set of all real numbers x for which the function has real values.

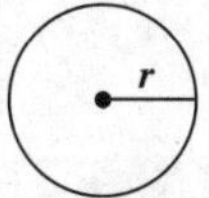

Radius of a circle $= r$
Area of a circle $= \pi r^2$
Circumference of a circle $= 2\pi r$

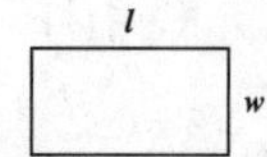

Area of a rectangle $=$ length $\times$ width $= lw$

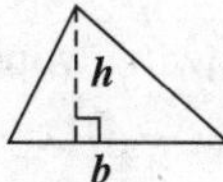

Area of a triangle $= \frac{1}{2} \times$ base $\times$ height $= \frac{1}{2}bh$

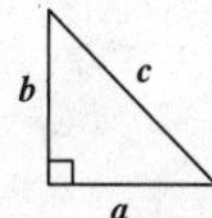

Pythagorean theorem: $a^2 + b^2 = c^2$

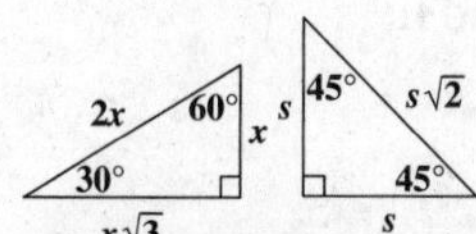

Special right triangles: 30-60-90 and 45-45-90

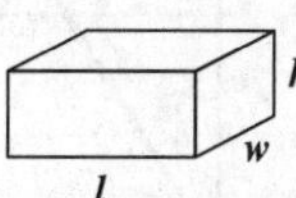

Volume of a box $=$ length $\times$ width $\times$ height $= lwh$

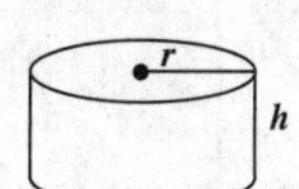

Volume of a cylinder $= \pi r^2 h$

Volume of a sphere $= \frac{4}{3}\pi r^3$

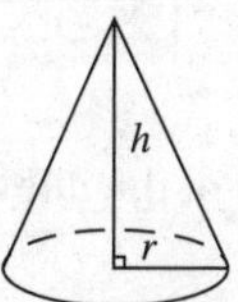

Volume of a cone $= \frac{1}{3}\pi r^2 h$

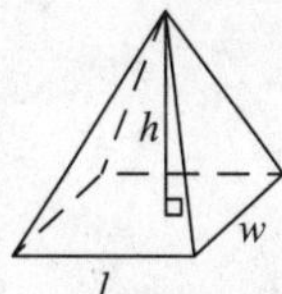

Volume of a pyramid $=$
$\frac{1}{3} \times$ length $\times$ width $\times$ height $= \frac{1}{3}$ lwh

PRACTICE TEST 2

0

0

Key Facts:

- **A circle has 360 degrees.**
- **There are 2π radians in a circle.**
- **There are 180 degrees in a triangle.**

1. What is an equivalent form of $(0.8a + 0.7b) - (1.4a - 0.3b)$?

(A) $2.2a + b$
(B) $-0.6a + b$
(C) $1.12a - .21b$
(D) $-0.6a - 0.4b$

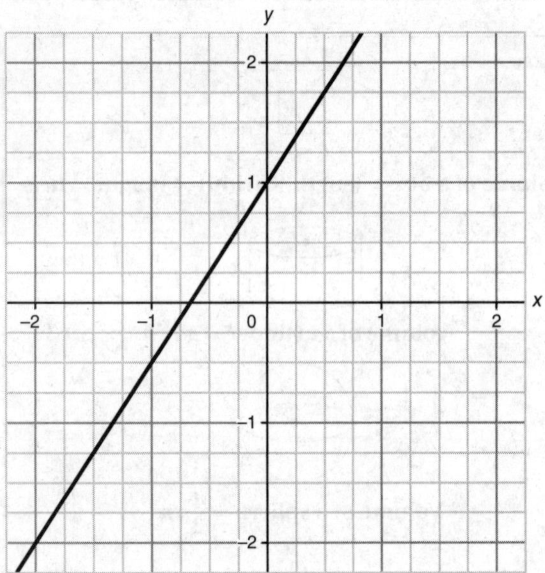

2. Based on the graph of the line above, what is its slope?

(A) $\frac{2}{3}$
(B) 1
(C) $\frac{3}{2}$
(D) $\frac{4}{3}$

3. The volume of a cylinder, v, is given by the equation $v = \pi r^2 h$, in which r is the radius of the cylinder and h is the height of the cylinder. What is the height in terms of the other variables?

(A) $h = \frac{v}{\pi r^2}$
(B) $h = \frac{\pi \sqrt{r}}{v}$
(C) $h = \frac{2\pi v}{r}$
(D) $h = \pi r^2 v$

4. If $y = x^2 - 13x + 40$ and $y = x - 9$, what is the value of x?

(A) -5
(B) -3
(C) 4
(D) 7

5. Which of these options is equivalent to the following expression?

$$(2y^2 - y) - (2y^2 + 2y)$$

(A) $4y^4 - 2y^2$
(B) $4y^2 - 2y$
(C) $-3y$
(D) $6y + 2$

6. Which of the following would be points at which the function $y = (x + 4)(x - 5)x$ intersects the x-axis?

I. $(-4, 0)$
II. $(5, 0)$
III. $(0, 0)$

(A) I only
(B) II only
(C) I and III only
(D) I, II, and III

x	f(x)
3	−1
6	0
9	1

7. For the linear function *f*, the table above shows some values of *x* and the corresponding values of *f*(*x*). Which of the following equations correctly defines the function?

(A) $f(x) = \frac{1}{3}x - 2$
(B) $f(x) = \frac{2}{3}x - 1$
(C) $f(x) = x - 6$
(D) $f(x) = 3x + 2$

8. $f(x) = kx - 3$

In the above function, when *x* is 2, $f(x) = -1$. What is the value of the constant *k*?

(A) −3
(B) 1
(C) 2
(D) 6

9. $B(h) = 1{,}000 \times 2^h$

The growth of a population of bacteria is modeled by the above function, in which $B(h)$ represents the number of bacteria after *h* hours. After how many hours will the population of bacteria be 8 times its initial number?

(A) 1 hour
(B) 2 hours
(C) 3 hours
(D) 4 hours

10. The solutions to this set of inequalities are found in which quadrant(s) of the *xy*-coordinate plane?

$$y > x + 1 \text{ and } y < -2x - 3$$

(A) Only quadrant 1
(B) Only quadrant 3
(C) Quadrants 1 and 4 only
(D) Quadrants 2 and 3 only

11. If a circle graphed in the *xy*-coordinate plane has a center at (3, 4) and intersects the origin, what is the equation of the circle?

(A) $(x - 3)^2 + (y - 4)^2 = 25$
(B) $(x + 3)^2 - (y + 4)^2 = 25$
(C) $x^2 + y^2 = 49$
(D) $x^2 + y^2 = 25$

12. When $2y^2x - 2x^2y = 60$ and the value of *x* is 3, what is the value of *y* given that *y* is positive?

(A) −6
(B) −2
(C) 1
(D) 5

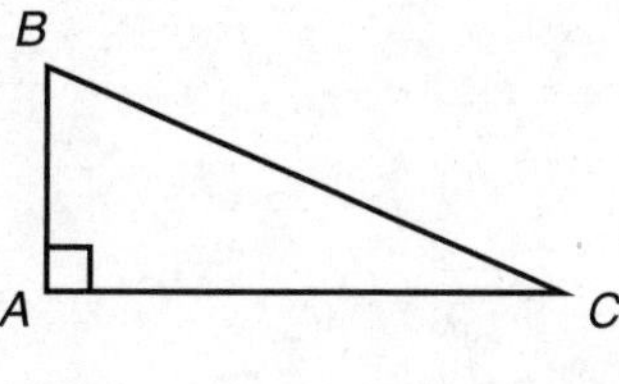

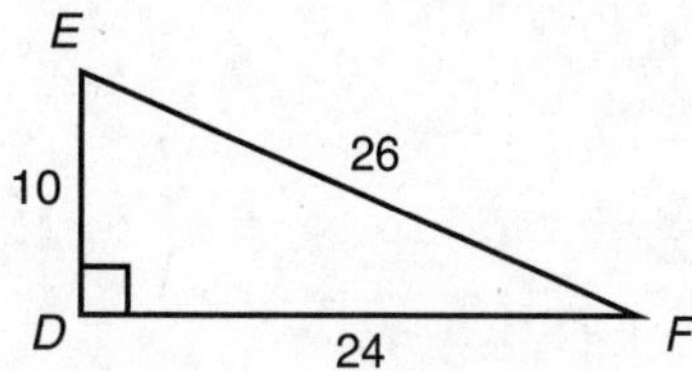

13. The above triangles *ABC* and *DEF* are similar to one another, with angle *B* corresponding to angle *E*.

What is the tangent of angle *C*?

(A) $\frac{5}{13}$
(B) $\frac{5}{12}$
(C) $\frac{10}{13}$
(D) $\frac{12}{13}$

0

14. What would be the value(s) of x that would be a solution or solutions to this equation?

$$\frac{x^2 - 4}{x - 2} = 4$$

(A) -2
(B) 2
(C) 4
(D) There are no solutions.

15. What is the vertex of a parabola with the equation $y = (x - 6)^2$?

(A) $(-6, 0)$
(B) $(0, 0)$
(C) $(6, 0)$
(D) $(0, 6)$

Student-Produced Response Directions

In questions 16–20, first solve the problem, and then enter your answer on the grid provided on the answer sheet. The instructions for entering your answers follow.

- First, write your answer in the boxes at the top of the grid.
- Second, you may grid your answer in the columns below the boxes.
- Use the fraction bar in the first row or the decimal point in the second row to enter fractions and decimals.

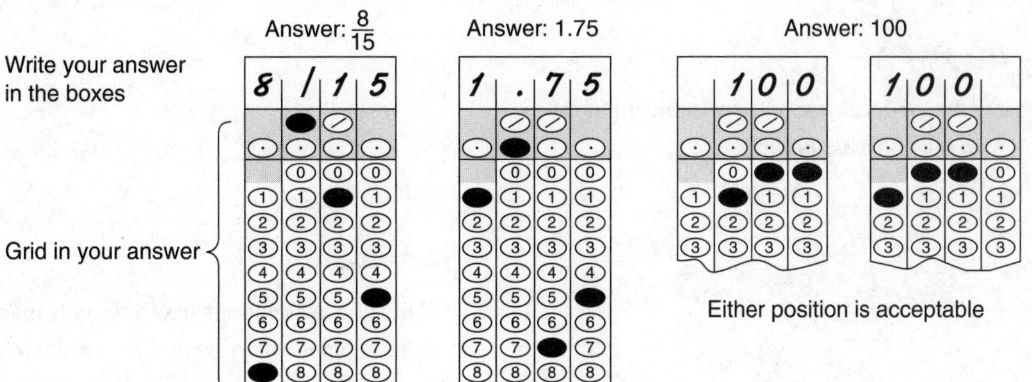

- Grid only one space in each column.
- Entering the answer in the boxes is recommended as an aid in gridding but is not required.
- The machine scoring your exam can read only what you grid, so you **must grid-in your answers correctly to get credit**.
- If a question has more than one correct answer, grid-in only one of them.
- The grid does not have a minus sign, so no answer can be negative.
- A mixed number *must* be converted to an improper fraction or a decimal before it is gridded. Enter $1\frac{1}{4}$ as $\frac{5}{4}$ or 1.25; the machine will interpret 11/4 as $\frac{11}{4}$ and mark it wrong.
- **All decimals must be entered as accurately as possible.** Here are three acceptable ways of gridding

$$\frac{3}{11} = 0.272727\ldots$$

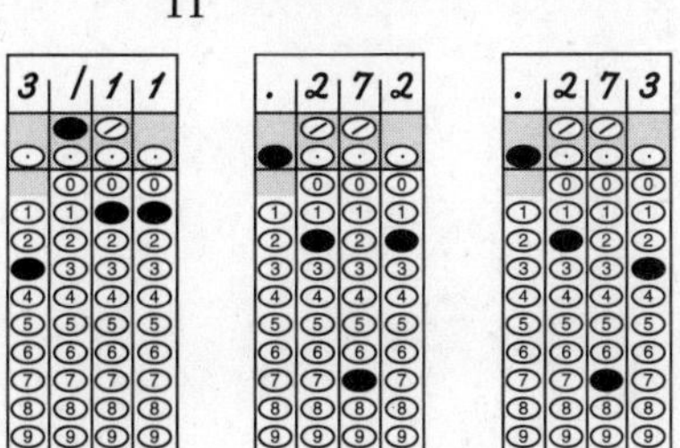

- Note that rounding to .273 is acceptable because you are using the full grid, but you would receive **no credit** for .3 or .27, because they are less accurate.

16. If $12x - 10 = 4$, what is $-5 + 6x$?

17. $y = 2x - 3$

What is the x-coordinate of the x-intercept of the line with the above equation?

18. For the function f as defined below, what is the value of $f(5)$?

$$f(x) = (x - 3)(x + 1)$$

19. On a map, 1 inch represents 3 miles in actual distance. If there is a rectangular plot of land on the map with a width of 2 inches and a length of 3 inches, what would be the actual area of the rectangular plot of land in square miles?

20. $-\frac{1}{4}x + \frac{1}{6}y = 12$

$2y = 3x + a$

If the above equations have infinitely many solutions, what is the value of the constant a?

STOP If there is still time remaining, you may review your answers.

MATH PRACTICE TEST 2 (CALCULATOR)

55 MINUTES, 38 QUESTIONS

DIRECTIONS: For questions 1–30, solve each problem and choose the best answer from the given options. Fill in the corresponding oval on your answer document. For questions 31–38, solve the problem and fill in the answer in the answer sheet grid. Please use any space in the test booklet to work out your answers.

Notes:

- You **CAN** use a calculator on this section.
- All variables and expressions represent real numbers, unless indicated otherwise.
- All figures are drawn to scale, unless indicated otherwise.
- All figures are in a plane, unless indicated otherwise.
- Unless indicated otherwise, the domain of a given function is the set of all real numbers x for which the function has real values.

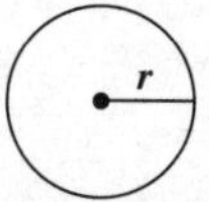

Radius of a circle = r
Area of a circle = πr^2
Circumference of a circle = $2\pi r$

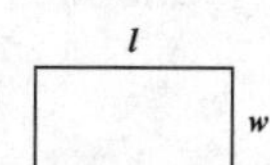

Area of a rectangle = length × width = lw

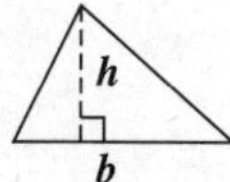

Area of a triangle = $\frac{1}{2}$ × base × height = $\frac{1}{2}bh$

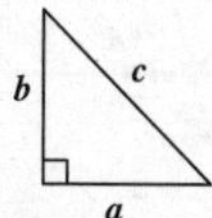

Pythagorean theorem: $a^2 + b^2 = c^2$

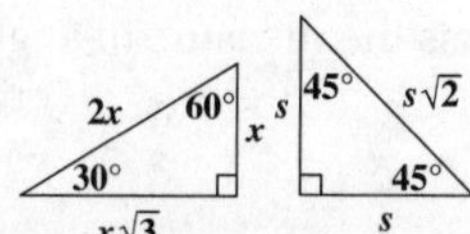

Special right triangles: 30-60-90 and 45-45-90

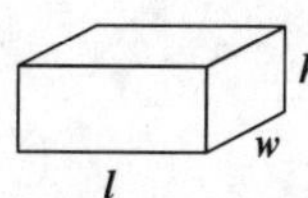

Volume of a box = length × width × height = lwh

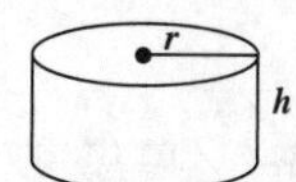

Volume of a cylinder = $\pi r^2 h$

Volume of a sphere = $\frac{4}{3}\pi r^3$

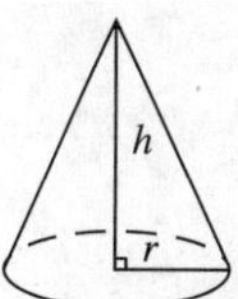

Volume of a cone = $\frac{1}{3}\pi r^2 h$

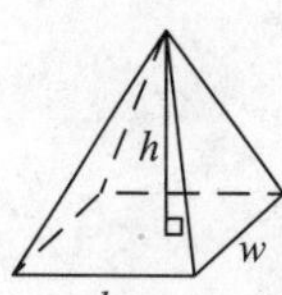

Volume of a pyramid = $\frac{1}{3}$ × length × width × height = $\frac{1}{3}$ lwh

PRACTICE TEST 2

Key Facts:

- **A circle has 360 degrees.**
- **There are 2π radians in a circle.**
- **There are 180 degrees in a triangle.**

1. Which of these is equivalent to $\sqrt[3]{a} \times a^{\frac{5}{3}}$?

   (A) $a^{\frac{2}{3}}$

   (B) $a^{\frac{4}{3}}$

   (C) a^2

   (D) a^5

2. The function g is defined by $g(x) = \frac{x^3}{2}$. What is the value of $g(-2)$?

   (A) -4

   (B) -2

   (C) -1

   (D) 4

3. The graph of $y = \frac{1}{2}x - 2$ in the xy-plane is a line. What is the y-intercept of this line?

   (A) -2.5

   (B) -2

   (C) $\frac{1}{2}$

   (D) 2

4. Voter turnout rates for different U.S. presidential elections are given in the following graph:

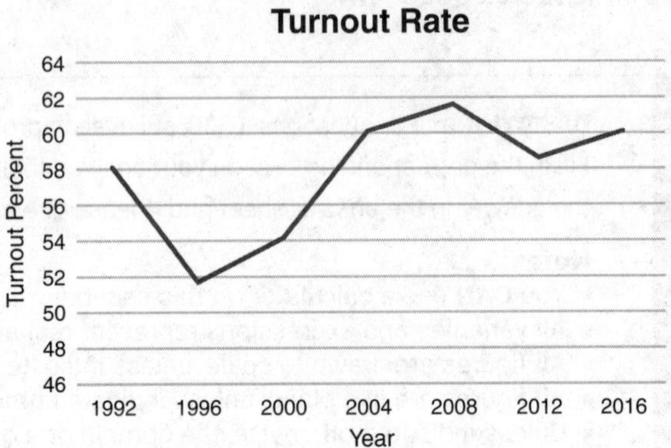

Source: *electionproject.org*

During what year was voter turnout the highest?

   (A) 1996

   (B) 2004

   (C) 2008

   (D) 2016

5. If $y = ax$, in which a is a constant, and $y = 16$ when $x = 8$, what is the value of x when y is -3?

   (A) -6

   (B) -1.5

   (C) 1

   (D) 8.5

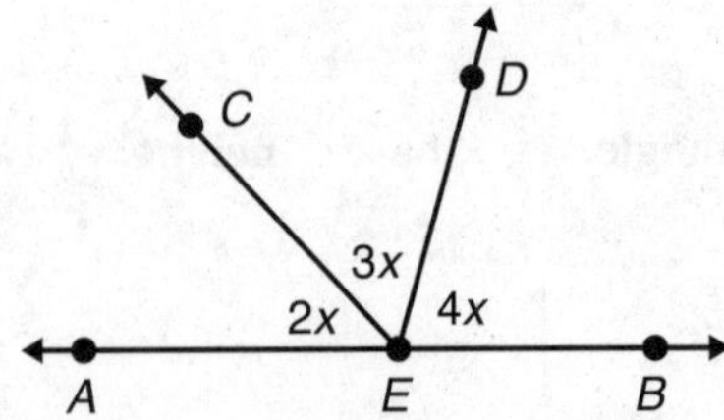

6. In the figure above, lines $\overline{AEB}$, $\overline{CE}$, and $\overline{DE}$ all intersect at point E and have measures as indicated. What is the measure of angle $\angle CED$?

   (A) 20°

   (B) 30°

   (C) 45°

   (D) 60°

7. $ax^2 + bx + c = 2x^2 + 16x + 32$

In the equation above, a, b, and c are all constants. What is the sum of a, b, and c?

(A) 48
(B) 50
(C) 52
(D) 64

8. $S(w) = 500 + 10w$

Ana receives an allowance of $10 per week. The function above shows how much money she will have in her savings account after w weeks, assuming she saves all of her allowance in the account. What does the number 500 represent in the function?

(A) The money in her account at the beginning of the time period
(B) The money in the account at the end of the time period
(C) The weekly increase in money in the account
(D) The net profit she receives after expenses

9. Samara drove her car on a 400-mile trip. If the first half of the trip took her 4 hours of driving to complete and the second half took her 6 hours of driving to complete, what was her average driving speed for the whole 400-mile trip?

(A) 20 miles per hour
(B) 35 miles per hour
(C) 40 miles per hour
(D) 80 miles per hour

	Appetizer	No Appetizer	Total
Dessert	15	35	50
No Dessert	25	25	50
Total	40	60	100

10. A restaurant tabulated 100 of its diners to record if the diner ordered an appetizer and/or a dessert with a meal. Based on the table above, what is the probability that if a diner ordered dessert, they would also order an appetizer?

(A) $\frac{1}{5}$
(B) $\frac{3}{10}$
(C) $\frac{3}{8}$
(D) $\frac{3}{7}$

11. If $y = 2x^2 - 7x$, what is a value for y when x and y are equal?

(A) -6
(B) -3
(C) 2
(D) 4

Questions 12–13 refer to the following information.

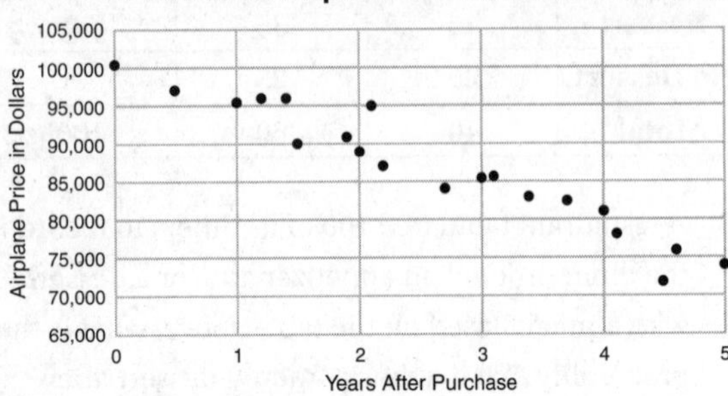

12. Based on the trend in the graph above, which of the following most closely approximates the value an airplane decreases each year?

(A) \$1,000
(B) \$2,500
(C) \$5,000
(D) \$7,500

13. If the airplane continues to decrease in value at a linear rate, at what year after purchase will the plane first closely approximate a value of zero dollars?

(A) 10 years after purchase
(B) 15 years after purchase
(C) 20 years after purchase
(D) 25 years after purchase

14. If x is increased by 400%, what is the result in terms of x?

(A) x
(B) $2x$
(C) $4x$
(D) $5x$

Total of Combined Spins	Number of Spins with That Total Value
2	1
3	2
4	2
5	4
6	5
7	6
8	7
9	4
10	3
11	4
12	2

15. Pete was playing a children's game that had a spinner with values 1–6; with each turn, he spins the spinner twice and finds the total. He tabulated the combined values of two spins from a total of 40 different turns as shown above. What fraction of all his combined spins were 6 or less?

(A) $\frac{1}{40}$
(B) $\frac{9}{40}$
(C) $\frac{13}{40}$
(D) $\frac{7}{20}$

16. Damon has a non-interest-bearing checking account that he sets up with an initial amount of \$200. Each year, he adds \$500 to the account on the first day of the year. If the function $C(y)$ represents the amount of money in the account after y years have passed since opening the account, which of the following best describes $C(y)$?

(A) An increasing linear function
(B) A decreasing linear function
(C) An increasing exponential function
(D) A decreasing exponential function

PRACTICE TEST 2

17. One hundred high school students who attended a Broadway theater performance were asked about their favorite form of live entertainment. A majority of the respondents said musical theater. What would be an accurate statement about this survey?

    (A) Over 50% of all high school students prefer musical theater.
    (B) Over 50% of the students at the high school closest to the theater where the show took place prefer musical theater.
    (C) Less than half of all high school students dislike musical theater.
    (D) The survey cannot be fairly generalized as to the entertainment preferences of all high school students.

Questions 18–19 refer to the following information.

The population of the greater metropolitan area of Mexico City is estimated to be 22,000,000 people at the end of the year 2020.

18. If the Mexico City area represented 17% of all of Mexico's population at the end of 2020, what would be the closest estimate of Mexico's total population?

    (A) 4,000,000
    (B) 26,000,000
    (C) 104,000,000
    (D) 129,000,000

19. If the population of Mexico City grows at 0.5% each year for the two years after 2020, how many additional residents will the Mexico City greater metropolitan area have at the end of 2022?

    (A) 110,000
    (B) 220,550
    (C) 1,100,000
    (D) 4,450,000

20. Susan blinks an average of 20 times per minute while awake. In the 16 hours she is awake in a day, how many times will she blink?

    (A) 320
    (B) 7,680
    (C) 12,400
    (D) 19,200

21. Troy is restocking his kitchen's inventory of coffee and tea. He would like to buy a combined total of 80 tea bags and instant coffee bags. Each tea bag costs \$0.50, and each instant coffee bag costs \$0.75. If Troy has a budget of \$55, which system of equations would represent the number of tea bags, T, and instant coffee bags, C, that he ordered?

    (A) $T + C = 80$
    $.50T + .75C = 55$

    (B) $.50T + .75C = 80$
    $T + C = 55$

    (C) $80T + 55C = 0.5$
    $T + C = 0.75$

    (D) $T - C = 80$
    $1.25(T + C) = 55$

Questions 22–23 refer to the following information.

Hugo's \$3,000 monthly budget is broken down in this table:

Rent	\$800
Car expenses	\$400
Student loans	\$300
Savings	\$250
Food	\$450
Utilities	\$250
Clothing	\$150
Miscellaneous	\$400

22. What fraction of Hugo's total budget is spent on clothing?

(A) $\frac{1}{20}$

(B) $\frac{1}{12}$

(C) $\frac{1}{10}$

(D) $\frac{1}{6}$

23. Hugo is trying to allocate more money into savings. If he cut his allocation toward miscellaneous expenses by half and allocated this amount to savings, by what percentage would his monthly savings increase?

(A) 20%

(B) 50%

(C) 65%

(D) 80%

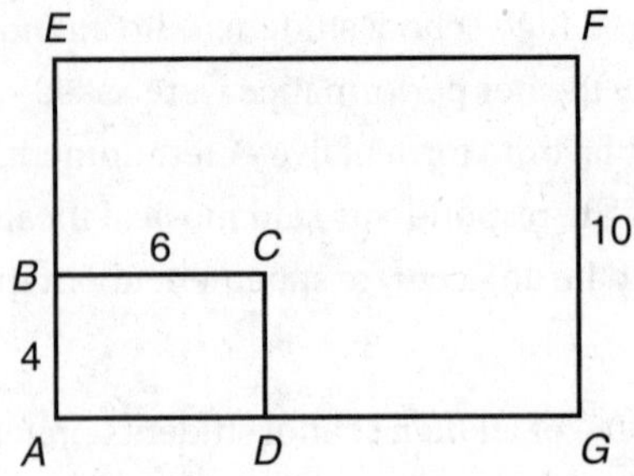

24. In the figure above, *ABCD* and *AEFG* are similar rectangles. If $\overline{AB}$ is 4 units long, $\overline{BC}$ is 6 units long, and $\overline{FG}$ is 10 units long, what is the perimeter of rectangle *AEFG*?

(A) 24 units

(B) 48 units

(C) 50 units

(D) 72 units

25. How many zeros will a line with the equation $y = k$ have in which k is a constant greater than zero?

(A) Zero

(B) One

(C) Two

(D) Cannot be determined from the given information

26. Out of all the 44 people to serve as president of the United States before the year 2020, 14 of them had previously been vice president of the United States. Which function expresses the relationship between the number of presidents, *P*, and vice presidents who became presidents, *V*?

(A) $V = 14P$

(B) $V = \frac{7}{22}P$

(C) $V = \frac{1}{14}P$

(D) $V = \frac{22}{7}P$

27. If a computer costs \$2,000 and depreciates (i.e., the value decreases) by the same amount each year, how much is the annual amount of depreciation if after 6 years the computer is worth \$800?

(A) \$80
(B) \$100
(C) \$200
(D) \$400

28. Julian and Maria are budgeting for their upcoming wedding reception. They are inviting people from each side of their families—J people from Julian's side of the family and M people from Maria's side of the family. They are planning on spending \$40 per person invited to the wedding reception. If they want to keep the cost of the wedding reception to less than \$18,000, and have more than 200 people in attendance, which system of inequalities would represent these conditions?

(A) $M + J \leq 200$
$40M + J \geq 18,000$

(B) $M + J > 40$
$18,000 + M + J > 200$

(C) $M + J > 18,000$
$\frac{M + J}{40} < 200$

(D) $M + J > 200$
$40(M + J) < 18,000$

29. Given that there are 5,280 feet in a mile, which of the following would most closely approximate 30 miles per hour in feet per second?

(A) 28 feet/second
(B) 44 feet/second
(C) 176 feet/second
(D) 158,400 feet/second

30. At a drink shop, each cup of coffee has 95 milligrams of caffeine, and each cup of tea has 26 milligrams of caffeine. Shantiel goes to the store and purchases only cups of coffee and tea. If the number of cups of coffee that Shantiel purchased was half the number of cups of tea that she purchased, and the total milligrams of caffeine in all the drinks she purchased was 735, how many cups of coffee did she purchase?

(A) 2
(B) 3
(C) 5
(D) 6

Student-Produced Response Directions

In questions 31-38, first solve the problem, and then enter your answer on the grid provided on the answer sheet. The instructions for entering your answers follow.

- First, write your answer in the boxes at the top of the grid.
- Second, you may grid your answer in the columns below the boxes.
- Use the fraction bar in the first row or the decimal point in the second row to enter fractions and decimals.

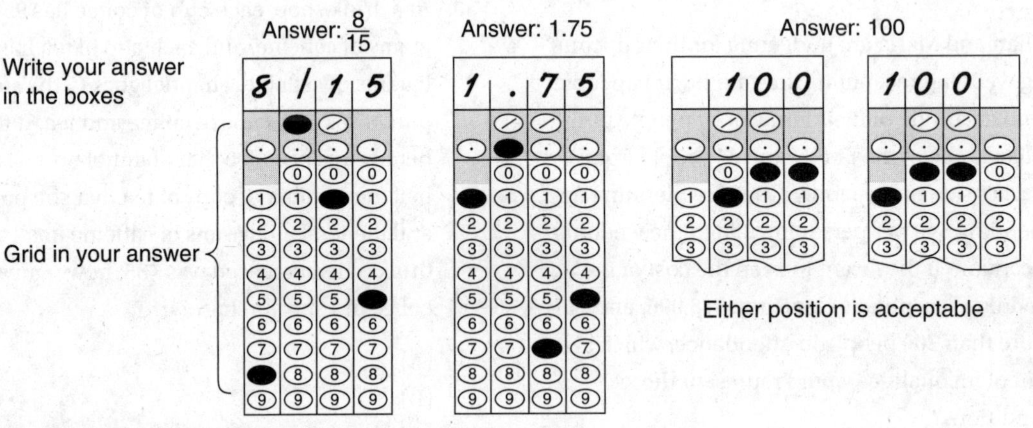

- Grid only one space in each column.
- Entering the answer in the boxes is recommended as an aid in gridding but is not required.
- The machine scoring your exam can read only what you grid, so you **must grid-in your answers correctly to get credit**.
- If a question has more than one correct answer, grid-in only one of them.
- The grid does not have a minus sign, so no answer can be negative.
- A mixed number *must* be converted to an improper fraction or a decimal before it is gridded. Enter $1\frac{1}{4}$ as $\frac{5}{4}$ or 1.25; the machine will interpret 11/4 as $\frac{11}{4}$ and mark it wrong.
- **All decimals must be entered as accurately as possible.** Here are three acceptable ways of gridding

$$\frac{3}{11} = 0.272727\ldots$$

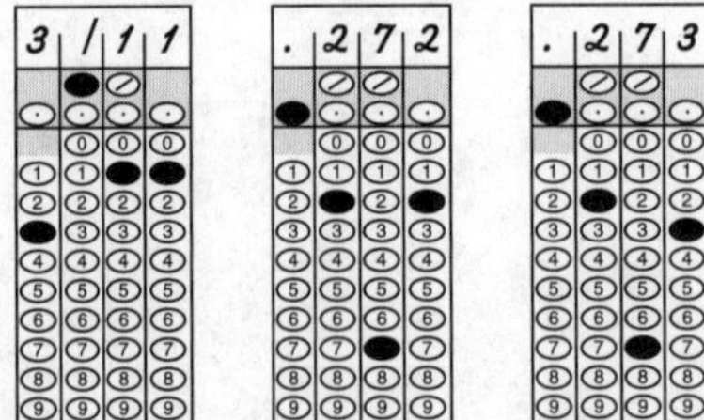

- Note that rounding to .273 is acceptable because you are using the full grid, but you would receive **no credit** for .3 or .27, because they are less accurate.

PRACTICE TEST 2

31. $(x + 2)^3 = 27$

What positive value of x would make the above equation true?

32. $2x - y = 6$
$3x + 2y = 23$

What is the value of y in the above system of equations?

33. $(x + a)(x + a) = x^2 + 8x + 16$

In the equation above, a is a positive constant. What is the value of a?

34. A recipe calls for 1 and $\frac{1}{3}$ cups of flour to make a pastry. There is enough flour to make a maximum of what quantity of pastries if the chef has 16 cups of flour?

Questions 35–36 refer to the following information.

Quiz Score (Out of 5 Points)	0 Correct	1 Correct	2 Correct	3 Correct	4 Correct	5 Correct
Class 1 Students' Scores	1	2	4	6	4	3
Class 2 Students' Scores	0	4	7	3	4	2

A teacher gave a 5-question quiz to 2 different classes. Class 1 and class 2 each have 20 students, and their quiz results are compiled in the table above.

35. What is the difference in the score ranges between class 1 and class 2?

36. What is the median quiz score of the combined set of both classes?

37. Mia wants to spend no more than \$500 on lodging for her upcoming trip. How many more additional whole nights could she stay at a hotel that cost \$70 per night compared to one that cost \$90 per night?

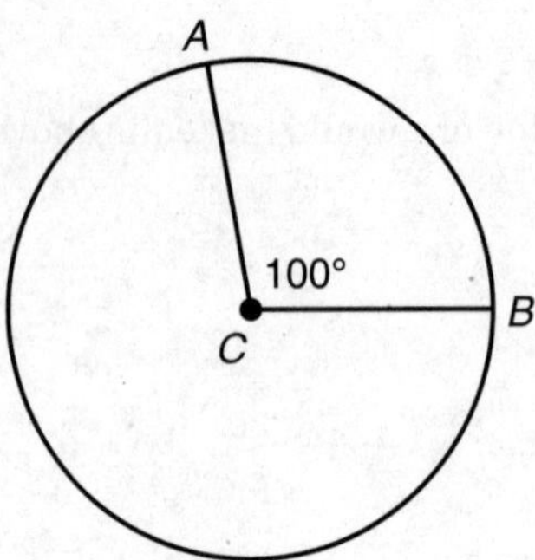

38. The circle graphed above has a center of C, a radius of 7 units, and a central angle $\angle ACB$ with a measure of $100°$. What is the area of the sector of the circle designated by $\angle ACB$ to the nearest whole square unit?

STOP If there is still time remaining, you may review your answers.

ANSWER KEY
Practice Test 2

Section 1: Reading

1. **A**
2. **D**
3. **B**
4. **B**
5. **D**
6. **A**
7. **B**
8. **C**
9. **C**
10. **B**
11. **D**
12. **D**
13. **B**
14. **C**
15. **C**
16. **A**
17. **D**
18. **D**
19. **C**
20. **D**
21. **B**
22. **A**
23. **D**
24. **C**
25. **C**
26. **C**
27. **B**
28. **D**
29. **D**
30. **C**
31. **B**
32. **D**
33. **D**
34. **C**
35. **C**
36. **D**
37. **D**
38. **A**
39. **B**
40. **C**
41. **A**
42. **B**
43. **A**
44. **A**
45. **D**
46. **D**
47. **B**
48. **B**
49. **A**
50. **D**
51. **B**
52. **A**

Section 2: Writing and Language

1. **D**
2. **B**
3. **B**
4. **A**
5. **C**
6. **D**
7. **C**
8. **C**
9. **B**
10. **D**
11. **D**
12. **D**
13. **D**
14. **A**
15. **A**
16. **C**
17. **C**
18. **A**
19. **D**
20. **B**
21. **B**
22. **A**
23. **A**
24. **C**
25. **B**
26. **A**
27. **C**
28. **B**
29. **D**
30. **A**
31. **C**
32. **B**
33. **A**
34. **B**
35. **A**
36. **A**
37. **C**
38. **C**
39. **D**
40. **C**
41. **A**
42. **D**
43. **A**
44. **D**

ANSWER KEY
Practice Test 2

Section 3: Math (No Calculator)

1. **B**
2. **C**
3. **A**
4. **D**
5. **C**
6. **D**
7. **A**
8. **B**
9. **C**
10. **D**
11. **A**
12. **D**
13. **B**
14. **D**
15. **C**
16. **2**
17. **1.5 or $\frac{3}{2}$**
18. **12**
19. **54**
20. **144**

Section 4: Math (Calculator)

1. **C**
2. **A**
3. **B**
4. **C**
5. **B**
6. **D**
7. **B**
8. **A**
9. **C**
10. **B**
11. **D**
12. **C**
13. **C**
14. **D**
15. **D**
16. **A**
17. **D**
18. **D**
19. **B**
20. **D**
21. **A**
22. **A**
23. **D**
24. **C**
25. **A**
26. **B**
27. **C**
28. **D**
29. **B**
30. **C**
31. **1**
32. **4**
33. **4**
34. **12**
35. **1**
36. **3**
37. **2**
38. **43**

SAT Scoring Chart

Tally the number of correct answers from the Reading section (out of 52), the Writing and Language section (out of 44), and the combined Math without and with calculator sections (out of 58). Match these numbers of correct answers to the find the Reading Test score, the Writing and Language Test score, and the Math section score.

Number of Correct Answers on Each Test Part (Reading, Writing/Language, Combined Math Sections)	Reading Test Score	Writing and Language Test Score	Math Section Score
0	10	10	200
1	10	10	200
2	10	10	210
3	10	11	220
4	11	11	230
5	12	12	250
6	13	13	270
7	13	14	280
8	14	14	300
9	15	15	310
10	16	16	320
11	16	16	340
12	17	17	350
13	17	17	360
14	18	18	370
15	18	18	380
16	19	18	390
17	19	19	400
18	20	19	410
19	20	20	420
20	21	20	430
21	21	21	440
22	22	21	450
23	22	22	460
24	23	23	470
25	23	23	480
26	24	24	490
27	24	24	500
28	25	25	500
29	25	25	510
30	26	26	520
31	26	27	520

(Continued)

Number of Correct Answers on Each Test Part (Reading, Writing/Language, Combined Math Sections)	Reading Test Score	Writing and Language Test Score	Math Section Score
32	27	27	530
33	28	28	540
34	28	29	540
35	29	29	550
36	29	30	560
37	30	31	570
38	30	31	580
39	31	32	580
40	31	33	590
41	31	34	600
42	32	36	610
43	32	38	610
44	33	40	620
45	33		630
46	34		640
47	35		650
48	36		660
49	36		670
50	37		680
51	39		690
52	40		700
53			710
54			730
55			750
56			770
57			790
58			800

Add the Reading Test score and the Writing and Language Test score:

________ (Reading Score) + ________ (Writing and Language Score) =

________ (Combined Reading and Writing and Language Score)

Then multiply the Combined Reading and Writing Language score by 10 to find your Evidence-Based Reading and Writing section score:

10 × ____________ (Combined Reading and Writing and Language Score) =

____________ **Evidence-Based Reading and Writing Score (between 200–800)**

The Math section score is also between 200–800. Get this from the table above.

_____________ **Math Section Score (between 200–800)**

Add the Evidence-Based Reading and Writing score and the Math section score to find your total SAT test score:

__________ Evidence-Based Reading and Writing Score +

__________ Math Section Score =

__________ **Total SAT Test Score (between 400–1600)**

Approximate your testing percentiles (1st–99th) using this chart:

Total Score	Section Score	Total Percentile	Evidence-Based Reading and Writing Percentile	Math Percentile
1600	800	99+	99+	99
1500	750	98	98	96
1400	700	94	94	91
1300	650	86	86	84
1200	600	74	73	75
1100	550	59	57	61
1000	500	41	40	42
900	450	25	24	27
800	400	11	11	15
700	350	3	3	5
600	300	1	1	1
500	250	1	1	1
400	200	1	1	1

Answers Explained

Section 1: Reading Test

Robinson Crusoe

1. **(A)** Crusoe is warned in the passage to take the ship's sinking as a sign to not pursue a seafaring life. However, he ignores this advice and begins to look for a seafaring voyage as shown in the last paragraph. This attitude is most clearly shown in choice **(A)**. Choice (B) is incorrect as this wisdom is given to him even though he does not seek it out. Choice (C) is incorrect as he listens to neither family, nor acquaintances. Choice (D) is incorrect as he clearly does consider the warnings while he is in London, prior to his searching out a voyage.

2. **(D)** The context of this sentence shows that even though the storm had begun to abate, the ship still would not have been able to reach land. This shows us that "abate" must mean to die down since if the storm were to die down, that would help the ship get closer to safety, even though the ship is too damaged to get all the way to shore. This makes choice **(D)** the best option as *subside* means "to die down." Choice (A) would be the opposite of "abate." Choices (B) and (C) do not have the correct meaning given the context of the sentence.

3. **(B)** What on the water would need to be ridden out? A storm. The ship ahead of them had ridden out the storm instead of sinking and can now come to their rescue. This means that "it" is referring to the storm that had been ridden out. The ship would not have had to ride out a boat, ship, or port, making choices (A), (C), and (D) incorrect.

4. **(B)** This paragraph explains that the men who were rescued from the sinking ship were given a place to stay and enough money to complete their journey. The citizens of the town were hospitable toward the men when they landed, making choice **(B)** the best option. There is no evidence within the paragraph that they were treated with scorn (looked down upon), envy, or humor, making the other choices incorrect.

5. **(D)** In the earlier quote, the captain says he would not step foot on another ship with the narrator for a thousand pounds, an enormous amount of money. The narrator explains this away in the later quote by saying that the man had only spoken in such a way because he was suffering from a great loss. The narrator clearly believes that this loss has led the captain to speak in an exaggerated manner. This makes choice **(D)** the best option. The reader might think the captain is being malicious, but the narrator does not, so choice (C) is incorrect. There is no evidence that the narrator believes that the captain is being convincing or disingenuous, making choices (A) and (B) incorrect.

6. **(A)** In the last paragraph, we see the narrator first concerned about shipwrecks, but again looking for a voyage after some time has passed. This best fits with choice **(A)**. Choice (B) is incorrect as the narrator seems determined to sail again. Choice (C) is incorrect as we are not aware of his financial situation after the wreck. Choice (D) is incorrect as we know the ship sank entirely.

7. **(B)** Directly after the shipwreck, the narrator says he is determined not to return home but rather to press on in his adventure. This makes choice **(B)** the best option. Choice (A) would be a good reason to return home—to reassure his father. Choice (C) is foreshadowing a possible bad future, but that does not deter the narrator. Choice (D) does not show his eventual decision to take back to the sea, but rather the conflict he faced in coming to that decision.

8. **(C)** This entire section of the passage is the warning of an older, much-experienced seafaring man. He tells the narrator not to return to the sea but rather to seek out a different future. This warning is an omen and causes the reader to understand just how dangerous it would be for the narrator to return to the sea. It foreshadows a dismal future, causing a sense of foreboding. This makes choice **(C)** correct. The other choices are not emotions that are conveyed in this section of the passage.

9. **(C)** This word is used within the context of the sentence to mean "find" or "encounter." The captain is warning the narrator that if he returns to the sea, he will "meet with nothing but disasters." The word *encounter* would fit best within the context to replace the word "meet." The narrator would not converse, remember, or compete with nothing but disasters.

10. **(B)** The question asks for proof that a character believes in ill omens. Don't make the mistake of thinking that character must be the narrator; we have no proof that the narrator believes in ill omens. Choice **(B)**, however, shows us that the captain does believes in such signs. He calls the shipwreck a "token" which, in the context, can mean an omen. He would not say such a thing if he did not believe in them himself. Choice (A) is spoken by this same character but does not show his belief in omens. Choices (C) and (D) show the narrator's conflict in deciding what to do, but do not reveal that he believes in omens.

Crop Rotation

11. **(D)** This passage discusses the benefits of crop rotation and the drawbacks of other soil management methods. The author concludes that crop rotation is still used today in soil management because it is safe and effective. This makes choice **(D)** the best option. Choice (A) is incorrect as crop rotation is not a planting method. Choice (B) is incorrect as the author clearly favors crop rotation over fertilization. Choice (C) is incorrect as fertilization is the more expensive option.

12. **(D)** The Native Americans discussed in the passage arranged their crops in a way that was physically advantageous, as described in the passage. The phrase in question shows that this physical advantage also gave a chemical advantage, even though the Native Americans may not have realized it. This makes choice **(D)** the best option. It is not choice (A) since the Native Americans did have a set way of planting. While choice (B) is factually correct, it is incorrect because the phrase in question does not demonstrate that. It is not choice (C) since there is no evidence in the passage of scientific concerns in earlier periods.

13. **(B)** Soil (dirt) cannot become physically tired like humans do, making choice (A) incorrect. Choices (C) and (D) are also emotions that are not attributable to soil. However, the context of the rest of the paragraph shows that dirt can become depleted of resources like nitrogen. This makes choice **(B)** the best option.

14. **(C)** The second paragraph of the passage notes that soil depletion can end the livelihood of the farmers. The farmer could lose his ability to earn money should the soil be too depleted. This makes choice **(C)** the best answer and choices (A), (B), and (D) less correct. While part-time gardeners, Native American leaders, and scientific researchers may experience some risk related to nitrogen depletion, they do not take on as much risk as a career farmer.

15. **(C)** Choice **(C)** is the best option as these lines show the dangers that nitrogen depletion can pose to farmers. The other options do not discuss the risk associated with depletion.

16. **(A)** In the previous sentence, the author claimed that fertilizer runoff could lead to negative results for humans. This example of the algae bloom causing a large population to have tainted water illustrates one situation in which this claim was correct. This makes choice **(A)** the best answer. Choice (B) is incorrect as this is a shortcoming of the fertilizer method, not crop rotation. Choice (C) is incorrect as this is just one single example; we have no evidence of a pattern of such algae blooms. Choice (D) is incorrect as this one instance of negative consequences does not prove that either fertilizer use or crop rotation are in decline.

17. **(D)** The author here is saying that because of the expense of newer technologies, crop rotation remains the main tool that farmers use for soil management. "Staple" therefore means "main." This makes choice **(D)** the best option as *principal* can mean "main." The author is not saying that crop rotation is consumable, fastened, or specific, making choices (A), (B), and (C) incorrect.

18. **(D)** In Table 1, we can see that grass-legume hay has the lowest yield per acre at two. This means that for each acre of seed planted, a farmer will only harvest two units at the end of the growing season. The other answers all have significantly higher yields meaning the farmer will harvest more per acre. Thus, choice **(D)** is the best option.

19. **(C)** We learn in the table that soybeans strip quite a bit of nitrogen from the soil at 103 pounds per acre removed. This means that the farmer would need to plant a nitrogen fixing plant in the next year to return the nitrogen to the soil. The beginning of Paragraph 3 tells us that legumes are nitrogen-fixing, which would solve the issue of there being a lack of nitrogen. This makes choice **(C)** the correct answer. None of the other options are shown to be nitrogen fixing crops.

20. **(D)** Choice **(D)** is the best answer as this is where the author tells us that legumes are nitrogen-fixing. Without this information, we would not be able to answer question 19. Choices (A), (B), and (C) all talk about other crops and crop rotation, but do not help the reader understand which crop would be nitrogen-fixing.

Stress and Love

21. **(B)** This phrase is used to describe the physical pain that people often feel after a "heart breaking" experience. This kind of pain is very common and has a biological reason behind it, making choice **(B)** the best answer. Choice (A) is incorrect as the term is not an allegory. Choice (C) is incorrect as the term refers to mild physical pain, not a severe heart attack. Choice (D) is incorrect as the event is physical as opposed to psychological.

22. **(A)** These terms are used in the first paragraph to introduce the reader to the idea of broken-heart syndrome. The passage goes on to explain how these terms can be based in scientific reality. This makes choice **(A)** the best option as the author is connecting these common phrases to what is discussed later in the passage. Choice (B) is incorrect as these phrases are not key research terminology. Choice (C) is incorrect as these terms do not show the author's personal heartbreak. Choice (D) is incorrect as the author is not considering objections at this point.

23. **(D)** This excerpt from the passage explains to the reader the reasons for the release of stress hormones. The author tells the reader the evolutionary reason the human body reacts in such a way and how current-day stressors are different than the stressors historical humans experienced. This makes choice **(D)** the best answer. Choice (A) is incorrect as animal attacks are used as an example of a stressor; they are not the main purpose of this paragraph. Choice (B) is incorrect as the author is saying that the human body's response to stress has remained the same, despite a change in stressors. Choice (C) is incorrect as there is no evidence in this paragraph of such a human adaptation.

24. **(C)** Within the context of the passage, "presents" is used to show what symptoms are present and associated with a given disease or physical issue. The patient "presents" certain symptoms. In this context, the best replacement would be *exhibits*, which makes choice **(C)** the best option. Choices (A), (B), and (D) are all closely related words that do not fit the context of the given sentence.

25. **(C)** If we examine the first sentence of the second to last paragraph, we see that broken-heart syndrome often looks like a heart attack with one key difference—there is no arterial blockage. That would mean that if we wished to tell the difference between the two, we could simply look for arterial blockage. If it were absent, we could conclude that the patient is suffering from broken-heart syndrome, not a heart attack. This makes choice **(C)** the best answer. Choice (A) is not discussed in the passage. Choices (B) and (D) are symptoms that the two conditions share and would therefore not be a good way to differentiate between the two.

26. **(C)** Mortality risk would be the risk of dying from broken-heart syndrome. The best evidence for mortality risk within the passage would be choice **(C)**, where the author says "Unlike a heart attack, broken-heart syndrome is rarely fatal and can even resolve itself within hours to weeks." This gives the reader solid information on the mortality risk of this syndrome. Choice (A) tells us who suffers from this syndrome, but not how fatal it is. Choice (B) tells of the difference in stressors over time but does not address the fatality rate of those stressors. Choice (D) looks to the future study of the heart but again does not address mortality rates.

27. **(B)** In the third to last paragraph, the author says, "While the exact mechanism behind broken-heart syndrome is not known, scientists believe it may be a defense mechanism." This shows us that the science is not settled on the matter, although there is a theory. This makes choice **(B)** the best answer. Choice (A) is not the correct answer as the science is not definitive, but rather still being researched. Choice (C) is incorrect as there is no evidence of polarization in the scientific community around this question. Choice (D) is incorrect as there is no reason for scientists or scientific knowledge to be paranoid.

28. **(D)** In the second to last paragraph, we learn that "consequences exemplify the importance of psychological health, as it can significantly affect one's physical health." This shows the reader that physical and psychological health are connected to one another, making choice **(D)** the best option. Choice (A) is the opposite of the relationship shown in the passage. Choices (B) and (C) do not accurately describe the relationship as it is portrayed in the passage.

29. **(D)** Choice **(D)** is the best option as it clearly shows that physical and psychological health affect one another and are therefore interconnected. Choice (A) does not describe the relationship between the two. Choice (B) shows a physical symptom of broken-heart syndrome, but does not show a relationship to psychological health. Choice (C) shows that it is likely a patient will physically heal from broken-heart syndrome, but it does not connect it to psychological health.

30. **(C)** In the final paragraph, the author says, "As research expands to understand the role of hormones on heart health . . ." This tells us that the research is not complete, but that it continues to expand as scientists continue to study. The implication is that the study is interdisciplinary—hormone scientists and heart scientists will have to work together. The research is assuredly not complete or unnecessary, making choices (A) and (B) incorrect. The research is not yet completed, so it cannot be obsolete (out of date), making choice (D) incorrect.

Arnett and Douglass

31. **(B)** In the first paragraph, it is made clear that Arnett is discussing former slaves. There is no indication of him switching the topic of the speech, which can lead the reader to assume that the "he" in the second paragraph is the former slave. This makes choice **(B)** the best answer. Within the context of the second paragraph, it becomes clear that Arnett is not discussing any white people as he talks about whites having 12 amendments and "we have had three." This makes it clear that answers (A), (C), and (D) would all be incorrect as Civil War generals, pilgrims, and political party leaders would have all been white.

32. **(D)** In the second paragraph, Arnett discusses the passage of the 13th, 14th, and 15th amendments and then mentions that as a result, "we have been on the platform and so, thank God, all the parties have a place on their platforms for us. Some of them have a very little place for us, but we have a place." This shows that each party is working to include the former slave population to at least some extent—some parties more than others. This makes choice **(D)** the best option. Choice (A) is incorrect as we have no evidence that any former slaves were accepted as party leaders. Choice (B) is incorrect as we have no evidence that political parties were trying to change the religion of any given group. Choice (C) is incorrect as there is no discussion of passing any amendments beyond the 15th.

33. **(D)** As shown in the explanation to question 32, choice **(D)** best shows that after the passage of the 13th, 14th, and 15th amendments, former slaves were at least partially represented in each party. Choice (A) asks a rhetorical question but does not show representation. Choice (B) shows the social involvement of former slaves historically, but not their representation in political parties. Choice (C) introduces the 13th, 14th, and 15th amendments, but does not explain the position of former slaves in political parties after their ratification.

34. **(C)** Looking at the lines before and after this excerpt can provide some context. The author says, "They cannot remain half slave and half free," and then clarifies afterward all the ways in which former slaves are still "half-and-half." Douglass mentions split schools and restricted voting specifically. In other words, Douglass is saying that until segregation ends, the black population remains "half slave and half free." With that in mind, then, we can see that "half-and-half" most closely means "segregated," making choice **(C)** the best option. *Equivalent* is the opposite of the intended meaning, making choice (B) incorrect. *Discounted* and *populist* do not convey Douglass's intended meaning, making choices (A) and (D) incorrect.

35. **(C)** As we can see in the very last sentence of the passage, Douglass believes that there will never be a better time for this change. He implies that the longer we wait, the more difficult it will be. Therefore, it makes sense that it should be addressed with urgency—it must be done now. He does not advocate for harshness or violence, making choices (A) and (B) incorrect. While it makes sense that he would encourage an intellectual approach, we do not have evidence of this encouragement in the passage, so choice (D) is incorrect.

36. **(D)** It is in the final few lines of the passage that we learn that Douglass sees no better time for change than the present. This leads to the sense of urgency in addressing the situation. Choice **(D)** is the option that highlights those lines and showcases the urgency. Choices (A), (B), and (C) simply show Douglass's feelings on the issue, but do not tell us how he would want to address the problem.

37. **(D)** In the context of this sentence, Douglass is saying the world may "sink back" or return to moral darkness. This makes choice **(D)** the best option as *regress* means "to revert to something worse." For example, it is a well-documented fact that students' math skills regress after long breaks from school. Since moral darkness is a bad thing, *regress* would fit the context perfectly whereas *submerge, excavate,* and *embed* would not, leaving choices (A), (B), and (C) incorrect.

38. **(A)** In formal writing, repetition is often used to emphasize a point. In this case, Douglass is emphasizing that the discussion will continue until the work is done. The number of times it is repeated showcases how very much work remains to be done, which makes choice **(A)** the best answer. Choice (B) is not correct as Douglass is not discussing oral traditions, but rather serious conversations that must take place. Choice (C) is not correct as Douglass is not addressing objections, but rather showing how much work is left. Choice (D) is not correct as he is saying that his beliefs will not change—the work needs to be done.

39. **(B)** The author of Passage 1 talks about the first 12 amendments as a group, saying that they belong to white people. He also groups the next 3 amendments together and says they belong to the former slaves. This grouping is not done in Passage 2, making choice **(B)** the best option. Choice (A) is how Passage 2 treats the amendments. Choices (C) and (D) are things both passages do.

40. **(C)** Passage 2 ends on an urgent and forceful tone—emphasizing that something must be done now to rectify the situation. The second passage also contains forceful language as Douglass insists time and again that the discussion will go on. In comparison, Passage 1 is much more hopeful. Arnett is much happier with the advancements that have already been made and sees even more hope for the future. He is much less forceful in the words he chooses. This means that choice **(C)** is the best option. Choices (A), (B), and (D) do not accurately describe the tone of Passage 2.

41. **(A)** While Passage 1 discusses what the slave must do internally, such as better economic management, Passage 2 discusses external societal factors that must change. This makes choice **(A)** the best answer. Choice (B) is incorrect as both passages agree that slaves should have political rights. Choice (C) is incorrect as gender equality is not addressed in the passages. Choice (D) is incorrect as at the time of the writing of these two passages, slavery had already been ended.

Car Safety

42. **(B)** If we look at the final sentences of this passage, we see the author's call to action: people must demand safety features that will protect everyone. Throughout the passage, the information given is leading up to this demand. This supports the idea that certain people are far less safe in cars. Her main objective, therefore, is to convince the reader that car safety must be made more equal. This makes choice **(B)** the best option. At no point does she describe how a crash test is run, so choice (A) is incorrect. She is not calling for the end of cars, but

rather for safer cars, so choice (C) is incorrect. She is not saying we should be more risk tolerant, but rather should reduce risk by having safer cars, so choice (D) is incorrect.

43. **(A)** As shown in the very first lines of the passage, the author believes that "our cars are much safer today than at any time in the past." This tells the reader that older cars were, in the eyes of the author, less safe: choice **(A)** is the best answer. The author does not address fuel efficiency, making choice (B) incorrect. The author would likely say that older cars were less likely to have seatbelts, making choice (C) incorrect. The author indicates that female test dummies were not used until 2003, making choice (D) incorrect.

44. **(A)** As quoted in the explanation to question 43, the first sentence of this passage most clearly shows that the author believes that older cars were less safe. Choice **(A)** is the best option. The other choices do not compare the safety of older and newer models of cars.

45. **(D)** Within the parenthesis, the author explains why regardless as to which option women use to adjust the driver's seat, it poses a safety risk: low visibility, too close to the airbag, inability to reach the pedals. This makes choice **(D)** the best option. The parenthetical information is not telling the reader how these adjustments are made, so choice (A) is incorrect. The parenthetical information is showing how car seating disadvantages women, making choices (B) and (C) incorrect.

46. **(D)** In the first paragraph, the author says that "crash test dummies are generally calibrated to measure injuries on people who fit the 50th percentile of men." If test dummies are set up in such a way, then it makes sense that safety features are engineered based on those crash results and those dummies. That would make an average male most safe in any given car accident. Choice **(D)** is the best answer. Choices (A), (B), and (C) do not include average-sized men, making those answers incorrect.

47. **(B)** As shown in the answer explanation to number 46, this quote most clearly tells the reader what demographic of people would be safest in a car accident. Choice **(B)** is the best answer. Choice (A) is discussing car safety in general, not for specific demographics, making it incorrect. Choice (C) shows a choice women make that results in lower car safety, but does not say who is the safest, making it incorrect. Choice (D) explains why certain demographics are less safe but does not give clear evidence for which demographic would be the safest, making it incorrect.

48. **(B)** The data within the passage shows that the greatest disparity in safety lies in leg safety with women being 70 to 80% more likely than men to suffer leg injuries. This makes choice **(B)** the best option. Choices (A) and (C) are incorrect as the passage makes clear that women are more likely to suffer certain types of injuries, including abdominal injuries. Choice (D) is incorrect as women are also more likely to suffer head injuries.

49. **(A)** In the context of the sentence, the author says that "safety ratings that are available to consumers should break down the safety of any given car for different demographics." This context tells us that the author wants an analysis of car safety for different demographics, making choice **(A)** the best option. The author is not talking about physically breaking something, making choices (B), (C), and (D) incorrect.

50. **(D)** Looking at the right-hand column in the table, we can see the total crash rate for various age groups. The lowest rate is in the 60–69 age group, which has a crash rate of just 1.2. This makes choice **(D)** the best answer. The other answer options are all age groups which have higher rates.

51. **(B)** If we look at the males in the age range of 30–59 on the table, we can see that they have a crash rate of 1.7 for every 100 million miles traveled. To get to 1 billion miles, we would have to multiply the 100 million by 10. We would then also multiply the 1.7 by 10 to get a total of 17 crashes per 1 billion miles traveled, making choice **(B)** correct. The other answers do not correctly calculate the accurate rate for 1 billion miles.

52. **(A)** We can see in the table that men have higher rates of crash involvement than women in every age range. It therefore might be argued that car safety engineers should focus on male safety more as males are the ones who more often need to be saved. This would be against what the author is arguing throughout the passage, but could be supported with the data. This makes choice **(A)** the best option. The passage does not discuss age-related safety, so choices (B) and (C) would be incorrect as they do not argue against the author. Choice (D) would support the author's message, not provide an argument against it and is therefore incorrect.

Section 2: Writing and Language Test

1. **(D)** Choice **(D)** correctly places commas around the parenthetical phrase that clarifies the scientific term. Choices (A) and (B) do not punctuate around the parenthetical phrase, while choice (C) uses inconsistent punctuation around the phrase.

2. **(B)** The term "bodies of freshwater" is rather broad, so having this clarification is helpful to the reader. It is not choice (A) because this is a clarification, not a rebuttal to an objection. It is not choices (C) or (D) because the addition should be made.

3. **(B)** There is no need for the wording "in addition" in the original sentences, because the second sentence provides a clarification of the first sentence. Choice **(B)** most concisely joins these two sentences together. Choice (A) has no pause. Choice (C) maintains the wordy transition, and choice (D) also has no break.

4. **(A)** "Have adapted" uses the correct verb tense of "adapted" and uses the plural form "have," making it consistent with the plural subject "platypuses." The other options either incorrectly use the singular "has" or the incorrect tense of "adapt."

5. **(C)** The first part of the sentence states that platypuses use their bills to sense the electricity that surrounds them—choice **(C)** is the only option that elaborates on this electrical sensory capacity.

6. **(D)** "Since" is the only transition that shows a cause-and-effect relationship between the fact that platypuses break down their food using gravel and dirt from the water and the fact that grinding plates in their bills enable this to take place. The other options do not show a cause-and-effect relationship.

7. **(C)** Choice **(C)** correctly uses commas to set aside the parenthetical phrase "which is a trait that is advantageous to the survival of the organism." Choices (A) and (B) do not set aside this parenthetical phrase, and choice (D) sets it aside using inconsistent punctuation.

8. **(C)** "Landscape" most appropriately describes the land in which the platypuses were prevalent. A panorama is more of a scenic view. A perspective is more of a point of view. Agriculture would not have been associated with the nonhuman activities so long ago.

9. **(B)** Choice **(B)** most concisely expresses the idea that there is a cause-and-effect relationship between the fact that marsupials could not dominate the water and the need for young marsupials to have caregivers very close by. The other options are all overly wordy.

10. **(D)** "In contrast" provides a proper transition that shows the oppositional relationship between the previous sentence about the extensive care requirements for typical marsupials and the adaptation that platypuses made by having eggs. The other options do not convey oppositional relationships.

11. **(D)** Sentence 2 would be most logically placed after sentence 5 because it would both elaborate on the information about the egg-laying process of platypuses and conclude the paragraph. All of the other potential placements would not make sense because it is not until sentence 5 that the author mentions the egg-laying of platypuses.

12. **(D)** Choice **(D)** best underscores that specialty is not all that important and therefore makes the point that prospective engineering students can be flexible with their particular engineering major. Choice (A) might lead the reader to think that mechanical engineering is the best possible engineering major. Choice (B) does not focus on engineering. And choice (C) would strongly lead the reader to think that petroleum engineering should be pursued if compensation is of importance.

13. **(D)** "Is" matches the singular subject "coursework." All of the other options use plural verbs.

14. **(A)** No change is needed in this situation because choice **(A)** expresses the idea most concisely. All of the other options add in unnecessary wording.

15. **(A)** Choice **(A)** puts the wording in the most logical sequence, helping the reader clearly understand what is being expressed. Choices (B) and (C) do not clarify the subject until later in the sentence, and choice (D) provides a convoluted claim of there being "goals that skills accomplish."

16. **(C)** Choice **(C)** logically leads to the example that clarifies a type of engineering that deals with a particular type of physical problem. The other options would not lead into a clarifying example.

17. **(C)** No punctuation is required in this sentence. Choice (A) does not have a complete sentence after the semicolon. Choice (B) uses the dash to provide an unnecessary, awkward pause. And choice (D) unnecessarily sets aside "an engineer" with commas, suggesting a parenthetical that is not needed; without "an engineer," the sentence would not make sense.

18. **(A)** The paragraph goes on to argue that since certain types of engineering are considered subdisciplines of broader types of engineering, it does not make sense to over-specialize as an undergraduate engineering student. So, choice **(A)** would most logically introduce this argument. Choice (B) is incorrect, since the paragraph does not focus on compensation. Choice (C) is incorrect, since the author does not argue that students should skip studying engineering all together in their undergraduate studies. And choice (D) is overly broad given the focus of the paragraph.

19. **(D)** A brief pause is needed after the introductory word "similarly". Choices (A) and (B) do not have this needed pause, and choice (C) unnecessarily introduces a semicolon when there is not a complete sentence before it.

20. **(B)** While all of the choices are in some way related to money or business, only "compensation" makes sense in terms of referring to the likely salaries that engineers could receive. "Expenditures" refers to general spending, "enterprises" refers to business activities, and "reimbursement" refers to receiving a refund for one's paid expenses.

21. **(B)** Choice **(B)** is the only option that focuses on financial rewards. Choice (A) focuses on flexibility in choosing a major. Choice (C) focuses on making connections while in college, and choice (D) emphasizes earning a well-rounded education.

22. **(A)** "Aptitude" refers to natural skill or ability, so this would make sense given the reference to math and science. Choice (B) does not make sense in referring to math and science abilities, and choices (C) and (D) are overly casual given the more formal tone of the essay.

23. **(A)** Choice **(A)** provides a comma between the dependent introductory clause and the independent clause that follows. Choice (B) does not have a complete sentence before the colon. Choice (C) does not have a complete sentence before the semicolon. Choice (D) unnecessarily uses a series of dashes to interrupt the phrasing of the sentence.

24. **(C)** "Someone else" is a singular subject that agrees with the singular verb "has." All of the other verbs are plural.

25. **(B)** "Receive" makes the most sense in this context, since the injured person is the recipient of help from people going by. "Inherit" would involve receiving something typically after someone's death. "Endure" is not associated with giving or receiving help, and "extract" would mean to take something out (like *extract a mineral from the earth*).

26. **(A)** Choice **(A)** expresses the intended idea without unnecessary wordiness. Choice (B) unnecessarily uses "confines of," since this is assumed if you are running through your local park. Choice (C) expresses the idea that the park is local in a wordy fashion, and choice (D) says "jogging" after already saying "running."

27. **(C)** This sentence would most logically be placed after sentence 5, since it would provide an answer to the rhetorical question asked in sentence 5. None of the other potential placements would have a question prior to this potential insertion.

28. **(B)** The paragraph focuses on laws that states have passed to help encourage people to help those in need without fear of lawsuits. Choice **(B)** effectively introduces this by acknowledging that many people make excuses to avoid helping; it asks how this situation can be improved. The other options are overly negative in terms of the author's description of human motivation—the feelings about helping others are best described as mixed, not extremely negative.

29. **(D)** "While" sets up a logical contrast within the sentence, underscoring that even though there are criticisms of these laws, they do in fact help minimize the negative effects of the bystander effect. None of the other options would set up a logical contrast.

30. **(A)** "Impacts" best fits the meaning needed in this context, since the author is referring to the negative consequences or effects of the bystander effect. Choices (B) and (C) are overly violent, and choice (D) is overly positive.

31. **(C)** A comma at the end of this independent clause maintains the parallel structure of punctuation found throughout the sentence as a whole. Choice (A) provides no break. Choice (B) inserts an unnecessary comma and inappropriately uses a semicolon. Choice (D) has an unnecessary comma and an inappropriate colon that would not precede a list or clarification.

32. **(B)** According to the first row of the first table, 18.0% of victims said that third-party involvement in their situation resulted in the helpful consequence of preventing injury. According to the first row of the second table, 1.1% of victims felt that third-party intervention resulted in the unhelpful consequence. All of the other options in some way use numbers that do not correspond to their descriptions in the table.

33. **(A)** The general point of the paragraph is that it is more helpful to intervene in some way when encountering a crime than to simply ignore it. Choice **(A)** is the only option that highlights the potential positive consequences of intervention—all of the other options highlight potentially negative consequences.

34. **(B)** *Are* is consistent with the plural subject "paintings" and matches the other verbs by being in the present tense. The other options are all singular verbs.

35. **(A)** There is no need for any punctuation to break up the long yet unified subject "What is not visible in these museums." All of the other options provide unnecessary interruptions with their punctuation.

36. **(A)** Without this insertion, the sentence will be vague in its description of how the majority of Renaissance art works were lost. This insertion gives specific details that elaborate on how the artworks came to be harmed. It is not choice (B) because it does not clarify a term that follows, but instead clarifies what comes before. It is not choices (C) or (D) because the selection should be inserted.

37. **(C)** The phrasing in choice **(C)** is parallel to the phrasing in the other listed items in the sentence: "what . . . how . . . where." The other options lack parallelism.

38. **(C)** The focus of this paragraph is on the restoration process itself, not on the colors that were used in Renaissance art, so the insertion would distract from the focus of the paragraph. This information was not stated elsewhere in the essay, making choice (D) incorrect. And it is not choices (A) or (B) because the sentence should not be inserted.

39. **(D)** This option provides a comma after the introductory dependent clause and the independent clause that follows. Choice (A) does not have a complete sentence before the semicolon. Choice (B) does not have a complete sentence before the colon. And choice (C) places the comma between the subject and the verb.

40. **(C)** When writing a comparison that starts with "not only," use "but also" to complete the thought. Choice **(C)** is the only option that provides this language.

41. **(A)** Choice **(A)** provides a comma between the introductory dependent clause and the independent clause that follows. Also, it uses concise, active language. Choice (B) uses the passive voice, and choices (C) and (D) put the words in an illogical sequence.

42. **(D)** The surrounding sentences use verbs that are in the present tense, like "can" and "have." So, "allows" is both consistent with the present tense and the singular subject of "method." The other options are not in the present tense.

43. **(A)** "If" sets up a logical relationship between the two parts of the sentence: *If* the restorationist is not skilled, the result is that the restoration attempt can be a disaster. The other transitions would not set up this logical relationship. Even though "because" and "since" can express cause and effect, they would not work because they would show that this is a definitive situation rather than a possibility.

44. **(D)** The passage in general argues that art restoration, when done carefully, can help us appreciate artworks created many years ago. So, choice **(D)**, which argues that art restoration is a risk worth taking, makes the most sense. Choices (A) and (B) are overly negative about the possibility of art restoration, and choice (C) does not focus on art restoration.

Section 3: Math Test (No Calculator)

1. **(B)**

$$(0.8a + 0.7b) - (1.4a - 0.3b) \rightarrow$$
$$0.8a + 0.7b - 1.4a + 0.3b \rightarrow$$
$$(0.8a - 1.4a) + (0.7b + 0.3b) \rightarrow$$
$$-0.6a + b$$

2. **(C)** Take two clearly identifiable points from the line: (0, 1) and (−2, −2). The slope is the change in y divided by the change in x:

$$\frac{y_2 - y_1}{x_2 - x_1} = \frac{-2 - 1}{-2 - 0} = \frac{-3}{-2} = \frac{3}{2}$$

3. **(A)** Manipulate the equation to isolate the height of the cylinder:

$$v = \pi r^2 h \rightarrow$$
$$\text{Divide both sides by } \pi r^2 \rightarrow$$
$$\frac{v}{\pi r^2} = h$$

This corresponds to choice **(A)**.

4. **(D)** Use substitution to solve. Since $y = x^2 - 13x + 40$ and $y = x - 9$, plug $x - 9$ in for y to the first equation:

$$y = x^2 - 13x + 40 \rightarrow$$
$$x - 9 = x^2 - 13x + 40 \rightarrow$$
$$0 = x^2 - 14x + 49 \rightarrow$$
$$0 = (x - 7)(x - 7) \rightarrow$$
$$x = 7$$

5. **(C)**

$$(2y^2 - y) - (2y^2 + 2y) \rightarrow$$
$$2y^2 - y - 2y^2 - 2y \rightarrow$$
$$-y - 2y = -3y$$

6. **(D)** All of the options have a y value of 0. So, look at what values of x will cause there to be a y value of 0, since a point that intersects the x-axis must have a y value of 0. In $y = (x + 4)(x - 5)x$, if x is 0, −4, or 5, the entire right side of the equation would be 0. Therefore, all three options would be points at which the function intersects the x-axis.

7. **(A)** The answers are all written in slope-intercept form, and they all have different slopes. So, calculate the slope of the linear function by using two points. We can use (6, 0) and (9, 1) since there is no negative value in the point, which could more easily lead to a careless error:

$$\frac{y_2 - y_1}{x_2 - x_1} = \frac{1 - 0}{9 - 6} = \frac{1}{3}$$

The only option with a slope of $\frac{1}{3}$ is choice **(A)**, $f(x) = \frac{1}{3}x - 2$.

8. **(B)** Since when x is 2, $f(x) = -1$, plug in the point $(2, -1)$ to the function to solve for the constant k:

$$f(x) = kx - 3 \rightarrow$$
$$-1 = k(2) - 3 \rightarrow$$
$$2 = k(2) \rightarrow$$
$$k = \frac{2}{2} = 1$$

This corresponds to choice **(B)**.

9. **(C)** The initial number of the bacteria can be found when you plug 0 in for h, since when $h = 0$ no time has passed.

$$1{,}000 \times 2^0 = 1{,}000 \times 1 = 1{,}000$$

Now, determine the value of h that would be needed to find a number of bacteria that is 8 times the initial value of 1,000: $8 \times 1{,}000 = 8{,}000$.

$$B(h) = 1{,}000 \times 2^h \rightarrow$$
$$8{,}000 = 1{,}000 \times 2^h \rightarrow$$
$$8 = 2^h \rightarrow 8 = 2^3$$

Since 8 is equal to 2 cubed, the correct value for h in this situation is 3 hours. If you do not remember that 8 is equal to 2 cubed, you could also plug in the answer choices to solve.

10. **(D)** The solution set of the two inequalities $y > x + 1$ and $y < -2x - 3$ and the quadrants of the coordinate plane are graphed below:

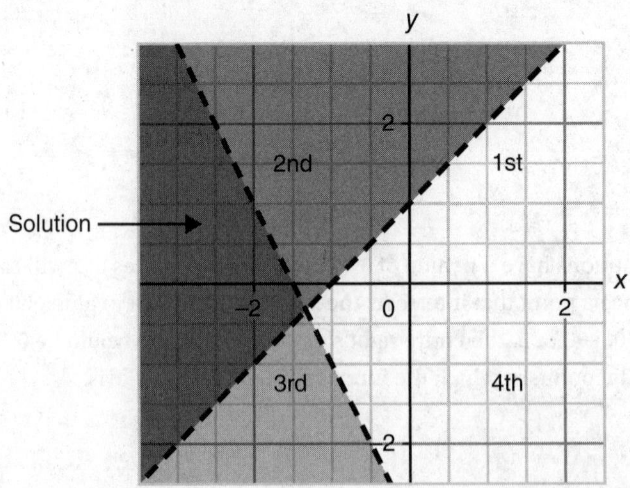

So, the solution set is in quadrants 2 and 3 only.

11. **(A)** A circle with a center at (3, 4) that intersects at the origin (0, 0) would look like this:

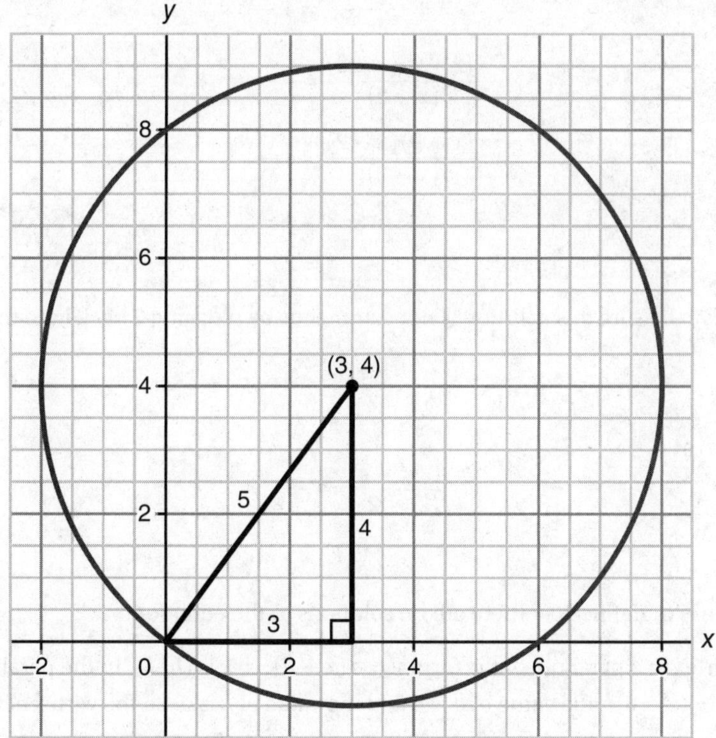

To find the radius, notice that you can inscribe a special 3-4-5 right triangle as shown above. The radius is therefore 5. The equation of a circle is $(x - h)^2 + (y - k)^2 = r^2$, in which (h, k) represents the center and r represents the radius. Plug in (3, 4) for the center and 5 for the radius to find the answer:

$$(x - h)^2 + (y - k)^2 = r^2 \rightarrow$$
$$(x - 3)^2 + (y - 4)^2 = 5^2 \rightarrow$$
$$(x - 3)^2 + (y - 4)^2 = 25$$

12. **(D)** Plug 3 in for x to solve for a positive value of y:

$$2y^2x - 2x^2y = 60 \rightarrow$$
$$2y^2(3) - 2(3^2)y = 60 \rightarrow$$
$$6y^2 - 18y = 60 \rightarrow$$
$$y^2 - 3y = 10 \rightarrow$$
$$y^2 - 3y - 10 = 0 \rightarrow$$
$$(y - 5)(y + 2) = 0$$

The two possible solutions for y are therefore 5 or -2. Choose the one that is *positive*: 5.

13. **(B)** Since the triangles are similar to one another, the ratios of the sides will be the same. So, the tangent of angle C will be the same as the tangent of angle F. The tangent of angle F is the opposite side ED divided by the adjacent side DF: $\frac{10}{24} = \frac{5}{12}$. This corresponds to choice **(B)**.

14. **(D)** What would be the value(s) of x that would be a solution or solutions to this function?

$$\frac{x^2-4}{x-2}=4 \rightarrow$$

$$\frac{(x+2)(x-2)}{(x-2)}=4 \rightarrow$$

$$\frac{(x+2)\cancel{(x-2)}}{\cancel{(x-2)}}=4 \rightarrow$$

$$x+2=4 \rightarrow$$

$$x=2$$

Now, check to be sure this solution is not extraneous by plugging 2 back in to the original equation:

$$\frac{x^2-4}{x-2}=4 \rightarrow$$

$$\frac{(2)^2-4}{(2)-2}=4 \rightarrow$$

$$\frac{0}{0}$$

The left side is undefined, so there are no solutions to the equation.

15. **(C)** The vertex in a parabola of the form $y=a(x-h)^2+k$ is (h, k). In the parabola with the equation $y=(x-6)^2$, the value of h is 6 and the value of k is 0. So the vertex of the parabola is (6, 0).

16. **2** Make things as easy as possible to solve for this expression: simply take half of the equation to find the value of $-5+6x$.

$$12x-10=4 \rightarrow$$

$$\frac{12x-10}{2}=\frac{4}{2} \rightarrow$$

$$6x-5=2 \rightarrow$$

$$-5+6x=2$$

17. **1.5 or $\frac{3}{2}$** The x-intercept of the equation is found when the y value of the point equals 0. So, plug 0 in for y to solve for the x-coordinate of the x-intercept.

$$y=2x-3 \rightarrow$$

$$0=2x-3 \rightarrow$$

$$3=2x \rightarrow$$

$$x=\frac{3}{2}$$

18. **12** Plug 5 in for x to solve for $f(5)$:

$$f(x)=(x-3)(x+1) \rightarrow$$

$$f(5)=(5-3)(5+1) \rightarrow$$

$$f(5)=2\times 6=12$$

PRACTICE TEST 2

19. **54** The width of 2 inches on the map corresponds to 6 miles in actual distance, and the length of 3 inches on the map corresponds to 9 miles in actual distance. So, multiply 6 by 9 to find the actual area of the rectangular plot of land:

$$6 \times 9 = 54 \text{ square miles}$$

20. **144** For the equations to have infinitely many solutions, they must be multiples of one another. Rearrange the equations so that the x and y terms match:

$$-\frac{1}{4}x + \frac{1}{6}y = 12$$

$$-3x + 2y = a$$

Notice that -3 is 12 times $-\frac{1}{4}$ and that 2 is 12 times $\frac{1}{6}$. So, multiply the 12 from the first equation by 12 to find the value of a in the second equation:

$$12 \times 12 = 144$$

So, $a = 144$.

Section 4: Math Test (Calculator)

1. **(C)** $\sqrt[3]{a} \times a^{\frac{5}{3}} = a^{\frac{1}{3}} \times a^{\frac{5}{3}} = a^{\left(\frac{1}{3}+\frac{5}{3}\right)} = a^{\frac{6}{3}} = a^2$

2. **(A)** Plug -2 in for x and solve:

$$g(x) = \frac{x^3}{2} \rightarrow$$

$$g(-2) = \frac{(-2)^3}{2} = \frac{-8}{2} = -4$$

3. **(B)** The line is already in slope-intercept form, $y = mx + b$, in which the b represents the y-intercept.

So, the y-intercept is -2.

4. **(C)** The voter turnout in the year 2008 was at nearly 62, making it the highest turnout for any of the years presented in the graph.

5. **(B)** First, use the ordered pair (8, 16) to solve for the value of the constant a:

$$y = ax \rightarrow$$

$$16 = a8 \rightarrow$$

$$\frac{16}{8} = a \rightarrow a = 2$$

Now, plug -3 in for y to the function that has the constant a as 2:

$$y = 2x \rightarrow$$

$$-3 = 2x \rightarrow$$

$$\frac{-3}{2} = x \rightarrow x = -1.5$$

So, the answer is choice **(B)**.

6. **(D)** All three of the angles will add up to 180, so set up an equation to solve for x:

$$2x + 3x + 4x = 180 \rightarrow$$

$$9x = 180 \rightarrow$$

$$x = 20$$

Since $\angle CED$ is equal to $3x$, multiply 3 by 20 to find the measure of the angle:

$$3 \times 20 = 60 \text{ degrees}$$

7. **(B)** Match the constants with the corresponding numbers on the other side of the equation. a equals 2, b equals 16, and c equals 32. Add these numbers together to find the sum of a, b, and c:

$$2 + 16 + 32 = 50$$

8. **(A)** In the function $S(w) = 500 + 10w$, when zero weeks have gone by, the value of w will be 0. Plugging 0 into the function for w, the amount of money she will have in her savings account will be 500. This represents how much money she has in the account when no weeks have gone by, so it corresponds to choice **(A)**, the money that is in her account at the beginning of the time period. Profit corresponds to revenue minus expenses, and the slope of 10 corresponds to the weekly increase in money in the account.

9. **(C)** The total amount of time that it took Samara to complete the trip is $4 + 6 = 10$ hours. Use the equation Distance = Rate × Time to work with this problem. The problem asks for the average speed, which corresponds to the rate. Using that equation, Rate $= \frac{\text{Distance}}{\text{Time}}$. Use 400 for the distance and 10 for the time to solve for the average rate over the entire trip:

$$\text{Rate} = \frac{\text{Distance}}{\text{Time}} \rightarrow$$

$$\text{Rate} = \frac{400 \text{ miles}}{10 \text{ hours}} = 40 \text{ mph}$$

10. **(B)** The number of diners who ordered a dessert is 50. Out of those 50, there were 15 diners who ordered an appetizer. Solve for the probability that a diner who ordered a dessert also ordered an appetizer by dividing 15 by 50:

$$\frac{15}{50} = \frac{3}{10}$$

11. **(D)** Plug x in for y to solve for what the value of the variables would be when they are equal:

$$y = 2x^2 - 7x \rightarrow$$

$$x = 2x^2 - 7x \rightarrow$$

$$8x = 2x^2 \rightarrow$$

$$4x = x^2 \rightarrow$$

$$4 = x$$

So, when the variables are equal, x and y would be 4.

12. **(C)**

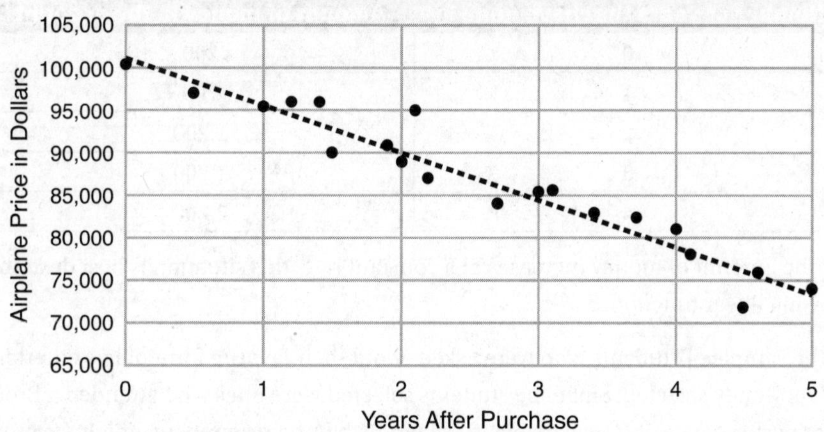

The line of best fit is sketched above. From year 0 to year 1, the price decreases by approximately \$5,000, going from about \$100,000 to about \$95,000. This rate of change remains constant throughout, so the best estimate for the amount that the value of an airplane decreases each year is about \$5,000.

13. **(C)** Based on the best-fit line that you can see in the previous solution, the amount that the value of an airplane decreases each year is approximately \$5,000. Since the initial cost of the airplane is approximately \$100,000, divide 100,000 by 5,000 to estimate when the plane value will closely approximate 0 dollars:

$$\frac{100,000}{5,000} = 20$$

So, 20 years after purchase the plane will closely approximate a value of 0 dollars.

14. **(D)** 400% of x is $4x$. This must be added to the original value of x to find the total value when x is increased by 400%: $4x + x = 5x$.

15. **(D)** The spins that had total values of 6 or less are bolded and italicized below:

Total of Combined Spins	Number of Spins with That Total Value
2	***1***
3	***2***
4	***2***
5	***4***
6	***5***
7	6
8	7
9	4
10	3
11	4
12	2

Out of the 40 total turns, there are therefore a total of $1 + 2 + 2 + 4 + 5 = 14$ turns in which Pete has a total of 6 or less. Find the fraction of the combined spins as follows:

$$\frac{14}{40} = \frac{7}{20}$$

16. **(A)** You might try visualizing what the amount of money in the account will be as each year goes by. Damon starts with \$200 in the account and adds \$500 each year:

Number of years that have gone by	Amount of money in the account
0	200
1	700
2	1,200
3	1,700
4	2,200

Since the amount of money increases at a constant rate, this situation is best described as an increasing linear function.

17. **(D)** The sample of students who were asked about their favorite form of live entertainment is not randomly selected. Since the students selected were ones who attended a Broadway theater performance, it is reasonable to conclude that the respondents might be more likely than the average student to prefer musical theater as a form of entertainment. So, the survey cannot be fairly generalized as to the entertainment preferences of all high school students.

18. **(D)** Since the Mexico City area represented 17% of the total population of Mexico, solve for the total population of Mexico, x, by using this equation:

$$0.17x = 22,000,000 \rightarrow$$

$$x = \frac{22,000,000}{0.17} \approx 129,000,000$$

19. **(B)** Use compound interest to solve:

$$A = P\left(1 + \frac{r}{n}\right)^{nt}$$

$A =$ Future Value, $P =$ Initial Value (Principal), $r =$ Interest Rate Expressed as a Decimal (r is positive if increasing, negative if decreasing), $t =$ Time, and $n =$ Number of Times Interest is Compounded over Time Period t

P will be 22,000,000, r will be 0.005, n will be 1 since the interest is compounded just once a year, and t will be 2 for the 2 years.

$$A = P\left(1 + \frac{r}{n}\right)^{nt} \rightarrow$$

$$A = (22,000,000)\left(1 + \frac{0.005}{1}\right)^{(1)(2)} \rightarrow$$

$$A = (22,000,000)(1.005)^2 = 22,220,550$$

The number of additional residents after the two years will therefore be:

$$22,220,550 - 22,000,000 = 220,550$$

Alternatively, the fact that Mexico City's population grows a .5% per year means that the next year, the population would be (1.005)(22,000,000), and the year after that, it would be (1.005)[(1.005)(22,000,000)], or 1.005^2(22,000,000) = 22,220,550. Thus, the population grew 22,220,550 − 22,000,000 = 220,550 in the two years.

20. **(D)** Find how many minutes there are in 16 hours:

$$16 \text{ hours} \times \frac{60 \text{ minutes}}{1 \text{ hour}} \rightarrow$$

$$16 \cancel{\text{hours}} \times \frac{60 \text{ minutes}}{1 \cancel{\text{hour}}} = 960 \text{ minutes}$$

Then, since Susan blinks 20 times per minute while awake, multiply 20 by 960 to find the total number of times she will blink:

$$20 \times 960 = 19,200$$

21. **(A)** The total number of tea bags T and coffee bags C that Troy will purchase is 80, so one equation will be $T + C = 80$. The total amount of money that Troy has budgeted is $55, and each tea bag costs $0.50 and each coffee bag costs $0.75. So, the second equation will show Troy's budget when he purchases T tea bags and C coffee bags: $.50T + .75C = 55$. Choice **(A)** is the correct answer since it has both of these equations.

22. **(A)** Hugo spends $150 a month on clothing out of a total monthly budget of $3,000. So, set this up as a fraction and simplify to find the fraction of Hugo's total budget that is spent on clothing:

$$\frac{150}{3000} = \frac{1}{20}$$

23. **(D)** Hugo spends $400 a month on miscellaneous expenses. If he cut this expenses by half and allocates all that he has cut to his savings, his savings would increase by $200 a month. Hugo is trying to allocate more money into savings. Now, calculate how large of an increase this additional $200 would be relative to the $250 he is currently saving:

$$\frac{200}{250} \times 100 = 80\%$$

So, he would increase his monthly savings by 80% if he were to make this change.

24. **(C)**

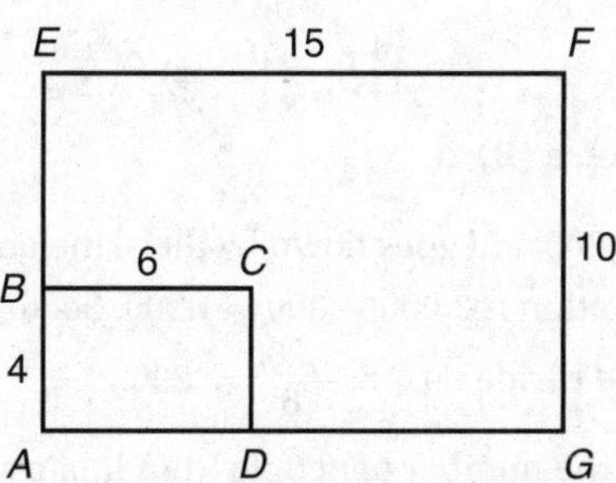

Since the rectangles are similar to one another, the sides are proportional. Therefore, the ratio of $\overline{EF}$ to $\overline{FG}$ will be the same as the ratio of $\overline{BC}$ to $\overline{AB}$. Call x the length of side $\overline{EF}$, and set up a proportion to solve:

$$\frac{x}{10} = \frac{6}{4} \rightarrow$$

$$x = \frac{10 \times 6}{4} = \frac{60}{4} = 15$$

Since $AEFG$ is a rectangle, there will be two sides of length 15 and two sides of length 10. Find the perimeter of the rectangle by adding the lengths of all these sides together:

$$15 + 15 + 10 + 10 = 50$$

25. **(A)** A line with the form $y = k$ will simply be a horizontal line. Since the constant k is greater than zero, it will not intersect the x-axis at all and will therefore have no zeros. For example, consider the equation $y = 2$. The graph of this line is given below:

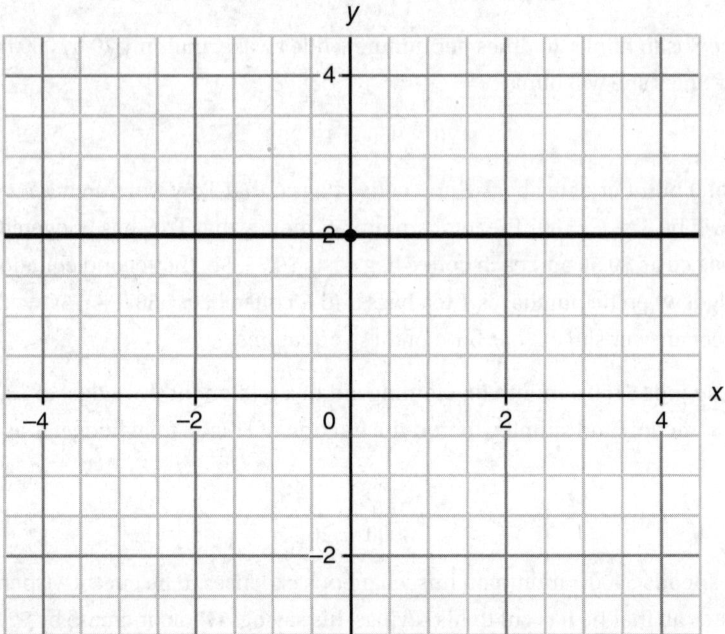

As you can see, the line is horizontal and will never intersect the x-axis.

26. **(B)** Fourteen out of the 44 people to serve as president of the United States prior to 2020 had previously been vice president. So, $\frac{14}{44}$ of the presidents had been vice presidents. Set up an equation expressing this as follows:

$$V = \frac{14}{44}P \rightarrow V = \frac{7}{22}P$$

Therefore, the answer is choice **(B)**.

27. **(C)** The computer costs \$2,000 and goes down by the same amount each year. After 6 years, the total amount of depreciation is 2,000 – 800 = 1,200. So, to find the annual amount of depreciation, take 1,200 and divide it by 6: $\frac{1{,}200}{6} = 200$.

28. **(D)** Given that J stands for the number of people from Julian's side of the family and that M stands for the number of people from Maria's side of the family, the first inequality should be $M + J > 200$, since they want to have more than 200 people in attendance. The second inequality represents the costs. The total cost for the reception should be less than \$18,000, and the cost for each invited guest is \$40. So, the second inequality should be $40(M + J) < 18{,}000$ to model this relationship. These two inequalities correspond to choice **(D)**.

29. **(B)** Use unit analysis to cancel out the necessary terms and convert the value to the required terms:

$$30\,\frac{\text{Miles}}{\text{Hour}} \times \frac{5{,}280 \text{ Feet}}{1 \text{ Mile}} \times \frac{1 \text{ Hour}}{3{,}600 \text{ Seconds}} \rightarrow$$

$$30\,\frac{\cancel{\text{Miles}}}{\cancel{\text{Hour}}} \times \frac{5{,}280 \text{ Feet}}{1\,\cancel{\text{Mile}}} \times \frac{1\,\cancel{\text{Hour}}}{3{,}600 \text{ Seconds}} \rightarrow$$

$$\frac{30 \times 5{,}280}{3{,}600} = 44\,\frac{\text{Feet}}{\text{Second}}$$

30. **(C)** Use C to represent the number of cups of coffee Shantiel purchased and T to represent the number of cups of tea purchased. Set up a system of equations to solve for C. First, since the number of cups of coffee is half the number of cups of tea, one equation would be $C = \frac{1}{2}T$. The second equation represents the milligrams of caffeine. Since there are 95 milligrams in each cup of coffee and 26 milligrams in each cup of tea, the equation would be $95C + 26T = 735$. Solve for C by using substitution from the first equation:

$$C = \frac{1}{2}T \rightarrow$$

$$2C = T$$

Now, substitute $2C$ in for T into the second equation, then solve for C:

$$95C + 26T = 735 \rightarrow$$

$$95C + 26(2C) = 735 \rightarrow$$

$$95C + 52C = 735 \rightarrow$$

$$147C = 735 \rightarrow$$

$$C = \frac{735}{147} = 5$$

So, she purchased 5 cups of coffee, which corresponds to choice **(C)**.

31. **1** Take the cube root of both sides of the equation, then solve for x:

$$(x + 2)^3 = 27 \rightarrow$$

$$\sqrt[3]{(x + 2)^3} = \sqrt[3]{27} \rightarrow$$

$$x + 2 = 3 \rightarrow$$

$$x = 1$$

32. **4** Use elimination to solve. If you multiply the first equation by 2 and add it to the second equation, you can eliminate the y variables:

$$2x - y = 6$$

$$3x + 2y = 23 \rightarrow$$

$$4x - 2y = 12$$

$$\underline{+3x + 2y = 23}$$

$$7x + 0 = 35$$

Then, solve for x:

$$7x = 35 \rightarrow$$

$$x = \frac{35}{7} = 5$$

Now, plug 5 back in for x to the first equation to solve for y:

$$2x - y = 6 \rightarrow$$

$$2(5) - y = 6 \rightarrow$$

$$10 - y = 6 \rightarrow$$

$$-y = -4 \rightarrow$$

$$y = 4$$

33. **4** Factor the right-hand side of the equation to see what number would correspond to a:

$$(x+a)(x+a) = x^2 + 8x + 16 \rightarrow$$
$$(x+a)(x+a) = (x+4)(x+4)$$

So, $a = 4$.

34. **12** Since each pastry calls for 1 and $\frac{1}{3}$ cups of flour, divide the total amount of flour, 16 cups, by 1 and $\frac{1}{3}$, which can also be expressed as $\frac{4}{3}$.

$$16 \div \frac{4}{3} \rightarrow$$

Multiply by the reciprocal $\rightarrow$

$$16 \times \frac{3}{4} = \frac{48}{4} = 12$$

35. **1** The range for class 1 can be found by taking the greatest score and subtracting the least score: $5 - 0 = 5$. Use a similar approach to find the score range for class 2 (be careful since no one has a score of 0, so the least score is actually 1): $5 - 1 = 4$. So the difference in the score ranges between the two classes is $5 - 4 = 1$.

36. **3** The combined set of both classes will have a total of 40 students, since there are 20 students in each class. So, the median of the set of both classes will be between the 20th and 21st terms when the numbers are put in order from least to greatest. There are a total of 18 values that are 2 or less, and then there are 9 values that are 3. So, the 20th and 21st terms will both be 3, making 3 the median of the combined set of scores.

37. **2** If Mia has a total budget of \$500, if she stays at a hotel that costs \$70 per night, the total number of whole nights she could stay is found by dividing 500 by 70, and looking just at the whole number to the left of the decimal point:

$\frac{500}{70} \approx 7.14$. So, she could stay 7 whole nights at the \$70 per night hotel.

Do a similar calculation to find the total number of whole nights she could stay at the \$90 per night hotel:

$\frac{500}{90} \approx 5.55$. Since she cannot stay for 0.55 nights, the total number of whole nights she could stay at the \$90 per night hotel is 5.

Now, subtract 5 from 7 to find the maximum number of additional whole nights that she could stay at the less expensive hotel:

$$7 - 5 = 2$$

38. **43** Since there are 360 degrees in a circle, the sector designated by $\angle ACB$ represents $\frac{100}{360}$ of the total area of the circle. The area for this circle is found using the formula πr^2, and the radius of the circle is 7. So, multiply the area of the circle by the fraction of the area that the sector represents to find the sector's area:

$$\pi 7^2 \times \frac{100}{360} = 42.74$$

This would be rounded to an area of 43, since that is the nearest whole square unit.

ANSWER SHEET
Practice Test 3

Section 1: Reading Test

1. Ⓐ Ⓑ Ⓒ Ⓓ	14. Ⓐ Ⓑ Ⓒ Ⓓ	27. Ⓐ Ⓑ Ⓒ Ⓓ	40. Ⓐ Ⓑ Ⓒ Ⓓ
2. Ⓐ Ⓑ Ⓒ Ⓓ	15. Ⓐ Ⓑ Ⓒ Ⓓ	28. Ⓐ Ⓑ Ⓒ Ⓓ	41. Ⓐ Ⓑ Ⓒ Ⓓ
3. Ⓐ Ⓑ Ⓒ Ⓓ	16. Ⓐ Ⓑ Ⓒ Ⓓ	29. Ⓐ Ⓑ Ⓒ Ⓓ	42. Ⓐ Ⓑ Ⓒ Ⓓ
4. Ⓐ Ⓑ Ⓒ Ⓓ	17. Ⓐ Ⓑ Ⓒ Ⓓ	30. Ⓐ Ⓑ Ⓒ Ⓓ	43. Ⓐ Ⓑ Ⓒ Ⓓ
5. Ⓐ Ⓑ Ⓒ Ⓓ	18. Ⓐ Ⓑ Ⓒ Ⓓ	31. Ⓐ Ⓑ Ⓒ Ⓓ	44. Ⓐ Ⓑ Ⓒ Ⓓ
6. Ⓐ Ⓑ Ⓒ Ⓓ	19. Ⓐ Ⓑ Ⓒ Ⓓ	32. Ⓐ Ⓑ Ⓒ Ⓓ	45. Ⓐ Ⓑ Ⓒ Ⓓ
7. Ⓐ Ⓑ Ⓒ Ⓓ	20. Ⓐ Ⓑ Ⓒ Ⓓ	33. Ⓐ Ⓑ Ⓒ Ⓓ	46. Ⓐ Ⓑ Ⓒ Ⓓ
8. Ⓐ Ⓑ Ⓒ Ⓓ	21. Ⓐ Ⓑ Ⓒ Ⓓ	34. Ⓐ Ⓑ Ⓒ Ⓓ	47. Ⓐ Ⓑ Ⓒ Ⓓ
9. Ⓐ Ⓑ Ⓒ Ⓓ	22. Ⓐ Ⓑ Ⓒ Ⓓ	35. Ⓐ Ⓑ Ⓒ Ⓓ	48. Ⓐ Ⓑ Ⓒ Ⓓ
10. Ⓐ Ⓑ Ⓒ Ⓓ	23. Ⓐ Ⓑ Ⓒ Ⓓ	36. Ⓐ Ⓑ Ⓒ Ⓓ	49. Ⓐ Ⓑ Ⓒ Ⓓ
11. Ⓐ Ⓑ Ⓒ Ⓓ	24. Ⓐ Ⓑ Ⓒ Ⓓ	37. Ⓐ Ⓑ Ⓒ Ⓓ	50. Ⓐ Ⓑ Ⓒ Ⓓ
12. Ⓐ Ⓑ Ⓒ Ⓓ	25. Ⓐ Ⓑ Ⓒ Ⓓ	38. Ⓐ Ⓑ Ⓒ Ⓓ	51. Ⓐ Ⓑ Ⓒ Ⓓ
13. Ⓐ Ⓑ Ⓒ Ⓓ	26. Ⓐ Ⓑ Ⓒ Ⓓ	39. Ⓐ Ⓑ Ⓒ Ⓓ	52. Ⓐ Ⓑ Ⓒ Ⓓ

Section 2: Writing and Language Test

1. Ⓐ Ⓑ Ⓒ Ⓓ	12. Ⓐ Ⓑ Ⓒ Ⓓ	23. Ⓐ Ⓑ Ⓒ Ⓓ	34. Ⓐ Ⓑ Ⓒ Ⓓ
2. Ⓐ Ⓑ Ⓒ Ⓓ	13. Ⓐ Ⓑ Ⓒ Ⓓ	24. Ⓐ Ⓑ Ⓒ Ⓓ	35. Ⓐ Ⓑ Ⓒ Ⓓ
3. Ⓐ Ⓑ Ⓒ Ⓓ	14. Ⓐ Ⓑ Ⓒ Ⓓ	25. Ⓐ Ⓑ Ⓒ Ⓓ	36. Ⓐ Ⓑ Ⓒ Ⓓ
4. Ⓐ Ⓑ Ⓒ Ⓓ	15. Ⓐ Ⓑ Ⓒ Ⓓ	26. Ⓐ Ⓑ Ⓒ Ⓓ	37. Ⓐ Ⓑ Ⓒ Ⓓ
5. Ⓐ Ⓑ Ⓒ Ⓓ	16. Ⓐ Ⓑ Ⓒ Ⓓ	27. Ⓐ Ⓑ Ⓒ Ⓓ	38. Ⓐ Ⓑ Ⓒ Ⓓ
6. Ⓐ Ⓑ Ⓒ Ⓓ	17. Ⓐ Ⓑ Ⓒ Ⓓ	28. Ⓐ Ⓑ Ⓒ Ⓓ	39. Ⓐ Ⓑ Ⓒ Ⓓ
7. Ⓐ Ⓑ Ⓒ Ⓓ	18. Ⓐ Ⓑ Ⓒ Ⓓ	29. Ⓐ Ⓑ Ⓒ Ⓓ	40. Ⓐ Ⓑ Ⓒ Ⓓ
8. Ⓐ Ⓑ Ⓒ Ⓓ	19. Ⓐ Ⓑ Ⓒ Ⓓ	30. Ⓐ Ⓑ Ⓒ Ⓓ	41. Ⓐ Ⓑ Ⓒ Ⓓ
9. Ⓐ Ⓑ Ⓒ Ⓓ	20. Ⓐ Ⓑ Ⓒ Ⓓ	31. Ⓐ Ⓑ Ⓒ Ⓓ	42. Ⓐ Ⓑ Ⓒ Ⓓ
10. Ⓐ Ⓑ Ⓒ Ⓓ	21. Ⓐ Ⓑ Ⓒ Ⓓ	32. Ⓐ Ⓑ Ⓒ Ⓓ	43. Ⓐ Ⓑ Ⓒ Ⓓ
11. Ⓐ Ⓑ Ⓒ Ⓓ	22. Ⓐ Ⓑ Ⓒ Ⓓ	33. Ⓐ Ⓑ Ⓒ Ⓓ	44. Ⓐ Ⓑ Ⓒ Ⓓ

ANSWER SHEET
Practice Test 3

Section 3: Math (No Calculator)

1. Ⓐ Ⓑ Ⓒ Ⓓ **5.** Ⓐ Ⓑ Ⓒ Ⓓ **9.** Ⓐ Ⓑ Ⓒ Ⓓ **13.** Ⓐ Ⓑ Ⓒ Ⓓ

2. Ⓐ Ⓑ Ⓒ Ⓓ **6.** Ⓐ Ⓑ Ⓒ Ⓓ **10.** Ⓐ Ⓑ Ⓒ Ⓓ **14.** Ⓐ Ⓑ Ⓒ Ⓓ

3. Ⓐ Ⓑ Ⓒ Ⓓ **7.** Ⓐ Ⓑ Ⓒ Ⓓ **11.** Ⓐ Ⓑ Ⓒ Ⓓ **15.** Ⓐ Ⓑ Ⓒ Ⓓ

4. Ⓐ Ⓑ Ⓒ Ⓓ **8.** Ⓐ Ⓑ Ⓒ Ⓓ **12.** Ⓐ Ⓑ Ⓒ Ⓓ

16.

17.

18.

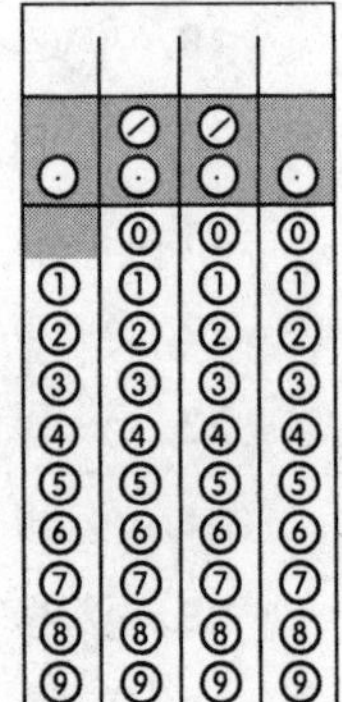

19.

20.

ANSWER SHEET
Practice Test 3

Section 4: Math (Calculator)

1. Ⓐ Ⓑ Ⓒ Ⓓ
2. Ⓐ Ⓑ Ⓒ Ⓓ
3. Ⓐ Ⓑ Ⓒ Ⓓ
4. Ⓐ Ⓑ Ⓒ Ⓓ
5. Ⓐ Ⓑ Ⓒ Ⓓ
6. Ⓐ Ⓑ Ⓒ Ⓓ
7. Ⓐ Ⓑ Ⓒ Ⓓ
8. Ⓐ Ⓑ Ⓒ Ⓓ
9. Ⓐ Ⓑ Ⓒ Ⓓ
10. Ⓐ Ⓑ Ⓒ Ⓓ
11. Ⓐ Ⓑ Ⓒ Ⓓ
12. Ⓐ Ⓑ Ⓒ Ⓓ
13. Ⓐ Ⓑ Ⓒ Ⓓ
14. Ⓐ Ⓑ Ⓒ Ⓓ
15. Ⓐ Ⓑ Ⓒ Ⓓ
16. Ⓐ Ⓑ Ⓒ Ⓓ
17. Ⓐ Ⓑ Ⓒ Ⓓ
18. Ⓐ Ⓑ Ⓒ Ⓓ
19. Ⓐ Ⓑ Ⓒ Ⓓ
20. Ⓐ Ⓑ Ⓒ Ⓓ
21. Ⓐ Ⓑ Ⓒ Ⓓ
22. Ⓐ Ⓑ Ⓒ Ⓓ
23. Ⓐ Ⓑ Ⓒ Ⓓ
24. Ⓐ Ⓑ Ⓒ Ⓓ
25. Ⓐ Ⓑ Ⓒ Ⓓ
26. Ⓐ Ⓑ Ⓒ Ⓓ
27. Ⓐ Ⓑ Ⓒ Ⓓ
28. Ⓐ Ⓑ Ⓒ Ⓓ
29. Ⓐ Ⓑ Ⓒ Ⓓ
30. Ⓐ Ⓑ Ⓒ Ⓓ

31.

32.

33.

34.

35.

36.

37.

38.

Practice Test 3

READING PRACTICE TEST 3

65 MINUTES, 52 QUESTIONS

DIRECTIONS: Each passage or pair of passages is accompanied by several questions. After reading the passage(s), choose the best answer to each question based on what is indicated explicitly or implicitly in the passage(s) or in the associated graphics.

Questions 1–10 are based on the following passage.

The following is an excerpt from the novel My Ántonia, *by Willa Cather, written in 1918.*

Last summer I happened to be crossing the plains of Iowa in a season of intense heat, and it was my good fortune to have for a traveling companion James Quayle Burden—Jim Burden, as we still call him in the West. He and I are old friends—we grew up together in the same Nebraska town—and we had much to say to each other. While the train flashed through never-ending miles of ripe wheat, by country towns and bright-flowered pastures and oak groves wilting in the sun, we sat in the observation car, where the woodwork was hot to the touch and red dust lay deep over everything. The dust and heat, the burning wind, reminded us of many things. We were talking about what it is like to spend one's childhood in little towns like these, buried in wheat and corn, under stimulating extremes of climate: burning summers when the world lies green and billowy beneath a brilliant sky, when one is fairly stifled in vegetation, in the color and smell of strong weeds and heavy harvests; blustery winters with little snow, when the whole country is stripped bare and gray as sheet-iron. We agreed that no one who had not grown up in a little prairie town could know anything about it. It was a kind of freemasonry, we said.

Although Jim Burden and I both live in New York, and are old friends, I do not see much of him there. He is legal counsel for one of the great Western railways, and is sometimes away from his New York office for weeks together. That is one reason why we do not often meet. Another is that I do not like his wife.

When Jim was still an obscure young lawyer, struggling to make his way in New York, his career was suddenly advanced by a brilliant marriage. Genevieve Whitney was the only daughter of a distinguished man. Her marriage with young Burden was the subject of sharp comment at the time. It was said she had been brutally jilted by her cousin, Rutland Whitney, and that she married this unknown man from the West out of bravado. She was a restless, headstrong girl, even then, who liked to astonish her friends. Later, when I knew her, she

0 0 0

was always doing something unexpected. She gave one of her town houses for a Suffrage headquarters, produced one of her own plays at the Princess Theater, was arrested for picketing during a garment-makers' strike, etc. I am never able to believe that she has much feeling for the causes to which she lends her name and her fleeting interest. She is handsome and energetic, but to me she seems unimpressionable and temperamentally incapable of enthusiasm. Her husband's quiet tastes irritate her, I think, and she finds it worthwhile to play the patroness to a group of young poets and painters of advanced ideas and mediocre ability. She has her own fortune and lives her own life. For some reason, she wishes to remain Mrs. James Burden.

As for Jim, no disappointments have been severe enough to chill his naturally romantic and ardent disposition. This disposition, though it often made him seem very funny when he was a boy, has been one of the strongest elements in his success. He loves with a personal passion the great country through which his railway runs and branches. His faith in it and his knowledge of it have played an important part in its development. He is always able to raise capital for new enterprises in Wyoming or Montana, and has helped young men out there to do remarkable things in mines and timber and oil. If a young man with an idea can once get Jim Burden's attention, can manage to accompany him when he goes off into the wilds hunting for lost parks or exploring new canyons, then the money which means action is usually forthcoming. Jim is still able to lose himself in those big Western dreams. Though he is over forty now, he meets new people and new enterprises with the impulsiveness by which his boyhood friends remember him. He never seems to me to grow older. His fresh color and sandy hair and quick-changing blue eyes are those of a young man.

1. Based on the context of the passage, what does the narrator most likely mean when she says "It was a kind of freemasonry" in lines 26–27?

(A) The culture in urban centers like New York is more complex than the cultures in rural areas.
(B) The architectural styles in rural areas are substantially different from those in large cities.
(C) Only those who have grown up in small prairie towns can fully understand what they are like.
(D) The workings of the weather systems in the Great Plains are nothing short of mysterious.

2. As used in line 40, "sharp" most closely means

(A) intense.
(B) stabbing.
(C) elegant.
(D) punctual.

3. According to the passage, the main characters currently primarily reside in

(A) a Western prairie town.
(B) New York.
(C) Wyoming.
(D) Montana.

4. It can reasonably be inferred from lines 35–38, ("When Jim... marriage") that the narrator likely believes that Jim married his wife

(A) out of a love for her intellect.
(B) because of professional ambition.
(C) due to his sincere love for her.
(D) given her sympathy for his poverty.

5. The narrator uses the third paragraph, lines 35–63, to portray James Burden's wife as someone who is
   (A) possessing of many redeeming qualities despite her lack of energy.
   (B) independent while having highly refined aesthetic sensibilities.
   (C) unimpressive and substantially different from her husband.
   (D) inspiring given her passion for social justice projects.

6. The narrator of the passage suggests that if Jim were to encounter an extremely difficult situation, he would most likely
   (A) be resilient and positive enough to overcome it.
   (B) use his vast inherited wealth to make the problem go away.
   (C) rely on his connections to bankers out West to amass financial resources.
   (D) give up due to his low tolerance for personal challenges.

7. Which option gives the best evidence for the answer to the previous question?
   (A) Lines 15–18 ("We were . . . climate")
   (B) Lines 35–38 ("When Jim . . . marriage")
   (C) Lines 64–66 ("As for . . . disposition")
   (D) Lines 73–77 ("He is . . . oil")

8. The narrator would most likely envision James Burden's wife as doing which of the following activities?
   (A) Extravagantly financing a charitable event for a cause for which she has a fleeting interest
   (B) Surprising her many friends by showcasing her impressive innate skills in music
   (C) Bettering herself intellectually by doing an in-depth self-study in world literature
   (D) Devoting herself to strengthening her relationship with her husband by engaging him in long daily conversations

9. Which selection from the passage provides the best evidence that Jim Burden had a positive attitude toward entrepreneurial investments?
   (A) Lines 57–60 ("Her husband's . . . ability")
   (B) Lines 66–69 ("This disposition . . . success")
   (C) Lines 73–77 ("He is . . . oil")
   (D) Lines 86–89 ("He never . . . man")

10. As used in line 83, "lose himself in" most closely means
   (A) become physically lost.
   (B) meet with defeat.
   (C) give all attention to.
   (D) experience deprivation with.

Questions 11–20 are based on the following passages.

These two passages analyze the principles of handwashing. Both were written in 2020.

Passage 1

When the first few doctors started to recommend handwashing to prevent infection, they were largely ridiculed. It seemed preposterous that soap (which had previously only been used to remove actual dirt) could be related to health. Germ theory had yet to be born, and people's understanding of the microscopic world was nonexistent. Soon, however, medical professionals began to realize that washing hands indeed improved patient results for surgeries: they had stumbled upon a life-saving technique. However, *why* handwashing saved lives remained an unsolved mystery for quite some time. Now, most small children can tell you that soap helps to wash away germs. The mechanisms that allow this to happen, though, remain unknown to the average layman.

Soap is made up of small molecules that have hydrophilic heads and hydrophobic tails; the hydrophilic heads are attracted to water, while the hydrophobic tails are repelled by water. The soap molecules, when dissolved in water, float around and can either act independently or can join with other soap molecules to form bubbles with all the molecules pointing their heads outward and their tails inward. With only the heads exposed, the soap bubbles are hydrophobic and "run away" from water.

Many bacteria look very similar. They are round organisms that often have four layers; the innermost and outermost are generally hydrophilic while the middle layers are generally hydrophobic. Because the outermost layer is hydrophilic, water alone will not be effective in washing away the molecule—the germs won't "run away" from water. However, when soap is added, the hydrophobic exterior of the soap bubble seeks out ways to avoid the water. The primary way of doing this is for the soap molecules to worm their way into the bacteria. This action by the soap breaks up the layers of the bacteria, causing their hydrophilic exteriors to be shattered, and allowing water into the hydrophobic layers of the molecule. Once broken up in such a manner, the bacteria can easily be rinsed away.

Passage 2

Handwashing *is* important, especially in people who have compromised immune systems or who know they have been exposed to germs against which they have no immunity. It is for this reason that all people are asked to wash their hands frequently during large outbreaks of communicable diseases. In daily life though, *excessive* handwashing, for the average person, can lead to long-term negative outcomes even while it prevents them from getting minor illnesses in the short term.

Because of the antimicrobial properties of soap, a thorough washing will take away almost all bacteria from a surface. Whether a person is washing their hands or wiping down their countertop, soap creates a sterile environment. This is crucial at times when pernicious bacteria are present (like when handling raw food or after using the restroom). However, living in a constantly sterile environment is, for the average person, not necessary.

Soap does not kill just bacteria that are fatal to humans. Instead, it works as an agent to remove *all* germs. Therefore, humans who over-wash have much less exposure to relatively harmless germs that their immune systems should be able to fend off. The human immune system gets stronger through exposure to germs. This system builds up antibodies to protect the body during future exposures.

This basic principle is what makes immunizations effective—the person being immunized is given a small dose of a "dead" virus so that their body can learn what it is and build up antibodies to fight it when they are exposed in "real life." However, when the immune system lacks exposure to any germs, no antibodies are built up. Consequently, when it is accidently exposed to a virus or other bacteria, it can't act against it and the person can become grievously ill from what otherwise might be an innocuous exposure.

The line between over-sterilization and under-sterilization seems to be a tight rope with falling on either side leading to disaster. However, with common sense and moderation, most healthy people can remain healthy with little effort: Wash your hands when you suspect you may have been exposed to something that could make you ill (raw meat, bathroom germs) and before you eat. The rest of the time, let less harmful germs interact with your immune system to keep you healthy.

11. The medical understanding of handwashing as presented in lines 1–12 ("When the... technique") can best be described as something that

(A) is ineffective given the available observational data.
(B) no doctors chose to recommend.
(C) was considered useful but not fully understood.
(D) was widely applied due to a solid theoretical concept.

12. As used in line 11, "stumbled upon" most closely means

(A) accidentally discovered.
(B) tripped on.
(C) thoroughly researched.
(D) expressed disappointment.

13. As described by Passage 1, the primary mechanism by which soap molecules clean hands covered in bacteria is by

(A) strengthening the hydrophilic surface of bacteria.
(B) dissolving bacteria into a less harmful solution.
(C) breaking up parts of the bacteria from within.
(D) joining with other soap molecules to absorb the bacteria.

14. Which option gives the best evidence for the answer to the previous question?

(A) Lines 21–26 ("The soap... inward")
(B) Lines 29–33 ("Many... hydrophobic")
(C) Lines 33–36 ("Because... water")
(D) Lines 41–46 ("This action... away")

15. The attitude of the author of Passage 2 toward germs is that they

(A) should be avoided at all costs.
(B) must be encountered to build bodily resilience.
(C) uniformly threaten the body's immune response.
(D) are not well understood by medical researchers.

16. Which option gives the best evidence for the answer to the previous question?

(A) Lines 47–50 ("Handwashing... immunity")
(B) Lines 58–60 ("Because of... surface")
(C) Lines 73–76 ("The human... exposures")
(D) Lines 89–91 ("The line... disaster")

17. As used in line 63, "crucial" most closely means

(A) severe.
(B) indifferent.
(C) authoritative.
(D) important.

18. The sentence in lines 77–82 ("This basic... life") primarily serves to

    (A) dispute the theoretical basis for a claim.
    (B) explain how patient education can lead to better health outcomes.
    (C) provide an analogy to explain a previous assertion.
    (D) cite scholarly sources in order to justify a hypothesis.

19. Which of the following best describes the relationship between the two passages?

    (A) Passage 1 presents the latest research findings on a topic, and Passage 2 critiques the methodology of the findings.
    (B) Passage 1 analyzes the theory behind why the assertions made in Passage 2 have a sound basis.
    (C) Passage 1 explains how a process works, and Passage 2 analyzes how this process should be implemented most effectively.
    (D) Passage 1 considers the history behind a belief system that Passage 2 chooses to embrace.

20. A problem that Passage 2 highlights that Passage 1 does not is

    (A) the potential danger of an artificially sterile environment.
    (B) the need to be aware of how bacteria is removed through handwashing.
    (C) how soap can play an important role in disease prevention.
    (D) how it is impossible to wash one's hands too much.

Questions 21–31 are based on the following passage and supplementary material.

Multi-Level Marketing, written in 2020.

Get-rich-quick schemes have probably existed since humans first used money to buy instead of goods to barter. Most have learned to be wary of people and organizations that claim to be an easy path to riches. However, in the 1950s a new type of scheme emerged disguised as a work or career opportunity, but was designed to pad the pockets of a select few. This effective setup targeted young women who found life at home to be boring after returning to domesticity post World War Two. It allowed a woman to feel like she was contributing financially to her family's well-being while still maintaining her role in the household. This sales system, called multi-level marketing (MLM), still pervades our society today, promising unsuspecting targets the chance at great wealth—for a cost.

Many people are familiar with MLMs by another name: pyramid schemes. Pyramid schemes involve one person getting two or three people to give him money by promising riches at a later time. Then, those two or three people each recruit a few more people who recruit a few more people in a never-ending stream: each person passes money up the pyramid toward the people near the top. MLMs are different from pyramid schemes in only one way—they sell things. From makeup and oils to weight loss pills and clothes, MLMs all have a product that they sell. People who sign up for an MLM must use their own money to purchase the products to then sell to their family and friends. This "investment" can involve shelling out thousands of dollars. More often than not, family and friends become tired of purchasing things they don't need; the consultants are left with piles of expensive goods they cannot sell.

0 0 0

So how do MLMs survive if most people have trouble selling to their small circle of family and friends? The real money comes from people buying in. In addition to selling items, consultants are encouraged to sign up new people to be consultants. Consultants get a percentage of what their "downline" (the people they signed up, and the people who then sign up with their new consultants) sells *or* buys. Consultants also earn incentives for signing up more and more people below them in the structure. What this means is that the first person in an area to join a new MLM may actually make a little money. However, the market quickly becomes saturated with the product, and having thirty or forty independent consultants in a small town means that no one is making many sales and everyone who wants to be a consultant already is one, leaving no way for new consultants to make money.

Consequently, only a tiny percent of people who buy into an MLM actually make money. Across the nation, 20 million adults generate about 36 billion dollars each year from MLMs. A self-reported survey by AARP shows that 74 percent of these 20 million make no money or actually *lose* money. About 13 percent made $1–$5,000 per year, leaving only thirteen percent of people making over $5,000 per year, most of whom still made less than $24,000 per year. Only one percent (the top of the pyramid) make anywhere near the riches they were promised. Of the people who join MLMs, 54 percent said that they felt they were misled by the company as to their chances at financial success.[1]

The MLMs explain this away by saying that those who fail simply aren't trying hard enough. They ignore market oversaturation. They ignore the fact that many people try so hard they lose family and friends who don't want to hear the pitch again. They ignore the fact that at some point there simply aren't enough people in a population to support more consultants. They instead target the young and the gullible. Young men and women fresh out of high school often receive letters in the mail promising a business opportunity. Young broke single parents are drawn in by people who they think are friends. The cycle continues with new MLMs popping up every year. No one has to be part of the cycle though. Avoiding these companies is simple—just ask two questions. Do I have to use my own money to purchase the products I'll be selling? Will I be rewarded for convincing people to join? If the answer to either of these questions is yes, leave. You are not going to get rich quick.

[1] Data gathered from: *www.aarp.org/content/dam/aarp/aarp_foundation/2018/pdf/AARPFResearchExecutiveSummaryFINAL101018.pdf*

Profits broken down in a classic no-product 8-ball (1-2-4-8) pyramid scheme:

Order of participants' entry into the scheme	Revenues to each participant at that level	Number of participants at that level
Initiator	$140,000	1
2nd participants entering the system	$120,000	2
3rd participants entering the system	$112,000	4
4th participants entering the system	$98,000	8
5th participants entering the system	$84,000	16
6th participants entering the system	$70,000	32
7th participants entering the system	$56,000	64
8th participants entering the system	$42,000	128
9th participants entering the system	$28,000	256
10th participants entering the system	$14,000	512
Total number of participants who would profit		1,023
Number of participants at the lower levels who would lose money		7,168
Total of all participants in the scheme		8,191
Percent who profit (assuming all those who profit reinvest in new cycles of the pryamid		12.49%
Percent who lose money at the 10th level		87.51%

* This includes all who participated, regardless of how many times.

** This is the number of participants who have cashed in at least once and some multiple times.

*** This assumes every profiting participant keeps investing in new pyramid cycles. The percentage profiting would be slightly higher or lower depending on how many participants dropped out and when.

Source: Corporate Survey from the Federal Trade Commission at ftc.gov

21. The main purpose of the passage is to

(A) help readers avoid a scheme by explaining how it works.

(B) show business owners how to successfully start a new enterprise.

(C) describe the primary way that most businesses today operate.

(D) consider different points of view on a controversial topic.

22. It can be reasonably be inferred from the passage that which of the following would be a pyramid scheme but not an MLM?

(A) Consultants are recruited to sell handmade products.

(B) New members do not sell products but rather just pass money, which flows up to the original member.

(C) Corporate advisors collect fees for their services.

(D) Illegal substances are sold for a greater value than it cost to produce them.

23. Which selection provides the best evidence that nonfinancial factors could motivate people to participate in an MLM?

    (A) Lines 3–5 ("Most... riches")
    (B) Lines 8–11 ("This effective... Two")
    (C) Lines 14–17 ("This sales... cost")
    (D) Lines 22–25 ("Then... stream")

24. As used in lines 33–34, "shelling out" most closely means

    (A) earning.
    (B) growing.
    (C) spending.
    (D) harvesting.

25. If someone were trying to showcase a participant in an MLM to convince others to join, it is most likely that the participant selected would be

    (A) a participant who invested considerable funds in purchasing products.
    (B) someone who took out a loan to gather funding to sign up.
    (C) a consultant in a small town that is saturated with other consultants.
    (D) one of the first to join the MLM.

26. Which option gives the best evidence for the answer to the previous question?

    (A) Lines 28–30 ("From makeup... sell")
    (B) Lines 33–34 ("This... dollars")
    (C) Lines 34–37 ("More often... sell")
    (D) Lines 48–51 ("What this... money")

27. The intention behind proponents of MLMs in using the phrase "explain this away" in line 73 is to

    (A) grant that their detractors have a valid point.
    (B) show their desire to provide greater detail.
    (C) minimize reasonable objections to their ideas.
    (D) undermine those who believe MLMs are worthwhile.

28. The author primarily uses the questions in lines 89–92 ("Do I... join") to provide readers with

    (A) questions to ask themselves before starting their own MLM.
    (B) helpful tools that will empower readers to make wise decisions.
    (C) ways to judge whether something is an MLM or just a pyramid scheme.
    (D) business advice to empower them to be savvy human resource managers.

29. In the pyramid scheme portrayed in the table, the number of participants in each subsequent entry to the scheme

    (A) doubles.
    (B) halves.
    (C) triples.
    (D) remains the same.

30. To the nearest whole percent, what percent of participants portrayed in all ten cycles of the scheme in the table made a profit?

    (A) 0%
    (B) 12%
    (C) 88%
    (D) 100%

31. An advocate for MLMs could most effectively critique the information in the accompanying table by pointing out that

    (A) the data is not from an authoritative source.
    (B) the initiator in a pyramid scheme actually makes quite a bit of money.
    (C) both MLMs and pyramid schemes depend on the participation of many people.
    (D) while it may be true for pyramid schemes, it is not applicable to product-based MLMs.

Questions 32–42 are based on the following passage.

The following is an adaptation of part of an address by Elizabeth Cady Stanton to the Judiciary Committees of the legislature of New York as she argued for the right of Black men and all women to vote in the election of delegates to the Constitutional Convention. The address was given January 23rd, 1867.

The wheel of progress moves onward, and man must, in the nature of things, throw off old customs, creeds and codes, as the snake sheds its skin in the new growth, and from the dead letters of the past, emerge into higher civilization. History shows that each generation has been marked by some new idea, alike tending to the greater freedom and equality of man; and those who, in their blindness or folly, have tried to block this onward march, have invariably been ground to powder. We see a signal instance of this in the summary manner in which an indignant people have ridden rough-shod over Andrew Johnson and his satellites—showing that even the head of a nation is nothing, but as he represents the leading ideas of his generation. They only are immortal who link the future to the past, and roll on the triumphal car of progress to the brighter and the better day.

The extension of suffrage is the political idea of our day, agitating alike the leading minds of both continents. The question of debate in the long past has been the rights of races. This, in our country, was settled by the war, when the Black man was declared free and worthy to bear arms in defense of the republic, and the last remnants of aristocracy were scattered before our Northern hosts like chaff in the whirlwind. We have now come to the broader idea of *individual* rights. An idea already ably debated in Congress and out, by Republicans, Democrats and Abolitionists, who, in common with the best writers and thinkers of the day the world over, base all rights of society and government on those of the individual. Each one of you has a right to everything in earth and air, on land and sea, to the whole world of thought, to all that is needful for soul and body, and there is no limit to the exercise of your rights, but in the infringement of the rights of another; and the moment you pass that limit you are on forbidden ground you violate the law of individual life, and breed disorder and confusion in the whole social system.

Where, gentlemen, did *you* get the right to deny the ballot to all women and Black men not worth $250? If this right of suffrage is not an individual right, from what abstract place and abstract body did you get it? Is this right of franchise a conventional arrangement, a privilege that society or government may grant or withhold at pleasure?...

The demand we today make, is not the idiosyncrasy of a few discontented minds, but a universal movement. Woman is everywhere throwing off the lethargy of ages, and is already close upon your heels in the whole realm of thought—in art, science, literature, and government. Everything heralds the dawn of the new era when moral power is to govern nations.

In asking you, Honorable Gentlemen, to extend suffrage to woman, we do not press on you the risk and responsibility of a new step, but simply to try a measure that has already proved wise and safe the world over. So long as political power was absolute and hereditary, woman shared it with man by birth. In Hungary and some provinces of France and Germany, women holding this inherited right confer their right of franchise on their husbands. In Ireland, Moravia, Canada, Austria, Australia, Holland, and Sweden some or all women can vote. There is a bill now before the British Parliament asking for household suffrage... Would you be willing to admit, gentlemen that women know

less, have less virtue, less pride and dignity of character under Republican institutions than in the despotisms and monarchies of the old world?...

I think, Honorable Gentlemen, I have given you facts enough to show that you need not hesitate to give the ballot to the women of New York on the ground that it is a new thing; for, as you see, the right has long ago been exercised by certain classes of women in many countries. And if it were a new thing, and had never been heard of before, that would yet be no argument against the experiment.

32. Stanton primarily focuses her argument on advancing the political rights of

(A) former American slaves.
(B) American women.
(C) those living in despotic regimes abroad.
(D) those living under monarchical systems.

33. In the first paragraph in lines 1–20 ("The wheel... better day"), Stanton primarily argues that

(A) recent events have demonstrated the inability of Andrew Johnson to effectively lead the United States.
(B) the march toward equality is inevitable and leaders should embrace, rather than fight, the coming changes.
(C) those who stand in the way of social progress should instead redouble their efforts to maintain the status quo.
(D) the examples of harmonious animals in nature should inspire humans to create a more just society.

34. The concept of human rights as Stanton describes them in lines 36–45 ("Each one... system") can best be described as

(A) having arbitrary limits—a necessary evil given the social chaos that would otherwise ensue.
(B) giving those in positions of power a fundamental right to violate the rights of others.
(C) protective of the environment, without any qualification given the particular geographical locale.
(D) generally universal, with limitations on who can have rights only causing confusion.

35. As used in line 44, "breed" most closely means

(A) create.
(B) sort.
(C) educate.
(D) organize.

36. Stanton mainly uses what approach in lines 46–53 ("Where... pleasure") to make her point?

(A) Rhetorical questions
(B) Statistical analysis
(C) Appeal to authority
(D) Personal anecdotes

37. Stanton argues that at the time of the passage's composition, the movement to extend political suffrage to women in the United States is

(A) in its infancy.
(B) unlikely to advance.
(C) widespread.
(D) successful.

38. Which option gives the best evidence for the answer to the previous question?

(A) Lines 31–36 ("An idea... individual")
(B) Lines 50–53 ("Is this... pleasure")
(C) Lines 54–56 ("The demand... movement")
(D) Lines 66–68 ("So long... birth")

39. As used in line 57, "throwing off" most closely means

    (A) tossing something toward.
    (B) ridding themselves of.
    (C) shaping in the style of.
    (D) agitating in favor of.

40. Stanton's argument in the paragraph in lines 62–80 ("In asking…world") can best be summarized as

    (A) despite fears that extending the right to vote to women in absolute monarchies, it has not led to the violent overthrow of the government.
    (B) other countries have the social structure and traditions that better empower them to allow female political participation than does the United States.
    (C) the United States should overhaul its political system, changing its form of government to either monarchy or despotism.
    (D) if women can participate politically in other countries and governmental systems, it makes sense for them to do so in the United States.

41. Which choice would best address the potential concern by Stanton's intended audience that what she is proposing is unprecedented?

    (A) Lines 1–6 ("The wheel…civilization")
    (B) Lines 17–20 ("They only…day")
    (C) Lines 56–61 ("Woman…nations")
    (D) Lines 81–86 ("I think…countries")

42. The main purpose of the final sentence of the essay in lines 87–89 ("And if…experiment") is to show that

    (A) the expansion of suffrage rights to women in other countries demonstrates how such an expansion would be unlikely to succeed in the United States.
    (B) more rigorous social experimentation is necessary before making fundamental changes to the social fabric of the United States.
    (C) the concept of voting rights for women is revolutionary, and it will take time for good examples of its implementation to emerge.
    (D) even if other countries had not previously extended suffrage to women, it would still make sense for the United States to do so.

Questions 43–52 are based on the following passage and supplementary material.

Tornados, written in 2020

While tornados have been reported on every continent except Antarctica, North America experiences the majority of the world-wide tornados each year. Over 1,000 tornados are reported most years in The United States alone, making tornados (especially severe ones) seem like a distinctly American issue. Most tornados are small and cause little damage. However, in North America, there is an area called Tornado Alley in which weather conditions are occasionally just right to spawn twisters that are miles wide and have wind speeds over 300 miles per hour. These massive storms can pick up whole houses and toss them about like toys in the hands of a child.

Even though the majority of severe storms are in the U.S., the conditions that create tornados can occur anywhere. Imagine flushing a toilet and watching the water swirl away. The conditions in the water of the toilet bowl are very similar to those that create a tornado in the air. Low pressure in the pipe pulls the water on top down to the bottom. However, since the point of pressure or suction is smaller than the surface of the water above, the water can't flow out in a straight line; instead, each molecule gets pushed to the side, into a spinning queue of other molecules waiting their turn to exit the toilet through the pipe.

The conditions that create a tornado are similar—low pressure is to blame. Generally, a tornado begins as a thunderstorm. Thunderstorms are normally brought on by a constant stream of warmer low-pressure air moving into an area. Thunderstorms are also full of energy (part of where lightning comes from) that accumulates as the water evaporates to form clouds. The more water evaporates, the more heat (energy) is created. Supercell thunderstorms are one of the largest categories of thunderstorm. While an average thunderstorm contains the energy equivalent of a small nuclear warhead, a supercell can have orders of magnitude more energy within it. In a supercell, if the updrafts created by low pressure are strong enough, a cycling motion can be created, just like in a toilet. Generally, this cycle starts out miles wide—a slow, gradual movement of cloud. Once one of these mesocyclones occurs, then the chances of a tornado forming increases drastically. About fifty percent of mesocyclones spawn at least one tornado. The low pressure forms a line of swirling cells, waiting for their chance to be pulled down through the "pipe." This causes the distinctive rope-like appearance that most people associate with tornados. Even when the conditions are right and a tornado forms, they fortunately don't always touch down on the ground. Quite often, tornados stay well above the ground, preventing widespread disaster. Only when they approach close to earth are they generally known to wreak havoc.

To classify the strength of a tornado, scientists and storm chasers rely on the Enhanced Fujita, or "EF" scale. This scale replaced its predecessor in 2007. While the two scales are similar, the EF scale is more precise than the F scale (i.e., "Fujita") previously in use. Tornados can be rated from EF 0 to EF 5, with 0 the least powerful and 5 the most powerful. These steps aren't measured as the storm occurs, as it is far too dangerous to measure storm intensity during the event. However, meteorologists use the EF scale to analyze the destruction left behind. They observe and catalog the damage done to 28 different categories of structure and nature to assign each storm an EF rating. By observing the damage, they can ascertain the strength of the wind, the path the tornado took, and the overall strength of the storm system.

With this observational knowledge, scientists and engineers can work on creating structures that help prevent deaths from tornados. No structure is safe from a strong storm, but basement shelters and other advice and features have been developed to help maximize the chances of human survival in even the strongest storms. With the continued study of tornado formation and destruction, humans are safer than ever before.

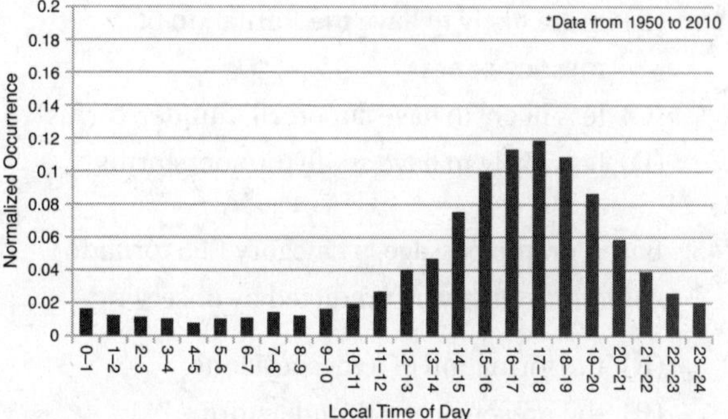

Source: *www1.ncdc.noaa.gov/pub/data/cmb/images/tornado/clim/US_nationa_timeofday.png*

Figure 1

PRACTICE TEST 3

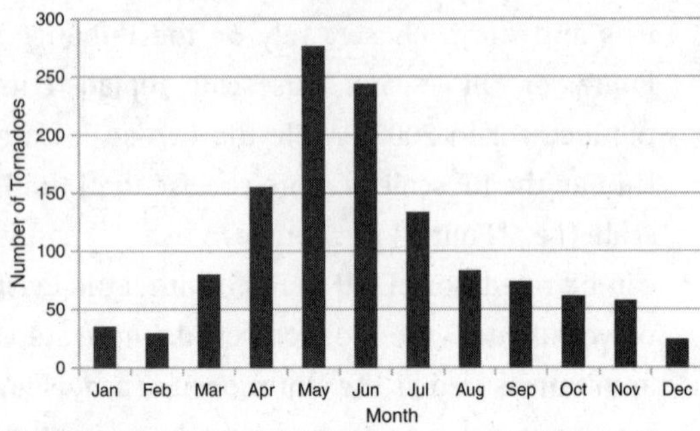

Source: *www1.ncdc.noaa.gov/pub/data/cmb/images/tornado/clim/tornadoes_bymonth.png*

Figure 2

43. What is the primary purpose of the passage?
    (A) To summarize the current general scientific understanding of tornados
    (B) To explain the importance of the newly implemented Enhanced Fujita scale
    (C) To consider the most promising avenues for further tornado research
    (D) To present the best options for keeping safe during a tornado

44. It can be reasonably inferred from the passage that when compared to the United States, another country in the world is
    (A) more likely to have unusually low-pressure weather systems.
    (B) more likely to have the formation of mesocyclones.
    (C) less likely to have supercell thunderstorms.
    (D) less likely to have small thunderstorms.

45. Based on the passage, a category EF5 tornado could most likely be predicted by observing
    (A) the formation of a mesocyclone.
    (B) the presence of a thunderstorm.
    (C) evaporation of water.
    (D) changes in air pressure.

46. Which option gives the best evidence for the answer to the previous question?
    (A) Lines 22–23 ("Low pressure... bottom")
    (B) Lines 32–34 ("Thunderstorms... area")
    (C) Lines 37–39 ("The more... created")
    (D) Lines 48–50 ("Once... drastically")

47. The author most likely uses the phrase "small nuclear warhead" in line 42 to help the reader visualize
    (A) the inevitable destruction associated with storms.
    (B) the radioactive effects of severe weather.
    (C) the immense power of a thunderstorm.
    (D) the influence of military planners on weather forecasting.

48. Based on the passage, the main difference between the Fujita and the Enhanced Fujita scales is
    (A) their association with tornados.
    (B) whether scientists have used them at some point.
    (C) which countries have chosen to adopt them.
    (D) the level of detail.

49. Which option gives the best evidence for the answer to the previous question?
    (A) Lines 63–66 ("To classify... 2007")
    (B) Lines 66–68 ("While the... use")
    (C) Lines 70–73 ("These steps... event")
    (D) Lines 75–77 ("They observe... rating")

50. As used in line 78, "ascertain" most closely means
    (A) regulate.
    (B) determine.
    (C) decide.
    (D) influence.

51. Based on Figure 1, at what time of day would a severe tornado be least likely to occur?

(A) 4:30 A.M.
(B) 9:30 A.M.
(C) 5:30 P.M.
(D) 10:30 P.M.

52. Based on both Figure 1 and Figure 2, which of the following set of conditions would be optimal for tornado formation?

(A) Midday in the summer
(B) Nighttime in the fall
(C) Sunset in the springtime
(D) Sunrise in the winter

STOP If there is still time remaining, you may review your answers.

WRITING AND LANGUAGE PRACTICE TEST 3

35 MINUTES, 44 QUESTIONS

DIRECTIONS: The passages below are each accompanied by several questions, some of which refer to an underlined portion in the passage, and some of which refer to the passage as a whole. For some questions, determine how the expression of ideas can be improved. For other questions, determine the best sentence structure, usage, or punctuation given the context. A passage or question may have an accompanying graphic that you will need to consider as you choose the best answer.

Choose the best answer to each question, considering what will optimize the writing quality and make the writing follow the conventions of standard written English. Some questions will have a "NO CHANGE" option that you can pick if you believe the best choice would be to leave the underlined portion as it is.

Questions 1–11 are based on the following passage.

Culinary Careers

Making something that is truly delicious for one's friends and family can be a formative experience that **1** leads one to pursue a career as a chef. While not everybody can be a celebrity chef with millions of television fans, there are many **2** boulevards to a fulfilling career in the food services industry.

To truly understand the food industry, one must dive into it headfirst. One can work part-time as a cook or a waiter at a local restaurant to see what the work entails. If one enjoys interacting with customers and making them happy, a face-to-face job in the front of the house may be suitable. **3** If one prefers hands-on work with ingredients, a job as a chef may be a good fit. For those who like both customer interaction and hands-on work, restaurants with open-kitchen concepts could be the ideal choice—chefs and customers can interact with one another directly.

1. (A) NO CHANGE
   (B) leading
   (C) have led
   (D) will have led

2. (A) NO CHANGE
   (B) promenades
   (C) thoroughfares
   (D) avenues

3. The writer is considering deleting the underlined sentence. Should the writer make this deletion?
   (A) Yes, because it is unnecessarily repetitive.
   (B) Yes, because it provides details not relevant to the overall point of the paragraph.
   (C) No, because it gives both a relevant statement and a logical transition.
   (D) No, because it gives both an important definition and addresses a likely objection.

4 The best way to achieve success as a chef is to pursue a formal culinary degree. There are many collegiate culinary programs; some lead to associate degrees, others to bachelor's degrees. Like with other artistic pursuits, arguably the best training comes from working as an apprentice with a master of the craft. Aspiring chefs may set up **5** a "stage" an unpaid internship, with a cook to learn new cooking methods from a highly respected professional. **6** Staging can be a win-win situation for both the aspiring chef and the mentor: The mentor receives help in the kitchen, and the aspiring chef acquires new skills that they can apply in a future position. Stages at prestigious restaurants can **7** cushion a chef's resume for future opportunities.

4. Which choice best introduces the topic of this paragraph?
   (A) NO CHANGE
   (B) It is vital to pair with a mentor who can guide one's culinary career.
   (C) Open-kitchen concepts are the way of the future, giving both chefs and patrons the interaction that leads to a great restaurant experience.
   (D) To pursue a career as a chef, a mixture of formal and informal schooling will lead to success.

5. (A) NO CHANGE
   (B) a "stage"—an unpaid internship—with
   (C) a "stage" an unpaid internship with
   (D) a "stage"—an unpaid internship: with

6. Which choice most effectively sets up the information provided in the next part of the sentence?
   (A) NO CHANGE
   (B) Culinary professionals use their formal education to pursue excellence:
   (C) It is important to have a collaborative atmosphere in order to create new cooking techniques:
   (D) While many chefs like to learn from others, some find the greatest culinary inspiration in more solitary pursuits:

7. (A) NO CHANGE
   (B) maintain
   (C) bolster
   (D) rebuild

{1} For those who have a passion for the food service **8** industry but may not want to work in a restaurant; there are many potential paths. {2} First, one could become a caterer, making food for weddings, parties, and corporate events. {3} Catering can be a good fit for those who would like to work as a chef on a more part-time basis, **9** but they could schedule their catering jobs around their family obligations. {4} Second, those who have passions both for science and for the culinary arts may enjoy food experimentation. {5} Finally, culinary instruction is a growing field given the many people who want to pursue cooking as **10** either a career and a hobby. {6} Ultimately, for those who love the business of making good food, there is truly an enormous menu of possible career options. **11**

8. (A) NO CHANGE
   (B) industry but may not want to work in a restaurant, there
   (C) industry, but may not want to work in a restaurant: there
   (D) industry—but may not want to work in a restaurant there

9. (A) NO CHANGE
   (B) which
   (C) while
   (D) as

10. (A) NO CHANGE
    (B) either a career or a hobby.
    (C) neither a career and a hobby.
    (D) neither a career nor a hobby.

11. The writer would like to add the following sentence to the paragraph.

    Corporations and universities have research positions for those who want to develop more nutritious and tasty food.

    The sentence would most logically be placed after
    (A) sentence 2.
    (B) sentence 3.
    (C) sentence 4.
    (D) sentence 5.

Questions 12–22 are based on the following passage and supplementary material.

The Replication Crisis in Psychology

The scientific method is the process that takes a hypothesis, tests it, and with careful observation, may lead to the discovery of new knowledge. ⓬ One of the key components of the scientific method is the ability to replicate findings. If the results of a scientific study can be replicated using the same methodology as the original experiment, then researchers can be much more certain about the experimental conclusions. If the results cannot be replicated, then scientists will assess the potential reasons for the inconsistency. Was there a statistical fluke with the original data? Was there an unknown variable ⓭ affecting the data in an unforeseen way? Or could the results have been fabricated to demonstrate a conclusion that was not warranted? The bottom line is that without consistent replication of experimental results, the original experimental study will be clouded ⓮ of uncertainty.

In 2010, psychologists became aware of the replication crisis in psychology. This was prompted by a study that claimed to show evidence of "precognition" ⓯. Given the questionable assertions from this research and the inability of other psychologists to replicate its results, researchers examined the problem of replication in psychology ⓰ more generally. After further investigation, it became clear that

12. (A) NO CHANGE
    (B) To replicate findings is, of the scientific method, one of the key components.
    (C) Of the scientific method to replicate findings is one of the key components.
    (D) Replicating findings of one of the components is, of the scientific method, key.

13. (A) NO CHANGE
    (B) effecting
    (C) affected
    (D) effected

14. (A) NO CHANGE
    (B) by
    (C) for
    (D) on

15. At this point, the writer is considering adding the following phrase to the end of the sentence, keeping the period at the end.

    —the ability to anticipate future events

    Should the writer make this addition here?
    (A) Yes, because it explains a research process.
    (B) Yes, because it defines an important term.
    (C) No, because it distracts from the main point of the paragraph.
    (D) No, because it provides an unrelated detail.

16. (A) NO CHANGE
    (B) more general.
    (C) general.
    (D) most general.

approximately 40 percent of psychological studies could not be adequately replicated. While this was not as much of an issue in psychological studies about human perception, it was more of a concern in studies that made claims about social interactions. **17** For instance decision fatigue, is the concept that willpower is a limited resource and using it drains from one's daily willpower reservoir. A study about decision fatigue led to several follow-up studies that failed to replicate the results of the original experiment.

This replication crisis does not mean that psychology is necessarily **18** unreliable, it would, however, be wise to refrain from running down a rabbit hole of follow-up studies and making grand claims about human nature on the basis of a single study. When findings do consistently replicate, then the results can be considered reliable and should **19** serving to a basis for further study. Also, psychological researchers should be more modest about the certainty of data that involves human behavior. After all, human behavior is more difficult to **20** impulsively measure than criteria that other scientific fields assess, like temperature or velocity. A recent analysis found that studies about social psychology could be replicated roughly a **21** half of the time, while studies about human cognition could be replicated about a third of the time. Given these concerns,

17. (A) NO CHANGE
    (B) For instance: decision fatigue is the concept that willpower is a limited resource, and using it drains from one's daily willpower reservoir.
    (C) For instance—decision fatigue—is the concept that willpower is a limited resource and using it drains from one's daily willpower reservoir.
    (D) For instance, decision fatigue is the concept that willpower is a limited resource, and using it drains from one's daily willpower reservoir.

18. (A) NO CHANGE
    (B) unreliable. It would however be wise to
    (C) unreliable; it would, however, be wise to
    (D) unreliable, it would however be wise to

19. (A) NO CHANGE
    (B) served as
    (C) serve as
    (D) serve to

20. (A) NO CHANGE
    (B) subjectively
    (C) irrationally
    (D) objectively

21. Which choice is best supported by the information in the chart?
    (A) NO CHANGE
    (B) third of the time, while studies about human cognition could be replicated about a quarter of the time.
    (C) quarter of the time, while studies about human cognition could be replicated about half the time.
    (D) quarter of the time, while studies about human cognition could be replicated about all of the time.

PRACTICE TEST 3

it is important that funding for replication of psychological experiments be increased to allow for a more rigorous foundation for research claims, particularly those that concern the psychology of **22** cognition.

22. Which choice most logically uses a trend from the chart to build off the point made in the earlier parts of the sentence?
   (A) NO CHANGE
   (B) learning.
   (C) memory.
   (D) social issues.

Reproducibility of Different Types of Psychological Science

Journal Name	Type of Research	Percent of Findings Replicated
Psychological Science	Social	29
Journal of Personality and Social Psychology	Social	23
Journal of Experimental Psychology: Learning, Memory, and Cognition	Cognitive	48
Psychological Science	Cognitive	53

Data adapted from the Noba Project, the Replication Crisis in Psychology. *https://nobaproject.com/modules/the-replication-crisis-in-psychology*

Questions 23–33 are based on the following passage.

Harlem Renaissance and Countee Cullen

The Harlem Renaissance, a period between the years 1918 and 1937, ㉓ <u>was</u> a revival of African American intellectual and artistic expression centered in Harlem, New York. Harlem contained the highest concentration of African American citizens in the world; this was a result of the Great Migration, ㉔ <u>the movement of African Americans from the South, to the Midwestern, and Northern regions of the United States.</u> In Harlem, a cultural Mecca for African Americans, talented artists congregated and collectively redefined Black culture. One such artist, Countee Cullen, was one of the most influential African American poets of his time ㉕ <u>given his residency in Harlem, a part of the greater New York City metropolitan area.</u>

23. (A) NO CHANGE
(B) were
(C) are
(D) had

24. (A) NO CHANGE
(B) the movement of African Americans, from the South to the Midwestern and Northern regions of the United States.
(C) the movement of African Americans from the South to the Midwestern and Northern regions of the United States.
(D) the movement of African Americans; from the South to the Midwestern and Northern regions of the United States.

25. Which choice best introduces the topic of the passage?
(A) NO CHANGE
(B) since historians believe he began his studies of poetry in elementary school.
(C) because he helped to break down racial barriers and stereotypes during the Harlem Renaissance.
(D) due to his leadership roles in nonviolent protest movements to end racial discrimination throughout the United States.

{1} Although not **26** much is known about Countee Cullens early life we know that he started writing poetry when he was fourteen years old. {2} When he was in high school at a predominantly white institution, Cullen excelled, despite being one of the few African American students who attended. {3} Additionally, he developed his talents and served as the editor of the high school newspaper and literary magazine and even won a local award for his poetry. {4} Later, he was accepted into New York University, where he received several awards; most notably, he won second place for the Witter Bynner Undergraduate Poetry Contest for his 1923 poem "The Ballad of the Brown Girl." {5} Following his graduation from New York University, Cullen became **27** a notorious poet with works like *Copper Sun* and *The Black Christ and Other Poems.* **28**

Cullen's work was focused on the acts of discrimination he faced because society perceived him as being solely African American, **29** if his having both African American and Caucasian heritage. In addition, Cullen embraced his biracial identity and expressed his opposition to segregation in his poems by combining social topics that pertained to African Americans with following traditional poetic structure, including Shakespearean sonnet form. **30** This drew

26. (A) NO CHANGE
    (B) much is known about Countee Cullen's early life,
    (C) much is known about Countee Cullens' early life—
    (D) much is known about Countee Cullens early life

27. (A) NO CHANGE
    (B) an imminent
    (C) an illustrated
    (D) a renowned

28. To make the paragraph most logical, sentence 3 should be placed
    (A) where it currently is.
    (B) after sentence 1.
    (C) after sentence 4.
    (D) after sentence 5.

29. (A) NO CHANGE
    (B) despite
    (C) whenever
    (D) DELETE the underlined portion.

30. At this point, the writer is considering adding the following sentence.

    The true identity of Shakespeare is sometimes disputed by historians.

    Should the writer make this addition here?

    (A) Yes, because it provides a helpful detail.
    (B) Yes, because it highlights an area that demands further investigation.
    (C) No, because it is overly speculative.
    (D) No, because it distracts from the focus of the paragraph.

criticism from other intellectuals and artists. One such artist was famous Harlem Renaissance poet and essayist Langston Hughes, who discussed his experiences with discrimination while adhering to standard Modernist writing techniques, characterized by experimental poetic form and style.

❸❶ Even though many considered his work to be controversial, Cullen continued with his originality and went on to receive more awards for his literature ❸❷ over any other African American poet of his time. ❸❸ He earned the praise of W.E.B. Du Bois. Du Bois described Countee Cullen as a talented poet who conveyed his authentic human experiences and remained true to his artistic freedom.

31. (A) NO CHANGE
    (B) And
    (C) Also,
    (D) Again,

32. (A) NO CHANGE
    (B) then any
    (C) with any
    (D) than any other

33. Which choice most effectively combines the sentences at the underline portion?
    (A) W.E.B. Du Bois; this was the person who described
    (B) W.E.B. Du Bois, who described
    (C) W.E.B. Du Bois, a man who went on to describe
    (D) W.E.B. Du Bois, therefore describing

Questions 34–44 are based on the following passage and supplementary material.

Family History and Vestibular Problems

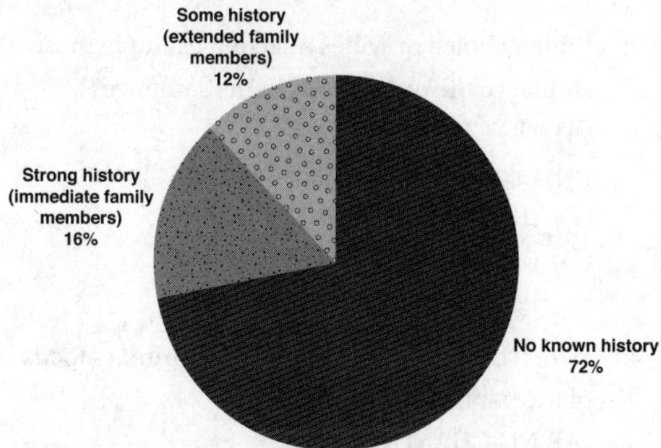

Data adapted from a Maladio.com survey on family history and vestibular disorders.

The Vestibular System

Like many bodily structures, the vestibular system is something most people do not consider (or even know exists) until it malfunctions. However, issues in the vestibular system can indeed be life-altering for many people. (34) In the critical functions of this system—providing balance and stability for the human body—any slight deviation from normal can result in constant nausea, vomiting, dizziness, and an inability to walk or stand. Some people have a family history of vestibular issues— (35) approximately 28% have a relative with some form of a vestibular problem. However, since a majority of those with vestibular problems do not have a relative who is known to suffer from such issues, (36) skeptics about the prevalence of vestibular problems should conduct more research.

The vestibular system is (37) residing in the inner ear and is comprised of three tubes on each side of the head. Each tube on the right has a corresponding tube on the left, making up three pairs. These pairs each have a certain job

34. (A) NO CHANGE
(B) As
(C) In contrast to
(D) Due to

35. Which of the following most effectively uses information from the graph to justify the point made earlier in the sentence?
(A) NO CHANGE
(B) in fact, the vast majority of people have no known history of vestibular problems.
(C) 12% of people have an extended relative who has vestibular issues.
(D) 16% of survey respondents indicate that they know someone who has had vestibular problems.

36. The writer wishes to indicate to the reader that vestibular issues are in fact widespread. Which of the following would best accomplish the writer's goal?
(A) NO CHANGE
(B) it would be helpful if doctors were more convincing during their patient interactions.
(C) new treatments for vestibular problems are being developed by researchers on a semi-regular basis.
(D) it is important to keep in mind that vestibular problems can happen to most anyone.

37. (A) NO CHANGE
(B) located
(C) lodged
(D) dwelling

in facilitating steady movement. They are called the right and left horizontal, anterior, and posterior semicircular canals. Filled (38) to liquid, the horizontal canals allow for stability when moving on a vertical axis (a ballerina spinning), while the anterior and posterior canals help with the frontal plane (39) (a gymnast flipping) and the sagittal plane (someone bowing in a dance). Each set of tubes is set up so that when the right is stimulated, the left is inhibited, and vice versa. This allows for stability in side-to-side movement.

(40) Stability in the inner ear is essential to overall bodily well-being. One of the most well-known complications from this system is known as "vertigo," in which people can experience severe dizziness at any change in altitude. They may also feel as if the room is moving and experience nausea, sweating, and vomiting. (41) These episodes, can be brought on by as little as a nod of the head. Vertigo can be caused by inner ear infections, vestibular migraines, and a host of other inner ear issues, (42) but it can also be caused by a simple weakness of the vestibular system.

38. (A) NO CHANGE
(B) in
(C) with
(D) about

39. Which choice provides a second example most similar to the one already in the sentence?
(A) NO CHANGE
(B) (a gymnast who happens to be flipping)
(C) (flipping a gymnast)
(D) (a gymnast)

40. Which choice best introduces the primary focus of the paragraph?
(A) NO CHANGE
(B) When any one part of this complicated system is compromised, people can experience life-altering effects.
(C) The vestibular system is known for the stability it offers the body, in spite of harmful environmental factors.
(D) People with compromised immune systems are far more likely to contract communicable diseases.

41. (A) NO CHANGE
(B) These episodes can be: brought on by as little as a nod of the head.
(C) These episodes can be brought on by as little as a nod of the head.
(D) These episodes can be brought on; by as little as a nod of the head.

42. (A) NO CHANGE
(B) in addition, they
(C) despite this situation, they
(D) they

Some humans have naturally weak vestibular systems. While people who lead an active life "exercise" this system quite **43** often (with gymnasts and ballerinas having all-star vestibular systems people) who just move around a decent amount in everyday life should have stronger systems than people who sit and watch TV or work on computers all day. Those who may be predisposed to vestibular system weakness can overcome their innate tendencies if they embrace **44** actively lively rather than sedentary lifestyles.

43. (A) NO CHANGE
    (B) often, with gymnasts and ballerinas having all-star vestibular systems—people
    (C) often, with gymnasts and ballerinas having all-star, vestibular systems people
    (D) often (with gymnasts and ballerinas having all-star vestibular systems), people

44. (A) NO CHANGE
    (B) animated and vigorous
    (C) active
    (D) energetically nimble

STOP If there is still time remaining, you may review your answers.

MATH TEST 3 (NO CALCULATOR)

25 MINUTES, 20 QUESTIONS

DIRECTIONS: For questions 1–15, solve each problem and choose the best answer from the given options. Fill in the corresponding oval on your answer document. For questions 16–20, solve the problem and fill in the answer in the answer sheet grid. Please use any space in the test booklet to work out your answers.

Notes:

- You CANNOT use a calculator on this section.
- All variables and expressions represent real numbers, unless indicated otherwise.
- All figures are drawn to scale, unless indicated otherwise.
- All figures are in a plane, unless indicated otherwise.
- Unless indicated otherwise, the domain of a given function is the set of all real numbers *x* for which the function has real values.

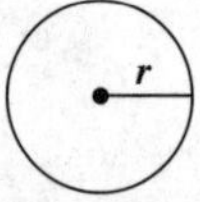

Radius of a circle = r
Area of a circle = πr^2
Circumference of a circle = $2\pi r$

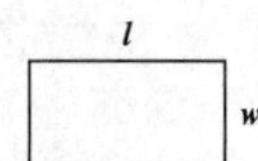

Area of a rectangle = length × width

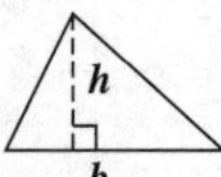

Area of a triangle = $\frac{1}{2}$ × base × height

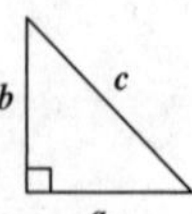

Pythagorean theorem: $a^2 + b^2 = c^2$

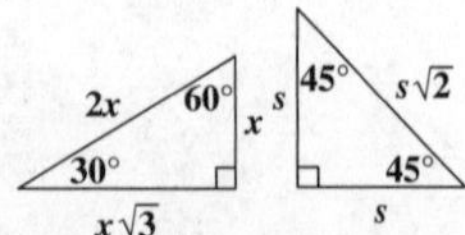

Special right triangles: 30-60-90 and 45-45-90

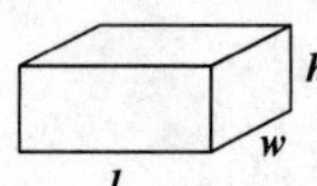

Volume of a box = length × width × height

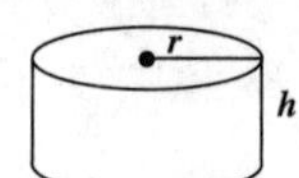

Volume of a cylinder = $\pi r^2 h$

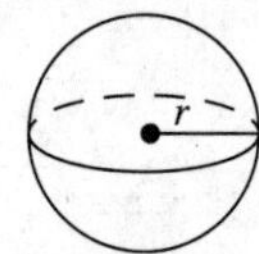

Volume of a sphere = $\frac{4}{3}\pi r^3$

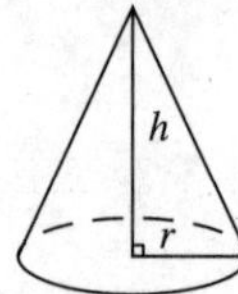

Volume of a cone = $\frac{1}{3}\pi r^2 h$

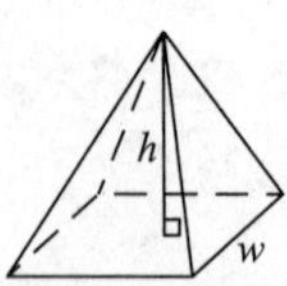

Volume of a pyramid = $\frac{1}{3}$ × length × width × height

PRACTICE TEST 3

Key Facts:

- **A circle has 360 degrees.**
- **There are 2π radians in a circle.**
- **There are 180 degrees in a triangle.**

1. If $x = 5$, what is $3(x + 2) - 2x$?

(A) 5
(B) 9
(C) 11
(D) 13

2. Mark consistently sleeps 8 hours during one day. Which expression gives the number of hours that Mark would sleep in *W* weeks?

(A) $56 \times W$
(B) $8 \times W$
(C) $8 + W$
(D) $56 + W$

3. If $x^3 = \frac{27}{8}$, what is the value of *x*?

(A) $\frac{1}{3}$
(B) $\frac{3}{4}$
(C) $\frac{3}{2}$
(D) $\frac{9}{4}$

4. If $5x + 2 = 4(x - 3)$, what is the value of *x*?

(A) -14
(B) -11
(C) -7
(D) 3

5. $\frac{x^2 - 9}{x - 3}$

Which of the following is equivalent to the above expression, in which $x \neq 3$?

(A) $x^2 - 2$
(B) $x^3 - 1$
(C) $x - 9$
(D) $x + 3$

6. A cylindrical tank has base with a diameter of 10 feet and a volume of 300π cubic feet. What is the height of this tank in feet?

(A) 8
(B) 10
(C) 12
(D) 16

x	0	1	2	3
$f(x)$	-5	-6	-7	-8

7. Which of the following functions defines the function $f(x)$ based on the values in the table above?

(A) $f(x) = -x - 5$
(B) $f(x) = -x - 3$
(C) $f(x) = x + 5$
(D) $f(x) = x - 8$

8. Consider the sum of the expressions $-x^2 + 4x - 3$ and $5x^2 - 2x + 8$. If the sum is written in the form $gx^2 + hx + k$, where *g*, *h*, and *k* are constants, what is the value of *k*?

(A) 1
(B) 3
(C) 4
(D) 5

9. If a line has a slope of 5 and a y-intercept of k, what is the value of k if the points (1, 8) and (3, 18) are in the line?

(A) 3
(B) 5
(C) 9
(D) 24

10. Kinetic energy, K, is calculated using the following formula, in which m = mass and v = velocity.

$$K=\frac{1}{2}mv^2$$

What is the velocity in terms of the other variables?

(A) $v=2Km$
(B) $v=\sqrt{\frac{2K}{m}}$
(C) $v=\sqrt{\frac{2m}{K}}$
(D) $v=2m^2\sqrt{K}$

11. If the function $f(x)=\frac{x^2+3}{2x}$ when $x\neq 0$, what is the value of $f(6)$?

(A) $-\frac{7}{3}$
(B) $\frac{2}{9}$
(C) 1
(D) $\frac{13}{4}$

12. $\sqrt{a^2-2a}$

Given that a is positive, what is the least possible value of a that would allow for a real value for the above expression?

(A) 1
(B) 2
(C) 3
(D) 5

13. For the system of inequalities $y\leq x+2$ and $y\leq -x+4$, when y is at its greatest possible value, what is the corresponding value of x?

(A) −6
(B) −2
(C) 1
(D) 4

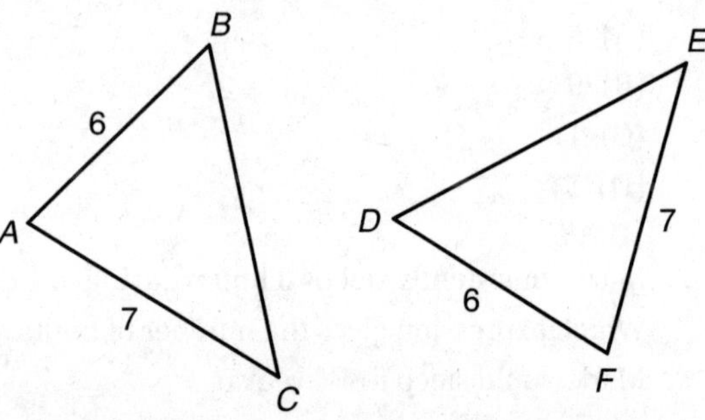

14. Triangles ABC and DEF both have sides of length 6 and 7 as shown above. Which of the following would, if true, be sufficient to prove that the triangles are congruent?

(A) That angle BAC equals angle DEF
(B) That angle CBA equals angle EDF
(C) That angle BAC equals angle DFE
(D) That angle ABC equals angle FED

15. What is the result when $4x^2-3x+2$ is divided by $x-3$?

(A) $4x-9$
(B) $12x^2+9$
(C) $2x-3+\frac{1}{(x-3)}$
(D) $4x+9+\frac{29}{(x-3)}$

PRACTICE TEST 3

Student-Produced Response Directions

In questions 16–20, first solve the problem, and then enter your answer on the grid provided on the answer sheet. The instructions for entering your answers follow.

- First, write your answer in the boxes at the top of the grid.
- Second, you may grid your answer in the columns below the boxes.
- Use the fraction bar in the first row or the decimal point in the second row to enter fractions and decimals.

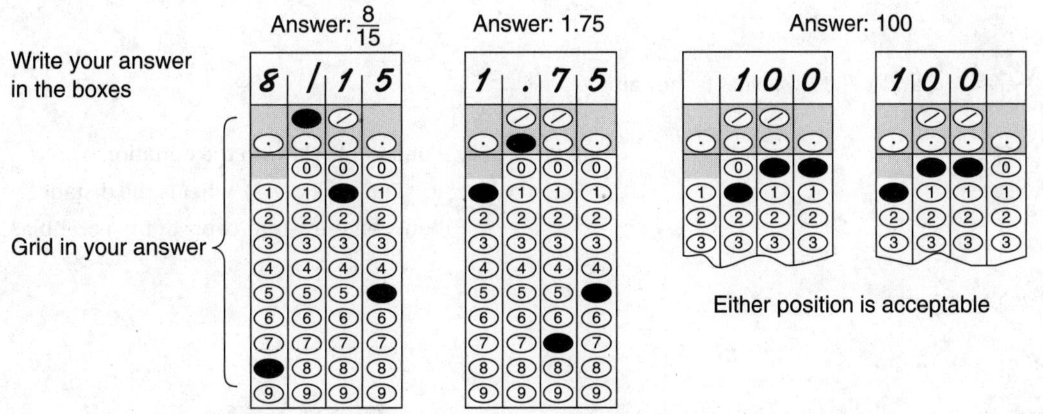

- Grid only one space in each column.
- Entering the answer in the boxes is recommended as an aid in gridding but is not required.
- The machine scoring your exam can read only what you grid, so you **must grid in your answers correctly to get credit.**
- If a question has more than one correct answer, grid in only one of them.
- The grid does not have a minus sign, so no answer can be negative.
- A mixed number *must* be converted to an improper fraction or a decimal before it is gridded. Enter $1\frac{1}{4}$ as $\frac{5}{4}$ or 1.25; the machine will interpret 11/4 as $\frac{11}{4}$ and mark it wrong.
- **All decimals must be entered as accurately as possible.** Here are three acceptable ways of gridding

$$\frac{3}{11} = 0.272727\ldots$$

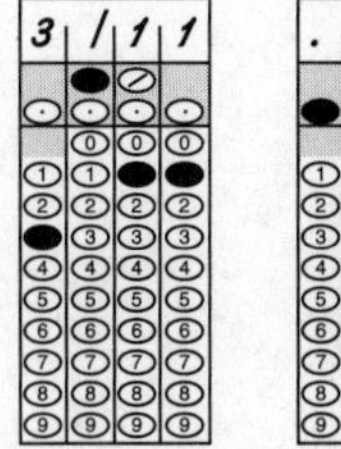
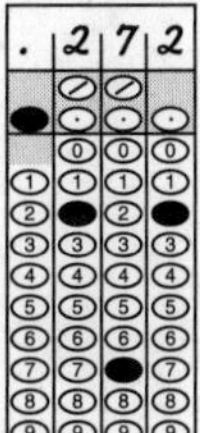
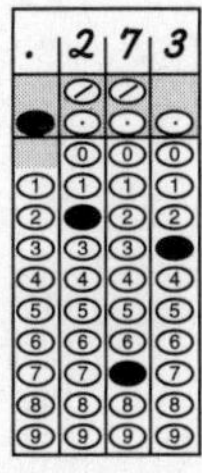

- Note that rounding to .273 is acceptable because you are using the full grid, but you would receive **no credit** for .3 or .27, because they are less accurate.

PRACTICE TEST 3

16. If $\frac{1}{3}(x - 2) = y$ and $x = 5$, what is the value of y?

17. If $\frac{x^2 - 4}{3} = 7$ and $x - 2 = 3$, what is the value of $x + 2$?

18. In the xy-plane, a line passes through the points (5, 0) and (0, 3). Another line is perpendicular to this line. What would be this perpendicular line's slope?

19. The measure of an angle is $\frac{2}{3}\pi$ radians. How many angles of this measure would be equivalent to 360 degrees?

20. For a parabola with the equation $y = 7(x - 5)(x + 2)$, what is the distance between the x-intercepts of the parabola?

STOP If there is still time remaining, you may review your answers.

MATH PRACTICE TEST 3 (CALCULATOR)

55 MINUTES, 38 QUESTIONS

DIRECTIONS: For questions 1–30, solve each problem and choose the best answer from the given options. Fill in the corresponding oval on your answer document. For questions 31–38, solve the problem and fill in the answer in the answer sheet grid. Please use any space in the test booklet to work out your answers.

Notes:
- You CAN use a calculator on this section.
- All variables and expressions represent real numbers, unless indicated otherwise.
- All figures are drawn to scale, unless indicated otherwise.
- All figures are in a plane, unless indicated otherwise.
- Unless indicated otherwise, the domain of a given function is the set of all real numbers x for which the function has real values.

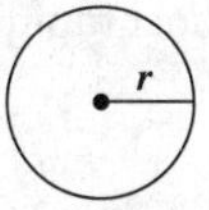

Radius of a circle $= r$
Area of a circle $= \pi r^2$
Circumference of a circle $= 2\pi r$

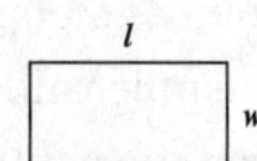

Area of a rectangle = length × width

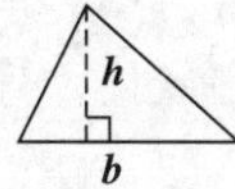

Area of a triangle $= \frac{1}{2} \times$ base $\times$ height

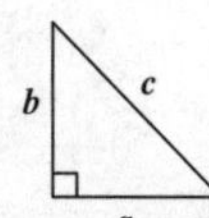

Pythagorean theorem: $a^2 + b^2 = c^2$

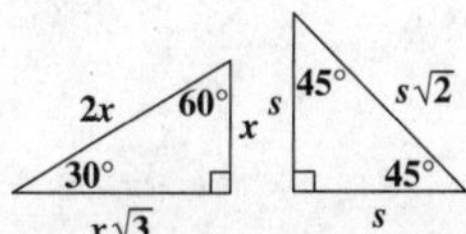

Special right triangles: 30-60-90 and 45-45-90

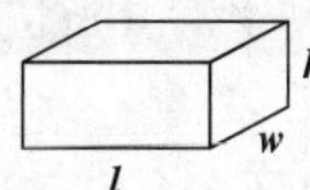

Volume of a box = length × width × height

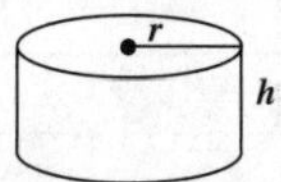

Volume of a cylinder $= \pi r^2 h$

Volume of a sphere $= \frac{4}{3}\pi r^3$

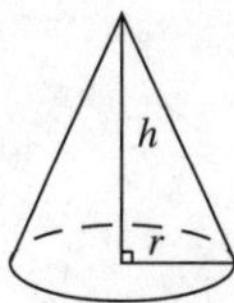

Volume of a cone $= \frac{1}{3}\pi r^2 h$

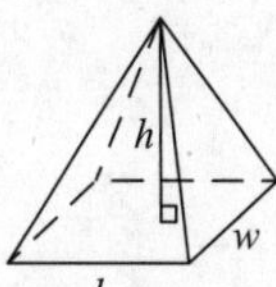

Volume of a pyramid $= \frac{1}{3} \times$ length $\times$ width $\times$ height

0

0

Key Facts:

- **A circle has 360 degrees.**
- **There are 2π radians in a circle.**
- **There are 180 degrees in a triangle.**

1. $-3(x^2 - 2x + 4)$ is equivalent to which of the following expressions?

(A) $3x^2 - 6x + 12$
(B) $-3x^2 + 6x - 12$
(C) $-3x^2 - 6x + 12$
(D) $-3x^2 - 6x - 12$

Letter Grade	Percentage of Students with That Grade
A (90–100%)	26
B (80–99%)	33
C (70–79%)	21
D (60–69%)	13
F (<60%)	7

2. The table above presents the percentage of students in a class with particular letter grades. What letter grade is the median grade for the class?

(A) A
(B) B
(C) C
(D) D

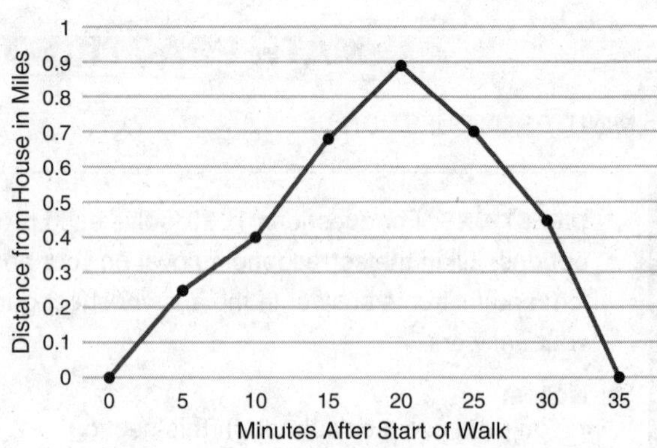

3. Tyrese takes a walk around his neighborhood. The distance he is in miles from his house at a particular number of minutes after beginning his walk is represented in the graph above. At what interval of time in his walk did the distance he is from his house decrease most rapidly?

(A) 0–5 minutes
(B) 15–20 minutes
(C) 25–30 minutes
(D) 30–35 minutes

4. If the city of Detroit has a population of 4,900 persons per square mile, and there are 139 square miles of land within the city, what would most closely approximate the total population of the city?

(A) 35,000
(B) 47,000
(C) 681,000
(D) 1,240,000

PRACTICE TEST 3

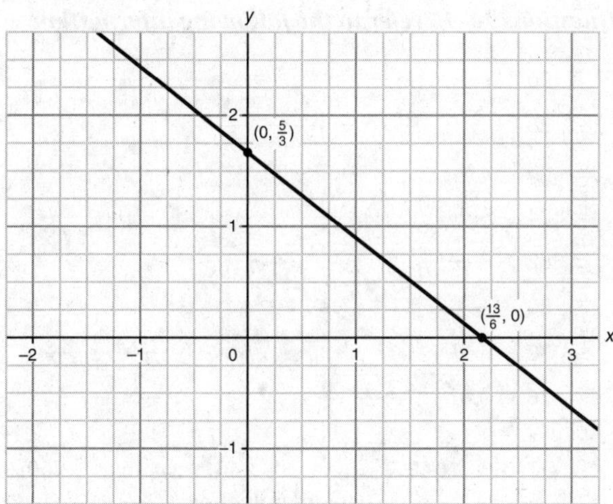

5. What is the slope of the line in the above graph in the *xy*-coordinate plane?

(A) $-\frac{13}{4}$

(B) $-\frac{10}{13}$

(C) $-\frac{1}{3}$

(D) $\frac{7}{4}$

6. An electrician charges \$50 per hour and a one-time fee of \$40 for an appointment. Which expression models the total amount charged for an appointment that is x hours long?

(A) $2{,}000x$

(B) $200x$

(C) $40x + 50$

(D) $40 + 50x$

7. What is the product of the solutions to the equation $0 = \left(x + \frac{1}{4}\right)\left(x - \frac{2}{3}\right)$?

(A) $-\frac{1}{12}$

(B) $-\frac{1}{6}$

(C) $\frac{1}{4}$

(D) $\frac{5}{12}$

8. At a certain college, 27% of all students majored in science or mathematics. If there were a total of 4,000 students at the college, how many of the students would have a science or mathematics major?

(A) 1,080

(B) 2,920

(C) 14,815

(D) 108,000

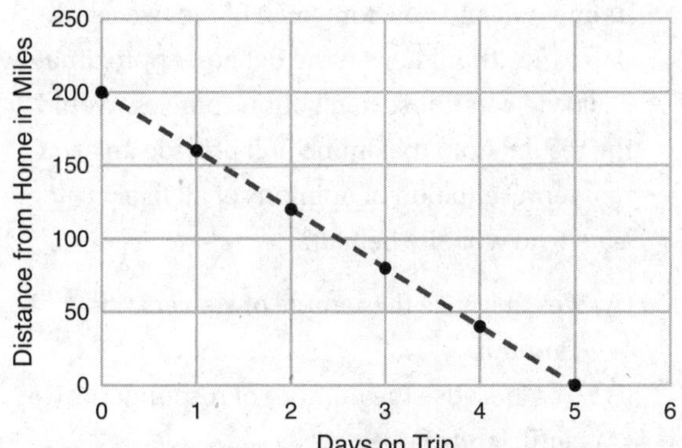

9. As shown in the graph above, a bicyclist records the distance from home that she is in miles over a five-day period. What is the bicyclist's daily change in distance from home?

(A) 20 miles

(B) 25 miles

(C) 35 miles

(D) 40 miles

10. A circle with an original area of 16π units is increased in its area by 56.25%. What is the radius of the new circle?

(A) 5 units

(B) 6 units

(C) 10 units

(D) 25 units

11. A line graphed in the *xy*-coordinate plane has a point (6, 8) and a slope of $\frac{2}{3}$. What is the *y*-intercept of this line?

(A) $-\frac{1}{3}$
(B) $\frac{8}{3}$
(C) 4
(D) 7

12. After a presidential debate, viewers could go to an online poll and vote for which of the two candidates they thought won the debate. Approximately 2,500 viewers chose to fill out responses. Would the results from the online poll provide an accurate representation of opinions of all likely voters as to who won the debate?

(A) Yes, because the sample of viewers was random.
(B) Yes, because the number of respondents was sufficiently large.
(C) No, because the respondents were self-selected instead of randomly selected.
(D) No, because the number of respondents was insufficient.

13. A fruit stand charges a different amount depending on the number of pieces of fruit in a box:

Number of Pieces of Fruit in the Box	Cost of Box
6	$13.40
12	$25.40
20	$41.40
32	$65.40

What function could be used to determine the total cost, *C*, of a box that has *x* pieces of fruit?

(A) $C(x) = -x + 2.40$
(B) $C(x) = 2x + 1.40$
(C) $C(x) = 1.4x + 3$
(D) $C(x) = 2.8x + 1$

Questions 14–15 refer to the following information.

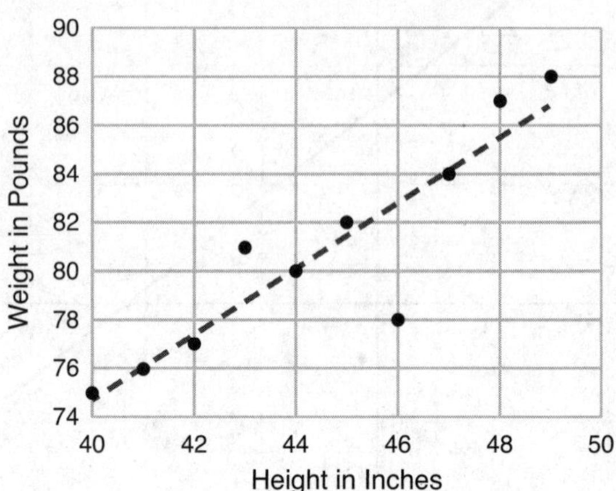

The height in inches and weight in pounds for several female orangutans is graphed in the scatter plot above.

14. Based on the data in the graph, which of these statements best summarizes the overall trend in the data?

(A) The greater the height of the orangutan, the greater the weight.
(B) The lower the height of the orangutan, the greater the weight.
(C) The greater the height of the orangutan, the lower the weight.
(D) The height and the weight of the orangutan are equivalent throughout the set of data.

15. Based on the trend of the best-fit line, what would most likely be the weight of an orangutan that is 50 inches tall, to the nearest pound?

(A) 76
(B) 80
(C) 88
(D) 104

PRACTICE TEST 3

16. A data set of 15 different numbers has a median of 25 and a mean of 30. If the smallest member of the set has 5 subtracted from it and the largest member has 20 added to it, while all the other elements remain the same, which of these is a correct statement?

(A) The standard deviation of the set changes more than the range of the set.
(B) The range of the set changes more than the standard deviation of the set.
(C) The range of the set remains the same.
(D) The standard deviation of the set remains the same.

17. In the *xy*-plane, which of these equations would shift the graph of $y = x^2 - 4$ upward five units?

(A) $y = x^2 - 5$
(B) $y = x^2 - 1$
(C) $y = x^2 + 1$
(D) $y = 5x^2 - 4$

18. $y \geq x + n$

When the ordered pair (2, 5) is a solution for (x, y) in the inequality above, what is the greatest possible value for n?

(A) 3
(B) 5
(C) 8
(D) 12

19. A new cell phone at a retailer normally sells for $300 plus an additional 7% sales tax. If the phone is on sale for 40% off the normal price (with the discount applied before tax is added), what would a customer pay for a phone, including sales tax?

(A) $122.80
(B) $128.40
(C) $192.60
(D) $449.40

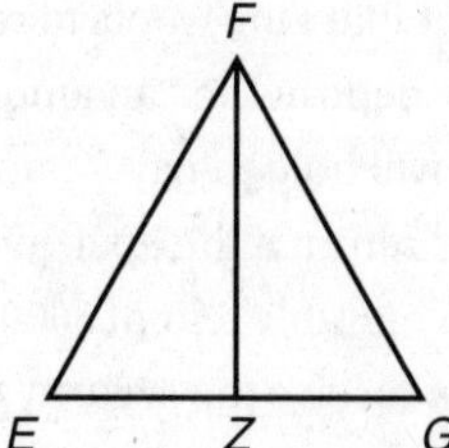

20. Triangle *EFG* is equilateral. If $\overline{EF}$ is 10 units long, and $\angle EFZ$ is 30°, what is the length of $\overline{FZ}$?

(A) $5\sqrt{3}$
(B) $5\sqrt{2}$
(C) 10
(D) $10\sqrt{2}$

21. A college meal plan charges a flat fee of $90 for a week of meals at the school cafeteria in which the student can get two meals a day; a third meal on a given day at the school cafeteria costs an extra $10. If Marcos has breakfast and lunch at the school cafeteria every day of the week, and dinner at the school cafeteria on just Monday through Thursday, how much will his food bill for the college be that week?

(A) $90
(B) $130
(C) $150
(D) $180

22. If $a - 3\sqrt{a} - 10 = 0$, and a is a real number, what is the value of a?

(A) -4
(B) 1
(C) 9
(D) 25

23. An apartment that Ling wants to rent requires an \$800 security deposit (i.e., an amount the apartment owner will hold to pay for any apartment damages and return if the apartment is in good shape) and a monthly rent of \$600. Assuming that Ling does *not* receive the security deposit back, after how many months will the average total monthly cost (including the security deposit) average out to \$700 per month?

(A) 2 months
(B) 3 months
(C) 5 months
(D) 8 months

x	y
1	2
2	$\frac{1}{2}$
3	$\frac{2}{9}$
4	$\frac{1}{8}$
5	$\frac{2}{25}$

24. As show in the table above, which function expresses the relationship between x and y?

(A) $y = \frac{2}{x^2}$
(B) $y = \frac{4}{x^2}$
(C) $y = \frac{1}{2}x^2$
(D) $y = \frac{1}{6}x^3$

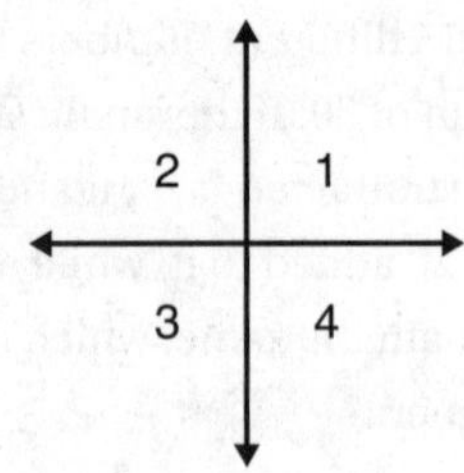

25. The solutions to the inequality $y \geq -x + 4$ will be in which quadrant(s) of the xy-coordinate plane?

(A) 1 and 2 only
(B) 3 and 4 only
(C) 1, 2, and 4 only
(D) All four quadrants

	Actually Has Illness	Actually Does Not Have Illness
Positive Test Result	5	20
Negative Test Result	0	800

26. If a randomly selected patient who participated in the study with the results given above has a positive test result, what is the probability that the result is a *false* positive?

(A) 0.5
(B) 0.8
(C) 0.9
(D) 1.2

27. A particular multivitamin provides 300 mg of calcium, giving 23% of the recommended daily value of calcium for an adult. If another multivitamin provides 210 mg of calcium, approximately what percent of a recommended daily value of calcium for an adult would it provide, to the nearest whole percent?

(A) 8%
(B) 16%
(C) 20%
(D) 44%

28. What values of x would make the product of $\frac{2}{x}$ and $\frac{3}{(x-1)}$ undefined?

(A) 0 only
(B) −1 only
(C) 0 and 1 only
(D) −1 and 0 only

	Bus	Walk	Total
Elementary	a	b	c
Middle	d	e	f
Total	80	70	150

29. Consider the information in the table above with the variables representing numerical values. There are twice as many elementary students as there are middle school students, and 60% of elementary students take the bus. How many middle school students walk to school?

(A) 20
(B) 30
(C) 40
(D) 60

30. $y = x(x-4)^2(x+3)^2$

In the above equation, how many unique x-intercepts does the graph of the function have?

(A) 0
(B) 1
(C) 3
(D) 5

Student-Produced Response Directions

In questions 31–38, first solve the problem, and then enter your answer on the grid provided on the answer sheet. The instructions for entering your answers follow.

- First, write your answer in the boxes at the top of the grid.
- Second, you may grid your answer in the columns below the boxes.
- Use the fraction bar in the first row or the decimal point in the second row to enter fractions and decimals.

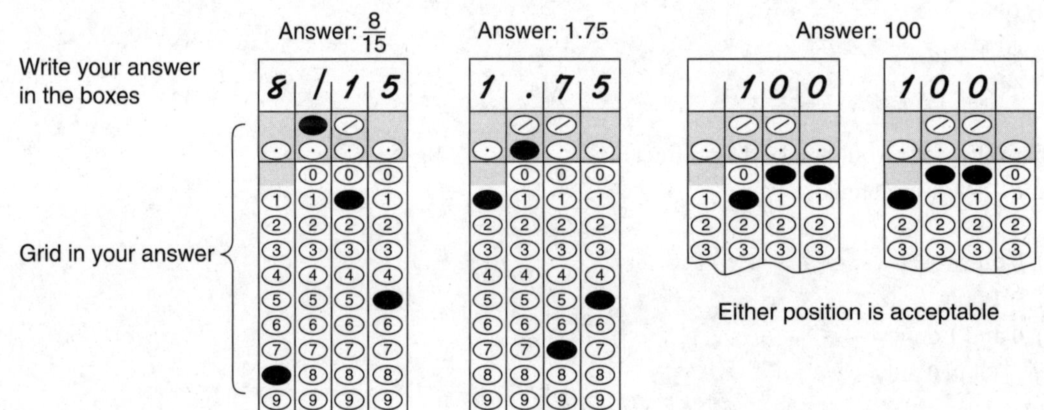

- Grid only one space in each column.
- Entering the answer in the boxes is recommended as an aid in gridding but is not required.
- The machine scoring your exam can read only what you grid, so you **must grid in your answers correctly to get credit**.
- If a question has more than one correct answer, grid in only one of them.
- The grid does not have a minus sign, so no answer can be negative.
- A mixed number *must* be converted to an improper fraction or a decimal before it is gridded. Enter $1\frac{1}{4}$ as $\frac{5}{4}$ or 1.25; the machine will interpret 11/4 as $\frac{11}{4}$ and mark it wrong.
- **All decimals must be entered as accurately as possible.** Here are three acceptable ways of gridding $\frac{3}{11} = 0.272727\ldots$

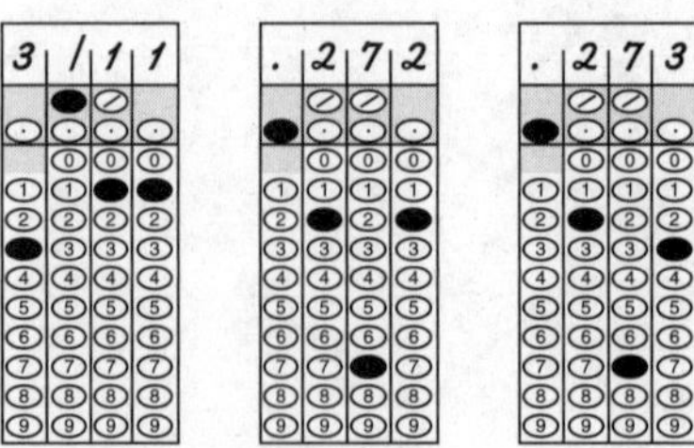

- Note that rounding to .273 is acceptable because you are using the full grid, but you would receive **no credit** for .3 or .27, because they are less accurate.

31. $B = 2P + 3E$

A bagel store charges \$2 for each plain bagel, P, and \$3 for each everything bagel, E. The equation above represents the total amount, B, that Samantha paid for a box of bagels. If the box cost a total of \$40 and Samantha purchased 4 everything bagels, how many plain bagels did she purchase?

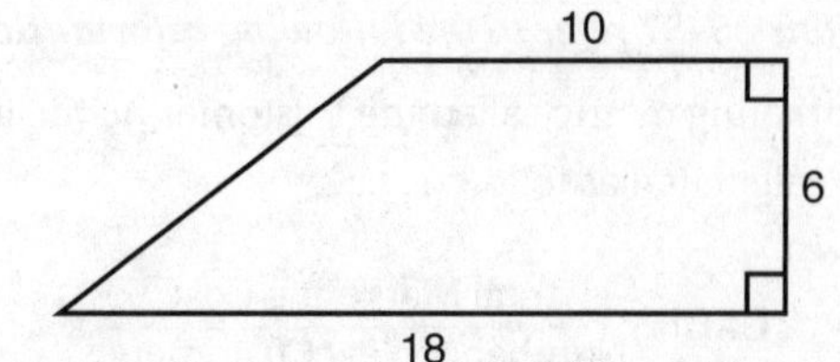

33. How many units is the perimeter of the above trapezoid?

32. $3x - 4y = -2$

$x + y = 11$

Given that (x, y) is a solution to the above system of equations, what is the value of x?

x	y
2	5
6	15
10	25

34. The relationship between the values in the table above can be expressed as the function $y = kx$, in which k is a constant value. What is the value of k?

Questions 35–37 refer to the following information.

The marketing metric called the Customer Acquisition Cost is calculated as follows:

$$CAC = \frac{\text{Total Marketing Cost}}{\text{Number of New Customers}}$$

Different marketing strategies and their total marketing costs and expected number of customers are given in this table.

Campaign Type	Total Marketing Cost	Number of New Customers
Online Ads	\$1,000	50
Radio Ads	\$1,600	45
Door-to-door Sales	\$800	20
One TV Ad	\$5,000	125

35. Based on the above information, what is the Customer Acquisition Cost in dollars for the door-to-door sales campaign?

36. Given the information in the table, how many more customers could the business acquire by spending an equivalent amount on repeated online ad campaigns instead of a single TV ad campaign?

37. What is the difference in customer acquisition cost between the door-to-door campaign and the TV campaign?

38. If $(x + 5)(x + 3) = ax^2 + bx + c$, in which a, b, and c are all constants, what is the value of c?

STOP If there is still time remaining, you may review your answers.

ANSWER KEY
Practice Test 3

Section 1: Reading

1. **C**	14. **D**	27. **C**	40. **D**
2. **A**	15. **B**	28. **B**	41. **D**
3. **B**	16. **C**	29. **A**	42. **D**
4. **B**	17. **D**	30. **B**	43. **A**
5. **C**	18. **C**	31. **D**	44. **C**
6. **A**	19. **C**	32. **B**	45. **A**
7. **C**	20. **A**	33. **B**	46. **D**
8. **A**	21. **A**	34. **D**	47. **C**
9. **C**	22. **B**	35. **A**	48. **D**
10. **C**	23. **B**	36. **A**	49. **B**
11. **C**	24. **C**	37. **C**	50. **B**
12. **A**	25. **D**	38. **C**	51. **A**
13. **C**	26. **D**	39. **B**	52. **C**

Section 2: Writing and Language

1. **A**	12. **A**	23. **A**	34. **D**
2. **D**	13. **A**	24. **C**	35. **A**
3. **C**	14. **B**	25. **C**	36. **D**
4. **D**	15. **B**	26. **B**	37. **B**
5. **B**	16. **A**	27. **D**	38. **C**
6. **A**	17. **D**	28. **A**	39. **A**
7. **C**	18. **C**	29. **B**	40. **B**
8. **B**	19. **C**	30. **D**	41. **C**
9. **D**	20. **D**	31. **A**	42. **A**
10. **B**	21. **C**	32. **D**	43. **D**
11. **C**	22. **D**	33. **B**	44. **C**

Section 3: Math (No Calculator)

1. **C**	6. **C**	11. **D**	16. **1**
2. **A**	7. **A**	12. **B**	17. **7**
3. **C**	8. **D**	13. **C**	18. $\frac{5}{3}$, **1.66, 1.67**
4. **A**	9. **A**	14. **C**	19. **3**
5. **D**	10. **B**	15. **D**	20. **7**

ANSWER KEY
Practice Test 3

Section 4: Math (Calculator)

1. **B**
2. **B**
3. **D**
4. **C**
5. **B**
6. **D**
7. **B**
8. **A**
9. **D**
10. **A**
11. **C**
12. **C**
13. **B**
14. **A**
15. **C**
16. **B**
17. **C**
18. **A**
19. **C**
20. **A**
21. **B**
22. **D**
23. **D**
24. **A**
25. **C**
26. **B**
27. **B**
28. **C**
29. **B**
30. **C**
31. **14**
32. **6**
33. **44**
34. **2.5 or $\frac{5}{2}$**
35. **40**
36. **125**
37. **0**
38. **15**

SAT Scoring Chart

Tally the number of correct answers from the Reading section (out of 52), the Writing and Language section (out of 44), and the combined Math without and with calculator sections (out of 58). Match these numbers of correct answers to the find the Reading Test score, the Writing and Language Test score, and the Math section score.

Number of Correct Answers on Each Test Part (Reading, Writing/Language, Combined Math Sections)	Reading Test Score	Writing and Language Test Score	Math Section Score
0	10	10	200
1	10	10	200
2	10	10	210
3	10	11	220
4	11	11	230
5	12	12	250
6	13	13	270
7	13	14	280
8	14	14	300
9	15	15	310
10	16	16	320
11	16	16	340
12	17	17	350
13	17	17	360
14	18	18	370
15	18	18	380
16	19	18	390
17	19	19	400
18	20	19	410
19	20	20	420
20	21	20	430
21	21	21	440
22	22	21	450
23	22	22	460
24	23	23	470
25	23	23	480
26	24	24	490
27	24	24	500
28	25	25	500
29	25	25	510
30	26	26	520

(Continued)

Number of Correct Answers on Each Test Part (Reading, Writing/Language, Combined Math Sections)	Reading Test Score	Writing and Language Test Score	Math Section Score
31	26	27	520
32	27	27	530
33	28	28	540
34	28	29	540
35	29	29	550
36	29	30	560
37	30	31	570
38	30	31	580
39	31	32	580
40	31	33	590
41	31	34	600
42	32	36	610
43	32	38	610
44	33	40	620
45	33		630
46	34		640
47	35		650
48	36		660
49	36		670
50	37		680
51	39		690
52	40		700
53			710
54			730
55			750
56			770
57			790
58			800

Add the Reading Test score and the Writing and Language Test scores:

________ (Reading Score) + ________ (Writing and Language Score) =

__________ (Combined Reading and Writing and Language Score)

Then multiply the Combined Reading and Writing Language score by 10 to find your Evidence-Based Reading and Writing section score:

10 × ___________ (Combined Reading and Writing and Language Score) =

_____________ **Evidence-Based Reading and Writing Score (between 200–800)**

The Math section score is also between 200–800. Get this from the table above.

________________ **Math Section Score (between 200–800)**

Add the Evidence-Based Reading and Writing score and the Math section score to find your total SAT test score:

____________ Evidence-Based Reading and Writing Score +

____________ Math Section Score =

____________ **Total SAT Test Score (between 400–1600)**

Approximate your testing percentiles (1st–99th) using this chart:

Total Score	Section Score	Total Percentile	Evidence-Based Reading and Writing Percentile	Math Percentile
1600	800	99+	99+	99
1500	750	98	98	96
1400	700	94	94	91
1300	650	86	86	84
1200	600	74	73	75
1100	550	59	57	61
1000	500	41	40	42
900	450	25	24	27
800	400	11	11	15
700	350	3	3	5
600	300	1	1	1
500	250	1	1	1
400	200	1	1	1

Answers Explained

Section 1: Reading Test

My Ántonia

1. **(C)** The sentence before this phrase says, "We agreed that no one who had not grown up in a little prairie town could know anything about it." The author then builds on this assertion with, "it was a kind of freemasonry." The author here is reiterating the idea that only a person who has experienced growing up in such a town would understand it. This makes choice **(C)** the best option. Choices (A), (B), and (D) do not explain this concept, but rather introduce unrelated details from the passage.

2. **(A)** Within this paragraph, it is explained that unlike Jim, Jim's wife is well known and has a lot of connections. She was supposed to marry her cousin, but he dumped her. It is implied that all of this was rather scandalous, leading to "sharp comment." We can infer, therefore, that the sharp comment would not lead to very nice discussions about the situation—harsh gossip would be another way of describing it. The definition of sharp, therefore is closest to *intense*, making choice **(A)** the best option. The author is not referring to the sharpness of a knife or other weapon, making choice (B) incorrect. The author is not referring to someone who is well dressed, so choice (C) is incorrect. The author is not referring to someone who is on time, so choice (D) is incorrect.

3. **(B)** We can see at the beginning of the second paragraph that "Jim Burden and I both live in New York." Choice **(B)** is clearly the correct answer. Choice (A) is where they grew up, but not where they live now. Choices (C) and (D) are contradicted when the passage says they live in New York.

4. **(B)** These lines tell us that Jim was struggling to make it in New York. Then, he had a "brilliant marriage." By the time the narrator and Jim are on the train, Jim is a well-known and wealthy lawyer. The connection to "the daughter of a distinguished man" helped Jim advance in life. The inference, then, is that Jim married his wife for her connections. This makes choice **(B)** the best answer—the narrator believes Jim married his wife to advance his career. Choices (A) and (C) are incorrect as there is no evidence that Jim and his wife share any love. Choice (D) is incorrect as we have no evidence that his wife sympathized with his poverty.

5. **(C)** In the third paragraph, Jim's wife is described as restless and headstrong and always doing something unexpected for the shock value. The narrator also says that "she is handsome and energetic, but to me she seems unimpressionable and temperamentally incapable of enthusiasm." In the next paragraph, the description of Jim is a stark contrast. He is described as having a "naturally romantic and ardent disposition" and then described further in a very favorable manner. This makes choice **(C)** correct. The narrator has directly said that the wife is unimpressive, and the comparison shows us how different the two people are. Choice (A) is incorrect as we do not see any redeeming qualities in the wife. Choice (B) is incorrect as the narrator does not share with us the wife's aesthetic sensibilities. Choice (D) is incorrect as the narrator does not find the wife inspiring, even though she gives her house for a suffragette society.

6. **(A)** In the final paragraph, Jim is described as a man who has a "naturally romantic and ardent disposition." Ardent, in this context, means enthusiastic. Jim, therefore, might be described as resilient and positive. Choice **(A)** is, therefore, the best option. Choice (B) is incorrect as Jim's wife has a large inheritance, not Jim. It is not choice (C)—Jim's bankers are back East. It is not choice (D) as the passage describes Jim as being a persistent man.

7. **(C)** As quoted in the previous answer explanation, choice **(C)** is the best evidence for the idea that Jim would meet difficulty with positivity and resilience. Choice (A) is part of the conversation between Jim and the narrator and does not show Jim's personality. Choice (B) shows how Jim's marriage advanced his career. However, his wife is still living and cannot marry again, which is not a viable avenue for him to overcome future difficulties. Choice (D) shows his reaction in a specific situation but does not give insight into how he handles difficulties in general.

8. **(A)** In the third paragraph, the reader can see the narrator's view of Mrs. Burden. The narrator says she did many things, not because she wanted them done, but merely to get a reaction out of her friends. This involved giving a home for a suffrage headquarters and being arrested for picketing during a strike. The narrator says about these incidents that "I am never able to believe that she has much feeling for the causes to which she lends her name and her fleeting interest." This makes choice **(A)** the best answer. Choices (B) and (C) are incorrect as the narrator does not share any details about her musical or literary abilities. Choice (D) is incorrect as it is heavily implied that she is not at all engaged in her marriage and that Mr. and Mrs. Burden lead separate lives.

9. **(C)** In the last paragraph, the author says "He is always able to raise capital for new enterprises... and has helped young men out there to do remarkable things in mines and timber and oil." This aligns with choice **(C)**. It shows how involved Jim is in entrepreneurial investments. Raising capital means raising money, so he is helping to fund entrepreneurs as they start their businesses in the West. He must, therefore, look upon such investments favorably. Choice (A) is about Mrs. Burden and does not show Jim's attitude toward investments. Choice (B) is about Mr. Burden's personality, not his attitude toward investments. Choice (D) discusses Mr. Burden's outward appearance, but again does not give insight to his attitude on personal investments.

10. **(C)** In this context the author is not talking about being physically lost, but rather about losing oneself in a big idea. The idea is that of being swept away or completely engrossed in "those big Western dreams." This makes choice **(C)** correct. Jim often "loses himself" or "gives all his attention to" these dreams. Choices (A) and (B) are different meanings of the word "lost." Choice (D) does not fit the intended message of the author.

Handwashing

11. **(C)** In the first paragraph of Passage 1, the reader learns that historically handwashing was used to remove dirt. Even once its usefulness in preventing disease was discovered, no one understood why it was helpful. Choice **(C)** is therefore the best answer as handwashing was seen as a good thing, but it was not fully understood. Choice (A) is incorrect as handwashing was always known to be effective at washing away dirt. Choice (B) is incorrect as some doctors *were* recommending it. Choice (D) is incorrect as it was widely applied despite a lack of theoretical understanding.

12. **(A)** In the context of the passage, no one is physically stumbling. Instead, this phrase is used to describe the accidental discovery of a lifesaving technique. This makes choice **(A)** the best option. Choice (B) implies a physical stumble and is therefore incorrect. Choice (C) is incorrect as this discovery was accidental and was not thoroughly researched. Choice (D) is incorrect as "stumbled upon" never implies the process of expressing disappointment.

13. **(C)** As we see at the end of the first passage, when soap and water meet bacteria, their hydrophilic exteriors are "shattered," which allows water into the molecule to wash the molecule away. This best fits with choice **(C)**—the bacteria are broken up and washed away. Choice (A) is incorrect as the very opposite is what occurs—the hydrophilic surface is broken, not strengthened. Choice (B) is incorrect as the bacteria break, but don't dissolve. Choice (D) is incorrect as there is no evidence that the bacteria work with soap to attack other bacteria.

14. **(D)** Choice **(D)** is the best option as it is in this reading selection that we learn the mechanism by which soap and water work together to break up and wash away bacteria. Choice (A) describes how soap molecules work together or independently, but not how they get rid of bacteria. Choice (B) is incorrect as it describes the physical properties of bacteria, but not how soap can clean them away. Choice (C) is incorrect as it tells us why water alone won't wash away bacteria but does not tell us why the addition of soap will wash away bacteria.

15. **(B)** In Passage 2, the author is very clear that over-washing is bad for human health since humans need to be exposed to bacteria so that they can "build up antibodies to protect the body during future exposures." Choice **(B)** best explains this conclusion by the author. Choice (A) is incorrect as the author feels that some germs are necessary for a healthy immune system. Choice (C) is incorrect as the author states that different germs pose different risks to people. Choice (D) is incorrect as there is no indication that the author of Passage 2 believes germs to not be understood by researchers.

16. **(C)** As quoted in the explanation to question 15, choice **(C)** best supports the author's belief that some germs must be encountered in order for a healthy immune system to exist. Choice (A) states why handwashing is important, not why germs are important. Choice (B) explains that washing removes bacteria, but not why bacteria are important. Choice (D) shows that the issue is complex, but again does not say why bacteria are important for human health.

17. **(D)** Within the context, the author is talking about how "crucial" it is to create a sterile environment after using the restroom or handling raw food. The best replacement word would be *important* as those are the times when it is most critical to clean away any bacteria. The other answer options do not fit within the context of the passage.

18. **(C)** This sentence helps to explain the importance of exposure to bacteria by referencing something most people are familiar with: vaccinations. This makes choice **(C)** the best option—the author has previously explained why bacteria are important, and now she is further clarifying with an analogy to a well-known concept. Choice (A) is incorrect as this is a clarification, not a dispute. Choice (B) is incorrect as the author is not clarifying the importance of patient education, but rather the importance of bacteria. Choice (D) is incorrect as there are no scholarly sources cited in this sentence.

19. **(C)** Passage 1 goes into detail about how soap and bacteria are structured and how they interact with each other during the process of washing. Passage 2 explains when and how much washing is effective. This makes choice **(C)** the best option. Choice (A) is incorrect as the findings in Passage 1 are not recent and Passage 2 is not critiquing a research

methodology. Choice (B) is incorrect as the assertion in Passage 2 (that over-washing is bad) is not addressed in Passage 1. Choice (D) is incorrect as this is not a belief system.

20. **(A)** Passage 2 clearly lays out the dangers of over-washing, something that Passage 1 does not address. This makes choice **(A)** the best option. Choice (B) is incorrect since Passage 1 addresses the mechanics of how bacteria are removed. Choice (C) is incorrect as both passages mention bacteria removal in the prevention of disease. Choice (D) is incorrect as Passage 2 directly says that it *is* possible to over-wash.

Multi-Level Marketing

21. **(A)** In the final paragraph of the passage, we can see the author's intent. Having explained to the audience why joining an MLM company is a bad idea, she gives a quick and simple way to identify and avoid such companies. She is clearly trying to help readers avoid being pulled into such a scheme. This makes choice **(A)** the best answer. Choice (B) is incorrect as the passage is not aimed at business owners. Choice (C) is incorrect as multi-level marketing is not the primary way that businesses operate—only some businesses operate in this manner. Choice (D) is incorrect since only one point of view is considered: the one against MLMs.

22. **(B)** In the second paragraph, the author shares the difference between a pyramid scheme and an MLM: MLMs sell things, whereas pyramid schemes do not. In choices (A), (C), and (D) thing are being sold. In choice (A), handmade products are being sold. In choice (C) services are being sold. In choice (D) illegal substances are being sold. Choice **(B)**, however, does not have anything for sale, making it likely to be a pyramid scheme, but not an MLM.

23. **(B)** In the first paragraph, the author describes why women originally joined MLMs in the post–World War II era, saying in part that, "This effective set up targeted young women who found life at home to be boring." This presents a nonfinancial motive for joining an MLM: Having something to do alleviates boredom. This makes choice **(B)** the best answer. Choice (A) is incorrect as in these lines we learn that most people are wary of and would stay away from an MLM scheme. Choice (C) is incorrect as these lines explain the extent of MLMs, but not a nonfinancial reason to join one. Choice (D) is incorrect as these lines explain how an MLM works, but again do not mention a nonfinancial reason a person would join one.

24. **(C)** In the context of the sentence, the author mentions an "investment" that involves "shelling out" thousands of dollars. This makes it clear that "shelling out" means "to spend." This makes choice **(C)** correct. The other choices do not mean "to spend" and are therefore not appropriate given the context of the sentence.

25. **(D)** The author makes it clear that the first few people who join an MLM company have the best odds at making a profit. This can be clearly seen when she says that "the first person in an area to join a new MLM may actually make a little money." This makes choice **(D)** the best option as someone who was successful would be the best person to showcase to bring in new recruits. Choice (A) is incorrect as there is no evidence that a bigger investment leads to a bigger payout. Choice (B) is incorrect as taking out a loan would mean a bigger investment, which again does not necessarily lead to a bigger payout. Choice (C) is incorrect as the author makes clear that once an area is saturated, it is very difficult, if not impossible, to make any money.

26. **(D)** Choice **(D)** is the best option as shown in the answer explanation for question 25. Choice (A) is incorrect as it simply explains what kind of products MLMs might sell. It does not explain what kind of participant would be best to showcase to get new recruits.

Choices (B) and (C) are incorrect as they would *not* be good people to showcase to get people to join an MLM.

27. **(C)** This phrase comes directly after information is provided that make MLMs appear in a very negative light. Of course, these companies need to do something to ensure that this negative light does not harm business. It makes sense, then, that they would minimize the objections being made. The phrase "explain this away" is how they try to rid their potential new clients of the objections. This best fits with choice **(C)**. Choice (A) is incorrect as the companies do not acknowledge the valid point of their opponents. Choice (B) is incorrect as we have no evidence that they do provide more detail—on the contrary, they seem to offer very basic explanations that put the blame on others. Choice (D) is incorrect as they would be trying to support, not undermine, those who believe MLMs are worthwhile.

28. **(B)** This last paragraph is trying to enable the reader to recognize and avoid MLMs. These questions are put forward as a kind of test—if the answer to either of them is yes, then a person should not join that company. This best fits with choice **(B)**. The passage is not discussing starting new MLMs, so choice (A) is incorrect. The questions are a tool to help people recognize MLMs, not distinguish between them and so choice (C) is incorrect. Choice (D) is incorrect as nothing in the passage is discussing human resource management.

29. **(A)** We can see on the far-right side of the table that the number of participants goes 1, 2, 4, 8, 16, and then continues in this pattern, doubling with each advancement. This makes choice **(A)** correct and the other choices incorrect.

30. **(B)** We can see in the data that there are 8,191 total participants, and of those participants 1,023 made a profit. This means that roughly 1/8 of the participants profited. One-eighth is 12 percent, making choice **(B)** correct. Also, the table explicitly states that 12.49% profited, so that would be closest to 12. Choice (A) is incorrect as we know that some people did profit. Choices (C) and (D) are far too high and are therefore incorrect.

31. **(D)** The label on this data is "profits broken down in a classic no-product 8-ball pyramid scheme." The "no-product" is an important qualifier as that is what differentiates this scheme from an MLM. A proponent of MLMs would likely point this out in defense of MLM companies, which have products that they sell. This makes choice **(D)** the best option. Choice (A) is incorrect as the data source is the Federal Trade Commission—a very reputable organization. Choice (B) is incorrect as the fact that a pyramid scheme initiator makes money does not defend MLMs. Choice (C) is incorrect as this fact would not defend MLMs but rather lump them in with pyramid schemes.

Voting Rights

32. **(B)** Stanton's primary focus is on the voting rights of women. Since we know from the introductory information that she is speaking to the legislature of New York, she must be talking about American women as that governmental body would not be able to give voting rights to the women of any other country. This makes choice **(B)** the best answer. The other answer choices are mentioned briefly in the passage but are not the focus of the argument.

33. **(B)** The first paragraph starts with the phrase "The wheel of progress moves onward." This part of the topic sentence sets up the rest of the paragraph to talk about what Stanton sees as inevitable progress and the embrace thereof. This makes choice **(B)** the best option. Andrew Johnson is only an example, not the main message, so choice (A) is incorrect. Choice (C) is the opposite of her message—she believes that people should embrace change and shift the status quo. Choice (D) is incorrect as she is not discussing animal examples.

34. **(D)** In these lines, Stanton tells the reader that each person has rights, but that our rights do not include the right to infringe on another's rights. This best fits with choice **(D)**. Stanton makes it clear that when people infringe on the rights of others, confusion ensues. Stanton does not believe that arbitrary (made up) limits exist, so choice (A) is wrong. She does not believe that any human may violate the rights of another, so choice (B) is wrong. She does not address the protection of the environment in any meaningful way, making choice (C) wrong.

35. **(A)** In this line "breed" is being used to mean "to start" disorder and confusion. This best fits with choice **(A)**. We could not say we would sort, educate, or organize disorder and confusion, so choices (B), (C), and (D) are incorrect.

36. **(A)** Rhetorical questions are questions that do not require an answer. They are asked not to garner an answer, but rather to make a point. We see several of these within this paragraph, making rhetorical questions the primary approach in this section. Choice **(A)** is therefore the best answer. Choice (B) is incorrect since there is no analysis of statistics, even though the number $250 is mentioned. Choice (C) is incorrect as there is no direct appeal to authority. Choice (D) is incorrect as Stanton at no point tells a personal anecdote (story).

37. **(C)** In the fourth paragraph, Stanton says, "The demand we today make, is... a universal movement." That demand is for suffrage—Stanton is saying that the suffrage movement is universal. This would mean that is very widespread, making choice **(C)** the best option. The movement has had the time to spread, so it is not in its infancy, making choice (A) incorrect. Stanton herself is pushing the movement forward, so she likely thinks it can advance, making choice (B) incorrect. If the movement had been successful, then Stanton would no longer feel the need to speak for women's suffrage, making choice (D) incorrect.

38. **(C)** As shown in the answer explanation to question 37, the excerpt from choice **(C)** best shows that Stanton sees the movement as widespread. Choice (A) is incorrect as it shows that the idea is debated in Congress, but that does not prove that it is widespread. Choice (B) is incorrect as it does not show how widespread the movement is, but merely explains the demands of the movement. Choice (D) is incorrect as it tells of some of the history of personal rights but does not prove that the suffragette movement is widespread.

39. **(B)** Within the context of the sentence, Stanton is using the term "throwing off" to show that women are removing or getting rid of their lethargy (sluggish sleepiness). This term could best be replaced with "rid themselves of," making choice **(B)** the best option. Choices (A), (C), and (D) do not mean to remove and are therefore incorrect.

40. **(D)** Within this paragraph, Stanton is reminding the audience that suffrage is not a new concept. She names many examples of other nations and groups of people that have allowed female suffrage. This best aligns with choice **(D)**. Choice (A) is incorrect as she does not bring up other countries to show that they have not been overthrown. Choice (B) is incorrect as Stanton is saying the very opposite—she implies that the U.S. (a democracy) should be better equipped to allow women the right to vote. Choice (C) is incorrect and can in no way be supported by this excerpt.

41. **(D)** Choice **(D)** is the best answer as Stanton clearly says that "the right has long ago been exercised by certain classes of women in many countries." This proves that giving women the right to vote would not be unprecedented (never done before). Choices (A), (B), and (C) do not offer such direct evidence of women being allowed to vote prior to this speech and therefore would not support the idea that suffrage for women is not unprecedented.

42. **(D)** The final sentence says that "if it were a new thing, and had never been heard of before, that would yet be no argument against the experiment." With this sentence Stanton is saying that even if suffrage had never been tried before anywhere in the world, that is still not a good reason not to try it now. This best fits with Choice **(D)**. Choice (A) is incorrect as she is not saying that suffrage is unlikely to succeed. Choice (B) is incorrect as she is calling for full suffrage, not smaller experiments. Choice (C) is incorrect as she does not feel women's voting rights are revolutionary as they have been established in many other countries already.

Tornados

43. **(A)** The passage gives a general understanding of tornados—it explains how they form, how they're studied, and how they're classified. This gives us an overall understanding of what the scientific community knows about tornados. This makes choice **(A)** the best answer. Choice (B) is incorrect as, while the EF scale is explained in one part of the passage, describing the EF scale is not the primary purpose of the passage. Choice (C) is incorrect as future research is only briefly mentioned; it is not the primary purpose of the passage. Choice (D) is incorrect as the passage does not give any sort of in-depth idea of how to keep safe during a tornado.

44. **(C)** The beginning of the second paragraph says that "the majority of severe storms are in the U.S." Severe storms that spawn tornados are known as supercells. Therefore, most supercells must be in the United States. The rest of the world would be less likely to have supercell storms. Choice **(C)** is therefore the best answer. The other answers do not accurately convey this relationship.

45. **(A)** In the third paragraph, the author says, "Once one of these mesocyclones occurs, then the chances of a tornado forming increases drastically." It would therefore be reasonable to infer that a tornado could be predicted once a mesocyclone was formed. This makes choice **(A)** the best answer. The other answer choices are not directly linked by the passage to the formation of a tornado. While tornados may occur at the same time as thunderstorms, the evaporation of water or changes in air pressure would not predict a tornado.

46. **(D)** As quoted in the explanation to question 45, the lines in choice **(D)** directly connect the formation of a mesocyclone to the increased chances of tornado formation. Choice (A) is incorrect as it explains how a tornado works, but not how to predict it. Choice (B) is incorrect as it tells us how a tornado begins, but again, doesn't tell us how to predict one. Choice (C) is incorrect as it describes the formation of a supercell, but not how to predict a tornado.

47. **(C)** In the context of the passage, the author is trying to help the reader visualize just how much energy there is. He could give a number in watts or volts, but those numbers wouldn't mean much to an average non-scientist reader. Instead, he uses something everyone has an idea of—a nuclear blast. This helps the reader visualize just how much energy there is and makes choice **(C)** the best option. Choice (A) is incorrect as he is not trying to explain the destruction of a storm. Choice (B) is incorrect as he never implies that severe weather might be radioactive. Choice (D) is incorrect as he is not trying to say that the military can influence the weather.

48. **(D)** In the fourth paragraph, the author says, "While the two scales are similar, the EF scale is more precise than the F scale." Greater precision implies a greater attention to detail, making choice **(D)** the best option. Choice (A) is incorrect as both scales are related to tornados. Choice (B) is incorrect as scientists have used both scales. Choice (C) is incorrect as we do not know where the different scales have been adopted.

49. **(B)** As quoted in the explanation to number 48, the lines in choice **(B)** best show that the EF scale is more attuned to detail than the F scale. Choice (A) introduces the EF scale but does not show the differences between the two scales. Choice (C) explains part of how the EF scale works but does not explain the difference between EF and F. Choice (D) explains how scientists use the EF scale to number tornados, but again it doesn't explain to the reader the difference between the two scales.

50. **(B)** Within the context of the sentence, we see that scientists use the damage to "ascertain," or "figure out," things about the tornado like its path, wind speed, and strength. The best choice to replace "ascertain" would be *determine*, which is choice **(B)**. The other choices would not work within the context to replace "ascertain."

51. **(A)** When we look at Figure 1, the lowest bar occurs from 4–5 A.M. This means that 4–5 A.M. has the lowest normalized occurrence of tornados: Tornados are least likely to occur at this time. This makes choice **(A)** the best option. All the other choices have higher rates of normalized occurrence and therefore, a higher chance of having a tornado.

52. **(C)** We can see in Figure 1 that the evening hours have the highest normalized occurrence rates of any time of day. We can see this in Figure 2 in the spring months of April, May, and June. Combined, this makes the evening hours in the spring the most likely time for a tornado to form. Choice **(C)** is the best option. The other options all have a lower likelihood of spawning a tornado.

Section 2: Writing and Language Test

1. **(A)** Choice **(A)** is consistent with the present tense used elsewhere in the sentence, as in the verbs "is" and "can." In addition, choice **(A)** is consistent with the singular subject, "experience." The other options do not maintain the correct tense or numerical agreement.

2. **(D)** "Avenues" can mean potential "paths" that one could take to becoming a culinary professional—it does not have to mean a literal road. The other options are commonly used to refer to actual roads and do not have the potential double meaning that "avenue" has.

3. **(C)** The previous sentence mentions the potential appeal of face-to-face jobs. The sentence that follows the sentence in question refers to both customer interaction and hands-on work. Without this sentence, there would not be a logical transition between the surrounding sentences. It is not choice (D) because it does not address a likely objection. It is not choices (A) or (B) because the sentence should not be deleted.

4. **(D)** The paragraph first mentions possible academic degrees that aspiring culinary professionals may earn, and then it discusses hands-on internships that students can do to learn from practicing culinary professionals. Choice **(D)** would therefore best introduce this paragraph since the paragraph discusses both formal and informal training. Choice (A) ignores informal training. Choice (B) ignores formal training. Choice (C) does not emphasize education.

5. **(B)** Choice **(B)** uses dashes to set aside the definition of what a stage is. Choice (A) only punctuates one side of the definition. Choice (C) does not provide any punctuation. Choice (D) inconsistently punctuates the definition.

6. **(A)** The next part of the sentence shows how both the mentor and the aspiring chef can benefit from working with one another. Therefore, it is most logical to emphasize how the relationship between them is mutually beneficial, as found in choice **(A)**. Choice (B) does

not emphasize the mutual benefit from collaboration. Choice (C) focuses on new cooking technique development instead of career advancement. Choice (D) contradicts the emphasis on the benefits of interpersonal collaboration.

7. **(C)** "Bolster" means "to solidify or build" in this context, making it the most logical option to refer to improving one's resume. "Cushion" and "rebuild" would suggest protecting one's career against a hardship, when the emphasis here is on positive growth. And "maintain" does not suggest growth but keeping things as they are.

8. **(B)** Choice (B) provides a comma after the long introductory dependent clause. Choice (A) does not have a complete sentence before the semicolon. Choice (C) inserts an unnecessary comma and does not have a complete sentence before the colon. And Choice (D) does not have the needed pause after "restaurant."

9. **(D)** "As" provides the needed transition to show cause-and-effect in this situation—the chef wants to work on a part-time basis *because* they could have more flexible scheduling. The other options do not show a cause-and-effect relationship.

10. **(B)** Based on the surrounding context, it is clear that the author is discussing cooking as a possibility for both a career and a hobby. Therefore, it would be most logical to go with "either...or" to clarify this. It is not choice (A) because "either" should be used with "or," not with "and." It is not choices (C) or (D) because these both use "neither."

11. **(C)** This sentence is most logically placed after sentence 4, since sentence 4 introduces the field of culinary experimentation, and this sentence would elaborate on how there are positions available for people with this intellectual interest. The other options would not be appropriate, as there would be no surrounding context about the possibility of food research.

12. **(A)** Choice (A) puts the words in the most logical sequence, clearly stating the subject of "scientific method" and following with the description of it. The other options all put the words in an illogical order.

13. **(A)** "Affect" is generally used as a verb, and "effect" is generally used as a noun. "Affecting" would be correct given the surrounding context. It is not "affected" because the word "that" would be needed before "affected" if it were used here. It is not choices (B) or (C) because these both use variations of "effect."

14. **(B)** "Clouded *by*" is the appropriate phrase given the context—it helps to emphasize the uncertainty surrounding the study. The other prepositions would not create a logical phrase given the context.

15. **(B)** The term "precognition" is not widely known, so having a definition of it at this point would be helpful to the reader. It is not choice (A) because there is not an explanation of a research process in this rather short phrase. It is not choices (C) or (D) because the phrase should be added.

16. **(A)** "More generally" appropriately uses the adverb "generally" to describe the verb "examined." The other options use adjectives instead of adverbs.

17. **(D)** Choice (D) places a comma after the introductory phrase and separates the two independent clauses in the sentence. Choice (A) provides no break after the introductory phrase "For instance." Choice (B) does not have a complete sentence before the colon. Choice (C) provides pauses in awkward locations such that the second comma separates the subject from the verb.

18. **(C)** Choice (C) provides a semicolon to break up the two independent clauses in the sentence. It also provides commas to surround the word "however," which provides a transition and could be removed from the sentence without making the sentence incomplete. Choices (A) and (D) create run-on sentences by using just use a comma to join two independent clauses. Choice (B) does not surround "however" with the needed punctuation.

19. **(C)** "Serve as" both maintains the present tense of the surrounding verbs and uses the correct preposition "as." Choices (A) and (B) do not use the right verb tense in this context, and choice (D) uses the incorrect preposition *to*.

20. **(D)** The sentence is focused on scientific measurement, so "objectively" would be most appropriate. The other options would not be used to describe high-quality scientific measurement.

21. **(C)** The percentages for the social science journals are 29 and 23, while the percentages for the cognitive journals are 48 and 53. The social science journals would therefore have replication about a quarter of the time while the cognitive journals would have replication about half of the time. The other answers do not have the correct corresponding fractions.

22. **(D)** The sentence states that there should be a more rigorous foundation for research claims. It would therefore be most logical to connect this to social issues, since, according to the table, social science research can be replicated only about 23–29% of the time. The other choices are all associated with cognition and would have a more rigorous foundation based on their higher reproducibility.

23. **(A)** "Was" is in the past tense and correctly matches up with the singular subject of "Harlem Renaissance." Choices (B) and (C) are plural verbs, and choice (D) would change the meaning of the sentence: It would no longer define what the Harlem Renaissance was.

24. **(C)** Choice **(C)** avoids unnecessary breaks that would interrupt the phrase. Choices (A) and (B) provide unneeded pauses, and choice (D) does not have a complete sentence after the semicolon.

25. **(C)** The passage goes on to discuss Cullen's biography in which the author highlights how Cullen was a trailblazer in the world of poetry and in working to end racial segregation. Choice **(C)** would be the most appropriate introduction to that information. Choices (A) and (B) focus just on specific elements of the passage instead of the passage as a whole. Choice (D) overstates Cullen's role—he did not lead nonviolent protest movements.

26. **(B)** Choice **(B)** is the only option to correctly use the apostrophe to show Cullen's possession of his early life. The other options either do not use the apostrophe at all or use it to show plural instead of singular possession.

27. **(D)** The passage as a whole describes Cullen in a positive light, so it makes sense to use "renowned," which means "respected." "Notorious" is too negative. "Imminent" describes something happening quickly. "Illustrated" is not supported by the passage since there is no mention of artwork accompanying his writings.

28. **(A)** The paragraph follows a chronological order, so having sentence 3 where it currently is makes the most sense. It would come after the first mention of his high school experience and before the discussion of his university experience. The other options would move this sentence out of chronological order.

29. **(B)** "Despite" shows a contrast between the fact that Cullen was perceived as being solely African American and the fact that he was biracial. The other options would not show this contrast.

30. **(D)** The focus of the paragraph is on Cullen's biography and his poetic development. While the passage mentions "Shakespearean sonnet form," this is not to discuss the biography of Shakespeare but to elaborate on the type of poetry that Cullen created. Having this insertion would distract from the focus of the paragraph. Choice (C) is incorrect because it does not provide any specific speculation as to the identity of Shakespeare. It is not choices (A) or (B) because the insertion should not be made.

31. **(A)** "Even though" is the only option that provides the needed contrast between the two parts of the sentence, showing that while many people thought that his writings were controversial, Cullen continued to push forward with his creations and earned recognition for his work. The other options do not provide the needed contrast.

32. **(D)** "Than any other" provides a logical comparison, using the word "than" and also providing "any other" to represent the other poets to whom Cullen is being compared. "Over" and "with" would not set up comparisons, and "then" is used for time, not comparisons.

33. **(B)** Since the first sentence in this pairing ends with "Du Bois," it would be repetitive to restate his name when the sentences are combined. Choice **(B)** avoids this repetition and logically joins the sentences together. Choices (A) and (C) have overly wordy language, and choice (D) has an illogical transition, "therefore."

34. **(D)** "Due to" provides a cause-and-effect transition between the major ideas in the sentence: Because the functions of the vestibular system are so critical, any deviation can cause negative health consequences. The other options do not provide the needed cause-and-effect connection.

35. **(A)** Choice **(A)** uses correct information from the graph to emphasize that a relatively high number of people have some family history of vestibular issues. Choice (B) would go against the point made in the first part of the sentence. Choice (C) does connect to family history but uses a less impressive statistic. Choice (D) does not relate to family history.

36. **(D)** Choice **(D)** best indicates that vestibular issues are widespread since it asserts that vestibular problems can happen to almost anyone. The other options do not focus on the widespread nature of vestibular issues.

37. **(B)** The sentence shows where in the body the vestibular system is found, so "located" is most appropriate. The other options would be more appropriate in referring to people and where they live instead of where a bodily system is located.

38. **(C)** Choice **(C)** uses the appropriate word "with" to make a commonly used phrase. The other possible prepositions would not make sense in this context.

39. **(A)** The first example in the sentence is "a ballerina spinning." "A gymnast flipping" most closely matches this style, maintaining parallelism. The other options do not maintain the order and word types found in the first example.

40. **(B)** The paragraph focuses on the problem of vertigo, which results from issues with the vestibular system. It is therefore logical to introduce this specific example with the general claim about the potential vulnerability of the vestibular system found in choice **(B)**. Choice (A) shifts the focus away from the overall vestibular system. Choice (C) is contradicted by the

later part of the paragraph that shows the potential fragility of the vestibular system. Choice (D) focuses on immune system compromise instead of the vestibular system.

41. **(C)** Choice (C) correctly avoids any unnecessary punctuation. Choice (A) separates the subject from the verb with a comma. Choice (B) uses the colon to provide an unneeded and awkward interruption. Choice (D) does not have a complete sentence after the semicolon.

42. **(A)** Choice (A) provides a needed contrast without excessive wordiness. Choice (B) would need a semicolon before "in addition" to avoid a run-on sentence. Choice (C) also would need a semicolon or period before "despite" to avoid a run-on. Choice (D) provides no contrasting language and would result in a run-on sentence.

43. **(D)** In choice (D), the parentheses set aside the clarification of the types of people who have extremely fine-tuned vestibular systems, and there is a comma to separate the dependent introductory clause from the independent clause that follows. Choice (A) does not have the needed comma to separate the beginning dependent clause from the rest of the sentence. Choice (B) uses inconsistent punctuation to set aside the parenthetical phrase. Choice (C) does not have a comma separating "systems" and "people" while having an unneeded comma after *all-star*. Since the adjectives "all-star" and "vestibular" must be in the order that they are written, no comma is needed to separate them.

44. **(C)** Choice (C) conveys the idea without repetition. All of the other options use repetitive description.

Section 3: Math Test (No Calculator)

1. **(C)** Plug 5 in for x into the expression to find its value:

$$3(x+2)-2x \rightarrow$$
$$3(5+2)-2(5) \rightarrow$$
$$3(7)-10=21-10=11$$

2. **(A)** There are 7 days in one week, so multiply the 8 hours Mark sleeps per day by 7 to find out the total number of hours he sleeps in a week: $7 \times 8 = 56$. Then, multiply 56 by the number of weeks, W, to find the number of hours that Mark would sleep in W weeks: $56 \times W$.

3. **(C)** Take the cube root of both sides of the equation to solve for x:

$$x^3=\frac{27}{8} \rightarrow$$
$$\sqrt[3]{x^3}=\sqrt[3]{\frac{27}{8}} \rightarrow$$
$$x=\frac{3}{2}$$

4. **(A)**

$$5x+2=4(x-3) \rightarrow$$
$$5x+2=4x-12 \rightarrow$$
$$x+2=-12 \rightarrow$$
$$x=-14$$

5. **(D)**

$$\frac{x^2-9}{x-3} \rightarrow \frac{(x+3)(x-3)}{x-3}=\frac{(x+3)\cancel{(x-3)}}{\cancel{x-3}}=x+3$$

PRACTICE TEST 3

6. **(C)** Use the volume formula for a cylinder, $V = \pi r^2 h$, in which r is the radius and h is the height. Note that this formula is provided in the formulas at the beginning of the section, so refer to it if you do not remember the formula. Since the tank has a base with a diameter of 10 feet, the radius will be 5. Plug the volume and the radius into the formula to solve for height:

$$V = \pi r^2 h \rightarrow$$
$$300\pi = \pi(5^2)h \rightarrow$$
$$300\pi = 25\pi h \rightarrow$$
$$\frac{300\pi}{25\pi} = h \rightarrow$$
$$12 = h$$

7. **(A)** Notice that the functions in the answer choices are all written in slope-intercept form and all have different y-intercepts. So, see what the y-intercept of the function is based on the values in the table. The y-intercept occurs when the function intersects the y-axis; points that are on the y-axis have an x value of 0. The point $(0, -5)$ is given in the table, indicating an x value of 0 when y is -5. So, the y-intercept of the function is -5 and the correct answer is choice **(A)**, since with the equation $f(x) = -x - 5$, it has a y-intercept of -5.

8. **(D)** Add the two functions together, combining like terms to put it in a simplified quadratic form:

$$\begin{array}{r} -x^2 + 4x - 3 \\ + \quad 5x^2 - 2x + 8 \\ \hline 4x^2 + 2x + 5 \end{array}$$

In this combined equation, the number 5 corresponds to the constant k, making choice **(D)** correct.

9. **(A)** The equation can be written in slope-intercept form, since it is a line. Use k as the y-intercept:

$$y = mx + b$$
$$y = 5x + k$$

Now, plug in a point—we can use (1, 8)—for x and y to solve for k:

$$y = 5x + k \rightarrow$$
$$8 = 5(1) + k \rightarrow$$
$$3 = k$$

10. **(B)** Manipulate the equation to isolate v:

$$K = \frac{1}{2}mv^2 \rightarrow$$
$$\frac{2K}{m} = v^2 \rightarrow$$
$$\sqrt{\frac{2K}{m}} = v$$

11. **(D)** Plug 6 in for x to solve for the value of $f(6)$:

$$f(x) = \frac{x^2 + 3}{2x} \rightarrow$$

$$f(6) = \frac{6^2 + 3}{2(6)} = \frac{36 + 3}{12} = \frac{39}{12} = \frac{13}{4}$$

12. **(B)** For there to be a real value for the expression, the numbers inside the square root sign must be zero or greater. Otherwise, you would be taking the square root of a negative number. The smallest number you can have without it being negative is 0, so set the expression within the square root sign as equal to 0 and solve for *a*:

$$a^2 - 2a = 0 \rightarrow$$
$$a^2 = 2a \rightarrow$$
$$a = 2$$

So, 2 is the least possible value of *a* that would allow for a real value of the expression.

13. **(C)** The greatest possible value for *y* occurs when $y = x + 2$, since that would maximize its value within the inequality. Set $x + 2$ equal to $-x + 4$, since the value of *y* would be at its maximum in both inequalities, and then solve for *x*:

$$x + 2 = -x + 4 \rightarrow$$
$$2x = 2 \rightarrow$$
$$x = 1$$

The correct answer is therefore choice **(C)**.

14. **(C)**

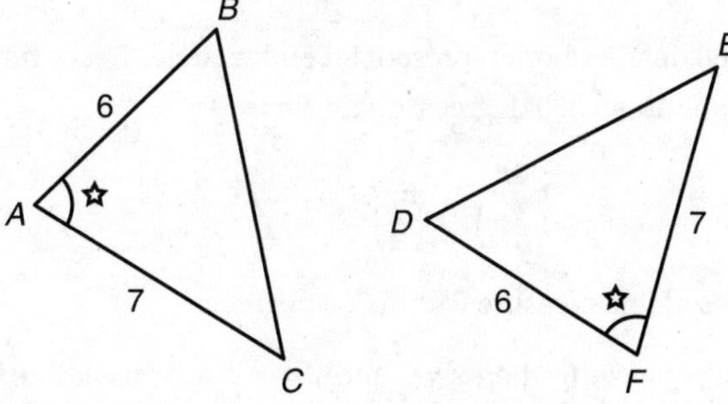

If angle *BAC* equals angle *DFE*, as labelled above, the triangles would be congruent because of the Side-Angle-Side theorem. This theorem states that if two sides and the angle formed by these two sides are equal to two sides and the included angle in another triangle, the two triangles are congruent.

15. **(D)** Use synthetic division to divide. Use 4, -3, and 2 as the values in the top of the synthetic division format, and use $+3$ to go through the synthetic division steps.

$$\begin{array}{c|ccc} 3 & 4 & -3 & 2 \\ & & 12 & 27 \\ \hline & 4 & 9 & 29 \end{array}$$

This results in $4x + 9 + \frac{29}{(x-3)}$, with $\frac{29}{(x-3)}$ as the remainder.

16. **1** Plug in 5 for *x* to the equation to solve for the value of *y*:

$$\frac{1}{3}(x-2) = y \rightarrow$$
$$\frac{1}{3}(5-2) = y \rightarrow$$
$$\frac{1}{3}(3) = 1 = y$$

PRACTICE TEST 3

17. **7** The expression $x^2 - 4$ can be rewritten as $(x + 2)(x - 2)$, enabling you to plug in 3 for $x - 2$ and solve for $x + 2$:

$$\frac{x^2 - 4}{3} = 7 \rightarrow$$
$$\frac{(x - 2)(x + 2)}{3} = 7 \rightarrow$$
$$\frac{3(x + 2)}{3} = 7 \rightarrow$$
$$x + 2 = 7$$

Alternatively, simply solve $x - 2 = 3$ for x, to get $x = 5$, and then substitute $x = 5$ for $x + 2$ to get 7.

18. $\mathbf{\frac{5}{3}}$**, 1.66, 1.67**

First, find the slope of the line comprised of the two points (5, 0) and (0, 3).

$$\text{slope} = \frac{y_2 - y_1}{x_2 - x_1} = \frac{3 - 0}{0 - 5} = -\frac{3}{5}$$

Now, take the negative reciprocal of $-\frac{3}{5}$ to find the slope of a line perpendicular to this one:

$$-\frac{3}{5} \rightarrow \text{Flip the fraction and multiply by } -1 \rightarrow \frac{5}{3}$$

19. **3** 2π radians and 360 degrees both represent an entire circle. To see how many angles of the measure of $\frac{2}{3}\pi$ radians are in 360 degrees, divide 2π by $\frac{2}{3}\pi$:

$$\frac{2\pi}{\left(\frac{2}{3}\pi\right)} = \frac{2}{\left(\frac{2}{3}\right)} = 2 \times \frac{3}{2} = 3$$

So, there are 3 angles of this measure within 360 degrees.

20. **7** The equation will equal zero when $x = 5$ and $x = -2$, as you can see below:

$$y = 7(x - 5)(x + 2) \rightarrow$$
$$y = 7(5 - 5)(5 + 2) \rightarrow$$
$$y = 7(0)(7) = 0$$

and

$$y = 7(-2 - 5)(-2 + 2) \rightarrow$$
$$y = 7(-2 - 5)(-2 + 2) \rightarrow$$
$$y = 7(-7)(0) = 0$$

So, the points (5, 0) and (−2, 0) are the x-intercepts of the parabola. Since the y values do not change, simply find the difference between the x values to find the distance between the x-intercepts:

$$5 - (-2) = 7$$

Section 4: Math Test (Calculator)

1. **(B)**

$$-3(x^2 - 2x + 4) \rightarrow$$

Distribute the $-3 \rightarrow$

$$-3x^2 + 6x - 12$$

2. **(B)** The total number of students in the class is $26 + 33 + 21 + 13 + 7 = 100$. So the median grade will be the average of the 50th and 51st term. The 50th and 51st terms, when the grades are put in order from least to greatest, are both B. So, the median grade for the class is B.

3. **(D)** The interval from 30–35 minutes has a decrease in distance of 0.45 miles. This is the greatest decrease in distance over any period of time portrayed in the graph, so choice **(D)** is the correct answer.

4. **(C)** Multiply the number of persons per square mile by the total number of square miles to find an approximation of the total population of the city:

$$4{,}900 \times 139 \approx 681{,}000$$

5. **(B)**

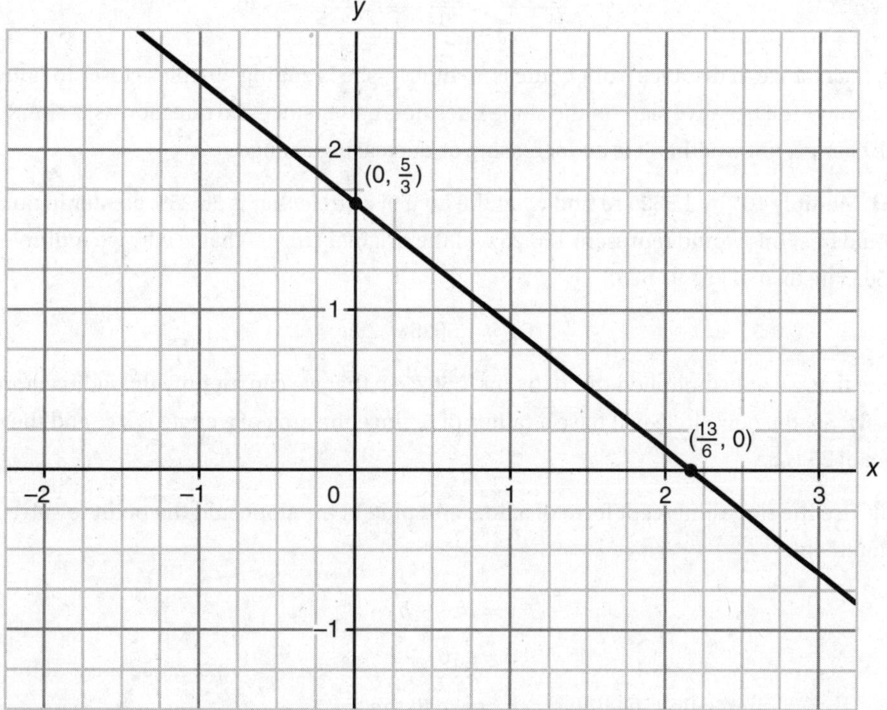

Take the change in *y* divided by the change in *x* to find the slope of the line. Use the points $\left(0, \frac{5}{3}\right)$ and $\left(\frac{13}{6}, 0\right)$, and the formula $slope = \frac{y_2 - y_1}{x_2 - x_1}$:

$$\frac{y_2 - y_1}{x_2 - x_1} = \frac{\frac{5}{3} - 0}{0 - \frac{13}{6}} = \frac{\frac{5}{3}}{-\frac{13}{6}} = \frac{5}{3} \times -\frac{6}{13} = -\frac{5 \times 2}{13} = -\frac{10}{13}$$

PRACTICE TEST 3

6. **(D)** The electrician will charge \$40 just to come to an appointment. Then, for each hour the electrician works, there is an additional charge of \$50. So, the correct expression is $40 + 50x$. You can verify this by plugging in a sample value. If the electrician comes for a 3-hour appointment, the total cost will be \$40 for the initial fee plus $3 \times 50 = 150$ for the hourly costs. This would be a total of \$190. Only choice **(D)** corresponds to this number when 3 is plugged in for x.

7. **(B)** The equation is already in a factored form that allows you to identify the solutions. If x is $-\frac{1}{4}$ or $\frac{2}{3}$, the value of the right-hand side of the equation would be zero. Therefore, these two numbers are solutions. So, multiply them together to find the product:

$$-\frac{1}{4} \times \frac{2}{3} = -\frac{2}{12} = -\frac{1}{6}$$

8. **(A)** Find 27% of 4,000 to see how many of the students would have a science or math major. Move the decimal point of 27 to the left two spots, then multiply this by 4,000 to find the number of students:

$$0.27 \times 4,000 = 1,080$$

9. **(D)** The daily change in distance from home is the same as the slope of this line. Pick two easily identifiable points, (0, 200) and (5, 0), and find the slope using the slope formula:

$$slope = \frac{y_2 - y_1}{x_2 - x_1} = \frac{200 - 0}{0 - 5} = \frac{200}{-5} = -40$$

So, the change in distance from home is 40 miles—she is getting 40 miles closer to home each day. The negative sign on the slope does not matter since the question asks simply for the change, not whether it is an increasing or decreasing change.

10. **(A)** Multiply 16π by 1.5625 to find what the area of a circle that is 56.25% greater in area would be. (This would represent 156.25% of the original circle—that is why we multiply by 1.5625 instead of just 0.5625.)

$$16\pi \times 1.5625 = 25\pi$$

Note that we only multplied the 16 by the 1.5625 so that we can identify the radius more easily. So, the new circle will have a radius of 5, since the area of a circle is πr^2 and the square root of 25 is 5.

11. **(C)** Use the slope-intercept form of a line, and plug in the slope and the point to solve for the y-intercept.

$$y = mx + b \rightarrow$$
$$8 = \frac{2}{3}(6) + b \rightarrow$$
$$8 = 4 + b \rightarrow$$
$$4 = b$$

So, the y-intercept of the line is 4.

12. **(C)** The number of respondents is sufficient to generalize on the voter preferences. However, the respondents were not randomly selected—they all chose to go to an online poll to vote for a particular candidate. People who chose to respond to the online poll are more likely enthusiastic about their political preferences; this self-selected group would therefore not accurately represent a cross-section of voters. The survey would have been more accurate if the respondents had been randomly selected instead of self-selected.

13. **(B)** The functions are all in slope-intercept form, and they all have different values for the slope. So, find the slope of the function by using the slope formula and plugging in two points. The cost corresponds to the *y* values and the pieces of fruit will be the *x* value. Use the points (6, 13.40) and (12, 25.40) in the slope formula:

$$slope = \frac{y_2 - y_1}{x_2 - x_1} = \frac{25.40 - 13.40}{12 - 6} = \frac{12}{6} = 2$$

The only option that has 2 as its slope is choice **(B)**. Alternatively, you could plug in values to the equations to see which one correctly models the numbers in the table.

14. **(A)** As the height of the orangutans increases, their weight also increases. Choice **(A)**, *The greater the height of the orangutan, the greater the weight,* correctly summarizes this trend.

15. **(C)** Sketch out the trend line to see what the weight would likely be if the height were at 50 inches:

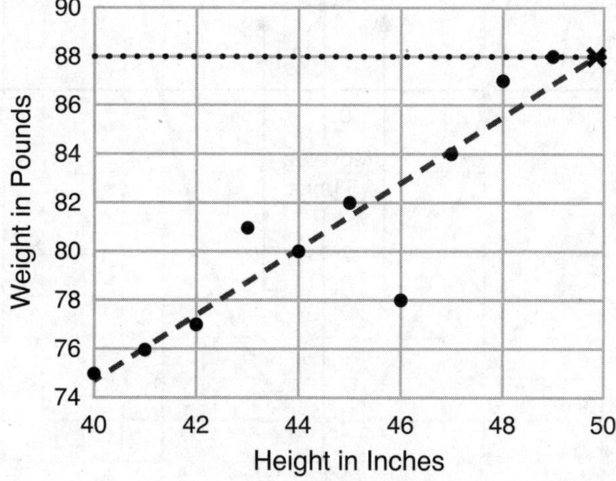

Eighty-eight pounds comes closest to the value, and fortunately the answer choices are far enough apart that it is not necessary to create an equation to model the situation. You can find a clear estimate by sketching it out as seen above.

16. **(B)** The range of the set (difference between the least and greatest terms) will increase by 25, since the smallest member of the set has 5 subtracted from it and the largest member has 20 added to it. The standard deviation (the deviation from the mean) would increase slightly with these changes, but not nearly as much as the range would since the values of the other 13 members of the set will remain constant. So, choice **(B)** is the correct answer.

17. **(C)** Add 5 to the equation to shift the equation upwards by 5 units:

$$y = x^2 - 4 \rightarrow y = x^2 - 4 + 5 \rightarrow y = x^2 + 1$$

You can see the effect of this translation in the graph below:

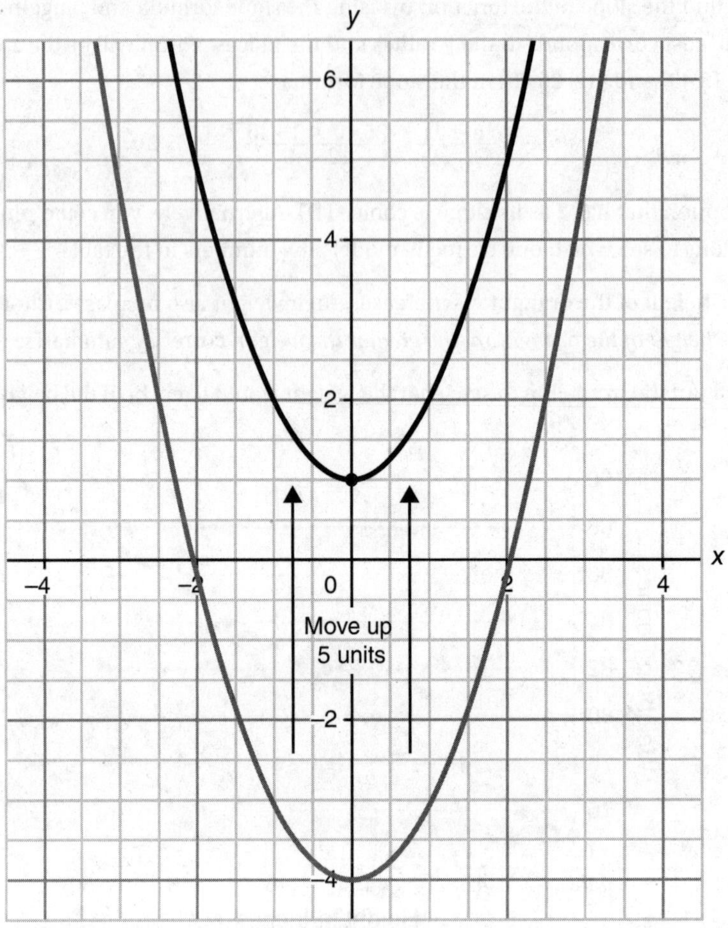

18. **(A)** Plug in 2 for x and 5 for y, since this ordered pair represents a solution to the inequality:

$$y \geq x + n \rightarrow$$
$$5 \geq 2 + n \rightarrow$$
$$3 \geq n$$

Since n must be less than or equal to 3, the greatest possible value for n is 3.

19. **(C)** Take 40% off of the $300 price. Use the formula

$$\text{Decreased Total} = (\text{Original Amount}) \times (1 - r)$$

in which r is the percentage expressed as a decimal to find the new total:

$$300 \times (1 - 0.40) = 300 \times 0.6 = 180$$

Now, add the 7% sales tax to the discounted price by using this formula:

$$\text{Increased Total} = (\text{Original Amount}) \times (1 + r)$$

in which r is the percentage of the sales tax.

$$180 \times (1 + 0.07) = 180 \times 1.07 = 192.60$$

So, the customer will pay $192.60 for the phone, including sales tax.

20. **(A)**

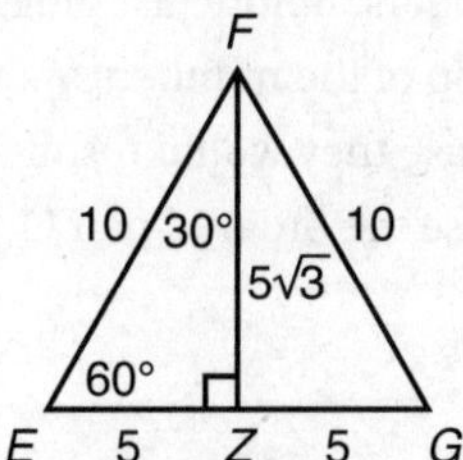

Since triangle *EFG* is equilateral, you can label $\angle FEZ$ as 60 degrees. This turns triangle *FEZ* into a special right triangle—a 30-60-90 triangle. The ratios of the sides in a 30-60-90 triangle are x, $\sqrt{3}\,x$, $2x$. So, the length of $\overline{FZ}$ will be $5\sqrt{3}$ since the x in this case is 5.

21. **(B)** Marcos has two meals each day that are covered by the \$90 flat fee. Then, he has a third meal on four days of the week—Monday through Thursday. Each of these four meals costs an additional \$10. So, add 90 and 4×10 to get the total amount he must pay for his food bill: $40 + 90 = 130$

22. **(D)** Factor the equation:

$$a - 3\sqrt{a} - 10 = 0 \rightarrow$$
$$(\sqrt{a} - 5)(\sqrt{a} + 2) = 0 \rightarrow$$

We cannot have an imaginary value for *a* since the problem states that *a* is a real number. So, ignore the part of the equation that has $\sqrt{a} + 2$, since for this to be true, we would need an imaginary solution. Just consider the part of the equation that has $\sqrt{a} - 5$, since you can solve for *a* and get a real number. $\sqrt{a} - 5$ must equal zero so that the value of the entire equation will be zero:

$$\sqrt{a} - 5 = 0 \rightarrow$$
$$\sqrt{a} = 5 \rightarrow$$
$$a = 25$$

So, choice **(D)** is correct.

Alternatively, substitute the answer choices into the equation to see which one works.

23. **(D)** Ling will have to pay both the \$800 security deposit and the \$600 per month rent. This will total the amount that Ling would pay at \$700 per month. So, you can set up an equation like this to solve for the number of months, *n*:

$$800 + 600n = 700n$$

Then, solve for *n*:

$$800 + 600n = 700n \rightarrow$$
$$800 = 100n \rightarrow$$
$$8 = n$$

So, Ling would need to rent the apartment for 8 months in order for the monthly cost to average out to \$700 per month.

Alternatively, you could notice that the \$800 security deposit must be divided over enough months to result in a \$100 per month increase in rent. $\frac{800}{100} = 8$, so it would take 8 months for the rent to average out as the problem stipulates.

24. **(A)** Try plugging in values from the table to determine which function correctly represents the relationship between the numbers. Before just plugging in numbers to every equation, think about the overall relationship of the numbers. As x increases, y decreases. So, choices (C) and (D) would not work because they would result in increasing functions. Then, you just need to try options (A) and (B). Use the ordered pair (1, 2) to see which of these would work:

$y = \frac{2}{x^2} \rightarrow 2 = \frac{2}{1^2}$, which is true.

$y = \frac{4}{x^2} \rightarrow 2 \neq \frac{4}{1^2}$, so choice (B) is incorrect.

Therefore, the correct function is in choice **(A)**.

25. **(C)**

The inequality $y \geq -x + 4$ can be graphed as follows:

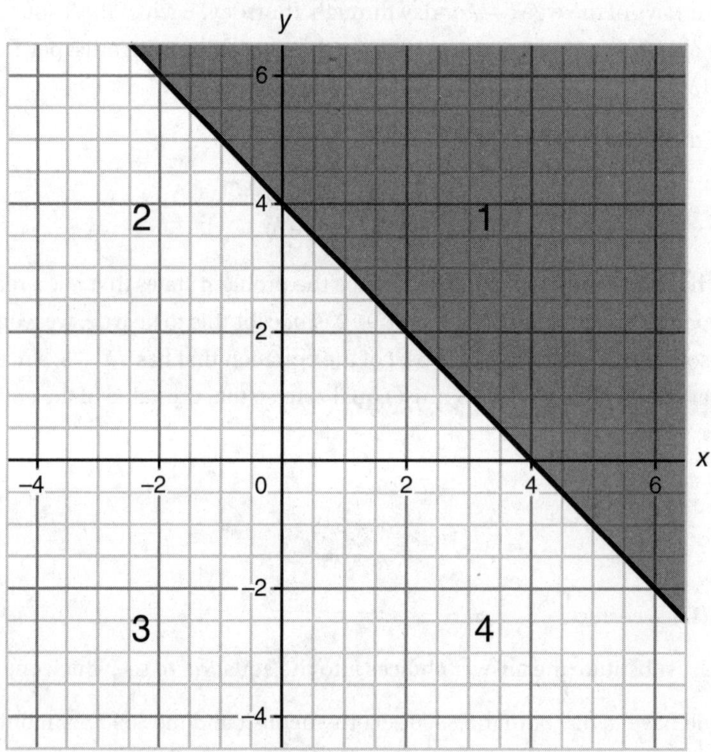

So, the solutions to the inequality will be in quadrants 1, 2, and 4 only.

26. **(B)** There are 25 patients who had a positive test result. Out of those 25 patients, 20 actually did not have the illness, meaning they had a false positive. So, divide 20 by 25 to find the probability that one of the positive test results was actually a false positive:

$$\frac{20}{25} = 0.8$$

27. **(B)** Since 23% of the recommended daily value of calcium for an adult is 300 mg, calculate the total recommended daily value of calcium for an adult, x, using this equation:

$$0.23x = 300 \rightarrow$$
$$x = \frac{300}{0.23} \approx 1{,}304$$

Now, find what percent of 1,304 that 210 is:

$$\frac{210}{1{,}304} \times 100 \approx 16\%$$

28. **(C)** The product of these two expressions will be undefined if the denominator of either expression is equal to zero. For $\frac{2}{x}$, if $x = 0$, the expression is undefined. For $\frac{3}{(x-1)}$, if $x = 1$, the expression is undefined since the denominator $x - 1$ would equal zero if $x = 1$. So, the correct answer is choice **(C)**.

29. **(B)** Since there are twice as many elementary students as middle school students, $c = 2f$ and $f = \frac{c}{2}$. The number of elementary students and middle school students is 150, so find the value of c:

$$c + f = 150 \rightarrow$$
$$c + \frac{c}{2} = 150 \rightarrow$$
$$1.5c = 150 \rightarrow c = 100$$

So, we know that c is 100.

Since 60% of elementary school students take the bus, find 60% of 100 to find the value for a: $0.6 \times 100 = 60$. Since the number of elementary school students is 100 total, subtract 60 from 100 to find the number of elementary school students who walk: $100 - 60 = 40$.

The total number of students who walk to school is 70 based on the table. So, find the number of middle school students who walk by subtracting 40 from 70:

$$70 - 40 = 30$$

To more easily visualize this, all the solved values for the variables are plugged into the spots in the table below:

	Bus	Walk	Total
Elementary	60	40	100
Middle	20	30	50
Total	80	70	150

30. **(C)** A selection of the function is graphed below:

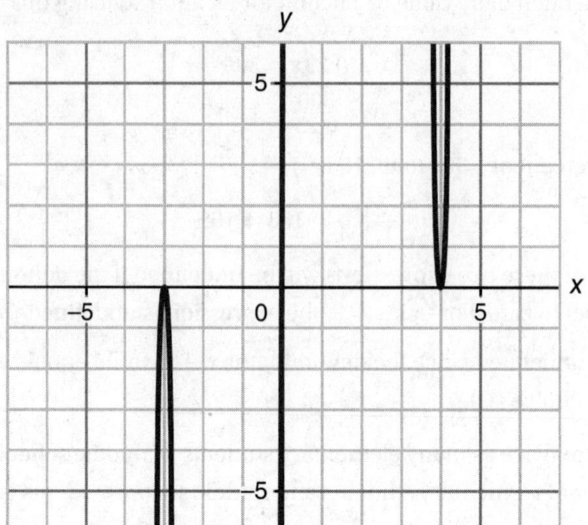

While the function has a high degree, it has only three unique x intercepts: 0, 4, and -3. You can see this by examining the equation to see what values of x would cause y to equal zero. If $x = 0$, $x = 4$, or $x = -3$, the value of y will be equal to zero.

31. **14** Plug 40 in for B and 4 in for E. Then solve for P:

$$B = 2P + 3E \rightarrow$$
$$40 = 2P + 3(4) \rightarrow$$
$$40 = 2P + 12 \rightarrow$$
$$40 - 12 = 2P \rightarrow$$
$$28 = 2P \rightarrow$$
$$P = 14$$

32. **6** You can use substitution to solve for x. Take the second equation and find the value of y in terms of x:

$$x + y = 11 \rightarrow$$
$$y = 11 - x$$

Then, substitute this in to the first equation to solve for x:

$$3x - 4y = -2 \rightarrow$$
$$3x - 4(11 - x) = -2 \rightarrow$$
$$3x - 44 + 4x = -2 \rightarrow$$
$$7x = 42 \rightarrow$$
$$x = 6$$

33. **44** Since this is a trapezoid, the top and bottom sides are parallel to one another. You can inscribe a right triangle within the trapezoid whose leg lengths are 8 (18 – 10) and 6. You can then find the length of the hypotenuse of the triangle (which is the fourth side of the trapezoid) by using the Pythagorean theorem:

$$a^2 + b^2 = c^2$$
$$6^2 + 8^2 = c^2$$
$$36 + 64 = c^2$$
$$100 = c^2$$
$$c = 10$$

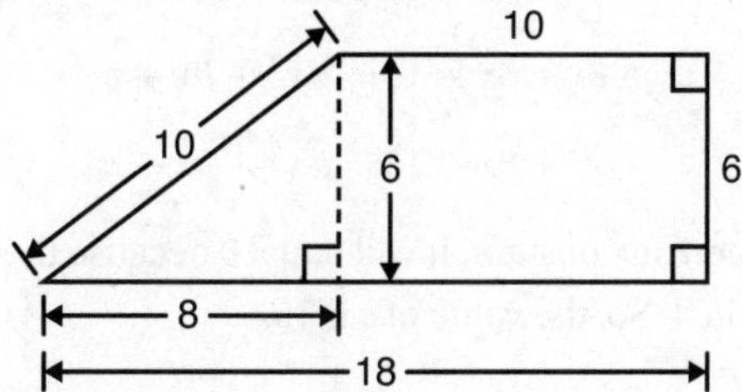

Then, add up the lengths of the sides to find the perimeter of the figure:

$$10 + 6 + 18 + 10 = 44$$

34. **2.5 or $\frac{5}{2}$** Pick an ordered pair—(2, 5) would work—and plug it in to the equation $y = kx$ to solve for the constant k:

$$y = kx \rightarrow$$
$$5 = k(2) \rightarrow$$
$$k = 2.5$$

35. **40** Since CAC $= \frac{\text{Total Marketing Cost}}{\text{Number of New Customers}}$, take the total marketing cost for the door-to-door sales campaign, \$800, and divide it by 20, the number of new customers:

$$\frac{800}{20} = 40$$

36. **125** The total marketing cost for a single TV ad campaign is \$5,000—this results in 125 new customers. An online ad campaign earns 50 new customers for every \$1,000 spent. \$1,000 goes into \$5,000 a total of 5 times, so multiply 50 by 5 to find out how many customers an online ad campaign would earn with the same budget as a single TV ad campaign:

$$50 \times 5 = 250$$

Now, subtract 125 from 250 to find how many more customers the business would acquire with the online ad campaign than with the TV ad campaign:

$$250 - 125 = 125$$

37. **0** $\text{CAC} = \frac{\text{Total Marketing Cost}}{\text{Number of New Customers}}$, so find the CAC for both the door-to-door and the TV campaign:

Door-to-door: $\frac{800}{20} = 40$

TV campaign: $\frac{5{,}000}{125} = 40$

So, the difference between the two customer acquisition costs is $40 - 40 = 0$.

38. **15**

$$(x + 5)(x + 3) = ax^2 + bx + c \rightarrow$$

$$x^2 + 3x + 5x + 15 = ax^2 + bx + c \rightarrow$$

$$x^2 + 8x + 15 = ax^2 + bx + c$$

Since 15 is the only numerical constant, it will equal c because the c term on the right-hand side does not have an x in it. So, the value of c is 15.

ANSWER SHEET
Practice Test 4

Section 1: Reading

1. Ⓐ Ⓑ Ⓒ Ⓓ	14. Ⓐ Ⓑ Ⓒ Ⓓ	27. Ⓐ Ⓑ Ⓒ Ⓓ	40. Ⓐ Ⓑ Ⓒ Ⓓ
2. Ⓐ Ⓑ Ⓒ Ⓓ	15. Ⓐ Ⓑ Ⓒ Ⓓ	28. Ⓐ Ⓑ Ⓒ Ⓓ	41. Ⓐ Ⓑ Ⓒ Ⓓ
3. Ⓐ Ⓑ Ⓒ Ⓓ	16. Ⓐ Ⓑ Ⓒ Ⓓ	29. Ⓐ Ⓑ Ⓒ Ⓓ	42. Ⓐ Ⓑ Ⓒ Ⓓ
4. Ⓐ Ⓑ Ⓒ Ⓓ	17. Ⓐ Ⓑ Ⓒ Ⓓ	30. Ⓐ Ⓑ Ⓒ Ⓓ	43. Ⓐ Ⓑ Ⓒ Ⓓ
5. Ⓐ Ⓑ Ⓒ Ⓓ	18. Ⓐ Ⓑ Ⓒ Ⓓ	31. Ⓐ Ⓑ Ⓒ Ⓓ	44. Ⓐ Ⓑ Ⓒ Ⓓ
6. Ⓐ Ⓑ Ⓒ Ⓓ	19. Ⓐ Ⓑ Ⓒ Ⓓ	32. Ⓐ Ⓑ Ⓒ Ⓓ	45. Ⓐ Ⓑ Ⓒ Ⓓ
7. Ⓐ Ⓑ Ⓒ Ⓓ	20. Ⓐ Ⓑ Ⓒ Ⓓ	33. Ⓐ Ⓑ Ⓒ Ⓓ	46. Ⓐ Ⓑ Ⓒ Ⓓ
8. Ⓐ Ⓑ Ⓒ Ⓓ	21. Ⓐ Ⓑ Ⓒ Ⓓ	34. Ⓐ Ⓑ Ⓒ Ⓓ	47. Ⓐ Ⓑ Ⓒ Ⓓ
9. Ⓐ Ⓑ Ⓒ Ⓓ	22. Ⓐ Ⓑ Ⓒ Ⓓ	35. Ⓐ Ⓑ Ⓒ Ⓓ	48. Ⓐ Ⓑ Ⓒ Ⓓ
10. Ⓐ Ⓑ Ⓒ Ⓓ	23. Ⓐ Ⓑ Ⓒ Ⓓ	36. Ⓐ Ⓑ Ⓒ Ⓓ	49. Ⓐ Ⓑ Ⓒ Ⓓ
11. Ⓐ Ⓑ Ⓒ Ⓓ	24. Ⓐ Ⓑ Ⓒ Ⓓ	37. Ⓐ Ⓑ Ⓒ Ⓓ	50. Ⓐ Ⓑ Ⓒ Ⓓ
12. Ⓐ Ⓑ Ⓒ Ⓓ	25. Ⓐ Ⓑ Ⓒ Ⓓ	38. Ⓐ Ⓑ Ⓒ Ⓓ	51. Ⓐ Ⓑ Ⓒ Ⓓ
13. Ⓐ Ⓑ Ⓒ Ⓓ	26. Ⓐ Ⓑ Ⓒ Ⓓ	39. Ⓐ Ⓑ Ⓒ Ⓓ	52. Ⓐ Ⓑ Ⓒ Ⓓ

Section 2: Writing and Language

1. Ⓐ Ⓑ Ⓒ Ⓓ	12. Ⓐ Ⓑ Ⓒ Ⓓ	23. Ⓐ Ⓑ Ⓒ Ⓓ	34. Ⓐ Ⓑ Ⓒ Ⓓ
2. Ⓐ Ⓑ Ⓒ Ⓓ	13. Ⓐ Ⓑ Ⓒ Ⓓ	24. Ⓐ Ⓑ Ⓒ Ⓓ	35. Ⓐ Ⓑ Ⓒ Ⓓ
3. Ⓐ Ⓑ Ⓒ Ⓓ	14. Ⓐ Ⓑ Ⓒ Ⓓ	25. Ⓐ Ⓑ Ⓒ Ⓓ	36. Ⓐ Ⓑ Ⓒ Ⓓ
4. Ⓐ Ⓑ Ⓒ Ⓓ	15. Ⓐ Ⓑ Ⓒ Ⓓ	26. Ⓐ Ⓑ Ⓒ Ⓓ	37. Ⓐ Ⓑ Ⓒ Ⓓ
5. Ⓐ Ⓑ Ⓒ Ⓓ	16. Ⓐ Ⓑ Ⓒ Ⓓ	27. Ⓐ Ⓑ Ⓒ Ⓓ	38. Ⓐ Ⓑ Ⓒ Ⓓ
6. Ⓐ Ⓑ Ⓒ Ⓓ	17. Ⓐ Ⓑ Ⓒ Ⓓ	28. Ⓐ Ⓑ Ⓒ Ⓓ	39. Ⓐ Ⓑ Ⓒ Ⓓ
7. Ⓐ Ⓑ Ⓒ Ⓓ	18. Ⓐ Ⓑ Ⓒ Ⓓ	29. Ⓐ Ⓑ Ⓒ Ⓓ	40. Ⓐ Ⓑ Ⓒ Ⓓ
8. Ⓐ Ⓑ Ⓒ Ⓓ	19. Ⓐ Ⓑ Ⓒ Ⓓ	30. Ⓐ Ⓑ Ⓒ Ⓓ	41. Ⓐ Ⓑ Ⓒ Ⓓ
9. Ⓐ Ⓑ Ⓒ Ⓓ	20. Ⓐ Ⓑ Ⓒ Ⓓ	31. Ⓐ Ⓑ Ⓒ Ⓓ	42. Ⓐ Ⓑ Ⓒ Ⓓ
10. Ⓐ Ⓑ Ⓒ Ⓓ	21. Ⓐ Ⓑ Ⓒ Ⓓ	32. Ⓐ Ⓑ Ⓒ Ⓓ	43. Ⓐ Ⓑ Ⓒ Ⓓ
11. Ⓐ Ⓑ Ⓒ Ⓓ	22. Ⓐ Ⓑ Ⓒ Ⓓ	33. Ⓐ Ⓑ Ⓒ Ⓓ	44. Ⓐ Ⓑ Ⓒ Ⓓ

ANSWER SHEET

Practice Test 4

Section 3: Math (No Calculator)

1. Ⓐ Ⓑ Ⓒ Ⓓ **5.** Ⓐ Ⓑ Ⓒ Ⓓ **9.** Ⓐ Ⓑ Ⓒ Ⓓ **13.** Ⓐ Ⓑ Ⓒ Ⓓ

2. Ⓐ Ⓑ Ⓒ Ⓓ **6.** Ⓐ Ⓑ Ⓒ Ⓓ **10.** Ⓐ Ⓑ Ⓒ Ⓓ **14.** Ⓐ Ⓑ Ⓒ Ⓓ

3. Ⓐ Ⓑ Ⓒ Ⓓ **7.** Ⓐ Ⓑ Ⓒ Ⓓ **11.** Ⓐ Ⓑ Ⓒ Ⓓ **15.** Ⓐ Ⓑ Ⓒ Ⓓ

4. Ⓐ Ⓑ Ⓒ Ⓓ **8.** Ⓐ Ⓑ Ⓒ Ⓓ **12.** Ⓐ Ⓑ Ⓒ Ⓓ

16.

17.

18.

19.

20.

ANSWER SHEET
Practice Test 4

Section 4: Math (Calculator)

1. Ⓐ Ⓑ Ⓒ Ⓓ
2. Ⓐ Ⓑ Ⓒ Ⓓ
3. Ⓐ Ⓑ Ⓒ Ⓓ
4. Ⓐ Ⓑ Ⓒ Ⓓ
5. Ⓐ Ⓑ Ⓒ Ⓓ
6. Ⓐ Ⓑ Ⓒ Ⓓ
7. Ⓐ Ⓑ Ⓒ Ⓓ
8. Ⓐ Ⓑ Ⓒ Ⓓ
9. Ⓐ Ⓑ Ⓒ Ⓓ
10. Ⓐ Ⓑ Ⓒ Ⓓ
11. Ⓐ Ⓑ Ⓒ Ⓓ
12. Ⓐ Ⓑ Ⓒ Ⓓ
13. Ⓐ Ⓑ Ⓒ Ⓓ
14. Ⓐ Ⓑ Ⓒ Ⓓ
15. Ⓐ Ⓑ Ⓒ Ⓓ
16. Ⓐ Ⓑ Ⓒ Ⓓ
17. Ⓐ Ⓑ Ⓒ Ⓓ
18. Ⓐ Ⓑ Ⓒ Ⓓ
19. Ⓐ Ⓑ Ⓒ Ⓓ
20. Ⓐ Ⓑ Ⓒ Ⓓ
21. Ⓐ Ⓑ Ⓒ Ⓓ
22. Ⓐ Ⓑ Ⓒ Ⓓ
23. Ⓐ Ⓑ Ⓒ Ⓓ
24. Ⓐ Ⓑ Ⓒ Ⓓ
25. Ⓐ Ⓑ Ⓒ Ⓓ
26. Ⓐ Ⓑ Ⓒ Ⓓ
27. Ⓐ Ⓑ Ⓒ Ⓓ
28. Ⓐ Ⓑ Ⓒ Ⓓ
29. Ⓐ Ⓑ Ⓒ Ⓓ
30. Ⓐ Ⓑ Ⓒ Ⓓ

31.

32.

33.

34.

35.

36.

37.

38.

Practice Test 4

READING PRACTICE TEST 4

65 MINUTES, 52 QUESTIONS

DIRECTIONS: Each passage or pair of passages is accompanied by several questions. After reading the passage(s), choose the best answer to each question based on what is indicated explicitly or implicitly in the passage(s) or in the associated graphics.

Questions 1–10 are based on the following passage.

This passage is from Our Mutual Friend, *by Charles Dickens, written in 1864. In it, a newly wealthy couple, the Veneerings, discuss their own situation as well as that of a newfound party companion, Mr. Twemlow.*

Mr. and Mrs. Veneering were brand-new people in a brand-new house in a brand-new quarter of London. Everything about the Veneerings was spick and span new. All their furniture was new, all their friends were new, all their servants were new, their plate was new, their carriage was new, their harness was new, their horses were new, their pictures were new, they themselves were new, they were as newly married as was lawfully compatible with their having a brand-new baby, and if they had set up a great-grandfather, he would have come home in matting from the Pantechnicon, without a scratch upon him, French polished to the crown of his head.

For, in the Veneering establishment, from the hall-chairs with the new coat of arms, to the grand pianoforte with the new action, and upstairs again to the new fire-escape, all things were in a state of high varnish and polish. And what was observable in the furniture, was observable in the Veneerings—the surface smelt a little too much of the workshop and was a trifle sticky.

There was an innocent piece of dinner-furniture that went upon easy castors and was kept over a livery stable-yard in Duke Street, Saint James's, when not in use, to whom the Veneerings were a source of blind confusion. The name of this article was Twemlow. Being first cousin to Lord Snigsworth, he was in frequent requisition, and at many houses might be said to represent the dining-table in its normal state. Mr. and Mrs. Veneering, for example, arranging a dinner, habitually started with Twemlow, and then put leaves[1] in him, or added guests to him. Sometimes, the table consisted of Twemlow and half a dozen leaves;

[1]A leaf is an extension to a table that can be unfolded, allowing more people to sit at the table.

0 0 0

sometimes, of Twemlow and a dozen leaves; sometimes, Twemlow was pulled out to his utmost extent of twenty leaves. Mr. and Mrs. Veneering on occasions of ceremony faced each other in the center of the board, and thus the parallel still held; for, it always happened that the more Twemlow was pulled out, the further he found himself from the center, and nearer to the sideboard at one end of the room, or the window-curtains at the other.

But, it was not this which steeped the feeble soul of Twemlow in confusion. This he was used to, and could take soundings of. The abyss to which he could find no bottom, and from which started forth the engrossing and ever-swelling difficulty of his life, was the insoluble question whether he was Veneering's oldest friend, or newest friend. To the excogitation of this problem, the harmless gentleman had devoted many anxious hours, both in his lodgings over the livery stable-yard, and in the cold gloom, favorable to meditation, of Saint James's Square. Thus Twemlow had first known Veneering at his club, where Veneering then knew nobody but the man who made them known to one another, who seemed to be the most intimate friend he had in the world, and whom he had known two days—the bond of union between their souls, the nefarious conduct of the committee respecting the cookery of a fillet of veal, having been accidentally cemented at that date. Immediately upon this, Twemlow received an invitation to dine with Veneering, and dined: the man being of the party. Immediately upon that, Twemlow received an invitation to dine with the man, and dined: Veneering being of the party. At the man's were a Member, an Engineer, a Payer-off of the National Debt, a Poem on Shakespeare, a Grievance, and a Public Office, who all seem to be utter strangers to Veneering. And yet immediately after that, Twemlow received an invitation to dine at Veneerings, expressly to meet the Member, the Engineer, the Payer-off of the National Debt, the Poem on Shakespeare, the Grievance, and the Public Office, and, dining, discovered that all of them were the most intimate friends Veneering had in the world, and that the wives of all of them (who were all there) were the objects of Mrs. Veneering's most devoted affection and tender confidence.

Thus it had come about, that Mr. Twemlow had said to himself in his lodgings, with his hand to his forehead: 'I must not think of this. This is enough to soften any man's brain,'—and yet was always thinking of it, and could never form a conclusion.

1. The personalities of the Veneerings can best be described as

   (A) reclusive.
   (B) altruistic.
   (C) inventive.
   (D) extroverted.

2. What is the effect of repeating the word "new" in the first paragraph (lines 1–24)?

   (A) To emphasize an idea
   (B) To build suspense
   (C) To clarify a point
   (D) To provide multiple perspectives

3. It can be reasonably inferred form lines 25–30 ("There was . . . confusion") that Twemlow

   (A) did not commit a crime of which he was accused.
   (B) had a difficult time understanding the Veneerings.
   (C) enjoyed the time he spent on introspection.
   (D) was a cunning manipulator of his neighbors.

4. Dickens most extensively uses the literary device of personification to compare people to

   (A) horses.
   (B) passenger carriages.
   (C) pieces of furniture.
   (D) apartments.

5. As used in line 32, "requisition" most closely means

   (A) sympathy.
   (B) despair.
   (C) demand.
   (D) leadership.

6. Dickens uses lines 30–38 to show that Twemlow was

   (A) someone around whom the Veneerings arranged their party guests.
   (B) a worthy guest simply on the strength of his own personality.
   (C) warmly appreciative of the friendships he had cultivated through the Veneerings.
   (D) largely interested in the superficial aspects of socializing instead of making deeper connections.

7. As portrayed in the passage, Twemlow struggles most deeply with the question of

   (A) how he could optimize his seating arrangement.
   (B) if he will be able to eat what is served at the dinner.
   (C) how deep is Veneering's friendship with him.
   (D) whether Veneering will use his connections to empower him.

8. Which option provides the best evidence for the answer to the previous question?

   (A) Lines 37–38 ("sometimes . . . leaves")
   (B) Lines 51–55 ("The abyss . . . friend")
   (C) Lines 66–69 ("the bond . . . date")
   (D) Lines 75–78 ("At the man's . . . Veneering")

9. Twemlow is best described as someone who has a clear tendency to engage in

   (A) showing up without an invitation.
   (B) horse training.
   (C) ceremonial pomp.
   (D) unhelpful rumination.

10. Which option provides the best evidence for the answer to the previous question?

   (A) Lines 25–30 ("There was . . . confusion")
   (B) Lines 41–44 ("Mr. and Mrs . . . held")
   (C) Lines 49–51 ("But . . . soundings of")
   (D) Lines 90–95 ("Thus it . . . conclusion")

Questions 11–21 are based on the following passage and supplementary material.

Investing and Diversification, written in 2020

The first introduction many students have to the world of investment and the stock market is through their American history class when they learn about the devastating stock market crash that led into the Great Depression, or the market crash that much led us into the more recent Great Recession. However, what is rarely impressed upon students is the success that the majority of people experience in the stock market when they invest intelligently over a long period of time. Indeed, most of those high school students will (hopefully) go on to have a retirement account that invests in the stock market, allowing them to comfortably cease work between the ages of 65 and 70. There are indeed outliers—people who invest poorly, who fail to diversify their portfolio, or who get in or get out at the wrong time—but for many people, investment is the surest way to a solid retirement.

The two basic keys to retiring comfortably are time and portfolio diversification. Time is enormously important and the essential reason why young people should be taught about responsible investment. Because investments build on themselves through interest accumulation and returns, it is vital to begin saving as soon as possible to allow for that interest to build on itself. If a person were to begin saving at age 25 with the goal of retiring with a million dollars, she would need to save about $4,500 each year. If she waits until age 35, she would need to save around $9,000 each year. Starting at 40 would mean even more money would be required to meet the goal—the amount of savings needed grows over a given time.

Portfolio diversification is the other essential element to a successful retirement. Here, the old adage "don't put all your eggs in one basket" really does hold true. There are thousands of stocks, bonds, and funds to choose from. If one portion of the market crashes, you do not want all your money to be there. Many people choose to bet on what they think "the next big thing" will be. These are the investors who lament that they didn't buy Google stock in the early 2000s. What they forget is that there were hundreds of companies like Google in that time frame, and only a few led to riches. It is these people who treat the market like a get rich quick scheme who end up losing everything.

So then, instead of going "all in" on the next big thing, people should work on spreading their money out, like a net to catch them if they fall. Young people have lots of time to recover from market crashes and can afford to be a little riskier with their investments. They can spend more money on stocks and mutual funds (which are stocks bundled together by a manager), while keeping some money in the safety of bonds (which work as the buyer lending money to a government or corporation that will pay it back with interest). As investors becomes older, though, they should slowly move their money away from the volatility of the high-risk, high-reward stock market and invest more and more in the low-risk, low-reward options offered to them. This helps prevent them from losing vast amounts of money just a few years before retirement when there is no time to recover.

Finally, when people understand the idea of time and diversification, they need one final thing to help them be successful in the marketplace: a sense of calm. Panic buying and selling is never a good idea. If an account was started early and properly diversified, even severe market downturns should not incite panic. Instead, clear-thinking investors will see that the market will correct; rather than "selling low," investors wait for the upswing (and maybe longer) in order to see the payout on their investments. Remaining calm is a skill that is easy to develop when people are properly prepared for anything. With this skill as the cherry on top of time and diversification, there is little reason that retirement would be out of reach for the average American.

Table 1 Portfolio variance is an estimation of the risk of a portfolio, with a higher number indicating a greater risk and a lower number indicating a lower risk.

Number of Stocks	Expected Portfolio Variance
1	46.6
2	26.8
4	16.9
6	13.7
8	12.0
10	11.0
20	9.0
50	7.8
100	7.5
1,000	7.1

Data gathered from Edwin Elton and Martin Gruber in their article "Risk Reduction and Portfolio Size: An Analytical Solution," published in The Journal of Business *in 1977.*

11. The author's intended audience for the essay is most likely
    (A) the general public.
    (B) people about to retire.
    (C) experienced investors.
    (D) mutual fund managers.

12. As used in line 14, "cease" most closely means
    (A) increase.
    (B) perform.
    (C) stop.
    (D) search for.

13. The sentence in lines 15–20 ("There are . . . retirement") mainly serves to acknowledge that
    (A) it is important to be mindful of the many possible shortcomings when thinking about investing.
    (B) even those who invest in a patient and diversified way are likely to experience difficulties in choosing stocks and bonds.
    (C) while there may be exceptions to successful investing, in general it is the best way to achieve financial security.
    (D) those who ultimately choose to invest are inevitably on the path to a comfortable retirement.

14. The author of the passage would most likely approve of which of the following individual investment approaches?
    (A) Someone in their 50s transfers most of his retirement assets to two high-performing stocks.
    (B) Someone in their 30s continues to consistently invest in a diverse group of stocks through contributions to mutual funds.
    (C) Someone in their 60s shifts all of his savings into the stock market so that he might have greater funds for later in life.
    (D) Someone in their 20s sells his investments during a stock market crash so that he might preserve his money for retirement.

15. Which option gives the best evidence for the answer to the previous question?
    (A) Lines 21–22 ("The two . . . diversification")
    (B) Lines 33–36 ("Starting . . . time")
    (C) Lines 63–68 ("As investors . . . to them")
    (D) Lines 77–81 ("Instead . . . investments")

16. Which choice best supports the idea that excessive greed can lead to negative outcomes when it comes to investing?
    (A) Lines 25–29 ("Because . . . itself")
    (B) Lines 41–43 ("If one . . . there")
    (C) Lines 49–51 ("It is these . . . everything")
    (D) Lines 82–84 ("Remaining . . . anything")

17. The author most likely uses the parenthetical phrases in lines 61–63 in order to
    (A) clarify the justification behind an investment recommendation.
    (B) define terms that may be unfamiliar to some readers.
    (C) explain how diversification is essential to strong investment performance.
    (D) show why investors should delegate asset management to others.

18. According to the passage, it is important for older investors to
    (A) eliminate the diversification in their portfolios.
    (B) secure greater returns through more stock allocations.
    (C) shift toward more conservative investments.
    (D) focus on maximizing stock and bond volatility.

19. The table best serves to support what idea the author of the passage advocates?
    (A) Avoiding panic buying and selling
    (B) Starting to invest at an early age
    (C) Portfolio diversification
    (D) Preventing another recession

20. According to the table, which of the following changes to one's stock portfolio would likely have the greatest impact on the portfolio's risk?
    (A) Having two stocks instead of just one
    (B) Having six stocks instead of four
    (C) Having 20 stocks instead of 10
    (D) Having 1,000 stocks instead of 100

21. Which statement is an appropriate generalization based on the data in the table?
    (A) The only way to successfully reduce portfolio variance is to increase the number of stocks in one's portfolio.
    (B) It is important to have a mixture of stocks, bonds, and cash in order to maximize one's investment performance.
    (C) One must be happy with large fluctuations in a portfolio's value to be willing to invest in the stock market.
    (D) After a certain point, diversification has diminishing returns as far as portfolio risk.

Questions 22–31 are based on the following passage.

"How can an understanding of bear biology help better treat human disease?" written in 2020

When it comes to the biological and biochemical building blocks of organisms, there's no mistake that humans are special. From our amazing defense mechanisms to our innate ability to adapt to different environments, the human body is quite phenomenal. However, perfection simply does not exist in nature, and thus the human body comes with a variety of flaws. For example, most humans can only dream of being able to filtrate harmful cholesterol from their blood without having to resort to strenuous exercise or, in more extreme cases, prescription medications. Understanding the mechanisms behind removing cholesterol from our bloodstream remains a relatively unknown mystery.

Many studies suggest that while exercising and having a healthy diet can drastically reduce the concentration of cholesterol in our blood, genes do play a crucial role in an individual's risk of cardiovascular disease. The strong role genes play in cholesterol processing is seen in bears, especially polar bears. Polar bears are among the most fat-obsessed members in the animal kingdom, yet they do not experience any cardiovascular complications. About half of a polar bear's weight is fat and its blood cholesterol levels are high enough that they would cause serious cardiovascular disease in humans; even so, heart attacks are not a concern for polar bears.

When analyzing the genes known to be involved in cardiovascular health, researchers discovered that bears have mutated genes that allow them to consume extremely fatty diets without affecting their cardiovascular health. The specific trait that allows bears to take cholesterol from their bloodstream and deposit it in other cells is called the APOB gene. Scientists are hopeful that study of this gene could help unlock new heart disease treatments for humans.

There is still much about the bear's body that is not fully understood. During hibernation, a bear's heart can stop beating for about 14 seconds at a time and then continue beating at varying heart beats from 5 to 60 beats per minute. Humans are not so fortunate—if a person's heart stopped for a mere 3 seconds, he or she would faint and go into cardiac arrest. During a heart attack, the heart becomes deprived of oxygen; when an area of the heart dies from said lack of oxygen, it is called an "infarct." After giving a pig heart bear hormones before a heart attack, it was found that the infarct areas were reduced by more than 50%. Further understanding the hormones and agents used during hibernation can greatly impact treatments in cardiovascular patients.

If humans were to lie around on a couch for a month and do nothing, they would lose about 30 to 40 percent of their muscle mass. This is most often seen in extremely ill patients. Bears, however, are able to maintain their muscle mass and keep their muscle tone despite lying around for 4 to 6 months at a time. Understanding how bears are able to do this can help find answers to help patients combat severe muscle mass loss during long stays at the hospital.

Immobility has many harmful effects on the human body, ranging from bone degradation to cardiac atrophy. This is often seen in astronauts who return from space. Even with workout equipment and hours of exercise completed, astronauts still suffer from cardiac atrophy as a response to immobility. During hibernation, bears do not experience cardiac atrophy—unraveling how bears are able to combat the harmful effects of long periods of immobilization could provide numerous benefits in human medicine.

Solving the mystery of how bears stay so healthy during hibernation can not only reshape our current understanding of cardiovascular illness, but also deepen our knowledge about various ways to keep the human body healthy as well. It is clear that bears are incredibly well-equipped to combat cardiovascular disease. It should come as no surprise if a future therapeutic or cure for human cardiovascular disease originates from these magnificent creatures.

22. The overall argument of the passage is that

    (A) medical researchers should learn from the successful adaptations that bears have made.
    (B) humans should model their lifestyles on the healthier, more natural ones of bears.
    (C) heart disease can best be treated with natural remedies instead of hospitalization.
    (D) veterinarians should conduct further studies on how to best remedy bear health problems.

23. To what does the author most strongly attribute the bears' ability to reduce cholesterol?

    (A) Their natural surroundings
    (B) Their ability to hibernate
    (C) Their genetic makeup
    (D) Their lack of muscle atrophy

24. Which option gives the best evidence for the answer to the previous question?

    (A) Lines 13–16 ("Understanding . . . mystery")
    (B) Lines 26–31 ("About half . . . bears")
    (C) Lines 32–37 ("When analyzing . . . health")
    (D) Lines 66–69 ("Understanding . . . hospital")

25. As used in line 41, "unlock" most closely means

    (A) undo.
    (B) discover.
    (C) unfasten.
    (D) liberate.

26. It can be reasonably inferred that if a doctor evaluated the fat levels in a blood sample from a bear, but mistakenly believed the blood to be from a human, the doctor would most likely

    (A) be relieved that the blood is relatively free of cholesterol.
    (B) be troubled at the low possibility of an infarct.
    (C) be mindful that cardiac atrophy was a strong possibility.
    (D) be concerned about the potential for heart disease.

27. Which option gives the best evidence for the answer to the previous question?

    (A) Lines 21–23 ("The strong . . . bears")
    (B) Lines 26–30 ("About half . . . humans")
    (C) Lines 50–53 ("During . . . infarct")
    (D) Lines 73–76 ("Even with . . . immobility")

28. According to the fourth paragraph in lines 43–59 ("There is . . . patients"), in what range of seconds stopped would the author most likely believe that a bear's heart could likely have problems?

    (A) Less than 14 seconds
    (B) More than 14 seconds
    (C) At exactly 5 seconds
    (D) At exactly 3 seconds

29. The author most likely includes the sentence in lines 53–56 ("After giving . . . 50%") because he believes that

    (A) reducing heart attacks in pigs is a major research priority.
    (B) human anatomy has important similarities to pig anatomy.
    (C) the lack of a significant result shows that research should go in a different direction.
    (D) bear hormones are important to increasing the frequency of heart disease in other animals.

30. As used in line 58, "impact" most closely means
    (A) influence.
    (B) strike.
    (C) harm.
    (D) ignore.

31. Which of the following findings, if true, would most significantly undermine the possibility of using research from bears to help astronauts, as mentioned in lines 70–81 ("Immobility . . . medicine")?
    (A) Bears are found to have more success than humans in reducing their muscle atrophy over extended periods of time.
    (B) Humans are unable to enter a state of hibernation like bears can.
    (C) Astronauts who performed no exercise while travelling in a spacecraft experienced greater muscle atrophy than astronauts who did exercise.
    (D) Bears that are placed in orbit in a spacecraft had a similar level of muscle atrophy as did humans in the same spacecraft.

Questions 32–42 are based on the following passages.

Passage 1 is a selection from Civil Disobedience *by Henry David Thoreau, written in 1849. Passage 2 is an adaptation from an account written by activist Bernice Johnson of the Student Nonviolent Coordinating Committee; she discusses her experience in being arrested for taking part in a nonviolent protest in December of 1961.*

Passage 1

Under a government which imprisons any unjustly, the true place for a just man is also a prison. The proper place today, the only place which Massachusetts has provided for her freer and less desponding spirits, is in her prisons, to be put out and locked out of the State by her own act, as they have already put themselves out by their principles. . .

If any think that their influence would be lost there, and their voices no longer afflict the ear of the State, that they would not be as an enemy within its walls, they do not know by how much truth is stronger than error, nor how much more eloquently and effectively he can combat injustice who has experienced a little in his own person. Cast your whole vote, not a strip of paper merely, but your whole influence. A minority is powerless while it conforms to the majority; it is not even a minority then; but it is irresistible when it clogs by its whole weight.

If the alternative is to keep all just men in prison, or give up war and slavery, the State will not hesitate which to choose. If a thousand men were not to pay their tax-bills this year, that would not be a violent and bloody measure, as it would be to pay them, and enable the State to commit violence and shed innocent blood. This is, in fact, the definition of a peaceable revolution, if any such is possible. If the tax-gatherer, or any other public officer, asks me, as one has done, "But what shall I do?" my answer is, "If you really wish to do anything, resign your office." When the subject has refused allegiance, and the officer has resigned his office, then the revolution is accomplished.

But even suppose blood should flow. Is there not a sort of blood shed when the conscience is wounded? Through this wound a man's real manhood and immortality flow out, and he bleeds to an everlasting death. I see this blood flowing now.

Passage 2

On Wednesday, December 13, 1961 at nine o'clock, I along with 75 other [protestors] marched down to City Hall where some three hundred persons were jailed the day before.

Upon reaching the jail we all kneeled down and prayed. . .

That same evening, around four, some three hundred [protestors] marched around City Hall without being disturbed. The second march held about thirty minutes later resulted in the arrest of the marchers, of which I was a member.

We, thirty-five women, spent the night in the National Guard Armory. We had to share restroom facilities with about thirty men who were also held there.

The next day we were taken to City Hall where we spent the next two nights. While at the National Guard Armory we refused to eat breakfast. The food at the jail, being supplied by the county, was terrible. We kept our spirits up by singing and praying. While we were in the city jail, Mr. Slater King was knocked into the bars because he gave his breakfast to an ill young lady.

On Saturday another group was arrested. While the arrests were being made all women and men were piled into a cell. We were then shipped out to the Lee County Stockade. We spent two nights there. While at the city jail we had to sleep on steel bunks. At the Stockade, however, we had bunks, and mattresses, but no bed linens. We had a table on which we ate.

On Sunday morning around four o'clock, twelve women held in the Newton jail were brought to the Stockade. They stayed there until we were brought to Albany for release Monday night. While in Leesburg we were allowed food, but not visitors from the outside. On Monday night at a quarter to nine we started out for Albany. We came home in silence. At the Leesburg jail we were joined by eight young men.

Upon arriving in Albany we were released and sent home. . .

I am none the worse for wear, and I would be willing to go through the whole thing again if necessary. I feel that all discomforts suffered were worth the cause for which we committed ourselves. The sleep I lost on a steel bed made me appreciate the bed I had at home, the slop I ate in jail made me think twice before criticizing what I had when I was at home.

32. The first sentence of Passage 1 in lines 1–3 primarily serves to

(A) declare the importance of incarceration.
(B) undermine the concept of moral governance.
(C) underscore an ethical paradox.
(D) contend that prisons are overcrowded.

33. As used in line 19, "irresistible" most closely means

(A) unstoppable.
(B) delightful.
(C) bothersome.
(D) obsolete.

34. According to lines 23–27 ("If a thousand . . . blood), Thoreau believes that

(A) the rates of taxation are overly high to enable economic prosperity.
(B) those who help fund conflict bear responsibility for the consequences.
(C) those who refuse to share in the financial responsibility of government should be held accountable.
(D) all citizens must do their part to support military finances.

35. The final paragraph of Passage 1 most strongly suggests that

(A) unless one is actually bleeding, the suffering is not significant.
(B) moral wounds can be just as significant as physical wounds.
(C) it is necessary to resort to violent methods when nonviolent ones do not succeed.
(D) those who draw the blood of others lack an ethical compass.

36. As described in Passage 2, the policies of the different prisons in which the narrator stayed were
    (A) artistically appreciative.
    (B) humane.
    (C) considerate.
    (D) inconsistent.

37. Which option gives the best evidence for the answer to the previous question?
    (A) Lines 42–45 ("On Wednesday . . . before")
    (B) Lines 53–56 ("We . . . held there")
    (C) Lines 70–73 ("While at . . . linens")
    (D) Lines 74–78 ("On Sunday . . . night")

38. As used in line 61, "kept" most closely means
    (A) maintained.
    (B) contained.
    (C) accumulated.
    (D) expended.

39. Based on Passage 2, Bernice Johnson would have most appreciated which of the following after being in prison?
    (A) Interesting books and magazines to read
    (B) Opportunities to interact with both males and females
    (C) A comfortable bed and a good meal
    (D) The chance to compose original songs

40. The relationship between the passages can best be summarized as which of the following?
    (A) Passage 1 and Passage 2 both contend that society is irreversibly unjust.
    (B) Passage 1 is more philosophical while Passage 2 is more descriptive.
    (C) Passage 1 relies on firsthand experiences to elaborate on the theories of Passage 2.
    (D) Passage 1 agrees with the ideas but not the methods advocated in Passage 2.

41. What aspect of Passage 2 would best exemplify Thoreau's idea in lines 21–23 ("If the alternative . . . choose")?
    (A) The evident overcrowding of the prisons and subsequent release of prisoners
    (B) The success of the government in deterring rebellious activity by making prisons inhospitable
    (C) The need to prevent prisoners from congregating with one another
    (D) The importance in having outside visitors in order to share firsthand accounts of injustice

42. Which selection provides the best evidence that Bernice Johnson's conclusion is intellectually aligned with Thoreau?
    (A) Lines 13–16 ("nor how . . . person")
    (B) Lines 27–29 ("This is . . . possible")
    (C) Lines 32–33 ("If the . . . office")
    (D) Lines 33–35 ("When the . . . accomplished")

Questions 43–52 are based on the following passage and supplementary material.

Cellular Metabolism, written in 2020

Cells, commonly known as the building blocks of life, vary widely in structure and function. They range from neurons that transmit signals to and throughout the brain, to skin cells that guard the body. Though each cell type has a different function, they all have one commonality—a need for energy to drive processes within the cell. To obtain this energy, cells must break down energy-containing compounds.

Almost all organisms begin this process through a series of chemical reactions collectively known as glycolysis. Glycolysis breaks down the energy molecule glucose, more commonly known as sugar. When glucose is absent, such as when fasting, cells can convert other molecules, such as carbohydrates, into glucose.

The longer the organism fasts, the more likely the body is to convert non-carbohydrates into glucose. While glycolysis is a necessary component of energy production, it does not produce much energy on its own. The products of glycolysis must be further broken down to produce the energy required to sustain life. The mechanism behind this second set of reactions depends on the organism and specific cell-type.

One of the many ways organisms can be categorized is based on oxygen consumption. Organisms that must consume oxygen to live are known as aerobic organisms, while those that do not need oxygen are considered anaerobic. Aerobic organisms derive most of their energy from a process known as cellular respiration. This process is oxygen-requiring and cannot be completed by anaerobic organisms. Cellular respiration produces eighteen times more energy units per glucose molecule consumed in glycolysis than the anaerobic alternative, fermentation. Yeast, an anaerobic organism, is known for undergoing ethanol fermentation. Because of this ability, more commonly known as alcohol fermentation, yeast is often used to make bread and alcohol.

Though fermentation does not require oxygen consumption, it is not solely limited to anaerobic organisms. Even humans sometimes undergo fermentation when oxygen supplies are low. This often occurs when the organism rapidly needs more energy than can be produced from cellular respiration alone. Some human cells undergo fermentation more often than others, depending on the cell's specific needs. One such example is during strenuous exercise, when oxygen demand for cellular respiration is unable to be met. This results in muscle cells undergoing lactic acid fermentation, which provides additional energy to prevent muscle fatigue.

Some cancer cells are also known to utilize fermentation, but, unlike healthy cells, they do so even when oxygen levels are normal. Because of this, they take in more glucose and produce more lactate than normal cells. This alternative metabolic pathway in cancer cells is known as the Warburg Effect. Though this was discovered almost a century ago, its function in promoting growth of cancer cells is still not known. Scientists have suggested that, because fermentation is a much faster process than cellular respiration, tumor cells may outcompete nearby normal cells by taking up the limited supply of glucose in the body. While an intriguing idea, this is only one of the many theories scientists have proposed. With many hoping to understand the Warburg Effect's role in cancer cell proliferation, research about this mystery will continue to grow.

Although many aerobic organisms can undergo fermentation, it is clear that aerobic organisms need cellular respiration to survive. Simply withholding oxygen from the body for more than a few seconds will trigger energy-deprived cells to send signals to the brain communicating the need for oxygen, a necessary molecule for cellular respiration. While it would make sense for the body to utilize fermentation processes to make up for this energy loss, the amount of energy produced per glucose molecule by fermentation is significantly lower than cellular respiration. Without this process, aerobic organisms are simply unable to provide the amount of energy needed to carry out the necessary functions of life.

Without metabolic processes such as glycolysis, fermentation, and cellular respiration, the many chemical reactions necessary for life would not be possible. Because of this, every cell, regardless of its function in an organism, must undergo metabolic processes to function. Due to the energy requirement for organisms

to survive, organisms, including humans, have developed many adaptations over the millennia, such as undergoing fermentation when oxygen-deprived, to ensure cells' needs for energy are met.

In a 2014 study on the Warburg Effect, researchers tested the change in glucose concentration over a period of one hour in various cancer cell lines. The average rate of change of glucose concentration in each cell-type is shown in Figure 1 below. An asterisk (*) denotes the cell tested is cancerous.

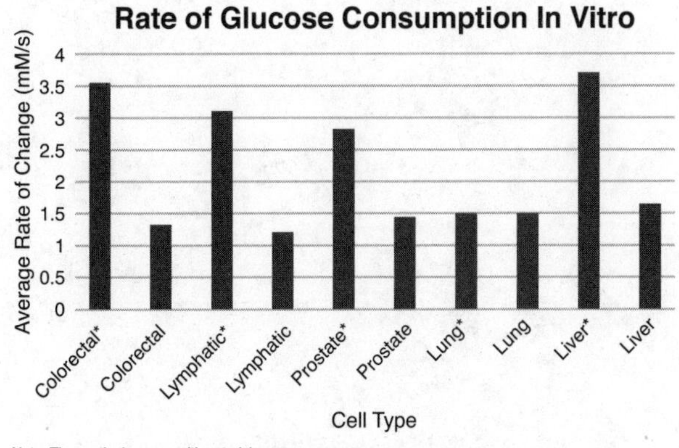

Figure 1

43. What is the main purpose of the passage?

(A) To introduce a scientific topic
(B) To explain the process of human respiration
(C) To outline the history of an innovation
(D) To explain the cause of a disease

44. Based on the passage, which of the following statements is most accurate?

(A) Glycolysis is more efficient than aerobic respiration.
(B) Aerobic respiration is more efficient than anaerobic fermentation.
(C) Ethanol fermentation is more efficient than alcohol fermentation.
(D) Anaerobic organisms are more complex than aerobic organisms.

45. Which option gives the best evidence for the answer to the previous question?

(A) Lines 12–14 ("Glycolysis . . . sugar")
(B) Lines 21–25 ("The products . . . cell-type")
(C) Lines 35–38 ("Cellular . . . fermentation")
(D) Lines 38–42 ("Yeast . . . alcohol")

46. The paragraph in lines 43–57 ("Though . . . fatigue") primarily serves to show that

(A) fermentation is the primary process whereby humans obtain energy.
(B) humans can use fermentation when extra energy is needed.
(C) vigorous exercise is a way to minimize the amount of fermentation that takes place.
(D) human muscles use fermentation instead of respiration to acquire energy.

47. As used in line 52–53, "strenuous" most closely means

(A) pessimistic.
(B) lethargic.
(C) apathetic.
(D) vigorous.

48. Based on the passage, the consensus among scientists regarding the link between the Warburg Effect and cancer cells is that

(A) there is a clear link.
(B) a link is a possibility.
(C) such a link is impossible.
(D) the idea of a link is outdated.

49. Which option gives the best evidence for the answer to the previous question?

(A) Lines 61–62 ("Because . . . cells")
(B) Lines 62–64 ("This alternative . . . Effect")
(C) Lines 67–71 ("Scientists . . . body")
(D) Lines 71–73 ("While . . . proposed")

50. As used in line 81, "trigger" most closely means
    (A) cause.
    (B) persuade.
    (C) harm.
    (D) deprive.

51. Based on the figure, when compared to the non-cancerous cells, the cancerous cells
    (A) have a generally greater average rate of change.
    (B) typically have a lower average rate of change.
    (C) have approximately the same rate of change.
    (D) are more likely to have a rate of change of zero.

52. Which aspect of the Warburg Effect does the figure best illustrate?
    (A) That tumors primarily rely on respiration for energy
    (B) That cancerous cells take in more glucose than noncancerous cells
    (C) That malignant cells are more likely to spread in major organ systems
    (D) That the liver is the organ most likely to become cancerous

STOP If there is still time remaining, you may review your answers.

WRITING AND LANGUAGE PRACTICE TEST 4

36 MINUTES, 44 QUESTIONS

DIRECTIONS: The passages below are each accompanied by several questions, some of which refer to an underlined portion in the passage, and some of which refer to the passage as a whole. For some questions, determine how the expression of ideas can be improved. For other questions, determine the best sentence structure, usage, or punctuation given the context. A passage or question may have an accompanying graphic that you will need to consider as you choose the best answer.

Choose the best answer to each question, considering what will optimize the writing quality and make the writing follow the conventions of standard written English. Some questions will have a "NO CHANGE" option that you can pick if you believe the best choice would be to leave the underlined portion as it is.

Questions 1–11 are based on the following passage.

Underwater Welding

Since its development in 1932 by Soviet engineer Konstantin Khrenov, marine welding has become a highly specialized and **1** monetary career. As the name suggests, marine welders construct or repair infrastructures like oil rigs and bridges underwater by welding them. Welding occurs when structures like metals or thermoplastics are heated to high temperatures and melted together, causing the structures to bind. Because the conditions to which underwater welders are exposed are different from **2** those that typical welders experience, underwater welders are specially trained to utilize techniques like dry hyperbaric or wet welding methods.

1. (A) NO CHANGE
   (B) exorbitant
   (C) budgetary
   (D) lucrative

2. (A) NO CHANGE
   (B) typical welders,
   (C) the experiences of typical welders,
   (D) welders,

In the dry hyperbaric method, welders are enclosed in a hyperbaric chamber known as a "habitat," a capsule-like structure with a pressure similar to that on the water's surface. Inside, the capsule pushes out water from the environment and replaces it with helium and oxygen, enabling the welder to breathe. **3** Larger welding projects typically require more time to finish, so, for example, a large-scale project involving an oil rig would likely require a bigger habitat than a pipeline project.

4 In contrast, the structure being welded is often kept in dry chambers while the welder constructs or repairs it (although the structures can also be worked on in wet environments). When the structure is in a dry chamber as opposed to a wet one, the welder does not have to buy special welding equipment designed for aquatic environments. **5** An advantage of using the dry hyperbaric method, is that the habitat protects the welder from the surrounding aquatic environment; **6** also, it would be disadvantageous that the habitats are often expensive since they are custom-made to accommodate the size of the welding project.

Another method of underwater welding is wet welding **7** in which the welder performs the welding without a habitat. Although wet welding is more

3. Which choice most effectively sets up the information that follows in the sentence?
   (A) NO CHANGE
   (B) The size of the habitat usually depends on the size of the project the welder needs to complete,
   (C) The budgets for underwater welding projects are often insufficient,
   (D) Robotic underwater welding techniques have made significant strides in recent years,

4. (A) NO CHANGE
   (B) Additionally,
   (C) Surprisingly,
   (D) As a result of this,

5. (A) NO CHANGE
   (B) An advantage of using, the dry hyperbaric method is
   (C) An advantage of using the dry hyperbaric method is
   (D) An advantage, of using the dry hyperbaric method, is

6. The writer wants to have a transition at this point that is both logical and consistent with the language in the first part of the sentence. Which choice most effectively accomplishes the writer's goal?
   (A) NO CHANGE
   (B) however, a disadvantage is
   (C) in fact, the major disadvantages are
   (D) disadvantages include

7. (A) NO CHANGE
   (B) so
   (C) that
   (D) of

cost-effective than dry hyperbaric welding because there is no **8** habitat required: this technique is more dangerous because it exposes the welder to the outside aquatic environment. But, because no habitat is needed to enclose the welder, **9** this technique enables the welder to freely move about the project.

Given the different methods associated with underwater welding, it is clear that this is a specialized and complicated field. **10** Because of this, welders with these skills are in demand by employers: regular welders have a job growth outlook of between 4 to 6 percent, but "because [underwater welders] are so uniquely skilled and there are comparatively so few of them," underwater welders have a much **11** more outrageous job growth outlook than normal welders.[2]

8. (A) NO CHANGE
   (B) habitat required, this technique
   (C) habitat required; this technique
   (D) habitat required. This technique

9. Which choice most effectively concludes the sentence by underscoring an advantage of the wet welding technique?
   (A) NO CHANGE
   (B) wet welding lacks the safety that other methods may provide.
   (C) welders may feel more comfortable with this approach.
   (D) welders must proceed with caution in the dangerous underwater environment.

10. At this point, the writer is considering inserting the following sentence.

    In addition, those who design underwater pipelines must be highly trained in addressing the unique circumstances found in an aquatic environment.

    Should the writer make this addition here?
    (A) Yes, because it provides a relevant detail.
    (B) Yes, because it explains an important design process.
    (C) No, because it shifts the focus away from underwater welding careers.
    (D) No, because it provides information already stated in the passage.

11. (A) NO CHANGE
    (B) more appreciative
    (C) more eminent
    (D) higher

[2]"Underwater Welding Outlook." ETI School of Skilled Trades. 28 June 2021. *https://eticampus.edu/welding-program/welding-career/underwater-welding-outlook/*

Questions 12–22 are based on the following passage.

Musical Musings

Music is something that fills our lives and confuses social scientists. We live in a very fortunate time when music **12** have always just a click away. However, historically, music was something that (other than singing) most people could not easily access. Unless people lived in or near a community that could make instruments and train musicians, professional musical performances were almost wholly unreachable. Yet still it was used in nearly every society ever studied. People sang, **13** beat on makeshift drums, whistled, and danced as far back in human history as we can trace. A few questions then arise. Where did music come from? What is it about humanity that puts music in us? **14** Is the piano a better instrument than the violin? Is it a language that we created?

The short answer is that we don't exactly know. The answer likely lies in the reason why certain music appeals to us. Why **15** are they that certain notes sound heavenly together while others make us cringe? Music is a combination of specific sound waves started and stopped at specific times. Some waves align nicely with one another or contrast nicely with one another, **16** while others are neither regularly

12. (A) NO CHANGE
(B) are
(C) is
(D) was

13. (A) NO CHANGE
(B) beat on makeshift drums
(C) beat on makeshift drums;
(D) beat, on makeshift drums

14. Which choice provides a similar question to the ones that surround it in this paragraph?
(A) NO CHANGE
(B) Is it a part of nature to which we are attuned?
(C) Do some people have natural talent for composition?
(D) Is it better to learn music from professionals or amateurs?

15. (A) NO CHANGE
(B) is it
(C) was it
(D) were they

16. (A) NO CHANGE
(B) because
(C) since
(D) DELETE the underlined portion.

contrasting nor matching. **(17)** Matching and nicely contrasting waves make music mathematically enjoyable. Moreover, they make music aesthetically appealing.

Heavy beats are another puzzle around music. Some scientists **(18)** know that humans like them because they mimic our heartbeat—the vital thrum of our bodies. Others think that humans enjoy them because they interrupt our thoughts, make it tougher to become preoccupied with distractions, and allow us to relax. Beats are so universally **(19)** love that babies will dance to them and hard of hearing people will seek out their vibrations. **(20)** These two things (the melodical notes and the beats), come together in music. Humans, since the very beginning of our species, have used them to express joy, sadness, heartache, love, and pain. They are woven into our lives, our history, and **(21)** our memories. People across the world dance to music at births, weddings, and funerals. They use music and dance at special ceremonies

17. Which choice most effectively combines the underlined sentences?
    (A) Matching waves, and also nicely contrasting waves, result in music that is both mathematically and aesthetically appealing.
    (B) Waves that both match and have a nice contrast cause music that is appealing to someone mathematically and aesthetically.
    (C) Waves, matching and in contrast, make mathematical and aesthetic music.
    (D) Matching and nicely contrasting waves make music mathematically and aesthetically appealing.

18. Which word is the most appropriate to use at this point, given the sentence that precedes it?
    (A) NO CHANGE
    (B) realize
    (C) hypothesize
    (D) understand

19. (A) NO CHANGE
    (B) loving
    (C) will love
    (D) loved

20. (A) NO CHANGE
    (B) These two things the melodical notes and the beats, come together
    (C) These two things—the melodical notes and the beats—come together
    (D) These two things—the melodical notes and the beats, come together

21. (A) NO CHANGE
    (B) their minds.
    (C) my mind.
    (D) your memories.

and celebrations in almost every culture. They hold up musicians as special, revered. And yet, despite all of this, we still don't really know if music is within us, something we created, or something we merely discovered.

I would argue it doesn't really matter. (22) Since music is only appreciated by certain people, it is not worthwhile to scientifically investigate the topic. Humanity and music are inseparable. It is a part of our lives as surely as birth and death. It flows through and around us and makes our lives more beautiful, more enjoyable, more comfortable, more relaxing, and more of everything good.

22. Which sentence most effectively connects the first sentence of the paragraph to the remainder of the paragraph?
(A) NO CHANGE
(B) After all, we cannot be certain as to how important music is to humanity.
(C) Perhaps my skepticism is unwarranted, but I feel very strongly about the irrelevance of music to most people.
(D) No matter where music came from, it is a part of us now.

Questions 23–33 are based on the following passage and supplementary material.

Mortgages

One of the most common ways that people can amass wealth is through (23) assembling equity in their homes. (24) While very few people have sufficient cash on hand to make an outright purchase of a home, many people are able to qualify for a mortgage—a loan that permits someone to take possession of a home, with the home serving as collateral for the loan until the loan is fully repaid. If home buyers are (25) sharp and intelligent, utilizing mortgages for a home purchase can be a wise choice.

{1} First, one should consider the term of the mortgage. {2} Most home mortgages are for 30-year or 15-year terms. {3} With a 30-year term, the monthly mortgage payment will be lower; however, it will take much longer for one to build up equity in the home. {4} A 15-year loan, on the other hand, can be paid off more quickly. {5} (26) You should be sure that the monthly mortgage payment is affordable, or one could run the risk of defaulting on the mortgage and having the home repossessed by the bank. (27)

Second, one should shop around for the best interest rate. It is important to understand the differences between fixed (28) interest rates, that remain constant throughout the term of the loan, and adjustable interest rates, which can change over time. One should be mindful of the historic trends in rates to be sure one

23. (A) NO CHANGE
(B) manufacturing
(C) building
(D) fabricating

24. (A) NO CHANGE
(B) Since
(C) And
(D) Because

25. (A) NO CHANGE
(B) savvy,
(C) discerning and insightful,
(D) gullible,

26. (A) NO CHANGE
(B) They
(C) He or she
(D) One

27. The writer wants to add the following sentence to the paragraph.

This is because most of the payments early on in a 30-year mortgage go toward paying interest instead of paying principal.

This sentence would most logically be placed immediately after
(A) sentence 1.
(B) sentence 3.
(C) sentence 4.
(D) sentence 5.

28. (A) NO CHANGE
(B) interest rates, which remain constant
(C) interest rates which remain constant
(D) interest rates; remain constant

is financing a home at the appropriate time. Between 2017 and 2021, mortgage rates on a 30-year fixed mortgage ranged from a little over (29) 0% to a little under 7%. So, a mortgage with a rate (30) of over 1% would likely be high for historical purposes.

(31) Third, it is important to look out for other mortgage payment expenses. Some loans may have points—these are up-front fees that allow the interest rate to be lower over the life of the loan. Points can be worthwhile if one plans on keeping the mortgage in place for many years, but they would be unwise if one plans on refinancing the mortgage a year or two into the loan. Also, monthly payments like home insurance and real estate taxes may be included, potentially raising the monthly costs by a significant sum.

(32) Finally explore any special mortgage programs, that may be available. First-time homebuyers may be eligible for loans with lower requirements for down payments. Teachers, law enforcement officers, firefighters, and emergency medical technicians may qualify for home buying incentives for purchasing houses in a revitalization area. (33) A clear understanding of everything a mortgage entails will enable homebuyers to make sound financial decisions.

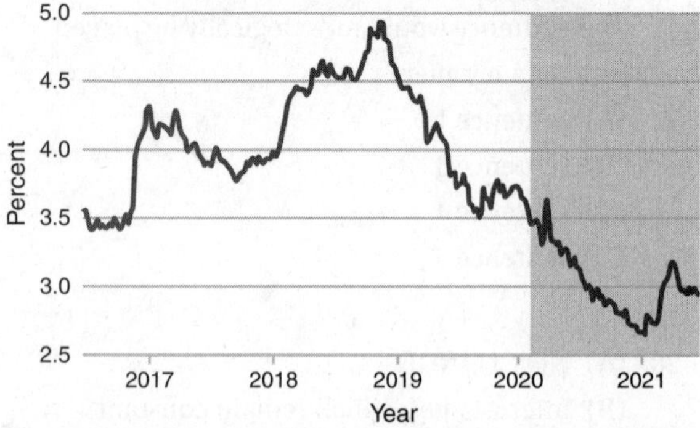

Freddie Mac, 30-Year Fixed Rate Mortgage Average in the United States [MORTGAGE30US], retrieved from FRED, Federal Reserve Bank of St. Louis; https://fred.stlouisfed.org/series/MORTGAGE30US, June 22, 2021.

29. Which choice best represents the data in the graph?
    (A) NO CHANGE
    (B) 1% to a little over 6%.
    (C) 2.5% to a little under 5%.
    (D) 4% to a little over 5%.

30. Which choice is best supported by the data in the graph?
    (A) NO CHANGE
    (B) of less than 2.5%
    (C) of less than 3.5%
    (D) of over 5%

31. Which choice best introduces the paragraph?
    (A) NO CHANGE
    (B) Next, it is vital to conduct thorough research before applying for a loan.
    (C) In contrast, many homebuyers do not have the credit scores they need to have favorable loan terms.
    (D) In addition, the interest costs of mortgages can make them prohibitively expensive for most homebuyers.

32. (A) NO CHANGE
    (B) Finally: explore any, special mortgage programs that may be available.
    (C) Finally explore any special mortgage programs; that may be available.
    (D) Finally, explore any special mortgage programs that may be available.

33. (A) NO CHANGE
    (B) Great knowledge
    (C) Awareness
    (D) Knowing what a mortgage may or may not involve based on your personal situation

Questions 34–44 are based on the following passage.

Servals

The most successful wildcats in the world are not the large feline predators (like ferocious lions and tigers) that people commonly think of. **34** The most successful wildcats in the world are actually small cats—specifically, African servals. African servals are found mainly in southern Africa and catch their prey successfully about 50 percent of the time. Servals are successful as hunters **35**.

Servals are medium-sized, gold-colored cats covered in darker patterns of stripes and spots. Having a lighter-colored coat with a darker pattern **36** make them more difficult to spot them. These unique markings allow the servals to blend into the waving grasses on the savannahs where they make their homes. Camouflaging into their habitat allows servals to approach their favorite prey without being **37** pictured.

One of the serval's greatest **38** adoptations is their sizeable, finely tuned ears. A serval's ears are large enough that it can discern the smallest noises in

34. At this point, the writer wants to insert a sentence that both underscores a contrast with the previous sentence and provides a transition to the following sentence. Which choice best accomplishes the writer's goal?
    (A) These animals are nowhere near as dangerous as a charging rhinoceros.
    (B) In fact, they are not big cats at all.
    (C) Common sense is not nearly as accurate as expert opinion.
    (D) Some people like to domesticate these large cats.

35. At this point, the writer is considering inserting the following.

    thanks to a number of evolutionary adaptations and the ability to consume a large variety of prey

    Should the writer make this addition here?
    (A) Yes, because it justifies a claim.
    (B) Yes, because it addresses a concern.
    (C) No, because it does not relate to the first part of the sentence.
    (D) No, because it provides an inappropriate conclusion to the paragraph.

36. (A) NO CHANGE
    (B) makes them
    (C) makes it
    (D) make it

37. (A) NO CHANGE
    (B) envisioned.
    (C) ignored.
    (D) detected.

38. (A) NO CHANGE
    (B) adaptations
    (C) adoptions
    (D) adaptings

the savannahs. Servals will listen **39** at holes in the ground, for the sound of burrowing, rodents scurrying, and then they will stick their long legs into the hole to scoop out the prey.

Rodents only make up a portion of a **40** serval's diet. Servals will also use their large ears to listen carefully for the flutter of bird wings overhead or the buzz of an insect nearby. At the precisely right moment, the servals will spring into **41** action, therefore relying on their powerful back legs to propel their two-foot-tall bodies over ten feet in the air.

Once their back legs have taken off from the ground, **42** they use there long front legs to snatch the bird or insect out of the sky. Even a serval's tail is adapted to jumping great heights. Servals have shorter than average tails for felines, making it possible for servals to jump high into the sky without risking injury from becoming tangled in a long tail.

Despite the servals' renowned skills, there is still one member of the feline family that reaches far beyond the rest—the domestic housecat. Housecats **43**, which are found in the homes of many Americans, are responsible for the killing of billions of native birds each year in the United States alone. This predation by housecats has led to the addition

39. (A) NO CHANGE
    (B) at holes in the ground—for the sound of burrowing
    (C) at holes in the ground for the sound of burrowing
    (D) at holes, in the ground for the sound of burrowing

40. (A) NO CHANGE
    (B) servals diets.
    (C) servals' diet.
    (D) serval's diets'.

41. (A) NO CHANGE
    (B) action; however, relying
    (C) action, relying
    (D) action; however relying

42. (A) NO CHANGE
    (B) use they're
    (C) using there
    (D) they use their

43. The writer is considering deleting the underlined phrase from the sentence. Should the writer make this deletion?
    (A) Yes, because it is an unnecessary detail.
    (B) Yes, because it contradicts what has previously been asserted.
    (C) No, because it defines a sophisticated term.
    (D) No, because it is essential to the main focus of the passage.

of many species of birds to the endangered species list, and some have even been driven to extinction. (44) Endangered species from the oceanic regions are increasingly prevalent, so the solution is just to keep our housecats contained inside and leave the hunting to their cousins in the wild.

44. Which choice best sets up the information in the rest of the sentence and provides a transition from the previous sentence?
(A) NO CHANGE
(B) It is clear to even the most casual observer that the key
(C) The easiest way to help the feathered members of our communities
(D) While some people may prefer dogs to cats, the conclusion

STOP If there is still time remaining, you may review your answers.

MATH PRACTICE TEST 4 (NO CALCULATOR)

25 MINUTES, 20 QUESTIONS

DIRECTIONS: For questions 1–15, solve each problem and choose the best answer from the given options. Fill in the corresponding oval on your answer document. For questions 16–20, solve the problem and fill in the answer in the answer sheet grid. Please use any space in the test booklet to work out your answers.

Notes:

- You **CANNOT** use a calculator on this section.
- All variables and expressions represent real numbers, unless indicated otherwise.
- All figures are drawn to scale, unless indicated otherwise.
- All figures are in a plane, unless indicated otherwise.
- Unless indicated otherwise, the domain of a given function is the set of all real numbers *x* for which the function has real values.

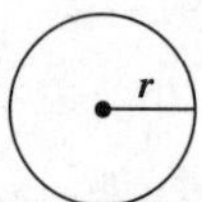

Radius of a circle = r
Area of a circle = πr^2
Circumference of a circle = $2\pi r$

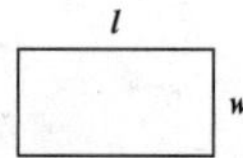

Area of a rectangle = length × width = lw

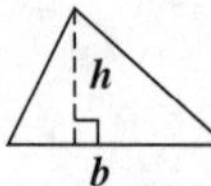

Area of a triangle = $\frac{1}{2}$ × base × height = $\frac{1}{2}bh$

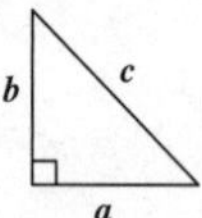

Pythagorean theorem: $a^2 + b^2 = c^2$

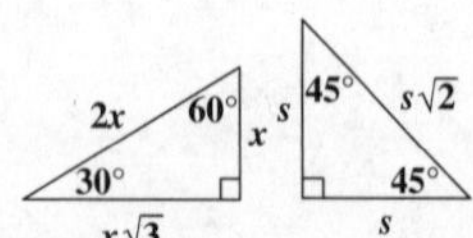

Special right triangles: 30-60-90 and 45-45-90

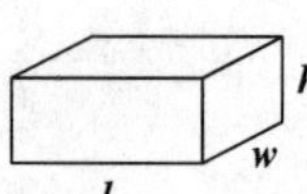

Volume of a box = length × width × height = lwh

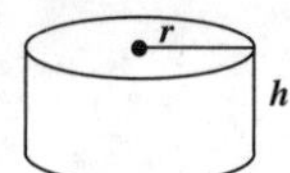

Volume of a cylinder = $\pi r^2 h$

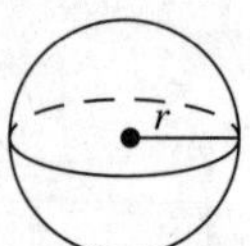

Volume of a sphere = $\frac{4}{3}\pi r^3$

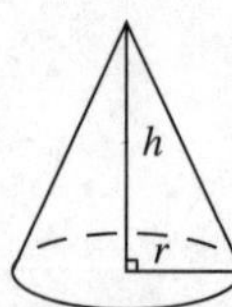

Volume of a cone = $\frac{1}{3}\pi r^2 h$

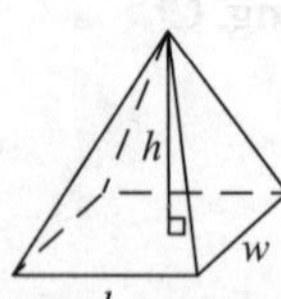

Volume of a pyramid = $\frac{1}{3}$ × length × width × height = $\frac{1}{3}$ lwh

Key Facts:

- **A circle has 360 degrees.**
- **There are 2π radians in a circle.**
- **There are 180 degrees in a triangle.**

1. $5(x + 1)(x - 1)$ is equivalent to which of the following expressions?

   (A) $5x^2 - 5$
   (B) $5x^2 + 5$
   (C) $5x^2 - 10x + 5$
   (D) $5x^2 + 10x - 5$

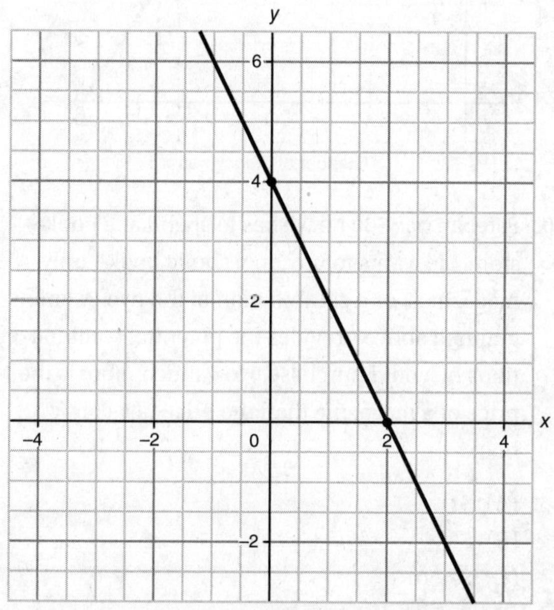

2. The graph of $y = mx + b$ is given above in the xy plane, in which m and b are constants. What is the value of b?

   (A) -2
   (B) $-\frac{1}{2}$
   (C) 2
   (D) 4

3. If $\frac{a+b}{5} = 6$, what is the value of $a + b$?

   (A) 4
   (B) 11
   (C) 30
   (D) 60

4. A line on the xy-coordinate plane passes through the point (6, 4) and the origin. What is the equation of the line?

   (A) $y = \frac{2}{3}x$
   (B) $y = \frac{3}{2}x$
   (C) $y = 2x$
   (D) $y = x + \frac{2}{3}$

5. If x is positive, which expression is equivalent to $\sqrt{64x^4}$?

   (A) $4x^2$
   (B) $8x^2$
   (C) $16x^2$
   (D) $32x^4$

$$\frac{2}{3}x - y = 4$$
$$\frac{1}{3}x + y = 3$$

6. Given the system of equations above, what is the value of x?

   (A) -4
   (B) -1
   (C) 5
   (D) 7

7. The gas tank of a certain car has a capacity of 20 gallons. A driver completely fills the gas tank. Her car averages 30 miles per gallon of gas. What would represent the number of gallons in her gas tank, G, after she has been driving for m miles after initially filling the tank?

(A) $G = 30 - \frac{m}{20}$
(B) $G = 20 - 30m$
(C) $G = 20 - \frac{m}{30}$
(D) $G = 30 - 20m$

8. $(x + y)^2 = 2(x + y) - 1$

In the equation above, what is the value of the sum of x and y?

(A) 1
(B) 2
(C) 5
(D) 6

9. In a right triangle with 3 distinct angles, the cosine of the smallest angle is $\frac{1}{4}$. What is the sine of the median angle?

(A) $\frac{1}{8}$
(B) $\frac{1}{4}$
(C) $\frac{3}{4}$
(D) $\frac{3}{2}$

0

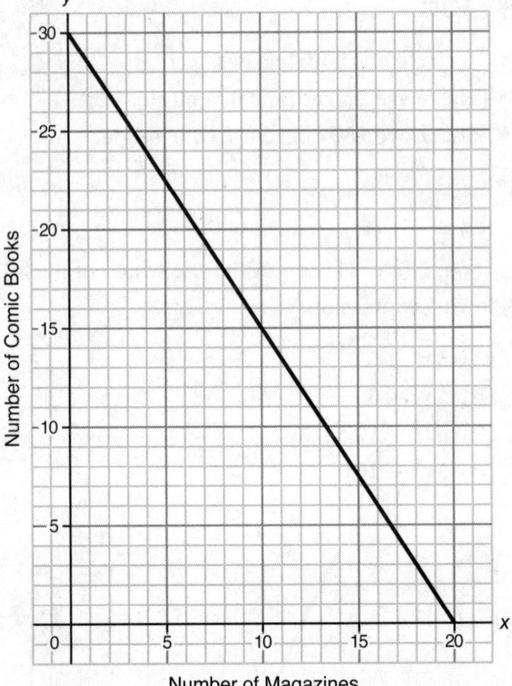

10. Esteban has $60 he wishes to spend at a bookstore. He wants to buy only comic books, only magazines, or a combination of the two. A line graphed above provides the potential combinations he could purchase. How much more is the price of a magazine than the price of a comic book?

(A) $1
(B) $2
(C) $2.50
(D) $3.20

$$2 = \frac{a}{x}$$

11. Given that in the above equation, a is a constant, for what value of x will the equation be undefined?

(A) -1
(B) 0
(C) 2
(D) 4

12. $\dfrac{a}{\left(\frac{1}{a}\right)+\left(\frac{b}{2}\right)}$ is equivalent to which of the following?

(A) $\dfrac{2a^2}{2+ab}$

(B) $\dfrac{2b^2}{a}$

(C) $\dfrac{a^2}{b}$

(D) $2a+2b$

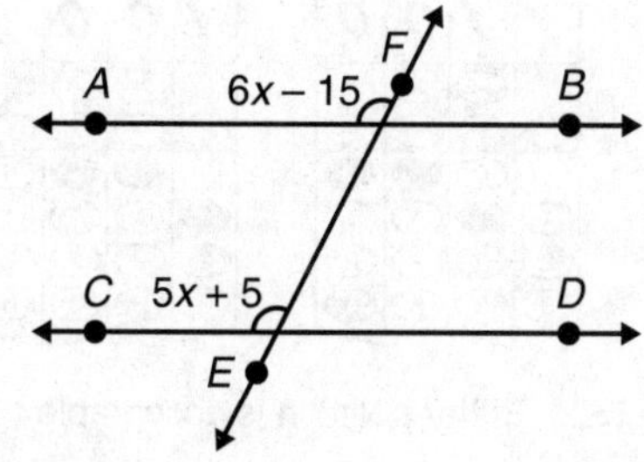

13. Lines AB and CD are parallel, and line EF intersects both lines. Two angles are marked with their angle measures in terms of x. What is the value of x?

(A) 5
(B) 8
(C) 15
(D) 20

14. $x=\sqrt{8x-12}$

What is/are the solution(s) to the equation above?

(A) 1.5 only
(B) 2 only
(C) 6 only
(D) Both 2 and 6

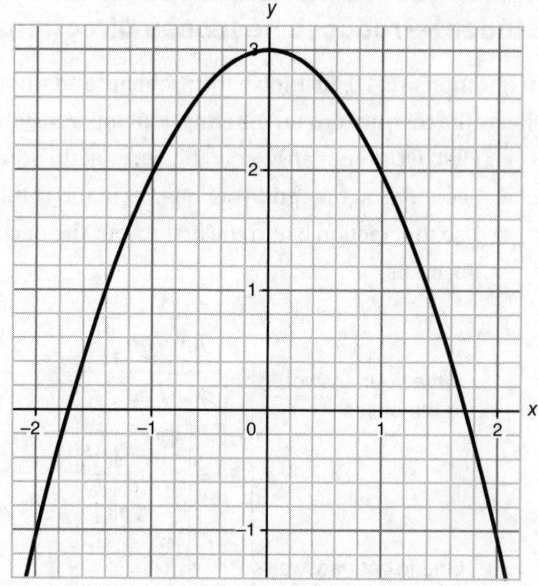

15. The above graph represents the reflection of which of the following functions across the x-axis?

(A) $f(x)=x^2+3$
(B) $f(x)=x^2-3$
(C) $f(x)=x^2+1.7$
(D) $f(x)=x^2-1.7$

Student-Produced Response Directions

In questions 16–20, first solve the problem, and then enter your answer on the grid provided on the answer sheet. The instructions for entering your answers follow.

- First, write your answer in the boxes at the top of the grid.
- Second, you may grid your answer in the columns below the boxes.
- Use the fraction bar in the first row or the decimal point in the second row to enter fractions and decimals.

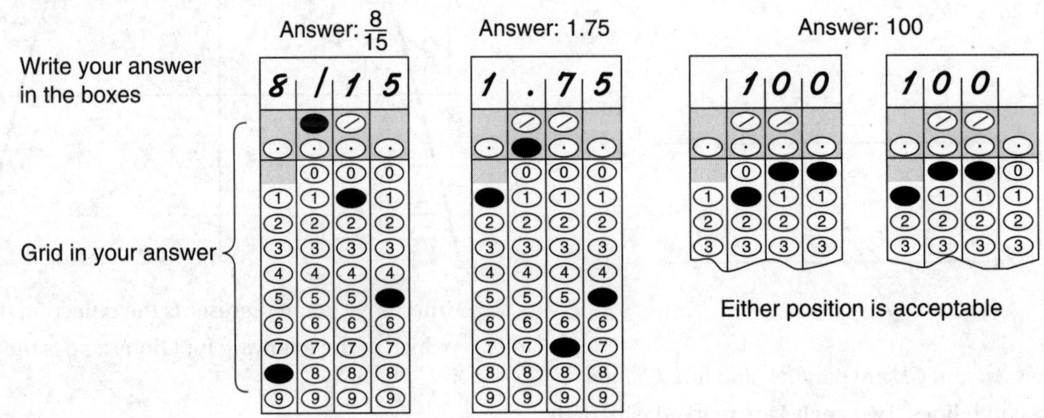

- Grid only one space in each column.
- Entering the answer in the boxes is recommended as an aid in gridding but is not required.
- The machine scoring your exam can read only what you grid, so you **must grid-in your answers correctly to get credit**.
- If a question has more than one correct answer, grid-in only one of them.
- The grid does not have a minus sign, so no answer can be negative.
- A mixed number *must* be converted to an improper fraction or a decimal before it is gridded. Enter $1\frac{1}{4}$ as $\frac{5}{4}$ or 1.25; the machine will interpret 11/4 as $\frac{11}{4}$ and mark it wrong.
- **All decimals must be entered as accurately as possible.** Here are three acceptable ways of gridding

$$\frac{3}{11} = 0.272727\ldots$$

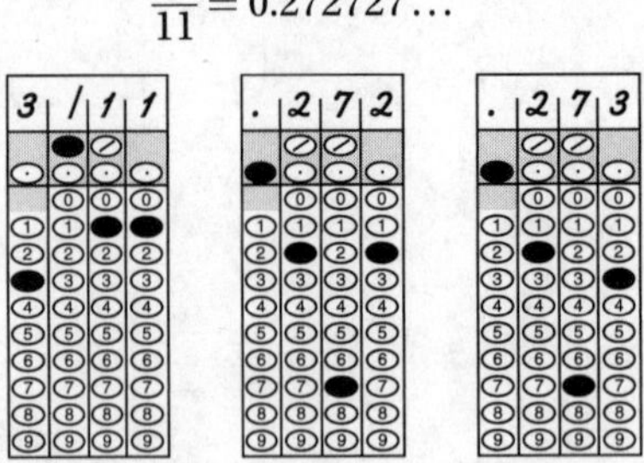

- Note that rounding to .273 is acceptable because you are using the full grid, but you would receive **no credit** for .3 or .27, because they are less accurate.

16. If $x = 5$, what is $\frac{2x}{5} + \frac{4x}{10}$?

17. If $3 = \frac{3}{2}(4x - 2y)$ and $y = \frac{1}{2}x$, what is the value of y?

18. If the volume of a right rectangular prism is 90 cubic inches, and the product of the length and width of the prism is 30 square inches, what is the height of the prism?

19. If $\frac{2x + 8}{k} = x + 4$ has infinitely many solutions, what is the value of k?

20. The expression $(12a - 13b)(12a + 13b)$ can be written in the form $ka^2 - jb^2$, in which k and j are constants. What is the sum of k and j?

STOP If there is still time remaining, you may review your answers.

MATH PRACTICE TEST 4 (CALCULATOR)

55 MINUTES, 38 QUESTIONS

DIRECTIONS: For questions 1–30, solve each problem and choose the best answer from the given options. Fill in the corresponding oval on your answer document. For questions 31–38, solve the problem and fill in the answer in the answer sheet grid. Please use any space in the test booklet to work out your answers.

Notes:

- You **CAN** use a calculator on this section.
- All variables and expressions represent real numbers, unless indicated otherwise.
- All figures are drawn to scale, unless indicated otherwise.
- All figures are in a plane, unless indicated otherwise.
- Unless indicated otherwise, the domain of a given function is the set of all real numbers x for which the function has real values.

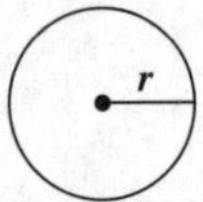

Radius of a circle = r
Area of a circle = πr^2
Circumference of a circle = $2\pi r$

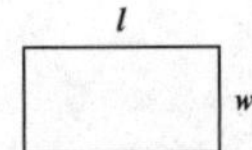

Area of a rectangle = length × width = lw

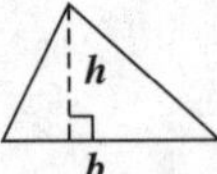

Area of a triangle = $\frac{1}{2}$ × base × height = $\frac{1}{2}bh$

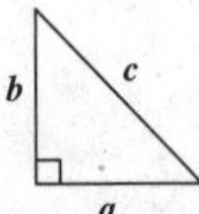

Pythagorean theorem: $a^2 + b^2 = c^2$

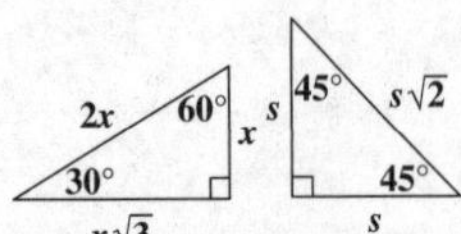

Special right triangles: 30-60-90 and 45-45-90

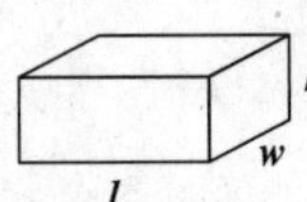

Volume of a box = length × width × height = lwh

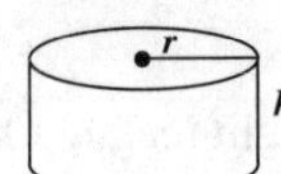

Volume of a cylinder = $\pi r^2 h$

Volume of a sphere = $\frac{4}{3}\pi r^3$

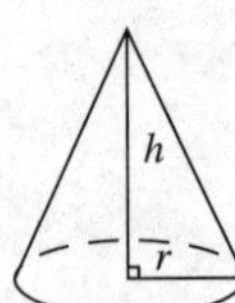

Volume of a cone = $\frac{1}{3}\pi r^2 h$

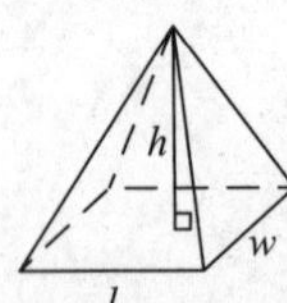

Volume of a pyramid = $\frac{1}{3}$ × length × width × height = $\frac{1}{3}$ lwh

Key Facts:

- **A circle has 360 degrees.**
- **There are 2π radians in a circle.**
- **There are 180 degrees in a triangle.**

1. In the line formed by the equation $y + 5 = 7x$, what is the value of the y-intercept?

(A) −5
(B) −1
(C) 5
(D) 7

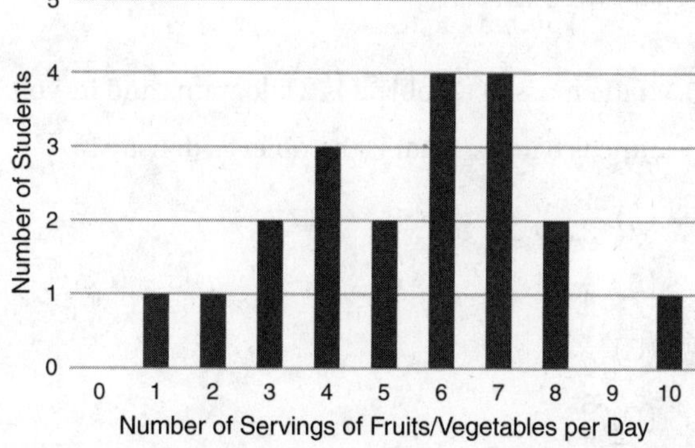

2. Twenty students were asked the combined total number of servings of fruits and vegetables they have each day. The results are presented in the histogram above. What is the median number of servings of fruits and vegetables consumed each day?

(A) 4
(B) 5
(C) 6
(D) 7

3. Which of the following is equivalent to $\frac{x^2 - 81}{x + 9}$?

(A) $x + 9$
(B) $x - 9$
(C) $x^2 - 3$
(D) $x^2 + 3$

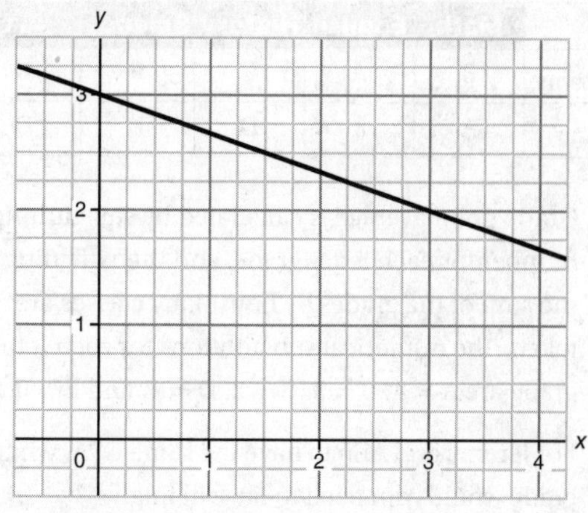

4. The graph of the line above is represented by which of the following equations?

(A) $y = 3x + 8$
(B) $y = \frac{1}{3}x - 4$
(C) $y = -\frac{1}{3}x + 3$
(D) $y = -3x + 6$

5. A food delivery service charges a $5 booking fee plus $0.75 for each mile driven from the pickup point to the delivery spot. If the delivery service charged a customer a total of $27.50, how far did the delivery driver travel from the pickup point to the customer's delivery spot?

(A) 10 miles
(B) 15 miles
(C) 20 miles
(D) 30 miles

	Math	English	History	Science	Art
Jeremy	B	A	C	F	B
Ann	A	?	D	B	D

6. Grade point average is calculated by substituting a number for each letter grade, and then dividing the sum of the grades by how many classes are taken. The numerical substitutions for each letter grade are A = 4, B = 3, C = 2, D = 1, and F = 0.

For Jeremy and Ann to have the same GPA, what grade would Ann need to have in English?

(A) B
(B) C
(C) D
(D) F

The table below provides the average hours of battery capacity for smartphones at an electronics store.

Hours of Capacity	Number of Phones at Store with That Capacity
20 hours	2
18 hours	7
16 hours	8
14 hours	4
10 hours	3
8 hours	5

7. Which of the quantities of the hours of phone battery capacity would be the smallest?

(A) Mode
(B) Mean
(C) Median
(D) Range

8. In the system of inequalities $y + 10 \leq 3x$ and $x \leq -y - 2$, what is the maximum value of y?

(A) -6
(B) -4
(C) 0
(D) 3

9. The cost function to sell x units of a good is $C(x) = F + Ux$, in which F is a constant representing the fixed cost and U is a constant representing the additional cost for each unit sold. The total cost of selling 10 units is $400, and the fixed cost is $100.

What is the total cost when 12 units are sold?

(A) $410
(B) $460
(C) $540
(D) $560

Questions 10–11 refer to the following information.

Density, mass, and volume are related by this formula:

$$Density = \frac{Mass}{Volume}$$

10. If the mass of an object is 2 kilograms and its volume is 8 liters, what is the object's density in $\frac{kg}{L}$?

(A) $\frac{1}{8}$
(B) $\frac{1}{4}$
(C) $\frac{1}{2}$
(D) $\frac{3}{4}$

11. Which statement correctly expresses a relationship among the variables in the density formula?

(A) If mass increases while volume remains constant, density will increase.
(B) If volume increases while mass remains constant, density will increase.
(C) If mass increases while volume remains constant, density will decrease.
(D) If volume decreases while mass remains constant, density will decrease.

12. Jie has a total of $30 to spend on snacks at a movie. A box of popcorn costs $5 and a drink costs $2. If Jie buys p boxes of popcorn and d drinks, which inequality represents the number of total boxes of popcorn and drinks Jie can buy, given that there is no sales tax and there is no need to spend money on anything else?

(A) $p + d \leq 7$
(B) $p + d + 7 \leq 30$
(C) $5p + 2d \leq 30$
(D) $32p > 37d$

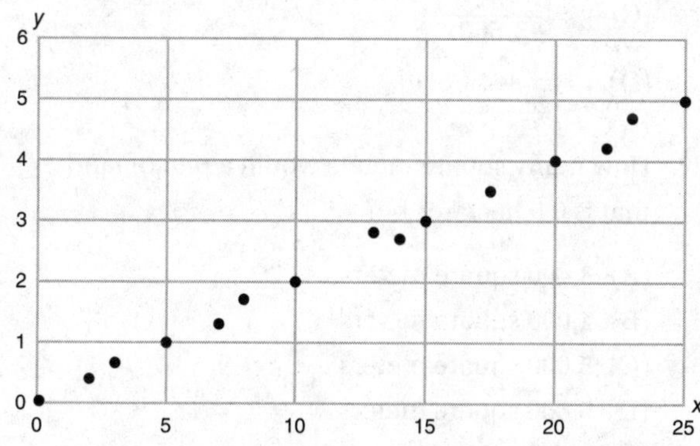

13. Which of the following would best approximate the equation for a best-fit line based on the values in the scatterplot graph above?

(A) $y = 0.1x$
(B) $y = 0.2x$
(C) $y = 0.3x$
(D) $y = 0.5x$

14. $0 = 2x^2 + x + k$

In the equation above, what value for the constant k would make it such that there is just one solution for x?

(A) $\frac{1}{8}$
(B) $\frac{1}{6}$
(C) $\frac{1}{2}$
(D) 4

Questions 15–17 refer to the following information.

The cost in dollars, C, and revenue in dollars, R, for a sandwich food truck that sells x sandwiches are given below.

$$R = 5x$$

$$C = 12{,}000 + x$$

15. What does the 12,000 most likely represent in the cost function?

(A) The variable cost associated with making each additional sandwich
(B) The total revenue from selling x sandwiches
(C) The net profit of operating the sandwich food truck
(D) The fixed cost of operating the sandwich food truck

16. What is the least number of sandwiches the truck must sell to make enough money to cover its costs and break even?

(A) 2,200
(B) 2,600
(C) 3,000
(D) 4,800

17. If the truck raises its price per sandwich to 6 dollars, by what percentage would revenue per sandwich increase?

(A) 20%
(B) 24%
(C) 28%
(D) 32%

18. Alani rode her bike a total of 120 miles on a hilly road. The route was $\frac{1}{3}$ uphill and $\frac{2}{3}$ downhill. If her speed going downhill was an average of 20 miles per hour and the entire biking time took a total of 8 hours, what was her average uphill speed?

    (A) 8 miles per hour
    (B) 10 miles per hour
    (C) 16 miles per hour
    (D) 28 mile per hour

19. What is the remainder when $4x^2 - 7x + 8$ is divided by $x - 2$?

    (A) -5
    (B) 3
    (C) $\frac{8}{x-2}$
    (D) $\frac{10}{x-2}$

20. A movie theater chain owner surveyed 100 filmgoers who had said they liked the prequel to a particular movie sequel that was about to be released. The owner found that in the private film showing, 70% liked this particular sequel. What would most reasonably be inferred from this information?

    (A) 70% of the general public liked the sequel to the movie.
    (B) 30% of the general public had no opinion on the quality of the sequel to this movie.
    (C) Those who like this particular movie's prequel are likely to like the movie's sequel.
    (D) Movie watchers generally like sequels to any movie that has a sequel made.

Questions 21–23 refer to the following information.

Unit	Equivalent Unit
1 hectare	10,000 square meters
1 acre	43,560 square feet
1 meter	3.281 feet

21. If x acres equal y square feet, what equation correctly expresses the relationship between x and y?

    (A) $y = 43,560x$
    (B) $y = \frac{x}{43,560}$
    (C) $y = \frac{1}{43,560x}$
    (D) $y = x + 43,560$

22. How many square meters would a plot of land that is 0.5 hectares be?

    (A) 3,400 square meters
    (B) 4,000 square meters
    (C) 5,000 square meters
    (D) 5,600 square meters

23. A 1-acre plot of land would be approximately how many hectares?

    (A) 0.404 hectares
    (B) 0.854 hectares
    (C) 1.329 hectares
    (D) 4.360 hectares

Votes in Favor of Tax Levy

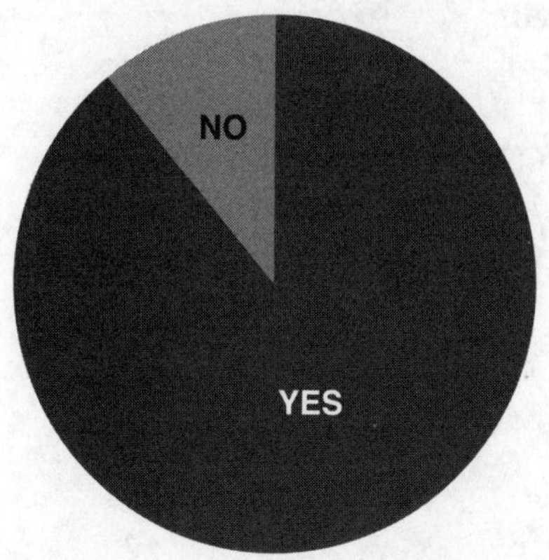

24. The above circle graph gives the percentages of 800 city residents who voted in favor of a tax levy ("YES") and those who voted against it ("NO"). If the central angle formed by the portion of the circle allocated to "NO" is 45°, how many of the residents voted "NO"?

(A) 90
(B) 100
(C) 110
(D) 120

Questions 25–26 refer to the following information.

Approximate Sources of U.S. Federal Government Revenue

Individual Income Tax	50%
Payroll Tax	36%
Corporate Income Tax	7%
Excise Tax	3%
Customs Duties	2%
Other	2%

25. If the total federal revenue in a given year were 3 trillion dollars, how much of the revenue would come from the payroll tax?

(A) 0.36 trillion dollars
(B) 0.72 trillion dollars
(C) 1.08 trillion dollars
(D) 8.33 trillion dollars

26. Suppose that over a period of 5 years, the revenue for the federal government increased from 3 trillion dollars to 4 trillion dollars. If the percent of revenue sources remained constant over this period, by how much would the revenue from customs duties increase?

(A) 8 billion dollars
(B) 14 billion dollars
(C) 16 billion dollars
(D) 20 billion dollars

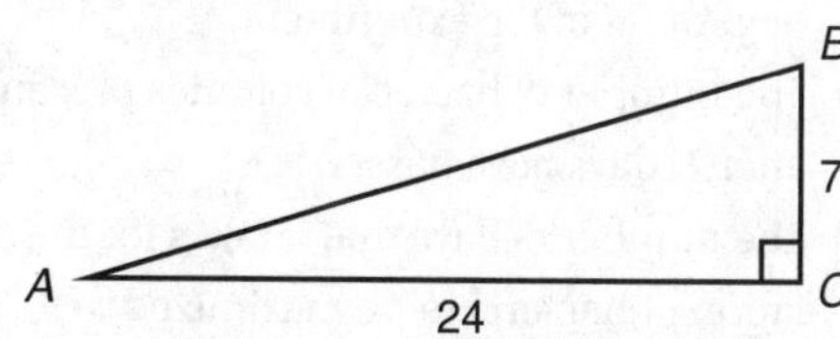

27. In triangle ABC above, $\overline{AC}$ is 24 units long and $\overline{BC}$ is 7 units long. What is the cosine of $\angle ABC$?

(A) $\frac{7}{25}$
(B) $\frac{7}{24}$
(C) $\frac{24}{27}$
(D) $\frac{25}{27}$

28. Two hot air balloons were initially at the same height in the air at 200 feet. After 10 minutes go by, one balloon's height has increased by 30% and the other balloon's height has decreased by 15%. At that point, how many feet apart in height would the two balloons be?

(A) 60 feet
(B) 70 feet
(C) 80 feet
(D) 90 feet

Questions 29–30 refer to the following information.

The spread of colonies of bacteria is modeled by this function, in which C is the total number of colonies and D is the number of days that have passed since the experiment began.

$$C(D) = 500(1.1)^D$$

29. What does the number 500 most likely represent in the function?

(A) The number of bacterial colonies at the beginning of the experiment
(B) The number of bacterial colonies present after D days have passed
(C) The number of days that it takes for the population of bacteria to be maximized
(D) The number of days that it takes for the population of bacteria to be minimized

30. Which of these functions would portray the number of bacterial colonies after H hours had passed?

(A) $C(H) = 500(24)^{(H)}$
(B) $C(H) = 500(1.1)^{(24H)}$
(C) $C(H) = 500(1.1)^{\left(\frac{H}{24}\right)}$
(D) $C(H) = 500(1.1)^{\left(\frac{24}{H}\right)}$

Student-Produced Response Directions

In questions 31–38, first solve the problem, and then enter your answer on the grid provided on the answer sheet. The instructions for entering your answers follow.

- First, write your answer in the boxes at the top of the grid.
- Second, you may grid your answer in the columns below the boxes.
- Use the fraction bar in the first row or the decimal point in the second row to enter fractions and decimals.

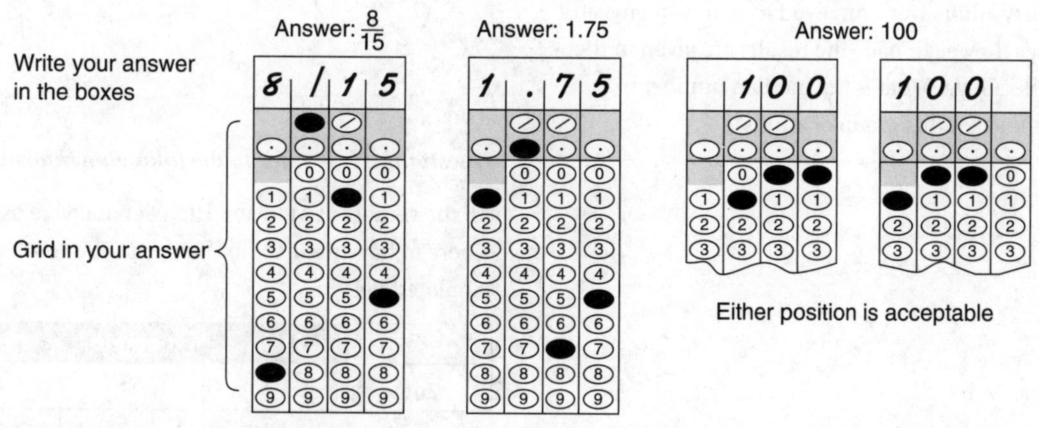

- Grid only one space in each column.
- Entering the answer in the boxes is recommended as an aid in gridding but is not required.
- The machine scoring your exam can read only what you grid, so you **must grid-in your answers correctly to get credit**.
- If a question has more than one correct answer, grid-in only one of them.
- The grid does not have a minus sign, so no answer can be negative.
- A mixed number *must* be converted to an improper fraction or a decimal before it is gridded. Enter $1\frac{1}{4}$ as $\frac{5}{4}$ or 1.25; the machine will interpret 11/4 as $\frac{11}{4}$ and mark it wrong.
- **All decimals must be entered as accurately as possible.** Here are three acceptable ways of gridding

$$\frac{3}{11} = 0.272727\ldots$$

3/11 .272 .273

- Note that rounding to .273 is acceptable because you are using the full grid, but you would receive **no credit** for .3 or .27, because they are less accurate.

Number of Siblings	Frequency
0	6
1	8
2	7
3	4
4	3
5 or more	2

31. Thirty adults were surveyed as to how many siblings they each had. The results are given in the table above. What is the median number of siblings for this group of adults?

32. If $x^{-3b} = \frac{1}{x^a}$, what is the value of $\frac{a}{b}$?

33. Central Park in New York City is a rectangle that is approximately 2.5 miles long and 0.5 miles wide. Based on this information, how many square kilometers, to the nearest hundredth of a square kilometer, is the area of Central Park, given that there are approximately 1.61 km in 1 mile?

34. A gasoline tank for a car has a capacity of 15 gallons. If gas costs $3 a gallon, how much would it cost in dollars to completely fill the gas tank if it already had 5 gallons of gasoline in it?

Questions 35–36 refer to the following information.

All the seniors at Madison High School were asked where to have their senior field trip. The results are tabulated below:

	Male	Female	Totals
Zoo	65	55	120
Waterpark	30	X	80
Totals	95	105	200

35. What is the value of the missing quantity X?

36. What percentage of all the seniors wanted to go to the zoo?

37. If an 80° arc on a circle measures 5 inches, what is the circumference of this circle in inches?

38. The function f has an equation of $f(x) = -(x + 3)(x - 5)$. For what value of x is the value of $f(x)$ at its maximum?

STOP If there is still time remaining, you may review your answers.

ANSWER KEY
Practice Test 4

Section 1: Reading

1. **D**
2. **A**
3. **B**
4. **C**
5. **C**
6. **A**
7. **C**
8. **B**
9. **D**
10. **D**
11. **A**
12. **C**
13. **C**
14. **B**
15. **A**
16. **C**
17. **B**
18. **C**
19. **C**
20. **A**
21. **D**
22. **A**
23. **C**
24. **C**
25. **B**
26. **D**
27. **B**
28. **B**
29. **B**
30. **A**
31. **D**
32. **C**
33. **A**
34. **B**
35. **B**
36. **D**
37. **C**
38. **A**
39. **C**
40. **B**
41. **A**
42. **A**
43. **A**
44. **B**
45. **C**
46. **B**
47. **D**
48. **B**
49. **D**
50. **A**
51. **A**
52. **B**

Section 2: Writing and Language

1. **D**
2. **A**
3. **B**
4. **B**
5. **C**
6. **B**
7. **A**
8. **B**
9. **A**
10. **C**
11. **D**
12. **C**
13. **A**
14. **B**
15. **B**
16. **A**
17. **D**
18. **C**
19. **D**
20. **C**
21. **A**
22. **D**
23. **C**
24. **A**
25. **B**
26. **D**
27. **B**
28. **B**
29. **C**
30. **D**
31. **A**
32. **D**
33. **A**
34. **B**
35. **A**
36. **C**
37. **D**
38. **B**
39. **C**
40. **A**
41. **C**
42. **D**
43. **A**
44. **C**

Section 3: Math (No Calculator)

1. **A**
2. **D**
3. **C**
4. **A**
5. **B**
6. **D**
7. **C**
8. **A**
9. **B**
10. **A**
11. **B**
12. **A**
13. **D**
14. **D**
15. **B**
16. **4**
17. $\frac{1}{3}$ **or .333**
18. **3**
19. **2**
20. **313**

ANSWER KEY
Practice Test 4

Section 4: Math (Calculator)

1. **A**
2. **C**
3. **B**
4. **C**
5. **D**
6. **A**
7. **D**
8. **B**
9. **B**
10. **B**
11. **A**
12. **C**
13. **B**
14. **A**
15. **D**
16. **C**
17. **A**
18. **B**
19. **D**
20. **C**
21. **A**
22. **C**
23. **A**
24. **B**
25. **C**
26. **D**
27. **A**
28. **D**
29. **A**
30. **C**
31. **2**
32. **3**
33. **3.24**
34. **30**
35. **50**
36. **60**
37. **22.5**
38. **1**

SAT Scoring Chart

Tally the number of correct answers from the Reading section (out of 52), the Writing and Language section (out of 44), and the combined Math without and with calculator sections (out of 58). Match these numbers of correct answers to the find the Reading Test score, the Writing and Language Test score, and the Math section score.

Number of Correct Answers on Each Test Part (Reading, Writing/Language, Combined Math Sections)	Reading Test Score	Writing and Language Test Score	Math Section Score
0	10	10	200
1	10	10	200
2	10	10	210
3	10	11	220
4	11	11	230
5	12	12	250
6	13	13	270
7	13	14	280
8	14	14	300
9	15	15	310
10	16	16	320
11	16	16	340
12	17	17	350
13	17	17	360
14	18	18	370
15	18	18	380
16	19	18	390
17	19	19	400
18	20	19	410
19	20	20	420
20	21	20	430
21	21	21	440
22	22	21	450
23	22	22	460
24	23	23	470
25	23	23	480
26	24	24	490
27	24	24	500
28	25	25	500
29	25	25	510
30	26	26	520

(Continued)

Number of Correct Answers on Each Test Part (Reading, Writing/Language, Combined Math Sections)	Reading Test Score	Writing and Language Test Score	Math Section Score
31	26	27	520
32	27	27	530
33	28	28	540
34	28	29	540
35	29	29	550
36	29	30	560
37	30	31	570
38	30	31	580
39	31	32	580
40	31	33	590
41	31	34	600
42	32	36	610
43	32	38	610
44	33	40	620
45	33		630
46	34		640
47	35		650
48	36		660
49	36		670
50	37		680
51	39		690
52	40		700
53			710
54			730
55			750
56			770
57			790
58			800

Add the Reading Test Score and the Writing and Language Test scores

________ (Reading Score) + ________ (Writing and Language Score) =

________ (Combined Reading and Writing and Language Score)

Then multiply the Combined Reading and Writing Language score by 10 to find your Evidence-Based Reading and Writing section score:

10 × ________ (Combined Reading and Writing and Language Score) =

________ **Evidence-Based Reading and Writing Score (between 200–800)**

The Math section score is also between 200–800. Get this from the table above.

____________ **Math Section Score (between 200–800)**

Add the Evidence-Based Reading and Writing score and the Math section score to find your total SAT test score:

__________ Evidence-Based Reading and Writing Score +

__________ Math Section Score =

__________ **Total SAT Test Score (between 400–1600)**

Approximate your testing percentiles (1st–99th) using this chart:

Total Score	Section Score	Total Percentile	Evidence-Based Reading and Writing Percentile	Math Percentile
1600	800	99+	99+	99
1500	750	98	98	96
1400	700	94	94	91
1300	650	86	86	84
1200	600	74	73	75
1100	550	59	57	61
1000	500	41	40	42
900	450	25	24	27
800	400	11	11	15
700	350	3	3	5
600	300	1	1	1
500	250	1	1	1
400	200	1	1	1

Answers Explained

Section 1: Reading Test

Our Mutual Friend

1. **(D)** Throughout the passage, the Veneerings are described as having many friends. They often have gatherings at their home where they entertain up to 20 guests. This would make the best answer choice **(D)**—extroverted. They are certainly not reclusive (hiding away from society), so choice (A) is incorrect. They are not described as altruistic (having a great concern for the well-being of others), so choice (B) is incorrect. The reader also has no evidence that they are a particularly inventive couple, making choice (C) incorrect.
2. **(A)** The main idea of this paragraph is that everything about the Veneerings is new. To emphasize this point, the author continually repeats the word "new" when describing them. This best fits with choice **(A)**. Choice (B) is incorrect as there is no suspense in this passage. Choice (C) is incorrect as the point is being emphasized, or hammered in, not clarified. Choice (D) is incorrect as only one perspective is offered—the perspective that the Veneerings are new.
3. **(B)** This passage starts by describing Twemlow and then by saying that to him, the Veneerings were "a source of blind confusion." This tells the reader that he had a hard time understanding them, which makes choice **(B)** the best option. This selection does not address any crime committed, which makes choice (A) incorrect. While Twemlow is later described as thinking about how he was confused by the Veneerings, this selection does not imply that he enjoyed thinking about it, making choice (C) incorrect. We have no evidence in this selection that Twemlow is manipulative, making choice (D) incorrect.
4. **(C)** In the second paragraph, the author compares Twemlow to a dinner table. He does this quite extensively going to great lengths to say where Twemlow is stored when not in use, and how he is used with various party sizes with various numbers of leaves added. There is no more extensive use of personification in the passage. This makes choice **(C)** correct—the author extensively compares people to pieces of furniture. Choices (A), (B), and (D) are incorrect as they are comparisons used far less extensively or not at all within the passage.
5. **(C)** Within the context, the word "requisition" is used to explain how often Twemlow is being "used" as a "dinner table." He (as a table) is "in frequent requisition" or "being used often." If he were describing Twemlow as a human, not a table, the author might say that "he is often invited to dinner parties as a guest." This best fits with choice **(C)**—Twemlow is in frequent demand. Choices (A) and (B) describe emotions, not the frequency of use and are therefore incorrect. Choice (D) is incorrect: Twemlow is not the leader as he is not the host of these parties—he is simply a guest.
6. **(A)** In the first sentence of this excerpt, we can see that "Mr. and Mrs. Veneering, for example, arranging a dinner, habitually started with Twemlow and then put leaves in him or added guests to him." Leaves are part of a table that makes the table longer so that more guests can be accommodated. In short, what this excerpt is saying is that the Veneerings would begin with Twemlow on their guest list and then build the rest of the guest list around him. This makes choice **(A)** the best answer. Choice (B) is incorrect as Twemlow is clearly described in the third paragraph as someone who was essential because of his connection to his cousin, not because of his own personality. Choice (C) is incorrect as he has many dinner invitations

regardless of his connections to the Veneerings. Choice (D) is incorrect as Twemlow seems to want to have deeper connections. This is shown in his genuine upset and confusion when he is unable to determine the nature of his relationship with the Veneerings.

7. **(C)** In the fourth paragraph, we learn that Twemlow is confused and that the source of his confusion and difficulty is "the insoluble question whether he was Veneering's oldest friend, or newest friend." This makes choice **(C)** the best answer as he struggles with how deep the friendship is. He is not concerned with details of a dinner party, so choices (A) and (B) are incorrect. He is not worried about people using him for his connections, so choice (D) is incorrect.

8. **(B)** As quoted in the explanation to question 7, choice **(B)** best shows Twemlow's concern over how deep his friendship with the Veneerings is. Choice (A) shows how the Veneerings use Twemlow at their dinner parties, but not what he is concerned about. Choice (C) describes the first time Twemlow met Mr. Veneering, but not what Twemlow is concerned about. Choice (D) shows who the two men spend time with, but again, does not illustrate Twemlow's concern.

9. **(D)** In the last paragraph, we see Twemlow trying to convince himself not to think any further about his relationship with the Veneerings. He believes that such ruminations are "enough to soften any man's brain." In other words, he does not find it to be helpful to think about it, yet he can't stop thinking about it. This best fits with choice **(D)**. Ruminations are thoughts; he is having unhelpful thoughts. Choices (A), (B), and (C) are incorrect as there is no evidence that Twemlow engages in any of these behaviors.

10. **(D)** Choice **(D)**, as quoted in the explanation to question 9, is the best evidence for the fact that Twemlow tends to engage in unhelpful ruminations. Choice (A) introduces the idea of Twemlow as a dinner table but does not give insight into his habits. Choice (B) shows one way the Veneerings used Twemlow, but again does not give insight into his habits. Choice (C) introduces the idea that Twemlow is confused but does not show the reader that he habitually spends time in unhelpful thinking.

Investing and Diversification

11. **(A)** In this essay, the author is giving very basic investment advice for a lifetime of investment. She explains when a person should start investing as well as how a portfolio may change over a lifetime. This indicates that she is speaking to the general public—anyone who would want to invest for retirement. This makes choice **(A)** the best option. She is not just speaking to people who are about to retire because it would be too late for them to use her advice. Therefore, choice (B) is wrong. She is also giving very basic advice, meaning she is likely not gearing the passage toward experienced money managers; therefore, choices (C) and (D) are wrong.

12. **(C)** In the context of the sentence, the author is talking about retirement. When people retire, they "cease" to work. Since retirement is when people leave their jobs to relax and pursue other projects, "cease" best means "stop." Choice **(C)** is the best option. Retirement does not mean to "increase," "perform," or "search for" work, making choices (A), (B), and (D) incorrect.

13. **(C)** The author here is qualifying her statement. She wants to enforce the idea that investment is a good idea for all people but that it can go wrong for people who do it poorly. She therefore gives some examples of situations in which investment can appear to have a negative outcome. This best fits with choice **(C)**; the author acknowledges that investments can go bad, but asserts that it is still the best retirement option. Choice (A) is incorrect as the author is not trying to caution people away from investing by talking about shortcomings. Choice (B) is incorrect as she is not discussing the difficulties associated with investing in specific areas, like stocks and bonds. Choice (D) is incorrect as the author makes it clear that there may be setbacks. Success is not inevitable.

14. **(B)** The first sentence of the second paragraph says that "the two basic keys to retiring comfortably are time and portfolio diversification." The author, therefore, would likely support an investment plan that included those two elements. Choice **(B)** best does this as it presents a relatively young person who has time and who is investing in a diverse group of stocks. Choices (A) and (C) are incorrect as those people are short on time and failing to diversify. Choice (D) is incorrect as that person has plenty of time but is withdrawing from the market and failing to invest.

15. **(A)** As we see in the explanation to question 14, the author believes that time and portfolio diversification are the most important keys to retirement planning. This is stated in the line selection in choice **(A)**. Choice (B) is incorrect as it explains what *not* to do (wait). Choice (C) is incorrect as it explains what to do as the investor ages, but not what the best strategy is for the rest of a person's life. Choice (D) warns against panicking, but that does not clarify what the best investment strategies would be.

16. **(C)** Choice **(C)** is the best option as these lines say that "people who treat the market like a get rich quick scheme . . . end up losing everything." The author is saying that the greed of wanting a quick path to riches leads to very negative outcomes. The other answer options do not address the issue of greedy investing.

17. **(B)** Within the parentheses in these lines, the author explains what mutual funds are and then what bonds are. She most likely does this to help readers unfamiliar with those particular investment options. This makes choice **(B)** the best answer option. She is clarifying certain terms, not justifying them, making choice (A) incorrect. She is explaining terms, not diversification, making choice (C) incorrect. She is not talking about delegating work, so choice (D) is incorrect.

18. **(C)** We can see in the second to last paragraph that the author says that "as investors become older . . . they should slowly move their money away from the volatility of the high-risk high-reward market and invest more and more in the low-risk low-reward options." Older investors should therefore be investing more in low-risk, conservative investments. This makes choice **(C)** correct. Choice (A) is incorrect as the author would say that diversification is always important. Choice (B) is incorrect as the author does not discuss stock allocations for older and younger investors. Choice (D) is incorrect as the author would not want anyone to maximize volatility (instability).

19. **(C)** In the table, we can see that the more stocks within a portfolio the lower the variance is. Variance is explained above the table as "an estimation of the risk of a portfolio, with a higher number indicating a greater risk." The author supports the idea of portfolio diversification, or the buying of multiple stocks. This aligns with the table, which shows that the more stocks that are owned, the lower the risk to the owner. The other options are not supported by the table.

20. **(A)** If we check the answers against the table, we can see the biggest drop in variance, and thus the biggest drop in risk, occurs as stocks owned go from one to two. This change cuts the variance nearly in half. The other choices still decrease the risk, but not by as much as choice **(A)**.

21. **(D)** As we can see in the table, the second stock bought has a huge effect on variance (risk). It nearly cuts the risk in half. However, at the bottom of the table when a portfolio goes from 100 stocks to 1,000 stocks, the variance barely changes—from 7.5 to 7.1. As the portfolio accumulates stocks, the addition of each new stock has less of an effect on the variance. This best supports choice **(D)**. Choice (A) is incorrect as the table does not indicate that adding stocks is the *only* way to decrease variance. Choice (B) is incorrect as the table only shows stocks—no generalizations can be made about bonds and cash. Choice (C) is incorrect as the table does not address portfolio value.

Bear Biology

22. **(A)** Throughout the passage, the author discusses the struggles humans face in their cardiovascular health and how bears' unique genetics help the bears avoid such struggles. The author also discusses how bear adaptations should be studied to help create medical advancements. This best fits with choice **(A)**. Choice (B) is incorrect as the author is not suggesting that humans change their lifestyles so that they eat fatty foods and sleep for months at a time. Choice (C) is incorrect as the author is not discussing natural remedies for humans, but rather a complex scientific study based on bear biology. Choice (D) is incorrect as the author thinks that medical researchers, not veterinarians, should study bears.

23. **(C)** As can be seen in the third paragraph, the author directly states that "bears have mutated genes that allow them to consume extremely fatty diets without affecting their cardiovascular health." This clearly means that the genetic makeup of the bear allows them to reduce their cholesterol. Choice **(C)** is therefore the best option. Choices (A), (B), and (D) are not as strongly supported by the passage as the reason bears can reduce their cholesterol.

24. **(C)** As is quoted in the answer explanation for question 23, the lines in choice **(C)** give the best evidence that it is the genetic makeup of the bears that allow them to reduce their cholesterol. Choice (A) is incorrect as it addresses human cholesterol removal, not bear cholesterol removal. Choice (B) is incorrect as it explains why bears' cholesterol intake is so high, but not why bears are so good at reducing it. Choice (D) is incorrect as it explains one of the benefits that could be gleaned from studying bears but does not explain how bears manage their cholesterol.

25. **(B)** Within the context of the sentence, the author says that "study of this gene could help unlock new heart disease treatments for humans." This context best fits with choice **(B)** as it is not discussing physically releasing something as choices (A), (C), and (D) imply. The best replacement word would be *discover*—studying the new gene could help discover new heart disease treatments.

26. **(D)** In the second paragraph, the author says that "about half of a polar bear's weight is fat and its blood cholesterol levels are high enough that they would cause serious cardiovascular disease in humans." Therefore, if a doctor mistook bear blood for human blood, he or she would likely be very concerned that the human has developed cardiovascular (heart) disease. This best aligns with choice **(D)**. Choice (A) is incorrect as the bear blood would not be free of cholesterol. Choice (B) is incorrect as infarcts are bad—a doctor would not be troubled if an infarct was unlikely. Choice (C) is incorrect as the passage link inactivity, not high cholesterol, to cardiac atrophy.

27. **(B)** As quoted in the explanation to question 26, these lines best show how a doctor would react if he or she mistook bear blood for human blood. The other answer options do not compare the two types of blood and can therefore not be used to infer how a doctor would react in this situation.

28. **(B)** The author says in this paragraph that "a bear's heart can stop beating for about 14 seconds at a time and then continue." This tells the reader that it is normal and not unhealthy for a bear's heart to stop for up to 14 seconds. Anything over 14 seconds, however, would be atypical and might very well cause issues for the bear. This makes choice **(B)** the best option. The other options would all be within the normal 14 second pauses that a bear's heart can make.

29. **(B)** This is the only time the author mentions pigs in the essay, which primarily discusses how scientists can improve human health by studying bears. It makes sense, then, that the author would assume that pig hearts are similar to human hearts and that if this treatment worked well on pig hearts that it would also work well on human hearts. This makes choice **(B)** the best answer. Choice (A) is incorrect as the author would likely think that studying human or bear hearts is more important. Choice (C) is incorrect as the author does not imply that this is not a significant result. Choice (D) is incorrect as he implies that this treatment could *decrease* the frequency of heart disease in other animals.

30. **(A)** As used in the context of the sentence, the author uses the word "impact" to talk about how hormones in hibernation can *influence* treatments in cardiovascular patients. This makes choice **(A)** the best option. The word "impact" is not being used in a physical sense; therefore, choices (B) and (C) are incorrect. The word "impact" is also not being used to mean ignore, making choice (D) incorrect.

31. **(D)** The issue that astronauts have, as described in the passage, is that they "suffer from cardiac atrophy as a response to immobility." The author explains that bears do not suffer from cardiac atrophy even after months of hibernation. The author therefore thinks that bears may be the key to solving cardiac atrophy in astronauts. If, however, bears have the same response to time in space that humans have, then this line of scientific inquiry would not be helpful. This makes choice **(D)** the best answer. Choice (A) is incorrect as this would be a good reason to further study bears and how they might help astronauts. Choice (B) is incorrect as the author is not a proponent of human hibernation. Choice (C) is incorrect as this does not relate to the study of bears to help astronauts.

Governments and Imprisonment

32. **(C)** The first sentence proclaims that when any government unjustly imprisons someone, then the only place for any just person is in prison. This is best described as a paradox (a statement that seems to contradict itself but may really be true). Thoreau goes on to explain this seemingly contradictory statement, making choice **(C)** the best option. Choice (A) is incorrect as Thoreau is not saying that incarceration (imprisonment) is important. Choice (B) is incorrect as Thoreau is not discussing moral governance, but rather governance that has become immoral. Choice (D) is incorrect as he does not say that prisons are overcrowded.

33. **(A)** Within this context, irresistible means "something that cannot be resisted," which best fits with choice **(A)**, unstoppable. Choices (B), (C), and (D) do not mean "something that cannot be resisted."

34. **(B)** Within this excerpt, Thoreau says that not paying taxes would *not* be violent and bloody, but paying them *is*. This is because paying taxes enables the State "to commit violence and shed innocent blood." He is saying that he believes that paying taxes helps to fund conflict, and, therefore, the taxpayers are responsible for that conflict. This best aligns with choice **(B)**. Choice (A) is incorrect as Thoreau is making a point about violence and injustice, not economic prosperity. Choices (C) and (D) are incorrect as he is advocating *not* paying taxes, not speaking about what should be done to those who don't pay taxes.

35. **(B)** In the final paragraph, Thoreau talks about a wounding of the conscience. He says that "through this wound a man's real manhood and immortality flow out, and he bleeds to an everlasting death." Thoreau believes, therefore, that a wounding of the conscience, or a moral wound, can cause death as surely as a physical wound. This supports choice **(B)** as the best answer. Choice (A) is incorrect as Thoreau does not think that physical bleeding is necessary for significant suffering. Choice (C) is incorrect as he is not talking about violence or non-violence in this paragraph. Choice (D) is incorrect as he is not trying to make any statement about those who draw the blood of others.

36. **(D)** The narrator in the second passage describes several different places where she was held or imprisoned. She describes the differences in part by saying "while at the city jail, we had to sleep on steel bunks. At the Stockade, however, we had bunks, and mattresses, but no bed linens." This comparison between the two places shows that they were indeed different or "inconsistent." There is no evidence that the holding cells were "artistically appreciative," so choice (A) is incorrect. The narrator describes terrible conditions, so they were not "humane" or "considerate" and choices (B) and (C) are incorrect.

37. **(C)** As quoted in the explanation to question 36, the lines in choice **(C)** best show that the different holding facilities were inconsistent. Choice (A) says that she was jailed but does not explain the differences in the facilities. Choices (B) and (D) describe one facility, but do not compare it to others.

38. **(A)** We are looking for a word that could replace "kept" in the context of "we kept our spirits up." The author is not talking about keeping something physical, so choices (B) and (C) are incorrect. The author is talking about keeping the spirits up, not getting rid of them, so choice (D) is incorrect. This leaves choice **(A)** as the best option. The prisoners "maintained" their spirits by singing.

39. **(C)** In the last paragraph, the narrator says that she lost sleep and ate slop. This leads the reader to the conclusion that when she was released, she would likely greatly appreciate a good bed and a good meal, making choice **(C)** the best option. There is no strong evidence that she missed having books and magazines, interaction opportunities, or composing songs more than she missed a comfortable bed and good food, making choices (A), (B), and (D) incorrect.

40. **(B)** The first passage sets up a moral and philosophical background to justify civil disobedience. The second passage describes the results of an act of civil disobedience. Therefore, the first is more philosophical while the second is more descriptive: Choice **(B)** is correct. Choice (A) is incorrect since neither author would say that the injustice is irreversible. Choice (C) is incorrect as it is Passage 2 that relies on firsthand experience. Choice (D) is incorrect as Thoreau would likely agree with the methods for Passage 2 as he advocates for just men going to jail to protest injustices.

41. **(A)** Thoreau says that "if the alternative is to keep all just men in prison, or give up war and slavery, the State will not hesitate which to choose." In other words, Thoreau is saying that the state would rather imprison all just men than to get rid of injustices. This is supported by the experience described in Passage 2 where the government would rather overcrowd holding cells with protestors than deal with the source of the protests. This makes choice **(A)** the best option. Choice (B) is incorrect as Thoreau is not describing protest deterrents in the first passage. Choice (C) is incorrect as Thoreau is not describing prison policies in the first passage. Choice (D) is incorrect as Thoreau is not talking about the importance of visitation in prison.

42. **(A)** Bernice Johnson concludes in her final paragraph that her horrible experience was worth it as "all the discomforts suffered were worth the cause for which we committed ourselves." Thoreau would agree that in the pursuit of justice discomforts such as jail stays are warranted. He says in the second paragraph that men are better able to combat injustice when they have experienced "a little in his own person." This makes choice **(A)** the best option. The other answer choices do not show how Thoreau would agree that being in jail could be a good thing for a cause.

Cellular Metabolism

43. **(A)** This passage gives a general overview of how a cell produces energy for different kinds of organisms. This best fits with choice **(A)**. The passage does briefly mention human respiration, but it is not the main purpose of the passage, therefore choice (B) is incorrect. The passage does not focus on history or on disease throughout, making choices (C) and (D) incorrect.

44. **(B)** In the third paragraph, the reader learns that "Cellular respiration produces eighteen times more energy units per glucose molecule consumed in glycolysis than the anerobic alternative, fermentation." This best supports choice **(B)**. Since cellular respiration produces more energy units per input, it can be said that cellular respiration is more efficient than the alternative: anaerobic fermentation. Choice (A) is incorrect as glycolysis is the process that comes before aerobic respiration or anaerobic fermentation and can therefore not be compared to aerobic respiration. Choice (C) is incorrect as it is directly contradicted by the passage. Choice (D) is incorrect as there is no indication in the passage as to the complexity of the organisms.

45. **(C)** As quoted in the answer explanation to the previous question, the lines provided in choice **(C)** best demonstrate that aerobic respiration is more efficient than anaerobic fermentation. Choices (A), (B), and (D) are incorrect as they do not compare the two methods of energy production.

46. **(B)** Throughout this paragraph, the author presents information to support his claim that fermentation is not solely limited to anaerobic organisms. In order to do this, he extensively explains the reasons why a human cell might use anaerobic fermentation. This best fits with choice **(B)**. Choice (A) is incorrect as it is respiration which is the *primary* process whereby humans obtain energy. Choice (C) is incorrect as the author says that vigorous exercise would increase the chance of fermentation taking place. Choice (D) is incorrect as the paragraph makes clear that when human muscles use fermentation it is *in addition* to respiration, not instead of it.

47. **(D)** In the context of the sentence, the author is talking about exercise so "strenuous" that the respiration isn't sufficient, and cells need to supplement with fermentation. This would be when cells are working the hardest, meaning a very *vigorous* workout. This makes choice **(D)** correct. Choices (A), (B), and (C) do not show hard work by the muscles.

48. **(B)** Readers learn in the passage that while the Warburg Effect is "an intriguing idea," it is "only one of the many theories scientists have proposed." This implies that it is possible that this idea is true, but it has not been proven, making choice **(B)** the best option. There is no clear link, making choice (A) incorrect, but such a link is not impossible, making choice (C) incorrect. This passage gives no indication that such an idea is outdated, making choice (D) incorrect.

49. **(D)** As quoted in the answer explanation to question 48, the uncertainty around the link is best shown in the lines given in choice **(D)**. The other answer options do not illustrate the possibility of this link.

50. **(A)** Within the context of the sentence, "trigger" is used to mean "cause them to activate." This best fits with choice **(A)**. Choice (B) is incorrect as "persuade" generally has a connotation of one party being reluctant, which is not the case here. Choices (C) and (D) are incorrect as there is no evidence that this process is harmful.

51. **(A)** In Figure 1, the cells with an asterisk are cancerous. The reader can learn this by reading the italicized paragraph above the figure. Every cancerous cell has a taller bar than the corresponding noncancerous cell. This shows the reader that cancerous cells have a higher average rate of change and makes choice **(A)** the best option. Choice (B) is the opposite of the relationship shown in Figure 1. Choice (C) is not supported by Figure 1 except in the lung cells. However, the question is asking about the figure as a whole, so choice (C) is incorrect. Choice (D) is incorrect as no cells on the table have a rate of change of zero.

52. **(B)** We can see in the table that the cancerous cells have a greater rate of glucose change. This is reinforced in the passage when the author says that "[cancer cells] take in more glucose and produce more lactate than normal cells." This is best explained in choice **(B)**. Choice (A) is the opposite of the facts given in the passage. Choice (C) is not addressed in the passage. Choice (D) is not an aspect of the Warburg Effect as explained in the passage.

Section 2: Writing and Language Test

1. **(D)** "Lucrative" suggests that marine welding would be a career that has a high salary. While the other options could be associated with money, they would not be logically applicable to this situation, in which the potential earnings from a career are described.

2. **(A)** Choice **(A)** sets up a logical comparison, with the "conditions" in the first part of the sentence compared to "those" in the second part of the sentence. Choices (B) and (D) would compare the conditions to people, which would be illogical. Choice (C) compares the conditions to "experiences," which also would not make sense.

3. **(B)** The sentence goes on to explain that a larger underwater project would require a bigger habitat than a smaller one. Choice **(B)** focuses on the size of the habitat and so would best set up the information that follows in the sentence. Choice (A) focuses on the time to build a habitat. Choice (C) focuses on the cost associated with building underwater welding projects. Choice (D) is not directly connected to the sentence's focus on habitat construction.

4. **(B)** "Additionally" is the most logical transition, since this paragraph provides another description of how the underwater welding process unfolds. The other transitions would not logically introduce a continuation of the examples.

5. **(C)** There is no need to break up the subject "advantage of using the dry hyperbaric method" and the verb "is." No commas are therefore needed.

6. **(B)** The transition "however" makes sense since the second part of the sentence provides a contrast with the first part, given that the first part focuses on an advantage and the second part on a disadvantage. Also, the use of "disadvantage" will be parallel to the use of "advantage" in the first part of the sentence. The other options do not have the proper transition and lack parallel structure.

7. **(A)** "In which" provides a connection between the broad notion of "wet welding" and the specific description of wet welding that follows. The other options use incorrect connecting words given the context.

8. **(B)** While the first part of the sentence is lengthy, it is still a dependent clause given that it begins with "Although." Therefore, a comma would be the appropriate punctuation to separate the dependent clause from the independent clause that follows. A colon, semicolon, and period would all require an independent clause beforehand.

9. **(A)** It would be most logical to elaborate on the advantage of the wet welding technique by explaining why it could be preferable to the habitat welding approach. Stating that the welder can move freely about the project accomplishes this goal. Choices (B) and (D) emphasize negative aspects of wet welding, and choice (C) is overly vague.

10. **(C)** The focus of the passage is on the career of underwater welding—this potential insertion would shift the focus to underwater pipeline design: It is not a relevant addition. It is not choice (D) because the information has not already been stated. It is not choices (A) or (B) because the sentence should not be added.

11. **(D)** Choice **(D)** concisely uses appropriate wording to describe the greater job growth outlook. The other options are overly wordy and do not use words that would be suitable to describe a greater job growth outlook.

12. **(C)** *Is* matches the present tense of other verbs in the surrounding context and matches the singular subject "music." Choices (A) and (B) are plural, and choice (D) is in the past tense.

13. **(A)** A comma after this phrase makes sense given that the phrase is one of several items in a list. Choice (B) provides no pause. Choice (C) incorrectly uses a semicolon to break up a list that is using commas to separate its items. Choice (D) uses a comma too early such that it breaks up the phrase.

14. **(B)** The other questions in the surrounding context ask big picture questions about the origins and fundamental nature of music. Choice **(B)** fits this general profile. Choice (A) focuses too specifically on a comparison of musical instruments. Choice (C) focuses on musical ability rather than music in general. And choice (D) shifts to musical education, instead of keeping with the broader emphasis of the paragraph.

15. **(B)** Choice **(B)** matches the present tense of the surrounding verbs and correctly uses the singular "is" to match up with asking about a singular situation. Choice (A) uses a plural verb, and choices (C) and (D) are in the past tense.

16. **(A)** "While" is the only option that gives a contrast between the first part of the sentence that mentions the nice alignment or contrast of some musical waves and the second part of the sentence that mentions waves that do not align or contrast in a regular fashion. Choices (B) and (C) show a cause-and-effect relationship, and choice (D) would remove an important transition.

17. **(D)** The two sentences are making two general points about matching and nicely contrasting waves—they make music both mathematically and aesthetically appealing. Choice **(D)** most concisely maintains this overall message. Choice (A) uses awkward punctuation, choice (B) is overly wordy, and choice (C) has awkward phrasing with "matching and in contrast" making the description less clear.

18. **(C)** The first sentence of the paragraph states that heavy beats present a "puzzle." It is therefore most sensible for the scientists to "hypothesize" about why humans like them. The other options all convey more certainty than would be warranted given the preceding sentence.

19. **(D)** "Loved" is the appropriate tense of the word "love" to describe the positive attitude that people have toward beats. "Loved" acts as an adjective in this context. "Love" and "will love" use verbs, and "loving" can be used as an adjective to describe how someone *gives* love, but not that something is itself appreciated.

20. **(C)** Choice **(C)** appropriately uses dashes to set aside the parenthetical phrase that clarifies what the two things are. Choice (A) has an unnecessary comma after the parentheses—the parentheses would be sufficient by themselves to set this phrase off to the side. Choice (B) does not have a comma before the parenthetical phrase, and choice (D) uses inconsistent punctuation around the parenthetical phrase.

21. **(A)** "Our memories" uses parallel phrasing to match the earlier listed items of "our lives" and "our history." The other options do not maintain this parallel phrasing.

22. **(D)** The remainder of the paragraph focuses on how humanity and music are inextricably linked to one another. Choice **(D)** would transition from the introductory sentence of the paragraph by acknowledging that we may not know where music originated. It then connects to the next part of the paragraph by stating that music is a part of us now. Choices (A) and (C) are overly negative about music given the context. Choice (B) is overly neutral.

23. **(C)** "Building" is the most appropriate word in this context to describe the process of accumulating wealth. The other words are all more associated with the physical construction of items and are not used to describe the wealth creation process.

24. **(A)** "While" correctly shows a contrast between the first part of the sentence, which states that few people can pay cash to directly purchase a home, and the second part of the sentence, which states that a mortgage is a viable way for many people to obtain a home. The other options do not show a contrast.

25. **(B)** "Savvy" is sufficient to express the economic smarts that home buyers should have. Choices (A) and (C) are repetitive, and "gullible" conveys the opposite of the needed meaning.

26. **(D)** "One" is consistent with the usage of "one" in sentences 1 and 3 of this paragraph. The other options are inconsistent with this wording.

27. **(B)** This sentence is most logically placed after sentence 3 because it clarifies why it takes longer to build up home equity with a 30-year mortgage than it does with a 15-year mortgage, helping to clarify the broad statement made in sentence 3. The other potential placements would not allow sentence 3 to be clarified.

28. **(B)** "Which" is used to set aside a nonessential description, while "that" is used at the beginning of an essential description. In this case, the clarification about the constancy of interest rates could be removed from the sentence and the sentence would still be logical. Therefore, surrounding the description of the fixed interest rates with commas make sense. It is not choice (A) because this is a nonessential description, and commas typically do not precede the word "that". It is not choice (C) because there is no pause before "which." It is not choice (D) because there is not a complete sentence after the semicolon.

29. **(C)** The *y*-axis on the graph ranges from a low of 2.5 percent to a high of 5.0 percent, so it is most logical to say that over this span of time, the rates on a 30-year mortgage will range between 2.5% and 5%. The other options do not properly represent the range of values portrayed in the graph.

30. **(D)** Since no interest rate in excess of 5% is portrayed in the graph, it makes sense that a mortgage rate of over 5% would be relatively high based on recent history. The other options are all too low based on the information in the graph.

31. **(A)** The two preceding paragraphs start with "First" and "Second," so it makes sense to maintain this parallel structure with the beginning of this paragraph. Choice **(A)** is the only option that does so. The other options introduce transitional words that do not match this parallel structure.

32. **(D)** A brief pause after the introductory word "Finally" is needed, and a comma provides just such a pause. Choices (A) and (C) do not have a pause after the introductory word, and choice (B) lacks a complete sentence before the colon.

33. **(A)** Choice **(A)** precisely clarifies the subject so that the reader fully understands what it is that will enable homebuyers to make sound financial decisions. Choices (B) and (C) are too vague, and choice (D) is too wordy.

34. **(B)** Choice **(B)** effectively shows a contrast with the previous sentence by clarifying that the most successful wildcats in the world are not big cats at all. This sentence also transitions to the following sentence by emphasizing the size of the cats. Choice (A) introduces an irrelevant detail about a different animal. Choice (C) is overly vague and disconnected from the current discussion. Choice (D) would connect to the previous sentence but not connect to the sentence that follows.

35. **(A)** Without this insertion, the sentence would simply declare that servals are successful as hunters without providing any details in support of this claim. Having this insertion would justify the claim about the success of servals as hunters. It is not choice (B) because it does not address a concern that readers may have about servals. It is not choices (C) or (D) because the insertion is in fact warranted.

36. **(C)** "Makes it" is most appropriate since the sentence is making the declaration that it is more difficult for the servals to be spotted. Also, "makes" is consistent with the singular "having a lighter colored coat." Choices (A) and (D) do not match up numerically with the subject, and choice (B) would not work in terms of making a declaration.

37. **(D)** Camouflage would prevent potential prey from spotting the approaching servals since the prey would not be able to detect the servals. "Pictured" and "envision" involve more hypothetical visualization, and "ignore" is the opposite of the intended meaning.

38. **(B)** An "adaptation" would mean a change that has gradually evolved for the serval to best survive; this would be the most logical wording at this point. Choices (A) and (D) are not generally accepted words, and choice (C) would be used to indicate the choice to care for a child or take up some other idea. Since the focus is on the survival of the serval rather than choices the serval might make, "adoption" does not make sense.

39. **(C)** No punctuation is needed to break up the phrase—any pause within the phrase would interrupt the full meaning that is expressing what the servals are doing. Choice (A) is too choppy, and choices (B) and (D) insert pauses at awkward points.

40. **(A)** Choice (A) uses the apostrophe to show that the singular *serval* possesses its diet. *Serval* must be singular since the word "a" precedes it. Choice (B) does not show possession, and choices (C) and (D) inappropriately use plural apostrophes on *servals'* and *diets'* respectively.

41. **(C)** No transitional word is needed in this situation, since the part of the sentence that follows the underlined portion is simply elaborating on how the servals will spring into action. The other options provide unnecessary transitional words.

42. **(D)** Choice **(D)** appropriately uses "they" as a subject and "their" to show possession. It is not choices (A) or (C) because "there" is used to indicate a location, not possession. It is not choice (B) because "they're" is a contraction that means "they are."

43. **(A)** By virtue of being called "housecats," these animals are already noted as being in the homes of people: This detail does not need to be inserted. It is not choice (B) because it is not contradictory, just unnecessarily repetitive and irrelevant. And it is not choices (C) or (D) because the phrase should not be included.

44. **(C)** The previous sentence focuses on how birds have been negatively affected by housecats, so choice **(C)** would logically provide a transition from the previous sentence. Choice **(C)** also effectively sets up the rest of the sentence, since it clarifies what readers can do to be of the most help to birds. It is not choice (A) because the surrounding sentences are not focused on aquatic animals. It is not choice (B) because this statement is rather vague. And it is not choice (D) because there is no mention of dogs in the surrounding context.

Section 3: Math Test (No Calculator)

1. **(A)**

$$5(x+1)(x-1) \rightarrow$$
$$5(x^2+x-x-1) \rightarrow$$
$$5(x^2-1) \rightarrow$$
$$5x^2-5$$

2. **(D)** Since $y = mx + b$ is the slope-intercept form of a line, the b represents the y-intercept. The line intercepts the y-axis at 4, so the value of b is 4.

3. **(C)** Solve for the value of $a + b$ as a whole:

$$\frac{a+b}{5} = 6 \rightarrow$$
$$a+b = 5 \times 6 \rightarrow$$
$$a+b = 30$$

4. **(A)** Since the equation passes through the origin, which has coordinates of (0, 0), the y-intercept of the line is 0. The slope of the line can be found by taking the change in y divided by the change in x for the two known points, (0, 0) and (6, 4):

$$slope = \frac{y_2 - y_1}{x_2 - x_1} = \frac{4 - 0}{6 - 0} = \frac{4}{6} = \frac{2}{3}$$

Now, put the equation into slope-intercept form for a line, $y = mx + b$: $y = \frac{2}{3}x$

5. **(B)** Take the square root of all the components under the square root sign:

$$\sqrt{64x^4} = \sqrt{(8 \times 8)(x^2 \times x^2)} = 8x^2$$

6. **(D)** Use elimination to solve for x, since the y terms can be easily cancelled:

$$\begin{aligned} \tfrac{2}{3}x - y &= 4 \\ + \quad \tfrac{1}{3}x + y &= 3 \\ \hline x + 0 &= 7 \end{aligned}$$

So, $x = 7$.

7. **(C)** After initially filling the tank, the driver will have a total of 20 gallons of gas. Since the car averages 30 miles per gallon of gas, each mile she drives will require $\frac{1}{30}$ of a gallon of gas. So, put this in the form of an equation to solve for G, the number of gallons in her gas tank after she has been driving for m miles:

$$G = 20 - \frac{m}{30}$$

8. **(A)** The sum of x and y can be expressed as $x + y$. Fortunately, $x + y$ is already expressed as a whole unit throughout the equation. So, just solve for $x + y$ as though you were solving for a whole variable.

$$(x + y)^2 = 2(x + y) - 1 \rightarrow$$
$$(x + y)^2 - 2(x + y) + 1 = 0$$
$$((x + y) - 1)((x + y) - 1) = 0$$

Thus, $x + y$ will equal 1 so that the value of the entire equation will equal zero.

9. **(B)** The largest angle in the triangle is 90 degrees. The median angle will be complementary to the smallest angle, since the median and smallest angles will add up to 90 degrees. Recall the rule that for two complementary angles, the sine of the first angle will equal the cosine of the second, and vice versa. So, the sine of the median angle will be the same as the cosine of the smallest angle, making the sine of the median angle equal to $\frac{1}{4}$.

10. **(A)** When Esteban purchases only comic books with his \$60, he can purchase 30 of them (this is the y-intercept of the line, when the x value is 0). Therefore, the price per comic book is $\frac{60}{30} = 2$ dollars. When he purchases only magazines, he can purchase 20 of them (this is the x-intercept of the line, when the y value is 0). Therefore, the price per magazine is $\frac{60}{20} = 3$ dollars. Find the difference in price between the two by subtracting 2 from 3: $3 - 2 = 1$. So, the price difference per comic book and per magazine is 1 dollar.

11. **(B)** When you divide a number by zero, you have an undefined result. Thus, when $x = 0$, the equation will be undefined since you would be dividing the constant a by 0.

12. **(A)** Get the least common denominator for the fractions on the bottom, and then simplify:

$$\frac{a}{\left(\frac{2}{2a}\right)+\left(\frac{ab}{2a}\right)} \rightarrow \frac{a}{\left(\frac{2+ab}{2a}\right)} \rightarrow \frac{a(2a)}{(2+ab)} \rightarrow \frac{2a^2}{2+ab}$$

13. **(D)** Since the lines AB and CD are parallel, the angles that have the x terms are equal to one another because they are corresponding angles. So, solve for x by setting the values for these angles equal to one another:

$$6x - 15 = 5x + 5 \rightarrow$$

$$6x = 5x + 20 \rightarrow$$

$$x = 20$$

14. **(D)** You could fairly easily solve this by plugging the values 1.5, 2, and 6 into the original equation to see that just 2 and 6 work. Algebraically, you can simplify and solve like this:

$$x = \sqrt{8x - 12} \rightarrow$$

$$x^2 = 8x - 12 \rightarrow$$

$$x^2 - 8x + 12 = 0 \rightarrow$$

$$(x-2)(x-6) = 0$$

So, 2 and 6 work for this. Check for extraneous solutions just to be sure, and you will find that both 2 and 6 still are fine.

15. **(B)** Since the graph of $y = -x^2 + 3$ is a parabola with a vertex at $(0, 3)$, the graph of its reflection has its vertex at $(0, -3)$ and has an equation $y = x^2 - 3$, as shown in the figure below:

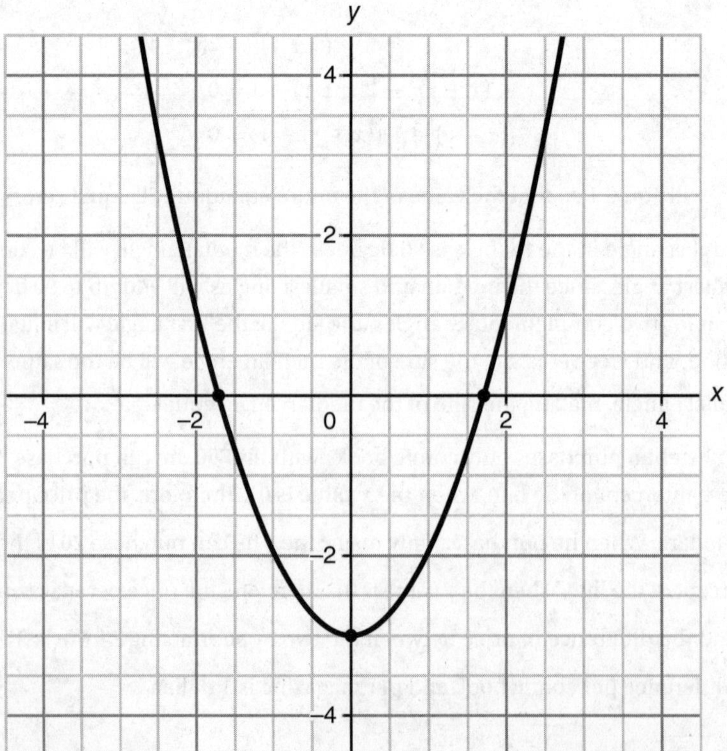

16. **4** Plug 5 in for x into the expression to solve for the value of the expression:

$$\frac{2x}{5} + \frac{4x}{10} \rightarrow$$

$$\frac{2(5)}{5} + \frac{4(5)}{10} \rightarrow$$

$$\frac{10}{5} + \frac{20}{10} \rightarrow$$

$$2 + 2 = 4$$

17. $\mathbf{\frac{1}{3}}$ **or .333** Use substitution to solve for y. Since $y = \frac{1}{2}x$, $x = 2y$. Plug $2y$ in for x into the first equation:

$$3 = \frac{3}{2}(4x - 2y) \rightarrow$$

$$3 = \frac{3}{2}(4(2y) - 2y) \rightarrow$$

$$3 = \frac{3}{2}(8y - 2y) \rightarrow$$

$$3 = \frac{3}{2}(6y) \rightarrow$$

$$3 = 9y \rightarrow$$

$$\frac{3}{9} = \frac{1}{3} = y$$

18. **3** The volume formula for a right rectangular prism is $L \times W \times H = V$. Since we already know the volume of the prism and the product of the length and width, we can set up a formula like this to solve for the prism's height:

$$L \times W \times H = V \rightarrow$$

$$30 \times H = 90 \rightarrow$$

$$H = \frac{90}{30} = 3$$

So, the height of the prism is 3 inches.

19. **2** For the equation to have infinitely many solutions, the expressions on both sides of the equation should be equivalent. Simplify the equation to see what value of k would be needed:

$$\frac{2x + 8}{k} = x + 4 \rightarrow$$

$$2\frac{x + 4}{k} = x + 4 \rightarrow$$

$$\frac{2}{k} = 1 \rightarrow$$

$$k = 2$$

20. **313** Simplify the expression to get it in the form $ka^2 - jb^2$:

$$(12a - 13b)(12a + 13b) \rightarrow$$

$$144a^2 + 156ab - 156ab - 169b^2 \rightarrow$$

$$144a^2 - 169b^2$$

So, the value of k is 144 and j is 169. Add them together to find the sum of k and j:

$$144 + 169 = 313$$

Section 4: Math Test (Calculator)

1. **(A)** Put the equation into slope-intercept form, $y = mx + b$, to solve for the value of the y-intercept, b:

$$y + 5 = 7x \rightarrow$$

$$y = 7x - 5$$

So, the value of the y-intercept is -5.

2. **(C)** Since there are 20 students, find the number of the servings by the 10th and 11th students to see the median of the set. The values are already in order, so you can see that the 10th and 11th terms are both 6. Therefore, the median of the set is 6.

3. **(B)**

$$\frac{x^2 - 81}{x + 9} \rightarrow$$

$$\frac{(x + 9)(x - 9)}{x + 9} \rightarrow$$

$$\frac{\cancel{(x + 9)}(x - 9)}{\cancel{x + 9}} \rightarrow$$

$$x - 9$$

4. **(C)** The solutions are all written in slope-intercept form and they all have different y-intercepts. So, identify the y-intercept—it is at 3. The only option that has 3 as its y-intercept is $y = -\frac{1}{3}x + 3$.

5. **(D)** First, subtract the \$5 booking fee from the total amount the customer paid, \$27.50:

$$27.50 - 5 = 22.50$$

Then, since each mile driven results in a \$0.75 charge, divide \$22.50 by \$0.75 to find how many miles the delivery driver drove:

$$\frac{22.50}{0.75} = 30$$

Thus, the driver drove a total of 30 miles from the pickup point to the customer's delivery spot.

6. **(A)** You can label the numerical values for the grades that Jeremy and Ann have:

	Math	English	History	Science	Art
Jeremy	B = 3	A = 4	C = 2	F = 0	B = 3
Ann	A = 4	?	D = 1	B = 3	D = 1

For Jeremy and Ann to have the same GPA, the sum of the numbers that correspond to their grades must be equivalent. Jeremy's sum is $3 + 4 + 2 + 0 + 3 = 12$. Ann's sum without the English grade is $4 + 1 + 3 + 1 = 9$. So, Ann will need 3 more points to have the same GPA as Jeremy. 3 points corresponds to a letter grade of B.

7. **(D)** The range, which is the difference between the least and greatest terms, would be 12 since $20 - 8 = 12$. The mode is the most frequent, and it would be 16 hours. The median is the middle term, which would also be 16 hours. And the mean would be the average, and it would be approximately 14.5. Rather than doing a tedious calculation to find the mean, you can estimate that it will be greater than 12 since the majority of the terms are 16 or greater. So, the range will be the least value.

8. **(B)** Plug the second inequality $x \leq -y - 2$ in to $y + 10 \leq 3x$ and simplify:

$$y + 10 \leq 3x \rightarrow$$
$$y + 10 \leq 3(-3y - 2) \rightarrow$$
$$y + 10 \leq -3y - 6 \rightarrow$$
$$4y + 10 \leq -6 \rightarrow$$
$$4y \leq -16 \rightarrow$$
$$y \leq -4$$

So, the largest possible value for y is found when $y = -4$.

9. **(B)** Use the first set of values to find the value of U. Plug in 10 for x, 400 for $C(x)$, and 100 for F, then solve for U:

$$C(x) = F + Ux \rightarrow$$
$$400 = 100 + U(10) \rightarrow$$
$$300 = U(10)$$
$$30 = U$$

Since the values of U and F are constant, use the function $C(x) = 100 + 30x$ to find the total cost when 12 units are sold:

$$C(x) = 100 + 30x \rightarrow$$
$$C(x) = 100 + 30(12) \rightarrow$$
$$C(x) = 100 + 360 = 460$$

So, the total cost for 12 units is $460.

10. **(B)** Use the density formula $Density = \frac{Mass}{Volume}$, plugging in 2 kilograms for the mass and 8 liters for the volume:

$$Density = \frac{Mass}{Volume} \rightarrow$$
$$Density = \frac{2}{8} = \frac{1}{4}$$

11. **(A)** Since mass is in the numerator and volume is in the denominator, if the mass increases while the volume remains the same, the density will increase. This can be seen by plugging in sample values. Suppose that the mass increases from 1 kg to 5 kg, while the volume remains at 1 liter. The density would increase from 1 kg/L to 5 kg/L. So, the relationship described in choice **(A)** is correct.

12. **(C)** Jie can spend no more than $30 on snacks at a movie. Each of the p boxes of popcorn costs $5, so the cost from the boxes of popcorn is $5p$. Each of the d drinks costs $2, so the costs from the drinks would be $2d$. The total costs from both the popcorn and drinks must be less than or equal to $30, so the inequality $5p + 2d \leq 30$ will correctly portray this situation.

13. **(B)** Since the equations are all in slope-intercept form and all have the *y*-intercept of zero, use the slope formula to find the slope of the line: $slope = \frac{y_2 - y_1}{x_2 - x_1}$.
Pick a couple of easily visible points to plug in to the equation: (0, 0), (5, 1). Now, plug these points into the slope formula to find the line's slope:

$$slope = \frac{y_2 - y_1}{x_2 - x_1} \rightarrow$$

$$slope = \frac{1 - 0}{5 - 0} = \frac{1}{5} = 0.2$$

The only option that has 0.2 for its slope is choice **(B)**: $y = 0.2x$.

14. **(A)** Use the quadratic formula, $x = \frac{-b \pm \sqrt{b^2 - 4ac}}{2a}$, to approach this. If the value of $b^2 - 4ac = 0$, there will be just one solution for *x*. Since the equation is already in quadratic form, the value of $a = 2$, $b = 1$, and $c = k$. Plug these values in to $b^2 - 4ac = 0$:

$$b^2 - 4ac = 0 \rightarrow$$

$$1^2 - 4(2)(k) = 0 \rightarrow$$

$$1 - 8k = 0 \rightarrow$$

$$1 = 8k \rightarrow$$

$$k = \frac{1}{8}$$

15. **(D)** The cost function $C = 12{,}000 + x$ shows the relationship between the number of sandwiches sold, *x*, and the total cost, *C*, for the truck. No matter how many sandwiches are sold, the truck will have expenses of $12,000 based on this equation. So, the $12,000 will represent the fixed cost of operating the sandwich truck.

16. **(C)** For the truck to break even, its costs must equal its revenue. So, set the revenue equation equal to the cost equation and solve for *x*:

$$5x = 12{,}000 + x \rightarrow$$

$$4x = 12{,}000 \rightarrow$$

$$x = \frac{12{,}000}{4} = 3{,}000$$

17. **(A)** Based on the revenue equation, $R = 5x$, the amount generated for each sandwich sold is $5. If the truck raises the price to $6, the price per sandwich would increase by $1. Find the percent change formula: $\frac{\text{New} - \text{Original}}{\text{Original}} \times 100 = \text{Percent Change}$.

$$\frac{6 - 5}{5} \times 100 = 0.2 \times 100 = 20\%$$

18. **(B)** Since $\frac{1}{3}$ of the route was uphill, Alani rode $\frac{1}{3} \times 120 = 40$ miles uphill. She would then ride $120 - 40 = 80$ miles downhill. Since her speed going downhill was an average of 20 miles per hour, find out how long she spent on the downhill portion of the journey by using the formula Distance = Rate × Time. Use 80 miles as the distance and 20 mph as the rate:

$$\text{Distance} = \text{Rate} \times \text{Time} \rightarrow$$

$$80 = 20 \times T \rightarrow$$

$$\frac{80}{20} = T \rightarrow$$

$$T = 4$$

Since Alani spent 4 hours going downhill, she would have to spend $8 - 4 = 4$ hours going uphill. Find the average uphill speed by dividing the distance she went uphill, 40 miles, by the amount of time she spent on the uphill portion of the journey, 4 hours:

$$\frac{40 \text{ miles}}{4 \text{ hours}} = 10 \text{ mph}$$

19. **(D)** Take the coefficients of the expression and use synthetic division to solve:

$$\begin{array}{r|rrr} 2 & 4 & -7 & 8 \\ & & 8 & 2 \\ \hline & 4 & 1 & 10 \end{array}$$

So, the result will be $4x + 1 + \frac{10}{x-2}$, and $\frac{10}{x-2}$ will be the remainder.

20. **(C)** The sample size of the survey is limited to just those filmgoers who liked the prequel to a particular movie sequel. This sample is not representative of the general public or of movie watchers in general—it only represents those filmgoers who liked a certain movie. So, the most reasonable conclusion to be drawn from this information is that those who like this particular movie's prequel are likely to like the movie's sequel.

21. **(A)** 1 acre equals 43,560 square feet, so since x represents the number of acres and y represents the number of square feet, the equation $y = 43{,}560x$ will correctly express the relationship between x and y.

22. **(C)** Since 1 hectare is equal to 10,000 square meters, set up a proportion to solve for the number of square meters that 0.5 hectares would be:

$$\frac{\text{Square Meters}}{\text{Hectares}} = \frac{x}{0.5} = \frac{10{,}000}{1} \rightarrow$$

$$x = 10{,}000 \times 0.5 = 5{,}000$$

23. **(A)** Since 1 meter is equal to 3.281 feet, 1 square meter would be equal to $3.281^2 \approx 10.76$ square feet.

Now, solve for the number of square meters in 1 acre:

$$\frac{43{,}560 \text{ square feet}}{1 \text{ acre}} \times \frac{1 \text{ square meter}}{10.76 \text{ square feet}} \rightarrow$$

$$\frac{43{,}560 \cancel{\text{square feet}}}{1 \text{ acre}} \times \frac{1 \text{ square meter}}{10.76 \cancel{\text{square feet}}} \rightarrow$$

$$\frac{43{,}560}{10.76} \approx 4{,}048.3 \ \frac{\text{square meters}}{\text{acre}}$$

Since there are 10,000 square meters in 1 hectare, use unit conversion to find the number of acres in 1 hectare:

$$4048.3 \text{ square meters} \times \frac{1 \text{ hectare}}{10{,}000 \text{ square meters}} \rightarrow$$

$$4048.3 \text{ \sout{square meters}} \times \frac{1 \text{ hectare}}{10{,}000 \text{ \sout{square meters}}} \rightarrow$$

$$\approx 0.404 \text{ hectares}$$

24. **(B)** Set up a proportion to solve for the number of residents, x, who voted no. There are 360 degrees total in a circle, so make the proportion have degrees on one side and residents on the other:

$$\frac{45}{360} = \frac{x}{800} \rightarrow$$

$$x = \frac{45 \times 800}{360} = 100$$

So, there are 100 residents who voted no on the levy.

25. **(C)** According to the table, 36% of the revenue comes from payroll tax. So, find 36% of 3 trillion dollars:

$$0.36 \times 3 = 1.08 \text{ trillion dollars}$$

26. **(D)** At the beginning of the five-year time period, the amount of money from customs duties would be 2% of 3 trillion:

$$0.02 \times 3 = 0.06 \text{ trillion}$$

At the end of the time period, the amount of money from customs duties would be 2% of 4 trillion:

$$0.02 \times 4 = 0.08 \text{ trillion}$$

The amount of money has increased by $0.08 - 0.06 = 0.02$ trillion. The answers all present the increase in billions of dollars. Since there are 1,000 billions in 1 trillion, multiply 0.02 trillion by 1,000 to find how many billions it is:

$$0.02 \times 1{,}000 = 20 \text{ billion}$$

27. **(A)** While you could solve for the length of $\overline{AB}$ by using the Pythagorean theorem, it will be easier if you recognize that this triangle represents a Pythagorean triple: 7, 24, and 25. With the hypotenuse at 25, the cosine of $\angle ABC$ will be:

$$\cos\theta = \frac{\text{Adjacent}}{\text{Hypotenuse}} = \frac{7}{25}$$

28. **(D)** The balloons both start at 200 feet in altitude. If one balloon increases its height by 30%, its new height will be $200 \times 1.3 = 260$ feet. If the other balloon decreases its height by 15%, its new height will be $200(1 - 0.15) = 200(.85) = 170$ feet. The different in height between the two balloons will then be $260 - 170 = 90$ feet.

29. **(A)** When the number of days $D = 0$, the value for $C(D)$ is going to be 500 since $500(1.1)^0 = 500 \times 1 = 500$. At the beginning of the experiment, zero days have gone by. So, the number 500 represents the number of bacterial colonies at the beginning of the experiment.

30. **(C)** There are 24 hours in one day, so H hours would represent $\frac{H}{24}$ of a day. Visualize this relationship by using a concrete number. If there were 12 hours, they would represent half of a day since $\frac{12}{24} = \frac{1}{2}$. Plug $\frac{H}{24}$ in for D to the equation to get the number of bacterial colonies after H hours had passed: $C(H) = 500(1.1)^{\left(\frac{H}{24}\right)}$.

31. **2** There are 30 adults, so the median will be the average of the 15th and 16th terms when the terms are placed in order from least to greatest. There are 6 adults with 0 siblings, 8 adults with 1 sibling, and 7 adults with 2 siblings. So, the 15th and 16th terms will both be 2, making 2 the correct answer for the median of the set.

32. **3**

$$x^{-3b} = \frac{1}{x^a} \rightarrow$$

$$\frac{1}{x^{3b}} = \frac{1}{x^a} \rightarrow$$

$$3b = a \rightarrow$$

$$3 = \frac{a}{b}$$

33. **3.24** Since there are approximately 1.61 km in 1 mile, in 1 square mile there would be approximately $1.61 \times 1.61 \approx 2.592$ square kilometers. In a rectangle that is 2.5 miles long and 0.5 miles wide, the area would be $2.5 \times 0.5 = 1.25$ square miles. Now, multiply 1.25 square miles by 2.592 to find the number of square kilometers in the park: $1.25 \times 2.592 = 3.24$ square kilometers, when rounded to the nearest hundredth of a square kilometer.

34. **30** If the gasoline tank has a capacity of 15 gallons and it already has 5 gallons of gas in it,to completely fill the tank, you would need $15 - 5 = 10$ gallons of gasoline. Since each gallon of gas costs $3, multiply the 10 gallons by $3 per gallon to get the total cost to fill the tank:

$$10 \times 3 = 30 \text{ dollars}$$

35. **50** Since the total number of students who prefer the waterpark is 80, and the number of male students is 30, subtract 30 from 80 to find the missing number X: $80 - 30 = 50$.

36. **60** There are 200 total seniors, 120 of whom want to go to the zoo. Find the percent of 200 that 120 represents:

$$\frac{120}{200} \times 100 = 60\%$$

37. **22.5** Since there are 360 degrees in a circle, and since the circumference corresponds to the entire distance around the circle, set up a proportion with degrees on one side and the length on the other, using C to represent the circumference:

$$\frac{80}{360} = \frac{5}{C} \rightarrow$$

$$C \times \frac{80}{360} = 5 \rightarrow$$

$$C = \frac{360 \times 5}{80} = 22.5$$

So, the circumference of the circle is 22.5 inches.

38. **1** The function has zeros at x values of -3 and 5 based on the equation. Also, the function has a negative coefficient, which means the direction of the function is downward. So, the maximum of the function will be found at an x value that is halfway between -3 and 5: $x = 1$. You can see this in the graph of the function below:

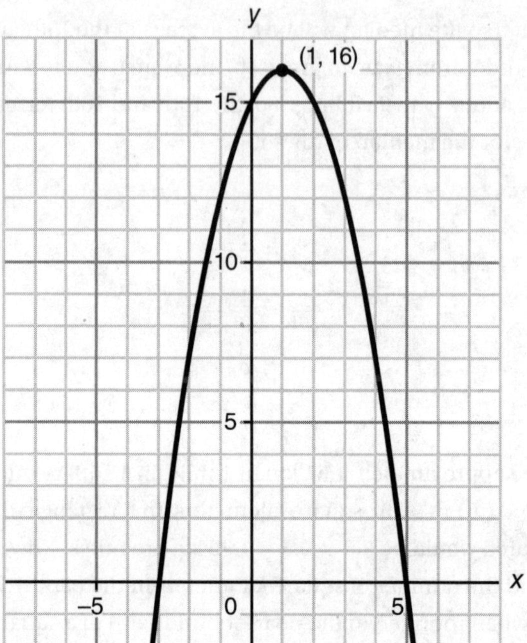

Appendix

SAT Vocabulary Index

50 Words Important to SAT Test Questions

Review these words if you find yourself having difficulty fully understanding what the SAT questions are asking.

Abstract

When something is *abstract* it doesn't exist in solid form. Ideas are *abstract.* This term often refers to theories.

Question: Which of the following best describes the *abstract* idea that the author is presenting throughout the second half of the passage?

Question explanation: In this question, you are being asked to sum up a non-concrete idea that the author is explaining in the latter part of the passage.

Accurate

Accurate just means to be correct or exact. An Olympic basketball player is likely *accurate* with her free throws, as in she makes them a majority of the time. She must be very exact.

Question: Which of the following options most *accurately* describes the author's purpose in the fifth paragraph?

Question explanation: You are being asked for the most exact and precise summation, not of the paragraph itself, but of the author's purpose within the paragraph.

Analogy

An *analogy* compares two things to one another without the words *like* or *as.*

Question: Which answer option best explains the *analogy* that the author introduces previously in this sentence?

Question explanation: If the sentence previously said, "Her face was a deep pool of emotion," the question is looking for the answer that best clarifies how a person's face can be a pool.

Anticipate

To *anticipate* something is to see it coming in advance. If you watch a movie in which the main character is crying while driving at night in the rain, you might *anticipate* that she will soon be in a car accident.

Question: As the author discusses the research that is to be conducted, what conclusion does he seem to *anticipate*?

Question explanation: This question is asking what the author thinks will happen when the research is conducted.

Appropriate

When something is *appropriate*, it is proper for the given situation. A black outfit is *appropriate* at a funeral, but not at a breezy summer picnic.

Question: Which of the following answers *appropriately* summarizes the author's key point in the second paragraph?

Question explanation: This question is asking which answer is the best or most proper summary of the key point. Make sure that your answer sums up the main idea and doesn't instead give the secondary or tertiary ideas presented.

Assumption/Assume

When you *assume* to know something, you are drawing conclusions based on less than suitable proof.

Question: What *assumptions* are made in the second paragraph as the author discusses the mating habits of flightless birds?

Question explanation: This question is asking you to understand what the author is taking for granted about the mating habits of flightless birds. He may not have evidence for something that he is *assuming* and basing his conclusion upon.

Attitude

The *attitude* of a passage may also be described as its tone or feeling. It is an emotion or style of the author. It is a way of thinking that is reflected in the words the author uses to convey her point. Her *attitude* may be calm, angry, upset, happy, content, or any number of others.

Question: What *tone* does the author establish through his use of words like "vengeful" and "merciless"?

Question explanation: This question wants you to examine the word choice of the author and choose what emotion or tone the author is conveying through those words. In this case, those words show anger and aggression.

Attribute

Attribute as a verb means to give credit or to show that something causes something else. You may *attribute* good grades to hard work or to good luck.

Question: The passage's writer *attributes* the change in business practices in 20th-century America to what phenomenon as discussed in the passage?

Question explanation: This question is asking for what the author thinks the cause of the phenomenon is.

Characterize

Characterizing is to tell or show the reader the traits or features of a person or thing. People and things can be *characterized* through dialogue or description.

Question: How does the author *characterize* the problem that Maria and Will are facing in the fifth paragraph?

Question explanation: This question is asking you to pick the answer that best describes the problem in light of how the author presents it in the fifth paragraph.

Claim

A *claim* is a statement of something believed by the author or speaker to be true, often without evidence. In scientific writing, the *claim* is made prior to evidence being used to support the claim.

Question: What *claim* is being supported by the evidence in lines 23–28?

Question explanation: This question isn't asking what the evidence is saying, but rather what the original *claim* was. Look before and after the presented lines to find the statement of a *claim* that needs the evidence.

Cohesion

Cohesion is when everything works well together to form a complete thought or action.

Question: Which of the following options best completes the sentence with full *cohesion* to the author's message in the first part of the paragraph?

Question explanation: This question wants you to pick the answer that best completes the thoughts set up by the author previously in the paragraph—make sure you're looking at enough context.

Combine

To mix two or more things together is to *combine* them.

Question: Which of the following options best *combines* the two sentences?

Question explanation: This question is asking you which of the answer options best turns two sentences into one. Look not just at punctuation, but also for active voice instead of passive voice as well as for the sentence to maintain the author's original intent.

Conclusion

The *conclusion* to a story is the end of that story. *Conclusion* will also often refer to the judgement made by looking at facts and data. A scientist may observe traffic data to come to the *conclusion* that a certain intersection needs a traffic light.

Question: The data in the chart supports what *conclusion* from the passage?

Question explanation: This question is asking which statement from the passage is supported by the data in the chart.

Confirm

To *confirm* something is to check on it to make sure it is true. For example, if you were to say you couldn't go to school due to illness, the school might call your parent or doctor to *confirm* your story.

Question: If inserted here, which of the following statements accurately uses the information from the graph to *confirm* the author's beliefs about the cause of low voter turnout?

Question explanation: You are trying to pick the answer option that correctly represents the information in the graph and shows that the author's opinion is indeed true.

Contradict

To *contradict* means to go against. If your teacher said that clouds are caused by magic gremlins in the sky, you might raise your hand to *contradict* him.

Question: A literary editor claims that this passage supports the use of nuclear power. What evidence from the passage would *contradict* the editor's claim?

Question explanation: This question is asking for the lines that show that the author does NOT support the use of nuclear power. This would *contradict* the editor's claim that the author DOES support it.

Contrast

When two things *contrast,* they are close to opposites from one another, or at least are very different. White snow *contrasts* nicely with a night sky, as does green grass against a red picnic blanket. Liberal and conservative ideologies are in *contrast* to one another, as are the wishes of parents who want you stay home and friends who want you to go out.

Question: In the passage, what is the central *contrasting* opinion to that which Anna Leah, the attorney for the defense, presents?

Question explanation: What opinion is presented that contradicts the opinion of the defense attorney?

Convey

To *convey* an idea means to get that idea across, to make it known, or to communicate it.

Question: What is the primary thought that is being *conveyed* by Mr. Knych in the third paragraph in regards to his daughter Emily?

Question explanation: What thought about his daughter is Mr. Knych making known?

Developmental Pattern

The *developmental pattern* of a passage is how the passage is laid out and how it progresses.

Question: Which choice best describes this passage's *developmental pattern*?

Question explanation: This question is asking you to sum up how the passage progresses and what the overall layout of that progression is.

Effective

When something is *effective,* it is working as it should to produce the desired result.

Question: Which of the answer options most *effectively* combines the two sentences?

Question explanation: In this case, you can simply replace the words "most effectively" with the word "best." Which of the answer options best combines the two sentences?

Emphasize

To *emphasize* something is to place importance or stress upon it. The italics on the word *emphasizes* the word in the sentence.

Question: Which of the options *emphasizes* the physical size of the man in question?

Question explanation: All the answers will likely be grammatically correct and punctuated correctly as well. Look for the one that best shows the reader what size the man is.

Establish

To *establish* something is to set it up on a firm foundation.

Question: Which of sentences, if inserted here, would best *establish* the serious tone that is carried throughout the passage?

Question explanation: Make sure you read the rest of the passage first to feel the tone for yourself. Then return to this question and pick the answer that best matches the seriousness that is evident throughout the passage.

Explicit

When something is *explicit,* it is clearly and directly stated.

Question: Which of the following options reflect the author's *explicit* feelings on living in the Midwest?

Question explanation: This question is asking you to sum up what the author clearly and directly stated about how they feel about living in the Midwest. The author may have implied things or you may be able to draw conclusions or make inferences, but those things weren't *explicitly* stated, and so should not be reflected in the answer.

Facilitate

To *facilitate* something is to help it come together or to make it simpler. Your teachers *facilitate* your education.

Question: What actions did the researchers take in order to *facilitate* the completion of the study after it had stalled?

Question explanation: This question is asking what the researchers did once the study faltered in order to get it moving once again toward completion.

Figurative

To speak in a *figurative* manner is the opposite of speaking literally. Whereas in literal language we speak directly and the words mean their actual meaning (the house is on fire, please call 911), in *figurative* language we use words to mean things other than their actual meaning (the band's lead singer is on fire right now).

Question: Which of the following answers are being used by the author in a *figurative* sense?

Question explanation: This question is asking about how the words are being used within the context of the passage. Go back and look at the sentence in which each of the four options is found. Is that word being used to mean something other than the dictionary definition? If so, it is *figurative*.

Figure

Generally, on the SAT the word *figure* is used to refer to a visual representation of data. It could be a graph, a table, a chart, or some other visual piece of information. These items will often be labeled as Table 1 or Figure 2, etc.

Question: Which of the following statements, if included in the passage, would best clarify the author's position by using information from the *figure*?

Question explanation: This question wants you to take information from the graph/table and use it to support the author's ideas.

Function

The *function* of a word, phrase, sentence, or paragraph is what that item does within the context it is used.

Question: What is the *function* of the phrase "as the crow flies" in line 97 in the context of the paragraph as a whole?

Question explanation: This question is asking you what that phrase is doing within the paragraph. It may be used to show that a character's journey is very long since they can't travel as the crow flies. Or maybe it's being used to indicate the path a character took to explain how they beat another character home. Maybe it's being used to help a scientific passage have a more conversational tone as it discusses animal migration patterns.

Implicit

Implicit means something is being said indirectly. It has the same root as the word *imply*. It is the opposite of *explicit*, which means to say something clearly and directly.

Question: Which of the following thoughts is *implicit* in the first passage and explicit in the second?

Question explanation: This question is asking you to compare the two passages and find an opinion that is stated directly in the second passage, but indirectly (or hinted at) in the first passage.

Imply

Imply means something is suggested without being directly stated. It is saying something in an indirect way.

Question: When the author states that "when lake pollution increases, the fish population declines," he is *implying* that:

Question explanation: This question is asking what the author is saying indirectly by putting these two statements next to each other. The answer would be that the author is *implying* that the pollution increase causes the fish population to decline.

Impression

An *impression* is how you view a person or thing—your thoughts, opinions, and ideas about them. If a teacher gives a pop quiz on the first day of school, you may form the *impression* that he is difficult, mean, or unreasonable.

Question: Through the use of words like "casual," "witty," and "informal" what *impression* is the author giving of Mr. Gimley's character?

Question explanation: This question is asking how the author wants you to view Mr. Gimley. The author chose those words to paint a certain picture of this character. What picture is it?

Indicate

Indicate means to show, often in a nonverbal manner. For example, when a person rides a bike, they may *indicate* a turn by extending an arm.

Question: How does the writer the passages *indicate* that people want to see what result from scientific studies?

Question explanation: This question is asking you to choose the answer that best reflects what people want to see from scientific studies. However, because the answer is *indicated* and not just stated by the author, there is a good chance the answer will not be a direct quote from the passage.

Infer

To *infer* means to suppose something that leads to a conclusion. It is different from *implying*, which hints at something, but doesn't conclude anything.

Question: It can be reasonably *inferred* from the passage that driving electric cars leads to what issue?

Question explanation: This question is asking us to draw a conclusion that is not directly stated in the passage. Which conclusion is most strongly supported by evidence from the passage?

Interpretation

An *interpretation* is how a certain person views a situation or idea. For example, five different people may read the Constitution and have five different *interpretations* of how it should be applied today.

Question: Which of the following best describes the author's *interpretation* of the results of the study?

Question explanation: Be careful here. The question isn't asking for the results themselves, but rather for what the author *interprets* from them. It is asking for the conclusion that the author draws based on the data.

Literal

To speak in a *literal* manner is the opposite of speaking figuratively. In *literal* language, we speak directly and the words mean their actual meaning (put down your pencils). In figurative language, we use words to mean things other than their actual meaning (it is raining cats and dogs).

Question: Which of the following answers are being used by the author in a *literal* sense?

Question explanation: This question is asking about how the words are being used within the context of the passage. Go back and look at the sentence in which each of the four options is found. Is that word being used to mean its dictionary meaning? If so, it is *literal*.

Maintain

To *maintain* something is to keep it the same over a period of time. *Maintaining* a car means to keep it in running order over time. *Maintaining* your GPA means keeping it at a steady level throughout high school.

Question: Which of the following sentences, if inserted here, would best complete the passage and *maintain* the tone as established by the author?

Question explanation: The question wants you to do two things. First, think about what the passage says and look for a good conclusion. Second, try to keep the tone the same as what has been used in the rest of the passage.

Parenthetical

The word *parenthetical* is related to the word *parentheses*. *Parenthetical* information is the information within the parentheses (the punctuation surrounding this phrase). *Parenthetical* information is generally not essential to the sentence.

Question: If the author were to remove the *parenthetical* information, what would the paragraph primarily loose?

Question explanation: If the information within the parentheses were removed, what would the paragraph be lacking?

Preceding

Preceding means coming before. Think of previews (before the movie) or prequels (the story before the story); *pre-* almost always means before.

Question: Which of the following sentences would best fit at the beginning of the *preceding* paragraph?

Question explanation: This question is likely marked in a small box at the end of a paragraph. It is that paragraph (the one before the box) to which the question is referring.

Previous

Previous has that same *pre-* beginning and means nearly the same thing as *preceding*. While *preceding* can sometimes mean much before, *previous* always means directly before.

Question: Which answer option, if inserted here, would best connect the author's message in this sentence to that in the *previous* sentence?

Question explanation: Pick the answer option that best transitions between the sentence directly before and the one directly after.

Primary

The adjective *primary* is used to show that the noun it describes is the most important in its category or that it came first.

Question: Which of the following options best describes Seth's *primary* objection to photographs?

Question explanation: Seth may have many objections to photographs. The answer you pick should be his main objection, or his strongest objection.

Propose

To *propose* something is to suggest it for the consideration and thought of others.

Question: What is the second author's response to the *proposed* solution to political corruption suggested in Passage 1?

Question explanation: First, find what Passage 1 wants to do to solve the issue of political corruption. Then look through Passage 2 to see what the author thinks about the solution.

Reasonable

Reasonable describes something fair or appropriate, something that no one would object to, or something that is not extreme.

Question: Which of the following is the most *reasonable* explanation for the sudden change of heart experienced by Levi's character in the second paragraph?

Question explanation: There could be a lot of hypothetical reasons why the character had a change of heart, from alien abduction to blackmail; however, the question is asking for a *reasonable* explanation. Which of the answers is most likely to be true based on what you know of the character and the situation in the passage?

Refer

Refer shares a root with the word *reference*. When an author *refers* to something, they are making a reference to it or, in simple terms, talking about it or mentioning it.

Question: The writer of the passage *refers* to Martin Luther King, Jr., in order to . . .

Question explanation: The question (or open-ended statement) is asking *why* the author brings up MLK. What purpose does it serve to mention it?

Reinforce (a claim)

To *reinforce* a claim is to back it up or support it.

Question: Which of the following options, if included here, would best *reinforce* the claim the author is making about the levels of salmon in the river during spawning season?

Question explanation: This question is asking you to pick the answer that would best support what the author is saying about the levels of salmon. Don't worry about the factual accuracy of the answers, just focus on which one, if true, would back the author up.

Relative

When something is *relative*, it is being considered in relation to something else. For example, you may have good grades *relative* to some of your classmates and bad grades *relative* to others. This book is long *relative* to some books and short *relative* to others.

Question: Which option best describes the tone of the final paragraph *relative* to the passage as a whole?

Question explanation: Compare the tone in the final paragraph to that of the rest of the passage. Is the final paragraph more hopeful, sad, direct, etc.?

Relevant

When something is *relevant*, it relates to the matter being presently discussed. A discussion of Jupiter's moons is interesting, but not *relevant* to a conversation about the book *Of Mice and Men*.

Question: Which of the following options, if inserted here, would be most *relevant* to the discussion of historical costuming in Hollywood that is found in the passage as a whole?

Question explanation: Which of the options is most on topic to the historical costuming discussion in the passage?

Serve (to)

In the context of most SAT questions, the *serve(s) to* can generally be thought of as "completes this action."

Question: Which of the options *serves to* complete the author's thought as it was begun previously in the sentence?

Question explanation: This question is asking which of the options acts to complete the author's thought.

Significant

Something *significant* could also be described as notable or important.

Question: Which of the following options would *significantly* change the author's original meaning?

Question explanation: Some of the options may slightly change the author's meaning. However, one of the answers will notably change the meaning, or change it a lot—which one is it?

Stylistic

Stylistic refers to the style of something. A designer would make *stylistic* choices so that her clothes reflect her chosen aesthetic.

Question: Which of the following sentences, if inserted here, would prove most *stylistically* consistent with the rest of the passage?

Question explanation: You're looking for the answer that best fits the design of the rest of the passage. Try to match tone as well as any other elements that you can.

Summary

A *summary* takes a lot of information and cuts it down to just a simple, to-the-point sentence or two.

Question: Which choice is the best *summary* of the author's main message in this passage?

Question explanation: What is the author's main message and how can we best sum it up in a nutshell? Make sure you get the answer that sums up the main message, not a small side message or something that is in the passage but not the primary idea.

Tone

Tone is how someone sounds. It is the emotion that shows through in their word and style choices. *Tone* may be formal, informal, happy, sad, anxious, excited, etc.

Question: What *tone* does the author adopt in the fifth paragraph as he discusses his childhood?

Question explanation: This question is asking you to look back to the fifth paragraph and identify how the word and style choices of the author show his feelings. Is he using very stilted formal language? Is he using a lot of slang? Does he pick happy or sad words? All of these together show us the *tone*.

Transition

A *transition* connects two things. It may be two paragraphs or it may be two sentences. When a question asks for the best *transition*, start by mentally summing up those two things and then consider which answer best connects those two things in a logical manner.

Question: Which of the following options establishes the best *transition* between the previous and current paragraph?

Question explanation: Which option best connects the two paragraphs?

250 Words Important to SAT Reading and Writing and Language Passages

Review these words if you find yourself coming across vocabulary in the Reading and Writing and Language passages that you do not know. Even though the SAT does emphasize determining the meaning of words in context, it is critical that you can make sense of the context by understanding frequent vocabulary.

Abject—Abject is often used to describe negative things and heighten the negativity. You might see loneliness, poverty, or sadness described as being abject. It describes the highest level of loneliness, poverty, or sadness a person could reach.

Example sentence: Having lost his wife to the bubonic plague, the young man fell into abject sadness that did not lift until life provided him with a new companion some 25 years later.

Abode—Put simply, an abode is a place where people live. It could be anything from a house, to a cave, to an apartment, to a van. If humans take shelter there, it can be called an abode.

Example sentence: "Welcome to my humble abode," said the nomad, as he lifted a flap to allow me entrance to his colorfully furnished canvas home.

Abstract—When something is abstract, it isn't concrete or tangible. It might exist as an idea only (the concept of gravity is abstract), or it might be something that you can touch but that represents ideas or feelings (like abstract art, which is art that does not depict real items).

Example sentence: She soon realized that while they often had long talks about the future, they were not concrete discussions. Rather, he discussed the future abstractly, as something he couldn't really see.

Acknowledge—To acknowledge someone or something is to notice it and make sure it knows that it has been noticed. If a student raises her hand during a lecture, a teacher may nod toward the student to acknowledge the student. That is, the head nod says, "I see you have your hand raised. Just a moment while I finish up my thought."

Example sentence: After training longer and harder than any of his teammates, the new tennis player was proud to receive the "most improved" award as an acknowledgement of all his hard work.

Adapt—To adapt is to change to fit the situation. If a fish is switched to a new tank, it may need a few days to adapt before going back to its more normal patterns of existence.

Example sentence: The sudden change of rules was very upsetting for the mock trial team, but soon they were hard at work adapting their strategy in order to best take advantage of the new situation.

Admonition—An admonition is the noun form of the word admonish. Therefore, an admonition is the scolding you might receive if you have done something wrong.

Example sentence: Having been caught with her hand in the cookie jar, the little girl hung her head and waited for the admonition she was sure she would receive from her parent.

Affluent—To be affluent is to be very well off financially.

Example sentence: Having grown up in an affluent home, John Smith was well accustomed to all the luxuries and sophistication of upper-class life.

Agitate—To agitate means to work up or disturb. The big post that is sometimes in the middle of a clothes washing machine is called an agitator because it helps work the soap into a lather. You might also agitate a human or animal by annoying them or frustrating them until they become all worked up.

Example sentence: As the baby's cries grew louder and louder, the other theatergoers became more and more agitated until someone was finally so fed up that he asked the parents to take the baby outside.

Aggrandize—If you notice the word *grand* in aggrandize, it may help you remember how this word is used. Generally, to aggrandize something is to make it grander; oftentimes people mentally aggrandize and think of things as grander than they really are.

Example sentence: Since they lived in different states, the young couple had spent a lot of time apart. When they finally saw each other again, they realized that they had each aggrandized the other, and were disappointed in the real person in front of them.

Aggregate—When discussing the aggregate (as a noun), you're talking about the whole, not the parts.
Aggregate can also be a verb in which you build up the parts to create a whole.

Example sentence: I've been very busy at work since my superior asked that I aggregate all the available data on consumer habits and present it as a complete report to the CEO.

Alternation—Alternating is simply taking turns. For example, you and your sibling might alternate doing the dishes so that no one has to do them two nights in a row. Alternation, then, is simply the noun form of the verb alternate.
Example sentence: The alternation of quarterbacks from one play to the next confused the opposing team and caused them to misread several plays, leading to our team scoring a touchdown.

Amicable—To be amicable with other people means to get along with them. It is a warm word often used to describe friendly, but not overly friendly, relationships with coworkers, neighbors, and other acquaintances.
Example sentence: After the hubbub from the move settled down, the roommates forged an amicable relationship. While never becoming close friends, they were more than happy to bring in the other's mail and to live in relative peace and harmony.

Analogous—When two things are analogous to each other, they can be compared to one another. Often, this comparison will help clarify something about one of the things being compared. Think of the word analogy when thinking about what analogous means.

Example sentence: Finding my missing phone was analogous to trying to find a needle in a haystack—it was pretty hopeless.

Analogy—An analogy is a comparison between two items using *like* or *as*.

Example analogy: The young boy's jealousy grew inside him like a little green monster, waiting to escape.

Anomaly—An anomaly is something strange or out of the usual pattern of things. If, for example, a very kind and sweet classmate lost their temper just one time, you might call that occurrence an anomaly.

Example sentence: The scientist assured the worried townspeople that the strange lights at night were merely a meteorological anomaly and not the signals of arriving aliens.

Antipathy—If you were to hate someone's guts, you might say you felt antipathy toward them. It is a very negative feeling toward another person or thing.

Example sentence: While he loved his wife very much, he felt nothing but antipathy toward his in-laws, which put a definite strain on their marriage.

Apparition—Apparition sounds like the word appear. An apparition is something that suddenly appears. Oftentimes, ghosts and other supernatural phenomena will be described as being apparitions.

Example sentence: The youth quaked as they heard a strange sound; they should have never broken into the abandoned house, which was full of apparitions.

Arbitrary—This word can usually be replaced with the word random.

Example sentence: The seating chart had previously been arbitrary, but the teacher had to be more deliberate in assigning seats during the second quarter so as to prevent cheating.

Ascertain—To ascertain something is to find it out or confirm it. For example, the police may hold a person for a certain amount of time while they try to ascertain the details of the crime committed.

Example sentence: The town waited with bated breath as the counters worked to ascertain the winner of the mayoral election.

Aspire—If someone were to tell you to "aspire to higher things," it might be interpreted as "dream big." Aspiring means working toward a lofty goal.

Example sentence: Though I'm only a yellow belt at the moment, I aspire to be a black belt in a few years.

Autocratic—An autocrat is someone in charge who has all the power. The czars in Russia, for example, were autocrats. There was no governmental power outside of them. Autocratic, then, is the adjectival form of autocrat—it can be used to describe someone who is acting like an autocrat.

Example sentence: Mrs. Nafziger is a very strict teacher and is quite autocratic in the way she runs her history classes.

Automated—Think about the word automatic. Automated means something has been changed to make it now automatic where as previously it was not. For example, a dishwasher would automate the dishwashing process.

Example sentence: The factory workers were very concerned about losing their jobs as more and more tasks around the plant were automated.

Beget—When you beget something, it means you take steps to bring that thing into existence. It can also refer to an action that leads to something. You might say that if you pass around a petition to bring chicken nuggets back to the cafeteria, you are trying to beget change. (Don't mess this word up with the similar-sounding word baguette, which is a long, thin loaf of French bread).

Example sentence: Planting seeds in the spring is the only way to beget a harvest in the fall.

Benevolent—To be benevolent is to be kind. Quite often, this word is used to describe elderly people who are willing to give away all they have and charities that work to better people's lives by giving.

Example sentence: When hard times hit the community, many people turned to the benevolent philanthropist who live just outside of town. It was well known that he would help everyone he could.

Bestow—To bestow something is to give it to someone. This is often use when giving titles and other honors.

Example sentence: After his heroic actions on the battlefield left him with grave injuries, the government bestowed upon the soldier the Purple Heart medal.

25

Biological—Biology is the study of life; biological is describing something related to the study of life or related to life itself. For example, if you are infected with bacteria, you could call how your body reacts a biological response.

Example sentence: When I broke my leg, my doctor explained the biological process my body would go through to bring about healing; it was really neat to learn!

Calibrate—To calibrate something is to adjust it so that it runs the way it should. This is especially applicable to machines that have readouts. If your car's speedometer tells you that you're going 30 miles per hour when you're really going 55 miles per hour, then you need to have your speedometer calibrated.

Example sentence: The old oven was in bad shape. When we set it to 350, it only reached 200. We called a repair person to calibrate the dial, and that fixed the problem.

Calisthenics—Calisthenics are a type of exercise that rely on body weight. They include push-ups, sit-ups, jumping jacks, and other simple movements that require no equipment.

Example sentence: While the elderly man was far past the point in life where he could lift heavy weights, he still stuck to the daily calisthenics routine that he had in the Army some 50 years earlier.

Capacity—The capacity of something is a measure of its ability. A room has a maximum capacity, which says how many people can be in that room. A car may have the capacity to go 150 miles per hour. A person could have the capacity to handle a difficult situation.

Example sentence: What the president was asking the man to do was far beyond his capacity; he would need to request backup.

Celestial—When something is celestial, it has to do with outer space.

Example sentence: When studying astronomy, it is helpful to have a celestial map for reference.

Censure—To censure someone is to give them a formal reprimand. Quite often, governments hand out censures to their members for having done something wrong, but not necessarily illegal.

Example sentence: The young representative received a censure after his foolish and dangerous antics were published by a respectable newspaper.

Circulation—Circulation is quite often thought of in relation to blood moving through the body, but it can refer to anything moving back and forth or around in a predictable pattern.

Example sentence: The circulation of rumors can be quite detrimental to a person's reputation.

Coerce—To coerce someone is to get them to do something by threat of force.

Example sentence: When asking nicely fails to work, bad people often turn to coercion to get what they want.

Cognition—Cognition is the ability to understand something. When people get older and develop dementia, quite often their cognition is negatively impacted.

Example sentence: Getting plenty of sleep is instrumental in increasing one's cognition.

Colloquial—The word colloquial almost always describes language. Colloquial language is everyday language. In English, for example, you probably use a lot of colloquial language with your friends, but likely speak a bit more properly to teachers and other adults.

Example sentence: When my turn came to speak to the foreign dignitary, I did my best to speak formally and avoid using colloquial language.

Commercial—Commercial has to do with the buying and selling of goods. For example, if you begin a commercial enterprise, you are likely setting out to go into business to buy, sell, create, or distribute goods.

Example sentence: Many companies now use overnight delivery to get their commercial goods to the customers who have ordered them.

Complementary—When something is complementary, it goes well with the thing around it.

Example sentence: Milk and cookies are complementary foods that I greatly enjoy eating simultaneously.

Complimentary—Something that is provided free of charge. Also, a compliment is a nice thing to say about someone.

Example sentence: Compliments about your excellent work cost the teacher nothing—they are complimentary.

Conflate—Oftentimes, we are warned not to conflate things. This means we need to keep the two things separate and not assume that they are the same idea. For example, in history class you may conflate the feminist movement and the suffragette movement. While they have some similarities, they aren't the same thing.

Example sentence: Be careful not to conflate infatuation and love. That is a surefire way to end up with a broken heart.

Conjure—To conjure is to bring something up. When telling a scary story, you may conjure up images that are terrifying to the listeners.

Example sentence: If a small child demands candy when you have none, you might reply, "I'm afraid I can't conjure up sweets out of thin air just because you want them."

Consensus—When everyone agrees, there is a consensus.

Example sentence: In government, rarely is there a consensus. Rather, there are a multitude of opinions vying to be heard.

Consequence—Consequences are the results of an action taken. There can be positive consequences, but more often this word is used to indicate a negative result or a punishment for negative actions.

Example sentence: If you fail to show up at practice, the consequence is that you don't get to play.

Conservator—A conservator is a person whose job it is to conserve or preserve something. This word could also be used to just mean a general guardian.

Example sentence: The art collection had a marvelous conservator who did all she could to ensure that the art would be enjoyed for many generations to come.

Constitution—We are likely all familiar with the governmental term constitution. But this word can also apply to someone's bodily health or how something is put together. Any of those three meanings could pop up on the SAT.

Example sentences: Since the constitution of the carriage was not very sturdy, a delegate was involved in an accident on his way to the Constitutional Convention. Luckily, the delegate had a strong personal constitution, and he recovered easily in just a few days.

Contingent—When something is contingent, it is relying on other factors to come to be. An outdoor field trip, for example, might be contingent on the weather.

Example sentence: I am planning on traveling to the capital to watch the soccer team play for the state title. That is contingent, of course, on us winning this last playoff game.

Conventional—When something is conventional, it follows the traditional rules that are set up. For example, a bride wearing white is very conventional while a bride wearing bright red would be unconventional.

Example sentence: My family tends to be very conventional at Thanksgiving. We always eat a turkey with stuffing, mashed potatoes, and a few side dishes, and then we have pumpkin pie for dessert.

Convey—To convey something is to get it across. You could convey a tin of cookies safely from your grandmother to your mother. If you are an effective public speaker, you can convey ideas from your mind to the minds of others.

Example sentence: Try as he might, the student teacher continually failed to convey his expectations to the class. This resulted in a rather disorderly classroom experience.

Convoke—Generally, the word convoke means to call a meeting.

Example sentence: Convoke the leaders of the nations; we must come together or we shall surely perish.

Convulsion—To convulse is a physical movement. Think of a person having a seizure—all of their muscles are convulsing. They are therefore having convulsions.

Example sentence: The audience stared in amazement as the snake charmer's snake exited the basket, its body racked with convulsions as it heard the mesmerizing music.

Cooperatively—You likely know the word cooperate. Cooperatively just means working in a cooperative manner.

Example sentence: During times of international crisis, it is best for governments to work cooperatively with one another.

50

Cultivate—To cultivate something is to bring it up or to try to make it grow or exist. Farmers cultivate crops. Your teachers try to cultivate in you a love of learning.

Example sentence: Holidays like the 4th of July, Labor Day, and Memorial Day all have a side effect of cultivating a sense of patriotism in the population.

Dawdle—To dawdle is to lag behind.

Example sentence: "Don't dawdle or you'll miss the school bus," the grandfather called, as he turned around to see what was taking his grandchild so long.

Decipher—To decipher something is to figure it out. A spy might decipher a special code, for instance.

Example sentence: The store clerk looked puzzled as he tried to decipher why the customer in front of him was so upset.

Deficient—When something is deficient, it isn't enough; it is lacking something. In the winter, people are often vitamin D deficient due to spending too much time indoors.

Example sentence: The young man, while highly educated, had no work ethic. Due to this deficiency, he was nearly unemployable.

Degrade—To degrade is to break something down slowly over time.

Example sentence: While the engine was still sound, the body of the car had degraded to the point where it was no longer safe to drive.

Demur—To demur is to politely say no to something or avoid it.

Example sentence: When offered a second helping of food, the man politely demurred since he already felt full.

Desolation—Desolation is total abandonment, emptiness, and destruction. Desolation occurs when everything of value and everything alive is destroyed.

Example sentence: War seemed more imminent each day, and families quickly began fleeing the city, worried at what seemed to be the certain desolation to come.

Despoil—Despoil is related to the phrase *the spoils of war*. The spoils of war are the things that invaders would take from the inhabitants upon victory. Pretty much anything of worth would be looted or plundered. To despoil is the act of taking away anything of value.

Example sentence: The greedy criminals broke into the historic mansion to despoil it.

Deter—To deter someone is to stop them from doing something.

Example sentence: The would-be bank robbers were deterred when they saw that security had been increased dramatically.

Disenfranchise—To disenfranchise is to take away someone's right to vote, or prevent them from using it.

Example sentence: For most of human history, women were disenfranchised.

Disparity—A disparity is an inequality or a difference between two things. For instance, there may be a disparity between the posted rules in a classroom and the rules that are actually enforced.

Example sentence: Small children are quick to point out any disparity between the dessert they receive and the dessert their brother or sister receives.

Disseminate—To disseminate is to pass out or to ensure the spread of something (quite often information).

Example sentence: At the end of the security meeting, the participants were asked not to disseminate the knowledge that they had acquired, since doing so could put people in harm's way.

Dissimilar—Things that are dissimilar are not the same (not similar).

Example sentence: While they had grown up in the same house, at the same time, with the same parents, the twins were quite dissimilar.

Diverge—When two things move apart, they diverge. (This is the opposite of when two things come together, which is when they converge.)

Example sentence: Quite often, when students graduate, they diverge from their friends and move on with life.

Doctrine—A doctrine is a sincerely held belief, often of the religious variety, but also political or other beliefs as well.

Example sentence: Some people do not stand for the pledge as it goes against their religious doctrine—this is their right under the First Amendment.

Doldrums—The word doldrums is often used to describe a time in which nothing happens. It is also used in sailing to describe an area of water that is not moving in which a sail boat would be trapped. Doldrums are never a good thing and can sometimes even be used to describe depression, boredom, and other negative mental states.

Example sentence: After his breakup, he entered a period of doldrums which lasted for several weeks.

Domestic—When something is described as domestic, it is related to the home. If someone hires domestic help, they are likely hiring someone to help take care of their house or something in it. It could be a gardener, maid, or cook.

Example sentence: Compared to the other families of 1900, their marriage was unconventional, with her working and bringing home a paycheck while he stayed home and attended to domestic matters.

Dominion—Dominion is control or authority over someone or something.

Example sentence: The king frequently exercised his dominion over the serfs to extract more and more work from them in less and less time.

Dubious—To be dubious is to be doubtful and uncertain.

Example sentence: While my friend was eager to explore the cave, I was much more dubious about doing so.

Earnest—When someone is earnest, they are showing that they are serious. They really believe what they are saying and they find it important that you understand that.

Example sentence: The young man spoke earnestly as he told her of his feelings and tried to convince her to accept his proposal.

Eddy—An eddy is when water or air moves swiftly in a circular motion.

Example sentence: The boat, caught in a persistent eddy, appeared to be lost forever.

Effectual—The word effectual means that the desired result has been achieved through that action.

Example sentence: I have found that asking for help is far more effectual than simply waiting for someone to offer.

Efficacy—The efficacy of something is how effective that thing is.

Example sentence: The efficacy of the treatment came into question when the wound became infected instead of healing.

Efficient—When something is efficient, it is done in the most direct way possible using the least amount of time and resources to get the best result.

Example sentence: Jennifer completed her errands quite efficiently and was back at home just an hour after she had left.

Embellish—To embellish is to add details or flair to something—either verbally or physically.

Example sentence: The seamstress told embellished tales of her youth while embellishing the wedding dress with thousands of tiny pearl beads.

75

Emit—Emit means to give off.

Example sentence: After having been sprayed by a skunk, the puppy emitted a horrid smell for several days to come.

Empathize—When you empathize with someone, you feel what they're feeling. You might empathize with a friend who had a terrible grade on a test, or with a family who needs some help getting enough food for a holiday meal.

Example sentence: The storm damage to the home caused an outpouring of support from their neighbors, who empathized with the now-struggling family.

Endearing—When people are endearing, they create warm feelings toward themselves. A person may have an endearing smile that makes you like them and feel kindly toward them.

Example sentence: When I joined my new school, I was seated next to a small girl with pigtails. She had the most endearing personality and we were soon great friends.

Endeavor—To endeavor is to try something. It can also be used as a noun, meaning "a try."

Example sentence: Once the rain stops, we will endeavor to get the garden planted.

Endow—To endow is to give. Quite often, this term is used to describe massive donations given to charities upon the death of a wealthy person. It can also talk about rights given to people just because of their birth or citizenship.

Example sentence: (From the Declaration of Independence) "We hold these truths to be self-evident, that all men are created equal, that they are endowed by their creator with certain unalienable rights, that among these are life, liberty, and the pursuit of happiness."

Enhance—To enhance something is to make it better or clearer. An umbrella enhances your experience of walking in the rain. Prescription glasses enhance your eyesight.

Example sentence: The coach added a few trick plays to the book in order to enhance our chances of success.

Enterprise—When you set out to do something, the process of doing it is an enterprise. This word often refers to big or difficult tasks. Think about the starship *Enterprise* from Star Trek—it has a very difficult mission: "To explore strange new worlds. To seek out new life and new civilizations. To boldly go where no man has gone before."

Example sentence: The process of building and moving to a whole new school in just a year was quite a difficult enterprise; however, the school board was committed to it as it was seen as the best option for the students' education.

Entice—To entice someone is to convince them to do something through the promise of reward (as opposed to coerce, which is through promise of harm). A cat can be enticed to come out from under the bed with a treat.

Example sentence: When the workers dragged their feet getting a project done, the manager enticed them to finish by promising an extra vacation day to whomever completed their portion first.

Entrenched—To be entrenched means to be dug in, to refuse to move, especially when it comes to thoughts and ideas. Think about how armies use trenches. They dig trenches, and then they can't easily move from the trenches without risking harm. The word entrenched comes from that idea.

Example sentence: Some people believe that debates are essentially useless since both parties often begin the debate already so entrenched in their ideas that they won't even listen to the other debater.

Ephemeral—Something ephemeral is very short-lived. It is fleeting and quickly gone.

Example sentence: The rainbow—one of the most beautiful natural phenomena—is quite ephemeral and generally disappears within just a few short minutes.

Evince—Evince is generally a verb meaning to show one's feelings.

Example sentence: The actions of the government as it tries and fails to help time and again evince anger and frustration.

Expenditure—An expenditure is a spending of money or other resources.

Example sentence: Buying all new china was an extravagant expenditure, but the noble felt it was necessary since he would be entertaining a duchess.

Explanatory—When something is explanatory, it explains something.

Example sentence: Quite often, students skip over explanatory examples and jump straight to the work; this is generally a mistake.

Extensive—When something is extensive, it is widespread or far-reaching. You might also say it is thorough.

Example sentence: Due to extensive cheating, the teacher shredded the tests and instead made each student meet with her for an oral examination of their knowledge.

Feature—A feature is a part of an item that is designed for a specific use. One feature of my car, for example, is a stereo system.

Example sentence: I was excited to check out all of the new features on my phone upgrade.

Feeble—To be feeble is to be weak.

Example sentence: The feeble elderly couple often needed their neighbors' help with the landscaping.

Fetter—To fetter is to hold someone or something back from what they want to do or accomplish.

Example sentence: While I love my parents, living under their rules often leaves me feeling fettered.

Finite—Finite is the opposite of infinite. When something is finite, it has a definitive beginning and ending.

Example sentence: The fact that the movie was finite saddened me—I wished it could go on and on forever.

Fiscal—When people describe things as fiscal (like the fiscal year), they are talking about money and the economy.

Example sentence: Because of excessive spending, the business was experiencing fiscal difficulties that threatened to bankrupt it.

Florid—Generally describing a person's face, this adjective means red or flushed.

Example sentence: Having run the 5K in brutal heat, the athlete rested with his florid face cradled in his hands.

Former—Former refers to the one before or in the past. The former president used to be the president, for example. If I give you two options and you choose the former, then you have chosen the first one that was given.

Example sentence: I was shocked when the former mayor of my town was revealed to be in the middle of a scandal, which plunged the town into a fiscal crisis.

Forum—A forum is a location or a meeting where people can talk about their thoughts, ideas, and opinions.

Example sentence: The teacher rearranged the desks into a circle to facilitate discussion and turn the classroom into a forum on governmental improvements.

Frantic—Frantic could also be expressed as desperate. When you are frantic about something, there is urgency to do all you can as you try to solve the problem.

Example sentence: The dog wandered off during the picnic, triggering a frantic search by all the family members.

Frequent—Frequent simply means often. When something happens frequently, it happens all the time.

Example sentence: His frequent tardiness led to a Saturday detention.

Fundamental—Fundamentals are basics. The fundamentals of reading would be learning the alphabet and phonics. The fundamentals of baseball are throwing, catching, and hitting.

Example sentence: After many in the class failed the math test because they weren't allowed to use calculators, the teacher made them return to fundamentals and practice adding, subtracting, multiplying, and dividing by hand.

100

Germinate—To germinate something is to take something with potential and make it start to grow. Quite often this term is used with seeds.

Example sentence: Part of the preschool's mission statement is "to germinate active and curious minds."

Glom—To glom is to attach to something (often in a blob-like manner).

Example sentence: Even despite continual cleaning, the boat was still covered in barnacles, which had glommed on to the hull.

Glut—A glut is a ridiculous abundance of something. It's having so much of something you don't even know what to do with it.

Example sentence: When the flood waters receded, there was a glut of carp left behind, flopping on the streets. The townspeople ate like kings that night and celebrated the day every year after with a Carp Festival.

Grievance—A grievance is a complaint. Think of it as something you would grieve over—something that makes you sad.

Example sentence: After the salesperson was seen taking a picture of my credit card, I felt it necessary to lodge a grievance against him as he was probably planning on stealing my identity.

Haggle—Haggling is the process two people go through as they exchange offers back and forth while trying to make a deal.

Example sentence: One reason I like garage sales so much is the opportunity to haggle with the seller and try to secure a better deal.

Ignominious—Something that is ignominious is undignified—it will likely cause the person experiencing it to feel shame or embarrassment.

Example sentence: My brother pulled the chair out from under me, causing me to sprawl on the ground in a very ignominious position.

Illegible—When something is illegible, it is unable to be read or understood.

Example sentence: With the prevalence of typing these days, many people have illegible handwriting due to lack of practice.

Immured—When someone is immured, they are held against their will in some way, often enclosed.

Example sentence: The young man felt trapped in the relationship, immured by his desire not to hurt her feelings.

Impel—To impel is to push or force someone to do something in some way.

Example sentence: Impelled by the fear of loneliness, many people resort to blind dates to try to find a companion.

Inapplicable—When something doesn't apply in a given situation, it is inapplicable. For example, you may have the quadratic equation memorized, which is great; however, that equation is inapplicable to many non-quadratic math problems.

Example sentence: While she had many skills, most of them were inapplicable to the current crisis; she would have to call for help.

Incomprehensible—Something that is incomprehensible is unable to be comprehended or understood.

Example sentence: The student's illegible handwriting and incomprehensible train of thought resulted in a very low grade on the essay.

Incontestable—Incontestable means unable to be contested. In other words, you can't dispute it or go against it.

Example sentence: The results of the election were incontestable; the candidate won by a landslide.

Incorporate—To incorporate is to fully include something. For example, you might incorporate an explanation of climate change into a paper on Antarctica.

Example sentence: The leader was harshly criticized when the press found out that he had failed to incorporate any women into the task force on family and children's rights.

Incredulous—When you're incredulous of something, you don't really believe it, or you have doubts about it.

Example sentence: The child looked at her friend incredulously when she tried to convince her that the monster was, in fact, not real.

Indifference—Indifference is that feeling of not feeling strongly about something one way or the other. You might feel indifference toward which teacher you get, or what you have for lunch, or any number of things.

Example sentence: Indifference is a dangerous emotion as it can lead to people drifting through life and never taking any risks or making any big decisions.

Indistinguishable—When two things are indistinguishable, they can't be told apart from one another: There are no distinguishing features.

Example sentence: Even though their mother could tell them apart, to everyone else the twins were indistinguishable.

Ineffective—When something is ineffective, it doesn't work. It doesn't have the effect it should.

Example sentence: Flushing ice cubes down the toilet is an ineffective strategy that kids try to ensure a snow day the next morning.

Inefficacious—This is pretty much the same as the previous word. Inefficacious just means not having the desired effect.

Example sentence: Studying can be inefficacious if you don't make sure to get rid of all distractions before beginning.

Inexorable—Inexorable is kind of like inevitable. It can't be avoided or stopped—it will occur no matter what.

Example sentence: The clock had been ticking constantly for the entire winter, counting out the inexorable passage of time.

Ingenious—For some reason, ingenious and genius mean the same thing.

Example sentence: The pirate queen was known for her ingenious plots to capture other ships.

Innumerable—When something is innumerable, it is unable to be counted. You'll notice *num* hidden away—this is also the root of the word number.

Example sentence: The grains of sand on the beach are truly innumerable.

Institution—An institution is an organization that has been created to fulfill a purpose (generally for the greater good). For example, governments, churches, and schools can all be examples of institutions. Generally, institutions are thought of as permanent or nearly impossible to get rid of.

Example sentence: Between churches, schools, and my mom's job as our small-town mayor, I often feel like I grew up in institutions.

Insurrection—An insurrection is a revolt or an uprising.

Example sentence: Though Catherine the Great is revered by Russians, the peasant insurrection during her time as ruler put a damper on her legacy.

Integrate—To integrate two or more things is to mix them together.

Example sentence: I don't remember the exact date, but at some point in seventh grade, the girls' lunch tables and the boys' lunch tables started to integrate and nothing was ever the same again.

Intend—Intend has to do with intentions. It's what you mean to do, not what you actually do. Every new year, many people intend to form new habits; what actually happens is a different story.

Example sentence: In the evenings, I always intend to get up early the next morning to increase my productivity. This rarely actually happens.

125

Intermittent—Intermittent just means off and on at a set interval.

Example sentence: The stoplight let cars proceed intermittently.

Intuitive—When something is intuitive, it is easy to use and figure out without directions. You can go based on your gut feeling and probably get it right.

Example sentence: While some people struggle to memorize math facts, other people find numbers to be intuitive and breeze through their classes.

Inherent—When something is inherent, it wasn't learned or created; it is naturally occurring. For example, some animals have an inherent fear of predators. You may have an inherent love of the color green or hatred of the smell of tomatoes.

Example sentence: As hard as they tried, my neighbors could not train their dog out of his inherent desire to dig holes.

Insolent—You might well get in trouble for acting insolent at school. Such behavior shows a general bad attitude, lack of respect, and overall grumpiness.

Example sentence: "Wouldn't you like to know," came the insolent reply from the teen when her father asked her why she had returned so late the night before.

Intolerable—When something is intolerable, you simply can't put up with (or tolerate) it.

Example sentence: "Your behavior is intolerable," her father responded before he grounded her.

Invasive—Think of the word invade. When something is invasive, it invades something or goes somewhere it isn't wanted.

Example sentence: Family get-togethers are always difficult since my great aunt likes to gossip; she goes around asking everyone highly invasive questions.

Inversion—To invert something is to turn it upside down. An inversion is the noun form of that word and means the act of turning upside down.

Example sentence: The scariest roller coaster in the park had the fastest speeds, the highest hills, and the most inversions.

Irk—When something irks you, it annoys you, but not in a major way. Someone leaving a dirty dish out, taking the middle piece of cake, not using their turn signal in traffic, or failing to do what they promised may irk you.

Example sentence: I was very irked when the teacher changed the assignment. While there was still plenty of time before the due date, I had already begun the research and had to change course due to the adjustments.

Labyrinth—Quite simply, a labyrinth is a maze.

Example sentence: Moving from a small family firm to a giant corporation was a big change, and I often found myself lost in the labyrinth of cubicles.

Laden—To be laden is to be weighed down with something physically. A shopping cart might be laden with groceries, for instance.

Example sentence: The mailman dreaded the holiday season when his bag became quite cumbersome to carry, laden as it was with packages full of presents.

Latter—Latter is the opposite of former. Former is the first thing mentioned, latter is the second or last.

Example sentence: I was given the option of either getting out of bed for school or getting grounded, and I foolishly choose the latter, which left me trapped at home over homecoming weekend.

Liaison—This is often used to mean a close connection or relationship. It can also mean a person who facilitates understanding between parties.

Example sentence: In the office, it was often my job to be a liaison between various parties.

Magnitude—The magnitude of something is how big it is.

Example sentence: My coworker seemed to have her head buried in the sand and didn't realize the magnitude of losing our biggest client.

Malice—Malice (*mal* at the beginning of the word means bad) is generally used to describe the feeling of one person wishing to do something harmful to another person.

Example sentence: It was a long-standing rivalry, and the malice off the field lead to overly aggressive behavior on the field, which resulted in the game being ended at halftime.

Malign—To malign someone is to say terrible things about them.

Example sentence: After he got a bad grade, he proceeded to malign the teacher to anyone who would listen.

Manifest—This can mean a variety of things. As a noun, it is a complete list. As a verb, it means to make appear or to make clear. As an adjective, it means obvious or clear.

Example sentence: The passenger manifest manifested to the detective the fact that the sought-after party was not on board the ship.

Manipulate—To manipulate something or someone is to change them to your liking. You might manipulate your parent's opinion on where to eat by casually mentioning pizza several times during the day. You might also manipulate clay into the shape of a vase.

Example sentence: While many people believe that data don't lie, in reality, data can be heavily manipulated to show just about whatever results are desired.

Mantra—A mantra is something that people repeat over and over to themselves in the hopes that it becomes true or as a means toward achieving a goal.

Example sentence: In the early days of January, people who appear to be just going about life are silently repeating their mantras in the hopes of fulfilling their New Years' resolutions.

Marginalize—This word refers to the action of making something less, often when it shouldn't be. A person's feelings may be marginalized or brushed away as not important.

Example sentence: The young girl always felt marginalized when her successful older siblings were around.

Meander—To meander is to wander in a non-straight line and with little or no haste or purpose.

Example sentence: If I get bored this afternoon, I may meander over to the park to see if anything is going on.

Mechanization—Mechanization is when something that used to be done by hand is now done by a machine.

Example sentence: Mechanization has caused great concern in the auto industry lately as workers have been laid off and their jobs replaced by robots.

Meddle—To meddle is to tamper with something, often human situations or emotions.

Example sentence: When my two best friends broke up, I tried to help them fix their relationship, but I only ended up making it worse. As my mom often says, "Meddling does no one any good."

Metastasize—When something metastasizes, it is spreading.

Example sentence: Luckily, the disease had been found before it metastasized, and so it appeared as if recovery were very likely.

Mire—To mire is to stick something down. When someone or something is mired, it can't be freed, but is stuck in a sticky situation either figuratively or literally.

Example sentence: I always cry during my favorite childhood book when the horse becomes mired in a bog and must be abandoned so that the quest can be completed.

Monotony—Monotony is the same thing over and over again.

Example sentence: As the semester progressed, I felt trapped in a scholastic monotony with nothing ever changing, each day exactly the same as the last.

150

Motivation—Motivation is what drives you. It's the feeling inside that makes you start that project, run that extra mile, or take the extra shift.

Example sentence: Since motivation was low, the teacher promised extra credit to the first student who turned in an "A"-worthy project.

Mundane—Something that is mundane is boring and normal. It's a regular everyday occurrence.

Example sentence: Until the fire alarms went off, it had just been a mundane Monday morning.

Mutable—Think about the math term permutation. A permutation has to do with all the different ways a set of numbers can be changed and rearranged into different orders. That root word *mut* generally has to do with change. Mutable describes something that is easy to or likely to change. Other words you might know with this root include mutate and commute.

Example sentence: The speaker was worried he would be unable to change the audience's minds, but it turned out they were much more mutable than he had anticipated.

Mystify—To mystify just means to confuse. Think about the word mystery with the same root. A mystery is confusing—mystifying someone confuses them.

Example sentence: The scientists were mystified at first as to the meaning of the data that they had collected.

Net—In describing pay, net pay is what is left after all taxes and fees are removed. In scientific terms, it could be what is left after all other considerations are removed. For example, when you weigh something and you remove the weight of the container, you are left with the net weight of what is in the container.

Example sentence: The charity race raised a net total of $3,500 after the administrative expenses and permit fees were paid out.

Notation—You know the word note; what you probably didn't realize is that it's a shortened version of notation. It's something you write to help you remember something or to convey information to another person.

Example sentence: By the time I bought the textbook, it had already had several other owners and the margins were filled with notations—some helpful, others decidedly not.

Nuance—A nuance is a subtle difference in the meaning or expression of something.

Example sentence: While the applicants responded to the question in a similar way, the nuances in their reactions helped the manager make a decision as to who would be a better fit for the job.

Null—Null means nothing; it's just another way of saying zero.

Example sentence: When the parties pass away, the contract becomes null and void.

Obliterate—To obliterate something is to completely and utterly destroy it beyond recognition.

Example sentence: The meteor obliterated the forest into which it crashed, scattering debris all over the countryside.

Obstinate—Obstinate is just the same as stubborn. It means refusing to give up even when wrong or faced with insurmountable forces against you.

Example sentence: Despite pleading, cajoling, and coercing, the young child obstinately refused to get in the bathtub.

Oscillate—To oscillate is to move back and forth in a predictable pattern at a set speed. The pendulum in a grandfather clock is a classic example of oscillation.

Example sentence: The oscillation of the carnival ride made me sick to my stomach.

Onerous—When something is onerous it is difficult to do, usually taking a lot of unpleasant work to complete.

Example sentence: As a veterinarian, I often have the onerous task of discussing expensive bills with clients.

Panacea—A panacea is a fix-all solution.

Example sentence: While most people view love as a panacea, I know from experience that it can't solve all problems.

Parasitic—Something that is parasitic attaches to something else and feeds off of it without giving anything back. This might be used to describe an actual parasite (like a tapeworm) or a person like the friend who always borrows money, but never returns it.

Example sentence: When one person would get wise to her parasitic ways, she would merely find someone else to leach the homework off of for the next few weeks.

Parity—Parity is equalness or being equal. It is the opposite of disparity, which is inequality.

Example sentence: Despite the parent's best efforts at parity, one of the children always felt that they had received less attention.

Paradox—A paradox is something that contradicts itself or sets up an impossible train of thought that never ends but always circles back on itself.

Example sentence: One of the most well-known paradoxes is the statement, "This statement is false."

Partake—To partake is the same as to participate. It is often used with food (to partake in a meal is to eat it) but can also be used with any given activity.

Example sentence: Even though I always insist I'm not hungry, my grandmother won't let me leave her home without partaking in at least one meal or snack with her and my grandfather.

Paternal—To be paternal is to act in a fatherly way. Paternal can also be used to describe things relating to fathers.

Example sentence: Even though I barely knew him, the old man acted in quite a paternal way to me and insisted on seeing me home safely when I became lost.

Permeate—To permeate is to soak through something, invading and saturating every part of it and leaving nothing untouched. Water permeates things in a flood, and smells permeate rooms and homes.

Example sentence: The smell of burned food permeated the kitchen as the family rushed to save their dinner.

Permutation—Remember the word mutable from above? Permutation has that same *mut* syllable indicating it's about change. Permutation has to do with all the different ways a set of items can be arranged in different orders. In how many ways can the order be changed?

Example sentence: In math class, the teacher explained permutations to us by making ten students line up in as many different ways as possible; the possibilities seemed endless.

Perpetual—Something that is perpetual is never-ending.

Example sentence: Life in the Arctic Circle is very difficult in the winter when whole communities are plunged into perpetual darkness for months on end.

Perspective—Your perspective is how you see things both literally (different seats in a theater have different perspectives of the stage) and figuratively (you and your parent may have different perspectives on your staying up until 3 A.M.).

Example sentence: Since he was the only young person in the office, he was often called into meetings to give a different perspective on various issues.

Perturb—To perturb is to disturb, but in an emotional way. A scary book or a strange person may perturb.

Example sentence: The teacher was quite perturbed by the actions of the small child, which were very out of character for a four-year-old.

Pervading—Pervading or pervade are often used as synonyms for permeate. Something (especially a smell) can be pervading when it permeates an area where it is not welcome.

Example sentence: The pervading smell was quite offensive to the students, who quickly jumped to open the windows.

Phenomena—Phenomena is the plural of the word phenomenon. A phenomenon is something that is known to exist or occur, the cause of which is often not clear. Planes going down in the Bermuda triangle is a well-known phenomenon.

Example sentence: A great crowd gathered to watch the strange phenomenon.

175

Pittance—A pittance is a pitiably small amount: not really enough to do anything with.

Example sentence: With her children and husband all gone, the widow somehow managed to live off the pittance given to her by neighborhood charities.

Plasticity—The plasticity of something is its ability to change and be molded.

Example sentence: The best time to learn a foreign language is when you're young; that's when you still have the most brain plasticity.

Plenipotentiary—A plenipotentiary is a person who has been given the authority to act on behalf of their country in foreign countries. Diplomats often act in this role, though true plenipotentiary power is rare.

Example sentence: During negotiations with France, Benjamin Franklin acted as a plenipotentiary for the United States.

Posterity—Posterity is the future of humankind: all of the people who will come in the future.

Example sentence: The collection of American historical artifacts at the museum is being carefully preserved for posterity.

Postulate—To postulate is to guess or to present an idea that is not proven. A TV personality may postulate that a certain person will be elected.

Example sentence: "Maybe there is a traffic jam," she postulated as she waited for her date who was very late.

Potent—Potent means very strong. Not physically, but of a high concentration. A smell or taste, for example, may be very potent.

Example sentence: As the potent fumes wafted through the laboratory, the alarms sounded to warn all the scientists to evacuate quickly.

Prattle—To prattle is to talk on and on while saying little of value.

Example sentence: Faced with an abundance of awkward silences, the young lady prattled endlessly to avoid the quiet.

Predecessor—The predecessor to something or someone is what came before. This word is often used to describe a person who held an office or job prior to the current office or job holder.

Example sentence: "My predecessor may have allowed talking in class, but I do not," the new teacher informed her students.

Preposterous—Something that is preposterous is so ridiculous as to be laughable.

Example sentence: The elderly man laughed and said "don't be preposterous," when his grandson suggested that he try the mechanical bull at the fair.

Primitive—Something that is primitive is very basic and not technologically advanced. For example, some might see flag signaling as a primitive form of long-distance communication.

Example sentence: Primitive computers took up whole buildings and had less computing power than the average flip phone does today.

Pristine—Something that is pristine is untouched and perfect. It is completely unmarred in any way.

Example sentence: One of my favorite sights is a field of pristine snow, untrampled by any animals or humans.

Proliferate—To proliferate is to grow, spread, and reproduce, often at a high rate of speed. Rumors tend to proliferate within schools, as do germs.

Example sentence: The weeds proliferated throughout the summer, and he quickly realized that having a pristine garden was impossible.

Promulgate—To promulgate an idea is to spread it around. There are a lot of programs, for example, that promulgate anti-bullying messages to students.

Example sentence: The man was asked to leave the gathering when he was heard to be promulgating his latest get-rich-quick scheme.

Province—A province is a geographical area under a government. Many countries have a province system instead of having states.

Example sentence: As a Canadian, I often simply respond with my province when Americans ask what state I'm from.

Proxy—A proxy is a substitute. A person standing in for another person can generally be called a proxy. In some situations, formal events like voting, getting married, and signing contracts can be done by proxy.

Example sentence: Since the CEO was incredibly busy that day, he had his assistant attend the board meeting to vote as his proxy.

Psychological—Things that are psychological have to do with the inner workings of our minds, which affect our feelings, emotions, and actions.

Example sentence: The doctor, having run out of tests to perform, came to the conclusion that the symptoms must have psychological causes.

Quarrel—To quarrel is to argue with someone. A quarrel is an argument.

Example sentence: The young nanny was constantly begging the children not to quarrel.

Rapacious—Someone who is rapacious is unable to be satisfied. They are very greedy and always looking to gain more of what they want.

Example sentence: The rapacious vultures searched for food all over the meadow.

Receptive—A person who is receptive is open to receiving things, quite often ideas.

Example sentence: While the student was nervous about asking to take the test again, the teacher was quite receptive to the idea.

Redress—Don't get tricked into thinking this word means to get dressed again. Instead, it means to fix or make a situation right where someone has been wronged.

Example sentence: The man who had been wrongfully imprisoned sought redress for his grievances.

Reluctant—To be reluctant is to act on the feeling of not wanting to do something. If you end up doing the thing, you do it in a manner that shows that you don't want to be doing it.

Example sentence: The teacher was reluctant to give up his Saturday to grade papers, but the students had already waited a week, so he sat down with his red pen and got started.

Remonstrate—To remonstrate is to object to something strongly or to speak out against something strongly.

Example sentence: The principal remonstrated the student's misbehavior.

Repression—Repression is the act of holding something down or back, especially ideas and movements.

Example sentence: The governmental repression of revolutionary societies became stronger each week.

Reverence—Reverence means showing great respect or a deep appreciation for something.

Example sentence: When entering the throne room, it is always necessary to show reverence for the king by bowing before him and kissing his ring.

Rhetoric—Rhetoric is the way in which people speak and argue to convey their points. Different people may have different styles of rhetoric: They may ask questions, they may use persuasive language, they may yell, they may trick. All of those are types of rhetoric.

Example sentence: The country quickly got tired of the candidates' loud rhetorical blustering.

200

Sanction—Sanction is a very interesting word as it has seemingly opposite meanings. Make sure you pay very close attention to the context. Sometimes sanction refers to officially approving or allowing something to happen. The school might sanction a dance, meaning it's officially approved by the administration. However, sanctions can also be negative—a penalty for something done that is bad. Usually the context of negative sanctions is legal; when the word is used in this manner, it often refers to one country placing sanctions on another country for things like human rights violations.

Example sentence: "Just know that I do not sanction this event," said the major when the town council voted to have the festival against her wishes.

Scuttling—Scuttling is a very specific type of movement. It's moving very quickly with tiny (often not smooth) steps. Think about how crabs may run along a beach—they're almost always scuttling.

Example sentence: The pickpocket checked over his shoulder one more time before scuttling down an alley with his ill-gotten gains.

Scenario—A scenario is the setup for a work of fiction, a book, movie, or play. It can also be any imagined situation that people put themselves in, such as discussing what could happen in the future or things that should have happened in the past.

Example sentence: My English teacher proposed an interesting scenario—what books would you take with you if you were stuck on a deserted island?

Seamless—Think of a shirt without seams—it's completely smooth and has no breaks in the fabric. When something is seamless, it is very smooth. This word is often used as a synonym for flawless.

Example sentence: The director was thrilled when the whole production came together seamlessly.

Sentiment—A sentiment is how you feel or what you say about something that has occurred.

Example sentence: While he expressed nice sentiments about being sorry, she couldn't bring herself to forgive his mistakes.

Sentinel—A sentinel is a soldier whose job it is to keep watch over something.

Example sentence: The sentinel rushed to the general with news of invaders.

Sequence—A sequence is the order that things are in or the order that they should be in.

Example sentence: The librarian got very upset when she found out that her assistant was shelving books in the wrong sequence.

Shingled—Something described as shingled would have the same layered look as the shingles on a roof.

Example sentence: As odd as it looked, shingled hair was quite popular in the early 2000s.

Skeptic—A skeptic is someone who is skeptical, or doubtful, of something.

Example sentence: Jack continued to power forward with his extravagant plans, despite the loud voices of his skeptics.

Sluggish—When described as sluggish, things are slow or moving like a slug.

Example sentence: I'm incredibly sluggish if I don't have any coffee in the morning.

Squalid—When described as squalid, things are run down, dirty, and often infested with vermin. This is often the result of war or poverty.

Example sentence: Despite her best efforts at fixing and cleaning, the apartment remained at best squalid and at worst unlivable.

Squelch—Squelch is an onomatopoeia; the word means the sound it makes. Squelch is the sound that might be made if you tried to pull your foot out of thick mud or if you stepped on a slug.

Example sentence: With soaking wet socks and shoes, every step squelched.

Stagnate—To stagnate is to stop moving forward. This is generally not physical movement.

Example sentence: The project had stagnated, which caused great concern with the management team.

Stewardship—A steward is someone who takes care of something. Stewardship, then, is the noun form of the act of taking care of something.

Example sentence: As the result of careful stewardship, the manor survived the 50 years of being boarded up with only a bit of dust to tell of the long emptiness.

Stupefied—To be stupefied is to be made temporarily stupid. This generally happens if something really sudden or unexpected occurs.

Example sentence: After witnessing the last-minute heartbreaking loss, many fans left the stadium with stupefied looks on their faces.

Subjugate—To subjugate a person or group of people is to put them under your total control. This is especially applicable in war-time situations when entire populations are conquered and subjugated.

Example sentence: The hero rode gallantly into town, determined to free the subjugated people.

Subordinate—Someone who is subordinate is lower in status, usually in a workplace. A worker is subordinate to the boss.

Example sentence: The hallmark of a good manager is when they treat their subordinates with care, kindness, and fairness.

Subsequent—Something that is subsequent comes after something else. For example, my birthday is subsequent to that of my older sibling.

Example sentence: After getting a D on the midterm, he resolved to study harder for any subsequent tests.

Substantial—When something is substantial, it is not insignificant, but almost the opposite. It is of an important size or amount.

Example sentence: The restaurant lost a substantial amount of money when it changed management.

Sufficient—When something is described as sufficient, it means that it is enough.

Example sentence: While I was doubtful that we'd have enough food to feed everyone, it ended up being a sufficient amount.

Supplemental—Something that is supplemental adds something unnecessary, but helpful, to something else. There may be supplemental information at the end of a chapter. A family may pay for a vacation with supplemental income from a part-time job.

Example sentence: The supplemental assistance from neighbors helped the family through tough times.

Sustenance—Sustenance is what sustains a person. Generally, this is used as a fancy word for food.

Example sentence: After having been shipwrecked for months, the sailors craved sustenance other than dried fish and leaves.

Swayed—To sway is to move slightly back and forth. However, this term can be used figuratively as well as literally. In an argument, you may have swayed your opponent. They didn't actually move back and forth, but maybe their opinions moved slightly.

Example sentence: As the boat swayed, I felt my stomach turn.

Symmetric—Something that is symmetric is the same on both sides. For example, if a person has a symmetrical face, then the left and right sides of their face would be identical.

Example sentence: By very definition, all circles must by symmetric in all directions.

Synthetic—Something that is synthetic is made artificially, not naturally.

Example sentence: Clothing made from synthetic material may last longer, but it also tends to breathe less, causing sweat, smells, and acne.

225

Sullen—To be sullen is to be grumpy and unenthusiastic. It is a type of bad mood wherein you do things only under protest. You might think of it as being related to sulking.

Example sentence: The sullen young man was often reprimanded by his mother for his bad attitude.

Tactile—Something that is tactile has to do with the sense of touch. A tactile sensation, for example, is a sensation of being touched in some way.

Example sentence: When I was young, I had a tactile disorder whereby the feeling of grass and other things against my skin caused me great distress.

Tangible—Something that is tangible can be seen and touched (as compared to the opposite intangible).

Example sentence: The tangible benefit of saving for retirement is obviously the money; the intangible benefit is peace of mind.

Tedious—Something that is tedious is repetitive and boring. It takes a long time and doesn't engage the mind.

Example sentence: The tedious task of hand stitching clothing is thankfully no longer necessary due to the advent of the sewing machine.

Tout—To tout is to aggressively try to sell something, to sing its praises to get someone to buy it.

Example sentence: I left quickly when I discovered the so-called party was just an excuse for the hostess to tout her overpriced essential oils.

Transaction—When something is a transaction, it has something to do with the purchase or exchange of goods or services.

Example sentence: The person she thought was her friend was really just interested in a transactional relationship.

Transit—To transit is to move from one place to another. As a noun, transit can also refer to a network of public busses, trains, and streetcars.

Example sentence: Since her car had broken down, she found it necessary to take public transit to work for a few weeks.

Traipsing—When one is traipsing, they are coming and going or moving in a carefree manner.

Example sentence: He finally had to put a stop to the children traipsing in and out of the house with their shoes covered in mud.

Tributary—A tributary is a stream or river upstream that feeds into a bigger river.

Example sentence: The Ohio River, while large, is just a tributary of the mighty Mississippi River.

Ubiquitous—When something is ubiquitous, it is found everywhere. It is common.

Example sentence: The flags were ubiquitous in the highly patriotic town.

Unassuming—When something or someone is unassuming, they are unthreatening and down to earth.

Example sentence: Everyone liked the high school principal. His unassuming nature made him easy to work with.

Unrequited—When feelings are unrequited, they are not returned in kind. This word is often used to describe one-sided love.

Example sentence: Driven mad by unrequited love, the story's heroine wandered the moors for the rest of her life and haunted her beloved after her death.

Unseemly—Something that is unseemly might otherwise be described as inappropriate for the situation.

Example sentence: While appropriate for milking cows, overalls are an unseemly choice for a fine French restaurant.

Unstinting—Something that is unstinting is given without pause or second thought.

Example sentence: My favorite teacher gave me unstinting support in my quest for academic excellence.

Unveil—To unveil is to reveal. Think of a bride walking down the aisle wearing her veil and then removing her veil to reveal her face to the groom.

Example sentence: The excitement was noticeable as the crowd waited for the mayor to unveil the new city monument.

Usurp—To usurp is to overthrow. This word is often used to discuss overthrowing governments and other authorities.

Example sentence: It is the duty of several agencies to find and arrest anyone who intends to usurp the government.

Validate—To validate something is to say that it is valid, true, or accurate. Quite often, businesses will validate parking. That is, they'll stamp the parking ticket to indicate that the person who parked had a true reason to be there.

Example sentence: Though the woman claimed that she owned the house, her words needed to be validated by calling the local public records office.

Vantage—Vantage is a spot with a good view to see what needs to be seen.

Example sentence: From their vantage point on the second story, they could see the whole parade while staying nice and warm.

Verifiable—Something that is verifiable is able to be verified, or proven correct. Facts are generally verifiable while opinions are not.

Example sentence: His alibi was not verifiable and so he was left on the list of suspects.

Vernacular—The vernacular is the common or slang terms that people in a given community use.

Example sentence: While parents might think it's rude or confusing, most students have vernacular terms that they and their friends use frequently.

Versatile—Something that is versatile can be used in many different ways.

Example sentence: Anytime you go camping you should take a good length of cording. It's a versatile tool that can help in many dangerous situations.

Vestigial—Something that is vestigial is a small left-behind part of something much bigger.

Example sentence: The one standing hut was the vestigial remains of a once-mighty empire.

Virtuous—Something that is virtuous has virtue, or a high sense of morality.

Example sentence: The virtuous young people refused to take part in the cheating ring that was quickly growing at their school.

Wayside—The wayside is exactly what it sounds like, the side of the road. This term is also often used in a figurative sense.

Example sentence: It is often a sad fact of life that when someone begins dating, their friends are pushed to the wayside.

Yearning—Yearning is to want something with all your heart. To crave it at the expense of all else.

Example sentence: Although the young man liked his hometown, he felt a sense of yearning for international travel.

Index

A

Abject, in word list, 956
Abode, in word list, 956
Absolute value, solving equations, 373–374
Abstract
  in vocabulary index, 947
  in word list, 956
Accommodations, for SAT, 4
Accurate, in vocabulary index, 947
Acknowledge, in word list, 956
Active reading
  demonstration of, 94–96
  strategies for, 92
Adapt, in word list, 957
Adjacent sides, in right triangles, 586–587
Adjectives, 242
Admonition, in word list, 957
Advanced drills (writing and language)
  comparative passages, 203–206
  fiction, 192–194
  historical documents, 198–200
  passages, 323–333
  science, 201–203
  social science, 194–197
Advanced math components
  common factoring patterns, 416–418
  completing the square, 434–435
  exponent rules, 421–422
  exponents and roots, 423–425
  extraneous solutions, 439–440
  identifying constants, 474
  interpreting functions, 475–478
  parabola graphing, 455–459
  plugging in the answers, 436–437
  polynomial graphs, 463–466
  polynomials and factoring, 414–417
  quadratic equations, 429–430
  quadratic formula, 432–433
  question type, 343
  square root method, 431–432
  synthetic division, 441–443
  term manipulation, 473–474
  transformations, 460–463
  undefined functions, 438–439
  zeros of a function, 452–454
Adverbs, conjunctive, 241–242
Affluent, in word list, 957
Aggrandize, in word list, 957
Aggregate, in word list, 957
Agitate, in word list, 957
Algebra
  distance, rate, and time, 388–389
  functions in table form, 390
  interpreting variables and constants, 389–390
  intersecting and overlapping lines, 405
  lines and slope, 403–409
  parallel lines, 406–409
  perpendicular lines, 406–409
  question type, 343
  slope-intercept, 404–405
  word problems, 386–388
Alternation, in word list, 957
Amicable, in word list, 957
Analogous, in word list, 958
Analogy
  in vocabulary index, 947
  in word list, 958
Analysis
  passage and paragraph, 293–296
  practice passage, 296–298
  question types, 90
Angles
  complementary, 588
  inscribed, 595–596
  measures in degrees, 575
  parallelogram, 577
  quadrilateral, 577
  rectangle, 577
  supplementary, 572–573
  vertical, 573
Anomaly, in word list, 958
Anticipate, in vocabulary index, 947
Antipathy, in word list, 958
Apostrophes, 248–250
Apparition, in word list, 958
Appropriate, in vocabulary index, 948
Arbitrary, in word list, 958
Arc length, 596
Area
  circle, 593–594
  equilateral triangle, 587–588
  formulas, 347, 557
  parallelogram, 560
  rectangle, 558
  sector area of a circle, 597–598
  surface, 561–563
  trapezoid, 561–563
  triangle, 558–559
  See also Formulas; Volume
Ascertain, in word list, 958
Aspire, in word list, 958
Assumption/assume, in vocabulary index, 948
Attitude, in vocabulary index, 948
Attribute, in vocabulary index, 948
Audiobooks, 103–104
Autocratic, in word list, 958
Automated, in word list, 958–959
Axis of symmetry, 455

B

Bar graphs, 532–533
Beget, in word list, 959
Benevolent, in word list, 959
Bestow, in word list, 959
Big picture
  question drills, 134–138
  question types, 90
Binomial, square of, 416
Biological, in word list, 959
Box
  formulas, 347
  volume, 563
Box plots, 538–539

C

Calculator
  algebra drill with, 610–612
  in math section, 343
  mixed math, 642–645
  problem solving and data analysis with, 632–634
Calibrate, in word list, 959
Calisthenics, in word list, 959
Capacity, in word list, 959
Celestial, in word list, 959
Censure, in word list, 960
Characterize, in vocabulary index, 948
Circle
  360 degrees, 594
  arc length, 596
  area, 593–594
  circumference, 594
  common unit, 600–601
  formulas, 347, 557, 598–599
  radians, 599–600
  radius and diameter, 593
  sector area, 597–598
Circulation, in word list, 960
Circumference, circle, 594
Claim, in vocabulary index, 948–949
Clarifying information, math, 349
Coerce, in word list, 960
Cognition, in word list, 960
Cohesion, in vocabulary index, 949
Colloquial, in word list, 960
Colons, 246–247
Combine, in vocabulary index, 949
Commas, 240–244
Commercial, in word list, 960
Common denominator, 362

Common factoring patterns, 416–418
Common unit circle, 600–601
Comparative passages
  advanced drills, 203–206
  question drills, 146–151, 180–183
  question types, 90
Complementary, in word list, 960
Complementary angles, sine and cosine, 588
Completing the square, 434–435
Complimentary, in word list, 960
Compound interest, 509–510
Comprehension, improving, 102–104
Concepts tested, in math section, 344
Conclusion, in vocabulary index, 949
Conclusions
  in reading, writing, and language passages, 288–289
  from survey data, 520–521
Cone
  formulas, 347
  volume, 557, 565
Confirm, in vocabulary index, 949
Conflate, in word list, 960
Conjunctive adverbs, 241–242
Conjure, in word list, 960
Connecting words, 218
Consensus, in word list, 960–961
Consequence, in word list, 961
Conservator, in word list, 961
Constants
  identifying, 474–475
  interpreting, 389–390, 543–545
Constitution, in word list, 961
Context, words in, 90
Contingent, in word list, 961
Contradict, in vocabulary index, 949
Contrast, in vocabulary index, 950
Conventional, in word list, 961
Convey
  in vocabulary index, 950
  in word list, 961
Convoke, in word list, 961
Convulsion, in word list, 961
Cooperatively, in word list, 961–962
Coordinating conjunctions, 241
Cosine, in right triangles, 586–587
Critical thinking
  question drills, 140–144
  question types, 90
Cubes
  difference of, 416–417
  sum of, 416
Cultivate, in word list, 962
Cylinder
  formulas, 347
  volume, 557, 564

D

Dashes, 247–248
Data analysis, question type, 343
Data and graphs, question type, 343
Data sets, range and standard deviation, 489–491
Dawdle, in word list, 962
Decay, linear, 540–542
Decipher, in word list, 962
Deficient, in word list, 962
Degrade, in word list, 962
Degree
  measures in, 575
  to radian conversions, 600–601
Demonstrations
  active reading, 94–96
  reading questions dos and don'ts, 96–99
Demur, in word list, 962
Denominator, 362
Dependent clause, 240
Desolation, in word list, 962
Despoil, in word list, 962
Deter, in word list, 962
Developmental pattern, in vocabulary index, 950
Diameter, circle, 593
Differences of squares, 416
Digital format, 3
Dimensional analysis, 497–498
Discriminant, 434, 607
Disenfranchise, in word list, 962
Disparity, in word list, 962–963
Disseminate, in word list, 963
Dissimilar, in word list, 963
Distance, rate, and time, math problems, 388–389
Diverge, in word list, 963
Doctrine, in word list, 963
Doldrums, in word list, 963
Domestic, in word list, 963
Dominion, in word list, 963
Drills, math
  additional math topics, 638–640
  advanced math no calculator, 620–622, 626–628
  algebra with calculator, 610–612
  algebra without calculator, 616–618
  area, perimeter, and volume, 567–569
  with calculator, 610–612, 632–634
  circles, 601–604
  exponents and roots, 425–427
  function interpretation and manipulation, 476–478, 481–483
  lines, angles, and triangles, 578–581
  lines and slope, 409–412
  measures of center, 491–493
  mixed math, 642–645
  polynomials and factoring, 417–419
  problem solving and data analysis, 511–513, 515–517
  problem solving and data analysis with calculator, 632–634
  problem solving, data analysis graphs, and data interpretation, 546–548, 550–554
  right triangles and trigonometry, 588–591
  solving advanced equations, 445–446, 448–450
  surveys, 521–524
  unit conversion, 498–499
  zeros, parabolas, and polynomial graphing, 468–471
Drills, reading
  advanced, 169–183
  big picture in reading, 134–138
  comparative in reading, 146–151
  comparative passages, 180–183
  critical thinking in reading, 140–144
  evidence in reading, 125–131
  fiction, 169–171
  full passage, 169–183
  function in reading, 119–123
  graph analysis, 161–166
  historical documents, 175–177
  inference in reading, 111–116
  interpretation in reading, 105–109
  passages 1 and 2, 180–183
  social science, 172–175
  words in context in reading, 153–158
Dubious, in word list, 963

E

Earnest, in word list, 963
Eddy, in word list, 963
Effective, in vocabulary index, 950
Effectual, in word list, 964
Efficacy, in word list, 964
Efficient, in word list, 964
Elimination
  concepts and formulas, 365–366
  solving equations, 368
Embellish, in word list, 964
Emit, in word list, 964
Empathize, in word list, 964
Emphasize, in vocabulary index, 950
Endearing, in word list, 964
Endeavor, in word list, 964
Endow, in word list, 964
English language learners, 4
Enhance, in word list, 964
Enterprise, in word list, 964–965
Entice, in word list, 965
Entrenched, in word list, 965
Ephemeral, in word list, 965
Equilateral triangles
  area, 587–588
  concepts of, 575
Equivalent equations, 405
Errors, common math, 344
Establish, in vocabulary index, 950
Evidence
  question drills, 125–131
  question types, 90
Evince, in word list, 965
Expenditure, in word list, 965
Explanatory, in word list, 965
Explicit, in vocabulary index, 950–951
Exponent rules, 421–422
Exponential growth and decay, 540–542

Exponents
MADSPM acronym, 421
and roots, 423–425
rules, 421–422
Extensive, in word list, 965
Extraneous solutions, 439–440

F
Facilitate, in vocabulary index, 951
Factoring, common patterns, 416–417
Feature, in word list, 965
Feeble, in word list, 965
Fetter, in word list, 965–966
Fiction/literature
advanced drills, 192–194
drill, 169–171
reading strategies for, 93
test structure, 89
Figurative, in vocabulary index, 951
Figure, in vocabulary index, 951
Finite, in word list, 966
First, outer, inner, last (FOIL) method, concepts and formulas, 359–360
Fiscal, in word list, 966
Florid, in word list, 966
FOIL method, 359–360
Format, digital, 3
Former, in word list, 966
Formulas
circle, 598–599
equivalent equations, 405
first, outer, inner, last (FOIL), 359–360
fractions, 362–364
math, 347
pyramid, 347
Pythagorean theorem, 347, 557
sheet, 556
slope, 403–404
slope-intercept, 404–405
See also Area; Volume
45-45-90 triangle, 557
Forum, in word list, 966
Fractions, concepts and formulas, 362–364
Frantic, in word list, 966
Frequent, in word list, 966
Function
identifying constants, 474–475
interpretation and manipulation, 473–476
interpreting, 475–476
interpreting constants and, 543–545
key word, 96
question drills, 119–123
question types, 90
in table form, 390, 390–391
undefined, 438–439
in vocabulary index, 951
zeros of a, 452–454
Function notation
concepts and formulas, 374–385
solving equations, 374–375
Fundamental, in word list, 966

G
Geometry, question type, 343
Germinate, in word list, 966
Glom, in word list, 966
Glut, in word list, 967
Goals, accomplishing, 293–294
Grammar knowledge, improving, 223–224
Grammar review
number and tense agreement, 231–232
punctuation, 240–253
subject-verb agreement, 225–226
verb agreement, 228
wordiness, 233–235, 237–239
Grammar rules, 222
Graph analysis
practice questions, 300–304
preparation for, 299
question drills, 161–166
question types, 90
in reading, 89
typical questions, 218
Graphing
function transformations, 460–463
parabolas, 455–459
Graphs
bar, 532–533
box plots, 538–539
of a function, 452–454
histograms, 532–535
interpretation, 527–528, 527–529
polynomial, 463–466
scatterplots, 529–532
visualizing polynomial, 463–467
Graphs and data, question type, 343
Graphs and data interpretation, probability, 525–526
Greatest common factor (GCF), concepts and formulas, 361–362
Grievance, in word list, 967
Growth
exponential, 540–542
linear, 540–542

H
Haggle, in word list, 967
Heart of algebra
See Algebra
Histograms, 532–535
Historical documents
advanced drills, 198–200
drill, 175–177
reading strategies for, 93
test structure, 89
Hypotenuse, in right triangles, 586–587

I
Ideas, developing, 294–295
Ignominious, in word list, 967
Illegible, in word list, 967
Imaginary numbers, essentials, 606–609
Imaginary solutions, 439
Immured, in word list, 967
Impel, in word list, 967
Implicit, in vocabulary index, 952
Imply, in vocabulary index, 952
Impression, in vocabulary index, 952
Inapplicable, in word list, 967
Incomprehensible, in word list, 967
Incontestable, in word list, 967
Incorporate, in word list, 968
Incredulous, in word list, 968
Independent clause, 240
Indicate, in vocabulary index, 952
Indifference, in word list, 968
Indistinguishable, in word list, 968
Ineffective, in word list, 968
Inefficacious, in word list, 968
Inequalities
concepts and formulas, 372–373
solving equations, 372
Inexorable, in word list, 968
Infer, in vocabulary index, 952
Inference
key word, 96
question drills, 111–116
question types, 90
Infinite solutions, pattern recognition, 366–367
Ingenious, in word list, 968
Inherent, in word list, 969
Innumerable, in word list, 968
Inscribed angle, 595–596
Insolent, in word list, 969
Institution, in word list, 968
Insurrection, in word list, 968
Integrate, in word list, 969
Intended meaning
logical comparisons, 259–260
modifier placement, 257–258
in word list, 969
Interest
compound, 509–510
simple, 508–509
Intermittent, in word list, 969
Internet archives, 102
Interpretation
question drills, 105–109
question types, 90
in vocabulary index, 953
Intersecting lines, 405
Intolerable, in word list, 969
Introduction, paragraph, 287–288
Intuitive, in word list, 969
Invasive, in word list, 969
Inversion, in word list, 969
Irk, in word list, 969
Isosceles triangles, 575–576

K
Key words, reading, 96

L
Labyrinth, in word list, 969–970
Laden, in word list, 970
Latter, in word list, 970
Least common multiple (LCM), concepts and formulas, 361
Liaison, in word list, 970
Library of Congress archives, 103

Library resources, 103
Linear decay, 540–542
Linear and exponential growth, 540–542
Line(s)
  intersecting and overlapping, 405
  parallel, 406–409
  perpendicular, 406–409
  slope-intercept, 404–405
Lists, 241, 246
Literal, in vocabulary index, 953
Literal meaning
  logical comparisons, 259–260
  modifier placement, 257–258
Logical comparisons, 259–260

M

MADSPM, exponent acronym, 421
Magnitude, in word list, 970
Maintain, in vocabulary index, 953
Malice, in word list, 970
Malign, in word list, 970
Manifest, in word list, 970
Manipulate, in word list, 970
Mantra, in word list, 970
Margin of error, 520
Marginalize, in word list, 970
Math
  calculator usage, 348
  clarifying information, 349
  dos and don'ts, 348–354
  fill-in questions, 346–347
  formulas, 347
  non-tested items, 343
  pacing, 348
  question types, 343
  scoring for, 345–346
  strategies for, 348–354
  test structure, 343–344
  See also Advanced math; Calculator; Math, additional topics; Math strategy tips; Percentages; Problem solving and data analysis
Math, additional topics
  angles, 572–573
  angles, triangles, and quadrilaterals, 575–578
  area, 558–563, 587–588
  circles, 593–600
  common unit circle points, 600
  degree to radian conversions, 600
  formulas, 557
  imaginary numbers, 606–609
  parallel lines, 406–409, 573–575
  perimeter, 569
  right triangles and trigonometry, 583–588
  volume, 563–567
Math errors, manipulating negative signs, 414
Math practice, word problems, 391–403
Math strategy tips
  common factoring patterns, 416
  constants, 474
  constant/variable meaning, 389
  drawings, 572
  expressions, 473
  geometric formulas, 557
  graph axis units, 527
  pattern recognition, 423–424
  percentage changes, 510
  polynomials, 414
  proportions, 496
  quadratic function, 442
  reading math questions, 444
  slope and line formulas, 408
  surveys, 519, 520
  system of equations, 368
  wording and math operations, 386
  zeros, parabolas, and polynomial graphing, 433
Mean, measure of center, 486–487
Meander, in word list, 970–971
Meaning, intended, 271–273
Measures in degrees, 575
Measures of center
  mean, 486–487
  median, 487–488
  mode, 488
  outliers, 488–489
  range, 489–491
  standard deviation, 489–491
Mechanization, in word list, 971
Meddle, in word list, 971
Median, measure of center, 487–488
Metastasize, in word list, 971
Mire, in word list, 971
Mode, measure of center, 488
Modifier placement, 257–258
Monotony, in word list, 971
Motivation, in word list, 971
Mundane, in word list, 971
Mutable, in word list, 971
Mystify, in word list, 971

N

Natural science, reading strategies for, 93
Negative reciprocals, 406
Net, in word list, 971
Nonfiction
  reading strategies for, 93
  test structure, 89
Non-tested items, 343
Not, key word, 96
Notation, in word list, 972
Nouns, 249
Nuance, in word list, 972
Null, in word list, 972
Number and tense agreement, 218, 231–232
Numerator, 362

O

Obliterate, in word list, 972
Obstinate, in word list, 972
Onerous, in word list, 972
Opposite, in right triangles, 586–587
Order of operations, concepts and formulas, 358–359
Organization
  conclusions, 288–289
  introduction, 287–288
  practice passage, 289–291
  sentence placement, 286
  sentences and paragraphs, 285–289
  setup information, 285
  See also Sentence structure
Oscillate, in word list, 972
Outliers, measures of center, 488–489
Overlapping lines, 405

P

Panacea, in word list, 972
Parabola
  completing the square, 434–435
  function transformations, 460–463
  graphing, 455–459
  visualizing polynomials, 463–466
  zeros of a function, 452–454
Paradox, in word list, 972
Paragraphs, organization, 285–289
Parallel lines
  concepts, 406–409
  and transversal, 573–575
Parallel structure, 255–256
Parallelogram
  angles, 577
  area, 560
Parasitic, in word list, 972
Parentheses, 251
Parenthetical, in vocabulary index, 953
Parenthetical phrase, 240–241, 247
Parity, in word list, 972
Partake, in word list, 973
Passage, order, 100–101
Passage and paragraph analysis
  accomplishing a goal, 293–294
  developing ideas, 294–295
  tone, 295–296
  typical questions, 218
Passage and paragraph organization, typical questions, 218
Passages 1 and 2
  drill, 180–183
  question types, 93–94
  reading strategies for, 93
  test structure, 89
  types of, 93–94
Paternal, in word list, 973
Pattern, developmental, 950
Pattern recognition
  concepts and formulas, 366–367
  exponents and, 423–424
  practice questions, 364
  solving equations, 368
PEMDAS, 358–359
Percentages
  compound interest, 509–510
  essentials, 502–505
  increase/decrease, 505–508
  simple interest, 508–509
Perimeter, 559, 569
Permeate, in word list, 973

Permutation, in word list, 973
Perpendicular lines, 406–409
Perpetual, in word list, 973
Perspective, in word list, 973
Perturb, in word list, 973
Pervading, in word list, 973
Phenomena, in word list, 973
Phrases, prepositional, 270–271
Pittance, in word list, 973
Plasticity, in word list, 974
Plenipotentiary, in word list, 974
Plugging in choices
  concepts and formulas, 367–372
  pattern recognition, 367–369
  solving equations, 369
Plural possession, 248–249
Podcasts, 103–104
Polygon, perimeter, 559
Polynomials
  common factoring patterns, 416–417
  graphing, 463–467
  manipulation, 414–416
  synthetic division, 441–442
  visualizing, 463–466
Posterity, in word list, 974
Postulate, in word list, 974
Potent, in word list, 974
Practice passage
  analysis, 296–298
  graph analysis, 300–304
  writing and language, 306–322, 315–317
  proper wording, 274–275
  punctuation, 252–253
  sentence structure, 266–268
  transitions, 281–283
Prattle, in word list, 974
Preceding, in vocabulary index, 953
Predecessor, in word list, 974
Preparation, for SAT, 7–8
Prepositional phrases, proper choice, 270–271
Preposterous, in word list, 974
Previous, in vocabulary index, 954
Primary
  key word, 96
  in vocabulary index, 954
Primitive, in word list, 974
Prism, right rectangular, 563
Pristine, in word list, 974
Problem solving and data analysis
  box plots, 538–539
  constants and functions, 543–546
  graph interpretation, 527–529
  graphs and data interpretation, 525–545
  histograms, 532–534
  linear and exponential growth, 540–543
  measures of center, 486–491
  percentages, 502–511
  probability, 525–526
  question type, 343
  scatterplots, 529–531
  surveys, 519–523
  tables, 535–538
  unit conversion, 496–498
Problem solving process, 344
Project Gutenberg, 102
Proliferate, in word list, 974
Promulgate, in word list, 975
Pronouns, 249
Proper tone, 271–273
Proper wording
  typical questions, 218
  words that confuse, 269–270
Propose, in vocabulary index, 954
Province, in word list, 975
Proxy, in word list, 975
Psychological, in word list, 975
Punctuation
  apostrophes, 248–250
  colons, 246–247
  commas, 240–244
  dashes, 247–248
  practice passage, 252–253
  pronouns, 249
  question marks, 251–252
  semicolons, 245–246
  sentence combinations, 261–264
  typical questions, 218
Purpose
  key word, 96
  question types, 90
Pyramid
  formulas, 347
  volume, 557, 565–567
Pythagorean theorem
  formulas, 347, 557
  right triangles, 583–585
Pythagorean triples, 584–585

Q

Quadratic equations, factoring, 429–430
Quadratic formula, 432
Quadratic functions
  completing the square, 434–435
  factoring quadratic equations, 429–430
  plugging in the answers, 436
  square root method, 431
  undefined functions, 438–439
Quadrilateral, angles, 577
Quarrel, in word list, 975
Question marks, 251–252
Question types
  data analysis, 343
  data and graphs, 343
  graph analysis, 90
  graphs and data, 343
  math, 343
  number and tense agreement, 218
  reading, 90

R

Radian conversions, 600–601
Radians, circle, 599–600
Radius, circle, 593
Random, sample size, 519
Range, measure of center, 489–491
Rapacious, in word list, 975
Reading
  comprehension improvement, 102–104
  passage order, 100–101
  question dos and don'ts, 96–99
  question order, 101
  scoring, 91
  strategies for, 92, 99–100
Reading drills
  big picture, 134–138
  comparative in reading, 146–151
  critical thinking, 140–144
  evidence, 125–131
  function, 119–123
  graph analysis, 161–166
  inference, 111–116
  interpretation, 105–109
  words in context, 153–158
Reasonable, in vocabulary index, 954
Receptive, in word list, 975
Reciprocals, negative, 406
Rectangle
  angles, 577
  area, 558
  formulas, 347, 557
Redress, in word list, 975
Refer, in vocabulary index, 954
Reflection, 462
Registration, for SAT, 4
Reinforce, in vocabulary index, 954
Relationship, linear, 540–542
Relative, in vocabulary index, 955
Relevant, in vocabulary index, 955
Reluctant, in word list, 975
Remonstrate, in word list, 975
Repression, in word list, 975
Reverence, in word list, 976
Rhetoric, in word list, 976
Right rectangular prism, 561, 563
Right triangles
  adjacent sides, 586–587
  opposite sides, 586–587
  Pythagorean theorem, 583–585
  sine, cosine, and tangent, 584–585
  special, 583–585
  and trigonometry, 583–588
  trigonometry, 588–591
Rise, in the slope of a line, 403–404
Roots
  exponents and, 423–425
  of a function, 452–454
Rotation, of a circle, 594
Rules, exponent, 421–422
Run, in the slope of a line, 403–404

S

Sample size, 519
Sampling methods, 519–520
Sanction, in word list, 976
SAT
  frequently asked questions, 3–8
  reading section structure, 89–91
Scatterplots, 529–532
Scenario, in word list, 976

Science
 advanced drills, 201–203
 drill, 178–180
 reading strategies for, 93
 test structure, 89
Scoring
 in math section, 343–346
 of SAT, 3–4
Scuttling, in word list, 976
Seamless, in word list, 976
Sector area, circle, 597–598
Semicolons, 245–246
Sentence combinations, 261–264
Sentence structure
 logical comparisons, 259–260
 modifier placement, 257–258
 organization, 285–289
 parallelism, 255–256
 placement, 286
 practice passage, 266–268
 sentence combinations, 261–264
 typical questions, 218
Sentiment, in word list, 976
Sequence, in word list, 976
Serve (to), in vocabulary index, 955
Setup information, for paragraphs, 285
Shingled, in word list, 976–977
Significant, in vocabulary index, 955
Similar triangles, 576–577
Simple interest, 508–509
Sine, in right triangles, 586–587
Singular possession, 248–249
Skeptic, in word list, 977
Slope formula, form of a line, 403–404
Sluggish, in word list, 977
Social science
 advanced drills, 194–197
 drill, 172–175
 reading strategies for, 93
 test structure, 89
Solving equations
 elimination, 365–366
 pattern recognition, 366–367
 practice drill, 375–385
 substitution, 364–365
Sphere
 formulas, 347
 volume, 557, 564–565
Squalid, in word list, 977
Square root
 method, 431
 of a negative number, 439
 negative number, 606–608
Square(s)
 angles, 577
 binomial, 416
 completing the, 434–435
 difference of, 416
Squelch, in word list, 977
Stagnate, in word list, 977
Standard deviation, measure of center, 489–491
Stewardship, in word list, 977
Strategies
 math, 348–354
 reading, 92, 94–101
Stupefied, in word list, 977
Stylistic, in vocabulary index, 955
Stylistic preferences, 222
Subjects, 241
Subject-verb agreement, 225–226
Subjugate, in word list, 977
Subordinate, in word list, 977
Subsequent, in word list, 977
Substantial, in word list, 977
Substitution, 364–365, 368
 concepts and formulas, 364–365
Sufficient, in word list, 977–978
Sullen, in word list, 978
Summary, in vocabulary index, 955
Supplemental, in word list, 978
Supplementary angles, 572–573
Surface area, 561–563
Surveys, sampling methods, 519–520
Sustenance, in word list, 978
Swayed, in word list, 978
Symmetric, in word list, 978
Symmetry, axis of, 455
Synthetic, in word list, 978
Synthetic division, 441–444

T

Table form, functions in, 390–391
Tables, 535–537
Tactile, in word list, 978
Tangent, in right triangles, 586–587
Tangible, in word list, 978
Tedious, in word list, 978
Tense agreement, 231–232
Test-taking strategies, 5–6
30-60-90 triangle, 557
360 degrees, circle, 594
Time
 for math, 343–344
 for reading passages, 99–100
Time allotment, reading section structure, 89
Time management, in math section, 343
Tone
 paragraph and passage analysis, 295–296
 proper, 271–273
 in vocabulary index, 956
Tout, in word list, 978–979
Trade publications, 103
Traipsing, in word list, 979
Transaction, in word list, 979
Transformations, functions in, 460–463
Transitions
 practice passage, 281–283
 sentence combinations, 261–264
 typical questions, 218
 in vocabulary index, 956
 in word list, 979
 wording, 277–279
Transversal, parallel lines and, 573–575
Trapezoid, area, 561–563
Triangle
 30-60-90 degree, 557
 45-45-90 degree, 557
 360 degrees, 594
 area, 558–559
 formulas, 347, 557
 isosceles, 575–576
 right, 586–587
Tributary, in word list, 979
Trigonometry
 question type, 343
 right triangles and, 588–591

U

Ubiquitous, in word list, 979
Unassuming, in word list, 979
Undefined functions, 438–439
Unit circle, 600
Unit conversion, 496–498
Unit-factor method, 497–498
Unrequired, in word list, 979
Unseemly, in word list, 979
Unstinting, in word list, 979
Unveil, in word list, 979
Usurp, in word list, 979

V

Validate, in word list, 980
Vantage, in word list, 980
Variables, in terms of other variables, 473–474
Variables and constants, interpreting, 389–390
Verb, 241
Verb agreement, 228
Verifiable, in word list, 980
Vernacular, in word list, 980
Versatile, in word list, 980
Vertical angles, 573
Vestigial, in word list, 980
Virtuous, in word list, 980
Visualizing polynomial graphs, 463–467
Vocabulary
 appendix, 951
 reading, 104
Volume
 box, 563
 cone, 565
 cylinder, 564
 formulas, 347, 557
 pyramid, 565–567
 right rectangular prism, 563
 sphere, 564–565
 See also Area; Formulas

W

Wayside, in word list, 980
Whisker plots, 538–539
Word choice, sentence combinations, 261–264
Word problems, setting up, 386–388
Wordiness
 practice questions, 237–239
 typical questions, 218
 in writing and language, 233–235

Wording, 218, 269–270
Words
  suitable, 271–273
  that confuse, 269–270
Words in context
  question drills, 153–158
  question types, 90
Writing and language
  dos and don'ts, 219–223
  scoring, 218–219
  test structure, 217–218

Y

Yearning, in word list, 980

Z

Zero solutions, pattern recognition, 367
Zeros, of a function, 452–454